BRASSEY'S ENCYCLOPEDIA OF LAND FORCES AND WARFARE

BRASSEY'S ENCYCLOPEDIA OF LAND FORCES AND WARFARE

Executive Editor

Col. Franklin D. Margiotta, USAF (Ret.), Ph.D.

Foreword by

Gen. Gordon R. Sullivan, USA (Ret.)

BRASSEY'S
Washington · London

Library of Congress Cataloging-in-Publication Data

International military and defense encyclopedia. Selections.
    Brassey's encyclopedia of land forces and warfare/executive
editor, Franklin D. Margiotta; foreword by Gordon R. Sullivan.
    p.   cm.
    Includes index.
    ISBN 1-57488-087-X
    1. Infantry—Encyclopedias.   2. Infantry drill and tactics—
Encyclopedias.   I. Margiotta, Franklin D.   II. Title.
    UD145.I58   1996
    355'.003—dc20   96–14299

First Edition

10 9 8 7 6 5 4 3 2 1

Printed in the United States of America

DEDICATION

The *International Military and Defense Encyclopedia* was dedicated to the memory of Morris Janowitz (1919–1988), the Distinguished Service Professor of Sociology, University of Chicago. Morris would have been pleased that the world finally had a comprehensive codification of knowledge about the military and defense, international in scope and authorship. For almost half a century, he focused his intellectual life on organizing the study of the military and issues of defense. Through his scholarship, his Inter-University Seminar on Armed Forces and Society, and his scholarly journal, Morris expanded the study of the military and society to all parts of the globe. He was brilliant at opening windows into defense establishments and let us all understand them better. Our only regret is that Morris Janowitz is no longer here to provide the scorching criticism and generous encouragement we always expected. It is only fitting that we continue to remember him upon the publication of *Brassey's Encyclopedia of Land Forces and Warfare*.

 An AUSA Book

The Association of the United States Army (AUSA) was founded in 1950 as a not-for-profit organization dedicated to education concerning the role of the U.S. Army, to providing material for military professional development, and to the promotion of proper recognition and appreciation of the profession of arms. Its constituencies include those who serve in the Army today, including Army National Guard, Army Reserve, and Army civilians, the retirees and veterans who have served in the past, and all their families. A large number of public-minded citizens and business leaders are also an important constituency. The association seeks to educate the public, elected and appointed officials, and leaders of the defense industry on crucial issues involving the adequacy of our national defense, particularly those issues affecting land warfare.

In 1988 the AUSA established within its existing organization a new entity known as the Institute of Land Warfare. Its purpose is to extend the educational work of the AUSA by sponsoring scholarly publications, to include books, monographs, and essays on key defense issues, as well as workshops and symposia. Among the volumes chosen for designation as "An AUSA Institute of Land Warfare Book" are both new texts and reprints of titles of enduring value that are no longer in print. Topics include history, policy issues, strategy, and tactics. Publication as an AUSA book does not necessarily indicate that the Association of the United States Army and the publisher agree with everything in the book, but does suggest that the AUSA and the publisher believe it will stimulate the thinking of AUSA members and others concerned about important issues.

INTERNATIONAL HONORARY ADVISORY BOARD OF *THE INTERNATIONAL MILITARY AND DEFENSE ENCYCLOPEDIA*

CONTENTS

FOREWORD

The impressive six-volume *International Military and Defense Encyclopedia* has been widely acclaimed in reviews describing it as an authoritative and indispensable work of reference in its fields. I am thus pleased to write the foreword to this smaller volume, *Brassey's Encyclopedia of Land Forces and Warfare*, which selects from the larger encyclopedia those articles related to land forces and warfare that have already been so useful to military professionals and scholars. The U.S. military services and U.S. government, as well as many foreign governments, bought significant quantities of the larger set for their libraries. This smaller encyclopedia of carefully selected articles now makes broadly available, at an affordable price, the most significant one-volume comprehensive collection of information on the subjects that consumed my life for more than thirty years.

The high quality of the publication is easily explained by the experience, expertise, and reputations of the editorial team that designed, compiled, edited, and wrote it. The editorial and advisory boards set new standards in their scope and academic quality and in their deliberate editorial choice to break free from a purely Western approach to the subject matter. I know well many members of these boards. I also find in these pages authoritative articles written by senior army officers from the United States, United Kingdom, Germany, and Egypt. They are joined by distinguished scientists and social scientists. Together they have created the premier reference on land warfare. I personally look forward to having this volume on my shelf as a comprehensive source of information, concepts, and ideas regarding both the enduring nature of warfare and its future. I recommend it to anyone who is interested in the art of war.

GEN. GORDON R. SULLIVAN, USA (RET.)
WASHINGTON, D.C.

PREFACE

Brassey's Encyclopedia of Land Forces and Warfare has a rich and unique history. It is the only English-language encyclopedia of land forces and warfare that was supported, advised, organized, and designed by distinguished international boards of military leaders and scholars and was written by subject area experts from throughout the world. It is the only such encyclopedia organized alphabetically in separate articles. It is a richer encyclopedia because its articles have been carefully selected out of the much larger six-volume work, the *International Military and Defense Encyclopedia (IMADE)*.

Brassey's and the Macmillan Publishing Company invested six years of effort and well over a million dollars in *IMADE*, which all seemed worthwhile when the extremely positive reviews and commentaries appeared. It rapidly became clear that the normally very critical reference reviewers had reinforced our notion that in *IMADE* our authors and editors had created something very significant. With the cooperation of Macmillan, it didn't take long for me to decide that it was incumbent upon Brassey's to make more readily available to the general public selected parts of the *International Military and Defense Encyclopedia*. While more than one third of the articles in this *Brassey's Encyclopedia of Land Forces and Warfare* come directly from *IMADE*'s land forces and warfare segments, the depth and breadth of our six-year effort permitted me to include almost one hundred more related articles by experts on subjects from areas such as technology, leadership, logistics, combat theory and operations, material and weapons, and more.

Because this encyclopedia owes its existence to *IMADE*, it is appropriate to follow the normal tradition in encyclopedic works in which the editor shares with the reader the logic of the encyclopedia's background and development. We will thus explain how we determined there was a need for the parent encyclopedia, how *IMADE* was defined and developed, and what aids we have built in to help the reader find information. We were confident enough to explore the daunting task of compiling this encyclopedia for three reasons: first, we are the oldest book publisher in these fields; second, we have published the largest collection of books by authors in these fields; and third, we are one of the few commercial publishing houses managed by former military officers with operational and combat experience, advanced academic and research experience, and worldwide contacts.

The Need for *IMADE*

To test further our initial research about the need for *IMADE*, Brassey's convened a two-day international conference of distinguished librarians, journalists, scholars, and active and former government and military officials. Strong expressions of support emerged from Mr. John Barry (senior national security correspondent, *Newsweek*); Col. John Collins, USA (Ret.), Ph.D. (senior defense analyst, U.S. Library of Congress); Col. Trevor N. Dupuy, USA (Ret.) (author and eventually editor-in-chief of *IMADE*); Jacques Gansler, Ph.D. (vice president, The Analytic Sciences Corp.); Gen. Paul Gorman, USA (Ret.) (former commander, U.S. Southern Command); Prof. William Kaufmann, Ph.D. (author; former DOD official; faculty member, MIT and Harvard University); Mr. John Keegan (author; defense editor, *Daily Telegraph*, London; faculty member, Oxford University); Col. Fred Kiley, USAF (Ret.) (director of research and press, National Defense University); Prof. Charles C. Moskos (faculty member, Northwestern University; chairman, Inter-University Seminar on Armed Forces and Society); Mr. Thomas Russell (director, National Defense University Library); and Mr. Steven Shaker (author; former Navy program analyst). Based upon this group's preliminary suggestions about content, we then began to define more precisely the purpose and scope of *IMADE*. The first step was to assess more carefully the potential audiences.

Defining and Developing *IMADE*

A wide range of potential users was identified. They included faculty and students in civilian high schools, universities, and educational institutions; private and government academies and military colleges, universities, and training organizations; active, reserve, and retired officers and enlisted personnel of the armed forces; and all levels of defense and military personnel in government agencies concerned with security and foreign policy issues. Researchers and staff of research institutes and organizations devoted to the study of security, foreign policy, defense, and the military would also find *IMADE* invaluable, as would all those involved in defense industries or areas affected by defense spending and procurement. Finally, the encyclopedia would serve as a ready reference guide for journalists and the knowledgeable, informed citizen wanting or needing information about the military and defense.

Brassey's then formed two distinguished boards. The honorary advisory board included British and Indian field marshals, a former chairman of the U.S. Joint Chiefs of Staff, a senior general from the People's Republic of China, and three leading civilian scholars from Germany, Japan, and the United States. Later, we added the former chairman of the Republic of Korea Joint Chiefs of Staff, the former commandant of the U.S. Marine Corps, the admiral of the fleet from the United Kingdom, and an internationally known scholar in the study of the military and society.

Next, we named an impressive editorial board of seventeen subject editors, each responsible for a subject area. They were experienced, prominent experts from three continents and seven countries. Selecting people of reputation and experience around the world was a start toward making *IMADE* international in scope and approach. We brought the editorial board to Virginia for a week of debate, discussion, and decision. This was a stimulating experience because of the quality of the individuals involved, their broad range of backgrounds, and the level at which most of them had actively participated in or studied the military and defense. The multicultural basis of *IMADE* was enhanced further by the selection of authors from seventeen countries and the richness of examples used in their articles. Depending on the subject, we sometimes found it essential to select board members and authors who were active duty or retired senior military officers, particularly those who had both operational and academic experience.

Many articles were written by people who have both lived and studied the military and defense subjects of which they wrote. Many of the authors have participated in combat operations. Their unique insights are not normally available to those outside military and defense establishments. Most authors have advanced degrees and academic and/or operational credentials. Collectively, they represent a distinguished international group of practitioners, warriors, scientists and engineers, former high-level commanders, researchers, and scholars.

We recognized the bias that could emerge from *IMADE's* publication in American English, management by Americans, and the weight of the United States in military and defense matters. The possibility of an unbalanced focus on things American was resisted in many ways. *IMADE* has almost sixty articles from authors from the United Kingdom; more than sixty by German authors; and thirty from Egyptian flag ranks. The advisory board, editorial board, and non-American subject editors also insisted on an international approach in articles. During editorial review, articles were returned to authors for examples beyond American or British experience.

This struggle to keep *IMADE* multicultural created significant editorial issues. Articles were written by authors whose English was their second language. At times, we contracted for translations into English. Some articles were revised or rewritten by English-capable associate editors, resulting in team authorship. Sometimes new authors replaced non-Americans if quality and agreement could not be reached. We generally respected the author's spelling of non-English words, especially those in Chinese and Russian. Fortunately, I was able to get assistance from colleagues met during my more than three decades of experience and education in air combat and operations, advanced academic study and teaching at the Air Force Academy and Air Command and Staff College (ACSC), research and publication, and management of large academic research organizations at ACSC and National Defense University.

Using *Brassey's Encyclopedia of Land Forces and Warfare*

This encyclopedia is presented alphabetically for the convenience of the reader, and a detailed index is presented at the end of the volume. The users of this encyclopedia will find it a rich source of information, but will be more successful if they take time at the beginning to understand the main aids we have put in for their benefit. Readers looking for information in a particular area should begin by looking up key words in the index and then scanning the entries to which they are referred. They can also use the significant cross-indexing, which details specialized areas that might be covered in other articles. Another aid is the detailed cross-referencing system to be found at the end of nearly every article, the "See Also" section. This refers the reader to related articles recommended by the authors and editors. Almost all articles conclude with a bibliography containing primary source material or longer, sometimes "classic" treatments of the subject.

The front matter of the volume is another valuable source of information: it lists the names and affiliations of the advisory board, subject editors/editorial board, associate editors, and authors. The alphabetical list of entries lists all articles in this encyclopedia and their authors.

These aids should help the reader find solid, objective information on virtually any major subject of land forces and warfare.

We wish you good and fruitful reading and research.

FRANKLIN D. MARGIOTTA, PH.D.
COLONEL, USAF (RET.)
EXECUTIVE EDITOR AND PUBLISHER
WASHINGTON, D.C.

ACKNOWLEDGMENTS

Hundreds of people are responsible for the development, quality, and publication of Brassey's *International Military and Defense Encyclopedia* (*IMADE*), from which *Brassey's Encyclopedia of Land Forces and Warfare* is drawn.

The first general recognition must go to the distinguished international group of military leaders, scholars, research and library experts (identified in the Preface) who strongly suggested in an exploratory meeting that *IMADE* would be a significant contribution to public information and education about the military and defense. They also emphasized that the mere collection of this material into one major work would be of great benefit. Their encouragement, preliminary advice on content, and suggestions on potential contributors sustained us through the next long six years.

We also must thank the International Honorary Advisory Board, which includes seven of the most senior military officials in the world and four of the most prominent scholars of military and defense matters. Their faith in and support of Brassey's and this project from the earliest days permitted us to attract experts from seventeen countries, whose work is displayed in the articles. Their advice on the selection of the editorial board and authors was especially helpful in broadening the international basis of the work.

The subject editors who formed the editorial board must be acknowledged for their diligence, their positive approach to *IMADE*, and their significant contributions to a better understanding of the military and defense. After helping to define the encyclopedia's scope, weight of effort, responsibilities, and topics, these subject editors signed up author-experts from around the world. They then reviewed and edited the articles, sometimes translating them into English. Without their efforts, this reference work would not exist. We must also recognize those brought on board late as associate editors who pitched in when deadlines neared and we needed to reevaluate and rewrite dozens of articles because of translation problems, late or incomplete work, or monumental changes in the world. Of great importance to this particular encyclopedia of land forces and warfare was the development work by *IMADE* subject editor for this area, Maj. Gen. Johannes Gerber of Germany.

Most important, of course, are the more than four hundred authors who generously wrote the expert articles, sometimes receiving a modest honorarium, sometimes prohibited by their governments from accepting any compensation. We hope that they will feel that this final product is worthy of their efforts.

The Brassey's and Macmillan staffs, too, deserve special mention. As associate director of publishing for reference works, Deirdre Murphy spent more than three years of her life working with authors and with senior subject editors while managing an impossibly large and complex encyclopedia project. Toward the middle stages, she was joined in these tasks by a first-class contract editor, Jack Hopper. Martha E. Rothenberg completed the contract editorial team and added her substantial skills in computers and database management to our effort. At different times during the six-year gestation period, we were helped by Christine E. Williams and Anne Stockdell. Carrie Burkett helped me start it all, and Elizabeth Ashley helped us finish. At Macmillan in New York, book production was managed with great professionalism by John Ball, Terri Dieli, and Benjamin Barros. I could not have spent the time I did on *IMADE* without our fine book publishing staff who stepped up their efforts and kept the book program alive and well: Don McKeon, associate director of publishing for books; Vicki Chamlee, production editor; and Kim Borchard, director of marketing and public relations.

Special recognition goes to Col. James B. Motley, USA (Ret.), who particularly assisted *IMADE* during the last six months of manuscript completion. Jim helped us smooth articles, chased authors and editors, rewrote certain articles, and assisted us with his management and organizational skills. He applied the skills and knowledge he learned in his combat, leadership, and academic assignments. We could not have finished on schedule without him.

LIST OF ARTICLES

CONTRIBUTORS

Mr. Lawrence J. Acchione
President, SENSCI Corporation
United States

Maj. Gen. Mamdouh H. Attiah
Egypt

Lt. Col. Dieter Bangert (Ret.), Ph.D.
Germany

Col. Rolf Bergmeier (Ret.)
NATO Headquarters Situation Center
Germany

Col. James D. Blundell, USA (Ret.)
Institute of Land Warfare, Association of
   the U.S. Army
United States

Lt. Col. Gert Bode
Germany

Lt. Col. Peter Bolte
Germany

Mr. Zeev Bonen, Ph.D.
Senior Research Fellow, The Neaman
   Institute
Israel

Maj. Keith E. Bonn, USA
United States

Col. John R. Brinkerhoff, USA (Ret.)
Former Deputy Assistant Secretary of
   Defense for Reserve Affairs
United States

Col. Ortwin Buchbender
Germany

Maj. Gen. Hermann Büschleb (Ret.)
Germany

Col. Nicholas H. Chavasse, USAF (Ret.)
United States

Mr. Charles Q. Cutshaw
Senior Scientific Technical Intelligence
   Analyst, USMC
United States

Prof. H. A. d'Assumpçao, Ph.D.
Chief Defence Scientist, Microwave
   Radar Division, Surveillance Research
   Laboratory, Dept. of Defence
Australia

Maj. Gen. Kheidr K. El Dahrawy (Ret.)
Professor, Nasser Higher Military
   Academy
Egypt

Maj. Gen. Alaa El Din Abdel Meguid
   Darwish (Ret.), Ph.D.
Defense Analyst
Egypt

Capt. Kevin Donohue, USA
Faculty, U.S. Military Academy
United States

Col. Trevor N. Dupuy, USA (Ret.)
Author and Media Military Analyst
United States

Contributors

Lt. Col. Sturmhard Eisenkeil
German Military Attaché, Hungary
Germany

Brig. Gen. Uzal W. Ent, USA (Ret.)
United States

Mr. Nikolaus Fiederling, Ph.D.
Dynamit Nobel
Germany

Mr. Abraham Flatau
United States

Air Vice Marshal Gabr Ali Gabr (Ret.)
Egypt

Mr. Reuven Gal, Ph.D.
Director, Israeli Institute for Military
   Studies
Israel

Col. Samuel Gardiner, USAF (Ret.)
Former Faculty, National War College
United States

Mr. Benjamin C. Garrett, Ph.D.
United States

Col. John F. Geraci, USA (Ret.)
United States

Maj. Gen. Johannes Gerber (Ret.)
Germany

Capt. Bruce I. Gudmundsson, USMC
Faculty, Marine Corps Command and
   Staff College
United States

Col. Oswald Hahn (Ret.), Ph.D.
Dept. of Economics, U.
   Erlangen-Nuernberg
Germany

Col. K. E. Hamburger, USA
Faculty, U.S. Military Academy
United States

Prof. Manfred Held, Ph.D.
Messerschmitt-Bölkow-Blohm GmbH
Germany

Brig. John Hemsley (Ret.)
Author
United Kingdom

Mr. Lloyd Hoffman
United States

Prof. Hans W. Hofman, Ph.D.
Universität der Bundeswehr
Germany

Mr. Axel Homburg, Ph.D.
Chairman, Dynamit Nobel
Germany

Mr. Daniel J. Hughes
United States

Col. Larry H. Ingraham, USA, M.S.
Neuropsychiatry, Walter Reed Army
   Institute of Research
United States

Mr. Robert F. Jackson
Engineering Director, British Aerospace
   Dynamics Ltd
United Kingdom

Maj. Gen. Carlo Jean, Italian Army
Ministry of Defense
Italy

Lt. Col. Friedrich K. Jeschonnek,
German Army
Germany

Mr. Curt Johnson
Military Historian
United States

Capt. Steven M. Jones, USA
Faculty, U.S. Military Academy
United States

Mr. Albert M. Karaba
Director of Engineering, Combat
  Vehicle Operations, Cadillac Gage
  Textron
United States

Mr. Anthony Kellett
Analyst, Dept. of National Defence
Canada

Col. Klaus Kleffner
Operations Division, SHAPE—Belgium
Germany

Col. Timothy E. Kline, USAF (Ret.)
United States

Brig. Gen. Heinz Kozak
National Defense Academy
Austria

Mr. Paul-Werner Krapke
Germany

Capt. Ulrich F. J. Kreuzfeld
Germany

Lt. Col. Manfred Kühr, German Army
Germany

Mr. William S. Lind
Director, Center for Cultural
  Conservatism, Free Congress
  Foundation
United States

Prof. Robert F. Lockman, Ph.D.
Economics Dept., U.S. Naval Academy
United States

Lt. Col. Timothy T. Lupfer, USA
United States

Lt. Col. Frederick M. Manning, USA
Division of Neuropsychiatry, Walter
  Reed Army Inst. of Research
United States

Col. Donald S. Marshall, USA (Ret.),
  Ph.D.
Peabody Museum
United States

Lt. Col. Albert D. McJoynt, USA (Ret.)
United States

Mr. David Messner, Ph.D.
Vice President, E-Systems, Garland
  Division
United States

Col. Christian Meyer-Plath, German
  Army
Commander, 30th Mechanized Infantry
  Brigade
Germany

Brig. Gen. Arie Mizrachi (Ret.)
President, Armaz Consulting, Ltd
Israel

Maj. Arno Möhl
Germany

Mr. Robert Moore
United States

Prof. Moustafa Aly Morsy Aly, Ph.D.
Egypt

Prof. Charles C. Moskos, Ph.D.
Dept. of Sociology, Northwestern U.
United States

Lt. Col. N. T. P. Murphy (Ret.)
United Kingdom

Lt. Col. Günther Nagel
Germany

Col. Roger H. Nye, USA (Ret.)
Former Faculty, U.S. Military Academy
United States

Col. Rod Paschall, USA (Ret.)
Former Commander, Delta Force
United States

Lt. Col. Günter Pauleit
Ministry of Defense
Germany

Mr. Ernest N. Petrick, Ph.D.
Consultant, General Dynamics Land
Systems Division
United States

Col. Francis M. Rush, Jr., USAF (Ret.)
Former Director, Sixth Quadrennial
Review of Military Compensation
United States

Maj. Gen. Ibrahim Ahmed Salem
Egypt

Mr. Hansjörg Schwalm
Federal College of Public Administration
Germany

Gen. Samir Hassan Mohammed Shalaby
(Ret.), Ph.D.
Egypt

Mr. D. H. Sinnott
Chief, Microwave Radar Division,
Surveillance Research Laboratory,
Defence Science and Technology
Organisation, Dept. of Defence
Australia

Brig. J. H. Skinner, U.K. (Ret.)
United Kingdom

Col. David A. Smith, USAF (Ret.)
United States

Maj. Gen. W. Stanford Smith, USA
(Ret.)
Military Analyst
United States

Gen. Donn A. Starry, USA (Ret.)
Former Commander, U.S. Army
Training and Doctrine Command
United States

Mr. George F. Steeg, Prof. Eng.
Former Vice President, Systems
Analysis, United Technologies Corp.
United States

Lt. Col. Ulrich Stork
Federal Armed Forces Office for Studies
and Exercises
Germany

Lt. Col. Gertmann Sude
Germany

Mr. John E. Tashjean, Ph.D.
President, Conflict Morphology, Inc.
United States

Lt. Gen. Franz Uhle-Wettler (Ret.),
Ph.D.
Former Commandant, NATO Defense
College
Germany

Brig. Gen. Reinhard Uhle-Wettler
Germany

Mr. Lutz Unterseher, Ph.D.
Independent Analyst, Studiengruppe
Alternative Sicherheitspolitik
Germany

Mr. Frank D. Verderame, Ph.D.
Former Assistant Director of Army
Research
United States

Cdr. Bruce W. Watson, USN (Ret.),
Ph.D.
Adjunct Faculty, Defense Intelligence
College
United States

Ms. Susan M. Watson
Author
United States

Mr. Ingo Wolfgang Weise, Ph.D.
General Director, Rheinmetall GmbH
Germany

Lt. Cdr. James T. Westwood, USN
(Ret.)
Defense Analyst
United States

Mr. Charles E. White, Ph.D.
United States

Capt. Leonard Wong, USA
Faculty, U.S. Military Academy
United States

Lt. Gen. William P. Yarborough, USA
(Ret.)
Former Commander, U.S. Army Special
Warfare Center
United States

BRASSEY'S ENCYCLOPEDIA OF LAND FORCES AND WARFARE

AIR ASSAULT

An air assault is an attack against a terrain feature or other objective held by enemy forces executed by a force carried to the place of attack by aircraft. Related terms are:

Airborne/airmobile/airlift operations: An air assault is a special type of airborne, airmobile, or airlift operation characterized by an assault on enemy forces immediately after the respective dedicated troops have landed from aircraft.

Raid: An air assault is a special type of raid in which the assault forces approach through the air.

Special operations: An air assault can be a special operation if conducted in line with, or as part of, unconventional warfare operations of operational or strategic importance.

Air attack: This is an attack against an objective by aircraft in order to destroy or to incapacitate it without taking permanent or temporary control of it. An air assault can be supported by an air attack.

Characteristics as a Special Form in Modern Warfare

After gaining the capability of exploiting the third dimension for fast movements, the old idea to launch a fast surprise attack unexpectedly through the air into the objective area became feasible. This led to air attacks and, later, air assaults. An air assault is the combination of a fast surprise approach through the air with a classic assault into or against an objective of significance in order to seize it—at least temporarily. Therefore, an air assault is a special form of attack characterized by speed, surprise, and approach through the air.

An air assault is seldom an autonomous or independent operation. It is usually carried out in support of major ground attacks or offensive operations by ground, air, or naval forces. It requires the close cooperation of air and ground elements. This cooperation makes it a complex matter with specific rules and principles. An air assault requires more coordination and preparation than ground-based operations or sea maneuvers. Its intensive organizational and material efforts will be undertaken only if the value of the objective justifies an air assault and cannot be achieved by a classic attack on the ground.

The objectives of an air assault can be to:

- take enemy positions, terrain features, or other targets in the front line behind natural or artificial obstacles (e.g., field and/or permanent fortifications, rivers);
- take protected/guarded objectives in the enemy's rear such as artillery, air defense or missile sites, nuclear or chemical assets, logistic installations, command posts, key terrain, and river crossings;
- hold seized terrain or objectives until relieved by ground forces or destroy these objectives;
- form an airhead/bridgehead after the initial assault and hold it until relieved by ground forces; and
- divert the enemy's attention from other sectors of the front or theater of war.

Depending on the intention and the level of employment, an air assault can be of tactical, operational, or strategic importance for the conduct of an operation, battle, campaign, or war. Principally, the following interrelations can be assumed among level, range of insertion, size of objective (including enemy strength), and assault force (Table 1).

An air assault is carried out in three major phases (see Fig. 1):

1. approach to the objective through the air and landing near, on, or inside the objective
2. final approach or assault to defeat the enemy and to carry out destruction or denial measures
3. relief by ground forces or extraction/withdrawal from the objective.

Principles

During all phases of an air assault the assault force and the transporting elements are vulnerable to enemy reaction, especially to air defense. The high likelihood of contact with an unexpected enemy makes the air assault an extremely risky operation. This requires the consideration of special principles in preparation and execution.

Preparations for assaults are often executed in a clandestine manner in order to make the assault fast, dynamic, unpredictable, and successful. Intelligence about the objective must be gathered with priority and analyzed in detail (e.g., enemy strength and available reserves, characteristics of the objective and its environment, landing sites, obstacles, weak points, weather, air defense). A permanent intelligence watch on the objective should be established until the end of the operation.

The selection of the assault force takes into consideration:

- strength of force in comparison with the enemy inside and around the objective
- own combat experience and morale
- requirement for experts such as artillery observers, ground liaison officers, engineers, intelligence experts
- appropriate air assets (one or more types of aircraft) for insertion

TABLE 1. *Interrelations Among Level, Range of Insertion, Objectives of Air Assault, and Size of Force*

LEVEL	RANGE OF INSERTION	OBJECTIVES	ASSAULT FORCE SIZE
Tactical	Frontline	Strong points	Platoon/company
		Bridges, sites	Platoon/company
		Fortifications, small	Platoon/company
		Fortifications, major	Battalion
	Enemy's rear up to	Command post	Platoon/company
	50 km (always in	Artillery sites	Company
	the area of respon-	Communication sites	Squad/platoon
	sibility of the task-	EW sites	Squad/platoon
	level)	Missile sites	Platoon/company
		Logistic installations	Company
Operational	Frontline	Bridgeheads	Battalion/brigade
		Fortifications	Company/battalion
	Enemy's rear up to	Airheads	Battalion
	150 km (always in	Major command posts	Company/battalion
	the area of respon-	Major logistic	Battalion
	sibility of the task-	installations	
	ing level giving	Airfields	Battalion/regiment
	consideration to the	River crossings/passes	Battalion/regiment
	range of airlift assets)	Key terrain	Battalion/regiment
		Nuclear assets	Platoon/company
		Islands	Battalion/regiment/ brigade
Strategic*	Theater of war	Government	Platoon to brigade-
	(maximum global	installations	size level
	war)	of strategic	(depending on
	(considering the range	importance	identified size
	of air assets)	Strategic nuclear	of enemy strength
		assets, POW	in/around
		camps, lockups	the objective)
		of hostages	

* In conjunction with conventional offensive or unconventional operations.

• logistic and medical support
• task organization, consideration of the objective and possible subobjectives.

The selection of the air assets considers the air situation, distance, weather, available air resources, qualifications of the aircrews, and available aircraft. Special emphasis is placed on support measures such as air escort, suppression of enemy air defense, electronic warfare (EW) support, and fire support from the ground or air.

The responsibility for the execution and support of the air assault should be clearly defined. All elements involved should be controlled by the same commander who is responsible for the air assault.

Operation plans for air assaults are more detailed than those for classic ground assaults and include detailed task organization down to the individual level, loading plans, ammunition and special equipment allocation, code words, al-

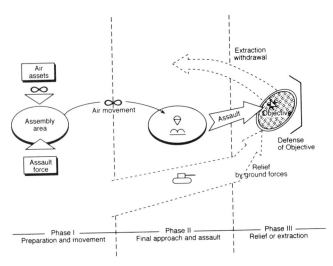

Figure 1. Major phases of an air assault.

ternate and emergency operations, target lists, communication rules, procedures to link up with ground forces or for exfiltration, evasion, and escape. In many armed forces, standing operating procedures (SOPs) for airborne/air assault/airmobile/airlift operations have been developed. Whenever and wherever possible air assault troops should be briefed in more detail about the assault than normal troops before an attack. In many cases it has proven worthwhile to build models of objectives and execute rehearsals before the assault.

Air Assault Forces

Suitable forces for the execution of the assault are specially trained air assault infantry; paratroopers (e.g., commando, special forces, and rangers); infantry; and mountain infantry. They might be reinforced by elements or individual members of the artillery, communications, engineer, technical, intelligence, medical, and/or reconnaissance forces, and staff personnel. The amount of preparation necessary to carry out an air assault depends on the experience and the training of the forces.

Air Support

The transport assets might be tactical transport aircraft for assault landings or parachute insertion, helicopters for assault landings, gliders (these have generally been replaced by helicopters), and ultralight aircraft (for small assault teams only).

Additional support can be provided by a ground attack by mechanized forces, air escort by interceptor aircraft, EW support for air defense suppression, attack helicopters, attack aircraft and gunships, and long-range artillery or missile fire.

Defense against Air Assaults

Since the first air assaults in history caught most defenders by surprise and proved a successful and effective method, most defense plans incorporate measures against air assaults and air landings.

Preventive measures against air assaults include the following:

- maintenance of reserves for counterattacks
- air observers at important objectives and at key points
- surveillance of possible landing sites
- allocation of air defense assets for area defense
- combat air patrols over key terrain or threatened areas
- electronic intelligence watch on enemy airborne forces and their air assets in the depth of the enemy area.

When an air assault is undertaken and in process, the defenders' air assets are employed to counter the transport and support elements in the air. Quick-reaction forces are used to attack the ground elements before or just after they have taken the objective, because air-landed assault troops are most vulnerable immediately after landing and debarkation.

History

In military history, the idea of air assault was born long before appropriate air assets were available. When Napoleon was massing his barges at Boulogne, it was quite seriously suggested that he should use balloons to carry his assault troops, or at least some of them, across the channel. One idea was for 2,500 balloons, each carrying four men, to be launched before the invasion by sea and to land in England a few hours in advance of the main body to cause confusion, if not complete surrender. The operation could not be carried out due to the lack of balloons, and the whole invasion was canceled because of other politico-military events on the continent.

Toward the end of World War I, U.S. general William Mitchell proposed a large-scale air assault behind the German front by the 1st U.S. Infantry Division to take the fortification of Metz. The plan was not executed because it was forestalled by the Armistice.

After the First World War, the development of mobile and mechanized warfare in Russia, Germany, and other nations was accompanied by the creation of parachute and glider formations, mainly to carry out air assaults. The first successful trials were executed in France, Poland, Germany, Italy, Japan, and the Soviet Union before the outbreak of World War II.

Along with the new tactics and operation of mechanized warfare, the Germans were the first to employ airborne assault forces in northern and western Europe. They did so with great surprise, shock to the defenders, and success for their own strategic intentions.

The circumstances under which the first operations were carried out gained the fascination of the public and the press. Other nations, especially those who lost the battles, copied the air assault posture and redeveloped it for their own purposes. These types of operations remain an extraordinary issue for the media and public whenever they occur.

The initial and most shocking air assault was launched in May 1940 against Belgium's modern fortification of Eben Emael by a glider-borne force of 100 men. Outnumbered six to one by the forces deployed around and inside the fort, the paratroopers proved able to blind and destroy part of the artillery systems. Within 48 hours the air assault force was reinforced by ground forces, and the commander of the fort—caught by surprise—agreed to surrender. The fall of Eben Emael was a shock to the Belgian army, which soon surrendered to the broad German ground attack.

Other major airborne attacks during the Second World War, such as those on Rotterdam, Corinth, Crete, Sicily, Normandy, Arnhem, and others in Southeast Asia, were combinations of air assaults and air landings. The heavy losses among the paratroopers and glider forces during the air assaults on Crete in 1941 clearly showed the risks inherent in airborne/air assault operations, especially if the assault is launched against a more-or-less prepared enemy on the ground. Therefore, the principle was established that air assault directly into the enemy should be avoided wherever possible and that, instead, airborne forces should be inserted behind the enemy lines into areas not controlled by major forces. If, however, it is impossible to avoid launching an air assault, the enemy must be totally suppressed during the landing and advance-to-attack phases.

After World War II, nearly all nations activated airborne, air assault, commando, and infantry units that were trained to execute air assaults. During this period forces of the colonial powers carried out air assaults against indigenous forces and so-called liberation armies.

During the Korean War (1950–53), the French Indochina War (1945–54), and the Arab-Israeli Wars (1956 and 1967), air assault operations were carried out by parachute insertion. During the Vietnam War (1965–73), the Israeli October War (1973), and the Rhodesian War (1968–79), helicopters were used for insertion of air assault forces. The tactics on the ground remained unchanged.

Two of these operations received wide publicity. One was an air assault launched to free U.S. prisoners of war from a camp near Hanoi in 1970 (Schemmer 1976). The other was an operation to free U.S. hostages held by Irani revolutionary guards in 1980 (Beckwith and Knox 1983). Both operations failed; the first, because the POWs had been moved to another camp, the latter because of deficiencies in air transport capabilities and aircrew skills. As a consequence, various improvements, especially in the United States, but also in other armed forces, were made that have enhanced the capability for air assaults.

The Israeli air assault against Entebbe, Uganda, in 1976 to free Israeli hostages in the hands of international terrorists proved the advantages of air assaults if the basic principles are considered and if surprise can be maintained until the final assault.

Soviet special forces and airborne forces executed various air assaults in Afghanistan.

Regardless of the difficulties and high risks involved, air assaults remain tactical, operational, and strategic (unconventional) warfare options for many armed forces today.

Major powers like the United States, the former USSR, the United Kingdom, France, Poland, India, Pakistan, Brazil, and Korea maintain major units whose elements are primarily dedicated to carry out air assaults or airborne operations.

The United States maintains ranger and airborne units including two airborne/airmobile divisions and one ranger regiment. Nearly all of the U.S. Marines combat units can be employed in air assault missions by helicopter.

In the former Soviet Union, each division had a motorized rifle battalion, specially trained for tactical air assaults, and each army had a motorized rifle regiment for executing tactical air assaults. At front level, air assault brigades consisting of air-mechanized parachute battalions and additional combat support were envisaged for conducting air assaults of operational importance. For strategic purposes, elements of eight Soviet airborne divisions and other special forces brigades (*Spetsnaz*) were capable of making air assaults. The composition of these forces varied.

Other countries have developed similar air assault concepts tailored to their tactical, operational, and strategic requirements. Wherever suitable they are already implemented in the war plans. NATO, in particular (when the Warsaw Pact was intact), expected various air assaults on tactical, operational, and strategic levels by Warsaw Pact airborne forces. This threat led to the development of rear area defense concepts and the employment of major combat formations in the rear echelons.

Air assault forces also have been identified in nearly all of the smaller developing countries. Their capabilities seem to be limited to only independent companies or battalions due to a shortage of air assets and limited strength.

Future Prospects

In the future, the air assault option will continue to play an important role for crisis management. Air assault elements might belong to intervention forces or to rapid deployment forces. Air assault options also might become part of Western defense strategy to threaten the potential aggressor's rear areas and force him to commit major forces to his own rear areas, thus preventing their use in frontline assaults. Small assault forces will be inserted by parachute or ultralight aircraft; major formations are likely to be inserted by landing helicopters or aircraft.

Air assault will not be limited to major conflicts, but also might be executed during low-intensity conflicts as well as against terrorists and criminal organizations. For the latter purpose, some nations have already formed airmobile police reaction forces.

FRIEDRICH K. JESCHONNEK

SEE ALSO: Airborne Land Forces; Army Aviation; Special Operations; Special Operations Forces.

Bibliography

Beckwith, C. E., and D. Knox. 1983. *Delta Force*. San Diego, New York, London: Harcourt-Brace-Jovanovich.
Gavin, J. 1963. *War and peace in the space age*. New York: Harper and Row.
Merglen, A. 1968. *Histoire et avenir des troupes aéroportées*. Grenoble: Arthaud.
Morzek, J. 1972. *The fall of Eben Emael*. New York, London: Hyde.
Morzik, F. 1965. *German air force airlift operations*. New York: Amo Papers.
Otway, B. H., trans. 1951. *Airborne forces*. London: War Office.
Schemmer, B. F. 1976. *The raid*. New York, London: Harper and Row.
Tugwell, M. A. J. 1971. *Airborne to battle*. London: Kimber.
Weeks, J. 1976. *Airborne equipment: A history of its development*. Newton Abbott, UK: David and Charles.
———. 1982. *The airborne soldier*. Poole, Dorset: Blandford Press.

AIRBORNE LAND FORCES

Airborne land forces are army combat forces that use the third dimension for airborne, air landing, and air assault operations. For air movement and for combat support they depend on air force or army aviation aircraft. They have tactical, operational, or strategic missions. Regardless of terrain characteristics, they will quickly deploy over great distances and, to the extent possible, be committed in surprise operations.

Their missions may include raids, security and surveillance, air assault, containment of enemy penetrations and breakthroughs, reinforcement or relief of committed forces, closing of gaps, and employment as operational and strategic reserve.

During aerial deployment airborne land forces require effective protection against the enemy's air force, attack helicopters, and air defense. Their limited ground mobility is increased by tactical vehicles carried with the deploying force and by organic or attached helicopters. Their special training and equipment make such forces particularly well-suited for close combat operations in urban areas, woods, jungle, and other difficult terrain. The development of airborne land forces began before World War II and is still going on. At present, there are three types of airborne land forces: airborne, airmobile, and air assault forces.

Airborne Forces

Airborne forces specialize in parachute assault and air landing operations. Air mobility is provided by transport aircraft, by gliders, or by helicopters. Combat and combat service support is provided by the air force or by organic or attached army aviation assets.

Organization, arms, and equipment are tailored to the requirements of airborne operations. The air transport capacities available limit the size, weight, and number of items that may be airlifted. Often air transport must be accomplished in several waves. If possible, the force will be organized into an air echelon transported by air and a ground echelon following the air echelon by land marches. The air echelon will primarily comprise the combat/fire-support elements, while the ground echelon primarily comprises the service-support elements.

Airborne forces have a high proportion of infantry. Weapons and equipment are mostly light and man-portable. Shoulder-fixed guided antitank and antiaircraft missiles are standard armament. Air-transportable light artillery as well as light armored and unarmored vehicles provide additional firepower and mobility in operations after the air landing but require air transport space.

Airborne Operations

Airborne forces will normally be committed only if time and the environment leave no other choice and when no other forces can carry out that mission. Another prerequisite is comprehensive and up-to-date intelligence. Operational security (OPSEC), deception, ruses, and surprise are other aspects critically important to success. Airborne forces will try to avoid frontal assaults and, instead, attempt to hit the enemy's weak spots in surprise operations, leaving him no time for preparation; they try to cut off the enemy's communications and disrupt the synchronization of his operations. This is done by attacks against the enemy flanks and rear, or by air landing/airdrop directly atop the objective.

Coup de main. A coup de main operation is executed by task-organized forces. It is an operation of very limited duration and should be accomplished by the time the enemy can institute effective countermeasures. A coup de main operation is conducted to seize or destroy key objectives, eliminate an adversary's command and control structure, or disrupt enemy defenses. It is often the opening phase of a major operation.

Tactical and operational missions. Forces from battalion to division size and larger conduct tactical and operational missions, such as preliminary attacks, flanking attacks, or deep attacks, or seize and hold key terrain. The decisive success must be achieved before the airborne operation turns into a regular battle fought in accordance with the principles applicable for all ground forces. The light armament and limited ground mobility of airborne forces are highly limiting. Airborne forces may also be retained as reserves to reinforce committed forces in critical situations or relieve them in position or by rearward passage of lines. They may also be employed as a gap filler, or to seal off enemy breakthroughs and to protect threatened flanks.

The limited mobility of airborne forces after air landings and the mostly light arms available in the initial battle frequently call for the seizure of airfields or the establishment of expedient airstrips to land vehicles, heavy weapons, supplies, and reserves. Apart from this, heavy loads are routinely dropped by cargo chutes. Another option is unassisted low-level flight delivery of resilient bulk supplies like food and ammunition. Heavy loads may also be transported by helicopter as external loads. Once on the ground, the mobility of airborne forces should be increased by providing them with helicopter assets.

PRINCIPLES

Thorough and detailed preparation is essential for these operations. Also indispensable, at least for a limited period of time and in local areas, are air superiority and the suppression of enemy air defenses along the air avenues of approach and in the landing zone. Effective and continuous air combat support, good communications, and, in most cases, cooperation with the ground forces will be required. Only an orchestrated combined-arms effort will ensure success. To prevent losses by friendly defensive fire while the force is airborne, clear airspace management and rapid identification of friendly elements are needed. If the landing takes place far from enemy forces, initial losses will be avoided, but this means giving up surprise and the crucial headstart. It is usually more promising to attack the enemy directly, leaving him no time for a concerted response. Airborne operations against a well-prepared and strong enemy have little chance of success and bring especially great losses.

AIRBORNE FORCES AND FLYING UNITS

Some believe the necessary close cooperation between flying units and airborne forces can be achieved only if both elements belong to the same branch of service. Whether or not airborne forces and flying units are integrated, it is logical that the airborne force should be stationed in the vicinity of airfields. Such stationing will decisively enhance coordination, training, and organization and improve responsiveness. The elements conducting the ground battle must know that they can rely on "their" pilots under enemy fire. They should develop an understanding for the technical aspects of the aircraft and flight conditions and understand the influence of weather conditions on airborne operations. Conversely, the personnel of the flying units should have a thorough knowledge and understanding of the conditions and tactical doctrine of the ground battle.

Airmobile Forces

Airmobile forces may be committed in support of airborne forces but may also operate independently. These forces are normally light division-size army forces. They are air-transportable with air force or army aviation assets. Frequently, their task is to expand successes and complete the mission of commandos or initial tactical/operational successes achieved by airborne forces. They specialize in air landings but they may also be used in a traditional role in the ground battle if required. Their equipment and doctrine are similar to that of light infantry with emphasis placed on antitank capability. Their heavy weapons and tactical vehicles require an extensive air transport effort by the air force or army aviation.

Air Assault Forces

Air assault units are combined-arms units of brigade and division size. All assets and forces required for airborne/air assault landings are organic to these units, and aviation assets are an integral part. This gives them high mobility. They conduct all types of offensive and defensive operations and are well-suited for operations in urbanized terrain, woods, jungles, and mountains, and for operations in extreme climates. They are capable of seizing and holding objectives or airheads. Only under extremely favorable conditions can they attack without support against armored or mechanized forces. They are primarily employed at the operational or strategic level. They can conduct independent operations, but are normally employed as elements of a larger force. The most prominent aspect of their operations is that they can concentrate forces with great firepower and momentum over great distances rapidly.

Historical Example: Operation Merkur (Scorcher)

The first operational airborne operation in military history was the capture of the island of Crete by the German Wehrmacht in World War II. Numerous tactical air landings in the campaigns in Scandinavia and the West in April and May 1940 had preceded it. In these actions, the Germans successfully seized important airfields, bridges, forts, and government institutions in Denmark, Holland, and Belgium and held them until the linkup with follow-on forces.

At the end of the Balkan campaign, on 20 May 1941, Crete was attacked by paratroopers of the 7th Air Division and mountain infantry of the 5th Mountain Division, under control of Gen. Kurt Student's XI Air Corps. The defenders—from Australia, Great Britain, Greece, and New Zealand—were superior in numbers, but short of equipment. The German attackers suffered high losses but seized the island within twelve days. Three methods of invasion were used: parachute jumping, glider assault landing, and air landing with transport aircraft. All of this took place by day. Tactically, it was a deliberate attack against a prepared defense. The parachute drops and glider landings were mostly atop or in the immediate vicinity of the objectives.

Additional naval transport had been planned. Naval support, however, was prevented by British naval superiority. Therefore, personnel, combat support, resupply, and medical support came almost exclusively by air.

PROBLEMS

The preparation and execution of air landings suffered from the following problems:

Great pressure of time. The beginning of the offensive against the Soviet Union (Operation Barbarossa) had been set for 22 June 1941, and that operation was to take precedence over all others.

Improvisation. Elements of the Luftwaffe's VIII Air Corps had been assigned other missions or had already been redeployed in preparation for the Russian campaign; as a result, the Luftwaffe ground elements for flight operations, air traffic control, maintenance, repair, refueling operations, and communications were inadequate.

Inadequate infrastructure. The only feasible airfields were mostly unprepared agricultural areas. At best they could be called improvised or expedient airfields and were suited only to a limited degree for such an operation. The clouds of dust caused by landing and takeoff of aircraft consequently upset the schedule of the operation and resulted in piecemeal commitment of the second wave in the afternoon of the first day of combat.

Logistical deployment problems and lack of service support forces. Most supplies, especially ammunition, POL, food, and gliders and transport vehicles, had to be moved over some 2,500 kilometers (1,550 mi.) from Germany to southern Greece by rail, ship, or air, with several transshipments; XI Air Corps had no organic logistics component and, therefore, had to organize a supply element from other units within one week.

Inadequate communications. Essential elements of the signal troops of the Fourth Air Force, assigned overall responsibility for Operation Merkur, had already been redeployed for the Russian invasion; as a result, the force had to rely primarily on wire communications, which were often disrupted by actions of resistance groups.

Deficiencies of the parachute force organization. During the past year the force had been expanded from five battalions, several companies, and the training establishment to four regiments plus corps and divisional units, and the buildup was not yet completed. Previous wartime experience had been limited to the aforementioned tactical operations in Denmark, Norway, Belgium, and Holland, but the troops had no experience in operational-level employment. Battalion, regimental, and division tactics, combined-arms operations, and cooperation with the air force for close air support had not been sufficiently practiced.

The technical development of the parachute corps was still in the early stages. Individual soldiers carried only a pistol, hand grenades, and explosives during the jump. Rifles and machine guns were stowed in special weapons containers and dropped separately. The parachutes and cargo platforms as well as the procedures for delivery of weapons, equipment, and heavy loads were sometimes inadequate—particularly in difficult terrain. Many of the radios and heavy weapons were damaged in the airdrop and rendered inoperative.

Deficiencies of air transportation forces. Air transport forces were unable to keep up with the development of the parachute forces. Only a small portion of available air transport was permanently assigned to XI Air Corps. Additional planes and crews were assembled from units from all corners of the Reich and few had experience in cooperation with, and airdropping of, parachute troops. The total capacity was just sufficient to transport in one wave half of the force that was to be airdropped. A Junkers Ju 52 aircraft could carry only twelve fully equipped and armed paratroopers. Large transport aircraft were not available.

Unclear picture of the enemy situation. Crete's defenders had excellent camouflage and fire discipline. Their location on the island permitted only aerial reconnaissance, the results of which were inadequate. Information on the enemy was hardly available; thus, the enemy was underestimated.

Failure to achieve surprise. The British had succeeded in deciphering the German radio code. They monitored the Luftwaffe's radio traffic and knew the German intentions and plans.

Moreover, it was impossible to keep the preparations for an air landing of such scale secret because they took place in occupied enemy territory. The well-functioning British intelligence service provided a steady input of information. The Luftwaffe first defeated the British air elements stationed on the island in a preparatory air battle that lasted about one week and thus gained absolute air superiority. Although this was essential, it further confirmed the intended German attack. The enemy knew the day and hour of the attack as did the German task organization.

British dominance of the sea. Since the British navy dominated the sea around Crete, seizure of one or more airfields on the island was essential for the success of the planned German attack. The commander of the British defense, New Zealand general Bernard C. Freyberg, was aware of this fact. He therefore concentrated on defending the airfields at Maleme, Rethymon, and Heraklion, Suda Bay with the village of Suda (important for his lines of naval communications), and the capital of Chania. This meant that defense efforts were concentrated exactly in the areas of the attacker's points of main effort.

OUTCOME

Despite these serious problems, Operation Merkur was a success. The well-prepared defenders, assisted by the Greek civilian population and armed and motivated by the British secret service, fought a battle that inflicted high losses on the Germans. Still, the defenders were forced to evacuate the island. The deciding factors included:

- organizational skills and initiative of the troops and staff in the preparation of the air landing;
- readiness to take risks on the part of the flying units of the Luftwaffe to provide good and continuous combat support;
- flexible command and control of the XI Air Corps in battle; shifting of the main effort to Maleme and the air landing of the 5th Mountain Division while the airfield was still under enemy fire; commitment of liaison teams, resupply and reserves;
- courage, fighting spirit, battle experience, and endurance of the parachute troops and the mountain infantry, and the initiative of the individual soldier in battle;
- shortages of equipment and the inexperience of the defenders.

The victory of the air-landed force definitely was attributable in part to superior leadership. The Germans call it "mission-oriented leadership." It means that any leader must know the intent of the higher command. Unit leaders to a large extent then act at their own discretion in accordance with this intent and within the framework of the mission, which delineates the objective and the means available. This enables them to react flexibly, to exploit favorable situations without delay, and to respond quickly to contingencies without waiting for orders. From the German point of view, the British system of "leading by orders" responded without flexibility and gave the landed paratroopers ample time. Counterattacks, though they were conducted methodically, normally came too late. Because air landings are always characterized by a greater extent of imponderables than normal ground operations, "mission-oriented leadership" seems the most effective means of control for airborne forces.

The island of Crete was captured in only twelve days by numerically inferior parachute and mountain infantry forces—some 22,000 versus 42,000 men—with heavy and continuous air support rendered under unfavorable conditions. The losses were high compared with the previous battles of the "Blitz," and even disastrous for some parachute units, but justifiable in relation to the overall success; losses were low in comparison with the subsequent Russian campaign. Operation Merkur showed the operational-level capabilities of airborne forces and opened a new chapter in the history of war.

BATTLE EXPERIENCES AND LESSONS LEARNED

Following Operation Merkur, German evaluation of the battle led to changes and new actions, such as the following:

1. reconstitution of the depleted parachute units
2. activation of new parachute units, including a Parachute School Battalion
3. activation of logistics units
4. improvement of in-service gliders, including installation of dive brake flaps and drag chutes for pinpoint landing after a dive; General Student coined the term "assault glider"
5. development and introduction of new transport gliders for greater loads, to include tanks and artillery pieces
6. improvement of cooperation with the Luftwaffe, especially for training and employment of special airborne observers for locating the planned drop zones and eliminating drop errors
7. training and employment of direction-finding teams to jump in first and then guide the follow-up transports to the drop zones
8. expedient communications procedures to make up for disrupted radio communications (e.g., black cloth strips with white letters some 70 cm high that could be photographed and read from the air)
9. upgrading of small arms and ammunition
10. improvement of jump procedure to make the soldiers combat ready immediately after removing their parachutes
11. development of special foods for arctic, temperate, and tropical climates.

By the spring of 1942, more than 30,000 fully trained paratroopers and some 1,200 modern gliders were available for new operational air landings, despite the fact that elements of the force had been employed in current operations in Russia and Africa and suffered further losses. In addition, two Italian divisions (an airborne division and the parachute division "Folgore") had been activated with German assistance and they would later give proof of superior bravery and true comradeship in arms.

Experience of the Allies in World War II

The American and the British armies carefully evaluated the German experiences and doctrine, and especially captured German documents, and immediately began to expand their small forces significantly. By 1942 they had strong and well-trained parachute forces for tactical and operational missions. They proved their value on the battlefields of North Africa, Sicily, Italy, the Far East, and France. The first major operation in which the new force was successfully employed at the operational level took place the night of 5–6 June 1944 in Normandy as part of Operation Overlord. The 101st and 82d U.S. Airborne divisions and the 6th British Airborne Division, employed to secure the flanks of the invasion zone north of Carentan and east of Caen, accomplished their missions and made an essential contribution to the success of the landing.

Post–World War II Developments

The French army developed the parachute assault tactics of its airborne forces to perfection during the war in Indochina from 1945 to 1954. In more than 150 airborne operations of forces from platoon to regiment size, the "Paras" gained legendary fame. In the Algerian War from 1954 to 1962, they were the first to prepare the way to modern air mobility with the use of helicopters for air landings.

U.S. forces developed the concept of the airmobile division in the Vietnam War from 1964 to 1973 with the 1st Cavalry Division (Airmobile), using massive helicopter operations for transportation and armed helicopters for combat support operations. This marked the birth of the attack helicopter and the air assault concept.

The Soviet Union carefully evaluated these wartime experiences and subsequently built a strong, efficient airborne force belonging to the Guard Forces (an elite unit of the Soviet army) that was capable of power projections worldwide. After the Vietnam War, the USSR developed an attack helicopter fleet that rivaled its American counterpart. In the Afghanistan War from 1979 to 1988, the Soviets took numerous losses of helicopters in the battle against the freedom fighters, who initially had only light arms but later received Stinger man-portable air defense missiles.

The Present

As of early 1991, the situation was characterized by rapid development of the airborne land forces of almost all large nations. Rapid technological progress in aeronautics had contributed to the use of the helicopter as an airborne weapons platform, and there was an emerging capability of airborne land forces to conduct independent operations.

THE SOVIET UNION

The Soviet Union, in early 1990, had eight airborne divisions, eight separate air assault brigades at front level, and a great number of battalion-size airborne forces at army level. The ground force divisions were assigned organic attack helicopter assets. The Mi-26 HALO transport helicopter has a capacity of 20 tons or 100 soldiers. New attack and antihelicopter helicopters were under development or awaiting introduction.

The Soviet Union also had a large air transport capacity in the air force, which could be augmented by civilian air transport assets (Aeroflot) when required. An example of the capability of the Soviet air transport fleet was the Antonov 124, a large, four-engine transport jet with a speed of 834 km/h (517 mph) and a capacity of 150 tons.

Tactical, operational, and strategic air landings, close air support with attack helicopters, and the employment of air/ground assault groups were elements of the offensive-oriented Soviet doctrine. Mixed helicopter units, including attack, multiple-purpose, and transport helicopters, supported by ground-attack aircraft and radio-electronic warfare assets played an important role. Helicopters were to conduct all kinds of offensive and defensive operations and also operate over enemy-occupied territory and within the range of threat weapon systems. Soviet helicopter protective measures included the use of armor, system redundancy, IR protection, a mix of weapons, and electronic countermeasures (ECM) and counter-countermeasures (ECCM).

With the concept of air/ground assault groups the Soviet Union also explored new methods. Attack helicopters, fighter-bombers, and airmobile infantry of at least regimental size were grouped together with mechanized ground forces under the direct control of the ground force commander to execute missions typical of advance forces, such as seizure of key terrain and attacks against the flanks and the rear.

The following options were considered for antihelicopter defense:

• proper siting of radar
• man-portable air defense missiles
• artillery-firing procedures to engage helicopters
• helicopters in an air-to-air combat role
• fighters in an antihelicopter role
• new munitions with proximity fuzes and large fragmentation radii fired from tanks and antitank guns.

The operations of the Soviet land forces were developed into an integrated air-land battle.

THE UNITED STATES

The U.S. Army has the 101st Airborne Division (Air Assault) as a mixed major unit, integrating under central control all ground forces and aviation units needed for independent operations. The units include three infantry brigades, one aviation brigade, one artillery brigade, and one support command. The organization is flexible enough to form mixed major air assault task forces tailored to a given mission. In addition, the army has the 82d Airborne Division for the traditional spectrum of operations (Fig. 1).

The integration of an aviation brigade into U.S. corps and divisions has resulted in a significant increase in combat power. The aviation brigade has attack, reconnaissance, multiple-purpose, and transport helicopters. The divisional aviation brigade has its own reconnaissance battalion, in which armored cavalry and its aviation elements are combined. This gives the brigade the necessary footing on the ground during separate operations and prevents unplanned clashes of the attack helicopters with enemy ground force defenses.

The main tasks of the aviation brigade are:
1. air attack in cooperation with ground forces, but also independently (this also includes combat operations in the depth of the area)
2. air assault of infantry additionally supported by attack helicopters
3. air-to-air engagement of enemy helicopters to protect the friendly operations
4. air transport of troops and aerial supply.

FRANCE

Similar to the American concept of rapid deployment forces, the French army has created the Force d'Action Rapide as a ready-reaction force consisting of five air-transportable divisions, with missions both overseas and in central Europe. An innovative development is the 4th Airmobile Division, which includes three attack helicopter regiments, one airborne regiment, and one aviation transport regiment. Employed as an operational reserve moved forward from the depth, this division can contain enemy breakthroughs and destroy them in

Figure 1. Paratroopers of the 82d Airborne Division, shown at Fort Bragg, N.C., in August 1990, make up the only fully airborne force still in service in the United States. (SOURCE: Robert F. Dorr Archives)

close cooperation with other forces. Operations are conducted by combined reconnaissance, antitank, and attack-helicopter assets.

GERMANY

The German army in World War II had been the role model and lead example for operational-level employment of airborne forces. It has now developed, after years of hesitation, a concept for concentrating its airmobile forces and for their future development, with the long-term goal of establishing two air-mechanized divisions as operational reserve.

WEAKNESSES OF AIRBORNE LAND FORCES

Airborne land forces still suffer from several weaknesses. The all-weather capability and night-flying capability of the in-service aircraft and the duration of operations are still limited. Aircraft vulnerability remains a serious operational concern and can be reduced only to a limited extent by the application of new materials for the airframe, electronic countermeasures (ECM) and ECCM, and active suppression of enemy air defenses. Friend-foe identification still poses a problem; the systems currently in use require further development. Organizing a continuous and up-to-date airspace management remains complicated and time-consuming. The ground element—the soldier fighting on foot—is still too vulnerable and immobile.

The Future of Airmobile Land Forces

AERONAUTICAL ENGINEERING

While the possibilities of improving ground vehicles are mostly exhausted, significant innovations appear in the aeronautical sector. As a result of research, new materials such as fiber compound materials and titanium will significantly reduce aircraft vulnerability. The use of "stealth" technology complicates identification, location, and engagement by reducing the radar, infrared, and laser as well as the acoustic and visual signature. By means of electronic countermeasures enemy reconnaissance and air defenses can be jammed, deceived, or neutralized. For example, advanced sensor missiles can lock on the radar emissions of enemy air defenses and destroy the emitting system. Electromagnetic pulse and electromagnetic interference protection will be part of new concepts. Survivability in a nuclear, biological, and chemical (NBC) environment will be improved by an overpressure atmosphere inside the aircraft and protective suits for the pilots, as well as by other measures.

A combination of VSTOL and tilt-rotor technology for aircraft can exploit the advantages of the fixed wing and the rotary wing in one aircraft. This would mean high speed and acceleration with independence from large and, thus, vulnerable runways. Use of satellites will revolutionize navigation. Electronic data and image transmission and digital map displays will improve command and control and significantly enhance the responsiveness of flying units. By means of image intensification and thermal imaging devices and use of terrain-avoidance/terrain-following radar, flight operations will be possible at night and with limited visibility. Identification systems not susceptible to interference will solve the problem of friend-foe identification. Mast-mounted sights for helicopters allow better use of cover during observation and engagement. Counter-rotating rotors give more lift and speed and eliminate the tail rotor. Better crash resistance will improve the chances of crew survival. Intelligent camouflage by a digital camouflage screen will improve protection of aircraft on the ground. Aerial refueling greatly expands the radius of action.

It will always be important to establish the right balance of armor protection and weight and to keep maintenance and repair performance and resources as low as possible. Only the large industrial nations can afford the high costs of aeronautic research and development. Smaller nations wishing to keep up will have to work cooperatively with each other or with the larger countries.

THE HELICOPTER AS A WEAPONS SYSTEM

Lasers and optical waveguide technology will likely be used for target location and engagement. Armament will consist of air-to-ground and air-to-air rockets and missiles as well as automatic guns with a variety of ammunition. Standoff weapons with submunitions and intelligent ammunition will complement the helicopter's offensive and defensive capabilities.

AIR TRANSPORT AIRCRAFT

The variety of transport aircraft is wide-ranging and continually developing. On the one hand are propeller aircraft with a weight-carrying capacity of some tons and extremely short landing and takeoff ability that can be used as assault transport aircraft and can take off and land also on makeshift airstrips. On the other hand are large jet-engine transport aircraft that can carry 100 tons or more, refuel in flight, and operate at speeds just below the speed of sound. The Soviet Antonov 225, developed from the Antonov 124, will have a payload capacity of 250 tons, with 6 engines and a speed of 800 km/h (500 mph).

A recent development is the American V-22 Osprey, a tilt-rotor aircraft that combines the efficient flight characteristics of a modern turboprop aircraft with the vertical takeoff and landing capabilities of a conventional helicopter. It will cruise at 275 knots (510 kph), carry combat payloads more than 1,000 nautical miles (1,852 km), and—with a flight ferry range of 2,100 nautical miles (3,889 km)—will be capable of self-deploying worldwide without aerial refueling.

The V-22 Osprey can supplement or replace the helicopter in many roles. It will be used for basic troop and cargo transport missions as well as for combat rescue, special warfare, assault support, medical evacuation, and the special requirements of the navy.

PARACHUTES

The rectangular ram air parachute with its cell design is an example of the possibilities for development of parachutes. Safe and quick release at both extremely high and extremely low drop altitudes and controllability of the parachutes expand and improve the spectrum of operational use.

LAND WARFARE IN THE FUTURE

The intensive use of the third dimension by land forces redistributes the classical elements of battle: fire and movement. The battle becomes highly dynamic. The time needed to move is reduced. Large forces with great firepower can be moved over great distances, concentrated, and dispersed again within a short time. The friendly area is better used and covered completely irrespective of tactical boundaries. Points of main effort can be established and shifted rapidly; gaps can be accepted without great risk, surveyed, and closed as required. Enemy breakthroughs can be contained more rapidly and destroyed by counterattacks. It is possible to attack the enemy on his own territory by overflying obstacles and barriers in surprise attacks. The third dimension will likely gain increased importance. The two-dimensional battlefield will be turned into three-dimensional battle space. Land warfare will assume a wholly different nature.

Airborne land forces and army aviation can be integrated into an air/land combat branch that will fight the air-land battle in the air, from the air, and on the ground. Units of this air-land combat branch will complement the battle of armored forces. They will conduct all kinds of offensive and defensive operations, normally in cooperation with other operational forces.

The battle in and from the air requires a main battle air vehicle (MBAV) whose different versions will be able to fulfill all tasks of the combined-arms combat. Its development might lead to "air mechanization." Maximum effectiveness can be obtained by concentrating the MBAV as an independent force. Parceling out the valuable MBAV to army divisions would repeat the mistake made in some nations at the beginning of World War II of parceling out tanks to infantry divisions. Success was finally achieved then by the creation of armored divisions.

Particular attention should be given to those elements of the force that are to fight the ground battle. Similar to mechanized infantry, a "heliborne infantry" force will dismount only if so dictated by the combat situation. Its operations might be continually supported by attack helicopters. The force will need new and effective weapons and armament that provide it with the necessary combat power, and it will need modern equipment for field fortifications and barriers. Reconnaissance, combat support, and resupply will be effected by air. For movements, these forces will mount their "laagered" aircraft. The primary weapon system of heliborne infantry will likely be the main battle air vehicle.

REINHARD UHLE-WETTLER

SEE ALSO: Air Assault; Army Aviation; Special Operations; Special Operations Forces.

Bibliography

Bellamy, C. H. 1987. *The future of land warfare*. London and Sydney: Croom Helm.
Galvin, J. R. 1969. *Air assault: The development of airmobile warfare*. New York: Hawthorn Books.
Glantz, D. M. 1984. *The Soviet airborne experience*. Research Survey no. 4. Combat

Studies Institute. U. S. Army Command and General Staff College. Washington, D.C.: Government Printing Office.
Merglen, A. 1968. *Histoire et avenir des troupes aéroportées*. Grenoble: B. Arthaud.
Mrazek, J. 1975. *The glider war*. London: Robert Hale; New York: St. Martin's Press.
v. Senger und Etterlin, F. 1983. New operational dimensions. *Journal of the Royal United Service Institute for Defence Studies*, June.
Simpkin, R. E. 1985. *Race to the swift*. London: Brassey's.
Winterbotham, F. 1975. *The Ultra secret*. New York: Dell Books.

AIR-LAND BATTLE

The United States Army's basic operational concept is called the air-land battle doctrine (ALB), a doctrine based on securing or retaining the initiative and exercising it aggressively to defeat the enemy. It was presented in *Field Manual (FM) 100–5: Operations* published on 20 August 1982. This manual established the rules for waging war at the operational level (division and army corps). For the purpose of this discussion, the author addresses the August 1982 version of *FM 100–5*. Since its initial introduction in 1976, *FM 100–5* has been revised about every five years. Revisions to the May 1986 version have been completed by the U.S. Army Training and Doctrine Command. Almost simultaneously with *FM 100–5*, the U.S. Army Training and Doctrine Command (TRADOC) published a paper entitled *Air-land Battle 2000*. Encompassing the period 1995–2015, this effort was intended to distinguish it as a future-oriented concept while referring to its roots in the ALB doctrine of the 1980s. Air-land battle 2000 was envisioned as a concept that would be the starting point for all future weapons acquisition, as well as future doctrine, force design, and training requirements. To eliminate the resulting confusion between the army's ALB doctrine and the air-land battle 2000 concept, in November 1983, TRADOC retitled the war-fighting concept for the twenty-first century *Army 21*.

To assess properly the 1982 *FM 100–5*, it is useful to note its predecessor's characteristics. The 1976 version, titled *Active Defense*, came under sharp criticism almost from the moment it was published. A group of American military thinkers known as the Military Reform Movement, both inside and outside of the armed forces, accused the manual and its doctrine of being tied to positional warfare, that is, being firepower-oriented to the detriment of mobile tactics, reactive to enemy action instead of emphasizing initiative, relying primarily on attrition through firepower exchange, and neglecting the teachings of the art of war.

This dissatisfaction with the army's operational doctrine led to the concepts of the *integrated battlefield*, which tried to combine nuclear and conventional operations, and the *extended battlefield*, which advocated an extension of operations far and deep into enemy territory. Both concepts depended heavily on the use of nuclear weapons for military purposes, thus causing considerable criticism.

In the late 1970s and early 1980s, the effect of emerging technologies became apparent, promising weapon delivery of remarkably increased accuracy and lethality, not only against point targets such as bridges and armored vehicles, but also against area targets such as armored formations. The effects of all these weapons were viewed by many as a substitute for low-yield nuclear weapons, thus reducing the emphasis on the use of nuclear weapons for tactical, military purposes.

Responsible authorities must have considered some of the dissatisfaction with the 1976 operational doctrine as justified, because a new *FM 100–5*, titled *Operations*, was issued six years later. It described how the army must conduct campaigns and battles in order to win; explained U.S. Army operational doctrine involving maneuver, firepower, movement, combined arms warfare, and cooperative actions with sister services and allies; and emphasized tactical flexibility and speed as well as mission orders, initiative among subordinates, and the spirit of the offense.

The thrust of the 1982 edition of *FM 100–5* is best captured by a quotation from chapter 2, "Combat Fundamentals":

> Army units will fight all types of operations to preserve and to exploit the initiative. They will attack the enemy in depth with fire and maneuver and synchronize all efforts to attain the objective. They will maintain the agility necessary to shift forces and fires to the point of enemy weakness. Our operations must be rapid, unpredictable, violent and disorienting to the enemy.

Success on the modern battlefield will depend on the basic tenets of air-land battle doctrine: initiative, depth, agility, and synchronization.

It is significant that *FM 100–5* placed the principles of war, and their application to classical and modern theory, at the foundation of the army's ALB doctrine. ALB was a return to the tried and true principles of experience in war.

In remarks to a group of TRADOC historians, one of the principal authors of the ALB doctrine, Gen. Donn A. Starry, U.S. Army (Retired) said:

> In a very broad sense, AirLand Battle is a grand offensive defense—one on the style fought so successfully by General George Washington in the revolution, with great skill and initial success by Lee and Jackson in the Civil War, and with striking success by MacArthur in World War II.

In addition to the examples identified by General Starry can now be added the brilliantly conceived and professionally executed multinational Persian Gulf ground campaign against Saddam Hussein.

In sum, it is important to remember that military doctrine is a set of attitudes about war conditioned by historical experience. Therefore, doctrine cannot promise too much nor suggest too little.

FRANZ UHLE-WETTLER

SEE ALSO: Doctrine; Joint Operations; Offense; Principles of War.

Bibliography

Starry, D. A. 1989. A perspective on American military thought. *Military Review*, July, pp. 9–10.

Romjue, J. L. 1984. *From active defense to airland battle: The development of U.S. Army doctrine, 1973–1982*. Ft. Monroe, Va.: U.S. Army Training and Doctrine Command (TRADOC).

U.S. Department of the Army. 1982. *Field manual 100–5: Operations.* Washington, D.C.: Government Printing Office.

AMMUNITION

Ammunition is "a device charged with explosives, propellants, pyrotechnics, initiating composition, or nuclear, biological, or chemical material for use in connection with defense or offense. Certain ammunition can be used for training, ceremonial, or nonoperational purposes" (U.S. Department of Defense 1987). Generally, ammunition for firearms may be divided into two categories: small caliber—usually less than 20mm to 40mm—and large caliber—usually greater than 20mm to 40mm. The categories overlap in the 20mm to 40mm range.

Small-Caliber Ammunition

There is a wide variety of small-caliber ammunition, virtually all of which is fixed—that is, the cartridge case is permanently attached to the projectile. Each round of small-caliber ammunition is an assembly of all components—the cartridge case, primer, propellant, and bullet (projectile) or shot—required to fire a weapon one time. A typical small-caliber cartridge with its components is shown in Figure 1.

The cartridge case, which holds the primer, the propellant, and the projec-

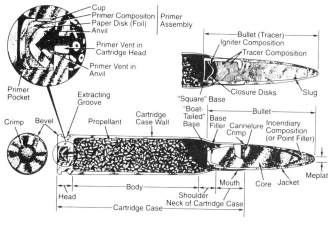

Figure 1. Cartridge terminology. (SOURCE: U.S. Army)

tile that is fired from the weapon, conforms to the shape of the specific weapon's chamber and is usually made of brass but may also be steel or some other material. The case also seals the weapon's barrel, so it must be sufficiently flexible first to expand and then to return to its approximate original size, permitting the extraction of the case and the insertion of a fresh round of ammunition. It must also be strong enough to withstand the great pressures generated by firing. Experimental weapons using caseless rounds have been developed, but none has yet seen widespread use. Heckler and Koch has developed a rifle, the G-11, that uses 4.7mm caseless ammunition. This rifle is scheduled to enter service with the German armed forces in 1992.

The primer of a round of ammunition is the assembly that fits in the center of the cartridge base and ignites the propellant when struck by the weapon's firing pin. Some cartridges, usually 20mm or larger, may use electric priming to speed ignition and improve reliability; this type is almost always used in aircraft. Rimfire priming is also used in some low-power ammunition; today, this is limited to .22-caliber bulleted breech (BB) caps; conical breech (CB) caps; and short, long, and long-rifle ammunition. All other mechanical primers consist of a primer cap, primer composition, and anvil. Most modern center-fire cartridges use Boxer priming, in which the anvil is integral to the primer assembly. Cartridges that are Berdan-primed have the primer anvil machined into the center of the primer pocket with two small flash holes on either side of the anvil. Ironically, Boxer priming, traditionally used in the United States, was invented by a British officer, Edward Boxer, while Berdan priming, more common in Europe, was invented by an American, Col. Hiram Berdan. Most primers today are made of noncorrosive materials so that the residue of the burned primer will not cause corrosion in the barrel of the weapon, a common problem prior to the 1950s. A primer is a mixture of ingredients extremely sensitive to shock; the most important characteristics are sensitivity, impulse, gas volume, and duration of flash.

The propellant is a low-explosive fine-grained substance that burns at a controlled rate and produces gases that expand with sufficient energy to propel a bullet out of the weapon's barrel. From the time firearms were invented until the late nineteenth century, black powder was used as the propellant. Black powder had several disadvantages: (1) it was very susceptible to moisture, which drastically changes its burning characteristics; (2) because it was a mixture of charcoal, sulphur, and saltpeter by volume, its explosive value was very dependent on the care with which it was mixed; (3) the manufacturing process of black powder required extreme care because the ingredients could explode during mixing; (4) when fired, black powder generates huge volumes of smoke, which obscured the battlefield and enabled the enemy to pinpoint the location of the shooter; and (5) black powder leaves a dense gummy residue when burned, requiring weapons to be cleaned frequently in order to remain operational. Black powder is still used in some artillery igniters, fuzes, and in other specialized ammunition applications.

Modern ammunition uses smokeless powder, which not only overcomes the problems associated with black powder but also makes possible the use of

small-caliber, high-velocity ammunition. Although it is called smokeless powder, the propellant that pushes the bullet down the bore of modern weapons is
neither smokeless nor truly a powder. The grains of modern powder are made
by an extrusion process into a variety of forms—flakes, rectangles, cylinders,
crosses, or any other desired shape. The shape of the powder grain is critical
because it determines the burn rate and thus the amount of pressure in the
weapon's barrel and therefore the velocity of the projectile. Velocities may be
as low as 45 meters (150 ft.) per second for mortar projectiles or as high as 1,200
meters (about 4,000 ft.) per second for some tank ammunition. The velocity of
most military rifle ammunition is between 750 and 900 meters (2,500 and 3,000
ft.) per second. The burn rate of the propellant must be carefully designed to
take advantage of the characteristics of the weapons in which the ammunition
will be used. If all propellants were to be burned before the bullet moved very
far down the barrel, undesirably high pressures would be generated. Thus,
most propellants are designed to burn at a given rate so that the powder is not
completely consumed until the bullet has traveled along approximately two-
thirds of the barrel. This results in a larger volume for the expanding gases with
a concomitant decrease in pressure.

Smokeless powders may be either single-based or double-based. Single-
based powders are composed primarily of nitrocellulose and are manufactured
by the "nitration of cotton" method. Double-based powders have nitroglycerin
added to the nitrocellulose, to form a gel or plastic-like substance, and small
quantities of stabilizers.

The bullet is the component of the cartridge that is fired from the weapon.
It may be a single projectile or, in rare instances, more than one projectile.
Shotgun cartridges usually fire a mass of round shot that may be of varying
sizes, depending on the purpose of the cartridge. Bullets are made of various
materials. At one time almost all bullets were made of a lead/tin alloy, but the
introduction of smokeless powder engendered several problems with lead bullets. First, lead-alloy bullets fired at high velocities do not readily engage the
rifling of a weapon's barrel and may in fact override the lands and grooves of the
bore, which leads to erratic accuracy. This phenomenon is called *swaging*.
Another problem associated with lead-alloy bullets fired in high-velocity military weapons is *leading*. As the bullet is swaged down the bore without engaging the rifling, it overrides the lands and grooves of the rifling, leaving a deposit
of lead in the barrel. This deposit, if not removed, may cause inaccuracy and
higher-than-desired pressures. Also, lead bullets tend to be easily deformed
prior to firing, causing malfunctions in feeding. Finally, lead bullets have a
relatively low penetrating capability. These problems led to the introduction of
what is termed *ball ammunition*. Such bullets have a lead-alloy core and a
gilding metal jacket, such as copper, that positively engages the rifling in the
weapon bore and can be fired without swaging. The most common military
small-caliber ammunition fires an armor-piercing (AP) bullet. This type of bullet consists of a gilding metal jacket surrounding a tungsten or molybdenum
steel core, with a point filler of lead alloy or incendiary mixture. The lead-alloy
point filler initially stresses the point of impact and supports the steel core so

that the latter has a good chance of penetrating without breaking up. About one-third of the way forward from the bullet base is the cannelure, a machined groove around the circumference of the bullet that is used to crimp the case to the bullet. Bullet bases are of two shapes, boat tail or square. The boat-tail design is better at velocities under 900 meters (3000 ft.) per second. At higher velocities, either design delivers adequate performance. Other common types of small-caliber bullets include incendiary, armor-piercing incendiary, and tracer bullets. All incendiary bullets function on impact; they are ignited by the heat generated when they strike their target. Incendiary bullets are derived from ball-bullet design; they are filled with an incendiary mixture ahead of the lead-alloy core. Armor-piercing incendiary (API) bullets have the incendiary mixture in front of their steel core. Tracer bullets are ignited by the cartridge propellant and allow the gunner to observe the path of the bullet. Tracers, however, do not burn for the full range of the bullet. Most 7.62mm bullets are limited to a trace length of approximately 1,500 meters (4,950 ft.). Tracers are usually used in machine-gun ammunition loaded in belts in which every fifth round is a tracer, with the other four rounds being AP or API.

Multiple bullets have been in existence since the early 1900s and consist of two or more bullets in one cartridge. Typical was the U.S. design of the late 1950s. These multiple bullets consisted of two 7.62mm rounds in one standard North Atlantic Treaty Organization (NATO) cartridge. The intent was to increase the odds of hitting a target with one shot. The first bullet had a conventional shape and a flat base; the second bullet's nose nested in the face of the first with the base of the second slightly slanted. The trajectories of both bullets were thus somewhat offset because the gases leaking past the offset base of the second bullet as it emerged from the muzzle of the rifle caused it to be slightly canted. The cant was carefully engineered so that the strike of both bullets was predictable over given ranges. The multiple bullet, however, was not particularly successful in service and was withdrawn by the late 1960s.

Cartridge cases are, with the exception of shotgun cartridges, usually made of brass, although steel is occasionally substituted. The cartridge case is drawn from flat brass stock in such a way that the thickness of the case tapers from base to mouth. Cases may be rimmed, semi-rimmed, or rimless. Most military cartridges have rimless cases. Rimless and semi-rimmed cases have an extraction groove around the circumference of the case head. In rimless cartridges, this is often mistakenly referred to as the cartridge rim, but rimless cartridges do not have a rim, only an extraction groove. Belted cases, rare in military cartridges, have a belt forward of the extracting groove to reinforce the case head against extremely high pressures. This type of case is usually associated with cartridges of very high power, such as the .300 Winchester Magnum or the .375 H&H Magnum. During the Vietnam conflict, some U.S. sniper teams used rifles of .300 Winchester Magnum caliber.

Complete rounds of small-caliber ammunition are classified according to purpose. The most common classifications are: AP, API, API tracer (API-T), ball, grenade launching, incendiary, tracer, blank, dummy, high-pressure test (HPT), match, practice, and shotgun. Ammunition is also color-coded to facilitate recognition. Representative NATO standard color codes for small-caliber ammunition are as follows:

AP	Black
API	Silver
API-T	Silver/Red
Ball	None

The principal types of small-caliber ammunition are listed below.

Ball. At one time the most common type of small-arms ammunition, ball ammunition has been largely supplanted by AP ammunition for combat use. Ball ammunition has a bullet of lead with a gliding metal jacket and is now used primarily for marksmanship training.

Armor piercing. AP ammunition has a hardened steel or tungsten carbide core behind a lead-point filler inside a gilding metal jacket. It is used against personnel and in larger calibers, such as 12.7mm and 20mm, against lightly armored vehicles. A variant of AP ammunition being developed in the United States is called "saboted light armor piercing" (SLAP) ammunition. It is being developed in 7.62mm and 12.7mm calibers and consists of a subcaliber penetrating projectile in a discarding sabot of light plastic—that is, the outer shell of plastic peels off the steel projectile after it leaves the muzzle of the weapon, allowing the projectile to continue. The light weight of these rounds gives them very high velocities and improved armor penetration over normal AP rounds.

Tracer. Tracer (T) ammunition is similar to ball ammunition, but the bullet has its rear portion replaced by a composition of magnesium powder and barium nitrate with metallic compounds added to provide colors. This is usually strontium nitrate, which produces a red color when the compound burns. It was developed originally for use by aircraft machine gunners and eventually came to be used in all machine guns.

Incendiary. Incendiary (I) ammunition is designed specifically to start a fire in a target. Like tracer ammunition, incendiary ammunition was originally designed for use in aircraft to set fire to enemy planes. Its use has gradually declined, as small-caliber weapons are rare in modern high-performance aircraft, which are often capable of flying faster than bullets of this type.

Armor-piercing incendiary and armor-piercing incendiary tracer. Both API and API-T ammunition combine the features their names imply. Like incendiary ammunition, both were designed for use against enemy aircraft, and again, both are becoming less common due to less frequent use of small-caliber weapons in aircraft.

Blank. Blank ammunition consists of a powder charge in a cartridge case with no bullet and is used for training, for simulating weapons fire, and in ceremonies.

Dummy. Dummy ammunition, also known as drill ammunition, is completely inert but looks like an actual round of ammunition. It is used for training, has no propellant or primer, and can usually be identified by holes or longitudinal grooves in the cartridge case. In Great Britain, dummy ammunition is used by weapons inspectors for testing the mechanical functions of weapons and is made of tool steel to precise tolerances.

High pressure test. HPT is similar to ball ammunition except that it has a heavier bullet and an excess propelling charge for proof-testing weapons. Firing of proof loads is performed with the weapon under a hood and the trigger pulled mechanically.

Rifle grenade. This ammunition is similar in appearance to blank ammunition but has distinguishing features to set it apart. It has no bullet but does have a large propellant charge designed to fire a grenade from the end of the rifle barrel. Rifle grenade cartridges are no longer widely used due to the development of rifle grenades that may be launched using standard AP ammunition.

Shotgun. This ammunition consists of a propelling charge; a load of shot, a projectile, or flechettes; and primer in a case of paper, plastic, or brass. The head of the cartridge, usually brass, contains the primer and encloses the propellant. On top of the propellant are several wads of paper or plastic, followed by the shot or other projectiles. The case may be closed by either placing a closing wad over the shot and rolling the case down tightly to seal it or, more commonly, crimping the case mouth over the shot. Military shotguns are usually loaded with 00 buckshot (.34 in.) or flechettes. A typical 12-gauge shotgun round will contain nine balls of 00 buckshot or twenty flechettes. Shotguns may also fire a solid ball or a rifled slug. Shotguns are especially useful in jungle warfare, where ranges of engagement seldom exceed 50 meters (165 ft.). Indeed, they were widely used by U.S. forces in Vietnam. Shotgun gauges are determined by the number of lead balls of the diameter of the bore required to weigh one pound. The exceptions to this rule are the .410 and 9mm shotguns, which have a bore diameter of .41 inch and 9mm, respectively. Shotgun gauges and bore diameters follow.

Shotgun gauge/Bore diameter

4 Gauge	.935 inch
8 Gauge	.835 inch
10 Gauge	.775 inch
12 Gauge	.729 inch
16 Gauge	.662 inch
20 Gauge	.615 inch
28 Gauge	.550 inch

Large-Caliber Ammunition

Large-caliber ammunition starts at 20mm to 40mm. At the lower end of the scale, from 20mm to approximately 75mm, large-caliber ammunition is usually fixed—that is, the projectile and case are permanently attached until the time of firing, similar to small-caliber ammunition. Larger-caliber ammunition may be semi-fixed or separate loading. In the former case, the projectile and case are separate but are put together prior to firing. In the latter, there is no case; instead, powder bags are used as the propellant. Separate-loading ammunition is employed only in the largest calibers of cannon either because of a need to vary the charge of propellant or because of handling requirements.

The basic types of large-caliber ammunition are high explosive, which has a filler of TNT or some other explosive; AP, which may be of either kinetic energy or chemical energy varieties; chemical, which also includes smoke and white phosphorus (WP) ammunition; canister, which has balls, flechettes, or other type of fragments in a matrix; and illuminating, which contains a magnesium flare and a parachute for lighting a battlefield at night. Within these categories are many varieties of ammunition. For the purposes of this discussion, large-caliber ammunition is divided into ammunition for guns and howitzers, ammunition for mortars, and ammunition for recoilless rifles.

Guns and Howitzers

High Explosive (Fig. 2). The high-explosive (HE) artillery shell is by far the most common in most military establishments; there are several types. Typically, an HE projectile is cylindrical, tapering to a point at the nose. The tapered portion is called the *ogive*, and the fuze is tapered to closely match the contour of the ogive. The *bourrelet* is a smooth, machined surface of the projectile just to the rear of the ogive; it rides the bore lands of the gun tube, supporting the projectile as long as it is in the tube. The rotating band is slightly larger than the bore of the gun and performs a number of functions, one of which is to impart spin to the projectile by engaging the lands and grooves of the bore. Another function is that it provides obturation, or sealing, thus preventing the propellant gases from blowing by the projectile as it travels down the bore. Some projectiles have a separate obturator. Finally, the rotating band provides a rear bearing surface for the projectile while it is in the bore of the gun.

Some projectiles also have a base cover or plug. The base cover is sheet steel and prevents hot gases from bleeding through the projectile body, which may be porous. Such an occurrence would ignite the projectile filler while it was still in the bore of the weapon, a highly undesirable event. Base plugs are employed in HE-improved conventional munitions projectiles that are base

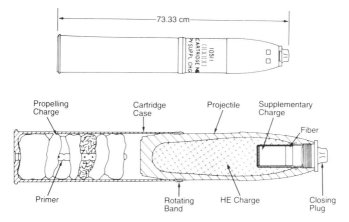

Figure 2. High-explosive round (semi-fixed). (Source: U.S. Army)

ejecting and in other projectiles, such as smoke, illuminating, and leaflet rounds.

Conventional HE shells are used to obtain demolition effects against materiel and fragmentation effects against both materiel and personnel. Fragmentation is a serious design consideration of the projectile engineer and is the result of the careful selection of explosive filler and metallic composition of the projectile body. An explosive of overly high brisance—the ability of an explosive to shatter a surrounding medium—will cause the projectile to shatter into fragments that are small and ineffective, as will a projectile body that is too brittle. An explosive that is of low brisance will result in fragments that are large and of low velocity and thereby of limited range. Projectile designers strive for a balance between explosive brisance and projectile metallurgy to deliver fragments of optimum size for the intended purpose. This is generally considered to be in the range of 150 to 750 grains for effects on both materiel and personnel. Most HE shells of conventional design, however, deliver no more than 60 to 75 percent of fragments in this range. This limitation led to the development of controlled-fragmentation projectiles in the late 1960s, in which fragmentation and explosive effects are optimized to achieve greater effectiveness than conventionally designed HE rounds.

Another type of HE projectile is the improved conventional munition (ICM). ICMs carry a number of submunitions—for example, grenades or mines—that are ejected from the base of the shell over the intended target or in an area in which targets might occur. Developments in this type of munition have resulted in a dual-purpose, improved conventional munition (DPICM) that is effective against both light armored vehicles and personnel. Developmental ICMs carry submunitions that, when ejected over the target, will seek out and destroy armored vehicles using millimeter-wave radar and infrared seekers. This type of munition is characteristic of the U.S. Army seek-and-destroy armor (SADARM) program, which utilizes either 155mm or 203mm projectiles to carry the SADARM submunitions.

Armor piercing. There are two basic types of AP ammunition: kinetic energy and chemical energy. The former defeats the armor by a combination of pressing, spiking, or punching its way through. Pressing fractures the armor by overstraining it; spiking defeats the armor by forcing the armor material aside as it strikes at a very high velocity; punching defeats the armor by punching its way through, actually pushing a plug the size of the projectile diameter out of the armor plate. A typical kinetic-energy AP round is a fin-stabilized, discarding-sabot tracer round (APFSDS-T). In this type, the weapon bore is unrifled, although APFSDS-T rounds are used in rifled guns. Smoothbore guns are capable of higher velocities because the problem of swaging is eliminated. The capability of a kinetic-energy projectile to defeat armor is a function of its weight and velocity; higher velocity generally results in greater penetration. When fired, the light metal sabot surrounding the arrow-shaped penetrator falls away, leaving the penetrator to fly to the target. Penetrators were originally made of tungsten alloy steel, but they are now constructed of depleted uranium, a very heavy alloy of uranium that has little radioactivity but is very hard and heavy in comparison to its overall size. Most smoothbore cannons are employed in tanks. The first was fitted to the Soviet T-62 in the 1960s, and such cannons have been adopted by the Bundeswehr in the Leopard II. The same 120mm gun used by the Germans is fitted to the U.S. M1A1 tank.

Chemical-energy ammunition is usually associated with shaped-charge (also known as hollow-charge) ammunition. The principle of the shaped charge lies in the fact that an explosive, usually cylindrical, with a cavity at one end will inflict more damage than an equivalent charge without the cavity. Most shaped-charge cavities are lined with a material such as copper. To achieve maximum effect, they are detonated some distance from their targets.

The shaped charge is detonated at its base. Detonation waves pass over the liner, causing it to collapse upon itself. When the collapsing liner reaches the axis of the detonating warhead, it forms two parts. A small portion forms a high-velocity jet while the bulk of the charge forms a slower moving but more massive slug. The jet is responsible for the deep penetration of the shaped charge. The jet itself varies in velocity along its length, with the tip moving at about 7,500 meters (25,000 ft.) per second while the base moves at approximately 1,500 meters (5,000 ft.) per second. This is caused by the mass of the liner increasing as it collapses while the amount of explosive remaining to move it decreases. Thus, the elements of the liner reach the axis of the charge at progressively lower velocities, which causes the formation of a jet with various velocities along its length.

When the jet strikes armor, or any material, it generates tremendously high pressures, typically 4^{10} pounds per square inch (psi), which cause both the target and the jet to deform hydrodynamically. The jet and material displaced from the target merge together and flow radially until the jet is used up or its velocity falls below a critical point and penetration ceases. The depth of penetration into a given material is directly proportional to the length of the jet and the square root of its density, which is considered to be the same as the original liner material. Depth of penetration is also dependent on the strength of the target material.

The more time a jet has to form the better, as it will have more time to lengthen and increase penetration. This is true, however, only up to a point, because once a certain jet length is reached, the jet separates into discrete particles that no longer stretch and the jet length becomes constant. Once this point is reached, penetration falls off because of an inherent asymmetry in shaped charges called "jet waver." In this phenomenon, the separate particles tend to follow different paths and thus do not contribute to the penetration already attained. This condition sets in very shortly after optimum standoff; this is why spaced armor and standoff devices are very effective against normal shaped charges. Reactive armor, which explodes on impact of a shaped-charge jet, is also effective because the jet is displaced and separated into particles. Several shaped-charge countermeasures against both spaced and reactive armor have been developed. One is a tandem-shaped-charge warhead in which a small charge makes the initial penetration and a larger charge follows to defeat the main armor.

The design of shaped charges compensates for the characteristics of the warhead or projectile into which they are fitted. For example, a shaped charge designed for a spinning projectile will have flutes on its surface to induce tangential velocity on detonation, which counteracts the spin of the projectile and increases penetration.

The pizeoelectric element in the tip of the standoff spike generates an electrical charge on impact. This charge flows back through the wire lead to the point-initiating base-detonating (PIBD) fuze and detonates the charge. This round is designated a high-explosive antitank tracer (HEAT-T).

A third type of antiarmor ammunition is the high-explosive squash head (HESH) projectile, also known as high-explosive plastic (HEP). This type of ammunition was originally developed for attacking concrete fortifications, but it later came to be used against armored fighting vehicles. Rather than actually penetrating the armor, the HESH round explodes against the armor, causing a huge amount of spalling on the opposite side of the armor plate. The fragments resulting from this spalling ricochet throughout the inside of the vehicle, wrecking the interior and killing or injuring the crew. It is still in use by many armies, and is particularly favored by the British, but it is less effective against composite armors than are other types of antiarmor ammunition.

The newest development in antiarmor cannon ammunition is the guided artillery round exemplified by the U.S. M712 Copperhead. In this type of projectile, a laser designator–equipped forward observer calls for a fire mission from a remote artillery unit. The projectile's code detector is keyed by the gun crew to match that of the observer. When the projectile is fired, fins are deployed by centrifugal force, and after a time delay, the main batteries activate and the projectile wings deploy. The projectile then receives and decodes the laser energy that is reflected from the target by the forward observer. It steers itself into a gliding intercept path to the target while the fuze electrically arms the warhead. When it hits the target, the Copperhead projectile functions as a conventional HEAT round.

Chemical ammunition is filled with a chemical agent such as mustard, a nerve agent, or some other type of chemical. It is usually associated with poison gas of some sort but may also include smoke ammunition such as white phosphorus. In most international treaty definitions chemical ammunition encompasses those munitions that deliver a substance intended for use in military operations to kill, seriously injure, or incapacitate personnel through physiological effects. Primary types of chemical ammunition in use today are nerve agents, either persistent (V-agent) or nonpersistent (G-agent); mustard (blister) agents; and tear gas. Binary nerve agent projectiles have also been developed. In these rounds, two chemicals, which by themselves are not poisonous, are contained in the same projectile. Once fired, the chemicals are mixed and transformed into a highly toxic nerve agent. Chemical ammunition has not been used on a wide scale by a major power since World War I. The United States, however, used tear gas in Vietnam, and there have been scattered reports of a chemical agent having been used by the Soviet Union in Afghanistan. Because chemical ammunition is relatively cheap, it has been used in several Third World conflicts, notably by Iraq in the recent Persian Gulf War against Iran.

Some countries also classify smoke ammunition as chemical munitions; for the sake of convenience they will be covered here, but they are not properly chemical ammunition. Smoke ammunition includes WP and a variety of screening smokes, such as hexachloroethane-zinc (HC). In addition to creating smoke, white phosphorus causes casualties and is effective as a high explosive. It burns on contact with air and can be extinguished only by immersion in water or by otherwise cutting off its air supply. Smoke shells are used for a variety of purposes, including spotting charges for artillery, but they are most commonly used to screen troops from enemy observation. Advances in smoke technology have given smoke shells new life as countermeasures against thermal imagers. These are referred to as multispectral smokes, because they cover more than one wavelength of the electromagnetic spectrum, including not only visible light but also infrared, ultraviolet, radio, and radar waves. Smoke projectiles may be of either the bursting or base-ejecting type; screening smokes are usually white while signaling smokes are various colors.

Traditionally, canister ammunition had no explosive charge and consisted of a projectile filled with a large number of slugs, balls, pellets, or flechettes enclosed in a light metal casing. It has been used for many years by artillery for close defense and in tank cannons against personnel. Conventional canister ammunition functions in a manner similar to that of a huge shotgun. The latest canister rounds may be filled with balls or flechettes. When fired, they eject forward from the projectile in a conical pattern propelled by a base charge. When loaded with flechettes, such modern canister rounds are often referred to as "beehive ammunition."

In one significant respect, the modern "beehive" and similar canister ammunition is really a version of a now-obsolete form of artillery ammunition called shrapnel. It was so named after its early nineteenth-century inventor, British general Sir Henry Shrapnel. The principal differences between shrapnel and the traditional canister are (1) an explosive charge in the shrapnel projectile shell permitted it to be a long-range version of canister; and (2) a time fuze set so as to detonate the internal explosive charge as the shrapnel projectile's trajectory approached the ground. In this way, the shrapnel projectile sprayed the contents of its shell against targets on the ground just before the projectile would otherwise strike the surface. The contents were usually steel or lead balls, often about 12 centimeters (almost 5 in.) in diameter. Shrapnel was the principal antipersonnel artillery ammunition of World War I. Toward the end of that war, however, shrapnel began to be displaced by an HE shell with a time fuze also set to detonate as the projectile approached the ground. It became evident that the jagged fragments from an HE shell were substantially more lethal—and thus more effective—than were the pellets of the shrapnel shell. Further, it was more cost-effective to use an HE shell for both antipersonnel and antimateriel targets. Except to use up old stocks of ammunition, shrapnel was little used in World War II, and it is not believed that (except for the "beehive version") shrapnel ammunition has been produced since about 1940.

The term *shrapnel* has been widely misused by nonartillerymen since the closing months of World War I. The origin of this misuse seems to have been reports by British surgeons on their treatment of wounds. Apparently aware that shrapnel had been the principal artillery ammunition against personnel, the surgeons began to refer to shell fragments as "shrapnel." This misuse of the word *shrapnel* was quickly adopted by journalists. And so it has become common practice to refer to shell fragments (quite incorrectly) as shrapnel and to wounds inflicted by such fragments as shrapnel wounds.

Another even-more-obsolete version of canister was grapeshot. These were large pellets, iron or lead, often about 2.5 centimeters (1 in.) in diameter, that were held together by a wire net or some adhesive compound rather than being enclosed in a container, as was canister. Grapeshot was a short-range antipersonnel ammunition, like canister, and was widely used in the eighteenth and early nineteenth centuries. It was certainly in use as late as the Mexican War (1846–48), and some grapeshot may have been used as late as the American Civil War.

Illuminating ammunition is used to light an area at night in order to detect targets. Illuminating projectiles are base ejecting and consist of an open-ended projectile filled with a magnesium compound attached to a parachute. The illuminant is packed in the forward position of the projectile with the parachute and its shroud lines toward the rear. A small ejecting charge of black powder is fired by a mechanical time fuze that expels the illuminating flare from the projectile while simultaneously igniting the flare's first-fire composition. As the flare is ejected from the projectile, the parachute deploys, allowing the flare to slowly descend. Typically, the luminosity of illuminating projectiles ranges from 450,000 to 1,000,000 candlepower lasting from 60 to 120 seconds depending on the size of the projectile and the composition of the flare.

Rocket-assisted and base-bleed artillery ammunition are described separately because of their unique characteristics. Both represent efforts to achieve greater range than possible with conventional projectiles, although each is a different approach to the problem. Rocket-assisted projectiles have a rocket motor to boost their range. The first efforts at rocket-assisted ammunition for artillery were undertaken by the Germans during World War II. They were able to achieve experimental ranges of up to 200 kilometers (120 mi.), although accuracy was poor. The latter has always been a problem for the rocket-assisted projectile (RAP) designer because the gradual consumption of the rocket's fuel during the flight of the projectile upsets the balance of the projectile, which results in pitching and yawing. The Germans solved this problem by placing the rocket motor in the center of the shell and venting it through side nozzles or through a long center tube. The yaw problem persists, however, because any deviation from trajectory at the time of rocket firing results in inaccuracy. RAP ammunition is a compromise.

Base-bleed projectiles represent another approach to extending the range of artillery projectiles. Base-bleed projectiles have a small chamber filled with propellant in the base of the projectile. This propellant ignites and "bleeds out" the base of the projectile, filling the low pressure area created by the passage of the round through the air and thereby reducing drag. The effect of base bleeding has been to extend by as much as 20 percent the range of 155mm artillery projectiles.

AMMUNITION FOR MORTARS

In the West, mortars are defined as muzzle-loaded, indirect-fire weapons that may have either a smooth or rifled bore, although the former is more common (Fig. 3). Mortars have shorter ranges than howitzers and employ a higher angle of fire. A mortar tube (barrel) is usually 10 to 20 calibers in length. A few large-caliber mortars, such as the Soviet 240mm mortar, are breech loaded. Most mortar projectiles are different from artillery ammunition in that they are "tear drop" shaped and fin stabilized. Because of this shape, mortar projectiles are often referred to as "bombs" even though they are not true bombs. The fin assembly is screwed into the base of the projectile. Mortar projectiles are also lighter in construction than artillery projectiles because chamber pressures and setback forces are far lower than in cannons and howitzers. Since most mortars are smoothbore, they have no rotating band and usually contact the bore of the weapon at two places. One is on the forward portion of the mortar projectile, where older mortar rounds had a series of machined bands called the gas check. More modern mortar projectiles have an obturator rather than a gas check. The

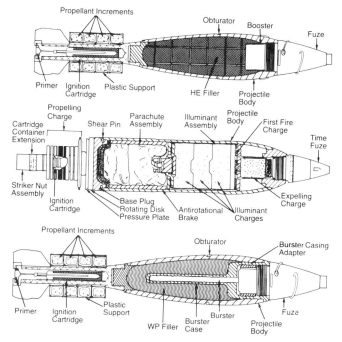

Figure 3. Typical mortar projectiles. (SOURCE: U.S. Army)

other bearing surface is the outside portion of the fins. A few mortars, such as the U.S. 4.2-inch (107mm) rifled mortar, use projectiles similar in appearance to artillery projectiles. This type of mortar projectile is spin stabilized rather than fin stabilized, but otherwise it has characteristics similar to "tear drop" mortar projectiles. Early versions of this type of projectile had rotating disks instead of bands, but the latest 107mm mortar projectiles have rotating bands and are very similar in appearance to artillery projectiles, except for the projectile base spike to retain the propellant increments. Mortars have been traditionally used as area weapons inasmuch as they lack the accuracy of guns and howitzers. Developments in munitions technology have resulted in mortar ammunition with a homing capability for use against armor. Mortar ammunition in this category includes the Bussard projectile manufactured by Diehl of West Germany; the Stryx munition by Saab-Scania of Sweden; and the Merlin terminally guided projectile produced by British Aerospace.

In their role as "the infantryman's artillery," mortars use a variety of ammunition similar to that used in artillery guns and howitzers. A panoply of munitions is available, from conventional HE to "smart munitions." Only direct-fire antitank ammunition is not available for mortars. With the widening use of the 120mm mortar as standard in most armies, it will be only a matter of time until ICMs and DPICMs find their way into mortar use.

The HE mortar in Figure 3 illustrates the construction of a typical mortar projectile. The mortar fuze is similar to that utilized in an artillery round. It may be of any one of a number of types. Like the artillery projectile, the mortar round has a steel body that carries the filler of explosives or other material. Unlike artillery projectiles, most mortar rounds have a fin assembly (includes the tail boom and fins). Inside the tail boom are a primer and an ignition cartridge that set off the propellant increments to launch the projectile out of the mortar tube. Like the separate bags of propellant and charges used in artillery ammunition, mortar increments are used to achieve variations in range. Virtually all mortar rounds, whether spin or fin stabilized, consist of a fuze, body, and tail boom. Those rounds that are spin stabilized lack fins.

The functioning of mortar rounds is different from artillery, or even small arms, in that the majority of mortars remains the only modern weapon that is muzzle loaded. Those few mortars that are breech loaded are very large caliber and are in service primarily with forces of the former Soviet Union and its allies. Having selected the appropriate charge for firing, the mortar man removes increments to adjust the range. The fuze is set, in the case of mechanical time or proximity fuzes, and the mortar round is dropped down the tube of the weapon, which contains a fixed firing pin in the base cap of the tube. When the projectile strikes the firing pin, the primer fires, igniting the ignition charge, which in turn ignites the propellant increments, firing the round.

Other than the firing procedure and the design of the projectile itself, the differences between mortar rounds and artillery projectiles is one of degree. The functioning of mortar and artillery projectiles after firing is similar and the range of munitions available for both is likewise congruent. As can be seen from the accompanying illustrations, the general designs of mortar rounds of HE, chemical, smoke, and illuminating types differ little from their artillery cousins. The newest developments in mortar ammunition are the antiarmor "smart munitions." Instead of being like the "area weapons" of the past, these mortar rounds are highly accurate projectiles that seek their targets through millimeter wave radar, infrared seeker, or semiactive laser sensors. In the case of the millimeter wave radar and infrared seekers, the round is fired toward an area where a target is known to be located. No further action on the part of the crew is necessary. Once over the target area, the seeker "looks down" onto the battlefield. When it acquires a target, the seeker "locks on" and guides the projectile to it using either wings or canards that are folded until after launch. These mortar rounds carry a shaped-charge warhead capable of defeating the top armor on almost any known tank. The functioning of this type of warhead is the same as that in HEAT ammunition.

AMMUNITION FOR RECOILLESS RIFLES

A final type of artillery ammunition is that for recoilless rifles. The projectiles for such weapons are similar to those fired from traditional guns and howitzers, but the functioning of the recoilless gun is quite different from any other, and as such it deserves mention.

A recoilless gun consists of a light artillery tube and a lightweight mount. Recoilless guns are typically employed by infantry as antitank artillery, although most fire a variety of ammunition. The tube is open at both ends. The recoil of fired rounds is counterbalanced by the thrust of gases generated by the burning of the propellant. The thrust of the burning gases acts as if it were a "rocket motor" to offset the recoil of the gun. Recoilless guns can be constructed in a far lighter configuration than other weapons of similar caliber. The lack of recoil and the light weight of the recoilless gun is offset somewhat by the back blast inherent in such weapons. In larger calibers, the back blast can be lethal to personnel who are caught in it.

While recoilless guns fire HE, HEAT, and other munitions, their propellant cases are different, characterized by many perforations to allow propellant gases to escape when the weapon is fired. Some recoilless gun ammunition uses a "blowout disk" instead of case perforations, but the effect is the same: release of propellant gases from the vent of the weapon.

Grenades

A grenade is a small explosive or chemical missile originally designed to be thrown by hand but currently capable of being fired from a variety of launchers that may be fitted to the end of a rifle or carbine barrel or attached underneath. In the latter instance, the grenade is a small cartridge of fixed ammunition in the 30mm to 40mm range. The projectile warhead contains an explosive, smoke, illuminating, or shot grenade. This type of weapon was originally developed in the 1960s for use with the U.S. M-79 grenade launcher, a single-shot weapon that resembles a single-barreled, break-open shotgun. Grenades launched from the end of a rifle barrel either are specifically designed as rifle grenades or are hand grenades adapted for the purpose. Traditionally, rifle grenades required the use of special cartridges, but developments have led to the introduction of "bullet trap" rifle grenades. While this concept is not new, previous efforts at firing rifle grenades using standard ammunition have not been especially successful. Generally, grenades are classified as either hand or rifle, but there are several variations of both types.

Hand grenades are among the oldest firearms, having been in use almost since the recorded advent of gunpowder. Early hand grenades were simply earthenware pots filled with black powder and a fuze that were dropped or thrown at the enemy. Such grenades were used to defend fortifications. By the seventeenth century, specialized grenadier units were formed to carry and throw grenades. Many such units later became elite elements within their national military establishment. All hand grenades consist of a body, a filler, and a fuze. Modern hand grenades are classified as to purpose and type. They may be offensive or defensive and may be classed as fragmentation, incendiary, smoke, or antitank (the last category is rare). Most grenades have a fixed delay fuze that is activated by a pull ring. There is a safety lever, or "spoon," on the fuze and it prevents fuze actuation until after the grenade leaves the thrower's hand. Once the safety lever flies off, most grenades explode in three to five seconds.

The idea of a "rifle" grenade is also old. The first concept for launching a grenade from a musket dates to the seventeenth century. The rifle grenade did not develop until the early years of the twentieth century when grenade cups were introduced to allow firing grenades from service rifles. Such a grenade cup, the British 6.5cm grenade launcher, was officially in service from 1917 to 1962. During World War II, rifle grenades were developed by the Germans and Americans. These were fitted to a "spigot" attached to the muzzle of the rifle. The grenade had a hollow-tail assembly with fins and appeared very similar to a small mortar projectile. In use, the hollow-tail assembly was placed over the launcher "spigot" and a special cartridge was used to launch it. Rifle grenades have been developed that allow the use of standard ammunition to fire them. Most modern Western rifles have standardized integral grenade adapters on their muzzles that have eliminated the need for a separate grenade adapter, as "bullet trap" rifle grenades have begun the elimination of grenade cartridges.

Offensive grenades contain a high-explosive charge in a thin container and do most of their damage by demolition or lethal shock rather than by fragmentation, although some offensive grenades have a fragmentation effect. In this case, the fragments are designed to be of a range that is less than the distance the grenade can be hand thrown to allow an advancing soldier to throw his grenade without having to take cover from its fragments. "Stun grenades," developed for use in antiterrorist operations, are a form of offensive grenade with a loud report and vivid flash. These temporarily disorient victims in the vicinity of the explosion. They do not produce fragmentation or lethal blast effects.

Defensive grenades contain a high-explosive charge in a metallic body and achieve their effects primarily through fragments. The grenadier must take cover when he throws this type of grenade to prevent wounding himself because the range of the fragments is greater than the distance the grenade can be thrown.

Smoke grenades, like artillery and mortar smoke rounds, are used for screening and signaling. White smoke grenades are almost universally of the HC or WP types. Colored smoke grenades come in a variety of colors for use in signaling, especially for air-ground operations. The most common colors are red, green, yellow, and violet. The chemical compounds used in smoke grenades are identical to those used in artillery and mortar ammunition.

Incendiary grenades are used for starting fires. They are filled with thermite, a compound of iron oxide and aluminum powder that burns at a temperature of approximately 2,000 degrees Celsius. Incendiary grenades are widely used to destroy artillery and mortars when their capture is imminent; all that is necessary is to drop them down the weapon's barrel. Otherwise, WP is better suited to general incendiary effect under battlefield conditions because of its more widespread effects and the fact that few materials found on the battlefield require 2,000 degrees Celsius to ignite them.

Antitank grenades are used against armored vehicles, but they are rare in modern armies. All consist of a shaped charge and a stabilizing mechanism. In the case of the Soviet RGK-3 antitank grenade, for example, a small drogue parachute keeps the warhead of the grenade oriented after it is thrown. Such hand-thrown antitank grenades have little effect against all but the most lightly armored vehicles. Antitank rifle grenades are in widespread use by many armies, but their effectiveness against modern tanks in other than flank or rear shots is marginal.

Rockets

A rocket is a self-propelled vehicle whose trajectory cannot be controlled while it is in flight. It is propelled by hot gases ejected to the rear by a motor or a burning charge. Rockets are among the oldest weapons, having been used in Asia since the fourteenth century and in Europe since the eighteenth century, in essentially the same form as today. Rockets are used in a variety of roles by modern military forces on air, sea, and land. Rockets are launched from aircraft against ground and sea targets; at one time they were also used against other aircraft, but guided missiles supplanted them in that role. Rockets are extensively used by ground forces in multiple-launch rocket systems (MLRSs). These systems launch from 12 to 40 individual rockets ranging in caliber from 122mm to 240mm. Their primary advantage over conventional artillery lies in their ability to saturate a target area with a large number of warheads in a very short period of time. One battery of Soviet BM-27 or U.S. MLRS rockets can fire 64 or 48 rockets, respectively, almost simultaneously, while a cannon battery can fire only 6 or 8 rounds at one time. The accuracy of modern rocket artillery has improved since World War II. As of the early 1990s, rockets are being equipped with a variety of warheads in addition to traditional HE. Some rocket launching systems include not only HE but also ICM, DPICM, chemical, and terminal homing warheads for use against armored vehicles. These warheads function as do those employed in cannon artillery projectiles.

Rockets are also used as antitank weapons, mostly as last-ditch defenses by infantry. Such weapons were employed beginning in World War II and have continued in use to the present time. Almost all antitank rockets employ HEAT warheads and are disposable—that is, the rocket and launcher are issued as a complete round of ammunition and the launcher is thrown away after firing. A notable exception is the Soviet RPG-7 system, which not only launches a HEAT rocket but can also fire a number of other rocket-propelled projectiles. A few other countries manufacture systems similar to the RPG-7, but all work much like the original and many are outright copies of this venerable and effective system. These rockets, of marginal effectiveness against modern tanks utilizing composite armors, are of great utility in urban combat and against snipers and weapons' emplacements.

CHARLES Q. CUTSHAW

SEE ALSO: Artillery, Rocket and Missile; Artillery, Tube; Fuze; Grenade; Gun, Antitank; Machine Gun; Missile, Antitank Guided; Mortar; Munitions and Explosives Technology Applications; Small Arms.

Bibliography

Campbell, C., ed. 1987. *Understanding military technology.* New York: Gallery Books.
Courtney-Green, P. R. 1991. *Ammunition for the land battle.* Vol. 6 of *Land warfare: Brassey's new battlefield weapons systems and technology series.* London: Brassey's.
Germershausen, R., et al. 1982. *Rheinmetall handbook on weaponry.* English ed. Frankfurt am Main: Broenners Druckeri Breidenstein GmbH.
Hogg, I. 1985. *The illustrated encyclopedia of ammunition.* Secaucus, N.J.: Chartwell Books.
———. 1988. *The illustrated encyclopedia of artillery.* Secaucus, N.J.: Chartwell Books.
Miller, D., and C. Foss. 1987. *Modern land combat.* New York: Portland House.
Ohart, T. 1947. *Elements of ammunition.* New York: Wiley.
Quick, J. 1973. *Dictionary of weapons and military terms.* New York: McGraw-Hill.
U.S. Department of Defense, Joint Chiefs of Staff. 1987. *Department of Defense dictionary of military and associated terms.* Washington, D.C.: Government Printing Office.

ARMOR

Armor serves to protect men and vehicles on land, at sea, and in the air by means of protective covering and specialized equipment. The term *armor* is used here as a collective term for all armored combat vehicles.

Historical Development

By the early Bronze Age (ca. 3500 B.C.) primitive fighting among groups of Paleolithic men had evolved to include concepts of organized warfare. Protection against rocks, clubs, and arrows was provided by handheld shields, often of leather stretched and hardened over wooden frames, but all-wood and wicker shields were also used. Protective covering was also developed for the head, torso, and legs.

The dagger and the sword were the first new weapons of the metallic era, and bronze-reinforced shields, helmets, breast plates, and greaves evolved to become entirely made of bronze and later of iron. Early armor extended to horses and chariots, small armored carts drawn by one or more armor-clad horses. Prior to about 700 B.C. chariots constituted the elite force of ancient armies. The great Kurusch (Cyrus) of Persia is supposed to have built chariots for twenty warriors, who dismounted to continue fighting. This early version of the armored personnel carrier shows that the concept of delivering men swiftly, and protected, into fighting is not new.

Although the designed use of protective armor in warfare is limited only by the imagination, in practical application it is limited by the physical or mechanical ability to transport it about the battlefield. Before the industrial revolution made mechanization possible, the weight of armor used in combat was no more than could be borne by man or animal. Interesting applications appeared: Germanic warriors in the time of Ceasar used barricades of wagons, maneuvering these in close formation to engage Roman forces; in Italy in 1335 Guido Da Vigerano, and in 1482 Leonardo Da Vinci, designed armored combat vehicles, but they were too heavy to be of practical use; the use of protective wagons was revived and used by the Hussites in the fifteenth century; in Korea (ca. 1592–99), an ironclad ship in the shape of a tortoise helped defeat a Japanese fleet.

By the end of the Middle Ages (ca. 1400–1500), refinements in metalworking had advanced to the point where further improvements to armor would be only marginal or would reduce mobility. Mounted knights, heavily clad in protective chain mail, armor plate, and helmets, their horses similarly encased, represented the elite shock troops of the day (Fig. 1). The evolution of weapons had generally surpassed the ability of armor to keep pace. The famous English longbow (of Welsh origin) had good penetrating power even at long ranges; crossbows were lethal at close range; determined Swiss pikemen could unseat a heavy cavalry charge. Most importantly, however, technology enabled the fielding of a new class of weapons—gunpowder cannon and small arms.

Gunpowder was known in China as early as the eleventh century and made its way to Europe via East-West trade routes in the thirteenth century. The first gunpowder cannons in Europe were used in the early 1300s; small arms made their appearance in the latter half of the century.

The use of gunpowder began a new era of warfare. The armor of knights could not withstand projectiles propelled by gunpowder. With cannons, muskets, mortars, and later rifles and modern artillery, it became possible to fight an enemy from increasingly greater distances. As technology progressed, the rate of fire, range, and penetration power increased and handling became easier. Body armor for man and beast, already heavily leveraged by its weight, could not keep pace. Thereafter, efforts to improve protection and maintain mobility focused on a revival of the chariot. Various experiments included: a

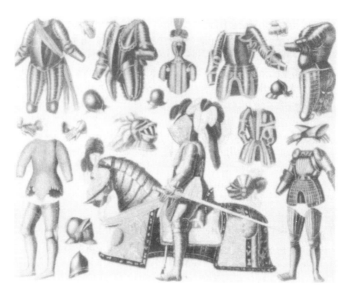

Figure 1. Examples of European armor in the Middle Ages.
(SOURCE: U.S. Library of Congress)

Scottish war chariot from the year 1456; a war chariot by Vaturio in 1472; a war chariot by Holzschuher in 1558; an armored steam tractor by Applegarth in 1886; and an armored wagon by Batter in 1888.

The object of these developmental efforts was to direct fire on the enemy and to make renewed use of mobility, which had brought the knight success. The power to move these vehicles, however, was insufficient. Muscle power was inadequate, and steam power was too cumbersome. The internal combustion engine would eventually improve to the point where it could provide a solution, but not until World War I.

With the introduction of the machine gun, in addition to the repeating rifle, the fire cadence of the individual soldier became equivalent to that of a whole company previously, and cover, or protection, from enemy fire increased dramatically in importance. The soldier dug his foxhole, and trench warfare began.

Otto's internal combustion engine led to Daimler's motor vehicle and soon to the idea of armoring the latter, thus making it a mobile means of combat. In the dynamics of modern combat, mobility had once again become significant. One of the first armored vehicles of modern times was built by Austro-Daimler in 1904. The prototype was remarkable for its revolving turret with built-in machine gun and all-wheel drive. It earned no recognition, however, and was never produced.

Ten years later, the Belgian army became the first to use vehicle-mounted machine guns in combat against attacking German troops. The Minerva armored fighting vehicle saw action in the autumn of 1914, and the British and French soon followed this example. The German supreme command did not decide to use this means of combat until 1916.

Because they lacked cross-country mobility, these armored vehicles were forced to stay on hard-surface roads, and street fighting did not provide opportunities to prove the value of these armored vehicles. These limitations were recognized before the war, and motivated Austrian first lieutenant Burstyn to develop a combat vehicle that was inspired by the idea of sliding bands, or caterpillars. These endless bands of wire netting mounted over two wheels offered armored vehicles a cross-country capability.

Burstyn's idea for a small, fast armored vehicle with caterpillar treads, however, was rejected by the same institutions that had rejected Daimler's fighting vehicle. Germany acknowledged the need for a chain-driven combat vehicle only after the British, under the code name "Tank," developed and fielded a treaded armored vehicle in World War I in 1916.

Development of the Tank

The British First Lord of the Admiralty, Winston Churchill, had the mobility of sea warfare in mind when he called for the development of "land ships" in 1915 to break the deadlocked trench warfare on the Western front. William Foster and E. D. Swinton conceived the first heavy battle tank. It weighed 27 tons, was adapted to the speed of marching soldiers, and was intended to accompany them when overcoming enemy field fortifications. Although their first use, at Flers-Courcelette on 15 September 1916, involved heavy losses because the crews were inexperienced, some tanks succeeded in making a deep penetration that reached their objectives and overpowered all resistance. This success led the army command to give orders for further production.

World War I Operational Doctrine and Technical Limitations

The introduction of tanks implied a return to mobile warfare. For the first time since the days of knights in armor, there was a sufficiently compact source of energy (the internal combustion engine) to make effective armored vehicles possible. The tank afforded protection against fire and made possible the penetration of the trench systems. This had the same effect on warfare as catapults of the early Middle Ages: fortifications were breached and provided the foot soldier with access to the defenders.

The first tanks had limited mobility and thus were confined to overcoming field fortifications while simultaneously holding down enemy infantry fire and affording covering fire to their own accompanying infantry. Although technology had broken the deadlock on the Western front, the infantry escort tank was developed on a narrow technical base: the motorized vehicle was not yet twenty years old, gear technology for heavy vehicles was very rudimentary, and the track and suspension configuration was based on that of U.S. Caterpillar farm tractors.

Interwar Period

After the end of the war, opinions on the operational potential of the tank diverged. Although the idea of tank warfare originated in Great Britain, no logical consequences followed their experience in combat. The British expert

Liddell Hart described modern operational possibilities for the tank, but prior to World War II all Western countries, with the exception of Germany, had forgone the opportunities inherent in the tank.

By contrast, the German Wehrmacht paid attention to the lessons of the war and the German general staff listened to the suggestions, proposals, and reflections of Liddell Hart. After Hitler's rearmament, a modern tank force was organized. General Guderian created independent tank divisions equipped with new combat tanks that were fast and well-armored. The objectives of mobility, firepower, and protection had been achieved, and German tanks, operating on roads or across country and formed into independent divisions, became tools for Hitler's lightning war (blitzkrieg).

In addition to combat tanks, the Wehrmacht produced combat vehicles, known as assault guns, to support the infantry. These assault guns emphasized firepower, were more lightly armored than combat tanks, and took over the task of accompanying the infantry during an attack. The idea was to use these guns, mounted in a mobile casemate, primarily against machine gun emplacements to open a breach for the infantry.

World War II

At the beginning of the war, antiarmor weapons and munitions technology had not kept pace with tank armor. As the penetrating power of shells fired from antitank guns improved, however, armor plating on tanks was also thickened and improved. This increase in armor led to an increase in weight, and some tanks at the end of the war weighed more than 70 tons. Because engine power did not keep up with increases in weight, tank mobility began to suffer. The development of the hollow-cone, or shaped-charge ammunition provided the capability to defeat even the most heavily armored tank by the end of the war.

On the Eastern front, the strengthening of the Russian adversary brought an end to the success of the blitzkrieg, and the war degenerated into defensive combat against advancing tanks, first on the Russian and then on the German side. The combat tank turned into an antitank means of combat. The criticism of Liddell Hart was: "The wastage of such an effective force as the tank corps, by using it to combat enemy tank forces, is as foolish as the chess-player who opens his game by disposing of the queens."

Both sides followed this criticism and developed vehicles on the basis of tanks, but without a turret and with a high-velocity gun mounted in a casemate. These weapons, well armored at the front, usually had better cannons than an equivalent battle tank, but the mounting restricted movement in traverse and they were not suited to unaided defense. These tank destroyers were known as the "best tank killers."

The fighting doctrine was not to engage in battles of long duration, but to conduct short operations of limited length and proportions. The basic principle was the formation of points of main effort (i.e., concentration of greatest fighting capacity at decisive points).

Post-World War II

During the war the effect of the tank corps had been considerable, but the concluding event—the dropping of two atomic bombs on Japan by the United States—brought a momentous turn to world history. For a time, the tank seemed to have lost significance; atomic weapons had made all others obsolete. The Soviet development of atomic weapons and intercontinental ballistic missiles to deliver them seemed to result in a nuclear standoff between East and West, but this view proved illusory. Tanks again became important: in a conventional war without nuclear weapons, tanks would be a critical feature; in a war with nuclear weapons, the tank offered the best protection against blast, heat, and radiation of nuclear bursts.

Tank designers reevaluated the parameter of mobility. Hit probability by ballistic missiles and rockets is largely dependent on the maneuverability and acceleration of the tank and on its dimensions or outline. The operating range of tanks was extended, and lower fuel consumption was emphasized even as engines became more powerful. Maintenance features received attention; high reliability and thus high availability were deemed necessary for defenders who might be outnumbered.

The parameter of firepower was also studied in terms of system stability during firing, and fire control. Accuracy at ranges beyond 2,000 meters (6,600 ft.) was improved, and sighting systems aided fast target acquisition. Emphasis was placed on improved munitions in terms of an increase in caliber and in the penetration and detonation characteristics of the warhead.

When the Bundeswehr recommended tank development, it emphasized protection through mobility, an example that was followed by other countries. New armor protection developed in the late 1960s (armored bulkhead plating, compound plating) was further strengthened by the use of reactive armor. With these technical advances in protective materials, aided by improved engines, the parameter values of mobility and of protection became equivalent for the first time. This, combined with improved firepower through better ammunition and electronic fire control systems, gives the present-day tank an almost inconceivable fighting value in the dynamic course of any future conflict.

The Tank and Combined-Arms Concepts

The original combat tanks were successful from a tactical point of view, but they were unable to hold their own for any length of time in captured territory without the coordinated support of other combat arms. The assistance in combat of infantry, artillery, engineers, scouts, and air support is vital to ensure the operational success of tank warfare.

INFANTRY

The British acquired the following basic knowledge from the first tank operations in World War I:

- The speed of the tank assault is determined by the accompanying infantry. A slow attack pace gave the defender time to take countermeasures in the depths of the battlefield.
- If the tank broke through without infantry, it became an easy target for the defender, especially if he could keep his nerve and had tank destroyer weapons at hand.

Successful attempts that breached defenses, therefore, were only successful if the infantry was brought up rapidly with the tanks and with necessary protection from small arms and shell bursts. The British experimentally developed the first armored personnel carrier (APC), the Mark IX. After World War I, the French were the first to construct a combat vehicle for transporting infantrymen on the basis of a 15-ton lorry. The armored plating contained apertures for firing during mounted combat.

Some early theories expounded noncooperative "all-tank" themes. In 1919 J. F. C. Fuller, then chief of staff of the British tank corps command, presented "Plan 1919," in which he defined the question of collaboration between tanks and infantry: "Up till now the prevailing theory for the tactical use of tanks revolved around the reconciliation of their strength with existing combat methods, i.e., with the infantry and artillery tactics. Indeed, the tank idea, which revolutionized warfare methods, was applied to a system it was destined to destroy." He concluded, "The infantry as equipped at present, will become first an auxiliary weapon and later an impracticable weapon on any territory which can be driven through by tanks." The crux of the statement was that the equipment of the infantry was unsatisfactory.

The German Wehrmacht did not accept this view and focused on turning infantrymen into motorized infantry. Using lightly armored semi-tracked vehicles, they were able to keep pace with tanks moving cross-country. The modern armored personnel carrier concept was born and gave the armored infantry the possibility for tank assault "instantly followed in quick succession by exploitation and supplementation" (Guderian). The combination and cooperation of the battle tank with the APC in the German Wehrmacht created the basis for the blitzkrieg successes.

After World War II, the Bundeswehr retained this concept. It was consistent with the experience of military organizers and with the ideas of the Anglo-American expeditionary corps, evolving from their experiences. Initially, the Bundeswehr used American equipment and vehicles, but soon began development of its own fully tracked armored personnel carrier, and later, the development of a German main battle tank.

By the 1970s, the concept of combining mechanized infantry in APCs with tank forces was well developed. The German Marder (the original Western armored personnel carrier) pioneered the concept with the Leopard I tank. The former Soviet Union's version of the APC, the multi-wheeled BTR-70, was used in a similar role. The U.S. M-113 was replaced in the 1980s by the M-2 and M-3 Bradley Infantry Fighting Vehicle (IFV) and Cavalry Fighting

Vehicle (CFV), and emphasis continued on cooperation between the two combat arms.

One drawback of mechanized and motorized infantry forces is the relatively light armor plating of APCs and IFVs. Increasing the armor protection is impractical for several reasons: cost; battlefield mobility; and vehicle size, or payload.

Armored personnel carriers are designed to carry an infantry squad of 8 to 12 soldiers. In the attack, it is important that the infantry be delivered into the breach made by tanks as quickly as possible. Armored and mechanized tactics have adapted so that the APCs follow the tanks instead of being commingled with them, where they would become initial targets for antiarmor systems. The U.S. Bradley has somewhat offset this, but it is still a far more vulnerable vehicle than a main battle tank.

Some critics have suggested that the proliferation of effective antitank weapons, especially antitank guided missiles (ATGM), will lead to the end of mobile tank warfare. The 1973 October War led to intensive analysis of the value of the combat tank in light of the numerous successes of antitank missiles. The French military historian Mischke implied that the tank had reached its limit of development and cost effectiveness. He cited that in the first 10 days of the October War 2,700 of 6,000 tanks involved had been destroyed.

Counterarguments that focused on tactical countermeasures for antitank defenses prevailed, however, and the Israelis succeeded in breaking through Arab antitank systems and restored the full mobility of their tanks. The prerequisite for the restoration of offensive mobility was the optimal collaboration of all arms, the infantry in particular. At the beginning of the war the cooperation of Israeli armor and infantry was minimal and lacked a strong collaborative structure. When this was changed and an effective structure implemented as a battlefield tactic, the war turned in favor of the Israelis.

ARTILLERY

Indirect-fire support units form the essential third leg of the combat triad of armor, infantry, and artillery. As a consequence of increasingly effective methods of counterbattery artillery fire, improvements in artillery protection resulted in lightly armored, self-propelled artillery howitzers.

Improvements in artillery-delivered munitions, such as scatterable mines and smart munitions, have been a cause of concern for tanks and APCs. Concepts for employment have varied and depend on the situation. To achieve surprise, German attacks in World War II often held the use of artillery until the last moment, or it was not used at all. Blitzkreig emphasized dive-bombers in providing fire support for attacking tanks, and surprise was often achieved because there was no extensive artillery preparation to give away the plan.

In contrast, extensive use of artillery fire in support of attacking armor and mechanized formations was used in Operation Desert Storm (February 1991). Artillery rockets were used in a counterbattery role and to scatter mines to deny Iraqi forces maneuverability. Howitzer fire suppressed Iraqi formations, pinning them so that tank-gun fire and infantry antitank guided missile fire could have maximum effect.

Armored, self-propelled mortars are also a feature of indirect fire-support weapons. At firing ranges of 6 to 8 kilometers (approx. 4 to 5 mi.) self-propelled mortars come into their own, with a firing efficiency greater than that of longer-range artillery pieces. Originally mounted in caterpillar-tracked chassis, they have evolved with all-around protection against shell splinters, small-arms fire, and possible nuclear, biological, and chemical (NBC) attack.

ENGINEERS

Antitank mines were one of the early devices used to stop or slow tanks and deny them use of terrain. Mines can be effective in destroying a tank, but often they take them out of action by damaging a tread, thus eliminating their mobility. Other methods of hindering tank advances involve tank ditches and traps and uncrossable blocks of concrete (dragon teeth).

To counter these obstacles, the support of combat engineers is necessary. Engineer tanks, equipped with dozer blades, mine-clearing flails or wheels, excavator shovels, and jib cranes, help to fill trenches, clear paths through mine fields, and breach obstacles. In defensive operations, engineer tanks can help prepare defilade fighting positions for tanks and APCs.

An interesting feature of combat engineer vehicles is the armored vehicle launched bridge (AVLB). The AVLB is a bridge-laying tank with the turret removed and replaced by a bridge with powered hydraulics to extend the frame in scissors or cantilever fashion. AVLBs have protection against small arms and shell fragments and can accommodate spans from 15 to 20 meters (50 to 66 ft.) over rivers and ditches.

ARMORED SCOUTS

Despite electronic, optronic, and optical reconnaissance by aircraft, drones, and satellites, the tank corps still cannot dispense with the human scout: the reconnaissance soldier. In mechanized fighting, the scout is equipped with an armored reconnaissance vehicle, a lightly armored combat vehicle that emphasizes silent operation, obstacle negotiations capabilities (e.g., fording, flotation, and water navigation), maneuverability, and a low profile.

The use of optical, optronic, and electronic sensors, combined with a long-range method of communication and precise navigation instruments, enable a scout patrol leader to carry out comprehensive missions and transmit findings quickly to appropriate command levels. Because reconnaissance vehicles are only lightly protected by armor plate, a good scout will avoid becoming involved in combat as far as possible.

The armament on reconnaissance vehicles varies from light machine guns to antitank missiles in accordance with different concepts for their use. The U.S. M-3 Bradley is used as a scouting vehicle with armored and mechanized forces and is designed to withstand more punishment than lighter scout vehicles such as the versatile French Panhard VBL. The M-3 also mounts TOW ATGMs, which can kill tanks at ranges exceeding 3,500 meters (approx. 2.5 mi.).

CLOSE AIR SUPPORT

Armored and mechanized forces derive a great benefit from the fire-support capability of attack helicopters and mission-specific aircraft such as the U.S. A-10 Warthog. By necessity, these flying machines cannot be too heavily armored, yet some armor plating around sensitive areas is incorporated into their design. More important is the contribution they make to the ground fighting forces by overcoming opposing armor and APCs with ATGMs, rockets, and rapid-firing mini-guns.

The value of attack helicopters is their high mobility and capability to deliver fire support quickly to different parts of the battlefield. Some modern concepts view the mobility advantage as permitting the tank to be replaced by the attack helicopter. In certain situations—surprise attack or where terrain is difficult—this may be partly true, but the attack helicopter is not intended to be an airborne replacement for the tank. Rather, the cooperation of this air arm with the ground arms remains as originally conceived.

OTHER ARMORED SUPPORT VEHICLES

With the possible exception of airborne and light infantry forces, armored protection of some sort has become ubiquitous in modern warfare. Armor plating has evolved from frontal shields on antitank guns of World War II to enclosures of the entire gun casemate mounted on a mobile platform today. Other armored fighting vehicles consist of self-propelled antitank missile launchers such as the combination BMP-1 with a Sagger ATGM mounted on top of its 73mm gun (Hungary) and self-propelled air defense tanks that use a search radar to acquire airborne targets and guide munitions to distances of 6 to 8 kilometers (approx. 4 to 5 mi.). In addition, there are armored recovery vehicles used to pull damaged tanks and APCs from the battlefield under fire and armored transport vehicles to deliver combat supplies to the fighting troops.

Combined-Arms Performance

The combat tank of today requires the support of other combat vehicles to guarantee an effective performance. In order to achieve optimal collaboration, the latter should have comparable mobility and protection. The combined armored forces should represent the synthesis of firepower, mobility, and protection. If one of the component arms lacks a particular characteristic, the combined force may be unable to fulfill its mission.

The main battle tank and the combat vehicles that support it can be the most potent tool in the hands of an aggressive commander. Operational possibilities of the combined armored force symbolize a potential for implementing aggressive policy; equally, they symbolize the ability to deter, or to defeat, such action.

Future Tank Development

Since their first use at Flers-Courcelette on 15 September 1916, tactics and technology have influenced, complemented, and made demands on the primary tank features of firepower, mobility, and protection. Early ammunition has moved from high-explosive to shaped-charge to high-velocity, kinetic-energy rounds with pinpoint accuracy at increasing ranges. Electro-optic technology has vastly improved target acquisition, firing speed, and accuracy. Mobility has improved with advances in automotive technology that has continually increased the power-to-weight ratio of internal combustion engines. Protection has improved in terms of armor thickness (initially), improved steel plating techniques, and design of sloping front and sides. Although perhaps at an optimal position vis-à-vis trade-offs between the key parameters, there seems still to be room for improvement.

Future improvements in firepower will come from several sources: improved auto-loading mechanisms; larger-caliber warheads; so-called smart munitions with target recognition microelectronic guidance systems; higher-speed kinetic-energy penetrators powered by new propulsion mechanisms; and advances in intelligence collection, filtering, fusion, and distribution systems.

Of these, auto-loaders are of particular interest because they can lead to a reduction in crew size and thus to a different tank configuration. The possibility of automating, or of semi-automating, other crew functions is also being researched. Also of interest are developments in electromagnetic, or rail, guns that have demonstrated the ability to hurl rounds at hypervelocity speeds approaching 10 kilometers (6.2 mi.) per second. Power requirements at present prohibit the development and fielding of a practical weapon, but should one become possible, it is difficult to imagine armor that might provide protection from such a weapon.

Advances in mobility will come from either a reduction in the overall weight of the armored vehicle or an increase in engine power for the same weight of engine; gears and power train components will have to keep pace. Developments in lighter-weight engines with ceramic materials and lighter metal alloys have shown promise, particularly for aircraft engines. These advances could extend to engines for ground mobility platforms. Reductions in the weight of armor while maintaining the same protective capability can also contribute to improved mobility.

New classes of composite materials are being researched and developed for use in many applications. Lightweight plastic composites are used in some armor plating; other types of composite materials have already been used for body armor, and extensions of this existing technology may find applications in armored vehicles. Improvements in reactive armor plating may also be developed and can be a defense against both kinetic-energy rounds and shaped-charge rounds.

One possible future for armored vehicles is the combination into one system of the tank and the armored personnel carrier. If the power-to-weight ratio of engines can be increased and composite armor can afford the same protection for less weight, and if crew size can be reduced, it will be possible to combine tank and APC in one vehicle. This concept would be a further development of the Israeli combat tank Merkava (Chariot). The Merkava, with its engine and drivetrain forward, features a tank turret and space in its rear for 6 to 8 infantrymen. Improvement on this idea is possible and would not mean a reduction in fighting value. In sum, it would be cheaper than fielding a tank and an infantry APC team and could perform the same cooperative mission.

PAUL-WERNER KRAPKE

SEE ALSO: Armored Ground Vehicle; Blitzkrieg; Gun, Antitank; Helicopter, Battlefield; Mechanized Warfare; Tank.

Bibliography

Albrecht, W. 1973. *Gunther Burstyn (1879–1945) und die Entwicklung der Panzer-waffe.* Osnabrück: Biblio-Verlag.
Chamberlain, P., and Ellis, C. 1972. *Britische und amerikanische Panzer des Zweiten Weltkrieges.* München: Verlag Lehmann.
Dupuy, R. E., and T. N. Dupuy. 1986. *The encyclopedia of military history.* 2d rev. ed. New York: Harper and Row.
Eimannsberger, L., Ritter von. 1934. *Der Kampfwagen.* München: I. F. Lehmann Verlag.
Foss, C. F. 1971. *Armoured vehicles of the world.* London: Allan.
Frentag, Taktische und oerative Verwendung moderner Tanks in der Roten Armee. 1932. *Militär-Wochenblatt,* no. 3.
Fuller, I. F. 1937. *Erinnerungen eines freimütigen Soldaten.* Stuttgart: Rowolt Verlag.
Gaulle, C. de. 1935. *Frankreichs Stossarmee.* Potsdam: Voggenreiter.
Guderian, H. 1937. *Die Panzertruppe und ihr Zusammenwirken mit den anderen Waffen.* Berlin: Union Verlag.
———. 1952. *Erinnerungen eines Soldaten.* London: Michael Joseph.
———. 1957. *Panzer-Marsch.* München: Schild Verlag.
Heigl's Taschenbuch der Tanks. 1971. Teil III: *Der Panzerkampf.* München: Verlag Lehmann.
Hillgruber, A. 1940–41. *Hitler's Strategie Politik und Kriegführung.* Koblenz: Bernard und Graefe.
Hubatsch, W. 1958. *Hitler's Weisungen für die Kriegführung.* Frankfurt/Main: Verlag für Wehrwesen.
Justrow, K. 1938. *Der technische Krieg.* Berlin: Claasen-Verlag.
Krapke, P. W. 1986. *Leopard 2, sein Werden und seine Leistungen.* Herford: Mittler und Sohn.
Liddell Hart, B. H. 1940. *Das Buch vom Heer.* Potsdam: Voggenreiter.
Miksche, F. O. 1941. *Blitzkrieg.* London: Faber and Faber.
Mostowenko, W. D. 1940. *Panzer gestern und heute.* Berlin: Deutscher Militärverlag.
Nehring, W. K. 1974. *Die Geschichte der Panzerwaffe von 1916–1945.* Stuttgart: Propyläen Verlag.
Ogorkiewicz, R. R. 1960. *Armour.* London: Stevens and Sons.
Spannenkrebs, W. 1939. *Angriff mit Panzerkampfwagen.* Oldenburg: Gerhard Stolling.

ARMORED GROUND VEHICLE

Armored ground vehicles include tanks, infantry fighting vehicles, many self-propelled artillery weapons, armored cars, personnel carriers, cargo carriers, recovery vehicles, and fire direction centers. Usually, the design, equipment, and production of specialized vehicles are adapted from the basic design of the armored personnel carrier (APC) (Fig. 1).

Figure 1. A Soviet BTR-50 amphibious-tracked APC used in training exercises with U.S. Army units. (SOURCE: Robert F. Dorr Archives; U.S. Army)

An important example of this flexibility of design is the armored infantry fighting vehicle (AIFV), which can be adapted to serve for close air defense; as an antitank missile carrier; as a command post carrying communications systems; as an ambulance for medical first aid and evacuation; as a minelayer; as a mortar carrier; as an artillery forward observation platform; as a field workshop and a recovery vehicle; and for internal security.

Specialized Vehicles

The following descriptions of five important categories of armored ground vehicles will serve to illustrate the broad range of highly specialized roles for which these vehicles can be adapted.

RECONNAISSANCE VEHICLE

Reconnaissance vehicles are wheeled or tracked armored vehicles designed primarily for scouting and reconnaissance, either by visual observation or through the use of other detection methods. The key characteristics of these vehicles are a high degree of mobility, capability for long-distance deployment, and the ability to maneuver over rough ground even under hostile fire. These requirements mandate a certain degree of survivability linked to protection, but design compromises are required because adding armor sufficient to protect against heavy fire could increase vehicle weight to such a level that cross-country mobility would be impaired.

At present, no ideal design for a universal reconnaissance vehicle exists, and compromises tend to consider mission requirements as determined by military doctrine. Generally, wheeled, rather than tracked, armored vehicles have come to be used for a variety of low-intensity missions such as scouting, liaison, communications, and surveillance. This is because of their greater speed and mobility when used along established road networks and trafficable terrain and their more economical production and operation. More heavily armored tracked reconnaissance vehicles tend to be used when doctrine stipulates a more active role in fighting and where terrain is more difficult.

Amphibious capabilities are of paramount importance for reconnaissance vehicles, which should be able to navigate water obstacles and "move" at high speed in water rather than merely "swim" as other wheeled and tracked vehicles do. Hence positive propulsion by propellers or water jets is required. In some versions, the vehicle has a second driving position aft, which enables another member of the crew to drive the vehicle backward for a short distance should it become necessary to immediately disengage from contact with heavily armed enemy units. Reduced width of such vehicles is an important consideration, given that they are often required to move through wooded or built-up areas.

These 3- to 5-ton vehicles can typically transport up to six men, including the driver. The provision of large windows of bulletproof glass helps drivers to drive comfortably. An automatic weapon can be fired from within the vehicle over a frontal arc or from a small turret at the expense of a limited increase in weight. This modification can be adapted so as to be employed in counter-reconnaissance.

ARMORED INFANTRY FIGHTING VEHICLE

Armored infantry fighting vehicles (AIFV) give the infantryman a level of mobility comparable to that of the main battle tank (MBT) and a substantial degree of protection from enemy fire. The AIFV may be equipped with light, medium, or heavy turrets, and a variety of armaments, depending on its role.

Turrets may be either one-man or two-man. The first type is smaller and lighter and thus suited to light vehicles. In this configuration, only the gunner can occupy the turret, while the commander remains in the hull with a limited field of vision. In a two-man turret, the commander can override the gunner for all combat functions, besides making use of the installed optics and command devices. Achieving this advantage entails greater dimensions, however, especially in width.

Turrets should have the same level of protection as the overall vehicle, or even higher, due to the inclination and thickness of the armor. They feature all-around vision blocks or periscopes for observation of the surrounding field. They can rotate 360 degrees continuously, which is accomplished manually, hydraulically, or electrically, depending on the weight of the turret.

AIFVs may be either wheeled or tracked. They are excellent platforms for different weapons, which can range from 100mm guns to 30-caliber coaxially mounted machine guns. Other popular armaments include antitank guided missiles, 25mm chain guns, and externally mounted grenade launchers. Some vehicles feature firing ports for individual weapons of the occupants.

The primary weapon on an AIFV is mounted and balanced about its trunnion on the front part of the turret. Weapon elevation is controlled through a gearbox (pinion and toothed arc), and traverse depends on the turret itself. Subsystems, such as magnification sights, thermal and infrared sights, and searchlights, are used to improve weapon effectiveness.

Consideration must be given to the weight and placement of the main armaments. Larger-caliber weapons require greater structural support and thus add to the weight of the AIFV, which in turn affects the weight of the vehicle's engine, transmission, and suspension systems. For example, high-pressure guns need about a 1.6-meter turret ring, which is best adapted only to heavy AIFVs (about 12 tons), while a 1.4-meter turret ring is suitable for lower-pressure guns and can be mounted in AIFVs of about 7 tons. Asymmetrical designs (e.g., offset mounting of the main gun) can impair amphibious operations through listing caused by uncorrected torque along the axis of movement of the vehicle.

Grenade launchers provide AIFVs, as well as tanks, armored personnel carriers, and other armored ground vehicles, with a unique and variable defensive capability. The launchers may fire smoke, phosphorus, tear gas, or illumination rounds in addition to antipersonnel grenades. They may also fire infrared and radar-jamming munitions. These are fired from inside the vehicle individually or in salvo and can form a considerable screen to conceal the vehicle as it safely changes position. Some armored vehicles are provided with smoke generators that can rapidly provide a dense smoke screen, which is produced by fuel being sprayed onto the exhaust outlet.

Many AIFVs are equipped to maintain a slight overpressure inside the vehicle. While this feature may complicate the design of the turret, it serves to prevent exposure of the crew and occupants to the conditions of nuclear, biological, and chemical (NBC) warfare.

Some sophisticated AIFVs are equipped similarly to the latest generation of main battle tanks, and even two-axis stabilization is being adapted to AIFVs. This system compensates for the vehicle's movement in roll, pitch, suspension travel, and tire behavior. Once so equipped, an AIFV turret lacks only adequate firepower to become an MBT turret.

INTERNAL SECURITY VEHICLE

Internal security vehicles are designed for missions involving territorial security, antiguerrilla combat, restoration of order, and repression of riots in urban areas. Their high maneuverability, wide range of vision, and special ancillary equipment give such vehicles outstanding performance characteristics. They feature large and comfortable interior space, which enables crews to remain on alert for several hours in the vehicle. These vehicles may be equipped with turrets fitted with a medium 12.7mm machine gun or a light 7.62mm machine gun. They are found in a 4×4 or 6×6 configuration, but tracked vehicles are absolutely unsuitable. The latter also have political disadvantages in that they are often confused with tanks. An amphibious capability is necessary only for coast or border patrol missions. Vehicles of this type can typically accommodate about ten men in the crew compartment.

To minimize the "dead zone" in front of the vehicle, the depression capability of the mounted machine gun may be as low as −12 degrees. These vehicles are usually also equipped with smoke and CS (tear gas) grenade launchers, searchlights, a magnifying telescope mounted coaxially with the weapon, all-around observation glass vision blocks, and episcopes or periscopes.

Vehicles intended for antiriot duty should be provided with protection of the engine air intake against flammable liquids, protection of the exhaust port, fuel tank locking, suppression of outside handles on doors and hatches, vision blocks with swiveling tight firing ports permitting protected firing from inside the vehicle, and CS protection. For repression of riots in urban areas such vehicles may be equipped with a hydraulic cleaning blade, windscreen shutter, tear gas dispenser, siren, outside public address system, rotating light, turret, video camera, and water cannon.

ARMORED WORKSHOP VEHICLE

The armored workshop vehicle transports mechanics and necessary spare parts and tools to the combat zone, where maintenance operations and first- and second-level repair can be performed under the full protection of an armored hull. The workshop is equipped with the necessary tools and equipment, such as a welding set, bench, toolboxes for mechanical and electrical repairs, and lifting gear. Also included are a vise, portable drilling machine, disk grinder, electric generator, and battery charger. Lightly damaged vehicles can thus be repaired and put back into operation without being towed to the rear. The workshop has both an external radio set and internal communications. It is also usually armed with a small-caliber machine gun. Mechanics can work in a standing position through two large roof hatches with about a 90-degree opening while being protected by the sides of the vehicle's hull. The same workshop can be fitted to a wheeled or a tracked vehicle.

RECOVERY VEHICLE

Armored recovery vehicles are used to evacuate partially disabled military vehicles suffering battle damage and those experiencing severe technical failures that cannot be repaired in place. Such inoperable equipment is extracted and towed to the rear, where a higher-level repair facility can deal with the problem.

Recovery vehicles have a hydraulically driven crane that can rotate within a minimum arc of 180 degrees to the rear and often a full 360 degrees. Two or four jacks, manually or hydraulically operated, provide additional stability for lifting, and heavier recovery vehicles may feature outriggers to widen the range of stable operations.

Ground clearance, fording ability, and a short turning radius are other important attributes of recovery vehicles. There are usually two driver's work stations, one on the vehicle for road travel, the other on the crane mechanism for movement about work sites and over rough terrain at low speed. These vehicles also mount various pulleys, wire, and tools to be used to facilitate recovery operations.

Mobility Characteristics

Regardless of the type of armored ground vehicle or its mission, its main purpose is to provide mobility to a military force. Since speed is one mainstay of mobility, military vehicles are designed to attain high speed both on hard-surface roads and on different kinds of cross-country terrain.

Another key element of mobility is traction. When roads and cross-country terrain are slippery—from ice, snow, sand, or mud—friction is often insufficient and the driving wheels or tracks spin in place instead of pushing the vehicle forward. This may combine with the reduced resistance to shear of certain soils to result in the sinking of the vehicle's tracks or tires and a mired, immobile vehicle.

Tracks are more effective than driving wheels in achieving traction. More driving wheels, however, will enhance a vehicle's mobility. The specific pressure of tracked vehicles on soil may be as low as 0.5 bar, but the lowest value using normal low-pressure tires is not less than 0.9 bar, and even deflating tires can only reduce the pressure to 0.7 bar.

Generally a vehicle's mobility can be improved by the following: (1) low specific soil pressure, so that the friction in the contact area plus the resistance to shear are enough to withstand the tractive force and thus sufficient to push the vehicle; (2) firm contact of the rolling driving element (track or wheel) with the terrain by transferring the weight of the vehicle via the elastic element of the suspension system (springs or torsion bars) so as to maintain this contact at all times; and (3) absence of the probability of spinning due to lack of adhesion in the contact areas. This can be achieved by positive connection of different components of the drive line through locking the interwheel and interaxle differentials during movement on slippery roads. Tracked vehicles have a distinct advantage in terms of these factors. The specific soil pressure is limited by the length of track contact and its width, and the contact with the ground is secured by the tracked vehicle's suspension system (road wheels and torsion bars).

Thus the track throughout its length can adapt its configuration to that of the terrain being traversed, something that cannot be achieved by wheeled vehicles. Multiaxle wheeled vehicle designers try to approach this configuration by increasing the number, width, and diameter of the wheels, by decreasing their inflation pressure, and by improving their tread pattern and applying independent suspension. By these means the design of 8 × 8 vehicles has realized a satisfying mobility despite its complexity; this seems to be the optimum possible solution.

The Map of Armored Vehicles

According to their function, armored vehicles differ widely in their characteristics, especially in weight and power. Weight depends mainly on the available interior room and the amount of armor protection, while the power depends on the resulting weight and the required dynamic performance. Even vehicles having similar functions have variations in these parameters, mainly combat weight and specific power (the power-to-weight ratio).

Infantry fighting vehicles, having taken over essential battlefield tasks formerly performed on foot, are capable of moving more rapidly when tanks cannot or need not be employed. They are able to keep up with tanks tactically, defend themselves, and even be used offensively against a light enemy. They are designed to discharge their embarked infantry from the rear of the vehicle for dismounted combat. They are armed with heavy small arms (a 20 to 30mm cannon) and antitank guided missiles, but arming these vehicles with powerful weapons has also left them with less room for carrying infantrymen and their equipment; thus fewer soldiers are available for dismounted action.

Tracked armored vehicles enable the infantry to follow the tanks, but unfortunately most of them as currently designed prevent the crew from firing their weapons without exposing themselves. Some versions have a one- or two-man turret or vision blocks and firing slots in the sides and rear of the vehicle; these permit infantry to fire their weapons from within the vehicle and also reduce the risk of their becoming claustrophobic or disoriented.

Clearly, the roles of infantry carriers and fighting vehicles are quite different. Infantry carriers must deliver infantry to their objective by a series of tactical bounds, while fighting vehicles must deliver them to suitable firing positions. The various factors deriving from the disparate missions have affected the design of the vehicles for performing them. For infantry carriers, the priority is to transport eight or ten soldiers rapidly and under maximum protection, then dismount them to go into action on foot. Such vehicles have suffered heavy losses when they tried to function as fighting vehicles.

Well-designed wheeled vehicles with independent suspension have the advantage of a lower silhouette than tracked vehicles, while their running gear enables them to operate effectively off the road as well as on it. They also provide the base vehicle for an entire family of variations.

In order to identify the main tendencies in combat weight and in power-to-weight ratio of existing armored vehicles, a survey was conducted of about 70 military armored vehicles fielded by the American, European, and Soviet armed forces. A specific power (power-to-weight ratio) versus weight diagram was then plotted for both armored wheeled vehicles and armored tracked vehicles. A number of considerations go into the design of the various systems considered, constituting a series of trade-offs, in effect a calculus of vehicle design.

Ultralight and light reconnaissance wheeled vehicles, for example, with their extremely light combat weight and small crew designed for conducting deep reconnaissance missions in the forward battlefield, lack the capability to conduct major engagements and must avoid such confrontations. They must have instead outstanding agility, mobility, and maneuverability. Conversely, medium and heavy reconnaissance and heavy reconnaissance/armored personnel carriers, although heavier in weight, may not need such high power.

On the other hand, infantry fighting vehicles have more offensive missions that necessitate an increased level of protection of the hull and turret, larger-caliber weaponry, more powerful observation and aiming devices, more ammunition stowage, and accurate tactical and navigation systems. All these in the aggregate result in an enormous increase in weight and thus require a corresponding increase in power to ensure adequate levels of mobility and maneuverability to perform their offensive tasks. These considerations are, to some extent, similar to those affecting main battle tanks.

Ultralight and light reconnaissance vehicles weighing up to five tons have high specific power to suit their missions of scouting, liaison, transportation of commanders, and surveillance patrols, all of which require high mobility and rapid maneuverability. This can be provided by 4×4 light vehicles of 3.0 to 5.5 tons with a power-to-weight ratio of about 20 to 34 horsepower per ton. Heavy reconnaissance vehicles sacrifice high dispensable dynamic performance to gain more room. Thus their weights range from 7.5 to 20 tons for 4×4 and up to 8×8 configurations, with lower power-to-weight ratios of about 13 to 27 horsepower per ton.

Armored personnel carriers have a similar character and similar power-to-weight ratios, as their main operating theater is often in the rear. Their configuration varies from 4×4 up to 8×8 with weights of 4 to 18 tons and power-to-weight ratios of 15 to 30 horsepower per ton. Since an infantry fighting vehicle's weight increases with the increase in its gun caliber and the addition of missiles, its power-to-weight ratio must increase correspondingly to maintain high mobility and maneuverability. These vehicles may be as heavy as 15 to 26 tons and have power-to-weight ratios of 10 to 22 horsepower per ton.

Tracked vehicles having the same function as comparable wheeled vehicles show the same tendencies. Increase in weight is accompanied by a decrease in power-to-weight ratio as the vehicle version shifts from reconnaissance to reconnaissance/armored personnel carrier to pure armored personnel carrier.

Monocoque Version of Armored Wheeled Vehicles

In the monocoque version of armored wheeled vehicles, the hull represents the infrastructure on which all the main drive line aggregates and components of the vehicle are mounted. These include the engine, transmission, axles, steering, and suspension. When all, or at least most, of the vital aggregates and components are installed within the hull armor, it is called an "all-in" design.

In this form the hull completely replaces the frame. As a result of eliminating the frame, the dead weight of the vehicle is considerably reduced; the saving can be added to the useful payload. At the same time, the design is not restricted by the classic frame. Consequently, road clearance can be increased, height reduced, the center of gravity lowered considerably, and the angles of approach and departure increased during the design process. The bottom of the hull of this version has a v-shape to provide additional protection against mines and a lower level that enables the crew to embark and disembark more easily and quickly. The v-shape also helps to reduce water resistance in the amphibious version, which can be equipped with propellers or water-jet pumps for propulsion in water.

In the monocoque version most suitable for armored military vehicles, the designer can make use of "leftover" places and pockets to arrange crew seating and their accommodations. The suspension can easily be adapted as independent and, since the axles and final drives are related to the sprung mass in this type of suspension, the comfort and riding quality of these vehicles are noticeably improved.

The hull may be covered by an armored roof to protect the crew. It may also be provided with hatches for observation by the commander and crew and for use as emergency exits. The sides of the hull may have as many vision blocks and firing ports as the number of crewmen. The windshield in front of the commander and driver, along with the crew vision blocks, are made of armored glass that provides the same degree of protection as the hull. All crew members, and especially the commander and driver, are afforded wide fields of vision with a minimum dead zone.

The level of protection afforded by the front part of such vehicles is usually higher than that on the sides and can withstand 7.62mm fire at a range of 30 meters.

NBC Protection

Ground forces are especially threatened by nuclear, biological, and chemical (NBC) warfare. Main battle tanks and most military armored vehicles, especially those subject to operation in the forward battle area, are provided with a sealed, airtight, and pressurized compartment that excludes the entry of radioactive dust, harmful chemicals, and microorganisms. Filtered fresh air is ducted to the crew compartment; crew members can thus maintain maximum efficiency since they can work freely without the need to wear respirators or breathing aids.

Air-Conditioning

NATO countries have been slow to adopt any form of air-conditioning on military vehicles, preferring to rely on forced air ventilation. Equipment intended for export to tropical areas, especially those characterized by high humidity, may have better marketability if it is air conditioned to maintain a more comfortable crew environment. This is particularly important in tightly closed vehicles designed to include NBC protective systems. These types of vehicles are subject to operation in a "closed down" mode for long periods in a contaminated environment. Under such conditions a satisfactory atmosphere for the crew cannot be achieved without air-conditioning. Ambient temperatures in certain tropical climates may reach 50 to 60 degrees centigrade in summer with accompanying humidity up to 90 percent. No human body can withstand such conditions for more than several minutes, much less work and fight effectively under them.

Various approaches have been devised to solve this problem, each a function of the characteristics and operating requirements of the vehicle being conditioned. The simplest solution is a direct descendent of the automobile air-conditioning system, that is, to drive the compressor off the vehicle engine and to locate the discrete components of the system in suitable places within and on the outside of the vehicle. If this approach is not taken, retrofitting installation costs for existing vehicles are certain to be high, and probably nonstandard components will have to be designed to fit into the "leftover" spaces. The main drawback of this design is that it can only operate when the vehicle engine is running. Also, if the system is designed and sized for operation at low engine speed, then it will have surplus capacity at higher engine speeds. Ambulance vehicles, in particular, should be fitted with air-conditioning systems. This provides a cooling capability that permits personnel survival in ambient or tropical humidity and desert solar loading. Compactness can be attained primarily by use of a high-efficiency heat exchanger.

An internal and completely independent power pack that is entirely protected within the armored hull may also be used, although such a system takes up considerable interior space. Usually it comprises a small 2- or 3-cylinder diesel engine using the same fuel as the vehicle engine but equipped with a separate fuel tank, its own battery starter, and a powerful alternator to drive the system's fans. The condenser of the system is cooled, together with its engine radiator, by the same fan through the same armored grill. An adjustable thermostat is provided for switching the system on and off automatically within a temperature range preset by the crew. The main feature of this independent version is that it can air-condition the vehicle even when the main engine is not running. This is important for ambulance, command post, internal security, and patrol vehicles. In both systems heating can be provided only when the vehicle engine is running.

Wheels versus Track

Practical experience has shown that ground pressure of a two-axle wheeled vehicle may amount to twice that of a tracked vehicle of the same weight. Therefore, and in order not to lose the other advantages of wheeled vehicles, the solution has been to provide more axles so as to maintain ground pressure within a range that could compete with tracked vehicles.

The mean maximum pressure is sometimes used as the unit of measure, rather than nominal ground pressure; the former is more critical, especially since the difference between the two figures is considerable for tracked vehicles with a small number of road wheels. Due to the provision of large tires and a tire inflation pressure control system, this approach is deemed acceptable.

On roads, the rolling resistance of tracked vehicles is double that of wheeled vehicles (0.04 times the tracked vehicle weight versus 0.02 times that of wheeled vehicles fitted with cross-country tires). Wheeled vehicles can cover longer distances on roads before they require refueling, especially if they are driven by diesel engines. They can also cover longer distances faster and with less fatigue for their occupants, since the vibrations generated by tires are negligible in comparison with those produced by tracks.

The suspension of tracked vehicles is simpler, lighter, and more compact than that of wheeled vehicles. Tracked vehicles are sprung by transverse torsion bars, which are lighter than springs. Tracked-vehicle wheel travel due to torsion bar suspension may be as much as 230 to 280 millimeters and even up to 380 millimeters in the case of hydropneumatic suspension.

Steering in tracked vehicles may depend on a clutch-and-brake system, formerly the standard. A controlled differential is now considered more effective, but it provides only one radius of steering.

It is generally accepted that the main battle tanks should be tracked rather than wheeled, but the same conclusion does not necessarily follow for light armored vehicles. The relative cross-country performance depends on vehicle weight. Within the weight range of the main battle tank, tracks are required, but the light weights of other armored vehicles may or may not favor wheels. Wheeled vehicles with up to eight driving wheels are, despite the accompanying steering and transmission difficulties, currently being produced. The low ground pressure that favored the track has also been achieved in wheeled vehicles by using large-diameter tires with a high loading capacity and central tire-pressure control that permits adjustment of tire pressure in accordance with the terrain being traversed. This system is both more convenient and easier than making adjustments in track tension. Also, if run-flat tires are used, then puncture of one or more tires will not immobilize the vehicle, whereas any track link damage does halt a tracked vehicle.

Other advantages of the wheeled armored vehicle include fuel economy and longer range, especially with diesel engines; high road speeds; simplicity; relative quietness; long service life as compared with track life, which rarely exceeds 4,000 kilometers (2,480 mi.); better riding quality, without the vibration associated with tracks; ability to be towed or recovered more easily; lower procurement and in-service costs; easier driver training; and higher mobility on semisoft terrain and hard surfaces. While 4×4 wheeled vehicles are inferior to tracks in their ability to cross wide trenches, 6×6 and 8×8 versions have approximately the same capability as tracked vehicles in this respect.

Wheeled vehicles have lighter armor protection than tracked vehicles. To be able to withstand 12.7mm, 14.5mm, and 20mm armor-piercing shells, wheeled armored vehicles would have to be brought up to combat weights that would result in unacceptably high ground pressure. Thus they are not a substitute for tracked armored vehicles. Rather, wheeled and tracked vehicles should be viewed as complementary, not competitive, and tailored according to the geographical characteristics of the theater of operations.

Semitracked vehicles, sometimes known as half-tracks, were first produced in large numbers in Germany by 1940. During the next five years the Americans quickly followed suit, producing some 40,000 half-tracks for themselves and their allies. None of these vehicles proved completely satisfactory, as they proved to be difficult to maintain, awkward to drive, of poor reliability, inadequate in cross-country mobility, and too expensive. It was reported, for example, that their cost per unit of weight was higher than a tank's. By 1944 the Allies had turned toward fully tracked and armored solutions based on the tank chassis.

Semitracked vehicles should probably be excluded from consideration for modern use, since they lack the respective advantages of wheeled and tracked vehicles while at the same time having many of the disadvantages of both.

Military Tires

Since the greater part of the distances covered by wheeled armored vehicles is on hard or dirt surfaces, their tires must have good resistance to abrasion and good adhesion even on wet roads.

Military tires cannot operate as close to their maximum load-carrying capacity as commercial tires because of "up sizing" to provide an extra margin of safety against possible structural failure, higher ground clearance, and extra flotation on yielding surfaces. Military applications also emphasize the importance of tire-ground contact area more than commercial uses. Military vehicle designers seek to improve mobility and agility by achieving the largest possible area of tire contact with the ground at the lowest possible inflation pressure, minimizing soil pressure while also limiting tire dimensions. Thus a single, wide, variable-pressure tire is often used on heavy military vehicles where an equivalent commercial vehicle would utilize a double tire.

Tire rubber will always remain vulnerable to penetration due to enemy action, ground litter, and debris. To counter this difficulty and become competitive with, and possibly to displace, metal tracked systems or solid rubber tires, pneumatic tires must provide good flotation and tractive characteristics and must have an acceptable degree of continued mobility in terms of distance and speed even after being punctured. This translates into a quick-escape capability of 30 to 50 kilometers (18.6 to 31 mi.) of travel at 40 to 50 kilometers per hour (25 to 31 mph) for heavy vehicles and 50 to 100 kilometers (31 to 62 mi.) at 50 to 70 kilometers per hour (31 to 43.4 mph) for light vehicles.

For medium and heavy vehicles (1,100 kg/tire or more), flat tires generate high internal heat that causes rapid breakdown and disintegration of the tire structure. One solution is to provide thick-wall, self-supporting tires that can bear the load without totally collapsing on the rim. Such tires use low-hysteresis, high-structure compounds that limit bending of tire walls as they go into compression with the basic casing reinforcement in tension. The base of the tire is held in the correct relationship with the rim by insertion of a reinforced rubber spacer. There is a penalty in terms of reduced shock absorption and flotation, especially in the deflated mode. An alternate solution involves filling the toroidal void within a tire with a rubber core that incorporates nitrogen-filled cavities within its structure.

The dominant advantage of radial tires is the extension of tread life that results from stabilization of the ground contact area, along with decreased rolling resistance and consequently reduced fuel consumption. In terms of run-flat capability, radial tires provide better performance, although this is not essential if a limited post-deflation performance is acceptable. When running on partially or fully deflated tires, serious failures of the inner tube can occur;

the valve can be torn from the tube by the increased rotational forces imposed and the increase in circumferential strain. Such failures are not present, of course, in tubeless tires.

Military requirements for tire performance have tended to concentrate on optimizing off-road capabilities and operation in soft soils, sand, mud, loose rock, and the like, often to the detriment of performance on hard surfaces. Unidirectional patterns of tire design are generally not favored, so as to avoid extra complications in tire fitting. Certain other designs have been found highly advantageous. A full run-flat design with an efficient bead-locking system, for example, has been evaluated as doubling tractive capability in snow when fully deflated. For optimum performance in loose sand (which has very poor shear strength), a high-flotation, low-pressure tire is required. A rounded-profile tire edge helps to avoid excessive sinkage due to milling into the sand when a spin occurs. But there are always trade-offs; such tires provide rather hard road performance in terms of abrasion resistance. Sectional height-to-width ratios for military vehicle tires vary from 0.3 to 0.7.

The provision of run-flat tires, together with a pressure-control system for them, on armored fighting vehicles and armored personnel carriers is indispensable on the modern battlefield, where these vehicles are continually subject to enemy action, and the need often arises for continued use of the tires even after they have been punctured; indeed for the vehicle to be able to cover a considerable distance at relatively high speed after punctures have occurred. The construction of run-flat tires does not adversely affect maneuverability of the vehicle. Only tubeless tires, however, can incorporate the run-flat emergency running ring, a solid rubber ring made from two different special types of rubber. Its base is reinforced with steel wire, which provides a good interference fit so that the ring remains in place on the rim even at high speed. The outer section of the running ring contains rubber tubes filled with a lubricating paste. In case of an emergency breakdown involving complete loss of air pressure inside the tire, the tire lowers down to the emergency running ring; under this pressure, the sections of the ring open. The lubricating tubes come free and are broken between the tire and the running ring. The "freed" lubrication reduces friction between the parts. Such rings are easy to fit, have a homogeneous structure without imbalance, incorporate safe-to-use lubricating tubes, and are extremely light.

Another type of run-flat tire uses a circular bead lock of molded rubber to keep the bead against the sides of the rim, regardless of low or zero tire pressure. It thus avoids tire separation and the entry of sand or other foreign matter into the tire casing. The contact surface is increased when tire pressure is reduced. The bead lock can be installed in either tubeless or tubed tire types; standard air valves are used.

A third type of run-flat tire uses an inner tube of cellular core manufactured with a specially processed elastomer. Each cell is independent and is inflated with some type of inert gas during manufacture. This system also includes a lubricant to prevent overheating while running flat.

Run-flat tires eliminate the need for a spare wheel, thus saving space and payload for military vehicles. Besides military utilization, such tires are useful for police vans and commercial armored cars.

Conclusion

Different types of armored ground vehicles, their characteristics, attributes, and performance comparisons have been described above. While the primary role of these vehicles varies greatly—direct combat assault, reconnaissance, communications, repair and recovery, medical aid—the common denominator is mobility: their ability to operate effectively over various road surfaces and different terrain.

In terms of mobility, these vehicles are divided into wheeled and tracked classes, each with its own particular advantages and disadvantages. Effective employment of armored ground vehicles in combat and combat support operations depends on using them in a complementary manner, rather than arguing the relative value of one over the other. In the final analysis, use of these vehicles by military forces will "depend on the situation," and the astute commander will organize all mobility assets accordingly.

MOUSTAFA ALY MORSY ALY

SEE ALSO: Armored Land Vehicle Technology Applications; Engine Technology, Ground Vehicle; Mechanized Warfare; Tank.

Bibliography

Bekker, M. 1980. Tracked vehicles: Terrain damage and economy. *International Off-Highway Meeting and Exhibition*, Milwaukee, Wis., September. SAE Technical Paper Series 800953.
Enrico, P. 1985. Scout and reconnaissance combat vehicles. *Military Technology* 9 (12):68–78.
Flume, W. 1987. Towards a new generation of wheeled vehicles. *Military Technology* 11 (11):115–17.
French, T. 1985. Tyres for the military. *Military Technology* 9 (4):36–41.
Howarth, M., and R. Ogorkiewicz. 1986. Tracked and wheeled light armoured vehicles. *International Defense Review*, editorial supplement 8:37, 40–47, 52–62.
Meckenheim, H. 1978. New multi-purpose amphibious armoured vehicles from EWK. *International Defense Review* 8:54–58.
Ogorkiewicz, R. 1986. Tracked and wheeled light armoured vehicles. *International Defense Review*, editorial supplement 8:19–23, 25–30, 31–34.
Vial, D. 1984. Armoured vehicles from Cardoen. *International Defense Review* 2:179–81.

ARMORED LAND VEHICLE TECHNOLOGY APPLICATIONS

The armored land vehicle traditionally leads the assault and affords breakthrough opportunities to the ground forces. The assault itself is a coordinated effort between air, land, and sometimes sea forces. The armored land vehicle as typified, for example, by the main battle tank and the armored infantry fighting vehicle is exposed to a large and increasing number and level of threats. The technology of the threats themselves is becoming increasingly diverse and lethal. The threats include: tank cannon; antitank guided missiles; free-flight rockets and guns; aircraft and artillery cannon; bombs and bomblets; high-energy lasers; electromagnetic radiation; nuclear, bacteriological, and chemical agents; and mines.

The application of new technologies to the armored land vehicle has as its purpose the provision of capabilities to overcome these threats and to improve the three principal functions that determine the effectiveness of the fighting vehicle: lethal firepower, crew and vehicle survivability, and mobility.

The mix and degree of lethality, survivability, and mobility in an armored vehicle varies according to the combat mission it is intended to perform—assault leader, fire support, reconnaissance, transport, and logistics—and the likely type of opposing weapons. Accordingly, vehicle design is tailored to provide the desired balance of these attributes for optimal mission effectiveness. As Table 1 shows, there is a wide range and mix of these attributes from tracked main battle tanks to wheeled armored personnel carriers.

Technology Applications

The application of technology requires an assessment of the technologies either presently or potentially available for the various components or subsystems that comprise the entire armored vehicle. (The subsystems include structure, armor, propulsion system, suspension, auxiliary automotive systems, armament, vetronics, fire control, command, control and communications, and nonballistic survivability.) These subsystems are then assessed for specific technologies that have application to future vehicles.

STRUCTURE

The hull (and the turret for turreted vehicles) provides the structure to accommodate the crew and the armament, ammunition, and automotive system and the integral armor that has traditionally provided protection against penetra-

TABLE 1. *Armored Vehicle Characteristics*

	WGT. (TONS)	ENG. HP	MAX. ROAD SPEED (MPH)	MAIN GUN CALIBER	CREW
U.S. M1A1 main battle tank	63	1,500	44	120mm	4
USSR 2S3 self-propelled howitzer	30	520	38	152mm	5
FRG Marder infantry fighting vehicle	32	600	46	20mm	9
USSR BTR-70 armored personnel carrier	12.6	240	50	14.5mm	2 + 9
UK Fox scout vehicle	6.7	190	65	30mm	3

tion. In many vehicles a cast-steel structure was used; but increasingly the trend is toward fabrications of welded rolled plates, with space allocated for the inclusion of armor and more recently provision for the addition of modular armor. The latter design approach is expected to predominate in the future because of the capability to modify or replace the armor as the threat changes or to accommodate to specific threats. In effect, the approach provides for a vehicle structure that serves as a carrier for the functioning components but with replaceable or modifiable protection levels.

Heavy armored vehicles are fabricated principally of ballistic steel, with aluminum used in certain applications. Plastics, such as polymer composites, are increasingly being investigated, initially for weight reduction applications but also as principal components of the structure or armor. Various candidate configurations for vehicle structures include those listed below:

- steel monocoque (welded)
- aluminum monocoque (welded)
- composite monocoque
- steel casting
- aluminum casting
- steel rib-stiffened
- aluminum rib-stiffened
- composite integral rib
- composite cored
- steel frame + aluminum skin
- aluminum frame + steel skin
- steel frame + composite skin
- aluminum frame + composite skin

Heavyweight vehicles are expected to continue to utilize structures principally of monocoque steel and aluminum, with selected application of steel castings; medium-weight vehicles, either rib-stiffened aluminum or rib-stiffened steel; and lighter vehicles, a combination of aluminum and composite materials. The trends will be influenced by progress in manufacturing technology, principally in the techniques of fabrication and fastening.

A significant past trend in armored land vehicles has been the steady growth in weight for virtually all types of vehicles as both the lethality and protection levels have been increased. This trend is expected to be reversed as new weight-saving technologies emerge, but also as some trade-offs in survivability are made in favor of lighter vehicles, particularly for airborne and rapid-response forces.

ARMOR

Reliable protection is required against a diversity of weapons, including armor-piercing kinetic-energy projectiles and shaped-charge ammunition. Each has a different effect on the armor and requires different protection mechanisms. Figure 1 is an armor technology tree delineating the threats to the armored

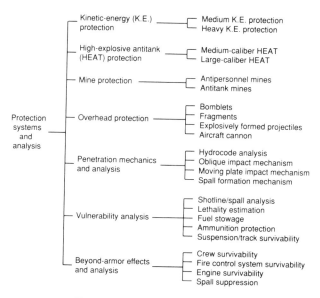

Figure 1. Armor technology tree.

vehicle and the analyses made in determining the final armor design. The armor is tailored for the range of threats included in the design requirements. The candidate armors and combinations of armors include passive solid or spaced-composite, various laminates, and reactive. Recognizing the constant technological battle between improved threats and improved armor, vehicle designers are reluctant to rely solely on integral armor, which requires a major vehicle rebuild to improve the armor protection. Future applications increasingly will utilize replaceable armor packages, either contained within cavities in the basic structure or attached to the structure. This approach is advantageous for several reasons:

• ease of incorporating improved armor technologies as they evolve
• ease of design upgrade for future threat changes
• the flexibility of changing vehicle armor protection levels to meet the battlefield threat environment
• the ability to minimize vehicle weight (operational efficiency) and maximize vehicle safety by removal of all armor (or only reactive armor) for certain operations such as training.

It is recognized that there is a limit to the amount of armor that can be applied for protection. As the lethal threat increases, the required weight of protective armor can become excessive.

Nontraditional methods of survivability and protection include techniques for signature reduction to avoid being detected and countermeasures to defeat threat sensors, as described further in the section entitled "Nonballistic Survivability."

PROPULSION SYSTEM

The propulsion system includes the entire power pack and drivetrain, from the primary power source at the engine to the final drives for the track sprockets. Included are the engine, transmission including provision for steering and braking, final drives, cooling for engine and transmission, air filter, inlet and exhaust ducting, ancillary power generation, batteries, fuel tanks, and other auxiliary equipment. The engine and the transmission represent the bulk of the propulsion system in terms of both volume and cost and are key factors in establishing the design of the vehicle. One of the principal requirements is a high power-to-weight ratio to minimize the space requirement.

Propulsion system technologies can be categorized into three major areas:
1. primary power source, which includes combustion energy engines, electrical energy, and fuel cells;
2. power transmission device to provide speed and torque control, steering and inhibitors, drivetrains to transfer power from transmissions to the vehicle sprocket/wheel; and
3. auxiliary systems, which include air-induction system, exhaust system, cooling system, fuel system, diagnostic systems, and other ancillary equipment.

While a large variety of engine-transmission combinations have been developed and used in armored land vehicles, the preferred engine has been a four-stroke cycle diesel engine, with more recent applications of gas turbines. The latter are compact and reliable, and start up easily under cold conditions, but have a higher fuel consumption than the diesel. Future trends indicate continued activity in improving the power-to-weight ratio. As shown in Figure 2 for main battle tanks, a steady growth has been experienced. The trend is expected to be applied to all components of the propulsion system with the

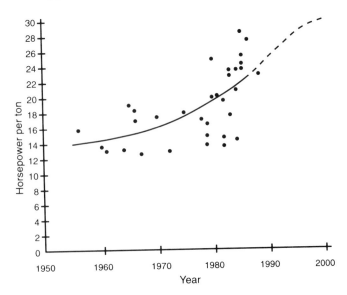

Figure 2. Power-to-weight ratios for main battle tanks.

objective of reducing the armored volume requirement. Current systems under development have the objective of a 40 percent reduction in volume and a 50 percent reduction in fuel consumption for equivalent power.

One negative effect of the increased power in land combat vehicles has been the dramatic increase in operational fuel requirements. Vigorous efforts to reduce fuel consumption will be a challenge for future technology. A combination of efforts is required—weight reduction, improved fuel efficiency, and operational choices in the mix and utilization of various types of combat vehicles. It is expected that the drive for increased power and weight will have to be modified to fit logistical and operational realities.

One of the most promising technologies for future propulsion systems is the application of electrical drive, particularly as electrical weaponry is developed and a significant electrical power generation capability is developed that can serve both the propulsion and the weapon system.

Many configurations for the electrical drive are possible. Perhaps the simplest version has individual motors at each sprocket, but a number of experimental and operational vehicles have been built and tested. Electrical drivetrains offer greater flexibility in design due to the modularization of electrical components and the lack of a rigid mechanical drivetrain. Critical component technologies that have shown marked progress are in the areas of power semiconductors, permanent magnet materials, and brushes for high current collection. Power storage devices have improved, and the entire field has profited from high-energy laser and space power programs. In particular, the promise of superconductivity at moderate to high temperatures, as that technology develops, will open the doors to electrical propulsion systems.

SUSPENSION SYSTEM

The suspension system, coupled with the track or wheel drive of the armored vehicle, is the critical element in effective transfer of power from the propulsion system to the tractive effort required for vehicle movement. The suspension consists of the springing and damping subsystems linking the hull with the wheel axles. The performance of the suspension system determines the stability of the vehicle platform, which in turn affects the degree of crew fatigue, vehicle speed over various terrains, accuracy of fire on the move, and, by absorbing impact energy, the service life of the vehicle components and mechanisms.

The majority of modern tracked armored vehicles utilizes a passive suspension system designed for a specific loading condition, frequently with some provisions for minor adjustment to the system for other operating conditions. For example, a tank may have torsion bars for springing and rotary hydraulic shock absorbers for damping. Each side of the vehicle incorporates a compensating idler with an adjustable track tension link, road arm stations with road arm, axle, and road wheel, and support rollers for top support and alignment of the track.

Some modern tanks incorporate external coil springs instead of torsion bars for the springing action in order to eliminate the weight and space occupied within the vehicle by a torsion bar system. A more recent advance is the use of pneumatic or hydropneumatic units external to the vehicle as the springing device. A further advantage is that the system can be made adaptive by modifying or adjusting the springing and damping with changes in the gas or hydraulic fluid and by relief pressure adjustment. The technology has made steady progress and it is anticipated that the next generation of armored vehicles will incorporate adaptive suspension systems. But the added cost and complexity will be a consideration in finalizing the vehicle design, and for some armored vehicles the passive system will continue to be adequate, particularly for locales where the traversing of difficult terrain is not a major requirement.

The highest level of suspension control technology is the incorporation of an active suspension with controlled changes in the springing and damping rates during dynamic vehicle operation based on sensor data from the terrain, suspension rates, and vehicle speed, all processed and controlled by an onboard computer.

The electromagnetic suspension system is an infant technology holding promise as progress is made in magnetic materials and in electric power generation and conditioning. With continued developmental effort on electrical drive and electrical weaponry, the prospects are excellent for this technology application to the suspension system as well.

The tracks consist most frequently of metallic track shoes connected by pins, usually in rubber bushings, with rubber pads on the shoes to reduce road damage. Tracks are high-mortality service items with relatively poor durability requiring frequent servicing, maintenance, and replacement. Tracks are by far the highest-operational-cost item for suspension systems and will gain the most from innovative design and from technological advances in rubber development.

The preceding discussion has emphasized the suspension system for the tracked combat vehicle, which is decidedly superior to the wheeled armored vehicle in terms of adverse terrain mobility and in combat survivability of the drive system. But for many combat-related roles, the wheeled vehicle has been and will continue to be employed. Wheeled vehicles are more economical to acquire and operate; have higher reliability, with component life four to five times that of the tracked vehicle; are less costly to maintain and repair; and can rely on national truck and automotive production bases. Both the armor and the armament can be equivalent to that of a tracked vehicle of similar weight, limited generally to 20 to 25 tons. Wheeled vehicles that operate at higher speeds on road marches are quieter and less fatiguing for the crew and consume less fuel than tracked vehicles. All of the suspension technologies for tracked vehicles are applicable to wheeled vehicles.

AUXILIARY AUTOMOTIVE SYSTEMS

In armored vehicles, the auxiliary systems most amenable to technology application are the fire detection and suppression system and the fire control system, which includes the gun and turret drive systems.

Automatic fire detection and suppression systems with provision for manual actuation are widely used in modern armored vehicles. Detectors sensitive to ultraviolet or infrared radiation rapidly sense the radiation emitted by flames, with a response time of two to three milliseconds. An electronic control unit processes the sensor signal data, interprets the data for such factors as false alarms, and activates the installed fire extinguishing system. In the past, carbon dioxide has been the principal suppressant for military vehicles, but modern vehicles use halogenated compounds that are two to three times more effective on a unit weight basis. Once the fire suppressant is released, it is effective in protecting the crew and the engine compartment. In terms of the application of new technology, principal effort will be in improving the detectors with regard to response time, false alarms, sensitivity to lens obscuration, and reliability.

Hydraulic pressure has traditionally been used for gun and turret drives at pressures most commonly in the 1,500- to 2,000-psi range. Other types of vehicles, such as modern construction equipment, operate at 3,000 to 6,000 psi, and some aircraft applications are being designed for 7,000 to 8,000 psi. In an armored vehicle, increased hydraulic pressure constitutes a hazard to personnel due to fire potentially endangering the crew from an equipment leak or a ballistic hit. Hydraulic systems constitute an ever-present danger in the vehicle, exacerbated as the pressures are increased to provide additional functions such as robotic hardware for ammunition auto-loaders. Technology application efforts are being directed at the development of nonflammable hydraulic fluids and the development of suitable materials and fabrication techniques for hydraulic hardware that is subjected to elevated pressures.

One approach being effected in some armored vehicles is to avoid the problem by totally eliminating hydraulic fluids and replacing hydraulic actuators and motors with electrical drives. Electrical gun turret drives have been designed and are operational, a trend which is expected to continue.

ARMAMENT

A wide range of armaments is carried by various land combat vehicles, including main tank guns, automatic cannon, cupola-mounted self-defense weapons, scatterable mine dispersers, field artillery armament, antitank missiles and guided munitions, air defense missiles, and mortars. One prevailing characteristic has been the growth increase in gun caliber over time and the continuing effort to increase muzzle velocity and the penetration capability of the projectile warhead. The effect on the vehicle has been weight growth due to the heavier guns and ammunition and to the increased armor required to afford self-protection against equivalent-threat weapons. At the same time, the requirements for improved fire control and gun stabilization systems have resulted in increased complexity of electronics and display systems. The overall lethality of the armored vehicle, therefore, is affected not only by the gun and ammunition but by the effectiveness of the gun control mechanisms.

New technologies applicable to main armament include principally liquid-propellant and electrical weapons.

From a vehicle viewpoint, liquid-propellant guns are advantageous because the liquid can be stowed in tanks in a more efficient manner than can individual solid propellants. On the other hand, the added valves, pumps, and piping increase vulnerability and complexity. Handling of projectiles is easier with elimination of the solid propellant. From the viewpoint of application of liquid gun technology, the effect on the overall vehicle system is expected to be positive. With proper design, the liquid propellant can be stored and compartmented for protection purposes, and the requirement for ammunition handling would be limited to the projectile, easing the handling and storage requirement. The promise would be even better if progress were made in the bipropellant-liquid approach, with one of the propellants being engine fuel, thereby easing somewhat the liquid handling problem. From an armored vehicle viewpoint, the development and incorporation of a liquid-propellant gun could be accommodated.

The application of the electrical gun, either electrothermal (ET) or electromagnetic (EM, either the rail or coil type), would have a much greater impact on the vehicle. The electrothermal gun uses a conventional gun tube with modified breech, which is easier to accommodate than the more radical reconfiguration required for the electromagnetic gun. The elimination of the chemical-propellant charge improves the survivability of the crew and vehicle, as well as reduces the logistics of ammunition supply, since only projectiles are required. Fuel logistics would be increased because more fuel would be required for the prime power source to provide the electrical energy for the gun.

From a technology application viewpoint, the development of electrical weaponry will provide the most significant change in future armored vehicles. The lethality of the system will increase. Radical changes will be possible in other subsystems, including the potential for electrical drive, electromagnetic suspension, even the possibility of electromagnetic protection. All of this potential is highly dependent on technological progress in efficient power generation and conditioning techniques. The drive toward electrical weapons, therefore, has an ancillary benefit—the parallel effort for technological progress in power generation and power conditioning techniques. Once those are in hand, additional electrically powered weaponry like lasers and microwave devices will be possible.

VETRONICS

Vetronics (*vehicle electronics*) is the major new technology to be applied to future armored land vehicles—the techniques of using modern computer systems to achieve precise control through electrical and electronic integration. These subsystems are becoming more complex and more costly than the automotive and armament subsystems in the current vehicles. Vetronics, initiated by the U.S. Army Tank Automotive Command in 1981 to develop a standard electronic and electrical architecture for all land combat vehicles, is a total systems integration approach to the electronic and electrical subsystems on a land vehicle, similar to avionics systems in aircraft. In the past, armored land vehicles, even those of more modern design, focused on the development of individual electronic subsystems without much thought to how vehicle integration would be accomplished. The result has been extensive use of hard wiring, manual actuation devices, and little capability for upgrading without a major retrofit of the vehicle. Vetronics utilizes a distributed architecture design and modular building blocks that allow efficient integration and the flexibility to accommodate change. Management of computer assets and automation of vehicle tasks are facilitated, as well as onboard fault diagnosis and prognosis.

One possible vetronics architecture showing functional allocation to subsystems is given in Figure 3. Variations of this generic architecture will be made for different vehicle types and to meet the degree of sophistication demanded by the mission. In this generic example, the data control and distribution subsystem manages the information flow between the crew stations and the subsystems, as well as between subsystems. The power generation and management subsystem distributes electrical power from the generator or batteries. The computer resources subsystem provides the automated data collection, manipulation, and control. The crew stations consist of controls and displays that allow the crew members to access and control all of the vehicle subsystems.

Figure 4 depicts the vetronic system's integrating elements: controls and displays, computers, and buses for digital communication. These basic elements provide the design flexibility needed to integrate easily mission-specific subsystems such as navigation, electro-optical, radar, etc. The advantage of this system is that the integrating elements can be replaced by improved units without altering the wiring systems, and additional units and displays can be installed as required for particular vehicles, for example, engine controls, additional threat sensors, communications equipment, command and control devices—whatever the design requires. The individual modules of the integrating elements will be designed so as to have application to a number of vehicle types, with the vehicle architecture software tailored for the specific application.

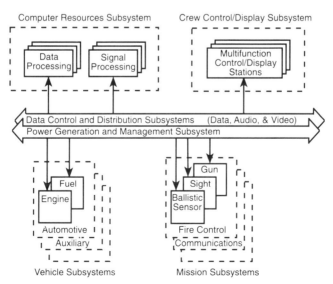

Figure 3. Vetronics generic systems architecture.

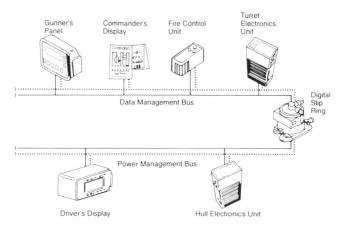

Figure 4. Some data and power management connections.

FIRE CONTROL

The lethality of a gun-firing armored vehicle requires an effective method of detecting the target by means of an onboard observation and sensing device and accurate laying of the gun with aiming devices. To increase gun-firing accuracy, corrections need also to be made for relative motion between the vehicle and the target, the environmental conditions, the condition of the gun, and ammunition type. All of these data are fed into an onboard digital computer that accurately controls gun pointing for putting a round on target. As technology has progressed, each generation of armored gun vehicle has increasingly utilized automatic inputs from sensors to the computer rather than mechanical inputs from the gunner.

A wide field of view is needed for surveillance of the battlefield, with capability for high magnification for target identification and enhanced target detection. Optical sights continue to be the preferred sighting device; however, other sensors such as infrared devices are the primary device in the case of night fighting. Active infrared searchlights have been employed but are readily detectable. Passive night-vision devices based on image intensification are in use but do not perform well on dark nights or in other poor-visibility conditions. Increasingly, armored vehicles are being equipped with thermal imaging devices in the 8- to 14-micrometer range to detect the radiation given off by target objects. The initial high cost of these sensors gradually has been reduced. As the technology improves, techniques for the integration of thermal with optical sights will be enhanced, as well as the wider application of the sighting devices to additional crew members, to remotely positioned sensors, and for robotic devices. Other types of sensors under development, and candidates for future technology application, include low-light-level television and millimeter-wave radar sensors. The latter are superior to infrared devices in battlefield operation with obscurants and smokes.

Once a target has been detected, the range to it must be ascertained and included in the ballistic computation. In early armored land vehicles, determination of range by eye under good conditions resulted in an error of about 15 percent of the range. The use of sight scales within the optics improved the acuracy to an 8 percent error. Further improved optical range finders utilizing the coincidence principle are in wide use, but more recently laser range finders with an error of about ± 10 meters (32 ft.) have dramatically improved accuracy and reduced the first-round engagement time. Development of laser range finders will continue, probably moving from the current neodymium-YAG laser to the CO laser for better smoke penetration.

Initially, ballistic computers were mechanical devices into which the gunner fed data such as ballistic firing conditions (charge conditions, gun tube wear, vehicle cant, angle of sight), meteorological conditions (wind direction and velocity, air temperature, atmospheric pressure), and speed and direction of target movement. Subsequently, automated electromechanical ballistic computers were developed, and today the fully digital ballistic computer has been placed in service on several vehicles. Coupled with the signal and data processing capabilities previously described with the development of the vetronics architecture, and the potential application of electrical drive for the gun and turret stabilization systems, the time required for first-round engagement will continue to be reduced.

Additional technology applications to the fire control system will include automated target acquisition and identification, improved techniques for target handoff from commander to gunner or from vehicle to vehicle, and automatic target tracking. The last already is being developed based on thermal sensors and will be the next principal addition to the fire control suite. With vision devices, automatic target acquisition is a processing function that automatically finds targets by searching an image to find localized areas that are most likely to be targets. Automatic target recognition is a software function based on a pattern recognition system to discriminate between targets. The technology will be applied as algorithms are developed and as computer processing capability increases. Laboratory devices already have been demonstrated and the onboard architecture system design will be able to accommodate the software functions.

COMMAND, CONTROL, AND COMMUNICATIONS

As rapid technological progress is made in all subsystems of the armored land vehicle, including increased mobility, higher weapon lethality with reduced times for engagement, improved first-round hit probability, and better protection mechanisms, the environment for the commander is changing to a high-paced battlefield with an overriding need for improved tactical and troop-leading procedures. The same technological progress being made in mechanical and electronic subsystems and in systems integration is required for the acquisition, processing, transmittal, and utilization of battlefield information. Four areas of technology development are anticipated: navigation, digital map display, enhanced communications, and tactical data processing.

Navigation systems are important to the control of armored land vehicles in battle and on the march. With good visibility and with adequate time, the use of maps and local topography features is adequate, but with poor visibility or in difficult terrain, automatic navigation systems are becoming a basic requirement. Navigation information is needed in combat situations to determine the route and disposition of troops and for the plotting of vehicle and troop movements. With advances in lethality, the use of purely visual devices and crew observation is becoming too hazardous; automatic techniques are required.

Navigation and position-reference systems of the self-contained passive gyroscopic type will be developed initially, with eventual coupling to satellite-based position-locator systems to provide increasingly accurate position information.

For topographical maps, the paper maps traditionally used will continue for certain applications. However, with the extensive electronic display and computer capabilities of future armored vehicles, maps can be generated using integrated computer graphics generators embedded into the vehicle host computer. It is anticipated that map generation and display technology will be included in the next-generation commander's display functions for armored land vehicles.

Communications equipment is the most critical component in the command function and in the control of armored combat vehicle forces. It also is the most vulnerable in view of threat jamming efforts and the volume of message traffic. Technology applications include improved data link security by encryption techniques and the use of data compression to provide for increased traffic and a reduction in the time of transmission.

Just as onboard data is processed and managed by the vetronics architecture design, a corresponding procedure will be developed for the handling and display of tactical data. Protocols for the handling of data at various levels of battle management (including and beyond the armored land vehicle level), such as formatting of messages and automatic transmittal and acknowledgment procedures tailored for specific mission roles, will be applied as the development of specifications, software, and hardware continues.

It is anticipated that tactical data processing will become a major effort because armored vehicles are increasingly being utilized as team members in combined operations. The lack of adequate command and control mechanisms otherwise would negate the progress made in individual vehicle capability and performance.

NONBALLISTIC SURVIVABILITY

In addition to the improvement of the armored land vehicle itself and of its components, a major effort is developing in the technology of avoiding detection and increasing vehicle and crew survivability by means other than the use of antiballistic armor. As the range of threats to the armored vehicle has expanded, the range of protective mechanisms under investigation and development similarly has been expanded, covering a diversity of techniques and technologies. The field is too broad for a detailed discussion, but a brief summary follows.

Active protection requires the detection of a threat and activation of a defeat mechanism. For example, an incoming missile can be detected and defeated by a countering blast warhead missile fired from the armored vehicle. Various techniques of passive protection are afforded by utilizing smoke or chaff generators to evade attack. The vehicle can be equipped with warning receivers to alert the crew to a threat, triggering either an automatic or a manually actuated response. With the variety of sensors and response mechanisms available, integration of the countermeasures is required and sensor fusion techniques will be applied. To avoid detection, a variety of signature-reduction methods can be employed, with initial emphasis on the infrared signature because of the large number of infrared threat sensors. NBC (nuclear, biological, chemical) protection is required for the crew. Several modern armored vehicles carry both collective and individual crew protection devices against chemical and bacteriological attack. Nuclear survivability techniques include gamma ray absorption devices, and, in most instances, armored vehicles are designed to resist electromagnetic pulses (EMP). Lasers and microwaves have as a first target the optical systems; various protective schemes are in development. As power levels increase, additional attention will be placed on protection for other components of the vehicle.

One of the greatest threats to the armored vehicle, and one of the most difficult to counter, is the mine, either self- or command-actuated. The technology for mine defeat is perhaps the least advanced. Traditional methods continue to be used for mine clearing or for mine lane marking. A great advance in nonballistic survivability would be the development of methods for neutralizing mines. Armored vehicles continue to be vulnerable to this threat.

Conclusion

The current trends in armored land vehicles will continue, with expanded technology applications in sensors, electronics, and computers, benefitting greatly from developments in more sophisticated weapons. Correspondingly, the sophistication and cost of the systems will increase, although major progress is expected in the ability to operate the vehicle with the inherent complexity transparent to the crew.

- Welded monocoque steel and aluminum structures will predominate, with increased application of polymer plastic composites. Armor packages will be replaceable to permit the upgrade of a vehicle's protective capabilities without requiring a complete vehicle rebuild. Emphasis will continue on reducing vehicle size and weight.
- The vehicle propulsion system will increasingly move to more compact designs with higher power-to-weight ratios to conserve armored volume. The growing overall fuel consumption due to weight and power growth in the vehicles will become a more significant factor in future design considerations, with greater emphasis on reversing the trend.
- The vehicle running gear, consisting of the suspension system and tracks or wheels, will continue to use mechanical springing with damping for many

applications, but the technology of adaptive suspensions and active suspensions with external hydropneumatic devices will be applied to selected high-performance vehicles.

- In terms of armament, higher-caliber main guns will appear in the next generation of fighting vehicles, but the promise of electrical weaponry in increasing lethality and in reducing the ammunition logistics burden is such that major effort is expected to continue and expand. Electrical power generation and conditioning are the key technologies; once they are achieved, it is expected that electrical drive for vehicle propulsion, electromagnetic suspensions, and electromagnetic protection systems will move to the demonstration phase.
- The continuing technological battle between improved lethality and improved protection has contributed to the growth in weight, complexity, and cost; all of these likely will continue but with more attention devoted to alternate solutions. A range of techniques to improve survivability by other than ballistic armor protection—for example, by such methods as reducing detectability, countermeasures, and active protection—are expected to receive greater emphasis.
- Major technology application in future vehicles will feature the expanded use of electronic devices and software architecture utilizing displays, automated controls, and a variety of aids to relieve the crew of tasks and improve the decision-making process. Data will be selectively distributed within the vehicle and between vehicles.

In summary, the technologies directly associated with the components and subsystems of the armored land vehicle, coupled with the wealth of technologies from other weapons developments, as well as the general progress in commercial fields, provide a host of opportunities for application to land combat vehicles. All are expected to continue to be candidates for consideration, requiring a selective process of determining the optimum combination of performance and cost suitable for each particular design.

E. N. Petrick

See Also: Armor; Armored Ground Vehicle; Engine Technology, Ground Vehicle; Mechanized Warfare; Tank.

Bibliography

Hilmes, R. 1987. *Main battle tanks: Developments in design since 1945.* Trans. R. Simpkin. London: Brassey's.
Nürnberger, W. 1981. Technical trends and possibilities for the armoured vehicles of the future. *Defence Today* 33/34:56ff.
Senger und Etterlin, F. M. von. 1983. *Tanks of the world.* London: Arms and Armour Press.
Zaloga, S., and J. Loop. 1982. *Modern American armour.* London: Arms and Armour Press.

ARMY AVIATION

Army aviation is a term applied to airmobile forces that belong to the ground forces as a branch of service in the armies of various countries.

The growing need of ground forces for operational, tactical, and logistic mobility necessitated the exploitation of the air dimension. The army aviation forces are equipped primarily with helicopters, also with some fixed-wing aircraft.

The spectrum of air mobile operations extends from liaison flights over friendly territory to the independent operation of an airmobile division with assault, antitank, escort, transport, C³ (command, control, and communications), and electronic warfare helicopters up to 300 kilometers (186 mi.) from a friendly base.

Historical Development

The origins of all air forces lie in the exploitation of "lighter than air" means, that is, balloons, which were anchored to the ground and were used to observe the battlefield. The first use of a tethered balloon for aerial reconnaissance occurred at Maubeuge, France, on 2 June 1794, when a French balloon was used to observe Austrian troops. Subsequently, balloons were used in many conflicts, including the U.S. Civil War (1861–65). Prior to World War I, individual army officers in various countries investigated the suitability of early aircraft for military purposes.

From the very start, aircraft were instruments for observation, reconnaissance, and the direction of artillery fire. Between World Wars I and II the already existing air forces, which had developed their own profile with pursuit and bomber aircraft, sought new fields of operation.

At the beginning of World War II, the German army (Wehrmacht) used the air force for tactical close support of army operations on the ground. In 1942, in the endeavor to accelerate target acquisition and adjustment of artillery fire, army aviation was founded in the United States and the army air corps in Great Britain. In the same year the Soviet Union combined its army and front air forces, which had been separate, into one air force.

In the period after World War II, several countries' armed forces began the use of helicopters. Although they were limited in performance, it soon became apparent that rotary-wing aircraft were ideal for supporting armies. This encouraged the formation of army aviation units in many countries. France supported its ground forces in the Indochinese and Algerian wars with her *Aviation Légère de l'Armée de Terre*. The United States made use of helicopters for the first time in the Korean War.

The extensive use of army aviation units came to the fore in the Vietnam War. With the deployment of the 1st Cavalry Division, for the first time a major airmobile unit was committed in a war. The massive use of helicopters for transport, logistics, reconnaissance, fire control, command, rescue, salvage, repeater stations, and messenger services increased their vulnerability to grounded antiaircraft defense and infantry fire.

Roles and Functions

ORGANIZATION

The organizational form of army aviation forces varies from nation to nation and is influenced by the number of missions of the ground forces requiring support, by the dimensions of threat, by the geographical features of the operational area, and by financial aspects of force structure.

With the introduction of antitank and assault helicopters equipped with efficient weapons, as well as observation and fire control systems with improved survival capacity, a radical change in the organization of larger armies took place, attributable to the increased significance of airmobile operations.

The outline of army aviation structures in four countries is described below. The current structure of U.S. army aviation focuses on the combat aviation brigade (CAB).

Each U.S. Army corps contains a CAB with two attack regiments, each with three battalions and a combat aviation regiment. The regimental attack helicopter battalions of the corps CAB are the corps commander's most mobile maneuver force, each with approximately 120 assault helicopters. Battalions of the combat aviation regiment perform combat, combat support, and combat service support tasks.

Depending on the type of division, the CAB comprises one or two attack helicopter battalions and assault helicopter companies and the divisional cavalry, with 97 or 131 helicopters, respectively.

The U.S. 101st Airborne (Air Assault) Division's battlefield mobility depends on the aviation brigade. The brigade in this division consists of four attack helicopter battalions, two assault helicopter battalions, and a command aviation battalion, with altogether approximately 350 helicopters.

In the Soviet Union, helicopters were originally subordinate to the transport and more particularly to the first-line air forces. As assault helicopters became an important element in the ground combat battle, and in close air support, an assault helicopter regiment with about 75 helicopters was provided at the army level. Similar regiments (with 20 helicopters each) were provided to divisions. Similar formations exist in other East European countries.

Of the Western countries, France undertook a radical alteration of its army aviation organization in 1985; the Force d'Action Rapide (FAR) was built up and the army light aviation (Aviation Légère de l'Armée de Terre—ALAT) was considerably reduced. Each French corps has a combat helicopter regiment with five squadrons and a light helicopter group with two squadrons. One of the five divisions of the FAR is the 4th Airmobile Division, which concentrates on the employment of 90 Gazelle helicopters, equipped with the antitank guided missile HOT. The three combat helicopter regiments have a total of 60 helicopters; in the command and support regiment there are 60 more, mainly Puma helicopters.

At approximately the same time that the army of the Federal Republic of Germany was reorganized, service introduction of the PAH-1 antitank helicopter weapon system made it necessary to reorganize army aviation as well. It is currently structured as follows: An army aviation command is assigned to each corps, with one helicopter regiment of 56 PAH-1, two transport helicopter regiments with 32 CH-53 and 48 UH-1D, and one army aviation squadron with 15 liaison and observation helicopters (LOH). Each division has one army aviation squadron with 10 LOH.

CAPABILITIES AND LIMITATIONS

The following list of functions illustrates the possibilities of army aviation: battlefield reconnaissance, aerial patrols, aerial observation and adjustment of indirect fire, command and control actions, aerial fire support for ground forces, day and night air assault operations, destruction of tanks and other combat vehicles, rear area combat operations, offensive and defensive air-to-air operations, deep attacks, electronic warfare, laying of minefields, radiological surveys and chemical reconnaissance operations, aerial radio relay, aerial resupply, aeromedical evacuation, and dispersion of riot control agents and smoke.

Army aviation is subject to several important restrictions: limited NBC protection and decontamination capabilities; vulnerability to air defense, aircraft, and artillery; personnel and maintenance requirements, which may preclude sustained 24-hours-a-day operations; and adverse weather, extreme heat and cold, and driving snow and sand, which may hinder operations.

EMPLOYMENT

The tactical use of aviation systems and forces differs little from classical ground fighting techniques. For example, army aviation forces seldom will fight alone; they will be employed alongside other combat and combat support arms.

Although employment on a tactical level was the rule over a long period of time, nowadays the larger-scope operational significance is rapidly taking over where numbers and equipment permit. No other branch of the services in the army is in a position to concentrate forces and firepower over long distances, at critical points, and so fast—and consequently with surprise effect—as is aviation.

Certain principles can be formulated for army aviation operations that apply in varying degrees depending on the situation. The requirement to fight as an integral part of the combined arms team on the battlefield is always applicable.

Employment as support for the armored or mechanized infantry forces is planned in advance in most combat situations. Possible conflicts with the artillery fire plan, air defense, and close air support should not only be avoided, but on the contrary should be turned to advantage. The capabilities of as many as possible of the troops fighting in the combined arms team should be optimized to maximum reciprocal advantage. For example, the helicopter flight course should not result in a reduction in the use of arms by the air defense system.

Army aviation is in a position not only to employ its own firepower but also for the manipulation and support of other firepower. The aerial transport of artillery guns, antitank and air defense commandos, engineer blocking forces, ammunition supplies, and maintenance teams are only a few examples. Irrespective of ground features, obstacles, and blockades, surprise, and consequently success, can be achieved even where the local situation favors the opponent.

Armed Helicopters

Armed helicopters are divided into categories according to the nature of the armament and the operational mission.

1. Relatively simple antitank helicopters (ATH), originally conceived as liaison and observation helicopters on which an air-to-ground, antitank guided missile system has been fitted, are generally used defensively and not usually armored (e.g., Bo 105 P, SA-342 Gazelle). They are used by many NATO countries.
2. Attack helicopters (AH), which have a more offensive range of operation depending on the weapons with which they are equipped (e.g., Mi-24, AH-64). This type of helicopter is found predominantly in the former Warsaw Pact countries but also is becoming increasingly popular in NATO countries.
3. Multirole helicopters that, depending on the situation, can conduct attack or transport functions (e.g., Mi-8, Lynx).

HELICOPTER ARMAMENT

Although U.S. Army and Marine Corps test groups began experimenting with various weapons on helicopters in the early 1950s, it was the French experience in Algeria, and shortly thereafter the American experience in Vietnam, that created the first specific needs.

At the beginning of the Algerian War, the vulnerability of the unarmed helicopters rapidly became apparent, particularly when hovering while engaged in enemy territory. CH-21 helicopters were subsequently armed with two containers for 18 68mm missiles, with two mobile 7.62mm machine guns mounted under the fuselage and with a 20mm gun in the cabin door.

With the large-scale introduction of American forces in Vietnam, it soon became evident that their utility helicopters required armament for self-defense. In 1967 the first attack helicopter, the AH-1G Huey Cobra, was used in Vietnam, equipped with a six-barreled 7.62mm machine gun or 40mm automatic grenade launcher. Up to 76 2.75-inch free-flight rockets can be carried under the body. A 20mm gun can also be used in a special turret.

ANTITANK MISSILES

Following the introduction of antitank missiles, their utilization by helicopters was investigated.

France tested the antitank missile SS-11 on its Alouette II as early as 1958, and the Soviet Union integrated the AT-3 missile (Sagger) into the Mi-1, Mi-2, and Mi-8 helicopters.

These missiles belong to the first generation, are wire guided, and require optical pursuit from the helicopter, which is not easy (manual command to line of sight—MACLOS principle).

The second generation of missiles used the semiautomatic target cover procedure SACLOS (semiautomatic command to line of sight), for which the control gunner follows the target with his sighting mechanism. The missile is tracked automatically, in the course of which an infrared sensor measures the divergence of the missile from the line of vision to the target and brings the missile on target by means of guiding signals through the wire.

The most common antitank missiles today are the TOW (tube-launched, optically tracked, wire-guided), manufactured by Hughes, and HOT (*haut subsonique, optiquement téléguidé, tiré d'un tube*), manufactured by Euromissile. Both work on the SACLOS principle.

The radio-controlled Soviet AT-6 and the Hellfire laser homing missile manufactured by Rockwell constitute further developments of second-generation missiles. Ranges vary between 3,750 meters (2.3 mi.) and 6,000 meters (3.7 mi.), with a penetration capacity of up to 700 millimeters (27 in.).

Antitank missiles of the third generation are currently being developed. These operate on a "fire-and-forget" principle.

OTHER MUNITIONS

Bombs. The dropping of bombs from helicopters has occurred only sporadically in recent conflicts.

Rockets. The customary helicopter armament since the Vietnam War is with rockets, usually with HE, HEAT, antiradar, and fragmentation warheads. However, 70mm FFARs (free flight aerial rockets) are also in use. These are able to carry hollow-charge sub-ammunition over a distance of 6,000 meters.

Cannons. Aircraft cannons are the usual armaments for assault helicopters, and views differ on their suitability for combating aerial targets. Commonly, 7.62mm ammunition is used, but Soviet helicopters use, in the main, 12.7mm, and other armies use 20mm with single-, double-, or triple-barreled guns. In Soviet helicopters, mobile machine guns built into the nose predominate, but fixed arrangements are more common elsewhere.

The engagement of helicopter against helicopter in air-to-air combat is being taken with increasing seriousness. Tests with high-cadency automatic cannons (up to 4,000 shots/min.) and rockets (Stinger, Blowpipe, etc.) have been underway for some time. The antitank missiles available are unsuitable from the point of view of construction. In the long run, only a fire-and-forget rocket with a range of 6,000 meters (3.7 mi.) or at least an autonomous end-phase guidance system comes into consideration.

Mines. Mine laying from helicopters has been applied by the Soviet army for a long time. The U.S. Army also has a scatterable mining system in use, and a considerably more efficient version is being tested as assembly for the ESSS (external stores support system) for the UH-60A Blackhawk. This could lay a minefield 1,000 meters by 30 meters (3,280 × 98 ft.) in 30 seconds.

AIDS FOR WEAPONS EMPLOYMENT

As a general principle, arms are dependent on auxiliary aids, including equipment for identification, for obtaining target data for fire control, for the selection of weapons and their activation, and above all for directing or guiding. Assault helicopters are frequently equipped with radar warning systems. Laser warning systems will have to follow.

Sighting mechanisms are increasingly being installed as mast-mounted sight (MMS). This allows the helicopter to remain below the horizon and yet observe and even attack on the far side without giving away its position. The MMS is mounted above the rotor disc and the images it sees are transferred electronically to the observer in the helicopter.

Very few helicopters at present have sighting mechanisms suitable for night and bad-weather flight. This presumably will not change soon in many countries for economic reasons. The introduction of night-vision glasses and instruments with forward-looking infrared (FLIR) or low-light-level television (LLLTV) has begun. The advanced attack helicopter AH-64 Apache possesses the most efficient target acquisition and designation system available to date, TADS (target acquisition and designation system), which can be used at night and to a certain extent under unfavorable weather conditions. TADS provides the gunner with a search, detection, and recognition capability with direct-view optics, television, or forward-looking infrared sighting systems. Once acquired, targets can be tracked manually or automatically for an autonomous attack with 30mm guns, rockets, or Hellfire missiles.

The pilot night-vision sensor (PNVS) is used by the pilot for night navigation and consists of an FLIR sensor system packaged in a rotating turret. The PNVS is slaved to the pilot's helmet display line-of-sight and provides imagery that allows the helicopter to be flown in a NOE (nap-of-the-earth) fashion.

Combat Operations

ANTITANK HELICOPTER (ATH) AND ATTACK HELICOPTER (AH) OPERATIONS

Operational procedures for ATH and AH are almost identical with regard to combat against armored weapons systems. However, in the 1990s there will be a considerable number of nonarmored AH in use in the NATO countries, although their operational capability against ATH will be restricted.

Both ATH and AH operate with ground combat forces, which they reinforce and support for a specific length of time. Depending on the situation, various ways of employing ATH or AH can be selected: maximum destruction, continuous attack, or phased employment. The maximum destruction technique employs all assets forward to provide massed firepower over a relatively wide area. This technique severely limits the capability to maintain continuous fire.

The advantage of the continuous attack technique is that one-half of the ATH or AH available will be fighting while the other half is being serviced. Thus an enemy can be engaged for a longer period of time without the need to break contact.

The third technique, phased employment, is a modified form of the continuous attack. After engagement of one company or echelon, a second is brought in. A third replaces the first unit requiring relief.

Companies or echelons usually consist of five to seven ATH and additional scout helicopters for reconnaissance and coordination, depending on the equipment of army aviation units.

Operations may take the following sequence:
1. flight from an assembly area to a holding area;
2. coordination with the forces requiring support or scout helicopters;
3. approach in NOE flight in battle positions, maintaining radio contact with the troops in position; and
4. ATH/AH conduct of fire action at the greatest possible fighting distance. Because of dissimilar observation capabilities, specific target designation procedures will be used only in exceptional cases.

Soviet army aviation units equipped with Mi-24 and Mi-8 AH concentrate largely on close air support (CAS) and pursuit operations. Thanks to their high disposable load of weapons, these helicopters are particularly suitable for CAS. Soviet attack helicopters are therefore in a position to release aircraft for other missions. As the Mi-24 is also able to transport eight soldiers, it can combine fire action with transport.

Important targets are tanks, armored infantry fighting vehicles, vehicles in general, emplacements, antitank weapons, and command positions. Further targets include assembly areas for combat and combat support forces and nuclear delivery means, as well as assaults on fortified positions with the aid of dropped troops.

Helicopters and aircraft engaged in CAS collaborate in the accomplishment of these tasks. Harmonization and collaboration with friendly CAS aircraft, artillery, missile troops, and maneuver units are essential for the effective identification, allocation, and combating of targets. These CAS tactics also require neutralization of the enemy's short-range air defense, aerial disposition, signals coordination, and identification systems.

Three types of fire support are open to helicopters: (1) preparation (firing prior to attack), (2) close support (firing during attack), and (3) escort (helicopters escort the attacking unit and combat any resulting targets). Friendly ground forces mark their positions with smoke to facilitate helicopter operations. Artillery observers illuminate targets for the helicopters using lasers.

Assault helicopter operations usually take place with flights composed of two sections, although other formations are possible. A flight can be stationed on an airfield 30 or more kilometers (19 mi.) away from the FLOT (forward line own troops). On being requested for support, the helicopters fly from the airfield to just before the combat area at a height of 100 to 150 meters (330 to 490 ft.) above ground. At this point they reduce their altitude to 5 to 10 meters (16 to 33 ft.). On target acquisition, the altitude is increased to a maximum of 100 meters in order to fire on the target. Targets are approached preferably at a gradient; this restricts the enemy's chances of air defense firing to a minimum. Combat begins at the greatest possible distance from the target. (Swatter can be launched from 3,500 meters [2.2 mi.], Spiral from 4,000 meters [2.5 mi.].) When engaged in combat against area targets, missiles can be fired at a maximum of 1,500 meters (0.9 mi.) and fire opened with 12.7mm machine guns at 1,000 meters (0.6 mi.). Disengagement occurs by veering sharply at very low altitude.

The most important operation for army aviation units equipped with the Soviet Mi-24 is presumably low-flying combined combat in conjunction with the mechanized infantry and CAS.

Deep-line Operations

Helicopters operating in depth in enemy-occupied territory are included in the doctrine of countries such as the United States and the former Soviet Union. Within the framework of the Air-land Battle doctrine, even rear area forces may be attacked and their commitment either decelerated or prevented.

Target fighting in depth requires adequate helicopter strength (e.g., the combat aviation brigade reinforced by the air force, artillery, and electronic countermeasures). Targets need not be confined to enemy fighting forces. "Soft" targets such as command and control or logistics elements are struck by attack helicopters. Airmobile reconnaissance and operations by dwindling daylight give the attacking forces a greater measure of safety. Depending on the depth and duration of a deep attack, it may be necessary to hold airmobile supply points with fuel and ammunition at the ready in the depths.

Deep-attack operations have high priority for Soviet assault helicopters. These operations comprise at least five combat missions: capture of bridgeheads near water; capture of important terrain; destruction of enemy nuclear delivery means; disruption of the enemy's reserves, command and communications networks, and logistics systems; and exploitation of nuclear and chemical impacts.

Soviet attack helicopters fulfill these missions by supporting the operational maneuver groups (OMGs), by raiding parties, and by helicopter *desant* (landings).

A Soviet OMG generally consists of a reinforced unit of division strength or larger, with extensive helicopter and aircraft support. Its task is to penetrate the enemy's defense on a narrow front and to destroy the defense system by attacking vulnerable targets in the enemy's rear. OMGs are threatened by enemy air attacks, multiple missile launcher and artillery systems, and counterattacks from ground forces. Attack and multipurpose helicopters are required for flexible fire support, reconnaissance of enemy troops, surveillance of open flanks, evacuation of casualties, material supplies, and for dropping airmobile assault landing forces to capture key terrain or crossing points prior to the arrival of the ground forces.

On completion of a certain mission, the helicopters can land on a base within the OMG forces, be prepared for further operations, carry out supporting missions, and finally return to bases behind the lines, which are some distance from the main forces of the OMG.

A helicopter *desant* takes place either as part of an OMG operation or as an independent undertaking initiated by an army to capture an obstacle or key terrain. The depth of thrust is determined by the expected speed of the ground forces detached to receive the airhead. A helicopter *desant* carried out as part of an OMG operation may comprise *desant* forces with the strength of a rifle regiment. Armies usually carry out *desant* in battalion strength, whereas divisions carry out *desant* in company strength. In accordance with the principles of operation, relief of the *desant* forces should take place within two to three hours (5 to 30 kilometers), but in Afghanistan assault landings with helicopters occurred up to 50 kilometers (31 mi.) ahead of the front lines. A Soviet helicopter *desant* begins by neutralizing the enemy's air defense with air force and artillery. A strike group of attack helicopters flies ahead, above the assault landing forces transporting the *desant* troops. A forward air controller in the strike group coordinates the air attack by the helicopters and ground fighting aircraft in the target area. The fire support from the ground attack fighters is stopped when the *desant* forces are about three minutes from the target area, although the assault helicopters continue to attack the target until the final phase of the assault landing.

AIR TRANSPORT OPERATIONS

This is the classical form of helicopter employment by army aviation. Air movement operations serve to support the combat, combat support, and logistics forces at points of main effort and are clearly distinct from air assault and airmobile operations. The task involved is the transport of troops, casualties, equipment, ammunition, fuel, and other supplies.

The volume of these operations can vary considerably. Depending on the situation, such transports may require protection by assault helicopters or aircraft.

SPECIAL OPERATIONS

Special operations are overt, clandestine, or covert military operations conducted during periods of peace or war. They are conducted in direct support of national and strategic objectives. They are outside the typical spectrum of the army aviation units, which provide flying equipment, mainly helicopters, and practice and carry out operational procedures with special forces. Air force assets, with their higher capacity, are also employed for these special operations. Operations can include unconventional warfare, intelligence and electronic warfare, strike, psychological warfare, and civil affairs.

AIR-TO-AIR COMBAT

The increasing number of helicopters, in particular assault helicopters, has led many nations to consider how these can be combated in the air by other aircraft.

Helicopters have a flight profile that makes it hard for ground radar to detect them and fire antiaircraft weapons to engage them in good time. Enemy helicopters and fixed-wing aircraft constitute the greatest danger for friendly helicopters at present. At close range, stabilized automatic cannons are wholly suitable for utilization against helicopters, and mounted machine guns are useful to a certain extent. Accuracy of fire and penetration capacity give satisfactory results only within a range of 3,000 meters (1.9 mi.). Unguided missiles are effective only against concentrations of helicopters. Antitank guided missiles are unsuitable due to their restricted lateral and vertical target tracking ability and long flight time. At best they can be employed only against helicopters that are maneuvering slowly.

Air-to-air missiles are regarded as the most effective means of combating helicopters. For this, the use of helicopters rather than fixed-wing aircraft with limited look-down/shoot-down potential has definite advantages.

For helicopter-against-helicopter combat, several maneuvers have evolved that are applied depending on the type of armament, the type of helicopter, and the operational area. Unlike fixed-wing aircraft, the helicopter conducts its maneuvers in the horizontal plane; even the slightest alteration in flight altitude can be decisive and can foil an attack or win a tactical advantage. Yo-yo, horizontal scissors, and wingover are maneuvers that are generally combined for use in attack and defense.

JOINT AIR ATTACK TEAM (JAAT) OPERATIONS

JAAT, used by the U.S. Army, provides for the combination of army aviation and air force aircraft to conduct independent operations or actions integrated into combined arms operations.

The advantage lies in the high mobility of A-10 aircraft and AH-64 helicopters, which are able to conduct night combat and have specialized equipment for antitank defense (Fig. 1).

Operations are directed against enemy penetrations, against sensitive forces in the depths, and against enemy air assaults or air-landed insertions in friendly territory toward the rear.

Airspace Management

Airspace management is necessary if a variety of participants will be using the airspace; an additional complication is that the airspace will also be monitored on the ground by air defense forces. It is an objective of airspace management to impose as few restrictions as possible on the utilizers, who may have partially conflicting interests.

Airspace management must contribute to the overall operational plan; a rigid system would be unable to accommodate changing situations. Certain altitudes, corridors, and zones are laid down in a plan and are binding on the different users. Army aviation, air defense, artillery, and air force units participate in this plan.

Generally speaking, helicopters fly below the monitored airspace on the

Figure 1. U.S. AH-64 Apache attack helicopter. (SOURCE: Robert F. Dorr Archives)

battlefield. They avoid entering zones especially protected by air defense and zones of planned artillery fire or CAS. However, the identification of aircraft remains a problem until a friend-foe identification system (IFF) is introduced.

Future Development of Army Aviation

Development in the years ahead will depend primarily on the future assessment of land warfare and consequently on the supporting role of army aviation.

Improved intelligence systems already render it almost impossible to conceal military movements whether by day or night or under bad weather conditions. Combat tanks will continue to exist in large numbers in most armies into the next century and will threaten their enemies with firepower and mobility. Their armament and armor will be improved; but the vulnerability of the drive mechanisms, tracks, and track rollers will remain. However, decisive improvements will be made in barrier systems and intelligent long-range ammunition, both costly items. Consequently, land warfare in the future will increasingly risk stagnation, subject to the availability of finances.

Use of the third dimension is also subject to these restrictions, although to a lesser extent. It may therefore be able to maintain and considerably improve its place in combined-arms combat as a highly mobile form of warfare that is independent of terrain and, increasingly, of visibility.

EQUIPMENT

It is generally agreed that present-day helicopters will not measure up to requirements beyond the year 2000 with respect to efficiency, survivability, and flight and combat effectiveness.

For armed helicopters, whose main task will be to intercept and repel tank attacks, future models need to be improved in the following ways:

• ability to fly NOE missions at night and in bad weather
• accurate all-weather navigation, target acquisition, and communications and identification systems
• maneuverability and sustainability of flight performance
• endurance in the 2.5- to 3-hour range
• lightweight weapon systems capable of engaging and defeating armor, ground defenses, and airborne targets
• up-to-date equipment enabling one-man operation.

In the 1990s the United States plans to introduce a new helicopter generation now known as the light helicopter experimental (LHX), which will come up to these and further requirements.

The U.S. Army will replace the helicopters UH-1M, OH-58C, OH-6A, AH-1G, and AH-1S with the LHX-SCAT (Scout/Attack). In addition to a multibarreled, turret-mounted Gatling automatic cannon, the SCAT version will also carry guided antitank missiles of type AGM-114 Hellfire, Stinger aerial target rockets, and nonguided missiles.

The LHX is to replace the OH-58A and UH-1H and will transport up to six fully equipped soldiers and/or payload. Its main task will be to transport fighter, antitank, and/or defense detachments as well as logistics transports in the battle area.

The former Soviet Union soon will introduce the Mi-28 as a replacement for the Mi-24. It can be assumed that this helicopter is at least equivalent to the American AH-64 and consequently possesses fire-and-forget systems for tank and aerial target combat.

For the countries of Western Europe it is highly unlikely that they will be able to equip armed helicopters to a similar extent in the foreseeable future, due to financial constraints. However, the helicopters being developed, such as the Franco-German joint production of antitank and escort/support helicopters (PAH-2/HAC) and the Italo-British production of a multirole combat helicopter (TONAL), constitute a considerable step forward toward a helicopter fleet that is independent of the United States.

The Boeing Vertol Company is working on a replacement for the CH-47 Chinook, a medium-weight assault transport helicopter. The design, known as army cargo rotorcraft (ACR), should be able to transport a load of approximately 14 tons over a distance of 500 kilometers (310 mi.) and take a maximum load of 40 tons.

Work is also being carried out in the United States on an advanced tilt-rotor aircraft, which is to fulfill multiple duties. This aircraft, named V-22, will position the two wingtip-mounted engines vertically for a helicopter-style takeoff and then progressively tilt the rotors forward for transition to forward flight. The tilt-rotor concept combines the low-speed flight of a helicopter with the speed and range of an airplane.

The role of such aircraft will be in intertheater and intratheater movement of troops with their vehicles, guns, and stores, flying over long distances at speed, direct to their operational locations.

DOCTRINE

The increasing number of armed and armored helicopters in many countries can be taken as an indication that helicopters will assume a more active role in combat than they have in the past.

The United States, the USSR, and France already have strong army aviation units that are able to conduct air assault and airmobile operations. Discussions are still in progress in some NATO countries as to the size and role of airborne mechanized units. However all acknowledge the great significance of such forces, in situations where insufficient armored operative reserves are available, if they are brought into play decisively, rapidly, and effectively.

ARNO MÖHL

SEE ALSO: Airborne Land Forces; Helicopter, Battlefield; Low-intensity Conflict: The Military Dimension; Special Operations Forces.

Bibliography

Gunston, B. 1986. *Modern fighting helicopters.* London: Salamander Books.
Harrison, P. 1985. *Military helicopters.* London: Brassey's.
Jane's all the world's aircraft, 1987–88. 1987. London: Jane's.

ARTILLERY

Modern artillery weapons play a dominant role in land combat. The effects of massed fire of these weapons combined with the shock action of armor and the ground-gaining ability of infantry are often decisive; artillery is the greatest killer on the battlefield.

The use of the word *artillery* predates the use of gunpowder and the development of guns and cannons. Many scholars consider the word to be a combination of *arcus*, bow, and *telum*, projectile. Others attribute the word to the Latin *ars tolendi*, or *ars* and *tirare*, meaning the art of catapulting or shooting, or *ars telorum*, the art of long-range weapons.

French fortress-builder Vauban (1633–1707) traces the word *artillery* to the old French *artillier*, to fortify or arm. German philologist Diez assumes an association with the Provençal word *artilha*, for fortification, and usage of the word was adopted into the German language by 1500.

Regardless of its derivation, the present-day definitions of *artillery* include the following: a general term, usually referring collectively to large-caliber gunpowder weapons (such as howitzers, cannons, and rockets), too large to be hand carried, and served by a crew (although all large, pregunpowder devices for firing missiles may be considered artillery); the branch of an army that is equipped with such weapons; and, in the Russian sense, the science of construction as well as the peculiarities and methods of implementation in combat of artillery weapons.

History

EARLY DEVELOPMENT TO THE FIRST GUNPOWDER WEAPONS

Pregunpowder throwing machines were known to the Assyrians (ca. 700 B.C.) and were employed by them against fortifications. It was several hundred years later, however, before the principles of engineering and mathematics were applied to advance the state of early catapults and ballistae—weapons using tension and/or torsion to propel various projectiles through a range of trajectories. Dionysius of Syracuse is considered by most historians to be the father of these early progenitors of modern artillery (399 B.C.).

The origins of the first firearms—weapons using the power of expanding gases from exploding gunpowder to shoot projectiles—are obscure. Gunpowder was introduced in China in the eleventh century and may have made its way to Europe via east-west trade routes in the mid-thirteenth century, although an Englishman, Roger Bacon, and a German monk, Berthold Schwarz, have been credited with its discovery. The Chinese used gunpowder in pyrotechnic weapons (rockets) and developed crude, cannon-like projectors, but it was the Europeans who invented the first gunpowder-operated cannon.

This development, in the early fourteenth century, became possible when advances in metalworking technology produced bronze and iron tubes strong enough to withstand the tremendous pressures generated by exploding gunpowder and rapidly expanding gases. The first cannons were bulbous, vase-shaped devices with a touchhole at the rear used to ignite the powder charge and a muzzle opening for loading and expelling a missile. Early projectiles varied from iron bolts and arrows, usually with some wadding at the base of the shaft to permit a closer fit in the tube, to round stones and later to iron and lead balls.

The first use of cannons in warfare may have been as early as 1326, when such weapons were described in a Florentine document. Austrians made their first use of cannons in an attack against Cividale in 1331, and the English used the weapon against the French in the Battle of Crécy in 1346. Other scholars point to the first use of guns at Metz in 1324 and agree to their later use at Algeciras in 1342. During this period, cannons became features in the English and French forces in the Hundred Years' War and became known throughout Europe.

EVOLVING DOCTRINE, TACTICS, AND TECHNOLOGY

As militaries became increasingly aware of the impact that cannons had on waging war, they began adapting the structure of their forces to accommodate the new weapons. Concurrently, tactics evolved to better suit the new capabilities, and arms makers sought to design and construct guns of varying size and arrangement.

In the early 1500s the collective term *gun*, which until then had applied to all equipment used for shooting (bow, crossbow, fire tubes, etc.), was restricted to heavy weapons. Later the name was used for each individual gun, often with a second name descriptive of the type of fire or tactical use. In the fourteenth and fifteenth centuries the crewmen of a gun became known as bombardiers, the word deriving from the Latin *bombus*, meaning a muffled sound. By contrast, cannons are managed by cannoneers or master gunners. The term *cannonier* was used in France as of 1411 and spread from there to the artillery of other countries.

During this period the art and craft of designing, manufacturing, and employing artillery were handed down exclusively from gunsmith to apprentice. Thus the circle of the initiated was intentionally kept small and knowledge was transferred by word of mouth and hands-on practice. The first books concerning artillery appeared toward the end of the sixteenth century.

In the 1400s the dukes of Burgundy, Philip the Good and his son Charles the Bold, who appointed noblemen as *maîtres d'artillerie*, were the first to include artillery in an army structure. They no longer used artillery guns individually in field battles but assembled them into batteries to increase the effects of their fire.

As technology and gun designs improved, cannons were transformed from simple iron tubes sealed at one end (muzzle loaders) on wooden frames (trestles) into early breech-loading cannons (although muzzle loaders remained a common feature of guns until the mid-nineteenth century). These were followed in the fifteenth century by gun barrels cast from copper or bronze, with trunnions to allow pivoting. These were mounted on wheeled gun carriages; thus the artillery gained mobility.

In addition to the destruction of fortifications, artillery could be employed in other tasks in the course of battle, such as shattering close formations of foot soldiers and horsemen. Stone, iron, and lead shot continued in use as ammunition; these were effective against walls and entrenchments, but against living targets they had effect only in the event of a direct hit. Therefore, antipersonnel ammunition (grape or canister) was developed and resembled large shotgun rounds. The range of this ammunition was less than that of a solid projectile but had a broader spread and was more effective against personnel targets.

As the weight-to-caliber ratio of guns decreased, mobility improved, resulting in the separation of field artillery from siege artillery. The field artillery, positioned in front of closed infantry formations at the commencement of battle, attempted to disrupt enemy formations. However, reinforcement of infantry weapons alone did not constitute a sufficient task for field artillery; greater scope was sought for these firearms.

Maurice of Orange (1567–1625) assigned some light guns to the infantry regiments in certain battles. Typically employed on the flanks, they reinforced musket fire and advanced as best they could with the musketeers.

Gustavus Adolphus (1594–1632) of Sweden, however, is considered the father of modern field artillery and of massed, mobile artillery fire. He devoted much time and effort to solving artillery mobility problems: gun weight was reduced by shortening the barrel and reducing the thickness of the tube;

improved, standardized gunpowder permitted greater accuracy despite the shortened barrel; calibers were standardized for heavy (24-pound), medium (12-pound), and light (3-pound) regimental guns. Equally important, Gustavus abandoned the practice of hiring civilian contract gunners and replaced them with his own soldiers, responsive to his discipline and training; thus he ensured far better command and control in battle.

A Frenchman, Vauban (1633–1707), dominated developments in both siege-craft and fortification. At a time when sieges were the most common activity of warfare, Vauban provided a systematic approach for attackers and their heavy siege artillery to blow a breach in walled fortifications and exploit the breach with an infantry assault. Likewise, he devoted much effort to designing fortifications that could withstand such attacks.

Toward the end of the eighteenth century, technological developments brought new artillery advances. Improvements in powder and more resistant metal alloys resulted in an increased range up to 600 meters (1,970 ft.) and a rate of fire of two shots per minute. Aiming and sighting devices were developed in France, and an era of more accurate artillery fire began.

Napoleon Bonaparte (1769–1821), who began his career as an artillery officer, owed his success in battle largely to his intensive use of artillery as the backbone of the postrevolutionary mass armies. An infantry attack was preceded by concentrations of artillery fire that were greater than ever before. The artillery of Napoleon's Imperial Guard, which he held in reserve at the beginning of a battle, wore down enemy infantry forces at the point of intended penetration: "My Artillery Guard decides the majority of battles. As I always have them at the ready, I can deploy them anywhere they are needed."

In this way artillery reserves, alongside infantry reserves, became a means in the hands of the commander to force an issue during the course of combat. The effectiveness of artillery was enhanced not only by ambitious tactics, but also by improved powder, which increased the effective range to 1,000 meters (3,280 ft.). To a greater extent fire was now delivered over the heads of friendly troops—artillery had become the dominant, and most lethal, combat arm.

Napoleon's influence on warfare extended to the middle of the nineteenth century, at which time the organization, doctrine, tactics, and weapons of militaries had come together in a congruent and optimal way. The arms of artillery, cavalry, and infantry combined on the battlefield in a consistent and effective manner; their weapons had achieved something nearing their technological potential. It was the end of one era and the beginning of another.

AGE OF TECHNOLOGICAL INNOVATION

The congruence of Napoleonic warfare was shattered in the mid-nineteenth century by the introduction of the conoidal bullet (minié ball) in battle during the Crimean War of 1853–56. Combined with technological developments in percussion ignition, breech loading, rifled barrels, and cartridge cases, the conoidal bullet initially provided a new firepower and lethality for the infantry. It was to have a profound effect on warfare. Military strategists such as the

Prussian chief of staff Helmuth von Moltke (1800–1891), recognizing its destructive power, began adapting tactical and strategic concepts.

The technological innovations applied equally to artillery. In autumn 1857 the Prussian army began to replace smoothbore guns with rifled barrels. The new steel gun, manufactured by the Krupp concern, used a crucible casting process and was breech loaded. The barrel had grooves and lands, enabling the projectile to be spin stabilized. The use of cast steel resulted not only in increased resistance of the material, but also in decreased wall thickness and therefore a reduction of the barrel's weight.

In 1877 the development of explosive gelatin and of smokeless powder made possible the manufacture of high-explosive charges for the shell and of guns that would not obscure battlefields with smoke. The rifled gun barrel and elongated shells with ranges up to 4,250 meters (14,000 ft.) resulted in greater accuracy of fire. Easy loading from the rear increased the rate of fire, and aiming devices continued to improve.

In the late nineteenth century the introduction of the field telephone permitted indirect fire. Artillery was now able to fire into the depth of the battlefield from defiladed positions, to transfer fire, and to have drastic effect on the course of combat. Massed targets, which had originally encouraged the introduction of artillery, gradually diminished as a result of all these developments, but artillery tactics and techniques had become so versatile and reliable that the enemy could be struck even in loose formation. The old cast-steel shells were gradually replaced by modern shrapnel and high-explosive (HE) ammunition.

Simplified loading, recoil mechanisms, and aiming devices increased the rate of fire to 8 to 10 shots per minute; the range was now up to 8,000 meters (26,000 ft.). Along with the development of guns came innovations in artillery ammunition. In 1897 the laminated shell produced an effect five times that previously achieved. Shrapnel ammunition with time fuzes was developed further. The time fuze caused the shell, filled with lead pellets, to explode while still in the air, projecting the pellets in the direction of the target. This effect was increased by fitting a booster charge and a pusher plate into the base of the shell casing. Shrapnel soon became the main shell for field guns.

ARTILLERY IN WORLD WAR I

By the beginning of World War I, artillery development had spawned a wide assortment of weapons in the world's militaries. Artillery was divided into light field artillery (drawn by horses or tractors), heavy field artillery, and heavy artillery/siege artillery (emplaced semipermanently). Corps and divisions had light field artillery and (where appropriate) mountain artillery; guns were of 65 to 77mm and howitzers were in the 105 to 122mm range. Howitzers of 120 to 155mm were available at corps and army level; the heavy artillery with guns, howitzers, and mortars above caliber 155mm was subordinate to the supreme command. Antiaircraft artillery and trench mortars existed only as experimental models or in very restricted numbers at the beginning of 1915.

In principle the main artillery function was to support infantry combat. Artillery fire was largely dependent on visual observation, and adjustment fire was followed by fire for effect. During the course of the war the artillery developed into the main firepower of the ground forces.

In support of infantry troops the most important task of the artillery was to suppress enemy firepower throughout the depth of the defense, to destroy defense installations, and thus to provide the infantry attack with a chance of success. To facilitate breakthrough operations, artillery was employed in large concentrations in the most important sectors. For example, the Germans used 1,051 guns (722 light, 329 heavy and very heavy) for the attack near Verdun on 12 February 1916, along a 25-kilometer (15.5-mi.) front—42 guns per kilometer of front, three times the artillery concentration of the defender. The German armies attacking at Chemin des Dames on 27 May 1918 used 5,263 guns along a 55-kilometer (34-mi.) front (95 guns per kilometer of front and a ratio of 3.7:1 against the defender). British troops attacking at Wytschaete on 7 June 1917 along a front width of 16 kilometers (9.9 mi.) had an artillery density of 140 guns per kilometer of front.

In trench warfare, artillery firepower afforded the defender high resistance; at the same time, it constituted the strongest and most reliable means of destroying the defense. As a result artillery duels and lengthy artillery preparations characterized the war. The German artillery preparations at Verdun in February 1916 lasted nine hours; the French fired on the Somme in July 1916 for seven days and in Flanders in July 1917 for sixteen days.

The heavily fortified nature of trench warfare, and the emergence of artillery as the dominant firepower weapon, challenged employment of these pieces. Both the railway as a means of transport for deploying and the tactical march with mainly horse-drawn transport could be easily observed, triggering countermeasures by the other side. The resulting battles of attrition and subsequent stalemates affected artillery organization and tactics. The numbers of howitzers and heavy artillery rose five- to tenfold. Flat-trajectory fire was unable to reach defiladed targets effectively, so new howitzers were introduced that fired at high angles of elevation (45 degrees or greater), thus enabling the destruction of protected enemy infantry.

Artillery observers on hills or tall buildings were often far from the infantry struggle and could not see operational details. For that reason, as well as to enable prompt compliance with infantry requests for fire support, artillery liaison units and forward observers were detached to the infantry. In this way collaboration between the two branches of the service became closer than before. Another need was for artillery to accompany the infantry. This requirement was met principally with 37mm guns and trench mortars. These weapons were intended to close the artillery's fire gap and constitute a sort of "pocket artillery" for the infantry.

In an attempt to regain tactical mobility on the battlefield, the Germans reorganized their field forces in the spring of 1917. The reform was based on the close relationship between fire and movement, but the fronts were already so firmly established by trenches that only limited movements were achieved on the battlefield.

Under such conditions, the objective of the artillery could not be the destruction of the enemy army, but merely the acquisition of territory. Even the introduction of tanks made little difference, particularly as no new guidelines were elaborated for their employment; they were spread wide apart rather like mobile machine-gun nests, in successive waves, with the object of supporting the infantry in the sporadic conquest of sectors. The introduction of armored vehicles led to the creation of antitank artillery.

Artillery observation facilities were improved by the use of tethered balloons and aircraft. Observers in the sky above the battlefield could see a larger area and direct artillery fire more effectively. The rapid development of aviation in general resulted in the creation of antiaircraft artillery. In 1918 the armies in action had approximately 4,200 guns for air defense. Special field guns on carriages were similarly used to combat aircraft.

New developments in artillery ammunition continued throughout the war. Shrapnel was replaced by a fragmenting or splinter-producing shell as the principal antipersonnel round. Special projectiles were developed: incendiary shells, smoke shells, and shells filled with chemical agents.

New methods and procedures for commanding and controlling artillery were developed. Forces were centralized at the outset of an operation and decentralized as combat progressed. This necessitated uniform fire control and good signal communications. Firing commands required precise calculations, as adjustment fire was abandoned in order to achieve surprise. Internal and external ballistic influences were increasingly taken into better account in such calculations. The groundwork for this was provided by newly created artillery meteorological services, which permitted calculation of the effects of wind currents on projectiles at different levels of ballistic trajectory. As a result, indirect fire could be placed on target areas with reasonable accuracy and effectiveness.

Despite various techniques for employing artillery fire, such as rolling barrages that moved ahead of attacking infantry formations, artillery firepower in World War I was unable to overcome the static, entrenched positions of the opponent. On the contrary, increasing consolidation of artillery contributed to the "freezing" of the fronts and to stronger underground positions and greater defensive depth. The element of movement was missing. The potential of the tank used with artillery fire support was never recognized.

BETWEEN THE WORLD WARS

Technological innovation of artillery weapons and procedural development of their uses continued after World War I, albeit with varied emphasis and focus in different countries. In the 1920s and 1930s artillery weapons were modernized and developed further in the countries of Western Europe, the United States, Japan, and the Soviet Union. Range, rate of fire, mobility, and firepower all increased, the result of new types of powder, semiautomatic and automatic breech mechanisms, motorization, and the introduction of self-propelled artillery. The heaviest and longest-range artillery were loaded onto specially designed artillery carriages.

The artillery branches of the armies of France, Italy, and Great Britain were to some extent neglected due to the fascination with emerging possibilities for employment of tanks and airplanes in battle. Germany, by contrast, increased its artillery from negligible quantities in the early 1930s to approximately 50,000 guns and mortars of varying caliber by the end of the decade. Soviet artillery consisted of about 67,000 guns and mortars.

Although the United States had only a small number of artillery weapons in 1939, this was to some extent made up for by an intensive production effort beginning in 1940. Even more important, however, was a new and revolutionary method of fire control developed at the U.S. Field Artillery School during the 1920s and 1930s. Using this new method, built around battalion fire-direction centers, U.S. artillery proved to be more effective than that of any other belligerent in World War II.

Basic artillery employment concepts evolved, such as the concentration of artillery fire in prioritized areas, close collaboration between infantry and tanks, use of artillery to combat tanks, and emphasis on achieving surprise. Surprise was to be achieved by dispensing with adjustment fire and placing accurate, effective fire on known target locations; simultaneous opening of fire from all batteries; using brief artillery preparations, even if this meant the enemy's positions were not completely destroyed; and by great artillery density and high rate of fire.

ARTILLERY IN WORLD WAR II

Although all major belligerents in World War II employed artillery, the German and Soviet experiences provide an excellent illustration of the use of artillery at that time.

The motorization and mechanization of armies, the development of tactical air forces, and progress in communications systems were all prerequisites for reestablishing mobility in combat, which had been frozen in World War I. These elements fathered the German "blitzkrieg"; the technical method called for the concentrated employment of the mechanized forces in collaboration with the air force while the remaining components, including the artillery, played a subordinate role in combat.

In Poland in 1939, and in the west in 1940, German tank units broke through the front and the motorized divisions that followed widened the breakthrough with artillery support. Dive-bombers joined in ground combat and destroyed enemy artillery firing positions, thus to a certain extent sparing the attacker the need to establish heavy artillery concentrations. Offensives were made with no prior artillery preparation, only with air support. It was typical of the blitzkrieg to select weak points where an issue could be decided with concentrated superiority, enabling rapid penetration into the depths of the defender's position. This led to tremendous dynamics between opposing forces in battle and to the creation of a much deeper battlefield. The artillery was unable to keep pace with this development, particularly the heavy artillery, which in most armies was still horse drawn. Movement, considered more important than fire, was the movement of motor-driven, mechanized units. The artillery of the German army played a minor role in the lightning campaigns in 1939 against Poland and

Norway, in 1940 against Western Europe, and in the 1941 Balkan campaign.

This situation was altered with the German attack on the Soviet Union that began in June 1941. After a series of successful battles of encirclement similar to the blitzkrieg, the mobility of the motorized units was drastically curtailed in early October due to the weather. The offensive drowned in mud, and then the Russian winter set in.

The greatest artillery concentration of World War II was accumulated on the German side in 1942 for the third attack on Sebastopol (93 batteries of heavy artillery, 88 batteries of light artillery, 24 mortar batteries, three detachments of self-propelled assault guns, including howitzer and mortar batteries with 305mm, 350mm, and 420mm weapons, two 600mm mortars, and the 800mm gun known as Dora). Approximately 12,500 shells of the heaviest caliber were fired.

In the summer of 1943 the density of the German artillery was 70 to 80 guns per kilometer of front, this in preparation for a renewed assault operation in the Kursk offensive. The artillery, despite its concentration, was unable to shatter the double-echelon Russian defense, and the main effort of attacking tanks and infantry was repulsed.

In the extensive Soviet operations that ensued as a strategic counterattack between 1943 and 1945, the Soviet artillery was employed en masse. Depending on the situation it supported attacking operations with successive concentrated fire, with the creeping barrage, and, in numerous cases, with the double creeping barrage. Soviet artillery density in the breakthrough sectors often amounted to 200 to 300 guns and mortars per kilometer of front. In the spring of 1945, approximately 45,000 Soviet guns, mortars, and missile launchers participated in the battle for Berlin.

The Soviet Supreme Command placed heavy emphasis on the production of artillery, and by the end of the war the Red Army had nearly 50 percent of all artillery in the world. The Soviets used artillery to accomplish operational objectives. By the end of 1942 artillery brigades and divisions began to appear; in 1943 a special artillery breakthrough corps was established. The artillery was increasingly centralized, which made rapid deployments more difficult but permitted numerical concentrations of weapons beyond what was possible in other armies.

A significant German contribution to artillery was the development of jet propulsion systems. On 3 October 1942 the first A-4 rocket was launched from the Peenemünde, Germany, test area. Its flight lasted 296 seconds and covered 192 kilometers (119 mi.), and it fell with a lateral deviation of 18 kilometers (11.2 mi.) from its target. Although even the long-range V-1 and V-2 weapons (V stands for *Vergeltungswaffe*, which means retaliatory weapon) were not able to alter the outcome of World War II, the creation of the jet propulsion system began a development that has decisively influenced artillery right up to the present.

Altogether World War II encouraged the all-around development of artillery, particularly antiaircraft artillery, antitank artillery, self-propelled artillery, and missile artillery.

Artillery Today

ROLES, MISSIONS, AND CONCEPTS

The role of artillery has changed since World War II. In that war artillery was characteristically used for direct-fire support of combat troops and containment of first-echelon enemy forces, including accompanying artillery units. Today, with better reconnaissance, greater range, and more effective ammunition, artillery is also in a position to contain and destroy the following echelons (reserves) of the major units and operational alliances.

This has served to broaden the operational focus of artillery support. In addition to providing direct-fire support for maneuver forces, artillery also focuses on neutralization of enemy artillery and other important targets throughout the depth of the battlefield. These latter missions are assigned to general-support artillery units. Overall, combat operations are influenced by the commander to the extent that he effectively neutralizes enemy troops (in echelon), heavy weapons, logistics installations, battle headquarters, and facilities so that the threat to friendly major units is diminished or crushed and the way opened for accomplishment of his own mission.

For the artillery, this complex role requires rapid and accurate target acquisition; conversion of reconnaissance information into firing data with minimum action and reaction time between location of and effective fire on the target; engagement of static and moving targets of various size and hardness with effective ammunition; and safeguarding one's own survival against attacks of any kind, including enemy artillery fire.

Of contemporary interest is that the Russians also consider artillery a science that comprises all knowledge of structure and organization, deployment and employment, development and manufacture, and military technology, as well as combat characteristics, firing procedures, and use in action. The spectrum corresponds to the components of the artillery training in Western armies but with somewhat different emphases.

ORGANIZATION

Artillery is found as a branch of the service in different countries in artillery formations and units of various sizes (division, brigade, detachment, regiment, battalion, battery). The size of the artillery force relative to the overall size of the armed forces varies from country to country. These differences reflect differences in military doctrine, operational concepts, tasks of the armed forces in general and of the artillery in particular, and the strategies of alliances and nations.

Historical experiences frequently affect operational thought. Changes in technology increasingly determine the internal organization and structure of artillery units, as well as the task assignment for the combined forces' effort within the general concept of the armed forces.

Western organizational concepts. The artillery of the Western armed forces is composed of artillery divisions, brigades, regiments, battalions, and batteries of firing and reconnaissance (target acquisition) artillery. For example, German artillery consists of detachments (corps level), regiments (division level), and battalions (brigade level). Western artillery formations are defined as corps, division, or brigade artillery, depending on their organizational assignment to major units. They support combat troops with conventional and atomic fire and by reconnaissance.

The use of reconnaissance artillery by Western armies provides basic data for firing during combat and contributes to the commander's estimate of developing situations. It covers terrain with technical reconnaissance means that include optical control means, flash-ranging apparatus, radar apparatus, sound-ranging systems, and reconnaissance aircraft (drones). Regardless of the time of day or weather, it locates targets in the area of interest of the senior commander, with the aim of conducting combat and as a basis for the operational activity of the firing artillery. In addition, it has the apparatus for ascertaining meterological data.

The firing artillery consists of tube and rocket artillery. Tube artillery includes barrel weapons of all kinds that are able to fire bomblet, high-explosive, and smoke ammunition. Weapon types include field howitzers and field guns of various range and caliber (field artillery), as well as armored and nonarmored self-propelled howitzers and guns. Field artillery includes towed guns, mounted guns, and self-propelled guns.

Warsaw Pact organizational concepts. The structure of artillery in the armies of the nations of Eastern Europe was dictated by the requirements and agreements set by the Warsaw Pact. Accordingly, all of these nations still have a similar organization, which is described here. They may evolve in varying forms over the coming decade.

The structure of artillery in these armies comprises the troop artillery and the reserve artillery of the supreme command. At army level the troop artillery consists of an artillery brigade with howitzers and a brigade with self-propelled guns, as well as a battalion for artillery reconnaissance.

Each motorized infantry division has an artillery regiment with armored howitzers and multiple rocket launchers and a battery of reconnaissance artillery. The armored divisions have fewer armored howitzers but are otherwise similarly equipped. Motorized infantry and tank regiments each have a battalion of armored howitzers.

The reserve artillery of the supreme command in each nation's forces consists of artillery and rocket launchers that are easily attached to support the general tactical and operational units. The front artillery division has four regiments consisting of field guns, howitzers, armored howitzers, and multiple rocket launchers, as well as three artillery reconnaissance battalions.

This artillery is employed for the qualitative and quantitative reinforcement of the troop artillery in the sector of main effort. This range of weapons is considered necessary for any extensive operational artillery maneuver and to allow for a high artillery density in the breakthrough sectors. According to doctrine, an attack is inconceivable without integrating the necessary support weapons into the attacking command. The air force, combat helicopters, and heavy artillery elements all constitute important means of support.

Since 1973 the artillery of these armies has been reinforced and modernized. The tube artillery has been reequipped with 122mm and 154mm armored howitzers, which have automatic fire control and data-transfer systems. This has increased the survivability and effectiveness of the artillery.

Command regulations have aimed at an artillery support ratio of 10:1 in the main effort sector. This is obtained by the concentrated use of the troop artillery of the divisions attacking in echelons and the army artillery brigade and with the help of artillery forces detached from the artillery front division (reserve artillery of the supreme command).

CONCEPT VARIATIONS AMONG ARMIES

In some armies, artillery includes mortars, recoilless guns, and launching installations for antitank weapons as well as air force/air-defense guns and rocket launchers. Some nations subdivide their artillery into light, medium, and heavy artillery, depending on the caliber or weight of the weapons. Light artillery is intended primarily for direct support of infantry and armor and includes cannons with calibers up to 105mm; the largest (and only) light artillery piece currently in the U.S. Army is the 105mm howitzer (see Fig. 1). Medium artillery includes weapons that range in size from 105mm to 155mm howitzers. Heavy artillery includes guns of at least 155mm and howitzers of larger calibers.

Rocket artillery is equipped with multiple rocket launchers and rocket launchers that fire guided or nonguided missiles. Multiple rocket launchers use bomblet, mine, splinter, and smoke rockets. The rocket artillery is able to obstruct sectors of terrain, especially against attacking enemy tanks.

Figure 1. A U.S. Army 105mm gun shielded by a camouflage net during the Korean War. (SOURCE: U.S. Library of Congress)

The artillery in national armed forces is either allocated decentrally to the various formations or centrally organized. An example of decentralized organization is the German Bundeswehr. Tube artillery battalions are assigned to the brigades, regiments with a field artillery battalion to the divisions, and a battalion with multiple rocket launchers to the reconnaissance battalions.

Other armies may have armored artillery battalions in the brigades and artillery regiments with tube weapons of various calibers on division level. In addition, the corps often has available comprehensive artillery forces that provide heavy artillery support and air defense for the divisions. This is the case in the British corps artillery division.

A similar situation exists in the corps of the U.S. forces stationed in Germany. In addition to the artillery of the armored and infantry divisions, the corps also has strong artillery forces available in brigade strength. This artillery organization, which is primarily for the central command, enables the commander to form points of main artillery effort at his own discretion.

TUBE ARTILLERY OR ROCKET ARTILLERY?

At present, a burning question concerning armament revolves around the relative values of rocket and tube artillery.

The advantages of rocket artillery include consistent action where area targets are involved, an increase in range with minimal technical expenditure, low gas pressures in the barrel of the rocket launcher, and therefore a thinner, lighter covering on the warhead. The interior of the barrel is larger, although the caliber is the same, which allows more space for ammunition than in the shell. Rocket artillery has lower personnel requirements (operating crew) and lower cost.

The disadvantages of the rocket are several. The dispersion of rounds on the target is greater than that of guns, firing positions are restricted, and they are farther from the target. No uninterrupted fire support is possible because usually it is best to have only one fire mission per firing position with preselected ammunition. Since rockets are easy to observe, the launch position is very vulnerable to enemy artillery, and there is usually no armored protection available for the crew.

The advantages of tube artillery include greater hit accuracy, faster firing sequence, faster target acquisition, and faster change in type of ammunition. Consequently, tube weapons are more suited for use against smaller area targets and moving targets.

With the current state of engineering, the two weapons systems complement each other. The decision to choose rocket launcher or gun must depend in the last instance on the future development of ammunition for use against hard targets. In the meantime, several armies in the Western alliance have also recognized the possibilities of multiple rocket launcher systems.

A significant step toward increasing conventional firepower was made with the introduction of the multiple launch rocket system (MLRS). This system, which was inspired by weapons used by both Germany and the USSR in World War II and developed in the United States, has several advantages: its three-man crew can continue to fire even under nuclear-biological-chemical conditions; the launcher can be adapted to fire rockets with different calibers or ranges and is therefore effective against targets of any hardness; it has a short reload time (up to three refills per launcher per hour); and its range of up to 40 kilometers (24.8 mi.) enables echelonment in depth, which means that not all firing units are compelled to change position, even if the enemy penetrates. The MLRS was used successfully by coalition forces during Operation Desert Storm (February 1991) against area targets and also as a counterbattery weapon.

ANTIARMOR ARTILLERY

Antitank, or antiarmor, artillery is that which combats armored vehicles by direct fire. This branch is equipped with antitank guns (towed) or with armored and nonarmored self-propelled guns, as well as recoilless guns and weapons carriers with antitank guided missiles. The most modern electronics are used in connection with these antitank guided missiles, which have ranges up to 4,000 meters (13,000 ft.). In modern armies, antitank helicopters are also equipped with these missiles.

Tanks and armored infantry fighting vehicles pose a constantly increasing threat due to their special armor, greater mobility, better firepower, improved ammunition, electronic fire control equipment, and longer ranges. This threat is steadily being countered by the increased effectiveness of antitank artillery. Special antitank fighting vehicles and antitank missile systems with longer range, as well as hand-carried "fire-and-forget" weapons, are under development. In some countries antitank artillery does not belong to the artillery branch but to the supported troops (armored corps, antitank corps, mechanized infantry).

AIR DEFENSE ARTILLERY

Air defense artillery is that part of the artillery used on the battlefield to combat enemy helicopters and aircraft with tube or rocket antiaircraft weapons. It is equipped with cannons that are towed or are carried on armored or nonarmored self-propelled carriages, as well as with towed or self-propelled rocket launchers. In modern armies the air defense weapons systems are autonomous with regard to target identification and tracking. In some armies this type of artillery is a separate branch of service, as an army air defense corps. In some nations air defense is a separate service, on a level with the army, navy, and air force. It conducts battle against aircraft at low to medium altitude and protects ground combat forces and artillery as well as important installations against enemy reconnaissance and air attacks.

COASTAL DEFENSE ARTILLERY

In a few nations rockets have been put to use for coastal defense and controlling sea straits. It is conceivable that the compulsion to minimize costs in national defense budgets will result in expansion of such use. The guided missiles of today are already able to safeguard and defend coast and sea routes effectively using available technology.

Tasks of Artillery within Different Forms of Combat

Within the combined arms effort the artillery supports other troops with indirect fire and reconnaissance. The principal task attributed to the artillery on a worldwide scale is the direct support of the combat forces (tanks, mechanized infantry). Consequently, the artillery is largely responsible for nonatomic firepower on the battlefield. It may also make use of atomic warheads, depending on what options are open to the commander. Thus this branch of the services is a decisive means for the operational command of the land forces to combat enemy forces in the depths of the battlefield or directly ahead of combat troops, with fire of any quality and density.

The range of the various weapons and reconnaissance systems and the ability to open or shift fire quickly and precisely on the battlefield can decide a battle. Defense is, in the first instance, a battle with fire. An army whose main form of combat is defense therefore requires strong firepower. The perspectives for successful defense are increased if long-range fire can prevent follow-up units from being moved up and causing heavy losses and if the effect of support weapons can be diminished.

The classical sphere of artillery action therefore lies in the area beyond that of the direct-fire weapons of frontline combat troops and out to the maximum range of the reconnaissance means, guns, and rockets. The artillery has technical reconnaissance means and weapons systems available that enable it to react quickly and fire effectively within this area at any time.

The early crushing of enemy forces as far as possible ahead of friendly front troops obviously results in fewer casualties for supported forces than if penetrations must be suppressed during the course of combat. It is therefore imperative that artillery be integrated in adequate strength with other ground and air forces for modern combat.

Russian theory. According to Russian theories, the attacking artillery has the following tasks in combat: crush the adversary's defensive fire capability, making way for motorized infantry and tank elements; shatter the enemy by breaking through its defense sectors; beat off enemy counterattacks (counterblows) together with other forces and means; engage the enemy while introducing the second echelon; support friendly forces in pursuit of the enemy and when confronted with water obstacles; and combat the enemy by supporting tactical air landings.

For an attack with penetration of the defense sectors, the artillery's actions take place in three related periods: (1) artillery preparation of the assault; (2) artillery support of the assault; and (3) artillery accompaniment of the troops exploiting a successful assault into the rear areas of the enemy's defense.

The main tasks of defensive artillery include the following: engagement of the enemy during its attack preparations as well as during the assembly and deployment of its troops; repulsion of enemy assaults in front of the foremost line of defense; attrition of enemy groups that have penetrated the defense, so that they cannot push forward into the depths and flanks; protection of boundaries, flanks, and sectors between defensive areas; attrition of enemy airborne troops and advancing reserves, and the disorganization of the enemy's military command; and support of friendly troops conducting counterattacks. Artillery counterpreparations and fire against enemy tanks are important parts of artillery defense action.

Western theory. According to Western doctrine, defense artillery should harrass enemy movement at an early stage and destroy or damage enemy elements as much as possible while they are preparing for attack. Later, it should block tank attacks and crush lightly armored and nonarmored enemy forces with fire. The enemy is to be struck with concentrated fire at penetration points, and open flanks should be controlled. In particular, enemy artillery that has engaged friendly antitank weapons or reserves should be neutralized or crushed.

Attacking artillery should provide constant support for friendly troops without restricting their movements. Concentrated firing is required where enemy forces most strongly hinder friendly assault operations. Fire protection before an attack is normal; artillery firing action may also commence simultaneously with the attack, particularly if surprise is desired.

When delaying tactics are applied, the artillery engages enemy forces with concentrated fire in the depths of the battlefield, decelerating the hostile advance by using heavy fire and supporting the combat troops in delaying positions. This should compel the enemy to deploy his forces, thus contributing to the delay.

Artillery of the Future

The entire spectrum of artillery tasks will benefit from anticipated technological developments. Since artillery is responsible for indirect fire in the combined arms effort, it will bear more responsibility than previously. Future artillery capabilities will counteract other achievements of modern technology, such as an eventual increase in the fighting power of the armored elements of the armed forces, an increase in their speed due to reduction of their specific weight, and reinforced hardness. The spheres of reconnaissance and fire coordination will be of particular importance.

Artillery reconnaissance, command, and fire control should be optimized in a combined system that includes coordination of close air support. This could be achieved by an artillery system with the following elements: reconnaissance/target acquisition; command/fire control; weapons system/surveying; and ammunition. The scope and responsibilities of each element are suggested below. Reconnaissance and target acquisition:

- regular reconnaissance of the battlefield in sufficient depth, day and night, and in any weather
- identification of targets as to type and activity, as well as location, with adequate accuracy
- passing on and evelation of information without loss of time; situation and target information on the spot

- provision of information in degree of detail adequate for the requirements of the respective level of command
- combined use of infrared, laser, heat image, dwarf wave (millimeter wave), and radar techniques.

Command and fire control:

- connection of the reconnaissance and acquisition systems with artillery command positions, fire control points, and weapons systems
- integration of the elements of reconnaissance, evaluation, tactical and technical fire control, weapons, and ammunition
- guarantee of short artillery reaction and response times.

Weapons systems and surveying:

- use of a variable mixture of artillery weapons, consisting of autonomous armored artillery guns and rocket launchers
- optimization of the range, rate of fire, and accuracy of artillery weapons and protection of the operating crew
- integration of artillery weapons into computer-assisted operational systems
- use of combat drones to continually seek, find, and directly engage targets.

Ammunition:

- development of ammunition to achieve maximum effect on armored targets
- use of bomblet ammunition and hollow-charge ammunition
- construction of fully guided missiles, ejected as subammunition, that approach and destroy individual targets
- construction of homing ammunition that probes the target area and fires a projectile as soon as a target appears.

Realization of these objectives depends on the degree of threat involved, on the operational and tactical concepts, and on the finances available in the defense budget.

The efficiency of the combined artillery effort can be increased in collaboration with modern technology to such an extent that this branch of the services can cope with all conceivable threats in the future. All in all, a new quality of artillery will result from the existence of three conditions: (1) the battlefield is totally under surveillance; (2) fire can be opened on any target that appears, without adjustment fire and without time delay; and (3) soft, semi-hard, and hard targets—in front of friendly troops, in the depths of the enemy, and across the whole breadth of the scene of action—can be effectively engaged with optimal and economic use of ammunition. Thus the commander possesses new possibilities for the use of artillery.

The role of artillery in the postnuclear age, with radiating weapons such as laser or electromagnetic weapons, has yet to be determined. In view of its technical know-how, the artillery will continue to bear heavy responsibility.

MANFRED KÜHR

SEE ALSO: Ammunition; Artillery, Rocket and Missile; Artillery, Tube; Blitz-krieg; Combat Support; Combined Arms; Firepower; Gun, Antitank; Gun Technology Applications; Land Warfare; Mechanized Warfare; Rocket, Anti-armor; Tank.

Bibliography

Cocino, A. 1971. Artillerie-Entwicklungen beim italienischen Heer. *Internationale Wehrrevue*, Jg. 4, Nr. 2:139–41.

Die Artillerie. 1986. *Entscheidende Waffe im Konventionellen Kampf in Allgemeine Schweizerische Militärzeitschrift*, Beih. Jg. 152, Nr. 7/8:3–22.

Dodd, N. 1973. Die Royal artillery des britischen Heeres. *Wehrkunde*, Jg. 22, lt. 5, 253–59.

Dupuy, R. E., and T. N. Dupuy. 1986. *The encyclopedia of military history.* 2d rev. ed. New York: Harper and Row.

Graf, K. 1987. Artillerie 2000. *Allgemeine Schweizerische Militärzeitschrift* Jg. 153, Nr. 4:229–32, und Nr. 6:377–8o.

Hahn, F. 1986. *Waffen und Geheimwaffen des deutschen Heeres* 1933–1945. Koblenz: Bernhard und Graefe Verlag.

International Institute for Strategic Studies. *The military balance.* Annual. London: Brassey's (U.K.).

Krug, H. 1982. *25 jahre Artillerie der Bundeswehr.* Friedberg: Podzun-Pallas-Verlag.

Manuel du gradé d'artillerie T. 1-3. 1952. Paris: Charles-Lavanzelle.

Mausbart, F. 1969. Die Entwicklung der Artillerie in den letzten 3o jahren. *Österreichische Militärische Zeitschrift* Jg. 7:22–32.

Ministère de la Défense Nationale. 1955. *Artillerie au combat.* Paris: Charles-Lavanzelle.

Neuzeitliche Artilleriesysteme. 1983. Forum der Deutschen Gesellschaft für Wehrtechnik an der Artillerieschule in Idar-Oberstein, 6–7 Oktober. Koblenz: Bernhard und Graefe Verlag.

Reid, W. 1976. *Arms through the ages.* New York: Harper and Row.

Ryan, J. W. 1982. *Guns, mortars and rockets.* Vol. 2 of *Brassey's battlefield weapon systems and technology.* London: Brassey's.

Speisebecher, W. 1977. *Taschenbuch für Artilleristen.* Koblenz: Wehr und Wissen Verlagsgesellschaft.

ARTILLERY, ROCKET AND MISSILE

Free flight rockets (FFRs) provide a means for delivering massive firepower in a short time, at long range, and from comparatively light equipment. Furthermore, they are ideally suited to the new range of improved submunitions being developed. Despite their logistical penalties and the ease with which they can be detected, there will probably be more FFR systems employed by Western armies in place of heavy guns.

FFRs characteristically receive all their guidance instructions prior to launch. A rocket may be conveniently broken down into two parts: the forward part, which contains the warhead, and the rear part, which contains the motor, the fuel propellant, and the combustion chamber. The gas produced by the burning propellant escapes out the rear of the rocket, imparting a forward thrust to the rocket itself. Because the mass of the escaping gases is less than the mass of the rocket, however, the rocket moves at a lower velocity than the gases. The fuel can be either liquid or solid. Liquid fuels have a higher energy content than solid fuels, but solid fuels are easier to produce and safer to handle. FFRs are generally less accurate than guns due to the effects of wind, thrust misalignment, and the variability of velocity after all the fuel has been burned (which will affect the range of the rocket). There are three ways to overcome the problems of stabilization: fin stabilization, spin stabilization, and a combination of the two.

ROCKET MOTOR (CASING)

A rocket motor for an FFR is simply a casing that provides a combustion chamber in which the propellant can burn. The rocket's forward end is closed and attached to the warhead. It contains an igniter and, at the rear end, a nozzle. The motor casing must be strong enough to withstand the high temperature and pressure reached during combustion. If the casing is susceptible to bending when the motor is fired, or if it is not geometrically precise, there can be problems in dispersion at the target. Cold-worked flow-forming manufacturing techniques have been used for rocket motor casings and have produced good results in terms of material strength and of precision in producing the required dimensions. Other manufacturing techniques include the use of glass fiber.

RANGE COVERAGE

The accuracy of free flight rocket systems has improved greatly since World War II, with system accuracies of 1 percent of range or better now attainable. Nevertheless these systems still cannot compete with conventional gun systems for many tasks, particularly close support, because of their inferior range coverage and reloading times. "Spoilers," or air brakes, can be used to increase the drag on a rocket in flight, modifying its trajectory and range at a given quadrant elevation. The French RAFALE 145mm rocket system, for example, has air brakes positioned between the tail fins. When necessary, these can be actuated at the launcher before firing so that they deploy at the same time as the folding fins as the rocket leaves the launcher. Their effect is to reduce the minimum range of the rocket from 18 kilometers to 10 kilometers (from 11 mi. to 6 mi.).

It is possible to design a rocket with sets of air brakes that present different surface areas so as to vary the range. However, the use of air brakes can be regarded as primarily a means of reducing minimum range rather than a method of achieving range coverage similar to that of a conventional multi-charge gun or howitzer. Mechanical loading systems have slashed FFR reloading times. The Italian FIROS-25 122mm rocket system, for example, is said to be able to reload 40 rockets in five minutes. Regardless of such advantages, it is highly unlikely that FFR systems will ever be able to match conventional gun systems or mortars at sustained fire rates.

WARHEADS

Free flight rockets and missiles (Fig. 1) can be adapted to carry a wide variety of warheads: nuclear (at calibers of 150mm and above), high explosive, chemical, preformed fragments, and submunitions (including terminally guided). They also have a greater degree of inherent flexibility than guns. A general feature of fin-stabilized rocket ammunition is that different types, weights, and sizes of warheads can be fitted to the same motor. Spin-stabilized rockets are more limited, because any alteration in warhead shape and weight may upset the stability of the rocket. Both fin-stabilized rockets and those stabilized by fin and spin combined also have warhead limitations, but the limits within which

Figure 1. U.S. Improved Lance missile. (SOURCE: Robert F. Dorr Archives)

the same launcher and motor can be used are much greater. Moreover, with some FFRs the fins are larger than required for stability purposes, permitting changes in the warhead with little or no difference in stability. Some launcher tubes with helical guide rails have been designed so that the warhead protrudes from the tube; in such cases the diameter of the tube does not limit the size of the warhead. Currently the trend is toward larger-caliber rockets firing to long ranges, with warhead flexibility being more a function of the rocket's ability to carry either a full-caliber warhead or submunitions.

LAUNCHERS

A rocket launcher serves to support and aim the rocket. A launcher in its simplest form may be expendable. Most modern launchers, however, are designed for reloading. Rocket launchers may be built to carry a single rocket or a number of rockets. Since a rocket moves forward by ejecting gases backward, there is no significant recoil on the mounting, apart from a small amount of friction between the rocket and its guide rails. To prevent recoil, the escaping gases must be allowed to pass unimpeded to the rear of the launcher. In practice, this is difficult to achieve because the escaping gases, in expanding, impinge on parts of the launcher, even though the net effect is small. Unlike a gun, there is no trunnion pull to consider; therefore, an increase in maximum range does not necessarily mean an increase in the weight of the launcher, as is often the case with a gun.

With no great recoil forces to be withstood, the mounting for a rocket system need be only as heavy and as strong as required to support—and in some cases to transport—the desired size, weight, and number of rockets. It is possible for an armored self-propelled rocket launcher such as MLRS (multiple launch rocket system) to transport and fire 12 rockets, each weighing more than 270 kilograms.

There are two main types of launcher: positive length or "rail launchers" and "zero length launchers." A zero length launcher is one in which the first motion of the rocket removes it from the restraint of the launcher. The purpose of a zero length launcher is simply to hold and point the rocket in the required direction; it does not influence the subsequent trajectory of the rocket. Although zero length launchers can be lighter and smaller than rail launchers, they are generally unsuited for FFR system applications because their use results in high initial dispersion. They are, however, normally employed for guided weapons systems.

In contrast, a positive length rail launcher is long enough to influence the flight of the rocket after it has begun to accelerate. The term *rail launcher* is used to describe a wide variety of launchers, including tubes and ramps as well as rails. Tubes seem to be favored in modern FFR system design because the tube can be used to provide protection for the rocket from shell fragments and small-arms fire. In addition, tubes can provide good support for the rocket as it accelerates on the launcher and can be readily adapted to impart spin.

In the following sections, a variety of rocket and missile artillery systems are described.

Rocket and Missile Artillery Systems

SOVIET 132MM BM-13-16 (16-ROUND) MULTIPLE ROCKET SYSTEM (MRS)

The 132mm BM-13-16 MRS was standardized in August 1941 in a configuration mounted on a Soviet ZIS-6 or an American 6×6 truck chassis. After World War II the launcher was mounted on the ZIL-15 6×6 truck chassis, the only model seen today. The system is no longer in frontline service in Eastern Europe, but it is used for training. Each Chinese artillery division has one rocket launcher regiment with 32 BM-13-16 (16-round) or 32 updated BM-14-16 (16-round) systems, or 32 Chinese BM-21 variants, or 32 of the more recently developed Chinese 130mm MRSs. The 132mm BM-13-16 can easily be distinguished from other Soviet MRSs, as the launcher uses rails rather than the frames or tubes common to all other Soviet postwar launchers. The launcher consists of eight shaped launcher rails with eight fin-stabilized rockets on the top and another eight underneath. Before launching, two stabilizer jacks are deployed at the rear of the vehicle. A full load of 16 rockets can be launched in seven to ten seconds.

The weapons system requires a crew of six and has a reload time of five to ten minutes. Its maximum range is 9,000 meters (5.6 mi.).

240MM BM-24 (12-ROUND) MULTIPLE ROCKET SYSTEM

The 240 BM-24 MRS was introduced into the Soviet army in the early 1950s as the replacement for the World War II 300mm BM-31-12, which by then had been found to have insufficient range. When originally introduced, the system was mounted on the rear of a ZIL-151 6×6 truck chassis. This was later replaced by the ZIL-157 6×6 chassis, distinguishable from the earlier model by its single rather than dual wheels and its central tire-pressure regulation system. Soviet tank divisions normally had the tracked 240mm (12-round) BM-24 MRS, whereas the Soviet motorized rifle division had the 122mm (40-round) BM-21 MRS. The lighter weapon has a barrel rather than frame launcher and is mounted on the rear of an AT-S medium tracked artillery launcher.

The BM-24's accuracy at two-thirds maximum range for projectile error is 61 meters (200 ft.) in range, 46 meters (150 ft.) in deflection, and 93 meters (305 ft.) CEP (circular error probable). At maximum range the corresponding figures are 40 meters (131 ft.), 95 meters (312 ft.), and 118 meters (387 ft.), respectively. The system has 12 launcher frames and a maximum range of 10,300 meters (6.4 mi.). Reload time is three to four minutes.

130MM M51 (32-ROUND) MULTIPLE ROCKET SYSTEM

The Czechoslovakian 130mm V51 MRS was developed in the 1950s and is a standard Praga V3S 6×6 truck chassis with the rocket launcher mounted in the rear. No armor protection is provided for the cab, so the launcher is traversed left or right before the rockets are launched. Spare rockets are carried in stowage boxes on either side of the hull under the launcher. The rockets are spin stabilized, and it is believed that a rocket with an increased range has been introduced in recent years. Austria uses the M51 launcher mounted on the rear of a Steyr 680 M3 6 × 6 truck (q.v.), and Romania uses it on the rear of a Soviet ZIL-151 or 157 truck. The 130mm M51 (32-round) is sometimes called the RM-180 and is issued on the basis of one battalion of 18 launchers to each motorized rifle division and tank division. The system includes 32 barrels. It has a maximum range of 8,200 meters (5.1 mi.) and a reload time of two minutes. The crew consists of six men.

250MM BM-25 (6-ROUND) MULTIPLE ROCKET SYSTEM

The 250mm BM-25 entered service with the Soviet army in the 1950s and is the largest caliber MRS to have been deployed since World War II by any member of the former Warsaw Pact. It is no longer in frontline service, but numbers are probably held in reserve. The system was used in combat by South Yemen against North Yemen.

The rocket is believed to use a storable liquid propellant and to have a range of around 55,900 meters (34.7 mi.). The launcher is mounted on the rear of a KRAZ-214 6 × 6 truck chassis. Before launching the rockets, two stabilizers are lowered at the rear of the vehicle and armored shutters are lowered over the windshield. The launcher has six launcher frames. It requires a crew of eight to 12.

122MM RM-70 (40-ROUND) MULTIPLE ROCKET SYSTEM

The Czechoslovakian 122mm RM-70 MRS, which also carries the Western designation M1972, was first seen in public during a parade in Czechoslovakia following the SHIELD-72 maneuvers. It was since identified with East German and Libyan units. The system is essentially an armored version of the Czech Tattra 813 8 × 8 truck fitted with the same launcher as the Soviet BM-12 MRS at the rear of the hull, with an additional hull for preparing firing positions and clearing obstacles. It is probable that the M1972 is fitted with a winch with a 20,000-kilogram capacity.

The M1972 is issued on the basis of one battalion of 18 in each of the motorized rifle divisions and tank divisions. Two basic types of fin-stabilized rocket can be fired by the M1972: the BM-21, a short rocket with a range of 11,000 meters (6.8 mi.), and a long rocket with a 20,380-meter (12.6-mi.) range. In addition, there is a combination of the short rocket with an additional rocket motor, producing a range of about 17,000 meters (10.5 mi.).

128MM YMRL 32 OGANJ (32-ROUND) MULTIPLE ROCKET SYSTEM

The YMRL 32 (its Western designation, for Yugoslav multiple rocket launcher, 32-barrel) was developed in the early 1970s to meet the requirements of the Yugoslav army. It is normally found in batteries of six launchers. The system performs a role similar to that of the Czech 122mm M1972 (40-round) MRS but has neither the armored cab nor the excellent cross-country performance of the Czech system. The YMRL 32 consists basically of an FAP 2220 BDS 6 × 4 forward control truck with a 32-barrel 128mm rocket launcher mounted at the rear of the hull. An additional pack of 32 rockets is located at the rear of the cab to provide the capability of rapid reloading. The system fires a 20-kilogram warhead, containing some 5,000 fragments that are lethal in a radius of more than 30 meters (98 ft.), to a range of 20,000 meters (12.4 mi.). A fuze with preselected super-quick, inertia, and delay options is standard. The rockets may be launched singly or in a ripple salvo; the latter takes a total of 18 seconds. Launching can be accomplished by manual, semiautomatic, or fully automatic means. Once the rockets have been launched, the launcher is traversed to the rear and depressed to the horizontal, permitting the reserve pack of 32 rockets to be mechanically loaded. This operation can be completed in two minutes. The system can be emplaced and commence firing in 20 seconds; in a total of only four or five minutes it can occupy a position, fire both loads, and be on the move again.

220MM BM-27 (16-ROUND) MULTIPLE ROCKET SYSTEM

The BM-27 was introduced into service with the Soviet army in 1977 and is thus sometimes referred to in the West as the M1977. The system was found in a multiple rocket launcher battalion consisting of a headquarters, one support battery, and three firing batteries (each with six BM-27s). These units were attached to the combined-arms army-level artillery brigades. In a tank army the artillery brigade was replaced by a regiment of three battalions of BM-27s. The system provides chemical, high-explosive, and submunitions (including fragmentation bomblet, incendiary bomblet, and minelet) support fire to maneuver units. The rocket weighs some 360 kilograms and has a range of 5 to 40 kilometers (3 to 25 mi.). The launcher is configured with one layer of four tubes and two layers of six tubes and is mounted on the ZIL-135 8 × 8 truck chassis. Four stabilizing jacks are used during firing. A rapid reload capability is provided by another ZIL-135 carrying 16 rockets and a single-round capacity reloading arm on its rear platform. Reloading time is an estimated 15 to 20 minutes.

122MM TYPE 81 (40-ROUND) MULTIPLE ROCKET SYSTEM

The Chinese are known to have in service a locally built modified version of the Soviet BM-21 122mm system. The 40-tube launcher is carried on a CQ261 Hongyan (a locally built variant of the French Berliet GB4) 6 × 6 truck chassis. The launcher tube is 3 meters (9.8 ft.) long; each 122mm round weighs 66.8 kilograms. The rocket has a maximum range of 20,580 meters (12.8 mi.).

The launcher can also be mounted on a 4 × 4 truck with an enlarged cab to accommodate the crew of four and 12 reload rounds. During firing the vehicle suspension system is locked. If necessary, the entire launching system can be removed from the vehicle and placed on a towing carriage. The launcher can be fired from within the cab or from a remote position. This vehicle-mounted version is designated the Type 81.

A pack model developed for use by airborne and mountain units weighs 281 kilograms in firing position and can be dismantled into manpack loads. A lighter version of the Type 63, recently developed, has been designated in the West as the Type 63-1. It is some 136 kilograms lighter than the basic model and is distinguishable from it by its smaller spoked road wheels and four banks of three rockets. Both high-explosive and incendiary rockets are used. China is also known to use the Soviet 132mm BM-13-16 and the 140mm BM-14-16, each of which is mounted on the rear of a ZIL-151 6 × 6 truck chassis. Each Chinese artillery division has one rocket launcher regiment with 32 MRSs.

EGYPTIAN MULTIPLE ROCKET SYSTEMS

The Egyptian army uses a number of rocket systems provided by Czechoslovakia and the Soviet Union, including the 122mm (40-round) BM-21, 130mm (32-round) M51, 132mm (16-round) BM-13-16, 140mm (16-round) BM-14-16, and 240mm (12-round) BM-24. A straight copy of the BM-21 system has also been produced by the SAKR factory. This system can be mounted as a 40-round launcher on a ZIL 6 × 6 truck chassis or as a 30-round launcher on a Soviet ZIL-131 or a Japanese Isuzu truck chassis.

The Egyptian army has also deployed locally made rocket launchers on tanks (two quadruple box-like launchers on either side of a T-62 turret) and on wheeled armored personnel carriers (a rectangular system of three superimposed quadruple rail launchers in the rear of a Walid 4 × 4 APC). The purpose of these systems is to lay smoke screens.

In May 1981 Egypt successfully tested in firing trials the SAKR-30, which is an indigenously developed 122mm multiple rocket launcher system with interfaces that allow it to be fired from the Soviet BM-21 launcher vehicle. The rockets that can be fired include one with an HE fragmentation warhead, an antitank submunition round containing five mines, and a submunition round containing either 28 antitank or 35 antipersonnel bomblets. An increase in range to 30 kilometers (18.6 mi.) has been achieved through use of an improved lightweight rocket motor and case and a composite bonded stargrain propellant.

Another system of the same caliber, designated the SAKR-18, has also been developed. It has a range of 18 kilometers (11 mi.) and fires a rocket that can be fitted with either of two warhead types—one carrying 28 antipersonnel bomblets, each with a lethal radius of 15 meters (49 ft.); the other including 21 antitank bomblets, each of which can pierce up to 80 millimeters (3.2 in.) of steel armor. The number of launcher tubes can be varied between 21 and 40.

Egypt has also developed the 12-round 80mm VAP light vehicle-mounted multiple rocket launcher system. The rocket has a range of 8 kilometers (5 mi.) and can be fitted with illumination or HE-fragmentation warheads. Fire is by remote control from an off-vehicle system.

U.S. MULTIPLE ROCKET SYSTEMS

From World War II to the 1980s, the United States employed only two multiple rocket systems: the M21 (24-round), which was phased out of service some years ago, and the M91 (45-round), which has been declared obsolete.

Early in 1976 the U.S. Army Missile Command initiated feasibility studies and concept formulation for a general support rocket system (GSRS) that would have a high rate of fire and would use a low-cost rocket that could be handled like a round of conventional ammunition. This system was designed for use against troops, light-equipment air-defense systems, and command centers.

Later directives reoriented the GSRS toward a standard NATO weapon to be developed and produced in both the United States and Europe. France, Italy, West Germany, and the United Kingdom signed a memorandum of understanding with the United States for joint development and production of the GSRS.

Following completion of a test firing competition in February 1980, the U.S. Army planned for procurement of 491 self-propelled launcher loaders, more than 362,000 tactical rockets, and supporting systems by 1990. Each system, now redesignated the multiple launch rocket system (MLRS), has two pods, each containing six rockets, that can quickly be replaced once the rockets have been fired.

The warhead-carrying rocket, with a range of about 45 kilometers (28 mi.; a German variant has a range of about 40 km, or 25 mi.), supports several different munitions. Among these are a German-developed mine-laying warhead, the AT2, which carries seven mine distribution canisters, and the M77 warhead, which delivers 644 explosive submunitions. The MLRS is mounted on a light armored vehicle based on the U.S. M2 infantry fighting vehicle (IFV), which has a crew of three. In extreme emergencies, one man can operate the entire system.

The MLRS had its baptism by fire in Operation Desert Storm in February 1991 and proved highly effective in counterfire against Iraqi artillery. According to Iraqi prisoners the MLRS's submunitions were called "steel rain" and were the most terrifying threat they faced.

Germany, Italy, and the United Kingdom collaborated on an FFR project for development of a weapon called RS80. The system was to have a range of 40 to 60 kilometers (25 to 37 mi.), depending on the warhead used, and was designed to complement conventional 155mm weapons systems. After the RS80 project was discontinued, the United Kingdom and Germany adopted the U.S. Army's MLRS, while the Italian firm SNIA Viscosa produced two other systems, the 51mm FIROS-6 and the 122mm FIROS-25. Although these three systems are by no means the only ones produced in the Western world, they are good examples of the state of the art at opposite ends of the performance spectrum. The FIROS-25 and other modern rocket systems are described below.

FIROS-25

The Italian FIROS-25 field rocket system is an area saturation weapons system based on the 122mm SNIA BPD unguided rocket. The launcher consists of two removable modules with twenty launch tubes each. The escort unit can carry four launch modules. Loading operations are carried out by removing the empty module with a jib crane fitted on the support vehicle, then installing a filled module ready to fire.

Rockets are available in two models with different maximum ranges. They can carry a variety of warheads, from the conventional types (HE, PFF, WP) to the submunition types dispensing antitank or antipersonnel mines and bomblets. The rocket has a single solid-propellant motor with a burn time of just under one second. The system is suitable for massed use or individual missions and can cover large-area targets in the 8- to 33-kilometer (5- to 20.5-mi.) zone.

A typical battery would consist of a command post equipped with a fire direction system, six firing units, and six escort units. The firing unit is a modular rocket launcher installed on a heavy 6×6 truck. The system comes in two versions: a standard version with a motorized manual movement system that is simple to operate and an automatic version equipped with an inertial navigator, a servo control system, and a ballistic computer. This firing unit configuration enables the crew to perform topographic and ballistic calculations and aiming procedures by means of an automatic control unit installed in the vehicle's cab.

110MM LIGHT ARTILLERY ROCKET SYSTEM (LARS)

The 110mm LARS was developed in the 1960s and accepted for service with the West German army in 1969. First production systems were delivered the following year. The prime contractor for the launcher was Wegmann and Company of Kassel, with GUF responsible for the rockets. The system has 36 launcher tubes and a range of 14,000 meters (8.7 mi.). It is called the Artillery Raketenwerken 110 SF by the German army and issued on the basis of one battery of eight launchers per division; each battery has two Fieldguard fire control systems (mounted on a 4×4 truck chassis) and a resupply vehicle carrying 144 rockets. There are 209 LARS in service with the German army.

The system has been upgraded from LARS-1 to LARS-2 over the past few years. The program has included a new fire control system, more rocket types, and mobility improvement achieved by fitting the launcher to a new MAN 6×6 truck chassis. An air-transportable, towed, two-wheel, 15-round launcher was also developed by Dynamit Nobel, but it was not adopted by the German army.

140MM TERUEL (40-ROUND) MULTIPLE ROCKET LAUNCHER SYSTEM

The 140mm Teruel-2 MRLS, which has a maximum range of 18,000 meters (11.2 mi.), was developed to replace an older MRS in service with the Spanish army. The launcher has two 2-round packs arranged in five rows of four launcher tubes each. Mounted on the rear hull of an IASA-Pegaso 6×6 truck chassis, the vehicle is fitted with an armored crew cab that can mount a light machine gun for local defense and antiaircraft purposes. The launcher is deployed in a battalion of three batteries, each with six firing units.

A Teruel-3 system with new longer-range rockets, effective to 28,000 meters (17.4 mi.), has also been developed. The new rocket is fitted with a double-grain solid-fuel motor that, when equipped with aerodynamic air brakes, allows three distinct trajectories to be flown while using the same firing elevation. The rockets also have pop-out fins for stabilization in flight. The warhead can be either high explosive or, in the case of the Teruel-3, a submunition-carrying warhead in five versions: 42 antipersonnel grenades filled with steel pellets; 28 hollow-charge grenades with contact fuzes that are capable of penetrating 110 millimeters (4.4 in.) of armor; six pressure-activated antitank mines including antidisturbance features; 21 smoke grenades that can each provide four minutes of smoke; or a number of antipersonnel mines. The rockets can be equipped with contact, proximity, or time fuzes. All six versions of the rocket can be mixed on the launcher, which has 40 barrels, and selected according to the target to be engaged. The minimum range for both Teruel-2 and Teruel-3 is 6,000 meters (3.7 mi.).

A resupply vehicle with four blocks of twenty Teruel-3 reload rounds or six blocks of Teruel-2 reload rounds is assigned to each system. Reloading is manual and takes five minutes. The time required to emplace a launcher is two minutes; to fire, 45 seconds; and to displace, another two minutes. The system has a crew of five or six men.

MAR 290MM MULTIPLE ROCKET SYSTEM

This Israeli 290mm artillery rocket has a 25,000-meter (15.5-mi.) range. In the mid-1960s it entered Israeli Defense Force (IDF) service mounted in frame racks, holding four rockets, mounted on Sherman tank chassis. The basic 290mm rocket weighs 600 kilograms at launch and carries a warhead weighing 320 kilograms. The tube launcher can fire four rockets in ten seconds. The MAR-290 system is still in IDF use, but it is now mounted on a new launching system using Centurion tank hulls as the platform and consisting of four launching tubes. On the turretless Centurion chassis, the four tubes are carried in a horizontal layer on a new superstructure positioned on the original turret ring. These tubes can be traversed through a full 360 degrees and through elevations ranging from 0 to +60 degrees. Each launching tube has a diameter of 700 millimeters (27.5 in.) to accommodate the rocket's tail span of 570 millimeters (22.5 in.).

160MM LAR MULTIPLE ROCKET LAUNCHER SYSTEM

Following the 1973 Yom Kippur War, the Israeli Ground Defense Force generated a requirement for an unguided rocket artillery system that could be rapidly deployed to engage large mechanized units supported by artillery and protected by sophisticated air defenses. The result was Israeli Military Industries' Light Artillery Rocket System 160, which anticipated combat in the 1982 Lebanon campaign.

This system consists of a tracked or wheeled all-terrain vehicle on which is mounted a multiple rocket launcher with expendable launch-pods that contain sealed-in fuzed 160mm rockets. The pods can be rapidly replaced from resupply vehicles after firing. The number of aluminum/fiberglass tubes per launch-pod container varies according to the size and type of platform vehicle used.

The 110-kilogram LAR 160 rocket is of the solid-propellant, wraparound fin-stabilized type. It carries a 50-kilogram warhead that can be changed to suit the mission. The types available include a cluster munition with 187 M42 bomblets, the FASCAM scatterable mine, chemical or biological agents, the Skeet "smart" antitank submunition, battlefield illumination, and adaptation of any 155mm howitzer shell payload if required. All the rounds use an M445 electronic time fuze that can be remotely set. The minimum and maximum firing ranges are 12 and 30 kilometers (7.4 and 18.6 mi.). The maximum number of tubes per pod is 25 for the system mounted on an M47 MBT chassis, although the more usual number is 13. In Israeli army service the LAR 160 is mounted on a modified M548 chassis and is deployed with the 240/290mm MRS already in service.

Conclusion

Artillery rockets and missiles, particularly in multiple launch configurations as discussed here, will continue to play a significant role on future battlefields. For example, senior officials, recognizing the value of rocket artillery used by the UN coalition forces in Operation Desert Storm, have recommended increasing the range as well as the use of MLRS.

Improved technology and international cooperation will enable this to occur, just as the same combination has helped solve the problem of accuracy. This will also contribute to an increased variety of warheads and submunitions employed by FFR, especially the new generation of "smart" munitions. The future of artillery rockets and missiles as part of combined arms forces seems assured.

ALAA EL DIN ABDEL MEGUID DARWISH

SEE ALSO: Artillery; Artillery, Tube; Explosives Technology, Conventional; Firepower.

Bibliography

Farrar, C. L., and D. W. Leeming. 1983. *Military ballistics: A basic manual.* Vol. 10 of *Battlefield weapons systems and technology.* London: Brassey's.
Jane's armour and artillery, 1987–1988. 1987. London: Jane's.
Pearson, P. F., and G. K. Otis. 1991. *Desert Storm fire support: Classic airland battle operations.* No. 91-2. Association of the United States Army Essay Series. Washington, D.C.: Brassey's (US).
Ryan, J. W. 1981. *Guns, mortars and rockets.* London: Brassey's.

ADDITIONAL SOURCES: *Military Technology; NATO's Sixteen Nations.*

ARTILLERY, TUBE

Some of the earliest devices for hurling projectiles at an enemy were catapults, trebuchets, and ballistae. They were simply mechanical implements for the sudden release of energy to propel projectiles. Modern artillery, in contrast, relies on the ability to harness the energy released by burning propellant to push the projectile to the required range.

The earliest cannon probably had wrought-iron barrels fashioned by lashing iron bars or staves around a white-hot metal core, then arranging equally hot wrought-iron hoops, which contracted when they cooled, over the staves. Some of the earliest cannons were breech loaded because this method of loading and obturation was favored by the manufacturing technique.

The standard of obturation in early versions proved unsatisfactory, however, and the breech-loading approach was dropped. The purpose of the barrel in those early guns was simply to provide a vessel for the burning propellant, which at that time was black powder, and to enable the projectile to be held and pointed in the right direction. In this regard they were truly forerunners of modern guns. But it was the use of black powder propellant that was perhaps the most significant innovation, for without it the cannon would not have been introduced.

During the fifteenth century, cannons with trunnions began to appear. These were short-stub axles fitted at the barrel's point of balance and about which the elevation and depression of the piece were effected. Obviously gunners were becoming interested in being able to vary, quickly and easily, the range achieved by their weapons.

Benjamin Robins (1707–51), an English mathematician and engineer, invented a device called the ballistic pendulum for use in determining muzzle velocity. Unfortunately, the manufacturing techniques available during Robins's lifetime were unable to cope with the production of a rifled cannon so as to prove his theories. Nevertheless, the application of ballistics had begun; well before this time, also, new concepts for the tactical employment of artillery weapons were being put into practice.

Before the time of Gustavus Adolphus (1594–1632), artillery was comparatively immobile, with its most common task being to demolish fortifications or to fire from prepared positions at an advancing enemy. Gustavus Adolphus introduced a new dimension to artillery with the use of light and mobile 4- and 9-pounder demiculverins to support his troops. Frederick the Great of Prussia (1712–86) followed this lead with his employment of artillery during the Seven Years' War, extending the concept to include horse artillery.

The eighteenth century saw the arrival of one of the most significant artillerists in history, Jean Baptiste de Gribeauval (1715–89). His reforms as the French inspector general of artillery were the basis of the artillery triumphs of the Napoleonic era. Among other initiatives, he grouped artillery resources into coastal/garrison, siege, and field elements. The United States Army adopted his system in 1809 and retained it until the 1840s. The improvement in techniques for the tactical employment of artillery was not at this time, however, accompanied by many significant developments in the design of guns.

The early nineteenth-century artillery pieces still lacked many of the refinements apparent in modern weapons. A typical gun was muzzle loaded, smooth bored, and lacking any efficient mechanism to stop it from careering backward upon firing. In the second half of the century, however, developments in gun design began to move swiftly. Before that time, guns had been able to fire from exposed positions on advancing infantry with relative security beyond ranges of about 400 meters (1,308 ft.), and beyond such ranges guns could be used to some advantage.

The invention of rifled small arms made gunners vulnerable at much greater ranges. At the same time, the logical extension of the innovation of rifling to artillery became apparent. The French and the Prussians had rifles in quantity before 1850; rifled field artillery was first employed in 1856.

After many earlier attempts to produce an efficient recoil mechanism, the

French came up with their now famous M1897 75mm field gun. The French 75 design included a hydropneumatic recoil mechanism capable of performing two important functions. It absorbed the recoil forces acting on the gun during firing and, unlike other methods under examination at the time, also returned the barrel to its original position. The design of the French 75mm recoil mechanism incorporated a hydraulic brake, which absorbed recoil by the action of forcing oil through a small orifice. The weapon had a high muzzle velocity, thus producing a flat trajectory that was thought to be desirable because it produced a wide spread of shrapnel at the target.

Modern artillery claims the distinction of being the "greatest killer on the battlefield," causing more injuries and personnel casualties to the enemy than other combat arms. That distinction has resulted partly from the continued improvements to artillery pieces to increase range, enhance the lethality of projectiles, and improve mobility, durability, and rates of fire. Selected examples of modern artillery weapons, both towed and self-propelled, are discussed on the following pages (see Fig. 1).

Towed Artillery

25-Pounder Field Gun (United Kingdom)

The 25-pounder field gun (Mk 1) was developed and produced in the late 1930s. Initially, many were mounted on 18-pounder field carriages and these were commonly known as 18/25-pounders. The first production 25-pounders with a humped box trail for towing (Mk 2) were completed in 1940. In 1942 the ordnance was fitted with a two-port Solothurn muzzle brake to enable it to fire an armor-piercing projectile with a higher muzzle velocity. This was designated the Mk 3 and is the only version likely to be encountered today.

The 25-pounder is an 87.6mm weapon with a vertical sliding breech mechanism. Served by a crew of six, it can elevate and depress in the range of +40

Figure 1. The M-198 155mm howitzer is a typical example of the modern towed artillery weapon. (Source: U.S. Department of Defense)

degrees/ − 5 degrees and traverse 8 degrees. Its rate of fire is five rounds per minute to a maximum range of 12,250 meters (7.6 mi.).

76MM MOUNTAIN GUN M48 (YUGOSLAVIA)

This weapon, often called the "Tito Gun," was developed in the post–World War II period specifically to meet the requirements of Yugoslav mountain units, although it can also be used as a field gun. Its low weight has attracted the attention of other countries, especially in the developing world, where weight, rather than range, is often the overriding consideration.

There are at least four variants of the M48, all of which have split trails, with each trail hinged in the center so that it can be folded forward 180 degrees for towing. The M48 (B-1) has pneumatic tires and a maximum towing speed of 60 kilometers per hour (km/h [37 mph]). It can also be towed by animals in tandem or be broken down into eight pack loads. The M48 (B-1A2) has light alloy wheels with solid rubber tires and a modified suspension, but a maximum towing speed of only 30 km/h (18 mph). Featuring a multi-baffle muzzle brake and hydraulic recoil system, the M48 has a rate of fire of 25 rounds per minute to a maximum range of 8,750 meters (5.5 mi.).

Ammunition for these guns is of the semi-fixed type with four charges. It is based on that used by the obsolete Soviet 76mm regimental gun M1927, which fired fixed ammunition. The high-explosive (HE) M55 projectile weighs 6.2 kilograms (13.7 lb.) and has a muzzle velocity of 222 to 398 meters per second (728 to 1,305 feet per second [ft./sec.]). The high-explosive antitank (HEAT) projectile, weighing 5.1 kilograms (11.2 lb.), will penetrate 100 millimeters (4 in.) of armor at a range of 450 meters (1,475 ft.). There is also a WP M60 smoke shell that weighs 6.2 kilograms.

85MM FIELD GUN TYPE 56 (CHINA)

The Soviet 85mm divisional gun D-44 was first supplied to China during the Korean War. China began production during the early 1960s under the designation Type 56. Some slight changes were made in the D-44 design to suit Chinese production methods, one being the location of a push rod firing device in the center of the elevating handwheel. The Type 56 does not appear to use the Soviet infrared searchlight and sight system.

Ammunition currently available for the Type 56 includes HE, HEAT-FS (fin stabilized), and high-explosive squash head (HESH). The only current projectile for which definite information is available is the HEAT-FS. Its direct-fire maximum range is 970 meters (3,180 ft.), at which range it will penetrate 100 millimeters (4 in.) of armor set at an angle of 65 degrees.

The Chinese army assigns 12 Type 56 guns to an artillery regiment. The weapon uses a double-baffle muzzle brake and has a hydraulic recoil system. The breech mechanism features a semiautomatic vertical sliding block. Maximum range is 15,650 meters (9.7 mi.). A crew of from six to eight serves the piece, which can elevate and depress in the range + 35 degrees/ − 7 degrees and traverse through 54 degrees. The rate of fire is 15 to 20 rounds per minute.

The gun can be towed at a maximum on-road speed of 60 kilometers per hour (37 mph).

100MM FIELD GUN (CHINA)

This gun, a copy of the 100mm Soviet BS-3 (M1944), is basically the same gun found on the SU-100 and T-54 tanks. It is being introduced to replace the 85mm Type 56 in border area artillery regiments. The gun is effective as a counterbattery artillery piece. The Soviet UBR-412 AP-T round is used in the antitank role, while the HE-FRAG UOF-412 round (with a point-detonating fuze Type 429) is also produced in China.

The gun has a double-baffle muzzle brake; an easily identified massive square-shaped breech system; a cradle-enclosed recoil system; and a vertical sliding-wedge breechblock operating semiautomatically. The breech ring apparently doubles for the long gun tube. The gun is simple and rugged. Eighteen such weapons are assigned to an artillery regiment, although they may be found mixed with the 85mm Type 56 at the army level.

The elevation and depression range is +45 degrees/−5 degrees and the gun can traverse about 50 degrees on its carriage. Its maximum range is 20,000 meters (12.4 mi.). Rate of fire is seven rounds per minute.

GIAT 105MM LG1 LIGHT GUN (FRANCE)

During the mid- to late 1960s, GIAT (Groupement Industriel des Armements Terrestres) developed the prototype of a 105mm light gun known as the Canon 105 LTR. The prototype was not further developed, but the formation of the French Rapid Action Force created a need to replace the French army's existing 105mm M101 and 105mm Model 56 pack howitzers. The Canon 105 LTR was thus revived during the mid-1980s and has now been replaced by an updated model known as the LG1.

The 105mm LG1 light gun is the result of a private venture developed by GIAT's Etablissement d'Etudes et de Fabrications d'Armement de Bourges. By early 1987 three prototypes had been produced. The LG1 follows the same general lines as the earlier LTR, using a split-trail carriage, a small shield, a barrel approximately 30 calibers long, and generally light construction. A circular firing jack is provided, and the barrel has a double-baffle muzzle brake and a vertical sliding-wedge breech mechanism. The time required to go into or out of action is 30 seconds.

The LG1 fires the standard HE M1 OE 105 projectile to a maximum range of 11,680 meters (7.2 mi.). Using an HE hollow-base OE 105 DTC projectile, it has a range of 15,000 meters (9.3 mi.); with the HE base bleed OE D105 DTC the range is 17,500 meters (10.8 mi.). In the direct-fire role the weapon can fire the HEAT OCC 105 projectile to an effective range of 1,000 meters (.62 mi.).

The LG1 can be towed by a jeep-type light vehicle. The crew is specified as seven, although the gun can be operated by a reduced crew of five. The gun can elevate and depress in the range +70 degrees/−5 degrees and traverse 40 degrees; its rate of fire is 12 rounds per minute.

105MM HOWITZER M102 (UNITED STATES)

The requirement for a light towed 105mm howitzer to replace the 105mm M101 was established in 1960. The howitzer, first used in combat in South Vietnam, subsequently underwent major successful modifications to solve design problems. Today the M102 is the standard 105mm howitzer of airborne and airmobile divisions and other selected units. Each M102 battalion consists of three batteries of six howitzers each. In 1985 the U.S. Army had a total of 526 M102 howitzers in its inventory.

The weapon has no muzzle brake or gun shield. It uses a hydropneumatic recoil system and a vertical sliding-wedge breech system. It weighs 1,496 kilograms (3,300 lb.). Light and flexible, it can elevate and depress in the range of +75 degrees/−5 degrees and traverse a full 360 degrees. Its rate of fire is 10 rounds per minute. Maximum range is 15,100 meters (9.4 mi.) with HERA M548 or 11,500 meters (7.1 ml.) with HE M1. A crew of eight serves the piece.

105MM LIGHT FIELD GUN MARK 2 (INDIA)

This Indian Ordnance Factories' weapon resembles the British 105mm Royal Ordnance light gun; both were derived from the same 105mm L13 gun used on the FV433 Abbot self-propelled gun. The first 105mm barrel developed in India from the British original was used on the 105mm Field Gun Mark 1. The Mark 2 uses tubular bow trails similar to those of the British 105mm light gun.

The Mark 2 was developed for use in various types of terrain, ranging from mountains to the desert. To reduce its weight, the system is constructed using light, high-strength alloy steels. The resultant weapon in action weighs 2,275 kilograms (5,005 lb.).

Normal towing position is with the barrel folded back across the trails. A 360-degree traversing platform is provided. The gun can be parachute dropped or transported by helicopter. It fires separate ammunition using an eight-charge system. Projectiles include HE, smoke, base ejection star, and HESH.

The Mark 2 has a double-baffle muzzle brake and a vertical sliding-breech system. It can elevate and depress in the range of +73 degrees/−5 degrees and traverse 10 degrees on its carriage (or 360 degrees on the platform). Its normal rate of fire is four rounds per minute; maximum range is 17,425 meters (10.8 mi.).

105MM KH178 LIGHT HOWITZER (SOUTH KOREA)

In the preliminary design stages of a new 105mm light howitzer for the South Korean army, the Kia Machine Tool Company procured examples of the British Royal Ordnance 105mm light gun and the West German Rheinmetall conversion of the American 105mm M101 howitzer. Aspects of both have been incorporated in the KH178 105mm light howitzer, production of which began in 1984. The weapon is now in service with the South Korean army.

The KH178 comprises the CN78 cannon, the RM78 recoil mechanism, the GG78 carriage, and a new fire control system. The barrel is 34 calibers long and fitted with a double-baffle muzzle brake. A horizontal sliding breechblock is used with a percussion firing mechanism.

The weapon can elevate and depress through the range +65 degrees/−5 degrees and traverse 45.5 degrees. It has a maximum rate of fire of 15 rounds per minute and a sustained rate of five rounds per minute. Its maximum range using HE is 14,700 meters (9.1 mi.); with RAP it can reach 18,000 meters (11.2 mi.).

122MM HOWITZER M1938 (M-30) (SOVIET UNION)

This weapon entered service with the Soviet army in 1939. Until introduction of the D-30 in the 1960s, it was the standard division howitzer of Warsaw Pact armies, issued on the basis of 36 per motorized rifle division (organized into two battalions of three batteries, each with six howitzers) and 54 per tank division (in 3 battalions).

The weapon's carriage is of the same riveted box-section split trail type used for the 152mm howitzer M1943 (D-1), but the latter can easily be distinguished from the 122mm weapon by its longer and fatter barrel with a double-baffle muzzle brake. The top half of the M1938's gun shield slopes to the rear; in the center is a section that slides upward so the weapon can be elevated. The gun has a hydraulic buffer recoil system and a hinged screw breech mechanism. A crew of eight serves the piece, which can be towed by a variety of tractors and 6x6 trucks. The weapon has a rate of fire of five to six rounds a minute; can be elevated and depressed through a range of +63.5 degrees/−3 degrees and traversed 49 degrees; and has a maximum range of 11,800 meters (7.3 mi.).

The M1938 fires a variety of case-type, variable charge, separate loading ammunition including FRAG-HE and HEAT. With the HEAT round it can penetrate 200 millimeters (8 in.) of armor at 0 degrees of obliquity.

The M1938 has also been manufactured in China as the Type 54 and Type 54-1. There it is issued on the basis of 12 per infantry and armored division.

122MM HOWITZER D-30 (SOVIET UNION)

This weapon was introduced into service with the Soviet army in the early 1960s as the replacement for the 122mm howitzer M1938 (M-30). Its main improvements over the earlier system are increased range and the ability to traverse quickly through 360 degrees.

The D-30 is towed muzzle first. Upon arrival at the battery position, the crew must first unlock the barrel traveling lock. A firing jack under the carriage is lowered, raising the wheels clear of the ground. Three trail ends are then staked down, and firing can commence. An unusual feature of the D-30 is that the recoil system is mounted over the barrel.

Some projectiles fired by the D-30 are interchangeable with those fired by the M-30, but the D-30 also fires a HEAT projectile of the nonrotating fin-stabilized type, which can penetrate 460 millimeters (18 in.) of armor at 0 degrees of obliquity and any range. There are also at least two chemical projectiles for the D-30: one containing sarin, the other viscous lewisite. In both cases the chemical agent is dispersed by a TNT bursting charge.

The D-30, with a crew of seven, uses a multibaffle muzzle brake and a semiautomatic vertical sliding breechblock mechanism. It can be elevated and depressed through the range +70 degrees/ −7 degrees and has a rate of fire of seven to eight rounds per minute. Maximum range is 15,400 meters (9.5 mi.) or, with RAP, 21,900 meters (13.6 mi.).

In the Soviet army the D-30 is issued on the basis of 36 per tank division (two battalions of 18 howitzers each) and 72 per motorized rifle division. The D-30 is also produced in China.

130MM FIELD GUN M-46 (SOVIET UNION)

This weapon, developed in the early 1950s, was first seen in public during the 1954 May Day parade. It replaced the 122mm M1931/37 (A-19) field gun and is ballistically similar to the 130mm guns used by the Soviet navy. The weapon uses a pepperpot muzzle brake and a hydraulic buffer and hydropneumatic recuperator recoil system. The breech mechanism is of the horizontal wedge sliding type. The weapon can be elevated and depressed through the range +45 degrees/ −2.5 degrees and traversed 50 degrees. It has a crew of nine, can sustain a rate of fire of five to six rounds a minute, and has a maximum range of 27,150 meters (16.8 mi.). The weapon can be towed by a variety of artillery tractors or tracked armored vehicles.

During travel the gun's barrel is withdrawn from the gun by a mechanism on the right trail, reducing the overall length. The carriage is a split-trail arrangement provided with a two-wheeled limber. The M-46 has direct-fire sights, including an active/passive night sight. Modified M-46s with a longer barrel, recuperator, and cradle appeared in Soviet army service in the mid-1970s. India has deployed a self-propelled model called the Catapult, based on the Vijavanta MBT chassis. The first 130mm field gun produced by China was the Type 59, a direct copy of the Soviet M-46.

The M-46 fires FRAG-HE and APC-T rounds. With the latter it can penetrate 230 millimeters (9.2 in.) of armor at a 1,000 meters. It also uses illuminating and smoke rounds and at least two chemical rounds filled with sarin and VX. An RAP is also known to be in service; it was used by Syria during the 1973 Middle East war. The SRC Group of companies, based in Belgium, has produced a conversion package to allow existing M-46 guns to accommodate a new 155mm barrel capable of firing ERFB ammunition.

In the Soviet army the M-46 is issued on the basis of 72 per artillery division (two brigades of 36 each). It is also found in Soviet army artillery brigades.

FACTORY 100 ARTILLERY SYSTEMS (EGYPT)

Abu Zaabal Engineering Industries, also known as Factory 100, has reverse engineered the Soviet 122mm D-30 towed howitzer and the Chinese 130mm Field Gun Type 59. The first D-30 was completed in Egypt early in 1984, with Royal Ordnance Nottingham providing some machined-part components that were completed in Egypt. The 122mm based on the D-30 is called the D-30-M by the Egyptians; the copy of the 130mm Type 59 is designated the M59-1M.

Factory 100 is also closely involved with Royal Ordnance Nottingham in upgunning the Soviet-supplied T-55 main battle tank with the 105mm L7A3 rifled gun and will also be involved in whichever of the two competing 122mm

D-30 self-propelled howitzers is eventually selected for production or coproduction in Egypt.

152MM HOWITZER M1943 (D-1) (SOVIET UNION)

This weapon was introduced into the Soviet army in 1943 as the replacement for the earlier 152mm Howitzer M1938 (M-10). The D-1 is basically a strengthened carriage and recoil system of the 122mm Howitzer M1938 (M-30) fitted with the ordnance of the 152mm Howitzer M1938 (M-10), but with the addition of a large double-baffle muzzle brake.

The D-1 has a hydraulic buffer and hydropneumatic recoil system and a hinged screw breech mechanism. It features a split-trail carriage and has a gun shield. The range of elevation and depression is +63.5 degrees/−3 degrees; the range of traverse, 35 degrees. Rate of fire is four rounds per minute and maximum range is 12,400 meters (7.7 mi.). The system requires a crew of seven.

The D-1 fires variable charge, case-type, separate loading ammunition, including FRAG-HE and CP rounds. There are also chemical, illuminating, smoke, semi-AP (which will penetrate 82 millimeters of armor at 1,000 meters) and HEAT (which will penetrate 300 millimeters of armor at 0 degrees obliquity and 1,000 meters) rounds available.

In the Soviet army the D-1 is being replaced by the 152mm self-propelled gun/howitzer 2S3.

SOLTAM 155MM M-71 GUN/HOWITZER (ISRAEL)

The Soltam M-71 is a further development of the Soltam 155mm M-68 Gun/Howitzer and uses the same recoil system, breech, and carriage. The main differences are that the M-71 has a longer barrel and is fitted with a rammer driven by compressed air. This permits rapid loading at all angles of elevation.

The system has a single-baffle muzzle brake, a hydropneumatic recoil system, a horizontal wedge breechblock, and a split-trail carriage. Total traverse is 84 degrees, while elevation and depression can be carried out in the +52 degree/−3 degree range. The sustained rate of fire is two rounds per minute and can be doubled for short periods of time. Maximum range is 23,500 meters (14.6 mi.). The weapon has a crew of eight.

155MM FIELD HOWITZER 70 (FH-70) (MULTINATIONAL)

In the early 1960s West Germany, the United Kingdom, and Italy agreed on a requirement for a new 155mm field howitzer that would be able to sustain a high rate of fire with a burst fire capability, have high mobility and be deployable with minimum effort, and achieve increased range and lethality by means of a new family of ammunition.

The United Kingdom became project leader for the FH-70. Trilateral responsibilities were assigned for production of various components and accessories.

The system has a double-baffle muzzle brake, a semiautomatic wedge breech mechanism, and a split-trail carriage. There is no gun shield. Elevation and depression can be carried out in the $+70$-degree/-5-degree range, and the weapon can traverse through 56 degrees. Normal rate of fire is six rounds per minute. With the standard projectile, maximum range is 24,700 meters (15.3 mi.). A crew of seven or eight is required.

The FH-70 can be towed using a variety of trucks and is air transportable in a Lockheed C-130 aircraft or slung beneath a CH-47D helicopter. A new family of 155mm ammunition significantly increases the range and lethality of both direct and indirect fire against armored targets. The FH-70 can also fire NATO standard ammunition, including the American Copperhead CLGP. The new family includes HE, smoke, and illuminating rounds. The ERP (extended range projectile) being actively considered for tri-national use is the American M549A1, which would increase the range of the FH-70 to more than 30,000 meters (18.6 mi.).

The Japanese Self-Defense Force has selected the FH-70 to replace its 155mm M114 towed howitzers. Production is being undertaken under license in Japan.

Rheinmetall has produced a 46-caliber length barrel that replaces the standard 39-caliber barrel and enables standard HE projectiles using charge 9 propellant to reach a range of 30,000 meters (18.6 mi.) and base bleed projectiles to a range of 36,000 meters (22.3 mi.). Existing FH-70 howitzers can be modified to this longer barrel FH-70R configuration without being sent back to the factory. Development trials of the modified version began in mid-1984. The FH-70R was shown at the 1986 British Army Equipment Exhibition.

155MM TOWED GUN TR (FRANCE)

This weapon (Le Cannon de 155mm Tracte), developed to meet the requirements of French motorized infantry divisions, has now started to replace the older 155mm Model 50 towed howitzers. The weapon was shown for the first time at the 1979 Satory Exhibition of Military Equipment. First production 155mm guns were completed in 1984, with the first 79 units delivered to the French army by 1988. A special version for possible NATO customers is now in the design stage. It will have a modified chamber configuration and the maximum elevation will be increased to 70 degrees.

A crew of eight is required to man this weapon's tractor and gun. In the self-propelled mode, the gunner doubles as driver. The gun has a double-baffle muzzle brake, a hydropneumatic recoil mechanism, a horizontal wedge breechblock, and a split-trail carriage. There is no gun shield. The gun can be elevated and depressed through a $+66$-degree/-7-degree range and traversed 65 degrees. Sustained rate of fire is two rounds per minute. Maximum range is 24,000 meters (14.9 mi.) using a hollow base projectile and 33,000 meters (20.5 mi.) with a rocket-assisted projectile.

5.5-INCH MEDIUM GUN (UNITED KINGDOM)

This weapon was developed by the Armament Research and Development Establishment in the late 1930s to meet a requirement for a 5-inch gun that could fire a projectile weighing 41 kilograms (90 lb.) to a maximum range of

14,600 meters (9.1 mi.). The gun entered production in 1941 and was first used in action in the Middle East the following year. It remained in British army service in diminishing numbers until 1978–80, when it was finally phased out and replaced by the 155mm FH-70.

In 1982 and 1983 four 5.5-inch medium guns were reintroduced into service with the British army at the Royal School of Artillery. The 5.5-inch gun has a hydropneumatic recoil system, an interrupted screw thread breech mechanism, and a split-trail carriage. There is no muzzle brake or gun shield. Elevation and depression can be carried out in the +45-degree/−5-degree range, and the weapon can traverse 60 degrees. Rate of fire is two rounds per minute; maximum range is 16,460 meters (10.2 mi.). The weapon requires a crew of ten.

180MM GUN S-23 (SOVIET UNION)

This gun was developed in the early 1950s from a naval weapon. It was first seen in public in the 1955 May Day parade in Moscow. During travel the barrel is withdrawn out of the gun to the rear and linked to the trails to reduce overall length. In action the S-23 is supported on a base that is retracted under the carriage during travel.

The weapon uses a pepperpot muzzle brake, a screw-type breech mechanism, and a split-trail carriage. It is towed by a heavy artillery tractor and requires a crew of 16. Elevation and depression range from +50 degrees to −2 degrees, while the weapon can traverse 44 degrees total.

The S-23 fires using a bag-type variable charge and several different types of separate loading ammunition including FRAG-HE, HE/RAP, a concrete-piercing projectile, and a 0.2 KT tactical nuclear shell. Its maximum range is 30,400 meters (18.8 mi.), increased to 43,800 meters (27.2 mi.) with the use of RAP. The weapon can sustain fire at one round per minute for short periods, but the sustained rate is one round every two minutes.

In the Soviet army the S-23 is issued on the basis of 12 weapons in the heavy artillery brigade of the artillery division.

8-INCH HOWITZER M115 (UNITED STATES)

Following World War I, the United States developed two 8-inch (203mm) howitzers, the M1920 and the M1920M1, that could traverse 360 degrees, elevate from 0 degrees to +65 degrees, and had a common carriage that could also be used for a 155mm gun. It was not until 1940, however, that modifications of these designs resulted in a standardized 8-inch howitzer (the M1) for U.S. forces. After World War II, the M1 was redesignated the Howitzer, Heavy, Towed: 8-inch: M115.

Capable of hurling a 90.72-kilogram (200-lb.) projectile to a range of 16,800 meters (10.4 mi.), the M115 can fire as fast as a round per minute, with a sustained rate of fire of one round every two minutes. The howitzer fires several different projectiles including HE, antipersonnel mine-dispersing, chemical (agent GB or VX), and nuclear (5- to 10-kiloton range).

The M115 has a hydropneumatic recoil system with an interrupted screw-stepped thread breech mechanism and a split trail with limber carriage. It is designed to be served by a crew of 14 and is towed by a tractor or 6×6 truck. A self-propelled version was developed during World War II, but is no longer in service.

The 8-inch howitzer saw service in Vietnam by U.S. forces in the 1960s and early 1970s, where it gained a reputation for uncanny accuracy. Today, it remains prominent as heavy artillery and can be found in corps artillery groups.

Self-propelled Artillery

122MM SELF-PROPELLED HOWITZER M-1974 (2S1) (SOVIET UNION)

This weapon is commonly known as the Gvozdika (Carnation), although NATO usually calls it the M-1974, referring to the year it was first seen in public. It entered service with the Soviet and Polish armies in 1971 and was first seen by Western observers at a parade in Poland in July 1974. In appearance it is similar to the American M109 self-propelled howitzer, which entered service in 1962.

The M-1974 is issued on the basis of 36 per artillery division, 36 per motorized rifle division, and 72 per tank division. It can be distinguished from the heavier 152mm self-propelled gun/howitzer M-1973, which has six road wheels and four return rollers, by its seven road wheels and the absence of return rollers.

The M-1974's main armament is a modified version of the 122mm D-30 towed howitzer. It has a semiautomatic vertical sliding wedge breechblock and a firing pin that can be recocked in the event of a misfire. A power rammer and extractor provide a higher rate of fire and permit loading at any angle of elevation. The maximum sustained rate of fire is five rounds per minute. The basic load of 40 rounds carried aboard is normally divided into 32 HE, six smoke, and two HEAT-FS. The HE projectile has a maximum range of 15,300 meters (9.5 mi), with HE/RAP, that can be extended to 21,900 meters (13.6 mi.). AP-HE, flechette, leaflet, and chemical projectiles are also available. The system requires a crew of four. It is amphibious and has a maximum road range of 500 kilometers (310 mi.). The turret has both electrical and manual controls and full 360-degree traverse. The range of elevation and depression is $+70$ degrees/-3 degrees.

152MM SELF-PROPELLED GUN (2S5) (SOVIET UNION)

Since 1978 the Soviet Union has deployed two new 152mm guns, one self-propelled and one towed. The SP version is believed to have reached full operational capability with the Soviet army in 1980. So far it has not been identified in service outside the Soviet army.

The self-propelled gun is based on the chassis of the GMZ minelayer or the 152mm M1973, with the weapon well to the rear in an unprotected mounting. The ordnance is fitted with a muzzle brake but does not have a fume extractor. A large spade is lowered at the hull before firing commences.

This weapon has a nuclear capability. Maximum range with a conventional HE round is 17,000 meters (10.5 mi.), increased to 37,000 meters (22.9 mi.)

with a rocket-assisted projectile. In addition to high-explosive and tactical nuclear projectiles, the 2S5 can also fire chemical, concrete-piercing, and improved conventional munitions.

203MM SELF-PROPELLED GUN M-1975 (2S7) (SOVIET UNION)

Soviet ground forces began receiving the M-1975 during 1975; reportedly some 400 have now been deployed, although fewer than half are aligned against NATO forces. This gun equips heavy artillery units at front level and is capable of firing nuclear projectiles. It is believed that an artillery regiment equipped with the M-1975 has 24 weapons organized in three batteries of eight weapons each.

The M-1975 is based on a large chassis that is probably the biggest armored vehicle currently in the Soviet inventory. An armored cab at the front can carry two to four crewmen. Immediately behind the cab is the engine compartment. The transmission is forward-mounted below the cab so as to power the forward track drive sprockets. The suspension is of a new type and features seven road wheels. Storage bins are located midway of the hull; the gun is mounted at the rear in the conventional manner. The gun is equipped with a form of power-assisted loading, with its operator seated in a crow's nest position at the left rear of the vehicle. At the extreme rear is a large hydraulically operated recoil spade. The M-1975 has no cover for the gun crew when in action. It is possible that a second tracked vehicle carries the ammunition and the bulk of the gun crew.

A maximum range of 30,000 meters (18.6 mi.) has been quoted for this gun. It is understood to have a maximum rate of fire of two rounds a minute and a sustained rate of one round every two minutes. Types of ammunition fired include high explosive and tactical nuclear.

240MM SELF-PROPELLED MORTAR M-1975 (2S4) (SOVIET UNION)

This Soviet army system is known in the West as the M-1975. It is normally retained at front or high command levels of control for special-purpose use, since it can fire a nuclear projectile. The system reached full operational capability in 1975 but has yet to appear in public. It is believed that each 240mm mortar regiment has from 36 to 54 systems.

The M-1975 consists of a much-modified GMZ tracked mine-laying vehicle on the hull rear. The mortar is carried complete with a base plate and is hydraulically lowered from its traveling position around a pivot on the rear of the hull. The base plate is hinged to the hull rear; when emplaced, the mortar barrel faces away from the hull. Probably some rounds are carried inside the vehicle hull and some form of assisted loading is provided. Rate of fire is estimated at one round a minute.

The 240mm mortar has a minimum range of 800 meters (0.5 mi.) and a maximum range of 9,700 meters (6 mi.); it is possible that the mortar barrel used on the M-1975 has an enhanced range of 12,700 meters (7.9 mi.). In addition to nuclear projectiles the mortar fires a high-explosive round weighing

130 kilograms (287 lb.) and a chemical projectile. A concrete-piercing round for use against urban targets has also been reported.

M109A1 (United States)

The M109A1 is basically the M109 fitted with a new and much longer barrel, an improved elevation and traversing system, and a strengthened suspension system. It fires an HE projectile to a range of 18,100 meters (11.2 mi.), compared with 14,600 meters (9.1 mi.) for the M109; an RAP extends that range to 24,000 meters (14.9 mi.). The weapon can also fire other projectiles including one filled with agent H/ HD, an HE round, a grenade-filled round, an antitank mine round, and an antipersonnel mine round.

M109A2 (United States)

This system entered production in 1978 with the first deliveries made early the following year. The major changes from the M109A1 include a redesigned rammer and improved recoil mechanism, engine operation warning devices, redesigned hatch and door latches, an improved hydraulic system, and a bustle designed to carry an additional 22 rounds of ammunition. The weapon can be elevated to +75 degrees and depressed to −3 degrees, while the turret can traverse 360 degrees. Turret control is both hydraulic and manual. In addition to the main armament there is a 12.7mm or 7.62mm machine gun for antiaircraft defense.

Manned by a crew of six and powered by a Detroit Diesel turbocharged engine developing 405 brake horsepower, the system has a maximum road speed of more than 90 km/h (56 mi.) and a maximum road range of some 354 kilometers (220 mi.). It can ford more than 1 meter of water, climb a 60 percent gradient, and span a trench 1.83 meters (6 ft.) wide. The cross-drive transmission has four forward and two reverse gears. Independent torsion bar suspension is provided.

155mm GCT Self-propelled Gun (France)

The GCT (Grande Cadence de Tir) was developed beginning in 1969 to meet a French army requirement for a self-propelled gun to replace the 105mm and 155mm self-propelled weapons then in service. First production GCTs were delivered in 1978—to Saudi Arabia. The weapon was officially selected by the French army in July 1979 and is now being deployed in five-gun batteries, with each regiment consisting of three batteries. The French army has an overall requirement for 190 GCTs.

The GCT basically consists of a modified AMX-30 main battle tank chassis fitted with a new turret and armed with a 155mm gun and an automatic loading system. The vehicle has a crew of four: the commander, gunner, loader, and driver.

The hull is almost identical to that of the AMX-30, with modifications that lighten the hull by 2,000 kilograms (4,400 lb.). The 105mm ammunition racks in the hull have been removed, and a 5KVA 28-volt generator and a ventilator system to supply the turret with cold air have been installed.

The system, powered by a Hispano-Suiza 12-cylinder water-cooled and supercharged multi-fuel engine developing 720 horsepower, has a maximum road speed of 60 km/h (37 mph). Maximum road range is 450 kilometers (279 mi.). The vehicle has five forward and five reverse gears and torsion bar suspension; it can ford more than 2 meters and climb a 60 percent gradient. Turret control is both hydraulic and manual; the turret can traverse 360 degrees. Gun elevation and depression are in the $+66$-degree/-4-degree range. Equipment includes a 7.62mm or 12.7mm machine gun for antiaircraft defense and two smoke dischargers.

OTO MELARA PALMARIA 155MM SELF-PROPELLED HOWITZER (ITALY, FOR EXPORT)

The Palmaria was developed beginning in 1977 by OTO Melara specifically for export. The first production vehicles were ready in 1982. The first customer, Libya, placed an order for 210 systems. Nigeria placed an early order for 25, while Argentina ordered 25 Palmaria turrets to be fitted on the TAM medium tank chassis. All were completed by late 1986.

The system's chassis is similar to the OF-40 main battle tank's, apart from the engine. The driver is seated at the front of the hull. The other four crew members (commander, gunner, charge handler, and magazine operator) are seated in the aluminum turret in the center of the hull. The commander, in the right forward part of the turret, has eight periscopes for all-around observation and a single-piece hatch cover that opens to the rear. Additional large rectangular hatches are on either side of the turret. A 7.62mm or 12.7mm antiaircraft machine gun can be mounted on the roof, and four smoke dischargers are mounted on either side of the turret.

The system has a maximum road speed of 60 km/h (37 mph) and a maximum cruising range of 500 kilometers (310 mi.). The power shifting transmission provides four forward and two reverse gears. Torsion bar suspension is used. The main gun can elevate and depress $+70$ degrees/-4 degrees and traverse 360 degrees.

M107 175MM SELF-PROPELLED GUN (UNITED STATES)

The U.S. M107 has a crew of five, can attain a maximum road speed of 56 km/h (35 mph), and has a maximum road range of 725 kilometers (450 mi.). The cross-drive transmission provides four forward and two reverse gears. Torsion bar suspension is utilized. Turret control is both hydraulic and manual, with an elevation and depression range of $+65$ degrees/-2 degrees and gun traverse of 30 degrees in each direction.

In the U.S. Army, M107s were deployed in battalions of twelve guns and were held at corps level. All M107s in U.S. corps were, by 1981, converted to M110A2s (see below). It is expected that other countries deploying the M107 will follow suit; Italy and the Netherlands have already effected such conversions.

M110A1 AND M110A2 (UNITED STATES)

In 1969 the United States Army Armament Command began development of a new version of the M110, one that would have longer range and fire a new family of improved ammunition. The result was standardized as the M110A1 and entered service in January 1977. It replaced both the M110 and the M107, which were phased out of service with the U.S. Army in Europe by 1980.

The M110A1 203mm howitzer has a new and much longer barrel, a direct-fire elbow telescope, and a chassis identical to the M110's. The M110A2, which was standardized in 1978, is the M110A1 fitted with a double-baffle muzzle brake. It can thus fire charge 9 of the M118A1 propelling charge, whereas the M110A1 can fire only up to charge 8.

The M110A1 and M110A2 have a crew of five. Their maximum road speed is 56 km/h (35 mph), using a Detroit Diesel 8-cylinder turbocharged engine, and maximum road range is 725 kilometers (450 mi.). The transmission provides four forward and two reverse gears. Torsion bar suspension is used. Turret control is both hydraulic and manual. The gun can be elevated and depressed through a +65-degree/−2-degree range and traversed 30 degrees to each side.

Conclusion

The U.S. Army envisages that a new artillery system will be required to follow the present M109 howitzer improvement program (HIP). It currently antici-pates that a new weapons system will be required from the late 1990s onward; that requirement is now generally known as the advanced field artillery system (AFAS). Although AFAS is still in its early stages, two guiding principles have been established: to reduce personnel-to-weapons system ratios and to enhance survivability. Other requirements include increased range, a higher rate of fire, and a smaller crew, all related to existing systems; mobility equal to other anticipated AFVs; a nuclear-hardened capability; and the ability to be carried in a C-141 transport aircraft. AFAS will also have to be "soldier friendly."

Technologies under investigation for possible inclusion in AFAS are robotics, artificial intelligence, a single-charge propellant system, liquid propellants, electromagnetic propulsion, and a chassis common with the projected future combat systems.

Electromagnetic (EM) and electrothermal (ET) propulsion systems hold par-ticular promise for the future of guns, especially in direct-fire roles. Conven-tional guns cannot push projectiles any faster than the 2-kilometers-per-second (km/sec.) (1.25 mps) expansion speed of solid propellants. Recent experiments have used electric power to achieve projectile (1.1-kg; 2.5-lb.) speeds in excess of 3 km/sec. (1.86 mps). While substantial challenges remain, a conceptual design for an electric 120mm gun with twice the kinetic energy of conventional guns has been developed. Where the future leads is tied to continuing research and development efforts.

ALAA EL DIN ABDEL MEGUID DARWISH

SEE ALSO: Artillery; Artillery, Rocket and Missile.

Bibliography

Jane's armour and artillery, 1988–1989. 1988. London: Jane's.
Metzgar, T. L. 1991. Electric guns. *National Defense.* Arlington, Va.: The American Defense Preparedness Association.

U.S. Dept. of Defense. 1988. *Soviet military power: An assessment of the threat.* Washington, D.C.: Dept. of Defense.

ADDITIONAL SOURCES: *Military Technology; NATO's Sixteen Nations.*

AUTOMATIC WEAPON

The need to provide individual soldiers with a weapon that enables them to engage numerous enemy targets for short periods led to the development of multiple-firing, rapid-firing, and automatic-firing weapons. True automatic fire is associated only with gunpowder weapons and depends upon either the energy generated by the expanding gases of the fired cartridge or recoil energy. The first fully automatic firearm was developed by Hiram Maxim—the father of the machine gun—in the late nineteenth century and gave soldiers the firepower they sought.

Britain's colonial forces first used Maxim guns in the Matabele War of 1893–94. In one engagement, 50 police of the Rhodesian Charter Company with only four machine guns fought off 5,000 Matabele warriors. Today, automatic weapons comprise rifles, submachine guns, machine guns, assault rifles, and various other weapons.

Operation of Automatic Weapons

Automatic firing is the process of feeding a cartridge, firing a round, and ejecting the casing, carried out by the mechanism of a weapon after a primary manual, electrical, or pneumatic cocking, and continuing as long as the trigger is held to the rear and there is still ammunition in the belt, feed strip, or magazine. The same process describes semiautomatic fire from self-loading weapons, except that the trigger is pulled once per shot and must be released between shots.

This sequence of operations, which leads from the firing of one round to the firing of the next, comprises a basic cycle that is common to almost all automatic weapons and a series of associated operations that vary with the weapon type. The energy required can come from only two sources: recoil energy or the energy that would otherwise be wasted as muzzle blast. These two sources of energy lead to one or another of the three methods used today in all automatic weapons: blowback, recoil, or gas operation.

BLOWBACK OPERATION

In this method of operation the energy required to carry out the cycle of operation is supplied to the bolt by the backward movement of the cartridge case caused by gas pressure. There are four systems of blowback operation: simple blowback, advanced primer ignition, delayed blowback, and blowback with a locked breech.

Simple blowback. This system in its simplest form allows for a totally unlocked breech and relies merely on the mass of the breechblock and the strength of the return spring to prevent the cartridge case from coming back too quickly after firing. This form of operation is suitable only where the cartridge is of low power relative to the weight of the breechblock. Simple blowback operations are effectively restricted to pistols and submachine guns.

Advanced primer ignition. More sophisticated blowback designs have been incorporated into large-caliber machine guns. These take advantage of the fact that a cartridge fired before being fully chambered allows half the available firing impulse to force the block back again. This in effect allows the breechblock to be made lighter. In such weapons the fixed firing pin of the simple blowback design is replaced by a controlled pin that strikes the cap at the desired point in the forward travel of the cartridge being chambered.

Delayed blowback. This method is also known as retarded blowback or hesitation blowback. Here, as in the previous blowback systems, the breechblock is not locked, but some mechanical delay is incorporated to ensure that the breechblock cannot move back so rapidly as to allow the unsupported cartridge case to emerge from the chamber while the pressure is still high. The delay may be achieved by means of a lever or by a system of rollers that must be forced out of engagement with the barrel extension before the breechblock can move backward.

Blowback with a locked breech. In this system the breechblock is physically locked to the receiver of the weapon during the time the pressure is high, then unlocked in time to allow the residual pressure to blow the breechblock to the rear. This allows for use of the lightest possible breechblock with a high-powered cartridge, but the timing of the breech opening is critical and the system tends to be expensive. It is also sensitive to variations in ammunition.

Advantages and disadvantages of blowback operation. The blowback method is cheap, simple, and reliable, and it allows for a configuration that makes for ease of changing barrels. Its disadvantages are that it allows no adjustment for power, fouling is left in the breech, and it is not suitable for vehicular use.

RECOIL OPERATION

In this method of operation the energy required to carry out the cycle of operations is supplied to the bolt by the rearward movement of the bolt and barrel, locked together, caused by gas pressure. The system differs from the blowback in having a fully locked breech and in having the barrel move back with the breechblock. There are two types of recoil operation: long recoil and short recoil.

Long recoil. In the long recoil system both the bolt and barrel recoil a distance that is greater than the length of the unfired round. This method produces a very slow rate of fire but is advantageous in those cases where it is important to minimize the forces exerted on the mounting. Except where that special requirement exists, this approach is rarely used.

Short recoil. Here the breechblock remains locked to the barrel only while the pressure is high. In practice, as with a round of rifle caliber, this involves a barrel travel of only a centimeter or so. This approach reduces the weight of the breechblock compared with that required in a blowback system. In smaller-caliber weapons, however, there is less recoil energy and the system will not function unless steps are taken to maximize the available energy and use it to best advantage.

Advantages and disadvantages. Machine guns based on recoil operation are particularly well suited for use in armored vehicles. They are generally sturdy, can have their rate of fire slowed down when desirable, and allow for easy change of barrels from the rear. A disadvantage is that there is no way of adjusting the power under adverse conditions.

GAS OPERATION

In this system of operation, the required energy is obtained from the pressure of gas tapped off from the barrel. The amount of gas required to operate a machine gun is not very great, and the effect on the pressure in the barrel—and hence on the velocity of the projectile—is correspondingly small.

The required gas can be tapped off anywhere between the breech and the muzzle, and examples can be found of every conceivable gas position. Different effects are obtained at different positions. At the muzzle the gas is at a relatively low pressure and is much cooler. As a result, more gas must be led off to obtain the same working force. Here too the carbon is desublimated, which results in a lot of fouling. The working parts can be light, but since they are so far from the breech they tend to be thin and spidery.

At the other extreme, a gun has been produced that has a hole in the chamber wall through which a small section of the brass cartridge is blown to release the gas to drive back a very short tappet. In general a compromise is made, with a tap-off point somewhere about 20 to 30 centimeters from the muzzle, depending on caliber and barrel length. The gas pressure obtained can be used in one of three ways to operate the gun: long- or short-stroke piston or direct gas operation.

Long-stroke piston operation. In this system the piston is connected directly to the breechblock and controls the position of the block at all times. This type of arrangement is found in by far the greatest number of modern machine guns. The piston tends to be long and heavy, and the resultant recoiling mass is considerable.

Short-stroke piston operation. Here the piston moves back a distance that can be as short as a millimeter or two, but it imparts its energy to an operating rod that forces the breechblock to the rear. This arrangement is found on the great majority of gas-operated rifles; because the operating rod and the bolt can be quite light, this system avoids large changes in the center of mass of the weapon during firing and thus tends to have less effect on the firer's aim than a long-stroke system.

Direct gas action. No piston at all is used in this method. The gas is tapped off from the barrel and ducted back along a tube, where it imparts energy to the bolt carrier. The direct gas action system produces the lightest possible moving mass, but it can also result in heavy fouling, because the gases cool in the duct and bolt carrier, depositing solid residue in a critically inaccessible area where the accumulation of carbon can lead to difficult and prolonged stoppages.

Advantages and disadvantages. Gas operation is the only system that can genuinely regulate the power available and control it according to the needs of the moment by means of a simple regulator. A disadvantage is that special modifications are needed to alter the gas system when it is used in an armored vehicle because of fouling and the emission of toxic fumes. Also, because of the mating of barrel and gas cylinder, barrel changes must be made in a forward direction, which is a disadvantage in an armored vehicle.

Conclusion

Automatic weapons vary in caliber, size, weight, and mission and are ubiquitous to militaries throughout the world. They are likely neither to disappear nor to change in the fundamental way in which they function. The rates at which they fire will remain the same (anywhere from a low of about 100 rounds per minute to as fast as many thousand rounds per minute), although some new developments in caseless ammunition promise to greatly increase firing rates for submachine guns and assault rifles. Other advances in lightweight, composite material technology and advances in munitions will contribute to the flexibility and lethality of automatic weapons.

SAMIR H. SHALABY

SEE ALSO: Machine Gun; Small Arms.

Bibliography

Jane's infantry weapons, 1984–1985. 1984. London: Jane's.
Reid, W. 1976. *Arms through the ages.* New York: Harper and Row.

B

BALLISTICS

Ballistics deals not only with the motion of projectiles, but also is linked closely with a variety of technologies. Essentially there are four fundamental phases of ballistics. Interior ballistics involves the initial propulsion, or what happens in the gun or launcher; intermediate ballistics studies and analyzes the complex events related to the initial projectile flight just out of the gun or launcher; exterior ballistics describes the flight motions and performance characteristics of the projectile; and terminal ballistics determines the effect of the projectile on the target.

Currently, ballistics is in transition: both traditional and newer technology projectiles are in the field. Basic stockpiles of ammunition for a large number of weapons systems still consist essentially of "dumb" projectiles. That means that these projectiles, both kinetic energy (KE) and high explosive (HE), do not incorporate means to alter their trajectories once they are launched, nor can they sense the target or recognize the type of target. The newer generation of projectiles, however, is being designed to include guidance and sensing.

Thus one can generally differentiate between projectile types by broadly designating them as dumb (or conventional), "competent," "smart," or "brilliant." These designations require brief explanations. Conventional is usually a traditional ballistic projectile (spin stabilized or fin stabilized), whether KE or HE. The projectile (other than perhaps its fuzing) does not include any electronic sensing or subsidiary propulsion and guidance.

A competent munition consists of a conventional projectile that has been somewhat upgraded by the addition of one or more smart devices so that the projectile has gained a multiple increase in utilization and effectiveness over its basic form.

A smart munition is designed to be based on guidance and/or sensors to allow it to have in-flight (trajectory) flexibility unattainable by a conventional ballistic projectile.

Brilliant munitions are technology extensions beyond smart. They integrate guidance, control, and various sensors in conjunction with algorithms and high-speed microprocessing to represent the most advanced form of the state of the art.

As technology relentlessly advances in scope and complexity, smaller and more cost-effective devices will drive the application and design of future projectiles. Ballistics will no longer be based on a series of firing tables involving muzzle velocity, elevation angles, and range. Automatic fire control systems will dominate and offer the user a variety of options.

The computer, with its ability to become increasingly miniaturized while providing high-speed data processing, will underlie a new style of ballistics. These will be a blending of the technologies between gun-launched projectiles and guided missiles. Of fundamental importance is the currently accepted methodology of using high-speed computing to analyze warhead designs and potential terminal (target) effectiveness with amazing accuracy. Warhead design is then integrated with appropriate sensor and fuze technologies. Concurrently, new materials are evaluated and selected for application (for example, sabots) and mating with the propulsion elements.

Wind tunnels and instrumented ballistic ranges are a traditional, proven, and continuous means for deriving the aerodynamic coefficients required for input into realistic six degrees of freedom (6 DOF) equations that, in turn, can be used to simulate external and mass effects upon flight stability and potential performance. These analyses are critical to achieving a successful ballistic item. The new field of computational fluid dynamics (CFD) is making strides and will provide an efficient method for design evaluation and performance prediction.

The increased use of high-speed, high-capacity computers is rapidly altering the overall traditional methodology of design, preliminary analysis, fabrication, testing, and performance analysis. What is strongly indicated is that much of the warhead design, flight performance, and terminal effects potential can be sufficiently well predicted from computer-based mathematical models so as to move more rapidly and confidently into building and testing the actual hardware. Nonetheless, gun-launched testing is still required, as is overall testing to verify system performance.

An anomaly continues to exist in ballistic testing, namely that small-scale ballistic systems (e.g., small arms and medium-caliber weapons) require testing of many thousands of rounds. By contrast, since the large-caliber and smart systems are individually expensive, relatively fewer numbers are actually tested. Thus, it is necessary to have highly instrumented test ranges and the supporting database to undertake the complete system analyses and associated acceptance decisions.

Interior Ballistics

Potentially, one of the ballistics areas for the next stage of significant improvement will be the efficiency of gun propulsion. This area divides into two diverse technologies. The first is in advanced propellant technology, specifically retaining the conventional gun design and obtaining substantial performance increments through use of different propellants. Examples are liquid, gelled, and a form of compacted conventional propellant referred to as "very high burn rate" (VHBR). These new propellants could add approximately 10 percent to 20 percent to the present muzzle velocities without completely changing the current gun systems.

The second technology trend relating to propulsion started about a decade ago with official support for a major research program based on electromagnetic propulsion. While this is still a long-term technology area, several new variations offer promise of intermediate performance improvement in a shorter time frame. These hybrids include electrothermal (ET), which combines electrical and chemical energy to launch conventional shapes at velocities significantly above the current standard, and combustion-augmented plasma (CAP).

Light gas guns are a major ballistics research tool for conducting hypervelocity-impact and penetration-design studies leading to future armor/antiarmor systems. Two-stage light gas guns are capable of launch velocities up to 7,620 meters per second (25,000 ft./sec.). These fundamental research tools provide the means for obtaining the database upon which major changes and resultant advances in ballistics technology are dependent. Research is trying to determine whether these laboratory fixtures can become actual military weapons by means of unique redesigns and by applying the latest in materials and other advanced components. This work will require some unusual design and engineering to reduce size, weight, and complexity to a point where the proposed system has attractive military potential.

Intermediate Ballistics

In intermediate ballistics studies, KE investigations involve the launch dynamics of saboted projectiles. Emphasis is on achieving uniform sabot discard, thereby minimizing the dispersion error due to launch asymmetries. This is a form of fine-tuning the round to achieve reduced dispersion at ever-increasing ranges, since improved propellants are resulting in increased muzzle velocity with shorter time of flight to greater ranges. This results in the need to reduce those contributions to the total dispersion.

Projectile Configurations

In addition to modifying current projectile shapes, such as adding on rocket boost to long-rod penetrators, extensive research is being undertaken to increase significantly the length-to-diameter (l/d) ratio of rod penetrators. However, practical limits to the l/d will have to be considered because of the dimensions of munitions storage compartments within various fighting vehicles.

Currently, consideration is being given to including a multipurpose projectile in the small family of tank ammunition. This projectile would serve in a variety of roles from antihelicopter, using a proximity fuze, to bunker-busting, antiarmor, and antipersonnel.

Future projectile designs will be required as launch velocities are increased and there is a need to extend the effective range of these projectiles. Designs to be evaluated could be tubular, ramjet, or low-drag conical nose shapes, as well as wave-rider configurations. Each of these designs offers specific advantages and will have to be applied accordingly. For example, tubular projectiles, while generally having low mass, also have very low drag and can be used for both combat and training missions. On the other hand, ramjet projectiles can provide increased kinetic energy and extended range.

Another approach will be the weight reduction of sabots so that additional energy can be imparted to the projectile and not lost through sabot discard. Rocket-assisted projectiles will be utilized to gain more downrange kinetic energy.

With so many tanks equipped with the 105mm cannon system, it would be economically feasible to use increased energy propellants and/or a rocket boost—initiated just out of the gun muzzle—to reduce time of flight to target while adding significantly to the downrange kinetic energy. If this approach proves to be relatively successful, simple, terminal correction means will be added. Later, in view of the longer-range performance potential, more intricate guidance will be incorporated, particularly against maneuvering targets. These systems become complex when integrated, however, and require very detailed engineering design analyses, as well as experimental verification.

One of the key challenges will be integrating multisensors and fuzing without affecting the necessary, or required, warhead volume. Considering the continuing miniaturization of sensors and electronic fuzing, this design and packaging efficiency should be attainable within the next two generations of smart munitions.

Partial Ballistic Flight Modes

Free-flight, unguided projectiles and munitions are becoming converted to several terminal trajectory modes. Examples of these are guided mortars, where the first portion of the trajectory is ballistic, followed by terminal guidance. Artillery shells are being developed to deliver sensor-fuzed munitions. The shell's free-flight trajectory places it in a desired target area, and then the submunitions are base ejected to disperse, search, and fire on the target from above. In a similar manner, medium artillery rocket systems launch carrier rockets in a ballistic mode to reach a target area and then eject terminally guided submunitions that can detect and fly to the target. This combination of ballistic ammunition and electronic technologies is also applicable for future aircraft-delivered stand-off weapon dispensers.

Aircraft-delivered Munitions

One specialty generally overlooked in ballistics is air-delivered munitions, particularly submunitions or bomblets carried by aircraft to the target area and then released. Currently, the aircraft has to launch the dispenser in a free-flight ballistic trajectory.

The present dispensers are capable of spinning, then opening, and releasing the bomblets above the target area. The effective area coverage is determined by the centrifugal force generated by the spinning dispenser. What is of concern is the vulnerability of the aircraft, in that it must approach and fly near (if not over) the target zone to achieve the required ballistic trajectory release. Future dispenser versions in research will have a long stand-off range capability. They will contain onboard thrust generators and guidance so that the delivery aircraft will be able to launch the dispenser farther from the target and thus be able to "launch and leave" while the powered dispenser seeks and homes in on the target area, much like an advanced cruise missile. However, until the "smarts" become smaller and very affordable, the bomblets will tend to be ballistic. Eventually, technology is expected to transition dumb munitions into competent munitions by applying basic sensors and through maneuvering or guidance means. At this point, self-dispersing bomblets or submunitions will no longer be a direct function of their former ballistic characteristics. Additionally, air-launched munition dispensers will share some of the flight and performance characteristics of cruise missiles.

Small Arms

The current technology trend is on improving the hit probability at ranges beyond 250 meters (820 ft.). Ballistic effort is focusing on multiple rounds launched per trigger pull to increase the dispersion in a relatively controlled area or target zone, thus increasing the probability of a hit. Both conventional projectiles and flechettes are being tested for this improved hit probability.

Caseless ammunition is continuing to be developed by a small segment of the small-arms community. Concurrent with a trend toward smaller, lightweight projectiles launched at higher muzzle velocities is a trend toward larger capacity magazines as a means of supporting the higher rate of fire or expenditure of ammunition.

A new trend in the ballistics of infantry weapons that is in its earliest stage is the concept of a small-arms shoulder-fired weapon that can launch an exploding projectile, or bursting munition, to ranges in excess of 500 meters (1,640 ft.). Since the impulse required for achieving this range is beyond the human factors' limit for that of normal rifle or grenade-launched munitions, this calls for a rocket-propelled grenade or an aeroballistic projectile whose shape can produce sufficient lift in flight, in conjunction with low drag, to result in a relatively flat trajectory and extended range. This technology trend also calls for a compact fire control system that computes range and time of flight and communicates to the fuzing to achieve either an airburst near the ground or a direct impact, whichever may be required by combat conditions.

The focal point of this technology trend is to reduce significantly the major deficiency in small-arms infantry weapons: the large number of bullets that must be fired to achieve an incapacitating hit. By developing a shoulder-launched explosive fragmentation projectile that has both a relatively flat trajectory and extended range, two key results accrue. Area coverage rather than point target accuracy is required, and a suppressive effect is achieved at a range well beyond that of current shoulder-fired infantry weapons. This unique requirement has emerged from the U.S. Army Infantry School study, *Small Arms Strategy—2000.*

Medium-Caliber Ballistics

Progress in medium-caliber ballistics is gradual, as this tends to be an area for continuing the conventional rather than for undertaking radical change.

A major effort is under way to apply finned-rod penetrators to the entire range of medium-caliber ammunition. The rods are scaled down from the kinetic-energy tank-penetrator designs. In the medium calibers the accuracy of the rods becomes very sensitive to the tolerances of the projectiles' components and to the uniformity of sabot discard. To achieve higher muzzle velocities for the rods to increase penetration at longer ranges, newer propellant formulations are being applied.

Another area of slow, but continuing, progress in medium-caliber ballistics is telescoped ammunition. The projectile is completely enclosed within a cylindrical case containing compacted (or consolidated) propellant. The key is to launch each projectile into the barrel at, or very close to, the same initial velocity so as to achieve near-uniform muzzle velocity from shot to shot. Current studies have shown that launch velocities of 1,525 meters per second (5,000 ft./sec.) and higher can be obtained. This performance, combined with the more efficient case geometry, results in a larger number of stowed rounds per given volume, making this area of ballistics technology attractive for future application for both aircraft and ground systems.

Larger Caliber—Tank Cannon

As discussed previously, one of the key goals in obtaining increased muzzle velocities is to be able to launch kinetic-energy rod-type projectiles having higher length-to-diameter (l/d) ratios. This area of ballistics includes the development of new sabots of lighter weight materials, mainly of stronger composites.

Further, in view of the increased emphasis on tank protection, and through new material combinations and the addition of reactive armor, it will not be surprising to see larger caliber tank cannons come into use. Alternatively, new hypervelocity gun designs may also be introduced, and this could signal a new family of projectiles combining the best features of both the kinetic-energy and high-explosive types. Additional emphasis is currently being placed on projectile designs having a form of dual warheads to overcome the protective use of reactive armor and to be able to penetrate the main target. Again, ballistics is being challenged by the measure/countermeasure aspect from continuing advancements in technology.

Larger Caliber—Artillery

The trend in long-range artillery delivering submunitions that can independently seek, acquire, and destroy armor will continue. The keys to further advancements in this area are cost effectiveness of the electronics and sensor sensitivity countermeasures.

Fire control will play a major role in the ballistics of artillery systems, particularly for self-propelled units. With the use of land navigational systems and auto-loaders it will be possible to increase significantly firepower effects.

As more sensor-electronic systems become part of projectile design, various control systems will be used in ballistics. For example, in tank weapons, command and control from the tank could correct and guide the projectile toward the target. In artillery, studies have shown that to achieve accuracy at long range, application of a form of the Global Positioning System (GPS), combined with an onboard correction system, could play a key role in future artillery tactics.

Advances in ballistics must be integrated with concurrent advances in guidance and control, target acquisition, and fire control.

Training Systems

During peacetime, additional emphasis is placed on low-cost training systems. Tank cannon training systems are starting to utilize subcaliber ammunition whose ballistics are designed to match the combat rounds to a reasonable range and then rapidly decelerate so as to not overfly the maximum range or safety limits.

In artillery, new training rounds are being developed that allow for an airburst and that have an acoustic signature similar to combat antipersonnel rounds. This will allow for appropriate troop training.

A current mortar training system uses scaled trajectories and simulates full-scale ammunition handling.

Materials

Various near and future weapons systems will use more high-strength lightweight materials. For example, there are programs under way to develop medium-caliber gun barrels of composite materials in combination with special ceramics.

Some calibers of cased ammunition will have thinner, stronger walls of new high-strength steel. Also, the development of high-strength plastic cartridge cases will significantly reduce weight.

Lightweight composite materials are being used to fabricate sabots. The reduction in weight will allow the payload (projectile) to be heavier or to be launched at a higher muzzle velocity.

As new gun designs, such as the electromagnetic gun or its variants, produce increased muzzle velocities, there will be a need for heat-resistant materials for the projectile nose and the leading edges of the fins. This will be necessary to eliminate or minimize the configurational asymmetries due to ablation from atmospheric heating and the resultant effect on dispersion.

All told, new materials and their applications will be a vital factor in future ballistic systems.

Miscellaneous

NAVAL SYSTEMS

In the area of naval defense, while the 20mm Gatling gun (Phalanx system) is an accepted ballistic weapon, the trend is toward an increased caliber system so that a larger projectile can be launched at higher muzzle velocity, have shorter time of flight to the target, and arrive with more kinetic energy to hit and damage the target.

Larger caliber naval guns will make use of improved fuzes, explosives, and materials. New projectile designs are under development, from submunition carriers to extended range configurations.

An extension of the long-range large gun role will be in the form of ship-launched cruise missiles. Potential payloads will include submunitions.

CASELESS AMMUNITION

There is a near-term trend to caseless or consumable ammunition. Accepted and in use for the large-caliber 120mm NATO tank ammunition, a similar methodology is being intensively developed by the Germans for small arms (for example, the German G11 rifle in 4.92mm). Other infantry weapons using caseless ammunition also are being studied.

LASERS

Research continues on laser weapons. Although feasibility studies have determined the lethality of laser weapons, it remains to be seen how rapidly the power supply and associated components can be packaged into a reasonably sized and militarily rugged mobile weapon platform.

Summary

The trends show continuing competition between gun systems and missile systems, with a gradual merging or combination of these technologies. Emphasis in the gun area will be on developing new interior ballistic systems such as electromagnetic and electrothermal. These systems are capable of launching projectiles at hypersonic velocities, but they need to reach practical size and weight limits to become useful weapons systems. In turn, the hypervelocities will result in new projectile shapes using heat-resistant materials and other components developed for the space program. Although the higher launch velocities will result in shorter times of flight, the use of command or terminal guidance may be necessary to ensure higher hit probabilities.

Concurrently the large investment in conventional ballistic systems represents a basis for product improvement in a variety of technical areas associated with ballistics. These range from more energetic propellants to the materials composing the projectiles (e.g., high-strength metals and lightweight composites for saboted kinetic-energy penetrators and the use of new materials in explosive warheads).

Much of the supporting research and development in ballistics is being done through the use of complex mathematical modeling programmed on some of the world's fastest and largest capacity computers. These high-speed computers enable designers to evaluate and predict the complete ballistic performance of advanced weapons systems, ranging from interior ballistics through flight and then terminal ballistic effectiveness. What was once done very slowly and in a separate or compartmented manner is now being approached in a more unified way. Nonetheless, despite emphasis on the in-laboratory aspects, verification of ballistic systems' performance must still be undertaken on highly instrumented and specialized test ranges.

It appears that competent, smart, and brilliant munitions will dominate in the coming era, leaving small arms and some of the medium-caliber areas as the remaining fields for high technology to enter. Fundamental operations' studies might show whether it is cost-effective to fully apply high technology to these lower calibers.

Again, weight, size, and muzzle velocities will be key factors in future launch systems, while what flies through the atmosphere will depend in great part upon advances in electronics, miniaturization, and onboard propulsion and guidance systems.

The guns-versus-missiles debate may gradually diminish as the best elements of a variety of technologies are integrated into future weapons systems. Ballistics will produce a powerful combination of free-flight and guided dynamics.

ABRAHAM FLATAU

SEE ALSO: Ammunition; Artillery; Artillery, Rocket and Missile; Artillery, Tube; Fuze; Gun Technology Applications; Mortar; Munitions and Explosives Technology Applications; Sensor Technology; Small Arms.

Bibliography

Defense Technical Information Center. 1974–. Proceedings of Hypervelocity Impact Symposiums, nos. 1–7.

Deitchman, S. J. 1987. Exploiting the revolution in conventional weapons. *Aerospace America* (June).

DeMeis, R. 1987. Looking ahead to tactical missiles. *Aerospace America* (June).

Farrar, C. L., et al. 1982. *Military ballistics*. London: Brassey's.

Flatau, A. 1982. Non-spinning projectile, U.S. Patent No. 4,337,911.

Goad, K. J., et al. 1982. *Ammunition*. London: Brassey's.

Hooten, T. 1986. More punch for the infantry: The intelligent mortar round. *Miltech* (4).

Lenaerts, J. 1987. Automatic grenade launchers and their role. *Miltech* (10).

Ryan, J. W. 1982. *Guns, mortars & rockets*. London: Brassey's.

Swift, H., et al. 1979. Feasibility of hypervelocity ordnance. *U.S. Army ARDC*. AD-E400 338. July.

U.S. Army Infantry School. 1986. *Small arms strategy—2000*. Fort Benning, Ga.: U.S. Army Infantry School.

Zukas, J. A. 1982. *Impact dynamics*. New York: Wiley.

BIOLOGICAL WARFARE

Biological warfare (BW) is the military use of harmful organisms as weapons against man, animals, and plants. Because it includes the use of such organisms as bacteria and germs, BW is often referred to as bacteriological or germ warfare. However, BW is broader than germ warfare alone, encompassing the deliberate and direct use of living organisms (biological pathogens) and their naturally occurring by-products, which are commonly called toxins, for military purposes.

Types

BIOLOGICAL PATHOGENS

Biological pathogens, disease-producing living organisms, can be divided into four categories: bacterial, fungal, rickettsial, and viral. Many pathogens have been studied for use militarily, and some of the more prominent ones are listed in Table 1.

Because pathogens are living organisms, they are difficult to employ militarily. Conventional delivery systems—air-burst rockets, air-dropped bombs, and tube-fired projectiles—often prove too harsh, destroying the organism before it can be disseminated on the battlefield. To overcome this limitation, special munitions have been developed. For example, ceramic bombs were successfully tested for use with fleas that had been infected with the bacterium *Yessinia pestis,* the causative agent for bubonic plague. Spray disseminators have also proven effective, as a variety of pathogens are readily spread through the air. Aerial spraying, however, is notoriously difficult to predict and control.

More often, pathogens have been spread by rather conventional means. For example, in 1763, Sir Jeffrey Amherst, commander in chief of British forces in North America during the French and Indian War, suggested that an attempt be made to spread smallpox among some disaffected Indian tribes. At his suggestion, two blankets and a handkerchief from a smallpox hospital were given to two Indian chiefs; the disease soon broke out among the tribes. Similarly, during World War I, German agents in the United States inoculated horses and mules that were destined for shipment to the Allies overseas with

TABLE 1. *Potential BW Agents—Pathogens*

CATEGORY	EXAMPLES
Bacterial	Anthrax, brucellosis, bubonic plague, cholera, glanders, tularemia, typhoid fever
Fungal	Coccidioidomycosis, agent C (*Sclerotium rolfei;* an antiplant agent)
Rickettsial	Q fever, Rocky Mountain spotted fever
Viral	Dengue fever, encephalitis, influenza, meningitis, psittacosis, Rift Valley fever, smallpox, yellow fever

highly infectious bacteria, including those causing glanders, a highly contagious and destructive equine disease. During World War II, the British stockpiled linseed cattle cakes, each of which contained a lethal dose of anthrax spores. The concept was to drop the cattle cakes from bombers onto German pastures where they would be found and eaten by the cattle. The cattle cakes were never used.

Another problem with pathogens is that, once disseminated, they are susceptible to destruction by such natural environmental factors as rain, extreme temperature, and sunlight. However, the extent to which these factors will reduce the BW threat depends on the specific pathogen. For example, Gruinard Island off the northwest coast of Scotland was the site of anthrax testing in 1942 and 1943. As a result of these tests, the island was contaminated with anthrax spores, which are resistant to weathering. Follow-up testing from 1947 to 1968 found no lessening of the contamination. Then, in 1986, active decontamination measures were taken, using herbicides to remove vegetation and a solution of formaldehyde in seawater to destroy the spores. In 1990, more than 45 years after the initial testing, Gruinard Island was finally declared safe and returned to civil ownership.

Research during the 1940s perfected freeze-drying, which is a useful technique for enhancing the durability of pathogens that might otherwise perish during prolonged storage, explosive dissemination, or exposure to the environment. Freeze-drying has been successfully applied to the development of improved pathogen-type BW munitions.

TOXINS

Toxins are poisons produced by microorganisms, plants, and animals. The parent organism need not be present for the toxin to be used, although it is required for toxin production. Some toxins associated with military use are listed in Table 2.

TABLE 2. *Potential BW Agents—Toxins*

NAME	SOURCE	EFFECTS
Botulinal toxin A	*Clostridium botulinum*	Dizziness, sore throat, and dry mouth followed by paralysis. Death by suffocation (respiratory paralysis) or heart failure.
Ricin	Castor bean plant	Nausea, vomiting, bloody diarrhea, and drowsiness. Death by kidney failure (uremia).
Saxitoxin (shellfish toxin)	Dinoflagellates	Tingling around face, loss of sensation in extremities. Death by paralysis.
Tricothecene mycotoxins	Fungus	Nausea, vomiting, diarrhea. Death by internal hemorrhaging.

Toxins have certain advantages for use as military weapons. First, they occur naturally and, consequently, tend to be easy to manufacture. Second, they are nonliving substances and are more stable than biological pathogens. Third, unlike pathogens, they require no special care or treatment for use as weapons. This allows them to be disseminated in combat through conventional spray and explosive devices. Fourth, and perhaps most significant, is the exceedingly high toxicity of selected toxins, for toxins include the most poisonous substances known.

Because toxins are by-products of living organisms, they are sometimes referred to as agents of biological origin. They fall between the categories of classical biological pathogens, such as anthrax and smallpox, and traditional chemical warfare agents, such as nerve gas and cyanide. Soviet military literature viewed toxins as a "third generation" of chemical warfare weapons, with cyanide and mustard gas being the first generation and nerve gas being the second. However, the USSR was a signatory to the 1972 BW Treaty, which treats toxins as BW materials.

Toxins are a public health menace because they occur naturally. An excellent example is staphylococcus enterotoxin B, the toxin responsible for most cases of ordinary food poisoning. The bacterium *Staphylococcus aureus* grows in many foods. As it grows, it forms the toxin, which is ingested when the food is consumed. In general, staphylococcus enterotoxin B is not lethal, but as little as 50 micrograms causes severe vomiting and diarrhea. Deliberate use of staphylococcus enterotoxin B for military purposes is possible, especially for harassment and in situations where the intent is to weaken the enemy's resistance.

A more potent poison found in foods is botulinal toxin A. It is a neurotoxin that causes the nervous system to accumulate acetylcholine in a manner similar to that produced by chemical warfare nerve agents. Botulinal toxin A is produced by the bacterium *Clostridium botulinum* and is the most poisonous substance known. The bacterium can grow and thrive in prepared foods such as sausage and spiced herring and is associated with improperly preserved food such as canned vegetables. A lethal dose for a human is estimated to be one microgram.

The high toxicity of botulinal toxin A has made it the subject of substantial research, including studies of its use with the military. During World War II, the British made a concerted effort, at their Porton Down laboratories, to isolate and develop strains of *Clostridium botulinum*, along with antidotes and treatments for each. A toxin mix was developed and given the code designation BTX. British MI6 is thought to have used a strain of botulinal toxin for the assassination of Reinhard Heydrich, Hitler's governor of Czechoslovakia and presumed heir.

The alleged use of botulinal toxin in the attack on Heydrich illustrates the role of toxins in limited attacks, rather than as weapons of mass destruction. Ricin, the toxin found in the seeds and leaves of the castor oil plant *Ricinus communis*, provides another example of this type of use. Patented by the United States in 1962 for use as a BW weapon, ricin has been confirmed as the BW agent responsible for the Bulgarian "Umbrella Murders" of the 1970s. In these operations, a ricin-impregnated metal ball was shot out of the tip of an umbrella. Two victims, Bulgarians who had fled that country's Communist regime, were positively identified as having been assaulted in this way.

Public attention to toxin warfare was rekindled during the 1980s when U.S. government sources reported evidence of tricothecene mycotoxins in samples of vegetation (leaves and plant stems) from Southeast Asia. Additional evidence of tricothecenes in alleged victims of BW attacks was also claimed. Reports from refugees spoke of rockets and aerial spraying attacks that released clouds of poisonous vapor over their villages. Because these clouds were often yellow in color and had small rainlike particles, the attacks were popularly dubbed "yellow rain."

Tricothecene mycotoxins develop naturally, owing to *Fusarium*-genera fungal contamination of such grains as wheat and corn. Key tricothecene mycotoxins include nivalenol, deoxynivalenol (also known as vomitoxin), and T-2. These substances were responsible for the Soviet crop blights of the 1930s, which killed thousands of people and tens of thousands of cattle and horses. Tricothecene mycotoxin contamination of grains continues to be a concern in agriculture worldwide.

Critics of the U.S. claims regarding the Southeast Asia yellow rain attacks have suggested that the tricothecenes were the result of a natural occurrence— that is, food contaminated by mold. One explanation, advanced by Matthew Meselson of Harvard and accepted by many, suggests that the yellow spots found in Southeast Asia were the natural excreta of bees, which are known to swarm and defecate in flight. Conclusive evidence of deliberate BW attacks using tricothecene mycotoxins is lacking. The controversy over yellow rain underscores the difficulties associated with BW verification.

Role of BW in Combat

The deliberate use of pathogens and toxins for military purposes is ancient. Poisoning the enemy's drinking water and hurling diseased corpses over the walls of fortified cities were tactics used by such military leaders as Solon and Alexander the Great. It is only in recent times that the use of BW agents has acquired a stigma. No modern nation has admitted employing BW against personnel in combat despite numerous allegations to the contrary.

Effective use of BW in combat is difficult, and results are often unpredictable. Four major factors complicate the use of BW:
1. Particulate nature of most BW agents makes controlled delivery on target difficult.
2. Delay between exposure and the onset of disease because of an inherent need for an incubation period ranging from hours to days means too much time is needed before results are seen.
3. Susceptibility to such weathering effects as rain, sunlight, and temperature extremes reduce the virulence of selected BW agents and remove them from the target.
4. Natural and acquired immunity against pathogens make it impossible to predict the exact numbers of casualties from any BW attack.

Consequently, BW today is primarily for harassment and special operations.

There is considerable speculation that covert dissemination of BW agents—as in the poisoning of municipal drinking water or infecting food supplies—might occur as a prelude to large-scale assaults. Such use would weaken the enemy while leaving his physical defenses untouched and, therefore, available for the occupying force. Such covert use accommodates the limitations of BW agents. Delivery is done directly rather than by munitions, and the delay between exposure and onset of symptoms becomes a planning factor for the follow-up attack. Adverse effects from the weather are minimized by direct delivery to a compatible source, such as food or water. And the strategic objective of weakening the enemy rather than total annihilation makes precise predictions of the number of casualties less critical.

Although large-scale use of BW is difficult, it has seen substantial use in modern times for special operations. For instance, the suicide pill carried by Francis Gary Powers, the pilot who flew the secret U-2 plane over the Soviet Union in 1960, contained the toxin-type BW agent saxitoxin, a poison found in shellfish that feed on a particular kind of plankton.

Novel Developments

In the 1980s, biotechnology and genetic engineering became commonplace, gaining public acceptance as methods for bettering mankind. Industry, government, and academic institutions began examining the various ways these new technologies could be used, from developing new crop strains to more effective vaccines. But the same techniques that hold promise for increased food production and improved health are also applicable to BW. For example, genetic engineering might be used to develop not only a new strain of a known biological pathogen, but also a vaccine for it. This would give one nation immunity while leaving a potential adversary open to attack by an agent against which they have no defenses. There is no evidence of such BW research, and the scientific community seems to be united in its opposition to it.

Proliferation

One of the grounds cited for opposing BW is the possibility of the agent getting out of control, as is said to have happened in the most celebrated recorded case of biological warfare. During the siege of the Genoese city Kaffa (now Feodosiya, Ukrainian Soviet Socialist Republic) in the mid-fourteenth century, the Mongols hurled the bodies of bubonic plague victims over the city walls. Genoese ships leaving that city may have carried the plague bacillus to Europe, thereby letting loose the massive epidemic known in history as the Black Death.

BW is, however, not confined to nations; the ability of terrorist groups and individuals to disseminate BW is an issue of considerable concern around the world. An episode in Oregon shows the ease with which the use of biological pathogens can spread. In September 1984, an epidemic of food poisoning was reported in Antelope, Oregon, and it was traced to the bacterium *Salomonella typhimurium*, which had contaminated foods at local restaurants. Sworn testimony by the leader of a religious community that existed near Antelope, the Bhagwan Shree Rajneesh, identified the episode as one of deliberate poisonings committed by one of his aides in retaliation against local residents who thought the religious community members were "different."

The spread of toxin-type BW agents to terrorist groups has been verified. In 1980, French police raided an operation of the German Red Army Faction at 41A Chaillot Street, Paris. What they found at that address was a simple but effective "bathtub" facility producing botulinal toxin A.

In 1972, the Bacteriological and Toxin Weapons Convention was signed by more than 70 nations. It prohibits the production, stockpiling, and development of biological weapons and requires the destruction of existing stockpiles. The overwhelming challenge for full implementation of this or any other BW treaty is a working means for both verifying compliance and punishing noncompliance when it occurs.

BENJAMIN C. GARRETT

SEE ALSO: Chemical Warfare.

Bibliography

Brophy, L. P., W. D. Miles, and R. C. Cochrane. 1959. *The chemical warfare service: From laboratory to field.* Washington, D.C.: Office of the Chief of Military History.

Cole, L. A. 1988. *Clouds of secrecy—The army's germ warfare tests over populated areas.* Totowa, N.J.: Rowman & Littlefield.

Compton, J. A. F. 1987. *Military chemical and biological agents: Chemical and toxicological properties.* Caldwell, N.J.: Telford Press.

Douglass, J. D., and N. C. Livingston. 1987. *America the vulnerable: The threat of chemical/biological warfare.* Lexington, Mass.: Lexington Press.

Gutman, W. E. 1986. Chemical and biological weapons: The silent killers. *Nuclear, Biological, and Chemical Defense and Technology International* 1(1):24–25.

Lundin, S. J., J. P. Perry Robinson, and R. Trapp. 1988. Chemical and biological warfare: Developments in 1987. In *SIPRI yearbook 1988: World armaments and disarmament.* Oxford: Oxford Univ. Press.

McDermott, J. 1987. *The killing winds—The menace of biological warfare.* New York: Arbor House.

Seagrave, S. 1981. *Yellow rain: A journey through the terror of chemical weapons.* New York: M. Evans.

Spiers, E. M. 1986. Following decon, anthrax island up for sale. *Nuclear, Biological, and Chemical Defense and Technology International* 1(4):11.

Taylor, L. B., and C. L. Taylor. 1985. *Chemical and biological warfare.* New York: Franklin Watts.

Williams, P., and D. Wallace. 1989. *Unit 731: Japan's secret biological warfare in World War II.* New York: Free Press.

BLITZKRIEG

Blitzkrieg ("lightning war"), a German word initially made popular by non-German observers of the Polish campaign of September 1939, has acquired over the years a very wide range of meanings and connotations. A number of historians examining the structure of the Nazi economy have detected the existence of a blitzkrieg strategy in the alleged systematic economic planning for a short war as part of an overall military strategy along the same lines. Disagreement on this point includes such basic issues as whether the Germans had any such intentions and whether they actually had an organized system to prepare for short wars and thus spare the economy the burdens of protracted struggle. Other writers interested in strategy and military operations have argued that the German army developed a strategy for rapid victories in aggressive wars.

A new version of this argument has sprung up in the recent military literature, primarily in the United States. A number of authors now argue for the existence of a particular system of tactics and operations designed to win battles and campaigns by disrupting and confusing the enemy, rather than by destroying him in traditional battles. (This view, in turn, has provided much of the conceptual framework both for the so-called military reform movement in the United States and for much of the doctrinal thought, both official and unofficial, in the U.S. Army.) Other historians characterize the entire period of mechanized warfare as the "blitzkrieg era," which extends at least to the 1980s and includes the Soviet approach to mobile warfare. Orthodox Marxist historians regard blitzkrieg as a broad set of efforts by the German imperialists of both world wars to achieve quick victory. All these points of view argue or assume that behind blitzkrieg lies some sort of grand design, whether in politics, economic planning, or military doctrine and methods. The reality belies all of these interpretations. Blitzkrieg was neither a policy nor an economic expedient, nor was it a military doctrine.

Nevertheless, the idea is widespread that Heinz Guderian and others created a radically new type of tactical and operational doctrine for the armored forces of the German army. Numerous historians, journalists, political scientists, and, most recently, American officers link this alleged blitzkrieg doctrine with the use of maneuver warfare to paralyze the enemy without fighting major battles. These authors have developed elaborate theories about the purposes and methods of blitzkrieg and have created a broad consensus in support of their conclusions. The pervasiveness of these views and their impact upon current military thought give the issue more than a purely academic significance (Hughes 1986).

Nature of German Doctrine

The most fundamental prerequisite for a proper understanding of blitzkrieg in any military sense is an appreciation of the essentials of German military doctrine in the period 1919–45. (As used here, *doctrine* means the army's philosophy of war and its most basic principles of conducting operations and fighting battles within that framework.) German doctrinal manuals contained broad statements of fundamental concepts for the commander to apply as the circumstances warranted. German doctrine had no universal principles of war, no lists of tenets or imperatives, and few if any stereotyped illustrations with maps, charts, or diagrams (see, e.g., *Truppenführung*, 1933). Despite this lack of rigidity and of concrete guidelines, German doctrine consistently established a coherent approach to warfare that was applicable to all units, motorized or otherwise. Thus the 1933 *Truppenführung*, written before the creation of large armored formations, provided a sufficiently flexible concept for the tank forces.

Two Types of War

German theory between 1919 and 1945 distinguished between two types of war, positional and mobile. Despite the experiences of the long positional warfare between 1914 and 1918, the great majority of German theorists consistently rejected this as a model for the future and instead envisioned a return to the traditions of Frederick, Moltke, and Schlieffen. In this view, World War I, with its static fronts, meticulously prepared set-piece attacks, and endless battles without decision was an aberration, an operational perversity (Rabenau 1940). This return to basic theories of mobile warfare became evident immediately after the end of the war. Although Gen. Hans von Seeckt and his colleagues and successors have shared the credit (or blame) for the return to theories of mobile warfare after 1918, the truth is more complex (Wallach 1986; Messenger 1976).

Seeckt and His Antecedents

Seeckt's alleged reinstitution of mobile warfare was not the major innovation that is sometimes pictured. His new basic regulation of 1921, *Führung und Gefecht*, was entirely within the broad framework of traditional German theory. By the time that manual was published, the new German army had long since sought alternatives to the positional warfare of 1914–18.

The German offensive methods of 1918 were above all an effort to restore mobility to the western front. The much-misunderstood assault unit tactics were thus a means to return to the traditional mobile warfare (Jochim 1927). World War I never entirely shook the German army's faith in its fundamental principles. As early as 1920, Wilhelm Balck had noted the basic correctness of German wartime tactics and called for a return to mobile warfare (Balck 1920). That same year, Baron Hugo von Freytag-Loringhoven, a leading prewar theoretician and official historian, noted the return to mobile warfare as the basis of postwar German theory. The leading semiofficial handbook of the immediate postwar period, Rohrbeck's *Taktik* (1922), based its entire discussion on the traditional distinction between mobile and positional warfare and confirmed the superiority of the former, even given the experiences of the past war.

Traditional Prussian Concepts

Seeckt's new manual of 1921, which officially confirmed the continuing dominance of the principle of mobility, thus came to an officer corps that had never strayed far from the Prussian army's traditional emphasis on rapid and decisive offensive action based upon mobility and firepower. This information is absolutely essential to an understanding of the developments between 1919 and 1939. Prussian military leaders had always believed that their military system was uniquely suited to the demands and opportunities of mobile warfare. The Prussian army based its preparations for mobile warfare upon rapid offensive action, swift decisions by commanders, initiative at all levels, independent action by subordinate commanders, risk taking, acceptance of high losses, exploitation of uncertainty, the dominance of moral factors, and improvisation. Through all these ran the absolute belief in the superiority of the German system of education and training and in the ability of the army to execute its theories on the battlefield. Mobile warfare was the integrating centerpiece of the entire Prussian system, both in 1921 when Seeckt took charge of the new *Reichsheer* and in the later years when mechanization provided the army with new means of achieving mobility.

World War II Doctrine

The seeds of the German tank army thus fell upon fertile ground that had been well prepared both by many decades of Prussian military tradition and by the theoretical framework put in place by Seeckt and others after World War I. The German army had no special blitzkrieg theory because it had no need for such a construct. Unlike the situation in France or Britain, establishment of a modern approach to mechanized warfare did not demand a revolution in the army's outlook. Although Guderian and Lutz developed a few broad ideas about the employment of large armored formations, no official theory existed in 1939.

Most of the popular studies of the German army, of blitzkrieg, and of tank warfare in general hold that the German army *did* have such a doctrine or strategy (Murray 1984). Beyond that generalization, however, no consensus exists, even on the most basic issues. Len Deighton's popular and influential study, for example, argued that this method involved attack on narrow fronts and concluded that the famous cauldron battles (*Kesselschlachten*) of World War II were not part of blitzkrieg (Deighton 1979). According to his concept, blitzkrieg occurred only in France in 1940 and applies only to the operations of Guderian's forces. Neither Deighton nor anyone else has offered any evidence that German methods or expectations in 1940 were any different from those of the 1939 campaign; in fact, there is strong evidence to the contrary (Jacobsen 1957). Messenger's book (1976) argues that the Germans accepted Fuller's concept of producing paralysis by attacking the enemy's command apparatus, a point broadly consistent with the views of the influential military reformer William Lind. Some current theorists have used these arguments to link blitzkrieg theory to recent concepts of "operational depths," "centers of gravity," and so forth (Tiberi 1985). None of these authors bases his arguments upon a doctrinal publication or regulation in the traditional sense.

GUDERIAN'S VIEWS

Guderian's views, although not decisive for the army's theory as a whole, merit attention in this context. Numerous authors have recorded Guderian's long struggle with what he regarded as excessively conservative superiors who for a number of years prevented him from creating large independent tank units to carry out his grand designs for an armored force (Guderian 1952). Guderian's own memoirs, among the most unreliable sources for the period, railed at length against Gen. Ludwig Beck and other enemies, who apparently included most of the General Staff. Nevertheless, neither Guderian's memoirs nor the considerable literature on the development of the German armored force have offered a clear picture of the goals and methods he envisioned for the armored units.

THE DISRUPTION MISINTERPRETATION

Partly as a result of this gap in the scholarly literature, a number of civilian authors and military writers have advanced what might be termed the "disruption theory" of blitzkrieg methods. In this view, the essence of the blitzkrieg operational concept was disruption of the enemy's command and control system and the collapse of his resistance without costly battles or lengthy campaigns. In this view, paralysis replaced destruction of the enemy as the primary goal of military operations. This concept has become the basis of much of the so-called military reform movement in the United States and has become a staple of much of the U.S. Army's official and unofficial views of maneuver warfare (Franz 1983; Tiberi 1985; Higgins 1985). In recent years, political scientists have increasingly based part of their theories on the organizational origins of strategy and military doctrine upon this view of blitzkrieg and maneuver and the contrast between these and the alleged attrition style of warfare.

THE ANNIHILATION PRINCIPLE

For an accurate appraisal of what the German army was really trying to achieve by its battles and operations, one must consider both the army's official regulations (*Truppenführung*) and the writings of the German theorists cited above. The most basic fact of German tactical and operational thought was the continuing emphasis upon annihilation of the enemy (Wallach 1986; Hughes 1986). The German army relied upon its traditional theories of mobile warfare to produce battles of annihilation. The goal of the entire process was the conduct of traditional battles of annihilation under the most favorable circumstances possible, not the avoidance of such battles. Armored formations proved to be a new means of mobility and increased firepower; they did not fundamentally change the German army's approach to warfare.

Guderian's own writings make this point quite clear, despite the very widespread practice of linking his name to the disruption idea. In an article published in the General Staff's journal in 1939, Guderian pointed out that in the attack, the main objective of the armored units must be the destruction of enemy obstacles, antitank defenses, artillery, and tank reserves. After that, the tank echelons that follow should turn their attention to helping to mop up the infantry combat zone (Guderian 1939).

This was a slightly more limited concept than that advanced earlier in an article reprinted in a small booklet in 1938. In the 1938 article, Guderian, again limiting his perspective to the sphere of tactics (the concept of *levels* of war was unknown in the German army prior to 1945), spoke of three echelons (*Treffen*) of friendly tanks in breaking through enemy lines. The first echelon should penetrate and destroy enemy staffs and reserves; the second should destroy enemy artillery; and the third was to attack enemy infantry units (Bradley 1978). These tasks were relevant in breakthrough battles and thus were purely tactical.

Guderian's treatment of the combined arms functions of armored forces in a broader perspective provides an interesting example of how easily armored theories fitted in with the traditional idea of German mobile warfare. In his discussion of combined arms actions, Guderian first quoted the British regulations on freeing tanks from excessively restrictive ties to the infantry, then referred to *Truppenführung* for official German views on the same point. As Guderian thus recognized, this fundamental regulation was and remained the basis of official theory (and doctrine in the German sense) (Guderian 1936, 1938). *Truppenführung* was thus a manual for annihilation using breakthrough. It was the opposite of a manual for armored disruption, especially since—at the time of its writing (1933)—the German army was still forbidden to possess tanks and even heavy weapons in the cavalry divisions.

Truppenführung, 1933

Truppenführung, written under the supervision of Gen. Ludwig Beck in 1931 and 1932, officially appeared in 1933 and remained the basic German regulation throughout World War II. This classic manual provided the fundamental framework for German theories of mobile warfare, tactical concepts, and the conduct of operations. Among the manual's most prominent themes was that of destruction of the enemy as the goal of battles and operations. In particular, *Truppenführung* outlined the major task of tank units as the destruction of enemy artillery and reserve forces to prevent stagnation of the front into positional warfare (Erfurth 1957).

The problems of trying to reconcile the post-1945 evaluations of blitzkrieg with the real principles of German theories of mobile warfare become clear when one compares these later views with Guderian's writings and with other contemporary works of German theory, both official and semiofficial. Jehuda Wallach, for example, has argued convincingly that *Truppenführung* was strictly in the tradition of Schlieffen's emphasis on battles of annihilation and flank attacks (Wallach 1986). East German scholarship on this point is equally solid and convincing, if one can go beyond the Marxist rhetoric. Michael Geyer, on the other hand, argues that the authors of *Truppenführung* had "distanced themselves" from Schlieffen's notions in their concepts of operations and their definition of annihilation. Geyer nevertheless recognizes the importance of mobile warfare as the basis of the manual (Geyer 1986).

Other examples of misunderstandings of basic concepts of mobile operations illustrate the difficulty of defining a blitzkrieg methodology. One recent author advocating the disruption theory of blitzkrieg has stressed that the German offensives called for breakthroughs on narrow fronts, followed by concentration in the enemy's rear, and again dispersion (Tiberi 1985). This view, borrowed from Deighton, has utterly no foundation in German theory. Guderian, in fact, rejected any such notion by logically insisting that breakthroughs must be as wide as possible in order to provide greater security along vulnerable flanks.

In a similar manner, a number of authors have argued that the Polish campaign and the Russian campaign were not examples of blitzkrieg because they relied upon the traditional *Kesselschlacht* born in the days of Moltke and Schlieffen. This notion is also at variance with the alleged psychological dislocation of the enemy, which so many regard as the core of blitzkrieg. Guderian himself always wrote of annihilation of the enemy in battle and, on at least one occasion, clearly rejected the idea of attaining victory through moral effects on the enemy. On the contrary, he said, the enemy resistance must be broken "through annihilation by fire of the enemy encountered in the area of attack" (Guderian 1936).

In any case, the basic methods and theories of the German armored forces underwent no significant changes from Poland through France to the early months of the Russian campaign. Blitzkrieg was a rapid victory of the German system of mobile warfare over some enemies. When that same system failed under the very different circumstances of Eastern Europe, no blitzkrieg occurred. On the battlefield and in the campaigns, blitzkrieg was a result or perhaps an *ex post facto* description of the result. It was never a tactical or an operational system.

DANIEL J. HUGHES

SEE ALSO: Combined Arms; Firepower; Principles of War; Strategy; Tactics.

Bibliography

Addington, L. 1971. *The blitzkrieg era and the German general staff 1865–1941*. New Brunswick, N.J.: Rutgers Univ. Press.
Balck, W. 1906. *Taktik*. 6 vols. Berlin: R. Eisenschmidt.
———. 1920. Entwicklung der Taktik der Infanterie. In *Militärische Lehren des Grossen Krieges*, ed. M. Schwarte. Berlin: E. S. Mittler.
Bradley, D. 1978. *Guderian und die Entstehungsgeschichte des modernen Blitzkrieges*. Osnabrück: Biblio. Verlag.
Deighton, L. 1979. *Blitzkrieg: From the rise of Hitler to the fall of Dunkirk*. New York: Ballantine Books.
Doughty, R. 1985. *The seeds of disaster: The development of French army doctrine 1919–1939*. Camden, Conn.: Archon Books.
Eimannsberger, L. von. 1938. *Der Kampfwagenkrieg*. 2d ed. Munich: J. F. Lehmans.
Erfurth, W. 1957. *Die Geschichte des deutschen Generalstabes von 1918 bis 1945*. Göttingen: Musterschmidt.
Franz, W. 1983. Maneuver: The dynamic element of combat. *Military Review* 63(5):2–12.
German War Ministry. 1921. *Führung und Gefecht der verbundenen Waffen*. Berlin: E. S. Mittler.
Geyer, M. 1986. German strategy in the age of machine warfare. In *Makers of modern strategy from Machiavelli to the nuclear age*, ed. P. Paret, 529–97. Princeton, N.J.: Princeton Univ. Press.
Guderian, H. 1936. Kraftfahrkampftruppen. *Militärwissenschaftliche Rundschau* 1(1).
———. 1938. *Die Panzertruppen und ihr Zusammenwirken mit den anderen Waffen*. Berlin: E. S. Mittler.
———. 1939. Schnelle Truppen einst und jetzt. *Militärwissenschaftliche Rundschau* 4(2).

————. 1952. *Panzer leader*. New York: Dutton.

Higgins, G. A. 1985. German and U.S. operational art: A contrast in maneuver. *Military Review* 65(10):22–29.

Hughes, D. J. 1986. Abuses of German military history. *Military Review* 65(12):66–77.

Jacobsen, H. A. 1957. *Fall Gelb. Der Kampf um den deutschen Operationsplan zur Westoffensive 1940*. Wiesbaden: Franz Steiner.

Jochim, T. 1927. *Die Vorbereitung des deutschen Heers für die grosse Schlacht in Frankreich im Frühjahr 1918*. Vol. 1. Berlin: E. S. Mittler.

Kroener, B. 1985. Squaring the circle: Blitzkrieg strategy and manpower shortage, 1939–1942. In *The German military in the age of total war*, ed. W. Deist, 202–303. Dover, N.H.: Berg Publisher.

Lind, W. 1984. The case for maneuver doctrine. In *The defense reform debate: Issues and analysis*, ed. A. A. Clark IV, P. W. Chiarelli, J. S. McKitrick, and J. W. Reed, 88–100. Baltimore: Johns Hopkins Univ. Press.

Macksey, K. 1976. *Guderian: Creator of the blitzkrieg*. New York: Stein and Day.

Mearsheimer, J. 1983. *Conventional deterrence*. Ithaca, N.Y.: Cornell Univ. Press.

Meckel, J. 1890. *Allgemeine Lehre von der Truppenführung im Kriege*. Berlin: E. S. Mittler.

Miksche, F. O. 1941. *Attack: A study of blitzkrieg tactics*. New York: Random House.

Milward, A. A. 1985. Der Einfluss ökonomischer und nichtökonomischer Faktoren auf die Strategie des Blitzkrieges. In *Wirtschaft und Rüstung am Vorabend des Zweiten Weltkrieges*, ed. F. Forstmeister and H. Volkmann, 189–201. Düsseldorf: Droste.

Murray, W. 1984. *The change in the European balance of power*. Princeton, N.J.: Princeton Univ. Press.

Rabenau, F. von. 1940. *Seeckt: Aus seinem Leben*. Leipzig: Hase and Koehler.

Rohrbeck, Major. 1922. *Entwickelung der Taktik im Weltkriege*. 2d ed. Berlin: E. S. Mittler.

Sternberg, F. 1938. *Germany and a lightning war*. Trans. E. Fitzgerald. London: Faber and Faber.

Tiberi, P. 1985. German versus Soviet blitzkrieg. *Military Review* 65(9):63–71.

Wallach, J. L. 1986 [1967]. *The dogma of the battle of annihilation*. Westport, N.Y.: Greenwood Press.

BRIEFINGS

The object of military briefings and presentations is to establish and foster personal communication between commanders and their staffs or between different staff sections. The purpose of a briefing is to save time by eliminating the need for a detailed study of the topic being discussed. Allowing questions and discussion both during and following the presentation provides further insights and clarification of the points presented.

Both a briefing and a presentation achieve the same purpose. The term *briefing*, however, is normally used when a small group is involved; a *presentation* implies a more formal setting with a larger group. Most briefings and presentations use visual aids (e.g., maps, transparencies, or slides) to illustrate the topic being discussed.

Briefings and presentations are intended to:

• provide routine or specific information concerning current developments that may have an impact on decisions and plans

• review a situation and present different courses of action
• obtain a decision.

Briefings and presentations are intended to save the commander time by presenting him with essential information on which to make a decision. They are normally given orally but on occasion a written brief may be used by the staff, often with flagged references to the original document and/or recommendation, to summarize a complex topic.

SEE ALSO: Directives, Orders, and Instructions.

Bibliography

U.S. Department of Defense, Joint Chiefs of Staff. 1987. *Department of Defense dictionary of military and associated terms.* Washington, D.C.: Government Printing Office.

C

CAVALRY

From about 1000 B.C. until the early twentieth century, cavalry—soldiery mounted on horses—was a major component of land armies. (The word *cavalry* is derived from the Latin word *cabullus*, meaning horse.) The use of the horse as a source of energy and means of transportation increased the speed, mobility, and maneuverability of land forces on the battlefield. With the introduction of gunpowder, however, the steadily increasing range, accuracy, and density of fire rendered horse cavalry more and more vulnerable and eventually useless. Moreover, since the early twentieth century, the internal combustion engine has provided greater energy, mobility, and maneuverability. Nowadays the term is purely symbolic, as in *sky cavalry* or *air cavalry*. The use of these expressions implies that the cavalry's military missions still exist but are carried out by units with other equipment and means of mobility. Although in some armies units of horse cavalry participate in certain ceremonial occasions, the history of the cavalry is a finished chapter.

Cavalry first appeared in battle as a result of the eternal search for superior speed and mobility. Among the missions of the cavalry were reconnaissance, rapid change of deployment area, rapid commitment of reserve units, cover for disengagement actions, and offensive operations requiring great energy and impact in order to overrun the enemy.

Horses were first used on the battlefield as power sources for chariots. By about 800 B.C, the Assyrians had begun to mount some warriors on horses. The warrior increased his general and cross-country mobility on horseback. However, he had neither saddle nor stirrups to steady his seat and was therefore usually equipped as an archer, since he was unable to use other weapons effectively. The first bridles allowed very limited control of the horse; obedience was enforced by leg pressure and spurs. Over time, a saddle evolved that provided more secure seating, and the stirrup came into being in Asia in the third century A.D., reaching Western Europe by the eighth century. This enabled a rider to use the lance and, later, to use muskets and pistols.

In ancient and feudal times, both horse and rider were protected by armor. This diminished the advantage won in speed and mobility. With the emergence of firearms—initially large-caliber weapons with low rates of fire—cavalry began to be equipped with clumsy, inaccurate early versions of pistols. As firearms became more accurate over greater distances, the versions supplied to cavalry also improved, but the use of firearms from horseback remained relatively inaccurate. This led to the development of dragoons, cavalrymen who rode to battle but dismounted to use their muskets. The introduction of entrenchment for protection, which began in the middle of the nineteenth century, could not be adapted to the horse. The significance of the cavalry as a means of mobility began to dwindle from this point and had virtually disappeared by World War I. Nevertheless, its use continued: there was no other mobility means available.

First indications that the horse could be replaced came with the introduction of the internal combustion engine on the battlefield. Thanks to its greater energy and efficiency, the engine was able to transport automatic weapons, at the same time providing gun crews with armored protection. Used in aircraft, the engine also made possible the use of the air space over the battlefield for medium- and long-range observation and reconnaissance, previously the exclusive province of the cavalry. Between the world wars, the growing debate as to relative value of horse cavalry or motorized units was temporarily resolved in a compromise, as evidenced in the German regulation "Truppenführung" in 1936. The army cavalry was composed of mounted units, horse-drawn artillery units, and motorized troops. Bicycle units were assigned to the mounted route columns. However, because the cavalry was extremely vulnerable to aerial attack, it had to be provided with a motorized air protection force. This precluded truly united operations. In general, battle on horseback was possible only when small detachments encountered enemy cavalry and when surprising a weak adversary during reconnaissance. The very nature of the army cavalry, and its inability to use entrenchments, excluded its use for defensive purposes.

There was hardly any use of cavalry in World War II. It was occasionally employed in combat against guerrillas on the steppes and in marshes and woods, areas in which it is still theoretically useful today. The end of the independent branch of the horse cavalry came on 4 April 1964, the date on which the last remaining cavalry units in the U.S. forces were transferred to armored formations.

With the exception of the armed riders in Mongolia in the thirteenth century, the proportion of cavalry in typical armies before the twentieth century ranged from one-third to one-half of the total forces. The larger the land forces, the smaller the proportional cavalry contingent. This was largely a consequence of economic considerations. A horse could not be trained for military purposes until it was 3 years old, and the training lasted two to three years. With a life span of twelve to fifteen years, a horse was fit for service for about ten years. Mounted armies required vast grasslands and farming areas to cultivate grain for fodder. Large numbers of grooms were required, as well as trainers for horse and rider. Extensive training, for both men and horses, was necessary for the cavalry to act as a cohesive force. If a surprise attack was to be effective, the three gaits (walk, trot, and gallop) had to be used uniformly and consistently by all. Speed and endurance could be increased by practice; for example, at a gallop, horse and rider might achieve 30 kilometers (19 mi.) per hour. Nevertheless, the efficiency of cavalry over the centuries was enhanced only marginally by increased training.

Replacements for losses were not always easy to find, either at home or in a foreign country. Numerous large depots, or remount stations, were maintained. Private horse-breeding concerns usually could not supply enough horses to meet military needs and had to be supplemented by establishments owned by the sovereigns or states. Different breeds were raised according to the military action planned or the demands of the region, from the frugal steppe pony to the heavy horse able to carry the knight in armor.

Thus, in the time of Charlemagne, a horse was worth eighteen to twenty cows. Possession of a force of cavalry was a valuable investment for the owner. To own cavalry meant to climb a higher rung of the social—and political—ladder.

Within the cavalry, a distinction was made between heavy and light units, depending on the weight and size of the horses and the arms of the rider. From the sixteenth to the nineteenth centuries, cuirassiers (successors to the medieval knights) were protected both front and back by armor, while hussars and dragoons were counted as light units. The distinction between cavalry that fought on horseback and cavalry that used the horse purely as means of transport was fluid. Toward the end of the cavalry era, the tactical formation in Europe was the squadron of 100 to 150 horses, with four squadrons combined in a regiment and two regiments in a brigade. (In the U.S. Army, three troops of about 100 horsemen each were combined in a squadron, with two or three squadrons to a regiment.) Over and above the regiment or brigade came the division, reinforced by mounted horse artillery batteries, engineers, and machine-gun detachments. (Horse artillery differed from standard horse-drawn artillery in that each cannoneer had his own mount.)

Prior to the introduction of gunpowder, the outcome of military conflicts on open ground in mobile warfare was determined by efficient and opportune commitment of the cavalry. Most successful commanders were also themselves great cavalry leaders, such as Alexander III (356–323 B.C.), Genghis Khan (A.D. 1167–1227), and Gustavus Adolphus (A.D. 1594–1632). Hannibal's (247–183 B.C.) victory at the battle of Cannae in 216 B.C. is recognized as an early and brilliant example of the tactical use of cavalry (Fig. 1). Other commanders had great cavalry leaders as subordinates, as Frederick II (1715–84) had in von Seydlitz (1721–73) and Napoleon I (1769–1821) had in Murat (1767–1815). The outcome of the Russian Civil War (1919–21) was largely decided by the commander of the Bolshevik cavalry, Budjenny (1883–1973).

The Industrial Revolution in the middle of the eighteenth century saw the introduction of accurate infantry rifles and automatic weapons. Their effect on the cavalry was not at first adequately recognized by military men. The battles of Mars la Tour and Sedan in the Franco-German War of 1870–71 demonstrate the high losses that cavalry suffered in battle from this point on.

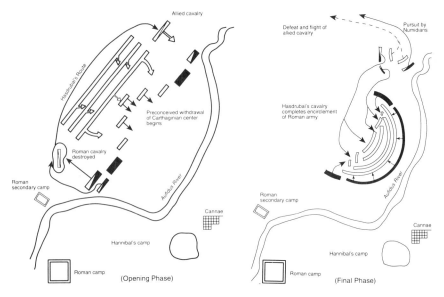

Figure 1. Hannibal employed cavalry to secure the advantage in the battle of Cannae (216 B.C.). (SOURCE: R. E. Dupuy and T. N. Dupuy, eds., The Encyclopedia of Military History [New York: Harper & Row, 1986], 66.)

Homage to the Cavalry Mount

The horse was used for more than three millennia on the battlefield. Man and horse drew close together in mutual dependence as they galloped across open fields, at times displaying both courage and fear. They shared hunger and thirst, cold and heat, and drought and rain. Technology, however, has made the use of horses for military purposes obsolete. No longer the pedestal for emperors or warriors, the horse today serves only for the delight of riders or for the edification of gamblers at racetracks.

JOHANNES GERBER

SEE ALSO: Armor; Army Aviation.

Bibliography

Basche, A. 1984. *Geschichte des Pferdes*. Stäfa, Salzburg, Sigloch: Edition Künzelsau.
Bülow, H. von. 1805. *Lehrsätze des neuern Krieges*. Berlin: Heinrich Fröhlich.
Denison, G. T. [1877] 1976. *A history of cavalry from the earliest times, with lessons for the future*. Reprint. Westport, Conn.: Greenwood Press.
Dupuy, R. E., and T. N. Dupuy. 1986. *The encyclopedia of military history*. New York: Harper and Row.
Ellis, J. 1978. *Cavalry: The history of mounted warfare*. Newton Abbot, England: Westbridge Books.
German Army. 1936. H.Dv. 300/1 *Truppenführung*. Berlin: Mittler.
Lawford, J., ed. 1976. *Calvary*. New York: Bobbs-Merrill.
Richter, K. C. 1978. *Die Geschichte der deutschen Kavallerie 1919–1945*. Stuttgart: Motorbuch-Verlag.

CHEMICAL WARFARE

Chemical warfare (CW) is the direct military use of chemicals to injure or kill humans, animals, or plants. Although the chemicals are commonly referred to as "poison gases," they can be in any physical state—gas, liquid, or solid.

Revulsion toward CW and debate as to its combat effectiveness have limited its use. Public concern over CW resurfaced in the late 1980s with revelations that Libya had constructed a CW production facility. These concerns were heightened by Iraq's pronouncements regarding its CW capabilities and willingness to wage CW.

CW Agents

CW chemicals are known as CW agents and are often categorized according to their effect. Because oftentimes their proper chemical names are hard to use, agents are frequently referred to by codes or symbols. Table 1 lists eight CW agent categories and gives examples of each with the symbols used by many Western nations, including the United States and United Kingdom.

NERVE AGENTS

Nerve agents keep the nervous system from functioning properly by inhibiting enzymes responsible for destroying acetylcholine, a body chemical vital to nerve signal transmission. This behavior is referred to as cholinesterase inhibition. Nerve agents cause acetylcholine to accumulate at nerve endings, and normal function becomes impossible.

The nerve agents are organophosphorus chemicals, or organophosphates. Their toxicity was first observed in 1932 and was exploited for use in pesticides to control insects and other pests. Organophosphates continue to be used commercially for that purpose.

The Germans recognized the potential military value of organophosphates in 1934 and, by the end of the Second World War, had synthesized three nerve

TABLE 1. *Chemicals Used by Military as CW Agents*

AGENT CATEGORY	COMMON MILITARY NAME (MILITARY CODE)
Nerve	tabun (GA), sarin (GB), soman (GD), VX, VR-55
Blister	distilled mustard or yperite (HD), lewisite (L), mustard/lewisite mixture (HL), nitrogen mustard (HN), phosgene oxime (CX)
Blood	hydrogen cyanide (AC), cyanogen chloride (CK), arsine (SA)
Choking	phosgene (CG), diphosgene (DP), chlorine
Incapacitating	BZ
Vomiting	Adamsite (DM)
Tear	CN, CS
Herbicide	Agent Blue, Agent Orange

agents deemed suitable for combat use. These compounds were named tabun, sarin, and soman. After the Allies captured the Germans' nerve agent stockpile, the compounds were given the code designations GA, GB, and GD, respectively. (Although the Germans amassed a large stockpile of these lethal chemicals, they never used nerve agents in combat.)

The discovery of the German nerve agents triggered considerable military research, with special interest in finding organophosphates with improved properties. By 1958 the Americans had selected an organophosphate known simply as VX. Soviet research produced VR-55, a compound similar to VX.

Early symptoms of nerve agent exposure include runny nose, drooling, pinpointing of the pupils (miosis), and muscle spasms. If untreated, nerve agent poisoning leads to paralysis, with death by suffocation. Atropine is the classical treatment to counteract nerve agents. It provides some protection against the excess acetylcholine that accumulates. In addition, chemicals called oximes that reverse cholinesterase inhibition are an effective antidote against some but not all nerve agents.

BLISTER AGENTS

Blister agents, or vesicants, cause wounds resembling those caused by burns. The first blister agent was distilled mustard (HD), named for its mustard-like odor. Although commonly called mustard gas, HD is normally a liquid or aerosol when dispersed in combat. Other blister agents include the nitrogen mustards (HN), lewisite (L), and phosgene oxime (CX).

Blistering and other burn-like injuries are common to all blister agents. Exposure to L and CX causes immediate and intense pain as well. A mixture of distilled mustard and lewisite (known as HL) extends the useful temperature range for HD, remaining liquid at temperatures where HD alone would freeze.

Blister agents can be lethal, causing dry-land drowning where the lungs fill up with fluids. Military interest in blister agents was sparked by their ability to disrupt routine combat operations. Depending on the weather, these agents routinely persist for hours to weeks, and some reports document persistence on the order of months and years. Such persistence demands extended wear of personal protective equipment, such as gloves, masks, boots, and clothing. Agent removal or rerouting to avoid contamination similarly disrupt operations.

Distilled mustard was used extensively during the First World War. Although its use proved indecisive militarily, it did spur research into blister agents and prompted many nations to build production facilities. By 1930 the British, Italians, French, Americans, Soviets, Japanese, and Spanish had constructed such facilities. Some use of blister agents occurred between the World Wars, notably by the Italians against the Ethiopians and by the French and Spanish against the Moroccans.

Although stockpiled throughout the Second World War, blister agent use was virtually nonexistent. Some large-scale Japanese use took place in China. A tragic episode of mass casualties occurred when the American cargo ship S.S. *John Harvey*, loaded with HD munitions, was damaged in an air raid while in the harbor at Bari, Italy. HD escaped from damaged munitions and contaminated both those escaping the sinking ship and civilians on shore.

BLOOD AGENTS

Blood agents inhibit proper use of oxygen by the body. They disrupt cellular energy production, and the resultant lack of oxygen causes cell respiration to cease. If that condition persists, all life processes come to an end.

Blood agents are among the most fast-acting of all poisons. Examples include hydrogen cyanide (AC) and arsine (SA). Use of cyanide and arsenic poisons has a long history, especially for assassinations. Military use was considered by the United States during the American Civil War (1861–65) and by the British during the Crimean War (1853–56). Practical battlefield use of blood agents was perfected during the First World War, and hydrogen cyanide was used extensively by the Germans during the Second World War for mass killings in their extermination camps.

CHOKING AGENTS

Choking agents primarily injure the eyes and the respiratory tract (nose, throat, and lungs). They cause the tissues to swell, making breathing difficult and leading to dry-land drowning. Chlorine and phosgene (CG) are choking agents as well as valued commercial chemicals. Both were used in the first CW attacks during the First World War and initial use was extensive. However, difficulties in controlling their release made them impractical as CW agents, and they came to be replaced by other chemicals, especially the blister agents.

INCAPACITATING AGENTS

Incapacitating agents are intended to make an enemy cease fighting without injury or death. They are intended to produce physiological or mental effects that render victims incapable of carrying out their military duties. As yet, no truly effective incapacitating agent has been found. The United States seriously considered using the hallucinogen BZ and briefly engaged in its manufacture. Testing proved BZ to be unsatisfactory, in part because exposure produced varied and unpredictable effects.

VOMITING AGENTS

Vomiting agents came out of British work during the First World War. These agents—typically arsenic-containing compounds—induce extreme nausea, leading to uncontrollable vomiting. The British used vomiting agents in North Russia against the Red Army in 1919.

Of low to moderate toxicity, vomiting agents were of significant interest for possible use in law-enforcement activities or riot control and saw some limited use for such purposes in the 1930s. By agreement, the Western nations banned the use of vomiting agents against civilians. There is no record of their combat use after 1920.

TEAR AGENTS

Tear agents, or lacrimators, cause copious tears to flow and irritate the skin. Because their effects are rapid but transitory, these agents are widely used for training, riot control, and other situations where long-term incapacitation is unacceptable. They can cause serious injury or death if used in confined spaces.

The tear agent CN was first prepared in Germany in 1871 and proposed as a CW agent by the United States in 1917. The war ended before it could be used, but it has since seen wide use. It is also the principal ingredient in Mace, a product marketed for personal protection.

HERBICIDES

Herbicides destroy vegetation and are important commercially for such applications as weed control. They have been considered for military use to destroy or limit crop production and to remove leaves from plants (defoliation). Some crop destruction by deliberate military use of herbicides occurred during the Vietnam War when the Americans used Agent Blue, an arsenic-containing chemical, to prevent grain formation in rice fields.

During this same period, the Americans also experimented with a variety of defoliants. They selected Agent Orange, which was employed to defoliate entire forests, thus denying their use by the enemy for cover and concealment. Agent Orange was formulated as a mixture of two chemically related herbicides, 2,4-D and 2,4,5-T. These mixtures were contaminated by dioxin, a toxic compound formed during 2,4-D and 2,4,5-T production. Its presence raised questions about possible adverse effects among both Americans exposed to Agent Orange and the people living in contaminated areas.

Related Developments

The major nations place little current emphasis on developing new CW agents. Since the mid-1960s, research has concentrated instead on ways to make existing agents more effective.

One means for enhancing effectiveness is to add a polymer. This mixing process modifies the agent's physical properties, especially viscosity (thickness), without altering its toxicity or chemical properties. The thickened agent is more difficult to remove and takes longer to evaporate; both these attributes increase the CW hazard.

Another development is the use of a binary system, which uses two chemicals that mix on contact to form a CW agent. In its ideal form, a binary system would have two chemicals of low toxicity that react completely to form a highly poisonous substance. In practice to date, the reaction is incomplete, and one or both chemicals are toxic, although less toxic than the CW agent itself.

A binary system has the advantage of less difficulty in storage, transportation, and handling. The United States investigated binary systems for producing the nerve agents GB and VX. Construction of production facilities has been placed on hold pending international negotiations aimed at multilateral reductions in CW capabilities.

A third means of enhancing CW agent performance is that of incorporating a chemical that degrades the protective measures used against CW attack. For instance, a chemical that quickly overcomes the protective ingredients in a gas mask filter might be mixed with a CW agent. The first chemical, called a mask penetrator or defeater, would destroy the filter, allowing the CW agent to get through and harm the individual wearing that mask.

Military Aspects

For various reasons, effective combat use of CW agents is difficult to predict. Wind speed and direction control CW agent spread upon release, and a shift in wind can bring the agent back upon the attacking force. Other weather conditions, such as sunlight, temperature, and precipitation, influence how long the CW contamination will persist. Topography and type of terrain influence CW agent spread and persistence once the target is hit. The level of preparedness of the intended target determines its ability to withstand an attack. For these reasons and others, military planners are disinclined to call for the use of CW agents.

Traditionally, CW agents were selected for their toxicity, with preference given to agents of the highest lethality. Recent examinations of CW, however, have noted its ability to bog down military operations and thus change the pace of battle. This change comes about in part because of required CW defensive measures. Such measures as burdensome individual protective gear, fully enclosed protective shelters, and labor-intensive means for detecting and neutralizing contamination are invoked by prudent commanders for operations in both a known CW environment and a suspected one (Fig. 1).

A cunning adversary might gain a tactical advantage by threatening to employ CW. This could prove particularly useful where the threatened force either possesses no CW retaliatory capability or chooses not to use its CW agents. In that situation, the adversary compels the threatened force to adopt burdensome protective measures, yet retains the upper hand by knowing when, where, and if such agents will be used.

Proliferation

Attempts have been made to control CW. The Geneva Protocol of 1925 prohibited first use (but not retaliatory use) of CW agents. More than 120 nations have joined in the signing of this treaty, including the United States, which delayed signing until 1975, and the Soviet Union.

Interpretation of the Geneva Protocol has proved troublesome. Some maintain that tear gas and defoliants are outside the protocol. Others argue that they are covered and consider the U.S. use of them during the Vietnam War to be CW. Disagreement continues, too, over whether the protocol covers the novel agents, such as mask penetrators and other compounds that are harmless to humans but render equipment useless.

Many nations, especially the United States and the former Soviet Union, are negotiating and implementing CW conventions that limit CW agent stockpiles

*Figure 1. Soldiers put on their protective gear during a simu-
lated gas attack on infantry division training grounds.* (SOURCE:
U.S. Army Signal Corps)

and stipulate conditions for on-site inspections of suspect production or storage
facilities. Major considerations for any such treaty are realistic verification procedures and means for punishing treaty violations.

More troublesome, perhaps, than control of CW capabilities possessed by
the major nations has been the issue of proliferation of CW capabilities in
lesser-developed nations. Obtaining the means for producing CW agents has
proved easy, as events in Libya in 1989 and Iraq in 1990 proved. In these two
instances, the host governments were able to obtain everything necessary for
CW weapon production through international trade. The similarity between
CW agents and well-known chemicals of commerce—especially pharmaceuti-
cals and pesticides—adds to the difficulties of controlling the potential for
chemical warfare.

BENJAMIN C. GARRETT

SEE ALSO: Biological Warfare.

Bibliography

Adams, V. 1990. *Chemical warfare, chemical disarmament.* Bloomington, Ind.: Indiana
   Univ. Press.
Compton, J. A. F. 1988. *Military chemical and biological agents: Chemical and toxico-
   logical properties.* Caldwell, N.J.: Telford Press.
Dunn, P. 1986. The chemical war. *Nuclear, biological, and chemical defense and tech-
   nology international* 1 (1):28–35.
Gripstad, B., ed. 1983. *FOA Orienterar OM: Chemical warfare agents.* Stockholm:
   Liber Förlang.
Kleber, B. E., and D. Birdsell. 1966. *The chemical warfare service: Chemicals in
   combat.* Washington, D.C.: Office of the Chief of Military History.

Lundin, S. J., J. P. Robinson, and R. Trapp. 1988. Chemical and biological warfare: Developments in 1987. In *SIPRI yearbook 1988: World armaments and disarmament*. Oxford: Oxford Univ. Press.

Robinson, J. P. 1985. *SIPRI chemical & biological warfare studies: 2. Chemical warfare arms control: A framework for considering policy alternatives*. London: Taylor and Francis.

Spiers, E. M. 1989. *Chemical weaponry: A continuing challenge*. New York: St. Martin's Press.

Taylor, L. B., and C. L. Taylor. 1985. *Chemical and biological warfare*. New York: Franklin Watts.

CLOSE AIR SUPPORT

Close air support is a tactical air mission normally performed by attack aircraft, fighters, or fighter-bombers. The mission has been accomplished on occasion by helicopters and bombers, and remotely piloted vehicles may one day dominate the mission area. Close air support is designed to apply heavy concentrations of air-delivered firepower needed for effective and timely support of ground forces. The mission includes air action against targets in close proximity to friendly ground forces; this requires integration of each air mission with the fire and movement of those forces. The same ordnance delivery platforms are said to be performing battlefield air interdiction when their attacks are not close to friendly ground forces. Close coordination is the hallmark of close-air-support operations.

Historical Development

The earliest stage of development occurred during the years 1917 to 1935. This first phase, described for convenience as the attack aviation era, was marked by air support activities in which agile single-seaters with machine guns performed the close-air-support mission. World War I had given airmen opportunities for experimentation and innovation. While most aviators wanted to concentrate on targets behind the lines, aiming for an independent striking role for the airplane, key ground commanders had more pressing concerns. One of these, Gen. John Joseph Pershing, thought the fragile airplane might have a mission of more immediacy. He asked his aviators to concentrate on ground support. The close air support provided by the Lewis machine gun mounted on canvas wings was not formidable, but it had a substantial psychological effect, and ground commanders believed the potential demonstrated was more than adequate to continue that emphasis after World War I. During that period, the term *attack* referred to any air-to-ground action. According to Pershing, aviators were to drive off enemy aircraft, provide information for infantry and artillery to facilitate maneuver and firepower applications, and provide direct attack when called upon by a ground commander. U.S. doctrine continues to emphasize the kind of close-air-support ideas articulated by Pershing and demonstrated by the "air-minded" Brig. Gen. William ("Billy") Mitchell. Mitchell had studied the thinking of British Sir Hugh ("Boom") Trenchard and was familiar with the visionary ideas of Italian general Giulio Douhet. An amalgam of conceptual schemes bore fruit in Mitchell's plans, but another nation had pioneered somewhat earlier the combat development of direct support to surface formations.

THE GERMAN EXAMPLE

Germany was first to demonstrate effective use of massed airpower in conjunction with ground operations. The great offensive of March 1918 included more than 300 aircraft operating in direct support of ground troops. For the first time, air and ground actions were fully coordinated. German air officers had practiced for several weeks well behind their lines. The decision to follow quick seizure of air superiority rapidly with hard-hitting air-to-surface attacks permitted significant gains by the infantry. The British use of aircraft against the German infantry to stop that offensive was equally significant. Mitchell learned from the German and British examples. At the St. Mihiel and Argonne offensives, he wedded the air arms of British, French, Italians, and Americans into a powerful concentration of more than 1,500 combat aircraft. The outcome was so successful that Mitchell never forgot the glory of those days. He later wrote of those operations, "Like any other military operation, concentration of force at the vital point is what counts."

TACTICS

The primary World War I tactic was to have a formation of aircraft make a level, low-altitude pass over the target. Having acquired visual contact, the formation returned for a wings-level strafing pass on the objective. Improved tactics were long in coming, but British experience in colonial wars in the 1920s and 1930s proved important to the air attack mission. Trenchard reestablished an independent air arm during the many small aerial campaigns of the empire between the world wars. Close air support was a primary task of aircraft in far-flung regions of the British Empire.

LIGHT BOMBERS AND FIGHTER-BOMBERS

In the late 1930s, light bombers appeared and initiated a phase best called the light- and medium-bomber period of close air support. More guns and more bombs were hung on aircraft like the German Do-17 and He-111 and the American B-25 and B-26. Heavily armed for aerial reconnaissance and direct support to surface operations, they were particularly effective in the World War II maritime theaters of the Mediterranean and Pacific. With long range and good loiter time, these formidable aircraft engaged surface targets with powerful effect. Only the appearance of the modern fighter could disrupt the mission successes won by these aircraft. The Zeros, Mustangs, Messerschmitts, and Focke-Wulfs, however, soon made life miserable for light and medium bombers. Toward the end of World War II, the awesome U.S. P-47 and P-51 and British Typhoon began to concentrate on bombing and strafing. Close-air-support successes won by fighters brought the fighter-bomber to the forefront of infantry consciousness. Again the Germans had pioneered the orchestration of fighter-bomber operations much earlier than the Allies. Luftwaffe successes in Poland and France in 1939 and 1940 proved apt models for close air support later in the war.

From 1950 until now, the central ideas of close air support have been codified in well-established doctrine. These are clearly described in various national publications and in the centerpiece of North Atlantic Treaty Organization (NATO) air manuals: ATP-27B, *Offensive Air Support*. Along with battlefield air interdiction, the close-air-support mission provides direct offensive firepower to the ground commander.

The Tactical Command System

The means of coordination is a solid system of command and control often known as TACCS, the tactical air command and control system (Fig. 1). Every nation employing close air support will use a version of the TACCS. The derivative principles are adaptable and flexible. Without some form of the TACCS, the close-air-support mission cannot develop into a robust and responsive form of air warfare that serves ground commanders involved in the stresses and emergencies of modern high-intensity combat.

THE AIR SUPPORT OPERATIONS CENTER (ASOC)

Integrated control is required to prevent catching friendly troops in the devastation wreaked by modern fighter-delivered weapons. Radio coordination for

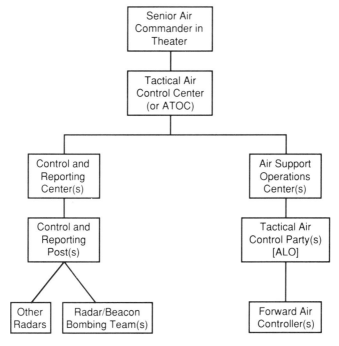

Figure 1. The generic TACCS elements for conducting close air support.

close-air-support missions is usually scripted, terse, yet manifold in its coverage of weather, target, friendly location, enemy dispositions, and egress procedures. In the target information checklist will be a "desired effect" recommendation. This information should be discussed by planners at a command and control node near or within the army corps or division-level tactical operations center. Information is passed to senior and supporting elements as well as to the fighters via the "air request net" (Fig. 2). In Europe and elsewhere, the node described above would be called an ASOC (air support operations center) and it would be closely aligned with a parent corps.

In addition to planning for close-air-support missions, the ASOC would have a part in coordinating daily activity in support of the corps engaged in ground combat operations.

THE TACC OR ATOC

The ASOC is subordinate to a theater-level node called the allied tactical operations center (ATOC) by NATO (or the tactical air control center [TACC] by the United States and Korea). This command center would supervise several ASOCs on a large front such as that of central Western Europe. But close-air-support direction and planning devolve to the ASOC in most cases. *Ipso facto*, the ASOC bears responsibility for direct support of field commanders. The bulk

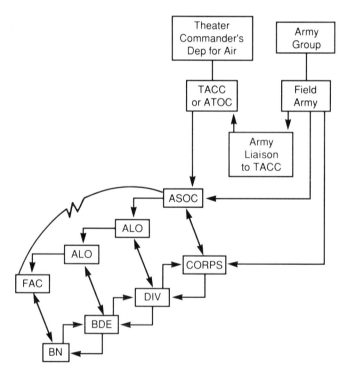

Figure 2. The air request net. CAS mission requests may pass up the army side via the chain of command or up the air side direct to the ASOC. For CAS, the ASOC is the hub of activity.

of such support is provided via the coordinating of TACPs (tactical air control parties). These units are nearly organic with surface formations at brigade level and below. TACPs must have the complete confidence of ground unit commanders and they form a key part of the staff planning done at those levels. They are equipped to pass requests to the ASOC and to the ATOC if necessary to provide requisite amounts of close air support. The ASOC serves as the parent to these TACPs and reiterates requests as necessary.

THE FORWARD AIR CONTROLLER

Some TACPs include airborne forward air controllers (FACs) who fly their own light planes, fighters, or helicopters to provide on-scene forward air control or, in high-density threat zones, forward air coordination just slightly removed from the target area. The airborne FAC's survivability is often difficult. Ground FACs accompany battalions and brigades in cases where airborne duties cannot be performed. Unlike the other tactical missions where control of an action or activity may be managed by a flight leader tied into a command post, close support requires continual positive control in the battle zone. Operation in close proximity to one's own forces requires positive control not only of the flight but also of each aircraft within the flight on each delivery attempt. The forward air controller (FAC) is responsible for ensuring that air-delivered munitions hit where the ground commander wants them to. The FAC is in the center of activity, observing impacts and securing safe approaches in the vicinity of friendly forces. While he shares mission responsibilities with the flight leader, the primary purpose for having a FAC on the scene is to avoid catastrophic mistakes (e.g., aircraft firing on friendly forces) that an uncoordinated mission could yield.

Close-air-support Operations

Close air support is hazardous. The zone of tactical employment includes the most lethal part of an enemy's air defense. Ringed with missiles, battered by guns, and distracted by the dust and debris of the modern battlefield, the close-air-support pilot faces a formidable task. Even with highly survivable aircraft that can hide behind terrain features, loiter offstage until committed, or absorb battle damage (such as the A-10 or Harrier), the mission is tough. More and more helicopters are joining the array of close air contributors and opponents. Tactics have evolved from straight-line ingresses to complicated moves. The constant stress of G forces and terrain-matching acrobatics make the employment of weapons less simple than in the past. The problem of delivery is the most difficult part of close air support. The position of friendly forces is the eternal concern of the attacker. Destruction by friendly air is the perpetual risk run by armor or infantry.

Success depends upon the planning and study preceding employment. Predelivery procedures must be mastered by aircrews very familiar with the friendly ground scheme of maneuver as well as the tactical situation of the supported force.

READINESS REQUIREMENTS

One troubling aspect of close air support is the degree of alert needed for an air force to respond quickly to army requests. Ordinarily there are two sources of attack aircraft for the close-air-support mission. The easiest posture to ensure adequate reaction time is the ground alert. Selected aircraft are armed and fueled in the corps' rear area awaiting emergencies that might generate an immediate request for close support. This is easy to maintain for long periods of low-intensity combat, and replacement aircraft can be swiftly set up to replace those that might be scrambled. The other posture is airborne alert. It is much more difficult to maintain over long periods yet provides even quicker responses in instances where an enemy strikes and disengages before ground-alert aircraft can react.

Both ground and airborne alerts have significant drawbacks. Ground alerts tie up significant resources available to air commanders, present lucrative counter-air targets to an enemy, and make aircraft tied down by such a commitment unavailable for other missions that could result in higher payoffs. Airborne alerts are also vulnerable to enemy attack and, while orbiting in air-to-surface configuration, close support aircraft are unable to reply in kind to an enemy fighter sweep. Bombs may be jettisoned to ensure survival, fuel is wasted, and use of afterburning to evade fighters leads to curtailment of the mission.

While airborne alerts may prove wasteful, they are preferable to a grounded air force. Only when fuel and other resources are stretched thin should ground alerts be considered an option for the air commander. An airborne alert is often pressed upon a beleaguered air commander by the sheer necessity of a rapid response. While costly in terms of resources, it has merit in tight combat situations and keeps the machines operating.

By far the best way to handle close-air-support requests is by diverting aircraft from other missions. Fighter-bombers en route to free-fire zones or to battlefield air interdiction targets can be redirected by an ATOC and handed off to an ASOC as needed, but this is not a simple process. It requires an agile command-and-control apparatus and can break down communications. The flexibility required to change the role of fighters relies on innovative pilots, adaptable munitions, and responsive mission planning. It is difficult to study a target while in flight and while being diverted, yet some close-air-support targets can be rapidly understood by aviators assisted by onboard information-processing equipment. Preplanning can ease the process, but ad hoc efforts run the risk of hasty thinking, poor navigation, and inaccurate weapons delivery. Preplanning must allow for introduction of general methods for handling variables in flight. Ingress and egress procedures should be standardized and selected on a match-and-mix basis. However, two variables cannot be predicted in advance—target acquisition and subsequent target area tactics. These must be assessed on a target-by-target basis.

THE THREAT

In Southeast Asia during the Vietnam War, nearly 80 percent of American combat losses were attributed to enemy guns. While missiles threaten close-air-support aircraft, the threat of gunfire remains the most vicious obstacle in the low-altitude environment where ordnance is delivered. The enemy can be expected to concentrate guns where friend and foe are locked in combat emergencies that draw down heavily on total air sorties slated to close support. Two forces cannot occupy the same path without one or both suffering a beating. Close air support posits just such a fight at the forward line of troops (FLOT). Electronic countermeasures and integration of friendly fire help the attacker. Nonetheless, the prospect for high attrition rates must be balanced against the combat emergency to which the close support sorties are directed.

WEATHER

The most serious obstacle to successful application of airpower in the close support area is bad weather. While the threat of enemy air defenses is lethal, the prospect of help to ground forces exists as long as aircraft are flying. Bad weather, however, can shut down air operations completely. Few aircraft are equipped with radar or beacon systems accurate enough to use bombs in close proximity to friendlies. It is possible, of course, to attempt such a mission in more benign or less cluttered environments where a miss will not matter. The single hit by a British Vulcan bomber on the runway of East Falklands was surrounded by misses. It was a remarkable hit, but it is doubtful if such a sortie would be attempted if one's own nation had deployed troops along the runway. The difference between close air support and all other missions is close contact. Weather makes it more difficult to retain positive control.

Poor visibility can also mar the close support effort. Haze and low clouds can mask terrain, hide enemy defenses, and make target acquisition difficult despite electronic aids. The position of the sun is also important, especially to fighter pilots. One instinctively depends on the sun, moon, and stars for orientation, and when they are obscured, orientation problems can occur.

Weather forecasts and analyses by the weather briefer have great import for every fighter pilot. In close support, the pilot's mission requires knowledge that might be of less concern to other mission planners.

TERRAIN

Ground features are extremely important to a tactician and can have a positive or negative effect on the success of close support. If the terrain allows approach to the target while shielding the aircraft from view or acquisition by target tracking radars, it will assist the pilot who uses tactics that take advantage of the terrain. On the other hand, if the terrain consists of long rolling hills or a steep valley, the pilot may be forced to adopt a tactic the enemy can surmise. Terrain that simplifies and amplifies the power of the defense can preclude the delivery accuracies expected by supported forces. If the target is too close to irregular terrain, final approach can be unacceptably hazardous. Most difficult terrain has some redeeming virtue that will enhance surprise or assist the pilot to acquire the target visually, if a visual acquisition is necessary.

MARKING THE TARGET

Modern technology has in some instances eliminated the need to mark the target with smoke, rockets, bombs, arrows, colored cloths, artillery impacts, or similar objects to attract the attention of FACs and fighter/attack pilots. Electronic means such as bombing beacons, flight direction by ground-based radars, and onboard radars with exotic computational assistance are available to locate and fix targets while timing the release of onboard munitions.

Despite the help of television cameras and target acquisition systems that work hand in glove with weapons wired into high-technology helmets, the target may still require marking for the safety of the supported side. Most often it is sufficient to mark the friendly position and then to relay the bearing of the enemy from that position. The target may be located by following key terrain features. Enemy surface-to-air fires may also mark his position. If the enemy remains concealed during the relatively short period of time a fast fighter-bomber spends in the target area, some kind of offsets and computer assistance may be useful if a system of positive marking cannot be employed. Certainly the smoke, fires, fumes, dust, and debris of the modern battlefield can obscure the exact location of a targeted enemy formation for considerable periods of time. Darkness, too, can mask an enemy's location, but a firefight in darkness might reveal the location of the enemy's fire line. Night illumination can be effective if the environment allows. Satellites and other sensors may provide positioning for flights while locating targets that cannot be marked by ordinary means.

Continuing Problems

Fluid land battles pose intricate and perplexing challenges to airmen attempting close air support. If the location of friendly troops is not known, confusion can result. The possibility of being shot down by friendly fire—always a risk in close support—is increased by imprecise understanding of the ground situation. But of far greater consequence is the danger of dropping ordnance on friendly forces. The positive-control aspect of close air support is designed to preclude just such an occurrence, which is often described as a "short round." The difficulty of pinpointing all elements of a friendly land force amplify the chances of short rounds when communications dissolve, when casualties eliminate unit leaders, and when heavy defenses damage aircraft engaged in the delivery of high explosives. This problem was highlighted during the 1991 Gulf War.

Close air support is a mission that frequently suffers from benign neglect or outright institutional denial. Limited budgets often squeeze future developments that might improve close support. Because army support is not the most welcomed occupation among airmen, close support may be underfunded, sacrificed to other mission requirements, or supported only under duress. It is a too-frequent claim by airmen that aircraft optimized for air superiority are adequate for close support. This is wishful thinking. Until air forces invest in close air support, armies will look to internal means for securing battlefield assistance; armed helicopters seem to be the method of choice. Army aviation will fill gaps created when air forces do not allocate resources to the close-air-support mission.

TIMOTHY E. KLINE

SEE ALSO: Blitzkrieg.

Bibliography

Fetzer, L., and R. Wagner. 1973. *The Soviet air force in World War II*. Garden City, N.Y.: Doubleday.
Hastings, M. 1984. *D-Day and the battle for Normandy*. New York: Simon and Schuster.
Hastings, M., and S. Jenkins. 1983. *The battle for the Falklands*. New York: Norton.
Mason, R. A., ed. 1986. *War in the third dimension*. London: Brassey's.
Walker, J. R. 1987. *Air-to-ground operations*. Vol. 2 of *Air power: Aircraft weapons systems and technology series*. London: Brassey's.

COALITION WARFARE

Coalition warfare is a confrontation involving an association of allied nations (or an armed political entity, such as a revolutionary or guerrilla movement) on one or both sides of a conflict. Military coalitions are usually based upon a formal and broader political alliance, or league, of independent, sovereign nations. However, military coalitions can also be temporary arrangements of expedience that have no basis other than to deal with an immediate, common threat to the coalition members.

Purposes for Coalition Warfare

Nations form coalitions for various reasons, and the specific reasons may differ among members of the same coalition. Generally, coalitions are perceived as collective arrangements necessary to confront a larger opponent, national or multinational. Such alliances may be initiated in anticipation of a future confrontation or in response to an immediate threat.

Coalitions impose risks and restrictions on member nations, and therefore the scope of an allied effort is usually carefully defined and limited to specific areas of cooperation and support and to specific, mutually agreed-upon objectives.

Coalitions may be formed for a wide range of goals, such as for economic cooperation, support of socio-cultural homogeneity, territorial exploitation, and security. Quite often, these goals overlap. If a coalition remains viable long enough, its objectives may change as the international situation changes.

While coalitions need not involve military actions, a significant number of international alliances have some implicit aspects of military cooperation. Coalitions with military goals do not always require formal military or political arrangements, and even fewer require coordinated employment of multinational military forces (i.e., combined operations). Coalitions for the conduct of warfare can be broadly categorized into "offensive" or "defensive" alliances.

OFFENSIVE COALITIONS

Offensive coalitions are formed to change an existing situation. The member nations agree to coordinate a scheme of mutually beneficial international actions—or inactions—at the expense of another nation or group of nations. Expansionism, either for territorial or economic domination, is normally the specific purpose.

Alliances to undertake an aggressive initiative are difficult to justify internationally. The 1956 Israeli, British, and French attack on Egypt (the Suez War) illustrates the difficulty of undertaking a blatantly hostile allied operation without some creditable facade. However, if the purpose is promoted as furthering the spread of "the right" religion or political philosophy, it is easier to justify. Often, the stated purpose of securing a more appropriate defensive geography for an anticipated threat is used to achieve a territorial advantage.

Offensive alliances are also formed for a major power to assist a subordinated state to gain independence. Examples are the 1778 French alliance with the American colonies against Britain, the 1858 alliance of France with the Kingdom of Piedmont against Austria, and the 1866 alliance of Prussia with Italy, also against Austria. The tradition continues with some large nations' support of "liberation movements," seeking to break from a colonial status, or "freedom fighters," where the insurgents seek a change of political leadership.

Many offensive alliances are dominated by a single nation, and most aggressor nations are confident in their own strength. Their allies are mainly for international support or to ensure the denial of potential allies to an enemy. Examples of the latter are Austria's alliances with France and Russia before confronting Prussia in 1756, and Prussia's alliances with Austria and Italy before precipitating the Franco-Prussian War in 1870. Often, their "allies" are merely border states or conquered countries that are coerced into participation. Examples are some of the eastern European countries submitting to Axis influence in World War II and the cooperation of countries in the Western Hemisphere with the many worldwide confrontations of the United States.

DEFENSIVE COALITIONS

Opposed to expansionism and domination is the coalition formed to defend the status quo against a perceived threat or actual military attack. These coalitions consist of nations seeking mutual, or collective, security. Such "defense" alliances seek strategic military advantage, in numbers and global positioning, as do offensive coalitions.

Alliances to protect the status quo, or at least to prevent change based on military conquest, can be viewed as regional or global. Regional coalitions are the most traditional arrangements. They played a major part in eighteenth- and nineteenth-century international politics, which involved networks seeking to "balance power" among contending groups of nations. These alliances were characterized by shifting allegiances and complex interconnections that, at times, led nations into unwanted wars. This was certainly a common perception held in respect to World War I. The concept of a global coalition to ensure stability began to develop after World War I but did not take root until after World War II with the United Nations (UN).

The two most significant UN military coalitions, those for the Korean War (1950–53) and the 1991 Gulf War, were fundamentally defensive but required offensive combat operations. Both were marked by strong U.S. political leadership and aggressive UN Security Council actions. Both wars attracted participation from a number of countries. The longer duration of the Korean conflict allowed an integrated command structure to develop, while no single, formal allied command emerged in the brief Gulf conflict. However, unity of effort was achieved in the Gulf War by the enormous efforts of U.S. senior political and military leaders, drawing heavily upon precedents derived from NATO and, most uniquely, from an array of regional arrangements developed through the U.S. Central Command (CENTCOM). This U.S. Unified Command, headquartered in the United States, was created to focus on and to prepare for contingencies in the Gulf theater, where the establishment of a formal allied structure was politically not acceptable. These two dramatic UN military coalitions, which involved open warfare, should not divert awareness from the very different, but nevertheless important, UN peacekeeping missions that have deployed throughout the world. Indeed, the latter role may take on even more importance in an emerging nonpolarized international environment.

There is not always a clear distinction between offensive and defensive alliances. Defensive coalitions are formed fundamentally to preserve an existing international order. Good examples would be the series of European coalitions against revolutionary and Napoleonic France in the late eighteenth and nineteenth centuries. Although these coalitions sought to overturn the status quo, they were against a recently established nonmonarchical France that was not acceptable to the major reigning states.

Manner of Participation

DEGREE OF FORMAL COMMITMENT

Military alliances vary as to the actions and contributions expected of its members. In earlier times, treaties usually required specific sizes of forces or amounts of money to be contributed. The North Atlantic Treaty Organization (NATO), however, obliges members only to take whatever action they deem necessary to reach a specific goal. This would make NATO ineffective if it were not for the establishment of active, multinational planning organizations that address strategies and force structuring.

LEVEL OF EFFORT

Coalitions can be further characterized by the level of effort, or manner of participation, of the member nations. The member states can participate throughout a spectrum of levels of effort, which can include assured inaction, diplomatic support, economic support, military assistance, parallel operations, and combined operations. The effort level is not necessarily fixed throughout the duration of the alliance. Often, one party may wait to see how the other prevails in its initial efforts—particularly so for revolutions—before committing itself. This was the case in the French *ancien régime* support of the revolt of the American colonies in the late eighteenth century.

Under certain conditions, nonmilitary support can be very effective. Of course, "nonmilitary support" is a technicality. Financial aid and the provision of vitally needed infrastructure resources allow the recipient to devote more of its own assets to its military effort. Nonmilitary support may be in the form of sanctuary basing for the recipient ally. This was common in recent wars of national liberation and counterinsurgency such as those in Vietnam, Latin America, and the Middle East. It can be especially effective if the giving ally is a strong power that cannot be attacked without a serious escalation of the war.

Military support to an ally can be almost undetectable when it commences from "noncombat" assistance. It often begins with money for arms and expands to advisers, logistical materiel, training, basing, intelligence sharing, and the direct transfer of weapons. U.S. support of Israel and Soviet support of Cuba are examples of military support not including combat support. The U.S. "Lend-Lease" program, which began supplying military supplies to Great Britain in early 1941, is a model of such support.

Coordinated (or parallel) military operations are the next level of effort. They may include multinational war councils and planning committees, but they do not include combined or interdependent employment of military forces. This would not exclude training exercises with mixed, or "combined," forces for the purpose of conveying confidence to some members of the coalition. Examples of this type of alliance are ANZUS (for the 1951 pact between Australia, New Zealand, and the United States) and the Inter-American Treaty of Reciprocal Assistance (Rio Treaty). With only a slight escalation of aid, however, the supporting ally can introduce military units into combat. This happened with the U.S. effort in support of South Vietnam.

The highest level of effort is combined operations and/or establishment of combined military planning headquarters with the assumption that integrated employment of combat units may take place.

Alliance Cohesion

Military alliances are fragile, and their effectiveness and durability are dependent upon factors that influence cohesion among the members.

SOCIOLOGICAL HOMOGENEITY

While they may be the most difficult to define and analyze, coalitions formed to preserve or to promote an ideology or a culture often prove to be immensely powerful. The ideology may be commonly held religious beliefs (Muslim *jihad* and Christian crusades of the past) or political-economic ideology (communism and capitalism of the twentieth century).

Cultural values (usually more specifically identified with language, racial, and ethnic groups) may not be easy to identify, but they do foster international alliances. It is possible that religious and political ideologies are the strongest catalysts in promoting coalitions. However, common cultural values appear to perpetuate enduring conditions for international cooperation. Western nations, and particularly the "English-speaking" nations, have exhibited the "family" syndrome; that is, they fight among themselves, but they usually unite against an "outside" culture. The North Atlantic Alliance of World War II was formed from a perceived need to preserve common cultural values.

COMMON PERCEPTION OF PURPOSE

The threat of an impending attack from a stronger enemy and clearly identified, near-term objectives help to unify an alliance. Overt warfare usually provides sufficient focus for allied unity. Maintaining a military alliance in peacetime is more challenging. NATO's success in this endeavor has been unusual and is due, to some extent, to the memory of democracies falling separately when they failed to stand together in the late 1930s. Part of NATO's success must also be attributed to a series of aggressive military ventures and arms buildup posturing by the Soviet Union.

SIMILAR GOVERNMENTAL STRUCTURES

While not essential to maintaining a wartime alliance, compatibility among the governing institutions and senior military planning institutions of member nations certainly support the cohesiveness of a coalition.

Observations

THE BENEFITS

The military significance of coalitions can be viewed in two forms: direct and indirect. Direct benefits to a coalition are greater resources (time and space as well as material and forces). These aspects also tend to make coalition wars longer or to create significant obstacles to immediate aggression. Indirect advantages are international moral and diplomatic support.

THE PROBLEMS

Coalitions make war complex and frustrating to leaders (especially to those of the more powerful member states). Alliances impose complications in decision making, usually requiring extensive coordination. Coalitions can bring added liabilities—new regional areas of weaker allies to defend and additional allied objectives to achieve before peace. In the end, coalitions make it difficult to achieve peace due to the varied interests of the partners.

Definite power relationships exist within coalitions, and these become more complex as the number of members increases. Relationships among partners usually change during the coalition. Incidents of arrogance and humiliation can easily occur and require statesmen and senior military leaders of a particular temperament.

There is some sacrifice of sovereign prerogatives and there are always questions of the intentions of allies. Beyond the common threat, there are possible unilateral ventures taken by one ally that may draw others into unwanted wars. This is why NATO members are careful to remind their partners with global interests of the regional limits of their particular Atlantic accord.

PERCEPTIONS

Official military histories are produced by national organizations and many writings on warfare are by authors seeking the acceptance of their citizen readers. Understandably, there is a strong propensity to appeal to national pride and, in turn, to perpetuate popular perceptions that lead to misconceptions about coalitions. National histories are often reluctant to acknowledge the contributions of alliance. A number of national leaders who served during the time of an alliance tend to excuse bad decisions as consequences of allied pressures at the time.

Conclusion

Memoirs and popular histories are replete with references to the difficulties that occur among allies. Much of the discord among allies is the same that exists among separate national military organizations (i.e., the egos of strong leaders and the pride of military units, which are not conducive to sharing the honors). However, the record indicates that coalitions are a "necessary evil" to prevail in most warfare.

The value of coalitions is easily apparent to small nations. However, in modern history regional powers have also developed an appreciation for coalitions following some costly confrontations that showed their disadvantage in relation to larger power balances. Some examples would be: France following the Franco-Prussian War, Great Britain after World War I, and Germany and the United States after World War II. Today a number of military coalitions exist without open warfare. One might ask, why would a strong power tie itself to a mutual defense agreement with one or more smaller, independent states? While there may be some economic advantages, the more important military reasons are apt to be: to secure "buffer" regions around itself, to maintain a force presence in strategic areas of the world, or to secure forward basing for flexibility in some unforeseen crisis.

The problems within coalitions, inherently complex undertakings, produce noticeable complaints, while the benefits receive little popular notice. It takes a serious and nonparochial reading of military history to appreciate that sustained military strength is not an island.

ALBERT D. MCJOYNT

SEE ALSO: Strategy.

Bibliography

Cerny, K., and H. Briefs, eds. 1965. *NATO in quest of cohesion*. Hoover Institution on War, Revolution, and Peace. New York: Praeger.

Dehio, L. 1963. *The precarious balance: The politics of power in Europe in world politics.* Boston: Little, Brown.

Farrar, L. 1973. *The short-war illusion.* Santa Barbara, Calif.: Clio Press.

Kennan, G. 1984. *The fateful alliance: France, Russia, and the coming of the First World War.* New York: Pantheon Books.

Langer, W. 1964. *European alliances and alignments, 1871–1890.* New York: Vintage.

Luard, E. 1987. *War in international society.* New Haven: Yale Univ. Press.

Morgan, R., and C. Bray, eds. 1986. *Partners and rivals in Western Europe: Britain, France, and Germany.* London: Gower.

Naidu, M. 1974. *Alliances and balance of power.* New York: St. Martin's Press.

Neilson, K., and R. Prete, eds. 1983. *Coalition warfare: An uneasy accord.* Mill Valley, Calif.: Wilfrid Laurier Univ. Press.

Wright, Q. 1965. *A study of war.* Chicago: Univ. of Chicago Press.

COMBAT EFFECTIVENESS

It is evident in the history of warfare that some military forces have been considerably more effective than others. The Macedonian army of Alexander the Great consistently defeated far larger Persian armies. Caesar, with a few Roman legions, conquered Gaul, defeating much larger forces of Gauls and Germans. Hernando Cortés, with about 500 Spanish soldiers, consistently defeated Aztec armies numbering in the thousands. The British conquered India with small forces that were invariably outnumbered by the native Indian armies. Although Germany was defeated in both world wars, German armies fought much larger Allied armies to a standstill for several years, until finally being overwhelmed by numerical superiority. And more recently, relatively small Israeli armies have consistently defeated far larger Arab armies.

In these examples, the Macedonian, Roman, Spanish, British, German, and Israeli armies were more effective in combat than their enemies. This raises two questions: (1) How much more effective were these armies than their opponents? (That is, can the effectiveness of superiority be quantified?) (2) Why were these armies more effective than their foes?

Quantifying Combat Effectiveness

Two eighteenth-century military theorists (Napoleon and Clausewitz) provided slightly different and incomplete, but generally consistent, answers to the first question.

Napoleon, in a letter to his brother, Joseph, in trying to teach him (unsuccessfully) to be an effective king of Spain, wrote: "The moral is to the physical as three is to one" (Napoleon 1858–70, 17, no. 14276). His meaning was that the quality of troops is three times more important than the numbers of the troops, or the quality or effectiveness of their weapons and equipment.

Clausewitz said that there are three major factors that determine the outcome of a battle: (1) numbers of troops (and weapons), (2) the circumstances of the battles (which side is attacking, which defending; the nature of the terrain;

the weather, etc.), and (3) the fighting value of the troops (which is a given quantity). Clausewitz never showed how he would calculate this "given quantity," but he obviously believed it was calculable (Clausewitz 1976, p. 194).

The calculation of "this fighting value of the troops" is not easy. A simple comparison of the strengths of the opponents is not sufficient. A defending force of 10,000 men may repulse an attacker of 20,000, but that does not mean that the defender is twice as effective as the attacker. Much of the defender's combat power may be due to the multiplicative effect of a defensive posture. As Clausewitz wrote, "Defense is the stronger form of combat" (1976, p. 84). The relative power is also affected by the nature of the terrain, by the weather, and by other factors.

Although a simple comparison of numerical strength will not provide an answer, it can help, and in one recent war a comparison of strengths is probably a true indication of relative combat effectiveness. In the 1973 Arab-Israeli War, Arabs and Israelis fought to a stalemate on two fronts (Dupuy 1984, pp. 387–584). On the Golan front 60,000 Israelis were opposed by 150,000 Arabs (mostly Syrians, plus a few Iraqis and Jordanians). Because of the stalemate, we can assume that these opponents were fairly closely matched in combat power. If so, the 60,000 Israelis were 2.5 times as effective as the 150,000 Arabs.

Similarly, on the Suez-Sinai front, approximately 200,000 Egyptians were opposed by about 100,000 Israelis. This suggests that the Israelis were 2.0 times as effective as the Egyptians. But the ratio of the casualty-inflicting capability of the Israelis was considerably more than 2.5 times that of the Syrians and their allies and considerably more than twice as great as that of the Egyptians.

In highly aggregated terms, on the Golan front the 60,000 Israelis inflicted about 10,000 casualties on the Syrians and their allies, while the 150,000 Arabs inflicted about 2,400 casualties on the Israelis. To put it more simply, 100 Israelis were inflicting 16.7 casualties on the Arabs, while 100 Arabs were inflicting 2.1 casualties on the Israelis. This is a ratio of 7.9 to 1.0 in casualty-inflicting capability. This must be compared with the 2.5 to 1.0 standoff capability.

On the Suez-Sinai front, the 100,000 Israelis inflicted about 16,500 casualties on the Egyptians, while 200,000 Egyptians had inflicted about 6,500 Israeli casualties. Or 100 Egyptians were inflicting 3.3 casualties on the Israelis, while 100 Israelis were inflicting 16.5 casualties on the Egyptians. Here the ratio is 5.0 to 1.0 in casualty-inflicting capability, much more than the 2.0 to 1.0 ratio in standoff ability.

In World War II, the ratio of the casualty-inflicting capability of the Germans to that of their opponents (Americans and British) was consistently between 1.4 to 1.0 and 1.5 to 1.0. Against the Russians, the casualty-inflicting capability ratio was about 7.5 to 1.0. One authority, however, suggests that the relative combat effectiveness ratio of the Germans to the Western Allies was about 1.2 to 1.0, and their relative combat effectiveness with respect to the Russians was about 2.5 to 1.0 (Dupuy 1987).

Dupuy (1987) also suggests that there is a consistent relationship between the calculated relative combat effectiveness value and the calculated ratio of casualty-inflicting capabilities (or lethalities). The relative effectiveness ratio appears to be approximately the square root of the lethality. On this basis, we can make the following comparisons:

	CEV	L	$\sqrt{L}$
Germans/Western Allies	1.2	1.5	1.2
Germans/Russians	2.5	7.5	2.7
Israelis/Syrians	2.5	7.9	2.8
Israelis/Egyptians	2.0	5.0	2.2

where:

CEV = Relative Combat Effectiveness Value
L = Lethality

This suggests that Napoleon was almost correct, but that it would be more precise to say that "the moral is the equivalent of the physical squared." It also shows how the fighting value of the troops is, as Clausewitz stated, "a given quantity."

Nature of Combat Effectiveness Superiority

There are three factors that account for the effectiveness superiority that more effective armies have over their enemies: technology, professionalism, and components of combat effectiveness.

TECHNOLOGY

In two of the six examples at the beginning of this article, the more effective force had better weapons and equipment. This disparity was substantial in the case of the Spanish versus the Aztecs; it was not so great but still significant in the case of the British against the Indians. There was little difference in weapons and equipment between the Macedonians and their enemies, the Romans and theirs, the Germans and the Allies, and the Israelis and the Arabs. However, even for the Spanish-Aztec and British-Indian conflicts, technology was not the only reason for the Spanish and British superiority.

PROFESSIONALISM

Professionalism may be the most important factor for effectiveness superiority in combat. The key can be found in the origins of the German combat effectiveness, which was the envy of the world for almost a century.

The Prussian army of 1806 was nearly indistinguishable from the powerful Prussian army led by Frederick the Great into the Seven Years' War. However, its performance was affected by two important factors. It lacked the leadership of Frederick, and it was a mid-eighteenth-century army in the nineteenth century. There had been some major changes in warfare in the previous quarter century due to the military impact of the American and French revolutions and the impact of the genius of Napoleon. The French emperor recognized both of these deficiencies of the Prussian army of 1806 when, early that year, he referred disparagingly to the Prussians as "the toy soldiers of Frederick the Great."

In the years just before the outbreak of war between France and Prussia, there were several Prussian military men who recognized the dangerous obsolescense of Prussian doctrine. The leader of these few realistic Prussian officers was Lt. Col. Gerhard von Scharnhorst, but his efforts to reform the army met with indifference or with scorn from most Prussian officers.

In a few hours on 14 October 1806, Napoleon confirmed his and Scharnhorst's evaluations of the weaknesses of the Prussian army by decisively defeating it on the battlefields of Jena and Auerstädt. The values of leadership, and particularly of genius, are hard to quantify, although there have been efforts. For instance, either Blücher or Wellington (it is attributed to both) said that Napoleon's presence on the battlefield was worth 40,000 men. But Napoleon was not present at Auerstädt, where 27,000 Frenchmen repulsed 63,000 Prussians. That was a ratio of 2.3 to 1.0. If we assume that defensive posture and the use of terrain gave the French a factor advantage of about 1.5, then their combat effectiveness superiority ratio was about 1.5 to 1.0.

After the Treaty of Tilsit, Prussian king Frederick William III grudgingly supported Scharnhorst in his attempt to reform the army. With his group of reformers (Gneisenau, Boyen, Grolmann, and Clausewitz being the principal ones), Scharnhorst reorganized the Prussian army, and particularly its leadership, by establishing the Prussian General Staff. It was this reorganized Prussian army, led by the General Staff, that later in the century won great victories over Austria-Hungary and France and that became the model for the subsequent German army. Its professionalism, centered in its General Staff, was the major reason for the combat effectiveness superiority of the German armies over their opponents in World Wars I and II.

The German soldiers were not braver, stronger, more intelligent, more highly motivated, or more warlike than their enemies. It was because the Germans had organized and prepared themselves for war more efficiently and more professionally than their opponents and thus were more effective in combat units. The superiority of the Germans was demonstrated consistently in both world wars: when they attacked, when they defended, when they had air superiority, when they did not, when they were successful, and when they were defeated. The Germans lost the wars because their enemies were able to assemble against them forces that outnumbered them by much more than their 1.2 combat effectiveness superiority (Dupuy 1984b).

It must also be stressed that the combat effectiveness difference between Israeli and Arab armies is not a measure of the worth, capability, or motivation of individual soldiers. Rather it is a reflection of the Israelis' ability to organize and prepare themselves for war more efficiently and professionally than their Arab opponents. The Arabs have never been able to accumulate enough numerical superiority on the battlefield to offset this Israeli CEV advantage.

It is a reasonable assumption that professionalism has been the key to combat effectiveness superiority wherever and whenever it has been manifested over the course of history.

COMPONENTS OF COMBAT EFFECTIVENESS

It has been suggested that the components of combat effectiveness are the intangible factors—behavioral or behavioral and physical—that relate to the performance of officers and men on the battlefield. Of the following list, the first four or five are probably the most important.

Leadership	Momentum
Training or experience	Technical command, con-
Morale	trol, communications
Cohesion	Intelligence
Logistical effectiveness	Initiative
Time and space	Chance

There is at present no known way to quantify these, but together they are the elements that make up the relative combat effectiveness ratios discussed above.

TREVOR N. DUPUY

Bibliography

Clausewitz, C. von. 1976. *On war.* Ed. and trans. M. Howard and P. Paret. Princeton, N.J.: Princeton Univ. Press.

Dupuy, T. N. 1984a. *Elusive victory: The Arab-Israeli wars, 1947–1974.* Fairfax, Va.: Hero Books.

———. 1984b. *A genius for war: The German army and general staff, 1807–1945.* Fairfax, Va.: Hero Books.

———. 1985. *Numbers, predictions, and war.* Rev. ed. Fairfax, Va.: Hero Books.

———. 1987. *Understanding war: History and theory of combat.* New York: Paragon House.

Napoléon I. 1858–70. *Correspondance de Napoléon Ier, publiée par ordre de l'Empereur Napoléon III.* 32 vols. Paris: Plon and Dumaine.

COMBAT MOTIVATION

Widespread interest in combat motivation and morale is a recent phenomenon. Prior to 1914 armies and navies generally took human factors for granted, and most commanders would have echoed Washington's contention that combat willingness derived from "natural bravery, hope of reward, and fear of punishment." However, some commanders, like Nelson and Napoleon, understood human nature and promoted motivation, recognizing (in Napoleon's words) that "in war the moral is to the material as three to one." The modern interest in combat behavior stems largely from the world wars, during each of which more than 65 million men were mobilized. Public familiarity with war has been allied with the military pursuit of effectiveness and with academic developments to produce a steady flow of studies of combat behavior, mostly relating to land warfare.

Surprisingly, this burgeoning literature was briefly paralleled by a widespread belief that technology and its accompanying managerial techniques would play a determinant role on the battlefield. However, recent military experiences from Vietnam to the Middle East and the Falklands/Malvinas has reaffirmed the importance of human factors in military effectiveness.

Motivation is essentially the "why" of behavior and concerns the needs and values that instigate goal-directed actions in an individual. Thus the term has connotations of choice and commitment. This article is institutional in focus, assessing the motivations that encourage (or discourage) compliant behavior within the context of military organization. Further, it will examine not only the combatant's motivations but also his behavior and the impact on both of battlefield conditions.

Individual and Social Factors

GROUP COHESION

The group is fundamental to most forms of human activity; it is especially so to combat. The importance to motivation of the "primary group"—the men in closest contact with the individual—has been well established since 1945. Thus, a higher rate of psychiatric breakdown and desertion has been found among poorly integrated men than among integrated men, while Israeli research shows that more heroic acts occur among tightly knit units than among less cohesive ones. Israeli psychologists have concluded that cohesion is one of the three principal immediate (battlefield) sources of combat motivation, along with leadership and self-preservation.

Studies of World War II American aircrews discovered that group membership was the primary motivator keeping the men flying. In warships, planes, and armored vehicles technical interdependence reinforces the cohesion engendered in combat; each member has restricted functions that must be followed to allow the crew to function as a whole, thereby further restricting the freedom of individual choice.

Individual self-concept is an important element of motivation. Most combatants want to be well regarded by their comrades, and some studies have shown that the fear of letting down comrades or subordinates can outweigh the fear of injury.

Cohesion does not invariably promote effectiveness. In that it represents a pragmatic response to a threatening situation—anxiety generally encourages association—cohesion can undermine task fulfillment where group survival acquires greater legitimacy than the military mission. Numerous examples of faked patrols, attacks on junior leaders, and discouragement of replacement enthusiasm indicate the potential of group bonds to degrade performance. One psychologist in Korea noted that a readiness to confer social approval in the absence of all-out effort resulted in reduced commitment. Similarly, group cohesion has been evident in units whose performance clearly reflected low motivation.

PERSONAL VALUES

Individual adherence to political, religious, or other values is a significant dimension of motivation. Soviet psychologists traditionally argued that morale is founded upon ideology, but while it has provided a focus of loyalty for a core of committed adherents, the World War II experience showed the importance as a motivator of an intense Russian patriotism. Evidence from Chinese prisoners in Korea suggests that intensive indoctrination helped to motivate the Communist forces. Equally, while nationalism appears to have strongly influenced the North Vietnamese Army (NVA) troops in the war in Vietnam, a thoroughly politicized cadre did infuse the NVA's three-man cells with a pro-organization culture. By contrast, ideology has not been a strong motivator for Western servicemen: only 5 percent of American enlisted men questioned in a 1944 survey cited ideological and patriotic motives as being the strongest behavioral influences. Nonetheless, a group's efforts to achieve certain goals are affected by the perceived legitimacy of those goals; therefore, public opinion, which modern technology readily communicates to the battlefield, can strongly influence motivation if it opposes national war aims.

In contrast with Iran and Afghanistan, religion has probably influenced the behavior of relatively few Western servicemen, although prayer has proven a valuable coping device for many. A few men, often professionals, will also be actuated by military ideals, such as those encapsulated in West Point's credo Duty, Honor, Country.

The probable smallness of the proportion of combatants adhering strongly to particular values is offset by the disproportionate influence on overall performance exerted by highly committed individuals, as the small Nazi element in Wehrmacht primary groups demonstrated.

REWARD AND RECOGNITION

Combat personnel expect some reward for their sacrifices. War has traditionally provided career mobility for military professionals, and a small number (including notables such as Winston Churchill) actively seek medals. In World War II the thrill and glamor of flying were complemented by commissions, extra pay, and training in a valuable civilian skill. Besides material rewards the combatant wants public recognition, in part as legitimatizing his efforts.

An inequitable distribution of rewards and inadequate recognition negatively affect morale. During the 1944 Burma campaign, Merrill's Marauders were demoralized by a lack of medals and commendations, and the lowly status of British and American infantrymen became a serious morale problem in 1944. By contrast, the Israelis deliberately accord their combat arms the highest prestige.

Organizational Reinforcement

MILITARY ORGANIZATION AND COHESION

Because cohesion generally enhances effectiveness but occasionally subverts military missions, armed forces seek to achieve congruence between group and organizational values. Policies that promote such congruence—such as assignment and leadership practices and efforts to build esprit de corps—are frequently reinforced by shared cultural values (such as Vietnamese nationalism) or common perceptions (for example, the Israelis' "no alternative" philosophy).

Social stability is central to cohesion—Napoleon claimed that he was defeated at Waterloo because his troops "had not eaten soup together long enough." A variety of organizational policies foster stability. The Israelis have used conscription effectively to promote cohesion, while in World War II the Germans exploited geographical roots to enhance bonding and tried to ensure that replacements were properly integrated into their companies before battle. The regimental system enhances stability in professional armies but tends to be swamped by mass mobilization and manpower shortages (as the Canadian and British armies discovered in 1944).

Navies have traditionally dispersed crews after voyages, a practice deplored by Nelson and still followed in the twentieth century. However, while at sea ships are communities apart, enforcing close duty and off-duty contacts, bonds that are further reinforced by natural as well as combat dangers. While army cohesion in Vietnam was adversely affected by one-year rotations, fixed tour lengths were vitally important in sustaining morale among World War II fliers.

Self-esteem is an important element in motivation and encourages individuals to behave according to the expectations of their peers or to some other standard. Unit pride is promoted in order to provide that standard, to develop esprit, and to channel cohesion into support of military objectives. Thus, British paratroopers in the Falklands/Malvinas were spurred by the memory of their battalion's epic stand at Arnhem in 1944.

LEADERSHIP

The leader's function is the fulfillment of unit missions. The dispersion of ground combat provides the soldier with opportunities for evasion, so army leaders must persuade their followers to accept military goals to ensure their compliant behavior. This link-pin role was exemplified by NVA cadre, who successfully fused group and army norms. Sailors' and fliers' choices are restricted by confinement in mobile steel shells, and the control of captains and pilots is correspondingly enhanced. Sailors have predetermined functions and generally little awareness of what fellow crew members are doing; only the captain knows the overall situation and can initiate action. Similarly, a World War II study noted that bomber pilots' responsibilities were increased by their being chiefly accountable for effectively discharging their planes' missions.

Confusion is characteristic of ground combat and, allied with danger, often induces paralysis. In such circumstances action can be contagious, given the tendency of people in threatening situations to emulate others. Followers tend to rate example the most important of leadership attributes, and the Israelis emphasize "follow me" leadership at the cost of high officer casualties. Generally, but not invariably, rank is a determinant of exemplary leadership, primarily due to training, to the pressures of responsibility, and to the appointed leader's control over operational communications. World War II American studies found officers had generally more favorable attitudes than enlisted men, and aircrews—which boasted a high proportion of officers—evinced notably strong morale.

When leader-follower contacts are infrequent (often the case in ground defensive actions), leadership operates by remote control rather than by visible example, depending on the climate previously established in the unit. Leader competence and concern are critical to that climate, because they give followers a sense of security.

TRAINING AND DISCIPLINE

Before 1914 training revolved around drill and was intended to inculcate obedience and automatic responses. Since then, the accent has been on realism (live fire and combat simulation), although drills are still taught to counter confusion. Effective training confers appropriate skills and builds teamwork and confidence. In World War II confidence was found to be the greatest factor in reducing fear among aircrews, and the Israelis have found a strong association between self-confidence and individual morale.

Surprise is a major demoralizer, and thus combatants need to form accurate preconceptions of combat. The British used the voyage to the Falklands/Malvinas as an opportunity for mental preparation, and group discussions on one ship helped the troops to come to terms with fear and strengthened cohesion. By contrast, the Argentinians were mentally unprepared for battle and evinced shock and surprise.

Military discipline implies compliance with organizational demands. Battlefield dispersion and mass mobilization have encouraged a trend away from formal discipline and toward self-discipline, whereby the combatant tries to achieve military objectives for his own reasons rather than under the threat of sanctions. This internalized discipline has a parallel in the functional discipline found in warships and planes, where teamwork in implementing predetermined tasks is vital to safety and success.

However, formal discipline has played a role in modern combat. Both the Soviets and Germans resorted to draconian discipline in World War II to discourage desertion, and more recently in Vietnam the NVA's surveillance system was extremely important in maintaining cohesion. There have been signs that the Soviets experimented with less coercive disciplinary forms in Afghanistan. There is also evidence that the reimposition of formal discipline when frontline units go into reserve helps to restore effectiveness.

Situational Influences

Combat generally differs appreciably from the combatant's preconceptions, and some of its elements—including danger, hardship, fatigue, weather, and success and failure—usually produce a motivational mutation from more general influences (such as ideology) to more immediate ones (leadership, for example).

Although it is difficult to prepare for danger, a number of preparatory measures, including cohesion-building and training realism, can offset its effects. However, severe hardship undoubtedly erodes motivation, as even dedicated NVA cadre demonstrated in the adverse conditions of 1965–67 in Vietnam. Fear is so pervasive, and friendly casualties so shocking, that rapid medical evacuation has become an important dimension of morale.

It is difficult to anticipate the confusion of battle, its surprising isolation, its unexpected noise (often equated with lethality), and the alternation of short bursts of intense activity along with long periods of waiting. Battle confusion is particularly acute for sailors below deck, and during the Falklands/Malvinas War the captain of HMS *Intrepid* found that his action broadcasts were valuable morale boosters.

Fatigue is inseparable from war but varies among services. The physical strain endured by soldiers is more prolonged and debilitating than that experienced by fliers, but the latter frequently suffer severe muscular and emotional tension from lengthy immobility. Airmen also confront a severe psychological strain in alternating rapidly between safety and extreme danger (a discontinuity that also affects stretcher-bearers).

Motivation is reinforced by a sense of achievement, and Montgomery considered success to be the best way to achieve high morale. Although success persuades combatants of their ability to cope, high morale is rarely separable from difficulty, and defeat is not always productive of demoralization, as the Germans showed after 1942. In fact, combat personnel may be more resistant than support troops to demoralization.

Combat Behavior

Combat behavior is the product of a complex interaction between motivation and situation and has traditionally been defined by its most overt manifestations, courage and fear. A small proportion of combatants is unusually aggressive—in World War II less than 1 percent of American pilots accounted for 30 to 40 percent of enemy aircraft destroyed in the air. By contrast, all armies have experienced combat refusals, whether physical or psychological in expression. Probably the majority of combatants are neither overly aggressive nor incapacitatingly fearful. Brought into the front lines by incremental steps, at each of which escape is socially or practically too extreme a response, the fighting man usually has little choice but to endure. As a British sailor commented of the Falklands/Malvinas War, "The ship itself helps: when the time comes the sailor must fight . . . there is no alternative."

Observers in World War II found a temporal dimension to combat performance. After an initial period of fearfulness and self-absorption, at about three weeks soldiers reached a peak of effectiveness, which lasted roughly a further week. Thereafter, increasing caution reflected progressive exhaustion. Likewise, among airmen a decline in combat motivation occurred with an increased number of missions. American soldiers in Vietnam displayed a similar rise, plateau, and decline in effectiveness during their one-year tours.

Until the 1973 Arab-Israeli War it was believed that, while any man too long subject to combat stress could suffer psychiatric breakdown, 25 to 30 days in the line was minimally required to produce such casualties. Recent experience indicates that intense combat will rapidly result in cases of battle shock. The proportion of psychiatric casualties to wounded among Israeli troops in the 1973 war was 30:100, indicating the impact such casualties can have on effectiveness. Fear itself is the critical ingredient in breakdown, but it is reinforced by such emotional and physical stresses as the loss of comrades, deprivation (especially of sleep and liquids), physical exertion, and domestic problems. Indirect fire and isolation also have been found to be predisposing factors, with unintegrated replacements being particularly susceptible to breakdown.

Combat stress can be mitigated by institutional means, such as cohesion-building and practices that facilitate leadership. For example, the volunteer status, efficient training, and high morale of American submarine crews in World War II resulted in a low rate of psychiatric casualties. Individual coping mechanisms such as activity (digging in or fighting back) are also valuable in palliating stress, as are confidence and a sense of control.

Conclusion

The combatant moving toward his first battle is characterized by a variety of motivations, but once under fire more immediate influences predominate, including group pressures, leadership, and self-preservation. Outright combat refusal is rare, and while relatively few men will go out of their way to further the mission, social, physical, and disciplinary pressures generally ensure that a majority of combatants will comply with military demands. Although fighting men often attempt to set some limit on the risks they will confront, once in combat the individual is prone to emulate the actions of others, and therefore his behavior may show some variation over time.

Military men often question the capacity of present and future generations to withstand combat's increased lethality, but greater dispersion and protection have thus far enabled humans to endure in battle. Nonetheless, the 1973 war in the Middle East indicated that future battles may be more intense than most hitherto experienced, resulting in early stress casualties. Behavior on the future battlefield will be redefined in other ways. A capability for continuous operations will exacerbate exhaustion, and the "automated battlefield" may affect leadership practices. Nuclear, biological, and chemical threats will enjoin protective clothing and dispersion, possibly undermining cohesion. Some nations have opened combat roles to women, who may therefore play a role on future battlefields.

Recent wars have shown that technology will not soon replace humans on the battlefield, and effectiveness will continue to be influenced by the shifting interrelationship of individual motivations, group dynamics, organizational requirements, and situational factors. As Patton remarked over 50 years ago, "Wars may be fought with weapons, but they are won by men."

[Note: The views expressed in this article are those of the author and do not necessarily represent the views of the Department of National Defence of Canada.]

ANTHONY KELLETT

SEE ALSO: Combat Stress; Discipline; Leadership; Morale.

Bibliography

Ellis, J. 1980. *The sharp end: The fighting man in World War II*. New York: Scribner's.

Gal, R. 1986. *A portrait of the Israeli soldier*. Westport, Conn.: Greenwood Press.

Grinker, R. R., and J. P. Spiegel. 1945. *Men under stress*. Philadelphia: Blakiston.

Henderson, W. D. 1979. *Why the Vietcong fought: A study of motivation and control in a modern army in combat*. Westport, Conn.: Greenwood Press.

———. 1985. *Cohesion. The human element in combat*. Washington, D.C.: National Defense Univ. Press.

Keegan, J. 1976. *The face of battle*. London: Jonathan Cape.

Kellett, A. 1982. *Combat motivation: The behavior of soldiers in battle*. Boston: Kluwer-Nijhoff.

Marshall, S. L. A. 1946. *Men against fire*. New York: William Morrow.

Rachman, S. J. 1978. *Fear and courage*. San Francisco: W. H. Freeman.

Richardson, F. M. 1978. *Fighting spirit. A study of psychological factors in war*. London: Leo Cooper.

Shils, E. A., and M. Janowitz. 1948. Cohesion and disintegration in the Wehrmacht in World War II. *Public Opinion Quarterly* 12: 280–315.

Stouffer, S. A., E. A. Suchman, L. C. DeVinney, S. A. Star, and R. M. Williams. 1949. *Studies in social psychology in World War II*. Vols. 1 and 2. Princeton, N.J.: Princeton Univ. Press.

COMBAT SERVICE SUPPORT

The term *combat service support* describes certain types of support provided to combat forces during their operational training and on operations. The discussion that follows concentrates upon its applicability and use in land forces.

The combat arms (armored, armored reconnaissance, infantry, and certain army aviation elements) and the combat support arms (artillery, combat engineers, and certain signals elements) require combat service support to sustain them in carrying out their operational tasks on the battlefield (or in peacetime training on ranges and exercises). Without service support in conditions of active combat, the capability and endurance of all fighting and supporting troops directly involved in the battle are rapidly depleted.

The operational functions that can be generally classified as services that support combat are listed in alphabetical order below.

Administration	Civil affairs
	Operational manpower planning
	Personnel services and management (during operations)
	Prisoners of war
	Refugees

Communications	Field courier services
	Field postal services
	Signals, telecommunications, cipher
Information	Information systems (manual and computerized)
	Intelligence services
	Meteorology
	Public relations
	Survey and maps

Logistics (see Logistics: A General Survey)	Catering and canteen services
	Constructional engineering
	Labor
	Maintenance
	Medical and associated services*
	Mobilization, reinforcement, and replacement systems
	Movement (logistic)
	Munitions and explosives: engineering and handling
	Quartering
	Supply
	Transportation

* These are also part of personnel services under administration, but the casualty evacuation and treatment system in war is included under Logistics.

The internal management of units is often categorized as a part of administration. It is omitted from this list because, as a function, it is undertaken in all units: combat, combat support, and combat service support units.

No method of classification is entirely tidy or accurate, and that used in the list above relates to no specific army. Also, the following comments are necessary:

1. Army aviation helicopters and signal communications are used for combat, combat support, and combat service support purposes.
2. Military police and intelligence services also will operate in all three roles.
3. Most logistic functions listed above are also organic to combat and combat support units (for example, tank battalions have integral supply platoons).
4. The basis for classifying combat service support cannot be strictly related to

geographical or physical disposition on the battlefield. One cannot say that all combat units are forward and all logistic units are in the rear. For example, under the heading of maintenance, forward repair and recovery teams may well find themselves operating at times nearer to the enemy than the tank or infantry battalions they support.

The list contains functions where the main task and main organization are external to active combat: for example, logistic support is provided mainly to the rear of combat and combat support units, and the greater part of signals support is deployed likewise. Nevertheless, "areas of main task" is a convenient criterion; although modern warfare often delineates no front lines and rear areas, the system is useful for classification purposes.

All the functions listed above are described in greater detail elsewhere in this publication.

J. H. SKINNER

SEE ALSO: Combat Support; Engineering, Military; Logistics: A General Survey; Maintenance; Meteorology, Military.

Bibliography

Historical Evaluation and Research Organization (HERO). 1966. *Historical analysis of wartime replacement requirements: Experience for selected major items of combat equipment.* 2 vols. Washington, D.C.: HERO.

Huston, J. A. 1967. *The sinews of war: Army logistics, 1775–1953.* Washington, D.C.: Government Printing Office.

U.S. Department of the Army. 1970. *Field Manual 101-10: Staff officers' field manual—organizational, technical, and logistic data.* Washington, D.C.: Government Printing Office.

COMBAT STRESS

In spite of the vast changes characterizing battlefields from ancient days to the modern time—changes in weapons systems, communications, transportation, tactics, scope, and duration—there is one aspect that underwent no change or modification. This is man's endurance of the horror of battle. Furthermore (as one noted warrior wrote to one noted historian), while "the principles of strategy and tactics, and the logistics are absurdly simple, it is the 'actualities of war'—the effects of tiredness, hunger, fear, lack of sleep, weather . . .—that make war so complicated and so difficult, and are usually so neglected by historians" (Connell 1965). Historical records notwithstanding, the issue of the stress of combat is, apparently, as old as combat itself.

Defining combat stress is a difficult task for several reasons. First, it is a multifaceted concept, comprising many dimensions and numerous variables. Second, "combat stress" can serve as either a cause (e.g., severe combat conditions) or a consequence (e.g., combat exhaustion). It can be viewed as objective stimuli (e.g., weather conditions, enemy fire, battlefield noises), as an observable response (e.g., fear, panic, breakdown), or as a subjective experience ("horror," "an exciting affair," "hell"). Thus, a proposed definition, albeit somewhat vague, is the following: *Combat stress is the accumulated effect of all the adverse conditions operating in combat, as they are appraised by the combatant and as they are reflected by his modes of response, ways of coping, and levels of performance.*

Combat Stress Conditions

The conglomeration of adverse conditions operating in combat can be categorized, schematically, into the following five categories:

1. *Physical factors:* Cold, heat, rain, snow, altitude, humidity, storms; extreme noise, density, compression, suppression, darkness, brightness; NBC (nuclear, biological, and chemical)-condition poisoned environment.
2. *Physiological factors:* Fatigue; lack of sleep, disturbed sleep; hunger; poor, cold, or monotonous food; lack of water; thirst; disturbed circadian rhythm.
3. *Battle-related factors:* Night versus day conditions; defensive versus offensive posture; surprise, unfamiliarity, uncertainty; monotony, prolonged anticipation, attrition; intensity of fire; duration of combat exposure; shortage of manpower, equipment, ammunition.
4. *Psychological factors:* Fear of death, being wounded, or captured; scenes of death, destruction, mutilation, violence; lack of confidence in equipment, leaders, group, oneself; lack of morale, bonding, and commitment.
5. *Personal factors:* Concerns about health and welfare of loved ones; marital, economic, or personal problems; weak personality, traumatic experience, sense of incompetence.

Several points should be emphasized regarding the above categorization. First, some of the above-mentioned factors, for example, climate conditions, are not necessarily born in combat, but they affect combat performance. When combatants are rapidly transported to a new and harsh environment with extreme weather conditions, they must first adjust or acclimatize to the new environment before performing at their optimum (Krueger 1991). Similarly, tank crews, fighter pilots, sailors, and many other types of combatants are all severely affected by physical conditions and environmental stressors that only add to the actual stresses of combat.

Second, for many of the combat stress conditions it is the cumulative, rather than the acute, impact that affects combat performance. A short exposure to extreme temperature, a single experience of prolonged sleep loss, or even a first encounter with one or two casualties may not have a significant impact on combat efficiency. However, sustained operations, repeated exposures to death and destruction, and accumulated fatigue and exhaustion become critical to soldiers' effectiveness.

A study of Allied soldiers in Normandy in 1944 attempted to assess a schematic curve (Fig. 1) of combat efficiency under prolonged combat stress (Swank and Marchand 1946). Other observers (Beebe and Appel 1958) of the Second World War estimate the average point at which "the doughboy completely wears out" to be in the region of 200 to 240 aggregate combat days.

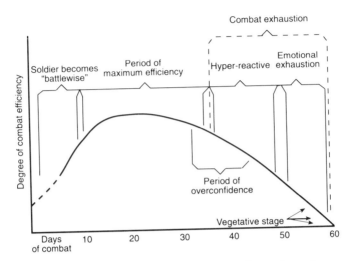

Figure 1. Assessment of combat efficiency under prolonged combat stress. (SOURCE: Swank and Marchand 1946)

Third, it should be noted that some of the above-listed combat conditions may serve as either stressors or supporters—depending on their particular interaction with the combatant. For example, while low morale and lack of unit cohesion can have devastating effects on combat soldiers, high morale and a cohesive unit may serve as "force multipliers" under combat conditions. The sight of mutilated bodies and other war atrocities may cause depression and incapacitation to some combatants, while for others they may strengthen fighting motivation and the will to take revenge and beat the enemy.

Finally, it is important to note that none of these factors directly determines the soldier's combat behavior (i.e., his responses, coping, and performance). Rather, they are mediated by other variables, mostly cognitive in nature, in molding and shaping the soldier's perception of the situation. Of paramount importance in the soldier's expectation or interpretation of the immediate situation are the roles his commanders and leaders play in providing the information concerning the impending military situation. Of equal importance is the soldier's previous experience and his sense of competence. Thus the way in which he is briefed before combat, interacting with his self-confidence, will strongly color his evaluation, or *appraisal*, of both the nature of his stress and his ability to handle it (Gal 1988).

Responses to Combat Stress

The individual's initial modes of response while confronting a combat situation reflect the immediate result of this process of cognitive appraisal. The responses may be divided into the traditional categories of physical, emotional, cognitive, and social.

PHYSICAL

These responses include autonomic changes (tachycardia, vasoconstriction, sweating, increased gastrointestinal motility); musculoskeletal (increased tonicity and perfusion of blood to muscle); gastrointestinal (nausea, vomiting, dry mouth, diarrhea); and glandular changes (release of medullary and cortical hormones from the adrenal glands, producing many of the foregoing effects).

EMOTIONAL

Emotional responses are expressed in a variety of affective reactions, varying from enthusiastic excitement to apprehensive fear, anxiety, or depression. In extreme cases, manic reactions and panic behavior may occur.

COGNITIVE

Included in these responses are distortion of perception with narrowing of attention span, hyperalertness to certain stimuli, and increased utilization of automatic or overlearned responses. More specifically, under conditions of sustained operations, combined with fatigue and sleep loss, the typical response is of degraded performance and mission effectiveness; reduced reaction time; decreased vigilance; and increasing difficulties in concentration and decision making.

SOCIAL

Social responses are characterized by increased dependency on leadership and need of affiliation, sometimes expressed by seeking reassurance and physical clustering. Negative aspects may be an increased tendency to make demands and irritability.

All of the above reactions are universal. Soldiers' modes of response under combat conditions are relatively involuntary or automatic, immediate and brief. In contrast, the combatant's ways of coping with the stress of combat are more flexible, relatively controllable, and may be delayed and prolonged.

Coping with Combat Stress

The most important aspect in soldiers' coping behavior under combat conditions is the active-passive dimension (Gal and Lazarus 1975). While activity conquers fear and enhances performance, passivity paralyzes the combatant and may result in a breakdown.

The active mode of coping may take various forms. During combat anticipation (almost always present on the battlefield), activity may take the form of preparation, checking gear and plans, last-minute details, and so on. Such activities serve as successful coping behavior since they discharge the accumulating tension and distract the individual from considering the death or wounding that may await him in battle. Activity, particularly when it takes the form of combat preparations, also gives the soldier a sense of mastery over the situation, thus diminishing anxiety.

During combat, the active coping mode is seen in purposeful, goal-oriented behavior by the combat soldier, such as seeking shelter, firing weaponry, and scanning or scouting the terrain. Similarly, the combat support soldier will stay active in his respective duties. The significance of this active mode is not only in a successful accomplishment of the mission; it is the most functional and effective behavior for the soldier's own well-being.

Inactivity, on the other hand, or complete passivity in the combat situation, is manifested by decreased movements, relative apathy to the surroundings and mission, and lack of initiative. A consequence of this unsuccessful coping mode is not only a failure to perform effectively but also a beginning of a psychological collapse, exhibited by increasing fatigue, mounting anxiety, and a sense of burnout. The ultimate result of a passive mode of coping may be a complete breakdown, whether labeled combat reaction, battle shock, or war neurosis. This breakdown occurs when the soldier's preoccupation with his own anxieties leads to complete incapacitation.

Combat Stress Reactions

Combat stress reactions (CSR) is the generic term for the various forms (i.e., psychic, somatic, or behavioral) of nonphysical casualties in combat (Noy 1991). It is a broad term that includes within its scope soldiers with preexisting mental disorders whose condition is reactivated or exacerbated by exposure to combat, soldiers who become psychologically dysfunctional because of their injuries or wounds, and soldiers who experience psychiatric breakdown under combat conditions.

The history of war and combat in the last century and a half has seen a variety of names and terms for CSR. In the American Civil War, if a soldier were chronically morose, lost his appetite and stamina, and were unable to function well, he was diagnosed as suffering from "nostalgia." In prerevolutionary Russia, medical officers were discussing "diseases of the soul" among their soldiers, while their American counterparts referred to the same syndrome as "neurasthenia." For World War I doctors, CSR casualties looked shocked, especially when stumbling out from the heavily bombarded trenches, hence the label "shell shock." As that long war ensued, a new term—"war neurosis"—evolved. These terms from World War I gave way to "combat fatigue" or "combat exhaustion" in World War II, reflecting the growing attention paid to the effects of excessive exposure to the demands of combat. Indeed, *every* soldier was thought to have his own breaking point if he remained in combat too long.

In the Korean conflict and later in the Vietnam War, incidence of classic CSR was reduced (partially due to rotation policies that limited the individual's degree of exposure to the stress of combat), but other forms of dysfunctional behavior (primarily substance abuse) were noted. A new generic term—"psychiatric casualties"—was assigned to include the wide range of stress-related disorders. Subsequently, growing numbers of delayed stress reactions in soldiers who had participated in those conflicts have become a major concern. The new term—"post traumatic stress disorder," known as PTSD—was established in 1980 by the American Psychiatric Association and was applied, among others, to war veterans with war-related behavioral disorders.

CSR is a covariant of battle casualties or combat intensity: the greater the intensity of battle—that is, the number of wounded and killed in action—the greater the number of CSR cases and the more rapid the onset of the disorder. Based on various war experiences, it can be predicted that in high-intensity conventional warfare, at least one CSR casualty will occur for every four battle casualties during the initial 30-day period (Chermol 1983). However, in some extreme cases of fierce battle (such as several operations in the Pacific theater in World War II), the percentage was almost one psychiatric CSR to every wounded soldier. Israeli researchers (Noy 1991) even reported a ratio of 1 wounded to 1.2 CSR casualties in a severely hit armor battalion in the Lebanon war of 1982. As to future battlefields, it is estimated that the psychiatric-to-battle-casualty ratios in a sustained nonconventional war will range from 1:3 to 1:2 for the first few days; for sustained nuclear, biological, and chemical (NBC) warfare, it is predicted that CSR casualties will far exceed other battle casualties (Chermol 1983).

Effects on Units

Obviously, combat stress affects not only individual combatants but also entire units. Systematic observations on fighting units, such as the conspicuous reports about the American soldier (Stouffer et al. 1949), suggest that continued engagement in combat, especially when casualty rates are high, adversely affects unit morale and combat motivation. When a combat unit is losing men and leaders, its tight-knit cohesiveness is at risk of loosening. Since unit cohesion is imperative both for combat performance and as a support system, deteriorated cohesion can be perilous for a fighting unit. New replacements, whether troops or leaders, only worsen the situation when they arrive amid fighting activities.

Extreme combat stress, however, not only impairs bonding and morale; in some cases it may result in the complete disintegration of a unit, caused by total exhaustion (of manpower, equipment, or fighting spirit) or panic and disbandment. One of the notorious examples of the latter is the panic reactions of the frontline brigades of two French divisions who were attacked by chlorine gas near Ypres, Belgium, on 22 April 1915. As the cloud of gas drew close to the French lines, men began dropping their rifles and running in every direction. Officers were powerless to stop them. A full-scale, contagious panic swept away entire units from the front line (Hammerman 1987).

Thus combat stress affects not only a whole unit's effectiveness and its ability to accomplish its missions, but foremost it jeopardizes the unit's morale, cohesion, leadership, and fighting spirit. These qualities are, in fact, the most important tools to prevent combat stress adversity.

Preventive and Treatment Measures

The most potent factors in preparing the soldier for the horrors of combat and maintaining him in the front are the very nature of the military organization—unit structure, leadership, discipline—and the soldier's own feeling of responsibility to the group. Most preventive measures do not occur in combat but long before. Realistic training, building confidence in one's equipment and in oneself, self-discipline, strong leadership, and high levels of morale and commitment are in fact the stress-inoculation provisions issued by the military organization to its combatants. Other factors, such as religion and patriotism, adequate information, and well-being at home, all play a role in counteracting the fear and coping with the stress of combat. However, the single most important factor that motivates men against fire, one that sustains men in combat and enables them to resist the effects of cumulative combat stress, is the desire not to let down one's fellow unit members and the powerful psychological support that men receive from their immediate primary group, that is, the squad, platoon, or company.

Indeed, it is also the power of the soldier's small unit that is utilized in managing acute CSR cases during war. The three most important principles for the traditional treatment of combat stress casualties were derived from World War I experiences (Salmon 1919) and are abbreviated as PIE: treatment should be in *proximity* to the unit and to the battle zone; intervention should occur *immediately* after the breakdown; and the *expectancy* of prompt return to the unit should be emphasized throughout the treatment.

Summary

The foregoing description of combat stress and its aftermath pertains primarily to conventional wars. The lessons learned regarding treatment, prevention, and coping with combat stress are mainly derived from actual experiences. However, no historical experience can safely prepare us for the potential impact of future warfare. While the combatant of tomorrow will basically be the same human being as his ancestor was, the battlefield of the future will impose much greater stress and demands. Weapons systems will become more and more lethal; NBC warfare will make lethality not only greater and faster, but will engender much greater uncertainty and unfamiliarity; and battles will extend over great distances—with no place to hide—and over long periods of time, with little opportunity to sleep or eat. Communication will be disrupted or destroyed, and leadership might be cut off from troops.

The answer to these growing demands is to improve preventive measures: increase soldiers' confidence in their equipment, in their leaders, and in themselves; strengthen unit morale, cohesion, and bonding among troops; and, most important, prepare leaders and troops who can cope effectively with uncertainty, who can tolerate ambiguity, and who can perceive, understand, and react to novelty.

REUVEN GAL

SEE ALSO: Leadership; Morale.

Bibliography

Beebe, G. W., and J. W. Appel. 1958. *Variation in psychological tolerance to ground combat in World War II*. Washington, D.C.: National Academy of Sciences.

Chermol, B. H. 1983. Psychiatric casualties in combat. *Military Review* 58, July, pp. 26–32.

Connell, J. 1965. Writing about soldiers. *Journal of the Royal United Services Institute* (Field-Marshal Lord Wavell to military historian Basil Liddel Hart), August, p. 244.

Gal, R. 1988. Psychological aspects of combat stress: A model derived from Israeli and other combat experiences. In *Proceedings of Sixth Users' Workshop on Combat Stress*, ed. A. D. Mangelsdorf. Report no. 88-003, August. Fort Sam Houston, Tex.: U.S. Army Health Care Studies and Clinical Investigation Activities.

Gal R., and R. S. Lazarus. 1975. The role of activity in anticipating and confronting stressful situations. *Journal of Human Stress* 1(4):4–20.

Hammerman, G. 1987. The psychological impact of chemical weapons on combat troops in World War I. In *Proceeding of Defence Nuclear Agency Symposium/Workshop on the Psychological Effects of Tactical Nuclear Warfare*, eds. B. H. Drum and R. H. Young, Technical Report, SAIC (contract no. DNA 001-86-C-0295), July.

Krueger, G. P. 1991. Environmental factors and military performance. In *Handbook of military psychology*, ed. R. Gal and A. D. Mangelsdorff. Chichester: Wiley.

Noy, S. 1991. Combat stress reactions. In *Handbook of military psychology*, ed. R. Gal and A. D. Mangelsdorff. Chichester: Wiley.

Salmon, T. W. 1919. The war neuroses and their lessons. *New York Journal of Medicine* 59:993–94.

Stouffer, S. A., L. C. DeVinney, S. A. Star, and R. M. Williams. 1949. *Studies in social psychology in World War II. Vol. 2, The American soldier: Combat and its aftermath*. Princeton, N.J.: Princeton Univ. Press.

Swank, R. L., and W. E. Marchand. 1946. Combat neuroses: The development of combat exhaustion. *Archives of Neurology and Psychiatry* 55:236–47.

COMBAT SUPPORT

Combat support today is an essential part of the conduct of battle. The classical concept of operations is always based on the elements of combat, combat support, and combat service support. A successful battle is possible only if combat power (consisting of combat and combat support forces) can be brought to the decisive point of the battle in such a way that, at least for a short time, one's own forces can be stronger than the opposing forces. Combat service support provides the logistical backbone needed to conduct and sustain the battle.

Through history combat support has increased in importance. In former times close combat was supported mainly by weapons such as spears and arrows or by creating or overcoming obstacles and fortifications. The art of building fortifications and overcoming them, together with the need to build roads and bridges for military movement, required a specialization that nowadays is generally provided by engineers. Defending fortresses or breaching walls required machines to throw heavier shells. This, and the requirement for heavy fire against enemy troops, led to the creation of modern artillery. The invention of gunpowder greatly increased possibilities for using fire support over longer distances.

The major combat support areas up to the nineteenth century were engineering and fire support. Indirect fire support became possible and effective with the introduction of the field telephone in the late nineteenth century. The beginning of the twentieth century brought new technologies to the support of war fighting. The airplane created the opportunity to use the third dimension for reconnaissance and the employment of weapons systems as well as the need to destroy those means. The detection of the electromagnetic spectrum made possible new types of communication but also created the need to destroy or deceive communication links. Development of the helicopter after World War II provided additional capabilities to support battle. Every form of combat support (such as construction or the delivery of firepower or ammunition) creates a need to protect against and to counter that capability. Modern warfare is a complicated web of all factors involved in the battle.

Elements of Combat Support

An official military definition of the term *combat support* is not available, but NATO defines *support* as "the action of a force, or position thereof, which aids, protects, complements, or sustains any other force" (NATO 1983). This definition is applicable also to the classic combat support units or forces that are common to every kind of operation on the battlefield. These include fire support, engineering support, and air defense.

In warfare under nuclear, chemical, or biological conditions, specialized units for nuclear, biological, and chemical (NBC) defense provide the necessary NBC warning and defense measures.

In addition to specialized units for combat support on the ground, airborne systems such as aircraft and helicopters can be used for combat support. For example, air forces can deliver weapons and ammunition for use against enemy forces on the ground. These types of air operations are called offensive air support. Armed helicopters can conduct the battle on their own or in support of the ground forces.

The third pillar of combat support is specific operations such as tactical reconnaissance, suppression of enemy air defense (SEAD), and electronic warfare (EW). These operations support combat but in more general terms. The ongoing efforts in these areas have a large impact on the battle as a whole but only partially influence combat at the lower levels.

Combined-Arms Battle

In former times only a few elements—infantry, cavalry, and artillery—played a major part in the battle. Even then, the timely coordination of their actions, including surprise, deception, and initiative, were the basic conditions for success. In modern warfare specialization has occurred even within the small units of the land forces. Riflemen, snipers, machine gunners, antitank gunners, engineers, and forward observers for mortars and artillery can be found at the platoon and company levels. A battalion commander has to coordinate a large number of activities in his area of responsibility. These can include: his own organic companies (infantry or tank), an attached company (infantry or tank), a specialized antitank platoon, elements of army air defense, artillery observers, engineers, a forward air controller for close air support, and commander of an attack helicopter unit. A profound understanding of the interdependency of these elements will allow him to make the best use of his own combat units and the attached combat support units.

The lowest unit level where one finds organic combat support is in the infantry battalion. For example, mortars provide indirect fire support over a distance of about 6,000 meters (6,600 yd.). Especially for the infantry battle, it is helpful to add to the normal direct-fire weapons system the capability of hitting the enemy hidden behind fortifications or obstacles.

Independent combat support units can be found in brigades in most of the Western armies and in regiments in the former Warsaw Pact armies. Dependent on their size and specialization, combat support forces are integrated at brigade, division, or corps level.

At brigade level there are normally the following combat support units: one artillery battalion, one engineer company, and one antitank company.

At division level there are one artillery regiment/brigade with several artillery battalions; one engineer battalion, with bridging capabilities; one army air defense battalion/regiment; one reconnaissance/cavalry battalion; and one NBC defense unit.

At corps level there are specialized artillery units, specialized engineer units, combat helicopter units, and electronic warfare units.

Depending on the type of battle, higher echelons may detach elements of their combat support units to lower echelons for direct support, or they may attach liaison elements to lower levels for the coordination of combat support systems during the battle. The act of providing combat support by detaching specific units for a mission is called reinforcement.

Combat Support Systems

Fire support, engineering support, air defense, and NBC defense constitute the major combat support systems.

FIRE SUPPORT

Fire support is defined as the collective use of indirect-fire weapons, armed aircraft, and all available target-acquisition assets. The aim of fire support is to suppress, neutralize, or destroy targets. In addition it can be used to disrupt, to disorganize and delay, to inflict attrition, to harass or interdict, or to deny the use of an area or location.

Fire-support systems usually consist of the following three elements:

1. *Target acquisition.* Numerous battlefield assets acquire targets for fire-support systems. These may include, among other things, reconnaissance elements, forward observers, radar, sound and flash means, electronic warfare results, forces in contact, air and naval elements, and photography.

2. *Weapons and ammunition.* These include mortars, artillery, offensive air support aircraft, armed helicopters, and naval gunfire weapons.

3. *Command, control, and coordination.* Fire-support systems include those functions that ensure responsive, safe, and effective fire support (e.g., communications, survey, meteorology, gunnery, logistics, mobility, security and protection, liaison, and positioning). Control elements are normally provided for forward units by representatives from the appropriate fire-support units. Fire support must be coordinated to ensure maximum efficiency. The more precious the fire-support weapons system or ammunition, the greater the need for accurate coordination in the target area.

The principal types of fire support are described below.

Mortar support. Mortars are infantry weapon systems of various calibers. They are loaded from the muzzle by letting the ammunition slide to the bottom of the tube for self-ignition. They can provide a large amount of responsive, accurate, and sustained fire and are ideal weapons for attacking close-in targets and those on reverse slopes. They are also, however, easily detected by enemy radar because of their projectiles' high trajectory and long time in flight.

Artillery support. Artillery provides fire support with guns, rocket launchers, howitzers, missiles, and in the future with unmanned air vehicles (UAV).

Artillery support has several major advantages: it can provide support under nearly all conditions of weather and terrain; its fire can be shifted and concentrated rapidly over large distances; it gives the supported commander the ability to engage targets in depth; and it fires a variety of ammunition.

Artillery fire support has the following main objectives: (1) direct fire support of combat forces at the forward line of one's own troops—the fire is directed by forward artillery observers and can have high accuracy and efficiency; (2) counterbattery fire to destroy enemy artillery forces including their target acquisition means; and (3) long-range fire against air defense systems, command posts, logistical installations, reserve forces, and choke points of the movement network (such as bridges, road crossings, and railroad systems). The attack of targets in depth requires appropriate target acquisition for fixed targets and real-time target acquisition for moving targets. Successful fire by artillery weapon systems against enemy follow-on forces may effectively disrupt and delay the enemy advance.

Offensive air support. Offensive air support is part of the tactical air support of land operations and consists of tactical air reconnaissance, battlefield air interdiction, and close air support.

Tactical air reconnaissance acquires information by employing visual observation and/or sensors in air vehicles.

Battlefield air interdiction (BAI) acts against enemy ground targets that can directly affect friendly forces. While battlefield air interdiction missions require coordination in joint planning, they may not require direct coordination during the execution phase. BAI missions are generally directed against enemy forces beyond the range of artillery fire.

Close air support (CAS) is directed against enemy targets that are close to friendly forces and requires integration of each air mission with the fire and movement of those forces. CAS missions are limited by visibility and weather restrictions, by vulnerability to enemy air defenses, and by delayed response times or limited time available in the target area.

The use of CAS in modern warfare will gradually be reduced. On the one hand, enemy army air defense is highly effective against sophisticated modern aircraft; on the other hand, BAI missions against valuable targets in depth may be more effective. Modernized artillery systems (e.g., better target acquisition and longer-range, precision-guided ammunition) and attack or combat helicopters may increasingly replace close air support.

Fire support by armed helicopters. In most armies a helicopter unit is considered a member of the combined arms combat team. That is, although it operates in the airspace above and adjacent to the battlefield, it is considered a maneuver unit much like its armor and infantry counterparts. When providing fire support to a land force commander, helicopter units are normally placed under the temporary control of the land commander. This relationship enhances the ability of the supported land commander to integrate the helicopter fire support into his overall battle plan. Helicopters can also be assigned an area of responsibility, much like that of armor and infantry units, where they will be required to monitor enemy activity and engage any enemy forces found in the area with antiarmor missiles, rockets, and cannon or machine-gun fire. Helicopter units additionally can provide rapid mobility for infantry and lightly mechanized forces in an air assault role. In this role, transport helicopters would be escorted by heavily armed attack helicopters. The capability of helicopters to provide close air support from forward, unprepared field locations, to concentrate their extensive fire power, and to provide air mobility for other combat and support forces make them a highly versatile and vital element on the modern battlefield.

Naval gunfire. Maritime forces may provide fire support to land forces in the vicinity of the coast or to amphibious operations. The main elements of naval gunfire are accuracy, long range, high rate, and volume of fire; large-caliber, wide-area coverage; and fire support under all weather conditions. Specific communications must be established to transmit target data to the fire control centers.

ENGINEERING SUPPORT

To ensure maneuverability for the successful conduct of operations, a major effort must be made to maintain the mobility of one's own forces and to reduce the mobility of the enemy. Engineers assist in maintaining mobility, carry out countermobility tasks, and improve the survivability of forces. Timely and economical use of engineer resources is essential to ensure completion of the large amount of engineering tasks.

Mobility tasks. Engineers alter the terrain to permit the movement of forces and to hinder enemy movement. Mobility tasks include engineer reconnaissance of obstacles and routes, assistance to other forces in the crossing of obstacles, repair of bridges and roads, construction of bridges with bridging equipment, and breaching and clearing of obstacles that are beyond the capacity of the supported combat troops themselves.

Countermobility tasks. Engineers create or improve obstacles to the enemy in ways that exceed the capacity of the supported combat troops, particularly by the laying of minefields. They also hinder enemy mobility by demolition.

Survivability tasks. Engineers carry out tasks that improve the survivability of friendly forces. Such tasks include the construction of field fortifications, weapons' emplacements, and shelters for combat, combat support, and combat service support forces.

AIR DEFENSE

The aim of air defense is to provide protection against air attack and air reconnaissance (by aircraft and helicopters), thus increasing freedom of action for friendly forces.

There are two types of air defense: active and passive. Active air defense aims at destroying or reducing the effectiveness of enemy air attack. It employs antiaircraft guns, electronic countermeasures, and surface-to-air guided missiles. Passive air defense plays an essential role in minimizing the effects of enemy air action. This includes use of cover, concealment and camouflage, dispersion, and protective construction. Passive air defense is an essential task for units at all levels.

Army air defense must be able to respond quickly to the fleeting nature of air targets and the short engagement time available. The variety of enemy aerial systems requires a mix of complementary air defense systems covering low and medium altitudes. Air defense must have sufficient mobility to provide adequate defense to both static and moving forces.

Terrain may influence mobility and radar coverage of air defense systems. Weather may affect the identification and engagement of enemy aircraft. Air defense systems need to be given priority when units are choosing suitable positions.

Units on the move are vulnerable to detection and subsequent attack by enemy aircraft or helicopters. Therefore air defense of such units is critical. It can be accomplished by providing units on the move with integrated air defense assets or by protecting their move with pre-positioned air defense forces along the route. Choke points and important crossing sites need continuous and effective air defense coverage, whenever possible with all-weather capabilities.

Because there are limited numbers of air defense units available to protect all forces, strict priorities must be set out for their tasks. Forces must be prepared to defend themselves against air attack using all available weapons. The range or airspace covered by modern weapons is so great that planning and execution of air defense operations must be both joint (land, sea, air) and multinational.

NUCLEAR, BIOLOGICAL, OR CHEMICAL (NBC) DEFENSE

NBC defense units support combat, combat support, and combat service support units by defensive measures under the threat of—or under conditions of—nuclear, biological, and chemical weapons' employment.

The tasks of NBC defense units are to support all forces in NBC defense; to reconnoiter contaminated terrain; to decontaminate personnel, equipment, and, to a limited degree, roads and military installations; and to set up an NBC reporting and warning system at various levels of command.

Effective NBC defense requires the following conditions:

• knowledge of the characteristics and effects of NBC weapons and the conditions under which they might be used
• knowledge of the potential enemy's delivery means and his current NBC doctrine
• well-conditioned troops with a high standard of personal hygiene
• high standard of individual and collective training in NBC measures
• detection, identification, and warning systems
• individual and collective protective equipment
• adequate medical support
• contamination control procedures, including avoidance, protection, and decontamination for personnel, supplies, and equipment
• NBC defense organization appropriate to the level of command.

Tasks in Support of the Battle

In addition to combat support provided by specialized combat support units and weapons systems, other tasks must be fulfilled that support the battle. They may or may not be executed by specialized units or systems. Some armies describe them as general tasks in combat. They comprise reconnaissance, suppression of enemy air defense, and electronic warfare.

RECONNAISSANCE

Reconnaissance is a mission to obtain, by visual observation or other detection methods, information about the activities and resources of the enemy or to secure data concerning the meteorological, hydrographic, or geographic characteristics of a particular area.

The primary objective of reconnaissance is to discover the type, strength, organization, behavior, and actions of enemy forces, their dispositions on the ground, and the direction and speed of their movements. Troop concentrations, firing positions of heavy weapons, nuclear delivery means, command posts, communication centers, field fortifications, barriers, and logistic installations are important reconnaissance targets.

Forces and means. Different forces and means available for reconnaissance purposes include the following:

- All troops carry out combat reconnaissance and report their findings.
- Armored reconnaissance units detect and keep in contact with the enemy. They often have to bypass or penetrate enemy forces. They obtain reconnaissance results by combat if necessary.
- Long-range reconnaissance forces reconnoiter in the depth of the enemy area.
- Target acquisition artillery conducts reconnaissance with its systems from friendly territory, and, with unmanned air vehicles, it penetrates into the enemy's area.
- Army air defense units conduct air surveillance, particularly of the lower airspace. They provide information on the local air situation.
- Signal intelligence forces operate on a wide front and deep into enemy territory. This type of reconnaissance is largely independent of the time of day and weather conditions. The more extensive and comprehensive the enemy's electronic emissions are, the better the results will be.
- Army aviation is responsive to the land force commander's requirements for information (subsequently processed into battlefield intelligence) about the terrain, climate, enemy dispositions/activities, route conditions, and so forth. This information is normally gathered and reported in a near-real-time manner to the land force battle staff. The degree of sophistication of army aviation's reconnaissance and information collection can vary from a pilot's report on visually acquired information to the use of more complex onboard systems such as electronic intelligence (ELINT) sensors, imaging and moving target indicating radar, night optics, and other electronic gathering systems.
- Air forces obtain a general view of the enemy within a short time through their fast and deep reconnaissance, providing immediate results. Visual observation, photographic reconnaissance, observation with photographic confirmation, and detection with electronic equipment are types of air reconnaissance.

Processing of reconnaissance results. Based on a reconnaissance plan the various levels of command employ their reconnaissance troops and means. The continuous flow of reconnaissance data will be processed within the headquarters to extract as quickly as possible results that can be used as primary reconnaissance for the decision-making process or in target acquisition for the immediate employment of weapon systems.

SUPPRESSION OF ENEMY AIR DEFENSE (SEAD)

A mix of SEAD measures is required to counter the variety of air defense measures that may be employed by the enemy. Only then can offensive air support missions, especially battlefield air interdiction and close air support, be flown effectively. The employment of helicopters over enemy territory also requires effective SEAD.

To suppress enemy air defense it is important to deny air defense target acquisition and the use of weapon systems to the enemy. Jamming or destruction of radar systems will prevent target acquisition. Indirect fire against the weapons systems will destroy them or at least interrupt their effective use for the time required to pass through the sector.

ELECTRONIC WARFARE (EW)

The purpose of electronic warfare is to reconnoiter and impair electromagnetic emissions of the enemy, to protect friendly electromagnetic emissions, and to deceive the enemy.

Army electronic warfare includes:

- signal (communications and electronic) intelligence
- electronic support measures
- electronic countermeasures
- electronic counter-countermeasures.

Electronic countermeasures in particular provide considerable support for the land battle. They are designed to jam the telecommunication links and the electronic detection, location, guidance, and control systems of the enemy, to impede his command and control and his reconnaissance, to mislead him by deception, and to render employment of his weapons more difficult. Used at the right time these countermeasures can considerably influence the course of the battle.

The execution of EW is primarily the task of signal troops. Electronic countermeasures are also employed by other arms and services, and electronic counter-countermeasures and protective measures are used by all units.

Coordination of Combat Support

The commander in any situation must know the combat support available to him, its capabilities, how best to employ it, and how its contribution can be adapted to his particular operation.

STAFF PROCEDURES

The operations order given to a commander usually contains the following parts: situation (enemy and own); mission (of the superior level); execution; logistics; and command and communications.

The part on execution contains the concept of the operations, the tasks assigned to the combat and combat support units, and coordinating measures. The operations order sets the framework for the freedom of action left to the commander and shows him which types of forces will support him.

Based on the situation and the combat and combat support forces available, the commander decides on his own concept of operations, including the main tasks for the combat support units and their coordination with the combat forces. Specific plans will be elaborated for the coordination and employment of artillery fire (fire plan) and for the construction of barriers (barrier plan).

COORDINATING MEASURES

Specific staff sections coordinate the employment of combat support means that cannot be placed at the exclusive disposal of subordinate commanders. Specialized staff officers assist the commanders at the various levels to employ these combat support forces and means most effectively. These forces mainly comprise additional artillery fire support, offensive air support, and support by attack/combat helicopters. Coordination is required for the efficient employment of NBC defense, army air defense, reconnaissance, suppression of enemy air defenses, and electronic warfare.

INTEROPERABILITY

To employ combat and combat support forces in the combined-arms battle requires a thorough understanding of these forces. Only by applying appropriate procedures will they be employed efficiently. In a multinational environment, interoperability is a prerequisite for the use of forces from one nation in support of those of another nation. Standardization and the establishment of agreed procedures facilitate the quick employment of forces for mutual support.

Technology

The modern equipment available to land forces continually increases the importance of combat support forces. Up to the nineteenth century infantry and cavalry were still the major components of the forces within a battle; artillery and engineer support could only marginally influence the outcome. During World War I the importance of artillery forces and engineers to the conduct of the battle increased significantly. Overwhelming firepower was used before combat forces were employed. The aim was to kill as much of the enemy as possible by indirect fire and to destroy his fortified positions. This massive use of firepower continued in World War II, was increased by large-scale air bombings, and culminated in the annihilation of hundreds of thousands of civilians by two nuclear bombs.

Modern warfare conditions allow the massive employment of conventional firepower only if one side has a large superiority. Weapons systems become more sophisticated and more expensive, and increasingly they facilitate the destruction of single targets. The circular error probable of long-range weapons systems is reduced by better guidance systems, and the hit probability will be increased by terminally guided warheads. Ammunition becomes ever more costly and therefore can no longer be stocked in huge quantities.

INDIRECT-FIRE SUPPORT

The major targets of indirect fire will be armored or semi-armored targets (e.g., battle tanks, armored combat vehicles, self-propelled artillery). For the disruption or delay of enemy forces the employment of barrier systems by rocket launch systems has great efficiency. Precise and real-time target acquisition is of utmost importance to achieve the maximum attrition with a minimum amount of ammunition. Modern technology, such as infrared and millimetric wave sensors, laser and directed-energy weapons, will have a great impact on future weapon systems.

ENGINEERING

The ability to establish barriers has been dramatically increased. Mine-laying methods (rocket launchers or tracked vehicles) allow the deployment of minefields over a large distance in a short time, even into enemy territory. Modern sensors will increase the ability to use hidden, single antitank weapons and allow the activation/deactivation of complete barrier systems.

AIR DEFENSE

High technology is increasingly needed by air defense units to match the capabilities of modern aircraft. This applies in particular to sectors for air surveillance and tracking sensors. Short reaction time, different flight profiles of enemy aircraft, and improved weaponry, in particular for longer ranges, require the full exploitation of future technology, especially in the field of electronics.

SUPPORT BY ATTACK AND COMBAT HELICOPTERS

Rapid advances are being made in composite-fiber construction of helicopter airframes and components that provide a less expensive, more easily repaired and maintained helicopter for combat operations. These new materials will enable helicopters to absorb more punishment, still accomplish their mission, and return to their bases. Additionally, advances in fire control now provide attack helicopters with the capability to fight at night and in the most adverse weather, as well as to integrate better their fire support with that of tactical air force aircraft. Substantial improvements have been, and are being, made with helicopter-launched munitions. Many of these munitions will evolve into fire-and-forget systems with improved lethality and enhanced accuracy.

Outlook

In the future the combined-arms battle will be the only way to conduct successful operations such as delay, defense, or attack. The main factor of the battle will no longer be a duel situation between battle tanks but will become the capability to combine combat and combat support systems into a flexible, highly mobile, and precise system. Achieving the best mix of target acquisition, direct and indirect fire, barriers, air defense, air mobility, and electronic warfare will require a great understanding of their employment principles, a highly flexible tactical concept, and excellent command, control, and communication systems.

Future technologies will reduce ever further the distinction between combat and combat support. A large array of highly precise ammunition affords the ability to destroy single enemy targets by indirect-fire weapons systems, thus supporting the tactical needs of the commander by hitting the enemy precisely at the right time and location. Nevertheless, only combat forces will remain capable of holding ground or regaining lost territory.

KLAUS KLEFFNER

SEE ALSO: Army Aviation; Artillery; Close Air Support; Engineering, Military; Ground Reconnaissance; Technology and Warfare.

Bibliography

NATO. 1983. *NATO glossary of terms and definitions.* AAP-6. Brussels: NATO Headquarters.
———. 1986. *Land force tactical doctrine.* ATP-35. Brussels: NATO Headquarters.

Sommer, D. 1989. Ein Wandel Kündigt sich an. *Truppenpraxis.* Bonn: Verlag Offene Worte.

U.S. Department of the Army. 1986. *Field manual 100-5: Operations.* Washington, D.C.: Government Printing Office.

Weitzel, H. 1989. Gefecht der verbundenen Waffen. Pt. 2, *Truppenpraxis.* Bonn: Verlag Offene Worte.

COMBINED ARMS

Combined arms in combined-arms operations means coordinated action by elements of different combat arms. The term is usually used in relation to combat activities at the tactical level, up to and including the division. The main characteristics of combined-arms combat are fire and movement. Effective employment of combined arms is assured by allocation of tasks in combat, as well as by training and education of personnel. The appropriate rules are provided as tactical operational principles in combat manuals.

Combined-arms combat has a centuries-old history. To effectively employ the weapons available (spears, swords, arrows) in a coordinated manner, an appropriate battle formation was necessary. This led initially to the employment of infantry, such as the Greek phalanx. With the development of war chariots and cavalry, a mobile element was added. The intention of military leaders was always to capitalize on the weaknesses of the opponent's battle formation and, at the same time, to improve the power and mobility of their own troops.

With the improvement of weapons and the introduction of the catapult and the arbalest (crossbow), combined arms and mobility changed in the eleventh and twelfth centuries. The forerunners of military engineers functioned as fortress constructors. The concept of combined arms was considerably influenced by the introduction of firearms in the fourteenth and fifteenth centuries. An optimum combination of firepower and mobility, together with an appropriate battle formation, led to the victory of the Swedes under their king Gustavus Adolphus (Gustavus II) near Breitenfeld on 7 September 1631 over the Catholic League Army under Tilly. Because of the battle's historical significance for combined-arms combat, an understanding of its essential characteristics is useful.

The most important weapon of the Swedish infantry was the musket. The pike, too, was a weapon of attack, but the main tasks of the pikemen were to protect the musketeers while they were loading and to fend off enemy cavalry. With its speed and shock power, the cavalry fulfilled two tactical functions: first, it prepared the way for the infantry; thereafter, it conducted the decisive thrust. The light artillery was assigned to the infantry brigades; the heavy artillery was positioned in front of the center. As a whole the organization, equipment, and training of the Swedish army were oriented toward an offensive employment of firearms. Gustavus Adolphus recognized that this required an optimum combination of the elements of firepower and mobility.

To this end, he developed forms of organization allowing combined arms combat and showing a degree of mobility and flexibility not known before that time, namely (1) the infantry brigade with supporting artillery and (2) the cavalry regiment with supporting infantry. These elements were suitable for the rapid conduct of attacks.

The further development of weapons technology in the succeeding centuries forced greater dispersion of battle formations. New branches of the military developed. Until World War II, however, the branches were organized as pure elements, except at divisional level. It was not until losses increased that mixed formations were created in the combat commands.

Combined-arms combat is characterized by the combat means employed, the development of which may change rapidly. This means that operational principles can become outdated very quickly. The development of new operational principles is time-consuming and involves the danger that tactical commanders may independently seek new and appropriate solutions. Such initiative leads almost inevitably to uncertainties and different views.

To employ combined arms as effectively as possible requires a thorough knowledge of the strengths and weaknesses of the different weapons systems and branches. They must be measured and evaluated in comparison with those of the opponent. The influences of time, weather, terrain, population, and the condition of the troops must be considered. Only by evaluating all these elements can combined arms be efficiently employed.

Employment in Tactical Combat Actions

The composition of combined arms is dependent on the objective of a tactical combat action.

In defensive operations, even if they are conducted dynamically, the point of main effort will be with the employment of armored and air defense weapons, as well as with obstacles. It is most important to compensate for weaknesses of the infantry by the strengths of armored forces and to prepare obstacles in such a manner that they do not impede later counterattacks.

In retrograde movements the more persistently the enemy is delayed and the more losses he incurs, the less important is the movement of the defending forces.

In offensive operations, it is decisive to coordinate the fire of both direct-fire combat troops and indirect-fire supporting units with the movement of the combat troops so that maximum power is concentrated at the point of decision. In all types of combat, combined arms must be employed in such a manner that the enemy's reserves and rear-area logistic assets are engaged as early as possible.

Movement, Fire, and Obstacles in the Combined Arms Battle

INFANTRY MOVEMENT

The capability of the infantry must be evaluated correctly, an extremely difficult task. For example, if employed together with other forces, it is important to know whether these are light, mechanized, armored, or special infantry forces like mountain infantry or paratroopers. To be able to develop the appropriate strengths effectively, the terrain and the environmental conditions must be favorable. To ensure the infantry maximum combat power, it must be equipped with a variety of weapons systems. Integrated weapons systems must be efficiently employed even at the lowest level: for example, the commander of an infantry fighting vehicle has control of its primary and secondary weapons (gun and machine gun), the infantrymen with their personal weapons, and antitank rockets or missiles. Efficient coordination of these varied systems has become so complicated that in the future it is likely that the characteristics of the single weapons system in an infantry fighting vehicle and a tank hunter-killer team will be optimized separately.

ARMOR

The infantry always requires support by other branches, and this is primarily the job of armor. Although the operational utility of main battle tanks (MBTs) was questioned because of the losses suffered at the hands of antitank guided missiles in the 1973 Arab-Israeli War, commanders in armies all over the world agree that the main battle tank will remain the principal factor in mobile combat. Accordingly, the protection (spaced, ceramic, and reactive armor, as well as protection against infrared and thermal reconnaissance and against nuclear, biological, and chemical weapons), mobility, and firepower of tanks are continuously improved. Advanced main battle tanks are capable of combining mobility with firepower by their ability to engage the enemy accurately while on the move. The first-hit probability is optimized by refinement of the gun stabilization system, the ranging systems, and the computer system for the firing data.

In battle against enemy tanks it is most important to establish a combination

Infantry forces and armored forces complement each other in all types of combat. Focusing on tank-infantry cooperation, it is apparent that infantry needs the mobile, protected firepower that tank and other armored systems can provide. This was the original reason for tank development, and it remains valid. On the other hand, tanks require infantry support. Such examples as the British in World War I (Cambrai) and the Israelis in the 1973 Arab-Israeli War demonstrate that tanks face an array of battlefield hazards that dictate the close support of infantry. Therefore, the two are mixed for appropriate combat missions. The disadvantages of this are that such attachments and detachments must be implemented separately and "team spirit" grows only slowly in command and employment of these integrated weapons systems. As a result, some armies in the East and the West now organically mix armored and infantry forces down to battalion level. Problems in logistics and training are outweighed by the advantage of having immediately available a smoothly coordinated instrument of combined arms for all types of combat.

In battle against enemy tanks it is most important to establish a combination of antitank systems of the infantry, tanks, antitank units, engineers, artillery, and air force and to commit those systems with mines, top-attack munitions, armor-piercing munitions, high-energy rounds, and other (intelligent) types of munitions at great distances. Sophisticated protection like reactive armor must be overcome by improved weapons systems, such as tandem warhead armor-piercing antitank missiles.

FIRE SUPPORT

The prerequisite for realizing movement is fire. It prepares and accompanies the attack. Technical developments allow firefights to be conducted over great distances. The improvement in ammunition as well as in target and firing procedures reduces the firing units down to a section or even to the single gun. Thus, the efficiency of integrated weapons systems is considerably enhanced. Armored artillery and mechanized artillery follow combat operations rapidly and take the opponent under fire with both point-blank and indirect fire.

This artillery was developed to attack multiple targets (soft, medium, and hard targets and airfields and bunkers) with ammunition that is optimized for the respective target (mines, bomblets, fuel air explosives, etc.). Thus the ammunition becomes very important in the combined arms battle and reduces the need to employ and endanger men. There is need for constant reevaluation of how man and technology can be integrated efficiently in the combined arms battle.

The most powerful type of weapon is the nuclear weapon. It imposes heavy losses on men and materiel and can drastically change the force ratio. This is less true of chemical and biological weapons, but these require protective measures that can have a restrictive effect on the employment of combined arms. The artillery is employed either as an integral component of the supported units or in separate supporting units. Most armies prefer a decentralized distribution, permitting flexible focus of firepower on points of main effort by attachments and detachments. However, the integration of artillery into combined arms units was especially utilized in the Warsaw Pact armies.

BARRIERS

The integration of obstacles into combined-arms operations has two objectives: slowing the movement of the opponent and reducing the size of the enemy force by attrition in all types of combat and especially in depth. Due to the technical capability of engineers, artillery, and air forces to lay antitank and antipersonnel mines quickly and over large areas, mine warfare in combined arms combat now receives increasing attention. Sensors considerably improve the effectiveness of mines and inhibit clearing. Thus the commitment of mine-clearing systems has to be planned and coordinated skillfully in time and space in wide-ranging operations.

Use of the Third Dimension in the Combined Arms Battle

Due to the high density of weapons systems on the battlefield and the efforts to increase mobility, many armies use the third dimension to an increasing extent for the employment of combined arms. In principle, there are two possible ways to achieve this: one is to allocate air assets on a limited basis, in both time and space, to the army, navy, or assault landing forces; the other is to integrate them organically at the tactical level, usually into the divisions.

The development of using the third dimension by employing rotary- and fixed-wing aircraft in cooperation with branches and weapons systems of the army deserves special attention. The advantage of the air forces is their ability to conduct missions within a short period of time and to change locations rapidly. As flying platforms, aircraft are suitable for reconnaissance (photo, infrared, radar, television, and electronic), antitank warfare, electronic warfare, artillery direction, mine warfare, logistics, casualty evacuation, and troop transportation, including heavy weapons and equipment.

The West German army, for example, optimized the role of the helicopter in the integration of the weapons systems with respect to antitank warfare. The Soviet armed forces strengthened its air assets in such a manner as to accomplish numerous individual tasks together with the weapons systems of the ground forces, as well as independent missions of airmobile forces conducting combined-arms combat limited in time and space. In close air support, combat helicopters and fighter-bombers are closely integrated with the artillery into the first support plan. As integrated weapons systems in the third dimension, they can undertake combat operations by themselves or together with ground forces into the depth of enemy space as early as possible. Figure 1 shows the organization chart of such a task force.

The initial phase of the 1982 Israeli invasion of Lebanon is a classic example of a rapidly conducted, fully mobile operation of combined arms with all services participating. The Israeli ground forces were efficiently supported by largely integrated weapons systems of air and naval forces. Many armies have drawn conclusions from this campaign. Thus, for the first time in 1985, the U.S. Marine Corps conducted a combined-arms exercise with all the services participating at brigade level. This exercise showed that the battalion is the basic unit for the employment of combined arms. Only there is it possible to achieve the maximum integration of weapons systems in changing combat situations; in changing environmental conditions; under conditions of communication elec-

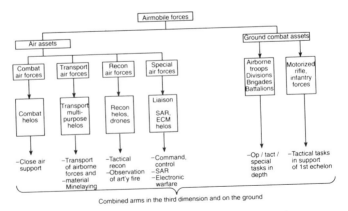

Figure 1. *Combined arms in an airmobile task force.*

tronics warfare; and under possible nuclear, biological, and chemical (NBC) warfare conditions. Since then, the technical developments and the pressure of the combat activities proceeding even more rapidly have involved an adjustment of the operational principles and the tables of organization and the tables of organization and equipment (TO & E). This can, again, be demonstrated by the example of an air mobile task force (AMTF) of the U.S. Marine Corps. The objective of this organization is to integrate weapons systems and branches even more efficiently for all types of combat. The AMTF possesses all elements of combined arms to enable it to act independently and to a limited extent with respect to time and space or to be supported by other weapons systems in major actions.

A similar organization is found in the so-called rapid reaction forces of different countries. In France, this is the Force d'Action Rapide (FAR); in Italy, the Forza di Pronto Intervento (Of.P.I.); in the United States, the Rapid Deployment Force (RDF). Their common feature is the integration of weapons systems and branches of the army, navy, and air force in a composition that is implemented according to the situation; the coordination of the integration of weapons systems is achieved to a maximum extent under unified command.

As the use of airpower has increased, the importance of air defense, together with integrated weapon systems, has increased. It is no longer sufficient for aircraft to protect combined-arms forces at the front; protection of the airspace in rear areas is also of great importance. The threat imposed by airborne weapon systems is complex and includes reconnaissance and combat drones, combat helicopters, and fighter-bombers as well as guided and unguided tactical missiles. In addition to close integration of air defense of all branches into combined arms combat, this required tactical missile/antitactical ballistic missile defensive power. A mixture of tube and rocket air defense weapons is required against low-flying aircraft. The Soviet antiair weapons system 2S6 (ZSU-30-2 Tunguska) is one solution. Examples from the Israeli invasion of Lebanon show clearly the vulnerability of target acquisition and target-tracking radars to electronic measures (EM) used for air-defense suppression (ADS) and the weapon effect involved. This requires an improvement of EM strength to avoid leaving gaps in combined arms that cannot be filled.

Electronic Warfare

This leads us to the role of electronic warfare in combined-arms combat. Each individual military commander must take appropriate and timely measures in order to successfully suppress enemy radioelectronic methods and to protect his own transmissions from enemy suppression. The effective employment of combined arms and the success of the force as a whole will largely depend on the outcome of these electronic combat operations.

In the former Warsaw Pact armies, electronic warfare served the additional purpose of reconnoitering enemy targets and engaging them immediately. This required new protective measures for weapons systems and facilities transmitting electromagnetic radiation. At the same time, this threat can result in limitations on the employment of combined arms.

Command and Control Organization

Combined-arms combat operations can be successful only with the close cooperation of all weapons systems and branches involved and with minimal time delays. The use of new technologies of information transfer and processing leads from combined arms to complete integration of all the components involved in combat. This battlefield management is based on merged command, control, communication, and intelligence systems (C^3I systems). Within this system, all the reconnaissance and weapons systems essential to combat as well as headquarters are linked with each other. The objective is to reduce the time factor as much as possible, that is, to minimize the time between recognizing and processing of a situation, preparing decisions for the operational order, and implementing the order.

It is most important to coordinate tactical movements of fire-support and combat support units horizontally and vertically in such a way that a maximum amount of combat power is always available for combat. For example, the success achieved by Field Marshal Rommel at Gazala in North Africa against the much stronger British Eighth Army of General Ritchie during World War II was based on the application of this principle. During the battle, General Ritchie never activated more than 10 to 20 percent of the forces of his army.

An example of a vertical synchronization is the reconnaissance/fire complex. Reconnaissance sensors of the forward observer, artillery detection devices, or electronic sensors deliver real-time target data to a fire-direction center. There, the firing data are automatically calculated and transmitted to a weapons system. Thus, only a minimum of time elapses between reconnaissance and the engagement of a target. In the former Soviet armed forces, this coordination at the tactical level was called RUK (*razvedyvatelno-Udarnyj-kompleks*) and at the operational level ROL (*razvedyvatelo-ognevoj-kompleks*). It was intended to achieve a considerable increase of weapon effectiveness with lesser forces and means than needed previously and within a shorter period of time. A fundamental change of the force ratio can considerably facilitate the subsequent movement of combat troops.

Comparable vertical combined-arms systems exist for the employment of air defense, engineers, communications, intelligence, and logistics.

The horizontal synchronization of all these measures links combat power to concentrated actions and integrates them with the tactical movements. For improved utilization of the third dimension, the tactical air forces were included in these procedures to an increasing extent.

The consistent buildup of the C^3I systems and their involvement with each other are essential prerequisites for speedy integration of combat actions against enemy forces in combined-arms combat. The objective is to gain the initiative in inflicting losses on the enemy at the front and in depth simultaneously, restricting his capabilities to employ his weapons and troops in a synchronized way. For this procedure, the air-land battle doctrine was developed by the U.S. armed forces and the follow-on forces attack (FOFA) doctrine by NATO.

STAFFS

Staffs are the instruments of the military commander that enable him to conduct combined-arms combat. In principle, there are two solutions for achieving coordinated employment of direct-fire, combat firepower, combat support (CS), and combat service support (CSS) units. In the first, the commander of a firepower, CS, or CSS unit is also the adviser of the commanding officer concerning all matters with respect to his branch. At the same time, he translates his intentions and decisions into orders to be given to his unit. This facilitates appropriate cooperation according to the situation in the conduct of combined-arms combat at the respective tactical level (horizontal synchronization). This solution is applied by most NATO armies.

The second solution provides the integration of a field grade officer in the staff for each branch and CSS activity. He carries out staff functions related to his specialized branch or activity but passes on the decisions and orders of the military commander to the CS and CSS unit commanders. The advantage of this system is that it facilitates attaching elements for reinforcement or shifting elements to establish a main effort at another place, thus changing the composition of combined arms rapidly and according to the situation. The disadvantage is that the intention of the superior commander cannot be transferred as rapidly to the CS or CSS unit. This can result in more details in the issuance of orders and in a more rigid command. This solution was used by the Warsaw Pact armies.

COMMAND BY ORDER OR BY MISSION

The dilemma of the employment of combined arms lies in the degree of centralization or decentralization of responsibility by order-type tactics on the one hand and mission-type tactics on the other. The effects of the German mission-type tactics in World War II are well known. However, the more complex combined arms become and the more rapidly and precisely the C^3I systems work, the more detailed must be the cooperation between individual weapons systems and branches that is planned by the military commander with respect to time and space. If, in combat, elements are unavailable in the vertical or horizontal synchronization and if the commanders of weapons systems and elements are dependent on their own resources, they are expected to act in the sense of the mission received and according to the intention of the superior commander. This requires initiative, readiness to take risks, and a cooperative attitude, as well as a full understanding of the process of coordinating weapons and force in the respective area of responsibility.

TRAINING

The inculcation of such capabilities in commanders and troops is the objective of training pursued by military commanders at all tactical levels. As a basis, the characteristics and capabilities and the strengths and weaknesses of all the individual elements of combined arms are taught, and the cooperation of the separate elements is practiced under difficult conditions. The British army uses training bases in Canada for its battle group training. It is increasingly difficult for many armies to find suitable training areas; on the one hand, more space is needed to accommodate the greater range of viable weapons while, on the other hand, available space is ever more constrained due to urbanization and budget limitations. Added to this is the rising cost of more sophisticated weapons and of employing them over larger areas. These problems have led to the development and use of simulation facilities for the conduct of combined-arms combat. At the same time, commanders and staffs are using computer models to simulate battlefield activities, from direct-fire individual weapons systems situations to the employment of troops in division and corps strengths.

DISCIPLINE AND MORALE

Sophisticated weapons systems and complex branches require disciplined troops. The soldier who shows strict external but essentially functional discipline must become a link in a chain of functions that must work as planned. Failure of an individual to perform as expected can lead to accidents or breakdowns of weapons systems.

Good morale, with the troops identifying themselves with the combat objectives, the army, and their country, improves their performance in combined-arms combat. Leadership ability and style can influence morale considerably. Knowing that they can depend upon a well-organized medical service can encourage troops as well (for example, the Israeli army in the Arab-Israeli War of 1967).

COMMAND SUPERVISION AND CONTROL

Command supervision and control contribute to the success of combined-arms combat. The more rapidly and comprehensively the responsible military commander can become aware of frictions, irregularities, losses, and success, the more efficiently he can react to them.

Above all, the commander must be aware of the primacy of the human factor in war. The human being is responsible for planning, organizing, and realizing the cooperation of combined arms and controls the results with his creative intellect, his will, his ideas, and his many weaknesses. Despite the high technology of weapons systems and command and control methods, leadership is an art, an activity that is based on character, efficiency, and spiritual power.

STURMHARD EISENKEIL

SEE ALSO: Air-land Battle; Blitzkrieg; Joint Operations; Mechanized Warfare.

Bibliography

Cardwell, T. A. 1985. Air land battle revisited. *Military Review*, September, pp. 4–13.
De Puy, W. E. 1984. The case for synchronization: Towards a balanced doctrine. *Army*, November.
Eshel, D. 1986. Modern inter-arms concepts IDF Organisation: The Yom Kippur war and after. *Defense Update*, 69.
Hanifen, T. C. 1986. The airmobile-mechanized task force. *Marine Corps Gazette*, August, pp. 56–60.

Maybee, J. S. 1985. The theory of combined-arms Lanchester-type model of warfare. *Naval Research Logistics Quarterly* 2:225–37.

Monteverde, R. 1985. The Soviet combined-arms reinforced battalion. *Military Technology*, October, pp. 180–87.

Onge, R. J. 1985. *The combined arms role of armored infantry.* Fort Leavenworth, Kans.: U.S. Army Command and General Staff College.

Reznichenko, V. G. 1984. *Taktika.* Moscow: Militärbuchverlag.

Ritschard, P. 1985. Über das Gefecht der Verbundenen Waffen. *Allgemeine Schweizer Militärzeitschrift*, 2–4.

Schaefer, W. 1985. Gepanzerte Kampftruppen-heute und morgen. *Wehrtechnik* 2:23–37.

Seredin, P. 1984. Osnovy obschtscherojskovogo boja (The combined arms doctrine). *Znamenosec* 2:24.

Starry, D. A. 1987. Combined arms. *Armor*, May, pp. 21–22.

U.S. Department of the Army. 1984. *Field manual 100-5: Operations.* Washington, D.C.: Government Printing Office.

Whitton, T. L. 1983. The changing role of air power in Soviet combined arms doctrine. *Air University Review*, March/April, pp. 180–87.

COMMAND

The word *command* has at least four military usages in the English language: as a noun denoting (1) the authority of an individual, (2) an order given by a commander, or (3) an organization or area under the command of an individual; and as a verb (4) denoting domination by weapons or observation from a superior position. American armed forces employ the third usage to name joint and uniservice commands, such as the U.S. European Command (EUCOM). This article will focus on the first of these usages, having to do with authority.

The North Atlantic Treaty Organization (NATO) offers the briefest statement of the meaning of command: "the authority vested in an individual of the armed forces for the direction, coordination, and control of military forces." The U.S. Joint Chiefs of Staff (U.S. Department of Defense 1987) prescribe a more precise definition of command:

> The authority that a commander in the military services lawfully exercises over subordinates by virtue of rank or assignment. Command includes the authority and responsibility for effectively using available resources and for planning the employment of, organizing, directing, coordinating, and controlling military forces for the accomplishment of assigned missions. It also includes responsibility for the health, welfare, morale, and discipline of assigned personnel.

Scope and Nature of Command

During the nineteenth and early twentieth centuries the Americans defined the legal and institutional limits of command authority (e.g., officers junior in rank should not command officers senior to them, staff members and aides should not assume the powers of the commander they assist, and specialists whose rank stems from their technical expertise, such as the Chief of Ordnance or Professors, U.S. Military Academy, should not command in the absence of designated commanders). The Americans also clearly defined the limits on the power of military commanders to control civilians and civil institutions in peacetime. Other Western democracies adopted similar strictures. As the twentieth century progressed, however, Communist nations and developing countries established considerably different patterns for the scope and nature of military command authority, although many of the developing countries adopted liberally from what they learned in the military schools of the Western democracies.

Most dictionaries state that to command is to "direct with authority." To command a military organization is to think and to make judgments, employing specialized knowledge and deciding what those commanded will and will not do. To command in wartime is to assume responsibility for taking and saving human lives. To command in peace and war is to direct how human beings will conduct themselves toward each other; as such, the commander sets moral standards and sees that they are obeyed. To command is to exercise an unusual concentration of power in one person—power begotten by specific legal ordination and energized by the will of a person to wield that power.

To command, therefore, is to think and decide, to feel and moralize, and to act and wield power. In the symbolism of the sage, to command is to direct with authority, using all the forces of the head, the heart, and the hand.

Uniqueness of the Command Experience

Whereas the acts of leading and managing can be generalized into the descriptive and analytical fields of leadership and management, there has been no development of a similar field called "commandership" or "commanderment," in which principles and theories are sufficiently identified and routinized as common to all command situations. Each command event is unique in its blend of personality, mission, environment, and power relationships. Only at the junior levels of command is there some commonality of experience among commanders.

For the purposes of this article, the company command, or its 150-man equivalent, is the largest "junior" command. "Senior" command extends upward from the battalion of 600 or its equivalent, through the division of 10,000 to 18,000 or its equivalent, to corps, army, joint, and combined commands. The term *very senior* command is reserved for three- and four-star flag officer billets, where responsibilities, roles, and tasks differ in both degree and kind from the commands subordinate to them.

Although he may be called "company commander," the peacetime commander at the junior level often lacks essential elements of a true command situation (i.e., insufficient concentration of power and autonomy of decision, absence of a staff, rapidly changing missions, and a lack of control over subordinate pay, discipline, administration, and related essentials for sustaining morale and efficiency). At the senior level, beginning with battalion command, however, these deficiencies in authority, mission, and structure are alleviated, and experience in a series of command and staff positions promotes a growing professionalism in the art of command. Some of these senior command skills still apply at the level of corps command and higher. However, the nature of the challenge begins to change at that level, and the response of the highest level commander is often measured by his creativity rather than his experience and by his rebalancing of the many roles that a commander must play.

Multiple Roles of the Commander

In order to carry out the functions envisioned in the American Joint Chiefs of Staff (JCS) description of the commander, he must be prepared to carry out many roles both in war and peace. The commander is at times a tactician and at other times a strategist or a master of the operational art. To carry out these roles he must also be the "technical expert of last resort" on the weapons and equipment of his military units, and he must have the knowledge and insights of the logistician.

In the violence of war the commander must be prepared to assume the role of the warrior, which has at least four challenges: (1) to be courageous in the face of great adversity; (2) to ensure that his soldiers will fight with courage and aggressiveness; (3) to wage war with the violence necessary to achieve victory; and (4) to restrain his use of that violence, in order to meet required standards of legality, morality, and justice. The commander must be both disciplinarian and moral arbiter for the troops in his command, insisting on standards of conduct and performance of duty that are consistent with mission accomplishment and demanding ethical standards that are intolerant of lying, cheating, stealing, and the unfair or degrading treatment of others.

The commander is the ultimate trainer of his younger and less experienced subordinates in military knowledge and skills. Not only must the commander be physically and mentally capable of withstanding great stress, he must also understand and enforce the requirements that lead to the good health and physical fitness of those he commands.

According to the JCS concept, the person in command must be a manager, if management is "the process of planning, organizing, coordinating, directing, and controlling resources to accomplish the organizational mission." The commander errs, however, if he limits his vision to management theory that is based on research in civilian institutions. Management literature is virtually silent on the commander's requirement to shoulder 24-hour responsibility for "employees," whose livelihood and motivation depend substantially on federal law and bureaucracy. The commander will not find in typical management theory the insights and values that can explain to soldiers why their unit is more important than they are, why it can be sacrificed to national need, and whether they may live or die in the process.

To command is to do more than lead soldiers, if military leadership is "a process by which a soldier influences others to accomplish the mission." The direct contact between leader and follower at the lower levels of command becomes more and more indirect as commanders become more senior and their commands more complex. At these levels, the role of leader finds itself in competition for time and attention among the many other roles expected of the senior commander.

To command, therefore, is to lead well when leadership is required and to manage well when management is called for. But a commander must also be a tactician and strategist, a technician and logistician, a warrior and moral arbiter, a disciplinarian, a trainer, and a soldier of great physical and mental endurance.

Senior Command in Military Organizations

The great military commanders of the past—Alexander the Great, Frederick II, Napoleon—usually exerted their authority as political heads of state as well as chiefs of their armed forces. In the late twentieth century this linkage is uncommon, except in certain Communist and developing nations. In the Western democracies the command function is carried out within military organizations, where commanders are assigned certain missions that are imposed on the military organization by duly constituted political authority. In recent years, the development of a theory of organizations and of a theory of systems within organizations has progressed to the point where the study of command has become intertwined with the study of organizations and systems.

It is useful to view a large command as an organizational system composed of interrelated parts, including units, committees, and groups that have official status but may not appear on organization charts. Thinking of a command as a system allows one to focus on the interdependencies of activities carried out by different individuals and units. This requires the senior commander to perform at least four essential tasks. The first involves giving the organization direction and priorities—a vision of what the organization and its mission should look like. The commander must focus forward and envision what is possible, set and articulate goals, and then motivate his people to achieve these goals. His second task involves defining relationships among subordinate elements, by answering questions such as: Who has directive power? Coordinating power? Responsibility to monitor? How much authority is delegated? Who provides liaison to whom?

The senior commander's third task involves his obligation to establish the organization's culture, that is, the pattern of values that guide the actions of personnel assigned to his command. These include not only the ethical principles of the military profession, such as duty, integrity, discipline, and courage, but also the broader moral principles that guide human beings in their relationships with each other, such as justice, obedience to law, and avoidance of murder, torture, stealing, and lying. His fourth major task is to establish effective information systems, each of which must get information from the right source, interpret it, process it into a form suitable for use by leaders at each echelon, distribute it at the right time, and store it for future use. Through these systems he is able to sense changes in the external and internal environment and make necessary adjustments.

How these four tasks are carried out varies with the conditions under which the commander exerts his authority. Is his mission to be accomplished in peacetime or in one of several wartime scenarios—low intensity, conventional, or nuclear? Is his command part of a national land, sea, or air service, or is it part of a joint or combined force? Is he commanding at the lowest senior level, the battalion or its equivalent, or is he at the very senior end of a progression of command assignments?

Modern Dilemmas of Senior Command

The 1990s find senior military commanders facing not only the traditional dilemmas of command but also new ones brought on by rapidly changing technological, political, and moral forces in the global environment. Among these ongoing dilemmas five deserve to be highlighted:

1. *Spectrum of conflict.* The growth of low-intensity warfare in the spectrum of conflict has presented new challenges to commanders whose training and experience have already changed from regional to global conventional and then to nuclear warfare. The insurgencies and proxy wars in Southeast Asia, Afghanistan, and the Middle East have heightened the requirements for commanders' understanding of the political and social ramifications of the application of military force to societal problems. Learning by commanders continues to go deeper into the military technology and organization that are most appropriate for low-intensity warfare and in the historical, religious, and language backgrounds of the regions where troops, aircraft, and ships may be deployed. The use of military forces to counter terrorism and the narcotics trade is a further extension of this trend that confronts military commanders.

2. *Fog of war.* World War II general G. S. Patton, Jr., wrote that if a commander waits for more complete information, he will never make a decision. Most successful commanders have underscored the importance of being able to sense the importance and meaning of a situation through the fog of misinformation and lack of critical information that has pervaded the battlefield and command post throughout history. The need for fast decisions has increased because of the enhanced speed of modern military equipment, rising lethality of weapons, and the networking of modern communications. This has led to a whole new technology of obtaining and interpreting data for the commander by electronic means available to him in mobile command vehicles. Yet, the vagueness of enemy intentions still remains, as do the riddles posed by geography, weather, and the lack of clear guidance from the commander's own superiors.

3. *The commander's intent.* The centralization of command and control at the highest levels has been encouraged by the technology of modern communications and the growth of large staffs who can assemble and assimilate great amounts of data. Running counter to this trend is the acknowledgment that modern warfare may result in the destruction of these communications and the wide dispersion of forces so that decentralization of command authority may be necessary. Therefore, many of the armed forces of the Western democracies

have renewed interest in training commanders to issue mission-type orders and to express their intent in future operations so that subordinate commanders can use their own initiative in achieving military goals.

4. *Creativity.* During the recent years of rapid change in military and naval technology, organizational structure, and types of warfare, there has been a continual search for doctrines that can provide a common understanding among commanders so that unity of effort and efficient fighting will be assured. The same conditions of rapid change, however, have increased the demand for creativity and imagination by wartime commanders. Biographers of history's great leaders cite their creativity—following a different vision—as central to their success. Although this creativity may depend on one's birthright and education before entering military life, there is common agreement that it is best developed in commanders by long and intensive personal study of the military profession and an interest in man's progress and failure through the centuries.

5. *Selection.* In most military organizations, junior commanders are selected by senior commanders. In a search for the best methods for selecting senior commanders, however, a variety of techniques have been tried, with many considered unsatisfactory. Commanders at the lieutenant colonel level have traditionally been selected by general officers, based on individual personnel records, direct contact, and advice from a variety of sources. In some military organizations, written examinations and interviews have been used; in some armies with small officer corps, special teams evaluate the performance of nominees in simulated command exercises. To ensure nondiscrimination on the grounds of race, sex, or religion, the American army changed to a system in the 1970s where special boards periodically selected battalion and brigade commanders on the basis of written reports of past performance and estimates of future potential. By the mid-1980s, "making the command list" became the strongest test of career success or failure in the minds of most officers, and good performance in these commands was deemed essential to promotion to general officer and access to higher command positions.

Whether or not battalion command should be a prerequisite for selection as a very senior officer is debatable. Karl von Clausewitz wrote: "There are Field Marshals who would not have shone at the head of a cavalry regiment, and vice versa." Very senior officers generally select from among the flag officers in their service those who should be promoted to higher command. Lateral entry by nonprofessionals is rarely permitted. Civilian authority plays a greater role in selection as one proceeds to the higher ranks. Very senior commanders might require approval by the commander in chief, head of state, and a national legislative body.

When selecting men and women for command, civil and military authorities seek indications that candidates can direct with authority in the many roles they must perform. While behavioral analysts have despaired of finding a set of personal characteristics or traits that are common to all commanders, historians and biographers continue to write in terms of traits or qualities of character, such as "resolution"—the persistence to stick at a task until victory is assured.

As commanders move through the senior ranks they should be measured by more sophisticated talents, such as their creativity, their capacity to imagine and articulate a vision for their commands, their abilities in indirect leadership as well as direct, their understanding of joint and combined operations and strategic policy, as well as the political and social consequences of applying military force to societal problems on a global scale.

When selecting commanders at the very senior level, authorities must fit individual personalities to each command position, knowing that in the past, for example, a Patton was not interchangeable with an Eisenhower. Command, especially at high levels, remains a unique phenomenon, each instance differing in its blend of personality and experience, mission, organizational structure, external environment, and power relationships.

ROGER H. NYE

SEE ALSO: Generalship; Leadership; Noncommissioned Officer; Officer; Rank and Insignia of Rank.

Bibliography

Nye, R. H. 1986. *The challenge of command.* Wayne, N.J.: Avery.
Smith, P. M. 1988. *Taking charge.* Wayne, N.J.: Avery.
U.S. Army War College. 1988. *Army command and management.* Carlisle Barracks, Pa.: Dept. of Command, Leadership, and Management.
U.S. Department of the Army. 1987. *Leadership and command at senior levels. FM 22–103.* Ft. Leavenworth, Kans.: USACAC.
U.S. Department of Defense. 1987. *Dictionary of military and associated terms.* JCS Pub 1. Washington, D.C.: Government Printing Office.
Van Creveld, M. 1985. *Command in war.* Boston: Harvard Univ. Press.
Zais, M. M. 1985. *Generalship and the art of senior command.* Ft. Leavenworth, Kans.: USACGSC.

COMMAND, CONTROL, COMMUNICATIONS, AND INTELLIGENCE (C^3I)

The grouping together of command, control, communications, and intelligence (C^3I) signifies the fact that in the modern era it would not be possible to separate in any way command and control from the important role played by communications as well as by intelligence.

The definition of C^3I is the ability of the commander on the battlefield to make the right decisions based on the status of both the enemy's and his own forces, to translate those decisions into commands and instructions, to transfer his directives in the fastest manner to his subordinates, and to ensure those directives are clearly understood. Once this process is finished, the commander must be able to receive feedback in real time to ensure his ability to deliver new orders and directives.

A major problem faced by every military leader since ancient times is how to make the best possible battlefield decisions. There are very few examples of a commander fully utilizing intelligence data about the enemy while, at the same time, having complete knowledge of the status of his own forces and complete control. One such example, however, is given in the Old Testament, Gideon's fight with the Midianites. Gideon had updated information regarding enemy status and morale (he personally sneaked into the enemy encampment), he knew the exact location and capability of his own soldiers (because he had selected them), and he had clear means of communication (the blowing of the ramshorn [shofar], which was the signal for "Follow me"). Using these three components, he won the battle.

Thus, in summarizing the command and control problem a military leader faces on the battlefield, we arrive at the following: victory in battle is a function of real-time knowledge of the enemy's status (which is obtained through intelligence) and the status of one's own forces as well as good control over one's forces.

Air, Naval, and Land Systems

Since ancient times, most wars have been decided by land forces, with air and naval forces primarily serving in support of land forces.

Of the three services, it is the naval and air control and communication systems that have reached a high state of technological development and been successfully tested in battle (e.g., the Israeli naval system during the 1973–74 Arab-Israeli War and the Israeli air system during the 1982 war in Lebanon). The reason is that, in comparison with the land battle, the number of factors involved in an air/naval battle are relatively limited.

In the case of an air battle, for example, the components involved are enemy planes, one's own planes, intelligence systems (radar, etc.), and the weapons' control system. Enemy planes, or even missiles, can be identified as soon as they take off from their bases or aircraft carriers using sophisticated intelligence systems. Friendly planes, satellites, and missiles can be accurately identified by navigational systems in each plane and with backup radar systems.

Control is precise through airborne warning and control systems (AWACS) and satellites of all kinds. The control of the air battle is, therefore, relatively uncomplicated, and the friendly/enemy status picture is available in real time, with satisfactory accuracy, on a screen in front of the pilot responsible for making the decision. This is also true in the case of a naval system. The naval battle zone is relatively clear and one can easily differentiate between friend and foe. Sailing speeds and weapons' characteristics of both sides are known. It is a relatively simple procedure to have the status picture compiled, analyzed, and brought to the commander who has to make the decisions.

The Land Battlefield

The land battle is much more complicated for purposes of command and control, comprehension, and administration. The reasons for this are:

1. Ground combat is for the most part continual and therefore exhausting to participants. Exhaustion and loss of mental acuity among commanders and soldiers may cause psychological strain and mental fatigue, thus making the decision-making process and the desire to accomplish the mission much more difficult.
2. Encounters with the enemy and fighting may take place in many areas simultaneously. These engagements are likely to be intense and highly destructive.
3. There is a great density of forces and troops operating in proximity to each other, thus the need for synchronization of battlefield activities.
4. Air and naval forces support the land forces, thus turning the land battlefield into a joint campaign.
5. Contradictions in the various command and control methods frequently occur—on one hand, centralization at the operational level; on the other hand, decentralization at the tactical level based on the initiative and resourcefulness of commanders.

Status of C^{3}I Systems

While there are a number of command and control systems available in the naval and air forces, and there have been serious breakthroughs in the land forces, there is as yet no system available worldwide upon which the land commander at the army, corps, division, or brigade level may fully rely. Command and control systems for land forces are in an advanced stage of development in a few armies, and, in some, they are even in the preliminary experimental and absorption stages.

A brief discussion of the main command and control systems available in the modern Western armies, their principles of operation, and their status as of the late 1980s follows.

U.S. Maneuver Control System

The U.S. Maneuver Control System (MCS) is designed to assist the commander and his staff by providing information on his own forces, the enemy's forces, and the characteristics of the battlefield. The MCS is a decision support system (DSS) that provides battlefield information by collecting, processing, and displaying data generated within the combat environment.

MCS is a hybrid system consisting of both fully militarized and nondevelopmental item (NDI) equipment. The tactical computer terminal (TCT) is a compact militarized, general-purpose data-processing, display, and communications terminal intended for army use in a variety of highly mobile tactical applications. It is designed to facilitate the collection, generation, review, analysis, and distribution of data. The TCT, with its floppy-disk memory, is located at the brigade level. At the division and corps levels there is a TCT (30A) with a bubble memory. A battalion terminal is provided as part of the Army Command and Control System (ACCS) project's hardware, which will extend MCS down to the battalion level. The MCS also consists of a digital voice communication interface module and a graphic-map display with a plasma panel.

HEROS

HEROS (Heeres Führungs Information System Operationsführung in Stäben) is a C³I system that was intended for the use of the Federal Republic of Germany's Bundeswehr, which provided automatic data-processing (ADP) support to headquarters through the Bundeswehr from brigade level upward. It was made up of three principal systems: HEROS 2/1, a mobile system intended for use in the field by headquarters at corps, division, and brigade level; HEROS 3, the static system used by the army staffs at various headquarters' locations; and the HEROS 5, which covers the territorial army static ADP needs.

HEROS cells at all levels have graphic displays with large-screen map displays limited to corps and division levels.

WAVELL

The British C³I development is the Wavell system, and it enables an ADP-supported fusion capability at division and corps levels. Wavell presents users with formatted or free text data regarding plans and orders, intelligence, current operations, terrain, order of battle, air defense cover, logistics, and so on. The system does not have a main display capability.

The data are a distillation of the detailed information from other data systems in such fields as electronic warfare, air defense, fire support, and logistic and combat support. As a common user system, data will be distributed using the U.K. packet switching bearer system known as Ptarmigan.

CATRIN

Italy's field communication and information system, designated CATRIN, has an integrated communications subsystem, SOTRIN; a battlefield survey and target acquisition subsystem, SORAO; and a tactical air target-acquisition and command and control subsystem, SOATCC.

BICES

In NATO, intelligence is the responsibility of individual country members. In an emergency, however, field commanders of different allied nations need to have integrated information available in real time, together with an initial analysis to enable them to make the best immediate use of their resources. One of the monumental problems in meeting this need is the technical incompatibility of the C³I systems of the different nations.

To provide a clear, up-to-date picture of the former Warsaw Pact's troop dispositions and movement, the Battlefield Information, Collection, and Exploitation System (BICES) was developed.

Sometimes called "the system of systems," BICES demonstrated NATO's resolution to improve standardization and interoperability in the tactical communications and ADP field.

The intention was for French, German, British, and U.S. army staff cells to interoperate, passing data to one another for storage and display on hardware provided by HEROS, Wavell, the French SACRA (System Automatique de Commandement et Renseignement de l'Avant), and the U.S. MCS.

DIFFERENT DEVELOPMENT APPROACHES

The development of such systems as the U.S. Tactical Operation System (TOS) failed mainly because of the overly comprehensive approach taken when deciding on system specifications. According to this approach, the command and control systems are required to answer the *entire* range of command and control needs in the modern battlefield. Another problem that contributed to the failure of the system's utilization was the lack of sufficient involvement of the users in the design of the system and its development stages.

A different approach to specification has been taken by some of the European armies and was adopted by the U.S. Army when specifying the MCS system. Called the evolutionary method, this approach is gradually realized in the field by performing only minimal functions at first, then gradually adding functions according to the rate of its absorption and the users' reactions. The specification and development approach of this method has been continually proving itself. Since it operates gradually, usually according to an ascending order of difficulty, it is based on a gradual realization of the system.

A comprehensive specification and development approach that aspires to specify a complete and wide system having maximum functions and extending to maximum areas in one go has failed in many attempts and has not yet proven itself.

PROBLEMS INHIBITING A SOLUTION IN THE LAND BATTLE

Specification (detail level). One of the main issues is the detail level at which the data should be brought to the commander who is to make the decisions. One might ask: Is it sufficient for the division commander to know events within a range of 30 kilometers (18 mi.) from the forward edge of the battle area (FEBA), or should he also be aware of expected threats at greater distances that might affect his combat zone? Is the division commander supposed to know the status of each platoon, every artillery battery, and every antitank force in his zone, or would it be sufficient for him to know only the location of his forces at battalion level? Wouldn't the lack of information regarding small forces prevent him from fully exploiting/utilizing tactical situations? Or wouldn't the saturation of details on the screen entirely block the picture and disable comprehension? Another question is whether every weapons system existing in the divisional sector should be specified, or would it be sufficient to rely on command and control subsystems for artillery support, for example?

Small closed loop/large open loop. Another issue lies in the operation of weapons systems. There are some weapons systems that would benefit from a closed-loop framework of operation—that is, the system acquires the target, immediately identifies it, and then destroys it with little or no decision making or input on the part of the operator. For example, fire control decisions can be subordinated to the operators of FIREFINDER (Artillery locating radar, TPQ-

37). Then, immediately after the radar has located a target, the system is engaged without the need for intermediate levels of command or decision making. But can or should intelligence means be subordinated to weapon means? What is the level of involvement required from the tactical level commander in decisions of this kind? Doesn't this closed-loop destruction of targets in effect constitute a waste and lack of control on the part of the commander over his resources? Such questions are at the core of the issue of the interface of man and machine.

Man-machine interface. A critical question is where does the involvement of the computer in the decision-making process end and the commander's reasoning begin?

The school of thought advocating the use of computers in decision making smooths the issue by referring to it as "recommendations." However, these recommendations resemble the "recommendations of the godfather" as they are virtually impossible to dispute and leave no alternative. The opposing school of thought claims that the role of the system is only to present the precise picture to the commander, who is the one to make the final decisions. The supporters of the first school of thought base their argument on commander's fatigue, the inability to consider the full range of details, the fact that vital facts may be left out during the decision-making process, and so on. Supporters of the second school of thought argue that there is no substitute for the commander's experience, natural intuition, and his ability to see, grasp, and comprehend the battlefield.

The main problem here is man's inability to solve with a computer problems in which there is a large uncertainty factor. Commanders on the land battlefield will find it difficult to order withdrawal just because the computer indicates a clear enemy advantage and recommends withdrawal. The commander himself, knowing his forces and the morale of his troops, trusts his experience and is confident that the human factor shall eventually triumph. It is evident that the commander will not always leave it up to a machine, no matter how technologically advanced it is, to make such an important decision.

Other problems inherent in using a computer are the effects of topographic and weather conditions, which are very difficult to display in an enemy/allied forces status.

THE DESIRABLE SOLUTION FOR THE FUTURE BATTLEFIELD

The command and control system of the future should be compatible at all levels, starting at the army level and ending at the battalion level. The system should also allow for the interface of existing aerial and marine systems in order to allow the execution of joint operations. At every level, the commander should have at his disposal a status picture, suitable for his specific level, displayed without it being too detailed or too comprehensive. This picture would enable commanders of all levels to make their decisions based upon the most accurate data available while at the same time relying on their combat experience and the confidence they have in their commanders and troops. The database would be the same for all levels and all subsystems. Once the commander made his decision, it would be immediately translated into orders, transferred through the command and control channels and, based on the common database, to all unit commanders who are supposed to receive and execute the orders and directions. At the same time, a control mechanism would become operational and notify the commander, in real time, of the extent to which his commands had been transferred to all the fighting troops of all forces. All the systems that can function in a closed-loop method and do not require the involvement of commanders in the higher levels for their operation would continue to operate as such. Subsystems, such as fire-support or logistic systems, would be independently operated while updating, in real time, the uniform database in order to enable commanders to make new decisions and distribute new directions or orders.

Summary

Command and control systems will undoubtedly be a major force multiplier on future battlefields. For the proper planning and operation of these systems, there is a clear need to distinguish sharply between the human factor and the capacity of the computer. The borderline is clear and runs between the display of data and the decision making. With the proper use of such an excellent auxiliary tool, an army might be able to implement command and control systems effectively and have a clear advantage on the future battlefield.

ARIE MIZRACHI

SEE ALSO: Command.

Bibliography

Elliott, R. D. 1989. The integrated tactical data network. *Signal* 43 (7):53–58.
Rechter, R. J., et al. 1989. ATCCS: An integrated C^3 environment. *Signal* 43 (10):181–90.
Rice, M. A., and A. J. Sammes. 1989. *Communications and information systems for battlefield command and control.* London: Brassey's.
U.S. Defense Communications Agency. 1987. Joint tactical command, control, and communications agency handbook 8000. *Joint Connectivity Handbook.* Washington, D.C.: Government Printing Office.
U.S. Joint Chiefs of Staff. 1987. JCS Pub. 1. *Dictionary of military and associated terms.* Washington, D.C.: Government Printing Office.
Wagner, L. C. 1989. Modernizing the army's C^3I. *Signal* 43 (5):29–34.

COMMAND POST

A command post is a location on the battlefield from which orders are given to control the actions of friendly forces. Command posts have changed considerably throughout history, largely in response to technological advances in communications and weaponry.

From antiquity into the nineteenth century, communication techniques remained basically the same; riders or runners carried written messages from the battlefield commander to his subordinates who were actively directing their units' maneuver. Simple commands might be conveyed by visual signals, such as flags or smoke, or audible signals, such as trumpet calls or drum rolls. In addition to signalers and runners, staff officers and deputies held various advisory or coordinative responsibilities; in a pitched battle, they might be housed in a shelter of some sort, often only a tent.

The battlefield commander typically placed his command post in a geographical position that was out of range of the enemy's weapons but that also afforded optimal observation of the battlefield. The limited range of weapons often allowed him to select a site quite close to the battlefield. If the enemy threatened to win, the command post was moved out of danger, which might cause a temporary loss of tactical control. Because communication techniques were so primitive, the battlefield commander had to personally observe the fighting to effectively control the battle.

The evolution of rifled cannons and explosive shells forced command posts farther and farther from the fighting. But as the telegraph, heliograph, and balloon were perfected, tactical control could be exercised even when the command post was out of sight of the battlefield.

The mass introduction of the machine gun and accurate indirect artillery fire had brought about even more substantial changes. At the same time, the battlefield commander's staff was growing ever larger in size because of the increasing complexity of modern military operations. World War I saw battlefield commanders relying on the reports of subordinates, plotting battle progress on a map, and communicating tactical instructions accordingly. With the limited introduction of the radio as a means of tactical communication, forward command posts could be established to allow the battlefield commander or his deputies to personally observe the battle while relying on communications and staff personnel at the main command post to coordinate and transmit instructions to friendly forces.

The vastly increased lethality of weapons and the concomitant jump in the complexity of warfare caused lower echelons of military organizations to begin establishing subordinate command posts. Now that troops were dispersed, especially in the defense, commanders down to platoon level created positions from which they could control their soldiers; standing up to bark orders was impossible in a hail of shrapnel and machine-gun fire. In the defense, orders down to squad level were often transmitted using electrically powered telephones, although couriers were still used when security was a must or when artillery cut the phone wires. On the western front, command posts were heavily protected and usually underground to ensure continual operation and control.

By the time of World War II, the growing lethality and range of weapons combined with the mass introduction of radios to remove command posts above the company level from the immediate battlefield. Forward command posts were often located in armored vehicles; messages were sent by radio or by couriers mounted in light vehicles or motorcycles, while staff at the main command post carried out detailed planning and coordination of future operations.

As of the early 1990s, high technology plays a prominent role in the fields of weapons, transportation, and communications. But the differing levels of technology and varying military doctrines of major modern armies have resulted in significantly different concepts of command posts.

The official doctrine of the U.S. Army and of most U.S.-style military organizations prohibits the establishment of command posts below the level of battalion. In practice, command posts are established down to platoon level. Each infantry or tank platoon has FM radios capable of transmitting effectively up to 11 kilometers (about 6½ mi.) or more, making controlled tactical dispersion possible. Typically, platoon command posts are established in the defense and in one or two dug-in fighting positions to protect the platoon leader, the platoon sergeant, the artillery forward observer, and the radio operators. Each squad is contacted by telephones wired to the command post. The platoon leader keeps a current situation map and sector sketches at his command post and controls both the direct fires of the machine guns and missile launchers and, through the forward observer, the indirect fires of supporting artillery and mortars. Because a platoon command post is located so near the enemy, tents are never used. In the attack, command is exercised on the move, either on foot or mounted in an armored fighting vehicle; no command post exists in the offensive mode at this level.

Company command posts are similar to their platoon-level counterparts, with a correspondingly higher level of sophistication (i.e., more radios, more telephones, and more attached personnel). Again, in the attack, command is exercised on the move.

Because of the much greater sophistication and complexity of operations above the company level, these command posts are typically much larger, more extensively manned, and in place during both offensive and defensive operations. Staff at these posts are principally concerned with tactical intelligence and operational affairs; personnel concerned with logistical and other support functions are often located closer to the supply trains.

U.S. doctrine calls for command posts to be established at four levels: battalion, brigade, division, and corps. At battalion level, a main command post, often called the Tactical Operations Center (TOC) is established, along with a temporary tactical command post to provide continuity of control during displacement of the TOC. Brigades establish main and tactical command posts but also must designate an alternate command post (usually that of a subordinate battalion) to be used if the main and tactical ones are disabled. Divisions and corps not only have main, tactical, and alternate command posts, they also establish rear command posts to control rear-area operations.

Because of the development of reliable, long-range, portable communication systems, the commander is rarely at the main command post during field operations. U.S. doctrine locates the commander where he can best influence the tactical actions being conducted. So long as he is in contact with his staff at the main command post, the commander can place himself with the unit that is the most immediately important to mission accomplishment. Sometimes the tactical command post is used as a forward control cell for the conduct of complicated operations.

The main command post is usually positioned several kilometers behind the command posts of the next lowest echelon—preferably as centrally as possible to be equally accessible to all subordinate commanders. However, the location of such command posts is always subject to the dictates of terrain and enemy action.

Figure 1 shows the configuration of a typical main command post at the brigade level. A good location affords cover and concealment. Two or three highly portable tents are configured beneath camouflage nets that deflect infrared light. A triple stack of concertina barbed wire is placed 40 meters (44 yds.) or so (beyond hand-grenade range) from the tents for security, and armed guards at the entrance limit access. Vehicles are dispersed away from the immediate area and camouflaged, and fighting positions are prepared nearby for security and to protect personnel against shrapnel in the event of an air attack.

Because a command post inevitably emits a considerable radio signal signature during combat operations, radios are mounted on vehicles parked at a distant location, usually several hundred meters away. The radios are wired to remote terminals within the main command post. Facsimile machines are similarly "remoted." If time permits, subordinate command posts are directly wired to the main command post to allow greater security of communications and to reduce the electronic signature.

The interior of the main command post is divided into different cells according to function. Part of the main command post comprises the actual command center. Maps portray the current friendly and enemy situations as well as planned future operations. Communications specialists operate the command and intelligence FM networks, and a duty officer and noncommissioned officer (NCO) coordinate the activity. In an adjacent compartment of the tent, the intelligence officer (S-2), the operations officer (S-3), the fire-support officer (FSO), and special staff officers, such as the chemical warfare officer, the signal

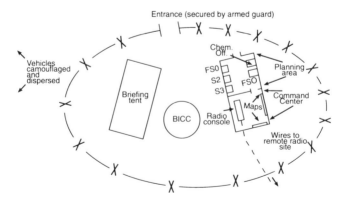

Figure 1. Typical configuration of brigade-level command post.

officer, and the U.S. Air Force air liaison officer (ALO), plan and coordinate conferences. Often, space is also allocated to liaison officers from supporting and attached units such as air defense artillery batteries, engineer companies, and army tactical aviation units.

In another, usually smaller, tent is the battlefield information collection center (BICC), where the S-2's staff collate and process information about the enemy; the relevant intelligence formed here is passed immediately into the command center.

Often, a third tent is used as a briefing area within a brigade's main command post. In peacetime exercises, the day's events usually are discussed in a major staff briefing to the commander each evening. During combat operations, this facility may be used to brief subordinate commanders on upcoming operations or to brief senior commanders on the current situation in the brigade. Some units dispense with the briefing tent altogether in combat situations and conduct all briefings in the command center.

The activities conducted at the main command post fall into two categories: current and planned operations. Assistant operations officers and NCOs monitor the activities of subordinate units and keep track of all significant events. A detailed journal tracks the time at which all communications are made and summarizes each message. Situation maps are continually updated with the latest information concerning unit locations and operations. Assistant intelligence officers and NCOs stay abreast of the enemy situation and post the most current intelligence available from the BICC on their maps and charts in the command center. The FSO and his assistants monitor fire missions conducted by friendly artillery and mortars and post damage reports as available. The chemical officer monitors the weather and updates the potential effects of both enemy and friendly chemical agents. The ALO, usually an experienced fighter pilot, advises about the current effects of enemy activity and weather on planned or available U.S. Air Force tactical air support missions. Thus, the commander has available all of the information he needs to make tactical decisions.

The S-2 and S-3 usually concern themselves with future operations. Based on foreseeable events and on the decisions and guidance of their commander, they formulate plans in conjunction with the personnel officer (S-1) and the logistics officer (S-4), both of whom come to the main command post from the brigade supply trains especially for such activities. The civil-military operations officer (S-5) and the officers of the special staff are also included to ensure that practical orders are ready to be issued at the appropriate times.

U.S. doctrine also establishes other types of command posts with special functions. For example, setting up a structure as complicated as a main command post is highly impractical during the initial phases of an amphibious or airborne/air assault operation. For such situations, an abbreviated command post, called a tactical or assault command post, is used. In mechanized units, these are usually located in specially modified armored personnel carriers; in more lightly equipped units, a brigade tactical command post is usually equipped with one or two light vehicles that are specially modified with several radios and room for compact map boards. The personnel complement usually includes the S-2 and S-3, the FSO, and a few assistants and communications specialists. This small cell carries on the immediate monitoring of the operations of the attacking battalions. Staff officers who are principally responsible for tactical planning and the formulation of orders enable the cell to control the rapidly developing situations common to assault operations. Once the situation stabilizes, the main command post is set up, and control is handed over as soon as practicable.

When the tactical situation dictates that the main command post should relocate, the tactical command post can be used to maintain continual operational control. Tactical command posts are located where they can communicate with all subordinate elements and with the main command post via their FM communications systems. When the main command post is dismantled, responsibility for control is passed to the personnel at the tactical command post. These personnel, usually assistant operations and intelligence officers with a few radio operators, then maintain tactical control and keep the journal up to date until the main command post is established at its new location.

Division and corps command posts operate in a similar manner but are much larger and more complex. Because of their size, they are extremely difficult to conceal from either aerial visual detection or from electronic identification. Consequently, they are frequently guarded by a company or more of infantry detached from the combat elements subordinate to them. In World War II, the forward command post of the Supreme Headquarters, Allied Expeditionary Forces, Europe, was guarded by an infantry battalion specially detailed for its role. Considerable air defense assets are often allocated for their protection.

The rear command posts established at division and corps level control rear-area operations including support functions such as personnel administration and logistics. These command posts also control rear-area security operations. The efficient conduct of such security operations is critical to the success of frontline troops during a counterinsurgency or when facing a threat from special operations units such as paratroopers or air assault brigades.

While command posts at the division and corps levels are capable of operation in a field environment, they are sometimes situated in built-up areas such as villages or towns. Not only can this allow a greater degree of protection and security, it also makes rapid relocation easier because there is no need to dismantle tents and other equipment.

Above the corps level, headquarters serve as command posts and are almost always located in permanent facilities. One exception to this rule, however, is the airborne command post. During amphibious or airborne/air assaults, temporary command posts are sometimes located in aircraft aloft in the vicinity of the area of operations. Modified UH-1 (Huey) or UH-60 (Blackhawk) helicopters sometimes serve as aerial tactical command posts, even down to the battalion level. Especially during low-intensity operations against a primitively equipped foe, these aircraft allow the commander and his staff to see the battlefield while remaining in tactical control of the units conducting the operation. When the antiaircraft threat is high, the use of such aircraft is obviously more limited.

Division-level staffs and higher sometimes use an aerial command post mounted in specially equipped C-130 or C-135 transport airplanes (for example, during the initial phases of Operation Urgent Fury in 1983). Once an appropriate area is secured and the situation stabilized, control is passed to a ground command post.

The doctrine of the former Soviet Union calls for several other types of command posts. Command observation posts are established, usually in armored vehicles, for the direct control of combat formations at the battalion level and below. At the regimental level and above, Soviet doctrine resembles that of the United States to the extent that they establish main, forward (tactical), alternate, and rear-area command posts. At the front level, auxiliary command posts are sometimes established so that the frontal headquarters can control a secondary operation. Practically all command posts at the division level and below consist of armored vehicles that can be rapidly moved and provide extensive protection from artillery bombardment. Like their Western counterparts, Soviet command posts are well camouflaged and dispersed, and significant air defense assets are devoted to protection. Unlike U.S. units, however, the Soviets establish rear command posts as far down as regimental level. This reflects their staff organization, which includes a deputy commander for rear services who coordinates the administrative and logistical activities that U.S.-style organizations assign to the S-1 and S-4. As a commander in charge of supply points, routes of movement within the rear area, the conduct of resupply activities, and rear-area security, the deputy for rear-area services has his own command post from the regimental level up to the frontal echelon. The Soviet doctrine also calls for employment of aerial command posts, usually in helicopters, to provide commanders at the division, army, and front levels with added flexibility for command and control during mobile operations.

In the twentieth century, the lethality of modern weapons has forced commanders to place their command posts in obscure and protected areas and to develop multiple command posts to ensure continuity of control in the event of catastrophic damage. The complex demands of high-technology warfare have expanded the size of staffs, and the size and composition of command posts have grown accordingly. Instant, reliable, long-range communications equipment enable commanders to conduct operations from tactical command posts well forward while retaining comprehensive control through the capabilities of the main command post.

Developments in high-technology information management and other types of automated control systems will undoubtedly influence prospects for the future of command posts. Computer-assisted graphics and recording devices, for example, may enhance the information flow from a largely automated (and therefore smaller) main command post to highly mobile, well-protected tactical command posts from which commanders may more rapidly and accurately transmit combat instructions. Weapons' lethality, advances in mobility, and the development of improved communications techniques will ensure the continued evolution of command post organization and activity.

KEITH E. BONN

SEE ALSO: Command; Command, Control, Communications, and Intelligence; Directives, Orders, and Instructions; Leadership; Planning, Military; Span of Control: Military Organizations and Operations; Tactics.

Bibliography

U.S. Department of the Army. 1984. *Field manual 100-2-1: The Soviet army— Operations and tactics.* Washington, D.C.: Government Printing Office.
————. 1984. *Field manual 101-5: Staff organization and operations.* Washington, D.C.: Government Printing Office.

COMMUNICATIONS, SIGNAL

An apt description of the situation surrounding the signal corps was provided by the German general Fellgiebel (born 1886 and sentenced to death in 1944 as a member of the resistance, he was instrumental in the development of the German signal, or communications, corps in the 1930s). He observed, "The Communications Corps has a hard time; you can't smell it and you don't hear it. People only realize it is there when it doesn't work any more." Because of the nature of its task, this branch can in no way be directly involved with glorious battles. From time immemorial, communications has had a serving function. The signal corps supports the command by establishing and maintaining communication links and by electronic warfare measures. This task of the signal corps in the past, present, and future is presented in this article.

History of the Signal Corps

In comparison with the other branches of the services, the signal corps has a relatively short history. In Germany, it was founded barely 90 years ago. It was not until the telegraph service was separated from the engineer corps in 1899 that it became an independent branch known as the "wireless corps." In most other countries, it originated in the mid- or late nineteenth century because a signal corps only became necessary with the advent of technical communications systems.

FROM ANCIENT TIMES TO THE EIGHTEENTH CENTURY

In ancient times and in the Middle Ages, armies were composed of a body of troops with a simple organizational structure. For centuries, warfare was characterized by serried battle array or the phalanx array; wars were decided by frontline battles. From his point of elevation, the commander in chief could direct his army, using messengers on horseback and trumpeters to convey his orders. However, movement of entire armies was possible only as long as they remained of limited size and were composed primarily of troops of one type of arms. Beginning in the sixteenth century, the expansion of armies and the deployment of several types of arms on the battle scene compelled changes in command. The strategist was no longer able to lead his army alone; he needed assistants in order to make coordinated use of several bodies of troops. This resulted in the development of a command organization, although the means of command remained basically unchanged.

In standing armies from the sixteenth to the eighteenth century, new weapons brought a dramatic change in warfare, but the means of command remained largely unchanged. Slow operational movements on the battlefield meant that the lack of speed—by modern standards—with which orders and reports were conveyed was of no great import. As in earlier times, commanders could observe battles from points of elevation. Command systems still consisted of the command organization: the commander in chief and his assistants, as well as the natural means of communication (e.g., running or mounted messengers), optical means of communication (e.g., flags), and acoustic means of communication (e.g., trumpets or signal guns).

NINETEENTH CENTURY

From the time of the French Revolution, at the end of the eighteenth century, the way was paved for the replacement of the old regular army by the conscripted mass army. Up until the end of the eighteenth century, individual soldiers had been occupied with the transfer of information—orders and messages. By contrast, the mass armies of the nineteenth century operated over a large area and could no longer be commanded from single points of elevation. Communicating links between the commander and the fighting soldiers became necessary. A special corps for the transfer of information became a requirement. Technical progress made during the nineteenth century gradually provided the material basis for this special corps.

The first invention of a technical means of communication was made at the beginning of the nineteenth century: the visual telegraph, invented by the three Chappe brothers of France. The telegraphs were erected on hills, high buildings, towers, or frameworks within sight of each other.

Napoleon was the first commander in chief to use optical telegraphs in his campaigns, introducing such equipment into his army and building telegraph stations, thus enabling the long-distance transfer of information, although of very limited content. Triggered by its successful use in the French army, the Prussian general staff constructed such a communications path linking Berlin to Trier.

These visual lines were either unsuitable or of only limited use for the command and control of armies on the move, with their extensive front lines, or for contacts among detached bodies of troops. In addition, the steadily increasing demand for greater speed and more reliability in the conveyance of information could not be met in the long run. Even though the visual telegraph system was an important invention, it was never important for the conveyance of information in the battle arena because it was stationary and dependent on weather conditions and daylight. Therefore, only minor changes occurred in the conveyance of information from the beginning of the military system until the first decades of the nineteenth century.

The modern transfer of information began in 1837 with the invention of the electrical telegraph by the American Samuel F. B. Morse. His telegraph was the first communication system able to convey information on an electromagnetic basis. This was a very significant improvement, as the conveyance of information over long distances was increased considerably in speed and volume compared with previous means. In subsequent years, numerous telegraph lines sprang up across the United States and Europe. The following events were important in the development of the military telegraph system:

- 1844—construction of the first Morse system electromagnetic telegraph link between Washington, D.C., and Baltimore, Maryland;
- 1846—construction of the first overhead telegraph line, operating with an electrical dial telegraph, in Prussia, between Berlin and Potsdam;
- 1854—in the Crimean War, the telegraph was important for the organization of supply services over a long distance, without the then-new apparatus, requests across the sea for the required supplies, and their timely delivery, would have been impossible;
- 1856—introduction of the electromagnetic field telegraph into the Prussian army and, in 1864, participation of two mobile field telegraph regiments, which had been set up a few years earlier in the campaign against Denmark;
- 1861–65—important and widespread use of military telegraphy in the American Civil War;
- In the wars of 1866 and 1870–71—operational command was influenced by the Morse telegraph, bridging the distance between central governments and commanders in chief.

The development of telephony by the American Alexander Graham Bell, in 1876, was another milestone in the evolution of communications systems.

Within a few years, telegraph systems appeared in many countries, first with bare wires, later with telegraph or low-frequency communication lines. In 1878 the first attempts were made to use the telephone (in military terminology known as the field telephone) during combat. Toward the end of the 1880s, the first serviceable field wire was successfully manufactured. Cable reels and carrying packs were developed for laying wire, and these are still in use today, with relatively little modification.

The construction of the first wireless radio sets by the Italian Guglielmo Marconi, around 1900, made a more advanced medium accessible, and this was soon put to use by the military.

The fighting forces of the world had come to recognize the importance of the conveyance of information for military missions. They backed up the development of communications techniques and set up telegraph units, which belonged for the most part—as, for example, in Germany, Russia, and England—to the engineering corps. The number of men and means involved grew constantly.

The rapid technical development soon had organizational repercussions. With the increasing demands on telegraphy, the engineering corps was soon overwhelmed by this additional assignment. Consequently, in Germany in 1899, the engineering corps was relieved of telegraphy. With the formation of an independent branch of the service, called the telegraph corps, the signal corps of the German army came into being.

First Half of the Twentieth Century

The importance of military communications continued to increase. Warships and aircraft were fitted with radio equipment. Divisions were equipped with long-range radio stations. Telegraphy, telephony, and radio were the primary means for transferring information. Nevertheless, the traditional means of communication—that is, for example, messengers on foot, horseback, bicycle, or motorcycle—as well as acoustic and visual means of communication were still in use.

During World War I, telephone connections were in wide use, although these proved susceptible to disruption in the increasing rigors of trench warfare. Toward the end of the Great War, wireless means of communication gradually took on the burden of military communications.

At this stage, considerable efforts were expended for the first time to intercept and analyze enemy radio messages and telephone conversations. In several countries, communications reconnaissance was organized for the first time.

In World War II, the construction of far-reaching, long-distance lines began. Incorporation of field-type amplifiers improved the speaking range in comparison with field wires. Cable laying was improved, so that wire connections could be made and maintained even if combat changed location.

Carrier frequency techniques and voice frequency telegraphy opened new horizons. Technology made the multiple use of cables possible—that is, several connections could be made via one cable. Many armies successfully used radio relays as their communications system. For example, in 1942, the German Wehrmacht managed to establish a radio relay link from Africa to Athens via Crete, using the available postal network to create a reliable voice connection, and on to Berlin. By comparison with World War I, the number of communications systems used by all armies had multiplied greatly.

Radio finally emerged as one of the main means of command. Between the two world wars, a system of command and control by radio had evolved in Germany that later proved to be excellent for the rapidly accomplished operations of the tank units. It was naturally of benefit that major unit commanders had recognized the value of radio. The German tank general Heinz Guderian is supposed to have stated: "Drive, radio, fire," still applicable to tank troops today.

In many countries, radio reconnaissance was steadily expanded, because it made an extremely important contribution to the assessment of situations and to targeting enemy units for attack.

After World War II, armies of the fifties and sixties generally made use of apparatus of a similar level of technical development to that used in the last years of the war. Radio relays and radio came to the fore, but wire communications still played an important role both for the connecting up of battle headquarters and also for long-distance communications. Since experience in World War II had shown that the command of operations over a vast area was no longer possible with single axially arranged wire/radio relay networks, the fighting forces devised a grid wire/radio relay communications system, as diagrammed in Figure 1.

The nature of high frequency (HF) and very high frequency (VHF) radio meant that a radio link could not be used by multiple subscribers. Therefore, radio networks could not be compared with the grid wire/radio relay. Radio links were established—and in general still are today—between battle headquarters on the various levels of command in an axial formation combined to form a radio circuit, as shown for a brigade command circuit in Figure 2.

During the 1970s, new equipment was introduced. Modern means commensurate with the latest technical developments took the place of outdated radio, radio-relay, and terminal apparatuses (telephone, teleprinters, exchanges).

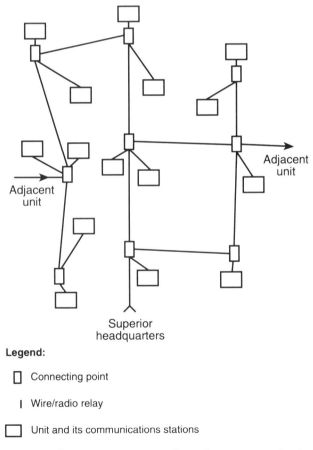

Legend:

☐ Connecting point

| Wire/radio relay

☐ Unit and its communications stations

Figure 1. Schematic presentation of a grid-type communications network.

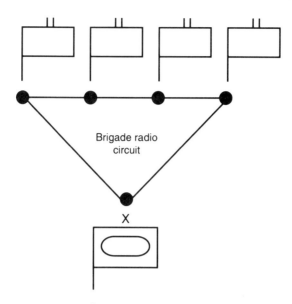

Figure 2. Schematic drawing of a radio circuit.

At the end of the seventies, some armies were outfitted with automated apparatus for long-distance telecommunications. This considerably accelerated telephone and teletype operations. As far as radio operations were concerned, radio-telephone and teletype fully replaced key transmitters. In particular, radio-teletype substantially augmented the efficiency of radio as a means of communication.

The history of the signal corps shows that this branch of the services was molded by technical development. Technology provided the prerequisites enabling the signal corps to fulfill its assignment.

The Signal Corps in the 1990s

COMMUNICATIONS SYSTEMS

It is the task of a signal communications service to establish and maintain the required communication links for all command levels, either by radio or wire/radio relay, as well as to set up and operate the signal installations.

Radio. Radio allows the fast establishment of communication and the transfer of information, even when on the move. It can be readily adapted to changes in the situation and the respective combat formation and is therefore the most important means of command where mobile operations are involved. The range of radio links is primarily dependent on the technical efficiency of the radio equipment and the propagation of the radio waves. Depending on the wavelengths, radio communications are assigned to various frequency ranges.

At present, military radio communications operate in the HF, VHF, and UHF (ultrahigh frequency) ranges.

The HF shortwave range includes frequencies from 3 to 30 megahertz (MHz). Long-distance telecommunications for radio-telephone, radio-teletype, and key radio transmission can be established rapidly and relatively easily via either ground or space waves.

In general, the use of VHF radio waves implies a range within line of sight—that is, roughly 50 kilometers (30 mi.). As a result, VHF radio links, although more reliable than HF radio links, have nevertheless a limited range. Consequently, armies make predominant use of the VHF range for surface-to-surface radio communications at the tactical level. At present, VHF radio communications are mainly of the radio-telephone and radio-teletype types and, increasingly, imagery and data apparatus. VHF radio links are the main means of command, conforming to army requirements and guaranteeing control of different branches of the services on the battlefield.

Owing to its limited range, UHF radio is restricted to surface-to-surface radio-telephone and surface-to-air radio-telephone communications—for example, within the framework of close air support of ground troops by tactical aircraft.

Wire and radio relay. To increase flexibility and chances of survival, wire and radio relay links are often combined to form networks. The interlinkage of wire and radio relay networks connects various levels of command with each other. The structure of the networks is determined in particular by the conduct of operations planned by a military force or service.

Because the construction of wire connections incurs great expense of both time and personnel, these are usually only laid in the field to extend other local communications links or to connect staff officers with telephone exchange facilities. Besides the field-type wire lines, the signal corps also employs, on a comparatively larger scale, fixed communications networks—that is, available communications lines, in particular postal networks. The following advantages accrue to communications via fixed networks:

- A large number of long-distance lines ("bunch of trunks") can be made available.
- Underground cables are well protected against the effects of weapons.

These advantages are counterbalanced by disadvantages:

- The switchboard, relay, and amplification installations, which are particularly susceptible to attack, are chiefly situated in towns and housed in buildings above ground.
- The repair of a fixed network requires special personnel and equipment and is time-consuming and infeasible with the means available to ordinary troops.

The serviceability of the fixed network in the theater of war decreases as the front line is approached.

To summarize, a fixed network can be assessed as:

- extremely beneficial in the liaison zone
- still very serviceable in the rear combat zone
- of little use in the forward combat zone because of the intensity of combat.

Greater distances can be spanned with radio relay than with wired radio. Special transmission equipment enables multiplexing as well as the simultaneous transmission of information in varying modes of operation (telephone, teletype, facsimile, and data transmission).

Increases in the mobility of armies, on land, sea, or in the air, as well as the growing demands as far as the quantity and quality of information transfers are concerned, forced the introduction of automated equipment for the conveyance of messages. As a consequence, in 1977 the German army introduced equipment for the automation of the corps' basic communications network. This became known as AutoKo (Automatisiertes Korpsstammnetz, or corps automatic basic communications network). The first phase of the project facilitated:

- self-dialing by the user
- the rapid erection and rapid alteration of the communications network
- the greater mobility of command posts thanks to comprehensive coverage by the communications system.

The principle behind the structure of this network is illustrated in Figure 3.

To conclude, signal communications are carried out by equipment that transmits speech, print, image, and data, as well as equipment that processes the information. Thanks to modern and operator-oriented technology, the equipment can usually be integrated into the workplace, greatly simplifying its use.

Speech is the dominant means of communication at all levels of command, allowing tactical commanders a personal influence on troops by telephone or radio messages.

The transmission of written information in teleprint (teletype) ensures that the originator and receiver have documentation. The utilization of facsimile equipment allows the transmission of drawings, texts, sketches, and so on with very little delay.

Thanks to the use of data-transmission equipment, staff officers can carry out operational tasks, communications, and report commitments as well as time-consuming routine activities much faster, more precisely, and more thoroughly than before.

EMPLOYMENT OF SIGNALS

The layout and choice of command posts by the major unit commander gives a basic outline for signal operations. The signals commander advises the major unit commander in all questions concerning communications, suggests contributions to be made by the communications service and electronic warfare in the operation order, and issues special directives for the signal corps, regulating details for the signals' assignment and its operation. He commands the signal troops subordinate to him.

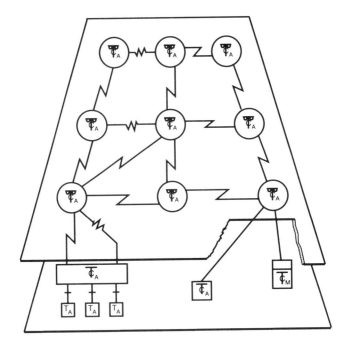

Legend:

Symbol	Description	Symbol	Description	Symbol	Description
𝄐ₐ	Access node	Tₐ	Dial telephone set	⌐Z—	Radio relay
𝄐ₐ	Trunk node	𝄐ₘ	Exchange (manual)	⌐W—	Wire communication

Figure 3. AutoKo network.

The signals commander has radio, wire, and radio-relay at his disposal as equivalent means of communication. He uses the means of communication so that, even when rapid changes of location or command channels occur, reliable communications links are available. This assignment is complicated by the effects of weapons and electronic war material, technical limits, weather, atmospherics, technical disturbances, and sabotage. Therefore, he strives to arrange several means of communications so that they overlap; this is called redundancy of communications.

The mode of operation depends on the level of command, the type of combat, and the degree of troop mobility. The following possibilities exist:

• exclusive use of radio
• exclusive use of wire/radio relay
• utilization of radio, with backup by wire/radio relay at points of main effort
• utilization of wire/radio relay, with backup by radio at points of main effort
• equivalent overlapping utilization of radio and wire/radio relay.

Communications links between staff and troops of superior or subordinate commands are established, maintained, and operated according to the following principles: from superior to subordinate headquarters, from the support to the supported unit, and among adjacent troops from left to right.

Characteristic features. The modes of attack, defense, and delaying actions set different priorities for signals operations.

Due to the rapidity of movements when attacking, radio is the main means of control. Prior to commencement of an attack, communications silence is usually imposed to conceal intentions. It is imperative for the success of an attack that radio communications with all subordinate and cooperating troops be available at any time after the line of departure has been crossed.

Signals commanders maintain reserves when attacking in order to deal with the continuous change in point of main effort, direction of attack, and formation.

Wire/radio relays are generally the most important means of communication for defense. The more mobile combat is, the more significant radio becomes.

It cannot be overemphasized that the main task of the signals commander is the correct and farsighted distribution of connecting points on the field. He must take into account the whole operational plan of the major unit commander, in particular deployment of troops, the key terrain, the fire and barrage plan, the point of main effort, and plans for counterattacks.

Where delaying tactics are involved, it is difficult to maintain communications links. Generally speaking, radio is then the main mode of command and control. Only the most important command posts are connected with wire/radio relay.

The signals commander must cooperate closely with the commanders of the delaying forces so the communications links can be dismantled at the right moment.

Depending on the level of command, for all types of combat, emphasis with regard to modes of communication is gradually transferring from wire/radio relay to radio the lower the level of command and the more mobile the combat is.

When on the march, communications silence prevails to camouflage the movements. All means of conveying information without using electromagnetic emissions have to be exploited. Messengers in motorized vehicles and helicopters are employed. Generally speaking, communications links (wire/radio relay) are ordered to reporting points.

If communications networks are overloaded and command is therefore in jeopardy, the major unit commander can order, for a limited time, restrictions for signals operation. This will ensure fast and safe transmission of information that is of importance for command purposes.

Communications security is a decisive factor for success in combat and for the survival of the troops. Therefore, information that is important to command is safeguarded by appropriate security procedures. The safest procedure is the electronic ciphering of speech, print, facsimile, and data. This enables plain text to be transferred into cryptotext—and vice versa—simultaneously with transmission of the information.

ELECTRONIC WARFARE

Electromagnetic emissions are subject to physical limitations. All armies take advantage of this "law of physics," even in times of peace, so as to gather and evaluate information about countries that can be classed as potential adversaries within the framework of electronic warfare. This is not forbidden by international law; only transmission frequencies per se are regulated. Therefore, each state is free to monitor radio transmissions and evaluate findings. In addition, electronic reconnaissance is a main instrument for military and political leaders in all countries for the early recognition of another country's intention to attack, both in peace and in times of crisis. The acquisition of information with electronic warfare methods, therefore, contributes to security and political stability in the world.

Electronic warfare comprises the following subsections:

- communications and electronic intelligence
- electronic support measures
- electronic countermeasures
- electronic counter-countermeasures.

Communications intelligence (COMINT) monitors and evaluates the wireless communications traffic of an adversary. The command then receives contributions toward assessment of the situation and, in time of war, indications that aid in firing on targets.

Electronic intelligence (ELINT) monitors and evaluates the emissions of an adversary's electrical noncommunications emitters, such as radar. In this way the command acquires knowledge about the adversary's weapons systems, in particular artillery and air defense weapons.

In the past, filing cards, paper, and pencils were the means available for evaluating the results of monitoring, whereas electronic data processing now enables a rapid and comprehensive evaluation. Tactical observations are finally reported to the major unit commander.

Passive listening, by electronic warfare support measures (ESM), aims to recognize an immediate threat at once and to counteract it with the appropriate measures. These may be alteration of the conduct of operations, utilization of weapons, and electronic countermeasures and counter-countermeasures.

Electronic countermeasures (ECM) include active interference and deception of the adversary by electronic means. The adversary's command and intelligence should be hampered and deployment of his weapons obstructed.

It is the objective of electronic interference to weaken the adversary's command capability and hinder the deployment of his weapons. Electronic deception by simulating, falsifying, or imitating communications traffic aims to mislead the adversary's communications intelligence.

To guarantee the command capability of friendly troops, all command levels must resort to appropriate electronic counter-countermeasures (ECCM). These aim to render the enemy's reconnaissance more difficult, as well as to protect one's own communications network and means of position finding and command. The most effective counter-countermeasure is radio silence. By maintaining radio silence, the major unit commander protects the troops under his command from enemy electronic measures. He can order radio silence altogether for all electronic means or separately for radio, radio relay, or radar. Radio silence involves restrictions and handicaps, so the commander must carefully consider whether the advantages of radio silence outweigh the disadvantages of forgoing signal communications.

Because of the utilization of modern electronics in command and weapon systems, all armies are dependent on the use and propagation of electromagnetic waves. The command capability of friendly troops and the efficiency of intelligence and weapons systems cannot be guaranteed without the utilization of modern electronics. For this reason, electronic warfare belongs to the most significant elements of combat, alongside fire, movement, and barriers; it has become an inseparable component for both sides.

Prospects

At the end of the 1980s, it was becoming apparent that signal corps were developing into one of the most technological branches of the services. Some possible trends of development are described below.

COMMUNICATIONS SYSTEMS

Fully automated digital systems will become increasingly important for exchange and transmission techniques. Digital communications systems are superior to the traditional analog systems, particularly with regard to the operational and economical aspects.

Furthermore, the technological capability of combining the exchange and multiplex functions and multichannel encryption have resulted in lower costs than in the past. Because cipher modules can be integrated into digital equipment, further possibilities of economizing result.

Where the transmission of information is concerned, existing beam waveguides made of glass or synthetic fibers are of increasing consequence, to the detriment of electrical wires such as traditional copper cables. The particular advantages of this new medium stem from its large bandwidth, very low attenuation, and high immunity to interference. Possibilities for its use are becoming apparent, particularly where a large volume of information has to be transmitted. This is especially the case for army battle headquarters.

Microwave technology is already an important component of modern military information systems. It has opened up new frequency ranges and therefore provides possible solutions for overcoming the existing difficulties in the HF, VHF, and UHF frequency bands caused by the bands being filled to capacity.

Other possible applications are headquarters communications and short-range communications between formations/units that are deployed within a small area or are stationary.

The susceptibility of conventional transmission procedures to interference can, in the future, be eliminated to a great extent by the introduction of information transfer systems that are largely immune to interference. This is especially true for radio communications, which are particularly sensitive to interference.

As a result of the utilization of modern technology (microelectronics, replacement of mechanical and electromechanical switching components with electrical ones, resistance to interference, and bulk encryption, for example), it will be possible to use radio equipment in a way similar to how equipment is currently used for entertainment electronics.

A new concept of operation in which radio communications are no longer headquarters-oriented but establish and operate reticularly with large area coverage seems possible in the future.

MEANS OF ELECTRONIC DATA PROCESSING

The command of the troops and the employment of modern and more efficient weapons and intelligence systems can no longer be mastered by traditional speech and teletype procedures alone, because ever-increasing volumes of information requiring decisions need to be processed. Computer-assisted information systems will consequently take on greater importance and facilitate command of the troops. It will be possible to save considerable time in the assessing of a situation and the planning and issuing of orders. Whereas much time was consumed monitoring and processing information when command procedures were not automated, which left very little time available for creative work, it is to be expected that this relationship will be reversed.

Furthermore, it is highly likely that future systems will be controlled so they can take over the strategy and methods of human beings in certain spheres. For example, systems for situation analysis on the battlefield, for the planning of command operations, or for decision making are conceivable. This can give rise to basic changes in command and control. The point will be to liberate commanders and staff officers from standardized formalities—that is, routine work—through the expedient employment of electronic data-processing systems, thus allowing them more time for creative initiative.

As it seems a basic characteristic of modern technology that the connection between signal and data-processing techniques becomes continually closer, it will probably not be expedient in the future to differentiate between the two from an organizational point of view. It seems obvious that the two should be combined.

IMPLICATIONS FOR PERSONNEL

It would appear that the future mission of the signal corps lies in the field of electronic data processing. The soldier of the signal corps, who in the past established communications for command posts, was superseded in the 1980s by the introduction of automated systems. The soldier of the signal corps in the future will be involved primarily in the construction and technical surveillance of modern communications systems and the use and operation of command information systems. This would imply, as a possible consequence, that training in communications techniques alone is no longer adequate for the future soldier in the signal corps. Training will have to be more comprehensive: in other words, it must be extended to cover data-processing and computer systems.

ORGANIZATIONAL IMPLICATIONS

Structural changes will inevitably unite the responsibility for communications and data techniques—for both organizational and operational reasons—and thus obtain a uniform branch of command support.

It is conceivable that signal corps will develop into a command services corps. The current main function, communications, could be supplanted by the functions of command, control, and communications (C^3). Far-reaching organizational measures cannot be excluded in the future if development in the field of electronics and in particular data processing continues with undiminished celerity and, if at the same time, economization is enforced. If technology can relieve command of a large proportion of routine affairs, and deal with a much greater volume of information than at present, this will guarantee better command support than at the present time. This could lead to a decrease in the levels of command. Nevertheless, it should be taken into account that command must remain feasible, without being fully dependent on technology, if success is to be achieved under conditions of war.

ULRICH STORK

SEE ALSO: Command, Control, Communications, and Intelligence; Electronic Warfare Technology Applications; Radar Technology Applications; Technology and Warfare.

Bibliography

Coker, K. R., and C. E. Rios. 1988. *A concise history of the U.S. Army Signal Corps.* Fort Gordon, Ga.: Office of the Command Historian, U.S. Army Signal Center and Fort Gordon.

Myer, C. R. 1982. *Division-level communications, 1962–1973.* Washington, D.C.: Government Printing Office.

Scheips, P. J., ed. 1980. *Military signal communications.* New York: Arno Press.

Torrieri, D. J. 1981. *Principles of military communication systems.* Dedham, Mass.: Artech House.

U.S. Department of the Army. 1969. *Historical sketch of the United States Army Signal Corps: 1860–1969.* Fort Monmouth, N.J.: U.S. Army Signal Corps.

———. 1985. *Division/corps information and communication flow analysis.* Fort Leavenworth, Kans.: Combined Arms Operations Research Activity, Scientific and Technical Support Directorate.

CONSUMPTION RATES, BATTLEFIELD

Consumption rates are a major factor of logistics; they are the assessment of the quantities of various materials that are consumed or expected to be consumed each day in combat. They can be defined as the average quantity of an item consumed or expended during a given time interval, expressed in quantities by the most appropriate unit of measurement.

The term *consumption rates* is commonly applied to the three basic battlefield consumables: rations, fuel for vehicles, and ammunition. These form the regular pattern of resupply and are delivered to combat organizations on a daily basis. Other requirements, such as reinforcements, vehicles, guns, and spare parts are supplied as they are needed, rather than on an automatic basis. This is reflected in the different terminology used for them: battle damage, battlefield attrition rates, casualties, battle wastage, or equipment replacement rates.

Rations

The term *rations* includes food, forage for animals, and such items as disinfectants, insecticides, and foot powder. It is normally the responsibility of the logistic staff to calculate how many rations are required and to implement their procurement, holding, and issue. The food element can be fresh food, tinned food, or composite ration packs. It is common practice to supply fresh food as long as possible.

Consumption rates of rations are easy to calculate, since they are based on the number of men taking part in an operation and the number of days or weeks for which supply is assumed to be required. The tactical conditions or type of combat has little effect on usage.

Fuel

Consumption rates of fuel for motor vehicles, aircraft, and ships are based on the planned usage or distance to be traveled. This calculation is straightforward and may be expressed in liters (gal.) per vehicle or as metric tons of fuel per aircraft or ship. The quantities required will often be aggregated into a daily total for an organization (i.e., so much per brigade or division).

In a mobile war, fuel will often be the largest item in the supply chain. Consumption calculations have to take into account ever-increasing mechanization of the battlefield and the introduction of larger, more powerful engines. This constant increase in fuel consumption is easily illustrated:

- Up to 1914, the standard measure of consumption was 10 kilograms (22 lb.) of forage per horse.
- In World War I (1914–18), consumption of fuel averaged less than 10 liters (2.6 gal.) a day per vehicle.
- In World War II (1939–45), a British Spitfire fighter aircraft used 205 liters (53.3 gal.) of fuel for each hour's flying.
- In the 1980s, an F-16 fighter aircraft used 4,550 liters (1,183 gal.) for each hour's flying, while a transport helicopter consumed more than 2,000 liters (520 gal.) an hour.

Ammunition

The supply of ammunition during operations is automatic and is designed to replace actual expenditure, which is revealed in daily returns to the appropriate headquarters. Since ammunition expenditure varies directly with the intensity of combat, there is considerable fluctuation in ammunition resupply.

From a knowledge of the quantities of ammunition expended during a long series of engagements, it is possible to produce average rates for "quiet," "contact," and "intense" periods of combat. The ratio among these rates may be 1:4:10–20—that is, intense rates may be ten or twenty times as much as quiet rates. These expenditure rates can be presented in various ways. One method often used is:

- rounds per gun per day for artillery and tanks
- rounds per division per week or month for such things as grenades, mortars, mines, and small-arms ammunition
- tons per division per month for explosives and demolition items.

In common with fuel, consumption rates for ammunition have risen continually in modern wars. Two major reasons for this have been the adoption of larger caliber weapons and faster rates of fire. The continual trend toward heavier consumption can be seen in the following figures:

- In the eighteenth century, a force of 40,000 men expended some five tons of munitions per day.
- In the Franco-Prussian War of 1870–71, the Prussian army fired an average of 199 rounds per gun over the duration of the war.
- In the first six weeks of World War I, the German army fired 1,000 rounds per gun.
- Over the four years of World War I, a German army corps consumed on average 40 tons of ammunition per day.
- In World War II, an American division consumed an average of 675 tons of ammunition and food per day. (Overall, the average combat division in this war consumed 400 tons of supplies per day.)
- In the 1950s, in Korea, a U.S. division consumed 1,000 tons of supplies per day.
- In the 1990s, it is anticipated that a U.S. division would use more than 3,450 short tons of ammunition per day.

New Factors in Consumption Rate Planning

The normal method of calculating consumption rates was to base them on the quantities consumed in recent combat augmented by projections of future usage. Over the last 30 years (1960–90), however, certain campaigns have highlighted different factors that have radically changed the basis of calculation.

Three wars are of significance: the Korean War of the 1950s, the Arab-Israeli War of 1973, and the Iran-Iraq War of the 1980s.

The Korean War was fought over rough, undeveloped terrain. After rapid movement in the initial stages, the war became static, resembling in some respects the trench warfare of World War I. Enormous quantities of ammunition were consumed by both sides over a period of years.

In 1973, the Arab-Israeli War between Israel and the forces of Syria and

Egypt highlighted a new aspect. This war lasted only eighteen days, but the intensity of the fighting was such that equipment attrition—that is, losses of tanks and guns—became the decisive factor.

In that campaign, a tank was destroyed every ten minutes and an aircraft knocked out every hour. Egypt and Syria started the war with 4,300 tanks; eighteen days later, they had only 1,746 left. More than one-third of their 1,250 aircraft were lost.

The Israelis lost 840 out of 2,000 tanks and 109 aircraft out of a force of 476. The Israelis started the campaign with six months' supply of fuel and ammunition, based on their experience of the 1967 war. At the end of eighteen days they were suffering severe shortages.

In direct contrast, the Iran-Iraq War of the 1980s has demonstrated that nations can still find themselves involved in static warfare. Although guided weapons systems and missiles were employed, the main ammunition consumption was still by conventional artillery.

It was the differences among these three campaigns that raised the question of the efficacy of logistic calculations based on classic consumption rates of ammunition, fuel, and rations. Although two of the wars demonstrated the continuing importance of the three commodities, the equipment attrition in the eighteen days of the October War caused other elements to be considered more closely.

After this campaign, military staffs started to look at two new factors: the cost and production complexities of new ammunition, especially guided missiles, and the likely attrition rates of major equipment like aircraft, tanks, and APCs.

One view currently held is that guided weapons (antiship, antitank, and antiaircraft missiles) are so accurate that they replace hundreds of shells. Therefore, on a simple mathematical ratio, a proportion of conventional ammunition can be replaced by a calculated number of missiles. The counterargument is that shells are comparatively cheap and easy to produce, while missiles are expensive, complex, and difficult to manufacture.

Planners have therefore started to consider whether it is possible to regard guided weapons in the same way as conventional ammunition. Can they be produced and supplied in combat in the same way? And can the normal methodology of calculating consumption rates be applied to them?

The second factor concerns equipment attrition rates. The fast, mobile action of the Arab-Israeli War showed that the deciding factor might not be the amount of shells and missiles a nation possessed, but the number of weapon platforms available to fire them. The logical conclusion of this view is whether it is worthwhile planning to resupply a specific number of tanks with ammunition if only half the tanks will be available to fire them.

Current Methods of Calculation

Although the term *consumption rates* has traditionally been applied to rations, fuel, and ammunition, nations have always made allowance for the replacement of tanks, guns, and aircraft lost in battle. This, however, has depended on a rate of loss that a nation was able to match from its reserves and its industrial base.

The Arab-Israeli War demonstrated two things. First, the loss of aircraft, tanks, and guns could be so heavy that no industrial base would be able to replace them at the rate they were being destroyed. And second, the loss could be so severe that it affected the calculations of ammunition consumption.

The theoretical solution is to expand industrial production to produce so many tanks, guns, and aircraft that there will always be sufficient amounts to keep the armed forces at their original level. The complexity and cost of modern equipment, however, mean that this answer is beyond the resources of even the wealthiest of nations. In any event, nations can no longer rely on a lengthy warning period during which new production lines can be established.

The current calculation of consumption rates, therefore, has to take into account the differences of usage between guided missiles and conventional ammunition and the likely heavy attrition rates of weapon platforms.

The solutions adopted by some nations is to calculate consumption rates on the types of engagement in which specific ammunition will be used and not on an estimate of the total number of rounds and missiles a division might fire in a day. This method involves bringing together two planning functions: the calculation of consumption rates (for consumables) and the planning of war reserve levels of major equipment. These tasks were dealt with separately in the past, but the Arab-Israeli War showed that they are interdependent. This is illustrated clearly by the new method of enumerating some munitions on a daily basis while others are calculated for the duration of a war.

New Categories of Consumption Rates

Some examples of this type of categorization are:

Level-of-effort munitions (applied to indirect-fire weapons like conventional artillery): Munitions for these weapons are calculated on the basis of a daily expenditure rate (the number of combat days and an assumed attrition rate) to counter targets the number of which is unknown.

Lifetime-oriented munitions: These are munitions, stocked for all direct-fire weapons (includes tanks and armored cars), that have a finite life in combat, which is defined as an average number of engagements; the requirement is the sum of munitions expended or lost by that equipment until it is destroyed.

Threat-oriented munitions: Munitions intended to neutralize a finite assessed threat and for which the total requirement is determined by an agreed mathematical model.

Target-oriented munitions: Munitions intended to neutralize a finite assessed number of targets and for which the total requirement is determined by an agreed mathematical model.

This is a radical change from previous methods of calculation. The old philosophy of consumption rates was open ended—that is, so long as an army, air force, or navy fought, it would consume ammunition and fuel at an assumed rate. These forecasts were altered as knowledge was obtained of combat characteristics, enemy tactics, and the effects of the terrain. They were based on an assumption of sufficient warning of a crisis to allow an increase in production of weapons systems and ammunition and that a campaign would be long enough for any necessary changes in consumption rates to be developed.

Three examples illustrate the new philosophy.

1. Consumption rates of lifetime-oriented munitions are based on three factors: a calculation of the number of tanks or armored cars that will be engaged in combat each day; the amount of ammunition they will expend in each engagement; and the number that will be destroyed each day. In effect the question of how much ammunition a force of tanks will use daily depends on an assessment of the number of tanks available to fire it.

2. Threat-oriented weapons include air-to-air missiles, surface-to-air missiles, and antiship missiles. Nations have usually worked out the specific threat they have to face (the number of enemy aircraft, divisions, and/or ships) and against which guided weapons/missiles will be employed. Using computer-based projections and combat simulation, a calculation is made of the total number of missiles required.

In this instance, the estimate of consumption rates becomes an estimate of war reserve stock levels, since it is not daily usage that is calculated but the total quantity needed in war.

3. Level-of-effort munitions—that is, conventional ammunition for artillery weapons—are still based on expected daily expenditure rates and include allowances for an unknown number of targets or engagements.

At the end of the twentieth century, the basis for calculating consumption rates for fuel and food remains much as it has always been. They are still vital components of military logistics, but assessment of expected usage is relatively straightforward.

By contrast, consumption rates for ammunition has become a complicated exercise. The Arab-Israeli War has persuaded some logisticians that consumption rates are now so dependent on equipment attrition that this is the only factor to be taken into account. A second complication is the reliance that is placed on guided weapons and, as a consequence, a tendency to reduce estimates of consumption of conventional munitions.

Future Methods of Assessment

There is no doubt that the advent of guided missiles has introduced a new element into the calculation of consumption rates, as has the crippling equipment losses of the Arab-Israeli War. Some military planners believe that this type of short, intense campaign will be the pattern of most future warfare.

If tanks and aircraft are consumed at the rate some strategists predict, and if guided weapons are as efficient as they hope, then consumption rates of food, rations, and conventional ammunition will indeed diminish in importance.

There are, however, other lessons of the Arab-Israeli War that are often overlooked. It took an average of 80 missiles to bring down each aircraft in that campaign, and, in one instance, a tank survived fourteen attacks by guided weapons. Furthermore, out of every five tanks they lost, the Israelis managed to repair three to return to combat.

A balance has to be drawn between excessive reliance on new technology and ignoring its implications. The prudent course is to prepare for the possibility of a short, intense campaign involving maximum usage of every type of guided missile and conventional ammunition. This planning must, however, always be undertaken with the realization that the conflict may last longer than expected. This has been the lesson of warfare throughout history, but it is too often forgotten.

What must not be forgotten is that no matter how long a conflict may last, consumption rates have to be calculated. Whether this applies only to rations, fuel, and ammunition or is extended to include the replacement of tanks and aircraft is unimportant. Efficient resupply of materiel and consumables depends on accurate calculation, and this is a basic requirement of military planning.

N. T. P. MURPHY

Bibliography

Great Britain. War Office. 1922. *Statistics of the military effort of the British Empire during the great war.* London: His Majesty's Stationery Office.

Historical Evaluation and Research Organization (HERO). 1966. *Historical analysis of wartime replacement requirements: Experience for selected major items of combat equipment.* 2 vols. Dunn Loring, Va.: HERO.

———. 1976. *Artillery survivability in modern war.* Dunn Loring, Va.: HERO.

Thayer, T. 1985. *The U.S. in Vietnam: War without fronts.* Boulder, Colo.: Westview Press.

Tholen, A. D., J. T. Goodley, and J. Seeley. 1970. *System for estimating materiel wartime attrition and replacement requirements.* 2 vols. McLean, Va.: Research Analysis Corporation (RAC).

U.S. Department of the Army. Headquarters. 1970. *Field Manual 101-10: Staff officers' field manual—Organizational, technical, and logistic data.* Washington, D.C.: Government Printing Office.

CONVENTIONAL WAR

There are few terms within the realm of military science that seem to be as clear as *conventional war*. It is used widely to denote wars fought with conventional means or in a conventional way. *Conventional* can be interpreted as "customary," leading to the common understanding of the term; that is, conventional war is "ordinary" war in that it is similar to wars fought in the past. However, apart from this "commonsense definition," there are no generally accepted scientific or political definitions.

Within the North Atlantic Treaty Organization (NATO) a conventional weapon is defined as "a weapon which is neither nuclear, biological nor chemical" (Joint Chiefs of Staff Pub. 1, 1987, Washington, D.C.: Government Printing Office).

On the other hand, the term *conventional* is often related only to *nonnuclear* as in the official definition of the U.S. Department of Defense for conventional forces, defined as "those forces capable of conducting operations using nonnuclear weapons." The *Dictionary of Military Terms* (Dupuy, Hayes, and Johnson 1986) primarily contrasts conventional with nonnuclear but admits that "chemical and biological weapons may also be considered unconventional." The dictionary also uses conventional "to distinguish operations of forces of a normal combat nature, as opposed to operations or forces of an insurgent or an insurgency."

The term *conventional war* is not in general use in Soviet military science. It is not defined in the *Soviet Military Encyclopedic Dictionary*. When the term is used, it is used to classify wars in terms of means of destruction and weapons (i.e., to distinguish between nuclear and nonnuclear wars).

Thus, it is only clear that a conventional war is a nonnuclear war. Other ways to distinguish conventional from nonconventional war must be the subject of further discussion.

Conventional Weapons

The easiest way to define conventional weapons is to include all weapons except those defined as nonconventional. There is only one category of weapons generally accepted as nonconventional: nuclear weapons systems.

The logic of this classification is questionable, however, because nuclear weapons are fully integrated in the armed forces of the major powers of the world. There are elaborate strategies and doctrines for the roles and functions of nuclear weapons in peace and in war. Training in the use of nuclear weapons and in protection against the effects of nuclear weapons is part of the normal military training of the armed forces of the nuclear powers. And the international law of war does not explicitly deal with nuclear weapons; their use is regulated by the same rules as are all other (conventional) weapons. Thus, the use of nuclear weapons would have to meet the basic requirements for a just war and for the conduct of a war (e.g., the principles of proportionality and discrimination). Therefore, it can be argued that, from the aspect of international law, a nuclear war must be considered a "normal," conventional war.

On the other hand, international law provides specific rules for dealing with weapons that often are considered conventional. This is especially true for biological and chemical weapons. Biological warfare is the object of the 1972 Convention of the Prohibition of the Development, Production, and Stockpiling of Bacteriological (Biological) and Toxin Weapons and on their Destruction. The use of "asphyxiating, poisonous or other gases, and of all analogous liquids, materials or devices" is outlawed by the 1925 Geneva Gas Protocol.

In addition, the use of means causing superfluous suffering has been prohibited since the 1868 St. Petersburg Declaration. This prohibition has been modified several times since; the last addition was the result of the 1980 Geneva Convention on prohibitions or restrictions on the use of certain conventional weapons, which may be deemed to be excessively injurious or to have indiscriminate effects. The 1980 convention restricts and partly prohibits the use of mines, incendiary weapons, and other devices.

The 1980 convention reflects the dilemma of the term *conventional weapon*: It is used without defining it, allowing the assumption that conventional weapons are those explicitly covered by international law. Based on this assumption, conventional weapons are nonnuclear—and nothing else.

Conventional Ways to Fight a War

Using the same approach as before, it is necessary to determine the meaning of nonconventional warfare. It is often suggested that guerrilla warfare, revolutionary warfare, and insurgency warfare are nonconventional (or "subconventional").

This classification seems somewhat contradictory when the commonsense meaning of conventional as customary is taken into account. The historical roots of insurgency warfare and all its related forms can be traced back at least 2,000 years, and these forms of war have outnumbered all other ("conventional") wars—especially in the last century. Would it be possible to consider such a phenomenon, which has occurred so often in recorded human history, as nonconventional?

Furthermore, since the 1977 Geneva Protocol II, the law of war is also explicitly applied to revolutionary or internal wars. Following the same logic as above, it must be suggested that insurgency wars (and similar forms) are also part of the wide realm of conventional war.

Such an approach also avoids the problem of distinguishing between low-intensity conflicts and conventional war. Due to the possible inclusion of low-level or small-scale conventional wars into the category of low-intensity conflicts, this would also cause difficulty in determining and defining the intensity levels of basically identical forms of war.

To be clear, the proposed inclusion of all nonnuclear wars under the term *conventional war* does not rule out the necessity for making distinctions between conflicts below the level of warfare and conventional wars. The term *subconventional conflicts* might be appropriate for conflicts below the level of warfare.

Future

It has been suggested that conventional wars might occur more often in the future. This suggestion is supported strongly by historic evidence during the 1980s, with wars in the Middle East, Far East, Africa, and Latin America.

There are other developments that also support this notion. The first is connected with nuclear strategy: While nuclear deterrence has proven successful in deterring nuclear war and wars between the superpowers, it has been unable to deter all forms of wars. This and the probable increasing withdrawal of the nuclear powers from areas they used to consider vital might lead to future attempts by lesser powers to use military means to resolve their conflicts.

Second, it has become widely accepted that nuclear wars cannot be won. It also has become clear that, if the use of force should be considered unavoidable, sole actions below the threshold of conventional war are not decisive in most cases. Therefore, seeking a military decision would be bound to the waging of a conventional war.

Third, the concept of using emerging technologies for the development of weapons systems is leading to new qualities of conventional weapons. The accuracy and lethality of such systems will be significantly increased, and emerging technologies may lead to a kind of weaponry not covered by current arms control measures. Scenarios and force structures might emerge in which extremely well-equipped infantry, not tanks or aircraft, will constitute the main thrust of decisive military action. In this case, all efforts to limit the probability of armed conflicts through arms control agreements might become obsolete; and future wars, which would be conventional in that they were nonnuclear, although very novel in other respects, might become more likely.

It is far too early to evaluate the likelihood of conventional wars in the future. The above-mentioned developments might increase their frequency, others might work the other way. One thing is certain: Conventional war has accompanied the development of mankind for ages—it appears unlikely that this course, as a phenomenon of human behavior, will change in the near future.

HEINZ KOZAK

SEE ALSO: Chemical Warfare; Land Warfare; Limited War.

Bibliography

Chandler, D. 1974. *The art of warfare on land.* London: Hamlyn Press.

Douglass, J. D., and A. M. Hoeber. 1981. *Conventional war and escalation—The Soviet view.* New York: National Security Information Center.

Dupuy, T. N. 1980. *The evolution of weapons and warfare.* New York: Bobbs-Merrill.

Dupuy, T. N., G. P. Hayes, and C. C. Johnson. 1986. *Dictionary of military terms: A guide to the language of warfare and military instructions.* New York: H. W. Wilson.

O'Brien, W. V. 1981. *The conduct of just and limited war.* New York: Praeger.

Ropp, T. 1962. *War in the modern world.* New York: Collier Books.

Small, M., and D. J. Singer. 1982. *Resort to arms, international and civil wars 1816–1980.* Beverly Hills, Calif.: Sage.

Walzer, M. 1977. *Just and unjust wars.* New York: Basic Books.

D

DECEPTION

Deception conceals one's intentions and capabilities. In addition, deception may attempt deliberately to mislead the adversary. Therefore, deception is one of the primary means to achieve surprise, which is one of the principles of war. It causes the adversary to react less rapidly and to employ his forces in a less than optimum manner. Sun Tzu (ca. 500 B.C.), the first known military author, concluded: "All warfare is based on deception. If you know the enemy and know yourself, you need not fear the result of a hundred battles. If you know yourself but not the enemy, for every victory gained you will suffer a defeat." Throughout history, deception has played a major role on the level of tactics and operations.

On the level of military policy and strategy, deception plays a different role. In this nuclear age, war prevention and, should prevention fail, war containment and termination are of paramount importance. Deterrence of potential aggressors, of unwarranted escalation, and of the continuation of war are necessary. They will only be achieved if credible resolve and visible capability dissuade the adversary from initiating or continuing dangerous actions. Therefore, in a strategic environment, deception can be counterproductive and may have disastrous consequences.

Deception—The Military Context

Surprise is one of the principles of war, one of the prerequisites for success in battle. It can be achieved by concealing one's capability and intention and by intentionally misleading the enemy. At a minimum, deception causes uncertainty in the opposing commander's mind and causes him to act and react less rapidly than necessary. This should allow friendly forces to stay one step ahead of the adversary's forces. In addition, if the enemy can be deceived, he will employ his forces ineffectively in the wrong place and in the wrong manner. He will attack where one's own forces are strongest and best prepared. His defenses may be strongest where one's own attack will not be launched. Deception, therefore, has been important for military actions since time immemorial.

Deception is used by all services, all branches, and at all levels. The individual soldier camouflages himself, his weapon, his vehicle, and his position.

271

Similarly, ships and aircraft are already being designed so that their radar and infrared signatures are less conspicuous. In addition, whenever necessary, they reduce electronic emittance and employ specific tactics to evade enemy sensors. Finally, many ships and aircraft are capable of employing specific means (e.g., chaff and flares) to actively deceive the enemy and his weaponry.

On a higher level, major operations are also normally supported by deception. Since the adversary will suspect such measures, all steps designed to deceive the enemy must be integrated, possibly into an elaborate cover and deception plan, to ensure that no contradictions occur and only one consistent story will be revealed to the enemy. Therefore, in the planning of major operations, it has often been advisable to appoint one authority for the planning and execution of deception.

Means of deception often employed are:

1. Electronic deception, which feeds false information to enemy sensors by establishing radio networks that do not reflect true headquarters and true units, by feigning unusually low or high levels of radio traffic, by planting false messages into an enemy network, or by controlled breaches of security.
2. Camouflage and concealment of one's capability and intention are the first steps toward active deception.
3. Feints are activities, such as local attacks with a limited objective, that have as their main purpose diversion of enemy attention away from the sector where the main effort will take place.
4. Demonstration is a show of force that does not seek to actually engage the enemy.
5. Displays seek to mislead enemy visual observation or enemy sensors by simulating military objects such as headquarters, airfields, reserve holding areas, artillery positions, depots, and so forth. Portrayals may use actual forces, repeatedly employed, to represent much larger forces.
6. Ruses of war also can cause the enemy to misinterpret what he actually notices. Examples are false flags, false uniforms, civilian clothes, use of captured enemy equipment, use of enemy recognition signs, and the like. The importance and widespread use of ruses are testified to by the fact that in about A.D. 85, Frontinus reported in his book *Strategemata* 583 historic events in which 484 different ruses or tricks were used.

Deception—The Strategic and Political Context

Throughout history, states have tried to deceive not only enemy field commanders, but the highest-ranking enemy military and political leaders as well. War plans, industrial and economic capabilities, and the time required for mobilization and deployment of forces to war stations are among the most jealously guarded secrets of state. In this way, countries also try to achieve surprise on the strategic level to improve their chances for victory.

It should be noted, however, that, throughout history, states have developed not only war-fighting capabilities, but also deterrent postures. In this way humanity is copying nature, since deterrent postures are widespread among animals, some of which attempt to deter adversaries by adopting an impressive posture. The armed forces of smaller states, especially, often have been deployed not only for war fighting, but also for deterring potential aggressors (e.g., Switzerland since about 1550 and Sweden in more recent times).

The traditional importance of deterrence has been reinforced by the advent of nuclear weapons and the simultaneous increase in the destructive power of modern conventional weaponry. In wars fought with modern conventional and nuclear weapons (even excluding chemical and biological weapons), neither side can be victorious; both will lose. Wherever such weapons are available, war prevention, war containment, and war termination are of paramount importance. These are among the missions given to military forces nowadays by governments. Deterrence is the cornerstone of the strategy developed by the North Atlantic Treaty Organization (NATO) and is agreed upon by all member governments.

Deterrence, however, cannot be effective if strategic deception of the enemy is carried to its logical extreme. Deterrence requires that one's capabilities and intentions not be concealed from the enemy. The enemy must be convinced that one's own strategy is to resist if attacked and that the resolve as well as the capability required by such a strategy are available. Only then can the adversary be deterred or persuaded that his aggression would cost him much more than he could possibly gain by aggression.

In an age of strategic deterrence, it is still necessary to conceal many details of one's military posture (e.g., war plans, nuclear targeting, radio codes, mobilization times, etc.). Such secrecy preserves that uncertainty concerning the specifics of the adversaries' reaction, which many regard as an integral component of any deterrent posture. A significant indication of the balance between deception and openness in strategic deterrence is the fact that the former Soviet Union and the United States agreed not to encode the radio traffic of their missile testing.

A strategy of deterrence requires that the adversary be convinced of one's defensive capability, of one's retaliatory capability, and of one's resolve to employ these capabilities should it become necessary. This restricts concealment—lest the adversary disbelieves one's resolve and capability. It also restricts, but does not prevent, attempts to deceive the adversary in that manner on a strictly military level.

FRANZ UHLE-WETTLER

Bibliography

Attiqur Rahman, M. 1981. *Reflections on the principles of surprise & deception*. Lahore: Wajidalis.

Bowyer, J. B. 1982. *Cheating: Deception in war & magic, games & sports, sex & religion, business & con games, politics & espionage, art & science*. New York: St. Martin's Press.

Erfurth, W. 1943. *Surprise*. Trans. S. T. Possony and D. Vilfroy. Harrisburg, Pa.: Military Service.

Handel, M. I. 1976. *Perception, deception, and surprise: The case of the Yom Kippur War*. Jerusalem: Hebrew Univ. of Jerusalem, Leonard Davis Institute for International Relations.

Weyde, E. 1965. *Die trojanische List: zur Theorie und Praxis der unkonventionellen Kriegführung.* Köln: Markus Verlag.
Whaley, B. 1969. *Stratagem: Deception and surprise in war.* Cambridge, Mass.: MIT Center of International Studies.
Wheeler, E. L. 1988. *Stratagem and the vocabulary of military trickery.* New York: E. J. Brill.

DEFENSE

In its most general sense, defense involves the protection of a country's territory, security, and the well-being of its people against hostile forces that may be threatening the borders or the territory of the defending country. Defense is also sometimes viewed as the opposite of offense, thus suggesting a more passive, protective posture, with less threat to another person, group, or country. Defense can also be dynamic and active, but its primary purpose is to prevent or mitigate rather than cause harm or damage. Defense implies reacting to and controlling or defeating another's initiative. This article describes defense at the tactical level of ground warfare; other articles address other aspects of defense.

In the military sense, defense implies resistance to an attack. Although defense is the opposite of offense, the two are closely associated, both operationally and tactically—although because it is intended to foil the onslaught of the attacker, defense is considered to be a less decisive type of military conflict. Whether an operation is offensive or defensive is more often determined by the aim than by the actual military action. Subsequently, an offensive action can on occasion be considered a defensive mission. However, good defense planning discourages or deters potential adversaries from attack.

On occasion, defensive operations require security forces to occupy forward positions. This protects major friendly units from surprise, repels enemy reconnaissance, and gives early warning of a pending attack. Defensive patterns may take a wide variety of forms: defense in depth, fortified, hasty, mobile, passive, and prepared.

Defense in depth is the organization of positions to provide mutual supporting fire within an assigned defensive sector. The intention is to gradually weaken the impact of an attack, to prevent penetration into the defense positions, and to facilitate the displacement of friendly reserve forces. *Fortified defense* is an extensive coordinated defense system with field fortifications and obstacles that allows the commander to position his weapons in such a manner as to maximize available firepower. *Hasty defense* is a type of defense established during contact with the enemy or when contact with the enemy is impending and there is little time for thorough preparations. *Mobile defense* utilizes a minimum of forces and uses fire and maneuver to establish whether an attack is pending and if so to canalize the enemy. *Passive defense* is limited to camouflage and the protection of the individual soldier and his equipment. *Prepared defense* is a system with prepared but not fortified positions.

It is important to distinguish at what level defense is used. For example, at the military-political level, defensive operations can include offensive actions to forestall a suspected enemy attack. At this level, defense presupposes a high degree of threat or at least a high fear of threat. At the operational level, the offensive use of major units may be required to conquer vital terrain or enemy positions so as to ensure a more effective defense. Operational planning focuses on establishing a campaign's major operation's long-term goals—for example, control of a geographical area, reestablishment of political boundaries, or the defeat of an enemy force in the theater of operations. At the tactical level (the conduct of battles within the context of campaigns/major operations, normally at the level of corps and below) counterattacks may become an imperative part of defense if strategic terrain has been lost.

Additional insights into defense regarding purpose, factors affecting success or failure, and the impact of climatic and topographical conditions follow.

The Essence of Defense

The purpose of defense is to spare one's own forces while exhausting the enemy's forces as much as possible. Defensive operations are intended to avoid offensive operations against the enemy, to gain time, to deny the enemy access to an area, and to inflict losses or defeat on an attacking force. It is important that one's own units are stronger at the end of defense operations than those of the enemy.

Compared with the attacker, the defender can be said to be static, in a fixed location. The attacker retains the initiative. He can dictate the type of combat, the time, place, and extent of combat action. Although a defense is never purely passive, the defender must endeavor to regain the initiative.

The essential factor of defense is fire. Taking full advantage of the ranges of all available weapons, fire should usually be opened as soon as possible and preferably while the enemy is making preparations for his attack. To disrupt the synchronization of the enemy's operation, it is important to increase the concentration of fire and engage targets as rapidly as possible.

The success or failure of defense is influenced by the geographical and topographical factors of the area to be defended. The defender has the advantage of being able to plan how to use the terrain best. In the case of local forces, the commander has an even better advantage in the fact that he has knowledge of the terrain and the population.

In regard to establishing defensive positions, a distinction should be made between inland and coastal states. An inland location is propitious for all-around defense. In order to ensure a friendly unit's safe passage through a defense position, the ideal placement of forces should be of circular shape and the external perimeter equally accessible to all units.

Within coastal states, the length and nature of the coast, as well as sea access, will dictate special defense measures. The depth of a country to the length of its coast will determine the extent and nature of coastal defense. Furthermore, the location with respect to the sea will have a determining influence on its maritime awareness and way of thinking. Countries with extensive coastlines are highly sensitive to the use of the coast in their defense planning.

Climatic and topographical conditions influence defense measures. For example, terrain that is impassable in summer may become passable in winter or vice versa. Weather conditions affect the speed with which military forces can construct weapons emplacements and defensive positions and lay mines; they are also important for aircraft and sea vessels. The use of natural terrain barriers and man-made obstacles to improve the natural structure of the terrain helps a defending commander to slow or canalize enemy movement and to protect friendly positions and maneuver.

Defense in the Post-Nuclear Age

STRATEGIC INTENTION AND OPERATIONAL PLANNING

Article 51 of the United Nations Charter permits countries to conduct individual and collective self-defense in the event of an armed attack, thus leading one to assume that countries would restrict their endeavors to the protection and preservation of their own territory. This, however, has not been the case as shown by the hundreds of wars that have been fought since the end of World War II. The reason for such a large number of wars may be that defense is organized along the same lines as attack. Fire and movement determine defense, specifically mobile defense. Because of the development of lethal stand-off weapons, fortresses or fortified installations no longer present a significant obstacle to an attacking force, perhaps serving only as border observation posts or as stationary hardened headquarters.

A mobile defense employs a combination of offensive and defensive action, and such a defense requires a relatively small deployed force. However, a force conducting a mobile defense must have mobility equal to or greater than the opposing force. It must also be capable of conducting a counterattack with a large reserve, preferably with tank and mechanized forces. Considerable battlefield depth is essential for a mobile defense, inasmuch as the enemy is allowed to advance to a position that exposes him to counterattack and envelopment by the mobile reserve.

Defense allows for the destruction of strong enemy forces as far forward as possible, for the retention of control of key terrain against an attack, and for the extra time to enable reinforcements to arrive. A defending commander will use his static forces (infantry) to delay, to cause attrition of, and to halt the attacking force and his mechanized forces (tanks) to conduct spoiling attacks and counterattacks to destroy enemy forces. Such actions will prevent the enemy from carrying out his attack as planned. An effective defense depends on firing all weapons as planned.

A commander is expected to attack the rear areas of the enemy's defensive positions so as to eliminate his artillery and to hinder the orderly moving up of his attacking forces and reserves. A successful defense requires the use of fire, obstacles, and movement. Combat power and fires should be used with surprise effect. The strength of the defender is to be seen in his expedient selection and use of terrain for offensive operations and positioning of obstacles, in conducting necessary movement, and in the use of cover and camouflage for friendly troops. The terrain should conceal friendly troops from the enemy's sight and impede his movements. On open ground and in country that is sparsely intersected, defense largely involves warding off the enemy's armed forces. Close country makes infantry combat easier and provides greater impediments for the aggressor. Possession of key terrain is considered essential for the success of defense. It should be maintained against attacks and regained if lost. The strength of the defense (firepower and obstacles) should be concentrated at the point(s) where the attacker's main threat is (are) expected. Reserves must be positioned where they can respond quickly to the enemy's main threat. The attack must be warded off in the defense area. Destruction of attacking tanks is of vital importance. A mobile defense often requires, in rapid succession, that terrain be held, the enemy be attacked, and, often, that the commander use some of his troops to delay the enemy.

Normally, a defense mission is of unlimited duration. Generally speaking, it is assumed that a defender has only limited forces and reserves available to fulfill the defense mission, whereas the attacker can replenish his assault forces with additional troops.

Infantry can only defend themselves in consolidated positions. Thus, they should launch counterattacks on fully covered terrain and with the support of heavy weapons, tanks, and supporting artillery. Missions assigned to the reserve forces include: counterattacking, containing the enemy if he has penetrated the positions of friendly units, and reinforcing forward defense units. In addition to tanks, the commander should retain an airmobile force capability as a reserve. In defense, particular importance is attached to engineers inasmuch as they must reinforce positions, lay obstacles, protect threatened flanks, and support other units by constructing field fortifications. Both field radios and telephones are essential for command and control of the forces in the defense area.

The forward edge of the defense area constitutes the forward boundary, whereas the rear edge limits the defensive commander's responsibility. The width of the defensive area depends on the enemy situation, the terrain, and type and number of troops available. How and with what forces the defense is to be conducted are covered in the plan of operations. This plan identifies the area to be defended, the key terrain, the combat organization of friendly forces, the coordination measures, and the use of reserves.

WORLDWIDE DEFENSE OF MATERIAL GOODS AND IMMATERIAL VALUES

The term *defense*, even in the military domain, is no longer viewed solely as warding off an enemy's attack on one's own territory or that of one's allies. The interdependence of the industrial nations makes their existence dependent on vital raw materials and the exchange of industrial goods. Hence, an attack on the sources of raw materials and connecting routes between the supplier and the consumer country is considered sufficient reason for defense.

Changes in the political situation in Europe have reduced the tension between East and West. The Warsaw Pact is now defunct. Nevertheless, developments in the field of technology still pose threats. These can be seen, in particular, in the ranges of unmanned missiles, which can be fired with high precision from any point on any target. Future defense will have to safeguard against such attacks.

For some countries, the immediate threat is not conventional attacks across their borders but the threat of ballistic missiles. Thus, intensive surveillance of airspace makes a combined defense front by all the previous branches of the services essential. For the foreseeable future, a country's territorial defense is likely to be increasingly focused on airspace. In the light of rapid developments in technology and weapons' proliferation, new defense structures are being considered, but as in the past, the transition will be gradual.

JOHANNES GERBER

SEE ALSO: Fortification; Offense; Principles of War; Tactics.

Bibliography

Afheldt, H. 1982. *Defensive Verteidigung.* Hamburg: Rowohlt Reinbek.

Aron, R. 1976. *Penser la guerre.* Paris: Edition Gallimond.

Clausewitz, C. von. 1832. *Vom Kriege.* 16. Aufl. 1952. Bonn: Ferd. Dümmler-Verlag.

De Puysegur. 1759. *Art de la guerre.* Paris: Charles-Antoine Jombert.

Drown, J. D., C. Drown, and K. Campbell. 1990. *A single European arms industry?* London: Brassey's.

Dupuy, T. N. 1987. *Understanding war.* New York: Paragon House.

Gerber, J. 1989. *Beiträge zur Praxis der Alternativen Verteidigung.* Münster-Hamburg: Lit Verlag.

Grin, J. 1990. *Military-technological choices and political implications, command and control in established NATO posture and a non-provocative defence.* Amsterdam: VU Univ. Press.

Hogg, I. 1981. *Fortification.* London: Orbis.

Mayers, T. K. 1990. *Understanding weapons and arms control.* McLean, Va.: Brassey's.

Molt, A. 1988. *Der Deutsche Festungsbau von der Memel zum Atlantik.* Friedberg: Podzun-Pallas.

Müller, H. 1880. *Geschichte des Festungskrieges.* Berlin: Verlag Robert Oppenheim.

Navias, M. 1990. *Ballistic missile proliferation in the Third World.* Adelphi Papers No. 252. London: Brassey's.

Palaschewski, T. 1989. *Geographie und Sicherheit.* Regensburg: Walhalla und Praetoria Verlag.

U.S. Department of the Army. 1982. *Field manual 100-5: Operations.* Washington, D.C.: Government Printing Office.

DEPLOYMENT

Deployment is a military term with several related meanings, of which the essence is the arranging of units in formation so that the greatest number of weapons can be brought to bear on the enemy.

In a strategic sense, deployment means the relocation of forces to desired areas of operation. It is this strategic aspect that has drawn public attention to the term *deployment*. For example, the deployment of nuclear forces or the deployment of tank formations close to a border can transmit significant political signals.

Aspects of Deployment

Deployment is characterized by political, economic, and military considerations.

POLITICAL CONSIDERATIONS

The deployment of nuclear weapons, in particular land-based nuclear weapons, has a tremendous political impact. The deployment of nuclear forces as a political measure can present such a serious threat to other countries that it destabilizes the political harmony within those countries and intensifies the political pressure. On the other hand, it may demonstrate the political will to counter any military pressure by military means (deterrence). The North Atlantic Treaty Organization (NATO) also uses the deployment of nuclear forces in various countries to demonstrate solidarity within the Western alliance, because all members must share the risk of a potential first nuclear strike launched by the enemy (risk-community).

The aforementioned considerations also apply to the deployment of non-nuclear forces. The deployment of ground and air forces close to a border may be a strong signal to a neighboring country. It may reflect a determination to counter immediately any military action launched by the neighbor (deterrence), but it may also be understood as a demonstration of political will to take the offensive in case of war.

Whether the deployment of military forces is perceived by the neighboring country as a threat or as a defensive posture depends on the number of units and the type of weapons. Therefore, peaceful movements sometimes call for a weapon-free zone on both sides of a border to ensure that the deployment of forces is not interpreted as an aggressive attitude.

ECONOMIC CONSIDERATIONS

The economic considerations are less obvious. However, they also contribute to the decision about the location of future garrisons and airfields, because the stationing of several thousand soldiers and their dependents can have a considerable economic impact, even on average-size towns.

MILITARY CONSIDERATIONS

Very often military arguments dominate the discussion on how to deploy military forces. In particular, after World War II the military arguments carried more weight than in discussions before World War I. Before World War I, the deployment phase of mobilization lasted two to three weeks, and there was ample time to correct any mal-deployment. Today, however, military planners are confronted with an enemy that can start an attack within days due to the high technical mobility of the forces. Therefore, military planners deploy land forces as close to the preplanned combat positions as possible to be able to counter the threat of a surprise attack. They argue that mal-deployment would cause serious, time-consuming transport problems in times of tension and crisis, in particular with regard to tank formations. Furthermore, the movement of land forces over long distances to their deployment area would interfere with the evacuation of the population to rear areas. Bringing mal-deployed forces forward would therefore increase the problems associated with uncontrolled movements of the population to the rear, especially in densely populated areas.

The geographical conditions that related to a confrontation between NATO and former Warsaw Pact countries focused public attention on the problem of deployment of military forces from a geostrategic point of view. While Warsaw Pact troops would have moved over relatively short land lines of communication, the bulk of NATO's reinforcements would have needed to cross the Atlantic Ocean and the English Channel in times of tension. Since it is not believed that NATO could maintain an effective defense with forces stationed in Europe, effective defense depended upon the timely arrival of substantial reinforcements from abroad. These reinforcement operations are very complex and require early political decisions to ensure the timely and coordinated availability of numerous military and civilian resources. The operations include the control of a pool of oceangoing merchant ships, the coordination of all military and civil aviation efforts, and the coordination of the use of ports and inland surface transport resources, as well as control of the supply of crude oil and petroleum products. Furthermore, long supply lines, caused by badly deployed storage sites, would add to the transport problems and extend the time needed to build up an uninterrupted flow of supply items.

To compensate for this geostrategic handicap, NATO has taken preventive measures to ensure rapid deployment of U.S., Canadian, and British forces to Europe. These include the rapid deployment of land forces whose major equipment is already pre-positioned in central Europe and the reinforcement of combat aircraft in Europe to the optimum levels that can be supported on European airfields.

As to naval forces, early and mission-consistent deployment is a fundamental prerequisite to achieve the requirements and objectives in the event of conflict. Poor deployment of naval forces would be particularly serious at the beginning of a war because it could delay an attempt to neutralize hostile naval forces by mine-laying operations or by blocking the exits of landlocked seas.

Summary and Conclusions

The deployment of military forces has always been practiced to achieve political goals. In particular, the deployment of naval forces has often been used in peacetime to demonstrate possible courses of action in case of a conflict, and this is today applicable to nuclear forces. In this respect, deployment of military forces in nonwar situations aims primarily at applying political pressure to force or prevent political actions.

Military considerations affecting deployment are secondary to political considerations. However, public debate or discussion about deployment often revolves around military arguments, particularly the need for sufficient time to compensate for the disadvantages of mal-deployed forces. In this context, the possibility of a surprise attack as a primary threat to mal-deployed forces is a major consideration. But it is sometimes argued that the problems of mal-deployment are overestimated because modern means of intelligence can detect hostile threatening movements, and because significant progress has been made in modern, industrialized countries to reduce the time needed for mobilization. Automated systems for registration and assignment planning, central management of mobilization, and computer-controlled movements contribute to a fast mobilization, as well as a prompt public call-up using radio broadcasts and TV. It is further argued that many undesired military impacts of mal-deployed forces can be compensated for with timely decisions by the political authorities. (This, of course, demands both political pre-science and determination.)

To summarize, deployment of forces is the result of political considerations and assumptions, military and economic arguments, as well as decisions made in the past.

Rolf Bergmeier

Bibliography

Dupuy, T. N., C. Johnson, and G. P. Hayes. 1986. *Dictionary of military terms.* New York: H. W. Wilson.
U.S. Joint Chiefs of Staff. 1963. *A Dictionary of United States military terms (JCS Pub-1).* Washington, D.C.: Public Affairs Press.

DESERT WARFARE

More than one-fifth of the earth's land area is desert; that is, it receives less than 25 centimeters (10 in.) of rainfall annually. Every continent except Europe includes a desert or deserts. Because of the inhospitable terrain and climatic conditions for both humans and machines, military operations in desert areas are generally conducted solely because that area or adjacent regions are of strategic importance. For example, the North African desert campaigns of World War II were directed at control of the Suez Canal area, a critical link in the world's sea transportation system and the gateway to the vast oil reserves of the Arabian Peninsula. Should these strategically critical resources have fallen under control of either side, it would have provided the controlling side with a singular strategic advantage. More recently, the campaigns and battles of the Arab-Israeli wars, since Israel's independence in 1948, have been fought primarily in deserts.

The world's most recent large-scale conflict, the 1991 Gulf War (Operation Desert Storm), which pitted U.S.-led coalition forces against Iraq, was also fought in the desert (along and on both sides of the Kuwait-Iraq border).

Desert Environments

Lack of fresh water is the single dominant characteristic common to the world's deserts. This condition leads to other common characteristics such as lack of vegetation.

Temperature extremes vary with latitude and season, from recorded high temperatures of 58°C (136°F) in northwest Mexico and in the Libyan Desert to subzero cold of − 45°C (50°F) in the Gobi Desert of eastern Asia. Day-to-night temperature fluctuations can range as much as 21°C (70°F).

TERRAIN

Desert regions have three types of terrain: mountain, rocky plateau, and sand or dune desert. Mountain deserts feature scattered areas of hills or mountains separated by flat dry basins, all generally barren. Higher elevations may rise rapidly from flat open areas to several hundred meters above sea level. In mountain deserts, most of the infrequent rain falls at the higher elevations. From there it runs off rapidly in flash floods (which erode deep gullies and ravines) and deposits gravel and sand around the flatland basins. Here the water evaporates rapidly, although it may remain long enough to support some vegetation, such as briefly blooming wildflowers.

Rocky plateau deserts have only slight variations in elevation, but there are extensive open areas covered with broken rock and sometimes with coarse gravel. There are deeply eroded steep-walled ravines called wadis in the Middle East and arroyos or canyons in the United States and Mexico. The Golan Heights in the area between Israel and Syria is a rocky plateau desert; its gigantic boulders and deep canyons make it a very hazardous place to move about.

Sandy or dune deserts are extensive flat areas covered by sand or fine gravel—the product of centuries of wind erosion. Dunes may reach heights of more than 300 meters (985 ft.) and extend for 25 kilometers (15.5 mi.). Vegetation, while sparse, varies from none at all to scrub growth 1 to 2 meters (3 to 7 ft.) high. The ability to move vehicles in such terrain is a function of the granularity of the sand and gravel. Large formations of vehicles can and have been hidden in the long valley-like intervals between dunes, which can serve as avenues of approach for military operations. The so-called ergs of the Sahara, the Empty Quarter of the Arabian Desert, some of the Californian and northern Mexican deserts in North America, the South African Kalahari Desert, and parts of the northern and north-central Sinai Peninsula deserts are examples of sandy or dune deserts. It was in such a desert that the principal and decisive operations of the 1991 Gulf War were conducted—the "end run" around Iraqi forces in northern Kuwait and southern Iraq by coalition forces led by the U.S. VII Corps.

CLIMATE AND WEATHER

Depending on latitude and season, desert temperatures range from very hot to very cold. The lack of vegetation and generally cloudless skies allow the earth to heat up during the day's bright sunlight and cool quickly to below freezing at night.

Desert winds of hurricane force are not uncommon. Windblown dust and sand can make life virtually intolerable, reduce visibility to a few meters, make vehicular operation and maintenance difficult, and make land navigation by anything but electronic means nearly impossible. Indeed, one of the most significant contributions of modern technology to the operations of coalition forces in the 1991 Gulf War was the Global Positioning System (GPS). A satellite-based electronic means for position location, it made possible precise location of one's position in an otherwise seemingly trackless waste.

WATER

Rain is infrequent and water is scarce in deserts. However, when rain does fall, it results in violent flash flooding because the runoff builds up very quickly.

There are rivers flowing through some desert areas. Rivers such as the Nile, the Colorado, and the Kuiseb in the Namib Desert of southwest Africa are fed by rainfall from areas outside the desert; thus the rivers survive despite high evaporation rates in the desert. These rivers have irrigation potential for lands adjacent to their banks.

There is also groundwater in some deserts. This appears in oases and near-surface wells. This water is subsurface seepage and may have traveled considerable distances. For example, water in a Saharan oasis may have fallen as rain in the highlands to the south before the time of Christ. Potable water supplies can never be taken for granted in the desert.

VISIBILITY

Windblown dust, low cloud density, and intense sunlight combine to produce unusually glaring bright light conditions during the daylight hours. While one can see for great distances, it is also common to grossly underestimate distance. Visibility can be degraded by shimmer—heated air rising from the land surface—and by mirage effects that distort the shape of objects, particularly in the vertical dimension.

Observation is best when accomplished from an elevation—hill, hummock, or dune top. Clear skies at night and high ambient light levels from the moon and starlight make good visibility possible, especially when using light- or image-intensification devices. From the Israeli-Syrian border along the Golan Heights, the Syrian capital of Damascus is nearly 65 kilometers (40 mi.) away, but it appears to be much closer. During the 1973 war, the complete array of Syrian forces moving to battle in the Golan Heights was clearly visible from Israeli Defense Force observation posts on the high ground above Kuneitra.

In both day and night operations, long-range visibility for target detection, acquisition, and fire direction can be significantly enhanced by infrared and other vision-enhancement devices. Primarily designed for night operations, they are also invaluable in daylight operations to reduce the mirage effects noted above. The fact that coalition forces, especially those of the United States, with U.S.-made equipment were equipped with the latest models of this modern technology added significantly to coalition success in Operation Desert Storm.

HABITATION

Deserts are generally uninhabited, although the Bedouins of the North African and Arabian deserts and the herdsmen of Israel's wilderness are exceptions. However, their population density is limited by the meager water supplies and scant vegetation for their flocks. Lizards, snakes, spiders, scorpions, centipedes, and many small invertebrates are found in quantity in deserts. Of these, desert snakes are the most dangerous to man.

The camel is the most well-known variety of specialized desert life. Camels are water-drinkers; they can drink and store up to 120 liters (27 gal.) of water at one time. Other mammals, such as gazelles, draw water from the sparse vegetation on which they graze. Smaller animals, such as rodents, burrow in the sand or under rocks during the daytime to prevent moisture loss, foraging at night. Fleas, ticks, and lice abound and are, as recorded in several soldiers' journals of desert warfare, a persistent nuisance.

Fighting in the Desert

PERSONNEL

The desert is a physically and emotionally fatiguing environment, but it is neutral—it treats friend and foe alike. Physical conditioning of the highest order, excellence of leadership (especially at the small-unit level), and high-quality individual and small-unit training are the key to survival and success in desert operations.

For personnel, acclimatization to extreme heat is probably the most important physical factor. The human body requires about two weeks to adjust to achieve and maintain efficiency in its cooling processes. A loss of 2.5 percent of body fluids (about 1.9 l, or 2 qt.) will reduce human efficiency by about 25 percent. A loss of 15 percent of the body weight (about 11 l, or 12 qt.) is usually fatal. Dehydration is rapid and can go unnoticed. Thus, it is essential to drink small amounts of water at frequent intervals. The several months of acclimatization afforded coalition forces during Operation Desert Shield, together with the opportunity for extensive training by units at division level and below in the very environment in which they would fight, in all likelihood contributed significantly to coalition success.

Remaining fully clothed is one way to inhibit dehydration. Full clothing also helps abate windburn and provides protection from windblown sand and dust. However, the need to protect against a chemical and biological weapons' threat by wearing protective overgarments can overburden the soldier with excess clothing—slowing work, increasing the risk of dehydration, and making normal operations very difficult.

EQUIPMENT

Desert environments affect equipment through several ways: soil trafficability, heat, light, sand and dust, temperature variations, static electricity, and wind.

Normally, tracked vehicles are better suited for desert operations than wheeled vehicles. The sand and rocks in the desert are the cause of the high suspension system maintenance rates, which are generally much higher than where other soils predominate. The Israeli Defense Force, for example, has traditionally employed its U.S.-built tanks (which feature live-tensioned track suspension systems) in operations in the Sinai Desert where sand and gravel soils occur. On the boulder-strewn Golan Heights, however, Israeli Defense Force British-made tanks (featuring dead-link track) perform much better and have historically been employed there. The Israeli-built Merkava tank has a suspension system designed to include the best features of both live- and dead-link track suspension. It is therefore a more versatile machine for Israeli needs than either its British- or U.S.-made predecessors.

Heat is always hard on automotive vehicles. In desert operations, temperature extremes and variations aggravate the problem. Plumbing problems with water-cooled engines in desert operations during World War II led U.S. vehicle engine designers to insist on air-cooled engines for heavy vehicles like tanks. Air-cooled engines are only a partial solution, however. With the advent of turbine engines in tanks, the principal problem became the cleaning of the air input to the engine sufficiently to reduce internal erosion of turbine operating parts. Despite this problem, the U.S.-made M1 Abrams tank, with a turbine engine, performed extremely well, largely reflecting extensive developmental testing of the tank in the deserts of the southwest United States, an environment similar to that encountered in the deserts of Iraq, Kuwait, and Saudi Arabia. The corrosion problem was in addition, however, to the continuing problem of cooling the oil. Also, vehicle batteries required frequent changes of electrolytes to hold their charge under desert heat.

Aircraft flying time and performance can be severely affected by the desert environment. This is particularly true for scout and attack helicopters that operate in or near the ground battle environment. Dust ingestion by engines and blade erosion from sand and dust were particular, although not unanticipated, problems in Operation Desert Storm. While operations in this environment should be expected to strain logistics systems, operationally it is possible to reduce the problem by limiting the amount of time at hover in ground effects and at flight-idle in the dust envelope. Both operational adjustments were successful in reducing environmental effects on helicopters during the 1991 Gulf War.

Desert ambient light—radiant light and its heat effects—are, potentially at least, detrimental to all materials affected by ultraviolet light.

Dust and sand are the greatest inhibitors to efficient functioning of vehicles and aircraft in the desert. Alone they abrade exposed surfaces, clog air-intake inlets, jam weapons, damage exposed electrical insulation, and accumulate in vehicle hulls and aircraft fuselages. Mixed with oils they form an abrasive sludge that can destroy the inside of an engine in minutes.

The temperature variations already described also result in many problems. These range from moisture condensation to changes in pressures inside pressurized systems (like pneumatic tires) to tube bending in tank gun barrels.

Static electricity potential is greater in the desert because of the absence of ground moisture. Secure grounding, especially during procedures such as hot refueling of helicopters, is another matter demanding close attention.

DESERT OPERATIONS

Operationally, the dune deserts, and to some extent rocky plateau deserts, invite battles of operational maneuver, long-range direct-fire battles with tank guns and antiarmor missile systems, and long-range antiaircraft system battles. Such battles demand quick, violent, and decisive action, because good visibility over long distances and the absence of large terrain features ensure a quick enemy response. Tactically, and to some extent operationally, surprise is difficult to achieve. When a defender goes to ground he gains significant advantages—cover and concealment are not easy to achieve in relatively flat country with sparse vegetation. Hidden among the Golan boulders, the Israeli defenders in the 1973 October War inflicted severe losses on the Syrian attackers. To take the initiative in battle, however, it is necessary to get up from the ground and move. If the enemy is even partially prepared this is a risky maneuver. As the Israelis attacked along the southern flank of the Golan Heights beginning on 8 October 1973, their losses rose dramatically. Tactically, then, desert warfare requires innovation to succeed without incurring excessive losses.

The almost lightning-like speed of the coalition attack against Iraqi forces in Operation Desert Storm resulted in a surprise attack—in time and in direction—against Iraqi forces who were dug in and expecting an attack generally from the south (to their front), which would have allowed them plenty of time to see and take aim. Confronted by a violent, sudden attack from the flank and rear, and taken by surprise, Iraqi tanks and other weapons were excellent targets as they tried to leave their dug-in positions and turn to confront their attackers.

Operationally, desert warfare both requires and makes possible the maximum effective use of long-range reconnaissance and surveillance and target-acquisition systems. These, linked with a comprehensive array of electronic warfare systems, were the cornerstone of Israeli success in the Bekaa Valley in the 1982 Operation "Peace for Galilee." During the critical early days of this operation, the Israelis destroyed all the Syrian surface-to-air missile sites in the valley and nearly 100 Soviet-made fixed-wing attack aircraft, with no Israeli Air Force losses. This helped make possible the defeat of two Syrian armored divisions deployed along the valley floor.

Operationally and tactically, in the modern world, desert warfare is mechanized warfare. It favors operations by the tank, armored infantry-fighting vehicle (Fig. 1), armored self-propelled artillery cannons, and armored reconnaissance vehicle. It is the mobility, survivability, and concentrated firepower of combined-arms organizations featuring these vehicles that make it possible both to fight in the desert and to take advantage of opportunities for initiative, maneuver, and decisive action that are provided by the desert.

Possibly never before in the history of battle has this been more dramatically

Figure 1. U.S. M-2 Bradley in the Arabian Desert, August 1990.
(SOURCE: *Army Times*)

demonstrated than in Operation Desert Storm. Tanks, artillery, airpower in deep and close attack (fixed-wing aircraft and helicopters), infantry, engineers, support forces of all types—in short, a well-coordinated combined-arms team—provided a dramatic demonstration of the decisive edge in battle afforded by well-trained, well-led, well-equipped, modern mechanized forces.

DONN A. STARRY

SEE ALSO: Geography, Military; Mechanized Warfare.

Bibliography

Barnett, C. 1961. *The desert generals.* New York: Viking Press.
Crisp, R. 1959. *The brazen chariots.* New York: W. W. Norton.
Herzog, C. 1975. *The war of atonement: October 1973.* Boston: Little, Brown.
Marshall, S. L. A. 1958. *Sinai victory.* New York: William Morrow.
Pitt, B. 1980. *The crucible of war: Western desert 1941.* London: Jonathan Cape.
———. 1982. *The crucible of war: Year of Alamein 1942.* London: Jonathan Cape.

DIRECTIVES, ORDERS, AND INSTRUCTIONS

The commander/staff/subordinate relationship is central to the executive function in any military organization. The dissemination of information, the dialogue between the commander and his staff, and the relaying of command decisions or information to subordinate units are all effected by directives, instructions, and orders. These means of communication differ and are characterized by one or more of the following factors:

- degree of formality required
- role, relationship, and organizational level of the issuing military headquarters and recipient
- amount of latitude to be allowed in interpretation
- time frame in which action is to be taken
- constraints that may be imposed by the general situation.

Irrespective of which means are used, the content needs to be well prepared and clearly presented and to follow certain basic principles of accuracy, conciseness, clarity, logic, relevance, and objectivity.

Directives

Military directives are categorized as follows:

- *Command* details areas of responsibilities, to include tasks and priorities.
- *Policy* is issued normally by a higher headquarters and provides the commander and staff with guidance on specific topics.
- *Planning* most often is issued before undertaking a tactical operation and is concerned with such matters as mission, organization, logistics, security, movement of units, intelligence requirements, and administration.

Orders

An order is the means by which a military commander conveys (normally through his staff) decisions to his subordinate for execution. Orders normally follow a written format that is readily recognizable. Standardization of orders provides clarity for the recipient and saves time in production by acting as an *aide-mémoire* for the drafting authority. When possible, annexes and appendixes are used for tabulations, maps, overlays, and other specific matters of detail. Appended material is integral to written orders.

Military orders may be given orally or in writing. They generally fall into one of five classifications: operation, warning, standing, routine, or administrative orders.

Operation orders. Operation orders can be issued in a number of ways. Written orders, which can be sent by courier or facsimile, may be produced in a standard format; in the form of a sketch, marked map, or map overlay; or as confirmatory notes following the issue of more detailed verbal orders. They are normally issued well in advance of the start of an operation. Once the operation has begun, subsequent orders are likely to be shorter and issued in the form of map overlays and/or verbal orders. In some nations, the latter are called fragmentary orders (FRAGORDS). The North Atlantic Treaty Organization (NATO), for example, uses FRAGORDS.

When operation orders are given orally, they are either given in person by the commander (or by his representative) to the recipient(s) or issued by radio or field telephone. At lower levels of army and air force tactical organizations, orders are almost always given orally. At higher levels a commander will usually only outline his general plan and concept of the operation and then let his staff develop the detailed aspects of the plan.

The format of operation orders differs by nation and often by branch of service (air, land, or sea). Within NATO, a standardization agreement has been reached to adopt a common format (Fig. 1) for operation orders. The main headings reflect the essential information that must be covered in any order.

Orders relating to certain operations (e.g., the guarding of a nuclear facility) may necessitate a particular format. In such situations, they should follow the same principles that apply to an operation order.

Warning orders. The purpose of a warning order is to save time; as such, it is anticipatory and forms one of the basic elements in effective battle procedure. A warning order from a higher headquarters to its subordinate units must be precise and may be sent by any secure means, either orally or in writing. It should contain sufficient details of a forthcoming operation to allow subordinate units, at all levels throughout the chain of command, proper preparation and planning time to carry out their mission, subject to receipt of more detailed orders. It is important to differentiate between those parts of the warning order that contain advance notice and those that require immediate action.

Information normally contained in a warning order includes:

- mission and concept of the operation
- tasks to be performed
- details of impending regrouping of forces
- movement instructions, to include time, changes to previous orders, and any preliminary preparations required (e.g., advance parties)
- administrative instructions
- time, location, and method of dissemination of detailed orders to follow
- request for acknowledgment.

Standing orders. There are many occasions when an order relates to a repetitive or routine military task that is undertaken by a different person or group for a set period of time. An example is the commander of the guard responsible for the security of a key installation. In such a case, a set of permanent standing orders is issued, rather than producing a new order every time the guard is changed.

Standing orders are designed to cover contingencies and have the legal standing of an operation order. It is the responsibility of the issuing authority to check frequently that such orders are current and relevant to changing situations and that the provisions are being complied with by those concerned.

In order to conduct routine military work efficiently, it is necessary in many cases to establish and follow certain basic operating instructions. These are in the nature of guidelines, which are normally incorporated into a set of standard operating procedures (SOPs). SOPs may apply to a wide range of predictable peacetime administrative functions such as office work, security training, transport and movement operations, and maintenance schedules. They also form part of wartime battle procedures by detailing responsibilities and instructions for certain combat activities (such as the composition of command echelons,

SECURITY CLASSIFICATION

Copy Number
Issuing Headquarters
Place
Date/Time Group
Reference Number

Type and serial number of order
References: Maps, charts, relevant documents
Time zone used
Task Organization

Situation	Enemy forces
	Friendly forces
	Commander's evaluation
Mission	A clear statement of the commander's operational aim
Execution	General outline (summary of plan)
	Specific tasks
	Task instructions for supporting elements
	Coordinating instructions
Service Support	Administrative and logistic arrangements (these may be produced separately as an administrative order)
Command and Signal	Communications
	Electronic equipment
	Locations of headquarters
	Liaison
	Recognition and identification instructions

Acknowledgment Instructions

Signature of Commander

Authentication:
Annexes:
Distribution:
SECURITY CLASSIFICATION

Figure 1. Example of main headings to be found in a typical operation order (based on NATO Standardization Agreement 2014).

reconnaissance groups, or advance and harbor parties; regrouping; convoy discipline; or the format and submission of casualty reports) and specifying the course of action to be taken in a given set of circumstances (such as defense against air and nuclear, biological, and chemical [NBC] attack). In sum, SOPs save time by detailing the action to be taken and by employing familiar procedures without waiting for specific orders.

Routine orders. Military commanders promulgate orders on a routine basis to deal with domestic and other internal matters relating to their command. These may be issued on a daily basis or less frequently as necessary. Routine orders deal with all day-to-day aspects of military life that are not already covered by a specific directive, standing order, or SOP and may be used to augment, amplify, or amend other orders and directives.

Administrative orders. As with an operation order, there will normally be a set sequence of headings for an administrative order. This is prepared by the commander's administrative staff and frequently produced as an annex or separate adjunct in support of a lengthy or complex operation order. Alternatively, it may be issued as an independent order relating specifically to administrative or logistic matters.

An administrative order will cover such diverse matters as the provision, direction, allocation, and coordination of transport movement planning and control, medical, materiel (e.g., ammunition, rations, fuel, and other combat supplies), maintenance support, finance (including requisition), welfare, ecclesiastical, and postal services.

Instructions

A commander's instructions differ from orders in that they are couched in general terms. An instruction aims to inform subordinates of the commander's overall intentions rather than direct a specific plan of action. The object is to allow the recipient to make his preparations and plans in advance, with a degree of latitude regarding the method for achieving the task. Usually instructions are issued in place of an operational order; however, they can be sent in advance of a formal order, or, in some cases, following an order, in response to rapid changes in a situation or to cover unforeseen contingencies. Instructions are often personally signed by the commander and addressed to the recipient by name. The circumstances in which instructions would normally be used are:

- when lack of information or a confused battle situation makes detailed written orders impracticable
- when the subordinate is a commander with an independent task or mission
- to meet possible contingencies where specific orders would be infeasible or inappropriate
- in cases where a commander wishes to influence events or to communicate further generalized intentions that do not justify detailed written orders.

Conclusion

The object of any military directive, order, or instruction is to disseminate the commander's decision, guidance, or intentions, in as unambiguous and timely a fashion as possible, to his subordinates for action and/or information.

JOHN HEMSLEY

SEE ALSO: Briefings; Command; Command, Control, Communications, and Intelligence; Field Service Regulations; Maps, Charts, and Symbols, Military.

Bibliography

Crocker, L. P. 1988. *The army officer's guide.* 4th ed. Harrisburg, Pa.: Stackpole Books.

Dupuy, T. N., C. C. Johnson, and G. P. Hayes. 1986. *Dictionary of military terms.* New York: H. W. Wilson.

Farrow, E. S. 1889. *Farrow's military encyclopedia.* New York: Farrow.

Scott, H. L. 1861. *Military dictionary.* New York: Van Nostrand.

U. S. Department of the Army. 1986. *Field manual 100-5: Operations.* Washington, D.C.: Government Printing Office.

U.S. Department of Defense, Joint Chiefs of Staff. 1987. *Department of Defense dictionary of military and associated terms.* Washington, D.C.: Government Printing Office.

DISCIPLINE

Military discipline has three meanings in U.S. usage. The first is punishment for violating orders or regulations. U.S. armed forces speak of judicial and nonjudicial punishment as disciplinary measures. The second meaning is obedience resulting from the fusion of individual and national interests. It is rooted in an individual's respect for the legal authority of superiors, respect for their leadership examples, and commitment to his comrades in arms. A well-disciplined soldier or sailor obeys out of internal commitment rather than from fear of external punishment. The third meaning of discipline is unified compliance with an explicit standard. When Americans speak of sleep discipline, water discipline, or noise discipline, for example, they refer to unit-wide obedience to prescribed practices.

Discipline makes the difference between an armed force and a mob. It enables an armed force to deliver a specified force to a specified target, at a specified time and place, in a specified manner. The desired result of discipline is maximum damage to enemy forces with minimum damage to friendly forces.

In battle, the opposite of discipline is demoralization and panic. In peace, the opposite of discipline is apathy and the inability to deploy when ordered. The seemingly simple task of moving a convoy requires hours of disciplined practice. Without good safety discipline, peacetime training accidents increase.

Whether discipline is ensured by fear-based external sanctions or by commitment-based internal sanctions depends on the technology of battle. External, fear-based discipline is most effective in mass formations where victory depends on maintaining the line of battle. On the cellular, fluid, contemporary battlefield, only internally based discipline is adequate for victory. The more dispersed the battlefield, the greater the need for individual initiative driven by an internal sense of commitment.

Closely aligned with the technology of the battlefield are the conditions of service and the capabilities of individual soldiers. Fear-based discipline has a long tradition in conscript armies in mass formations. The more complex the weapons, however, the more time required for their mastery and the less likely that conscripts will master them in the time available for their training.

Further, conscripts drawn from the lowest levels of the ability pool do not have sufficient mental abilities to master these weapons. Conversely, external fear-based discipline is less necessary or desirable with brighter and more capable service members; internal, commitment-based discipline is needed.

The killing power of modern weapons requires dispersal of troops on a cellular, dynamic, individualized battlefield. Victory increasingly depends on discipline based on individual commitment rather than on fear. Military discipline in the future will have more to do with leadership than with the law. It will be more concerned with incentives like morale, cohesion, and teamwork than with coercion such as threats of punishment.

Larry H. Ingraham

See Also: Combat Effectiveness; Combat Motivation; Leadership; Morale.

Bibliography

Farrow, E. W. 1885. *Farrow's military encyclopedia.* New York: E. W. Farrow.

Kellett, A. 1982. *Combat motivation: The behavior of soldiers in battle.* Boston: Kluwer-Nijhoff.

Shafritz, J. M., T. J. A. Shafritz, and D. B. Robertson. 1989. *The facts on file dictionary of military science.* New York: Facts on File.

Touras, P., B. W. Watson, and S. M. Watson, eds. 1991. *United States Army: A dictionary.* New York: Garland.

U.S. Department of the Army, Headquarters. 1990. *Field manual 22–100: Military leadership.* Washington, D.C.: Government Printing Office.

DOCTRINE

There is no internationally accepted formal definition of the concept of doctrine. In the military, doctrine is viewed in terms of strategy and tactics, is the basis for both academic training and field exercises, and is, in some cases, the military's forecast of future activities and events. Its most critical military application is how forces will fight in combat operations.

Military organizations and the nature of military operations relate to group, rather than individual, activities. It is essential, for example, that members of an infantry squad or platoon operate as a team. Thus, the formal use of doctrine—"this is the way we do it"—is an absolute military requirement. The fundamental definition derives from Middle English usage from the Latin *doctrina* (teaching, learning, instruction) and from the term *doctor*. In current usage, *doctrine* means "something taught; teaching," often expanded to the more specific "something taught as principles or creed; a rule, theory or principle of law; or an official statement of a nation's policy" (Neufeldt and Guralnik 1988).

Thoughtful modern military scholars explicitly appreciate the role and function of doctrine. For example, Wayne Hughes in *Fleet Tactics* states that "doctrine is the glue of tactics" (1986, p. 28). In another context he notes that "doctrine is the unifying agent that provides for collective action in time of war." In short, doctrine provides a common reference point, language, and purpose, uniting the actions of many diverse elements into a team effort.

Students of command and control systems recognize that doctrine is a large part of the system used by commanders to control actions and activities of their troops. The ideal military situation with respect to doctrine was perhaps best expressed by a senior German army officer who said doctrine "is a collective term for the operational concepts according to which military forces act." But doctrine and its dynamics, as shown in the subsequent discussion, are much more than a collection of operational concepts.

Military Characterizations of *Doctrine*

Doctrine is defined in the *Dictionary of Military Terms* as "fundamental principles by which the military forces or elements thereof guide their actions in support of national objectives. It is authoritative but requires judgement in application" (JCS 1984).

NATO uses the same basic definition, but drops the modifying terms *or elements thereof* and *national*. These definitions are not precise enough to reflect actual use by military persons or institutions. In this regard, three points need to be made. First, individuals vary widely in their use of the term *doctrine*, even within a single service in a single nation's defense establishment. Second, there are variations between a national military establishment's formal statements regarding the term *doctrine* and the national practice. Finally, the particularly dynamic nature of military activity is frequently overlooked. Doctrine must change and adapt, relating training approaches to the requirements of future combat operations as opposed to focusing on battles of the past. Discussion of these points follows.

One cannot assume that all the military leaders of a given nation or armed service regard military doctrine in a similar light. A brief study of actual usage of the term during the 1980s by senior U.S. military officers provides the following examples (to be compared with the U.S. Department of Defense definition):

• "Doctrine is not what is 'written in the book,' but what people believe in and act upon."
• "Doctrine should not survive 'contact with the enemy'; commanders in the field must adapt doctrine to circumstances; doctrine is a dialogue."

- "There was too much doctrine—we took what was best [when creating a new U.S. major force structure]."

National practice in regard to military doctrine is often the subject of stereotype and witticism. For example, two wall posters, passed along and posted on the office walls by American military study groups, bear these words:

- (attributed to a Russian document) "One of the serious problems in planning against American doctrine is that the Americans do not read their manuals, nor do they feel any obligations to follow their doctrine."
- (attributed to a German general officer) "The reason that the American Army does so well in wartime, is that war is chaos, and the American Army practices chaos on a daily basis."

American military officers may well appreciate the germs of truth in the above. Some may also subscribe to the widespread notion that, since "the Germans have no word for doctrine," they must have no doctrine. On the other hand, much of the U.S. Army's planning on how to "fight outnumbered and win" against manifestly superior numbers of heavily armed Soviet forces is based upon a belief that the Soviet military is so "doctrinaire" (overly imbued with following doctrine) that it can be beaten by forces whose officers (at battalion and company levels) are allowed to take initiatives. By using freedom of initiative U.S. forces expect to be able to predict and counter a doctrine-bound opponent.

Perhaps the most critical factor in developing and applying doctrine is comprehension of its relation to varied situations and the evolving and changing nature of war. Doctrine must respond to change. No one appreciated this more than did Clausewitz, who noted how Frederick the Great's adherence to an earlier, immensely successful doctrine (of drill or tactics) ensured the terrible destruction of the over-confident Prussian army. Clausewitz's biographer describes superb eyewitness accounts of the dynamics of doctrine, complete with alternative remedies (Parkinson 1971).

The issue of adaptation emphasizes the fact that doctrine is, in part, a distillation of lessons learned from history. Unless a nation or a military service has people with the vision to adapt these lessons to future threats and environments, its doctrine will always be looking back, refighting the last war, rather than anticipating the future.

Part of the difficulty in developing future-oriented doctrine is what Clausewitz describes as the problem of "friction" in battle. Doctrine cannot fully anticipate the pace of combat activity that stems from the realities of death and destruction caused by the enemy, nor does it often effectively relate to human weaknesses of men under fire. Another problem is the issue of weaponry. For example, the U.S. Army's operational doctrine in *Field Manual 100-5* depends upon having certain weapons' capabilities available to meet the needs of the Air-land Battle. Reality is that these weapons were not available when the doctrine was promulgated, nor will they be in the hands of army personnel for some time to come, despite the fact that other weapons (which the newer weapons were to replace) have been removed from service.

Formal Meanings and East-West Usage

The discussion thus far has focused on requirements for, and variations in, general definitions of the term *doctrine*. Although many military authors and discussants consider doctrine in its specific military sense, their discussions tend to use the general term without the "military" modifier. The Soviets, in their professional *Dictionary of Military Terms* (1965 version), explicitly refer to "military doctrine," *voyennaya doktrina*. Furthermore, their definition begins at the national level:

> A nation's officially accepted system of scientifically founded views on the nature of modern wars and the use of armed forces in them, and also on the requirements arising from these views regarding the country and its armed forces being made ready for war. . . . Military doctrine has two aspects, political and military-technical. The basic tenets of a military doctrine are determined by a nation's political and military leadership according to the socio-political order, the country's level of economic, scientific and technological development, and the armed forces' combat materiel, with due regard to the conclusions of military science and the views of the probable enemy.

Notwithstanding events of the early 1990s that may have affected the Soviet definition of *doctrine*, major distinctions stand out in comparing the Soviet ("Eastern") with the U.S. DOD/IADB ("Western") definitions. The Eastern definition highlights the *nation's* system and the *socio-political*, economic, technological, and materiel aspects over the "military science" conclusions. It speaks of the "views of the probable enemy"—which the Western does not—and seemingly offers scope for flexibility in application. Although the two definitions are set forth at different levels of abstraction, there is no mistaking the difference in emphases. The Eastern definition is explicit in the doctrinal subservience of the military's role to the overall national approach, together with its dominance of things political and economic. The Western definition speaks only of national objectives, without use of the terms *political* or *economic* but does explicitly note the aspect of judgment.

Discussions between U.S. and Soviet senior military officers regarding changes in Soviet military doctrine have stimulated widespread media, military, and political discussion as to the nature of the changes. These changes could lead to a new Soviet military doctrine or, at least, to a better understanding of what has already evolved.

Doctrinal Acceptance

It is evident that doctrine must be authoritative. The source of transmittal (the teacher) must have some authority if doctrine is to be accepted. While existence of the term *doctrinaire* implies that there can be a "too acceptable" aspect of doctrine, there are indeed some fundamental human behavioral problems in establishing an operative doctrine. The source of the doctrine must have a basis in present knowledge or an enforceable authority. This can be a particular problem when those responsible for executing actions according to doctrine are perceived as lacking in wisdom or being resistant to change—a charge often leveled at the military professional. It is a problem also when there is no general recognition of the need for change from an existing doctrine or without a specific stimulus for change (such as continual loss in battle). Also, when a particular stimulus has provoked change, but no official imprimatur has been placed on the new approach, there are likely to be many alternative views among the members of a democratic or pluralistic society.

Military commanders and staff officers charged with training are the first audience for whom the planners in Western society must orient their approach. In addition to developing realistic means of teaching a revised doctrine, the military planners must consider integration of its aspects in actual application, including the development or revision of standard operating instructions and procedural manuals.

Doctrinal Development

The need for a better understanding of the nature of military doctrine, a more precise definition of it, and a more effective way of developing and disseminating it has been pointed out by U.S. Air Force general Holley (1979). This goal has been subsequently addressed in descriptive form in the U.S. Army's doctrinal manual, *Field Manual 100-5: Operations* (May 1986, p. 6). Such generalized statements provide a framework for the significant professional public input concepts offered by other military authors (Cardwell 1984, DePuy 1988, McInnis 1988). There is ample material available to provide a framework for both process and substance in keeping dynamic the various national and armed service military doctrines.

However, much less material exists that indicates that the more difficult issues of interservice (joint), as well as international coalition military forces doctrine, are as well understood or as amenable to future evolutionary development. Perhaps the most difficult task of all is incorporating doctrine at the various levels of command on a high-technology battlefield. Exemplary military commanders may evolve better approaches to fighting, but the issues of determining which are the best solutions, integrating them into formal doctrine, disseminating it, and informing and training the troops in the "new way" present unimaginable difficulties.

The critical significance of having, promulgating, and testing the right doctrine—for sustainment as well as fighting against unforeseen opponents as well as traditional foes—to meet the needs of future conflicts is clear. Future military commanders and planners will be confronted with major challenges in developing doctrine to meet the perceived needs of changing times. Dealing with such issues as maneuver warfare versus firepower and equipment orientations, rapid deployable forces, the development of new weapons, reduced manpower, and a decreasing military budget will further compound the development and implementation of new doctrine.

Future

The primary focus in the evolution, testing, dissemination, and practice of doctrine must concentrate on understanding the nature of the principles and dynamics involved. Developers of doctrine must not be deluded by traditional techniques and tactical applications that have more form than substance nor develop a doctrine to face an illusory threat. Such overstress can lead to reliance upon obsolete images instead of contemporary reality.

DONALD S. MARSHALL

SEE ALSO: Command; Command, Control, Communications, and Intelligence; Leadership.

Bibliography

Alger, J. I. 1985. *Definitions and doctrine of the military art.* The West Point Military History Service Series. Garden City Park, N.Y.: Avery.

Cardwell, T. A. 1984. One step beyond—AirLand Battle doctrine not dogma. *Military Review* April, pp. 45–53.

DePuy, W. E. 1988. Concepts of operation: The heart of command, the tool of doctrine. *Army* August, pp. 26–40.

Holley, I. B., Jr. 1979. The doctrinal process: Some suggested steps. *Military Review* April, pp. 2–13.

Hughes, W. P., Jr. 1986. *Fleet tactics: Theory and practice.* Annapolis, Md.: U.S. Naval Institute Press.

Joint Chiefs of Staff (JCS). 1984. *Department of Defense dictionary of military terms* (incorporating the NATO and IADB dictionaries), JCS Pub #1. Washington, D.C.: Government Printing Office.

McInnis, C. W. 1988. Sustainment doctrine—Not keeping pace with AirLand Battle doctrine. *Military Review* February, pp. 22–29.

Neufeldt, V., and D. B. Guralnik, eds. 1988. *Webster's new world dictionary of American English.* 3d College ed. New York: Webster's New World.

Parkinson, R. 1971. *Clausewitz: A biography.* New York: Stein and Day.

Soviet Faculty of the General Staff Academy. 1965. *Dictionary of basic military terms: A Soviet view.* Trans. by the DGIS Multilingual Section, Translation Bureau, Secretary of State Dept., Ottawa. Washington, D.C.: Government Printing Office.

United States Army. 1986. *Field manual 100-5: Operations.* Washington, D.C.: Government Printing Office.

E

ECHELON

Echelon is a generic term describing an arrangement of a body of troops, ships, or aircraft to establish a certain sequence like a series of steps; it can also describe organizations that may or may not be staggered in depth and at different levels.

Echelon may refer to

- a subdivision of a headquarters/command, such as the forward and rear echelons
- a level of command—for example, a brigade is a lower echelon than a division; an army corps is a higher echelon than a division
- a fraction of a force with a principal combat mission—that is, an attack echelon, a support echelon, a rear echelon
- a level within the maintenance system
- a tactical formation in which the elements of a force are laterally distributed and staged sequentially to the rear, as in the formation of Epaminondas at leuctra in 371 B.C. and Frederick the Great at Leuthen in 1757
- an element of the formation of forces for battle.

If used in the last context, the term is almost exclusively confined to Soviet or Warsaw Pact literature, and it is this particular connotation that is the main topic of the following discussion, since only the former Soviet Union developed a system of echelons to suit its strategic, operational, and tactical needs. Used in this sense, the last meaning is more important than the other five.

The organization of an order of battle may involve more than one echelon: one-half to two-thirds (or more) of a unit may form the first echelon, to be followed by a second or even a third echelon. Unlike the use of reserves, the commitment of the second or third echelon will depend on a predetermined point in time or a predetermined situation and a predetermined objective.

In addition to a second echelon, reserves may be established at all levels of command. But they will normally not exceed 10 to 15 percent of a unit or formation.

Linguistic Roots and Usage

The word *echelon* is derived from the French *échelon*, which means the rung of a ladder. In French military parlance, the verb *échelonner* primarily suggests the staggering of forces in depth. The same word is used in Russian. In German, the word *echelon* was used particularly during the last century but has been replaced by the German *Staffel*.

If used in the West, *echelon* contains both an Eastern and Western connotation. If used correctly in a Western environment, it suggests a sequence of staggered steps or bodies of troops; however, if applied to the Eastern military system, the West follows the terminology of the East, where it is defined as an element in the formation of forces for battle.

WESTERN USAGE AND HISTORICAL DEVELOPMENT

As commonly used in the West, the principal meaning of *echelonment* is a staggered sequence of bodies of troops, which can be formed either in columns or in lines (Fig. 1).

The first known use of echelonment in battle was by the Theban general Epaminondas in his major victory over the Spartans at Leuctra in 371 B.C. (Fig. 2). Epaminondas, whose army was outnumbered, used echelonment as a means of "refusing" his right flank. This permitted the reinforced Theban left wing to strike with superior numbers against the Spartans' right, while the thin Theban lines echeloned to the right posed a continuing threat to the Spartans' center and left, holding them in position while the battle was decided to their right. Once Epaminondas's left wing had overwhelmed the Spartan right, it wheeled, to hit the remaining Spartans in their exposed flank. The echeloned Theban units then came up to engage the Spartans to their front, while the Spartans were being enveloped and destroyed from the right.

Alexander the Great, most of whose battles were against numerically superior foes, usually employed echelonment in his advance to battle, for the same reason as Epaminondas. The same was true for Frederick the Great. Echelonment was the most significant feature in his great victory over the Austrians at Leuthen in 1757.

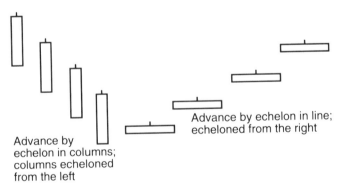

Advance by echelon in columns; columns echeloned from the left

Advance by echelon in line; echeloned from the right

Figure 1. Echelonment.

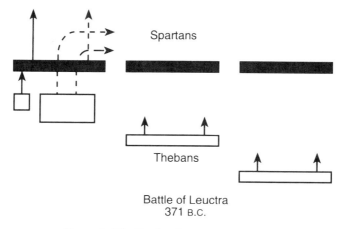

Battle of Leuctra
371 B.C.

Figure 2. The Battle of Leuctra (371 B.C.).

EASTERN USAGE AND HISTORICAL DEVELOPMENT

Eastern usage of the word not only refers to its own elements in the formation of forces for battle, but also describes Western reserves, especially at the tactical and operational levels, which tends to confuse the widely different meanings of reserve and echelon. In fact, echelon is a portion of a force with a *predetermined* mission, and the commander at a higher echelon (level) has no power to use this force freely. *Reserve,* on the other hand, is that portion of a force that a higher command may use *at its own discretion.* Soviet military literature frequently fails to make this distinction, although authoritative Soviet publications such as the *Soviet Military Encyclopedia* from 1986 do adopt this differentiation.

The forward deployment of forces in columns for purposes of strategic concentration was known throughout the eighteenth century as *échelonnement.* This term at least partially describes today's meaning in Eastern terminology, since the second or third formation in a column frequently had to take over the mission and role of the column's first formation if the latter had suffered excessive losses from enemy action. Already in the early years of existence of the Soviet Union (between 1922 and 1936), Soviet military thinkers, such as Frunze, Triandafilow, and Tukhachevsky, developed a system of echelons.

The disastrous experience of the first two years of the German-Soviet war, however, had shown that any rigid employment of two echelons in attack and defense, even when supported by a freely available reserve, could not cope with rapidly changing situations. It highlighted the dilemma of a conflict between the organization of forces into echelons—providing thrust to an attack through the timely introduction of a second echelon into the assault sector— and the necessity of having to take the second echelon forces from the total of forces available to the commander. This resulted in a weakening of the first echelon and frequently led to a situation where the attacker's echelons were defeated one by one.

Therefore, rules in line with the enemy's defensive preparations were developed. For example, weak defenses with only a few strong points and a lack of depth were attacked only by one echelon and few reserves in order to have the maximum forces on the front line for achieving quick and decisive victory. On the other hand, it was believed that if a well-organized defense in depth was encountered, up to three echelons were needed to provide the necessary punch for an attack. This highly differentiated formation of forces for battle was implemented at all levels of command. Naturally, and depending on the situation and the geographic conditions, a great number of combinations were possible.

In another example, at front (army group) level, the attack could be planned with only one echelon, so that all armies were at the line of contact, while corps or divisions within the armies could attack with two or more echelons, and at the regimental level the commander might choose to commit just one echelon. This system lent extraordinary flexibility to the attacker.

At the end of World War II, however, Soviet attacking forces, in principle, consisted of two echelons with artillery and antiaircraft artillery groups according to the level of command of the attacking formation, plus an antitank reserve and an engineer reserve (so-called special reserves). Normally, the artillery of the second and third echelons was moved up to support the first echelon right from the outset.

In 1983, the Soviets stated (*Encyclopedic Military Dictionary*):

Offensive operations at front level cover:

- first and follow-on offensive operations of the armies of the first echelon (according to some directions, possible also as defensive operations),
- offensive operations of the second-echelon armies,
- combat actions of the rocket troops and the artillery of the front,
- combat actions of frontal aviation and of air defense units of the front,
- combat actions of special reserves of the front,
- combat actions of reserves of the front.

This statement still holds true.

Mission of Echelons

Echelons may be formed at all levels of command. According to the different tasks at, for example, the strategic or tactical level, the missions of first, second, or other echelons will be different. There are, however, principles that are common to all levels, and these may be summarized as:

the first echelon has to break through the main defensive positions of the enemy and destroy the bulk of the enemy forces, including his reserves. Artillery formations of higher echelons (levels of command) and of the second echelon will participate in this task.

The second echelon has to take over from the first echelon to continue to exploit the former's initial success along the main axis of attack, to seize and destroy defensive positions in depth, and to repulse enemy counterattacks. If the first echelon fails to accomplish its task, it may be relieved by the second echelon.

The final success of an attack crucially depends on the correct choice of the second echelon's timely engagement. If committed too early, the engagement will not generate an uninterrupted thrust against an already exhausted enemy, since it will reduce the time during which the enemy is under constant pressure and it will be impossible to bring to bear the maximum strength of the combined echelons. If committed too late, the enemy will capitalize on the spacing between the two echelons by reorganizing its defense, by creating new reserves, and by launching counterattacks.

There are three major possibilities of committing the second echelon: (1) on one of the flanks of the first echelon; (2) in the space between two formations of the first echelon; and (3) passing through the first echelon that leads the attack. The first and second possibilities are the ones that were frequently used in Warsaw Pact maneuvers and exercises, while the third possibility is generally described as too complicated and as offering the enemy ample opportunity to concentrate firepower on the massed formations; this, in turn, will create confusion on the attacker's side.

Doctrine

As stated earlier, only the former Soviet Union and its former allies use *echelon* as a standard term to describe the arrangement of forces or the formation of forces for battle; the context is almost exclusively that of an offensive or attack.

The reason for this has a historical background. Experience has long taught the Russians that in order to achieve victory over a generally better-trained and frequently better-equipped enemy, the Russian army had to rely on its sheer mass of soldiers. Of course, Russia could afford the loss of enormous quantities of its territory, thus trading space for time, but the lesson learned by the Russians was that, in order to win the war, they had to attack. And these attacks at the tactical level, or offensives at the operational and strategic levels, became more successful as more and more troops attacked and were committed wave after wave.

It was these masses, organized in depth, that were able to generate the necessary uninterrupted thrust against the enemy, thus virtually drowning the enemy's initiative, rendering him first breathless, then exhausted, and finally defeated.

These basic facts were lessons not only learned from wars against more modern, better-commanded, and better-equipped forces, such as the Swedish forces under Charles XII or the French forces under Napoleon, but they were also often instrumental in expanding the Russian Empire toward the east and the south. Later, the Red Army learned the same facts during the Russian Civil War. But the new Communist ideology had added one new reason to an old concept: now the goal was no longer the expansion of the empire but the conquest of the world for the sake of progress and humanity. Defense proved to be an even more inappropriate way to accomplish this task.

Thus, early Soviet military thinkers, such as Marshal Tukhachevsky, focused their ideas on organizing Soviet forces in depth for offensive actions, combined with mechanized formations for quick exploitation. The second half of World War II proved his thoughts correct. For example, the evolution of the density of attacking forces in breakthrough sectors from 1942 to 1945 and the ratio between attacking and defending troops in the same sectors clearly demonstrate this dual effort: to strive for numerical superiority and to organize forces in depth (Table 1).

After the war, the combined experiences of the Russian Empire, the civil war, and the first and second half of the Great Patriotic War led the Soviet Union to conceive a doctrine that provided for forces strong enough to carry the war into an enemy's territory, to defeat the enemy's forces there, and to occupy it.

It is difficult to assess the military value of the employment of second echelons, on the one hand, and of reserves, on the other hand. In war, the decision of a military leader as to how to organize his forces for battle will always depend on a variety of factors, such as terrain, weather, daylight, type of own forces, strength in manpower and armaments, type of forthcoming operation (offensive/defensive), possibility of surprise, and the opposing forces. Above all, his decision should be influenced by the ratio of forces. In reality, however, it is the leader's military education and, therefore, the doctrine of his national military forces that will influence him most.

But, as stated before, this doctrine itself is the result of a nation's experiences and perceptions and is therefore something that will not easily be changed. Nevertheless, certain principles can be derived from this discussion:

> If there is an overall scarcity of military assets, the appropriate way to preserve a certain degree of flexibility, and, therefore, the necessary freedom of action, is to move the bulk of the forces to the front while keeping strong reserves at the discretion of the commander. Under conditions of scarce assets, this principle applies to both the defensive and offensive. The advantage of this rather simple organization lies in the total freedom of the responsible commander to decide time, place, and mission

TABLE 1. *Change in Density of Attacking Soviet Forces in Breakthrough Sectors, 1942–45*

	1942 (Stalingrad)	1943 (Kursk)	1944 (Belorussia)	1945 (Vistula)
Average break-through sector in kilometers	2.8	5.0	4.6	4.45
Battalions per kilometer in break-through sectors	2.3	5.6	5.0	23.25
Soviet:German strength ratios in break-through sectors				
—battalions	3.75:1	7.73:1	8.4:1	7.45:1
—guns/mortars	7.75:1	12.1:1	8.1:1	10.1:1
—tanks	6.0:1	6.93:1	5.25:1	3.9:1

for the commitment of his reserve. The disadvantage lies in the implicit all-or-nothing character of this commitment. If the commander, while committing his reserve to battle, is unable to create a new reserve, however small, he will subsequently find himself without any means to react should his plan fail.

Where military assets are relatively abundant, the best choice, especially for attack, will undoubtedly be to adopt an organization with two or more echelons plus a small reserve. The disadvantage of this choice is that the second or third echelons, with their predetermined missions, must be committed to battle with extraordinary precision in terms of place and time to avoid ineffectiveness (premature commitment) or a situation where echelon after echelon will be defeated (delayed commitment).

The enormous advantage of this principle is simply that, given numerically superior forces and organization in depth, the enemy will not have time to react with the necessary freedom of option on the basis of sufficiently available reserves. The attacker—at least at the tactical level—need not even probe for weak points in the enemy's defensive positions; he might, instead, be able to create such points through the wise commitment of his echelons.

Since May 1987, the Soviet Union claimed that it had altered its doctrine to one of "sufficiency to defend." As of mid-1991, it remains to be seen the extent to which this change in words will be followed by a change in the strength and structure of its armed forces.

CHRISTIAN MEYER-PLATH

SEE ALSO: Deployment; Doctrine; Reserves.

Bibliography

Conner, A. Z., and R. G. Poirier. 1983. Soviet strategic reserves. The forgotten dimension. *Military Review* 11:28–40.

Erickson, J., L. Hansen, and W. Schneider. 1986. Soviet operational forces. In *Soviet ground forces: An operational assessment*, pp. 51–103, 139–40, 249–57. Boulder, Colo.: Westview Press.

Glantz, D. M. 1983. Soviet operational formation for battle: A perspective. *Military Review* 2:2–12.

Kirjan, M. M. 1978. Armeeangriffsoperation. *Sowjetische Militärenzyklopedie* 2:63–73.

Militärakademie M. W. Frunze. 1961. *Die Entwicklung der Taktik der Sowjetarmee im Großen Vaterländischen Krieg.* (*Razvitie taktiki sovetskoj armii v gody velikoj otečestvennoj vojny 1941–1945*). Berlin: Deutscher Militärverlag.

Pleiner, H. 1980. Angriffsverfahren in Ost und West (Teil I). *Truppendienst* 2:145–51.

———. 1980. Angriffsverfahren in Ost und West (Teil II). *Truppendienst* 3:257–63.

Rimski-Korsakow, N. 1981. Grundlagen des modernen Angriffsgefechts. *Militärwesen* 8:31–34.

Vigor, P. H. 1982. Soviet echeloning. *Military Review* 8:69–74.

EDUCATION, MILITARY

As the nature of warfare evolved from conflict between massed soldiers with hand weapons to high-technology land, sea, and air battles, the education and training of military personnel became more complex and more important.

The sophisticated skills of almost all military personnel today have required significant improvements in institutions, qualifications of faculty and trainers, methods of imparting military knowledge, and the time required to attain proficiency. This has been true in all nations, although levels of sophistication in the training process vary with the resources available.

As a result, the time of military personnel today is principally occupied with training in individual and team skills except, of course, when engaged in military operations. Even then, respites from combat action are seized as opportunities for training to correct deficiencies observed in action.

World War II offers proof of the importance of standardized training for military personnel. The rapid expansion of the U. S. Army required formation of many new divisions built around cadres assembled from existing units. Because all personnel had been trained in the same manner, the new units were able to organize themselves and prepare for combat action rapidly under the same principles of strategy and tactics.

Definition of Terms

Although superficially the terms *military education* and *military training* might seem synonymous, they are not. Education is an all-inclusive term of which training is a major element. This is true in the civilian world as well as in the military. Vocational education or training for a career is part of the curriculum of most college and university programs. Definitions in published military works differ only slightly.

The U.S. Department of Defense (1988) defines *military education* as "the systematic instruction of individuals in subjects which will enhance their knowledge of the science and art of war." Obviously, many of these subjects are broad based and go well beyond the teaching of skills involved in military training.

As the complexity and sophistication of military education has increased, a new term has come into use, *professional military education* (PME); it is defined as instruction that provides officers with the skills, knowledge, and understanding that enable them to make sound decisions in progressively more demanding command and staff positions within the national security environment. In the United States, PME is formally organized at primary, intermediate, senior, and general/flag officer levels and emphasizes the joint nature of warfare.

The U.S. definition of military training is "the instruction of personnel to enhance their capacity to perform specific military functions and tasks; the exercise of one or more military units conducted to enhance their combat readiness."

A somewhat more specific definition of *military training* is "the process of preparing military individuals and units to perform their assigned functions and missions, particularly to prepare for combat and wartime functions. Covering every aspect of military activity, training is the principal occupation of military forces when not actually engaged in combat."

This definition makes it clear that military training applies to both individuals and units, whereas military education applies to the individual.

Historical Background

The beginnings of formalized military training, even for officers, came in the late seventeenth and early eighteenth centuries and then only as a result of the development of military science and the art of war.

In the Greek city-states, military leaders were highly educated men, but that education was cultural rather than military in nature. During the Middle Ages, military commanders were normally knights. Their education or training began early with lessons in handling a lance while sitting astride a wooden horse. Knights fought under the command of barons, and their advancement depended more on social standing than on demonstration of military skills.

Military education and training for officers was a major factor in the evolution of the professional officer. Training was originally limited to technical services but spread to combat strategy and tactics. This came several hundred years after university education of other professionals, such as doctors, lawyers, and clergymen, became commonplace. The early style of combat—massed blocks of troops using weapons of limited range—did not seem to require special skills. The evolution of longer-range weapons and more widely dispersed combat units required effective communication for command and control. The need for special training in military arts became apparent.

In the seventeenth century, some prominent Dutch, French, and Spanish commanders set up private military academies to train young men who applied for officer posts in their headquarters. Those academies were soon brought under government control. Their training courses were expanded in the eighteenth century into military and naval schools at several locations in Europe. These developments had parallels in the civilian world, as the Age of Enlightenment resulted in opening of schools for many civilian technical specialties. The enlightenment of the period also led to the publication of military textbooks in most European languages, which were studied by future military leaders as part of their general education.

These early military academies did not achieve the status of the academies of today. Until the nineteenth century, commissions were still issued to members of the nobility without any requirement that they have formal military schooling.

For personnel who had already won their commissions, advanced military training did not emerge until late in the eighteenth century. Because war was becoming more complicated, it was necessary to organize general staffs and begin to think about training for all personnel.

In the nineteenth century, education and training of officers and noncommissioned officers became generally recognized and gradually advanced along professional lines, albeit slowly. Warfare came to be recognized as a science as well as an art, including a body of professional knowledge to be learned by its practitioners. The U.S. Military and Naval academies came into being to develop a professional officer corps.

By the late nineteenth century, Austria, England, France, Germany, and Italy had established schools for officers and noncommissioned officers. In the British army, a director general of military education managed the entire program. In the United States every post, camp, and station were required to maintain schools to train officers and enlisted personnel.

The formalized military education system of the Soviet Union dates from the 1917 revolution. It includes three levels of military education: higher, secondary, and elementary, ranging from broad senior service education to the elementary training of individuals as team members.

The twentieth century has seen even greater changes in the nature of warfare than were experienced previously. The atomic bomb in World War II and the subsequent rapid advance of military technology increased the requirement for sophisticated technical training, not only for officers but also for enlisted personnel, especially noncommissioned officers. This has led generally to centralized control of the curricula of training and to the need for education of more officers in the principles of joint force operations to coordinate land, sea, and air actions.

Education

Military education is a step-by-step process in the case of both officers and enlisted personnel. The process applies in all countries but will vary greatly through combinations of courses, lengthened or shortened phases, and limitations of resources.

OFFICER EDUCATION

Officers are expected to have a broad-based general education. In some countries, notably the United States, officers must have a baccalaureate degree. Some who were commissioned without a college degree in the past are expected to get the degree while in the service. A further emphasis of the importance given to a broad education is the fact that many officers are offered the opportunity to attend civilian institutions to work toward graduate degrees early in their military careers.

The first phase of an officer's military education is the precommissioning. This may be through a military or naval academy; a civilian college offering military, aerospace, or naval science course options; or an officer candidate school. In wartime, officers are sometimes appointed directly from the enlisted ranks in combat, with required formal education and training to be gained later.

After commissioning, regardless of the source of the commission, most officers must attend a primary-level or basic course at their branch of service (e.g., infantry, artillery, military police) to qualify them for service with troops. Later, officers attend an advanced course at their branch school to qualify them for service at a somewhat higher level within their branch. Officers who are selected for further advancement next attend an intermediate-level command and staff course. The final level of schooling is the senior service college. Many, but not all, of its graduates attain flag rank. These levels of officer education are discussed in a later section of this article.

ENLISTED EDUCATION

With increased use of high-technology weapons and support systems, enlisted personnel also need more formalized education and training. All military services rely on noncommissioned officers both as operators of complex equipment and systems and as supervisors of teams or crews who operate the equipment.

All newly enlisted or inducted personnel must satisfactorily complete prescribed levels of training, starting with basic training to acquaint the recruit with the differences between civilian and military life and to teach the fundamentals of the military organization.

Individual skill training follows, after which further skill training is required for career advancement. Individuals who are selected for higher noncommissioned officer positions usually get formal leadership training in an academic environment such as the NCO Academy. This kind of broad-based instruction qualifies as education under our definitions and is discussed in a later section.

Recruit Training

Throughout the world, the initial exposure to military life is usually regarded as one of the most nerve-racking, physically demanding experiences of one's life. It may be a highly disciplined process to transform a civilian into a soldier, sailor, or airman in a relatively short time. This training is usually referred to as basic training or boot camp and lasts from five to ten weeks.

Basic training acquaints the recruit with the rudiments of military life, starting with discipline and customs of the service. It includes instruction on first aid and sanitation, which are essential to individuals' survival under field conditions. The individual also must master the use of a personal weapon, with emphasis on marksmanship and on care and cleaning of the weapon. Basic training also includes instruction of the individual as a member of a team such as a rifle squad, a weapon crew, or a logistical support activity. The length of this first phase of military training varies by service and by the overall training program of each nation's armed forces.

Even in this elementary form of training, current technology provides simulators and training devices that allow more individuals to get simultaneous exposure to expert instruction. High-technology training packages, such as interactive computer programs, are used to assist local instructors and upgrade the quality of training at many locations. Such equipment is coming into wider use, achieving economies through increased efficiency and reduced costs of equipment and ammunition for training.

Initial Skill Training

Immediately following basic training or boot camp, each individual must receive initial skill training to qualify him or her for a specific type of military job.

This phase of military training is like apprentice training in the civilian world.

The length of initial skill training varies greatly, depending mainly on the complexity of the job for which the individual is training. It may be only a few weeks for an infantry rifleman or many months for a complex assignment such as cryptography clerk. This phase may take place at the same installation as the basic training, or it may be at a different post or station where specialized equipment is available. The culmination of this phase is the award to the individual of a skill code, such as a military occupational specialty (MOS). This is a coded entry in the individual's personnel records identifying him or her as qualified to perform the duties of a specific job. The term *MOS* is not universally used, but some skill identifier is used for the same purpose in all forces.

Award of the MOS is roughly equivalent to completion of apprentice training in civilian occupations. As in civilian life, such individuals need additional training to enhance their capabilities on the job. In military initial skill training, some jobs may require proficiency in as many as 200 separate tasks. It may be impossible to acquire proficiency in all 200 during initial skill training. The remaining unlearned tasks then may be mastered after assignment to a unit or to a navy ship at sea. This is accomplished through on-the-job training that is facilitated through "exported training" materials supplied by the training installation. Such training is supervised by the immediate superior of the individual at his post, station, or ship. The normal practice is to combine formal instruction with on-the-job training.

Continuation/Upgrade/Midcareer Training

As the individual progresses in a military career, additional training is required to advance particular skills and to enable him or her to receive promotions in grade. This phase of training may be termed continuation, upgrade, or midcareer training. It usually comes after the individual has demonstrated competency in an assigned job (MOS) over a period of years through the journeyman phase and has shown a desire to continue a military career.

This level of training is intended for mid-level noncommissioned or petty officers. In the past, such courses were primarily technical in nature for support personnel in such fields as logistics and leadership oriented for noncommissioned officers of the combat arms. In recent years some services have combined the two types of courses to ensure that all NCOs receive both advanced technical instruction and leadership training.

Some armed forces maintain strict relationships between completion of these courses and promotions to higher grades. The rationale is that noncommissioned officers cannot properly supervise lower-grade individuals unless they are at least acquainted with the tasks they must supervise and proficient in many of them. The armed forces that do not maintain such hard-and-fast rules for promotion emphasize that soldiers, sailors, and airmen can advance their skill levels through on-the-job training as well as through formal courses.

This level of training for noncommissioned personnel is particularly difficult for national guard and reserve personnel, who are not serving full-time in the military. Some courses are so long that they jeopardize the individual's relationship with his or her civilian employer. Other methods must be found to solve this problem. (See Reserve Component Education and Training below.)

Leadership Training

In some countries, notably the United States, leadership training is taught in formal, curriculum-based courses for noncommissioned and petty officers who are entrusted with increasing levels of enlisted responsibility. These enlisted personnel are expected to be—and are—adept at solving more and more complex problems, particularly in the personnel field, to conserve the time of their commanders.

A second form of leadership training takes place every day in every unit as personnel observe the methods of their senior noncommissioned officers and see them as role models. This informal leadership training is fully as important as the formal courses in the academic environment. Both types combine to provide the knowledge and the inspiration to succeed.

Unit Training

In addition to qualification and advanced training of individuals, there remains the essential task of training units to operate as teams and as elements of still larger military forces. This type of training begins early in the experience of the individual as a member of a squad or on a crew-served weapons team. However, unit commanders and staff officers at all levels need experience in organizing for combat and conducting combat operations. This can only be gained through unit training that progresses up the levels of command to include major maneuvers and exercises involving land, sea, and air forces.

Some valuable command and staff experience can be gained through command post exercises conducted by skilled trainers without the main body of troops. A carefully drawn scenario overseen by qualified supervisors can test staff officers on the principles of information collection and analysis, plan preparation, staff coordination, and reporting to the commander. The critique conducted by the supervisor at the conclusion of such exercises provides valuable lists of "lessons learned" for commanders and staff officers.

Simulators and training devices can add to the realism of such exercises. Even as low as the battalion level, the U.S. Army has developed an automated command post exercise training device known as Army Training Battle Simulation System (ARTBASS). This system is used to train and evaluate battalion commanders and their staffs. ARTBASS is a real-time free-play, interactive combat simulation driven by a digital computer simulation system. Putting commanders and staff officers through this type of training exercise improves their command post procedures and techniques, improves the decision-making process, and develops unit self-confidence. The ARTBASS system is mobile, and its use by multiple units increases its cost-effectiveness.

Despite the value of such exercises, commanders and staff officers also need the experience of training exercises with troop participation. In the ground forces, for example, a battalion commander needs to see firsthand the effects of decisions. A commander who orders a battalion to move from a bivouac to an attack position estimates the time required; but actual execution by the troops provides the experience that builds confidence in making similar decisions when leading those troops into combat.

The same principles apply at each level of command and in all types of forces. In the navy, the captain of a single ship needs to experience the maneuver of the ship through teamwork of its crew resulting from his or her commands. Naval task force commanders and fleet commanders gain the same kind of experience through major exercises at sea. The same principles apply in air forces with squadron, wing, and major air force commanders and staffs gaining similar experience.

For senior commanders, joint force exercises on a large scale are particularly valuable experiences in the event of a major war. Although these large exercises provide some useful experience for soldiers, sailors, and airmen, their training value applies almost exclusively to the commanders and staff officers.

Professional Military Education (PME)

Increased use of high-technology weapons systems and increased importance of integrating land, sea, and air forces have placed greater emphasis on the professional nature of military education of officers.

In the United States this has led to continued reexamination of the military education institutions, their curricula and faculty, and their relationships to each other and to an officer's career pattern. So great has been this interest in military education that the U.S. Congress conducted a major review of the military education system in 1989. The House of Representatives Armed Services Committee produced a lengthy report covering all the training installations along with a series of recommendations.

The first recommendation in this congressional report was that the Department of Defense "establish a PME framework for Department of Defense schools that specifies and relates the primary educational objectives at each PME level." Other recommendations included adding more civilian faculty members, placing greater stress on joint operations, and establishing a position of director of military education on the staff of the chairman of the Joint Chiefs of Staff.

These recommendations, along with internal reviews within the Department of Defense, resulted in a more formalized approach to professional military education, including preparation of officers for duty assignments involving joint forces.

Professional military education, defined above, is conducted at a series of increasingly complex and demanding levels. It addresses the military, political, economic, social, and psychological dimensions of national security with varying degrees of emphasis on the planning and conduct of war, organization of the armed forces, joint and combined operations, force employment and deployment concepts, and military leadership. Increasing emphasis is placed on joint matters relating to the integrated employment of land, sea, and air forces.

PRECOMMISSIONING EDUCATION

Education at the precommissioning level is conducted at the service academies, civilian colleges offering military options (known in the United States as Reserve Officers Training Corps, or ROTC), and officer candidate schools or officer training schools.

Regardless of the source of commission, new officers receive the same commission and have the same status and rank upon entry on active duty. However, the nature of the precommissioning education varies considerably.

The service academies, especially in the United States, were originally intended to develop officers for combat service while providing them with a broad general education. Hence the military aspects of a service academy education were somewhat more focused than the military part of the ROTC curriculum at a civilian college, which offered that program as a set of course options leading to a reserve commission. In recent years this difference has narrowed. The service academies commission officers in the service and support branches as well as the combat arms. Even more recently in the United States, women have attended all of the service academies, thus further emphasizing the broad role of the academies to produce officers for all types of service.

The U.S. ROTC programs also have changed in recent years. There are separate programs for the army, navy, and air force. These programs have never been limited to producing officers for the reserve components, but the numbers receiving regular commissions were very small for many years. Recently, the need for more officers in the active components has led to increased regular commissions from ROTC programs. Their curricula have been strengthened accordingly, and their graduates have been able to compete successfully with academy graduates for promotion.

As a source of commissioned officers, officer candidate schools can increase or decrease their enrollments rapidly to meet changing demands for new officers. Their courses are highly intensive over a relatively short period, as short as thirteen weeks. This type of course is designed to convert a noncommissioned officer into a commissioned officer through a highly disciplined program that instills the difference in responsibilities and teaches the fundamental skills required of an individual as a second lieutenant or ensign. Individuals so commissioned gain additional military education later through the normal progression of courses and experience of all officers.

All precommissioning education focuses on the rudiments of military science such as service missions and organization, military history, and conceptual awareness of the levels of war. At this formative stage, the student begins the process of thinking about joint military operations.

PRIMARY-LEVEL PME

Primary-level PME consists of basic and advanced branch schools. In addition, it includes certain courses or programs of a specialized nature such as intelligence, logistics, and systems management. This level of education is intended to provide the officer with the fundamental knowledge required for service in his or her basic service branch or combat specialty, such as infantry, surface warfare, or civil engineering.

Professional military education at this level enhances leadership and decision-making ability and improves management and communication skills. It includes tactical employment of military units to achieve specific battlefield objectives. Students begin to learn how each service supports the missions of the others in joint operations.

INTERMEDIATE-LEVEL PME

Intermediate-level PME instruction generally includes the command and staff colleges of the four military services. These institutions focus on large-unit war fighting and expand student understanding of the employment of joint forces at the tactical level of war. It also seeks to develop the officer's analytic capabilities and creative thought processes.

The curricula include theater-level operations, combined-arms/composite warfare expertise, and an introduction to national military strategy (defined as employment of armed forces to secure objectives of national policy by force or threat of force) and national security strategy (defined as the use of political, economic, and psychological powers, together with armed forces, in peace or war to secure national objectives).

In the United States, this level of PME also includes an Armed Forces Staff College whose curriculum addresses joint staff operations in detail.

SENIOR-LEVEL PME

The focus of education at senior-level PME is on strategy—the plan that translates power into the achievement of national objectives. These courses are intended to enrich the cadre of national strategic thinkers. Institutions offering this level of education are the war colleges of the armed forces—army, navy, and air force. In the United States, this level is also offered through curricula more oriented toward joint service at the National War College and the Industrial College of the Armed Forces.

The joint curriculum at the war colleges includes national military capabilities and command structure, joint doctrine, joint planning, joint and combined operations, campaign planning, and joint and combined warfare in the theater context.

The U.S. National War College stresses national security strategy. The U.S. Industrial College of the Armed Forces stresses the resource component of national power and its integration into national security strategy. Graduates of both colleges meet the educational requirements for designation by the secretary of defense as joint specialty officers and for assignment to major joint forces commands.

Because of the importance of joint force operations, senior service colleges now normally include students of other services in their classes. Faculties have been broadened to include more civilian instructors as well as faculty members from the other armed forces.

GENERAL AND FLAG OFFICER EDUCATION

Officers of general or flag rank get additional professional military education to enhance their ability to function at the highest levels. Officers selected for promotion to flag rank usually are required to attend courses to reinforce their understanding of joint matters and national security strategy, which they will need for the rest of their careers. The principles of personal interaction with senior commanders in joint and combined operations with other services and with allies are stressed.

A variety of joint and service seminars and short courses are offered for general officers to keep their expertise up to date and to expand their ability to function in a joint or allied environment.

Senior general or flag officers provide civilian leadership with military advice needed to formulate national security strategy. Professional military education emphasizes for these officers the synthesis of national military strategy with national security strategy and the synthesis of national security strategy with national policy-making requirements.

EXCHANGES AMONG NATIONS

It is common for allied nations to arrange exchange training opportunities, especially of officers in the professional military education programs. Many officers of U.S.–allied nations have attended U.S. command and staff colleges and senior service colleges, and many others have participated in seminars and short courses on subjects in which the allied nations have common interests.

Other exchange training opportunities exist through assignment of individual U.S. officers to units of allied nations for a regular tour of duty. This provides a valuable exchange of tactical and technical expertise and is especially useful in the event of future multinational operations.

Even in the reserve components, exchange training of officers has grown in recent years. For example, U.S. and German reserve officer exchange training takes place under formal agreements. Similar exchange arrangements for reserve officers exist between the United States and France and the United Kingdom.

Reserve Component Education and Training

As nations seek to control defense budgets, they place great reliance on reserve component and national guard troops. The part-time nature of these forces makes them less costly but also makes effective training more difficult. Yet, because these forces are expected to be available on short notice, effective training is a vital requirement.

A particularly difficult problem is the training of reserve units and individuals at occasional assemblies in their home cities. Typically these sessions, referred to in the United States as inactive duty training, are held on weekends to minimize conflict with civilian jobs. The training problem stems in part from the difficulty of making effective use of all the time available. Each assembly must include some administrative time at the beginning and end of each duty period, regardless of its length. Individuals also must remember the instruction from the previous session when the instructor resumes. The two-day weekend training assembly has proven more efficient than the previous system of evening classes, which for practical reasons could not last longer than four hours.

Because the education and training process for both officers and enlisted personnel involves a series of schools and special courses of varying lengths, these part-time military personnel face serious problems of absences from their civilian employment and time away from families. In addition, military pay is often lower than the individual's civilian pay. Some employers grant time off with pay for their employees on reserve training duty or make up the difference between their military and civilian pay.

In the United States a National Committee for Employer Support of the Guard and Reserve has several thousand volunteers who assist in solving individual employer problems and conduct information programs designed to show employers that members of the reserve are gaining experience that makes them more valuable to their civilian employer. The program has been highly successful.

The armed forces are dealing with the reserve training problem in a variety of ways. For example, to ensure maximum attendance at annual training (usually two or three weeks) early notice of the dates helps employers plan temporary replacement of reservists.

Specialized courses required for both officer and enlisted reservists are sometimes rearranged into two or more segments to shorten the periods away from home. In some cases courses can be broken into segments that can be covered in a series of weekends, sometimes taught at the home station near the reservist's residence. Such adaptation is particularly suited to the use of newly developed simulators and training devices.

If reserve component officers are to meld effectively into the active forces upon mobilization, they must receive substantially the same professional education as regular officers. This difficult standard has been achieved in the United States through the creation of courses designed to take the reserve officer through the required levels of education with somewhat abridged curricula and a combination of nonresident and resident instruction.

Army reserve forces schools located throughout the United States provide instruction for both officer and enlisted reserve personnel from the level of advanced individual enlisted training to the command and general staff college level. The latter course includes both weekend and evening classes at the reserve school and short tours of active duty for certain course work.

Even the senior service college course of the U.S. Army and U.S. Air Force can be taken in a similar fashion, with some work done in nonresident status and some in short sessions at the war colleges.

Managing Education and Training

Because training consumes such a large part of the time of military personnel and requires such a large investment in facilities and instructor personnel, management of the education and training program and budgeting for its costs are major Department of Defense responsibilities.

As many as 10 percent of all military personnel may be undergoing formal education and training every day of the year. Specific numbers of students must be calculated based on the requirements for individual training to determine budgets each year. In addition, funds must be budgeted for instructors and other military and civilian personnel in support of training as well as for operations and maintenance and training-related procurement.

The "training load" is defined as the average number of students and trainees participating in formal individual training and education courses during the fiscal year. This figure is expressed in student/trainee man-years.

The requirement for training is derived from the need to replace losses in each skill required in the military force structure. Losses through separations, promotions, and other causes are projected for various points in the future and compared to the projected inventory of trained personnel. The deficit in each skill becomes a demand for an output of trained personnel. A phased input of students to the training establishment is then scheduled so that trained personnel in each skill and at each skill level are available at the proper time to replace the losses. The resulting workload establishes the training load.

The workload applies only to individual training, and it must be calculated for each skill and skill level in each of the armed forces to arrive at total figures for budget purposes. Unit training is not included in these calculations because it is included in operating budgets.

In the United States detailed calculations of individual training requirements with full justifications must be submitted to Congress annually as part of the budget process. Typical training loads for the active forces are about 200,000 man-years. Most of this training load is directly related to accessions of non–prior-service personnel. For the active forces, about 20 percent is recruit training, 58 percent specialized skill training, and 9 percent officer acquisition training.

Individual training requires manpower to conduct and support instruction, manage military schools and training centers, maintain training bases, and provide support to students and to military staff members and their dependents. In the United States this requires about 176,000 personnel, about one-third of whom are civilians.

Budgeting for the mammoth education and training activity must be precise to ensure that the training output can meet needs throughout the budget year. The budget includes the following twelve categories: recruit training; officer acquisition training; specialized skill training; flight training; professional development education; army one-station unit training; medical training; base operating support and direct training support; management headquarters; permanent-change-of-station costs for training; temporary duty costs for training; and reserve component pay and allowances.

From a national perspective, effective military education and training programs are essential to ensure that operational forces are manned with personnel who are fully qualified for their jobs. Since no nation can predict when or where war may break out or count on an extended period for mobilization and training, all must have ongoing, formalized training programs to ensure that operational units will be capable of carrying out national security missions in peace or war.

Future Trends

As combat and support systems make greater use of high technology and warfare becomes invariably a joint operation involving land, sea, and air forces, education and training assume increasing importance. A single error of judgment by a commander can have cataclysmic results. Effective education and training can minimize such errors.

Nations of all sizes face the same problems. Limited resources make solutions more difficult. Imaginative methods can be found to provide such training in cost-effective ways. A small cadre of trained military educators, possibly getting their own training from a larger allied nation, can devise training packages that can be used to train other trainers and can be distributed to training installations throughout the country.

Simulators and training aids are expensive initially, especially those that use interactive computers, but eventually they save money. The cost of such training aids is decreasing as they come into wider use.

For smaller countries, manufacturers are designing technical training materials that allow users to start small with a basic set that will remain useful as additional capabilities are added. These manufacturers are now holding training conferences at various locations so that potential buyers can see what is available and how it can be procured in stages.

Many leading military officers see simulators and complex training devices playing leading roles in solving these critical training issues throughout the world.

W. STANFORD SMITH

SEE ALSO: Personnel; Reserve Components.

Bibliography

Doeringer, P. B., ed. 1981. *Workplace perspectives on education and training*. Boston, The Hague, and London: Martinus Nijhoff.
Gander, T. J., ed. 1988. *Jane's military training systems, 1988–89*. Coulsdon, Surrey, UK: Jane's Information Group.
Great Soviet encyclopedia. Trans. of the 3d ed. 1973. New York: Macmillan.
U.S. Department of Defense. 1988. JCS Pub. 1. *Dictionary of military and associated terms*. Washington, D.C.: Public Affairs Press.
————. 1989. *Military manpower training report*. Washington, D.C.: Office of the Assistant Secretary of Defense (Force Management and Personnel).
Van Creveld, M. 1990. *The training of officers*. New York: Free Press.

ELECTRONIC WARFARE TECHNOLOGY APPLICATIONS

The range and speed of modern weapons and the pace and scope of modern combat depend on electronics. Electronic systems provide target detection, designation, and fire control for weapons, navigation and motion control for weapons platforms, and communications and information for battle management. Electronic warfare (EW) is a never-ending technological and operational contest. It is the battle for supremacy between the electronics of the weapons systems and the countermeasures devised to defeat and degrade these weapons systems.

Systems engineering is the point of view taken in the material that follows. The emphasis is on application of the technology rather than on the technology itself. This discussion is based on the principles of EW; it is largely independent of specific equipment and vehicles. Electronic devices and equipment have undergone dramatic changes since World War II, and they will continue to change; but the principles will remain the same.

To prevail in modern combat one must control the electronic environment on which sensor, communication, and information systems depend for operation. Control includes preservation of a force's offensive and defensive sensor, communication, and information capabilities, as well as denial of comparable capabilities to opponents.

The applications of technology to electronic countermeasures (ECM) include: jamming techniques used to deny opponents' capabilities and electronic counter-countermeasures (ECCM), such as the jamming avoidance techniques used to protect one's force capabilities from opponents' jamming. These techniques have come to be called electronic warfare. EW is encompassed in the broader concept of electronic combat (EC), which includes operational philosophy, strategy, and doctrine.

The technologies most commonly considered involve the electromagnetic spectrum: radio and radar, infrared (IR), optical, and ultraviolet (UV) frequencies (or wavelengths). Also included are acoustics, which have great importance in undersea warfare and increasing importance in short-range land warfare.

The benefit of EW must ultimately be expressed in terms of combat mission success, such as more intelligence gained without detection, more weapons on target, more combat missions generated for a given force size, and more effective battle management. Because EW capability increases the cost and complexity of a force, EW must demonstrate a benefit greater than would be provided by a larger force without EW at the same total cost.

Development of EW

The development of EW during and following World War II has followed the pattern of physics-based military technologies.

EW DEVELOPMENT HISTORICALLY DRIVEN BY RADAR

Over this time period, radar has been a prime example of "combined radical change" in the sense of Bonen's Battlefield Systems Evolution Paths. Radar technology grew to pervade all phases of military operations, leading to a quantitative and qualitative expansion of offensive and defensive capabilities, as well as organizational changes in force structure. For this reason, radar countermeasures became the principal interest of EW practitioners worldwide and absorbed the major share of EW funding, personnel, and facilities.

INCREASING ATTENTION TO NON-RADAR EW

Although examples of jamming and deception of communications and navigation systems preceded the advent of radar, they (and other portions of the electromagnetic spectrum such as IR and visual) have only recently begun to receive an increasing share of development resources. Visual countermeasures have existed for centuries in the form of camouflage, but television technology has created electro-optic (EO) surveillance and fire control applications, thus creating an opportunity for EW.

OPERATIONS ANALYSIS CRITICAL TO EW DEVELOPMENT

"For every measure there is a countermeasure" is the war cry of the EW practitioner. It applies to both countermeasures and counter-countermeasures. With the advancement of technology, EW has become limited only by imagination and cost. It is fiscally impractical to apply every advance in technology to its fullest by developing every conceivable countermeasure to every one of the opponent's measures. The ability to assess the relative benefit of EW techniques, equipment, and tactics over a wide range of combat situations is critical to the development and fielding of successful EW capabilities.

While EW performance assessment is critical, it is also more difficult than for most combat systems. Where possible, EW must operate against the fundamental attributes of an opponent's equipment, system, or operational practice. Where the opportunity presents itself, EW can exploit design, implementation, and doctrinal weaknesses in the opponent's capabilities.

The greatest difficulty in assessment occurs in developing the necessary understanding of attributes and exploitabilities of the opposing forces. The range of potential opponents can include major powers and developing countries, while combat situations can range from nuclear to subconventional. Intelligence about an opponent's system and force capabilities will always be incomplete and usually late.

Another major difficulty occurs in developing the personnel and physical assets for testing EW methods and equipment. Equipment against which EW can be tested may be difficult and expensive to acquire and operate and also of questionable fidelity. The deployment and control of surrogate assets on a scale approaching that of actual combat will seldom, if ever, be practical and will also be of questionable fidelity. In the case of weapons effects, live firing against expensive targets must be used sparingly, if at all.

Cost and time usually prohibit dealing with these two key issues—uncertainty and fidelity of detail—by permutations of real-life (surrogate) testing. The most effective approach is the extensive use of simulation, modeling, and other analytical tools of operations research to work out the key fundamental issues. Live testing, and/or the results of training and actual operational results, can be used to confirm or refute the operations analysis and the resulting fundamental relationships and interactions.

This combined analytical and experimental approach to developing a fundamental store of knowledge facilitates responding to the appearance of new and unexpected equipment, tactics, and doctrine. The alternative of dealing with new situations by extrapolating the results of live testing against a single point victim system and employment surrogates is more vulnerable to error and slower in responsiveness to change.

Principles of Radar EW

Many of the physical principles that apply to EW against radar also pertain to the other EW disciplines. An understanding of these principles is important for understanding how technology is applied to EW in general, as well as to radar.

THE RADAR EQUATION

Radar performance is described by the well-known radar equation

$$P_s = \frac{P_t G_t^2 \, L^2 \, \sigma}{D^4 \, 16\pi^2 \, 4\pi}. \tag{1}$$

This is the monostatic form of the radar equation, which assumes the receiver and transmitter are co-located. It ignores atmospheric and meteorological attenuation, ground propagation effects, and signal detection criteria as a function of signal processing and display, where:

P_t = radar transmitter power
P_s = signal power at the radar antenna terminals
G_t = radar (transmit = receive) antenna gain
L = wavelength of the radar transmitter frequency
σ = radar cross section of the target
D = distance from radar antenna to target

All are expressed in consistent units. Gain is expressed as a numeric ratio.

The radar homing missile system is a common example of bistatic radar. The radar transmitter at the launcher position illuminates the target. The radar receiver on the missile seeks the signal reflected from the target. The squared antenna gain term of monostatic equation (1) becomes the product of the antenna gains for the illuminator and the seeker. The fourth-power range term becomes the product of the squared-range terms for the illuminator-to-target and seeker-to-target ranges.

FUNDAMENTAL RADAR-EW SIGNAL RELATIONSHIPS

The radar equation is a convenient basis for developing the following fundamental signal relationships in EW. The performance of a radar jammer of constant power, which might be used as ECM aboard a target for self-screening (range denial) or self-protection, is given by

$$P_{j/s} = \frac{P_e G_e D^2 \, 4\pi}{P_t G_t \, \sigma} \tag{2}$$

where $P_{j/s}$ is the jam-to-signal power ratio at the radar receiver terminals, and P_e and G_e are the ECM transmitter power and antenna gain, respectively. $P_{j/s}$ is a fundamental criterion for jammer performance. One measure of effectiveness (MOE) for EW techniques is the $P_{j/s}$ required for their success.

The $P_{j/s}$ performance of a linear transponder jammer, which might be used as ECM aboard a target for self-protection or off the target as a decoy, is given by

$$P_{j/s} = \frac{G_e^2 G_x L^2}{4\pi\sigma} \tag{3}$$

where G_x is the gain of the transponder in its linear (unsaturated) region of operation. At saturation, the performance of the transponder is governed by equation (2).

The $P_{j/s}$ performance for an off-target platform using constant power to screen the detection of a target platform from a radar is given by

$$P_{j/s} = \frac{P_e G_e \, 4\pi \, D_t^4}{P_t G_t \, \sigma \, D_j^2} \tag{4}$$

where D_t is the distance from the radar to the target, and D_j is the distance from the radar to the jamming platform.

The minimum incident signal on the ECM receiver aboard a target at the maximum target detection range of the radar is given by

$$P_{sd}^2 = \frac{G_e^2 L^2 \, P_{sm} P_t}{4\pi\sigma} \tag{5}$$

where P_{sd} is the ECM signal power at maximum radar detection range for target radar cross section σ, and P_{sm} is the minimum detectable radar signal power, both referred to the respective antenna terminals.

PERFORMANCE SCALING RULES

Because of the large dynamic ranges of the parameters involved, EW practitioners are accustomed to dealing with equations (1) to (5) in decibel (db) values, where the value in decibels is given by 10 log (value/reference). The reference for each value is generally in consistent Système Internationale d'Unités (SI) meter-kilogram-second (MKS) units: meters for wavelength, watts for power, square meters for radar cross section, and unity for gain.

For two-way propagation, or fourth-power exponents such as radar detection range, equation results scale as a 40-decibel change in signal power per decade (10:1) of radar range change and 12 decibels per octave (2:1) of range. For one-way propagation, or square law equations such as $P_{j/s}$, results scale as a

20-decibel per decade and 6-decibel per octave change in $P_{j/s}$ for change in range.

The use of these scaling rules is illustrated by applying them to the issue of stealth, or low-observable, technology. Reducing the radar cross section of a platform by 12 decibels will reduce the range at which it is detected by radar by a factor of two (one octave). It will also improve (decrease) by a factor of four (two octaves) the range at which the platform and its jammer can approach a radar while maintaining a specified $P_{j/s}$. Conversely, reducing radar detection range by a factor of 10 requires a radar cross section reduction of 40 decibels. A factor of 10 reduction in the range at which a jammer can maintain a specified $P_{j/s}$ requires a 20-decibel reduction in radar cross section.

FUNCTIONAL CLASSES OF RADAR

The application of EW technology and techniques is dependent on the class of the victim radar and its military function, as well as the radar technology itself. For purposes of discussion, it is convenient to group the radars used in direct support of offensive and defensive military operations into three functional classes:

1. *Surveillance*—characterized by a large volume of coverage, moderate accuracy in determining target coordinates, and a military function of early detection, location, and sometimes classification of a very large number of targets.
2. *Target acquisition*—characterized by a large volume of coverage, coordinate accuracy, and target-handling capacity responsive to the weapons system for which they designate and assign targets.
3. *Fire control*—characterized by a limited field of view, high coordinate accuracy, and highly continuous tracking for a relatively small number of targets (often only one). The specifics of target tracking are responsive to the types of weapons to be controlled. For example, weapons that require a prediction computation, such as artillery and command-guided systems used against moving targets, may require target range to achieve a hit. In contrast, homing weapons may not require target range to achieve a hit.

In some cases, the three functions are performed in three separate pieces of equipment connected by communications. In other cases, two or three of the functions may be combined into operating modes in one piece of equipment. The functionality, as well as the hardware, must be considered in designing successful EW.

Table 1 demonstrates the need for identifying radar functions in EW design and in performance test and evaluation. The surveillance and target acquisition functions have their primary influence on setting the number of engagements a vehicle will encounter. The fire control function is the primary determinant of the probability of a hit or kill in an engagement.

Countermeasures to surveillance, acquisition, and communications functions include screening, jamming, and stealth and have the greatest effect on the number of engagements. Countermeasures to the fire control functions, such as self-protection jamming, have the greatest effect on the probability of a kill in an engagement. Some countermeasures can influence both. Decoys can saturate the defenses, affecting the number of engagements, as well as deflect a fire control system from the target it is engaging. (See Table 1.)

CATEGORIES OF RADAR EW

Two broad classes of EW can be identified. One, called onboard EW, is performed from the platform that is the target of a radar. It is designed to achieve situation awareness from, and deny or corrupt information to, radar illuminating the target itself. The other, off-board EW, is performed from a separate location to deny radar information on many targets over a wide area or volume. In some cases, off-board EW is performed from platforms that can provide situation awareness and battle management for the targets being screened.

In another dimension, there are two categories of EW equipment and operations: jamming and decoying. Both can be implemented on board, off board, or in combination. Onboard jammers and simple onboard decoys (which become off board when launched) are used for self-defense against fire control radars. Off-board jammers and more complex off-board decoys (e.g., those on remotely controlled or piloted vehicles) are used to delay and confuse surveillance and target designation radars. On-board jammers can be used in combination to provide mutual support.

Principles of Communications EW

Communications EW is the detection, classification, and response to communications signals. Some consider communications intelligence as a part of communications EW. Intelligence is derived from communications intercepted by cryptologic activities. These include encryption and decryption, signals analysis, traffic analysis, and analysis of communications' content. Cryptologic activities are not covered.

FUNDAMENTAL SIGNAL RELATIONSHIPS

For radar, the receiver and the transmitter of the jamming victim are most often at the same location. In communications, the transmitter and receiver are separated.

Most radar applications operate under conditions where propagation can be represented by the line-of-sight equations in the section "Principles of Radar EW" above. The radio frequency propagation of many communications is gov-

TABLE 1. *Survival Probability (%): Number of Engagements (N) versus Single Engagement Probability of Kill (SEPK)*

SEPK	N		
	1	*2*	*4*
0.64	36%	13%	2%
0.32	68%	46%	21%
0.16	84%	71%	50%

erned by earth effects. For example, at and near the frequencies designated high frequency (HF, 3–30 MHz), radio waves propagate beyond the horizon. They curve to follow the earth and reflect from the ionosphere. At these and higher frequencies, the siting of communications antennas causes their patterns to be dominated by the effects of the earth's surface.

The difference between line-of-sight and over-the-horizon propagation is one of detail. The separation between transmitter and receiver in communications provides a fundamental distinction between communications EW and radar EW. The EW objective is to jam the receiver. The transmitter affects the jamming power requirement and provides a reference signal. It is therefore instructive to examine the line-of-sight communications jamming equation.

The $P_{j/s}$ for communications jamming is given by

$$P_{j/s} = \frac{P_e G_e D_c^2}{P_t G_t D_e^2} \tag{6}$$

where:

P_e, G_e = ECM transmitter power and antenna gain,
P_t, G_t = radio transmitter power and antenna gain,
D_c = distance from communications transmitter to receiver, and
D_e = distance from ECM transmitter to communications receiver.

In many cases, the antenna gains are roughly equal, so the expression can be simplified to

$$P_{j/s} = \frac{P_e D_c^2}{P_t D_e^2} \tag{7}$$

By inspection, a 10-decibel power advantage of the jammer transmitter over the radio transmitter gives a $P_{j/s} = 10$ decibels when the radio and jammer transmitters are equidistant from the receiver. The performance scaling rules (see Performance Scaling Rules above) can be applied to show that $P_{j/s}$ scales as an increase of 20 decibels per decade of increase in the distance ratio D_c / D_e.

FUNCTIONAL CLASSES OF COMMUNICATIONS

As in radar, EW technology and techniques are dependent on communications functions. They are also dependent on the types of communications and the types of technologies employed. The functional classes are: (1) broadcast, with one transmitter and many receivers; (2) point-to-point, with one transmitter and one receiver; and (3) net, with multiple transmitters and receivers, a net control station, and operating protocol.

The classes of radio technologies are single channel, which uses one radio frequency for one connection between two points; and multichannel, which uses one radio frequency for multiple connections between two points. The amplitude, frequency, and phase of the radio frequency signal may be modulated to carry information, and more than one channel of information can be carried on a signal by multiplexing. A further technical distinction can be made between frequency ranges that are restricted to line-of-sight paths (above about 100 MHz) and those that support long over-the-horizon paths (below about 30 MHz).

CATEGORIES OF COMMUNICATIONS EW

The two broad categories of communications EW are jamming and deception. Unlike the radar categories, there is no fundamental distinction between on board and off board. The jamming platform need only be located so that P_{V_s} is large enough to overpower the radio technology in use. Deception does not require overpowering the victim communications signals. Deception need only exceed the receiver thresholds of the victim receivers or at most match the normal signal levels in such receivers.

The different classes and categories of communications influence the operational use of EW. It is a common mistake to measure target size by the number of radios to be jammed. The more useful measurement is the number of radio frequencies to be jammed.

Some classes of communications are always important, others only if certain conditions are met. Multichannel communications are almost always associated with command posts and other command activities and are therefore universally important. Only about 10 percent of single-channel radio nets may be operationally important (e.g., the maneuver unit command and control nets of a division). Broadcast frequencies may or may not be operationally significant.

As in the case of radar EW, communications EW priorities and the likelihood of effectiveness must be evaluated by using the methods of operations research. Simulation and modeling are particularly useful in assessing alternatives and in exploring the effects of geographical separation and backup means of communications.

Infrared and Electro-optical (IR/EO) EW

The range, accuracy, and all-weather day-night utility of radar have revolutionized military operations. On the other hand, the use of radar does have disadvantages. Radar denies the military element of surprise to the user and is susceptible to countermeasures from the target and its environment. Military systems that use the infrared, visual, and higher portions of the electromagnetic spectrum gain many of the benefits of radar while avoiding some of the penalties.

PRINCIPLES OF IR/EO EW

Three fundamental characteristics distinguish IR/EO sensors from radar: (1) IR/EO sensors are passive (i.e., they depend on target reflection of ambient energy or on the contrast between target energy and ambient background energy); (2) two or more spatially separated IR/EO sensors are required to measure target range and velocity; and (3) they have a narrow instantaneous angular field of view compared with a typical radar antenna beamwidth.

The absence of a transmitter is a key advantage against EW. A transmitter would provide warning, as well as a reference signal for jamming. The inability of IR/EO to discriminate in range and velocity provides false target EW opportunities. On the other hand, the narrow IR/EO field of view discriminates against poorly positioned decoys and other off-board countermeasures.

The new field of laser detection and ranging (ladar) is an exception to the general statement that IR/EO systems do not use transmitters. Illumination by a ladar would provide a warning, but ladar can provide range and velocity information.

The operational and EW implications of ladar are not yet well defined, but the highly collimated laser beam presents a constraint on each side. Operational applications will be limited by the field of view. EW warning and jamming at tactical ranges will require an array of detectors and transmitters. The nature of the array will be determined by the relationship of ladar spot size to the target size.

Fundamental IR/EO Signal Relationships

Although the same principles apply for both radio and IR/EO electromagnetic propagation calculations, there are important differences in practice. The range performance of IR/EO systems always depends on contrast with background radiation. For radar performance, contrast is an issue only in clutter and is a function of range and velocity gating. Atmospheric attenuation is always a complex factor in IR/EO; it is a major factor for radar only at the high microwave and millimeter wavelengths. Finally, the terminology is different. The IR/EO viewpoint is governed by detector equivalent temperature and area, signal flux density, and target/background spectral radiance, or luminance. The radar viewpoint has adopted the convention of antenna gains, spatial spreading loss, receiver noise figures, clutter in resolution cells, and radar cross section as a function of wavelength.

Functional Classes of IR/EO Systems

Two of the three classes of radar system functions are convenient for IR/EO: surveillance and fire control. The narrow instantaneous field of view of IR/EO sensors limits surveillance coverage but inherently provides accurate target designation. Wide coverage can be achieved by scanning, but scanning causes high revisit time. Wide coverage can also be achieved by multiple detectors and parallel processing (the "fly's eye"), with a penalty of complexity and cost. The narrow field of view of IR/EO fire control sensors demands a higher accuracy of target designation than required by radar fire control sensors.

Without range or velocity discrimination, IR/EO systems must use signal processing to separate targets from background. This processing takes two forms. One is spectral filtering, which discriminates between the wavelengths of target radiation and reflection from background characteristics. The other is spatial filtering, which discriminates the size and shape of targets from backgrounds that are extended and diffuse.

Categories of IR/EO EW

The on-board and off-board classes of EW apply to IR/EO as well as to radar. The absence of IR/EO transmitters and the narrow field of view of IR/EO sensors affect the objectives of IR/EO EW. There will be no warning of surveillance and fire control activities. Off-board jamming will not be effective unless it is within the narrow IR/EO sensor field of view. Onboard jamming will not be effective against surveillance systems. If onboard jamming affords contrast to ambient background, it may aid detection and location by a surveillance system.

Decoys and false targets will be effective against surveillance systems, and against fire control when in the field of view of the sensor. On-board jamming can be effective against fire control. To be effective, the wavelength and other signal characteristics of the decoys, false targets, and jamming must be accepted by the spectral and spatial filtering of the victim system. The kinematics of short-range missiles cause another constraint. The time window for deploying decoys to deflect a missile seeker from its target is very small.

In the case of an on-board jammer and an IR seeker, the match of jammer signal modulation and tracker spatial filtering is important. The reticles that provide spatial filtering have undergone continued and diversified development since the original Sidewinder missile tracking reticle. An IR jammer loses effectiveness without *a priori* knowledge of the specific reticles it must counter.

EW Today and Tomorrow: Revolution and Evolution

Two revolutions with potentially conflicting directions are taking place today. One is the chip revolution: very large-scale integration (VLSI), very high-speed integrated circuits (VHSIC), and monolithic microwave integrated circuits (MMIC). Stealth, or low-observable technology, represents the second revolution. The first gives the EW designer the capacity to realize EW system objectives that could only be dreamed of twenty years ago. The second, along with the evolution caused by the success of past EW, calls into question many of the EW objectives of twenty years ago. Stealth causes dramatic changes in the requirements and constraints that the EW designer must meet. It also forces the vehicle designer to understand issues that were formerly the exclusive province of the EW designer.

The Stealth Revolution

Stealth work is still cloaked in secrecy, but some of the central issues can be inferred from basic physical principles. Low-observable design involves control of a vehicle's structural and operational observables (e.g., radar cross section and engine exhaust), control of sensor interfaces (e.g., antennas), and sensor radiations (e.g., radar and communications).

The first set of observables is controlled by shaping the vehicle, selecting appropriate construction materials, and adding materials and features to achieve the desired effects. Sensor interfaces may use materials that have different reflecting and emitting characteristics than the vehicle structure itself. Signals from radars, communications, and navigation can be detected and used for location of the vehicle. The latter two areas may represent constraints in observability that must be traded off with the vehicle design itself in order to achieve a balance between stealth cost and overall performance. Trade-offs will usually include multiple attributes such as IR signature, visibility, and acoustic levels, as well as radar cross section.

Reduction in radar cross section has six effects on EW system design. It reduces the transmitter power needed to achieve a specified $P_{1/s}$ at a specified range (equations [2] and [4]). It reduces the transmitter power required of a decoy (equation [3]). It reduces the onboard receiver sensitivity needed to detect the radar signal at its reduced (by stealth) maximum range (equation [5]). It influences the distribution of jammer power from the antennas to complement radar cross section characteristics. It places constraints on the size and type of antenna used and possibly on the characteristics of the ECM signal itself. And finally, the reduced range will usually change the engagement envelope of the weapons system to be countered.

Special precautions must be taken to minimize the radar cross section of sensor antennas and other radio frequency (RF) interfaces. Sensor design must consider low probability of intercept (LPI) waveforms such as frequency hopping and direct sequence spread spectrum. The concept of LPI should be used with caution, especially for long-range radars. For any signal, there is a range at which it can be detected even with a mismatched receiver. The concept of limited range of intercept (LRI) is often more useful.

SIGNAL PROCESSING AND THE CHIP REVOLUTION

The chip revolution makes possible ever-increasing capability in a given volume or shrinking size and weight for a given capability. The growth in power and the decrease in size of the personal computer and the hand calculator are dramatic examples. Small vehicles can carry computer power and processing speed that permit the processing of hundreds of thousands of arriving pulses, along with continuous wave (CW) signals. Signal processing for EW can be partitioned into three primary functions: detection, classification, and response. Response may be an aural or visual output, a physical reaction such as maneuver or dispensing of an expendable, or modulation of the jamming transmitter. Modulation will be designed and chosen during operations to interrupt or corrupt the signals and signal processing of the victim electronic systems.

Detection comprises the reception of a signal and the recognition that the signal is present in the receiver. For example, the sensitivity requirements of equation (5) must be met for radar.

The first stages of all types of receivers may include a radio frequency passband, an RF amplifier, and an RF distribution network. A crystal video receiver consists of a diode detector followed by a pulse amplifier.

A superheterodyne receiver (a highly sensitive and selective radio receiver) performs the following tasks: conversion of a signal to an intermediate frequency (IF) using a local oscillator and a mixer, IF amplification, and IF detection of the signal envelope and its frequency or phase modulation. The channelized receiver has several variations. In principle, all are superheterodyne receivers organized to divide the RF passband into sub-bands, each of which is then further subdivided into channels. These receiver types are all capable of recovering the modulation on the received signals, as well as detecting their presence. The superheterodyne types also measure signal RF.

An instantaneous-frequency-measurement (IFM) receiver usually acts directly on the RF with a wide bandwidth frequency discriminator. The compressive receiver uses a mixer and linearly frequency modulated local oscillator to convert the received signal into a very short pulse. These receiver types detect the presence of a signal and measure its RF. They depend on the complementary use of the other receiver types for recovery of signal modulation.

The variety of receiver types reflects the technology used to optimize trade-offs in probability of intercept, bandwidth coverage, recovery of signal modulation, and speed of detection. New technologies involving Bragg cells, surface acoustic waves, and acoustic charge transport devices are being explored. The goals for these new approaches are reduced size and power consumption, as well as improved performance.

Classification is the processing of the detected information to identify the function and type of equipment that is the source of the signal. If possible, the result should indicate the weapon and the military unit or echelon with which the signal is associated. It may also be possible to identify the operational status of the weapon (e.g., searching or shooting) and the unit (e.g., static or on the move).

Classification can be based on detailed knowledge of signal properties and parameters or on gross information such as duty cycle of appearance. The greater the dependence on detailed knowledge, the greater the susceptibility to decoying and deception. The design challenge is to rely on fundamental characteristics to the greatest extent possible, while maintaining the capability to exploit details when expedient.

Response uses detection and classification as one input for taking the appropriate EW action. Other inputs are *a priori* knowledge of victim susceptibilities, situational and operational priorities, and EW system characteristics. Detection and classification can provide discrimination among classes of threats, such as search versus fire control radars and net versus point-to-point radios.

For example, radar jamming could be selected from among noise, false target, and responsive techniques. Communications and navigation jamming could be selected from among noise, deception, and intrusion techniques.

Within each of these classes of techniques there are specific categories for further selection. Perhaps the widest diversity occurs in responsive techniques for fire control radar. These include range and velocity gate pull off used against the radar target selection signal channels and various modulations used against radar conical scan, track-while-scan, and monopulse angle target tracking signal channels.

For jamming, one measure of effectiveness is jam-to-signal power ratio in the victim receiver. It is usually designated as $Pj/_s$. Each jamming technique is characterized by a range of $Pj/_s$ required for effectiveness.

Noise jamming techniques against radar and amplitude-modulated radio are usually considered effective at a $Pj/_s$ of about 10 decibels (decibels = 10 log power ratio). Signal capture techniques against radar target selection channels and frequency modulated (FM) radio are typically about 6 decibels less. Signal capture techniques against radar target angle channels and antijam radios are typically at least 6 decibels more. $Pj/_s$ values are situation dependent. They must be determined analytically and confirmed experimentally.

False target and intrusion techniques can be effective at a $Pj/_s$ of 0 decibels (1:1 ratio) or less. These techniques attempt to match victim electronic signal characteristics and do not require capture of a channel for effectiveness. Depending on the accuracy of match, this type of jamming needs only to be above the threshold of the victim receiver's signal processing.

Revolutionary results in detection are being achieved with MMIC. Complete receivers, and in some cases transmitter-receivers, can be created on a single chip. These chips provide small size, reproducibility through avoidance of labor-intensive construction and testing, and elimination of loss-inducing failure-prone connections. The modern acoustic wave and charge transport technology also lends itself to MMIC and holds promise for even more dramatic results.

From the description of classification and response, it is clear that what the imagination can design is limited only by processing power and memory. It is possible to assimilate hundreds of signals and tag their time and frequency components (e.g., pulses and other modulations) with their frequency and angle of arrival. These can be classified, compared with known data, and a course of action taken automatically or recommended to an operator. One example is called power management: the automatic selective ECM response with nearly instantaneous antenna-beam steering. Antenna-beam steering provides gain to improve $Pj/_s$ and decreases the sector of observability. Selective response provides the appropriate ECM techniques for each radar type. Responses are prioritized in the order of threat urgency. The number and types of response are controlled to remain within the power capacity of the jammers. In addition to power management, processing can provide cuing for operational responses such as avoidance maneuvers and antiradiation missiles.

EVOLUTIONARY RESPONSE TO PAST EW SUCCESSES

The chip revolution provides the EW designer with powerful capabilities. It also makes it easy to attempt more elegant solutions to yesterday's problems. In many cases, EW successes have caused fundamental changes to be made in the nature of the threat.

As an example of evolutionary response to the success of jamming, the effectiveness of defensive electronic countermeasures (DECM) has succeeded in making sequential lobing angle tracking obsolete. Primary threats today use simultaneous lobing (e.g., some form of monopulse), which is insensitive to modulations from the target in the form of jamming. While there are techniques for disrupting monopulse, they favor off-board, rather than onboard, applications.

As an example of evolutionary response to the success of passive detection, the onboard radar warning receivers that provide situation awareness make effective use of large-scale integrated circuits. The existence of these receivers has driven radar-guided weapons to shorter radiation times in order to provide less and even insufficient warning. Alternatives to radar guidance, such as IR, can eliminate radar warning completely.

IMPORTANT ISSUES FOR THE FUTURE

The revolutions of the past have focused on hardware and on onboard equipment and techniques. Measures of effectiveness have concentrated on single vehicles and single EW disciplines. EW contributions to force effectiveness have been based on aggregating single-vehicle survivability results.

Although major strides in devices using VLSI and MMIC will continue, future focus for their application is likely to be on software and on off-board and coordinated equipment and techniques. The issue of expanding radar warning to encompass threat warning for all types of missiles remains. It may be the only major remaining self-protection area where an onboard hardware development could provide the answer.

Measures of effectiveness are likely to involve the activities of multiple vehicles. EW contributions must be related more directly to combat effectiveness.

The increasing complexity of the electronic environment and the necessary speed of response to threats will require more intelligent software. Stealth will require greater control of ECM responses. Perhaps artificial intelligence solutions will be one of the future revolutions.

As stealth succeeds in reducing radar detection ranges, other sensors will gain importance. For example, surface-based electro-acoustic sensors may regain operational importance in some situations.

Stealth will make off-board countermeasures more feasible and favored. Monopulse radar angle tracking will make off-board countermeasures necessary in many cases. The chip revolution will facilitate very small, smart, and power-efficient decoys. These two factors could converge to make unmanned vehicles more important for both decoying and off-board jamming.

Off-board techniques and concepts will provide an opportunity for coordinated countermeasures and situation awareness using multiple platforms. Analysis, development, and training will depend heavily on simulation and modeling because of the complexity and cost of live operations. Simulation and modeling may also be the answer to increasing budget pressures. Electronic warfare programs will ultimately have to be justified in trade-offs with weapons programs in terms of their relative contribution to combat effectiveness.

GEORGE F. STEEG

SEE ALSO: Radar Technology Applications.

Bibliography

Fomichev, K. I., and A. I. Leonov. 1986. Interference tolerance of monopulse radars. In *Monopulse Radar*, trans. W. F. Barton, 223–80. Norwood, Mass.: Artech House.
Hartman, R., ed. 1988. *International countermeasures handbook*. Palo Alto, Calif.: EW Communications.
Herskovitz, S., ed. 1988. *EW design engineers handbook*. Norwood, Mass.: Horizon House.
Jones, R. V. 1978. *The wizard war*. New York: Coward, McCann, and Geoghegan.

Price, A. 1967. *Instruments of darkness.* London: William Kimber.
———. 1984. *History of U.S. electronic warfare.* Vol. 1. Washington, D.C.: Association of Old Crows.
———. 1989. *History of U.S. electronic warfare.* Vol. 2. Washington, D.C.: Association of Old Crows.
Schleher, D. C. 1986. *Introduction to electronic warfare.* Norwood, Mass.: Artech House.
Shustov, L. N., and S. A. Vakin. 1969. *Principles of jamming and electronic reconnaissance.* Trans. U.S. Department of Commerce Information Clearinghouse. Springfield, Va.
Steeg, G. F. 1978. Principles of airborne self-defense ECM systems. *Journal of Electronic Defense* Sept.–Oct., pp. 53–60.
———. 1988. Stealth and the straight through repeater. *Journal of Electronic Defense* May, pp. 53–57.
Van Brunt, L. B. 1978. *Applied ECM.* Vol. 1. Dunn Loring, Va.: EW Engineering.
———. 1982. *Applied ECM.* Vol. 2. Dunn Loring, Va.: EW Engineering.

ENGINE TECHNOLOGY, GROUND VEHICLE

Ground vehicle military engine applications range in power level from 50 kilowatts to as high as 1,200 kilowatts. This market is currently dominated by the diesel (compression ignition) engine, with spark ignition engines still being selected for light-duty application. In its M1 main battle tank (MBT), however, the United States has fielded a Brayton cycle (gas turbine) that is unique.

Data provided on weights, thermal efficiency, and air consumption for various engine types show general trends, but the wide variability of engines in the same class and the overlapping characteristics of various types of engines suggest that broad general conclusions should be avoided and each engine judged on its individual merits.

The principal factors that define an engine's efficiency and success in a vehicle are highly dependent on type of installation and installation losses. Installation factors dominate an engine's selection and how it operates.

Militarized commercial engines dominate the power train market below 500 kilowatts, principally because of cost advantages that accrue from the adoption of high-production-volume engines.

The key focus of advanced developments in the military engines is on the following areas:

- higher engine power density
- improved thermal efficiency
- integrated power packs
- reduced coolant heat rejection.

Historical Engine Selection

Primary power sources for ground combat and logistic vehicles are, for the majority of modern vehicles, limited to *spark ignition (gasoline, or petrol),* used in light-duty and dated medium- and heavy-duty applications; and *compression ignition (diesel)*, used in medium- and heavy-duty applications.

The only major exception to this generalization is the U.S. Army's adoption of a gas turbine (Brayton cycle) engine in its M1 main battle tank (MBT). All of the above engines use liquid hydrocarbon fuels.

The diesel engine currently dominates modern military ground vehicle power generation, having overcome the dominance of the spark ignition engines that were the accepted standard until the mid-1950s. Except for specialized applications, the diesel engine is likely to hold its competitive edge in fuel economy, safety, reliability, and overall operating economics into the 1990s.

Engine Characteristics

Ranges of engine characteristics that are considered practical today for viable ground vehicle prime-mover applications follow.

THERMAL EFFICIENCY

When comparing thermal efficiency ranges of various engine types (e.g., spark ignition, diesel cycle, Brayton cycle—with or without heat recovery—and sterling cycle) based on the higher heating value of hydrocarbon fuels, there is a wide disparity in the characteristics of engines of the same type. This disparity makes it necessary to evaluate each engine's unique efficiency characteristic rather than draw sweeping generalities based upon one or two engines in a class. As discussed in greater detail later in the article, parasitic and ancillary losses in many cases control the overall efficiency of the military power train.

POWER LEVELS

Power levels of all engines, independent of size or type, are controlled by their ability to draw in air and fuel in appropriate mixture ratios and convert their chemical reaction into mechanical work. In the case of displacement-type engines (reciprocating piston and rotary), this is achieved by varying the displacement per unit time (RPM) or intake air charge density. In the case of Brayton cycle engines the variables are air-swallowing capacity, flow path efficiency, and peak cycle temperature.

Assuming an appropriate fuel delivery system, output levels are then controlled by the air-swallowing capacity and specific air consumption of engines. Values and ranges for various cycles now commonly used are given in Table 1.

Because the combustion air must be clean for all cycles, there is some motivation, particularly in dirty air environments, to favor engines that obtain the

TABLE 1. *Commonly Used Values and Ranges for Various Cycles*

ENGINE TYPE	U.S. UNITS	METRIC UNITS
Spark ignition	450–550 HP sec./lb.	750–900 kw sec./g
Diesel cycle	275–375 HP sec./lb.	460–625 kw sec./g
Brayton cycle	75–200 HP sec./lb.	125–335 kw sec./g

highest power levels from the least air mass so as to minimize the volume, weight, and complexity of air cleaning systems.

Specific weight. Weights of engines have shown steady reductions in all areas, with displacement-type engine weights showing the most progress for transportation applications. However, there is a wide divergence in characteristics of engines in the same class, which makes it difficult to draw general conclusions about engine weights. The push for lighter and smaller commercial automotive products has pushed the specific weights of spark ignition engines to levels of less than half those generally seen as recently as ten to fifteen years ago in the U.S. market.

Types of fuels. Table 2 provides general characteristics of present and potential fuels considered for military power plants. The first column provides the higher heating value (HHV) in BTUs per kilogram, while the second provides a constant (K) to convert BSFC (brake specific fuel consumption) to thermal efficiency using the formula:

$$\text{Thermal efficiency} = K/BSFC$$

The right-hand column indicates the compelling reason for the continued popularity of hydrocarbon liquid fuels. Although other fuels that are richer in hydrogen offer more energy per unit weight, their specific volume limits their usefulness in military vehicles.

The Engine in a Vehicle Environment

Road Horsepower Requirements

The wheel or sprocket horsepower required to operate a vehicle at a selected ground speed is expressed in kilowatt/ton to allow extrapolation to various weight classes. On a level, paved road a tracked vehicle requires twice the power of a wheeled vehicle. However, neither a wheel nor a sprocket is sensitive to the type of engine delivering the power. What is significant are the losses through the vehicle power train before it reaches the sprocket or wheels. It is these losses, which vary with engine type and installation variables, that establish the overall fuel efficiency of the vehicle.

Power Losses between the Engine and Output

Significant power losses occur because of inherent engine losses caused by the installation and inefficiencies in the drivetrain transmitting the engine power

TABLE 2. *Characteristics of Common Fuels*

	BTUs/kg	K	BTUs/cu. cm
Gasoline	46,500	.1215	9,000 (liquid)
Diesel	44,000	.1275	8,950 (liquid)
Methane	52,500	.1071	9.6 (gas)
Ethane	49,000	.1143	16.8 (gas)
Propane	47,500	.1180	6,225 (liquid)
Hydrogen	134,000	.0419	3.1 (gas)
Methanol	22,700	.2476	4,550 (liquid)

to the wheels. Table 3 provides a range of those losses, together with the principal causal factors.

What becomes obvious in a review of Table 3 is the significance of installation effects and parasitic losses on the output power and load factors that prime movers (engines) must overcome. As a consequence of the dominance of these factors, generally outside the control of engine producers, an engine's reputation can be tainted or enhanced based on the installation's quality.

ECONOMICS OF ENGINES IN MILITARY VEHICLES

Inasmuch as no military vehicles in Western countries are produced in volumes of more than 10,000 per year, producing engines specifically for the military market is normally considered only when an adaptable engine is not commer-

TABLE 3. *Power Loss Factors in Typical Engine Installations*

TYPE	CAUSAL FACTORS	PERCENTAGE RANGE
Engine Losses:		
Induction Pressure	Ambient pressure, Armored grill drops, Air cleaner losses, Induction plumbing	0–7
Air temperature	Ambient temperature, Recirculation, Heat transfer	0–5
Fuel temperature	Ambient temperature, Pump volumetric eff., Heat transfer	0–6
Exhaust pressure	Muffler/plumbing losses, Grill losses, Exhaust flow	0–5
Electrical power	Hotel* load, System efficiency, Maximum load	1–7
Hydraulic power	Hotel* load, Maximum load, System efficiency	0–3
Cooling power	Heat rejection, Ambient requirements, Fan and drive effic., Cooler effectiveness, Grill losses	5–20
Transmission Losses	Torque converter ratio, Spin and lube losses, Mechanical losses, Steering type (tracked)	6–30
Differential/final drive losses	No. gear meshes, No. alignment joints, Spin losses, Mechanical losses	3–7

* Hotel = housekeeping and service functions, e.g., electrical supply, air-conditioning.

cially available. The break point between military adaptations of commercial engines and unique military designs is in the 500-kilowatt range.

This same distribution of high-volume commercial and unique military engine types leads to a wide disparity in costs for engines on a dollars-per-kilowatt basis, with commercially available engines from 100 to 350 kilowatt (diesel engine dominated) ranging from US$25 to US$35 per kilowatt whereas military unique engines in the 500- and 1,200-kilowatt class range from US$125 to US$300 per kilowatt. Obviously there is strong motivation to find adaptable commercial engines for military applications. Since these commercial engines meet the marketplace demands for reliability and economy, or else they would not be commercially viable, their selection and success are driven by installation factors.

Engine Developments

REDUCED HEAT REJECTION

Examination of the heat balance of a typical diesel engine in the late 1970s would have produced the results at rated power shown in Figure 1.

What is interesting about the energy balance is not only the thermal efficiency but also the fact that only the losses to the exhaust and power output are dissipated without the expenditure of some additional energy, which is generated by the engine. Historically this cooling power varies from 5 to 8 percent of the output power in military and on-highway trucks to as much as 15 to 18 percent in "under-armor" power pack installations.

What becomes obvious, of course, is that reduction of heat rejection to the engine's coolant (and inefficiencies in other under-hood/armor components) can make it possible to reduce cooling fan power. An additional claim is that a percentage of this reduced heat rejection ends up as additional power.

To reduce heat rejection to the coolant there are several approaches available:
1. cool the heat-wetted combustion areas with induction air
2. bring material temperatures in the combustion-wetted zone up to or near the mean cycle temperature of the combustion process
3. reduce the mean cycle temperature of the process
4. improve the mechanical and pumping efficiency of the hardware.

Approaches 1 and 3 are used to some degree in most engines and are provided either as excess combustion air not required for the cycle or as induction cooling.

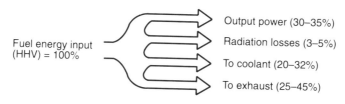

Fuel energy input (HHV) = 100%

Output power (30–35%)
Radiation losses (3–5%)
To coolant (20–32%)
To exhaust (25–45%)

Figure 1. Heat balance of a typical diesel engine in the late 1970s.

Approach 2 is being pursued through the use of several thermal barrier coatings and components. Areas being addressed are in the combustion-wetted zones and the exhaust ports. This has proved successful in reducing heat rejection but usually is accompanied by a reduction in the engine's induction air swallowing capacity of 5 to 15 percent and the necessity to readdress the combustion chamber geometry and fuel delivery characteristics.

Reduction in the mean cycle temperature (approach 3) can also be accomplished by retarding the initiation of combustion within certain restraints. Excessive retarding, however, can result in increased heat rejection if there is a significant change in the wetted area during the period of peak heat release.

Approach 4 is an attractive approach, since typical engines operate at mechanical efficiencies of between 75 and 85 percent. There is strong motivation to address this area, since there is an exponential return from improvements made here. The contrived example in Table 4 illustrates the advantages that can accrue from mechanical efficiency improvements.

In summary, although to date the results are mixed, there is good reason to believe that heat rejection to the coolant as a percentage of output energy can be reduced on typical engines from the present .9 to .65 BTU per minute BHP to as low as .35 to .40 BTU per minute BHP by the late 1990s.

IMPROVED THERMAL EFFICIENCY

A review of Table 5 provides an indication of the amounts of fuel energy potentially available to convert to power. To judge the potential for improvement, two typical diesel engines are compared to provide an indication of the ranges in thermal efficiency and other heat balance characteristics.

Obviously the engines in Table 5 are very different, with significantly different roles. Engine number 1 is a low-speed, highly efficient open chamber diesel engine built to operate over a narrow speed range with a life expectancy of twenty or more years. The number 2 engine is in a medium-duty automotive application requiring light weight, low inertia, and a very broad speed range. Because of its relatively short life (ten years), low initial cost is a prime driver. Depending on one's point of view, one can conclude from these examples that diesel engines are the most or least efficient class of engines available.

It is more important to compare the two engines and determine what factors in the number 1 engine provide nearly equal power at 70 percent of the

TABLE 4. *How Improved Mechanical Efficiency Enhances Engine Characteristics*

	EXISTING	IMPROVED	CHANGE
Engine power	80 Kw	85 Kw	+6.25
Mech./pumping effic.	80%	85%	+6.25
Thermal efficiency	35%	39.4%	+6.25
Rejection ratio*	.66	.585	−11.4

* Rejection ratio = $\dfrac{\text{Energy to coolant}}{\text{Energy to power}}$

TABLE 5. *Heat Balance Comparison of Two Typical Diesel Engines*

SPECIFIC AREA	ENGINE NO. 1	ENGINE NO. 2
Fuel energy (HHV)	100%	100%
Output power	41%	29%
Radiation	5%	5%
To coolant	22%	28%
To exhaust	32%	38%

number 2 engine's fuel rate. Using this as a guide, we can then broadly define strategies being used to improve fuel economy in piston engines.

1. The *number 1 engine* operates over a narrow speed range, and camshaft events are matched to this range, minimizing pumping losses. The *number 2 engine* operates over a broad speed range with camshaft events compromised to achieve this broad requirement.

2. The *number 1 engine*'s combustion system is relatively quiescent and employs a very high-pressure fuel injection system to ensure good fuel/air combustion mixing. The *number 2 engine* employs a very low-cost fuel delivery system that does not provide good fuel/air mixing. The mixing is accomplished by creating a high-turbulence combustion process that further increases pumping work.

3. The *number 1 engine* is heavy and of large displacement with low average piston speed, minimizing mechanical and pumping losses. The *number 2 engine* is a lighter, smaller displacement engine with high piston speed and high mechanical and pumping losses.

4. The *number 1 engine*, because of its heavy, robust structure, operates at higher combustion pressures and thus more closely approaches a constant volume combustion process. The *number 2 engine*, because of its high-turbulence combustion system and mechanical constraints due to its lighter structure, has a somewhat slower heat release and the combustion process is less efficient.

5. The *number 1 engine* is not presented with a wide range of operating environments, and thus lubrication and coolant pumping losses are minimized and starting requirements are simplified. The *number 2 engine* is confronted with a wide range of ambients, lubrication, and coolant conditions for which margin must be provided. Compression ratio is compromised at the expense of thermal efficiency to address white smoke, starting requirements, and a low noise level in the passenger area.

6. The *number 1 engine* has a very modest transient response requirement. With rotating inertia being of minimal concern and its robust construction and inherent stiffness, which minimize distortion, clearances are more closely optimized for minimal friction. The *number 2 engine*'s lighter weight and higher transient response requirements result in a more mechanically flexible construction with less optimized clearances and more lubrication and friction losses.

If each of the above differences is considered, together with many others outside the scope of this brief article, it is possible to define the forms of advanced developments that already provide military-adapted engines approaching the characteristics of the number 1 engine in much more adaptable form than the example. They are:

- more versatile fuel delivery systems
- induction systems and camshaft events with wider engine speed range capability
- significant reductions in piston ring and main bearing losses
- lower coolant and lubrication pumping losses.

The search for improved efficiency continues, with the principal focus on high-mileage commercial vehicles, where the payoff in fuel savings is significant. From the standpoint of total military vehicles, the logistics support for a combat organization can add 15 to 30 percent more vehicles, operating 400 to 500 kilometers per day; thus high-mileage commercial vehicles provide an attractive option.

INTEGRATED POWER PACKS

In the late 1970s, several vehicle studies compared U.S. and European designs with Soviet design practices, particularly as they related to armored vehicles. The reports, though not providing startling new revelations, provided comparisons of weights and volumes of various functional groups in a documented and well-formatted manner and became an influence for change in armored vehicle design philosophy as it relates to the power pack.

U.S. and European power packs employed a significantly larger percentage of the vehicle's volume than the Soviet counterpart, a difference even further magnified by comparing the relative size of the vehicles. What was more disturbing was the fact that the discrepancy between the Soviet and Western designs was widening with each generation of vehicles.

When the differences were reviewed, they were found to be clearly related to two major functional differences in the vehicles: (1) more cooling margin in Western vehicles and (2) a more sophisticated transmission in Western vehicles. Whatever the reasons, it was generally acknowledged that with today's kinetic-energy and shaped-charge penetration capability, and the resulting increased armor array density requirements, a smaller power pack was of high priority. The other obvious spur to serious study in this area was the likelihood that a more integrated power pack could address the system losses discussed previously.

The United States is actively pursuing an integrated power pack program that is attempting to reduce the volume by 50 percent when compared to existing Western countries' armored vehicle power pack installations. This, combined with previously discussed evolving technologies, would offer the opportunity of further reducing volume by addressing cooling and fuel volumes in an armored vehicle while not sacrificing the vehicle range, cooling margin, and other amenities of U.S. installations. Two likely secondary (and not trivial) benefits that could accrue from this program are a reduced logistic supply requirement (fuel) and a lower maintenance burden (improved reliability).

The latter of these secondary benefits has been demonstrated by West German power packs, with their integration of air cleaning and cooling packages on the engine/transmission.

HIGHER ENGINE POWER DENSITY

An examination of automotive spark ignition engines of the mid-1970s would have revealed only a small number of engines employing turbocharging or four valves per cylinder. The opposite was true in the motorcycle field, where very high speed and four valves were the norm rather than the exception. The motorcycle engine outputs of 50 kilowatts per liter of the 1970s have become the accepted standard of advanced spark ignition automotive engines today.

Whether diesel engines will follow this high-speed trend is highly speculative because of the injection system costs associated with such a speed increase. It is clearly a trend to adopt improved breathing with four valves per cylinder, however. In any case, it is demonstrated technology for diesel engines to operate at 50 kilowatts per liter or more in military installations. Two-cycle engines and four-cycle engines are available at 37 kilowatts per liter of swept volume today, with 45 kilowatts per liter engines for military application under development. These developments, using evolutionary piston engine technology, ensure a secure future for the diesel piston engine through the 1990s.

There are several engines outside the diesel piston engine category that offer significant volume (and weight) reductions, which promise potential for the future in specialized roles. Notable examples are rotary engines and nonregenerative turbine engines.

Rotary engines entered the market in the 1960s but have yet to achieve application in a military vehicle role, despite the fact that in commercial service some engines are achieving as much as 2,000 to more than 3,000 hours of service before overhaul. This slow acceptance is in part because development has been slow in the use of less volatile fuels than gasoline and because most vehicle integrators remember the poor experience in fuel consumption and seal life from the early 1970s. The progress being reported today suggests that in the late 1990s it may become the engine of choice in military applications where compact size, modest operating hour requirements, and outputs in excess of 600 kilowatts are requirements.

Surprising to some are the possible military applications of nonregenerative turbine engines, where extremely high power density is required in military vehicles for a limited percentage of the vehicle's operating time. Such limited period of operation as a supplemental source of power overcomes the engine's basic fuel consumption disadvantages.

The engine's high rotative speed becomes an asset where electrical power generation requirements are involved, since more compact high-speed generators result. Applications such as supplemental electrical vehicle drives and high-energy weapons systems could well benefit from such an application.

ALBERT M. KARABA

SEE ALSO: Armored Ground Vehicle; Ground Reconnaissance; Mechanized Warfare.

Bibliography

The literature suggested below is readily available through the Society of Automotive Engineers' offices in Warrendale, Pa. 15096-0001.

SP-785. Adiabatic engines: Worldwide progress.
SP-768. Rotary engine design: Analysis and developments.
SP-780. Power boost: Light, medium, and heavy duty engines.
PT-33. Advances in two-stroke cycle engine technology.

ENGINEERING, MILITARY

Within the scope of land warfare, military engineering comprises tasks designed to facilitate the movement of friendly forces, prevent or impede enemy movements, enhance the protection of friendly forces against enemy fire, and perform damage repair.

In many countries military engineering (M.E.) also comprises military construction engineering, movements, and transportation. Large armies have forces especially trained and equipped to accomplish these tasks. They are referred to as engineers, *Pioniertruppe*, or *génie*. (In the following paragraphs they are most often referred to as engineers; only when describing national particularities are the respective national terms used.)

Frequently, small states adopted not only the designation but also the definition of military engineering terms used by the military powers that dominated them or whose forces they used as a model. Therefore, in the following discussion of military engineering, the nations included will be only those that have been important military powers in the past, or are members of the North Atlantic Treaty Organization (NATO), or were members of the Warsaw Pact (WP).

Historical Development

It was not until the twentieth century that military engineering could be clearly defined. For centuries there had been a variety of engineer tasks, in many cases performed by separate organizations, that were not all equally valued. In most cases there was no distinction between the tasks of military and civil engineering.

ANCIENT WORLD

The history of military engineering goes back to ancient times. In the armies of the nations of antiquity that were situated in the Mediterranean area there were special detachments commanded by military builders to perform fortification, siege warfare, and bridging tasks. The Palestinian town of Jericho is considered the oldest fortified place known in history; its walls, constructed to a high technical level, were erected about 8000 B.C. As early as the fifth century

B.C. the Greeks used catapults, battering rams, and mobile siege towers. In 514 B.C. the Persian Emperor Darius had a 700-meter-long floating bridge constructed across the Bosphorus. During his military campaign against India (327 B.C.), Alexander the Great was accompanied by the first bridge train mentioned in historical records.

The most important works of military engineering in ancient times were those of the Romans. They put scientific knowledge to practical use for the benefit of military technology. As talented organizers, they established a highly developed engineer corps in their army. As of 230 B.C. all engineer officers were sent to a technical school for training on the construction and employment of siege and defense machines, surveying, road and bridge construction, mining, and the construction of obstacles and fortifications. Such works were performed by special units, *fabri* (Latin *fabricari* = to construct, build), which were employed throughout the Roman Empire, especially in the provinces of Gallia, Germania, and Brittania north of the Alps. Their main tasks included construction of fortified camps (*castellum*), road and bridge construction, and the fortification of the frontier lines (*limes*).

MIDDLE AGES AND EARLY MODERN TIMES

The tradition of Roman engineering was continued by the Muslim Arabs who conquered North Africa and Spain in the seventh century. They adopted from the Romans what seemed useful to them for conducting their expeditions. Not only the Arabs, but also the Byzantines preserved a rich tradition of military engineering during the Middle Ages. The Byzantines developed "Greek fire," a liquid incendiary (whose formula has been lost but which probably included resin, naptha, saltpeter, and caustic lime) used in firebombs and primitive flamethrowers. It was also used successfully against Christian knights during the Crusades.

In the medieval military system in Europe, which had emerged from the chaos of the Dark Ages and was based on the twin concepts of feudalism (personal loyalties to a lord) and manorialism (land granted in exchange for service), there was no room for military engineering. The castles of noblemen and knights were constructed and maintained by peasants, and the fortification of towns was the responsibility of guilds and workmen in the building trades.

It was only when gunpowder was invented and artillery was introduced in the armies of the fifteenth and sixteenth centuries, which superseded the armies of knights, that specialists were required to perform specific technical tasks. Craftsmen and country folk were recruited for that purpose, or, if not available in sufficient numbers, they were pressed to join the army: bridge builders and helpers to construct bridges, miners for digging tunnels, peasants for putting up entrenchments. In 1555, for example, the grand master of the Teutonic Order in Prussia, Albrecht von Hohenzollern, issued a war order governing the establishment of a detachment of peasants who were employed for trenching and were required to make *gabions*, dig gun emplacements, and fortify camps. The detachment consisted of twelve work crews, was commanded by a trench master, and was attached to the artillery.

During the Thirty Years' War (1618–48), military bridging operations gained particular importance in large-scale campaigns. In 1632, after cavalry troops had forded the Lech River and established a bridgehead during the Battle of the Lech, King Gustavus Adolphus of Sweden had a 100-meter bridge constructed across the river near the village of Rain in Bavaria. Then the army crossed the river with supporting fire provided by 72 guns, which were concealed by a smoke screen generated by smoldering wet straw.

The artillery, which was the actual technical branch of the army, was organized in a civilian manner: in guilds, just like craftsmen, with artificers and gunners. The construction of fortifications became increasingly important. Fortifications (bastions) protected friendly forces against artillery fire and provided covered positions for the guns.

STANDING ARMIES

As a result of the Thirty Years' War, more or less sovereign states were established within the German Empire, and France and Austria (the Holy Roman Empire) attained a dominant position in Central Europe. These states required armies with allegiance to the state sovereign as a token of their independent power and political ambitions. Armies of mercenaries had proven unreliable as a means of political power, mainly because of their moral and ethical decadence. This role could only be played by professional armies established and trained in peacetime. To achieve this goal, the state had to be centrally organized in an absolutist fashion. The French form of government, under Louis XIV (1643–1715), was adopted by almost every nation in Europe. Thus, the absolutist standing armies were formed.

Progress in technology was followed by strong specialization. France again provided the model: Apart from the infantry and cavalry, the artillery also was formed from a body organized in guilds into a separate branch within the army. Special units were established for military engineering as well: sapper, mining, and bridging units. At the same time, the corps of engineer officers was formed.

"Sappers" were named after the "saps" (approach trenches) that were dug from the positions of friendly forces toward the enemy during siege operations. From these approach trenches two or three parallel trenches were constructed at ever closer distances to the enemy fortifications, with special emplacements being provided for siege guns. The parallel trench dug last served as a jump-off position for assault troops. The sappers' equipment consisted mainly of axes, shovels, and picks, which also provided them with the means for route construction.

The miners' mission was to dig tunnels under the walls of fortified places and to emplace strong mines (demolition charges) to make breaches that would allow the assault troops to penetrate the fortifications. As a rule, sappers and miners were attached to the artillery, since their work had to be coordinated with the fire of the guns.

Pontoniers assembled bridges made of prefabricated pontoons (floating structures resembling small boats) with long planks mounted on top for crossing operations. Pontoon bridges were assembled starting on the near bank and proceeding across the river, with the pontoons being attached one after the other and connected to an overhead anchor cable, which had been stretched across the river to keep the pontoons at a right angle to the current. The load-carrying capacity of these floating bridges was calculated so as to make sure they could be used even by heavy artillery pieces.

The engineer officers emerged from the military builders of the armies of mercenaries. At first they consisted of civilians who were specialists in the field of construction and consequently were enlisted as officers from the start; later, special training was provided in civil and military engineering at the expense of the sovereigns. The engineer officers' tasks included the construction of fortresses as part of fortification systems, as well as the construction of important buildings. Foremost among them was Johann Balthasar Neumann (1687–1753), an engineer officer employed by the prince bishop of Würzburg. Not only was he an inspector of fortresses in the service of several German sovereigns, but he was also the creator of the residence of Würzburg and the Vierzehnheiligen pilgrimage church on the Main River.

In France Marshal Sébastien Le Prestre de Vauban (1633–1707) had a decisive influence on military engineering. His writings on fortification and siege-craft detailed the systems adopted by all European nations through the end of the eighteenth century. During Vauban's era a sapper company (1671) and a mining company (1673) were established in France.

In Austria a company of boat and bridge crews was activated in 1683 to conduct military transport operations during the Turkish Wars along the Danube and its tributaries through the provinces of the Austrian Empire where the road network was poorly developed. Their equipment included gunboats called *tschaikas;* the boat crews were referred to as *tschaikists.* In addition, there were pontoon units to assist in river crossing operations. Mining detachments were established within the artillery branch in 1717, and in 1760 they were combined with the sappers to form the *génie* corps.

Czar Peter I of Russia issued a decree in 1712 authorizing the establishment of an already-existing engineer company and a pontoon command. As early as 1701 an engineer school had been founded in Moscow. The officers and units also were employed for developing the backward Russian Empire and for constructing the new capital of St. Petersburg.

In 1722 a company of military artificers made Gibraltar into a fortress for the rising naval and colonial power of Great Britain.

Prussia, the new military power, at first attributed little importance to military engineering. Although the number of engineer officers in the service was large, they were held in low esteem. The noble officers showed little understanding of technical problems and looked down on the bourgeois engineer officers. Sapper, mining, and pontoon units were activated only in war and disbanded after the war ended. The engineer regiment of Walrave, established in 1742, was turned into a fusilier regiment in 1747.

In the War of Independence waged by the British colonies in North America (1775–83), a shortage of personnel qualified to perform engineer tasks soon made itself felt in the rebel American army. In this situation the Congress of the young nation turned to France, asking for assistance in activating a corps of engineers. The reason for this may have been political calculation and the necessity to take action: France and Great Britain were traditional enemies, and French military engineering was considered the most developed at that time. In 1776 the French established the first sapper and mining units in America. In 1777 the Frenchman Louis du Portail (American spelling: Duportail) was appointed chief engineer with the rank of general by the Congress. Congress authorized funds for establishing three engineer companies in 1778. In 1779 the Corps of Engineers was integrated officially into the army.

In sum, military engineering emerged from civilian organizations that were integrated into the armies. Any technical units formed during this process either originated from the artillery or were established to operate in conjunction with the artillery. Later they became separate units, with tasks that became more and more different from each other. Only the U.S. Army combined these units in one branch under a single command. There were no doubts as to the value of engineering, yet it was often regarded as an inferior occupation. In the standing armies of the eighteenth century, the glorious traditions of the infantry and cavalry regiments were too dominant. It was only in the United States—a young nation without a tradition in its own right—that military engineering was made the responsibility of a separate branch. The engineer schools developed along similar lines. While they had achieved a high standard and provided training in architecture, surveying, cartography, and so forth, their achievements did not receive the merit they deserved.

NINETEENTH CENTURY

The French Revolution in 1789 brought the era of standing armies to an end. They were superseded by people's armies that were based on compulsory military service and therefore had more personnel at their disposal. The armies of regular soldiers (volunteers) in Great Britain and the United States were also augmented; in Britain because of commitments in the colonies and in the United States because of the need to develop and secure the frontier in the West. Consequently, reorganization of military engineering became mandatory in all armies, although different methods were used by the various nations to that end.

The French National Convention formed the Corps du Génie as a separate branch of the army in 1790. As early as 1793 an engineer company was assigned to each division, and in 1800 the engineers received a technical command of their own when the position of Général du Génie was established.

Prussia followed a similar course. In 1809, as a result of the army reorganization program, a royal decree was issued that combined engineer officers, pontoniers, sappers, and miners into one branch and placed them under the direct command of the general staff. The plan to make this corps an elite unit closely attached to the general staff—with the chief of the general staff being also the chief of the engineer staff—could be realized for a short time only.

Austria adhered to its principle of separating missions and branches of the army. In 1809, after a series of reorganizations, an engineer battalion was activated in addition to the existing pontoon and *tschaikist* units and the *génie* corps. The Austrian Aulic War Council, however, did not provide for a single command body for these units.

In Great Britain, the Royal Artificers had developed into the Corps of Royal Sappers and Miners by 1812, with the engineer officers in the Corps of Royal Engineers continuing to exist. Not until 1855 were these two organizations amalgamated to form the Royal Engineers. In the Napoleonic Wars of Liberation (1813–14) the Russian engineer corps consisted of no fewer than 40 engineer companies. Personnel replacement was provided by regular replacement battalions.

In the United States, after a short period of forming one branch with the artillery in 1794, the U.S. Army Corps of Engineers was established in 1802. In addition to constructing fortifications and providing engineer services in the field, they also were assigned civil engineering tasks, including the surveying of national routes and canals and designing bridges, lighthouses, and a number of military and government buildings (e.g., the U.S. Military Academy at West Point and the dome of the Capitol in Washington, D.C.). When the topographical service was integrated into the Corps of Engineers in 1813, the engineers were assigned the task of producing maps of the United States's territory. In 1819 the Corps of Engineers took part in the first expedition to explore the West.

Thus, after some 300 years of historical development, military engineering became a mission assigned to one particular branch in all armies, a branch that continued to develop through the planning of fortifications and in the wars of the nineteenth century. From then on military engineering included the following tasks: mobility, countermobility, and special tasks.

Yet, because no engineer doctrine defined these tasks, the organization of troops still lacked a uniform concept. There were tasks to be performed in peacetime and tasks to be performed in wartime, and these affected the availability of engineer forces. Peacetime tasks included the design and construction of fortresses, assistance in the planning of transport facilities, and topographic support. Wartime tasks were divided into two fields. First, engineers provided support in the theater of operations, that is, engineer services in the field (emplaced obstacles and performed demolitions) as well as sapping and mining during sieges. Sapping and mining became less important when artillery became more effective. Second, engineers provided support during troop movements and in rear areas; that is, they constructed floating and expedient bridges, constructed and repaired roads and railroads, and operated railroads.

Engineer battalions and regiments consisting of sapper, mining, and pontoon companies were established to accomplish these tasks, and they were assigned to divisions as required. Since unimpeded movements during initial deployment and the ensuing campaign were given great importance, additional bridging equipment stores were established as bridge trains to be augmented by the personnel required when war began. The most well-known bridging equipment was the "Birago" bridge (1841), named after its inventor, which was introduced into all German-speaking armies and on which the design of all military bridging equipment was based until World War II. The system consisted of two half-pontoons that could be transported on two trucks along with the material required for the bridge superstructure and accessories and that could be used for assembling bridges of various load classifications.

In order to use railroad lines for military purposes and to operate military railroads, railroad sections were established at the general headquarters (Prussia in 1864, France in 1889), and railroad detachments were activated, which were normally provided personnel only after mobilization.

Thus equipped, the new army branch proved its efficiency during the wars of the nineteenth century. The successful siege of Sevastopol in the Crimean War (1854–55) was mainly due to the commitment of the three French Regiments du Génie. In the German-Danish War in 1864 Prussian engineers contributed much to the successful assault on the "Düppler Schanzen" and to the Alsensund crossing operation. During the Boer War (1899–1901) in South Africa, particularly high demands were made on the British Royal Engineers; the British employed 250 officers and 5,000 enlisted men to construct bridges, carry out demolitions, construct railroad lines, and build and maintain their blockhouse–barbed wire barrier lines.

Special engineer tasks included testing the suitability of new technical methods for military purposes, such as captive and free balloons, telegraph service as a means of communication, searchlights for battlefield illumination during nighttime, and the testing of aircraft for observation and aerial combat (Great Britain, Germany, and France). Thus, new branches emerged from the corps of engineers: signal troops and the air force.

Because the training provided at military academies was not sufficient for the variety of tasks to be accomplished, separate training schools for engineer officers were established at an early stage: in England and the United States in 1802, in France as early as 1794, and in Prussia in 1812. Enlisted men were trained in their units, with the emphasis on manual and technical skills rather than on infantry fighting techniques. It was not until the end of the century—during the epoch of imperialist hegemony—that the emphasis (mainly in European armies) was shifted to mobile combat, with stress on offensive capabilities. Engineer forces were increased in number, equipped with more efficient bridging equipment, and provided with mine launchers (mortars), hand grenades, and demolition charges. Army organizations dispensed with companies consisting of troops of one particular branch only. The field engineer service company became the standard type. Training in infantry fighting techniques was intensified. The all-around engineer came into being.

World Wars I and II

In World War I (1914–18) the tasks and equipment of the engineer forces of all the belligerent states changed considerably. During mobilization their strength increased about four times on average (from 21,000 to 80,000 men in the German Empire). The transition to trench warfare gave rise to new military engineering tasks. Therefore, flamethrower and mine-launcher detachments as well as troops for gas warfare were established. Mining companies were activated to conduct subterranean mining operations. In addition, a large number of construction battalions were required in the rear areas. There was close cooperation between infantry and engineer units in both defensive and offensive operations. This gave rise to assault battalions, which were to penetrate enemy positions by conducting raids with strong support provided by mine launchers or to take key terrain from the enemy. Barrier operations and the construction of fortified positions gained considerable importance. Large wire obstacles and antipersonnel mines were used to enhance the defense, but they also restricted the movements of friendly forces. In 1918 antitank mines were used against British tanks for the first time (they had been developed by the British Royal Engineers).

The conventional pattern of war had changed completely. It was no longer the military campaign with movements of troops, battles waged on open fields, and the encirclement of key fortifications that determined the course of war, but rather the permanent exchange of blows between armies consisting of millions of soldiers committed in trench warfare. The threat to soldiers was increased by new military equipment such as tanks and combat aircraft.

Lessons learned and the opportunities provided by the increasing mechanization and motorization of forces had to be taken into account in the development of military engineering after 1918. The following tasks became most important for the engineers: provide direct support to the infantry to protect them against enemy weapons, improve terrain to counter attacking infantry and tanks, breach man-made and natural obstacles in offense, support the provision of supplies behind the front line, and maintain routes for transporting men and materiel in rear areas.

Some armies, however, failed to draw the necessary conclusions from this definition of military engineering. While the Red Army, which was activated after the October Revolution (1917) in the young Soviet Union, as of 1919 had a large number of engineer units, the emphasis was on using technology for all kinds of construction purposes. Consequently, the fielding of construction machinery was stepped up. In 1932 the total machine power available was only 5,000 horsepower, but by 1934 it had increased to 95,000 horsepower. Similar objectives were pursued by Great Britain and the United States. In France military engineering was based on a purely defensive concept resulting in the construction of the Maginot line, a fortification built in the 1930s along the Franco-German border that consisted of an echeloned, inflexible barrier system of reinforced concrete bunkers and obstacles effective against vehicles. The elite of the French engineers and numerous regiments were used during the construction phase.

The German Wehrmacht pursued a different course. *Army Regulation TF 33 Truppenführung* (Command and Control of Forces), which was published in 1933, specified for the first time the tasks to be accomplished by the various branches of the army in battle. Engineer tasks included the following:

1. cooperate with tanks in the offense
2. support attacking infantry in breaching and clearing obstacles and in assaulting fortified positions
3. prepare the terrain for supply and evacuation
4. block enemy withdrawal routes and repair roads and bridges in the rear of pursued enemy forces
5. construct obstacles in the glacis, provide obstructions and lines of communication
6. block enemy forces in front of and between defense lines during delay operations
7. improve roads, construct bridges, and conduct river-crossing operations.

The missions assigned to the engineers were marked by a distinct change: mobile warfare instead of static warfare, with offensive operations to be conducted by tanks advancing at high speed followed by infantry forces. Furthermore, military engineering included planning fortifications along the border, constructing a transportation network suitable for military purposes, and constructing air-raid shelters.

German engineer organization was geared to this overall concept. Engineers were divided into motorized, armored, mountain, airborne, railroad, and construction engineers, as well as construction troops. Additional engineer staff sections were formed on army and army-group levels. By the beginning of World War II in 1939, 100 engineer battalions had been activated. The civil labor organization Todt and the National Labor Service were employed in support of engineer units. In the course of the war, the Allied powers (United States, Great Britain, and the Soviet Union) increasingly adopted the German concept of engineer mission and organization. Moreover, new tasks emerged for Allied engineer forces: construct and improve expedient port facilities after the landing operations in Africa, in the Pacific, and in Europe to ensure the supply flow from the United States; install a pipeline system; and construct tank storage depots and combat airfields. During the last years of the war, German engineers were used exclusively for barrier operations: minefields, demolitions, and destruction of roads, bridges, and railroad tracks.

Military technology played an increasingly important role in accomplishing engineer tasks with all forces involved in the war. The engineers were provided with armored personnel carriers for the protection of troops, armored bridge layers to enable them to keep abreast of lead elements of the attack, military bridging equipment, assault and landing boats, field railroads, cranes, tracked dozers, antitank and antipersonnel mines, and shaped charges, as well as mine-detection and mine-clearing equipment. In addition there were many different kinds of construction machinery to build field fortifications and shelters for protection against enemy fire.

Military Engineering in East and West after 1945

In 1949 the two largest military alliances of the postwar period were founded: the North Atlantic Treaty Organization (NATO) and the Warsaw Pact (WP).

Offensive combat was emphasized by WP forces; defensive combat was emphasized by NATO.

NORTH ATLANTIC TREATY ORGANIZATION

Within NATO, military engineering comprises national tasks to be accomplished in the home countries of the allied armies (territorial defense) and joint tasks to be performed in those countries where forces are stationed in accordance with the NATO Status of Forces Agreement. Military engineering is part of the national military defense contributing to the preparation and accomplishment of military defense tasks.

Preparatory tasks include the planning, construction, and maintenance of various kinds of military facilities (military infrastructure) in the home countries and the central area of the joint defense effort (i.e., the Federal Republic of Germany) and the preparation of barrier operations in peacetime (Wallmeister organization). The principal tasks in wartime include providing support to combat troops in the field, maintaining the freedom of operation in the rear areas, and the all-arms engineer missions, which provide nonengineer units with the capability to emplace obstacles with organic assets.

Planning staffs accomplish preparatory tasks in peacetime. They make plans for barracks, depots, air bases, naval ports, missile sites, and obstacle fittings in roads and bridges. In Great Britain special troops are employed to construct and repair runways; in the United States the Corps of Engineers is also responsible for supervising public construction projects; and in Germany there is close cooperation between military headquarters and civilian construction authorities.

Engineer staffs and troops, which are divided into combat engineer, engineer support, and special engineer units, are provided to support combat forces (armored troops and infantry). These units are organic to the respective levels of command (Fig. 1). At brigade level, armored engineer companies, which are capable of providing direct combat support, are committed. Each division has an engineer battalion, and its companies support the brigades in combat. At corps level there are special engineer battalions (barrier emplacement, amphibious, floating bridge, and heavy equipment battalions) that are attached to the divisions at the points of main effort.

Their principal tasks are:

1. *Countermobility:* to impede enemy movements by emplacing obstacles effective mainly against mechanized forces;
2. *Mobility:* to support the movement of friendly forces when negotiating or breaching man-made or natural obstacles;
3. *Survivability:* to provide protection for friendly forces in the field by constructing field fortifications and implementing special camouflage and deception measures.

Moreover, engineer battalions employed in the rear areas contribute to maintaining freedom of operation by performing damage repair and operating and repairing the pipeline system.

Emplacing obstacles is the most important engineer task. The antitank mine is the principal type of munition used for that purpose. Minefields can be em-

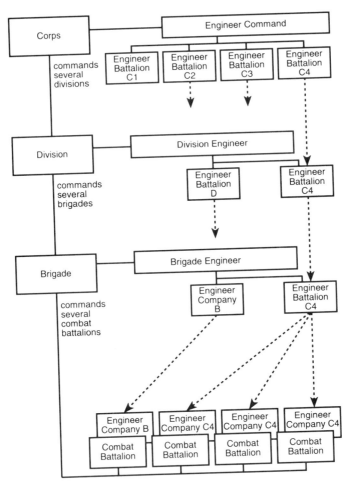

Figure 1. Allocation of engineers to levels of command within NATO and their command and control relationship for employment.

placed using placed mines, scatterable mines with selectable laid life, or off-route mines with horizontal action. Modern mine delivery systems can emplace these minefields in a short time and with very little manpower. The German mine launcher Skorpion is the most modern delivery system currently available. Two launchers can lay a 1,500-meter (1,640-yd.) minefield with 1,200 antitank mines in fifteen minutes. Artillery rocket launchers also can be used for remote delivery of scatterable mines. Constructed obstacles, such as wire obstacles and antitank ditches, as well as such demolition obstacles as cratering obstacles and bridge destruction are used to complement the defensive barrier system.

Mobility includes negotiating obstacles, waterways, and terrain gaps. In many cases minefields must be breached using mechanical and explosive means, such as the mine-clearing tank and linear charges (mine-clearing line charges). Waterways are negotiated using light crossing means (pneumatic and assault boats), armored vehicle–launched bridges, fixed bridges that are built across the river without requiring intermediate supports, and rafts and bridges made up of amphibious vehicles and pontoons. With armored and nonarmored construction machines capable of clearing, loading, and bulldozing, engineers can both breach man-made and natural obstacles and construct positions for dismounted infantry and emplacements for tanks and guns.

In rear areas engineer battalions with special equipment repair roads and destroyed and devastated areas and operate pipeline pumping stations and tank farms for petrol, oil, and lubricants (POL) supply.

A number of standardization agreements have been concluded among the allied nations to ensure that NATO military engineering concepts and procedures are generally accepted by all nations. This applies to combat support in particular. Chief engineers at allied headquarters and engineer commanders at corps, division, and brigade levels plan engineer employment and advise commanders on the allocation of engineer resources.

Warsaw Pact (WP)

Warsaw Pact military doctrine (prior to dissolution of the WP in 1991) was directed by Soviet military doctrine, which defines *military engineering* as a generic term comprising the provision of engineer support for combat operations, special training of engineers, and all-arms engineer training. (For the following description Warsaw Pact terminology will be used to illustrate WP engineer doctrine.) Military engineering also includes tasks in support of national economy and disaster control operations (e.g., the nuclear accident at the Chernobyl reactor in 1986). A sufficient amount of engineer support is provided to ensure success in battle. It comprises planning, organization, and employment of engineer resources. These tasks are based on a detailed analysis of military operations and engineer employment in World War II. In a pragmatic approach, the principles of command and control established for German engineers in the Wehrmacht by *Army Regulation TF 33* have been adopted by the Soviet Union. As opposed to NATO, where military engineering has been standardized by mutual agreements, the other WP nations accepted Soviet military engineering for their forces without any changes.

Soviet military engineering includes
1. conducting engineer reconnaissance of enemy forces and the terrain
2. creating gaps in man-made and natural obstacles
3. applying engineering techniques for terrain improvement
4. preparing, constructing, and maintaining movement routes
5. providing support during river-crossing operations
6. constructing obstacles and setting off demolitions
7. providing camouflage
8. assisting in damage-control operations after nuclear strikes carried out by the enemy.

In principle, the provision of engineer support is an all-arms task. Engineer forces are employed to accomplish complex tasks requiring special training and engineer knowledge and techniques. They are available in great numbers at all levels of command from front (army group) down to the regiments (Fig. 2). They are organized in general engineering, reconnaissance, road construction, landing/crossing operations, pontoon bridging, field construction, camouflage,

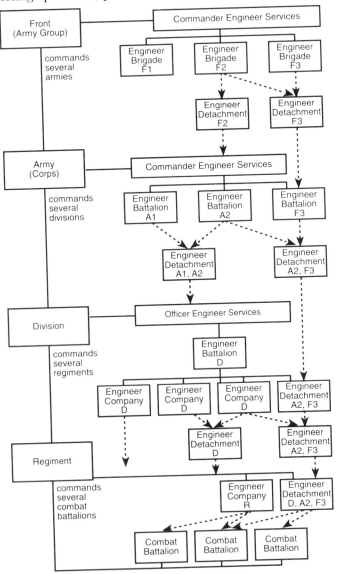

Figure 2. Allocation of engineers to levels of command within the Warsaw Pact and their detachment for "engineer-technical service."

and maintenance units. A particular feature of engineer units is that they normally comprise several elements. As opposed to NATO, where "pure" engineer units are normally committed forward, WP forces formed mission-oriented detachments consisting of various elements to be employed forward.

The main task of WP engineers was to provide mobility support for friendly forces. Engineer reconnaissance was conducted before every operation, and the engineers were equipped with special devices for that purpose (e.g., to locate enemy minefields). Mine-clearing equipment mounted on tanks was used to breach minefields. Engineer construction equipment was used to clear and bulldoze passages through or around obstacles. Mobility detachments were special types consisting of reconnaissance, obstacle-clearing, road construction, and bridge construction teams. Self-propelled rafts and pontoon sets for raft and bridge assembly were used for river-crossing operations.

Mines are emplaced with mechanical minelayers and helicopter-mounted systems and by artillery (remote delivery). Entrenching machines are used to dig positions, which are revetted with prefabricated material for use by dismounted infantry. Mobile barrier detachments, consisting of mine-laying, construction machinery, bridging, and demolition parties are employed for flank protection and at temporary defense lines. In rear areas special units are employed for concrete construction and woodworking.

The planning, command, and control of engineer operations are complex. At division and regiment level it rests with the officer of engineering; at front and army level it is a task of the chief of the engineer service (who is at the same time the commander of engineer forces). Although engineer troops and resources at various command levels are required to operate jointly during the operations planned by these officers, command authority nevertheless rests with their parent units. Command is also exercised by the officer of engineering. Before making important decisions, he must obtain confirmation from his higher engineer commander.

Future Developments

The more modern the means available for mobility and countermobility missions, the faster engineer forces will be able to react to rapidly changing situations in combat and to provide direct combat support without delay. Computer systems will be used to support planning, data flow, and task documentation. Military engineering will become the most important ally of the combat forces in the combined-arms battle. The engineers' area of responsibility will be concentrated on the combat zone.

There are two decisive factors regarding future military engineering. First, relying on state-of-the-art methods might mean that armies neglect a soldier's personal skills and his ability to improvise in accomplishing engineer missions. Second, the fact that planning and employment means are becoming more and more expensive and funds are becoming scarce may necessitate a reevaluation of the current doctrine of mobile combat in favor of combat based more on static operations. This might result in new and different tasks to be accomplished by the engineers.

ULRICH KREUZFELD

SEE ALSO: Mine Warfare, Land; Siege.

Bibliography

American Military Institute. 1982. *Military engineering and technology: Papers presented at the 1982 American Military Institute annual meeting.* Manhattan, Kans.: MA/AH Pub.

Boyd, D. 1965. *The Royal Engineers.* London: Leo Cooper.

Bundesministerium für Landesverteidigung, ed. 1984. *1684–1984 300 Jahre Pioniertruppe in österreich.* Vienna: Bundesministerium für Landesverteidigung.

Cook, F. D. 1973. *The Canadian military engineer, 1973: A brief history of the Canadian military engineers, 1610 to 1973.* Vedder Crossing, B.C.: Canadian Forces School of Military Engineering, CFB Chilliwack.

Erbe, J. 1987. Pioniere: eine Truppengattung im Wandel. *Wehrtechnik* no. 2/88:36–40.

Great Britain, Army. 1974. *Military engineering.* London: Her Majesty's Stationery Office.

Headquarters, U.S. Army Corps of Engineers. n.d. *The history of the U.S. Army Corps of Engineers.* Washington, D.C.: Government Printing Office.

Militärverlag der DDR, ed. 1973. *Militärlexikon.* East Berlin: Militärverlag der DDR.

Petter, P. 1963. *Pioniere.* Darmstadt: Wehr und Wissen Verlagsanstalt.

Porter, W. 1951. *History of the Corps of Royal Engineers.* Chatham, Eng.: Royal Engineers Institute.

Reidel, R. 1968. *Pionierdienst.* Berlin: Deutscher Militärverlag.

Roche, J. 1983. *Le génie: Ses origines, son evolution, ses titres de gloire.* Angers: École d'application du génie.

Varenyshev, B. V. 1982. *Voenno-inzhenernaia podgotovka.* Moscow: Voen. izd-vo Ministerstva oborony SSSR.

ENLISTED PERSONNEL

Enlisted personnel are members of the armed forces who are not commissioned officers or commissioned warrant officers. They make up the majority of the world's military services and are required to accomplish assigned missions under the command of commissioned officers with formally conferred rank and authority. The terms *rank* and *grade* are usually synonymous, but officers are often said to hold rank whereas enlisted personnel are said to hold grades or ratings. The term *grade* can also refer to authorized pay levels for both enlisted personnel and officers.

Strictly speaking, the term *enlisted* applies to individuals who volunteer for military service by enrolling or enlisting for a period of time or term of service and not to those who have been drafted, conscripted, or in any other way compelled to serve involuntarily. It applies to any branch of military service— land, sea, or air—and to all individuals whether on active duty or in reserve, militia, or of paramilitary status. The term can also be applied to members of irregular, guerrilla, and revolutionary forces. Common synonyms for enlisted personnel are soldiers, sailors, marines, airmen, troops, the ranks (as in rank and file), ratings, crew, and men (as in "officers and men"). The uniforms of enlisted personnel usually differ from those of officers in color and style according to branch of service and generally display less brass, gold braid, and other embellishments.

Enlisted personnel advance through grades by training, experience, longevity or seniority, examination, and merit. These grades can be equated across services in a hierarchy of authority if not strictly by title. Typical grade categories for land and air forces are private, corporal, and sergeant; for sea services, seamen, petty officers, and chief petty officers. Grades above private and airman are called *noncommissioned officers* (NCOs) and those above seaman are *petty officers*. In some services, warrant officer (noncommissioned) is the highest grade of enlisted personnel.

Robert F. Lockman

See Also: Education, Military; Personnel; Rank and Insignia of Rank; Reserve Components; Soldier.

Bibliography

Binkin, M., and S. J. Bach. 1977. *Women in the military*. Washington, D.C.: Brookings.

Binkin, M. and M. J. Eitelberg. 1982. *Blacks in the military*. Washington, D.C.: Brookings.

Berryman, S. E. 1986. Images and realities: The social composition of nineteenth- and twentieth-century enlisted forces. In *Life in the rank and file*, ed. D. Segal and H. W. Sinaiko, pp. 9–32. McLean, Va.: Pergamon–Brassey's.

Guides Muller. 1983. *Le citoyen, la défense, le service national, les reserves*. Issy-les-Moulineaux, France: OcebuR.

Harries-Jenkins, G. 1986. Role images, military attitudes, and the enlisted culture in Great Britain. In *Life in the rank and file*. McLean, Va.: Pergamon-Brassey's.

Hendes, J. A. 1989. Personal communication. Area Language Studies Dept., U.S. Naval Academy, Annapolis, Md.

International Institute for Strategic Studies. 1991. *The military balance 1991–1992*. London: Brassey's.

Janowitz, M. and R. W. Little. 1974. *Sociology and the military establishment*. Beverly Hills/London: Sage.

Keegan, J. 1983. *World armies*. Detroit, Mich.: Gale Research.

Keep, J. L. H. 1981. Catherine's veterans. *Slavonic and East European Review* 59 (3):385–96.

Landrum, R. 1980. *National service in West Germany and France*. Washington, D.C. Potomac Institute.

Lang, K. 1972. *Military institutions and the sociology of war*. Beverly Hills, Calif.: Sage.

Lee, D. T. Y. 1989. Personnel communication. Area Language Studies Dept., U.S. Naval Academy, Annapolis, Md.

OASD (Office of the Assistant Secretary of Defense [Force Management and Personnel]). 1988. *Department of Defense military manpower training report FY 1988*. Washington, D.C.: Government Printing Office.

OSD (Office of the Secretary of Defense). 1988. *Annual report to the Congress fiscal year 1989*. Washington, D.C.: Government Printing Office.

Polmar, N. 1986. *Guide to the Soviet navy*. Annapolis, Md.: U.S. Naval Institute Press.

Pruner, L. 1989. Personnel communication. Area Language Studies Dept., U.S. Naval Academy, Annapolis, Md.

Service National. 1984. *Français, Voici votre armée*, no. 35. Paris: Service d'Information et de Rélations Publiques des Armées.

ENVELOPMENT

Envelopment is a form of offensive maneuver "that seeks to apply strength against weakness" (U.S. Dept. of the Army 1986). In an envelopment, the attacker avoids the defender's front (where he is strongest) and maneuvers around or against one or both of the defender's flanks, where the defender is weak, and sometimes against his rear, where he is weakest. During an envelopment, the attacker also launches a secondary (holding) attack against the defender's front that is intended to hold or fix his frontline elements in place so he cannot maneuver against the threat to his flank and/or rear.

An envelopment usually involves more risk than a frontal assault (mainly because it involves some division of the attacking force) but is generally less costly in lives, promises greater success, and is frequently decisive. Envelopments can be tactical on the one hand or strategic or operational on the other.

Single Envelopment

In a single envelopment, the attacking force maneuvers its main effort around or against the defender's flank. Such an envelopment is often called a flanking movement or flank attack (Fig. 1). Successful envelopment depends largely on the ability of the attacker to identify and take advantage of an assailable flank before the defender can react to protect his vulnerability. Available flanks can be found in meeting engagements, counterattacks, gaps, or weak points in the defense or following a penetration. History is replete with examples of single envelopments, among them the battles of Leuctra (371 B.C.), Leuthen (1757), and Second Bull Run (1862).

Double Envelopment

In a double envelopment, the attacking force maneuvers against both flanks of the defender (Fig. 1). Such an attack requires close coordination and precise timing because the deeper an enveloping attack goes into an enemy's flank, the greater the danger that the attacker will himself be enveloped. Classic double envelopments occurred at Marathon (490 B.C.), Cannae (216 B.C.), Cowpens (1781), and Isandhlwana (1879).

Strategic Envelopment

An envelopment can also be a form of strategic or operational maneuver. In a strategic (or operational) envelopment, the attacking force passes around the defender's position to strike deep in his rear. Napoleon's successful maneuver against the Austrians at Ulm in 1805 was a famous instance of this technique.

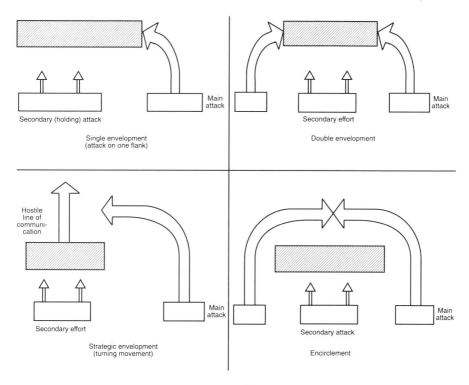

Figure 1. Types of envelopment.

The Schlieffen Plan of 1914 was an unsuccessful attempt to envelop the French armies strategically. The strategic envelopment is often called a turning movement (Fig. 1) because the attacker intends to make the defender's position untenable, usually by threatening his lines of communication, and thus to turn him from his position. The United States X Corps executed a classic strategic envelopment, or turning movement, in Korea in 1950 when it landed at Inchon, turning the North Korean positions on the Pusan perimeter. This maneuver was also used against Iraq by UN coalition forces in the 1991 Gulf War. In some cases (as at Ulm) a double envelopment results in encirclement of the enemy (Fig. 1). An encirclement can be the result of either a tactical or a strategic envelopment. For example, if the attacking forces conducting a tactical double envelopment meet in the defender's rear, cutting his ground routes of reinforcement and evacuation, an encirclement also occurs. Encirclement of the enemy is the consummation of an envelopment attack. While instances of encirclement are rare, the battles of Sedan (1870), Tannenberg (1914), and Stalingrad (1942–43) are famous examples in modern times.

Future Developments

Because successful envelopment is usually decisive, it will probably remain the preferred form of maneuver among future battlefield commanders. Turning the enemy's flank typically requires less initial combat power than other forms of maneuver, generally threatens the enemy's lines of communication, and nearly always has a greater effect on an enemy's morale than does a frontal assault. With the advent of airborne forces and helicopters, a vertical envelopment from above has also become possible. Moreover, because of their ability to create gaps and flanks, nuclear and chemical weapons have increased the likelihood of envelopment in future battle.

CHARLES E. WHITE

SEE ALSO: Air Assault; Defense; Maneuver; Offense; Tactics.

Bibliography

Bond, P. S., and E. H. Crounch. 1923. *Tactics: The practical art of leading troops in war.* Annapolis, Md.: New Military Library.
Culmann, F. 1922. *Cours de tactique général d'après l'expérience de la Grande Guerre.* Paris: Charles Lavauzelle.
Foertsch, H. 1940. *The art of modern warfare.* New York: Veritas Press.
U.S. Department of the Army. 1986. *Field manual 100-5: Operations.* Washington, D.C.: Department of the Army.

EXERCISES

The U.S. Department of Defense defines *exercise* as a military maneuver or simulated wartime operation involving planning, preparation, and execution. It is carried out for the purpose of training and evaluation. It may be a combined, joint, or single-service exercise, depending on participating organizations.

Exercises provide both a means of evaluating the skill with which commanders and forces are able to carry out existing tactics and doctrine and a means of judging the effectiveness of those tactics and doctrine.

Types of Exercises

The full range of military forces takes part in exercises: conventional and nuclear forces and ground, naval, and air forces. There are three main types of military exercises: (1) command post exercises, (2) field exercises, and (3) combination command post and field exercises.

The U.S. Department of Defense defines a command post exercise (CPX) as an exercise, in which the forces are simulated, that involves the commander, his staff, and communications between and within headquarters.

A field training exercise (FTX) is defined as an exercise conducted in the field under simulated war conditions in which troops and armament of one side are actually present, while those of the other side may be imaginary or in outline.

The final type of exercise is usually the largest in terms of numbers of participating individuals and headquarters; it combines the elements of a command post exercise and a field training exercise.

RELATED ACTIVITIES

Notwithstanding the above definitions, distinctions are often blurred between exercises and certain other military training activities, such as war games and simulated combat operations carried out at dedicated training ranges.

War games. Exercises are frequently referred to as "war games" by the press and even by military officials. Both command post exercises and war games involve attempts to simulate the wartime activities of commanders and headquarters' staffs; in both cases simulated operations must be carried out against intelligent, active adversaries.

Nevertheless, command post exercises and war games are generally distinguishable. The most important difference is the degree to which exercises emphasize execution while war games emphasize strategic, operational, and tactical decision making. The goals of the two activities are different. Exercises are used primarily as vehicles through which commanders and forces can be trained and evaluated. In contrast, war games are intended primarily to provide participants with opportunities for gaining strategic, operational, and tactical insights.

In summary, exercises focus on how activities are accomplished. War games focus on understanding what should be done.

Combat training centers. Distinguishing between field exercises and certain other unit training activities is more difficult. Perhaps the most dubious distinction is that sometimes made between field exercises that take place on nonmilitary public and private lands and similar activities carried out within military installations. The latter activities include, for example, simulated combat operations conducted at the U.S. Army's network of combat training centers and the U.S. Air Force's network of combat training ranges.

Training at such specialized facilities offers several advantages over off-base field exercises. In off-base field exercises, simulated enemy forces tend to be present in small numbers if at all, while units operating at modern combat training centers face relatively large, specially trained aggressor ground and air units. Because they take place at permanent facilities, operations at combat training centers can make wider use of various new electronic training aids. For example, units training at the army's National Training Center at Fort Irwin, California, are equipped with a laser system that allows "hits" on opposing forces to be accurately simulated.

Rehearsals. An exercise intended as preparation for a particular planned military operation is sometimes referred to as a rehearsal. The U.S. Marine Corps, for example, defines a rehearsal as that phase of an amphibious operation in which one or more exercises are conducted by the amphibious task force under conditions approximating those of the contemplated amphibious operation.

PUBLIC INTERFACE PROBLEMS

One great advantage of training on military-controlled lands is that it creates fewer public interface problems. Off-base field exercises may interfere with activities of the local civilian population, cause damage to private property, and cause local environmental damage. U.S. Army field exercises in Germany, for instance, in the 1980s typically caused US$50 million worth of damage to private property each year. Even operations on military-controlled lands may be constrained by local civilian concerns about such problems as noise pollution, but these constraints are likely to be significantly less severe than those imposed on off-base field exercises.

ADVANTAGES OF OFF-BASE FIELD EXERCISES

Off-base field exercises have some important advantages over operations at specialized training centers. Perhaps the most important, from a purely military perspective, is that in contrast to simulations at training centers, off-base exercises can be conducted over the very ground on which the future war being prepared for is most likely to be fought. In essence, this kind of realism must be weighed against the kind of increased realism possible through the use of sophisticated electronic instrumentation available at specialized training centers.

Off-base field exercises are also necessary to train and evaluate logistics support capabilities. By their very nature, long-range logistics support missions cannot be tested in simulators restricted to particular bases.

In addition, the fact that off-base exercises can be conducted in areas of potential future conflict heightens their usefulness as political and diplomatic instruments.

Political Significance

Military exercises are used not only to test and improve military capabilities but also as a means of sending political messages. It is not uncommon for an exercise's political purposes to equal or surpass in importance its purely military significance.

In ways, the cold war relationship between the East and West was expressed in exercise terms. Both the United States and the former USSR exercised naval forces to demonstrate their capability to project power worldwide. When Romania seemed to be straying from the Warsaw Pact, the USSR used exercises to express its concern. When the Berlin Wall was erected in 1961, the United States used exercises to show that it would continue to defend the city and the right of access to the city.

Exercises may be conducted on a routine basis to demonstrate support for long-standing political commitments. U.S. exercises conducted annually in Europe and South Korea fall into this category. Exercises can also be held on a more or less ad hoc basis as part of specific diplomatic initiatives. An example of this type would be the Soviet exercise conducted along the Soviet-Polish border in 1980, which was part of a larger diplomatic effort to persuade the Polish government to crack down on the Solidarity trade union.

While U.S. exercises held in Europe, South Korea, and other foreign areas undoubtedly serve political purposes, they are nevertheless carried out in a manner intended to make them useful devices for training and evaluation. By comparison, exercises conducted by forces of the former Soviet Union and many other countries tend to reflect a largely political or public relations orientation down to the lowest levels of execution. One manifestation of this emphasis on appearance over realism is the degree to which the Soviets typically restricted weapons and equipment usage in their exercises.

In the press releases associated with Warsaw Pact exercises in the 1970s and 1980s, it was easy to see the emphasis on appearance over training and evaluation. It was not unusual, for example, to read the description of a river-crossing operation in which Polish engineers prepared the crossing for an East German unit while being defended by Soviet air defense units. This kind of multinational integration during the difficult task of a river crossing would be very unlikely in actual combat.

Confidence-building Measures

A number of agreements have been negotiated that are intended to reduce the danger that an exercise might be used to mask actual preparations for war or that a war might arise inadvertently due to misunderstandings or miscalculations related to the conduct of an exercise. Traditionally, the former has been the major concern. A case in point occurred in 1968 when the Soviet Union invaded Czechoslovakia using forces nominally mobilized and readied for exercise purposes.

The most significant confidence-building measures (CBMs) related to military exercises involve forces in Europe. Since the end of World War II, Europe has played host to the largest concentration of military exercises in the world. In the mid-1980s, as many as 250,000 troops were involved in NATO's annual series of exercises played out across Europe. Typically a total of about 80,000 Soviet troops each year took part in European exercises.

The first CBMs relating to European exercises were agreed to in 1975 at the Helsinki Conference on Security and Cooperation in Europe (CSCE). Signed by most of the countries of Europe as well as the United States, Canada, and the Soviet Union, this agreement required among other things prior notification of any exercise involving more than 25,000 troops. The treaty also encouraged the signatories to invite foreign observers to attend these exercises. These CBMs were strengthened at the Stockholm CSCE meeting in 1986; a still more comprehensive set of CBMs was negotiated as part of the 1990 CSCE agreement.

The most noteworthy CBMs involving naval exercises are those associated with the Incidents at Sea agreement signed by the United States and the Soviet Union in 1972. This agreement is widely credited with reducing the number of collisions and other incidents involving U.S. and Soviet naval forces. In 1989, the United States and the Soviet Union signed the Dangerous Military Activities agreement, which committed both countries to take a number of additional precautions when they had military forces operating in proximity to each other.

NATO and Warsaw Pact Field Exercises

The size and number of NATO and former Warsaw Pact off-base field exercises in Europe declined toward the end of the 1980s. In 1987 NATO conducted seventeen field exercises large enough to require notification under the terms of the Stockholm agreement, while the Warsaw Pact conducted 25 (generally smaller) such exercises. By 1990, the number of notified NATO exercises dropped to ten and notified Warsaw Pact exercises decreased to seven.

In both cases, budgetary pressures and the general perception of the unlikeliness of a war in Europe were responsible for the decline in number and size of field exercises. The decline was also closely tied to the virtual disintegration of the Warsaw Pact as a military alllliance.

Future Trends

Like other training activities, exercises provide a means of improving readiness. Ideally, exercises supplement and complement other training and readiness activities, such as specialized individual training and nonexercise-related flight training missions. During times of budget constraints, exercises compete with these alternative types of training for scarce funds.

In the future both field exercises and simulations carried out at combat training centers may give way increasingly to the use of electronic simulators. One motivating factor is the high cost of operating modern weapons systems, whether off base or at training centers. Other factors could be equally important. Increasing urbanization, environmental sensitivity, and other changes are reducing the amount of land and airspace available for conducting field exercises. At the same time, because of the vast increase in range of many weapons, the area required to conduct realistic field exercises has increased. The combination of these trends will almost inevitably compromise the level of realism that can be achieved in field exercises. Thus, in the future electronic simulators may offer advantages over field exercises in terms not only of cost but also of realism.

Nevertheless, field exercises will probably always remain an important element in military training programs. It is likely to be years before military establishments outside the United States and other Western countries will have significant access to sophisticated electronic simulator technologies. Moreover, even if electronic simulators are eventually able to achieve the level of realism they apparently promise, they will never be able to replace field exercises entirely.

No matter how technically capable electronic simulators may become, confidence in the ability of forces to effectively perform complex support and combat activities—involving large numbers and diverse types of troops—can be achieved only through the use of field exercises. Moreover, electronic simulators can never replicate the political functions performed by field exercises.

SAMUEL B. GARDINER

SEE ALSO: Joint Operations.

Bibliography

Demers, W. A., and J. Kitfield. 1989. Training in Europe: Fenced in. *Military Forum* July, pp. 46–52.

Traxler, V. 1989. The CSCE negotiation in Vienna: Background and prospects. *NATO Review* October, pp. 5–10.

EXPLOSIVES TECHNOLOGY, CONVENTIONAL

The art of explosives technology consists of manufacturing dangerous substances in such a way that their designed effect—a violent liberation of shock waves, pressure, or heat—is manifested only when wanted. In all other circumstances the explosive substance or article must be safe to handle. Balancing the opposing requirements of safety and explosive properties is a challenge for the scientists and engineers engaged in this field.

Generally Accepted Safety Standards

Hazard Divisions and Storage Compatibility Groups

All regulations regarding safe conditions in manufacturing, storing, and shipping explosives consider the sensitivity of large quantities of explosive substances, or articles containing such substances, to locally generated sources of initiation. The generally accepted United Nations (UN) classification system divides explosive substances or articles into five hazard divisions:

Division 1.1   Substances and articles that have a mass explosion hazard

Division 1.2   Substances and articles that have a projection hazard but not a mass explosion hazard

Division 1.3   Substances and articles that have a fire hazard and either a minor blast hazard or a minor projection hazard or both, but not a mass explosion hazard

Division 1.4   Substances and articles that present no significant hazard

Division 1.5   Very insensitive substances that have a mass explosion hazard

The assignment to a particular hazard division is important for determination of minimum distances between buildings that house dangerous materials (see next section) and of transport regulations.

The UN system makes further distinctions reflecting possible dangerous interactions between different types of explosives. The so-called compatibility groups differentiate, for instance, among the following:

A: Primary explosive substances

C: Propellant explosive substances or other deflagrating explosive substances or articles containing such explosive substances

D: Secondary detonating explosive substances or black powder or articles containing a secondary detonating explosive substance, in each case without means of initiation and without a propelling charge, or articles containing a primary explosive substance and containing two or more effective protective features.

The UN system lists twelve compatibility groups. Explosives are considered compatible if they can be stored and transported together without significantly increasing either the probability of an accident or, for a given quantity, the magnitude of the effects of such an accident. It is easy to understand why specific combinations—for example A and C—are not permitted to be stored and shipped together.

CONSTRUCTION OF BUILDINGS TO HOUSE DANGEROUS SUBSTANCES

The construction of buildings that are to contain explosives depends upon the type and mass of explosive stored and the hazards from other explosive stocks nearby. With slowly deflagrating substances, the major hazard is heat radiation. The rise in pressure is small and slow and can easily be vented by doors, windows, or frangible walls designed as blowout areas. With rapidly deflagrating matter, the action of pressure on the building has a more dynamic character. Therefore, it may be difficult to design effective venting mechanisms, but it is possible to prevent a deflagration-to-detonation transition reaction from occurring.

The effect of a detonation of high explosives on a building is different from the effect of deflagration. The main effect of a detonation is extremely high pressure, which stresses the construction material in a time shorter than its natural vibrational period. There is no way to reduce the action of the shock wave on the structures by venting mechanisms. The incident shock wave will then be multiply reflected, followed by rarefaction waves, which amplify the demolition power of the detonation. The effect is determined by the mass conversion rate, which is a product of detonation velocity, density, and reacting surface of the explosive.

Buildings in an explosives factory are threatened not only by the explosives inside but also by the explosion of other buildings in the vicinity. In the latter case the resistance of a building depends upon its stability against the impulse of the shock wave. This impulse is related to the mass of the explosive and the distance to the explosion site and decreases by a cubic root law. Since there is an empirical relation between resistance against static pressure and the dynamic pressure of the shock wave, one can estimate the stability of structures against detonative stress arising from explosions of neighboring buildings.

Light construction, as was used in the early days of explosives manufacturing, can be used only for buildings not threatened by neighboring buildings, but it has the advantage that no heavy objects are projected in the case of an explosion.

Buildings with a light blowout area have more stably constructed roofs and walls, normally in skeleton design. When using cubicles in a row, the wall between two storage cubicles must be constructed in a solid, resistant manner; alternatively, storage rooms should be separated by cubicles that contain no explosive matter. Even better is a sandwich design, in which the space between storage cubicles is filled with sand.

For buildings threatened also by other buildings in the vicinity, the best design seems to be massive walls and roof together with a blowout area, or earth-covered construction. In this case the protection against shock waves and flying debris from the outside is optimized, but an event from inside the building may result in a number of large and heavy objects being projected.

Earth dams around a building are of only limited value for suppression of shock waves. Their main effect is protection against flying objects. It is important to know that blast waves flow over and around a barricade, while shock waves are reflected and can travel around corners. In addition, experiments have shown that, in front of a building with a blowout area and an earth dam, the effect of an explosion is about 30 percent higher than normal.

SAFETY DISTANCES

The safety distances between buildings containing explosives are determined by the hazard division of the explosives, the mass of explosive matter, and the protective means of the buildings themselves. The design of structures and barricades is reflected by the risk factor k, which is used to calculate minimum distances between buildings. For practical use there exist risk factor tables for all types of explosives and protection designs from which one may easily evaluate minimum distances without a deeper understanding of the theory behind the numbers.

AUTOMATION AND REMOTE CONTROL

Automation and remote control are the best ways to minimize risk to employees. Nowadays all manipulations with explosive matter can be remotely controlled, but for economic reasons remote control is used for only the more critical processing steps. This is true especially for the continuous production of nitric acid esters such as nitroglycerine, which is one of the most dangerous chemicals. Remote control is also used for explosives with a high ignition sensitivity such as propellants, ignition mixtures, or initiating explosives. Modern video techniques and measuring devices allow monitoring of safety and quality simultaneously. Moreover, all data can be handled by computers, which provide a powerful tool for quality assessment.

EQUIPMENT AND ENERGY SUPPLY

All regulations concerning the manufacture of explosives seek to prevent unintended accumulations of explosives at sites where they are not supposed to be and also to prevent any source of energy sufficient for setting the explosive on fire or causing a detonation. All equipment must be of a material that produces no sparks by friction or impact. All fasteners, such as bolts, screws, or nuts, must be secured against loosening. Friction of machine parts must be minimized, and pressure buildup must be vented as soon as possible. The accumulation of explosive dust in heating elements, ventilators, filters, or pipelines must be prevented. Coatings on floors and walls must not react with the explosive to generate other dangerous substances, such as with picric acid, where metals or even paint can produce mechanically sensitive picrates.

All buildings need efficient lightning protection and means to prevent electrostatic charging of personnel and equipment. Electrically driven equipment must be designed not to initiate explosions. Explosive gases or dust create additional risks, and these hazards also have to be considered. Furnaces are not permitted in buildings containing explosive matter.

In addition to these points, there are long lists of applicable regulations, which are similar in most countries.

Production of Selected Explosives

In general terms, the large field of explosive substances is divided into primary explosives, which detonate rather easily by mechanical or thermal stress but normally show no large energy output, and secondary explosives, which are comparably less sensitive and therefore need the shock wave of the detonation of a primary explosive to achieve detonation. (See Fig. 1 for the chemical structure of the explosives discussed below.)

Examples of primary explosives are lead azide and lead styphnate; their preparation is described below.

Typical classes of secondary explosives are nitric acid esters, or the reaction products of nitric acid with alcohols, the most famous of which are nitroglycerine and PETN (pentaerythritol tetranitrate). All of these compounds contain a C-O-NO_2 group. TNT (trinitrotoluene) is a member of the important class of aromatic nitro compounds, which carry the NO_2 group directly attached to the aromatic ring carbon atom. These compounds are chemically very stable and possess high energy. Nitramines are nitrated amines and have an N-NO_2 bond. They are nearly as stable as aromatic nitro compounds but have explosive powers well in the range of nitric acid esters. Cyclic nitramines, such as RDX (cyclonite) and HMX, contain the amine nitrogen as a member of the ring. These compounds are among the most powerful explosives in military use.

LEAD AZIDE AND LEAD STYPHNATE

Lead azide has become the most important initiating explosive for both military and commercial uses. It is prepared by reaction of lead nitrate or lead acetate with sodium azide in alkaline solution to prevent formation of explosive and toxic hydrogen azide. The mechanical sensitivity of lead azide, especially its friction sensitivity, is highly dependent on the crystal form. Since the early days of investigation, when lead azide was recrystallized from water, it has been known that the substance can explode even during crystallization. A considerable amount of work has been done to reduce the sensitivity to a level where the two requirements, performance and safety, are both met.

To get a less sensitive product one may stir the reaction mixture intensively, adjust the reaction temperature, adjust the concentrations, and add compounds that modify the size and shape of the crystals. Dextrin has been used in this way together with, for example, sodium ferrocyanide or sodium tartrate. Polyvinyl alcohol, however, is more efficient. With sodium hydroxide the formation of lead hydroxide or basic lead azide, both of which work as a diluent and phlegmatizer, can be controlled.

In batch production, only some few kilograms of lead azide are prepared at one time. In the Meissner continuous manufacture method the solutions of lead nitrate and sodium azide are combined on top of a reaction column that, on its lower end, has an outlet valve with a means for air agitation to prevent settling

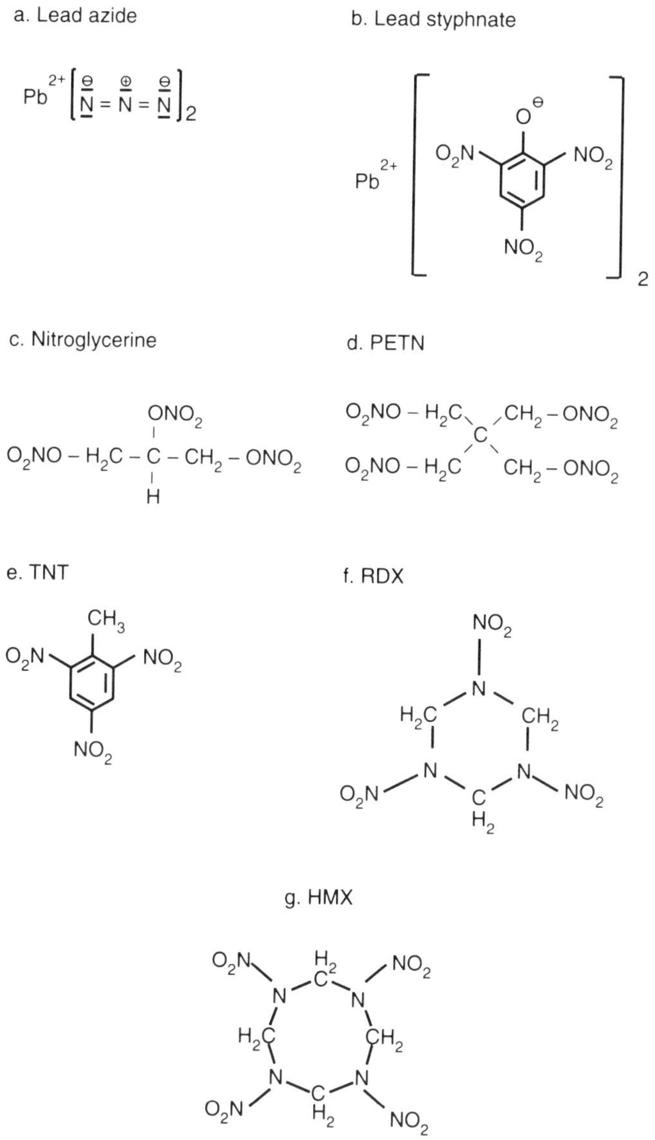

a. Lead azide

b. Lead styphnate

$$Pb^{2+} \left[\underset{\ominus}{\underset{|}{N}} = \underset{\oplus}{N} = \underset{\ominus}{\underset{|}{N}} \right]_2$$

c. Nitroglycerine

d. PETN

$$O_2NO - H_2C - \underset{\underset{H}{|}}{\overset{\overset{ONO_2}{|}}{C}} - CH_2 - ONO_2$$

e. TNT

f. RDX

g. HMX

Figure 1. Chemical structure of selected explosives.

of solid material. During their progress through the column the solutions react and form solid lead azide, which is then collected on filters, washed, dried, and sieved.

Special attention must be paid to the removal of azide in waste waters. This is done by reaction with sodium nitrate and nitric acid to give essentially the nitrates and nitrogen oxide.

Although lead azide is mechanically extremely sensitive, its performance in practical use as a primer or detonator is improved by the addition of specific compounds, depending on the intended application. Lead styphnate (see below) lowers the ignition temperature in detonators, whereas tetracene increases the impact sensitivity. Modern initiating systems also may contain potassium chlorate, ground glass, or antimony sulfide, together with phlegmatizers and binders.

Lead styphnate has poor initiation efficiency, but it is much more readily ignited by flame or spark than lead azide. Lead styphnate cannot be prepared directly from lead nitrate with styphnic acid (trinitroresorcinol), because this would result in the formation of basic lead styphnate, which has considerably weaker initiating power. In a two-step process, magnesium oxide reacts with styphnic acid to give water and magnesium styphnate, to which is added lead nitrate. The product is then filtered, washed, and dried as usual.

NITROGLYCERINE

Nitroglycerine is the esterification product of the trifunctional alcohol, glycerine, with nitric acid. To bring about the reaction, it is necessary to have in the system sulfuric acid, which reacts with nitric acid to produce the chemically active intermediate responsible for the esterification and takes up the water formed during reaction. The ratio of the two acids and the quantity of mixed acid used are a compromise between yield and solubility of nitroglycerine in spent acid. The specific values of the reactants depend upon the process used.

The production of nitroglycerine has to solve the problems that arise from the extremely high mechanical sensitivity of the substance and the chemical instability of both the impure material and the waste acid. As the reaction is highly exothermic, proper cooling is necessary to provide safe conditions and optimum yields. The addition of glycerine to the nitrating acid mixture must be done with appropriate stirring to prevent local superheating, followed by heat releasing oxidations, which could speed up to an explosion.

The nitroglycerine formed in the reaction is, to a small extent, soluble in the spent acid; the main quantity is formed as an emulsion, from which the oily nitroglycerine separates as the upper layer when the mixture is no longer stirred. After about one hour the separation is nearly complete and the two phases must be collected individually and purified. Great care must be taken to bring about a complete separation of the two phases, because contamination of nitroglycerine with acid is hazardous and leads to a self-accelerating decomposition reaction resulting in an explosion. On the other hand, the waste acid itself is chemically unstable (see below), and any nitroglycerine not dissolved in the acid separates in later processing stages and decomposes until in the worst case it results in an explosion.

Nitroglycerine is washed several times with warm water, sodium bicarbonate solution, and again with water to get rid of any traces of acid, which destabilize the product. The spent acid contains emulsified nitroglycerine, which separates in the course of time, and dissolved nitroglycerine. The solubility depends mainly upon temperature, water content, and nitric acid content. At about 14 percent water content, nitroglycerine has a solubility minimum. With additional water, the spent acid is brought to a state where no more nitroglycerine will separate. This acid is then stored until it is denitrated by a sort of distillation in which nitric acid is evaporated at the top of a column and sulfuric acid is collected at the bottom.

Spent acid is chemically unstable because the nitric acid therein oxidizes the organic components present and forms nitrogen oxides. These reactions are self-accelerating and can lead to a sudden eruption of gas and heat, resulting in an explosion of the tank. Therefore, storage of spent acid before denitration should be limited to a short time, and temperature and nitrogen oxide content must be checked regularly.

The safest way to manufacture nitroglycerine is to use a continuous process in which the quantity of nitroglycerine present at one site is minimized. The first continuous process was developed in 1930 by Schmid and Meissner. They used a flow reactor, which at first contains spent acid and is fed with glycerine and nitrating acid in the proper ratio. The mixture then overflows into a separator, where nitroglycerine settles on top and is emulsified in water or diluted sodium bicarbonate solution by means of an injector. In this form it is brought to the first washing tower, which contains glass rings and sieve plates. Compressed air is introduced to bring about thorough mixing of nitroglycerine and water. On top of the column the emulsion runs into another separator, where nitroglycerine settles at the bottom and is again emulsified by a second injector and brought to the next washing tower. This process is alternately continued until the pure nitroglycerine is collected. The water runs from the top of the individual separators through pipelines with baffle plates, where additional nitroglycerine is collected. The water may be used again or neutralized and discarded.

The process developed by Biazzi uses a somewhat similar flow reactor, but the separator has a special feature. It is a shallow vessel with a conical bottom and top, into which the emulsion is fed tangentially. This results in the emulsion circulating slowly relative to the contents of the separator: namely acid at the bottom, above it nitroglycerine, and water at the top. This slow motion promotes the separation.

The injector nitrating process of Nilssen and Brunnberg of NAB in Sweden makes use of spent acid, which is mixed with twice the volume of normal mixed acid and cooled to 0°C. The acid is pumped into the injector, which sucks glycerine from a storage tank. The emitted heat of reaction warms the nitrator up to 45 or 50°C. The nitroglycerine then is in the form of a nonexplosive emulsion. As the mixture immediately flows to a cooling device, where it is rapidly cooled to 15°C, the thermal stress upon the nitroglycerine is small. The emulsion then runs into a high-speed centrifugal separator. The separated nitroglycerine is then emulsified in another injector and washed several times as described above.

Most of these processes and their modifications are automatic and remotely controlled. The nitroglycerine is transported as a nonexplosive emulsion in water to storage locations, where it is stored underwater. When it is used for the production of explosives, it is again transported as an emulsion to the mixing location, where it is separated from the water in small vessels and weighed and dosed automatically.

This technology has made it possible to manufacture nitroglycerine at a level of safety comparable to the production of ordinary nonhazardous chemicals. Nevertheless, the process needs an untiring awareness of the material handled and thorough control of the equipment.

PETN

Pentaerythritol tetranitrate (PETN), a solid nitric acid ester, has a very high chemical stability compared with other members of this class, especially liquids such as nitroglycerine. It is also far more stable mechanically, but its sensitivity to shock waves is very high. Therefore it is one of the most easily ignited solid explosives in use.

PETN is manufactured continuously by feeding pentaerythritol into a reactor containing concentrated nitric acid. The highly exothermic reaction is conducted at 15 to 20°C. For safety reasons the ratio of the reactants is one part pentaerythritol to five to eight parts acid. The reaction mixture runs by an overflow process into a second reactor, where it is cooled to 10°C. This material then passes into a diluter, where it is diluted by water with cooling to bring about precipitation of PETN. The suspension then flows to one of two vacuum filters, which are filled alternately, one being filled while the other is in operation. The crude product is washed with water, recrystallized from acetone, and finally dried.

TNT

Trinitrotoluene (TNT) came into military use in 1902. During World Wars I and II it was the most important explosive used. Because of its low mechanical and thermal sensitivity and high chemical stability, it is among the safest explosive to handle. In contrast to most other explosives, it melts without decomposition; since the melting point is 81°C, TNT can easily be cast into shells or other cases.

TNT is the final product of a three-step reaction of toluene with a mixture of nitric and sulfuric acid. The second and third nitration steps need increasing temperatures and acid concentrations. Therefore, spent acids of later steps can be used for previous nitration steps. Modern continuous production uses a series of nitrators and separators connected in line. Each nitrator is fed with the substance to be nitrated (toluene, mono-, or dinitrotoluene), fresh acid, and spent acid from the next step (except for the last step). The emulsion of formed nitro compound and acid then flows to a separator; here the organic material separates at the top and is transferred to the next nitration reactor, whereas the acid flows back to the previous nitrator and is mixed there with fresh acid. The crude, molten TNT from the last separator is cooled with cold water until it crystallizes. The impurities, which concentrate on the surface of the crystals, are then dissolved by aqueous sodium sulfite, which does not affect the solid TNT. After filtration of the liquid, the TNT is washed with hot water, dried with hot air, and finally flaked. To accomplish this, the lower part of a cooled rotating steel drum dips into the molten TNT. The TNT solidifies on the rotating drum and is scraped off as flakes with a knife.

RDX AND HMX

RDX, or cyclonite, is a six-membered ring with carbon and nitrogen atoms alternating. Each nitrogen atom is additionally attached to a nitro group, whereas each carbon atom binds two hydrogen atoms. HMX is the next higher homologue, containing one more carbon nitrogen group. These heterocyclic nitramines have outstanding properties as military explosives, since they possess chemical stabilities not much lower than those of aromatic nitro compounds but considerably higher explosive power. Owing to their very high detonation velocity, they are used where a maximum of brisance is required, for instance, in hollow-charge ammunition.

The formation of these compounds is very complex and cannot be discussed in detail here. Some older methods used the reaction of hexamethylenetetramine (hexamine) with concentrated nitric acid. Besides the formation of RDX, many by-products were formed that lowered the yield drastically and made the process dangerous, since their stability was considerably lower than that of RDX. The greatest danger was in the spent acid.

Hexamine contains six methylene groups and four amino groups. To form two molecules of RDX, two additional amino groups are required; these are introduced in the form of ammonium nitrate. This mixture can be heated to about 80°C without risk of explosion, whereas mixtures without ammonium nitrate may be dangerous just above 25°C.

Hexamine can be prepared in situ when paraformaldehyde and ammonium nitrate react with each other and the water formed is taken up by acetic anhydride, which is then transformed into acetic acid. At the same step nitric acid is liberated and then reacts with hexamine to form RDX. Among several by-products, HMX is also formed.

The industrially used method was developed independently by Bachmann in the United States and by Knoeffler and Apel in Germany (KA method). In a first step, hexamine is reacted with 30 percent nitric acid to form hexaminedinitrate, which then is added to a mixture of ammonium nitrate, acetic anhydride, and nitric acid. This method takes advantage of the fact that the methylene and part of the amino groups required are offered in the dehydrated form; therefore less anhydride is needed. HMX is an important by-product and can be made the main product by proper adjustment of the reaction conditions. In heating with hot aqueous borax solution, to which sodium hydroxide is continuously added, the RDX is destroyed, whereas HMX is not affected. This material then is filtered, washed, and recrystallized from nitromethane.

Processing

Most explosives in military use are confined in cases, such as in shells or bombs. Therefore, they must be suitable for the processing techniques used: namely pressing, casting, or extruding.

For pressing high explosives some material such as wax or graphite is added to reduce the mechanical sensitivity and the sliding friction. Plastic binders can be used to improve mechanical stability of the pressed body. Complex forms are pressed in steps.

Casting is possible only for explosives that melt without decomposition. The most important such compound is TNT, with its low melting point at 81°C. One major drawback is the high reduction of volume when TNT solidifies. Air bubbles can be prevented by controlling the temperature curve or by vibrating the case. Casting can also be performed with suspensions of solid explosives in molten TNT. Most widely used are combinations of TNT with RDX (Composition B), with PETN (Pentolite), with aluminum (Tritonal), or with combinations of these explosives. Great care must be taken to prevent sedimentation of solid particles and thus separation of the mixture.

Extrusion is used for double- or triple-base solid propellants, which contain nitroglycerine and nitrocellulose. Nitroglycerine works both as an energetic compound and as a plasticizer. Modern continuously operating technologies use screw extruders for the processing of these propellants.

NIKOLAUS FIEDERLING
AXEL HOMBURG

Bibliography

Cook, M. A. 1958. *The science of high explosives.* New York: Reinhold.

Glassman, I. 1987. *Combustion.* New York: Academic Press.

Jarrett, D. E. 1968. Derivation of the British explosives safety distances. *Annals of New York Academy of Sciences* 152:18–35.

Lingens, P., J. Prior, H. Brachert, and H. J. Symanski. 1982. Sprengstoffe. In *Ullmanns Encyklopädie der technischen Chemie*, 4th ed., vol. 21. Weinheim: Verlag Chemie.

United Nations. 1988. *Recommendations on the transport of dangerous goods.* New York: United Nations.

Urbanski, T. 1983. *Chemistry and technology of explosives.* Oxford: Pergamon.

FIELD SERVICE REGULATIONS

Field service regulations (FSR) are official publications issued by general staffs or similar agencies for the guidance of officers responsible for the conduct of military campaigns on land. They contain little information about the employment of particular weapons or the internal functioning of military units (i.e., the "technical" level of war). Instead, field service regulations are concerned with integrating the actions of various units to produce a desired effect on the enemy (i.e., the tactical and operational levels of war).

Prior to the mid-nineteenth century, guidance for the conduct of military campaigns was limited to the ad hoc, often hand-written, guidelines that commanders in chief provided for their senior commanders. (Frederick the Great's *Instructions to My Generals* is a classic example of this type of work.) The development of general staffs, permanent all-arms formations (divisions and corps), and the concept of the military campaign as a distinct level of war created both the need and the means for giving these regulations a more permanent character.

Origins and Development

The first document that fits clearly into the category of field service regulations is the 1867 memorandum of the Prussian field marshal Helmuth von Moltke (the Elder), *From the Regulations for Higher Troop Commanders*. This memorandum, inspired by Moltke's victorious campaign against the Austrian army in Bohemia in 1866, promulgated his vision of the ideal battle—a concentric attack by armies that have traveled to the battlefield by separate routes. "When the operations have been so directed that the enemy is attacked simultaneously on the front and the flank," Moltke wrote, "then strategy has accomplished all that it is capable of and great results must follow."

Subsequent German field service regulations followed the pattern set by Moltke. True to his ideal of a campaign of grand maneuvers culminating in a decisive encirclement of the enemy's main army, these later editions of the German field service regulations contained a number of passages lifted verbatim from the text of *From the Regulations for Higher Troop Commanders*. Despite this strong chain of continuity, however, each version of the German field service regulations was the product of a great deal of original thought on the part of the author, who usually was the serving chief of the general staff.

As the originators of both the modern general staff and the concept of field service regulations, the Prussians had many imitators. The British field service regulations of the early twentieth century were patterned after contemporary German models. The 1941 edition of *Field Manual 100-5: Operations*, the first volume of three-volume field service regulations of the U.S. Army, was a close copy of *Truppenführung*, the 1933 edition of the German field service regulations (300-1); many paragraphs of the former were, in fact, verbatim translations of the German edition.

The Visionary Tradition

While field service regulations in the German tradition served primarily to codify actual experience, a number of armies have issued field service regulations that described campaigns employing weapons not yet available and operational concepts not yet in practice. The most striking example of this class of field service regulation is *PU-36*, a Soviet manual published in 1936. This work, written by a closely knit team of imaginative officers and heavily influenced by the thinking of the current chief of staff of the Red Army, Marshal Tukhachevsky, recommended deep strikes by mechanized combined-arms forces supported by aircraft, parachutists, and chemical attacks. Although at the time of the manual's publication the Red Army consisted almost entirely of foot-mobile infantry, horse cavalry, and horse-drawn artillery, *PU-36* provided the doctrine used by the Soviets in the blitzkrieg campaigns of 1943–44 that won for them their World War II battle against Germany.

American contemporaries of Tukhachevsky also used field service regulations as a means of preparing their service to practice a style of warfare for which the equipment had been neither designed nor procured. Beginning in 1931, a number of farsighted U.S. Marines began work on a manual that described amphibious operations that bore a remarkable resemblance to those of World War II. Armed only with the lessons of the failed British operation at Gallipoli in World War I and their own experience in landing on undefended beaches, these marines produced the *Tentative Manual for Landing Operations* that was to set the pace for American amphibious operations for the next half-century.

The British general J. F. C. Fuller also moved a step ahead in his *Lectures on FSR III (Operations Between Mechanized Forces)*, published as a book in 1932. At a time when neither Great Britain nor any of her potential adversaries possessed tanks in any significant numbers, Fuller used the format of the then-current field service regulations of the British Army to sketch out his vision of future battles in which the armies of both belligerents consisted entirely of fleets of armored vehicles.

The Technical Tradition

Armies without a strong tradition of operational art have often allowed their field service regulations to degenerate into handbooks dealing with the technical aspects of war and, in some extreme cases, with administrative details. The Nationalist Chinese field service regulations of 1934 provide a good example of this type of manual. Although the first paragraph of this work states that "battle is to be considered an army's chief object," none of the subsequent paragraphs give any indication of how a battle is to be fought or how battles are to be combined into a military campaign. Instead, the manual expounds on such banalities as the posting of sentries, the billeting of troops, the issue of rations, and the proper format for messages and war diaries.

The 1976 edition of U.S. Army *Field Manual 100-5: Operations*, is another example of field service regulations that make no mention of the art of fighting campaigns. Despite its name, the 1976 version of *FM 100-5* dealt neither with operational art nor, strictly speaking, with tactics. The main purpose of the work was to promulgate a number of techniques that were thought to be essential to the army's execution of its then-current policy of "active defense." The 1976 edition is thus full of information about tank-on-tank combat, the effectiveness of specific weapons systems, and specific recommendations about how American armored and mechanized infantry units should fight their Soviet-bloc counterparts.

The 1982 and 1986 editions of *FM 100-5* constituted a radical departure from the 1976 edition. With their heavy emphasis on operational maneuver, these manuals have much in common with field service regulations of the German tradition—particularly the 1941 edition of *FM 100-5*. In addition, the 1982 and 1986 editions have a bit of the visionary flavor of *PU-36*.

A New Paradigm

Traditionally, field service regulations have dealt primarily with conventional war. Guerrilla campaigns, counterinsurgency campaigns, and other military actions at the low end of the spectrum of conflict have consequently received little attention. The U.S. Marine Corps has recently attempted to remedy this defect with Fleet Marine Force Manual 1, *Warfighting*. Approved in March of 1989 and intended to serve as the keystone of an entirely new series of doctrinal publications, this manual provides general guidance for a whole range of military efforts—from nuclear war to surgical strikes and from conventional war against a major power to action against terrorists or guerrillas.

The organization and style of *Warfighting* constitute a further departure from traditional field service regulations. Designed to be read cover to cover, the manual is short (88 pages) and written in a lively, nonbureaucratic style. While its words have the authority of official doctrine, the arguments presented are buttressed with footnotes. More significantly, *Warfighting* contains no information about procedures, command relationships, or organization. Rather, it promulgates a philosophy of military action and leaves the details to other manuals and reference publications.

The Future

Field service regulations have traditionally assumed a clear distinction between strategy (a gray area where soldiers and statesmen share responsibilities) and the operational art (a purely military sphere). Today that distinction has little validity. Commando raids, the support and suppression of guerrillas and terrorists, dealing with civil unrest, and peacekeeping are all common military activities that make units as small as squads a direct link between political ends and violent means. Neither the organization of armies nor field service regulations have yet taken this into account, but both may in the coming decades.

BRUCE I. GUDMUNDSSON

SEE ALSO: Air-land Battle; Doctrine; Theory of Combat.

Bibliography

Beck, L. 1955. *Studien.* Stuttgart: Koehler Verlag.
Romjue, J. 1984. *From active defense to air land battle: The development of army doctrine, 1973–1982.* Ft. Monroe, Va.: U.S. Army Training and Doctrine Command.
Simpkin, R. 1987. *Deep battle: The brainchild of Marshal Tukhachevski.* London: Brassey's.

FIREPOWER

Firepower is the battlefield capability of a military force to deliver fire—the lethal end products of munitions—against an enemy.

The word *firepower* can be used either to refer to the fire that is delivered by a military force or to the quality or effectiveness of the fire that is delivered. It can also be used, although less frequently, to refer to any explosive or missile that causes damage to the target. In its most common sense, however, and that which will be discussed here, it is the amount or quantity of fire that may be delivered by a military force, unit, weapons system, or some clearly defined entity such as a fort or a position. This amount may be measured in any of a number of ways—such as volume (number of rounds), weight, or explosive potential—and is often (but not necessarily) thought of as a rate in relation to a period of time.

The combat capabilities of two military forces, or units, are often compared in terms of their respective firepower. For instance, in the days of sailing warships, the strength of a fighting vessel could be inferred from the number of guns it carried, and this number was cited explicitly whenever reference was made to the vessel. (Reference to "the American frigate USS *Constitution* (44)" meant that it was designed to carry 44 guns. Its captain often increased the designed strength by mounting additional guns on the gun decks, however, an American practice denounced by British opponents.) The firepower of a ship—or squadron or fleet—could be defined somewhat more precisely by the weight, in pounds, of all the projectiles of a broadside, of the combined broadsides, or of the combined total of projectiles from all guns carried, which was usually about double the weight of a broadside. (A broadside was the onetime firing of one round, or projectile, from each of the guns on one side of a warship; thus, there were usually 22 guns in the broadside of the *Constitution*.)

Measuring the firepower of a ground combat force is more complicated than it is for a naval force because there is a greater variety of weapons types regularly employed in land combat and because there is an almost infinite number of possible variations in the proportions of the different weapons in a force. The complications have increased as modern technology has brought about a proliferation in types of weapons. Prior to the twentieth century, the approximate strength (or firepower) of a military force was usually described in terms of the number of infantrymen (each equipped with a small arm, usually a musket or a rifled musket), the number of cannons (usually without distinguishing different types or calibers of guns, howitzers, or mortars), and the number of cavalrymen (or "sabres," even though some of these were often lancers). Cavalrymen armed with hand-to-hand weapons were not elements of firepower; although dragoons, equipped with muskets or rifles to be used when fighting dismounted, obviously had firepower potential.

Suppression

Firepower has two principal effects. The first, in the pre–World War I words of French marshal (then colonel) Henri Pétain, "Fire kills!" In other words, firepower inflicts casualties or destruction upon the target. The second, and perhaps more important effect, is suppression.

Suppression is a psychological phenomenon, resulting from the fear induced in human beings who are, or believe themselves to be, the targets of firepower. They instinctively seek cover from the hostile fire. When they take any kind of action that might expose them to the hostile fire, their movements are cautious, careful, and usually slow. (If the person believes it will reduce the time of exposure to the enemy fire, the movement may be rapid, but it is a fleeting rapidity, invariably punctuating periods of inactivity or reduced activity.)

Obviously, the effectiveness of a person who is suppressed is degraded. It is generally acknowledged that the suppressive effect of firepower degrades the performance of a hostile military force more than does the casualty-producing effect of that firepower.

There is no known way to eliminate the suppressive effect of hostile firepower. The degrading effect of suppression, however, can be minimized to some extent by training and discipline. Despite being suppressed, well-trained soldiers can perform their battlefield duties better than those with less, or less effective, training. Discipline, which is a by-product of training, inculcates in a soldier a sense of duty that enables him to work with some effectiveness under fire, particularly if he is a member of a unit that performs its functions as a cohesive team.

Fire Superiority

On battlefields, the relative firepower capabilities of opposing forces are determined in a very practical fashion. Fairly early in an encounter, one side or the other gains "fire superiority." This phenomenon reflects the ability of one side, because of greater volume, weight, accuracy of fire, or some combination of these, to impose more of a suppressive effect on the opponent than the opponent is able to impose in return. It may also reflect the ability of a better-trained, better-disciplined force to offset the theoretical firepower superiority of a hostile force simply because the suppressive effect of the enemy's greater firepower is not as great as the effect of its own, lesser, firepower upon the enemy.

A military force with fire superiority is by definition less suppressed than its opponent. The force that has fire superiority has a greater ability to maneuver and is able to seize the initiative and to undertake offensive operations. Fire superiority, therefore, is an absolute precondition to a successful offensive or attack.

Firepower Comparisons

For purposes of planning—or of prediction—it is essential for the military planner to make an assessment of the opponent's relative firepower in advance of combat operations. Otherwise, the planner would be forced to wait and depend, when it is almost certainly too late, upon the battlefield measurement inherent in the phenomenon of fire superiority. While some generals, and some staffs, have, in the past, enjoyed considerable success in making such assessments, the history of warfare is replete with instances in which inaccurate assessments have led to rash actions and catastrophic blunders. Over the course of history, military men have unceasingly endeavored to improve the accuracy of their predictive assessments.

The problem in making such predictive assessments of the relative strengths of naval or ground forces has been one of relating, and equating, the relative effectiveness of different kinds of firepower. For many years, there was no reliable, scientific way to compare the relative effectiveness of small-arms bullets, cannon balls, and high-explosive projectiles or to compare the effectiveness of such weapons with that of such nonfirepower weapons as bayonets and cavalry sabers or lances. Even more difficult is equating the effectiveness of ground weapons located on battlefields with that of air support weapons, which appear fleetingly, but devastatingly, over battlefields.

The need for such comparisons became more urgent with the introduction of war games, or *kriegspiel*, into the training and planning processes of armies, beginning with the Prussian army early in the nineteenth century. For more than a century, war gamers had to be satisfied with making general comparisons between different kinds of units and leaving it up to the military experience and judgment of umpires to decide the relative firepower capabilities of units under the circumstances of the battle being simulated. The umpires' decisions were particularly crucial—and often disputed—in the assessment of the relative firepower of opposing combined-arms units or formations.

The same problem of assessing firepower capabilities of opposing units was encountered in field exercises, where the practical effects of firepower superiority could only be estimated. Again, the only solution was to leave it up to umpires to determine relative firepower capabilities and thus to award fire superiority to one side or the other on the basis of dubiously substantiable military judgment—more often than not by officers with limited military experience.

Firepower Scores

In the United States Army, it was the need to provide guidance to umpires in field exercises that led to the first serious effort to quantify the effects of weapons. This was done in various documents and manuals produced in the 1960s and crystallized in *Field Manual FM 105–5: Maneuver Control.* Six criteria were presented in these documents and in the field manual as the basis for a comprehensive listing of firepower scores of existing weapons: (1) sustained rates of fire; (2) effective width of burst; (3) fragmentation area; (4) exposure and density of targets; (5) effectiveness in comparison with other weapons, and (6) distinction between direct-fire, point target weapons, on the one hand, and indirect-fire area weapons, on the other.

Questions or objections could have been raised about this approach but were not. For instance, what was the practical distinction between the effective width of burst and fragmentation area? An artilleryman might have wondered if there was any difference in the value of an indirect-fire weapon used against an area target and its value when used against a point target. One needs to remember, however, that the purpose of the firepower scores derived by this method was merely to provide umpires in field exercises with some means of quickly and crudely evaluating the firepower capabilities of opposing military forces in field exercises. This they got from the scores listed in the manual. They had little or no interest in the analytical method whereby these scores were derived. While the actual utility of the specific firepower scores to individual umpires may be doubtful, their very existence was an important contribution to the realism and utility of such exercises.

Furthermore, the firepower scores were a quantification of firepower, which would eventually have utility for other kinds of war gaming. This, however, was not immediately apparent to military operations research (OR) analysts who needed such quantification.

Soon after World War II, military OR analysts began to recognize that their quantitative approach to analysis provided a basis for improving the old techniques of war gaming. The advent of the computer provided both tools and incentives to seek greater precision in the quantification and representation of firepower in war games. At the same time, the term *war game* was less used for the new, and largely computerized, products of this effort and was reserved for exercises in which teams of people opposed each other in nonquantitative interactions. Quantified, and increasingly computerized, representations of combat were now usually referred to as combat models or simulations.

With few exceptions, the model designers were OR analysts who eagerly built their models and simulations around one of two sets of equations that had

TABLE 1. Comparative Operational Lethality Indices during Different Historical Periods

Weapons	TLI Values	Ancient or Medieval	17th Cent.	18th Cent.	Napoleonic Wars	American Civil War	World War I	World War II	1975
Dispersion factor		1	5	10	20	25	250	3,000	4,000
Hand-to-hand	23	23	4.6	2.3	1.1	0.9	0.09	0.007	0.006
Javelin	19	19	—	—	—	—	—	—	—
Ordinary bow	21	21	7.2	3.6	—	—	—	—	—
Longbow	36	36	6.6	—	—	—	—	—	—
Crossbow	33	33	2.0	—	—	—	—	—	—
Harquebus	10	—	3.8	—	—	—	—	—	—
17th-century musket	19	—	—	—	—	—	—	—	—
18th-century flintlock	43	—	8.6	4.3	2.2	1.7	—	—	—
Early 19th-century rifle	36	—	—	3.6	1.8	1.4	—	—	—
Mid-19th-century rifle	102	—	—	—	—	4.1	—	—	—
Late-19th-century rifle	153	—	—	—	—	6.1	0.61	0.050	—
Springfield model 1903 rifle	495	—	—	—	—	—	1.98	0.170	0.120
World War I machine gun	3,463	—	—	—	—	—	14.00	1.150	0.870
World War II machine gun	4,973	—	—	—	—	—	—	1.660	.240

16th-century 12-pdr cannon	43	43	8.6	—	—	—	—	—	—
17th-century 12-pdr cannon	224	—	45.0	22.0	—	—	—	—	—
Gribeauval 12-pdr cannon	940	—	—	94.0	47.0	38.0	—	—	—
French 75mm gun	386,530	—	—	—	—	—	1,546.00	129.000	97.000
155mm GPF	912,428	—	—	—	—	—	3,650.00	304.000	228.000
105mm howitzer	657,215	—	—	—	—	—	—	219.000	164.000
155mm "Long Tom"	1,180,681	—	—	—	—	—	—	394.000	295.000
World War I tank	34,636	—	—	—	—	—	139.00	12.000	—
World War II medium tank	935,458	—	—	—	—	—	—	312.000	234.000
World War I fighter-bomber	31,909	—	—	—	—	—	128.00	11.000	—
World War II fighter-bomber	1,245,789	—	—	—	—	—	—	415.000	311.000
V-2 ballistic missile	3,338,370	—	—	—	—	—	—	1,113.000	835.000
20 Kt. nuclear airburst	49,086,000	—	—	—	—	—	—	16,362.000	12,272.000
One megaton nuclear airburst	695,385,000	—	—	—	—	—	—	231,795.000	173,846.000

been formulated nearly half a century earlier by a British aeronautical engineer, Frederick William Lanchester, on the eve of World War I. (Almost simultaneously, a similar set of equations was being developed by a Russian mathematician, Osipov. The basic concept of the Lanchester Equations had been suggested in an article in an American naval professional journal almost ten years earlier and had been described in practical terms by Karl von Clausewitz in the early 1830s.) In essence, the Lanchester Equations postulated a mathematical relationship between the firepower of two opposing forces and the casualties they inflicted on each other. It was essential for models based upon the Lanchester Equations to have some relatively precise (and hopefully accurate, although the analysts did not worry too much about that) method of representing firepower.

The model designers seized upon the firepower scores used for the guidance of umpires in field exercises as the means of achieving the necessary quantitative precision. It was not long, however, before the designers and the users of these models began to express considerable dissatisfaction with these firepower scores. There were various reasons for this dissatisfaction, but most important was the inability of the scores to reflect the fact that, in reality, the effectiveness of the weapons varied from one combat situation to another, and a single number representation of a weapon's capability was intellectually unsatisfactory. Subsequently, in the 1960s and 1970s, firepower scores came to be supplanted by scoring techniques called weapons effectiveness indexes (WEIs) and weapons unit values (WUVs), which were combined into a system called WEI-WUVs.

There was not much more satisfaction with the WEI-WUVs than there had been with the firepower scores, and various other methods of representing firepower were introduced, none of which gained enthusiastic endorsement. Perhaps the most widely used of these alternative systems was one called armored division equivalent (ADE). This was in reality a return (without significant improvement) to the old and relatively crude method of expressing firepower in early war games by means of unit comparison.

Lethality

In the mid-1960s, a system for quantifying the lethality of weapons was developed in the United States. This system attempted to relate the effectiveness of all weapons, from antiquity to the present, to each other by means of a scoring system that combined consideration of rate of strikes (whether by firepower or nonfirepower weapons), targets per strike, range, accuracy, reliability, mobility, and protection. When applied to the characteristics of a weapon theoretically employed against an infinite array of targets, each occupying one square meter (approx. 10 sq. ft.), this system calculated the number of targets that would be destroyed by the weapon in one hour. This number was then considered the theoretical lethality index (TLI) of the weapon.

The TLI methodology demonstrated that continuing improvements in weapons technology, beginning early in the seventeenth century, had brought about dramatic increases in the theoretical lethality of firepower weapons. This was logical to anyone familiar with the manner in which technology has been applied to weapons over the past four centuries. Table 1 shows TLI values for typical weapons over the course of history. It was difficult, however, to reconcile these steadily and exponentially increasing lethality values with a persistent historical fact: daily casualty rates for military forces exposed to hostile firepower have steadily declined over those same four centuries.

It was subsequently recognized that there was another historical phenomenon that had accompanied the declining casualty rates of modern history: dispersion of troops on the battlefield has steadily increased over these same four centuries, apparently related to the steadily increasing lethality of firepower.

When the TLI values are modified by one additional factor, which reflects standard dispersion patterns for a historical era, the resulting values are consistent with the declining casualty rates. This is further shown in Table 1, where the TLI values of the weapons listed are modified for different historical eras by factor values reflecting the then-current tactical dispersion patterns of military forces. The values resulting from this application of a dispersion factor to the TLIs are known as operational lethality indices, or OLIs. These OLIs provide to operations research analysts, and others concerned with the concept of firepower, a precise and apparently realistically accurate measurement of the actual application of firepower on a battlefield.

Trevor N. Dupuy

See Also: Land Forces, Effectiveness and Efficiency of; Maneuver.

Bibliography

Dupuy, T. N. 1985. *Numbers, predictions, and war*. Rev. ed. Fairfax, Va.: HERO Books.
——. 1987. *Understanding war: History and theory of combat*. New York: Paragon House.
Hughes, B. P. 1975. *Firepower: Weapons effectiveness on the battlefield, 1630–1850*. New York: Scribner's.
U.S. Department of the Army. 1973. *Field Manual 105-5: Maneuver control*. Washington, D.C.: Government Printing Office.

FLAMETHROWER

Flamethrowers are weapons that project and ignite incendiary fuels. First known in history by the name "Greek fire," early versions used a mixture of sulphur, pitch, niter, petroleum, and other substances to burn enemy ships and installations. Flamethrowers were employed in both land and naval warfare at least as early as the seventh century by the Byzantines, who called them "liquid fire."

The modern flamethrower operates by projecting a stream of burning incendiary fluid from a nozzle under pressure of about 13 to 30 atmospheres. The rate of fuel discharge may vary from 2 to 20 liters (0.5 to 5 gal.) per second, depending on the size of the flamethrower employed. A variety of ignition systems may be used, including electric sparks, pyrotechnics, and mechanical ignition systems. Early flamethrowers used unthickened fuels. When a thickened fuel, known as napalm, was introduced into use during World War II, the range of the flamethrower was doubled. As napalm is forced through the flamethrower's nozzle, the jelly momentarily becomes liquid, then regains its viscosity after the shearing force is removed.

Flamethrowers consist of three principal components: an incendiary agent, the means of ignition, and a delivery system for conveying the flame to the target. The incendiary agent may be either a scatter type, which is most effective against readily combustible targets, or the direct casualty type used against personnel. There are four groups of incendiary agents: metal incendiaries, pyrotechnic incendiaries, pyrophoric incendiaries, and oil-based incendiaries. Certain additives are used to increase the destructive effect of the incendiary agents as well as to modify their flow properties, prolong their burning times, and increase their burning temperatures. At the outset of World War II rubber was the most commonly used thickening agent. Later it was found that certain soaps had a number of advantages as additives. When napalm was discovered, in 1942, it proved to be a superior additive when mixed with gasoline.

Tactical Employment

Modern flamethrowers are carried by foot soldiers, armored fighting vehicles, rockets, helicopters, and boats. They are used mainly on the offense but are also employed in defense. The objective in both postures is to assist troops in close combat, such as the attack and defense of bunkers and other defensive structures (Fig. 1).

Flamethrowers project lethal streams of burning liquid over obstacles, around corners and into crevices, into narrow openings, and inside walled fortifications and pillboxes. They are equally effective in rugged and broken terrain and where other weapons fail to dislodge defenders from tenaciously held positions and caves and tunnels.

Flamethrowers are also used to attack areas containing well-concealed defenses whose precise location is not known. Sprayed napalm can burn away camouflage to reveal the enemy. As offensive weapons, flamethrowers are also used to destroy pockets of organized resistance left behind by the main body of enemy troops and to reveal suspected ambush positions. Equally useful opportunities for employment of flamethrowers occur in defense, advances, meeting engagements, and withdrawals, especially in jungle and urban fighting.

TACTICAL AND TECHNICAL DRAWBACKS

The range of flamethrowers is much shorter than that of small-arms fire, necessitating ample cover, fire, and smoke for their effective employment. Their fuel capacity is limited, and their operation may fail unless they completely saturate the target with flame. To this end, several flamethrowers may have to

Figure 1. Chinese forces storm Tengchung, 1931–37. (SOURCE: Imperial War Museum, London)

be employed simultaneously on the same target. Portable flamethrowers are rather heavy and cumbersome, making them less maneuverable. The coordination required between different operating crews, and with their fire-support and cover units, increases the complexity of operations involving flamethrowers and reduces the number of occasions for their successful use in battle. The fire of flamethrowers remains in the target area for some minutes, but if target effect is required for a longer time many flamethrowers may have to be employed, and a nearby refueling point for flamethrowers may even have to be established. Finally, there are the effects of wind, which may interfere with the effective employment of flamethrowers; head winds shorten the range of such weapons, while flanking winds can deflect the flames from their target.

Types of Flamethrowers

The two principal types of flamethrower are man-portable and mechanized. The man-portable flamethrower is carried on the back of a foot soldier. It consists of a tank of thickened fuel or napalm, another tank of compressed air, and a nozzle and igniter system through which the thickened fuel, unthickened gasoline, or napalm is ejected. A typical portable weapon weighs about 25 kilograms (55 lb.) and holds about 11.2 kilograms (25 lb.) of fuel or 15 liters (4 gal.) of napalm. Napalm, a common fuel, can be projected to a distance of about 25 meters (80 ft.) in either a single 8-second burst or a series of shorter bursts.

Mechanized flamethrowers have longer ranges, reaching in some cases as far as 200 meters (660 ft.). They can hold as much as 1,300 liters (343 gal.) of napalm, enough to fuel a sustained burst of 1 minute or several shorter bursts.

Incendiary rockets fired from portable launchers are beginning to replace portable flamethrowers in some of their battlefield roles.

Post–World War II Developments

The Swiss multishot SIFRAG "S" 55 was introduced about 1957. It weighs 20 kilograms (44 lb.) and has a fuel capacity of 18 liters (4.7 gal.). This weapon incorporates a new ignition system featuring ten pyrotechnic cartridges in a magazine from which they can be fired automatically. It also has an improved range of up to 80 meters (260 ft.) with the use of thickened fuel.

The U.S. M-202A1 portable flamethrower illustrates the trend toward compatible weapon systems such that a single weapon can be used to launch a variety of warheads. This modern weapon can also launch antitank rocket-assisted projectiles. It fires up to four small rockets, each containing 6 liters (1.6 gal.) of TPA (polyisobutylene-thickened retiethylaluminum), to a range of several hundred meters. The agent ignites on impact rather than at the nozzle of the weapon, as was the case with earlier types. When fully loaded the system weighs about 12 kilograms (26 lb.). It can place bursts of flame over a radius of 10 to 20 meters (30 to 65 ft.) for a period of 8 to 9 seconds.

The U.S. Navy has mounted flame guns (the same weapons used in the M-67 flamethrower tank) on patrol boats for use against targets on riverbanks. They are housed in two flame-tank cupolas built into the foredeck of the patrol craft. The hold of the vessel can accommodate up to 100 gallons of napalm fuel for the weapons, whose range is about 200 meters (660 ft.).

Taking a different approach, West Germany has produced smaller systems that use one small disposable fuel container with a capacity of about 1.8 liters (0.5 gal.). The system has a range of 40 meters (130 ft.). The Germans also have a weapon consisting of a small, handheld tube launcher that fires an incendiary grenade. The grenade is derived from the Blend-Brandt Handgranate (BBH), an incendiary grenade containing a mixture of red phosphorus and a metallic powder such as aluminum. When ignited, it produces a ball of fire that causes severe burns and thick smoke.

The French LEP-58 flamethrower weighs 7.5 kilograms (16.5 lb.) and has a capacity of 3 liters (0.8 gal.) of fuel. It can fire one or two shots to a range of about 45 meters (150 ft.). The Italians have a light and efficient portable flamethrower that is also easy to operate. It consists of a tank assembly, a flexible hose, and a flame gun. Its range is more than 60 meters (200 ft.).

The LPO-50 flamethrower is the standard flame weapon that was used by Warsaw Pact armies. It consists of a tank group, hose, and gun group. There are three tanks, each topped by a pressure-relief valve and a cap for the filling aperture, which also contains the chamber for the pressurizing cartridge. Ignition in this system is achieved through the use of a slow-burning pyrotechnic cartridge, three of which are grouped below the muzzle of the flame gun. When the trigger is depressed, energy is supplied from a power pack of four dry cells to one of the ignition cartridges. This weapon's tank capacity is 3.3 liters (0.9 gal.), sufficient to support a 2- to 3-second burst.

Mechanized flamethrowers of the lighter type are exemplified by the U.S. M-132, which is a flame weapon mounted in a converted M-113 armored personnel carrier. Its flame gun has a range of up to 210 meters (690 ft.) and a maximum firing duration of 32 seconds. A heavier type weapon is the M-67A1/ A2, which is based on a converted M-48 medium tank. A dummy 90mm gun barrel, provided with holes in its sides for ventilation and holes and drop shields in the bottom for drainage, houses an M7A1-6 flame gun. This system has a fuel capacity of about 1,500 liters (400 gal.) of napalm, a range of up to 250 meters (820 ft.), and a single-shot maximum duration of 61 seconds. The XM-551 Sheridan armored airborne assault vehicle, which has a 152mm gun, will also be produced in a flamethrower version. It will thus be able to use encapsulated flame rounds in addition to Shillelagh missiles and conventional rounds.

MAMDOUH H. ATTIYA

SEE ALSO: Jungle Warfare; Land Warfare; Siege.

Bibliography

Hogg, J., ed. 1987. *Jane's infantry weapons.* London: Jane's.
SIPRI. 1971. *The problem of chemical and biological weapons.* Vol. 1, *The rise of CW weapons.* Stockholm: SIPRI.
———. 1978. *Anti-personnel weapons.* Stockholm: SIPRI.

FORCE STRUCTURE

The concept of force structure is the central idea around which most of the armies, navies, and air forces in the world are designed, formed, and supported. A force structure is the set of military units in an armed force or in all of the armed forces of a nation and describes, in part, the potential military capability of the armed force or nation. It is correct to refer, for example, to the force structure of the U.S. Army or the British navy and to the force structure of France or Russia.

Military units are battalions, companies and batteries, ships, squadrons, and any other organizational entity that is called a unit. Aggregations or sets of units are organizations (associated by a common commander) and forces (associated by a common mission). A force structure may be considered a set of forces, although the exact size and composition of a force depend on the mission and situation. A force structure may be regarded as a set of units of various types from which organizations and forces may be created to accomplish military missions.

Force structure is one of three elements of force posture, the other two being location and readiness. Force posture is an expression of the peacetime ability of a military force to accomplish wartime missions. Location is relative to the place where the wartime mission will occur—in the potential combat zone, in the probable theater of operations, or in a rear area. Readiness in its physical sense is the extent to which the force structure units have their wartime authorizations of people and equipment on hand in peacetime. Force posture can be expensive because the more that the location and readiness of a force structure conform to wartime demands, the more money it takes to support that force structure in peacetime.

In order to reduce the fiscal and manpower burdens of supporting military forces, units within a force structure are commonly placed in peacetime into different components—active, reserve, and standby (cadre)—each with a different mix of full-time, part-time, and augmentation personnel. The total force structure potentially available for combat operations includes all of the units from these three components plus additional units that may be formed upon mobilization.

The size of a force structure is described by its structure strength—the aggregate of the total wartime authorized personnel strength of each unit in the force structure. Describing the size of a force structure in terms of military personnel authorized or assigned in peacetime is inaccurate. It is advantageous to use structure strength to compare the sizes of different or alternative force structures because it is independent of peacetime economies, relates entirely to potential wartime operations, and establishes the demands that the personnel and supply systems must plan to meet during wartime. It is useful for some purposes to describe the content of a force structure in terms of the major organizations or items of equipment it contains. A navy can be described by the numbers and types of battle groups or combatant ships it includes; an air force, by the numbers and types of aircraft wings or squadrons; and an army, by the numbers and types of combat divisions or battalions. Strategic nuclear forces usually are described by the numbers and types of nuclear delivery vehicles they contain. Merely listing major organizations or equipment items, however, fails to capture the contribution and cost of the many diverse support units required to sustain the combat operations of the ships, squadrons, and combat battalions; nor does it convey an idea of the total size of a force structure.

The concept of force structure facilitates explicit recognition of demands for the military and civilian personnel to man the units, for the materiel to equip the units, and for the consumable supplies needed to train and operate the units. It allows military planners to make estimates of combat capability and net assessments of relative combat power, and it makes possible the rational design of military forces to provide maximum combat power for a given set of resources.

JOHN R. BRINKERHOFF

SEE ALSO: Organization, Army; Reserve Components.

FORMATION

In military usage, the term *formation* has three meanings. First, a formation is a military unit of division size or larger. Second, a formation is a specific and stylized array or grouping of fighting personnel and/or equipment, deployed so as to maximize combat power while still providing security, flexibility, and rapid response. Third, a formation is a military drill team.

Formation as a Unit

Examples of formations as units include divisions, consisting of several brigades, and army corps comprising a number of divisions and corps troops units. The term *formation* in this context was originally limited to U.S. and British usage but has become relatively common in NATO as well. The term *field* or *fighting formation* normally describes a force engaged in combat, thus operating under field and active service conditions. A formation is usually commanded by a major general or higher ranking officer. The following are the principal land force formations.

DIVISION

A division consists of a headquarters, two or more brigades (or regiments in the former Soviet ground forces and other armies), and divisional troops units. Divisional troops units provide the formation with combat support and combat service support but are not part of the constituent brigades. They may be allotted in direct support of one or more of the brigades for an operation or for a specified period of time. As an organization, a division is larger than a brigade but smaller than an army corps.

In some armed forces, the basic fighting formation is the division; in others, it is the brigade. In most, the divisions incorporate combat, combat support, and combat service support units permanently under their command; this gives the division, as a fighting force, an ensured degree of tactical autonomy and logistic self-sufficiency. There are exceptions, and some armies organize divisions as tactical groupings of combat units with most support and combat service support held permanently at the army corps level and allotted to support divisions directly when necessary.

The most common divisional nomenclatures include armored or tank; armored infantry, mechanized infantry, or motorized rifle; infantry; air assault; airborne; and mountain.

The term *division* is also used to signify a branch or department of headquarters staff, such as the armaments and standardization division of the international military staff at NATO headquarters. It is manned on a single-service, joint, or combined basis.

ARMY CORPS

An army corps consists of a headquarters, two or more divisions, and corps troops units. Corps troops units provide the corps with combat support and combat service support but are not components of one of the divisions. These units may be allotted to one or more of the divisions for an operation or a specified time period. In most modern armies, two or more corps form a field army. In NATO, however, there are no field armies, and combinations of two or more army corps are called army groups. (In the Warsaw Pact, the equivalent of an army corps was an army, although a Warsaw Pact army usually contained four or five divisions.)

FIELD ARMY

A field army consists of a headquarters, two or more army corps, and army troops. Army troops provide combat (rear-area defense), combat support (such as missile and deep-penetration patrol units), and combat service support (rear communications, information, logistic, and administrative facilities). These are not part of the corps but may be allotted to indirect support of one or more corps for an operation or specified time period. As an organization, a field army is larger than an army corps and smaller than an army group. In NATO, there are no field armies; several corps are combined to form an army group. (In the Warsaw Pact, there was no direct equivalent to a field army.)

ARMY GROUP

An army group is a formation composed of a headquarters and two or more field armies. In NATO, however, an army group takes the place of the field army and consists of a combined (multinational) headquarters and several national army corps under a designated allied commander. (In the Warsaw Pact, the formation equivalent to an army group was called a front.)

Formation as an Array

In modern land warfare, the use of particular formations on the battlefield has become rare, and what remains has become nearly indistinguishable from small-unit tactics. The use of formations has persisted in aerial and naval combat.

AERIAL FORMATION

The increased range and lethality of modern aerial weapons have forced a greater dispersion of combat aircraft in aerial battle. It is unlikely that air forces will return to rigid formations that maximize the bombers' defense capabilities, such as the U.S. Army Air Corps "box" formation of World War II.

Despite these considerations, some aerial formations remain important. For example, most bombing missions require that attacking aircraft remain in visual contact to ensure that they arrive at the target concurrently to maximize their effect. To reduce the possibility of mishap or confusion, most air forces have developed standard bomber formations that ensure a particular place for each aircraft.

Similarly, fighter aircraft usually operate in flights of four, consisting of two leaders and their respective wingmen. Some types of aircraft operate in formations only under certain circumstances. Transport aircraft, for instance, resort to flying in formation only when a large number of them must arrive over their destination concurrently, such as when they conduct an airborne assault. In these situations, formations must be carefully maintained so that all aircraft can complete their missions without interfering with one another.

NAVAL FORMATION

Traditionally, naval warships have maneuvered and fought in a line-ahead formation. This not only simplifies command and control, but also allows for maximum use of the ships' guns, especially those mounted in turrets. Consideration of the line-ahead formation reveals that a line of ships crossing ahead of or behind another line at a 90-degree angle enjoys a great superiority of available firepower. This tactic is called "crossing the T"; its use in naval battles has often been decisive, as in the U.S. naval victory against the Japanese at the Battle of Surigao Strait in the Philippines on 24–25 October 1944. Modern missile-armed warships do not use formations as often as their gun-armed predecessors.

Employment of warships in specific roles, such as destroyers and cruisers protecting an aircraft carrier or escort vessels shepherding a convoy of transports, is properly an issue of naval tactics.

Drill Formation

Drill formations are intended to organize troops and move them in an orderly fashion. Some formations are highly disciplined, such as the formation of units passing in review on a parade field. Field marching formations vary in organization depending on whether speed of advance, troop protection, or another factor has highest priority. Finally, informal formations are used when any number of troops are moved from one place to another, such as from a barracks to a mess hall. Such formations contribute to maintaining discipline and ensure order when large numbers of troops are positioned in relatively close quarters.

J. H. SKINNER
JOHN F. GERACI

SEE ALSO: Organization, Army; Tactics.

Bibliography

Dupuy, R. E., and T. N. Dupuy. 1985. *The encyclopedia of military history.* 2d ed., rev. New York: Harper and Row.
Hackett, J. 1983. *The profession of arms.* New York: Macmillan.
Keegan, J. 1987. *The mask of command.* New York: Viking Penguin.
Perret, G. 1989. *A country made by war.* New York: Random House.

FORTIFICATION

The history of fortification began millennia ago when man first modified the surface of the earth for defensive purposes. Structures built for defense evolved in response to the technological development of arms. Simultaneously, fortifications stimulated the invention and production of weapons. As the latter became more effective, fortifications grew to giant forms, although they have never been invincible. Some theorists assert that fortresses are obsolete; others point to the records of World War II, the Arab-Israeli wars, and the Iran-Iraq War to insist that fortifications today are as important as they ever were.

Prehistoric Man and Warfare

It is likely that in prehistoric times—before the time of written records—war did not exist. During that period men were completely occupied with daily survival and had no spare time for planned acts of violence against fellow men. Population was sparse. Brawls among members of a family or between different tribes were probably spontaneous. Small groups of people, each consisting of a few families, moved over the surface of the earth, always fighting for subsistence.

This changed greatly during the following period of cultural evolution. The domestication of animals and the beginnings of agriculture allowed people to gather in settlements, no longer completely dependent upon their individual physical abilities. Rules and structures for social life developed. With a larger, settled community came the gradual differentiation of roles and specialization of work. This in turn led to the evolution of class structure and the emergence of leaders—sometimes religious—who claimed authority over others and eventually fostered resentment and rebellion. The origin of walls is often explained as having a religious source. Many holy areas had distinguishing marks formed by rows of stones. These formed borderlines and symbolized blockades to evil spirits, bad gods, and other negative apparitions, preventing them from penetrating the sanctuary. Man learned that building even higher walls could prevent his own species from entering.

Over time rulers built residences or temples and often fortified them with ramparts or trenches. It is probable that these strongholds originally served to protect the rulers from their people rather than as a refuge for the local people in time of danger.

Stockades, walls, trenches, and towers on the periphery of prehistoric settlements came into existence at about the same time the residences of princes and priests were fortified. Both psychological and social factors doubtless played a part in these origins of fortification.

With larger congregations of population and the rise of authority came the inclination to spread rule and influence into neighboring areas. Fortifications then took on the larger role of protecting a community from external raids or reprisal. The existence of ancient palisades, ramparts, trenches, and towers is an early result of the rise of war and thereby enables us to determine the beginnings of organized armed conflict.

Beginnings of Fortification

For a long time the early use of defensive structures was thought to have occurred about 4000–3000 B.C. It was associated with the formation of states of some breadth and importance with power concentrated in the cities.

The results of archaeological research at Jericho, in Palestine, have overturned all former assumptions. Beginning in the 1860s, several expeditions searched for the famed "Walls of Jericho" that tumbled down when Joshua ordered the trumpets of the Israelites to be blown. The early expeditions failed to locate the walls, but in the early 1950s researchers under the direction of British archaeologist Kathleen Kenyon made a sensational find. A stone rampart about 6 meters (20 ft.) high with a trench in front of it (width: 9.5 meters [31 ft.]; depth: more than 2 meters [6.5 ft.]) were excavated. The remains of a tower, probably a little later in origin than the aforementioned fortifications, were found behind them. Close examination of all discoveries in the area showed Jericho to have been an extraordinarily old community (first settlement: 9637–7770 B.C.). Fortifications were dated about 8340 B.C. (plus or minus 100 years). With that, the history of fortification had a new date of beginning. The archaeological discoveries prove that in preceramic periods man was already building significant structures for defense.

Ruling Principles of Fortification

Fortifications take no active part in fighting. They are components of strategic and tactical plans and actions of warfare. The main aims of their existence and use are:

- blockade of access to the defended space
- protection of defenders against enemy weapons (shelter)
- improvement of effects of the defenders' weapons
- use as observation platforms.

Early fortifications show all these characteristics. Walls and obstacles prevented the enemy from entering the castle or town; sheltered the fighters on the ramparts from the stones, javelins, and arrows of the besiegers; and enhanced the defenders' weapons by using the force of gravity resulting from the defenders' position above the attackers. We may call the first rule the blocking-of-access principle (which includes the advantages of a higher position).

This principle favors the defenders. It is likely that the early development of protective personal armament for warriors was strongly inspired and promoted by this situation. The invention of helmets, shields, and other body armor may have been a reaction to the efficiency of the missiles thrown from fortifications. These improvements in turn led to changes in principles of fortification. The improved protection of the bodies of attacking warriors, especially the use of shields, greatly diminished the superiority of the defenders. With movable cover, besiegers could approach fortifications with less risk. The reaction to this new and dangerous situation can be stated in the *latus-apertu* principle (from Latin *latus*, wide, and *apertus*, open, or uncovered). This principle is a completion of the blocking-of-access principle. It indicates a special arrangement of the component parts of the fortification system. The salients of the ramparts or principal towers in the system of walls gave opportunity not only to fight the attacker's front but to threaten him from many directions. The closer he came to the wall in front of him, the greater was the chance to attack his flank or even his back. He was unable to protect himself against the projectiles that now could reach him from many sides.

The rise of the *latus-apertu* principle marks the end of the elementary development in the construction of fortifications. Nearly all fortresses or fortified lines were built fundamentally in consideration of the two principles described above. Only modifications, without changes of the elementary systems, can be stated.

Ancient Fortification

EGYPT

Ancient Egypt had few fortresses or fortified cities, due to its geographical pseudo-insularity. Remains of fortifications that predate the unification of the empire along the Nile under the rule of pharaohs indicate instability of power and internal conflicts. Following unification under a supreme power, castles, fortresses, and fortified towns either were not erected or vanished. Those that did exist, in general, served against foreign enemies. Egypt had natural defenses formed by the deserts in the west, the Mediterranean in the north, and the Red Sea in the east; the southern borders and the Sinai Peninsula formed the weak points of the system of natural barriers. The threat to the southern regions was minimal; the primitive tribes living in ancient Sudan posed little threat to the armed forces of the pharaoh. Small garrisons of soldiers acting as border police were stationed in forts of clay and wood. Remains of three such forts have been found near Wadi Halfa.

Against invasions via the Sinai, Egypt built a glacis by conquering Palestine, Lebanon, Jordan, and the greater part of Syria. The garrisons in the occupied cities of this buffer zone acted only as outposts. They observed enemy actions and defended the fortified places until the main army of the pharaoh advanced from Egypt. If bypassed by attackers, the garrisons remained a threat to the rear and flanks of the invaders.

MESOPOTAMIA

Mesopotamia, the fertile land around the Euphrates and Tigris rivers, has been the objective of numerous invasions by nearby peoples and tribes from early times. The inhabitants were forced to prepare the defense of their homes and other properties. The topography was unfavorable for defense. The river plains lack elevation and thus offer no ideal positions for fortification. Only the numerous swamps and sheets of water helped to offset this deficiency. The urban fortifications of Mesopotamia, to compensate for the weakness of their positions, had especially strong, high walls and towers of brick. Today we can still admire these enormous ramparts and towers or at least their impressive ruins—for example those of Babylon, erected about 600–560 B.C.

INDIA

In the Indus valley, another region with long cultural traditions, archaeologists discovered defensive installations of cities dating back to about 2300 B.C. The fortifications were not in the form of walls surrounding the settlements. Rather, the houses were walled in and built like a close ring of fortresses around the citadel or castle of the king or governor.

The *Arthashastra* (Book of Government and Life in the World) is a voluminous work by a Brahman named Kautalya who presumably served under King Chandragupta (321–297 B.C.) as minister and counselor. It describes in detail the construction of fortifications for castles and cities (see Figure 1). Kautalya is one of the earliest authorities on the architecture of engineering works for defensive purposes.

CHINA

According to present archaeological knowledge, walled cities existed in China before 1500 B.C. The ramparts were built of bricks and formed in a strict square. In many places, new and larger walls had to be constructed in consequence of population growth. Exact distances between the older walls and the new ones show that Chinese architects used mathematical surveying methods in ancient times. The walls of Nanjing, built in the fourteenth century while the city was China's capital, still exist; with a total length of 30 kilometers (18.6 mi.), they are the longest urban walls in the world.

China's other famous fortification, the Great Wall, will be discussed later.

GREECE

Greece, the mother of European-Atlantic culture, contributed surprisingly little to the development of fortification. This is mainly due to topography and mentality. Castles built of huge stones in pre-Hellenic eras, such as the Mycenaean period (about 1600 B.C.), give an impression of being constructed by giants. But later, many cities and towns were not fortified at all. They usually had a citadel (acropolis), for which sufficient protection was afforded by its high elevation with narrow passes that could be defended easily by a few fighters. Athens trusted in its "wooden walls," the ships of its fleet. The Spartans defended their country by their "human walls," the army. These haughty strategic views proved dangerous when in 480 B.C. the Persian king Xerxes invaded Greece. The combined operation of the Persian army and fleet left Athens

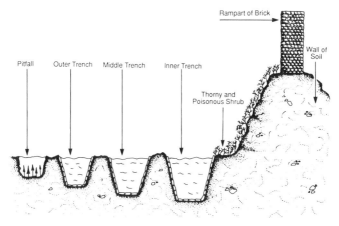

Figure 1. Sketch of urban fortifications in India according to the Arthashastra (*about 300* B.C.). (SOURCE: Schwalm, 1986)

defenseless. Its land forces were inferior to those of the intruders and unable to hold the unfortified city. Athens was evacuated and taken by the Persians without striking a blow.

After the retreat of the Persians following their defeat at sea, Themistocles (Athens's leader and victor in the naval battle of Salamis) ordered the city fortified. In a short time an urban wall made of brick was erected. The urgency of the work can be seen in the use of tombstones from Athens's cemeteries for the foundation of the walls. Between 461 and 445 B.C. Athens's defensive structures were greatly enlarged by construction of the famous "long walls." These enclosed a large area of Attica, the land between Athens and the sea.

Even the Spartans finally learned the advantages of fortification, but their efforts were insufficient to stop the Roman conquerors (about 200 B.C.).

ROMAN MILITARY INFRASTRUCTURE

The Roman Empire was founded and preserved by military force. The legions of the republic and later of the emperors guarded the expanded borders of the provinces against raids and invasion. They fulfilled this task effectively with the help of military infrastructure in the form of fortified borderlines, castles along these lines, and legion camps. The fortified borderlines in Germany and Scotland (Limes and Hadrian's Wall) were not actually meant for defensive action. These fortifications, formed by dry trenches and walls bearing palisades, were intended to deter invaders. Towers stood along the fortified lines at intervals that made light signals or other signs possible. Fortified camps in the borderline system served as garrisons for the patrols along the walls and the guards in the towers. They could even withstand attack and siege, having strong ramparts and towers bearing catapults for stones, arrows, and javelins.

The actual defense of the borders of the empire was entrusted to the legions in the camps. Integrated into the borderline system or situated at some distance in the interior, the camps were a combination of fortress and barracks. They could accommodate some 20,000 soldiers, the horses of cavalry units, the supply lines, and the provisions of food, feed, equipment, and weapons. From here the legions advanced toward invading tribes or armies, which thus were in a bad position, having the legions before them and the troops of the border defenses in the rear.

The legion camps and the border castles were true copies of the Roman bivouacs in their arrangement of buildings and lines of fortification. The marching order of the legions for halts before dark or in case of approaching hostile forces assigned the quick setup of the tents in strict order. The soldiers were to dig out a dry trench, pile up the soil to a wall behind, and fortify it with palisades. The latter, with the equipment for the work, were carried on the march by horses, donkeys or mules, or by the soldiers themselves. Legion camps and castles (see Figure 2), functioning as fortresses, had stronger ramparts and trenches, with towers at especially vulnerable points such as the corners of the quadrangular garrisons or at the gates (usually four). The gates were protected by *claviculae* (little hooks), salient walls that were connected with the ramparts and ran in front

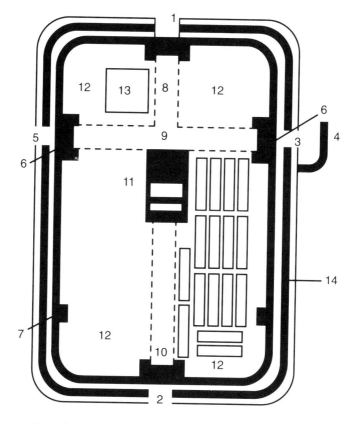

1 Porta Praetoria   8 Via Praetoria
2 Porta Decumana   9 Via Principalis
3 Porta Principalis Dextra   10 Via Decumana
4 Clavicula   11 Praetorium and Principia
5 Porta Prinicipalis Sinistra 12 Location of barracks
6 Gateway Towers   13 Horreum
7 Tower   14 Walls and ditches

Figure 2. Sketch of a Roman castle of the Limes. (SOURCE: Schwalm, 1982)

of the gates. They made it possible to engage from several sides an enemy who tried to attack the gates (*latus-apertu* principle).

The fortification systems of the Romans were simple and effective. At first constructed of clay and wood, they were later built of stone. All forms of fortification reflected the strict military order of the empire. Serving as bases of provision and rear cover for the armies, they also offered excellent protection in case of siege. They influenced the military infrastructure of the Middle Ages.

CELTIC FORTIFICATION

The Celtic tribes and clans were originally settled in the upper Rhine Valley. Beginning in the fifth century B.C. they spread over vast parts of Europe, reaching even the periphery of the continent (Ireland and Scotland) and Asia Minor (Turkey). They held their conquests not only by the bravery and ferocity of their warriors but also by their superior ability to build fortifications around their towns and the seats of their princes.

The Celts' method of constructing walls is called *murus gallicus*. It is known to us not only from archaeological research but also from Caesar's description in his report on his campaigns in Gaul (France), *De Bello Gallico*. Caesar praised the beauty and effectiveness of the Celtic walls. Constructed of clay and wood, they had an exterior facing of stone. The construction provided not only protection against fire but also firmness and elasticity at the same time, and it could absorb the blows of siege weapons. It may be assumed that the Celts' use of stones as building elements influenced Roman military architecture after the wars in Gaul (58–51 B.C.). The Celts also gained advantage by building their fortifications along ideal topographic lines. Their walls and ramparts, therefore, lacked the exactitude of Roman constructions.

AFRICA

The oldest and most remarkable African fortifications, other than the fortified Arab cities and castles of northern Africa, are those of Great Zimbabwe in the southern part of the continent. Dating from the tenth to the sixteenth centuries, they feature impressively thick walls that form outer and inner rings of defense for an acropolis or citadel. The interior of the fortified settlement is further divided by walls that, in conjunction with the fortified gateways, afforded a most impressive and effective defense of every area.

AMERICA

Pre-Columbian America's fortifications are comparable to megalithic forms of construction in Asia (China) and Europe (for example, Mycenae). Important fortified sites existed in Bolivia (Acapana) and Peru (Machu Picchu, Cuzco, Allantaylambo).

Fortification in the Middle East

The neolithic era of fortification in Europe, characterized by relatively primitive blockades that provided refuge in time of war, ended with the Celts. Overcome by the Romans, the Celtic population of central and western Europe was overrun by migrating Germanic tribes after the retreat of the Romans, which ended about A.D. 401. Some Germanic tribes settled there; others, pushed forward by following waves of their kin from northern and eastern directions, finally spread over the western parts of former Celtic and Roman territories.

The Germanic population in general disliked fortifications, and there were few castles or walled settlements. Noblemen often fortified their residences with two rows of palisades, the space between them filled with soil and stones. The same kind of fortification was used for ring walls on hills, which served as a refuge for the population, their cattle, and goods in time of war. The Germans originally made no use of the Roman infrastructure, which they had often taken intact due to the sudden retreat of the former defenders. In many cases the German conquerors settled close to former Roman towns, using them as sources of building material for their own houses, barns, and stables and even for churches after they became Christians.

Change came as a result of Viking raids and invasions during the ninth and tenth centuries. These sea warriors from Denmark, Norway, and Sweden not only threatened the coastal areas of Germany, the British Isles, the Netherlands, Belgium, France, Spain, Portugal, and Italy; their shallow-draft boats enabled them to sail or row up navigable rivers into the interior. The aversion to fortifications of the leaders and population of the threatened areas had disastrous consequences. They became helpless victims of the sudden and brutal strikes of the robbing and burning intruders.

In Germany early in the tenth century a further danger arose in the form of Hungarian raids nearly every year. These invaders on horseback rode far into the north and west.

As a result of these threats, defensive measures were taken everywhere. The nobility built castles on elevations close to their rural homes, which were often abandoned. Villages and towns built defensive walls and obstacles. Preserved parts of Roman military infrastructure, especially the fortifications of former Roman cities, were repaired and sustained. The importance of these places grew as they became centers of defense.

MEDIEVAL FORTIFICATION TECHNIQUES

The fortifications of the early Middle Ages were primitive. They were usually oval in shape, following the contours of high ground. Built of soil and wood palisades, they were a throwback compared with Roman military architecture. The art of fortification had to be learned anew. The remains and ruins of Roman infrastructure served as examples. The builders of early medieval European defense works often did not entirely trust their stone walls and, therefore, secured them by excavating trenches and erecting walls with palisades in front of them.

The political consequences of the proliferation of fortifications all over Europe were remarkable. Not only could the castles and walled towns be defended against foreign enemies, they also provided opportunities for greater independence. For example, a prince could no longer simply force his will and aims upon a town or city in his territory; he had to establish his rule and influence there by negotiation and treaty. If they did not accept a noble's aims and conditions, the burghers of the medieval fortified towns could defend their position and keep the nobleman and his armed men out.

The kings of medieval Europe took advantage of this urban independence by bestowing the right of freedom to towns and cities as a political instrument to limit the powers of the nobility. This privilege protected, above all, the right to fortify the town or city with ramparts, gates, and towers. This improved the position of the kings in their perpetual struggles with the dukes, counts, and barons of their territories.

Medieval castles were the spectacular manifestation of the feudal system.

Like cities and towns, the fortified seats of the nobility granted a great deal of independence and self-determination to their owners and inhabitants. A castle was both a fortress and a residence. While in superficial appearance there was great diversity, the basic components of castle construction were relatively uniform all over Europe. Using easily defended positions on hills, islands, or other advantageous places, the castles' chief defense was their walls. These were protected by trenches or moats located in front of the walls, where excavation was possible, and where they were needed. Especially high walls protected sites easily accessible from the hillside plateau and acted as a massive shield against bombardment by stones and other missiles. The dominant part of every castle was the mighty *donjon*, or keep. Unless it was a part of the system of ramparts in the peripheral defense system of the castle, the donjon played no active part in defense, but served as a center for observation and command. It was the place of last refuge and ultimate defense. The gates, inevitably the most vulnerable points of the complete system, were protected by towers and, when possible, by drawbridges. The donjon usually overlooked the gates, an example of the *latus-apertu* principle, enabling the defenders to attack intruders from above and from all sides.

The fortifications of towns had the same fundamental components. Often a citadel or castle in the center of the city, or sometimes with one or two sides integrated into the city walls, was the place of ultimate defense, similar to the donjon of a castle. All medieval ramparts bore parapets giving a salient position to the defenders and thereby enabling them to shoot at besiegers who approached the wall. Towers in the line of the ramparts reinforced the strength of the fortification and the possible measures of resistance.

DECLINE OF CASTLES AND WALLED TOWNS

The siege techniques used by the Greeks and Romans had reached high standards, but this knowledge was lost after the fall of the Roman Empire. Sieges in early medieval times were primitive. As a consequence of the Crusades (between 1096 and 1270), the lost abilities and experiences were learned anew by the Europeans from the Byzantines and the Arabs, who had preserved them. In reaction to this greater threat in Europe, old fortifications were merely strengthened, not constructed in new forms. The loss of security affected by the new techniques of siege was considerable.

The deadly stroke to the fortifications, and to all kinds of engineering works for defensive purposes, was the introduction of gunpowder into Europe in the fourteenth century. Usable for blasting or as a propellant for projectiles fired from guns, it rendered even the strongest constructions destructible. The first reaction was to seek security in extremely thick walls, but this had limited success. A better solution was offered by a new method of construction. Inclined angles of the walls diminished the effectiveness of bombardment. The image of fortifications altered considerably. The height of defensive works no longer provided advantage; fortifications were built closer to the ground, in some cases even embedded into it.

The political consequences of this development were significant. Fortifications could be overcome more easily. The lesser nobility, unable to defend their strongholds, lost influence and independence. Fortified cities suffered the same fate and were unable to adapt their defense to the new reality mainly because of the enormous costs of construction. Only large, rich cities had sufficient money and workers to modernize their fortifications. Rural towns gave up maintaining their now useless towers and walls, sometimes exploiting them for cheap building material.

The supremacy of central monarchies was now imposed in Europe. Fortifications were seen as necessary elements of national defense under direction and control of the ruling kings or dukes. To support their generally aggressive policy, aimed at continual territorial expansion, rulers used cities with up-to-date defenses as bases for operations. High costs forced them to fortify only strategically important places. The engineering works for these were enormous. Glacis, walls, trenches, and platforms for defensive batteries surrounded the fortresses, forming "baroque stars," so-called because of the form of the zigzag of bulwarks and bastions. This zigzag in itself bore the advantages of the *latus-apertu* principle; approaching enemy forces were fired upon from several directions. All the fortresses of this time give an impression of impregnability; some indeed were never taken by siege or storm. This must be seen as good fortune, for in reality the efficiency of artillery weapons was growing steadily and only fortunate circumstances or the impatience of the besiegers saved fortified places.

After the end of feudalism, warfare became the duty of professional soldiers whose knowledge in handling arms was much greater than that of the levies in former times. At the same time, the expenditure for armed forces increased immensely. Therefore, commanders tried to defeat hostile forces quickly in open battle and thus avoid the high expense and great risks and losses of prolonged siege. So fortress cities gradually lost importance, although they continued to form an element in strategic systems by posing a threat to the lines of communication of invading enemy forces. At least some of these had to be manned for the observation of the fortresses, and this manpower was often grievously missed in case of battle.

The old fortifications around cities had a strongly confining effect. The economic development that began late in the seventeenth century demanded space for expansion, which was hindered by the ring of walls, turrets, bulwarks, and bastions. An early result was the change in construction of city dwelling houses, most of which had previously had one story. Three-story and even higher city houses were built to compensate for lack of ground space. In most cases, rapid growth of cities led to an abandonment of their fortified defense. Military developments in the eighteenth and nineteenth centuries initiated modern warfare, which was characterized by greater mobility and the expansion of war theaters to include large areas of countries in armed conflict.

Beginning in the sixteenth century structures were built that can be called "pure fortresses." They included a residential area that was populated only by the members of the garrison, their relatives, and other people connected with the forces. These fortresses existed only for military (i.e., strategic and tactical) purposes. France in particular tried to secure its frontier using a system of such fortresses in combination with fortified cities.

All the pure fortresses were surrounded by fortifications constructed to the highest standards, with great strength and admirable geometric exactitude; the size of the fortifications was greatly disproportionate to the size of the defended inner space. Constructed by the famous military architect Maréchal Sebastien Le Prestre de Vauban (1633–1707), the fortresses still impress by their vastness and their strict yet beautiful trace. Nevertheless, even these giant works were superseded. The chief obstacle to the successful utilization of localized fortifications in warfare was the power and efficiency of heavy siege artillery (battering guns).

Fortification in Modern Times

By the seventeenth century the era of the fortress was ending, although many military leaders maintained that it still had tactical and strategic uses. One means employed to counteract the far-reaching effects of attacking artillery was to construct a ring of forts (smaller fortresses) around the actual (main) fortress or fortified city. Defensive fire from these kept the enemy artillery at a distance. This system greatly extended the fortified area. Effective bombardment range reached 3 to 4 kilometers (2 to 3 mi.) in the early decades of the nineteenth century. Taking into account the range of guns, the distance between a main fortress and its forward forts in the second half of the century was 7 to 8 kilometers (4 to 5 mi.). The enormous space between the outer forts and the fortress had to be left free of buildings and cleared of trees and elevations that might affect observation and fire. This cleared area, called the "rayon," could at best be used for agricultural purposes. Yet the growing range of artillery weapons overcame all natural and technical obstacles. Even locating fortresses on islands did not afford security. For example, Fort Sumter, located on an island in the harbor of Charleston, South Carolina, capitulated in 1861 after bombardment by Confederate forces from the surrounding shores during the American Civil War.

New and better construction materials were tried as a counter to bombardment, but long and intensive fire neutralized any advantages.

The remaining effectiveness of localized forces ended abruptly when warfare became three-dimensional—that is, when attack from the air exposed newly vulnerable surfaces. This absolute end was symbolized in May 1940 by the conquest of the Belgian fort Eben-Emael during World War II by a German airborne assault.

Fortification for Linear Defense

Fortifications for linear defense have a long tradition. Doubtless the most famous fortified line of defense is the Chinese or Great Wall in the People's Republic of China. Originally, it was an uninterrupted system of forts that protected the frontier of the Chinese Empire against invasions from the north and west. It was finished as a complete barrier about the year 214 B.C. In subsequent centuries it was extended to a length of 2,200 kilometers (1,360 mi.). Its purpose was to hold off the nomadic tribes of the deserts and prairies of Mongolia. In the wars against the Hsiung-nu (Huns), beginning in 133 B.C., the Great Wall was lengthened to the west. The Ming emperors (1368–1644) restored the fortifications, using stone as building material, since many of them had been destroyed or fallen into ruin due to invasion or neglect.

Other ancient fortifications for linear defense are the Median Wall and the aforementioned Long Walls of Athens. The Median Wall was erected about 600 B.C. in a place where the courses of the Euphrates and Tigris rivers run relatively close. The wall protected the access toward Babylon, thus strengthening the fortifications of that great city. The latter secured the area of Attica between Athens and the sea.

The fortifications of long lines by the Romans are described above. Although minor works were built later, no major systems of defense formed by uninterrupted fortifications of remarkable length were constructed until the nineteenth century.

A revival is seen in France's measures to secure its border with Germany after the war of 1870–71. The fortifications had not yet reached a final state of construction when World War I broke out. They proved ineffective due to the strategy chosen by the Germans, who avoided frontal assaults on the fortification system west of the Rhine and instead outflanked it by marching north of it through neutral Belgium.

As a consequence France erected the Maginot line between 1929 and 1932 (see Figure 3). Constructed as a system of barriers and defensive works, the centers of gravity of the line were formed by strong, heavily armed artillery towers. Antitank barriers were installed in the advanced areas to protect against that new weapon, and designers, seeking an invulnerable system, placed components underground whenever possible. Again, the fortifications proved useless in the defense of French territory when the quick, outflanking march of German armies in World War II avoided direct confrontation at the line of fortifications.

Hitler's West Wall (Siegfried Line), built in 1938–39, consisted of a system of artificial barriers against tanks and infantry, including an average of 22 bunkers and fortified artillery emplacements for each kilometer of length. The line was erected mainly for strategic purposes, meant to protect Germany's rear from attacks by France and Britain during its war against Poland.

Other long fortified lines about the same time were the Stalin Line in Russia, the Czechoslovak Line (built to defend that country against Germany shortly before World War II), and the Mannerheim Line to protect the southeastern frontier of Finland against an anticipated Soviet attack.

The Atlantic Wall, Hitler's defense against an invasion by the Allies in World War II, reached from Denmark to the Spanish border. At 3,500 kilometers (2,170 mi.) it was the longest fortification for linear defense ever built. In most parts of the line, field fortifications were of minor strength; only points presumed to be likely targets of Allied actions were secured by strong bunkers with heavy armament.

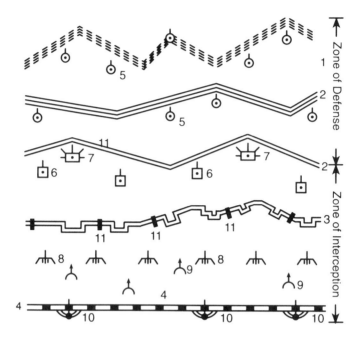

1.	Forward line of obstacles	7.	Emplacements (turrets),
2.	Wire entanglement (high voltage)		first category
3.	Prepared trenches (infantry)	8.	Emplacements for medium
4.	Railroad with sidings for heavy		and heavy artillery
	railroad artillery	9.	Air defense
5.	Emplacements (turrets),		emplacements
	third category	10.	Heavy railroad artillery
6.	Emplacements (turrets),	11.	Bomb-proof dugouts
	second category		

Figure 3. Linear defense in echelons (Maginot line). (SOURCE: Schwalm, 1982)

It is debatable whether any fortification built for linear defense met the aims set for it. Such lines needed strong forces for their defense and these were scattered over a great distance, so the strength of the defense force at a certain point of assault by enemy forces was limited. The longer the linear fortification, the more this effect was increased. Furthermore, even the longest fortifications usually could be outflanked.

Fortification and Architecture

The architecture of fortresses or fortified cities of the Baroque era shows a brilliant beauty in its trace. Planning and construction of defensive works aimed at gaining advantage and strength in combat against attackers and besiegers. At the same time, fortifications were a demonstration of the power and glory of their constructors. The ground plan, the position of the components in the system, their shape, and decoration could not be formed by a simple builder. Architects well acquainted with knowledge of defense and siege, of attack and counterattack, had to plan and construct useful installations that also showed beauty and harmony. It is no surprise that in late medieval times the architecture of fortifications became a profession not only of military engineers but also of renowned artists.

Albrecht Dürer (1471–1528), who is by far better known as an engraver, was also strongly occupied with theoretical studies and designs of fortifications. His work reflects the influence of the Italian architecture of his time.

A sixteenth-century architect of remarkable works in theoretical methods of fortification was Reinhard Count of Solms-Lich (1491–1562). His designs were greatly influenced by Dürer's. The most famous architect of fortifications of his time was Daniel Specklin (1536–89). Like Albrecht Dürer, he was impressed by the Italian defensive systems of the sixteenth century, and he followed in his designs the principles, shapes, and methods of Dürer's theoretical designs. His fortifications of Sélestat, Hagenau, Colmar, Strasbourg (all in Alsace), Ulm, Ingolstadt (both in Bavaria), and Basel (Switzerland) had great influence on French military architecture of the seventeenth century. So, a direct line of inspiration leads from Dürer to the pure fortresses of Vauban, the greatest designer of defensive constructions and systems.

Italian military architecture of the fifteenth and sixteenth centuries was the root of all modern fortifications, displaying the fundamental principles that govern the defense of places. Numerous Italian designers of castles, citadels, city fortifications, and fortresses inspired the Italian, French, German, and other European military architects of later centuries; several were especially ingenious and influential: Guiliano da Sangallo (1445–1516), Francesco di Giorgio (1439–1501), Michele Sanmicheli (1484–1559), and the genius Leonardo da Vinci (1452–1519). The latter, like Dürer, combined the professions of great artist and architect of military installations.

Conclusion

From their beginnings, fortifications continually changed form and shape in reaction to inventions that threatened their usefulness. At the same time, they stimulated such inventions by their mere presence or by the strength and resistance they showed against siege or attack.

Cases of destruction or occupation of defensive works and fortified places by assault are few in comparison with the number of such installations. Military leaders have usually tried to avoid the loss of time, the toil, and the high losses incurred in sieges. Treason and neglect were probably the most serious enemies of fortifications and their defenders until the modern era of heavy artillery and aerial attack. The field fortifications—the trenches, foxholes, rifle pits, wire entanglements, and so forth—of modern position warfare form installations comparable to the old fortifications; they follow the same governing principles and methods but are only primitive copies of the preceding works and lack their impressive power. Therefore, they can be considered a symbol of retrograde movement. Antonio Cassi-Ramelli entitled his book on the history of military architecture *Dalle Caverne ai Rifugi Blindati* (From Caverns to the Bunkers). In it he expressed the remarkable progress of civilization. Crawling out of the caverns of prehistoric times, man by his invention has progressed to a stage where he must crawl into the concrete caverns of modern times to gain a chance of survival. Hope remains that the air-raid shelters of our times may not be the ultimate refuge of mankind—the last fortification, from which he dares not venture.

HANSJÖRG SCHWALM

SEE ALSO: Artillery; Defense; Mine Warfare, Land; Offense; Siege.

Bibliography

Caesar, J. 1983. *The Gallic wars.* Trans. J. Warrington. Norwalk, Conn.: Easton Press.
Cassi-Ramelli, A. 1964. *Dalle caverne ai rifugi blindati.* Milan: Nuova Accademia Editrice.
Kenyon, K. M. 1967. *Archäologie im Heiligen Land.* Neukirchen-Vluyn: Neukirchener Verlag des Erziehungsvereins.
Mumford, L. 1961. *The city in history.* New York: Harcourt, Brace and World.
Neumann, H. 1988. *Festungsbaukunst und Festungsbautechnik.* Koblenz: Bernard and Graefe.
Schwalm, H. 1982. *Militärbauten.* Heidelberg; R. v. Decker's Verlag.
———. 1986. *Die Rolle des indischen Kreigswesens vor und während der Herrschaft Chandraguptas und seines Ministers Kautalya.* Osnabrück: Biblio Verlag.
Toy, S. [1939] 1985. *Castles: Their construction and history.* Reprint. New York: Dover Publications.

FRATRICIDE

In nonlethal environments, military and civilian, accidents resulting in injury or death are commonplace. In combat many casualties result from "friendly fire," a phenomenon called "fratricide" or "amicicide." In the vast majority of cases the casualties to friendly troops were unintended; in some few instances, they have been the tragic by-product of an intentional act.

The incidence of fratricide in military operations is not known and probably cannot be known with any degree of certainty. Casualty accounting categorizes casualties by type (whether killed, wounded, or captured/missing in action) and medical/surgical accounting categorizes casualties by causative agent (bullet, shell fragment, etc.). In most instances it is impossible to know, much less to record, whether the causative agent was "friendly" or enemy. Thus, evidence of fratricide is anecdotal.

The author of the only study of fratricide estimated that "casualties attributable to friendly fire in modern war constitute a statistically insignificant portion of total casualties (perhaps less than 2 percent)" (Shrader 1982, p. vii). It should be noted, however, that in certain operations incidents of fratricide have accounted for significant numbers of casualties.

Causes of Fratricide

In his examination of incidents of fratricide, Shrader found that human error was the "primary cause of most . . . incidents" (Shrader 1982, pp. 106–7). The possibility of error is present in all human affairs, since man is a fallible being. However, the possibility of error is increased by combat.

The single element that separates actual combat from all human attempts to replicate it, such as war games or training exercises, is the lethality of the environment—that all-pervasive, debilitating danger that affects the soldier physically, psychologically, and psychosomatically. In such an environment the friction of war is at work, and, in Clausewitz's words, "the simplest thing is difficult" (Clausewitz 1976, p. 119) and the possibilities of human error are multiplied many times.

One object of military training and of drill and procedures is to provide a framework of activity patterns that will assist the soldier to overcome the propensity for error and to continue to perform well under highly stressful circumstances. Combat experience also helps the soldier cope with disorienting, stressful stimuli, if only by making them familiar.

Even veteran soldiers who are well trained and inured to combat, however, may find themselves involved in fratricide situations.

Accidental, Unintentional Fratricide

Fratricide is probably best known generally in connection with important historical events. For example, it is well known that Confederate general Thomas J. (Stonewall) Jackson was mortally wounded by the muskets of his own men when returning from a reconnaissance at the Battle of Chancellorsville (2 May 1863). Jackson's loss was an incalculable blow to the Confederacy. Less well known is that Confederate general Albert Sidney Johnston likely received his fatal wound from friendly fire at Shiloh (6 April 1862). Johnston was the highest-ranking officer killed in action during the Civil War.

In recent times, one of the most spectacular and devastating fratricide incidents on record occurred when Lt. Gen. Lesley J. McNair, chief of U.S. Army Ground Forces, and more than 100 others, mostly men of the U.S. 30th Infantry Division, were killed by the Allied "carpet bombing" that preceded the Normandy breakout (Operation Cobra, 24–25 July 1944). Similar bombing incidents in Normandy occurred during Operation Totalize on the Caen-Falaise road (7–8 August 1944; more than 150 Canadian and Polish casualties) and near Falaise (14 August; 400 Canadian and Polish casualties).

In Italy the Allied aerial bombardment of the Cassino-Venafro area on 15 March 1943 resulted in nearly 400 casualties among friendly troops. Also, air-ground attacks by Allied fighter-bombers during the Anzio breakout (Operation Buffalo) in late May 1944 resulted in heavy casualties among men of the U.S. 1st Armored and 3d Infantry divisions.

In all these cases except Cassino-Venafro it may be assumed that both aviators and ground troops were experienced personnel who had observed the procedures intended to prevent such occurrences. This was not sufficient to prevent them from occurring. In each instance, lessons were learned that could be applied to future operations.

These are some of the more striking instances of fratricide in modern war. Each case involved air attacks on ground troops. Fratricide incidents involving artillery fire, antiaircraft fire, and small-arms and heavy weapons fire are probably more common but less destructive in terms of numbers of casualties and so are less remarked on.

Intentional Fratricide

On 15 March 1781 at the crisis of the Battle of Guilford Court House, North Carolina, British commander Lord Charles Cornwallis ordered his artillery to fire grapeshot into a desperate melee of British and American troops. The fire drove off the Americans and allowed the British time to reform, but many British soldiers were made casualties by it. This was a case of intentional fratricide; Cornwallis was severely criticized, but the order probably saved his army. It may thus be excusable as a "greater good."

Similar situations have arisen in modern times when commanders have called in friendly artillery fire on their own positions in an attempt to annihilate enemy troops either in or closing on those positions. In World War I and World War II, infantry attacking behind "rolling" artillery barrages often closed on the artillery danger zone themselves, accepting casualties from friendly fire, so as to be on the enemy as soon as possible after the barrage had moved on.

Conclusion

Fratricide is an unavoidable aspect of warfare. Training and experience may lessen its impact, but incidents in recent conflicts in the Falklands/Malvinas, Panama, and the 1991 Gulf War have shown that it has not been overcome by technological advantages. Military planners must take this into account, particularly when contemplating the employment of weapons of mass destruction. Some analysts have speculated that the safest place on a future battlefield may be as close to an enemy as possible; the possibility of intentional fratricide in extreme situations may cause some rethinking of this thesis.

CURT JOHNSON

SEE ALSO: Friction; Rules of Engagement.

Bibliography

Bryan, C. D. B. 1976. *Friendly fire.* New York: Putnam.
Clausewitz, C. von. 1976. *On war.* Ed. and trans. M. Howard and P. Paret. Princeton, N.J.: Princeton Univ. Press.
Percin, A. 1921. *Le massacre de notre infanterie, 1914–1918.* Paris: Albin Michel.
Shrader, C. R. 1982. *Amicicide: The problem of friendly fire in modern war.* Research Survey #1. Fort Leavenworth, Kans.: U.S. Army Command and General Staff College, Combat Studies Institute.

FRICTION

Perfect execution is a utopia; friction is the reality. Friction works against force and purpose. The more mechanistic, rationalistic, or abstract a scheme (military, political, or politico-military), the more the scheme needs realistic correction by the concept of friction.

Although Clausewitz (1780–1831) seems to have been the first to use *friction* in a military sense, this meaning of the term has acquired English-language currency only in the closing decades of the twentieth century. Friction now matters to commanders because it affects important aspects of their tasks.

First and most traditionally, friction is thought of as an obstacle or even a threat to the execution of orders and plans, or at least as an extra cost. In the words of Clausewitz:

> Countless minor incidents—the kind you can never really foresee—combine to lower the general level of performance, so that one always falls far short of the intended goal. . . . Friction is the only concept that more or less corresponds to the factors that distinguish real war from war on paper. (Clausewitz 1984, p. 119)

Second, and since the advent and diffusion of nuclear weapons, friction takes on an additional aspect. Friction now also means the threat of politically unintended escalation or other undesired military initiative. Here the reins must be shortened, for the severity of a potential blunder is much higher than its degree of probability. This newer aspect of friction is reinforced by two independent trends. One, international law has greatly restricted the traditional right of belligerence (*jus ad bellum*) through provisions of the United Nations Charter. This is one reason for the frequency of police actions, presence missions, undeclared hostilities, and crises (Lebow 1988). Two, progress in surveillance and communications technology makes close and real-time supervision of even remote theaters and commanders more feasible than ever before. This new aspect of friction as a threat to the control of forces underlies concern with fail-safe designs and procedures, permissive action links, communications with ballistic-missile submarines, computer failures, and escalation dynamics (Smoker and Bradley 1988).

Very generally, the higher the headquarters, the greater the concern with friction should be. Not the least reason for this is that headquarters themselves generate friction (e.g., the rivalry between Bradley and Montgomery was a serious problem for Eisenhower in France after Normandy).

Tripartite Theory

There are three fundamental forms or sources of friction: internal, hostile, and environmental, or a combination.

Internal friction is inherent in the military and the government. This aspect of the matter, including chance effects, is best known and least controversial.

A message may be misrouted, an allied document or directive may be mistranslated, a corps commander may be injured; for example, General Billotte on 21 May 1940, was in an automobile accident that left him in a coma and deprived the Allied First Group of Armies in Belgium of overall command for a day and a half (Benoist-Mechin 1963, p. 129).

Friction also derives from the enemy, both from wartime interactions and even from prewar measures. Discussing the causes of culmination of an invasion, Clausewitz points out that "the moment an invader enters enemy territory, the nature of the operational theater changes. It becomes hostile. It must be occupied, for the invader can control it only to the extent that he has done so; but this creates difficulties for the entire machine, which will inevitably weaken its effectiveness" (1984, p. 567). Before and during an invasion, the enemy's measures of secrecy and security create the friction of doubt—possibly even some kinds of polarization—in one's own decision process.

The environment, both natural and international, is also a source of friction. Day and night, fog, wind and wave, heat and cold, currents and storms, rain, snow, ice, mud, moisture, typhoons dangerous to ships, ports, and airbases, sandstorms, bird strikes against aircraft, and diseases are all natural phenomena. Such things matter greatly to sailors, airmen, soldiers, medics, and logisticians. Weather and nature, in short, rarely help, but often hinder or even prevent, some operations. Clausewitz links friction to chance, adduces weather as a form of chance presumably because it is relatively unpredictable, and illustrates the important effects that friction so defined can have on tactics and engagements (Clausewitz 1984, p. 120).

The international environment includes allies and neutrals. They ordinarily have aims and capabilities of their own. How much those matter is a question with potentially far-reaching ramifications going well beyond mere "bean counts" of capabilities. Depending upon the war in question, allies and neutrals can hold some, much, most, or all of the balance of power. It can also happen that an ally, seeing his stronger partner make large gains, will take adventurist initiatives, which may or may not succeed. Underlying the topic of allies and neutrals is the generality that communications with them are rarely perfectly and wholly frank, which opens the door to miscalculation and unpleasant surprises.

These three fundamental sources of friction—internal, hostile, and environmental—make possible, at least in principle, a fourth and derivative kind of friction. This is the hostile exploitation—or even manipulation—of internal or environmental friction (or both). Tacticians long ago discovered that a night attack maximized a defender's confusion. Tactical air, armor raids, and special forces are means for maximizing friction. A day-by-day account of the fall of France in 1940 is replete with varieties of friction (Benoist-Mechin 1963, esp. pp. 92, 193, 235, 243, 261, 270, 336, 339).

Friction is clearly a composite phenomenon. Its three fundamental forms have no unity. Hence there follows the important conclusion that friction *as a whole* is intrinsically uncontrolled. Military organizations will try to cope with friction as they are able to know and foresee (see section on Coping with

Friction), but on the whole, such treatment is symptomatic rather than cura-tive. Friction remains a "joker" in the pack.

Related Issues

Tripartite theory is, epistemologically speaking, a commonsense reflection on the course of military thought since Clausewitz. The evolution of Clausewitz's thinking about friction is summarized by Paret (Clausewitz 1984, pp. 16–18). As Clausewitz borrowed the term *culmination* from the astronomers, so he took *friction* from the physicists. The laws of friction in physics had been known partly since Da Vinci and more fully, later. The physicists' concept of damped oscil-lation may have suggested to Clausewitz the simile for friction, namely, that ac-tion in war is like walking in water: extra effort is required. This comparison shows that Clausewitz recognized friction other than the internal variety.

Although Clausewitz—neither a sailor nor an airman—had experienced the snow and cold of the Russian winter of 1812, he is almost totally silent about weather as an operational or theater-level consideration. He cites the disrup-tive effects of weather at the tactical level but adds that weather is rarely decisive. As late as World War II, the mud periods (*rasputiza*) of Russian springs and autumns substantially hindered operations (Schinzer 1981). When a truck drives through mud, its fuel consumption increases dramatically, me-chanical breakdowns multiply disastrously, and the logistical system as well as POL supplies are put to the test. Environmental friction can hardly be more obvious. For weather-related railroad problems of the German attack on Russia in 1941, see Schüler's *Logistik im Russlandfeldzug* (1987).

Possibly the neglect of weather as operational or theater-level friction on the part of Clausewitz (as distinguished from tactical and battle friction) has en-couraged neglect of environmental friction in general. According to some, friction is due exclusively to internal causes. This has been called the "vertical" dimension of friction. A contrary view stresses the "horizontal" dimension, meaning friction due to hostile action and interactions with internal friction.

There is a second issue bearing strongly on the scope of the concept of friction. Not only combat but military planning as well may belong to the domain of friction. For the combat aspect, Clausewitz must again be quoted:

> This tremendous friction, which cannot, as in mechanics, be reduced to a few points, is everywhere in contact with chance, and brings about effects that cannot be measured, just because they are largely due to chance. One, for example, is the weather. Fog can prevent the enemy from being seen in time, a gun from firing when it should, a report from reaching the commanding officer. Rain can prevent a battalion from ar-riving, make another late by keeping it not three but eight hours on the march, ruin a cavalry charge by bogging the horses down in mud, etc. (Clausewitz 1984, p. 120)

The general intent of this passage is clear. A pervasive and unpredictable threat hangs over all combat. The magnitude of the threat is left unspecified; as noted previously, Clausewitz also says that weather is rarely decisive of engagements. Weather, however, is only one element in the concept of friction. The general import is that friction is a hindering medium, a negative force multiplier.

An important complementarity emerges in the work of T. Fabyanic. Friction will be encountered in combat; it also presents a challenge to the planner. Analyzing the planning of the Eighth Air Force for the raid on Schweinfurt on 14 October 1943, Colonel Fabyanic concluded as follows:

> By *"collective risk"* we mean *the sum of the potential difficulties inherent in any spectrum of assumptions*. To repeat . . . the planners recognized that there were certain positive and negative aspects in each one of [their] assumptions. If the positive outweighed the negative, they tended to accept the assumption as fact. *By so doing, they ignored the cumulative effect of the residual negative aspects in each of these assumptions*. All of the assumptions were interrelated; *none* could be separated from the whole. But the planners attempted to do that. *And by not allowing the potential difficulties to accumulate, they fostered a highly erroneous conclusion about what strategic attack could do*. In short, they grossly oversimplified a very complex equation of offense and defense, a situation that, regrettably, is not uncommon in the annals of military history. (Fabyanic 1983, pp. 22–23)

There are two characteristics common to the phenomena analyzed by Clausewitz and Fabyanic. First, *multiple* factors (e.g., weather, chance) are at work jointly, in the same direction. Second, their effect is *adverse*. In a word, then, this aspect of friction may be characterized as adverse or negative military synergistics. Note, however, that this covers *only* the traditional, prenuclear aspect of friction as distinguished from others in the introduction of this article.

Reports of friction are scattered throughout military memoirs and histories; there is little systematic literature even of a descriptive nature. International or comparative treatment of friction seems largely nonexistent; for the three American services since World War II, however, a promising study is in preparation.

Friction in Concepts of War

Turning from friction to its theoretical environment, two necessities seem self-evident. A theory of war is radically defective if it ignores friction; conversely, any theoretical treatment of friction must be linked with other important aspects of the theory of war. The three fundamental sources of friction overlap with the major themes of a theory of war.

Internal, hostile, and derivative forms of friction bear, in principle, on perceptions and decisions about war aims (e.g., wars of overthrow, limited wars), outbreak scenarios, efficiency of attack and defense, management of escalation, the center or centers of gravity, culmination processes and decisions at the culminating point, moral(e) factors, and considerations of war termination and peace. International-environmental forms of friction bear, in principle, on war aims, outbreak scenarios, escalation options, third-party perceptions of culmination, considerations at the culmination point, and war termination and peace.

This sketch, however, deals only with concepts of war at the level of *Kriegstheorie*, that is, the dynamics primarily *internal* to war. In addition, concepts of war exist as "metatheory" to *Kriegstheorie*; some examples are religious and crusading ideas of war, international-law concepts of war, and historical materialism. Tolstoy's metatheory of war in *War and Peace* is discussed below. In general, these metatheories of war so predate *Kriegstheorie* (especially in its classic, Clausewitzian form) and are so weak in military content that any relation to the concept of friction is slight to negligible.

One major exception to this lacuna derives, not surprisingly, from reflection on the wars of the Napoleonic era. The fact that Napoleon united in himself the functions of head of state, supreme commander, theater commander, and often corps commander dramatized the topic of agency underlying all concern with friction. On the other hand, retrospection after 1815 showed the interactions and action-reaction cycles to which even Napoleon became subject. Not surprisingly, then, views might differ on the question of control. Tolstoy, projecting his populist or antielitist preconceptions, denied the possibility of control and depicted it as an illusion. As popular forces confronted post-1815 restoration monarchies in repeated revolutions (1830–31, 1848), the class mechanics of historical materialism portrayed war as a technique either of conquest or of revolution. As the preferred side, the proletariat was entitled to inevitable victory; all attention tended to center on outbreak scenarios of either revolution or war. The conduct and dynamics of war, which raise the question of friction, never came into view. Only the moral factor, *justa causa*, mattered after—and before—an outbreak.

Clausewitz, as distinct from these two schools of thought, took up an intermediate position. He emphasized the importance of genius and constancy in the commander (Tashjean 1986). Thereby he differed from the Tolstoyan thesis that control is an illusion. Clausewitz also differed from the Marxist notion that, ultimately, *social forces alone* matter in history; that is, all major evolution is *necessary* and only minor change is *contingent* upon individual personality. The Clausewitzian *Feldherr* (CINC, head of state) is the instrument of statecraft. Ever encountering chance and friction, he exerts control and direction despite them.

Coping with Friction

Training has always been an important countermeasure to friction. Plato in his *Laws* made detailed provisions for major and minor military exercises regardless of weather, with maximum possible realism, a variety of battle scenarios, and legal immunity for exercise-related homicide.

The spirit and logic of these provisions are close to modern military practice. Japanese army divisions proved quickly adaptable to a strange operating environment when the troops, after embarking for Malaya, were given a well-researched and very specific instruction booklet (Tsuji 1960, ch. 2, appendix 1). Reflection on American experience at the Kasserine Pass in 1943 and other first battles has prompted comparative historical studies of such battles, given fears of no-warning first battles (Heller and Stofft 1986). U.S. forces have also institutionalized an order-of-magnitude increase in training realism at the Army National Training Center and the air force's comparable center at Nellis Air Force Base. The long German tradition of *Auftragstaktik* has come in for serious study in the English-speaking world (Simpkin 1985, pp. 227–29). A major difficulty is that even for a relatively rich nation such as the United States, there are limits to exercises above the tactical level—"in practical reality, the fielding of sufficient troops to execute a live corps level test is not affordable" (Hollis 1988, p. 29).

Technology is the second great countermeasure to friction. It necessarily involves design limitations, costs, and logistics and may well increase maintenance burdens.

Concerning these two great countermeasures to friction, training and technology, a sobering comment is implicit in the Clausewitzian view that combat experience *alone* is the "lubricant" that reduces friction (Clausewitz 1984, p. 122). This may explain, in part, the importance of "laboratory" wars such as the Spanish Civil War and, in some respects such as air mobility, the second Vietnam War.

JOHN E. TASHJEAN

SEE ALSO: Tactics.

Bibliography

Benoist-Mechin, J. 1963. *Sixty days that shook the West: The fall of France, 1940.* New York: Putnam.

Clausewitz, C. von. 1984. *On war.* Ed. and trans. M. Howard and P. Paret. Princeton, N.J.: Princeton Univ. Press.

Fabyanic, T. A. 1983. Notes from a videotape of a lecture, "Development of airpower between the wars (part 1)," delivered 3 February 1983 to Air Command and Staff College, Maxwell Air Force Base, Ala.

Heller, C. E., and W. A. Stofft, eds. 1986. *America's first battles, 1776–1965.* Lawrence, Kans.: Univ. Press of Kansas.

Hollis, W. W. 1988. Analysis in support of the acquisition process. *Signal* 42(July):29–31.

Lebow, R. N. 1988. Clausewitz and crisis stability. *Political Science Quarterly* 103(Spring):81–110.

Schinzer, D. 1981. Verluste im Gefecht—in Kriegsgeschichte und Operations-Research. *Wehrwiss. Rundschau,* May–June, pp. 84–87.

Simpkin, R. E. 1985. *Race to the swift: Thoughts on twenty-first century warfare.* London: Brassey's.

Smoker, P., and M. Bradley, eds. 1988. Accidental nuclear war. In *Current Research on Peace and Violence,* vol. 11, nos. 1–2, pp. 1–79.

Tashjean, J. E. 1986. The ideal general of General von Clausewitz. *RUSI Journal of Defense Studies* 131(December):75–76.

Tsuji, M. 1960. *Singapore: The Japanese version.* New York: St. Martin's Press.

FRONT

The U.S. Department of Defense *Dictionary of Military Terms* provides the following definitions of the term *front*.

> *Front* (DoD, NATO, IADB) 1. The lateral space occupied by an element measured from the extremity of one flank to the extremity of the other flank. 2. The direction of the enemy. 3. The line of contact of two opposing forces. 4. When a combat situation does not exist or is not assumed, the direction toward which the command is faced.

In a broad sense, a front is a line. On the battlefield it extends, for the purpose of this discussion, from right to left and connects all soldiers or units deployed side by side facing the enemy. The front line may be neither straight nor uniform but is formed based on the terrain, which may be characterized by rivers, villages, valleys, or hills.

Independent of the type of combat, the organization of the front is of major significance. Gaps in the front provide the enemy with the opportunity to smash or breach the front. Smashing the front means an interruption in the front line caused by an enemy attack, leading to losses of ground and of one's own troops. Breaching of the front occurs when superior enemy troops force the defender's own troops to carry out temporary or permanent evasive movements within limited areas, without, however, destroying the organization of the front.

Troop Deployment

Operationally, all combat troops are considered qualified for deployment in the front. Although they retain their permanent organization status, they may be attached out to other organizations on a temporary basis to form combined-arms units (corps, divisions, brigades). In order to prevent gaps along the front, special measures must be taken, which in most cases consist of the establishment of liaison teams between the adjacent flanks of the major units. Coordination points at unit boundaries are established where liaison teams will meet at fixed dates and times.

Types of units well suited for deployment to the front include armored infantry, rifle infantry, mountain infantry, or paratroopers. Because of their mobility, armored forces can participate in establishing the front and also serve as a reserve (strike) force. Artillery units support forward-deployed combat troops at the front by observation and fire support. Engineers, antiaircraft units, and reconnaissance forces also provide support to those forces deployed across the front.

A Historical Perspective

Since ancient times, army leaders have used fronts in organizing their troops across the width of battlegrounds. In some instances, a front was smashed when a commander, in an attempt to surround the enemy, thinned out his troops in at least one place across the front, thus creating a gap. This decision provided the enemy an opportunity to make an attack toward the gap, providing the conditions for victory. The battle of Gaugamela, where the forces of Alexander the Great and the Persian army of Darius clashed in 331 B.C., is an excellent example. The left flank of Alexander's troops was almost completely split by a Persian frontal attack, and Alexander's base was plundered. At the same time, the extended Persian left flank started to encircle Alexander's front from the right. It was only behind his right flank that Alexander was able to stop this move. In the forward Persian phalanx, the front was overstretched, with a break in the line to the left of center. Alexander, recognizing this, made a surprise attack toward the gap. His attack was successful, resulting in Darius's departure from the battlefield in panic. This was the signal for the Persian forces in the center of the line to flee. It was only a matter of time before the other Persian troops were also defeated.

The Germanic warriors and the armies of the knights of the Middle Ages did not understand the concept of a front. They fought man to man and relied only on their bravery and skill. It was not until the fourteenth century and later that the mercenaries rediscovered the closed army formation, where numerous soldiers stood or advanced closely side by side and one behind the other while trying to kill the enemy in close combat—with pikes in the early days and later with muskets or guns.

In eighteenth-century Europe, this type of warfare was systematized. For example, in the era of Frederick II of Prussia, regiments and battalions were kept in a close front line in both attack and defense. When gaps developed between units—often caused by the varying terrain—reserve units were used to close them. Front gaps could arise during a battle at several places simultaneously or subsequently. In the 1805 battle of Austerlitz, Napoleon, the commander, was quicker than his opponents to recognize and take advantage of the gaps in the enemy's front.

In the early years, the appearance of a front depended on the tactics in the approach of the troops. Fronts could only be organized on clearly observable battlegrounds. It was not until the nineteenth century, when mass armies were mobilized, that importance was attached to the organization of the front on a large scale. This applied not only to the battleground itself, but also to the duration of a campaign.

Not until World War I did the front gain strategic importance. Following the battle of the Marne in 1914, the western front extended from Alsace to the North Sea. The two hostile forces were able to hold it nearly stationary for four years, even though it was repeatedly breached and moved. Because of the weapons capabilities of that time, none of the parties was able to break the enemy's front. In contrast, there was no coherently organized front on the East European battlefields. The vastness of the terrain was ideal for mobile warfare, but fronts were created only in certain areas, for limited periods of time, during partial encounters with enemy forces.

Mobile warfare characterized the early years of World War II because of

Germany's superiority in modern equipment and leadership. Fronts formed were continually smashed. With the adjustment of tactical approaches, the increase in the Allies' troops, and their superiority in weapons technology on the ground and in the air, fronts were formed all over the war theater. From 1943 on, these fronts were strategically broken in places, but not on a large scale until the last twelve months of the war. By then the Allies' superiority ranged from a combat ratio of 1:5 to 1:20, thus deciding the outcome of the war. Up until the collapse of the German Army Group Center in White Russia in July 1944 and the defeat of the German armies in August 1944 after the June landing of the Allies in Normandy, German troops had allowed themselves to be forced into creating fronts and had been able to hold their front line. But after 1944 permanent losses of ground—from the Don and Volga rivers to the Vistula River and from the English Channel to the borders of the German Reich—followed.

Fronts have not been recorded in wars outside Europe since 1960. Neither on the Falkland Islands/Islas Malvinas nor in Afghanistan were fronts formed. In Vietnam, and during the Palestine campaigns, only exceptional and temporary formations deserved designation as a front. In the mobile warfare of the future, armies will probably operate on battlefields that have no fronts; guerrilla warfare is a typical example of such a war.

HERMANN BÜSCHLEB

SEE ALSO: Defense; Geography, Military; Tactics.

Bibliography

Addington, L. H. 1984. *The patterns of war since the eighteenth century.* Bloomington: Indiana Univ. Press.
Clausewitz, C. von. *On war.* 1984. Ed. and trans. M. Howard and P. Paret. Princeton, N.J.: Princeton Univ. Press.
Keegan, J. 1989. *The Second World War.* New York: Penguin Books.
Tippelskirch, K. von. 1954. *Geschichte des zweiten Weltriegs.* Bonn: Athenaeum Verlag.
Weith, A. 1970. *Russia at war, 1941–1945.* New York: Avon (Discus Books).

FUZE

A fuze is a device with explosive components designed to initiate a fire train or detonation in an ammunition item by means of electrical energy, chemical action, mechanical timing, hydrostatic pressure, impact, or a combination of these. The term *fuze* should not be confused with *fuse*, which is limited to a cord that consists of a flexible fabric or plastic tube with a core of low or high explosive. It is used in demolition work and in blasting.

Fuzes are used to initiate the explosion or chain of events leading to the functioning of all types of ammunition, including artillery and mortar projectiles, grenades, mines, missile warheads, and bombs. Fuzes perform a number of functions that include safing (keeping the munition safe for storing), handling (including mishandling), launching, and emplacing. A fuze also arms a munition by sensing the environment associated with its actual use. The fuze arms the munition by aligning explosive trains, closing switches, or performing other functions to ready the munition for firing. Finally, a fuze fires a munition by sensing the point in space and time at which the munition is intended to detonate, then causing detonation. Fuzes range from relatively simple mechanisms in hand grenades to complex radar fuzes of missile warheads. In the latter case, a fuze may consist of a number of interconnected components, placed throughout the munition, that compose a fuzing system.

Types of Fuzes

Fuzes are categorized by their use (for example, in a bomb or an artillery projectile); by their purpose, such as armor piercing; by their application, such as air-to-air; or by their action, such as point detonating or mechanically timed. Fuzes also may be categorized by their location in the munition (e.g., in the nose or base). Another way to categorize fuzes is by function, such as mechanical or electrical. The U.S. Army categorizes munition fuzes into two broad classes: bursting and cargo carrying. Common fuze categories are listed below.

T	Time
MT	Mechanical Time
MTSQ	Mechanical Time and Superquick
PD	Point Detonating
PIBD	Point Initiating, Base Detonating
BD	Base Detonating
VT	Proximity (variable timed)
ET	Electric Time
MO	Multi-option

It should be noted that different terminology is used in different nations. For example, a fuze labeled point detonating by Americans would be labeled a percussion, direct-action fuze by the British. The same fuze might also be termed an *impact* or *contact fuze*. While terms differ from country to country, descriptions of fuze functions are similar.

Impact or *contact* fuzes (Fig. 1) are actuated by physical contact with a target. This class of fuze includes PD fuzes located in the nose of the projectile that function on impact with the target or, following impact, by a timed delay. Impact fuzes also include BD fuzes, which are located in a projectile's base, and function after a short (typically approximately 0.25-second) delay (Fig. 2). Such fuzes are generally used in antiarmor projectiles where the fuze must be protected as the projectile penetrates the armor. In shaped charges, PIBD fuzes are used. The nose of the projectile contains a piezoelectric crystal that, when crushed upon impact with the target, generates an electric current sufficient to detonate the base fuze, which in turn initiates the shaped (hollow) charge.

Impact fuzes are classed as superquick, non-delay, and delay. In superquick

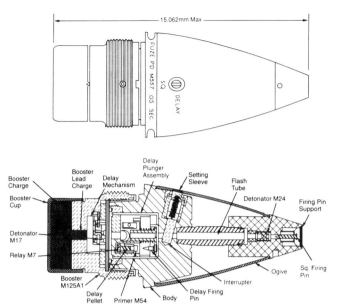

Figure 1. Typical impact fuze (PD). (SOURCE: U.S. Army)

fuzes the nose fuze causes initiation of the bursting charge in less than 100 microseconds. In non-delay fuzes there is no intentional delay designed into the fuze, but there is likely to be an inherent delay due to the internal components of the fuze that initiate the explosive train. Delay fuzes contain intentional delay elements that retard the initiation of the explosive train for a period of time after target impact. In projectiles intended for antiarmor or concrete piercing, the delay is generally a fraction of a second, which allows the projectile time to reach the desired penetration depth prior to initiation of the explosive train. Delay elements may be incorporated into either PD or BD fuzes. In some applications, such as bombs and naval mines, longer delays are required. In many cases, delays of hours or days after impact or emplacement are designed into the fuze. Many fuzes of this type have adjustable delay elements, and most have anti-removal devices that are actuated along with the fuze to

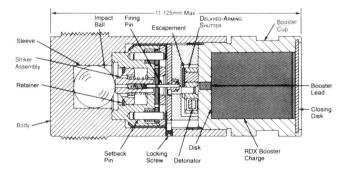

Figure 2. Typical BD fuze. (SOURCE: U.S. Army)

discourage an enemy from defuzing the munition in which they are used. Highly trained, hazardous-duty military personnel specialize in disarming unexploded munitions. Called "explosive ordnance disposal," this unique skill was developed into an art by the British in World War II.

Time fuzes (Fig. 3) function after an elapsed time subsequent to arming or impact. The timing mechanism may use mechanical, electrical, pyrotechnic, chemical, radiological, or other methods to measure elapsed time. These fuzes are used to initiate a munition at some desired point after launch, drop, or emplacement; they usually can be set by the user for a predetermined interval from fractions of a second to days. Most such fuzes have applications in illuminating, beehive, and special-purpose projectiles as well as in grenades, mines, and bombs. A typical artillery projectile time fuze can be set for up to 200 seconds' delay after tube firing.

Proximity fuzes, also known as influence fuzes and VT (variably timed) fuzes, were one of the scientific developments that altered the conduct of war in the twentieth century. This class of fuzes initiates an explosive train when the fuze senses that it is in proximity to a target. The idea of a proximity fuze was first suggested by Swedish designers in the late 1930s using photoelectric cells as the sensing mechanism. The British pursued the idea into production for use in antiaircraft rockets, although the photoelectrically fuzed munitions they developed were of use only during daylight. The concept of a radar proximity fuze was conceived in the United Kingdom, but the exigencies of war prevented the British from conducting the necessary research and development, and the concept was passed to the United States. There, Dr. Vannevar Bush and a team of researchers designed and built the first proximity fuze, which incorporated

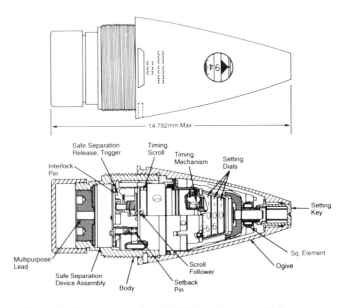

Figure 3. Typical time fuze (MTSQ). (SOURCE: U.S. Army)

a small radar set into a package small and rugged enough to be fired from a cannon. The first proximity fuzes were used against Japanese aircraft in the Pacific in 1943, where there was no chance that a dud would fall into the hands of the enemy. Later they were used against German aircraft over England with devastating effect. Their first use against German troops on land was on 16 December 1944 during the Battle of the Bulge, and it proved instrumental in halting the German offensive. Early VT fuzes were larger than their conventional counterparts and thus occupied more space in a projectile. This reduced explosive effectiveness somewhat but was compensated for by the accuracy of the fuze. Modern proximity fuzes, much smaller than those used in World War II, are just as effective and currently cost little more than conventional fuzes.

Modern proximity fuzes (Fig. 4) fall into two categories. Active proximity fuzes are initiated by reflected electromagnetic waves that emanate from the fuze and are reflected off its target. This category includes fuzes used against aircraft and those optimized for ground use. Passive proximity fuzes are initiated by an effect produced by the target itself, such as infrared radiation or magnetic signature.

Command fuzes are those in which the action that causes the fuze to function comes from outside the fuze and its munition. The action is deliberately communicated to the fuze by electrical, mechanical, or other means. Such fuzes are typically used in mines, booby traps, and other munitions requiring remote detonation.

Combination fuzes incorporate more than one of the types already discussed, with one as primary and the other as secondary.

Nonexplosive fuzes are generally used in training and practice munitions or in dummy munitions. A training or practice fuze is an exact duplicate of the service fuze modified for use in training exercises. This type of fuze may be completely inert or may have its explosive charge replaced by a spotting charge. A dummy fuze is completely inert and is a more or less accurate replica of a service fuze. Dummy fuzes generally provide the shape, weight, and center of gravity of a given service fuze.

Multi-option fuzes are currently being fielded for use with mortars and ar-

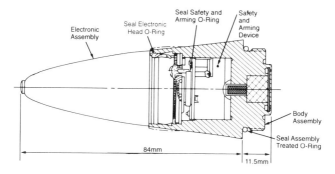

Figure 4. VT fuze. (SOURCE: U.S. Army)

tillery munitions. These fuzes may be set to function as proximity, impact, or delay fuzes.

Components of Fuzes

Fuzes have a number of common components, regardless of application. The most complex fuzes are those used in artillery munitions because not only are they subjected to much greater forces than fuzes in other applications, but they must also function with a reliability approaching 100 percent. The most common fuze components are energy sources, energy storage devices, bore and muzzle area safety devices, detonator safeties, switching elements for initiating the detonation, detonation means, and explosive trains.

Energy sources may be required not only to provide the energy necessary to initiate the explosive train, but also to power the components of an electronic fuze. Energy sources include pulse generators, which contain a small magnet and armature that generates electricity as a result of projectile rotation; piezo-electric elements, which function only on impact but which also may produce electricity throughout a projectile's trajectory as a result of mechanical pressure applied to the elements; thermal batteries, which are initiated on firing the projectile or missile; solid-electrolyte batteries; and mechanical springs or clockwork.

Fuze safeties ensure that a munition to which a fuze is affixed does not function until the desired point in time. In artillery fuzes, special consideration is given to ensuring that the fuze does not function while still in the bore of the cannon nor just after having left the muzzle. The latter protection is especially important in conditions of high humidity and rain. In many fuzes, the arm function is prevented by a mechanism that precludes arming until a set number of projectile revolutions have occurred. This not only provides in-bore safety but also prevents arming until the projectile has traveled some distance from the cannon. Other systems depend on setback forces for functioning. Systems of this type usually require not only an initial setback from the firing of the weapon but also acceleration over a specific time. In-bore safety also may be provided by a pin that is released by setback forces and rides the surface of the bore until the projectile leaves the muzzle of the cannon or mortar. Once outside the weapon bore, the pin is ejected—either by centrifugal force or by a spring, or both—and the munition is armed.

Detonator safeties are universal in modern fuzes; they ensure that the detonator of the fuze cannot function until after the munition has been fired. This is accomplished either by a physical barrier between the firing mechanism and the detonator or by maintaining the detonator in an out-of-line position with respect to the firing mechanism until after setback occurs. The detonator safety also may be incorporated as part of the safety mechanisms.

Once the detonator has moved into position or the barriers between it and the firing mechanism have been removed, the fuze is armed and detonation can be initiated. This function is frequently performed by switching mechanisms such as a double-ballistic nose cap. In this switching mechanism, two caps are insulated from each other during flight. When the outer cap is deformed in any way, it closes the firing circuit. This type of switch ensures that the fuze functions at almost any angle. Other switching mechanisms include acceleration or vibration switches that sense motion of a predetermined type, such as an abrupt change in direction caused by a ricochet. Regardless of type, the purpose of these switching mechanisms is to close the firing circuit in fuzes that require an electrical impulse to initiate the explosive train.

Many fuzes, especially those in antiaircraft and air-to-air munitions, are not allowed to fall to the ground in an armed state. Such munitions therefore use fuzes that incorporate a self-destruction mechanism. These mechanisms function either by a short-delay powder train in the fuze or by a spin delay in which the fuze will not function as long as a certain spin rate and centrifugal force are maintained. Once the spin rate slows, normally after a few seconds' flight, centrifugal force is no longer sufficient to prevent the fuze from functioning and the firing pin is allowed to strike the detonator, initiating the explosive train.

Fuzes initiate the explosive train in a munition by way of a detonator, which may be one of two types: electrical or mechanical. Mechanical detonators have a charge that is sensitive to friction or impact. Once the fuze functions, the detonator is stabbed by a firing pin; this action fires the detonator charge and ignites a booster charge used for initial detonation of the main charge. Electrical detonators function by heating a wire, by vaporizing a metallic layer at an arc point, or by passing a current through a conductive initial detonating charge. Like mechanical detonating charges, electrical ones usually require supplemental or booster charges to ensure reliable functioning. This is necessary because the detonator is usually kept as small as possible due to design considerations with respect to fuze volume and safety in maintaining a minimum quantity of sensitive explosive in the fuze.

Functioning of Fuzes

The functioning of any modern fuze is a complicated process encompassing all of the components described above. Figure 3 illustrates a current-production U.S. MTSQ fuze type typical in its functioning. The M582 fuze illustrated is produced for the U.S. armed forces.

The M582 fuze contains a mechanical clockwork mechanism that is set, with a special fuze setter or a common flat-tipped screwdriver, to function at any time between 2 and 200 seconds. The setting key is in the nose of the fuze and the time set is viewed on three dials through a window in the side of the fuze ogive. The first dial, closest to the fuze nose, indicates hundreds of seconds. A triangle indicates that no time is set. The second dial shows tens of seconds, and the third shows seconds and tenths of seconds. The superquick and timing elements are contained in the nose section threaded onto a steel fuze body containing the safe-separation arming element and the detonator. The timing mechanism and the safe-separation element are prevented from aligning before a predetermined projectile spin is attained by centrifugally operated lock pins. These are prevented from moving by setback pins until the munition is fired.

The arming mechanism also has a spin-actuated rotor that blocks the detonator prior to arming. An additional safety feature is a scroll follower that restrains the movement of the firing pin by interlocking with the arming mechanism. It is apparent from the description of this fuze that great effort has been made in its design to ensure that it is as safe as possible and that it will not function until the desired moment.

When the weapon is fired, setback withdraws the lock pins from the centrifugal detents blocking the timing and arming mechanisms. When the projectile reaches a spin rate of 1,800 rpm, the centrifugal pins withdraw, allowing the timing mechanism to actuate. The safety arming rotor is released by the scroll follower approximately three seconds before the time set on the fuze to allow final arming. Once set time is achieved, the scroll follower releases the firing pin, firing the detonator. If superquick impact functioning is desired, the gun crew turns the setting one-quarter turn counterclockwise prior to firing, to set the number "98" in the fuze window.

Fuze Design

Fuze design is usually initiated by a requirement from a military user who specifies the desired capability. Fuzes may be incorporated as a part of the design of a new weapons system or munition. Safety and reliability are inseparable in Western fuze designs; the fuze must function as intended, but it must function under none but prescribed conditions. These requirements usually are specified statistically by the military end user, with reliability determined by the probability that the fuze will function for a specified period under stated conditions. Safety also is described statistically, but the approach is different than for reliability. In most nations, the principle is that of a "fail-safe" mechanism, which means that any sequence of events other than those that constitute normal operation will result in failure to detonate. The steps in fuze design are preliminary design and layout, dimensional design and calculations, model testing and revision, safety and reliability testing, and final acceptance. The ideal fuze design will incorporate reliability, safety in handling, long storage life, simple construction, compactness, safety and ease of manufacture and loading, and economy in production. Most military fuzes are both detonator safe and bore safe and are designed with two independent safing features to prevent any unintended detonation before a munition is fired or emplaced.

Many fuzes also incorporate a self-destruction feature to minimize damage to friendly forces. Self-destruction may be accomplished by any of a number of timing mechanisms already discussed, which will explode the munition in the case of missing the target or failure of the primary fuze mode.

CHARLES Q. CUTSHAW

SEE ALSO: Ammunition; Artillery, Rocket and Missile; Artillery, Tube; Grenade; Mortar.

Bibliography

Germershausen, R., et al. 1982. *Rheinmetall handbook on weaponry.* English ed. Frankfurt am Main: Broenners Druckeri Breidenstein GmbH.

Hogg, I. 1985. *The illustrated encyclopedia of ammunition.* Secaucus, N.J.: Chartwell Books.

Johnson, C. 1976. *Artillery.* London: Octopus Books.

Quick, J. 1973. *Dictionary of weapons and military terms.* New York: McGraw-Hill.

U.S. Department of Defense, Joint Chiefs of Staff. 1987. *Department of Defense dictionary of military and associated terms.* Washington, D.C.: Government Printing Office.

G

GENERALSHIP

As used originally, the term *generalship* involved those duties, responsibilities, and attributes required of a general officer during the conduct of active campaigns. In more recent times, the term has come to encompass all the functions carried out by general officers in modern armies including, but not limited to, directing wartime activities. Most theorists include the functions of leadership, management, and command of military organizations larger than brigades. Additionally, the modern analyst usually includes such activities as high-level staff responsibilities: analysis, planning, and organization and training of military organizations in peacetime. Less often included, but frequently assumed as components of generalship, are such functions as liaison with and advice to the civilian leadership of governments and even functioning as a civil government official in some cases. According to W. Duane's *A Military Dictionary* (1810):

> *The natural qualities of a general*, are a martial genius, a solid judgment, a healthy robust constitution, intrepidity and presence of mind on critical occasions, indefatigability in business, goodness of heart, liberality, a reasonable age; if too young, he may want experience and prudence; if too old, he may not have vivacity enough. His conduct must be uniform, his temper affable but inflexible in maintaining the police and discipline of an army.
>
> *Acquired qualities of a general* should be secrecy, justice, sobriety, temperance, knowledge of the art of war from theory and practice, the art of commanding, and speaking with precision and exactness, great attention to preserve the lives and supply the wants of the soldiers, and a constant study of the characters of the officers of his army, that he may employ them according to their talents. . . . His experience inspires his army with confidence, and an assurance of victory; and his good qualities, by creating respect, augment his authority. . . . He ought to be fond of glory, to have an aversion to flattery, to render himself beloved, and to keep a strict discipline and regular submission.

History of Generalship

Much of the early study of generalship relied on historical analysis of famous generals of antiquity, often drawing up lists of "Great Captains" who were assumed to display all the attributes necessary for success as general officers. Such lists usually began with Alexander and included such luminaries as Hannibal, Caesar, Gustavus Adolphus, Marlborough, Eugene, Frederick the Great, Napoleon, and Wellington. Often the compilers of such lists drew conclusions as to characteristics or traits necessary for generalship.

In addition to the Great Captains school of generalship, virtually every military theorist to the present day has tried to define the qualities generals should have. Sun Tzu, Machiavelli, Clausewitz, and Jomini are among the better-known theorists whose aphorisms and advice on generalship have been most widely cited.

The study of leadership from the historical perspective reached its zenith in the period following World War I, when dozens of veterans of that war wrote their reminiscences and advice on leadership and generalship. The scientific study of human behavior accelerated in the period before World War II, and the behavioralist approach to the study of leadership surged during and after that war. With the ascendancy of behavioral science approaches in the period following World War II, the concept of attributes or traits of leadership became more and more discredited and the historical study of leadership and generalship declined as a discipline.

As of 1990, behavioral scientists and historians have been moving toward more of a synthesis on generalship and, in fact, often incorporate one another's findings into their literature. Few of these studies would be likely to use one approach to the exclusion of the other.

Modern Theories of Generalship

Both scientific and historical studies of generalship tend to identify a mixture of psychological, intellectual, and physical components necessary for success as a general officer. These components are drawn from the functions of leadership and management, at which a general must be adept; often the separate function of command is included.

Until recent times, it would have been impossible for a general to be successful without being an effective leader; even in 1990 it is extremely rare to find a successful general officer who would not be seen first as an accomplished leader. Leadership in this context is the process of working with people, developing their attitudes and values so that they will attain an appropriate goal. Given the size of the organizations generals lead, they can personally lead only a few soldiers at a time—their staffs and soldiers in their proximity, for example. As a consequence, generals must often exert leadership through subordinate layers of command. The ways in which generals have successfully or unsuccessfully exerted such leadership are often featured in historical studies of generals. Anecdotes such as Napoleon's calling experienced veterans by name to encourage units before battle and Eisenhower talking to camouflage-painted paratroopers before the Normandy invasion are contrasted with Haig's refusal to visit the slaughter in the trenches of World War I. Scientific studies of senior leadership likewise stress the importance of a general officer's imprinting his personality on his unit and describe ways in which it can be accomplished.

The study of generalship in earlier times seldom would have stressed management skill as being a talent equal to leadership skill as a requisite for success. Such is not the case at the beginning of the 1990s—management is usually considered of equal and in some respects of paramount importance for effectiveness as a general officer. In retrospect, it would seem that this was always the case. Studies have shown that Alexander's operational concepts were predicated in large part on his logistic requirements. Napoleon's acumen in the same field has been analyzed as an essential component in many of his successes, just as his logistic problems contributed immeasurably to his failure in Russia.

Management is less difficult to define and analyze than are the more intangible ramifications of leadership. The management skills of the military are more closely related to those of the world of business and bureaucracy than is military leadership to its other forms. The latter fact may partially account for the stress on management as a component of generalship in recent times. At any rate, few theorists argue that it is less than a *sine qua non* for effective generalship. Management deals with the scientific planning, apportionment, and use of resources of all kinds. In modern warfare, for which World War II has been the predominant case study since 1945, the successful apportionment and use of resources by the Allies brought them success on the battlefields of Europe and the Pacific, just as resource problems and logistic shortcomings contributed to the ultimate failures of both Germany and Japan. In that war, the management accomplishments of dozens of generals who never commanded forces in the field contributed as much to ultimate victory as did the better-known field commands of generals such as Omar Bradley, Bernard Law Montgomery, and Carl Spaatz. As a result, management threatened at times to eclipse leadership in the study of generalship in the decade following World War II.

Command is the third component that most authorities would recognize as a function of generalship, although some theorists subsume it in the other two. Some successful generals might never exercise command in the traditional sense—such generals as Brehon Somervell, who apportioned resources for the American army in World War II, never commanded units on campaign, for example. Command encompasses the overlapping functions of leadership and management and focuses on the effectiveness of the unit or organization.

When one moves from the functions of generalship to the qualities, attributes, or traits needed by general officers, there is much less agreement among theorists. From the chroniclers of the Great Captains to the 1990s, each analyst has his or her own list of requirements without which a general is bound to fail—such items as intellect, imagination, knowledge, creativity, judgment, experience, objectivity, *coup d'oeil*, communication skills, character, temper-

ament, willpower, ambition, physical and moral courage, integrity, persever-
ance, boldness, resilience, tenacity, adaptability, human relations skills,
technical skills, physical fitness, good health, youth, and luck. Some of these
are clearly contradictory—a youthful general is unlikely to have a great deal of
experience or refined judgment, for example. Some, such as character, are
virtually undefinable or unidentifiable, however real they may be. Still others
are self-explanatory or not particularly helpful. From a historical perspective,
one could quickly name generals lacking in several of these traits, although it
would be hard to find many successful generals who displayed none of them.
Nonetheless, keeping the lack of agreement among the experts in mind, a few
of these attributes are worth discussing.

Almost all students of generalship would agree on intelligence as a critical
attribute of a successful general. Intellect gives the capacity to grasp concepts
and to improvise solutions. When combined with imagination, it allows for
vision and creative problem solving. As a Russian general stated, "A battle takes
place twice: first in thought, then in reality." Napoleon expressed similar
thoughts, and the elder Moltke said that no plan survives the first engagement,
implying that a talent for improvisation is invaluable to any general.

Intellect enhances the ability to make the most of experience. Frederick the
Great cited his mule who had experienced many campaigns but knew no more
of war than after his first. Through study of military theory, history, and contemporary doctrine, the general with intelligence and imagination can learn not
only from his own experiences but from the experiences of others. In generalship, intellect implies common sense—the native good judgment that allows
for discerning evaluation of alternatives.

Most writers on generalship mention strength of character as an essential
attribute. Character, one of the less easily definable traits, refers to the aggregate of moral qualities distinguishing an individual's development, usually becoming more fixed with maturity. Thus a general's character would tend to
manifest itself in all aspects of his personality and in all that he does. It is most
often remarked on in such towering individuals as George Washington, Robert
E. Lee, and George Marshall, but it can be identified, if not precisely measured, in lesser mortals.

Courage, both physical and moral, is most evident in campaigning, but is
equally essential for a general in less hazardous situations. Examples such as
Ulysses Grant riding the front lines unperturbed by the bullets whizzing around
him or of "Vinegar Joe" Stilwell marching out of Burma with his defeated
troops, heartening the soldiers they commanded, come most easily to mind. In
many respects, however, they are overshadowed by such displays of moral
courage as Eisenhower ordering the Normandy landings against heavy odds
and with the possibility of catastrophic losses, yet assuming full personal responsibility. Napoleon referred to this sort of moral courage as "two o'clock in
the morning courage."

In virtually all modern armies, the soldiers who make up the army are the
general's most valuable and irreplaceable resource and his greatest challenge
both to lead and to manage. For this reason, all studies place a high premium on

a general's skills in human relations and communication. Anecdotes abound of how a general could assess his soldiers—their strengths, weaknesses, morale, and capabilities—and then impose his will on them through his ability to communicate with them. Whether in the stirring rhetoric of Douglas MacArthur, the earthy and calculated profanity of George Patton, or the back-to-the-wall bluntness of Walton Walker in the Pusan Perimeter, the effective general evokes reserves of tenacity and spirit that his soldiers often do not know they possess.

The technical skills required of a general in modern war are more difficult to assess. Alexander's prowess with the horse and weapons of his day were a prerequisite for success in the warfare he practiced. A modern general's skill with the weapons of war is more problematical. Although no one insists that a general must—or could—be able to operate all the weapons of a modern battlefield, a general must thoroughly understand their capabilities and limitations. It is likely that he will have been expert with some of the weapons to have risen to his position. Yet some commanders in modern armies have been criticized as being preoccupied with their own technical expertise at the expense of the vision required to employ the weapons and army as a team. As modern information-processing capabilities become more sophisticated and refined, the danger of fixating on technology rather than capabilities will pose an increasing risk.

The health and physical fitness of generals have always been important, but they have received additional attention in studies of generalship. George Marshall's biographer reported that, as chief of staff of the American army in World War II, Marshall had to relieve more generals for health or fitness reasons than for any other. Some authors add mental fitness as a component of physical fitness; certainly history reveals many generals who lost the edge on their opponent for what can only be explained as lack of mental toughness.

Training of General Officers

Until the latter part of the twentieth century, there has been no systematic method to train general officers. Since the American difficulties in the Vietnam War, more attention has been given to how general officers should be selected and trained for their responsibilities. Leadership institutes have been established, senior leadership manuals written, and both behavioral and historical studies of generalship have proliferated. The U.S. Army has developed methods for evaluating and training operational general staffs separately from their units. These efforts promise more precise scientific analysis of generalship in the future.

K. E. HAMBURGER

SEE ALSO: Command; Leadership; Span of Control: Military Organizations and Operations.

Bibliography

Barnett, C., ed. 1989. *Hitler's generals.* New York: Grove Weidenfeld.
Bausum, H. S., ed. 1986, 1987, 1988. *The John Biggs Cincinnati lectures in military leadership and command.* Lexington, Va.: VMI Foundation.

Creveld, M. van. 1985. *Command in war.* Cambridge: Harvard University Press.

Fuller, J. F. C. 1936. *Generalship: Its diseases and their cure.* Harrisburg, Pa.: Military Service.

———. 1957. *Grant and Lee: A study in personality and command.* Bloomington: Indiana Univ. Press.

Rommel, E. 1953. *The Rommel papers.* New York: Harcourt, Brace.

Slim, W. J. 1961. *Defeat into victory.* New York: David McKay.

U.S. Department of the Army. 1987. *Field manual 22-103: Leadership and command at senior levels.* Washington, D.C.: Department of the Army.

Wavell, A. 1941. *Generals and generalship.* New York: Macmillan.

Zais, M. M. 1985. *Generalship and the art of senior command: Historical and scientific perspectives.* Thesis. U.S. Army Command and General Staff College. Ft. Leavenworth, Kans.

GEOGRAPHY, MILITARY

Military geography is that part of military science that deals with the characteristics of the area of operations as they relate to military missions and forces. Military geography is the application of the geographic method of analysis to military problems.

Geography

Geography is the science that deals with the spatial distribution of phenomena at or near the surface of the earth. Geography is used to explain the patterns and relationships of natural and human phenomena: people and the artifacts of their cultures, animals, vegetation, climate, oceans, and landforms. These patterns and relationships are significant only in terms of a problem to be solved. Geography may be broken down into branches according to the type of problem being addressed. Economic geography covers the spatial distribution of factories and ports and the movement of goods and dollars among various locations. Human geography covers the way in which people live and relate to their environment. Urban geography covers the relationships among the different parts of cities. Political geography covers patterns among nation-states or other political entities. Physical geography covers the natural features of the earth's surface, such as rivers, mountains, plains, storms, and soil. Finally, geography is concerned with regions defined by the nature and scope of the problem being addressed. The geographic method of analysis seeks to define appropriate regions and explain the spatial distribution of phenomena in the region in the context of a problem.

Military Geography

Military geography is applied in regions defined by the missions of the military forces. Military geography is subdivided into four major branches: terrain analysis; theater analysis; geopolitics; and topical military geography. The first three of these may be related to the tripartite division of military art as follows:

LEVEL OF WARFARE	SCOPE	BRANCH OF MILITARY GEOGRAPHY
Strategy	Global	Geopolitics
Operational art	Theater of operations	Theater analysis
Tactics	Battlefield	Terrain analysis

TERRAIN ANALYSIS

Terrain analysis is used to determine the effect of the natural and manmade features of an area of operations on tactical military operations. It includes consideration of natural phenomena such as landforms, relief, drainage patterns, vegetation, animal and insect life, and surface materials. It includes consideration of works of man such as buildings, roads, railroads, airfields, dams, pipelines, and cultivation, but it does not usually consider humans in the area of interest. Terrain analysis may also include consideration of weather and climate.

Terms other than *terrain analysis* are also used to describe the application of military geography at the tactical level. *Terrain appreciation* is often used interchangeably with terrain analysis, although it implies a narrower and deeper study of the landforms of the area. *Terrain intelligence* implies more emphasis on basic data compilation than on mission-oriented analysis. *Military topography* was used formerly to mean the study of landforms from a military viewpoint, but now it refers primarily to map making and map reading. *Topography* still means the landforms of an area.

Terrain analysis is mission oriented. The area of operations is defined by the mission, and the significance of a terrain feature will vary depending on the nature of the mission. For example, a hill or a river has a different significance if the mission is to defend rather than to attack.

Terrain analysis is dynamic. The evolving military situation constantly changes missions and viewpoints and thus constantly changes the significance of the terrain for the military commander. Changes in military weapons and technology can also alter the relative significance of terrain features. A river, which was a formidable barrier, can become a trivial problem with the introduction of improved combat bridging equipment. A distant target, which was not worth considering, can become important with the introduction of long-range weapons. The terrain itself also changes. It is modified by natural forces such as erosion and earthquakes, and it is also modified by man's construction of roads, airfields, and bridges. It is modified by military operations from the effects of troop movements, artillery fire, air strikes, and demolition of structures.

The military components of terrain analysis are:
1. *Obstacles:* terrain features that slow down or stop momentarily the movement of either enemy or friendly forces.
2. *Fields of fire:* the tendency of an area to facilitate or hinder direct fire by flat-trajectory weapons and missiles.

3. *Observation:* the tendency of an area to permit or deny visual or sensor detection of the enemy.
4. *Concealment:* the tendency of an area to facilitate avoiding observation by the enemy.
5. *Cover:* the tendency of an area to afford protection against being hit by enemy direct-fire weapons and missiles.
6. *Routes of communication:* roads or paths for movement of troops and vehicles.

An essential element of terrain analysis is the definition and interpretation of the spatial relationships among terrain features. For example, if the military mission is to seize a crossroads, several factors must be noted: the precise location of the crossroads, the distance and direction of the crossroads from the military unit, the characteristics of the intervening ground, and the relative position of terrain features (i.e., whether they will help or hinder the unit in accomplishing its mission). All of these factors must be taken into account along with the capabilities of the unit's weapons, equipment, and troops, to determine not only the time it will take to accomplish the mission, but also whether the mission can be accomplished at all.

Terrain analysis also varies according to the level at which it is carried out. Smaller units use a greater level of detail than larger units. For an individual rifleman or gunner, for example, a single tree or a small hill or hollow offering cover and concealment are of paramount interest. At the rifle company level, however, a clearing or the next ridgeline are the significant terrain features and fields of fire, the primary concern. At the infantry or tank battalion level, the commander's interest is in obstacles such as villages, forests, or streams, while at the division level routes of communication may be the most important features.

Terrain is evaluated differently by different commanders, depending on the type and extent of influence the terrain will have on their units. A tank company commander, for example, with great organic tactical mobility will draw different conclusions about an area than the conclusions drawn by an airborne rifle company commander with few or no vehicles. An air assault division commander with several hundred helicopters will draw different conclusions about the nature of his area of operations than would an armored division commander with several hundred tanks. Each commander must perform terrain analysis that is appropriate for the mission, role, and circumstances of the unit.

THEATER ANALYSIS

Theater analysis, or strategic area analysis, is the application of military geography at the level of operational art. Theater analysis is used to describe the influence on military operations of the characteristics of an actual or potential theater of war.

Theater analysis, unlike terrain analysis, does include humans in its consideration of natural and manmade features in the theater of operations. The occupancy patterns of human activity, consisting of towns, agricultural areas, roads, railroads, and airfields are of interest, as well as landforms, drainage, vegetation, and climate.

There is also a difference in scale between theater analysis and terrain analysis. Theater analysis takes into account the entire area of operations; terrain analysis has a more restricted or localized viewpoint. To the division commander, a river is an obstacle either to be crossed or defended. To the theater commander, the same river is only part of a total pattern of drainage indicating likely defensive positions or avenues of approach for an offensive. The principles are the same, and the influence of the river is likely to be similar, but the scale is different.

Theater area analysis also tends to be less mission oriented than terrain analysis. At the theater and army group levels, missions are generally stated in broad terms, significant mission changes occur infrequently, and the planning cycle may be several weeks or months. For an army corps, the planning cycle may be several days or a few weeks; for a rifle company it may be measured in minutes.

Theater analysis tends to be more predictive than terrain analysis. Estimates used in the planning process at the theater headquarters must predict the impact of the area of operations on operations several weeks or months in the future. Terrain analysis deals with the immediate impact; theater analysis, with future impact.

The intelligence sections of theater headquarters or major land, air, or naval headquarters in the theater are responsible for theater analysis. In peacetime, the primary activity of theater analysis is compilation of data on the physical and human characteristics of the theater of operations. This includes descriptions of landforms and underlying geology, climatic data, distribution of vegetation and fauna, and demographic data. Special studies are made of trafficability, highway networks, railroads, ports, navigation channels and straits, airfields, airways, pipelines, power and communications networks, urban and built-up areas, and other characteristics of interest.

Theater analyses provide the basis for planning military operations in the theater. If the winter will be severe enough to require special clothing, that will have to be taken into account in planning the campaign. If the cloud cover will restrict air operations, that has to be considered in planning the kind and amount of air force units to be employed. If the terrain in a particular location is unsuitable for tanks, that should be taken into consideration when organizing the forces for combat. The presence of civilians has implications for nuclear and conventional fire-support planning. The impact of refugees on the movement of troops and supplies may cause a diversion of resources. All of these factors must be taken into account in theater analysis.

Finally, the spatial perspective is an essential element of theater analysis. Because the distances are greater and the times longer, the interaction of space-time factors with military forces becomes more important at the level of operational art (theater analysis) than at the tactical level (terrain analysis). This is particularly true for selection of targets for battlefield or long-range interdiction, major defensive positions, or offensive axes of advance. Properly conducted, the theater analysis constitutes a complete application of geographic method to the military problem.

GEOPOLITICS

The application of military geography at the strategic or global level is called geopolitics. Geopolitics integrates political, diplomatic, sociological, economic, and military considerations into an overall strategic approach. Geopolitics is concerned with relative power among nations and coalitions. It includes consideration of the foundations of national power: population, industry, commerce, financial status, internal stability, resources, and national will, as well as military forces.

The essence of geopolitics is consideration of the size, shape, location, and characteristics of nations with respect to one another. History offers numerous examples of the importance of location and terrain. Poland, a nation between two great powers but without natural lines of defense, has suffered repeated invasions. Switzerland has remained neutral and untouched through several major wars in its alpine bastion. The United States, secure from invasion and remote from Europe, needed only a small navy and an even smaller army from 1865 to 1917. Japan, lacking a large land area and raw materials, sought security by expanding into China and Southeast Asia.

Geopolitics recognizes tension between nations that are maritime powers and those that are land-based powers. Alfred Thayer Mahan advanced the concept of maritime power based largely on the experience of the British, who, invulnerable to invasion from the European continent, ruled a global empire for 140 years by virtue of a superior navy and a substantial merchant marine. In 1904 Sir Harold Mackinder identified the plains of Russia as the Heartland of Europe and predicted eventual global supremacy for the ruler of the Heartland. In Germany before World War II, Karl Haushofer bolstered German war aims by asserting that a combination of Germany, Russia, and Japan was unbeatable. Hitler's invasion of the Soviet Union, against Haushofer's advice, forced a coalition between the maritime power of the British Empire and the United States and the land power of the Soviet Union that led ultimately to the defeat of Germany in 1945. In 1943 Nicholas Spykman advanced the concept of the Rimlands in opposition to the Heartland concept. According to Spykman, a combination of the economic and industrial superiority of the Rimlands—the United States, Western Europe, and the nations of the Pacific basin—would be more powerful than the Soviet Heartland.

Geopolitics is a major element of military strategic thinking in the nuclear age. Geopolitical concepts of relative location and power are important in maintaining a global balance of power by coalitions between the superpowers and the medium powers. Geopolitical ideas underlie the current debate in the United States between advocates of a maritime strategy and adherents of a coalition (land-based) strategy. Geopolitics helps to understand how future changes in the relative power of nations will affect potential military operations.

TOPICAL MILITARY GEOGRAPHY

Topical military geography covers a particular, well-defined type of phenomena (a topic) on a worldwide basis. The major military applications of topical geography are:

Environmental studies. Environmental studies of climate, vegetation, and fauna are important in providing the correct equipment and training for military forces to be employed in various parts of the world. Troops employed in arctic regions need to be trained and equipped differently from troops employed in low-latitude deserts. This kind of topical military geography is often employed in the research and development process as new equipment, clothing, and supplies are developed.

Military geology. Geology is a scientific discipline dealing with the nature of the rock formations underlying the surface of the earth. Military geology provides a sound basis for protective construction for cover against conventional or nuclear explosions. It is also used to locate sources of water. Military geology is sometimes considered to be separate from military geography.

Geodesy. Geodesy is the science of global earth measurement that allows the precise location of points on the surface of the earth. Surveying, geodesy on a smaller scale, has been important in military operations since the introduction of field telegraphy allowed the use of indirect-fire control with artillery. The advent of nuclear weapons and very long-range missiles has increased the importance of knowing the exact location of potential targets.

Military topography. Military topography originally meant the study of the impact of landforms on military operations, but the term now applies to the making and, particularly, the reading, of maps. Topographic maps are a representation of a portion of the earth's surface, usually of a land area, and include a means to represent altitude or relief. Relief is the difference between the high points and low points of landforms in the area. Relief is shown on a topographic map by contour lines that connect points of equal elevation, by color tinting, by shading, or by hachure marks to depict mountains and other elevated landforms.

Cartography. Cartography is the science of making maps, including topographic maps, aerial charts, and naval charts. Aerial charts provide a representation of the land or sea surface, emphasizing recognizable landmarks and information on navigational aids and airfields. Navigational charts provide a representation of sea or ocean areas, coastal areas, water depth in coastal areas, and hazards and aids to navigation.

Influence of the Area of Operations on Warfare

The characteristics of the area of operations have had enormous influence on the nature of combat and warfare throughout the ages. Generally, the confluence of terrain and technology on the battlefield has determined tactics. The nature of the theater of operations has been the primary basis for campaign planning and execution. Time and distance relationships among various regions of the world along with considerations of resources and statecraft have determined strategy. The nature of the terrain and weather affects all forms of warfare. The most obvious influence is on land warfare, but air and naval warfare are also influenced by the nature of the surface of the earth.

Armies fight on and must conform to the nature of the earth's surface. Therefore, military commanders and planners must appreciate the interaction of men and equipment with the terrain and weather. Streams and forests are both barriers and avenues of advance and supply; mountains are both barriers and bastions; gaps and passes historically have had great military significance; hills are easy to cross and easy to defend; dry plateaus resemble the sea and favor rapid, mobile warfare; wet plateaus are rugged and make it difficult for military forces to move rapidly; and the boundary between land and sea—the coasts—is important for amphibious warfare and for access to the interior. Man-made structures have become increasingly important both as objectives and as defensive positions. Intimate knowledge of landforms and how to take advantage of them is a valuable tool for accomplishing a military mission.

Air and naval forces do not fight on land, but they are both dependent ultimately on land bases, although the nuclear-powered aircraft carrier and its nuclear-powered escorts may operate for extended periods of time without returning to base. So it is important to understand what influence the land will have on military operations by air and naval forces. Air forces fight from and over land, and their concerns in the area of operations are the suitability of the land for airfields and the adequacy of supporting roads and railroads. The nature of the terrain also influences the tactics and munitions that are appropriate to attack ground targets, particularly for low-flying aircraft such as helicopters and close-support attack aircraft. Despite great advances in high-technology navigation systems, aviators may have to rely sometimes on recognition of terrain features to locate themselves and their targets.

Navies also must learn the lay of the land. The nature of coastlines determines the availability of safe harbors and anchorages, for storms remain a dangerous foe for ships at sea. The distance of naval combat from supporting bases is still a major factor in planning and implementing naval warfare, although the time that a fleet can remain at sea without resupply has increased. The configuration of the ocean bottom is a major factor in undersea warfare. Even space warfare would be influenced by the wind patterns of the atmosphere and the shape and nature of the earth below.

WORLD WAR II

World War II was a truly global war, which necessitated an appreciation for military geography by both sides. Although the major land battles early in the war were fought in Europe, ultimately the Allies also conducted major ground campaigns in the Middle East, the Mediterranean area, China, Burma, the southwest Pacific, the central Pacific, and Manchuria. The nature of the war in each of these major theaters was dictated by the relative priority of the theater for resources and by the terrain and climate. Combat occurred in frozen mountains in Italy, on hot deserts in North Africa, across the stormy North Atlantic, on the vast ocean expanses of the Pacific, and in the moist tropical rain forests of Burma. The Allies had to produce uniforms and equipment, tactics, and techniques suitable for operations under these varied conditions. That they did this successfully reflects the best use of military geography until the Persian Gulf War of 1990–91.

On the tactical level, there were pluses and minuses. The Allies planned carefully for the breakout of armed forces from the landing areas secured by the Normandy invasion in June 1944. However, the planners had paid insufficient attention to the implications of the local hedgerows. These were formidable stone walls overgrown with thick vegetation and were characteristic of that part of France. It took a field expedient, attaching blades to tanks to clear out the hedgerows, to free the British and American armies to move to the Rhine.

Earlier, in May 1940 the Germans and the French did take note of a terrain feature—the Ardennes Forest—but drew different conclusions. To the French the Ardennes was an obstacle impassable to vehicles and worthy only of a light defense; to the Germans the Ardennes was an avenue of attack capable of handling the main effort of the German blitzkrieg.

In North Africa the Germans under Rommel and the British under Montgomery each adapted their operations to the realities of the desert, but in different ways. Rommel operated on a shoestring with rapid mobility and improvisation to take advantage of the ease of movement over most of the area. Montgomery adopted a mobile defense backed with air superiority, which could strike the Germans and Italians almost at will. Ultimately, the British prevailed when the Germans could not resupply their fighting forces.

In Russia, the Soviets learned from their earlier war with the Finns and adapted their clothing and tactics to snow and ice while the Germans froze and bogged down in the mire.

In the Pacific, the Japanese underestimated the ability of the U.S. construction troops to carve airfields and ports out of what was thought to be impassable and unusable terrain. This lack of appreciation of the capability of 1940s technology to alter the terrain cost the Japanese heavily as they were repeatedly outflanked during General MacArthur's island-hopping campaigns.

At the Ardennes Forest late in 1945 weather played an important role in the ability of the Allies to hold back the last desperate offensive by the Germans. The U.S. troops holding out in Bastogne were cut off from supplies and air support for several days because of bad weather, but when the clouds cleared, the U.S. and British planes were able to do their job and help defeat the Germans decisively. Terrain and weather were important elements during World War II.

KOREAN WAR

The invasion of South Korea by North Korea brought on some of the fiercest land fighting of the modern era. Korea was an infantryman's war. The navy supported and shelled, and the air forces attacked the North Koreans almost unchallenged. They both played important roles in the war, but the nature of the terrain in Korea was such that the outcome had to be decided on the ground.

Except for the western plain and small areas on the coast, Korea is a mountainous country with high relief. Relief is a measure of the difference in elevation between high points and low points and indicates the ruggedness of the land. Korea is a land of steep slopes, long ridges, and narrow valleys. Initially, the North Koreans took advantage of the roads and railroads to move swiftly southward with their tanks and trucks.

The U.S. forces, thrown unprepared into the breach, at first failed to appreciate the significance of the terrain; they moved in the valleys, which invited ambush and defeat. Adding to their misery was the cold and snowy weather for which the U.S. troops were also unprepared, with respect to both clothing and tactics. The North Koreans and the Chinese, however, took advantage of the terrain and weather. They fought at night in the worst weather, keeping to the ground and moving along the ridgelines to bring plunging fire to bear on the road-bound Americans in the valleys below. Fighting desperately, the U.S. and Republic of Korea (ROK) forces gradually adapted to the terrain and weather. They learned to fight on the ridges and make sure they had the high ground. They used artillery to attack North Korean troops dug into defensive positions high in the mountains. They learned how to live and fight in cold weather. Eventually, they fought their opponents to a military and political draw. The early stages of the Korean War illustrate the consequences of a lack of attention to military geography. Things that should have been known were not, and lives and battles were lost as a consequence.

Vietnam War

The terrain and weather of Southeast Asia had a major impact on the Vietnam War, and the time and distance of the area of operations from the United States influenced the strategy and the outcome of the war. The long distances involved increased the difficulties of establishing and maintaining the logistical pipelines of supplies and replacements. While the materiel problem was solved by the application of massive resources, the distance of Vietnam from the United States made the problem appear remote and may have contributed to the loss of public support that eventually ended the war without the United States having achieved its strategic objectives.

The nature of the theater had a definite influence on campaign planning. The three major regions of Vietnam where U.S. and allied troops fought were the northern coastal plain, the Central Highlands, and the Mekong Delta. At the outset the U.S. campaign plan was to find and defeat decisively the North Vietnamese forces while simultaneously conducting counterinsurgency operations against the Vietcong. This led the United States to distribute its forces across the nation more or less in proportion to the population rather than to the threat. Key terrain was defined tactically and not for the entire theater, and the option of closing off the border between South and North Vietnam extending into Laos was not pursued aggressively or with overwhelming force. Although the United States consistently won on the battlefield, the campaign turned into a war of attrition, which was won by North Vietnam as the United States lost its will to fight.

At the tactical level, the rugged and mountainous terrain in the Central Highlands and the heavy rainfall in the Mekong Delta slowed the tempo of operations and made it difficult for the United States to bring to bear fully its advantage in modern weapons. The thick vegetation of the triple canopy rain forest diminished the effects of air attacks and made bomb damage assessment difficult. The vegetation also offered the attacking North Vietnamese and Viet-cong the advantage of concealment, which they used to great effect in am-bushes. The United States responded by removing the protective vegetation, cutting down the trees and killing them with chemical defoliants.

Fighting a new kind of warfare without fronts, the U.S. and South Vietnam-ese forces tried to overcome the terrain with new technology—primarily heli-copters. This worked to a certain extent and made it possible for the U.S. and South Vietnamese forces to win almost all tactical engagements. After losing a few early battles conclusively, however, the North Vietnamese refused to stand and fight in decisive battles. They appreciated the nature of the terrain and took advantage of it to build combat power slowly and steadily under the conceal-ment offered by the terrain until they had sufficient force to defeat the South Vietnamese forces in conventional combat. The U.S. and South Vietnamese forces fought well and won most of the time but in the end were defeated by the terrain and the will of their opponent.

Persian Gulf War

The Persian Gulf War took place in a region entirely different from Southeast Asia. The terrain in Kuwait, Saudi Arabia, and Iraq is desert with low eleva-tions, little vegetation, and little rainfall.

Kuwait is 7,000 miles from the United States, but the United States had for several years been building a capability to project its armed forces rapidly to just such a remote location. Airlift, sealift, and pre-positioned equipment and supplies were on hand when President Bush decided to commit U.S. forces to defend Saudi Arabia and then to free Kuwait from Iraq. The strategic time and distance factors, however, did cause great anxiety for the U.S. commanders who were forced to wait for several weeks until the U.S. and coalition forces were sufficient to defend Saudi Arabia and another several weeks until enough forces had been assembled in the theater to take the offensive.

From a theater viewpoint, the man-made features of Saudi Arabia were critical to the success of the U.S. and coalition forces. Saudi Arabia had con-structed modern airfields, ports, and roads in the northern area near Kuwait and Iraq in anticipation of this contingency. The availability of these facilities was crucial to the success of the U.S. buildup and resupply operations. If these facilities had not been available, it would have been much more difficult—and perhaps impossible—for the coalition forces to have done what they did. The shallow seas of the Persian Gulf and the coastal islands off the coast of Kuwait made naval operations difficult and contributed significantly to the decision to make an amphibious operation a feint rather than a real attack.

Tactically, the lack of cover and concealment for the Iraqi forces was very important. The U.S. and coalition aircraft, having beaten the Iraqi air forces, could attack ground targets that could not hide. Although there were some problems due to unfavorable weather, in general the area was ideal for air operations. The mobility afforded ground vehicles in the desert areas west of Kuwait made possible the gigantic single envelopment that struck deep into Iraq and then turned to cut off the Iraqi Republican Guard from behind. Although the Iraqis sought to create artificial obstacles, they found it a difficult task since lacking terrain favorable for the defense. Finally, modern high-technology tank guns and missiles were at their best in the flat terrain and able to fire accurately at long ranges over excellent fields of fire. The success of the United States and the coalition against Iraq is evidence of sound appreciation of the terrain and weather in the area of operations and illustrates the application of military geography at its best.

Overall Characteristics of Military Geography

Military geography is mission oriented. The mere compilation of data on a military theater or area of operations does not constitute an application of military geography. The essential nature of the geographic process comes into play only when the spatial relationships and impacts of the area are interpreted in light of a mission. If the mission changes, the effect of the features of the area of operations changes also.

Military geography is part of the commander's planning process. The planning process begins when a new mission is received from higher headquarters. After the commander has analyzed and elaborated on the mission, the next step is to make an estimate of the situation. The estimate of the situation includes consideration of the mission, friendly forces, enemy forces, and a military geographic analysis of the characteristics of the area of operations. Alternative courses of action to accomplish the mission are drawn up and evaluated. The commander decides upon a course of action and issues orders to that effect. The products of the planning process are missions for subordinate units. The receipt of these new missions at lower levels in turn initiates a new cycle of military planning, including additional estimates of the situation and geographic analyses of new areas of operations.

The area of operations is the geographic region defined by the military mission. It comprises the area directly influenced by the forces and weapons under the control of the commander. It includes the area occupied by the opposing enemy force, terrain features designated as objectives to be seized or held, area held by adjacent friendly units, and the support area of the military organization itself. The commander needs to know everything about the area of operations and is also interested in major events in a larger area of interest, which includes the area of operations. The commander may assign reconnaissance resources to report on the area of interest or request intelligence on the area of interest from higher headquarters.

Military geography is an element of military intelligence and the responsibility of the staff intelligence officer. The compilation of data on natural and man-made terrain features and on human factors in a theater or area of operations usually is performed by intelligence sections and organizations. In intelligence terms, combat intelligence corresponds to terrain analysis, and strategic intelligence corresponds to theater analysis.

Military geography is three-dimensional. Warfare takes place in the oceans below the earth's surface and in the atmosphere above the earth's surface, as well as on the surface. Time and distance factors and the importance of relative positions take on different meanings when it is possible to deliver munitions by aircraft or missile or observe from a satellite. Submarines, aircraft, and satellites in earth orbit, with the possibility of manned space stations, must be considered in making the estimate of the situation. The area of operations is in reality a three-dimensional volume ranging from below the surface of the earth to the outer boundary of inner space.

Military geography uses the latest in modern technology and methodology. Earth satellites are used in geodesy and cartography. Aerial and space photography is used in cartography, terrain analysis, and theater analysis. Computers are used to calculate time and space factors and target locations and to compile, manage, and analyze geographic data. Modern methods of mathematical, statistical, and spatial analysis are applied to military geographic problems.

Problems of Military Geography

There is a general lack of knowledge about military geography. All military forces employ the various elements of military geography, but most of them do not realize that they are using military geography. Terrain analysis is always part of tactical doctrine. Theater analysis is an accepted part of the intelligence process. Geopolitics is employed in politico-military strategic studies. These applications of military geography often are used without an appreciation for the spatial viewpoint of geographic analysis.

Military geography is seldom taught as a unified discipline. Terrain analysis and theater analysis are taught in military schools as part of courses on tactics or intelligence, and the elements of geopolitics are taught at war colleges. The essential appreciation of geography as a discipline unified by the process of spatial analysis, however, has been lost.

The inclusion of area analysis in the intelligence staff function has the advantage of providing a sponsor for this activity. It has the disadvantage of reinforcing the tendency of commanders and operations officers to concentrate on enemy and friendly forces and ignore or relegate to secondary importance the characteristics of the area of operations.

Value of Military Geography

Military geography has had substantial impact on military combat in the past. The Russian winter played a part in defeating both Napoleon and Hitler. The defensible landforms (*cuestas*) north of Paris helped France stop the invading Germans in 1914. The hedgerows of Normandy stalled the Allied advance in

1944. The vastness of China thwarted Japanese attempts at military domination in the 1930s. The nature of the Persian Gulf area made it possible for U.S. technology to crush the Iraqi army overwhelmingly in short order. It is logical to believe that military geography will also have a substantial impact on combat in the future.

The value of military geography is that it integrates the effects of the area of operations by a process of spatial analysis. Military geography does not live up to its potential because it is seldom applied by trained geographers or by military personnel who understand geographic method. Even so, the ideas and concepts of geography are now, more than ever, essential to the planning and conduct of military operations.

JOHN R. BRINKERHOFF

SEE ALSO: Deception; Maps, Charts, and Symbols, Military; Theater of War.

Bibliography

Able, R. F., M. G. Marcus, and J. M. Olson, eds. 1992. *Geography's inner worlds: Pervasive themes in contemporary American geography.* New Brunswick, N.J.: Rutgers Univ. Press.
Faringdon, H. 1986. *Confrontation: The strategic geography of NATO and the Warsaw Pact.* London and New York: Routledge and Kegan Paul.
Gray, C. S. 1988. *The geopolitics of super power.* Lexington, Ky.: Univ. of Kentucky Press.
Hartshorne, R. 1962. *Perspective on the nature of geography.* Association of American Geographers. Chicago: Rand McNally.
James, P. E., and C. F. Jones, eds. 1954. *American geography: Inventory and prospect.* Association of American Geographers. Syracuse, N.Y.: Syracuse Univ. Press.
O'Sullivan P., and J. W. Miller. 1983. *The geography of warfare.* New York: St. Martin's Press.
Rosen, S. J. 1977. *Military geography and the military balance in the Arab-Israeli conflict.* Jerusalem: Hebrew Univ.
Zoppo, C. E., and C. Zorgbibe. 1985. *On geopolitics: Classical and nuclear.* NATO Advanced Science Institutes Studies. Dordrecht: Martinus Nijhoff.
U.S. Department of the Army. 1972. *Field manual 30–10: Military geographic intelligence (terrain).* Washington, D.C.: Government Printing Office.

GRENADE

Grenades provide soldiers on the battlefield with a cheap but lethal weapon suitable for use in a variety of situations, both on the attack and in defense. There are two main types of grenades: hand grenades, which the soldier throws by hand, and others that are fired from attachments to the soldier's rifle.

Hand grenades are used primarily by infantry soldiers and special troops (rangers, commandos, and parachutists). They are small in size, light in weight, and easily thrown by hand. The many types of hand grenades include defensive, offensive, smoke, antitank, illumination, and tear gas.

Rifle grenades are designed to be fired without the need for additional equipment. Again there are many types; they include antipersonnel, antitank, smoke, illumination, and dual-purpose antipersonnel.

Hand Grenades

Table 1 sets forth the main characteristics of the two primary types of hand grenades, those designed for defensive and those for offensive use.

Defensive hand grenades are used by infantry soldiers who throw them and then remain under cover, thereby causing heavy casualties among attacking forces.

Offensive hand grenades are used by assaulting infantry. They throw these grenades while continuing to move forward, seeking to daze and demoralize the defenders while creating suitable conditions for gaining temporary advantages and pressing home the assault. Such grenades are used in assaulting buildings, strong points, and other defensive positions.

Multipurpose (defensive and offensive) hand grenades have characteristics such that they can be used in both defensive and offensive action. For use in the defensive mode, a steel fragmentation casing may be fitted over the grenade's body. For offense only the basic grenade is used, primarily for its blast and shock effect.

Smoke-generating grenades are made of tinned steel and are capable of producing smoke in different colors (typically white, green, red, yellow, or gray) that lasts for one to two minutes. Some smoke grenades contain white phosphorus and produce not only smoke but also incendiary effects.

Antitank hand grenades are used at close ranges (15 to 20 m). These are antiarmor grenades that can pierce steel up to 75 to 100 mm thick. The effective fragments have a range of 20 meters (approx. 65 ft.). Such grenades are used by infantry from protected defensive positions against armored vehicles and may also be effectively employed by guerrillas and by militia units engaged in street fighting.

Illuminating grenades are designed to illuminate the surrounding area up to a radius of 100 meters (328 ft.). Burning time is about 45 seconds. They are used for observation of a particular area.

Tear gas (riot control) hand grenades are cylindrical grenades with a body made of tinned rolled plate. They can be thrown about 40 meters (approx. 130 ft.). The fuze is initiated to puncture a gas cartridge, which produces a stream

TABLE 1. *Characteristics of Defensive and Offensive Grenades*

CHARACTERISTIC	DEFENSIVE	OFFENSIVE
Effectiveness	Danger area 5–15m	Morale effect
Range of throwing	25–30m	up to 40 m
Mechanism	Time-fuzed (3.6–4.5 sec.)	Impact-fuzed
Fragmentation	About 3,500 steel balls, each 2.5–3mm in diameter	Very light fragments causing considerable blast effect
Weight	Heavy (309–486 gm)	Light (220–309 gm)

of tear gas for about one minute. These grenades are used mainly for control of civil disturbances.

Rifle Grenades

Antipersonnel rifle grenades come in two types, each described below.

Short-range antipersonnel rifle grenades have a maximum range of 300 meters (approx. 985 ft.) and produce a large number of fragments. The affected area is 20 meters (approx. 65 ft.) in diameter. Such a grenade is light, weighing not more than 341 grams, which enables the soldier to carry a number of them without limiting his mobility. It can be fired from a standing or prone position because of its light recoil. The weapon may be used effectively against small groups of enemy in the open, against buildings and bunkers, and in defilade positions.

Long-range antipersonnel grenades are fitted with a rocket propellant that ignites automatically when the grenade is fired, thus extending the range up to 650 meters (approx. 2,150 ft.) and the dangerous area up to a 40-meter (130-ft.) diameter. They can be fired from a standing or prone position while holding the rifle at a 45-degree angle, enabling the soldier to engage hidden targets behind barriers and in effect allowing the rifle to perform the function of a light mortar.

Antitank rifle grenades can pierce steel to a depth of 25 centimeters (approx. 10 in.). Their weight does not exceed 350 grams, so a soldier can carry several without impairing his mobility. They are fitted with a marked sight graduated from 50 meters to 200 meters (165 to 650 ft.), which is the maximum range of this grenade. They are noted for accuracy, have very low recoil, and can be used successfully to cover the distance beyond antitank hand-grenade range (more than 50 m) and the dead area that antitank missiles cannot reach (out to 200 m).

Smoke-generating rifle grenades produce a persistent and intense opaque smoke. They are effective for some 80 seconds at ranges of 50 to 300 meters (165 to 985 ft.) from the firer. The grenade weighs about 470 grams. A soldier can launch up to five grenades per minute. Versions are available that produce red, green, yellow, or white smoke, so that the resultant smoke can be used for either spotting or screening.

Illuminating rifle grenades produce an intense yellow illumination for about 30 seconds as a flare slowly descends by parachute after having been deployed at an angle of 80 degrees and a height of 100 meters (328 ft.). The grenade weighs 420 grams.

Dual-purpose antipersonnel grenades are designed so that they can be either thrown by hand or launched from a rifle with the use of a regular ball cartridge. For the latter purpose the tail of the grenade is fitted with a bullet trap. The grenade is also time fuzed, making air bursts possible. Maximum range is 225 meters (approx. 740 ft.). Each round weighs 615 grams and produces about 500 fragments. The weapon may be employed either offensively or defensively by changing the ball of the grenade in accordance with the desired effect.

SAMIR HASSAN SHALABY

SEE ALSO: Ammunition; Firepower; Mortar; Munitions and Explosives Technology Applications; Small Arms.

Bibliography

Chamberlain, P., and T. Gander. 1976. *Allied pistols, rifles and grenades.* New York: Arco Books.

———. 1977. *Axis pistols, rifles and grenades.* New York: Arco Books.

Hogg, I. V. 1977. *The encyclopedia of infantry weapons of World War II.* New York: Thomas Y. Crowell.

Jane's infantry weapons, 1983–84. 1983. London: Jane's.

Rosser-Owen, D. 1986. *Vietnam weapons handbook.* Wellingborough, U.K.: Patrick Stephens.

GROUND RECONNAISSANCE

Ground reconnaissance, a military function and craft, is the examination or observation of an area or specific location to gain militarily significant information. Information gained can be of a tactical or a strategic nature and may include enemy strengths, activities, and dispositions; the nature of terrain; obstacles to movement; results of friendly actions; and likely routes of approach. Strategic ground reconnaissance may be aimed at learning a target population's attitudes, social conditions, economic and political activities, and receptivity to friendly forces. Ground reconnaissance may be accomplished by combat action, overt observation, or stealth; the latter method is often referred to as "scouting." Ground reconnaissance is of ancient origin and has always been important to military commanders. The absence of an adequate ground reconnaissance can be fatal to a plan's execution, a commander's performance, or the conduct of war itself. For much of recorded history, there was little distinction made between reconnaissance and what would later become known as intelligence. Although air and satellite reconnaissance have greatly extended the ability of military staffs to determine an area's status and the condition of an enemy force, ground reconnaissance is expected to retain its prominence and importance in military affairs.

Strategic and tactical ground reconnaissance differ in several ways. Tactical ground reconnaissance is almost always conducted just prior to or in the midst of combat operations. Strategic ground reconnaissance may be conducted during peacetime as well as during war. The two forms of ground reconnaissance also differ in scope. Strategic ground reconnaissance may reveal general demographic patterns, such as how a population is settled within a large terrain corridor. The tactical reconnaissance product may deal only with the disposition of buildings in a particular village or the relation of a road junction to a hill. Information produced by these two forms of reconnaissance is used in different ways. The results of strategic ground reconnaissance are likely to be used in assessments that can influence both policy choices and national strategic options. On the other hand, tactical information may be of use only to an infantry company commander. Normally, there is also a distinction in permanence; strategic products may remain current for decades while information derived from a tactical ground reconnaissance may only be useful for a matter of hours.

Ideally, information gained from ground reconnaissance is integrated with other information to produce a refined, final intelligence product. But on occasion, ground reconnaissance is the sole basis for action. Both strategic and tactical ground reconnaissance are often accompanied by efforts to acquire information through technical means: satellite surveillance systems with photographic, radar, infrared, and electronic intercept sensors; air photography; and supplementary sources such as human intelligence and research of pertinent literature. When all of this information is integrated, analyzed, and combined in a single document it is usually called "finished" intelligence. Therefore, the product of ground reconnaissance can be an integral part of finished intelligence, information ready for either the policy maker or the military field commander. However, the results of ground reconnaissance may be so timely, persuasive, and important that a commander may take dramatic action on the basis of one reconnaissance report alone. Such a report was made in 1945 providing American commanders with the surprising knowledge of light defenses around the Remagen Bridge over the Rhine River. Discovery of the German failure to destroy this bridge and the bold Allied action in exploiting this weakness probably shortened the Second World War in Europe by several weeks.

The very nature of ground reconnaissance—a trusted subordinate reporting from the actual scene of interest—can be far more convincing to a commander than a photograph that might not discriminate between actual weapons systems and decoys, an agent who could be operating for the other side, or an electronic surveillance report that may only reflect sound enemy communications discipline. For these reasons, ground reconnaissance will likely be valued over many other forms of intelligence gathering for years to come.

Although ground reconnaissance has its advantages, it also has some distinct drawbacks. In most cases, ground reconnaissance is a much slower process than air or satellite reconnaissance. In addition, the latter two forms can cover much wider expanses of territory and can place terrain and troop dispositions deep in the enemy rear under friendly surveillance. These areas are likely to be beyond the practical reach of friendly ground reconnaissance units. However, a sound ground reconnaissance performance can result in taking prisoners, thus gaining information about the enemy's will to fight. Furthermore, a skilled member of a reconnaissance unit may be able to determine enemy strengths, habits, and past activities on a battlefield simply by reading tracks, noting terrain marks, and observing refuse left by opposition forces. Ground reconnaissance forces may be used, on the one hand, to provoke enemy reactions, reactions that might reveal strengths and weaknesses as well as unit dispositions. On the other hand, a poorly executed ground reconnaissance can reveal one's own intentions. If an attacker concentrates his reconnaissance forces at a likely point of attack, the defender may determine his opponent's design in time to reinforce a critical weak point.

Through the years a number of patterns have developed around ground reconnaissance activities, and future shaping trends can be discerned. Several distinct types of ground reconnaissance have evolved, each with its own characteristics. The historic use of light cavalry to conduct reconnaissance was almost universal, but industrialized nations began replacing these units with armored organizations in the twentieth century. Standard, well-known defensive techniques have been established to deny an opponent the opportunity to gain potentially damaging information through ground reconnaissance. Thus this field of military lore has developed like others, a cat-and-mouse game of moves and countermoves. Eastern nations (China, Vietnam, etc.) have often concentrated reconnaissance missions, training, and capabilities in foot-mobile units. On occasion, they have accomplished combat reconnaissance by use of their clandestine intelligence organizations.

Several evolutionary trends are emerging. Until recently, ground reconnaissance was shifting toward units using helicopters. Helicopters, of course, speed the process of moving to and returning from a target area. Often these units land and recover reconnaissance troops who have performed their classic role on foot. However, helicopters are becoming increasingly vulnerable to shoulder-fired infantry antiaircraft missiles. Highly trained special operations forces are gradually being given more and more reconnaissance tasks, often of a strategic nature. In a different kind of change, the information explosion, growth in the knowledge industry, and ever-expanding computer-assisted means to manage information are making quiet research and mundane staff work an increasingly valuable tool in strategic ground reconnaissance.

Historical Background

The function of ground reconnaissance has been associated with military affairs and warfare since the earliest recorded times. The biblical phrase for ground reconnaissance was "spying out the land." Moses used these words to describe the task for some of his followers in the land of Canaan. The word *reconnaissance* has evolved from the Old French word for "recognize"; this implies that the hearer of a reconnaissance report would know an area although he had never laid eyes on it. Early descriptions of warfare made no distinction between intelligence and reconnaissance. Indeed, the distinction was only firmly established in military literature during the latter part of the nineteenth century and the early part of the twentieth.

The simple requirements of receiving a general's instructions, proceeding to the area in question, and returning to render the anticipated report put a premium on speed. It is therefore not surprising that the reconnaissance craft has been associated with cavalry organizations. The Mongols were particularly adept at reconnaissance, sending specially picked riders hundreds of miles into an adversary's territory well in advance of an approaching army. The reports from these cavalrymen formed the primary basis for a Mongol commander's decision. This type of ground reconnaissance lasted well into the twentieth century. It was exhibited by camel-borne raiders coming from Saudi Arabia in formations of as many as 2,000 riders to pillage and loot Iraq as late as 1929. The techniques used by these warlike bedouin tribes included a general mounted reconnaissance to establish the locations of probable grazing areas, a more specific search maybe a month later, and a detailed reconnaissance the night before a raid on hapless shepherds and their flocks. These traditional reconnaissance techniques, witnessed and recorded by twentieth-century British military authorities, are believed to be little different from the methods used by reconnaissance elements of Genghis Khan's great army hundreds of years before.

Most modern-day distinctions among various types of tactical reconnaissance and counter-reconnaissance techniques and the current fundamentals of strategic ground reconnaissance can be dated from the nineteenth century. Napoleon was noted for the organized collection of written material and maps. He regularly gave his ambassadors detailed tasks for acquiring specific information and he made systematic observations during his own travels. All of this data and information were developed on regions where Bonaparte believed future military campaigns might occur. In effect, he was conducting strategic ground reconnaissance and was rarely without a considerable wealth of vital information for contingencies. Later, military attachés, collection agencies, and large, complex intelligence staffs would duplicate the basic procedures Napoleon developed.

The Gettysburg campaign during the American Civil War provides examples of reconnaissance and counter-reconnaissance techniques that today's professional soldier can easily recognize. In the early summer of 1863 the Confederate commander, Gen. Robert E. Lee, directed his cavalry commander, Gen. J. E. B. Stuart, to screen the initial Confederate move northward. Stuart executed his screening mission well, placing his horsemen between the Union army and the advancing Southerners. Stuart's cavalrymen largely prevented their own line of widespread outposts and patrols from being penetrated by Union reconnaissance forces. Stuart's screen thereby secured Lee's flank and provided him with information on Union movements. Despite the fact that the Union cavalry under Gen. Alfred Pleasonton had just been reorganized into balanced teams of cavalry, horse artillery, and rapidly moving infantry, the Union commander, Gen. George Meade, learned little of Lee's move from Pleasonton's force. However, hilltop Union observation and signal posts along Lee's route of advance provided Meade with another form of reconnaissance—battlefield observation. As a result of this and other sources, the Union commander was well advised of Lee's progress. When Stuart went on his futile and ill-advised raid toward Washington, Lee was deprived of a substantial part of his reconnaissance force. Moreover, Stuart's late arrival at the Gettysburg battlefield may have contributed to Lee's imperfect understanding of Union dispositions. The lack of an adequate reconnaissance is considered by some to be a major factor in Lee's defeat, and a better use of reconnaissance figured heavily in the survival of Meade's Army of the Potomac.

Modern Ground Reconnaissance

Twentieth-century reconnaissance forces perform many of the same tasks their forebears did, but their accouterments and weapons are quite different. Horse cavalry proved to be extremely vulnerable to modern firepower during World War I, a conflict that saw the rapid development of air reconnaissance. The airplane seemed to make ground reconnaissance a thing of the past. However, the radio-equipped tank and lightly armored wheeled vehicle were also created. With the growing reliability and improved cross-country mobility of these vehicles, ground reconnaissance reclaimed its importance on World War II battlefields.

It retained its prominence in the various wars of the Middle East, the Vietnam War, and beyond. Although some armies favor thin-skinned, speedy armored vehicles for reconnaissance tasks, others, like the U.S. Army, are partial to the use of combined arms teams with main battle tanks, self-propelled artillery, and mechanized infantry formations. This heavy type of organization is capable of conducting stand-up battles with substantial enemy formations, allowing American commanders to readily determine an opponent's actual strength and weapons' positions. In addition, a hefty reconnaissance formation can easily brush aside or roll through light resistance, contributing to the rapid advance of the main body. Also, heavy armored cavalry forces can confuse an attacking opponent by portraying an apparent main line of a defense when, in fact, the attacker is actually probing a relatively thin cavalry screen, well in advance of the primary defense position.

The penalty for this type of weighty reconnaissance structure, of course, is that it is every bit as expensive, every bit as heavy and difficult to move strategically, and just as difficult to maintain as a standard armored or mechanized infantry formation. In the later stages of the Vietnam War, however, when Hanoi increasingly sent regularly organized infantry units to South Vietnam, the heavily equipped American armored cavalry units proved particularly useful in a reconnaissance-in-force role. Ranging about the flat, thinly forested area north of Saigon known as War Zones C and D and in the Central Highlands region of South Vietnam, these units covered vast areas of territory in a short amount of time, often discovering North Vietnamese forces. In most instances, the speed of reinforcement that these armor forces exhibited ensured that Communist units were quickly outnumbered, outgunned, and overcome. In the rare cases where the North Vietnamese held the upper hand, the cavalrymen completed their reconnaissance-in-force role by maintaining contact with their enemies until artillery and air-supported infantry formations could be transported to the contact site.

Without a substantial industrial base to equip large armor formations, some nations in the Eastern Hemisphere became adept at foot-mobile reconnaissance. During the Korean War, China's army used "line crossers," reconnaissance troops who in some instances were dressed as South Korean peasants or soldiers. Line crossers infiltrated United Nations positions during darkness and returned to their own headquarters with detailed, tactically significant information. During the Vietnam War, North Vietnamese and Vietcong troops mimicked their Chinese counterparts but improved on the technique by recruiting and training local civilians, some of whom worked at U.S. or South Vietnamese installations. North Vietnamese Army sappers, especially, won the respect and admiration of their adversaries by their daring reconnaissance feats. Stripped almost naked, these brave soldiers would crawl through barbed wire and minefields nightly, weeks before an attack, in order to accurately locate communications bunkers, ammunition stocks, and weapons' positions. When the Communist assault was finally launched, Americans were invariably surprised at the precision of North Vietnamese mortarmen and the unerring way the Northerners found the critical installations. This proficiency was, of course, attributable to well-executed, painstaking ground reconnaissance.

The Vietnam War also brought about wide-ranging developments in the use of helicopters for ground reconnaissance. Early in the war, Americans experimented with a technique that was initially known as the "eagle flight." In time, the eagle flight was transformed into a standard U.S. Army organization with well-tested doctrine. These organizations, "aero scout" platoons, usually had three helicopter-borne rifle squads with accompanying helicopters armed with machine guns and rockets. Rifle squad members were often landed or let down by ropes into difficult, heavily forested terrain to conduct detailed searches while the armed helicopters hovered overhead, ready to assist the foot soldiers should an enemy unit be discovered. Upon finding an enemy unit, the infantrymen would try to maintain contact with their adversaries. If outnumbered, the scouts had to break off the engagement and be recovered by transport helicopters. The aero scout platoon leader then called in larger infantry units, air strikes, and artillery fire. These units were perhaps misnamed as scout units because they rarely gained information through stealth.

Even less stealthy was the use of the armed helicopters in a reconnaissance-by-fire role. In this type of action, air cavalry units would fly over a suspected enemy area and fire their rockets or machine guns at likely hiding places, hoping to draw return fire from Communist units. Occasionally, Vietcong and North Vietnamese units would rise to the bait, firing at the probing armed helicopters. Normally this type of reaction came from an erroneous belief on the part of the Communists that their hiding spots had been discovered by the Americans. On being fired upon, the air cavalrymen would bring in enormous amounts of firepower.

Americans have considerable twentieth-century experience in classic ground reconnaissance using stealth, particularly in Asia. The World War II Burma campaign was characterized by a brilliant use of reconnaissance on the part of the Office of Strategic Services Detachment 101. Operating deep in the Burmese jungle, the detachment provided allied air forces with detailed, accurate information on heavily camouflaged and concealed Japanese troop dispositions and facilities. During the Korean War, U.S. Army units employed and directed upward of 20,000 Koreans mostly in intelligence-gathering roles deep in the rear of Chinese and North Korean lines. Based on islands off the coasts of North

Korea, these organizations supplied UN forces with a steady stream of target information for naval bombardment and air strikes and produced hundreds of prisoners of war for interrogation by American and South Korean intelligence officers.

This traditional type of reconnaissance role was repeated during the Vietnam War. From 1962 until 1972, American Special Forces units recruited, trained, and led thousands of Southeast Asians on reconnaissance missions. Normally, the tasks for these units of mixed nationality involved only the acquisition of information, not combat. In these cases, weapons were used only in self-defense, a means to break contact and escape capture. The steady expansion of these Special Forces reconnaissance units was accompanied by the battlefield activation of American Long-Range Reconnaissance Patrol units. Operating under the control of corps headquarters, these all-U.S. forces provided corps commanders with timely information on Communist dispositions in the later phases of the war.

Some of the world's special operations forces are trained and occasionally used in strategic ground reconnaissance. While most reconnaissance patrols led by the American Special Forces during the Vietnam War were gathering information in South Vietnam for tactical purposes, others were employed in more of a strategic role. For instance, U.S. Special Forces teams assigned to the Studies and Observation Group of the U.S. Military Assistance Command Vietnam (MACV-SOG) conducted extended-duration missions in Laos, defining the extent, organization, and functioning of the Ho Chi Minh Trail, Hanoi's primary line of communication to South Vietnam. These reconnaissance teams were brought to Laos either by parachute or by helicopter and their explorations along the trail complex sometimes lasted for as much as two weeks. During the Falklands/Malvinas War, the British Special Air Service (SAS) was employed in a somewhat different fashion, keeping Argentine forces under constant surveillance prior to the start of British landings and the subsequent recapture of the islands. Although details are sketchy, the former Soviet Spetsnaz forces are believed to have had a strategic ground reconnaissance role among their other duties. Members of these units are reported to have visited Allied installations in Western Europe, gathering information for their wartime tasks. Targeted facilities were believed to include command and control bunkers, ammunition storage sites, North Atlantic Treaty Organization (NATO) missile units, and critical airfields.

While strategic ground reconnaissance may on occasion be accomplished by dramatic and daring operations in war, most of the world's activity in this esoteric field is carried on in peace by large bureaucracies. Both military attachés and the employees of civilian intelligence services are daily engaged in acquiring volumes of information of military utility in potentially hostile countries or in regions where combat operations might be anticipated. The type of information collected includes details about airfields—details that would be of use whether the facility were to be either used or destroyed. For example, it is important to know the thickness of the concrete forming the runways and taxiways. Knowledge of that thickness is essential so that appropriate ordnance can be chosen for the airfield's destruction; it is equally important when a plan involves the facility's capture and use, because insubstantial construction might rule out the basing of heavy cargo aircraft. Ground commanders need to know the availability and volume of potable water supplies in a region. The construction and security arrangements of headquarters, storage sites, port facilities, and other such facilities have to be examined and calculated or estimated. The demands of amphibious operations require the examination of beaches for a determination of slopes, soil and sand characteristics, navigation hazards, and typical wave heights. Bridges must be examined for their ability to support heavy armored vehicles and logistic traffic. All of this information and much more are being collected daily by many nations conducting strategic ground reconnaissance in preparation for military operations.

Principles of Tactical Ground Combat Reconnaissance

While the armed forces of some nations may proffer little attention to formal principles of ground tactical reconnaissance, there is general agreement among professionals on what leads to the successful performance of such missions. These principles include orientation on the objective, rapid and accurate reporting, retention of the freedom to maneuver, gaining and maintaining contact, and rapid development of a contact. Of course, the principles do not apply to reconnaissance missions conducted with stealth, the true scouting tasks.

Orient on the objective. This principle merely states the seemingly obvious necessity of remaining fixed on the physical object of the mission. If the reconnaissance mission is to determine the suitability of a road as an avenue of approach, the roadway, its bridges, and the surrounding commanding terrain must be thoroughly examined for obstacles or enemy forces. However, if the mission deals with the location and description of an enemy force, a reconnaissance unit must orient on the opponent's formation even if it is moving. The reconnaissance leader must position his unit where it can best observe the enemy and survive.

Develop rapid and accurate reporting. Although reconnaissance is a broad function, its prime purpose is usually the development of information, and information is useless unless it is presented to the decision maker in an accurate and timely fashion. Complete reconnaissance reports normally answer the questions who, what, when, where, and how.

Retain the freedom to maneuver. This principle is a reminder for reconnaissance leaders to position their units so that escape can be effected if a superior enemy force is encountered. Normally, a reconnaissance mission does not include decisive engagements. The purpose is most often to gather information so other friendly elements can win in battle.

Gain and maintain contact. This rule of thumb applies only to reconnaissance units whose task is to locate and temporarily fix enemy forces so that other, more powerful friendly forces can be brought to bear.

Develop the situation rapidly. The emphasis here is to make the maximum use of time and resources. Combat reconnaissance leaders should not be deterred by distractions, minor obstacles, or scanty resistance.

Types of Tactical Ground Reconnaissance Operations

There are a number of different types and forms of ground reconnaissance operations. It is not surprising that some types include ancillary tasks of preventing an enemy's reconnaissance of friendly forces.

Scouting. Usually accomplished on foot, scouting involves obtaining information by stealth. Ideally, the scout sees without being seen. And, since the word *scout* stems from an Old French word meaning "to listen," a scout presumably listens without being heard.

Route reconnaissance. Armored cavalry units are well suited for this task. The product of the route reconnaissance is detailed information on every possible obstacle to the use of a route by a friendly force. The route may be a road or a general direction of advance. Obviously, enemy strengths, unit compositions, and locations are of vital importance, but so too are bridge capacities and unoccupied but commanding terrain features.

Screening. This reconnaissance task is usually accomplished by placing outposts or widely separated units in front or on the flank of a larger force. The purpose is to prevent the larger force from being surprised. It might be accomplished either during movement or in static situations. One task of the screening force is to prevent enemy reconnaissance forces from penetrating the screen, thereby depriving an opponent of useful information. A large screening force, perhaps two or more armored cavalry regiments, might be called a covering force.

Zone reconnaissance. Considered by many professionals to be the most time-consuming and painstaking type of reconnaissance, zone reconnaissance requires the reconnaissance unit to examine all ground intervening two boundaries, usually terrain features such as rivers or ridgelines. Reports concern roads, enemy activity, obstacles, and other pertinent information for the entire designated area.

Area reconnaissance. Area reconnaissance examines a particular region, often a suspicious town site or forest. This type of reconnaissance is often conducted by dismounted armored cavalry units or the infantry squads of an aero scout platoon.

Commander's reconnaissance. This is the reconnaissance of an area, route, objective, or prospective defensive position by a unit commander.

Engineer reconnaissance. This type of reconnaissance is usually accomplished in friendly held territory. Military engineers conduct reconnaissance operations to assess future construction work or road or bridge repair or to gather information to advise a commander on the tactical or logistical feasibility of a course of action.

Reconnaissance in force. A reconnaissance operation conducted in force seeks to obtain information and to challenge and test enemy forces. Units conducting this type of mission are normally prepared to seize the initiative and capture critical terrain, overpower light opposition, and exploit success. Along a broad front, a reconnaissance in force may consist of simultaneous, strong probes at several points. The great danger in this kind of reconnaissance is that the probing force can be trapped, pinned down in decisive combat, and destroyed before help arrives.

River reconnaissance. A mission of this type usually involves determination of likely crossing sites. The emphasis here is on steepness of banks, structure of the river bottom to identify shallow, fordable bodies of water, and typical current speeds. In the last case, it should be noted that knowledge of the average current speeds of European rivers has been instrumental in the design of amphibious combat vehicles.

Beach reconnaissance. A sound beach reconnaissance is a time-consuming task, but skilled reconnaissance teams have conducted this type of mission during the hours of darkness and under the noses of enemy forces. The purpose is to gain critical information for possible amphibious operations. The slope and composition of the beach, wave heights, underwater obstacles, nearby commanding terrain, enemy reinforcement times, and other types of information are vital to the work of amphibious warfare planners.

The Future of Ground Reconnaissance

Although it is impossible to predict the future, some distinct trends can be discerned in the realm of strategic reconnaissance; yet at the same time, the development of tactical reconnaissance seems to be reaching a crossroads. In the main, the future of strategic ground reconnaissance appears to lie in the continued evolution of special operations forces and increasingly effective staff research and information management. The growth of both civilian and military intelligence bureaucracies will probably continue, and that growth will undoubtedly be accompanied by mounting data banks of militarily significant information. It is unlikely that acquisition efforts will diminish; thus each region of the world that can conceivably be exposed to military operations will be subjected to constant scrutiny by overt and covert collection agents from many countries. Concurrently, the globe is undergoing a rapidly accelerating explosion of information: books, magazines, videotapes, travel tips, travelers' tales, maps, interviews, and news reports. These are only some of the apparently countless sources in the information flood. Some knowledge industry products are useful to military staffs interested in terrain, targets, and facilities—all part and parcel of strategic ground reconnaissance. Thus, the collection, analysis, and cataloging of open source information is likely to continue expanding. This information revolution has developed side by side with the steadily improving computer-assisted information management field. The latter greatly facilitates efficient storage and responsive retrieval of militarily useful information. The desktop publishing phenomenon, together with quick computer-drafted graphics, makes rapid publication of easily understood intelligence products feasible. Accordingly, this rather pedestrian, staff labor–produced part of strategic ground reconnaissance can be expected to grow in importance, use, and value.

Another aspect of strategic ground reconnaissance, the use of special operations forces to acquire important concealed or protected information, may also be expected to grow. In part, the reason for this growth is that the distinction between war and peace will probably remain blurred. Declarations of war seem to be a subject for historical study, so some military tasks, including strategic ground reconnaissance, are constantly under way. For example, Soviet Spetsnaz troops were probably not the only special operations forces who visit their planned wartime targets wearing civilian attire. This condition, a legacy of the Cold War, has resulted in the virtual elimination of another distinction, the once-sharp division between soldier and clandestine agent. The use of special operations forces to conduct strategic ground reconnaissance missions either in combat or before fighting has begun can be expected to continue apace.

The expansion of strategic ground reconnaissance may be accompanied by a reduction in mounted tactical ground reconnaissance. The primary reason for this possibility is that the tools for such reconnaissance—tanks and helicopters—are becoming increasingly vulnerable to hand held antitank and antiaircraft missiles. From their initial battlefield appearance in the 1970s, shoulder-fired or man-portable, passive seeker missiles have rapidly gained effectiveness. In the late 1990s and the early years of the twenty-first century, these weapons can feature spoof-proof multiple seekers, tandem warheads, and variable flight profiles. The coming infantry antitank missile, for example, may seek its prey by sensing heat, millimeter wave emissions, acoustic signals, or magnetic distortions. The path of this missile will probably be programmed so that it weaves its way to the target, spoiling the aim of counterweapons. It will likely maneuver for a top or rear attack approach in the last few meters of flight, depending on the thickness of the tank's armor. This approach selection will probably be a gunner's option.

The foot soldier may also be equipped with shoulder-fired antiaircraft weapons of vastly improved effectiveness. Some idea of the impact of these weapons on a battlefield was glimpsed during the war in Afghanistan. The weapon used there, the American Stinger, was a relatively early and crude model. By the mid-1990s, the U.S. Stinger and its Russian equivalent may have more than just simple infrared sensors, and they will probably be able to discriminate between decoy flares and their intended targets.

These approaching innovations may shift the emphasis of tactical ground reconnaissance back to foot-mobile scouts and away from mounted reconnaissance elements. Whatever the future brings, the importance of ground reconnaissance in all its forms can be expected to continue well into the twenty-first century and beyond.

ROD PASCHALL

SEE ALSO: Cavalry; Intelligence, Tactical; Principles of War; Tactics.

Bibliography

Burgess, W. H. 1990. *Inside Spetsnaz: Soviet special operations.* Novato, Calif.: Presidio Press.

Chambers, J. 1976. *The devil's horsemen: The Mongol invasion of Europe.* New York: Atheneum.

Chandler, D. 1966. *The campaigns of Napoleon: The mind and method of history's greatest soldier.* New York: Macmillan.

Cleaver, F., et. al. 1955. *UN partisan warfare in Korea, 1951–1954.* Baltimore, Md.: Johns Hopkins Univ. Press.

Davidson, P. B. 1988. *Vietnam at war: The history.* Novato, Calif.: Presidio Press.

England, J. W. 1987. *Long range patrol operations: Reconnaissance, combat and special operations.* Boulder, Colo.: Paladin Press.

Gavin, J. 1955. Cavalry and I don't mean horses. *Armor* 63 (3).

Glubb, J. B. 1960. *War in the desert: An RAF frontier campaign.* New York: W. W. Norton.

Gugeler, R. A. 1954. *Combat actions in Korea.* Washington, D.C.: Association of the U.S. Army.

Hastings, M., and S. Jenkins. 1983. *The battle for the Falklands.* New York: W. W. Norton.

Jones, A. 1987. *The art of war in the Western world.* Urbana, Ill.: Univ. of Illinois Press.

Peers, W. R., and D. Brelis. 1963. *Behind the Burma road: The story of America's most successful guerrilla force.* Boston: Little, Brown.

Pike, D. 1986. *PAVN: People's Army of Vietnam.* Novato, Calif.: Presidio Press.

Stanton, S. L. 1985. *Green Berets at war: U.S. Army Special Forces in Southeast Asia, 1956–1975.* Novato, Calif.: Presidio Press.

Stevens, P. H. 1969. *Search out the land: A history of American military scouts.* Chicago: Rand McNally.

Sumner, E. M. 1944. *Modern reconnaissance: A collection of articles from the Cavalry Journal.* Harrisburg, Pa.: Military Service.

U.S. Army. 1981. *Field manual 17–95: Cavalry.* Washington, D.C.: Government Printing Office.

———. 1982. *Field manual 17–35: Aero scout procedures.* Washington, D.C.: Government Printing Office.

———. 1986. *Field manual 100–5: Operations.* Washington, D.C.: Government Printing Office.

Wagner, A. L. 1893. *The service of security and information.* Kansas City, Kans.: Hudson-Kimberly.

GUN, ANTITANK

After the Allies introduced the tank in battle in 1916, German soldiers had to find a means to negate it. Some types of German machine-gun ammunition were found to be effective against the relatively thin armor of the early British

Mark I tank, and artillery and mortars of the day also proved effective when fire was accurately placed. The first gun specifically designed to defeat tanks, however, was a modified German Mauser—a high-powered, bolt-action rifle. Increased in size to fire a 13mm bullet at 900 m/sec. (3,000 ft./sec.), could be used by infantrymen and proved sufficient to defeat the armored vehicles used in World War I.

In the years between World War I and the onset of World War II, many gun designers and manufacturers attempted to produce weapons capable of destroying tanks by using the armor-penetrating power of a kinetic-energy round. The British "Boys Rifle," Mark 1, named for one of its principal designers, Captain Boys, is one such example. Likely the best weapon of its kind, the Boys Rifle was completed in 1936 and fielded in 1937. It fired a 0.55-inch steel-cored bullet at 990 m/sec. (3,250 ft./sec.) and could penetrate armor to a thickness of 20 millimeters (0.8 in.) at a distance of 250 meters (825 ft.). Since the average tank armor at the time was about 15 millimeters (0.6 in.) thick, the Boys Rifle stood an excellent chance to defeat any tank of the day.

Tank armor, however, was greatly improved in the few years just prior to the German blitzkrieg attack against the Allies in May 1940, and small-caliber antitank guns were no longer very effective. The effectiveness of large-caliber guns was also problematic until the introduction of the hollow-charge explosive warhead. This new warhead, made with a cone of explosive lined with metal such that on detonation the blast is focused and a jet of the molten metal is propelled at speeds of about 6,000 m/sec. (20,000 ft./sec.), provided a means to effectively engage more thickly armored tanks. Hollow-, or shaped-, charge explosive technology was adapted to both antitank guns and rockets.

Of the numerous guns used in an antitank role in World War II, the most famous was Germany's "88." Originally developed for use against aircraft, the 88mm artillery piece proved deadly effective against all but the heaviest, most thickly armored tanks. The United States had no equivalent, and the British 6-pounder was underpowered. Only the Soviet 76mm gun came close.

During World War II, Swedish weapon designers began work on a recoilless antitank gun. Unlike the breech-loading, recoil-operated antitank guns that fire an explosive shell from a cartridge, recoilless guns have the propellant charge housed in the weapon itself. On firing, a disk of plastic (or a similar substance) at the base of the propellant case ruptures, permitting the rearward exhaust of propellant gas and other counterweight material (e.g., water, iron filings). The mass and velocity of rearward-exhausting material imparts a balancing forward velocity on the mass of the shell, allowing recoilless operation.

Recoilless guns are substantially lighter than their recoil-operated cousins. A typical recoilless system can weigh about 18 kilograms (40 lb.) compared to a typical recoil system that can weigh 13 times as much. Both types of systems permit effective engagement of targets to similar ranges—out to about 1,000 meters (3,300 ft.).

One of the more successful recoilless antitank guns, developed in the mid-1970s, is the Swedish weapon, the RCL Carl-Gustaf M2 (discussed below). It fires an 84mm projectile to an effective range of 450 meters (1,485 ft.) against tanks and 1,000 meters (3,300 ft.) against troops in the open.

Because of their light weight, relative simplicity, and ease of manufacture, recoilless weapons have provided interesting possibilities in the conduct of warfare. One example is a disposable gun, manufactured by the firm of Raikka in Finland and discussed later in this section.

Antitank guns of both types are in use in most militaries around the globe. The following discussion provides a variety of examples of contemporary systems, the predecessors of which first saw action in World War I.

MINIMAN LIGHT ANTIARMOR WEAPON (SWEDEN)

The Swedish Miniman is a one-shot throwaway, recoilless gun issued to infantrymen to provide them with an effective defense against close-in tanks. It arrives in the forward area with its projectile already in place. The user has only to estimate range and speed, cock the firing mechanism, lay on the target, and fire.

The weapon's barrel is made of filament-wound fiber. An attached label provides illustrated instructions for applying the correct lead to a moving target. The gunner need only judge the range (up to 150 meters [495 ft.]) to the nearest 25 meters (82.5 ft.) and the target's speed as very slow, slow, or fast, according to parameters provided.

The HEAT (high-explosive antitank) shell includes a distance tube at the front, made of alloy, which establishes the standoff distance; the shell body with copper liner and a shaped charge of octol; and a stabilizing tube of light alloy in the rear of which are four slots forming flaps that, forced out by gas pressure, form four fins to stabilize the shell.

When this shell strikes a target, the body is compressed, the piezo pushes the firing button forward, the firing rod goes rearward, and the pin ignites the primer. The resulting flame travels down an ignition transmission line to the igniting and propelling charges. The shaped-charge warhead is initiated from the rear. The resulting jet can penetrate up to 340 millimeters (13.6 in.) of armor plate.

The 74mm weapon weighs 2.9 kilograms (6.4 lb.) when loaded and has a range of 150 meters (495 ft.) against moving targets and 250 meters (825 ft.) against stationary ones.

M72 LAW (LIGHTWEIGHT MULTIPURPOSE ASSAULT WEAPON) (UNITED STATES)

The U.S. M72 is light, short when configured in the carrying mode, and expendable after firing. Its small size makes it easy to carry, while its low weight—3.2 kilograms (7 lb.)—does not add appreciably to the existing considerable load of infantry soldiers. The M72's multipurpose capability is also unique in this class of antiarmor weapons systems. Its accuracy, safety, and reliability give the combat soldier a highly effective short-range assault weapon. On both operational grounds and considerations of cost-effectiveness, this weapon is impressive, including its performance, acquisition cost, and training and logistics factors.

SPG-9 73MM RECOILLESS GUN (USSR)

The SPG-9 is a lightweight antitank gun normally carried by two men, crewed by four men, and mounted on a tripod for firing. It can be towed using a small two-wheeled carriage. It is used by motorized rifle battalions of the former Soviet army and is also in service in Bulgaria, East Germany, Hungary, and Poland. The weapon fires a fin-stabilized round with a HEAT warhead. The projectile is also given a slow spin inside the barrel by means of offset holes in the launching charge. The propellant charge is carried in a case attached behind the fins, thus making for a very long round. Not only does this system produce a high muzzle velocity, but the projectile is subsequently rocket-assisted, further increasing velocity to some 700 m/sec. (2,310 ft./sec.).

The launcher weighs 47.5 kilograms. The weapon is normally quad-mounted in sets of four tubes. The system has a maximum range of 1,300 meters (4,290 ft.) and can penetrate more than 390 millimeters (15.6 in.) of armor.

RAIKKA RECOILLESS GUN (FINLAND)

The firm of Raikka has developed a novel and interesting series of antitank recoilless guns. In their arrangement, the barrel is a plain tube into the center of which is inserted the cartridge. These barrels may be either smoothbore or rifled. On firing, the shell goes forward and an equivalent weight of another substance is blown backward, thus balancing the recoil. Raikka offers a range of such guns in calibers of 41, 55, 81, 120, and 150mm. The 41mm and 55mm weapons are man portable; the 81mm size comes in both man-portable and mounted versions; and the larger calibers are mounted. The 120mm version has a fin-stabilized high-velocity APDS round (HVAPDS [FS]). It is claimed that this projectile can achieve velocities of 1,500 m/sec. (4,950 ft./sec.) and is effective beyond 1,000 meters (3,300 ft.) against main battle tanks.

Multiple versions are produced, and their characteristics differ very greatly from one to the other. The smallest man-portable weapon, the 41mm, weighs 3 kilograms (6.6 lb.) and has an effective range of 200 meters (660 ft.). At the upper end of the spectrum, the 150mm mounted weapon weighs 1,200 kilograms (2,640 lb.), uses a round weighing 42 kilograms (92.4 lb.), and has an effective range of more than 1 kilometer. Two different versions of the 120mm weapon weigh 1,500 kilograms (3,300 lb.) and have ranges of 1.5 kilometers (4.95 ft.) or greater.

It might appear that the firm is a little late in producing these guns since most armies are phasing out the recoilless principle as a type of main launcher of antitank projectiles, but it may yet turn out that there is more to these guns than at first appears.

85MM ANTITANK GUN D-48 (USSR)

The 85mm antitank gun D-48 was originally given the Western designation 100mm field gun following its first appearance in the 1955 May Day parade in

Moscow. Subsequent investigation determined that the weapon was in fact a special high-performance 85mm gun designed by the FF Petrov design bureau as a replacement for the 100mm field gun M1944 (BS-3) for use in antitank warfare.

The D-48 is a towed weapon served by a six-man crew. It has a range of 18,970 meters (20,867 yd.) and can fire at a sustained rate of eight to nine rounds per minute or a maximum rate of 15 rounds per minute. The gun has a 54-degree traverse.

The ammunition for the D-48 was developed for high performance by necking down the cases for 100mm to accommodate a new 85mm projectile. Two basic forms of projectile were developed: a full-caliber, hard-core, high-velocity, armor-piercing (HVAP) projectile and at least one type of high-explosive round. Soviet references mention an armor-piercing (AP) projectile weighing 9.3 kilograms (20.5 lb.), an HE projectile weighing 9.7 kilograms (21.3 lb.), and a muzzle velocity of more than 1,000 m/sec. (3,300 ft./sec.). If the AP projectile is fired at that velocity, the corresponding HVAP would be fired at nearly 1,200 m/sec. (3,960 ft./sec.). Estimated penetration could then be about 190 millimeters (7.6 in.) for AP and 240 millimeters (9.6 in.) for HVAP at a range of 1,000 meters (3,300 ft.) and incidence of degrees.

The D-48 was replaced in the Soviet antitank elements of artillery formations during the mid-1960s by the 100mm antitank gun T-12, a very long barreled gun with the entire recoil system located over the breech area. A single castor wheel assists in bringing the weapon into and out of action; during travel the breech is clamped between twin box-section trails. The D-48 can be fitted with an infrared night-vision device. It is most likely that the D-48 served as the basis for the 86mm gun D-70 mounted on the ASU-85 airborne assault gun.

85MM ANTITANK GUN TYPE 56 (PEOPLE'S REPUBLIC OF CHINA)

The Type 56 is towed by a 4 × 4 truck and served by a crew of six to eight men. Its maximum range is 15,650 meters (10.7 mi.) or, with HEAT ammunition, 970 meters (0.6 mi.). The gun can traverse 54 degrees, elevate to +35 degrees, and depress to −7 degrees. It features a double-baffle muzzle brake and a recoil system employing a hydraulic recoil buffer and hydropneumatic recuperator. The breech mechanism is a semiautomatic vertical sliding block and the carriage, a split tubular trail. The weapon can sustain a rate of fire of 15 to 20 rounds per minute. Its traveling weight is 1,750 kilograms (3,850 lb.).

ASU-85 85MM AIR-TRANSPORTABLE SELF-PROPELLED ANTITANK GUN (USSR)

ASU was the Soviet designation for airborne assault gun. This weapon is deployed only with air assault divisions and is air transportable in the AN-12 Cub aircraft. Many of the automotive components for ASU-85 are identical to those used in the PT-76 light amphibious tank, although the ASU-85 has no amphibious capability. It can, however, ford to a depth of 1.1 meters (3.6 ft.).

The ASU-85 has infrared night-vision equipment and is probably fitted with a nuclear, biological, and chemical (NBC) defense system. Its main armament consists of an 85mm gun mounted in the glacis plate, slightly offset to the left of the centerline. The weapon has a double-baffle muzzle brake and a fume extractor. Mounted coaxially to the right of the main armament is a 7.62mm SCMT machine gun; some later versions have been observed with a 12.7mm DSHKM machine gun mounted on the roof for antiaircraft defense. Mounted over the main armament is an infrared searchlight that moves in elevation and traverse with the gun. The main weapon can elevate to +15 degrees, depress to −4 degrees, and traverse to 12 degrees. Both elevation and traverse are manual.

The main armament, the D-70 85mm gun, appears to be a variant of the D-48 85mm towed antitank gun. Served by a crew of four, it fires AP, HE, or HVAP projectiles at a muzzle velocity of more than 1,000 m/sec. (3,300 ft./sec.). Some systems have been fitted with a bank of smoke dischargers over the top of the hull at the rear; these can launch smoke grenades over the frontal arc of the ASU-85. The vehicle has a manual transmission and is powered by a 240-horsepower diesel engine (some later production models may have a 280-hp engine) and can attain maximum road speeds of 45 kilometers per hour (km/h [27 mph]).

90MM ANTITANK GUN MODELS 50 AND 57 (SWITZERLAND)

The Swiss army currently employs two towed antitank guns, the Model 50 Panzerabwehrkanone (or Pak 50, for short) and the Model 57 (or Pak 57). Both weapons have a two-wheel split-trail carriage with a small fixed spade mounted at the end of each trail. The Model 50 is fitted with a flat shield with its lower portion sloping forward at an angle of about 45 degrees; the Model 57 has a smaller curved shield. The Model 50 is towed muzzle first with the split trails folded into the vertical position to reduce the overall length of the weapon. In the firing position the towing attachment is removed and mounted on the rear of the shield. On the Model 57 the complete barrel, mount, and shield are swung through 180 degrees so that they rest over the trails. Both weapons are fitted with a day and night sight. They are served by a crew of five and can be towed by a jeep or Land Rover–type vehicle.

The Model 50 fires a HEAT projectile weighing 1.95 kilograms (4.3 lb.); the Model 57, a 2.7-kilogram (5.9-lb.) HEAT projectile. These will penetrate 250 millimeters (10 in.) of armor. Both have a muzzle velocity of 600 m/sec. (1,980 ft./sec.) and a maximum range of 4,000 meters (13,200 ft.), a normal rate of fire of six rounds per minute, and a maximum rate of fire of 20 rounds per minute. In 1983, the Swiss Ministry of Defense announced that new HEAT ammunition for these weapons had been developed by Bofors of Sweden and that production was being undertaken under license in Switzerland by the federal ammunition factory at Altdorf. The Model 57 is also fitted with an American 12.7mm ranging machine gun, added after the weapon was introduced into service with the Swiss army.

90MM MECAR KENERGA 90/46 ANTITANK GUN (BELGIUM)

The Kenerga 90/46 antitank gun features low recoil, an approximately 6-ton trunnion load, and light construction, making it particularly well suited for use with light armored vehicles and small gun carriages. Its semiautomatic breech is of the classical horizontal sliding block type. The recoil system consists of a two-stage muzzle brake that reduces recoil energy by some 70 percent, an optimized hydraulic recoil cylinder, and a hydropneumatic recuperator. A shield is available to provide a degree of crew protection against small arms and shrapnel. The weapon can fire a range of projectiles, including APFSDS-T, HEAT-T, HESH-T, WP smoke, and canister. It can achieve a maximum rate of fire of 10 rounds per minute and a sustained rate of seven rounds per minute. Its range of traverse is 54 degrees.

100MM ANTITANK GUN T-12 (USSR)

The smoothbore T-12 is the replacement for the 85mm antitank gun D-48. The fin-stabilized nonrotating APFSDS and HEAT projectiles fired by the T-12 resemble those fired by the 115mm gun of the T-62 main battle tank. The weapon fires an APFSDS projectile weighing 5.5 kilograms (12.1 lb.) and having a muzzle velocity of 1,500 m/sec. (4,540 ft./sec.) that is capable of penetrating 406 millimeters (16.2 in.) of armor at zero degrees' incidence and at a range of 500 meters (1,650 ft.); and a HEAT projectile weighing 9.5 kilograms (20.9 lb.) that develops a muzzle velocity of 990 m/sec. (3,267 ft./sec.) and can penetrate 400 millimeters (16 in.) of armor at an incidence of 0 degrees.

The T-12, served by a crew of six, has a split trail carriage and a gun shield. It utilizes a pepper-pot muzzle brake. The weapon can traverse through 27 degrees, elevate to +20 degrees, and depress to −10 degrees. Its rate of fire is 10 rounds per minute. Maximum effective range is 900 to 1,200 meters (2,970 to 3,960 ft.).

The T-12 reached full operational capability with the Soviet army in 1965. A slightly modified version, known in the West as the T-12A, was called the MT-12 by the East German army. It differs from the basic T-12 in that it weighs slightly more and uses a different tire specification. The T-12 was issued in the Soviet army on the basis of 12 guns (two batteries, each with six guns) in the antitank battalion of the motorized rifle division and 36 guns (two battalions, each having 18 guns) in independent antitank regiments.

100MM ANTITANK GUN TYPE 86 (PEOPLE'S REPUBLIC OF CHINA)

The Type 86 antitank gun appears to be a modification of the 85mm field gun Type 56, incorporating a new ordnance and recoil system. The smoothbore Type 86 gun features a distinctive muzzle brake. The breech mechanism has a vertical sliding block. The sighting mechanism is located to the left of the gun; a night-vision device is also available. The carriage uses split trails, with a castor wheel on the left trail leg to assist in bringing the gun into action. A shield with sloping sides is also provided.

The overall weapon weighs 3,600 kilograms (8,052 lb.) in traveling configuration. It has a maximum range of 13,650 meters (8.5 mi.) and a traverse of 50 degrees. Although the Type 86 is primarily an antitank weapon, it can also be used in an indirect-fire role, although potential range is limited by the maximum gun elevation of +38 degrees. The maximum rate of fire is quoted as eight to 10 rounds per minute.

105mm Noricum Antitank Gun ATGN 105 (Germany)

The Noricum ATGN 105 was originally developed as a mobile trail mount for the long recoil Noricum 105mm system and its associated ammunition, but the manufacturer realized that there might be a market for a 105mm antitank gun using existing 105mm L7/M68 tank gun ammunition. The result was the development of this gun, mounted on a split-trail, single-axle, two-wheeled carriage. The split trail has cranked, box-type trail legs of welded steel that are fitted with fixed trail spades. For towing, the barrel can be rotated through 180 degrees and folded over the trail legs. Recoil length is 590 millimeters (23.6 in.) and the weight of the complete gun 3,900 kilograms (8,580 lb.).

The ATGN 105 can fire all standard NATO 105mm L7/M68 tank gun ammunition, including HEAT and APDS, as well as the Noricum NP 105 A2 APFSDS round. Developed jointly with Hirtenberger GmbH, that projectile is made of Tungalloy 176 FA, uses a long rod penetrator, and develops a muzzle velocity of 1,485 m/sec. (4,900.5 ft./sec.).

106mm Self-propelled Recoilless Gun Type 60 (Japan)

Following successful employment of jeep-mounted recoilless rifles by the U.S. Army in the Korean War, the Japanese Ground Self-Defense Force issued a requirement for a self-propelled tracked recoilless gun, specifying that it was to be equipped with two recoilless rifles that could be raised hydraulically (with additional manual controls for emergency use) and have a crew of three, a loaded weight of 5,000 kilograms (11,000 lb.), an air-cooled diesel engine, and a maximum road speed of more than 55 km/h (33 mph.).

Prototype development and testing of the system in the mid- to late 1950s were fraught with difficulties, including engines overheating and steering mechanisms behaving poorly. After modifications, the weapon was accepted into service in 1960. Subsequent improvements have been made to increase engine power from 110 horsepower at 2,300 rpm to 150 horsepower at 2,800 rpm. Something on the order of 250 Type 60s have been produced with production ending in fiscal year 1979.

The type 60 is armed with two 106mm recoilless rifles that have an effective range of 1,100 meters (3,360 ft.). A 12.7mm spotting rifle assists with aiming the parallel-mounted recoilless rifles, further assisted by a 75-centimeter (30-in.) stereo range finder and an infrared night sight. The Type 60 has a three-man crew consisting of driver, loader, and commander and can carry a combination of eight HEAT or HE rounds. Special tracks give the vehicle a cross-snow capability, but there is no amphibious capability or NBC protection.

Jagdpanzer Kanone JPZ 4–5 Self-propelled Antitank Gun (West Germany)

When the West German army was formed, it issued a requirement for a 90mm self-propelled antitank gun—or tank destroyer, as the Germans normally call this kind of weapon. The first vehicle intended to meet this requirement was basically a Swiss-designed HS-30 armored personnel carrier with a 90mm gun ball mounted in the glacis plate. In trials, this approach did not meet with success, so development of a new system began. This time a chassis was developed that could be used for a number of basic vehicles, including the Jagdpanzer Rakete, a reconnaissance tank (which was subsequently developed to the prototype stage but not put into production); an MICV, which eventually became the Marder; and various other supporting vehicles. Three series of prototypes of the self-propelled antitank gun were built between 1960 and 1965. The prototypes were followed by 750 production vehicles completed between 1965 and 1967, half being built by Hanomag and half by Henschel.

The weapon is served by a crew of four. It has a combat weight of 27,500 kilograms (60,500 lb.). Powered by a 500-horsepower diesel engine, it has a road range of 400 kilometers (240 mi.) and a maximum road speed of 70 km/h (42 mph.).

The vehicle's 90mm gun, which fires the same ammunition as the M47 and M48 tanks, is mounted in the glacis plate, slightly offset to the left of center. The barrel is fitted with a double-baffle muzzle brake and a fume extractor. It can elevate and depress to $+15$ degrees/-8 degrees and traverse through 30 degrees. Both elevation and traverse are manual. The gun fires HEAT-T and HESH-T projectiles of a maximum effective range of 2,000 meters (6,600 ft.) at a maximum rate of fire of 12 rounds per minute.

Mounted coaxially with the main armament is a 7.62mm MG3 machine gun. A similar weapon mounted at the commander's station for antiaircraft use can also be removed and fitted at the loader's station. Mounted on the rear of the fighting compartment are eight electrically operated smoke dischargers that fire forward over the front of the vehicle. Mounted over the main armament is an infrared and white searchlight that can be removed and stowed at the rear of the hull when desired. The Jagdpanzer Kanone is also equipped with infrared night-vision equipment and an NBC defense system. The basic vehicle can ford to a depth of 1.4 meters (4.6 ft.) without modification and to 2.1 meters (6.9 ft.) with use of a fording kit. Some 160 of these systems have been rebuilt to a Jaguar 2 configuration and fitted with the Hughes TOW ATGW system with AN/TAS-4 night sight. Some have also been used in the role of an observation post with the 90mm gun removed.

Conclusion

Although their importance in antiarmor fighting—once dominant—has diminished, antitank guns will remain in service around the world for the foreseeable future. Many military commanders recognize the tactical capability of antitank guns to complement other antiarmor systems and that their effect in urban fighting can be greater than that of weapons that must be guided to a target and have relatively slower projectile speeds. They also tend to be less expensive to produce and field and so will remain popular with countries of limited resources or war-fighting requirements.

ALAA EL DIN ABDEL MEGUID DARWISH

SEE ALSO: Armor; Mechanized Warfare; Missile, Antitank Guided; Rocket, Antiarmor; Tank.

Bibliography

Hogg, I. V. 1977. *The encyclopedia of infantry weapons of World War II.* New York: Thomas Y. Crowell.
Jane's armour and artillery, 1988–89. 1988. London: Jane's.
Reid, W. 1976. *Arms through the ages.* New York: Harper and Row.
ADDITIONAL SOURCES: *Armada International; Military Technology; NATO's Sixteen Nations.*

GUN TECHNOLOGY APPLICATIONS

Gunpowder for use as a propellant was known in China as early as the eleventh century and, according to Franciscan friar Roger Bacon, has been known in western Europe since 1249. About 60 years later, the Europeans learned how to harness that explosive energy to accelerate a projectile. References to the "hand pipe" in the city of Aachen chronicles of 1338 describe a device still recognizable as a gun (Fig. 1).

Since the first appearance of that primitive firepot, a wide variety of firearms has been developed, from slow match to flintlock and from small revolver to the heaviest siege guns. All are based on the same principle: the tube is loaded with powder and projectile, and the ignition charge is actuated by means of sparks, causing deflagration that propels the projectile.

During the nineteenth century, firearms' development progressed enormously. The impact-sensitive percussion cap was introduced in 1807, to be succeeded by the paper cartridge, breech loading, and the metal case with center firing. The final step on the road to automatic weapons was taken in the

Figure 1. Firing of a hand pipe. (SOURCE: City Chronicles of Aachen, City Museum, Aachen, Germany)

United States by Richard Gatling, who, in 1862, developed the first operable machine gun. This was followed in 1884 by the recoil-operated Maxim and in 1892 by the Hotchkiss gas pressure–driven system. Cast bronze muzzle-loading guns were then replaced by steel breech loaders with rifled barrels; the recoil gun subsequently led to a higher rate of fire. Black powder was replaced by the smokeless and residue-free nitrocellulose powder in 1884. Table 1 lists a variety of modern guns, from handguns to heavy artillery, categorized according to size, form, and function. Some of the features and processes associated with operating a firearm are shown in Table 2.

Basic Operation and Assembly of a Gun

The gun barrel (Fig. 2) is the tube in which gas pressure accelerates the projectile. The projectile is propelled through the muzzle with a certain velocity and in a certain direction. The rear end of the tube is closed gas tight, and ammunition is loaded through the breech there. Between the projectile base and the rear of the tube is the "chamber" that holds the propellant and ignition device. The ignition device is actuated through the breech.

A "round" of ammunition is inserted into the chamber through the breech. The breech is then closed, and the igniter element is actuated by a mechanical blow or electrically. This actuates the primer charge, evenly igniting the propellant. The time between the firing pin impact and the start of propellant deflagration is less than one millisecond in small-caliber weapons and up to tens of milliseconds in large-caliber systems. Ignition transforms the propellant charge into gas.

The pressure created by the hot propellant gas expanding between the tube's rear end and the projectile base drives the projectile with increasing velocity down the tube until it exits through the muzzle. The characteristic in-bore pressure distribution (Fig. 3) from ignition until total propellant transformation into gas is controlled by contrary facts:

1. Transformation velocity increases at rising pressure, resulting in further pressure increase.

TABLE 1. *Types of Modern Guns*

CATEGORY	EXAMPLES
Handguns	Revolver, pistol, rifle, machine pistol, machine gun
Machine guns	Revolver, Gatling gun
Automatic guns	Recoil-operated, gas-pressure-operated, mass locked weapons (blowback), externally powered
Artillery guns	Field howitzers, field guns, mountain guns, fortification guns, naval guns
Tank guns	Tank guns
Antiaircraft guns	Antiaircraft guns
Special guns	Mortars, recoilless guns

TABLE 2. *Functional Sequence of Guns*

Gun	Ammunition transport, chambering, closing, firing, opening, case removal
Ammunition	Propellant ignition, in-bore acceleration, ballistic flight, effect on target
Aiming means	Target assignment, target acquisition, aiming, observation, correction
Mount	Gun ammunition transport, weapon mounting, absorption/deflection of firing forces

2. The projectile converts gas pressure into kinetic energy, which results in pressure decrease. Simultaneously, as the projectile moves down the tube, the space available for the gas to expand increases, resulting in further pressure decrease.

Normally, the in-bore gas pressure rises to a peak over the projectile travel and then drops until final combustion is achieved. Thereafter, pressure keeps dropping according to a polytropic expansion.

Ideally, propellant deflagration should be completed when the projectile is as far toward the muzzle as possible. The acceleration of the projectile takes place over a very short distance but creates up to 10^5 g loads. Projectile velocity at the muzzle can reach more than 1,700 m/sec. (about 1 mi./sec.) at maximum gas pressures in excess of 6,000 bar and temperatures of up to 4,000 degrees Kelvin.

The chemical energy released when the propellant is ignited is consumed as follows:

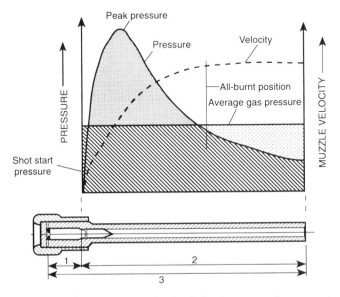

Figure 2. *Schematic view of a loaded tube—typical pressure/ time, velocity/time curves.* (SOURCE: Rheinmetall)

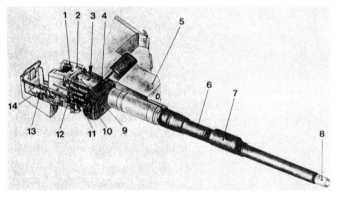

1. Breech-block with wedge
2. Buffer
3. Barrel brake, LH
4. Cradle
5. Shield with sealing
6. Thermal sleeve
7. Bore evacuator

8. Tube
9. Cradle tube
10. Recuperator
11. Emergency trigger
12. Barrel brake, RH
13. Recoil indicator
14. Spent case box

Figure 3. Smoothbore tank gun (120 mm). (SOURCE: Rheinmetall)

Projectile motion	33%
Frictional losses	3%
Propellant gas motion	4%
Heat loss to gun and projectile	20%
Heat retained by propellant gases	40%
Total propellant energy released	100%

Accordingly, only one-third of the chemically bound propellant energy is used for actual projectile propulsion; the rest is lost primarily to gas dynamics and heat buildup.

BARREL

The gun barrel consists of the tube, the breech system, the firing mechanism (and, if necessary, the muzzle brake), the bore evacuator, and the thermal shroud.

Tube. The tube is divided into two areas: at the rear is the chamber, which tapers at the front to enclose the cartridge case neck, and the narrower tunnel of the bore, through which the projectile is propelled. The inner diameter of the bore, measured in millimeters, is the caliber of the gun. The bore is rifled along its length; that is, it has grooves that extend helically toward the muzzle to impart spin to the projectile as it travels down the bore. This spin stabilizes the projectile in its trajectory.

Gun bores may also be smooth; these are simpler and easier to produce and have been used in mortars to fire relatively slow-moving, fin-stabilized rounds.

Since the 1960s, smoothbore technology has also gained the edge in tank guns, because modern high-speed, armor-penetrating projectiles can develop their full potential only when fin stabilized (see Fig. 3). In addition, the smoothbore surface allows higher thermal loads (i.e., peak gas pressure and temperature) and less erosion (i.e., wear life) when fired.

The tube wall thickness is determined by the gas-pressure load and should decrease toward the muzzle. Tube rigidity must be high enough to avoid any uncontrollable oscillations (longitudinal, lateral, twisting) that might have negative influence on firing accuracy.

With the rapid advances in weapons technology during the nineteenth century, cast bronze, cast iron, and cast steel tubes became obsolete. Today, forged or centrifugally cast monobloc tubes are used for smaller-caliber weapons. For high-performance guns, blanks are specially produced using extremely hard heat-treated vacuum-melted steel alloys with optimized properties. Special tube designs have been developed, such as built-up (multilayered) tubes, monobloc autofrettage tubes with interchangeable inner liners (where only the worn-out liner is replaced), and easily and quickly replaceable tubes.

A tube is subjected to many stresses during system operation, including:

• radial and tangential stresses due to gas pressure
• longitudinal stresses due to rotating band pressure
• torsional stresses due to projectile rotation
• bending stresses due to the tube's own weight.

Radial and tangential stresses exerted during firing are unevenly distributed across the tube diameter from the inside to the outside. This is compensated by autofrettage, which loads and evenly distributes residual stresses through the tube wall when firing. This technology facilitates (1) higher peak gas pressures, (2) better barrel dimensioning, and (3) very high fatigue life.

Tube heating can be a problem in rapid-firing guns, and special measures must be taken to carry off heat since barrel wear grows as the temperature increases, as does the risk of propellant "cook off." Preventive measures are water-cooled tubes, radiating ribs, fast and easy tube interchange, and heavier tubes with higher heat absorption capability.

Thermal shrouds (sleeves) are used on especially long tubes because the tubes tend to bend at higher temperature differences due to one-sided (solar) heating or cooling; this reduces accuracy. Thermal shrouds prevent such temperature influences.

A bore evacuator is a device that removes residual in-bore propellant smoke through the muzzle, thus avoiding blowback into the crew space when the breech is opened for reloading. In closed weapons stations, the bore evacuator or smoke absorber is mounted on the tube. The bore evacuator uses the ejector principle. As soon as the projectile has passed the absorber holes, which are canted toward the muzzle, part of the propellant gas fills the absorber pot and builds up pressure. As pressure in the tube decreases, these gases expand back into the bore and also wash out residues from the tube's rear through the muzzle.

Tube service life is determined by wear life and fatigue life. Wear life is reached when mechanical drive and propellant gas erosion deteriorate a gun so that it can no longer meet performance requirements. Wear life depends on the type of projectile, muzzle velocity, propellant charge, tube temperature, rate of fire, and so on. Wear can be reduced by hard chrome plating of the bore surface, use of propellant additives, and (in small-caliber weapons) cold forming of rifling. Drawn or rifled tubes have, at identical stress loads, a shorter wear life than smoothbore tubes.

Fatigue life is reached when materials fatigue and can result in spontaneous tube destruction. This is caused by microscopic cracks at the materials' grain boundaries that grow and eventually attain "critical crack depth." Autofrettage increases the weapon's life up to three times the original number of rounds. Highly stressed guns (tank guns) usually reach *wear* life sooner, whereas less stressed howitzer tubes reach *fatigue* life earlier. Highly stressed tubes usually are designed so that they can rapidly be exchanged; examples are machine-gun tubes with rapid locks and tank gun tubes with bayonet thread between breech-block and tube.

Breech (bolt). A certain sequence of operations is necessary to fire multiple rounds:
1. chamber the cartridge,
2. lock the breech or bolt,
3. actuate the firing mechanism,
4. fire,
5. unlock the breech or bolt,
6. extract the empty cartridge case from chamber,
7. store the actuating energy for breech or bolt,
8. eject the spent cartridge case,
9. chamber the new cartridge.

Automatic weapons perform these steps automatically; other weapons may be partly automated so that certain operations have to be performed manually.

Actuation of the breech or bolt system facilitates the repetition of rounds being fired. Its tasks are:

• gas-proof sealing of the tube rear
• initiation of propellant ignition
• absorption of gas pressure
• extraction and ejection of cartridge case
• chambering of new cartridge for next round (in automatic weapons only).

Breech or bolt systems can be quite different and are determined by rate of fire, caliber, and ammunition type. Breech systems include the closed, screw, and wedge types.

The simplest form of breech is the tube closed at one end. This closed breech form is as old as the gun itself and today is used only in mortars. At the closed end the mortar has a fixed firing pin onto which the round and its percussion cap drop.

In the mid-nineteenth century, the screw-type breech was developed, which made breech loading possible. A bayonet-threaded plug is manually or mechanically swung into the bore axis and screwed into the tube. Due to the use of an elastic obturator, this breech system is well suited to firing ammunition with bulk charges. This design depends on an obturating mushroom that protrudes into the chamber and, using gas pressure, compresses the elastic obturator.

The wedge-type breech developed later in the nineteenth century is a rectangular block that, by simply moving in a breechblock recess vertically to the bore center axis, closes or opens the rear tube end for loading. The wedge-type breech is simple in design and operating sequence and, in connection with a ring obturator, can also be used to fire ammunition without a sealing metal case. The ring obturator consists of a base ring plus an actual obturator that seals the breech by being forced against the barrel wall and wedge when under pressure.

Generally, ammunition is manually chambered in both breech types. Chambering may be partly automated using loading aids (flick ramming). In the future, fully automated chambering due to automatic loaders will gain ground even with large-caliber guns.

The simple operating sequence of the wedge-type breech is very fast and suitable for automation: driven by the tube recoil after firing, the breech opens, ejects the spent case, retorques the closing mechanism, and automatically closes after the new round is chambered.

Automatic Weapons

Very early revolvers were first tested in the Middle Ages. By about 1715, Puckel had developed the basic principle of the revolver weapon; following invention of the percussion cap in 1807, Samuel Colt used Puckel's principle in designing his own famous revolver in 1835. Introduction of the metal-cased cartridge in the mid-nineteenth century led to the development of the automatic weapon with constant ammunition feeding. Over time, numerous variations emerged.

In 1862, the rapid-fire gun developed by Richard Gatling was presented. It was a multibarrel system with a rotating barrel arrangement driven manually by a crank. This was the first automatic rotary action cannon in which the cylinder was reloaded during firing. Hiram Maxim followed in 1884 with the first self-actuating machine gun with a linear oscillating bolt system operating on the recoil principle, and in 1892, J. M. Hotchkiss developed the first gas-operated automatic weapon. Only at the end of World War II did the German company Mauser develop the Colt-equivalent revolver gun with a single fixed tube.

Modern automatic weapons' developments are based principally on the three main types of bolt action: rotating, linear, and lateral action. The functional round-to-round sequence of an automatic weapon (including the drive for simple ammunition feeding) employs energy that is provided either from outside (external power), manually, or mechanically; or from the propellant charge (self-driven), by tube recoil, case-base pressure, or gas pressure.

The simplest form of external drive is found in the repeating rifle. Here, the bolt is cycled manually. The Gatling gun derived its energy from a manually powered crank. Modern machine guns use an external motor, either electric, pneumatic, or hydraulic.

The self-actuating method uses energy derived from the propellant charge; this is obtained via tube recoil (see Fig. 4), directly from gas pressure, tapped from the barrel, or direct via the case acting on the bolt.

The main advantages of externally powered systems are smooth and uniform bolt motion and a controllable rate of fire due to drive speed. A disadvantage is the need for external energy, plus the fact that Gatling guns do not immediately reach their full rate of fire.

The main advantages of self-powered systems are independence from external energy, high and immediately available rate of fire, and sufficient energy in gas-pressure operation for belt pull without affecting the rate of fire. Disadvantages are rough bolt motion and the difficulty in controlling such a low rate of fire.

ROTATING BOLTS

Revolver/Gatling principle. Weapons with a rotating bolt system have a chambered cylinder that holds the cartridges. In revolvers and revolver guns, this loaded cylinder rotates at the end of a single tube (gas sealing), whereas in the Gatling gun, each chamber is affixed to its own tube.

The rotating cylinders are loaded by transport stars and cartridge pushers. The pushers also extract the spent cases after firing. The rotating bolt action and the arrangements of multiple chambers facilitate a high rate of fire. Rotary guns differ in both their cylinder cycling and their drive mode. While the Gatling, due to its rigid cylinder/barrel assembly connection, can fire while rotating, the revolver gun must be at rest when fired. The revolver gun taps the gas used to cycle the cylinder and feeds ammunition from the rigid tube. This driving mode creates problems in a Gatling gun because of the rotating tube assembly. Therefore, Gatling guns are mostly externally powered, either electrically, hydraulically, or pneumatically.

Roller breech. The roller breech or tilt cylinder is a special form of the rotary bolt principle especially suited for caseless ammunition. The roller breech pivots with the chamber back and forth from firing position to feeding position. It is gas-pressure operated and seals the chamber via telescoping sleeves. This new functional principle was designed by Heckler and Koch especially for the caseless ammunition of their G11 rifle.

Linear bolt. The essential features of this bolt are that it moves horizontally to chamber a cartridge, locks with the tube, ignites the cartridge, and ejects the spent case as it recoils. The energy required for this bolt movement can be provided either externally or through self-actuation. In the latter case, the bolt is forced backward by gas pressure of the round being fired; this simultaneously torques a spring that provides the return action. As the bolt motion is buffered and diverted, a new cartridge is inserted, and the returning bolt pushes it into

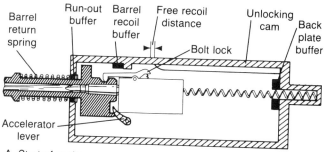

A. Start of cycle

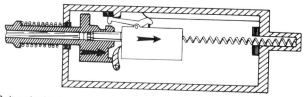

B. Bolt unlocked; acceleration starts

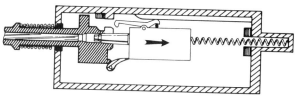

C. Acceleration completed

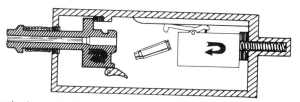

D. Barrel rebounding from recoil buffer; bolt rebounding from back plate buffer

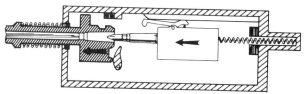

E. Bolt loading fresh cartridge

Figure 4. Recoil loader with short recoil. (SOURCE: C. J. Marchant Smith and P. R. Haslam, *Small Arms and Cannons*, London: Brassey's, 1982, p. 145)

the chamber and locks. In externally powered systems, the closing spring is not necessary, since the bolt motion is forced.

Most automatic weapons designed for multipurpose applications and mounts, from machine pistol to heavy guns, operate with the linear bolt action. Only when higher rates of fire (more than 1,000 rounds/min.) are required is the linear bolt replaced by the faster revolver or Gatling principle. The main difference between these two systems is their motion and functional sequence: the steps in revolver and Gatling guns are staggered but parallel while they are in sequence in a linear moving action.

Lateral bolt. The lateral bolt is a special version of the linear bolt in which a feeder transports the cartridge laterally and a laterally moving wedge locks the tube. This version is especially suitable for self-operating guns because of its smooth performance.

BOLT ACTUATION

There are four basic means of bolt driving: the recoil loader with long and short tube recoil, the case-base loader using the cartridge case with simple or delayed-action bolt, the gas-pressure loader that taps gas directly from the tube, and the externally powered gun.

The tube recoil loader has a tube that is loosely seated in the weapon housing. When the gun is fired, gas pressure forces the locked tube and bolt backward. With long tube recoil, the tube pushes the bolt backward to the return point, whereas with the short tube recoil, an additional accelerator is used to drive the bolt backward. Short recoil systems often use a recoil booster at the muzzle to increase the recoil force and improve the rate of fire; this also is called reverse muzzle brake action. The recoil loader is a very robust design; however, the rate of fire can be varied only by design measures.

The simplest automatic weapons are driven by the cartridge case base and are "semi-locked" by the dynamic mass of the bolt. There are two types of case-base loaders: the simple dynamic mass bolt with high mass for locking and the delayed action bolt with a lightweight mass. The latter type compensates for the missing weight necessary for secure locking by energy transfer, assisted by an accelerator for part of the two-part bolt. Because of the interference during the acceleration phase, this locking mode is also called "semirigid." The simplicity of this drive and locking mode makes case-base loaders attractive for use in machine pistols and machine guns.

The gas-pressure loader taps a portion of the propellant gas directly from the tube and uses it to activate a piston, which unlocks the bolt from the receiver housing and drives the bolt backward. Gas-pressure loaders have a number of advantages: the timing of actions and the amount of gas (nozzle cross section) can be adapted to system functions and the rate of fire can—within a certain range—easily be varied. Most modern automatic weapons are driven by this method.

Externally powered guns with linear bolts use a chain or other mechanical means to actuate the to-and-fro motion of the bolt. The motor drives the bolt throughout the whole cycle. Advantages of this system are its variable rate of fire based on the drive speed and the uniform and function-adequate controllable bolt movement (feeding, simple and safe locking, case removal, etc.); one disadvantage is its dependency on external energy.

FUNCTIONAL SAFETY

To avoid hazards in weapons system and handling, safety features are provided that prevent unintentional firing (trigger) and ensure that the tube and bolt are securely locked during firing.

Locking and ignition. A number of methods are available to lock the bolt either directly to the tube (in recoil-operated systems) or to the housing (in fixed tube systems). The semi-locking system—the simplest system—uses the kinetic mass effect of battery firing. Semirigid locking also uses the kinetic mass effect, but the bolt is lighter and more complex. The missing mass is replaced by transformed recoil momentum. Both semi-locking and semirigid locking facilitate the very simple bolt actuation via the cartridge case base. Rigid or form-fit locking can be achieved by screw-type lock, supporting lugs, support rollers, balls, or similar supporting elements, or by a lateral bolt. Rigid locking provides a high degree of safety. The supporting-lug bolt locks quickly and is favored in high-rate-of-fire systems. Under certain conditions, the bolt tends to jump, due to the front-end impact on the tube rear, causing premature unlocking. By employing special delay elements, this danger can be avoided.

Triggering system. The trigger is manually or electromagnetically (solenoid) actuated to initiate firing. Ignition of the cartridge is usually performed by a spring-loaded firing pin or electric current. Prevention of unintentional firing is of the utmost importance and ignition must start only after the bolt is securely locked. In systems with lateral bolt function, the bolt is held by the trigger in the ready-to-release rear position during firing interruption.

Closed bolt weapon systems "park" the bolt in the rear position, whereas in the open bolt mode, the bolt is locked in the forward position and cartridge ignition is separately controlled. Open bolt systems are used only when utmost precision in rate of fire and accuracy is required.

AMMUNITION FEEDING

Automated ammunition feeding systems called "loaders" (in large-caliber weapons) are required in single-shot weapons to increase the rate of fire, minimize crew size, and compensate for munition weight, or allow for remote weapon system control. The degree of automation in single-shot weapons' feeding covers the range from loading aids to remote-controlled fully automatic loaders.

Feeding systems for automatic weapons are considered an integral, functional part of the weapon. Cartridges can be fed in limited number by magazine; in the case of a larger supply, they can be contained in a "linkless feed system" or be fed linked in belts. If transport distance is not excessive, the feed mechanism (which transports a cartridge into chambering position) is driven mostly through tube recoil, weapon recoil, or gas pressure. Modern multipurpose weapons are equipped with alternating feeders, allowing different types of cartridges to be selected for different missions.

Carriages or Mounts

The "gun" comprises the actual ordnance together with the carriage or mount. The carriage or mount consists of an array of assemblies to support the ordnance when firing. The carriage absorbs or deflects occurring forces as well as mounting the ordnance and aiming and training the tube. It may also be used to transport ordnance and ammunition.

Carriages/mounts and their assembly groups can be configured differently, depending on their use: for ground- or surface-based guns, there are static or semi-static, mobile or self-propelled mounts; for guns based on aircraft, the mounting platform aims the gun system.

The main assembly of a carriage or mounting, the superstructure (Fig. 5), consists of the top carriage, the elevating and traversing gears, the balancing gears, the cradle, the recoil system, and the sighting device. These elements are used to mount and train the gun and to absorb and deflect the firing stresses. The main parts of the basic structure are the bottom carriage, the trials and articulation system, the platforms, the spades, and the wheels, axles, and so forth. Of course, handguns and rifles have the simplest mounts: the user.

The carriages of more complex gun systems (e.g., artillery pieces or the main guns of tanks) incorporate subsystems to aid in tube elevation, gun traverse and lay, and gun stabilization. These subsystems are respectively known as cradles, laying gear, and stabilization units.

Cradles support the mass of the gun tube at rest and during firing and facilitate tube elevation (or depression) about its trunnions. As the trunnions provide the pivot point for the tube, their location and the use of counter-

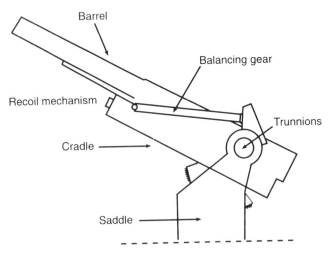

Figure 5. Superstructure of the conventional gun. (SOURCE: J. W. Ryan, *Guns, Mortars and Rockets*, London: Brassey's, 1981)

weights are important considerations in gun design, since artillery weapons are generally used for indirect high- or low-angle fire, and tank guns are used more in direct-fire roles.

Laying gear may comprise various combinations of gears, threaded spindles, or hydraulic cylinders and is used to adjust the elevation and traverse of the gun so that the trajectory of the projectile will intercept the sighted target. Gun stabilization systems, on the other hand, permit accurate laying of a gun while mounted on a moving platform, usually ships or armored vehicles. More complex, modern stabilization subsystems use ballistic computers and compensate for elevation, roll, and transverse motion.

ABSORPTION/DEFLECTION OF FIRING FORCES

Recoil force. The gas pressure accelerating the projectile must, as a counterforce acting on the breech, be absorbed by the mount. The dimensions of the mount must be adequate to absorb and deflect the recoil forces. The forces at the elevating mass are transmitted to the saddle via trunnions, elevating gear, and equilibrators. In systems with a recoiling tube, the recoil forces acting on the tube are transformed into reverse acceleration of the tube—recoiling mass. The kinetic energy of the recoiling mass is absorbed during recoil travel by a hydraulic tube recoil brake.

Recoil energy acting on the mount can be reduced further by increasing the weight of the recoiling mass, using muzzle brakes, and employing out-of-battery firing. Special-purpose guns may use low-recoil or recoilless systems.

The recoil system consists of a recoil brake, the recuperator, and a slider rail in the cradle. A recoil system must provide for uniform and vibration-free action and, when firing, a secure resting of the mount to avoid delays in firing sequence due to extensive readjustments. In general, only hydraulic brakes are used. They are connected with the recoiling mass and the cradle. Inside the brake unit, hydraulic fluid is pressed through an opening in the piston and converted into heat. By design, hydraulic brakes can be tuned to the exact loads of a mount, depending on the length of recoil and the elevation, so that an almost constant mount load is maintained throughout the recoil travel. After firing, the recuperator brings the tube back into rest position. The tube recoil energy is pneumatically or hydropneumatically accumulated.

The braking force to be absorbed by the mount is inversely proportional to the recoiling mass; that is, at identical recoil force the mount is less stressed by a heavier recoiling mass. To minimize mount stress during firing the principle of out-of-battery firing also can be applied: gas pressure is countered by the forward impulse of the recoiling mass in single-shot systems, the interrupted counter-recoil in automatic cannons (the next round is fired before the weapon is back in battery position), or the forward impulse (kinetic energy) of the bolt mass. Accordingly, the mount loads or the mass of the bolt can be smaller.

Muzzle brakes significantly reduce mount stresses by deflecting the gases expanding through the muzzle over impact surfaces, thus pulling the tube forward. Muzzle brakes with an efficiency of 35 percent are most practical, since greater efficiencies would create considerable crew hazards from sound pressure and dust.

Recoilless guns use propellant gas effects to compensate for recoil force. The tube is open at the rear end, where a nozzle is attached, and part of the gases are exhausted through this nozzle. When the impulse of these gases is equal to the projectile impulse, there is no tube recoil and no recoil system is required (which makes the tube much lighter). One disadvantage is that rear safety is restricted because of the exhaust gases, especially because overall pressure must be higher to propel the projectile. Physically, the recoilless gun is a transitional step to a rocket, which carries propulsion and housing and is self-propelling.

Projectile Propulsion

The metal case contains and protects the cartridge (which consists of projectile, propellant charge, and igniter) and securely seals the breech (or bolt) when the gun is fired. The case is made of brass, steel, or aluminum; it must be gas-pressure resistant and have the elasticity required for obturation and sufficient resilience for extraction.

The main disadvantage is that it is inconvenient: although it was a prerequisite for developing rapid-fire weapons, the case is used only once; it is expensive, heavy, and voluminous; and it must be removed after firing. Various configurations of cartridges are known: the conventional cartridge with metal case, the cartridge with combustible case (and stub case, as in the Leopard 2 main battle tank), caseless ammunition, the mortar grenade, and the split-loading case (howitzer ammunition).

Although the first patents for systems without metal cases date back to 1891, fully or semi-combustible cases or even caseless solutions have only recently been achieved. The combustible case—a mixture of paper, felt, and nitro-cellulose—is (for the 120mm smoothbore gun—the main armament of modern Western tanks) still equipped with a metal stub case to provide absolutely safe obturation at high operating gas pressures.

Caseless ammunition is still being developed. Such munitions are cheaper, up to 50 percent lighter, up to 30 percent smaller, and allow a higher charge density. Furthermore, eliminating empty case removal facilitates the round-to-round cycle of operations considerably.

Until recently, efforts to develop caseless ammunition have failed because of problems such as obturation, cook-off (self-ignition in hot chambers), rigidity, and the difficulty in removing an unspent, chambered cartridge. But some developments show promise: for example, the cartridge for the G11 Heckler and Koch automatic rifle manufactured by the German company Dynamit Nobel.

The simple mortar grenade functions fairly well as caseless ammunition; because it is muzzle loaded, no rear obturation problems exist. In-bore obturation between the projectile and the tube wall is solved by means of a specially designed obturating ring that is forced against the tube walls by gas pressure.

Range, aside from tube elevation, is adjusted by incrementally adding propellant charge units.

Large-caliber artillery guns normally use separately loaded (split) ammunition. Projectile, propellant charge, and primer are separately loaded because the amount of propellant needed depends on the range and elevation (in modern howitzers, up to ten bags or modules may be needed). Moreover, the individual projectile alone can be exceedingly heavy.

Future Technology

Modern weapons that use standard propellant powder are technologically mature; developmental quantum jumps can hardly be expected. However, with an efficiency of over 30 percent, their ease of handling, and their ability to immediately fire without pre-warming, they are good and reliable machines.

However, one disadvantage has not yet been eliminated: the mean gas pressure is only 40 to 50 percent of the true peak pressure. Thus, the launcher and the projectile must be designed to withstand very high peak pressures. A lower peak pressure with a tendency toward a constant pressure/time curve would be very desirable.

The search for alternate solutions to the conventional powder gun began during World War II. Today, intensive efforts are under way to achieve chemical propulsion with liquid propellants and electric propulsion.

LIQUID PROPELLANTS

Compared with standard propellant powder, liquid propellants (LP) for projectile acceleration have certain advantages in system technology, such as a continuously overlapping range in howitzers and mortars because of infinitely variable propellant injection and the elimination of the cartridge case in tank guns, which permits the protected storage of LP, use of the same propellant for all types of rounds, more favorable silhouettes for main battle tanks, and so forth.

Liquid propulsion systems under development include propulsion with liquid monopropellants containing fuel and oxidizer in one liquid and propulsion with liquid bipropellants, which store oxidizer and fuel separately.

Two versions of propellant injection are known: bulk loading, in which the propellant is pumped into the chamber prior to firing, and regenerative loading, in which the propellant is injected into the chamber during combustion. The regenerative mode may require greater technical efforts, but the defined injection during combustion gives it the advantage of a more favorable pressure curve development tending toward even pressure distribution. At constant projectile acceleration at lower peak pressure, the stress loads on mount and projectile would be significantly reduced.

ELECTRIC GUN

Higher projectile velocities are required in air defense because of ever-shorter engagement times, for increased penetration to defeat the modern tank targets with kinetic-energy projectiles, and so on. But the projectile velocity achievable with a current powder gun physically cannot be increased significantly. New methods for propulsion must be found in order to keep up with the development of potential targets. One option is the electric gun, which achieves considerably higher velocities than conventional guns.

The first patents were granted early in this century to the Norwegian physicist Kristian Birkelund. However, so far all efforts to develop a weapons system have failed because of a lack of suitable energy storage. Still, test systems have accelerated smaller projectiles to a velocity of over 4,000 m/sec. A usable system will require additional research on the storage of sufficiently high-energy, pulse-forming, launchers, or projectile configurations for those velocity regimes.

ACCELERATION METHODS

For the most part three alternative acceleration methods are being investigated: the coil gun, the rail gun, and the electrothermal gun. The coil and rail guns accelerate the projectile by electromagnetic force. They differ in the way the magnetic field is generated. The electrothermal gun accelerates the projectile in a similar way to a conventional gun—that is, by high gas pressure: a plasma burner creates an electric arc that vaporizes a suitable material, such as polyethylene, thus creating a high-pressure plasma. These principles or a hybrid electrochemical solution will probably be the future technology applied in hypervelocity guns.

INGO WOLFGANG WEISE

SEE ALSO: Ammunition; Artillery, Tube; Automatic Weapon; Explosives Technology, Conventional; Machine Gun; Munitions and Explosives Technology Applications; Technology and Warfare.

Bibliography

Canby, C. 1964. *Geschichte der Waffe*. Switzerland: Editions Rencontre and Erik Nitsche International.

Handbook on weaponry. 1982. Rheinmetall. Frankfurt am Main: Brönners Druckerei Breidenstein GmbH.

Lee, R. G. 1981. *Introduction to battlefield weapons systems and technology.* London: Brassey's.

Marchant Smith, C. J., and P. R. Haslam. 1982. *Small arms and cannons.* London: Brassey's.

Ryan, J. W. 1981. *Guns, mortars and rockets.* London: Brassey's.

H

HELICOPTER, BATTLEFIELD

The battlefield helicopter is an important component of the weapons of modern warfare. It now performs a variety of jobs formerly performed only by transport and fighter-bomber aviation as well as jobs that are unique to the helicopter. Battlefield helicopters can carry troops and their equipment—even heavy vehicles and light tanks—beyond the front and into the enemy's rear areas. They can render fire and general support for ground troops as well as hunt enemy helicopters. The diverse use of battlefield helicopters has greatly increased the mobility of ground troops.

Contemporary battlefield helicopters are of numerous types, from light observation and liaison ships to heavy lift and flying cranes, from unarmed utility carriers to lavishly armed attack systems. This article deals with the types of battlefield helicopters; their characteristics, roles, and missions; and the tactics they use to carry out such missions in combat.

Types

Battlefield helicopters are those helicopters that carry out their missions in the battlefield area, both over friendly terrain and behind the enemy's front lines. In most countries that possess a helicopter force, they are typically formed into units of the army and air force. According to their missions, capabilities, equipment, and armament, battlefield helicopters are classified as transport/general purpose and heavy lift, multirole, or attack.

Transport/General Purpose and Heavy Lift

The helicopters in this group have spacious, well-equipped cabins for accomplishing the lift mission plus external load capabilities. The payload of ships of this type varies greatly. Medium transports such as the SA 330 Puma and the Boeing Vertol 114 (CH-47D) can lift 16 to 44 fully equipped soldiers or about 2,976 to 12,600 kilograms (6,614 to 28,000 lb.) of externally slung cargo. Heavy lift helicopters, typified by the Soviet Mi-6 "Hook" and Mi-26 "Halo," have a lift capability of 70 to 100 soldiers or 12,000 kilograms (26,400 lb.) of internal cargo or 20,000 kilograms (44,000 lb.) of externally slung cargo. Helicopters in the transport/general-purpose and heavy lift category usually accomplish one or more of the following missions: helicopter assault, troop and cargo lift, aerial resupply, heavy lift, search and rescue, and medical evacuation.

MULTIROLE HELICOPTERS

These are ships that can perform more than one mission, either with the provision of additional equipment or by being manufactured in different versions. Examples are the Mil Mi-8 Hip, the Sikorsky S-70, the Westland Lynx, and the Aerospatiale 365. Some armed versions of multipurpose helicopters are considered attack helicopters and will be discussed in that category.

According to their capabilities and equipment, multirole helicopters can carry out more than one of the following missions: assault, scouting and target acquisition, search and rescue, electronic warfare, chemical reconnaissance, mine laying and clearing, airborne command and control, and others.

ATTACK HELICOPTERS

These are armed ships capable of attacking and destroying ground targets such as tanks and artillery. The category includes both armed versions of multirole helicopters and helicopters specifically designed for the attack role.

Modified light multirole helicopters include such systems as the SA 342 Gazelle and the Hughes 500 MD armed with antitank missiles, rocket pods, and heavy machine guns. Heavier modified types include the Bell 209/AH-1S Cobra and the Mi-24 Hind. These helicopters, designed from the outset as attack ships, are intended primarily for the antitank role.

In addition to the attack role, the armed multirole helicopter can carry out a variety of missions, such as general reconnaissance, scouting, observation, control of artillery fire, and liaison. The specifically designed attack helicopters, represented by such systems as the AH-64 Apache and the Mi-28 Havoc, are intended mainly for the attack role, although the latter is able to engage enemy helicopters as well.

The armament of helicopters in this group varies according to type but generally includes antitank missiles (wire or laser guided), unguided rockets mounted in pods, and either cannons or machine guns. Equipment can include advanced navigation systems, target acquisition/designation sights, laser spot trackers, laser range finders/designators, FLIR (forward-looking infrared), and computerized fire control systems as well as night-vision sensors, direct view optics, and television cameras. Infrared jammers, radar jammers, chaff dispensers, and passive radar warning receivers are also usually provided.

Roles, Missions, and Tactics

The battlefield helicopter is now regarded as an important weapon in its own right. It has an offensive capability even though at times it is used in a defensive situation. Its use, roles, and missions depend on the military doctrine of the user nation, the helicopter's capabilities, and the battlefield situation—especially the air defense environment. The key roles are fire support, general support, helicopter assault, and antihelicopter defense. (The primary characteristics of modern and advanced battlefield helicopters expected to be in service in the 1990s are shown in Tables 1 through 3.)

FIRE SUPPORT

As with fixed-wing aircraft, helicopter attack gunships with advanced weapons systems can provide for effective fire support for friendly ground troops. The Western allies use attack helicopters mainly in the antitank role, while the Soviet Union and its allies made wider use of such systems to provide fire support for tank and motorized infantry units as well as for heliborne forces. These helicopters, integrated into combined-arms groups, would have attacked enemy defensive areas, supported the advance of friendly troops, provided flank security, disrupted the movement of enemy reserves, and destroyed enemy tanks.

Attack helicopters are expected to play a major role in future conflicts, whoever the contending parties may be, but they are very vulnerable to air defense weapons, which requires them to take measures for secure completion of their missions.

During offensive operations, helicopter fire support is essential to create favorable conditions for breaking through an enemy's system of defenses, which have evolved to the point where they are highly resistant to conventional attack.

The helicopter, along with fixed-wing aircraft, works to accomplish air attack against enemy reserves, overrun tactical nuclear weapon delivery systems, and pursue withdrawing enemy forces. While fixed-wing aircraft are dealing with assigned targets in the operational depth of the enemy defenses, attack helicopters concentrate their efforts on the enemy's tactical zone of defense, mainly against enemy tanks, antitank weapons, artillery, and rocket launchers.

As the offensive develops, attack helicopters must secure the commitment of second-echelon formations and protect their flanks against enemy tanks and antitank weapons.

In defensive operations, attack helicopters usually participate in preventive strikes or counterpreparations against enemy first-echelon tanks, launching their attack from behind the friendly front line. With the onset of the enemy offensive, attack helicopters direct extensive fires against advancing enemy tanks and self-propelled guns, concentrating their efforts on filling gaps between friendly formations and protecting their flanks until reserves and second echelons can get into position.

Attack helicopters usually work in cooperation with the army antitank reserve so as to increase antitank capabilities in the threatened direction, seeking to stop advancing enemy tanks at a certain line of defense. Should the enemy seek to bypass the antitank position by a turning maneuver, the attack helicopters move to hinder enemy movement so that friendly antitank reserves can move to new blocking positions in the path of the enemy advance. Attack helicopters may also strike the enemy's flanks to force him in a certain direction where he will become more vulnerable to ground antitank weapons.

TABLE 1. *Characteristics of Assault/Transport and Heavy Lift Helicopters*

PARAMETER	AEROSPATIALE AS332 SUPER PUMA M	BOEING VERTOL 114 CH-47D CHINOOK	MIL Mi-17 HIP H	MIL Mi-26 HALO	BOEING VERTOL XCH-62/CH62
Origin	France 1978	U.S. 1979	USSR 1981	USSR 1977	U.S. 1975
Type	Medium transport	Transport	Assault transport	Heavy airlift transport	Heavy airlift
Engine	2 1,780 shp Turbomeca Makila 1A	2 3,750 shp Lycoming T55-L-712	2 1,900 shp Istov TV3-117 MT	2 11,400 shp Lotarev D-136 turbines	2 8,000 shp Allison T701
Rotor diameter	15.3 + m (51 + ft.)	18 m (60 ft.)	20.9 – m (70 – ft.)	31.5 m (105 ft.)	27.5 m (92 ft.)
Payload	22 troops or 4,500-kg (9,900-lb.) cargo	44 troops or 12,712-kg (27,966-lb.) cargo sling-loaded	32 troops or 4,000-kg (8,800-lb.) internal cargo	100 troops or 19,842-kg (44,092-lb.) internal or external cargo	55 troops or 18,000-kg (40,000-lb.) cargo sling-loaded
Maximum speed	294 kph (184 mph)	293 kph (183 mph)	248 kph (155 mph)	293 kph (183 mph)	Not available
Ceiling	5,905 m (19,684 ft.)	4,500 m (15,000 ft.)	4,920 m (16,400 ft.)	4,530 m (15,100 ft.)	Not available
Range	630 km (394 mi.)	387 km (242 mi.)	944 km (590 mi.) with reserve tanks	800 km (500 mi.)	Not available

TABLE 2. Characteristics of Multirole Helicopters

PARAMETER	MIL MI-24 HIND D	AGUSTA 109 A (MK 11)	WESTLAND LYNX (AH MK1)	SIKORSKY S-70 (UH-60A BLACKHAWK)	AEROSPATIALE SA 365 PANTHER	MBB-KAWASAKI BK 117 (A-3 M)
Origin	USSR 1971	Italy 1975	U.K. 1976	U.S. 1978	France 1984	Germany/Japan 1985
Type	Armed assault	General purpose multirole	General purpose multirole	Combat assault transport	Day/night attack/transport	Multirole armed
Engines	2 2,200 shp Istov TV3-117	2 420 shp Allison 250-C20B	2 900 shp Rolls Royce BS360 Gem	2 1,543 shp GE T700	2 838 shp Turbomeca TM333	2 550 shp Avco Lycoming LTS 101-650 B-1
Rotor diameter	16.7 m (56 ft.)	10.8 m (36 ft.)	12.6 m (42 ft.)	16.2 m (54 ft.)	11.7 m (39 ft.)	10.8 m (36 ft.)
Maximum weight	10,913 kg (24,250 lb.)	2,579 kg (5,732 lb.)	4,715 kg (10,478 lb.)	7,410 kg (16,468 lb.)	4,068 kg (9,040 lb.)	3,175 kg (7,055 lb.)
Maximum speed	318 kph (199 mph)	309 kph (193 mph)	280 kph (175 mph)	358 kph (224 mph)	278 kph (174 mph)	246 kph (154 mph)
Ceiling	4,425 m (14,750 ft.)	4,500 m (15,000 ft.)	Not available	5,700 m (19,000 ft.)	5,904 m (19,680 ft.)	1,350 m (4,500 ft.)
Range	746 km (466 mi.)	662 km (414 mi.)	677 km (420 mi.)	597 km (373 mi.)	746 km (466 mi.)	490 km (306 mi.)
Capacity	4 crew plus 8 troops	2 crew plus 6 troops	2 crew plus 10 troops	2 crew plus 11 troops	Pilot plus 8 troops	2 crew plus 10 troops
Armament	4-barrel 12.7mm MG(E), 2-barrel 23mm cannon (F), 2-barrel 30mm cannon, 4 rocket pods, and 4 ATM	8 TOW or AAMs; scout 2 podded 12.7mm and 2 pintle-mounted 7.62mm machine guns	8 TOW missiles, or podded machine guns, rockets, etc.	2 7.62mm M60 machine guns + 12 Hellfire missiles or gun (rocket pods or M56 mine dispenser)	8 HOT missiles or podded rockets, machine guns, other	1 12.7mm gun + HOT or TOW missiles or podded rockets, machine guns, other

TABLE 3. *Characteristics of Attack Helicopters*

PARAMETER	McDONNELL DOUGLAS AH-64A APACHE	AGUSTA A129 MANGUSTA	MIL MI-28 HAVOC (EST.)
Origin	U.S. 1975	Italy 1983	USSR ca. 1982–83
Engines	2 1,690 shp GE T700-GE-701	2 952 shp Rolls Royce Gem 2MK 1004D	2 2,200 shp Istov TV3-117
Rotor diameter	14.4 m (48 ft.)	11.7 m (39 ft.)	16.7 m (56 ft.)
Weight	7,949 kg (17,665 lb.)	3,671 kg (8,157 lb.)	9,027 kg (20,060 lb.)
Maximum speed	376 kph (235 mph)	269 kph (168 mph)	368 kph (230 mph)
Ceiling	6,150 m (20,500 ft.)	2,355 m (7,850 ft.)	Not available
Range	606 km (379 mi.)	744 km (465 mi.)	238 km (149 mi.)
Armament	1 30mm cannon plus 16 Hellfire missiles or 76 2.75-in. rockets in pods	8 HOT or TOW missiles plus podded 7.62mm or 12.7mm machine gun or rockets, other	Antitank and air-to-air missiles, 23mm gun turret

While counterattacking in this manner, attack helicopters participate in fire preparation, just as they do in the offense, and provide security for the commitment of the counterattack forces against enemy tanks and antitank weapons.

In both offensive and defensive operations, coordination and cooperation with friendly fixed-wing aircraft, antitank weapons, missile troops, artillery, and air defense weapons are essential. Strikes by attack helicopters and friendly ground weapons are coordinated through distribution of targets and the timing of strikes. Friendly maneuver elements must mark their positions with visual aids to assist their own attack helicopters. Artillery observation posts may also use lasers to illuminate targets for attack helicopters.

When supporting ground troops, attack helicopters usually operate from forward airfields located some 48 kilometers (30 mi.) behind the front lines. Resupply landing sites are also prepared and stocked at about half that distance from the front but out of enemy artillery range. In planning attack helicopter combat actions in offensive operations, special attention must be given to the nature of the terrain so as to select covered waiting and combat areas. In defensive operations, such areas, as well as ambush/attack positions, are selected to the front and on the flanks. The combat areas selected must provide for covered maneuvers between the ambush/attack positions. Attack helicopters typically deploy in small groups, although never less than two together, in combat/waiting areas that provide an unobserved route to preselected ambush/attack positions.

Helicopter fire support may be provided in several different forms, including preplanned strikes, on-call close support, free hunt, and ambush. Preplanned strikes are used mainly in the phases of fire/air preparation and commitment of the counterattack force in defensive operations. On-call fire support and the free hunt can be used in all phases of operations to hinder and repel the enemy while on defense or to overcome his most highly resistant positions in the offense. The ambush is used mainly while in defensive positions, independently, or in cooperation with ground antitank weapons along the direction of the enemy's approach and on his flanks. The ambush may also be used to repel an enemy counterattack during offensive operations.

Helicopters launch their weapons in two ways, from the hovering position and from dive attack. Missiles can be launched in either way, but the dive attack is usually used for rocket launching and gun firing. The hovering method is used where there is cover in the attack position. In open areas, dive attack is preferable, especially in desert areas where hovering causes sand clouds that interfere with visibility and reveal the helicopter's position.

Typical combat formations used by attack helicopters are organized around scout groups and strike groups. The scout group is used for reconnaissance of the combat area, target acquisition, and assignment and coordination of combat actions of strike groups. The scout group may select the attack positions or use previously selected positions. The scout group may also call for artillery and fixed-wing aircraft support.

In addition to their armament, scout group helicopters are usually equipped with advanced avionics systems such as night vision, target acquisition and designation, and navigation and artillery fire control systems. The scout group comprises approximately one-third of the combat formation force; the strike group constitutes the main body of the combat formation.

When delivering preplanned or on-call strikes, attack helicopters fly directly from advanced airfields or resupply sites to the assigned combat area, timing it so that they arrive just after suppression of enemy air defense weapons in the target area by friendly artillery or fixed-wing aircraft. The scout element arrives a few minutes before the strike force, which waits under cover in the combat area.

After the scout group reconnoiters the target area, the strike group moves to attack positions as directed by the scouts. Upon acquiring visual contact with its targets, the strike group launches its attack as directed; usually this begins with firing missiles from the hovering position (unless in desert terrain), followed by rockets and guns fired using dive attacks. To launch a dive attack, the helicopter performs a rapid climb followed by a brief attack run, then aims and fires its rockets while at the same time spraying the target area with gunfire so as to suppress return fire; this is followed by a hard down break and disengagement.

When engaged in the free hunt, attack helicopters traverse an assigned area, searching for enemy advanced/reconnaissance tanks that may be seeking a way around friendly antitank positions or trying to approach from the flank. Attack helicopters typically use combat flight formations when in the free hunt area. While a search-and-strike pair flies in a zigzag manner at minimum altitude and optimum speed, the leader brings up the rear at a distance that ensures good visual contact and mutual fire support. The zigzagging and frequent changes of position in the formation maximize the chance of spotting concealed targets. The flight leader suppresses enemy antiaircraft weapons on the flanks of the combat flight formation. Then, having contact with the enemy targets, the strike pair launches the attack according to the flight leader's instructions.

In the ambush, attack helicopters deploy to an assigned waiting/combat area that has been selected because it provides an unobserved run to the planned ambush positions into which they will move just before launching their attacks. Once in the ambush position, the helicopters observe advancing enemy tanks and select their targets. If the helicopters have mast-mounted sights, they will be able to operate with only the sights visible to the enemy.

To launch missiles (such as the Hughes BGM-71 TOW), the helicopters may need to break cover, with either a pop-up or a pop-sideways maneuver, to allow the missiles to clear the cover. This prelaunch maneuver may not be necessary if the missile is designed to be launched at an angle so that it will clear the cover. During the missile's flight, the helicopters resume their former positions with just the sight exposed, waiting until the missiles strike their targets. Then they repeat the attacks until such time as enemy fire approaches their positions.

With the mast-mounted sight, helicopters armed with the laser-homing Hellfire missile can even keep their rotor behind cover while launching their weapons in a "fire-and-forget" mode.

GENERAL SUPPORT

The helicopter general-support role comprises a group of missions that include general reconnaissance, scouting and target acquisition, chemical reconnaissance, artillery spotting, search and rescue, aerial command post, laying of smoke screens, mine sowing, and logistic and electronic warfare support.

The rapid changes and confusion typical of the battlefield environment may make it necessary to use helicopters for reconnoitering the situation along the front, to carry out scouting and target acquisition, and to insert ground reconnaissance teams into critical areas.

The helicopter's involvement in these missions will depend on the specific battlefield situation. For example, it would not be wise to use a helicopter for reconnaissance missions over enemy troops in a well-defended front with numerous antiaircraft weapons, especially when there is a suitable alternative such as the remote piloted vehicle (RPV), which is cheaper and less vulnerable under those circumstances. But in such missions as scouting and target acquisition, as well as chemical reconnaissance, there are few alternatives to the helicopter. On a front that is heavily infested with air defenses, scouting might be carried out from behind the friendly front line beyond the range of enemy air defense weapons. Insertion of chemical reconnaissance teams into contaminated areas, however, would require helicopters to operate behind enemy lines.

Scouting is essential for security, for directing attack helicopters to their targets, and for suppressing enemy antiaircraft weapons with artillery or fixed-wing aircraft strikes. The importance of scouting increases when the mission is to protect the flanks and to provide security for the commitment of second-echelon formations.

When the friendly force is engaged in exploiting chemical or nuclear strikes, helicopters are used to insert reconnaissance teams in the contaminated areas. Samples of the air may be collected during the helicopter's flight over the contaminated area, and survey teams can be landed within 15 minutes after the chemical or nuclear strike. Forward observers can perform their mission from helicopters behind friendly front lines.

Search and rescue, on the battlefield usually the location and extraction of bailed-out and crashed air crews, has long been one of the helicopter's missions. Helicopters assigned to this mission are maintained at an advanced state of readiness, equipped with search and rescue equipment, and on call around the clock.

The helicopter may also be used as an airborne command and control post. These helicopters must have wide cabins to provide a suitable place for the commander and his staff and special equipment for command and control. Such helicopters can also be used by commanders to control live-fire maneuvers and for radio relay.

Helicopters may also be used efficiently to lay smoke screens by using on-board pyrotechnic generators or by dropping smoke pots at low altitude. A single helicopter, such as the Mi-8 Hip, can, using some 24 BDSL-15 smoke pots, produce a 5-kilometer (3-mi.) smoke screen that will last for 15 minutes. These screens can be used to cover such friendly combat activities as hovering missile attacks, landing of assault helicopters behind enemy lines, and the maneuvering of ground elements.

Battlefield helicopters are also used for mine-sowing and mine-clearing operations. Two Hip helicopters, each carrying about 400 antitank mines, can lay their load in less than fifteen minutes while cruising at 25 kilometers (15 mi.) per hour. The importance of the helicopter's mine-sowing capability increases in critical situations, such as when it is necessary to hamper the rapid advance of enemy troops and tanks or to rapidly emplace coastal defenses against impending amphibious operations. Helicopters can also clear minefields by towing a device to detonate the mines.

Helicopter logistical support comprises mainly transport, supply, and medical evacuation missions. Such missions can be carried out behind friendly lines or across enemy front lines. Helicopters are used for logistical support behind friendly lines only when time is critical or when the helicopter is the only means that can complete the mission. Behind enemy lines, the helicopter's logistical support is provided mainly to heliborne assault troops or to troops encircled by enemy forces. In such cases, strong air protection must be provided for the logistical helicopters.

Electronic warfare support is usually carried out by helicopters from behind the friendly front line. Some helicopter versions, such as the Hip-K and EH-60A, are specially equipped for electronic warfare and intelligence.

HELICOPTER ASSAULT: THE SOVIET VIEW

Many nations expect to use heliborne operations extensively in future conflicts. Their aim is to increase the mobility and rate of advance of friendly troops, doing this in particular by attacking the enemy rear and thereby loosening and disrupting his system of defense. Many nations have thus organized heliborne forces, usually consisting of units of airborne troops and air-lifted motorized infantry units.

With their unique capabilities, helicopters play different roles in such heliborne operations. They can carry troops to an assigned area behind enemy lines without the complications of a parachute drop and the special training it requires. In addition, helicopters can provide the heliborne assault with most of the air support it requires, whether fire support or general support.

Employment of the helicopter assault has special importance in jungle terrain and on mountainous or desert battlefields where troop mobility is limited by the road network and combat involves fierce fighting to seize communications, road hubs, and key mountain passes.

Depending on the purpose of the operation, the strength of the heliborne force, and the depth of its penetration, helicopter assaults may (according to Soviet doctrine) be classified as operational, tactical, or special, as follows:

1. An operational assault is usually carried out by a heliborne brigade force to assist attacking troops in accomplishing operational missions according to the general concept of the operation.
2. A tactical assault is carried out by a heliborne force, varying in size from company to battalion, to accomplish tactical missions in combat of a field army's first-echelon divisions.
3. A special assault is usually carried out by a ranger force, varying in size from a squad to a company, to accomplish reconnaissance and sabotage missions. Special assaults may be carried out to both tactical and operational depth of enemy defenses.

In general, the helicopter assault aims to complete one or more of the following combat tasks: destruction of enemy tactical nuclear delivery means; seizure of river bridgeheads; seizure of vital territory; disruption of enemy reserves, command and control networks, and logistics systems; and exploitation of nuclear or chemical strikes.

A heliborne assault is initiated from a departure area where the heliborne force is loaded. The departure area is a suitable landing area for helicopters, usually 30 to 50 kilometers (18 to 30 mi.) behind the friendly front line and within the zones protected by antiaircraft weapons. It should include shelters, camouflage, and so on.

To minimize their vulnerability in the open departure area, especially when operating in desert terrain, helicopters arrive at the departure area to board the attacking force only 10 or 15 minutes before loading. The loading is then usually carried out under the protection of fighter aircraft.

Helicopters take off from the departure area in flights or squadrons, although night takeoffs are usually carried out in flights to minimize the requirement for lights on the ground and aboard the helicopters.

Under the protection of fighters, the helicopters' combat formation flies to the landing zone at very low altitude and in two groups, the landing group and the support group. The former makes the heliborne force landing, while the second includes scout and attack helicopters.

The scout helicopters fly far enough ahead of the landing group to permit reconnoitering the situation along the flight route and at the landing zone. Attack helicopters maintain contact with the landing group, flying ahead and along the flanks of its formation.

As the landing group approaches the enemy front line, friendly artillery and fighter-bombers, with coordinated fires, suppress enemy antiaircraft weapons along the flight route. When they reach the enemy lines, the attack helicopters, flying ahead and on the flanks of the landing group, suppress the revealed enemy antiaircraft weapons.

When they approach the landing zone (5 to 10 minutes before the helicopters land), the fighter-bombers suppress antiaircraft weapons in the landing zone and destroy any enemy tanks and artillery near it (out to a distance of approximately 15 kilometers [9 mi.] from the landing sites). Meanwhile, the density of friendly fighters in the air alert zones is increased so as to protect the combat operations of both the helicopters and fighter-bombers.

The landing zone should have been cleared of resistance by the fighter-bombers before arrival of the helicopters. If not, the attack helicopters must accomplish this, clearing the landing zone before arrival of the transport helicopters.

The landing group approaches the landing zone with the assistance of its navigational aids and the guidance provided by the scouting helicopters. As the transport helicopters approach the landing zone, the intervals between flights and squadrons are reduced so as to minimize the time needed for landing and disembarking and also the space required for landing sites.

In general, an area of 500 square meters (600 sq. yds.) is sufficient to land a medium transport helicopter brigade of 36 helicopters simultaneously, although the area must be doubled for a night landing. A helicopter brigade needs three landing sites for each squadron. Upon arriving at the landing sites, the transport helicopters land in squadrons using a direct approach. Disembarking is carried out as quickly as possible so the helicopters stay on the ground for the shortest time.

While the troops are disembarking and the heliborne force is assembling, the scout helicopters fly over the landing zone, in a radius of not more than 5 to 10 kilometers (3 to 6 mi.) from the landing sites, searching for any enemy weapons that might threaten the landing and assembly; if any are located, the scouts direct attack helicopters to destroy them.

After landing and disembarkation have been completed, the helicopters return to their home airfields by means of a less vulnerable flight route. In the case of an airborne raid, however, the helicopters must return to pick up the raiding party as soon as the mission has been accomplished.

ANTIHELICOPTER DEFENSE

It is widely believed that the best counter to the helicopter is an air combat helicopter, or helicopter hunter, armed for the task and faster and more agile than the enemy ship. A helicopter such as this, with a well-trained crew, will be able to tackle enemy battlefield helicopters in their own ultra-low-level environment, accomplishing its mission by either offensive or defensive combat actions.

Offensive combat action is aimed primarily at detecting and destroying the multithreat attack helicopter, which implies the need for wide and continuous reconnaissance activity. The defensive concept, on the other hand, means self-protection and the protection of other friendly helicopters and tank units against both enemy helicopter hunters and attack helicopters, respectively. This is the approach now receiving the most emphasis, especially by Western allies.

Self-protection against enemy helicopters seeking duels can be achieved by arming friendly helicopters with effective long-range weapons and air-to-air missiles, as well as by providing such helicopters with protective systems. But unarmed friendly helicopters, and those that do not possess suitable air-to-air weapons, will need aerial protection against the enemy helicopter hunter. This can be achieved by escorting friendly helicopters during their flight and mission accomplishment, using for this purpose suitable other helicopters having air-to-air combat capabilities, supported by electronic countermeasures, and competitive with the enemy helicopters.

Protection of friendly tank units against enemy attack helicopters can be accomplished by helicopter patrols carried out in the expected direction of the enemy's approach and along the flanks of the tank units to be protected. Such patrols must be carried out at a distance of not less than one-and-a-half times the missile range of the enemy helicopters. In the offense, this protection will be even more necessary during the phases of repelling counterattacks and commitment of the second echelon. In the defense, the need for this air protection will increase when moving tank reserves and during commitment of the second echelon to conduct a counterattack.

Compared with fixed-wing aircraft, a helicopter's aerial combat is more difficult. In order to engage and destroy an enemy helicopter, three important and difficult steps must be accomplished successfully even before firing or launching missiles. These are detection, identification, and getting into firing position.

In the modern battlefield environment, helicopters can survive only by sticking to the terrain and using natural and artificial cover. During low-level flight, both visibility and observation are considerably reduced. This means that, without airborne radar, detection and identification will take place mainly by surprise and at short range. Thus, the pilot will not have time to assume a firing position before he is sighted by the enemy.

At short distances—from 1,000 to 1,500 meters (3,300 to 4,950 ft.)—reaction speed is the decisive factor. If the friendly pilot succeeds in gaining a good firing position before being detected by the enemy, he will then have a good chance of destroying his opponent. Otherwise, he must resort to speed and to vertical and horizontal maneuvers to overcome the enemy, a more difficult task under those circumstances.

Several maneuvers have been developed for use in aerial combat by helicopters. They include acceleration and deceleration in horizontal flight, dive attack and pulling out, turns in dive attack followed by wingovers with high-pulled turns, horizontal backward flight, upward flight and spirals under acceleration, and yoyos at low altitude with side slip and rapid transition to stationary hover. Such maneuvers require a helicopter specifically designed and armed for the mission.

Future

With the continual development of the helicopter's capabilities, its importance as a potent force on the battlefield will increase. Advanced helicopters such as the Havoc, Apache, and the forthcoming Hokum and LHX/SCAT (light helicopter experimental/scout attack), with their impressive speed, lethal weapons, and great agility and flexibility, will play a decisive role in future conflicts.

As reliance on attack helicopters increases for antiarmor battles, the indicators point toward the helicopter hunter as a good response. As long ago as September 1979, Major General Belove foresaw the future of the helicopter when he wrote in *Soviet Military Review* that, "like tank battles of the past wars, a future war between well-equipped armies is bound to involve helicopter battles."

GABR ALY GABR

SEE ALSO: Air Assault; Airborne Land Forces; Army Aviation.

Bibliography

Apostolo, G. 1984. *World encyclopedia of civil and military helicopters*. London: Willow.
Chant, C., et al. 1977. Helicopter warfare. In *The encyclopedia of air warfare*, pp. 240–47. London: Salamander.
Gunston, B. 1984. *Modern fighting aircraft*. London: Salamander.
———, and M. Spick. 1986. *Modern fighting helicopters*. London: Salamander.
Illustrated encyclopedia of aviation. 1979. London: Cavendish.
Jane's all the world's aircraft, 1986–1987. 1986. London: Jane's.
Jane's all the world's aircraft, 1987–1988. 1987. London: Jane's.
Polmar, N., and F. Kennedy. 1981. *Military helicopters of the world*. London: Arms and Armour.
Soviet helicopters: Design, development and tactics. 1983. London: Jane's.
ADDITIONAL SOURCES: *International Defense Review; Military Technology*.

INFANTRY

Foot soldiers have been an important part of armies as long as wars have been conducted.

History

The armies of Sparta won undying fame fighting on foot with spears, and the legions of Rome conquered the peoples of the Mediterranean, the Near East, and Western Europe marching and fighting on foot. But in summer 378, the Roman emperor Valens attacked the Visigoth army of Fritigern outside Adrianople. Fritigern called on his nearby Alan and Ostrogoth allies, whose cavalry (armored horsemen) arrived while Valens's army was still deploying. The barbarian cavalry drove off the Roman cavalry and then struck the Roman foot soldiers from flank and rear. The surrounded Romans were slaughtered, and Valens was killed. Adrianople marked the demise of the Roman foot soldier and demonstrated the tactical power of cavalry.

THE MIDDLE AGES

During the Middle Ages, armies underwent a fundamental change: the ancient military system composed of freemen came under the feudal social system. Each feudal lord commanded his own army, which was built on a main striking force of armored horsemen (knights). As these knights were expensive to equip and train, they were supplied by wealthy landowners.

The decline of noble support for the knights coincided with the rise of *landsknecht* armies. (This initiative came from the Swiss confederates, who used well-trained foot soldiers to defeat armored knights.) The Germans gave the name *landsknecht* to this new version of the ancient Macedonian phalanx. The *landsknecht* forces were among the ablest foot soldiers of the late Middle Ages.

DEVELOPMENT OF INFANTRY

The modern term *infantry* is a relic of the Middle Ages. A knight or man-at-arms was followed into battle by retainers, who usually fought on foot and were recruited from tenants of his estate. Because the knight was both commander and patron, these retainers were often called *enfants* or *infante*, "children." Later, *infantry* became a term applied to all foot soldiers.

During the seventeenth and eighteenth centuries, the Netherlands became the forerunner for establishing standing armies composed of mercenaries and recruited natives. The Dutch military structure developed by Maurice of Orange created a trained professional army with the infantry as the prime component.

The Dutch soldier, especially the infantryman, was subject to drill, coercion, and draconian penalties for the pettiest offenses. Individualism and initiative were not in demand in the common soldier; the combat drill aimed at exact execution of precise commands and perfection in the control of fire and maneuver. Nothing is more characteristic of the art of war of that time than the statement of a Prussian general who said: "It is true that 76 steps per minute have been prescribed for marching, but upon careful deliberation and frequent observation I have come to the conclusion that 75 steps per minute are even better."

Over time, the infantry was subdivided into groups of specialists. There were the grenadiers—hand-grenade throwers—who were considered "the core of the infantry." They were specifically selected and reliable assault troops, who in most cases were seasoned by long service. Musketeers originally were soldiers armed with matchlock muskets but the term eventually became the generic name for the common soldier.

In contrast to the musketeers, the pikemen, foot soldiers armed with a pike for close combat, were regarded as gentlemen. Fusiliers, originally artillery train guards, were equipped with flintlock muskets. Jaegers, trained hunters and foresters employed as scouts and sharpshooters, were employed in irregular warfare, skirmishing, security tasks, and reconnaissance. The success of such volunteer riflemen in the American War of Independence led other nations—particularly France—to develop those troops as part of the "light infantry."

At the end of the eighteenth century, wars continued to be won by professional armies in battles with the proper employment of the infantry.

THE AGE OF REVOLUTION

When the masses of France were mobilized during the French Revolution, there was no time to train troops in the traditional way. However, like the American volunteers, the French troops had greater mobility and made better use of the terrain. Their use of columns echeloned in depth proved successful against the attacking armies, which were arrayed in lines according to prescribed regulations.

The revolutionary demand for liberty, fraternity, and equality changed the principles of military command and control and affected tactics as well as *esprit de corps*. The new *esprit* required superiors to treat their soldiers humanely and soldiers to be prepared to serve. The victories of revolutionary armed forces over the professional armies of the ruling order bear testimony to the success of this approach (again, the American War of Independence is an excellent example).

The rising nationalism connected with humane treatment by officers and noncommissioned officers contributed considerably to the success of the French troops and especially of the infantry. Napoleon's great victories strengthened that motivation.

The Prussians and the British who defeated the French at Waterloo had learned their lesson from Napoleon. The Prussian general Neithardt von Gneisenau described the light infantryman as follows:

> Ease in the individual, mobility, presence and agility of mind, skill in using all facilities as cover for himself or to the disadvantage of the enemy, jumping over ditches, fences, hedges and walls, running, correct target shooting, unnoticed creeping up and away, approaching and withdrawing with the speed of a horse, leaving no hiding place, no rock unnoticed to send the hitting bullet to the careless enemy.

Those demands are still valid today.

In his work *Vom Kriege*, Gen. Karl von Clausewitz emphasized the importance of the infantry when he discussed combat actions:

> An engagement consists of two essentially different components: the destructive power of firearms, and hand-to-hand, or individual, combat. The latter in turn can be used for either attack or defense (words employed here in an absolute sense, for we are speaking in the broadest terms). Artillery is effective only through the destructive power of fire; cavalry only by way of individual combat; infantry by both these means.

That is, the infantry is the only branch of service that combines both attack and defense, and it is thus (at least in the eyes of infantrymen) superior to both artillery and cavalry. As a logical consequence, Clausewitz stated that "Infantry is the main branch of the service; the other two are supplementary."

The reform of the armed forces in Europe at the beginning of the nineteenth century was largely a consequence of political development. With the end of absolutism and of mercenary armies, citizens were soldiers and soldiers were citizens. The professional situation changed for the military leader as well. Noble descent was no longer the key to advancement in the armed forces, but was superseded by knowledge and education in peacetime and bravery in wartime. The increasing number of citizens available for military service and the continued improvement of weapons led to reorganization in all armies.

Moreover, the growth of technology in the armed forces was unstoppable. The introduction of the cone-shaped rifle bullet (the "Minié ball") in the mid-nineteenth century more than tripled the effective range of infantry fire, from under 250 yards to over 800, with a sharp increase in accuracy. By the 1860s (especially in the American Civil War), infantry firearms inflicted more than three-quarters of all battlefield casualties. The increased lethality of these firearms forced greater dispersion on the battlefield, from an average of one soldier per 200 square meters in Napoleon's time to one per 257 square meters in the American Civil War.

WORLD WAR I

The lethal potential of technology first became apparent during World War I. Infantrymen discovered, especially on the western front, that courage was no longer sufficient to decide the battle. The firepower of artillery and the deadly effect of machine guns forced the foot soldiers of the belligerents to take cover. World War I produced a new type of infantryman: the individual fighter specifically trained and equipped for his task. Soldiers began the war carrying rifle, bayonet, and pistol; by the end, they carried steel helmet, knapsack, spade, gas mask, and hand grenades. Flamethrowers and satchel charges were supplemented by light and heavy machine guns and portable heavy weapons such as mortars and mine launchers.

The tank was first employed by the Allies in 1917 as an armored infantry escort vehicle. It indicated a solution to the stalemate of trench warfare. A successful attack against an enemy in trenches and behind deeply echeloned obstacles was possible only with specifically trained assault battalions after heavy preparatory fire, often lasting several days. This suggested that artillery, not infantry, played the decisive part in war. The attack of infantry formations in dense skirmish lines was abandoned. Neither the armies of the Central European powers nor the Allied forces could cope with the high losses of the offensives during the initial months of war.

The bitter experiences of the years 1914–18 introduced a new epoch of infantry tactics and training. British officers such as General Fuller and the former captain and military author Liddell Hart demanded the organizational combination of armored and infantry units. Liddell Hart asserted that the infantry must become mobile on light armored combat vehicles to ensure cooperation with the tanks. German general Heinz Guderian pursued that idea and developed a balanced composition of personnel for the German armored (*panzer*) divisions.

WORLD WAR II

Until the outbreak of World War II, the basic idea of motorizing infantry divisions had been implemented only in individual cases. But the ever-increasing use of technology required more extensive logistical support. In the infantry divisions of World War I, more than 80 percent of the military personnel fought on the front lines; in World War II, there were as many as three supporters for every "fighter."

The use of mobile troops by the German Wehrmacht eventually influenced the course of the war. A combination of tanks and infantry formations in the initial phase ensured the success of the blitzkrieg campaigns. The motorization of combat troops allowed Germany to move large numbers of troops rapidly on the battlefield, thus achieving superiority. However, the blitzkrieg successes would have been impossible without the cooperation of the German air force.

On the other side, the Allies quickly learned their lesson. The achievements of the British infantry in the desert war in North Africa, the resilience and toughness of the Russian soldiers in the Battle of Stalingrad, the bloody fights of the American marines in recapturing the islands of the Pacific region from the determined Japanese unequivocally demonstrated General Montgomery's claim that "without infantry you can do nothing, absolutely nothing."

British field marshal Wavell wrote in *The Times* in April 1945

> We should be aware of three facts. Firstly, all battles and all wars are won by the infantryman in the long run. Secondly, the infantryman always carries the main burden of the fight, his losses are higher, he suffers to a greater extent from adverse conditions and from physical exhaustion than the other branches of service. Thirdly, the skills of the infantryman in modern warfare are less stereotyped and much more difficult to acquire than those of the other branches of service. With almost every step he takes, and with everything he does on the battlefield the infantryman must put his independence and intelligence to the test. Therefore, we should employ those among our personnel with the greatest intelligence and persistence in the infantry.

The most important changes that World War II wrought upon the infantry were caused by the mechanization of the armed forces and the ever-improving weapons technology. Compensation included changed tactics, improved protection, new organizational structures, and improved training. During World War I, chemical agents (gas) had become a new threat to the infantryman employed forward in the trench; the battle tank became the main enemy of the infantryman in World War II. Consequently, every effort was made to develop new armor-piercing defense weapons.

Special troops of different designations developed within the infantry branch. The *Grenadiere* and later *Panzergrenadiere* units of the German armed forces, equipped with armored personnel carriers, corresponded to the armored infantry of the U.S. Army. They had the task of protecting main battle tanks against enemy infantry and were to a certain extent able to fight in both mounted and dismounted modes. The Soviet Red Army had "desant" infantry units in their tank forces that were mounted on battle tanks during attack operations and conquered terrain after a successful breach of breakthrough. Most armies employed specialized infantry including paratrooper, ranger (commando), and mountain troops. Another costly lesson was learned from the toll of lives paid primarily by frontline infantry. Human lives became valued, especially those of well-trained specialists; manpower increasingly would be replaced by technology and materiel. But the principal statement of the German regulation on *Truppenführung* ("military leadership command") remains valid, especially for the infantry: "In spite of all sophisticated technical means, man is the decisive element in battle."

Infantry Today

Today's infantry retains the virtues of the warrior, yet is more integrated with other branches. Modern war presents complex and diverse scenarios, such as fighting against regular military forces; combating guerrilla forces, partisans, and terrorists; civil war; and covert warfare. Moreover, it is subject to additional exogenous factors such as fighting in built-up areas, in the jungle, in the mountains, in the desert, or in large-scale amphibious operations. Although a "world war" between the great powers becomes more improbable, local and limited conflicts are increasingly frequent and virulent, requiring mobile, conventionally equipped task forces.

GERMAN INFANTRY

The German Federal Armed Forces are typical of a number of "special infantry forces" developed by several nations for almost every possible condition. The infantry comes under the collective term of armored and nonarmored combat troops. Rifle troops, mountain infantry troops, and parachute troops belong to the nonarmored combat troops, and the armored infantry troops belong to the armored combat troops. The term *infantry* itself is used in German service regulations almost exclusively in connection with the rifle troops. Each branch of service has specific tasks.

Armored infantry. The armored infantry troops are the most combat-effective and versatile infantry branch of service within the Field Army. They have the task of fighting against infantry and of combating light armored combat vehicles and main battle tanks. In addition, they can operate in close coordination with the armored troops.

The way armored infantry fight is influenced by armored personnel carriers, like the German Marder. Its cross-country and deep-fording capabilities permit employment of the armored infantry in many kinds of terrain. Its speed allows rapid concentration and dispersal of forces and thus provides additional protection against enemy weapons, especially against artillery fire. Its armor protects against hand weapons, to a limited extent against gunfire up to a caliber of 20mm, and against the effects of artillery shell fragments and blast. It also makes mounted combat possible even after nuclear, biological, or chemical weapons have been used. Armored infantry troops also carry 20mm secondary weapons that can use two types of ammunition and can be employed against armored and nonarmored targets. Long-range antitank missiles, machine guns, portable antitank weapons, and small arms complete the weaponry of the armored infantry.

Depending on mission, situation, and terrain, armored infantry troops may fight mounted or dismounted. In mobile operations, the infantry always fights in close proximity to its armored personnel carriers in order to make use of their mobility, firepower, and protection from enemy small-arms fire. Armored infantry troops fight on foot to destroy the enemy in close combat during attack operations or to defend decisive portions of terrain.

In conducting operations with various organizations, for example, brigades, combat groups, or regiments, the infantry forces must be organized so that they can be employed in mobile operations together with other mobile armored forces and antitank forces in attack, defense, and delay operations. The armored infantry forces are organized in battalions comprising a headquarters and supply company, two or three armored infantry companies, and an armored mortar company or a tank company. Battalions in turn make up armored brigades and armored infantry brigades.

Motorized infantry troops. Motorized infantry troops fight on foot, although they are equipped with armored or nonarmored vehicles to achieve greater mobility. Their primary task is to fight in built-up areas, in woods, and in swampy areas. Such terrain reduces the effectiveness of armored combat units and requires units with relatively large personnel strength.

The mission of motorized infantry troops is twofold. First, they must hold terrain from prepared positions and thus facilitate mobile operations of armored combat units during defensive operations. Second, they must dislodge the enemy from his positions, often engaging in close combat and often under the cover of darkness to create the preconditions for the employment of armored combat units in achieving a breakthrough and in pursuing the enemy.

To withstand attacks from armored combat vehicles, motorized infantry battalions are equipped with antitank rocket weapons systems. Motorized infantry units and armored infantry units employ the same small-arms equipment. Because of improved air mobility, motorized infantry units, like parachute units, can be rapidly employed by transport helicopters as a mobile reserve. Motorized infantry forces are particularly suited to guarding and securing important facilities in the rear area and to defending them in case of enemy attack. They are also used in counterraid operations against penetrated dispersed enemy forces or against spetsnaz (Soviet Special Forces). Motorized infantry normally operate on foot, often in difficult terrain, and rely on surprise attacks against the enemy.

Prospects

For centuries the infantry has adapted to new technical developments. In future conflicts, as in the past, the infantryman will play a decisive part. Infantry units must be optimally organized, equipped, and trained for numerous missions.

The specialization of the past generation will continue. Organization in smaller formations, units, and subunits will enable better command and control, and electronic command and control will play an important role.

Despite the most sophisticated technology, man will continue to be the main carrier of the fight. The individual soldier's power of resistance and ability will continue to be necessary. Both depend on hard, demanding training.

PETER BOLTE

SEE ALSO: Artillery; Cavalry; Combined Arms; Jungle Warfare; Land Warfare; Mechanized Warfare.

Bibliography

Bohrmann, K. 1983. Schützenpanzer für die moderne Infanterie. In *Heere International.* Bonn: Verlag E. S. Mittler u. Sohn.

Clausewitz, C. von. [1834] 1934. *Vom Kriege.* Berlin: Vier Falken Verlag.

Liddell Hart, B. H. 1966. *Lebenserinnerungen (deutsche Ubersetzung)*. Düsseldorf: Econ-Verlag GmbH.

Heeresdienstvorschrift. 1988. *Das Panzergrenadierbataillon*. Bonn: BMVg.

INTELLIGENCE, MILITARY

Military intelligence (hereafter generally referred to as intelligence) is a primary function in war; it runs throughout all command echelons and the entire conflict spectrum. Intelligence is absolutely essential for the rational conduct of war and as such is one of the oldest functions in the political/military arena. Military intelligence has an offensive side, usually called intelligence, and a defensive side, usually called counterintelligence.

Before defining *intelligence*, it is necessary to define two other terms as they will be used in this article: *war* and *military forces*. *War* is used here as Clausewitz defined it, "the mere continuation of policy [politics] by other means" (Clausewitz 1968, p. 119). It is important to recognize that what is being considered is armed conflict that supports political objectives. *Military forces* are defined as unique organizations created and maintained by a society for the primary purpose of threatening to apply, or actually applying, destructive force against other societies (normally concentrated on their military forces) in support of political objectives.

Intelligence is both a product and a process and, at a minimum, is the systematic, planned, and objective-oriented (i.e., nonrandom) collection, analysis, and dissemination of processed information from either open or denied sources, performed either openly or clandestinely. The very fact that such activity is being undertaken may be either openly acknowledged or kept secret. In all cases the key difference between intelligence and information is the processing involved. Data that has not been processed—that is, has not been analyzed in some fashion—is information, not intelligence. Intelligence is a continual process of mutually supporting, repeating cycles (collection-analysis-reporting) that must be directed, as production is not automatic. The denial of select information to unauthorized persons is both security and counterintelligence. The clandestine collection of information is a proper intelligence function, but covert operations and deception are not intelligence functions. Covert operations are a specific type of operation where a primary objective is to keep the action organization's identity secret, either by maintaining absolute secrecy or by deliberately identifying another organization as the actor. Although covert operations are often associated with the intelligence community, it is important to remember that clandestine collection and covert operations are completely different; only the former is a proper intelligence function.

Deception is a second major military function that is often erroneously considered an intelligence function. Deception is a function planned and executed by the operations officer. In essence, deception is the plan (i.e., the deliberate intent) to take advantage of an enemy's specifically induced or influenced behavior. The inducement of desired behavior requires using intelligence, but intelligence is a supporting element, not the executing element.

General Definition

The term *intelligence* has been misunderstood and misused throughout history because people often define intelligence based more on their own background than on a real understanding of the whole.

OFTEN DEFINED BY PROCESS

Of the three intelligence processes—collection, analysis, and dissemination—the most common definition is based on the most widely discussed: collection. Collection is not intelligence, any more than the other two taken separately are intelligence. Collection itself is only the beginning, although it is the most intriguing and in the popular media the most often portrayed. Spying and espionage are thus erroneously popularized as intelligence. In fact, spying is a form of collection that involves the use of humans as the collecting mechanism; espionage is the act of spying when obtaining denied (i.e., protected) information. The obtaining of this information is also called clandestine collection.

Spies come in two general categories, covert and overt. The covert spy is the type most often thought of in conversation and portrayed in movies and novels. This type of spy is most successful when never detected and when retired in total anonymity.

While espionage was for centuries the primary intelligence collection method, a new set of systems has clearly become dominant. Much of the imagery, including new and private corporation multispectral capabilities, is based on satellites. While they are expensive to build and operate, satellites have such advantages in terms of access that significant amounts of money and numbers of personnel are now devoted to their development and operation and the exploitation of their products. Because of this cost and the extraordinarily important access of satellite collectors, intelligence is a significant contributor to space's role as a new theater of military operations.

The second intelligence process, analysis, is rarely used to define intelligence, especially by the public media, because analysts do not make operational decisions, either political or military. The operational decision and the movement of political or military forces are the dramatic efforts. The analyst's contribution is not dramatic enough to capture the public's imagination nor is it the result. Only rarely are intelligence analysts and analyses a major element in the popular media. Two notable film exceptions are the movies *Midway* and *Sink the Bismarck*. In *Midway*, the supremely important work of naval cryptanalysts and order of battle analysts is shown clearly. In *Sink the Bismarck*, the key roles of intelligence analysis and dissemination are shown quite well.

The most common portrayal of analysis is in the detective genre. The detective slowly pieces together the puzzle, but he also has two key advantages over the intelligence analyst. First, the detective performs all three parts of the intelligence process—collection, analysis, and dissemination. Second, the detective is able to take direct action on his intelligence, the chase and arrest, as he is also an operational decision maker.

This third element, dissemination, is the generally forgotten element. This is a major problem, as no matter how thoroughly information is collected and analyzed into intelligence, if the results cannot be transmitted to the proper recipient in a timely fashion, the entire process has been a waste. Dissemination is largely a communications problem, and today this means electronic communications using satellites. In this manner, intelligence has again greatly contributed to space's role as a new theater of military operations.

OFTEN DEFINED BY SOURCE

Intelligence is often defined in terms of its source: for example, human intelligence (HUMINT), signal intelligence (SIGINT), and imagery intelligence (IMINT). This definition by source is as misleading and incorrect as defining by process. The three "INTs" are not in themselves intelligence; they are primary sources of information and as such are primary areas of collection activity. Until analysis is performed, all three provide only potentials that may become intelligence. That is to say, the information contained in an image or in an intercepted signal, or gathered by a human collector, is not yet "intelligence."

OFTEN DEFINED BY CONSUMER ECHELON

Intelligence is often defined in terms of the level of the primary consumer: strategic, operational, or tactical. Strategic refers to that which can in itself dominate a country's overall military situation, cause a major shift in military conditions, and win or lose a war. Operational is the next level down and refers to what is commonly called the theater in geographic terms and the campaign in operational terms. Tactical is the lowest element and includes everything below the operational level. If one were to look for a historical example, the American Civil War provides all three. The Federal Anaconda Plan, with the objective of physically isolating the Confederate states by blockading the entire Confederate coastline and controlling the Mississippi River, was strategic in nature. Within this, Federal operations under Gen. Ulysses S. Grant to capture Vicksburg were operational in nature, as at the time he commanded only one Federal army and was operating in one theater in order to fulfill the strategic requirement of controlling the Mississippi River. And further, within this campaign, the initial Federal assault on the city's main defenses was a tactical move involving select forces in an attempt to quickly gain the immediate objective, the capture of Vicksburg—which in turn accomplished the operational objective by eliminating the last Confederate stronghold on the river, thus contributing to the strategic objective of physically isolating the Confederacy.

OFTEN DEFINED BY SUBJECT AREA ORIENTATION

Intelligence is often defined in terms of subject area, such as political, economic, diplomatic, or military. At best, subject area orientation is a useful modifier but is in no way a definition of intelligence. Intelligence is intelligence regardless of subject area.

CORRECT GENERAL DEFINITION OF INTELLIGENCE

Having eliminated the common, but incorrect, ways intelligence is defined, the following specific definition is provided. Intelligence is both a product and a process and, at the minimum, is the systematic, planned, and objective-oriented (i.e., nonrandom) collection, analysis, and dissemination of information based on open or denied sources.

The Intelligence Process

The intelligence process, collection-analysis-dissemination, is also often called the intelligence cycle. This cycle is repetitive, planned, objective oriented, and interdependent.

The cycle is repetitive because the need for intelligence exists before war, during war, and again before the next war. Since there is neither a guarantee that another war will not break out nor knowledge of when and where it will occur, the cycle must continue. The cycle is also repetitive in that deterrence requires continuous intelligence activity by all interested parties.

The cycle is objective oriented; that is, intelligence production should never be random or self-generating. Intelligence should always be produced to support decision making. This requirement includes the need to maintain databases, which are the foundation of analysis. Inherent in remaining objective oriented is planning, but planning itself is not a separate intelligence function.

The processes of the cycle (collection-analysis-dissemination) are interdependent; each element is dependent on the other two for meaning. Collection is required to provide adequate raw material for analysis, analysis is required to transform raw material into an intelligence product, and dissemination is required to give the product utility. All three are also interdependent in that each informs the other as to its own current needs and accomplishments. Thus collection can be continued or redirected, new analysis needs can be determined, and all can know what has been disseminated.

COLLECTION

Collection is the deliberate, planned acquisition of information. The oldest form of collection is HUMINT; spying and reconnaissance are some of the oldest recorded human activities. The newest form of collection is satellite-based imagery and signal collection. This activity has excited a great deal of interest, especially as it relates to nuclear arms control verification and issues. Debate over the ability to monitor nuclear arms control agreements from space has raged for several years and will likely continue, with much of the debate fueled by media claims on both sides.

In general, three things should be kept in mind when participating in or observing a debate involving intelligence. First, collection alone is not intelligence: analysis must be performed successfully. Second, even when adequate, accurate, and timely intelligence is produced and disseminated, a decision maker must still make a proper decision (intelligence by itself accomplishes nothing). Third, collection is best when it is multisource; some combination of open and denied sources from more than one collection element provides the best opportunity to support superior analysis and detect deception.

ANALYSIS

Analysis, often overlooked, is the central intelligence function, transforming collected information into intelligence. It is the most difficult, and therefore the most challenging, part of the cycle. The difficulty is caused by the combination of two major factors. One is a lack of information—sufficient information rarely exists in a single place; even when it does, there is usually insufficient time to recognize it and incorporate it into truly complete intelligence. A second factor is the difficulty in recognizing and separating useful information from background "noise." The successful Japanese surprise attack on Pearl Harbor in 1941 is an outstanding example of what can happen when these difficulties are not overcome; the American intelligence effort prior to the Battle of Midway is an exception that illustrates what can happen when these factors are overcome. However, intelligence alone never wins; it is the correct use of intelligence by the commander that supports winning.

One of the main reasons that analysis is often not recognized as the central intelligence function is that it is almost impossible to quantify. This limits the ability to measure analysis, and it tends to be considered a zero-sum situation (i.e., the analysis is judged either correct or erroneous). This is not a useful way to look at analysis, which is always based on incomplete or dated information. Sometimes important information is not received in time to be used. Thus, a logical and rational analysis can still draw the wrong conclusions, one of the main reasons that intelligence is often so poorly regarded.

A related reason that analysis is so often not recognized as the central intelligence function is the fact that, historically, senior decision makers have tended to believe themselves to be superior intelligence analysts. This may have worked when one was analyzing manageable volumes of information from only a few sources and the commander could see the entire battlefield. Today, however, collection systems are more complex, sources are manifold, the volume of information is almost unmanageable, and the battlefield has expanded greatly. This combination makes it impossible for senior commanders to function successfully as their own best analysts.

DISSEMINATION

Dissemination is generally the forgotten element of the intelligence process because it is primarily a communications problem. Dissemination of intelligence must compete with all other activities for communications support. The problem worsens as both operations and intelligence continue to develop more data to transmit. For example, intelligence has developed new collection capabilities, such as digital imagery, that require more capable communications systems.

Military Intelligence

Military intelligence is all of the above applied to foreign countries, foreign military organizations, and the geography of possible military operations areas.

INTELLIGENCE GIVES WAR ITS RATIONAL FRAMEWORK

The fundamental reason intelligence is so important and central a capability, and therefore a primary function in war, is that intelligence is what makes going to and conducting war a rational act. There are ranges of intelligence forms and qualities; the more sophisticated the military, the more important the role of discrete, formal intelligence analysis may be in war-making decisions. It is also possible for arrogance, anger, and ideology to become overriding factors, but in the overwhelming majority of cases the final engagement decision, whether offensive or defensive, is made with some expectation of victory, and an intelligence assessment is the foundation of that calculation. This victory expectation is based primarily on some success probability calculation, with this calculation's minimum requirements being self-knowledge, knowledge of which way third parties may or may not participate, and knowledge of the enemy's military capability and probable objectives. The last two points require intelligence obtained through collection and analysis.

It should be noted that the victory expectation, while an essential element, is not normally sufficient in itself to decide to go to war. At a minimum, societies must also make some type of cost-benefit ratio calculation that accounts for such things as the war's potential internal political and social consequences. What may make perfect sense in an international context could be too expensive internally. This calculation is necessary to avoid political Pyrrhic victories.

INTELLIGENCE AS A PRIMARY COMMAND FUNCTION

Because intelligence is a primary command function central to the rational conduct of war, it has been the last primary function spun off to professional specialists. Until World War I, Western military forces did not have separate full-time professional intelligence organizations. The U.S. Army did not have a General Staff Military Intelligence Section until 1918 or an all-source integrated intelligence officers branch until the 1960s. Intelligence is designated a command function in the U.S. Army's *Field Manual 100-5: Operations* (U.S. Dept. of Army 1986), which states that "obtaining useful intelligence prior to the initiation of operations is a vital task." Even today the United States Joint Staff does not have a statutory and formally appointed full-time director J-2 (intelligence). The director of the Defense Intelligence Agency (DIA) is designated to serve as the J-2, and the DIA, through its directorate, which is assigned current intelligence and Joint Staff support responsibility, provides direct support to the Joint Chiefs of Staff. Additionally, the director of the DIA coordinates and functionally manages the defense intelligence budget through his position as the director of the General Defense Intelligence Budget Staff. Each of the services and all the unified and specified commands do have a senior intelligence staff officer designated.

THE INFORMATION WAR

Since purposeful war, as opposed to anarchy or criminal terrorism, implies objective-oriented, nonrandom, applied violence, such basic decisions as where, when, and how many personnel to move, when to engage, and when to disengage are dominated by intelligence. Otherwise, these basic decisions would be made in near total ignorance during war in general, and combat in particular, and would become random events unconnected to any objective. Such purposeful conduct of war has also always included the desire of commanders to control their own forces, neutralize the enemy's forces, and determine the war's outcome. Successfully accomplishing these three basics is dependent on several things, but knowledge of the enemy ranks high.

Clearly, the contribution of intelligence to campaigns has varied. For instance, Russian intelligence operations in East Prussia in 1914 were clearly inadequate, in stark contrast to the vitally important British integration of ULTRA and the Double Cross System during World War II. Additionally, the intelligence system may be either well organized and formal or, as in George Washington's time, somewhat rudimentary. Intelligence systems often have been faulty and have produced poor-quality results. But intelligence remains the foundation of a rational conduct of war because intelligence is the source of knowledge about the enemy and the terrain, two of the three primary elements that make up the commander's situational awareness. *Terrain* in this sense refers to more than just the ground over and on which units will operate; rather, it refers to the totality of the operating environment, what the Germans call the *Umwelt*, or the surrounding world situation.

In this context there are really two wars occurring simultaneously, a physical war and an information war. The information war is continuous; it generally intensifies before the physical war, continues during the physical war, and then continues during the peace until the next outbreak of physical war. The information war is both offensive and defensive. The offensive side is intelligence (the gaining of knowledge and understanding) and deception (the planned exploitation of self-generated information deliberately provided to the enemy). The defensive side is counterintelligence and security, which deny true knowledge and understanding.

Military Intelligence's Historically Pervasive Nature

Military intelligence is one of the oldest of political/military functions. The presence and nature of all military forces throughout history have been directly influenced by military intelligence. This influence begins with the most basic decision of all, whether or not to have a military force.

THE NEED FOR AND NATURE OF MILITARY FORCES

An intelligence-based, threat-assessment-driven, self-defense requirement is one of the two fundamental reasons for having armed forces. If there is no threat, no significant military force is required. Any society satisfied with its territory and economy, and not threatened externally, historically either has no military force or has one of no real consequence. This condition is extremely rare, however, as almost all peoples or states either have had external enemies or have been dissatisfied with their condition. A few exceptions are Eskimos,

Laplanders, some periods in Pharaonic Egypt, and Japan during parts of the Tokugawa Shogunate. Contemporary Iceland and Luxembourg are unusual in that they have virtually no indigenous military. While they have no significant military forces themselves, they are members of a major alliance where an attack on one is considered an attack on all.

The foundation of the first reason for having military forces, a threat perception, is an intelligence-based assessment of potential enemies. This assessment, along with one's own culture, one's geopolitical situation, and the geography of potential operating areas, determines the nature of one's military force.

HISTORICAL EXAMPLES

Since organized war has been written about, intelligence has been considered a key function. And while accurate and timely intelligence has not, in itself, guaranteed victory, its absence has almost always contributed significantly to defeat. This contribution generally has been in the form of an enemy's successful surprise, and the desire to gain surprise and at the same time avoid being surprised has been a primary command objective since the beginning of organized war.

While integrated multisource intelligence operations have appeared irregularly in history (e.g., Walsingham's in Elizabethan England), the widespread development of permanent, professional, all-source military intelligence organizations is relatively new. This is rather puzzling, given that intelligence in political and military events is recorded in some of the earliest documents of civilization. Cryptology, the science of encoding and decoding information, for instance, dates back at least 3,000 years, with China the only high civilization of antiquity not known to have developed any real cryptography. The Old Testament contains numerous stories of Hebrew spying activities in Palestine, and the *Arthasastra* (321–300 B.C.), an Indian classical work on statecraft, describes widespread espionage services in India.

PROFESSIONAL RECOGNITION OF THE IMPORTANCE OF INTELLIGENCE

From the earliest times, the Great Captains, other successful practitioners of the military art, and respected military theorists have recognized intelligence as a key function of war. Some examples will illustrate this point.

Sun Tzu. Sun Tzu's first chapter in *The Art of War* is entitled "Estimates," clearly indicating the fundamental nature of intelligence in war. His second statement in this chapter is, "Therefore, appraise it [war] in terms of the five fundamental factors and make comparisons of the seven elements later named. So you may assess its essentials" (Sun Tzu 1963, p. 63). He then lists these factors as moral influence, weather, terrain, command, and doctrine. Only after this assessment is made is the state committed to war and a general appointed. This assessment is what the Soviets would call a correlation of forces and means calculation.

Sun Tzu's next major point is often quoted, "All warfare is based on deception" (*Ibid.*, p. 66). Deception is based on intelligence and requires fooling the enemy commander, generally by also fooling his intelligence organization, in order to succeed. This applies even if the commander is his own intelligence organization. Sun Tzu further states, ". . . What is supreme in war is to attack the enemy's strategy" (*Ibid.*, p. 77). Thus, while one may be able physically to blunder into an opponent, it is far less likely that one will accidently attack an enemy's strategy. Attacking an enemy's strategy requires an understanding of one's opponent, and such an understanding is derived from intelligence. He goes on to make the following fundamental points:

> . . . know the enemy and know yourself; in a hundred battles you will never be in peril. . . . When you are ignorant of the enemy but know yourself, your chances of winning or losing are equal. . . . If ignorant both of your enemy and of yourself, you are certain in every battle to be in peril. (*Ibid.*, p. 84)

Sun Tzu concludes his book with a chapter on the employment of secret agents. He makes the main point very clear when he writes,

> . . . the reason the enlightened prince and the wise general conquer the enemy whenever they move and their achievements surpass those of ordinary men is foreknowledge [and] what is called "foreknowledge" cannot be elicited from spirits, nor from gods, nor by analogy with past events, nor from calculations. It must be obtained from men who know the enemy situation. (*Ibid.*, pp. 145–46)

The Strategikon. In the great Byzantine book on military strategy and tactics, *The Strategikon* (attributed to the Emperor Maurice [*r.* 582–602]), intelligence is mentioned prominently several times. In Book 7 it is written, "That general is wise who before entering into war carefully studies the enemy, [and] can guard against his strong points and take advantage of his weaknesses." It is also mentioned that the general is enjoined to ensure that every continuous effort be made "to obtain information about the enemy's movements, their strength and organization, and thus be in a position to prevent being surprised by them."

Machiavelli. Machiavelli, in *The Prince*, makes the point that some capability as a military intelligence analyst is an essential part of being a commander: ". . . with a knowledge of [the] geography of one particular province one can easily acquire knowledge of the geography of others. The prince who lacks this knowledge also lacks the first qualification of a good commander" (Machiavelli 1981, p. 89). In *The Art of War*, he discusses the importance of avoiding surprise through proper intelligence operations and states, ". . . such knowledge (of proper intelligence) is absolutely necessary to anyone anxious to be perfectly instructed in the art of war" (Machiavelli 1965, p. 142).

Marshal de Saxe. Marshal de Saxe, in *My Reveries on the Art of War*, states, "Too much attention cannot be paid to spies and guides. Montecuculli says they are like eyes and are equally necessary to a general. He is right. Too much money cannot be spent to get good ones" (Saxe 1985, p. 291).

Frederick the Great. Frederick the Great, in both *On the Art of War* and *Instruction . . . for His Generals*, emphasized intelligence. In *On the Art of War*, he states in the chapter on strategy that,

> above all, you must pay attention to the nature of the country where you wage war . . . it is therefore necessary, first of all, that those wishing to formulate a campaign plan have an accurate knowledge of the enemy forces and of the assistance he can expect from his allies. He must compare the enemy forces with his own and with those his friends can furnish him, in order to judge what kind of war he will want to undertake. (Frederick the Great 1966, p. 307)

In his *Instruction . . . for His Generals*, he wrote:

> Knowledge of the country is to a general what a rifle is to an infantryman and what the rules of arithmetic are to a geometrician. If he does not know the country he will do nothing but make gross mistakes. Without this knowledge his projects, be they otherwise admirable, become ridiculous and often impracticable. Therefore study the country where you are going to act. (Frederick the Great, 1985, pp. 338–39)

Napoleon. Napoleon in his *Maxims* states in No. 2, "A plan of campaign should anticipate everything which the enemy can do, and contain within itself the means of thwarting him" (Bonaparte 1985, p. 407). In No. 79 he states, "The first principle of a general-in-chief is to calculate what he must do, to see if he has all the means to surmount the obstacles which the enemy can oppose him and, when he has made his decision, to do everything to overcome him" (*Ibid.*, p. 433).

Jomini. In Article XLII, "Reconnaissance," in his great book, *The Art of War*, Jomini writes,

> One of the surest ways of forming good combinations in war should be to order movements only after obtaining perfect information of the enemy's proceedings. In fact, how can any man say what he should do himself, if he is ignorant of what his adversary is about? As it is unquestionably of the highest importance to gain this information, so it is a thing of the utmost difficulty, not to say impossibility: and this is one of the chief causes of the great difference between the theory and the practice of war. (Jomini 1968, p. 245)

He is stating here that the acquisition of adequate intelligence and the exercise of command using that intelligence are the meaningful differences between actually conducting war and just theorizing about war. He concludes the article with a timeless four-point summary on intelligence:

> 1. A general should neglect no means of gaining information of the enemy's movements, and, for this purpose, should make use of reconnaissance, spies, bodies of light troops commanded by capable officers,

signals, and questioning deserters and prisoners. [Be vigorous in using all possible information sources.]

2. By multiplying the means of obtaining information: for no matter how imperfect and contradictory they may be, the truth may be sifted from them. [Multiple sources are essential.]

3. Perfect reliance should be placed on none of these means. [This should always be borne in mind, with the gross overreliance on ULTRA in Europe that aided the Germans in the 1944 Ardennes surprise being an instructive example.]

4. As it is impossible to obtain exact information by the methods mentioned, a general should never move without arranging several courses of action for himself, based upon probable hypotheses that the relative situation of the armies enables him to make, and never losing sight of the principles of the art. (*Ibid.*, p. 250)

The key points here are that, while intelligence is a key factor, it will never be sufficient in itself, and a commander must maintain operational flexibility and never paralyze himself by continually waiting for just a bit more intelligence before moving.

Clausewitz. In *On War* (Book 1, Chapter 6, "Information in War"), Clausewitz opens the chapter by defining information as ". . . all the knowledge which we have of the enemy and his country: Therefore, in fact, the foundation of all our ideas and actions" (Clausewitz 1968, p. 162).

Triandafilov. The highly respected Russian military thinker, Triandafilov, in his 1929 book, *Nature of the Operations of Modern Armies*, in the section on command and control problems, states:

> . . . it would be erroneous to look upon operational art as some sort of bookkeeping effort, it would be incorrect to convert operational decisions into simple arithmetic multiplication. The material required for every specific case depends not only on the properties of the weapons and arithmetic figures characterizing the length of the front, on the operational and tactical density of the enemy front, how well his positions are fortified, the quality of both the resources and the enemy troops and commanders. These data change too much. The art of the leader is to calculate the operational significance of these changing situational elements correctly and to determine the correct material and personnel resources required to accomplish a given specific mission. (Triandafilov 1929, p. 205)

Clearly inherent and assumed present in this process is adequate intelligence.

Tukhachevsky. Marshal Tukhachevsky, in the 1936 *Red Army Regulations*, begins his command control this way: "The essence of command and control lies in thorough reconnaissance . . ." (Tukhachevsky 1985, p. 167).

Mao Tse-tung. Mao Tse-tung, in *On Guerrilla Warfare,* states that "intelligence is the decisive factor in planning guerrilla operations" (Mao Tse-tung 1961, p. 22). This point should always be kept in mind given that some today consider this to once again be an age of "limited wars."

Changing Nature of Military Intelligence

The nature of intelligence is changing to meet new, more time-sensitive requirements that are being driven by the rapidly increasing lethality of weapons, the increasing operational tempo, and the enormous spatial expansion of the battlefield. Emerging "smart" and "brilliant" weapons, increasing battlefield application of artificial intelligence, improving deception capabilities, and most important of all, increasing battlefield firepower and mobility are all combining to shorten radically decision times at all command levels. This includes air combat and war at sea. As command decision time is continually reduced, the nature of the intelligence requirement is changing; it is now more demanding in terms of time and accuracy. There is less time available to recover from a bad decision and less ability to absorb rising damage levels.

As intelligence increases in importance it also becomes more and more sophisticated, raising its complexity and cost.

Intelligence Is Often Misunderstood, Misused, and Distrusted

The public misunderstanding and mistrust of intelligence are a peculiarly Western condition, with the American public being one of the most mistrustful. There are several reasons for this extreme position relative to other Western societies; history is perhaps the most important.

U.S. Experience in the Intelligence Field

The American political system is largely derived from the British and, to a lesser extent, liberal French political philosophy and experience. English experience with absolute monarchy, civil war, and the subsequent rise of Parliament clearly established the legislature's ascendancy. However, there is one major difference between the European systems and the U.S. system as far as intelligence is concerned. In Europe, royal intelligence systems were generally continued under democratic control. In the United States, no system existed until the Civil War required extensive military intelligence and counterintelligence, and both capabilities were virtually eliminated after the war. There was an almost total gap in American military intelligence capability until World War I required a major domestic counterintelligence effort, largely aimed at preventing sabotage, that was mounted under Justice Department and War Department control. At the same time both the army and the navy had to develop major military intelligence capabilities almost from scratch. Again, the military intelligence systems were largely dismantled after the war. The only notable foreign intelligence effort between 1919 and 1941 was the SIGINT support of the Washington Naval Conference, 1921–22.

The Second World War again required the establishment of major military intelligence and counterintelligence capabilities. While sabotage in the United States was not a major German or Japanese effort, espionage was. The postwar environment, popularly known as the Cold War, was the first time in American history that a major postwar intelligence and counterintelligence effort was maintained. Despite the dissolution of the Warsaw Pact and the Soviet Empire, this intelligence effort remains massive and has become a major budget expense. The sheer size, complexity, and cost of this effort bring intelligence and counterintelligence to the public's attention. Another major reason for the American public's mistrust of intelligence is that successful intelligence operations require secrecy and security, both of which clash with the American concept of an open society.

THE NEED FOR SECRECY AND SECURITY

All intelligence operations depend on secrecy and security for success. Therefore, intelligence inherently contains a great irony based on the fact that the more important the operation, the more important are secrecy and security. The irony is that the more successful an intelligence operation, the less is known about that operation; only intelligence failures become widely known. Therefore, the public, whose support is essential, never learns of successes, but only of failures and abuses. This creates a one-sided situation in which, unlike the police or the Federal Bureau of Investigation, the intelligence community cannot present its counterbalancing successes in order to assist informed debate and defend itself. In effect, the Western intelligence communities, and especially the American one, must struggle with a public that has at best a media-generated caricature of intelligence.

DIRECTED MISUSE AND ABUSE OF INTELLIGENCE CAPABILITIES

Americans have experienced sufficient cause for wariness about how the intelligence community is sometimes used. This wariness is largely based on administration-directed misuse and abuse of intelligence capabilities, the vast majority of which occurred during the turbulent 1960s and early 1970s and were directly related to popular opposition to the Vietnam War. The illegal collection and use of communications intercepts, the filming of demonstrations, and the creation of counterintelligence databases on Americans have been well documented. These activities have had a major impact on the public, and they must always be kept in mind when trying to understand military intelligence and its proper role in American society. Clearly, in peacetime, military intelligence organizations have two proper domestic roles. One is the conduct of personal background investigations on personnel being considered for access to classified information. The second is assisting in the security of classified information and facilities. In wartime there is a proper and larger role for military counterintelligence in defending against espionage and sabotage. The exact boundaries of this role must be determined according to the situation.

COVERT OPERATIONS AND INTELLIGENCE

The formal, informal, and improper mixing of covert operations and police functions within intelligence organizations and operations has contributed greatly to the current situation of widespread public distrust of intelligence organizations. As previously stated, covert operations are not an intelligence function. In America, this situation really exists only within the Central Intelligence Agency (CIA), and this combination is by statute. In real terms, however, this mixing of two major and separate functions creates an adverse public environment for the intelligence side of the CIA. While there is significant public understanding of the need for foreign intelligence, there is significantly less support for covert operations. This means that covert operation controversies reflect adversely on intelligence as a whole, thereby significantly and adversely affecting public opinion. In an open society this argues powerfully for a separation of intelligence and covert operations.

THE POWER OF INTELLIGENCE

Finally, intelligence is knowledge and knowledge is power, and the misuse and abuse of power are as old as mankind itself. Nothing inherent in intelligence is going to ease this, and it is therefore incumbent on all concerned to keep this in mind and guard against misuse and abuse of intelligence and counterintelligence.

LLOYD HOFFMAN

SEE ALSO: Command, Control, Communications, and Intelligence; Deception; Strategy; Tactics.

Bibliography

Barron, J. 1984. *KGB*. New York: Reader's Digest Press.
Bonaparte, N. 1985. Military maxims. In *Roots of strategy*, ed. T. R. Phillips. Harrisburg, Pa.: Stackpole.
Brissaud, A. 1974. *The Nazi secret service*. New York: W. W. Norton.
Clausewitz, C. von. 1968. *On war*, ed. Anatol Rapoport. Baltimore, Md.: Penguin Books.
Cline, R. S. 1981. *The CIA under Reagan, Bush, and Casey*. Washington, D.C.: Acropolis.
Constantinides, G. C. 1983. *Intelligence and espionage: An analytical bibliography*. Boulder, Colo.: Westview.
Corson, W. R. 1977. *The armies of ignorance*. New York: Dial Press.
Dziak, J. J. 1988. *Chekisty*. Lexington, Mass.: Lexington Books.
Eisenberg, D., U. Dan, and E. Landau. 1978. *The Mossad*. New York: Paddington.
Finnegan, J. P. 1984. *Military intelligence: A picture history*. Arlington,Va.: History Office, U.S. Army Intelligence and Security Command.
Frederick the Great. 1966. *The art of war*. Glencoe, Ill.: Free Press.
———. 1985. Instruction of Frederick the Great for his generals. In *Roots of Strategy*, ed. T. R. Phillips. Harrisburg, Pa.: Stackpole.
Garlinski, J. 1979. *The Enigma war*. New York: Scribner's.
Godson, R., ed. 1990. *Intelligence requirements for the 1990's*. Lexington, Mass.: Lexington Books.
Holmes, W. J. 1979. *Double-edged secrets*. Annapolis, Md.: U.S. Naval Institute Press.
Innes, B. 1966. *The book of spies*. London: Bancroft.
Jomini, A. 1968. *The art of war*. Westport, Conn.: Greenwood Press.
Kahn, D. 1967. *The code breakers*. New York: Macmillan.
Kennedy, W. V., ed. 1983. *Intelligence warfare*. New York: Crescent Books.
Laqueur, W. 1985. *A world of secrets*. New York: Basic Books.

Levite, A. 1987. *Intelligence and strategic surprises*. New York: Columbia University.

Machiavelli, N. 1965. *The art of war*. Indianapolis: Bobbs-Merrill.

———. 1981. *The prince*. New York: Penguin Books.

Mao Tse-tung. 1961. *On guerrilla warfare*, ed. S. B. Griffith. New York: Praeger.

Platt, W. 1957. *Strategic intelligence production*. New York: Praeger.

Read, A., and D. Fisher. 1985. *Colonel Z*. New York: Viking.

Roosevelt, K. 1976. *War report of the OSS, Vols. 1 and 2*. New York: Walker.

Rowan, R. W. 1937. *The story of secret service*. New York: Doubleday.

Saxe, M. de. 1985. My reveries on the art of war. In *Roots of strategy*, ed. T. R. Phillips. Harrisburg, Pa.: Stackpole.

Scholars' Guide to Intelligence Literature: Bibliography of the Russell J. Bowan Collection in the Joseph Mark Lauinger Memorial Library. Washington, D.C.: Georgetown University.

Schwien, E. E. 1936. Combat intelligence. *The Infantry Journal*, Washington, D.C.

Sheldon. R. M. 1990. Tinker, tailor, Caesar, spy. Unpublished manuscript.

Stanley, R. M. 1981. *World War II photo intelligence*. New York: Scribner's.

Sun Tzu. 1963. *The art of war*. Ed. and trans. S. B. Griffith. Oxford: Oxford Univ. Press.

Triandafilov, V. K. 1929. *Nature of the operations of modern armies*. Moscow-Leningrad: State Publishing House.

Troy, T. F. 1981. *Donovan and the CIA*. East Haven, Conn.: Aletheia Press (distr. InBook).

Tukhachevsky, M. 1985. Quoted by R. Simpkin in *Deep battle*. Washington, D.C.: Pergamon-Brassey's.

U.S. Department of the Army. 1986. *Field manual 100-5: Operations*. Washington, D.C.: Government Printing Office.

Van Der Rhoer, E. 1978. *Deadly magic*. New York: Scribner's.

Winterbotham, F. W. 1974. *The Ultra secret*. New York: Harper and Row.

Wright, P. 1987. *Spycatcher*. New York: Viking.

INTELLIGENCE, TACTICAL

Military intelligence may be categorized, in narrowing order of scope, as strategic, operational, or tactical. Strategic intelligence serves planning at the broadest, usually international, levels; operational intelligence serves planning within a theater of war or on a front as a whole; and tactical intelligence, sometimes known as *combat intelligence*, focuses on the planning and conduct of battle.

In combat situations, modern field commanders must have a clear understanding of both the enemy and the environment. It is the task of tactical intelligence to collect such crucial information through techniques that include ground and aerial surveillance; spying (or human intelligence, HUMINT) and reconnaissance; technical intelligence of various types (e.g., signals intelligence, or SIGINT; imagery intelligence, or IMINT); counterintelligence (CI); interrogation; and sensory data obtained from target-acquisition and night-observation devices. Tactical intelligence also comprises the analysis and effective dissemination of information and decisions based on that information throughout the command structure.

The distinctive purviews of strategic, operational, and tactical intelligence do not prevent them from overlapping. For example, tools that are used primarily in strategic and operational contexts are often employed selectively in tactical situations: maps and charts of terrain, climate, or infrastructure; data on capabilities of enemy systems; political and cultural information; and so on. This is particularly so in low-intensity conflicts (LICs), because such conflicts are frequently motivated and constrained by complex political and cultural considerations. Although tactical intelligence is the beneficiary of substantial amounts of strategic and operational intelligence (i.e., it receives data from other levels), it also provides information used to make strategic and operational estimates through on-the-ground data gathering such as interrogations, descriptions of new enemy equipment or techniques, and so on.

Tactical Intelligence in Western Militaries

Before delving into the division of command responsibilities and the specific development of tactical intelligence in the combat context, it may be useful to see how tactical intelligence conceptualizes the information it must gather, the targets it may confront, and the conditions under which it must operate. Note that the terms used here are those of the United States, although they are generally analogous to those used by most Western military forces (Soviet and Soviet-inspired tactical intelligence is discussed at the end of this article). All military forces use specially trained tactical intelligence and counterintelligence personnel and equipment.

Concepts of Tactical Intelligence

Modern battle tends to be multidimensional; hence, commanders often must consider its ground, air, and sea aspects concurrently. For example, at a minimum, naval commanders must consider both the sea and air aspects of battle; ground commanders, the ground and air aspects.

As one way of managing the multidimensionality of battle, tactical intelligence divides the combat area into three distinctive zones. The first is the *area of operations* (AO), which is the portion of the battle area necessary for the actual military operations of the command involved. The second is the *area of influence*, which is the geographic area in which the commander directly influences operations by maneuver or fire support. Finally, the *area of interest* comprises the two other areas as well as adjacent territory that extends the objectives of current or planned operations into enemy territory. Each of the areas is viewed in terms of width, depth, airspace, and time. The areas may vary in size depending mainly on the size of the command and whether the force is in the attack or defense mode (see Fig. 1).

Commanders further classify tactical intelligence information in the following subcategories:

- *Order of battle (OB) intelligence*—Identification, strength, command structure, disposition of personnel, units, and equipment of a military force
- *Technical intelligence*—Identification, including the description, capabilities, and limitations of enemy materiel

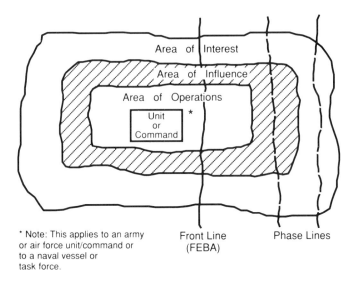

* Note: This applies to an army
or air force unit/command or
to a naval vessel or
task force.

Front Line
(FEBA)

Phase Lines

Figure 1. Battlefield areas. (SOURCE: Adapted from *U.S. Army Field Manual 34-1*, illus. p. 1–2; and *U.S. Army Field Manual 34-3*, illus. p. 1–3)

- *Target intelligence*—Detection, identification, and location of a target with sufficient accuracy and detail to permit the effective employment of weapons
- *Terrain/weather intelligence*—Data and analysis of terrain conditions in light of current and projected weather conditions and the consequences for friendly and enemy movement, communication, and combat

The targets of intelligence fall into four general subcategories: (1) *movers*, or moving elements; (2) *emitters*, such as communications systems; (3) *shooters*, or weapons systems; and (4) *sitters*, or stationary targets, such as command posts or logistical installations.

COMMAND ORGANIZATION OF TACTICAL INTELLIGENCE

The basic echelons of command are the company (or unit), the battalion, the brigade (or regiment), and the division. Each echelon has a structure of assigned, attached, or supporting intelligence/electronic warfare (IEW) personnel.

Company/unit level. At the company level, tactical intelligence devices from a variety of sources: from *organic* (i.e., officially assigned) on-the-ground resources (troops and patrols) and from technical and supporting elements such as ground surveillance radars (GSRs), fire-support teams, or remotely employed sensors (REMS). For aircraft, the basic tools of collection are the observations of flight personnel and radar or other targeting information. Naval units use sight, radar, sonar, and fire-control equipment. The time-critical nature of combat intelligence at this level means that company or unit commanders serve as the directors, coordinators, producers, and executors of intelligence operations within their units, directing placement of sensors, establishing outposts, and using patrol and troop reports.

Battalion level. At the battalion level, the IEW coordinators are the battalion intelligence and operations officers and their staffs. (In the U.S. Army these officers are known as the S2 and S3, respectively, at the battalion, regimental, or brigade level; as G2 and G3 at the division or higher echelons; and as J2 and J3 on joint staffs.) The S2, the intelligence officer, coordinates combat information and reconnaissance and surveillance operations. The S3, the operations officer, is responsible for electronic warfare (EW) and operations security (OPSEC).

Each frontline battalion in the U.S. Army has a Battalion Information Coordination Center (BICC) working for the S2. The BICC prepares reconnaissance and surveillance plans, information intelligence collection plans, and other plans as required. It employs maneuver companies, scout units, fire-support teams, GSR, and other available units to collect information. It forwards requests to higher or adjacent echelons for information and support that a battalion cannot provide.

The commanders of organic units or of units supporting the battalion are the executors of the battalion. Reconnaissance patrols, the organic battalion scout unit, GSR, REMS, and fire-support teams are employed by the executors to gather information for the S2, S3, and BICC.

Brigade/regiment level. At the brigade or regimental level, the S2 and S3 are again the principal coordinators of IEW operations. The S2 at this level also may have limited counterintelligence duties.

Producers include the BICC, the IEW support element, and a collection and jamming element. BICC responsibilities at this level include:
1. developing and coordinating the collection plan;
2. preparing and transmitting tasking messages and reports for information;
3. developing data for the brigade/regimental S2's intelligence estimate;
4. developing and maintaining the intelligence database;
5. processing intelligence;
6. disseminating combat information and intelligence; and
7. providing intelligence support to EW and OPSEC.

IEW and collection and jamming support are provided by special military intelligence formations from higher echelons.

These producers combine to provide coordinated IEW support responsive to the commander's needs. Analysis at this level, to include Intelligence Preparation of the Battlefield (IPB—a U.S. Army term), is limited.

Executors include subordinate battalions, direct support field and air defense artillery, engineer elements, and attached or direct support intelligence elements, which include interrogation teams.

The battalions, supporting artillery, and engineer units all perform reconnaissance, surveillance, and target-acquisition operations. Artillery radar locates enemy direct-fire systems, forward observers collect information, air defense units observe enemy aircraft, and all report information on routes, tactics, types, and numbers. Engineers provide information on terrain, obstacles, and enemy activities. OPSEC is monitored and evaluated by teams or individuals especially trained in OPSEC and CI.

Division

Division coordinators are the divisional intelligence officer (G2) and operations officer (G3), supported by their respective staffs. The G2 may have the added responsibility of formulating division document and personnel security policy. The G3 may formulate similar EW and OPSEC policy and may manage EW and OPSEC operations.

The division G2 section closely coordinates and directs intelligence, CI, special security, weather reporting, and eingeer reporting operations. The G2 operations element coordinates with the G3 operations element and fire-support element to ensure that intelligence and CI operations are integrated to support the commander's scheme of maneuver and fire-support targeting. The G2 also directs IPB and target value analysis efforts within the command.

Division-level producers include intelligence collection and dissemination personnel, information processing personnel (who perform divisional IPB, as well as OPSEC, EW, and weather and terrain analysis), and field artillery and air defense artillery personnel.

The principal executor at division level is an attached military intelligence battalion (in the U.S. Army) or a similar command or elements in other armies (see Figs. 2 and 3).

Development of Tactical Intelligence on the Battlefield

Intelligence preparation of the battlefield is a systematic approach used by the United States to develop combat intelligence. Different national military forces use logical and systematic processes of their own to develop combat intelligence.

IPB is a continual, systematic process of analyzing the enemy, weather, and terrain of a specific geographic area. IPB analysis is based on graphics such as annotated military maps, multilayered overlays, gridded photomaps, microfilm, and large-scale map substitutes, all capable of display on a computer terminal. Battlefield area analysis and intelligence estimates are not replaced by graphics but are converted to them whenever possible.

IPB, according to U.S. Army doctrine, entails five functions: (1) battlefield area evaluation, (2) terrain analysis, (3) weather analysis, (4) threat evaluation, and (5) integration of enemy doctrine with weather and terrain data.

The data developed by the first four of these functions are reduced to templates, one for each of the functions. The process orients on the AO and area of interest of the command concerned.

IPB function 1—Battlefield area evaluation. This evaluation process focuses on information about the enemy, terrain, and weather in a specific geographic area (the command's AO and area of interest). The dimensions of these areas are given in terms of width, depth, airspace, and time. The size of the areas is based on an evaluation of the command's mission, the enemy, terrain, troops available, and time. A lower command may recommend the sizes of its areas of operation and interest, but the actual size will be designated by higher headquarters (division, corps, etc.).

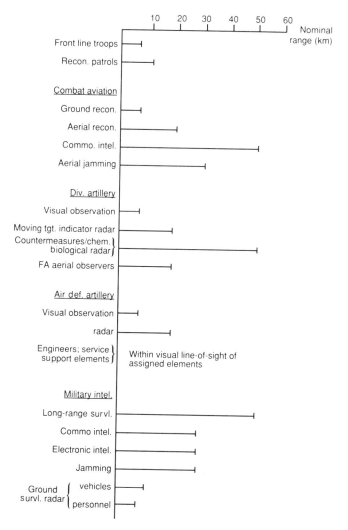

Figure 2. Division information resources.(SOURCE: Adapted from "Intelligence and Electronic Warfare Operations," *U.S. Army Field Manual 34-1*, July 1987, illus. pp. 2-36, 2-37)

IPB function 2—Terrain analysis. This function addresses the military aspects of the terrain and their effects on both friendly and enemy capabilities to shoot, move, and communicate. Terrain analysis concentrates on several key features.

First, *observation and fields of fire* is primarily visual and electronic line-of-sight analysis. *Concealment* is protection from enemy observation. *Cover* is protection from the effects of enemy fire. *Obstacles* are natural and artificial terrain features that impede, channel, stop, or divert military movement. Since they directly influence mobility, they are the most important considerations in terrain analysis.

The second is *key terrain*—any feature or area that, if seized or controlled,

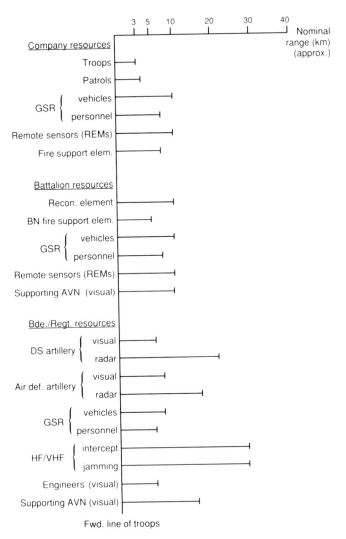

Figure 3. Company-brigade/regiment information resources.
(SOURCE: Adapted from "Intelligence and Electronic Warfare
Operations," *U.S. Army Field Manual 34-1,* illus. pp. 2-23, 2-25,
2-29)

will give a marked advantage in the conduct of operations to either command.
The determination of key terrain is dependent on the echelon of command, the
mission, the enemy, and the situation. For example, a relatively small hill that
dominates an area of operation of a platoon or company is key to those echelons,
but may not be significant to a brigade or division.

Third are *avenues of approach,* which are air, ground, or sea routes by which
a force can reach an objective or key terrain (or area). Historic examples of sea
avenues of approach are Flying Fish Channel, the approach to Inchon, Korea
(Korean War); and the Straits of Tsushima (Russo-Japanese War, 1904–5).

Avenues of approach are evaluated in terms of their (1) potential to support maneuver, (2) degree of channelization, (3) obstacles, (4) concealment and cover, (5) observation and fields of fire, and (6) access to the terrain and adjacent avenues.

To make effective use of terrain data, intelligence personnel prepare a terrain factor matrix and a series of overlays to develop a graphic database of terrain. This matrix facilitates threat integration and guides the selection of terrain and weather factor overlays needed to analyze the terrain. Terrain overlays portray the military aspects of terrain in the AO.

The final step of terrain analysis is to select the avenue of approach that supports friendly and enemy capabilities to move, shoot, and communicate.

The terrain factor matrix matches:

Functions of:
Observation and fields of fire
Concealment and cover
Assembly areas
Key terrain
Ground and air avenues of
 approach
Weapons sites
DZ (drop zone) and LZ (loading zone)
Maneuver
Barriers and fortifications
Lines of communication/main supply
 routes
Lines of sight
Communication and EW sites

Against such factors as:
Surface configuration (slope)
 and materials (soils)
Vegetation
Obstacles (linear)
Weather effects on terrain
Transportation
Built-up areas
Surface drainage (hydrology)

IPB function 3—Weather analysis. Since weather has a significant impact on both friendly and enemy capabilities, weather analysis is critical. In addition, because the weather has a tremendous effect on the terrain, terrain and weather analysis are inseparable. A weather matrix may compare:

Intelligence uses or applications of:
Observation and fields of fire
Artillery emplacements
Concealment
Camouflage
Ground/air avenues of approach
Cross-country movement
Fording sites
Air DZ
Helicopter/STOL/VTOL LZ/PZ
Lines of communication/main
 supply routes
Nuclear/biological/chemical operations
Lines of sight (radio/radar)
Remote sensor emplacement
Infiltration routes

To factors of:
Temperature
Humidity
Intervisibility
Surface winds
Precipitation
Snow/ice cover
Winds aloft
Cloud data
Light data
Severe weather
Fog

IPB function 4—Threat evaluation. This is a detailed study of enemy forces, their composition and organization, tactical doctrine, weapons and equipment, and supporting battlefield functional systems. The objective of this evaluation is to determine enemy capabilities and how they operate as set out by their doctrine and training. This evaluation is accomplished by using a doctrinal template matrix and doctrinal templates. It also includes an evaluation of high-value targets and troop movement rates, judged within the constraints of the terrain and weather.

The matrix examines types of enemy battlefield weapons, communications, radio electronic combat, reconnaissance, rear services, command and control of division- and regiment-level formations, and engineers. These battle systems are applied against types of enemy combat actions (march, meeting engagement, river crossing, attack against a defending enemy, pursuit, hasty defense, and prepared defense).

IPB function 5—Integration of enemy doctrine. Threat integration is accomplished by the sequential development of situation, event, and decision templates. Since a situation template depicts enemy positions for just one instant in time, a series of templates may be needed to depict how the enemy changes his position during the conduct of an operation. The event template is created after the analyst has decided on the probable enemy course of action. The event template provides the information needed to project what events are likely to occur relative to enemy courses of action. As an enemy moves along an avenue or corridor he will be required by the terrain, weather, and tactics to do certain things at certain times and places. Understanding this, the analyst can select individual areas of interest where he expects certain activities or events of tactical significance to occur. Activity, or lack of it, confirms or denies the enemy course of action. The event analysis matrixing in the U.S. Army is normally performed at division or higher levels.

Knowing in advance what the enemy can do and comparing it with what he is doing, the analyst has a basis for predicting what the enemy next intends to do. This information provides the basis for cuing intelligence collection and constructing decision support templates.

Ultimately, the objective of threat integration is to provide options for the commander to defeat the enemy. The Decision Support Template (DST) is developed specifically to aid the commander in decision making. The DST does not dictate decisions to the commander, but it does indicate points where tactical decisions are required. It relates events, activities, and targets of the event template to the commander's decision requirements. The DST is, basically, a combination graphic intelligence estimate and operations plan.

The DST is developed by overlaying the event template, war-gaming enemy courses of action, and placing decision points on the template at points where the commander must decide which course of action to pursue, either to affect the enemy course of action or to change a friendly course of action (such as attack by fire, maneuver, or employment of electronic warfare). Target areas are also selected. There are areas or points where interdiction of enemy forces by maneuver, fires, or jamming will eliminate or reduce a particular enemy capability, cause the enemy to abandon a particular course of action, or require the use of unusual support to continue operations. Some decision points and target areas may be independent, whereas others are associated with one another.

Time phasing is included in this template to illustrate potential enemy movement at his doctrinal rates, as modified by terrain and weather. Potential maneuver corridors are also depicted in the graphics. Other information which may be shown includes key terrain, combat force ratios, or a depiction of how the enemy may have to deploy within each avenue.

In sum, IPB provides one logical and systematic approach to developing military intelligence.

Soviet Intelligence Doctrine

The intelligence doctrine of the former Soviet Union is followed by a number of nations and has affected U.S. and other NATO intelligence and counterintelligence efforts. This doctrine embodies the same three general types of intelligence as U.S. doctrine—strategic, operational, and tactical.

Ground commanders acquire information about opposing forces by means of intelligence collection and target acquisition. The methods they employ to obtain information are basically the same as those employed by other nations. A basic tenet of this doctrine is rapid success. This requires commanders to have timely information on weather, terrain, and the enemy.

The Soviets had an excellent intelligence collection, analysis, and dissemination capability. This capability was organic to all echelons from regiment to front. The results of reconnaissance below the regiment level were passed up to that level, or above, for evaluation.

The most important element of combat support under this doctrine is reconnaissance, which is defined as all measures taken to collect information on:

• nuclear weapons and other means of mass destruction
• formations
• organization for combat
• intentions
• weather and terrain of the specific area of future operations.

This doctrine emphasizes maximum use of firepower and mobility, which means that target acquisition must be accurate and rapid. Tactical reconnaissance is carried out to varying depths by specialized units as well as by regular troop units.

The various collection methods often overlap and are redundant. Reconnaissance is considered effective only if it is conducted actively, aggressively, and continuously. Timeliness, reliability, and accuracy of information are stressed.

Aviation units organic to Soviet fronts performed air reconnaissance employ-

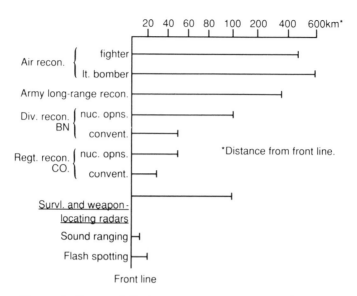

Figure 4. Range of Soviet reconnaissance means. (SOURCE: Adapted from "Intelligence and Electronic Warfare Operations," *U.S. Army Field Manual 34-1*, illus. pp. 4-4)

ing visual, photo, infrared, radar, and signal intelligence capabilities. These aircraft were armed and could attack any ground target. High-priority targets could often be engaged within two hours of detection.

The Soviets had extensive radio and radar intercept capabilities. Intercept units were deployed just behind leading maneuver regiments. Their target-acquisition radar could intercept electronic emissions approximately 25 kilometers (15.5 mi.) forward of their troops. Very high frequency (VHF) could reach about 40 kilometers, high frequency (HF) ground wave about 80 kilometers, and HF sky wave was unlimited. Airborne interception greatly extended these ranges. "Clear" traffic was evaluated and exploited immediately, but decryption was normally very slow.

The Soviet direction-finding capability was equal to that for intercept. Targets within artillery range would be attacked within minutes of location. Front, army, and division artillery units had organic target-acquisition units.

Soviet divisions had organic reconnaissance battalions that often operated a day's march ahead of the main body. Regiments on the march used battalion-size advance guards. The advance guard battalion sent a company forward and that company usually deployed a reinforced platoon forward as a reconnaissance patrol. Engineer, artillery, and chemical reconnaissance elements were cross-attached to leading reconnaissance units in the advance.

A hallmark of the Soviet tactical intelligence effort was aggressive patrolling and the employment of outposts, raids, and ambushes (see Fig. 4; compare Figs. 2 and 3).

UZAL W. ENT

SEE ALSO: Security Classification; Surveillance and Target Acquisition Equipment.

Bibliography

Campbell, S. 1987. Celtic cross IV. *Military Intelligence*, March, pp. 21, 48. (U.S. Army Intelligence Center and School, Ft. Huachuca, Ariz.)

Eldridge, J. L. C. 1987. Exploiting Soviet vulnerabilities by the brigade and task force. *Military Intelligence*, June, pp. 42–44, 47. (U.S. Army Intelligence Center and School, Ft. Huachuca, Ariz.)

———. 1988. OPFOR in the defense. *Military Intelligence*, January, pp. 38–39. (U.S. Army Intelligence Center and School, Ft. Huachuca, Ariz.)

Ivanov, D. A., V. P. Seval'yev, and P. V. Shemansky. 1969. *Fundamentals of tactical command and control: A Soviet view.* Trans. U.S. Air Force. Soviet Military Thought Series, no. 18. Washington, D.C.: U.S. Air Force.

Levesque, R. W. 1987. LIC doctrine and intelligence. *Military Intelligence*, October, pp. 32–34. (U.S. Army Intelligence Center and School, Ft. Huachuca, Ariz.)

Rundle, S. L. 1987. Battalion task force counter-reconnaissance. *Military Intelligence*, March, pp. 38–40. (U.S. Army Intelligence Center and School, Ft. Huachuca, Ariz.)

Saint, C. E. 1987. Intelligence rquirements at the operational level of war. *Military Intelligence*, March, pp. 6, 48. (U.S. Army Intelligence Center and School, Ft. Huachuca, Ariz.)

U.S. Department of Army. 1987. *Field manual 34–1: Intelligence and electronic warfare operations.* Washington, D.C.: Department of the Army.

JOINT OPERATION

A joint operation employs elements from two or more military services of the same nation to accomplish a designated task. Until recent emphasis required a distinction, the term *joint* was often used interchangeably to connote combined (allied) operations, and the term *combined* was sometimes used by the British to designate the multiservice (joint) aspect of amphibious operations. The term *unified* is frequently used in the same context as *joint* in current literature. While joint operations are not new, the conditions of modern military operations compel greater analysis and formal preparation for such undertakings.

The concept of joint operations addresses the need for unity of direction or control over military forces that are distinguished by the specialization of their particular arms (weapons systems). Unity of direction is important where specialized separation of arms exists within branches, or similar subdivisions, of armed services of nations with sophisticated defense establishments. For example, armies have combat components of artillery, infantry, armor, and so forth; navies have surface, air, and submarine forces; and air forces possess bomber, fighter, and transport forces. Intraservice and interservice unity of direction are addressed differently due to the differences in institutional authority of military services and of joint, or unified, national defense establishments. This article concerns interservice operations.

Most modern nations have three main armed services: army, navy, and air force. In addition, several nations have one or two other services, marines and coast guard, which are so integrated into the naval structure, particularly in wartime, that their operational employment with naval forces is not technically considered joint.

Procedures for establishing unity of direction over national armed services differ among nations. The political makeup of governments provides different national authority to implement uniform policy over their respective armed services. Institutional interests and professional perceptions play significant roles in unifying the organization and procedures of traditional armed services.

Historical Precedent

Earliest warfare exhibited specialization in combat forces. Spearmen, archers, cavalry, and numerous other weapons specialists made up the land armies of ancient forces. Coordinated employment of these mixed military forces often marked the more successful armies.

An additional challenge to achieving unity of effort in military operations was introduced when land forces required support from naval contingents. Early naval support was confined to transport of and resupply of ground forces (or interdiction of the enemy's supply). Naval power was seldom perceived separately from its role in support of the projection of land power. As ships deployed farther from coastal waters, however, functional differences became more pronounced between naval and land army skills. Eventually, institutional responsibilities for the administration of national armies and navies became distinctly separate, as did the perspectives of the respective military commanders.

WARFARE UNTIL WORLD WAR I

Early military operations were not directed by standing unified establishments. Yet numerous land and sea expeditions possessed unity of purpose in the planning and direction of operations. Cooperation was usually achieved through a war council of admirals and generals to devise coordinated (joint) operational plans. The apparent simplicity in directing these joint operations can be attributed to two factors: (1) the forces were small enough that personal leadership and team spirit could prevail, and (2) conflicting institutional interests between the naval and land forces had not yet emerged as dominant issues. If cooperation were lacking, it had to do more with the personalities of the commanders than with any rivalry between the army or navy as institutions.

Joint land-naval operations gradually expanded from the late eighteenth to the early twentieth century. Most amphibious operations were simply "administrative off-loadings" and did not require immediate assault against fortified positions. The improvement of naval gunnery, however, allowed the navy to provide artillery fire support to forces within range in coastal areas. Naval bombardment in support of land operations was conducted at the Battle of the Dunes (1658) and in the Crimean War, the American Civil War, and the Dardanelles (Gallipoli) Campaign in World War I, to cite but a few examples.

Revolutionary advancements in naval capabilities—iron construction, steam-powered engines, improved range and accuracy of guns—supported by the advocacy of sea power as a national strategy further separated doctrinal concepts held by land and naval leaders. A new sea power concept was articulated in Alfred Thayer Mahan's theories, which proposed that many national interests could be achieved by the sea arm alone. The sea power theory was used often to support an alternative to armies and, thereby, justify an enlargement of naval strength at the expense of allocation of resources to land forces.

POST–WORLD WAR I

In the United States, following World War I there was a great deal of rivalry between the services and among the specialized arms and branches within the services themselves. The war had been marked by considerable unity of effort in making the air arm, then part of the land forces, responsive to the ground forces. As components of the armies, the new air arm sought more recognition as an independent service and soon succeeded in doing so: at the end of the war in England and shortly thereafter in Italy and Germany. The war set in motion other schisms in the military. Armor advocates in the ground forces may not have sought independence, but they certainly proposed dramatic restructuring of combat formations. In navies, naval aviation pushed for dramatic new concepts in the conduct of surface naval combat. The U.S. Marine Corps pursued an identity independent from both the navy and the army.

The introduction of air forces significantly disturbed interservice and intraservice unity. The degree of functional specialization called for in growing army and naval aviation establishments intensified the industrial-technological changes already taking place in armed forces. Claims were made for airpower that were analogous to those made for sea power. Prophets of airpower, such as Douhet (Italy), Trenchard (England), and Mitchell (United States), argued for the distinctive role of air operations in war and for independent air forces. Two major industrial nations established separate air arms prior to 1940: England, the Royal Air Force (RAF); and Germany, the Luftwaffe. In the United States, the army air forces expanded in organizational status and received considerable backing in civilian, industrial, and political circles. The Japanese, U.S., and British navies developed distinct seaborne aviation components.

Traditional army and naval institutions found themselves challenged. Military establishments, particularly in the Western democratic nations, were compelled to debate and to justify their requests for resources. These debates focused ultimately on national budget decisions. Military services sought to support their positions in doctrine—authoritative statements of fundamental principles, which guide military actions. There were at least as many doctrines as there were advocates of a special military arm or service.

Competition for a share of the military budget became a competition of doctrines. This meant that services' roles and missions were in contention, whether they were singular, collateral, or supporting. The services' doctrinal struggles affected cooperative performance in that precedence of any single joint venture could become an issue in later military doctrinal debate.

Joint relationships between military services were also influenced by management changes in governments, which had been emerging since the middle of the nineteenth century. In earlier times, individuals had influenced the preparation and the direction of military forces, but the growth of national armies and the industrialization of weapons' manufacture introduced a complexity into the supervision of military establishments that was far beyond the capability of single individuals or small committees. The true impact of this change was not fully perceived until the world wars of the twentieth century. Armies and navies devised extensive staff systems to manage the increasing logistical demands of maintaining and directing forces. On the eve of World War II, the Germans held a special advantage. Building upon the heritage of the proven Prussian General Staff, Germany had an integrated, senior military staff (although largely army-dominated) for unified planning and direction of the nation's armed forces.

Although the German High Command was not immune to the parochialism and bureaucratic resistance to change found in most military institutions, it did have an institutional system for structured analysis of military requirements and, thereby, a potential to grasp the changes in technology and to plan and direct integrated employment of specialized arms. Like all national military institutions, the German command made some initial mistakes that had to be corrected as the war developed. Nevertheless, in the sphere of land operations, the effectiveness of the German High Command was dramatically impressive at the outset of the Second World War.

Joint Operations in World War II

Technological advances in weapons resulted in combat capabilities that propelled joint operations as a paramount military concern in World War II. It became evident that there was some truth in most of the separate service doctrines, but the most meaningful doctrines were those that harmonized the varied services' capabilities with a theater commander's operational objectives.

GERMAN BLITZKRIEG AND DIRECTION OF JOINT OPERATIONS

One of the most striking, modern manifestations of joint operations—an effective blend of land and air forces—was the German blitzkrieg. The concept called for a swift-moving, armor-led thrust supported by tightly coordinated tactical air bombardment and often integrated with airborne drops. The concept included an early counterair effort and subsequent direct support of the ground offensive by air forces.

German amphibious landings in Norway and the early airborne operations showed a sound concept for the mutual support of the joint arms. The early, spectacular successes probably encouraged later attempts to execute such operations with inadequate supporting resources—such as the airborne operation against Crete. Airborne operations by both sides were probably the most innovative and demanding joint undertakings in the war.

The German High Command did not show as extensive an understanding of strategic air warfare as it did of tactical air. This shortcoming can be partly explained by the German leadership's early perception that the war would be short and its failure to anticipate the development of counterair and offensive air capabilities by the Allies in response to their early reverses. The German armed forces rapidly adjusted their strategic air offensive and air defenses to counter the Allies' efforts. In both cases, German military exertions were compromised by erratic political dictates and were not solely failures of direction by the joint military staff.

DEVELOPMENT OF AMPHIBIOUS OPERATIONS

Amphibious operations became one of the most distinctive joint operational accomplishments of the war. This complex operation was crucial to the Allies' victories in both the European and Pacific theaters of war. The size and intensity of these operations were without precedent.

Japan, Great Britain, and the United States had conducted amphibious exercises and developed necessary landing craft prior to the war. The U.S. Marine Corps had prepared the basic doctrine upon which the U.S. amphibious operations were based throughout the war. The fundamental tenet of the doctrine addressed procedures for coordinated, supporting firepower and the command and control arrangements while establishing lodgment ashore.

Early British amphibious operations were limited to commando raids due to lack of resources, but they were assimilated easily into the Anglo-American operations in Africa and the Mediterranean. With considerably more resources, the Americans conducted a Pacific theater strategy based primarily on amphibious operations with army and marine corps forces. The Allies were well prepared for the Normandy landing of 1944, the ultimate amphibious invasion and demonstration of joint (and combined) operations up to that time. Although technically an amphibious operation, the Normandy invasion had a distinct supporting air operations component. Local air superiority, deep air interdiction, and airborne delivery of some army units were essential to its success.

One of the serious controversies among the armed services in amphibious operations was the priority of effort given to naval bombardment and direct air support from either naval forces or the U.S. Army Air Forces (USAAF). On more than one occasion in the Pacific area, U.S. naval units withdrew from the provision of direct offshore support in order to engage enemy naval forces. The navy's priority was first to ensure control of the sea. In a similar vein, USAAF and RAF leaders were reluctant to divert their strategic counterair bombing campaign in order to provide concentrated, direct air support to the Normandy landings.

World War II proved how dependent amphibious operations were upon control of the local airspace. This was especially so in noting the reverses in Japanese amphibious offensive and defensive operations that corresponded to their losses in naval aircraft carriers and island airbases. On a global basis, the Second World War was an air-land-sea war, a fact quickly recognized by the Allied strategic military planners.

DIRECT AIR SUPPORT OF GROUND OPERATIONS

Allied air forces began World War II with many of their air leaders committed to strategic bombing and with little experience in providing closely coordinated, air-to-ground firepower support to the armies. Allied unpreparedness for air-ground operations proved costly in North Africa. Allied joint air-ground operations improved throughout the war. The USAAF were greatly assisted by the independent RAF, which provided leadership in the early European tactical air operations. Based on considerable prewar doctrine development, the U.S. Naval and Marine Corps aviation was prepared to give close support to amphibious forces and performed effectively in the Pacific theaters.

The major concepts for direct air support to army forces emerged from the Allies' operations in which highly fluid combat situations limited opportunities for preplanned air strikes. Aided by radio communications, joint fire control and coordination posts were established and air liaison officers were deployed with many ground units. The air liaison officers assisted ground commanders in planning air support requirements, coordinated requests for air support with army artillery, and provided battlefield direction of tactical aircraft tasked to provide direct fire support. A range of tactical air missions evolved as part of most army theater operations. Air missions were categorized as: close air support, interdiction, sector air defense, reconnaissance, and tactical airlift.

World War II produced a wide range of air-land operations for which commanders and staffs were not fully prepared. The principle of central control of theater air assets generally prevailed even though it was challenged by several ground commanders of subtheater-level units. Airspace control over combat zones and identification procedures between land and air forces remained serious problems, which led to many tragic errors of friendly forces shooting and bombing one another. Concepts for airborne operations had not been developed to the extent that they had been for amphibious undertakings. Most obvious was recognition that effective interservice operations depended on forceful direction by senior officers with joint strategic vision. The fast pace of modern warfare reduced reliance on battlefield team spirit to make interservice coordination imperative.

ORGANIZATION FOR PLANNING AND DIRECTING JOINT OPERATIONS

Devising a structure for strategic direction of worldwide, joint operations was a challenge to the democratic governments of Great Britain and the United States—nations that carried the major responsibility for the Allied global efforts. Both nations had a tradition of being suspicious of concentrated military power and fostered strongly independent armed services. The British, however, had had a Chiefs of Staff (COS) committee, consisting of the senior officers of each of the three services, for joint planning since 1924. The combined Anglo-American alliance necessitated balanced senior national military structures. Therefore, the United States created, by executive order, the Joint Chiefs of Staff. This joint body served as the senior advisers to the nation's commander in chief and as U.S. members of the Allied Combined Chiefs of Staff.

Concurrently, for the first time, the United States organized military field operating forces on an interservice (joint) basis. This structure was most evident in the United States–dominated Pacific theater of operations. In the European theater, the U.S. joint command was incorporated into the Allied military combined (and inherently joint) command structure.

The Joint Chiefs of Staff and joint theater command structures did not eliminate interservice rivalry (or as some wish to describe it—creative rivalry). Although interservice differences continued during the war years, the effects were abated by the more unifying factor of a national threat and by the abundant U.S. national defense budget. Many of the tensions among services concerned fear of setting precedents that could affect declared service doctrine. Issues developed over marines commanding army forces and vice versa, naval firepower support of the army, the role of the USAAF in strategic bombardment versus ground support, and so forth. A significant number of interservice problems that arose, however, were due to the personalities of key personnel, honest misunderstandings, and simple mistakes caused by the confusion of war.

Near the end of the war, it was well accepted, even by the early advocates of airpower, that modern warfare was predominantly executed through joint campaigns and operations. The atomic bombs delivered on Japan by strategic air forces introduced a new era of debate concerning roles and missions of military services.

Post–World War II

During the Cold War era following the Second World War a high level of military activity continued for most of the major nations of the world. Preparedness for nuclear war eclipsed balanced national defense planning and awarded high priority to those military services and systems that could deliver such weapons. Airpower, at least for a while, held a favored position in defense budgets, but eventually the other services acquired nuclear weapons and gained a viable part of the nuclear mission. Despite the resulting nuclear standoff between the superpowers, military forces continued to be employed in regional, conventional wars and in special operations involving the joint employment of armed forces.

Two major factors influenced joint operations following World War II: the nature of the different governmental systems of the two superpowers, the Soviet Union and the United States; and the increasing complexity of military operations due to rapidly changing developments in weapons technology.

A description of the former Soviet military system is covered elsewhere in this encyclopedia. For the purposes of this article, it is only necessary to recognize that the basic concept of central authority inherent in the Soviet political system contributed to unity of direction over their forces. Unity imposed in this manner, however, does not ensure a balanced perspective over the various options permitted by the separate arms. In spite of the very large and modern independent navy and air force, the Soviet unified command's fundamental perception of warfare appeared heavily land oriented. Soviet navy and air forces were not perceived to be as influential in formulating independent doctrine as are their counterparts in the West.

The Soviet doctrine for dedicated aviation support to ground forces was similar to that of the German World War II blitzkrieg. The Soviets also dedicated land-based air in support of their naval forces. Separate strategic rocket and air forces existed as well as multipurpose air forces for theater (front) army commanders. Soviet doctrine, which emphasized integrated planning and direction of air and ground forces within defined theaters of military operations, appeared to counterbalance the parceling out of dedicated forces.

The diversity in Western, democratic nations makes it impossible to describe how each addresses joint operations. This article will emphasize developments in the United States since its military posture is the broadest in scope in terms of types of weapons, forces, and geographical commitments. American military organizational and procedural developments for joint military activity are indicative of those adopted by most of the industrialized Western nations. It must be noted that many other Western nations have led in improving aspects of joint operations. This has been particularly the case for nations such as Great Britain and Israel, which have engaged in frequent, limited armed conflicts.

THE AMERICAN EXPERIENCE

World War II left a legacy of joint armed services cooperation and military organization. Legislative actions quickly recognized the Joint Chiefs of Staff and created major geographical and unified theater commands with the 1947 National Security Act. The act also created the U.S. Air Force (USAF) as an independent armed service, a civilian secretary to administer a national defense establishment, a National Security Council, and a Central Intelligence Agency. The main thrust of the 1947 act was to create the structure for unity of direction over the nation's defense establishment. The act also established a framework, if not a mandate, for interagency coordination among civilian and military elements of the executive branch. The 1947 National Security Act, and a series of subsequent amendments, significantly influenced the policy and organization for the nation's military joint actions.

In spite of the unification of defense organizations, the American political and military leaderships were reluctant to accept or to promote joint activities below the most senior levels of defense. American supremacy in nuclear weapons encouraged for a period the belief that World War II experience would be irrelevant in the future. The air force and navy clashed over their roles in the strategic delivery of nuclear weapons. Both had the means for strategic deployment (using aircraft carriers or overseas air bases) and the issue was never really resolved even with the introduction of intercontinental bombers and missiles. It remains a shared navy and air force operation linked by a system for joint target planning.

America's loss of the nuclear monopoly and the occurrence of the Korean War (1950–55) were reminders that conventional war was still possible. American forces in Korea were led by military leaders and many unit commanders with World War II experience. This permitted many procedures for joint operations to be taken up from where they were in 1945 and to be developed further. Interservice operational techniques—particularly air-to-ground offensive support—were considerably refined. A structure for Tactical Air Control Systems (TACS) was formed that remains the basis for most theater air-land operations.

As old problems were solved, new issues arose. Korea saw the intensified struggle between the doctrines of the USAF and naval/marine aviation as to command and control of theater air assets. This remained an unresolved issue throughout America's next conventional war in Vietnam (1960–73).

Vietnam witnessed a high degree of successful joint operations in the theater. Unfortunately, bureaucratic budget and doctrine arguments in the Pentagon often overshadowed the cooperation on the battlefields in southeast Asia. Highly coordinated, supporting air firepower (strategic and tactical) and airlift (fixed-wing and helicopter) became integrated parts of most major in-theater operations.

Besides the major wars of Korea and Vietnam, the United States employed forces in several joint contingency operations. The general analysis of most of these engagements has been critical of the readiness of the army, air, and naval forces in conducting joint operations. The criticism is not directed at the commanders and the forces in the field but, rather, at programming, planning, and preparation of the forces. These observations, along with congressional frustration with interservice confrontations reflected in military advice from the senior programming and budgeting headquarters, have led to military reorganization initiatives by the U.S. Congress.

Organization for National Defense

An important backdrop to U.S. joint operations is the organization and structure for the overall direction of national defense. The U.S. national defense establishment is the product of several amendments to the 1947 National Security Act.

A 1949 Defense Reorganization Act strengthened the authority of the secretary of defense and created a chairman of the Joint Chiefs of Staff (JCS). The Reorganization Act of 1958 created two separate chains of command: an operational chain from the secretary of defense, through the JCS, to the combatant commands; and an administrative support chain from the Secretary of Defense to the military departments. Recently, the Reorganization Act of 1986 designated the chairman of the JCS as the principal military adviser (instead of the JCS corporately). The act provided for more direct involvement of the chairman, Joint Staff, and unified/specified commanders in the budget process. The act also called for the specific preparation of officers to perform joint duties.

Joint Military Organization and Arrangements

Since World War II, Americans have debated organizing the military for effective unified multiservice planning and operations. There was never a strong suggestion to go as far as Canada did in 1964, in a complete unification of all services (which, some evidence suggests, did not remove fundamental interservice struggles). Most Western democratic nations follow the British and U.S. pattern of a single civilian-headed defense department, or ministry, over the separate army, navy, and air forces.

In the United States, the services exist under the Defense Department along with separate joint military establishments. The joint military establishments have two main parts. One is a senior military advisory and strategic planning establishment in the tradition of the World War II Joint Chiefs of Staff. The other military part is the fighting structure—combatant (for the most part joint) commands.

The Joint Chiefs of Staff is made up of the chiefs of the armed services and a chairman (Fig. 1). They are served by a joint staff of officers from all services. They are not commanders, but chiefs, and advisers to the civilian authorities.

The Unified and Specified Command System is designed to ensure unity of effort over the planning and direction of military operations. The system separates responsibility for operations from that for logistical and administrative support, both of which are responsibilities of the separate armed services.

Figure 1. The Joint Chiefs of Staff on 6 August 1991. Pictured from left to right are Gen. Carl E. Mundy, USMC; Gen. Gordon R. Sullivan, USA; Gen. Merrill A. McPeak, USAF; Adm. Frank B. Kelso, USN; Gen. Colin L. Powell, USA, Chairman; and Adm. David E. Jeremiah, USN, Vice Chairman. (SOURCE: U.S. Department of Defense)

Responsibility for the conduct of operations rests with commanders of unified and specified commands, who are designated "commanders in chief" (CINCs) and are responsible directly to the secretary of defense for mission accomplishment. In turn, the secretary is responsible to the president of the United States. CINCs normally exercise operational command over their tactical forces through their subordinate service component commanders.

Unified commands are composed of component forces of two or more services to perform broad, continuing missions. The headquarters of unified commands are made up of integrated joint staffs. Unified commands are generally responsible for a specific geographical area.

Specified commands are composed of forces primarily from a single service to perform a broad, continuing mission. Their relationship to the secretary of defense and the JCS is the same as for unified commands.

A Joint Task Force (JTF) is a force composed of elements from one or more of the services to perform a specific mission or to function as part of the broader mission of a unified command. Some unified commands have standing JTFs. As a rule, a JTF is formed to accomplish a mission of limited duration. They are usually used to conduct special operations in contingencies.

Many other joint structures exist as activities reporting to the Department of Defense or as ad hoc arrangements between services. Various activities coordinate logistical support and doctrinal development, which still remain the responsibilities of the separate services. Some examples are: army–air force agreements focused around tactical air support and the development of rotary-wing systems by the army, and USAF Tactical Air Command and U.S. Army Doctrine Development Command (TAC-TRADOC) working groups, and Joint Assessment and Initiatives Office (1983–86).

TACTICAL PROCEDURES FOR JOINT COMBAT OPERATIONS

As mentioned earlier, World War II forced the development of procedures for joint combat such as amphibious, air-to-ground, and air defense operations. Initially, the responsibility for development and improvement of joint doctrine was with the services, working in coordination to derive mutually agreed positions. The progress made by interservice initiatives in joint doctrine was limited, however, and as a result there has been increased involvement of the Joint Staff and influence from the unified commanders in such matters.

There are a few broad concepts that have been proven in several confrontations and remain basic themes in planning and conducting joint operations:

1. *Coordination and control of offensive firepower* in direct support of ground operations are difficult enough when the army is using its organic artillery, but particularly challenging when using air-delivered support. A primary concern in control of close air support of ground forces is to ensure that enemy troops, not friendly troops, are attacked, or that supporting aircraft are not mistakenly fired upon by friendly air defenses. Planning for such strikes is usually based upon fire-support coordination procedures established by the ground commander. Various means employed to guide air strikes are use of ground signal panels and smoke, designation of fire-free zones, and employment of ground and airborne forward air controllers to provide radioed directions to the striking aircraft.

2. *Airspace control* over the combat zone is vested in a single authority designated by the joint force commander. The heavy traffic of air vehicles over the modern battlefield has necessitated management of airspace sectors, much as if it were a major civilian air terminal. The purpose of this control is not only to separate friendly air- and ground-launched missiles, but also to facilitate air defense.

3. *Headquarters' liaison officers* have long been recognized as essential for joint planning when the air, sea, and ground command centers are separated. Many war plans are basically prepared in peacetime and coordinated among separated service component headquarters. Effective execution of these plans depends upon sound understanding of the separate service perspectives during the initial planning. The importance of liaison officers at separate component service combat control centers is also essential. Colocation of service component theater, and subtheater, wartime headquarters (joint command and control centers) is another option being explored in various theater areas.

4. *Amphibious operations* have two distinct command phases. The naval amphibious force commander will retain command of all operations until a lodgment ashore is fully established. At that time, the ground force commander assumes command of forces ashore. With the increased operational ranges of land-based air, most amphibious operations are now triservice ventures.

5. *Special theater assets are centrally managed* and not committed piece-

meal. This most frequently applies to air support assets, but the concept extends to other high-value/limited-quantity systems on the modern battlefield. The principle ensures their maximum impact in accomplishing missions critical to the theater as a whole.

6. *Appreciation of the integrated aspects of a theater-level campaign,* as a whole, is represented in many recent concepts of operational art and air-land battle. Such concepts are drawn from some long-held military theories but are necessarily being recast in terms of modern weapons and service roles.

General Observations

The current environment for addressing joint operations is unsettled. Obviously, expanding the authority of unified defense establishments is accomplished at the expense of the separate services. There are questions as to the need for more unified organization merely to obtain an effective unified approach to operations. Will emphasis on unity constrain the important ability of having a constant review of alternative options in conducting combat operations? Will unified direction suppress initiatives of the separate armed services to fully exploit the potential of their particular combat specialties? In addressing such questions on joint military operations some significant observations are worth noting.

CRITICISMS AND PROBLEMS

Admittedly, even historically successful joint operations have had their share of problems arising from interservice rivalries: jealousy in command arrangements, wasteful duplication of effort, complexity in plans so that every service has a part, and arrogance in one service underestimating the capabilities of another. Each military specialty tends to cultivate fervent attitudes supporting its particular functional area. Such attitudes foster a two-sided dilemma. On the positive side, there is an aggressive effort to exploit the specialty to its fullest potential. The negative side is that it encourages dangerous pursuit of preferred courses of action by a commander in ignorance of other services' perceptions and procedures.

REDUNDANCY: A MILITARY HEDGE

In reality, political strategy undergoes frequent and sudden changes (as a result of such events as turnover of government leaders, international crisis, etc.), and as a result military planners must seek to develop broad capabilities to respond to a variety of contingencies.

In peacetime, efficiency experts decry (but military history frequently vindicates) duplicate efforts. Alternative capabilities often are the "secret weapon" permitting a commander to do what the enemy did not anticipate. The United States has benefited from having available capabilities for one service based upon independent initiatives pursued by another. Examples would be the marine corps's development of amphibious concepts used by the army in World War II, and tactical air support aircraft (F-4 and A-7) developed by the navy and used by the USAF in Vietnam. Nevertheless, given the value of multiple developments, it is hard to justify the lack of interoperable tactical communications equipment, as was reported in the 1983 Grenada operation.

Whatever its value, multiservice approaches need to be guided by a single focus. To some degree, command organization has structured some unity in formal operational planning and direction of joint combat forces. As called for in the recent U.S. Defense Act, however, there remains the challenge to prepare officers with a joint perspective, despite years of specialized experience in their respective services.

ALBERT D. McJOYNT

SEE ALSO: Blitzkrieg; Close Air Support; Combined Arms; Command, Control, Communications, and Intelligence; Doctrine.

Bibliography

Creswell, J. 1976. *Generals and admirals: The story of amphibious command.* Westport, Conn.: Greenwood Press.

Davis, R. G. 1987. *The 31 initiatives.* Washington, D.C.: Office of Air Force History.

Dupuy, T. N. 1977. *A genius for war, the German army and general staff, 1807–1945.* London: MacDonald and Jane's.

Fergusson, B. 1961. *The watery maze, the story of combined operations.* New York: Holt, Rinehart and Winston.

Fuller, J. F. C. 1970. *The decisive battles of the western world.* 2 vols. London: Paladin.

Galland, A. 1954. *The first and the last, the rise and fall of the German fighter forces, 1938–1945.* Trans. M. Savill. New York: Ballantine Books.

Hansell, H. S., Jr. 1980. *The air plan that defeated Hitler.* New York: Arno Press.

Hittle, J. D. 1949. *The military staff, its development and history.* Harrisburg, Pa.: Military Service.

Millet, A. R. et al. 1986. *The reorganization of the joint chiefs of staff: A critical analysis.* McLean, Va.: Pergamon-Brassey's.

Momyer, W. W. 1978. *Air power in three wars (WWII, Korea, Vietnam).* Washington, D.C.: U.S. Air Force.

Pogue, F. C. 1973. *Organizer of victory, 1943–1945.* Vol. 3 of *George C. Marshall.* 3 vols. New York: Viking.

Richmond, H. 1941. *Amphibious warfare in British history.* Exeter, U.K.: A. Wheaton.

Toth, J. E. 1986. *Higher direction of military action.* Washington, D.C.: National Defense Univ. Press.

Turner, G. B., ed. 1953. *A history of military affairs in western society since the eighteenth century.* New York: Harcourt, Brace.

U.S. Department of the Army. 1984. *Field manual 101–5: Staff organization and operations.* Washington, D.C.: Government Printing Office.

———. 1986. *Field manual 100–5: Operations.* Washington, D.C.: Government Printing Office.

U.S. Department of Defense, Joint Chiefs of Staff. 1986. *Unified action armed forces (UNAAF).* JCS Pub. 2. Washington, D.C.: Government Printing Office.

JUNGLE WARFARE

More than three-quarters of the earth's land surface that lies between the latitudes of the Tropic of Cancer (lat. 22°30′N) and the Tropic of Capricorn (lat. 22°30′S) is jungle. These areas receive an average of more than 180 centimeters

(70 in.) of rainfall annually. They include the vast basins of the world's great tropical rivers—the Amazon in South America, the Congo in Africa, and the Chindwin-Irrawaddy, Salween, and Mekong rivers in Southeast Asia. Many military operations of the past 50 years have taken place in the Southeast Asian jungle as well as in the Micronesian and Melanesian islands of the southwest Pacific. These include operations by the Japanese and by the Allies in World War II and, more recently, United States and allied operations in Vietnam and Cambodia. Jungles are generally important only because their location can provide or prevent access to regions or resources of strategic importance. In addition, however, political circumstances may necessitate military operations in jungle areas (e.g., Vietnam).

The first Japanese operations of World War II were carried out primarily to drive the Americans, British, Australians, Dutch, and French out of the western and southwestern Pacific and to secure control of the oil resources of Indonesia, which were critical to Japan. Subsequent Allied operations were conducted to regain a strategic presence in the area, deny Japan access to the oil, and stop Japanese expansionism. Operations carried out in places such as Tarawa, Saipan, Buna, and others either reduced Japanese control over the area, bypassed and made noneffective a Japanese force, or provided forward basing—especially airfields—for further pursuit of the strategy to regain control and contain the Japanese. Operationally and tactically, this required battles and campaigns in the jungles of the region.

Jungle Environments

TERRAIN

There are two types of jungles: tropical (equatorial) and subtropical. The former generally receive 150 to 350 centimeters (60 to 140 in.) of annual rainfall and have no marked seasonal variations in temperature, which averages 20°C to 30°C (68°F to 86°F) day to night year-round. The Amazon and Congo basins, Sumatra, and some South Pacific islands are characteristic.

Subtropical jungles are generally found along the windward coasts of land areas not more than 10 degrees north or south of the equator. There is usually a monsoon climate (i.e., a seasonal change in the prevailing wind direction that brings alternately wet and dry seasons) and vegetation patterns that are different from those in tropical forests. Typical subtropical jungles are found in Vietnam, Burma, the Philippines, Central America, and the Caribbean islands.

Jungle terrain is dominated by the presence of large amounts of water, which in turn generates vegetation. Jungles, tropical and subtropical, include dense forests, grasslands, cultivated areas, and swamps. In primary tropical forests, large evergreen trees form interlocking canopies from a few meters to nearly 100 meters in height. In some jungles, it is possible to operate helicopters under and between these layers. Because tree canopies shut out sunlight, the forest floor is less heavily overgrown than might be expected. However, ground observation is generally limited to no more than 50 meters (55 yd.).

In semitropical jungles a mixture of evergreen and deciduous trees allows more sunlight to reach the forest floor. In turn, this permits development of denser undergrowth than in many tropical forests.

Common to most jungle areas, but especially to subtropical jungles, are swamps (mangrove and palm), savanna grasslands, fields of bamboo 20 meters (65 ft.) high, and rice paddies.

Many Pacific islands are merely the above-surface part of undersea mountains, and thus rapid increases in elevation over short distances are not uncommon. Elevations in island areas vary from sea-level atolls like Kwajalein to several-thousand-meter mountains in the Solomon Islands and New Guinea. Roads and tracks, areas flat enough for airfields, and areas to accommodate forward supply bases are generally found along the coasts. Occasionally, for operational or tactical reasons, it may be necessary to occupy the hills in order to control the important lowland areas.

In Southeast Asia, the subtropical areas of Vietnam, Thailand, Burma, and Malaysia feature large alluvial plains (the deltas of the large river systems) and intensive rice culture along the coasts and in the river deltas. Soil conditions vary from delta silt to volcanic mountain structures, making movement difficult, especially for vehicles.

CLIMATE AND WEATHER

A benign temperature range and frequent rainfall are the primary characteristics of jungle areas. Southeast Asia and some adjacent island areas have a monsoon climate—a seasonal change of the prevailing wind direction. In the summer, onshore winds pick up moisture from the sea, which is the source of the heavy monsoon rainfalls. Reversing direction in winter, the prevailing winds bring drier air from the interior of the large land masses and, although temperatures remain high—except in mountainous regions—there is some relief from the constant rainfall.

HABITATION

Jungles are heavily populated with many species and varieties of birds, mammals, and reptiles. In larger land areas—Southeast Asia in particular—there are elephants, tigers, large and small simians, lizards, and many kinds of snakes. Human habitation is generally found along the coastlines and waterways, although there is a fairly large population of nomadic tribesmen, the Montagnards, in the highlands of the Indochina Peninsula. Deep jungles have become attractive hidden refuges for dissident revolutionary groups attempting to overthrow established authorities. The Hukbalahaps in the Philippines, Malaysian insurgents in Malaysia, the Vietminh (and later the Vietcong) in Vietnam, and insurgent groups in Borneo have all provided the established governments with a reason to take political-military action against them.

Fighting in Jungles

After the defeat of the Japanese Combined Fleet at Midway in early June 1942, it was believed that the Japanese could only continue offensive action in one area—the southwest Pacific. It therefore became imperative for the Allies to seize the initiative in that area, primarily to protect the lines of communication to Australia and to stop the spread of Japanese control over oil-rich Indonesia. Given those considerations, it would ultimately be necessary to neutralize the Japanese air and naval base at Rabaul. Thus, within two months of the battle at Midway, Allied and Japanese forces were fighting in the mountains and jungles of New Guinea and, not long after, in the rain forests of Guadalcanal. Jungle fighting taxed the resources of all combatants—their physical stamina, courage, and patience. Like the desert, the jungle is neutral—it treats friend and foe alike. Its dense vegetation provides cover and concealment for both sides, its insects and reptiles bother each side equally, and its debilitating climate saps the strength and resolve of all combatants. It is a place, like the desert, where excellent physical conditioning, high-quality small-unit leadership, and tough, demanding, relevant small-unit training are critical—even for survival, let alone for success.

In the first six months of the jungle war, the Allies took the initiative. However, after Guadalcanal and Papua, it took another fourteen months before Rabaul could be isolated by the seizure of the Admiralty Islands. During those months some of the toughest, most demanding tactical battles of the war were fought. It was exclusively an infantry war, foot soldiers on the ground hacking and struggling through jungle and over mountains. The few tanks were only for support of infantry.

Similar combat occurred in Southeast Asia at the start of World War II when the Japanese infantry swept across the Indochina Peninsula, through Malaya, Thailand, and much of Burma, after capturing Singapore from the rear. To regain this ground, and to support China over the famous Burma Road, the Allies found it necessary to reenter the jungles with infantry and win back meter by meter what had been lost. Battle was difficult in the rain forests, and this left a legacy in the minds of its participants. U.S. perceptions of the World War II Pacific jungle war were at the root of many of the causes for a less than satisfactory outcome for U.S. forces at the tactical and operational levels in Vietnam. In World War II, no armored divisions had tracked across Pacific islands or up forest trails toward Japan, and no leaders of armored units achieved professional fame in jungle battles. Therefore, institutional wisdom saw the jungle as a place where tanks and mechanized units simply could not go. Thus, when deploying forces to Vietnam, after replacing the French in 1954, the United States relied heavily on infantry divisions, initially leaving behind the armored cavalry and tank units that had become organic to infantry divisions following World War II. Provided instead was a new capability in force employment—the helicopter. After experiments with heliborne infantry, many in the U.S. Army believed that airmobile infantry was the answer to the need for mobility so dramatically felt in World War II jungle operations.

To some extent that was true. However, it was quickly apparent that moving troops by helicopter had some inherent disadvantages. Primary among these was a lack of sure knowledge of the terrain and the enemy by the troops and leaders who had been moved quickly by helicopter to respond to a situation. In addition, air mobility of foot infantry left the infantry no more tactical mobility than before, once on the ground. In fact, the enemy often proved more tactically mobile than the heliborne infantry because the enemy lived in the swamps and jungle and learned to use them to his advantage.

The Indochina Peninsula, Vietnam in particular, is not a land totally unsuited to mobile mechanized warfare. More than 45 percent of the terrain can be traveled by mechanized units year-round. Mechanized units—Vietnamese, U.S., and allied—operated successfully in every geographic region. The most severe limitations were encountered in the Mekong Delta to the south and in the mountain areas of the Central Highlands.

Most of the Mekong Delta is at or below sea level and rarely more than 4 meters (13 ft.) above. It is wet, extensively cultivated, and crisscrossed with kilometers of water courses—rivers, streams, and canals. Vehicular and foot traffic is restricted to the tops of dikes, dams, and a few raised roads.

In contrast, the jungle-covered Central Highlands to the north (part of the Annamite chain) have peaks as high as 2,600 meters (8,500 ft.) and are heavily forested with tropical evergreen and giant bamboo. Vehicles can travel in most areas after the vegetation is cleared, but movement on a one- or two-vehicle front is vulnerable to an ambush.

The other regions of Vietnam—coastal plain, piedmont, and plateau—include rice paddies, rubber plantations, cultivated fields, and jungle. These areas can be negotiated by mechanized forces about 80 percent of the time. The summer monsoon winds of Indochina blow out of the Indian Ocean June through Sep-

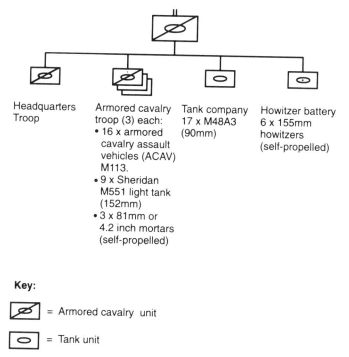

Headquarters Troop

Armored cavalry troop (3) each:
• 16 x armored cavalry assault vehicles (ACAV) M113.
• 9 x Sheridan M551 light tank (152mm)
• 3 x 81mm or 4.2 inch mortars (self-propelled)

Tank company 17 x M48A3 (90mm)

Howitzer battery 6 x 155mm howitzers (self-propelled)

Key:

= Armored cavalry unit

= Tank unit

Figure 1. Armored cavalry squadron (ca. 1969–70). (SOURCE: U.S. Army circa 1970)

tember, rise against the western slopes of the central mountains, and cause a wet season in the Mekong Delta, the piedmont, and most of the Western Highlands and plateau. From November to February, onshore northeast winds bring wet season conditions to the northern third of the country.

In 1967, a U.S. Army study team evaluated mechanized and armor operations and opportunities in Vietnam and concluded that tanks could move in about 60 percent of the country in the dry season and about 46 percent of the country in the wet season. Lighter armored vehicles (recce vehicles and personnel carriers) could move in about 65 percent of the country year-round.

In addition, it was determined that the U.S. Army armored cavalry squadron (Fig. 1)—a unique unit including organic recce vehicles and self-propelled howitzers and mortars—was the most versatile unit in the inventory. It proved far more cost-effective in terms of casualties and operating expenses than the airmobile infantry with its requirements for extensive helicopter support.

Mobility—strategic, operational, and tactical—is the key to seizing the initiative and so to success in jungle warfare. Modern technology is providing the equipment—helicopters, large transport aircraft, and armored vehicles that outperform their World War II predecessors by orders of magnitude, and more flexible reconnaissance, surveillance, and target-acquisition systems—to make mobility at all levels of jungle warfare a reality. Thus, jungle warfare is likely to become more complex than just combat among foot soldiers.

DONN A. STARRY

SEE ALSO: Geography, Military.

Bibliography

Hough, F. O., and J. A. Crown. 1952. *The campaign on New Britain.* Washington, D.C.: Government Printing Office.

Perrett, B. 1989. *Desert warfare: From its Roman origins to the Gulf conflict.* London: Patrick Stevens.

Slim, W. 1956. *Defeat into victory.* London: Cassell.

Starry, D. A. 1977. *Mounted combat in Vietnam.* Washington, D.C.: U.S. Department of the Army.

U.S. Department of the Army. 1982. *Field manual 90–5: Jungle operations.* Washington, D.C.: U.S. Department of the Army.

U.S. War Department, Historical Division. 1945. *The Admiralties: Operations of the 1st Cavalry Division, 29 February–18 May 1944.* Washington, D.C.: Government Printing Office.

L

LAND FORCES, EFFECTIVENESS AND EFFICIENCY OF

Factors influencing the effectiveness and efficiency of land forces (and criteria for their measurement) are of lasting, vital importance with regard to many problems in defense, such as

- selection and operation of weapons systems
- allocation of resources in the design and operation of military units within a given or planned force structure
- planning of force structure
- assessments of adversarial force structures to derive correct and appropriate evaluations of threats and the means to cope with them in war
- design and assessment of arms control proposals
- the operational planning for and control of military forces in peace and war.

For each of these problem areas, it is sometimes assumed that decision makers hold in their heads an implicit model of how the numerous, interdependent, and stochastic factors influence effectiveness and efficiency of land forces.

In general, one can say:

- technical progress contributes to a dramatic increase in the number of relevant influencing factors;
- selection of effectiveness criteria that satisfy numerous objectives is a difficult problem that includes the risk of making serious mistakes, in particular when considering the problem in too narrow a context;
- great military leaders distinguish themselves by being able to select and promote, from a disturbing variety, essential factors influencing effectiveness;
- computer-based models are being employed apace for purposes of analysis, planning, assessment, and training. A new generation of hardware systems in conjunction with new programming methods and software tools, in particular the employment of expert system technology, promises to contribute to an ever-increasing utilization of model-based analysis of military effectiveness.

Definitions and General Observations

Effectiveness is the degree to which given objectives are satisfied or missions accomplished as production or output. Efficiency is the ratio of that degree of accomplishment to the several possible costs in terms of inputs and throughputs.

A problem of practical significance for military force effectiveness is that objectives (or missions) usually represent only partial objectives or tasks within a complex, multidimensional, hierarchical system of sometimes poorly structured and frequently competing relationships. In addition, services rendered by military forces cannot be assessed by means of free-market mechanisms. Unless one is satisfied with assessments of simple input parameters, such as numbers of available tanks, soldiers, tooth-to-tail ratios, mobilization rate, and so on, one needs to have more or less complex dynamic process models to assess approximately, and off-line, real performance. Assessment criteria applied in a particular situation depend significantly on control level and situations. Also, objectives and missions may differ considerably between peacetime and wartime employments.

Figure 1 is a schematic of the assessment process at various hierarchical levels. Input data are related to the conflict scenario and to the adversary's military forces such as individual weapon and support systems, command, control, communications, and intelligence (C^3I) systems, personnel, combat units, and so on. Depending on objectives and missions, real or simulated combat interactions transform state variables of combat systems and provide state changes (e.g., losses in personnel and materiel or the gains/losses of terrain) as output.

From objectives/missions criteria may be derived both input as well as output values for assessing the extent to which objectives are accomplished. Input and output values at two or more hierarchical levels may be aggregated to serve as input values for assessments on a higher hierarchical level.

While input-oriented assessments apply static computational procedures and comparisons (frequently using linear-additive assessment functions) or use merely implicit or fuzzy models, output-oriented assessments are based more often on complex dynamic models of combat by means of which the dynamic

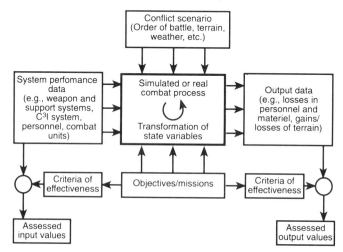

Figure 1. Schematic representation of the assessment process.

interactions in battle are simulated. For analysis, planning, and assessment of problems in defense, such models are highly significant, because in peacetime they represent practically the only way to obtain reproducible information on the effectiveness and efficiency of systems, structures, and concepts. This is because field trials and maneuvers usually do not present very credible models of combat, since safety requirements demand rather artificial circumstances and restrictions.

In what follows, important criteria for the assessment of effectiveness and efficiency of land forces are described. In doing so, distinctions are made between various hierarchical command and control levels on the one hand and input- and output-oriented values on the other.

Table 1 provides examples of important effectiveness criteria at various command and control levels that will be discussed in more detail below.

Effectiveness Criteria on the Weapons System Level

As important characteristics and indicators of performance, input-oriented effectiveness criteria of a typical army weapons system such as a main battle tank or a combat vehicle serve the assessment of such characteristics as firepower, mobility, and protection. Additional factors are related to reliability and availability as well as to certain restrictions (e.g., dimension and weight thresholds for rail and air transport). The degree to which these criteria are met by the weapon system are frequently compared to its cost, which in addition to research and development costs include primarily the procurement and operation costs.

Criteria such as firepower, mobility, and protection cannot be measured as such. Rather, they are the manifestation of some kind of an aggregation process at the basis of which performance parameters are assessed. With regard to mobility, such performance parameters may be a land vehicle's maximum velocity in various types of terrain; its acceleration time from a stationary position to maximum cross-country speed; its range, ground pressure, and the underwater mobility and river crossing capability; admissible gradient angles in terrain, and others. Similarly, the firepower of a combat vehicle is characterized by its type of main and secondary weapons (caliber, initial velocity, firing rate, range, etc.), type of ammunition and onboard supplies, the fire control system, and the available sensors. Protection afforded by a combat vehicle is determined by its silhouette, means of concealment (such as smoke dispensers), weapon-firing signatures, shape, armor protection as well as means to reduce or control damage (e.g., fire extinguishers, redundant components, active armor).

Input-oriented assessment on the weapons system level carries with it the risk that individual technical characteristics of high performance such as maximum cross-country speed, caliber of the main weapon, thickness of front armor, and availability of additional armor will be considered indicative of a high combat effectiveness that may not materialize under battle conditions. For this reason, an output-oriented assessment based on computer models of battle dynamics is usually preferred. At the weapons system level, these comprise

TABLE 1. *Examples of Effectiveness Criteria at Various Command and Control Levels*

LEVEL	INPUT-ORIENTED CRITERIA	OUTPUT-ORIENTED CRITERIA
Weapons system	Firepower Mobility Protection Reliability Availability Cost	Absolute or relative losses Losses over time Force ratios Loss ratios Consumption rates
Tactical (KP, BN, BG)	No. and type and organization of combat units No. and type of direct- and indirect-fire weapons Personnel: degree of presence, training status Combat support equipment	Tactical firing rates, kill probabilities, killer-victim scoreboards Relative losses of personnel and materiel Gains or losses in terrain Loss-exchange ratios Cost-effectiveness
Operational (division, corps, army group, theater)	No. and type and organization of combat, support, and combat service support Unit fill and mobilization rates Training status of reserves Data referring to logistics and C^3I systems	Capability to perform given operational missions Survivability and flexibility of combat, combat support, logistics, and C^3I systems Degree to which operational control can be maintained
Strategic/political	Global measures of defense economics Comparative enumerations of individual weapons systems Weapons system categories or unit types Weighted effectiveness indices (e.g., FPS, WEV, ADE)	Local, regional, or global force ratios over time Sustainability Degree of crisis, arms race, conventional and/or deterrence stability

mostly one-sided models; that is, they consider static target arrays that must be neutralized within a given period. To a limited degree, two-sided models, in the form of stochastic duels between two or more opponents, are also being applied to generate output parameters such as mutual draw-down curves for individual weapons systems, the development of force ratios, or loss over time.

It is frequently argued that these simple one- and two-sided models at the weapons system level usually disregard tactical factors (such as movement behavior), the impact of combat support systems (combined-arms combat), enemy behavior, terrain effects, and other issues. Furthermore, there is the risk of suboptimization in the sense of taking the support and command and control prerequisites for their successful employment for granted rather than explicitly considering the trade-offs between the respective weapons system under study and its peripheral systems. Thus, it follows that the effectiveness of a weapons system should be assessed in a larger tactical, operational, and finally strategic context. This is because individual weapons systems must be assessed in terms of their contribution to the accomplishment of national and alliance security objectives. This ideal complicates the assessment problem. Solutions satisfactory in every respect have yet to be found.

Effectiveness Criteria on the Tactical Level

In addition to assessment of weapons systems in the context of a tactical unit, tactical-level evaluations consider the organization of personnel and materiel within combat units with regard to their capability to perform given missions in battle.

Input-oriented parameters for the characterization of tactical-level combat units are, among others, unit types, peace- and wartime organization, number and type of direct- and indirect-fire weapons, personnel, training status, availability, communications, and engineering equipment.

Implicit conclusions are drawn from such data with regard to the combat power or capability of a land warfare unit for performing certain tactical missions. These are then contrasted with such input data as the required investment cost, the operating cost, and others.

The application of output-oriented effectiveness criteria on the tactical level requires combat simulation models that imitate the battle of the respective units (including combat support systems) in certain standard scenarios—that is, scenarios defined by combat modes, terrain types, weather conditions, and presumed types of opposing units.

In contrast to the pure duel situations on the weapons system level, these simulations emphasize the weapons system mix (i.e., the combined-arms combat in relevant tactical situations and terrain types). Thus, the respective combat simulation models must be able to distinguish between mounted and dismounted combat, account for synergisms of direct- and indirect-fire weapons systems, as well as take into account combat engineers, antiaircraft, communication, and other combat support systems.

Typical output-oriented effectiveness criteria for tactical analysis are:

- killer-victim scoreboards, duel frequencies, tactical firing rates, and kill probabilities versus certain enemy weapons systems;
- relative losses of personnel and materiel;
- relative gains or losses of terrain;
- relative change in force ratios;
- relative loss-exchange ratios;
- required operational depth for the attrition of a given number of attacking enemy units;
- relative cost-effectiveness;
- variance of the above parameters for purposes of risk assessment; and
- sensitivity or robustness of a tactical unit or mix of tactical units vis-à-vis changes in scenario parameters such as enemy type, terrain type, and weather conditions.

As an example of an output-oriented tactical-level assessment, the reader is referred to Hofmann, Huber, and Steiger (1985), which discusses simulation experiments designed to test cost-effectiveness of battalion-size "reactive" defense modules in comparison with the traditional "active" modules prevalent in general-purpose forces. The simulation experiments included four variants of active and more than ten differently designed reactive modules equipped with presently fielded weapons in a variety of circumstances by means of the tactical (battalion/regiment)-level model BASIS. The latter is a stochastic, Monte Carlo battle simulation model that permits closed simulations of battalion-size ground forces defending against a sequence of regimental-size attack forces and accounts for organic as well as higher-echelon fire support. It explicitly models each combat vehicle and dismounted infantry down to antitank teams. The effects of each shot are simulated, including the associated visibility degradation. The experiments take place in digital models of several pieces of real estate in Europe's central region. The terrain models use a grid size of 50 by 50 meters (55 by 55 yds.) and 10 centimeters' (4 in.) altitude resolution and accounts for natural and artificial obstacles and vegetation.

As an example, Figure 2 shows selected results derived from several hundred combat simulation experiments in terms of the relative cost-effectiveness over the relative operational depth required for the attrition of three consecutively attacking Soviet motor rifle regiments in a specific terrain in Bavaria and good visibility conditions. Cost-effectiveness is defined as the ratio of effectiveness to investment cost, with effectiveness being measured in terms of the relative loss-exchange ratio of attacker versus defender. For both cost-effectiveness and cost, the values are multiples of the values that resulted for the active module that turned out to be the most cost effective of the four active variants tested in the respective scenario.

The reactive modules are battalion-size forces specifically designed for defensive operations in the terrain prevalent within their respective area of operation and incapable of incursions into the opponent's territory, while the active modules are general-purpose battalions designed for employment in all combat modes including offense.

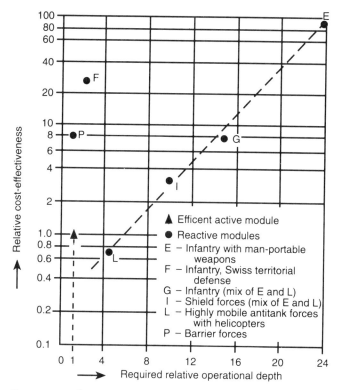

Figure 2. Relative cost-effectiveness of battalion-size defense modules over the relative operational depth required for the attrition of three consecutively attacking motor rifle regiments under standard scenario conditions.

The trend line established by the modules E, G, I, and L reflects primarily differences in type and density of antiarmor weapons deployed within the area to be defended. At the upper end, E represents infantry teams with limited mobility equipped with man-portable weapons. At the lower end, L represents highly mobile antitank teams equipped with helicopters. G and I have a mix of both. The direct-fire weapon density differs by a factor of more than four between E and L.

In addition to a weapon density 2.5 to 3 times that of module L, modules F and P are distinguished by a high degree of passive protection afforded through strong points (F) and field fortifications (P) assembled prior to combat from commercially available prefabricated structures stored in the vicinity of their usage. Thus, these modules turned out to be fairly robust against preparatory artillery fire, effects of which are not included in Figure 2.

From the above, it may be seen that the number of factors influencing the tactical level is considerably higher than on the weapons system level. This is due not only to the increased number of sometimes very different weapons systems, but also to the introduction of additional tactical variables such as battle plans and to the impact of combat support elements.

Typical results of combat simulation experiments on this level show that:

- tactics frequently dominate the impact of technical parameters of individual weapons systems,
- variance caused by a change in tactical variables usually exceeds the variance caused by other (technical) variables,
- identical weapons systems exhibit divergent combat-effectiveness parameters depending on the type of tactical unit within which they are employed, and
- effectiveness of a unit is not necessarily increased by introducing a few new high-quality weapons.

In addition to the parameters explicitly incorporated in the model, a comprehensive evaluation often requires the consideration of additional factors not easily modeled or measured. Such factors relate to dirty battlefield effects (impact of dust, dirt, noise, etc.); impact of fatigue; morale; leadership; and so on.

Effectiveness Criteria on the Operational Level

At the operational level—that is, division up to theater—the principal task of a military commander is the spatial and timely deployment of forces in such a manner that interim politico-military objectives are satisfied by maximizing mission accomplishment. In peacetime, the operational-level problem implies an allocation of resources provided to the military so that the prerequisites are created for an optimal employment of forces in wartime. In addition, other objectives usually have to be considered—such as those that may result from the political environment (e.g., alliance policy), stability requirements, the desire for arms control, and others. Thus, in addition to the input- and output-oriented criteria discussed above, a series of further criteria comes into play that result in a more comprehensive assessment appropriate to the operational milieu.

In addition to evaluation of combat and combat support units in the main combat postures, operational-level assessment addresses primarily issues related to mobilization and deployment planning, C^3I, combat service support (including medical services), sustainability, and flexibility.

Accordingly, input-oriented effectiveness criteria reflect equipment quality, unit fill rates, mobilization rates and training status of reserves and combat service support units, the mobilization system (distances between peacetime and wartime deployment positions, street and train capacity), the logistics system (logistic range, supply loads, transportation, maintenance, and repair capability), the C^3I system and its components of intelligence (width and depth of reconnaissance areas of the respective units, number and type of sensors, detection probabilities versus various target types, interference resistance, reliability, etc.), communications (type of system, average message transmission times, redundancies, etc.), and the very command and control elements that are usually described in terms of technical factors (such as vulnerability, reliability, turnaround times, etc.).

With respect to output-oriented effectiveness criteria, the complexity of modeling is confusing at this level. Based on the evaluation of expert opinion on "What comprise the significant factors of land combat?" Marshall (1986) has listed more than 100 significant factors ranging from accuracy, advance rate factors, aims and intentions, air superiority, and artillery, among others, to terrain, time, training, visibility, vulnerability, weapon system variables, weapons system interactions, and weather. Marshall concludes that:

> There is little consensus among individual practitioners as to what comprises the principal factors of military combat; indeed, there are significant issues involved in determining just what is a "factor" of combat and what are other components and descriptions in this area.

Many seemingly different terms for "significant/major factors" of combat are similar enough to be considered as one. Their frequency of nomination leads to the following order of priority: firepower, C^3 (including leadership and initiative), environment, human factors, strength (force ratio), intelligence, logistics, mobility, tactics (deployment), miscellaneous, chance, surprise, posture, attacker/defender, and political involvement.

In a tactical and operational context, the authors of *Land Force Tactical Doctrine—ATP35(A)* (NATO 1984, Chapt. 1) distinguish seventeen fundamentals to which armies have adhered in order to achieve their objectives: "Rapidly changing technology and capabilities have altered the emphasis and application of these but the fundamentals themselves remain constant." They are: human factors (leadership, morale, initiative, flexibility, endurance), selection and maintenance of the aim, freedom of action, aggressive action, concentration of effort, economy of force, mobility, maneuver, surprise, intelligence, simplicity, maintenance of forces, flexibility, cooperation, administration, security, and protection.

For main combat modes, additional factors of particular importance are: *defensive operations* (intelligence, use of terrain, depth, mutual support, concentration of combat power, maneuver, firepower, electronic warfare, collusion, offensive action, and reserves); *delaying operations* (intelligence, maneuver, terrain, time, space, and aggressive actions); and *offensive operations* (intelligence, audacity, surprise, concentration, speed, control, depth, security, maneuver). Similar factors are described by Clausewitz in *On War* (1984).

Complexities in modeling are increased by various technical, tactical, operational, and other factors. Variables are interdependent, and their relative importance varies with the scenarios under study. Furthermore, the dynamical battle simulation models on this level need to consider, in addition to the combat processes, the areas of mobilization, combat support, logistics, C^3I, and others. Their processing times must permit simulating a large number of options within a short period of time.

Modeling has progressed considerably in the past few years. Deficiencies remain, however, because military systems analysis emphasizes studies on single weapons systems and tactical levels, which simplifies the modeling. On the operational level, the most common dynamic analysis tool has been the computer-based war game, a technique requiring considerable personnel resources. Therefore, a new generation of fast, closed (without a man-in-the-loop) combat simulation models is being developed. These new models will be implemented on powerful computing systems and will take advantage of modern expert system technologies.

The need for such models is increasingly recognized as many historical examples show that tactical effectiveness (defined as the sum of all capabilities that contribute to the combat unit's lethality and survivability) will not compensate for poor operational effectiveness, which depends on both—that is, tactical effectiveness and commanders' concepts of operations (Hosmer 1988).

With regard to output-oriented effectiveness criteria, the operational level distinguishes the following:

- capability of a given force structure to neutralize forward echelons of an attacking force
- capability to regain lost territory
- maximum penetration depth of attacking enemy units prior to restoration of territorial status quo ante
- fraction of enemy weapons systems neutralized prior to their arrival on the battlefield and the associated time delays (e.g., for the assessment of follow-on-forces-attack [FOFA] concepts)
- degree of survivability and flexibility of combat, combat support, logistics, and C^3I systems or of particular combat functions such as antitank and air defense, movement impairment (barriers)
- degree to which operational control can be maintained in rear combat zones;
- sustainability of various force structures
- number and robustness of operational decision alternatives for various force structures vis-à-vis given operational options of the enemy
- values of variance for the above criteria for the assessment of risk associated with the various decision alternatives.

Effectiveness Criteria on the Strategic Level

In addition to the contribution of the various military services, analyses at the strategic level must consider additional aspects and variables such as civilian defense of a country, available population, industrial potential, alliance structure, the depth of the area of operations, and the length and exposure of lines of communication. Similar to the other levels of analysis, strategic objectives represent guidelines for the selection of effectiveness and efficiency criteria. These objectives are related to:

- improving regional or local force ratios;
- maintaining or improving crisis, arms race, conventional and/or deterrence stability;
- lifting the nuclear threshold through an improvement of conventional defense capabilities by means of technical, tactical, operational, and structural means within given defense budgets;

- providing for a balanced force structure capable of attaining these strategic objectives; and
- ensuring personnel and materiel preparedness.

Generally accepted dynamic conflict models do not exist at this level, so input-oriented effectiveness criteria dominate assessments. It is the domain of the various static force balance assessments that are frequently discussed in the open literature. These comparisons evaluate force balances in terms of: (1) global measures of defense economics (such as the fraction of gross national product spent on defense, men under arms in time of peace and war compared with the total population of a state, degree of protection provided to the general population and others); (2) comparative enumerations of individual weapon systems (e.g., tanks, armored combat vehicles, antitank weapons), weapon system categories (e.g., armored combat vehicles, air defense systems, artillery systems), or unit types (e.g., tank division, armored infantry division); or (3) weighted effectiveness indices such as firepower scores (FPS), weapons' effectiveness values (WEV), weighted unit values (WUV), or armored division equivalents (ADE).

From the foregoing, (2) and (3) may also be applied to operational-level analyses. Attempts are being made to incorporate, among others, command and control and logistics factors into the assessment.

Weighting factors are usually based on judgment and intuitions conditioned by experience. There are, however, serious shortcomings, such as the assumption of utility independence of the weighted parameters, which is obvious from frequent usage of linear and additive utility functions (Hofmann and Huber 1983, p. 153).

Output-oriented effectiveness comparisons on the military strategic level remain based largely on highly aggregated and fairly simple analytical conflict models. For as long as the aggregated input data and implicit assumptions of such aggregated models cannot be qualified by means of a hierarchy of conflict simulation models, results are of limited value. Simple models that are not sufficiently based on empirical evidence incur the risk that the complexity of the underlying problems will be overlooked, leading to faulty interpretations and to pretending an accuracy not found in reality.

Demonstration of variances and risks is considered an essential contribution of military systems analysis on the strategic level. Uncertainty in assessment of force potentials represents not only a source of mistakes (such as inappropriate allocations of considerable resources) but also, depending on the risk attitude of opponents, a probability of crises erupting into military conflict.

Problems in Effectiveness Criteria

The selection of appropriate objectives and effectiveness criteria represents a difficult problem requiring diligence and experience in military systems analysis.

This is especially true due to the lack of sufficiently detailed theater-level models on the one hand and the described disadvantages of aggregated models on the other. Therefore, the present approach is generally one of piecemeal analysis, which involves a risk of suboptimization.

In this context, mistakes frequently made in the criteria selection shall be discussed as per McKean (1970).

IGNORING ABSOLUTE SCALE OF OBJECTIVE OR COST

A common efficiency criterion is the ratio of achievement-of-objective to cost. For example, a problem may concern the selection of an antitank weapon. In a battle on battalion or brigade level, one antitank system may destroy, on the average, 5 tanks at a cost of US$1 million (i.e., an achievement-to-cost ratio of 5:1). In the same situation, another weapons system is assumed to neutralize 50 tanks at a cost of US$20 million (i.e., a ratio of 2.5:1).

Based on the ratio criterion, the first weapons system would be superior. Nevertheless, this choice might be suboptimal because the capability to neutralize 50 tanks in a certain situation—that is, the capability to thwart the attack of a regiment—can justify the additional cost of US$19 million, considering associated tactical and operational effects.

SETTING THE WRONG OBJECTIVE OR SCALE OF OBJECTIVE

A common criterion in most effectiveness problems is to maximize achievement-of-objective for a given cost or conversely to minimize the cost of achieving a specified objective. Choices between these two criteria depend on whether it is the cost or the objective that can be fixed with the greater degree of correctness.

Figure 3 shows the assumed functional relationship between the selected effectiveness criterion (e.g., number of tanks neutralized per unit time) and the required cost for two alternative systems. If we assume the cost restriction to be k_1, system 1 is preferable; for the cost restriction k_2, it is system 2. And vice

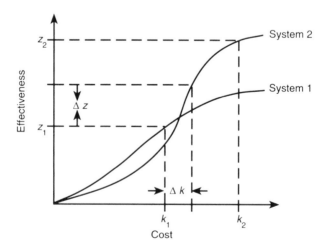

Figure 3. Functional relationship between effectiveness and cost for two alternative systems.

versa: for a required effectiveness, Z_1, system 1 is preferable, while the effectiveness Z_2 is satisfied by system 2 only. This serves to show how sensitive is the choice of a required degree of effectiveness or how fine is the definition of a cost threshold with regard to choice alternatives. Furthermore, use of fixed-cost or effectiveness thresholds may result in inefficient expenditures or inefficient savings.

This problem is illustrated in Figure 3. If the cost limit k_1 is increased by a relatively small margin Δk, one would select not only a different system, but also obtain a significant increase ΔZ in effectiveness. Thus, cost savings Δk could be considered inefficient. In addition, the convex-concave shape of utility functions typical for most military systems leads to another effect: compensation of cost overruns by means of numerical reductions that result in cost savings Δk that are frequently associated with a significant loss of overall effectiveness.

IGNORING UNCERTAINTY OR RISK

Uncertainty is an essential element in war. Its sources are manifold—for example, occurrence of chance events, lack of situation information, weather, deceptions and dissembly, composition of enemy forces, possible enemy countermeasures, one's own and/or the enemy's objectives, operational employment, and so on.

This means that results based on expected values (e.g., in the form of the mean number of neutralized targets) represent average results, at best, associated with a fairly low probability of occurrence in some cases. It is important that robustness of solutions vis-à-vis results that differ from average results is considered—that is, risks associated with certain decisions. This, in turn, means that assessment models must be capable of generating distributions on the essential assessment parameters rather than merely on expected values. For this reason, modern architectures of battle simulation models attempt to provide deterministic expected values as well as stochastic values. Because of favorable processing times, expected value permits simulating a large number of parametric evaluations, while the more time-consuming stochastic (Monte Carlo) version is applied to determine outcome distributions on interesting parameter constellations.

IGNORING EFFECTS ON OTHER WEAPON SYSTEMS OR OPERATIONS

A frequent mistake is using criteria that do not measure the effects on other systems or operations. For example, a combat unit that satisfies the requirements for a given defensive mission and also offers the potential for being employed in flank attacks (so that the enemy must provide for additional means in order to protect against the threat to its flanks) has a higher combat potential than a unit that is restricted to a defensive mission only. The same holds true for multirole weapons systems versus single-role systems.

INSUFFICIENT OR WRONG COST DATA

With regard to costs, there are several sources of error, such as the neglect of entire cost categories (e.g., personnel and maintenance costs); systematic underestimation of procurement cost (especially by the producers of systems); considering sunk costs instead of incremental or additional costs (i.e., additional net resource drain that would be incurred by each alternative); neglect of discounting effects (i.e., the fact that expenditures are done at different points in time) as well as disregard for additional resource expenditures that are not easily expressed in monetary terms. For example, assessment of expected personnel losses and the consequences is a largely unsolved problem.

IGNORING THE TIME DIMENSION

The impact of time is usually *the* decisive criterion at all levels of analysis. For example, on the tactical level, the requirement to neutralize a given number of attacking combat vehicles at minimal cost may be quite irrelevant. Capability to do this within a time period of, for example, ten to fifteen minutes might be the decisive criterion for denying the success of an attack.

In summary, the definition of relevant and practical effectiveness and efficiency criteria within the context of a given problem statement requires great diligence and experience in military systems analysis. Frequently, it is only the result of a long analysis process. "The point is that the only way to choose criteria is to undertake analysis, the pitfall is to believe the contrary" (Quade 1970, p. 304).

Future Developments

Selection, procurement, and employment of weapons systems as well as the transformation of technical innovations into appropriate tactical and operational concepts have traditionally presented a great challenge to military leadership. This is because, in peacetime, conservative attitudes usually dominate land forces to the extent that armies are always inclined to prepare for past wars. Thus, tactical requirements and specifications for new weapons and support systems tend to be based on scenarios and employment doctrines that have little relevance. This attitude is of grave consequence at a time when technical progress is accelerating and the potential of new technologies is increasing considerably.

For this reason, the tools of analysis must be improved through the development of a new generation of closed simulation models on the levels of operational control (up to theater) that are sufficiently detailed and empirically well founded. Modern concepts of systems analysis and computer science are about to provide the prerequisites for such an improvement. A new generation of extremely capable computing systems that provide multiprocess and parallel processing capability as well as good graphic interfaces, new programming methods and languages, improved software tools, and the employment of expert system technologies comprise the new dynamic assessment environment.

Such models will be employed not just for more adequate assessment of new technologies, new tactical and operational concepts, arms control proposals, and others; they may also be integrated into computer-based operational C^3I systems to be used as command and staff simulators for training commanders and staffs.

If it is correct that tactical and operational variables significantly determine the outcome of battles, as do weapons systems and well-trained troops, then the training of commanders and their staffs by means of simulations attains more significance the fewer opportunities there are to acquire real experience.

HANS W. HOFMANN

SEE ALSO: Combined Arms; Land Warfare; Span of Control: Military Organizations and Operations.

Bibliography

Clausewitz, C. von. 1984. *On war.* Ed. and trans. M. Howard and P. Paret. Princeton, N.J.: Princeton Univ. Press.

Dunnigan, J. F. 1983. *How to make war.* New York: Quill.

Helmbold, R. L., and A. A. Khan. 1986. Combat history analysis study effort (CHASE): Progress report for the period August 1984–June 1985. Bethesda, Md.: U.S. Army Concepts Analysis Agency.

Hofmann, H. W., and R. K. Huber. 1983. Systemanalytischer Ansatz zur Zielplanung am Beispiel der Verteidigungsplanung. In *Wirtschaftliche Landesvorsorge im Rahmen der Sicherheitspolitik,* ed. P. Stähly, pp. 149–62. Stuttgart: Haupt Bern.

———. 1988. *On the role of new technologies for conventional stability in Europe.* Report S-8802. Munich: Federal Armed Forces Univ.

Hofmann, H. W., R. K. Huber, and K. Steiger. 1985. On reactive defense options—A comparative systems analysis of alternatives for the initial defense against the first strategic echelon of the Warsaw Pact in Central Europe. In *Modeling and analysis of conventional defense in Europe: Assessment of improvement options,* ed. R. K. Huber, pp. 97–139. London: Plenum.

Hosmer, B. C. 1988. Operational art: The importance of the operational level of war. *Phalanx* 23 (no. 3).

Hughes, W. P., ed. 1984. *Military modeling.* Washington, D.C.: Military Operations Research Society.

Marshall, D. 1986. The factors and structure of combat—A revisit. Paper presented at the 3d International Symposium on Military Operations Research, Shrivenham, Swindon, U.K.

McKean, R. N. 1970. Criteria. In *Analysis for military decisions—The Rand lectures on systems analysis,* ed. E. S. Quade, pp. 81–91. London: North-Holland Amsterdam.

NATO. 1984. *Land force tactical doctrine—ATP-35(A).* Military Agency for Standardization. Brussels: NATO.

Quade, E. S. 1970. Pitfalls in systems analysis. In *Analysis for military decisions—The Rand lectures on systems analysis,* ed. E. S. Quade, pp. 300–16. London: North-Holland Amsterdam.

LAND WARFARE

Land warfare is the organized use of military force by a nation-state to achieve political, economic, or social objectives. Military force is used directly to defeat the military forces of an adversary or indirectly—by threat—to cause an adversary to modify its political, economic, social, or military behavior. Trained and disciplined individuals are organized into military units that employ a variety of weapons in a coordinated fashion to subdue an enemy military force.

Land warfare is multidimensional. It involves the integration and maneuver of military formations (personnel, vehicles, weaponry, logistics, and communications) and the application of firepower (direct and indirect, air and naval) in a coordinated fashion to exploit an adversary's weaknesses and avoid his strengths, so that assigned objectives are accomplished with minimum expenditure of resources. Battles are orchestrated to accomplish campaign objectives that are aimed at winning wars to accomplish strategic objectives. To achieve those strategic objectives, land power, sea power, and airpower must be fully interdependent.

Changes in technology have played a central role (and will continue to do so) in developing the doctrine and tactics of land warfare. The development of the bow allowed combatants to distance themselves from each other for the first time. That distance did not change again until the invention of gunpowder. The ability to fire a projectile further separated combatants, and that distance has continued to grow over the last 1,500 years. The 1991 war in the Persian Gulf served notice to land armies worldwide that targets to be engaged will be at even greater distances and that the human face of the enemy increasingly will be replaced by a blip on an electronic device. Factors that are influencing the conduct of modern land warfare include the electronic battlefield; the increased use and coordination of joint and combined operations; the improved lethality and accuracy of weapons; an array of strategic, operational, and tactical sensors and detectors; the increased maneuverability of forces; the technological sophistication of lesser military powers; and growing requirements for rapid reaction capabilities at the strategic, operational, and tactical levels.

Historical Evolution

The tactics of land warfare emerged from the conflicts of the earliest civilizations. Opponents probably first engaged in personal, brutal, hand-to-hand combat using their bare hands. The first rudimentary handheld weapons were stones, clubs, and stone-head axes. Instruments that thrust objects at adversaries from afar—slings and bows, javelins and spears—further improved lethality while giving some protection by placing distance between combatants. Thus began the cycle of using advancing technology to improve the instruments of war. Improved weaponry meant a gain in advantage over an enemy force, which could lead to victory on the battlefield or, in modern parlance, deter the adversary from entering the fray.

The history and evolution of land warfare revolves around a number of factors: the tactical genius of a few great military leaders; the specific technological breakthroughs with potential military application; the overall modernization and industrialization of societies; and the developing art and science of land warfare as it has grown through analysis of battles, strategic principles, and proven or evolutionary doctrine.

ANCIENT ROOTS OF LAND WARFARE

Although many early societies engaged in land warfare, the Assyrians left one of the earliest records of their weaponry, tactics, and battlefield engagements.

As early as 1000 B.C., the Assyrians had made extensive use of military formations of soldiers armed with bows and arrows, spears and slings, on foot, on horseback, and in horse-drawn chariots. Formations of soldiers on foot and horseback would simultaneously launch a mass of projectiles—arrows, spears, and stones—against the enemy and then maneuver in a prescribed formation and direction to complete the task of subduing or destroying the remaining enemy forces.

Two elements of the Assyrians' military prowess continue to be fundamental to an effective military force today. The first factor is the combined use of massive firepower and maneuver of forces to overwhelm and demoralize the enemy. This psychological dimension of warfare at the level of the individual soldier's willingness to fight underlies such battlefield tactics as the employment of the sniper, shock action, blitzkreig, carpet bombing, and artillery raids. The second factor is related to the Assyrians' use of more readily available iron in lieu of bronze on the tips of arrows and spears and on body armor to improve personal protection from enemy projectiles and swords. The timely recognition and application of technology to land warfare can have a deterrent psychological effect on the enemy, as well as affecting the outcome of the battle.

While the Assyrians and Persians perfected the utility of massed firepower and maneuver, the Greeks countered with extensive use of large, advancing infantry formations of well-disciplined soldiers who were each protected by a large shield and armed with a particularly long, iron-pointed spear. They used this formation to overcome the shock effects of Persian massed fires, similar to those used by the Assyrians, at Marathon in 490 B.C. "With the spears of the first five or six rows of men protruding beyond the front rank to create a deadly hedge of iron points, the phalanx advanced to battle at a steady pace, protected from missiles by heavy shields, and ground [its] way through the enemy formation like a chopping machine" (Kendall 1957).

The Romans improved on the phalanx by making it a more flexible legion of smaller, spaced units and using spears that could be thrown by a soldier bearing a larger shield for greater protection. The legion was modified later to adapt to the need for better leadership and a more professional army in the far-reaching Roman empire. This professional army was recruited from the entire population, organized into 100-man cohorts, led by a professional soldier or centurion, and paid and equipped by the state. This last innovation would continue to come and go throughout the ages.

The ancient civilizations of the Mediterranean region and of China also contributed great strategists who have had lasting effects on the art and science of warfare. Their contributions to strategy, operational art, and tactics remain relevant to contemporary land warfare doctrine.

THE ANCIENT STRATEGISTS AND GREAT CAPTAINS

As ancient tribal behaviors coalesced into more complex societies, the emerging city-states were charged with securing the interests of their citizens. Individuals served in their respective armies through either conscription or civil obligation. To survive, these ancient societies had to conquer or be conquered.

Consequently, they relied heavily on the skills of their military leaders, many of whom today remain central to our understanding of warfare and land warfare in particular.

Among these ancient generals were Sun Tzu (ca. 500 B.C.), who enunciated well-defined fundamentals of war that underlie modern principles; Alexander the Great (ca. 300 B.C.), who conquered the civilized world from Persia to Egypt to India, adapting firepower, maneuver, and organization to surprise his enemies; Hannibal (ca. 200 B.C.), the Carthaginian, who made the strategic maneuver of crossing the Alps into Italy, thus avoiding the Romans' major force, and subsequently moving his force through foreboding terrain to surprise and defeat a force of Roman legions; and Julius Caesar (ca. 50 B.C.), who demonstrated a genius for adapting the tactics of the legion to the terrain and the enemy's formations and deployments and engendering a discipline that ensured the commitment of forces to battle at the decisive time and place.

At the close of the last millennium B.C., the ancient Great Captains had secured their places of prominence in the study of military strategy, art, and tactics that underlie land warfare. The next Great Captains would not emerge until late into the second millennium A.D.: Gustavus Adolphus of Sweden (seventeenth century); Marlborough of England (eighteenth century); the Prussian, Frederick the Great (eighteenth century); and Napoleon (nineteenth century).

TRANSITION TO MODERN LAND WARFARE

In the first millennium A.D., emerging tactics included the use of horsemen (cavalry), light infantry, and heavy infantry, to be employed in various combinations and weightings. The extent of body armor covering head, chest, arms, and legs varied, as did the size and weight of shields and weaponry (javelin, spear, ax, dagger, sword, bow).

How armies fought also depended on the weaponry and tactics of adversaries. In the western Roman Empire at the start of the millennium, the response to continual barbarian raids on outposts was static defense; in the eastern Byzantine portion of the empire, cavalry prevailed by A.D. 500. The Byzantines codified their doctrine of warfare, focusing on defense in depth and conservation of resources (especially trained and expensive cavalry).

England and the western European tribes and enclaves of civilization were subject to Viking raids. To survive, they organized into protective fiefdoms and made extensive use of fortifications—at first, large earth and timber enclosures and, later, walled castle keeps and cities. Siege warfare was common, and the techniques and equipment used to penetrate walls and engage distant targets became increasingly sophisticated.

Feudal armies were usually temporary, brought together for a particular purpose and then disbanded. They varied in size, on the average 5,000 to 10,000 men. Local vassals were eventually replaced by paid soldiers (mercenaries); as the strength of armies became more predictable, longer campaigns could be conducted. Through invasions and counter-invasions among France, England, and later Spain, and as a result of the Crusades and the Hundred

Years' War, individuals built power bases and monarchies emerged. At first, the weapons of war and tactics of ancient periods were reinvented. However, with the advent of gunpowder, the relative lethality of infantry and cavalry changed forever; musket replaced bow, and cannon replaced catapult.

The Impact of Technology on Land Warfare

Before the invention of gunpowder, land warfare was fought in a destructive, personal manner and at closer quarters. As crude weapons were gradually replaced by more effective devices, the nature of land warfare changed. Early man made only relatively simple advances in weaponry over several thousand years. But as man's ingenuity advanced through the first millennium A.D., significant advances in weaponry occurred more frequently.

The short bow, sling, and javelin brought about significant changes in how land wars were fought. Chariots gave archers and javelin throwers a mobile and stable platform from which to launch their projectiles. The use of helmet, breastplate, shin guards, and shield in combination with a spear, ax, or sword and of lightly equipped soldiers on horseback (cavalry) continued well into the second millennium A.D. The effectiveness of this early weaponry was dependent on the mobility, maneuverability, and discipline of the military formation. Fortified defensive works of earth and stone were essential to the survival of entire city-states and date from the earliest periods. These fortresses were besieged by armies using fighting towers, battering rams, catapults, and flame-tipped arrows and other flame devices.

During the first millennium A.D., the role of the soldier on horseback was enhanced by the use of saddle and stirrup, which provided a stable platform and leverage to use weapons while mounted. The cavalryman replaced the two-horsed chariot, which was an economical move in terms of the number of fighters per horse and the forage required for horses. Both the longbow (which required a well-trained archer to launch up to six arrows per minute to a range of 200 yd.) and the crossbow (which required less training and discipline and had a rate of fire of one to two arrows per minute to a range of 130 yd.) assumed prominent positions for organized use on the battlefield soon after the start of the second millennium A.D. (Macksey 1973). The use of gunpowder emerged soon thereafter.

GUNPOWDER AND THE INDUSTRIAL REVOLUTION

Over the centuries, weapons' development focused on improving three elements: range, accuracy, and rate of fire. With the advent of gunpowder-propelled projectiles on the battlefield in the 1400s, science became a tool of the military in the search for ways to inflict more significant casualties on opponents. For the next 400 years, the sophistication and diversification of cannon, artillery, musket, pistol, and rifle revolutionized the conduct of land warfare. With each new invention—the cylindroconoidal bullet, improved explosives, smokeless powders, the fuze, shrapnel, rifling (to increase range and accuracy), breech-loading artillery, the repeating rifle, and the machine gun—

rates of fire and the vulnerability of soldiers to long-range fire increased dramatically. The industrial revolution meant these weapons could be manufactured in mass quantities. The railroad, telegraph, and internal combustion engine brought military units a degree of mobility and responsiveness unimagined a century earlier (Garden 1989).

The leap in technology and invention in the nineteenth century continued the trend toward large land armies and greater casualties, as evident in the American Civil War and the Russo-Japanese War. World War I brought the artillery barrage, the machine gun, infantry attacks on entrenched enemy forces, and limited use of chemical weapons. World War I also saw the introduction of the airplane and the first armored vehicle (the tank) to be used in modern warfare to overcome the limitations of trench warfare (Macksey 1973). These two weapons systems have influenced land warfare in an unprecedented fashion. The pace and lethality of military operations were greatly accelerated by these weapons systems and by the application of electronics, including radar, high-speed communications, and encryption, in World War II.

The enhanced ability of opposing military forces to maneuver, employ firepower, and protect their resources brought about new operational methods involving the close coordination of airpower (strategic bombing and close air support) and landpower (rapid-moving armor units and artillery preparations) to engage an opposing force at its most vulnerable location and avoid its strengths. This form of warfare was used with great success by the Germans in World War II, to a lesser extent by the Allies.

MODERN TECHNOLOGY

The weapons systems of land warfare that emerged from World War II set the framework for weapons to follow. In spite of its power, the atomic bomb has proven unusable in a ground war. The potential for escalation, side effects of radiation, and political intervention have negated a direct role for nuclear weapons in land warfare. Instead, technology has focused on improvements to traditional applications of energy in weaponry and the vehicles that propel them.

The microminiaturization of equipment components, the microprocessor and computer, the development of sensors and detectors that respond to wide ranges of the electromagnetic spectrum (infrared and laser), electronic countermeasures, near-real-time dissemination of information, ground positioning systems, satellites, lasers, increased lethality of and accuracy of warheads, improved armor and munitions using depleted uranium, and countless related technological adaptations are having a profound effect on warfare. Targets can be detected, tracked, and engaged at ranges that far exceed those of World War II.

The high levels of reliability, protection, and lethality that have been attained can be illustrated by the modern battle tank. The performance of the U.S. Army M1A1 main battle tank in the 1991 war with Iraq reflects technological improvements applied to an established weapons system. After 100 hours of offensive operations, the tank's operational readiness exceeded 90 percent. In a night movement of 300 tanks across open desert, all of the tanks arrived at the destination. Several M1A1 tanks received direct hits from anti-tank rounds and sustained no damage, attesting to the effectiveness of special armor. The tank's thermal night sight allowed crews to see enemy tanks through smoke from oil well fires, use the laser range finder, maintain gun stabilization on the move, and destroy targets at ranges that exceeded 3,000 meters (9,900 ft.). The state-of-the-art antitank round fired by the 120mm gun of the M1A1 was able to fire through berms protecting enemy tanks and still destroy Soviet-origin T-72 tanks.

Modern land warfare uses technologically advanced systems at the level of the individual soldier to enhance fire-support weapons. The individual soldier can be armed with night-vision equipment to allow him to "see daylight." He is also equipped with laser devices to designate targets for engagement by artillery and armed helicopters, and he is armed with individual antitank weapons that can launch smart rounds that stay on target until impact. He can engage enemy helicopters and aircraft using a shoulder-fired, heat-seeking antiaircraft missile and can locate his position within a few feet by using a hand-held global plotting device that receives satellite information.

Artillery weapons fire "smart rounds" that can seek out and destroy tanks from overhead and scatter antipersonnel and antitank mines. Radar systems can "backtrack" the path of enemy projectiles to the artillery location and automatically provide coordinates for counterartillery fires. Aircraft are used in traditional logistical and close-air-support roles. However, the armed helicopter is able to maneuver and engage enemy armor day or night using smart antitank missiles that respond to laser designation and infrared emissions.

Technology will continue to improve the overall capabilities of traditional land weapons systems. However, the limitations of technology and the man-machine interface will require continual attention. Success in warfare depends heavily on the ability of individuals to use weapons and information systems under battlefield conditions while maintaining the flexibility to adapt and take advantage of changing conditions. The advantages and economies of automation and robotics will have to be balanced with the human ability to process selective information to make good decisions—by a tank gunner's choice of target or a corps commander's timing of an attack.

Conceptual Foundation of Modern Land Warfare

The conduct of land warfare rests on three fundamental piers of analysis: strategy, operational art, and tactics. Successful military strategy achieves national and alliance political aims at the lowest possible cost in lives and national resources. Operational art translates those aims into effective military operations and campaigns. Sound tactics win battles and engagements that produce successful campaigns and operations (Department of the Army 1986).

In addition to these three components, modern land warfare doctrine reflects the precepts of ancient and modern theorists and strategists as reflected in principles of war and combat power (the ability to fight a war).

The classical principles of war were best articulated by British major general

J. F. C. Fuller during World War I. They remain valid today and are summarized below:

- Direct every military operation toward a clearly defined, decisive, and attainable objective.
- Seize, retain, and exploit the initiative.
- Concentrate combat power at the decisive place and time.
- Allocate minimum essential combat power to secondary efforts.
- Place the enemy in a position of disadvantage through the flexible application of combat power.
- For every objective, ensure unity of effort under one responsible commander.
- Never permit the enemy to acquire an unexpected advantage.
- Strike the enemy at a time or place, or in a manner, for which he is unprepared.
- Prepare clear, uncomplicated plans and clear, concise orders to ensure thorough understanding.

Combat power measures the effect of maneuver, firepower, protection, and leadership, which are defined as follows:

- *Maneuver* is the movement of forces in relation to the enemy to secure or retain positional advantage. It can involve concentrating forces at the critical point to achieve surprise and dominance over enemy forces; it also can be achieved by allowing the enemy to move into a disadvantageous position.
- Maneuver is linked to *firepower* to defeat the enemy's ability and will to fight; however, firepower can also be used independently of maneuver to destroy, delay, or disrupt uncommitted enemy forces.
- *Protection* involves the retention of fighting capabilities so they can be applied at the decisive time and place; this involves actions (such as camouflage, deception, dispersal, and air defense) to counter the enemy's ability to locate friendly forces and use firepower and maneuver against them.
- Competent and confident *leadership* provides purpose, direction, and motivation in land warfare.

Battlefield success is measured by the extent to which it accomplishes the operational goals of a campaign. In turn, the campaign is not successful unless the national security strategic objectives are met. Thus, clear statements of strategic purpose are essential. The effective application of combat power on the battlefield is defined in terms of doctrine.

MODERN BATTLEFIELD DOCTRINE

Battlefield doctrine addresses how to use combat power at the operational and tactical levels of warfare. Modern battlefield doctrine prescribes that friendly forces should gain and retain the initiative, act faster than the enemy, synchronize battlefield activities to produce maximum combat power, and operate in depth of space, time, and resources to win the battle.

The linear battlefield dominated the major land wars of the twentieth century. Trench warfare and the use of massive artillery fires in World War I resulted in mutual attrition and high casualties. World War II provided greater opportunities for coordination of mobile forces and firepower to gain the advantage over opposing forces; however, the linearity of the battlefield and heavy casualties still dominated, and rapid victory was elusive. However, the battlefield of the late twentieth century, as demonstrated in 1991 in the ejection of Iraqi forces from Kuwait (Operation Desert Storm), involves fast-paced, fluid operations. Depending on the assigned mission, units conduct close, deep, and rear operations.

Close operations involve units that are committed to battle, including support such as artillery, air defense, reconnaissance, and logistical units. At the operational level, close operations involve the activities of corps comprising divisions. At the tactical level, the subordinate units of the division, the brigades and battalions, fight battles (which can involve deep and rear operations as well). Close operations include maneuver, close combat (including close air support), indirect fire support (artillery or naval gunfire), combat support and combat service support of fighting units, and the necessary command and control (leadership and coordination) to ensure victory.

Modern battlefield doctrine incorporates deep operations to shape the operational situation in which later close operations will occur. Deep operations, which are not new to modern land warfare doctrine, include interdicting enemy supplies, reserves, and communications to minimize their impact on a current or future battle. With the increasing mobility and firepower available to modern tactical-level units, the ability of deep operations to influence the outcomes of battles and ensure early victory continues to grow. Deep operations are undertaken only against those enemy capabilities that can directly affect the conduct of friendly operations. They include deception operations, deep surveillance and target acquisition, interdiction by firepower and maneuver forces, and electronic warfare to disrupt enemy command, control, and communications.

Close and deep operations are closely coordinated with rear operations, which comprise activities to ensure freedom of maneuver and continuity of planned operations or opportunities to exploit success. Friendly reserve forces and fire support are positioned to successfully move and engage enemy formations while remaining secure from enemy observation or attack. Sufficient logistical support and services are conserved, without decreasing the support to currently engaged units, to ensure the sustainment of the reserves if committed.

These categories of operations reflect the fluid and nonlinear nature of the modern battlefield and provide a framework for the development of battle plans. Battle success depends ultimately on the ingenuity of the commanders, the readiness and training of individual soldiers and units, and their ability and flexibility to adapt to rapidly changing situations.

ORGANIZATION FOR LAND WARFARE

The doctrine of the modern battlefield is practiced by organizations within a designated operational area. Military operations are carried out in accordance with the strategic objectives established by national or international command authorities. A definite set of boundaries is established, rules of engagement are defined, and specific objectives are established. Land warfare operations are conducted in a theater of operations in coordination with air and sea forces (joint operations), to include the armed forces of allied countries (combined operations). A joint commander is designated who is responsible for coordinating all activities in the conduct of the campaign, to include all air, sea, and land forces operations. In a joint or combined command, a commander is designated for each of the air, sea, and land components. In a combined operation with forces from other countries, the joint commander may also be the combined commander, or a separate commander can be designated.

In the U.S. military, land forces at the operational level, where objectives are related to the accomplishment of specific strategic objectives, are organized into corps. One or more corps can operate under a theater army commander, who is responsible to the overall joint/combined commander. At the corps level, the operational objectives of the campaign are accomplished through the operations of subordinate tactical divisions: brigades and subordinate battalions and companies fight the battles and engagements.

The types of units assigned to each of these levels of organization—theater, corps, division, brigade—will depend on the overall purpose of the operation, the geographical location, the terrain and weather to be encountered, the sophistication of infrastructure in the theater of operation (i.e., ports, airfields, roadways), constraints of resources and time, and, most important, the threat of enemy forces and their capabilities. Each level of organization is task organized to ensure the capabilities and functions necessary to achieve the objectives of the operation. Tactical-level combat units rarely operate as pure organizations; rather, they are augmented (task organized) with other types of units into a task force to take advantage of the combined effects of their capabilities.

Divisions are major ground combat units that have the command and control capabilities (commanders, staff, communications) to effectively plan for and implement operational plans at the tactical level. At this level, tactical missions are assigned, operational orders are developed and implemented, and the battle is fought by assigned units. Operational orders include clear statements of missions to be accomplished, a scheme of maneuver, a visualization of the operation, controls on the movement and firepower of units, assignment of different types of fire support (i.e., close air support, artillery support, naval gunfire support, air defense), priorities regarding transportation, allocation of fuel and ammunition, intelligence information, missions and actions of adjacent friendly units, and time lines for the start of the operation.

The number of personnel and units in a division will depend on the assigned mission, the operational environment, and the capabilities needed to defeat enemy forces. The number of personnel can range from 10,000 to 30,000. The units assigned to the division, like those assigned at the higher corps level and at subordinate brigade, battalion, and company levels, are categorized by their major functions: combat, combat support, and combat service support. Combat units include armor, mechanized, light infantry, air assault, and airborne. Each of these units has unique capabilities that makes it appropriate singularly or in combination with other types of units to conduct a ground operation. Combat support units include artillery, aviation, engineer, and air defense. Combat service support units include medical, transportation, supply, and construction.

LOGISTICAL SUPPORT

The combat service support units are often neglected in the study of land warfare. Their role is to support the deployment, movement, and sustainment of combat organizations. Functions involved include construction and transport; fuel, water, food, and ammunition resupply; and provision of spare parts and maintenance of equipment and weapons systems. The logistical situation and the support units involved will weigh heavily in decisions regarding the deployment of military forces.

Figure 1 portrays the Kuwait theater of operations that existed at the start of the Operation Desert Storm ground war in February 1991. To emphasize the important role of combat service support and logistical support, only the major combat service support units are displayed. Each of the divisions (displayed to the far right) has its own internal support command to meet short-term supply, maintenance, and medical needs. The corps-level logistical support structure includes a corps support command (COSCOM) for each of the corps (XVIII and VII Corps) that provides a corps support group to support each division; in addition, a corps support group supports other units in the corps area. Each corps support group has a maintenance battalion, a supply and service battalion, and a transportation battalion. To the left are theater-level support units, including ammunition, fuel, spare parts, and transportation.

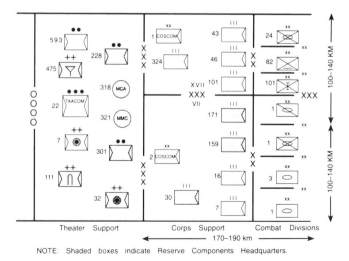

Figure 1. Operation Desert Storm: Kuwait theater of operations, 20 February 1991. (SOURCE: Association of the U.S. Army, 1991b.)

Land Warfare in the 1990s: Operation Desert Storm

States resort to warfare for many reasons: to promote and spread a political or religious ideology; to gain territory for resources and space for a growing population; to protect national interests in another region; and to conquer. In modern parlance, the reasons for going to war are usually expressed in terms of securing national, regional, or other international interests.

A case study can lend understanding to modern land warfare and particularly to its complexity in light of the spread of technology and the availability of sophisticated weapons to adversaries. It can also provide some vision of how wars will be fought in the future. The 1990–91 war in the Persian Gulf, which involved Iraq, the United States, and a coalition of other countries, involved a definable threat to the national interests of several countries; international political, economic, and military cooperation and United Nations legitimacy; the use of strategic assets; definable operational campaigns; and the use of advanced weaponry and systems that had not been proven in combat.

THE STRATEGIC SETTING

Severely strapped for international exchange following an eight-year war with Iran, Iraq pressured Kuwait and other OPEC nations to raise oil prices and to reduce production. It accused the Kuwaitis of digging oil wells on Iraqi territory and extracting more than US$2 billion worth of oil, for which Iraq demanded compensation. Iraq also sought Kuwaiti oil fields near the Iraqi border and demanded a lease of Kuwait islands to gain a seaport on the Persian Gulf.

By late July 1990, Iraq had positioned a large force of troops along the Kuwaiti border. On 2 August, the Iraqi army invaded Kuwait and gained full control of the emirate within one day. That move was promptly condemned by the U.N. Security Council, which demanded the immediate withdrawal of Iraq's forces from Kuwait—a measure that Iraq chose to defy.

By 6 August, with Iraqi forces disposed along the Kuwaiti–Saudi Arabian border and postured for a possible attack on Saudi Arabia, the United Nations authorized worldwide economic sanctions against Iraq. Saudi Arabia, fearing imminent attack, requested assistance in defense of Saudi territory. Thereafter, support from the United States and many other countries moved at a rapid pace. The United States deployed land, air, and sea forces to the Persian Gulf region to deter or defend against an Iraqi invasion of Saudi Arabia. On 7 August, Operation Desert Shield officially began. A 2,300-man contingent of the U.S. Army's 82d Airborne Division immediately deployed by air. On 8 August, Iraq publicly annexed Kuwait and declared it a province of Iraq. The U.N. Security Council took positive and immediate action by approving a resolution that demanded unconditional and immediate withdrawal of Iraq's army.

OPERATION DESERT SHIELD

The national security objectives of Operation Desert Shield as outlined by the American president were:

- to protect the lives of American citizens
- to deter and, if necessary, repel further Iraqi aggression
- to effect the immediate, complete, and unconditional withdrawal of all Iraqi forces from Kuwait
- to restore the legitimate government of Kuwait.

Rapid deployment of forces from all the services proceeded. The first requirement was to deter any further encroachment by Iraqi forces. U.S. naval forces in the region were reinforced and tactical air forces were moved to the theater of operations. Additional mobile light ground forces, including Marine elements and the balance of the 82d Airborne Division, were also moved to the region. Troops of air assault and heavier armored and mechanized divisions, as well as air defense and corps support units, were airlifted to the Gulf, while combat equipment followed in the largest sealift of combat forces since World War II. To provide required combat and combat service support, units from the reserve components of all services were called to active duty. Also, equipment on pre-positioned ships deployed to the region.

Thirty-seven nations sent military forces or medical teams to the region. Ten nations pledged more than US$50 billion to defray the costs of the operation.

All U.S. forces deployed in Desert Shield came under the command of the commander in chief of U.S. Central Command (USCENTCOM). USCENTCOM operated with the Saudi Joint Forces commander through a Coordination and Communications Center. Initially, British forces were under U.S. operational control and French forces under Saudi control.

Arab and coalition forces were initially positioned behind the Saudi task forces arrayed along the Saudi–Kuwaiti border. The forces that were deployed by air were in place in the first weeks of August; the others arrived in increments through October. The major pacing factor for subsequent movements was the availability of airlift and sealift, with the equipment moving by sea and the troops flying to Saudi Arabia in time to marry up with their equipment. By early November, there was sufficient combat capability to provide an effective defense of Saudi Arabia.

Iraq continued to build its forces in the Kuwaiti theater to more than 400,000 troops, to include mass construction of hardened bunkers, tank traps, minefields, and miles of earthen walls to reinforce positions along the frontier of Saudi Arabia. On 8 November, it was decided to develop an offensive capability with sufficient combat power to force the Iraqis out of Kuwait. At that point, the U.S. VII Corps from Europe and armored, mechanized, and support units from the United States were ordered to deploy, and the call-up of additional reserve units of all services was started. Toward the end of November, these units began to move, reaching full combat readiness in Saudi Arabia by early February.

In the first 80 days, more than 170,000 people and more than 160,000 tons of cargo were moved to Saudi Arabia by air from the United States. More than 7,500,000 square feet of cargo and equipment were moved by sea. By the time the coalition forces began the offensive on 17 January 1991, the United States had shipped some 460,000 tons of ammunition, 300,000 desert camouflage uniforms, 200,000 tires, and 150 million military meals to sustain the 540,000 soldiers, sailors, airmen, and marines deployed.

OPERATION DESERT STORM

The United Nations established a deadline of 15 January for Iraq to withdraw its forces from Kuwait and authorized member nations to employ all necessary means to evict them if they did not withdraw. The Iraqis did not withdraw by the deadline. On 17 January 1991, Operation Desert Shield became Operation Desert Storm when the coalition initiated combat operations.

The initial phase, the air campaign, was intensive. The coalition forces employed its air resources—including armed helicopters, cruise missiles, and at least eighteen types of land- and sea-based aircraft—to maximum advantage. Electronic jammers, sophisticated sensors, night-vision devices, and precision bombing technology destroyed Iraq's strategic capability.

Coalition air superiority was achieved early in the operation. The campaign was directed against Iraqi ground forces facing coalition units across the Kuwaiti–Saudi Arabian border. Thousands of sorties were flown each day, attacking targets of military importance such as missile sites; command and control centers; telecommunications facilities; power-generating plants; airfields and runways; aircraft storage shelters; bridges; Iraqi troop positions; and chemical, biological, and nuclear weapon development and production facilities. Air sorties against Iraqi military targets were conducted by U.S., Saudi, Kuwaiti, British, French, Canadian, Bahraini, Qatari, and Italian forces. The air and sea offensive continued for 38 days with a constant, around-the-clock bombardment that brought the war to Iraq.

Despite the high priority given to locating and destroying Iraqi Scud ballistic missile launchers, missile attacks continued throughout the period, although in decreasing numbers. The Scuds were intended as terror weapons against civilian targets and were never a serious military threat. U.S. Army Patriot missiles were used for the first time to defeat other missiles in a combat situation.

THE GROUND WAR

Two corps of more than 200,000 troops and thousands of tons of equipment started moving to the western part of Saudi Arabia on 17 January under the cover of air, sea, and artillery bombardments. Repositioning for a ground attack into Iraq and Kuwait was under way.

Sufficient fuel, ammunition, spare parts, water, and food were moved as much as 300 miles to establish a 60-day supply in preparation for the coming ground offensive. Special Forces teams were inserted deep into Iraq to perform strategic reconnaissance and to report on troop movements. By 16 February, American and coalition forces were in positions spanning a distance of more than 300 miles along the Saudi border.

Throughout this phase of the war, numerous feints, probes, and mock attacks were conducted by various elements of the coalition forces. On several occasions, the navy and marines rehearsed invasions from the sea and throughout maintained a large presence in Gulf waters off the shores of Kuwait. The American and coalition land forces executed reconnaissance missions all along the fortified borders of Kuwait and Iraq. By concentrating their forces along the southern Kuwaiti border and by fortifying the beaches east of Kuwait City, the Iraqis made it clear that they expected a headlong attack into their most heavily fortified areas.

By mid-February, the emphasis of the air campaign was clearly shifting to inflict maximum damage on Iraqi troop formations and defensive positions, softening them for the pending ground attack. By now, the U.S. Army had more than 250,000 troops in the Persian Gulf area. Its combat elements were poised for the attack.

At 4:00 A.M. (Gulf time), 24 February 1991, the coalition forces launched the largest successful ground campaign since World War II. Along a 300-mile front, they rolled into Kuwait and Iraq to engage the world's fourth largest army. One hundred hours later, on 28 February, the coalition declared a temporary cease-fire.

Having maneuvered over 300 miles westward to reposition ground forces composed of two corps for the attack into Iraq and Kuwait, U.S. and coalition forces were positioned as portrayed in Figure 2. XVIII Corps included the 82d Airborne and 101st Airborne divisions, 3d Armored Cavalry Regiment, the 24th Infantry Division (Mechanized), and the French 6th Light Armored Division. Further east, VII Corps included the 1st and 3d Armored divisions, the 2d Armored Cavalry Regiment, and the British 1st Armored Division. Near the confluence of the Saudi-Iraqi-Kuwaiti borders were the 1st Infantry Division (Mechanized) and the 1st Cavalry Division. To their right was a pan-Arab force consisting of Saudi, Kuwaiti, Egyptian, and Syrian units at the western edge of the Saudi-Kuwaiti border. The 2d Marine Division and a brigade of the 2d Armored Division were positioned to the east of the pan-Arab force; the 1st Marine Division anchored the right flank. Two additional Saudi task forces were prepared to advance up the Persian Gulf coast, while marines of the 4th and 5th Expeditionary brigades were poised for amphibious operations off the Kuwaiti coast. Earlier, a number of Special Forces teams had been inserted deep in Iraq to track enemy movements and especially to locate Scud missile sites.

The ground war started with two simultaneous attacks: one in the east, where pan-Arab forces and U.S. Marines breached the first line of Iraqi defenses and drove up the coast toward Kuwait City, and the other, 300 miles west, consisted of the French 6th Light Armored Division and one brigade of the 82d Airborne Division attacking 90 miles into Iraq to seize the airfield at Salman and establish a security screen for the western flank. At the same time, the marines in the Gulf, aided by intense naval gunfire, feinted an assault against Iraqi forces dug in along Kuwait's coast. Similarly, two brigades of the 1st Cavalry Division attacked about a dozen miles up the Wadi al Batin against sporadic resistance.

At 8:00 A.M., 23 February, the 101st Airborne Division launched the largest air assault operation in military history more than 70 miles into Iraq and then

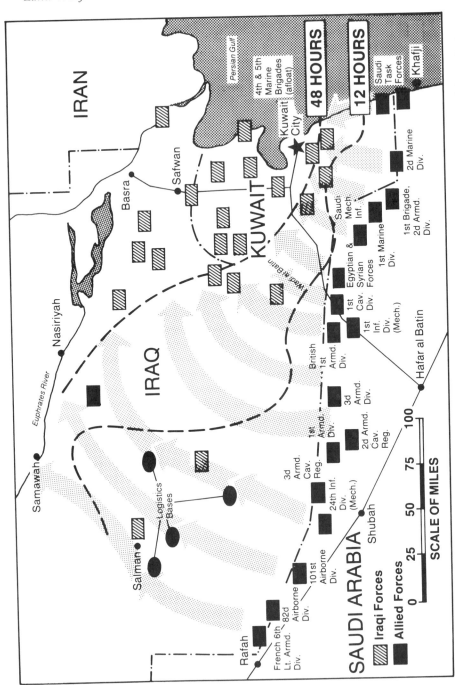

Figure 2. Operation Desert Storm: U.S. and coalition ground forces positioned for attack. (SOURCE: Association of the U.S. Army, 1991b.)

continued the attack to the Euphrates River. That afternoon, the 3d Armored Cavalry Regiment and the 24th Infantry Division (Mechanized) attacked north into Iraq.

In VII Corps's sector, the 1st Infantry Division breached Iraqi defensive positions and attacked north, followed by the British 1st Armored Division. The 2d Armored Cavalry Regiment and the 1st and 3d Armored divisions attacked rapidly, bypassing hundreds of enemy positions. Along the coast, Saudi-led coalition forces breached defensive barriers and joined the marines in the attack on Kuwait City. By the end of 24 February, all major coalition forces were engaged.

On 26 February, elements of the XVIII Airborne Corps and VII Corps maneuvered to the east to trap and destroy what was left of the Iraqi forces. Having driven almost 100 miles into Iraq, the 24th Infantry Division and the 3d Armored Cavalry Regiment turned toward Basra to cut off retreating Iraqi forces. VII Corps units turned east to attack the Iraqi reserve. During the night, VII Corps, which now included the 1st Cavalry Division, conducted a coordinated attack and destroyed two Iraqi divisions. The 1st and 2d Marine divisions also reached the outskirts of Kuwait City and fought for control of the international airport.

On 27 February, Kuwait was liberated. By the time a suspension of offensive combat operations was declared (at 8:00 A.M., 28 February 1991, Gulf time), U.S. and coalition forces had destroyed or rendered ineffective 43 Iraqi divisions, captured more than 80,000 prisoners, and destroyed or damaged 4,000 tanks, 2,100 artillery pieces, 1,800 armored personnel carriers, 7 helicopters, and 103 Iraqi aircraft.

The United Nations worked out the details of the formal cease-fire agreement, which was accepted by Iraq on 6 April and proclaimed on 10 April. Included in the U.N. action was the authorization of a 1,440-member observer team to oversee a newly created demilitarized zone (DMZ) between Kuwait and Iraq. Operation Desert Storm, preceded by Operation Desert Shield, became Operation Provide Comfort as some 13,000 coalition military personnel—including about 9,000 U.S. troops—turned their attention to giving food, shelter, and medical care to the refugees.

As U.S. and coalition forces redeployed, their troops in the DMZ were relieved by U.N. forces; the refugee support effort in the south was accepted by the Saudis. In the north, Operation Provide Comfort—support for the Kurdish refugees, much of which was rendered through Turkey—became the responsibility of the U.S. European Command.

Desert Shield and Desert Storm were the largest operational tests of modern military forces and doctrine since World War II.

The Future of Land Warfare

Land warfare, as the Desert Shield and Desert Storm operations indicate, involves the coordinated use of all military resources at a nation's disposal to achieve specific national objectives. The strategic, operational, and tactical settings of land warfare are shaped by airpower and sea power. Once strategically deployed and operationally positioned, the land power component is charged with carrying the fight to the enemy land forces and dislodging them from the area of contention. Throughout, airpower and sea power continue to play a major role in maintaining supremacy in the skies and on the seas.

Ancient and medieval history and the technological impact of the industrial, atomic, and electronic ages have forged today's military doctrine. Operation Desert Storm reconfirmed many of the principles of war and provided some vision of land wars yet to be fought. Some of the parameters of future land warfare might be as follows:

- Early deployment of military forces, particularly land forces, to the area of contention is the clearest signal of national resolve in a crisis. An accompanying clear statement of the purpose and objectives of the military operation provides a framework for strategic and operational planning and judicious use of national resources.
- Developing nations have access to sophisticated, high-tech weaponry and, especially in the face of overwhelming opposing forces, are prepared to employ them to achieve national goals and resolve disputes with neighbors.
- Land forces are the major military resource of most countries. Therefore, nations will continue to use land warfare as the predominant instrument of military force, particularly at lower levels of conflict.
- A vast array of sensors is now available to detect, locate, and engage targets. Future land warfare may see most enemy capabilities engaged and rendered ineffective long before they can be maneuvered and employed.
- Operational doctrine will be broadened to more thoroughly encompass activities short of war, such as peacekeeping, refugee support and security, and environmental disaster relief.
- The interdependence of nations' interests and the number of nations with sophisticated armed forces point toward greater use of limited, multinational coalitions in future land wars. Temporary, opposing regional coalitions and more permanent international forces will probably be necessary to pool limited and complementary resources to mount a military operation.
- The accuracy and lethality of weapons available to opposing military forces will continue to improve. Successful and economical employment of these expensive and sophisticated weapons will depend on the skill of the individuals and crews that employ them. While modern technology will provide "smart weapons," simplicity of use will drive their success in battle engagements.

JAMES D. BLUNDELL

SEE ALSO: Airborne Land Forces; Armor; Army Aviation; Artillery; Close Air Support; Coalition Warfare; Combined Arms; Conventional War; Envelopment; Firepower; Infantry; Limited War; Low-intensity Conflict: The Military Dimension; Maneuver; Mechanized Warfare; Principles of War; Tactics; Tank.

Bibliography

Association of the U.S. Army. 1991a. *The U.S. Army in Operation Desert Storm: An overview.* Arlington, Va.: AUSA Institute of Land Warfare.
————. 1991b. *Operations Desert Shield and Desert Storm: The logistics perspective.* Arlington, Va.: AUSA Institute of Land Warfare.
Bellamy, C. 1987. *The future of land warfare.* New York: St. Martin's Press.
Gabriel, R. A. 1990. *The culture of war: Invention and early development.* Westport, Conn.: Greenwood Press.
Garden, T. 1989. *The technology trap: Science and the military.* London: Brassey's.
Jones, A. 1987. *The art of war in the western world.* Oxford: Oxford Univ. Press.
Kendall, P. 1957. *The story of land warfare.* Westport, Conn.: Greenwood Press.
Liddell Hart, B. H. 1991. *Strategy.* New York: Penguin Books.
Macksey, K. 1973. *The Guinness history of land warfare.* Enfield, England: Guinness Superlatives.
U.S. Department of the Army. 1986. *Field manual 100-5: Operations.* Washington, D.C.: Government Printing Office.

LEADERSHIP

Leadership may be defined simply as the process of influencing others. Given the indispensable role of leadership in all cultures throughout history, people have long sought to understand what makes some leaders more effective than others. Nevertheless, the "secret" of good leadership continues to elude explanation.

Part of the difficulty lies in the variety of influence processes that may be called leadership. Valuable insights about political leaders might have no relevance to a gang leader organizing fellow prisoners; a leadership technique that works for the minister of a church might fail for an environmental activist. Yet, all these people are leaders.

This article deals specifically with organizational leadership, since a focused discussion may permit more precise conclusions about the essential nature of leadership.

Organizational leadership is the process of influencing human behavior to accomplish the organization's goals. This definition can apply to any organization including the military. An organizational leader is appointed by the organization and is not necessarily the same person who would emerge from the group as the group's leader or who might be elected by the subordinates.

Leadership and Management

The difference between leadership and management has been discussed at great length. The continuing debate is fueled in part by cultural biases about the meaning of these words that favor "leaders" over "managers." The word *leadership* conjures mental images of a charismatic and visionary war hero, while the word *management* implies a desk-ridden planner, and we constantly hear pleas for more leaders and fewer managers.

Yet leadership appears to be a subset of management. Leadership concerns interpersonal influence processes; management refers to the coordination and application of all resources, including people. A successful military leader must practice both management and leadership. A useful discussion will examine the difference between the skills of leadership and management, which are not inherent in character or personality but instead can be learned. Soviet marshal Georgi Zhukov noted that commanding troops "embraces a wide range of military-political, moral, material, and psychological factors" and that study of all of these factors is critical to success.

Approaches to Leadership

The notion that inherent character attributes enhance leadership potential led British field marshal Sir Archibald P. Wavell to conclude that "no amount of learning will make a man a leader unless he has the natural qualities of one." These traits have been the subject of considerable study and speculation. The most often cited characteristics include physical and moral courage, integrity, loyalty, dependability, ambition, unselfishness, enthusiasm, intelligence, endurance, initiative, self-discipline, tact, and physical attractiveness. Yet there are effective leaders who lack many of these traits and ineffective leaders who have these traits in abundance. There are many glaring exceptions to anyone's list of necessary leader characteristics: Napoleon was short, American Civil War general James Longstreet graduated near the bottom of his West Point class, Alexander the Great killed his best friend in a fit of drunken rage, and Adm. Ernest J. King had an extremely abrasive personality. Yet all these men were extraordinarily effective military leaders.

Noting this incongruity, social scientists have criticized the historically based studies of leadership, arguing that a complete picture cannot be gained merely by cataloging the characteristics of the leader. Applying the scientific method of inquiry, they have attempted to capture leadership in the form of testable, supportable principles. Greatly influenced by behavioral psychology, they have sought to understand not what an effective leader *is* but what an effective leader *does*.

Patterns of leader behaviors frequently are referred to as leadership "styles." The most-often discussed leadership styles are "task oriented" and "people oriented." A leader using a task-oriented style tends to structure his and the subordinates' roles toward accomplishment of the mission, often making decisions for the group. A leader using a people-oriented style is friendly and supportive, listens to subordinates, and may also seek their input. These behaviors are not mutually exclusive opposites; in fact, leaders frequently have a capacity for displaying varying degrees of both styles simultaneously.

Some leadership theorists have argued that the "one best style" of leadership is that in which the leader demonstrates high degrees of both styles simultaneously (Yukl 1989). Unfortunately, evidence to support this claim has been scarce. While it has been generally demonstrated that people-oriented behaviors consistently improve subordinates' satisfaction, neither style, nor any combination of the two, can generate group productivity or effectiveness.

Still, even a thorough understanding of what the leader is (through characteristics or traits) and what the leader does (through observable behaviors) does not give a complete picture of leadership. Recent leadership theories have included "situational" variables such as the task, the subordinates, and the effect of the external environment.

These situational theories and models of leadership suggest that effective leader behavior depends on such factors as how difficult or routine the task is, how motivated the subordinates are, and how well prepared they are to accomplish the task. For instance, a highly effective drill instructor might fail miserably if he uses the same repertoire of behaviors to organize a battalion picnic that proved so successful in pushing soldiers through the obstacle course. For an effective leader, then, the question is not which style or behaviors to use, but under what circumstances to employ certain leader behaviors.

Subordinate Reactions to Leadership

Leadership is a process of interpersonal interaction; therefore, it is imperative to understand how the subordinates perceive themselves, their task, and their leader. Changing a soldier's behavior is relatively easy; military leaders are generally imbued with enough power and authority to get subordinates to comply with the leaders' orders to avoid punishment or to obtain status, promotion, recognition, and so forth. But is compliance enough? Xenophon noted 2,300 years ago that "willing obedience always beats forced obedience." Obviously, if the subordinates are committed to the leader or the mission, the likelihood of success increases. Therefore, an effective leader wants to do more than change behaviors; he wants to change attitudes. As General Eisenhower put it, "I would rather try to persuade a man to go along, because once I have persuaded him, he will stick. If I scare him, he will stay just as long as he is scared, and then he is gone."

Recent theories of "transformational" leadership attempt to understand how leaders induce followers to move beyond mere compliance. These theories suggest that the best leaders are able to persuade their followers to transcend basic selfish needs and emotions, often by articulating a vision and setting an example that appeals to higher values such as liberty, justice, fraternity, patriotism, or equality. Subordinates' reactions to a leader's attempt to influence them depend on whether they perceive the leader to be relying on position power or personal power.

Position power is a function of the leader's ability to issue rewards and punishments due to the leader's role-vested authority in the organizational hierarchy; more simply, it is the expectation that the leader will be obeyed because he, by virtue of his rank, can demand obedience. Such power is not limited to a military commander's authority to convene a court-martial or award a medal. For instance, Alexander the Great graciously rewarded his victorious soldiers with extended leaves and a general cancellation of debts. The Vietcong lacked the resources of either Alexander or their American foe. However, relying upon the importance to fellow soldiers of recognition and esteem, they frequently punished itinerants through *kiem thao*, public group criticism. During the 1990–1991 occupation of Kuwait, Iraqi leaders became increasingly reliant on the threat of summary executions for any soldiers who attempted to desert their positions.

Unlike position power, *personal power* is not a derivative of the leader's rank or position. Personal power is based on the leader's expertise or skill as well as the leader's ability to cultivate the trust, respect, and admiration of the followers. The word *charismatic* is frequently applied to a leader who is able to influence followers with some set of personal characteristics or behaviors, although there is still much debate about exactly what charisma is and whether leaders can consciously develop it.

Marshal Aleksandr Suvorov, the founder of the modern Russian Army, displayed tremendous personal power. To the consternation of his fellow officers, Suvorov talked, ate, and slept with his soldiers. In the eighteenth-century Russian Army, few officers were willing to talk to the common soldier, even if they could (since most officers had been raised to speak French rather than Russian). As a result, Suvorov quickly endeared himself to the Russian soldiers; his lifetime of brilliant campaign successes was ample testimony to his soldiers' dedication.

The Israeli Defense Forces (IDF) have institutionalized a unique model for ensuring that leaders have personal power. Unlike most of the world's military organizations, the IDF promotes leaders only "from the ranks." Hence, the leader at any level—squad, platoon, regiment—is the best soldier in that unit. Furthermore, the basic tenet of leadership for an Israeli leader is to lead from the front, which may help account for the enormous respect that the Israeli soldiers almost always have for their leaders (as well as the extremely high casualty rates among officers and NCOs).

Position power and personal power elicit different responses from subordinates. Leaders may depend on position power to get public compliance to their influence. At least while they are supervised, subordinates will behave so as to avoid punishment or gain reward. This type of influence is good only as long as the leadership can supervise and sanction, for the soldiers' hearts will not be in the mission. Many of the Iraqi soldiers who carried out their duties during the 1991 Gulf War only under the threat of execution surrendered after offering only brief token resistance to the multinational force confronting them.

If the leader has personal power, followers are more likely to trust and accept that leader's influence, either because the leader knows best or because the subordinates identify with the leader. In such cases, the subordinates will surpass mere compliance—they will be committed to achieving the organization's goal. Consider the esteem that the Confederate soldiers of the American Civil War had for their commander Gen. Robert E. Lee. The Confederate soldiers' attachment to their commander in chief was nowhere more evident than at the battle of Spotsylvania Courthouse, where a Union attack threatened to overwhelm the Confederate position. General Lee, sensing the precarious situation, rode forward to personally lead a desperate counterattack. The distraught Confederate soldiers, fearing for their commander's safety, shouted,

"General Lee to the rear!" Lee relented, and the counterattack went forward without him.

One method of gaining commitment is ensuring the followers understand and believe in what they are doing. Gen. George Washington considered it essential that leaders "impress upon the mind of every man, from the first to the lowest, the importance of the cause and what it is they are contending for." Mao Tse-tung also considered the commitment of his followers essential. When he found that his soldiers' lack of education was hindering his ability to convey his vision of a Communist China, Mao had women wear placards of Chinese characters on their backs. While his Army marched, many soldiers in the column would eventually memorize enough to be able to read and write. The former Soviet army's reliance on the *zampolit* (political officer) is, at least in part, a recognition of how imperative it is that soldiers understand *why* they serve, fight, and die.

Cultural Differences in Leadership

Societal or cultural background frequently dictates the nature of the relationship between leader and follower. The relative importance of status between leaders and followers may vary from culture to culture. Many countries have an entrenched class system that closely parallels the social status of different ranks. (For example, in certain traditional European models, officership is the prerogative of the privileged class.) In countries such as North Korea, a harsh totalitarian political system socializes people to willingly submit to the authority of the leader. In the armies of these societies, subordinates are often less likely to respond effectively to a democratic or participative leader style.

In a culture with a high level of collectivism, the leader is more capable of transcending subordinate self-interest for the good of the organization. The fearsome Mangoday of Genghis Khan's army turned the tide of pitched battles with their shocking suicidal tactics. More recently, Japanese kamikaze pilots in World War II willingly went to their certain deaths to fulfill the ultimate warrior ethic.

Leaders must understand and accept cultural differences when working with a different culture's military organization. For instance, to the credit of Baron von Steuben, this professional Prussian officer did not attempt to shape the young Continental American army to mimic the European conscript armies of the time. Frederick the Great had a highly proficient system of discipline based on the notion that the troops needed to fear their leaders more than they feared the enemy. Von Steuben, however, had to adjust his training after noting that American conscripts expected to be treated with much more dignity than their European counterparts, had a zeal for individualism, and wanted to know what they were fighting for.

Leaders in Action

It is dangerous to draw conclusions about effective leadership solely on anecdotes and historical snapshots of successful leaders. The most obvious limitation is that examples can be found to support any and every belief about what makes an effective leader, so such examples can prove nothing. Also, historical examples are generally available only for the leadership of successful high-level wartime combat commanders; the leadership stories of lower-ranking leaders are less frequently available. There is also less information available about successful leadership back from the action of the front line. Little is known about the many excellent NCOs and officers who died doing their job, never having the chance to become famous and merit biographical recognition. Nevertheless, these examples can illustrate and help give context to what might otherwise be a rather theoretical and unexciting discussion.

It is virtually a prerequisite for any discussion of successful combat leadership to document heroic leadership in battle, but setting the example through selfless sacrifice can also be demonstrated away from the battlefield. While commander of a tank brigade in World War I, Col. George S. Patton, Jr., was observing 37mm gun practice. A round exploded in one gun's muzzle, wounding some soldiers. The next round fired from this gun exploded in the breech, killing the gunner. Fearing that the troops would lose confidence in their equipment, Colonel Patton went to the gun and personally fired the next three rounds without incident.

Effective leaders also must possess and demonstrate tactical and technical expertise. Followers are much more likely to respond favorably to a leader who will win battles and keep soldiers alive. Field Marshal Erwin Rommel distinguished himself as one of Germany's finest small-unit leaders on the French, Italian, and Romanian fronts in World War I. When he captured his lessons in the 1937 book *Infantrie Greift an* (Infantry Attacks), his demonstrated tactical genius caught the eye of the German leadership, to include Hitler himself. Rommel's expertise was genuine; in combat from 1940 until his death in 1944, he built a singular reputation that distinguishes him as one of the great military leaders of all time.

Good leaders also establish challenging goals and standards and build effective teams. One of Adm. Ernest King's first leadership challenges as a new ensign was to take over a division of 40 sailors on board the USS *Cincinnati*. Morale was quite low, and the desertion rate was extremely high. King took advantage of an impending gunnery competition to challenge his sailors. The sailors, responding with vigor to King's enthusiasm and self-confidence, won the competition. Morale, cohesion, and pride in King's division soared, and young Ensign King's reputation as a winner was launched.

Effective leaders are in touch with their subordinates. Although the claim is almost certainly exaggerated, Julius Caesar reportedly could recognize every man in his legions by name. During inspections and speeches, Napoleon also showed the ability to single out campaign veterans by name, asking about their families and other personal details (although an adjutant's advance briefing aided his recognition). Good leaders also have sought to understand the concerns of their soldiers. According to Shakespeare, an incognito King Henry V made rounds of the English campfires the night before the battle of Agincourt, seeking to learn the soldiers' thoughts and fears.

Beyond understanding the troops, the effective leader must provide for their well-being. Although this is often interpreted as providing the troops with material comforts, Rommel pointed out that "the best form of 'welfare' for the troops is first-class training, for this saves unnecessary casualties." Taking care of soldiers also means ensuring that they have the support they need to do their job. A young Col. George C. Marshall, as a division operations officer in World War I, discovered that his division's system for publishing orders to lower commands was so slow that the battalions, companies, and platoons of the division seldom had time to conduct a reconnaissance prior to attack time. Marshall directed his staff to send orders over the phone, instead of by messenger. He weighed the increased security risk against the advantage an extra two hours would give subordinate commands in preparing for the next day's operation. Marshall's action demonstrated not only a concern for subordinates, but a willingness to take initiative.

There are many examples of leaders giving inspirational speeches—*Feldherrnrede*—before battle, or at critical moments; Napoleon, always sensitive to the human element of command, noted that "a man does not have himself killed for a few half-pence a day or for a petty distinction. You must speak to the soul in order to electrify the man." Although assembling large bodies of soldiers before battle may now be tactically impractical, modern commanders can take advantage of other means to communicate their confidence and high expectations in soldiers. Gen. H. Norman Schwarzkopf, commander of Allied efforts during the Persian Gulf War, had an inspirational note delivered to each American soldier at the onset of the ground offensive. In this message, Schwarzkopf incited his soldiers to be "the thunder and lightning of Desert Storm."

Leadership Challenges in Future Warfare

Leaders in future wars will be confronted with a proliferation of weapons of mass destruction (nuclear, chemical, and biological); advances in the acquisition capability, lethality, range, and accuracy of weapons systems; sophisticated electronic warfare and counterwarfare measures; increased mobility of weapons systems; and an enhanced capacity to fight at night and in any weather. The increased lethality of warfare and the reduction in military forces due to both economic and political initiatives will disperse military forces on the battlefield more than ever before. Furthermore, as technology has made the "deep" battle a reality, it can no longer be assumed that combat is restricted to a relatively shallow battle zone at the forward edge of the battle area.

It is important for leaders to understand that social dynamics play a critical role: soldiers in imminent danger seek the companionship of fellow soldiers. Such support will be more difficult to ensure on the dispersed battlefield of the future. This isolation will be heightened when soldiers must fight at night or wear nuclear, biological, or chemical protective gear.

Both isolation and uncertainty may be amplified by the loss of communications with other units, a real possibility as battlefield distances increase and electronic warfare is employed. Uncertainty also will be fed by the increased mobility of troop and weapons carriers, which will increase the likelihood of surprise and impel more abrupt shifts on the already fluid battlefield.

The anxiety produced by increased isolation, lack of mental or physical down-time, heightened uncertainty, and reduced reaction time will place a tremendous strain on the individual soldier. The future battlefield leader will have to be able to shield his soldiers from these numbing effects by building a high degree of unit cohesion, which can be strengthened by increasing the soldiers' interaction and communication, establishing unique norms and symbols, creating a sense of unit identity, providing tough challenges that require teamwork to succeed, and rewarding unit success while punishing unit failure.

The future leader also must understand how to manage stress. Redundancy of functions (to include leadership) should be worked into unit training to ensure that every soldier receives adequate rest periods. Soldiers must have the opportunity to interact, to talk about their fears with one another. The unit must be well trained, even overtrained, in peacetime, so that proficient performance becomes a reflex reaction. Furthermore, the more similar the peacetime training conditions are to combat, the greater the likelihood that soldiers will not be overwhelmed by the reality of combat.

There is a relationship between unit cohesion and the ability to withstand stress. During the 1973 October War, Israel reacted to the Arab surprise attack by sending reserve tank crews to the front lines before the units had a chance to organize into their normal combat teams. These tank crews were in combat before they had even met each other. When later compared with organic tank crews, these rapidly assembled units had a profoundly higher rate of stress-related psychiatric casualties (Gal 1986).

Because of the reduced reaction time necessary from more-dispersed forces and the less-reliable communications between them, junior leaders (company-grade officers and NCOs) must be developed and prepared to make independent decisions. On the fluid modern battlefield, it is impossible for a commander to issue specific orders for every possible contingency; subordinates must have the willingness and ability to take action without requesting guidance or permission from headquarters. This philosophy of *Auftragstaktik*, as it was called by the Prussian Army of a century ago, encourages junior leaders to seize the initiative in accordance with their commander's intent. It is unlikely that a leader in combat will suddenly be rendered able to implement *auftragstaktik*, build a cohesive team, and manage stress. These capabilities are best developed before the battle. As a Chinese proverb suggests, "The more you sweat in peace, the less you bleed in war."

Future Trends in Leadership

Leadership theorists have begun to recognize that senior- and junior-level leaders may require different skills. Senior-level leaders must become adept at managing increasingly complex organizational systems. While face-to-face, direct leadership remains important, senior leaders must work through levels of subordinate leaders to influence subordinates indirectly. Thus, necessary leadership skills will not be the same in all levels of an organization. Organizations will have to adapt by ensuring that effective junior leaders receive the additional developmental experiences and training needed to become effective senior leaders.

As technology has flourished, the military increasingly needs better-educated soldiers who can effectively operate complex systems. Furthermore, the current size reductions in many armed forces will make recruitment more selective. As a result, incoming members of the armed forces probably will be better educated than in the past. The soldiers of the future may have different capabilities, needs, and aspirations and will require well-educated and technically competent leadership. Leaders themselves will have to balance competing demands to assume the specialized management functions of a technical leader along with the more traditional roles of troop leadership.

With smaller armed forces and a move toward all-volunteer staffing, the balance between those recruits who view the military as an occupation and those who view it as a profession becomes a key issue for leaders. Those who view the military as a profession would value intangible rewards such as duty, country, sacrifice, or patriotism; those who view it as an occupation would expect financial compensation and a quality of life comparable to that provided by a civilian occupation. Leaders should note that soldiers who subscribe to one model will be motivated by different rewards than those who take the opposite view.

Finally, the moral-ethical dimension of leadership has received increasing attention. Leaders influence their command's ethical climate by the way they administer rewards and punishments, establish goals and competitions, issue guidelines, and manage stress (U.S. Military Academy 1988). When subordinates act unethically, leaders can reasonably be held responsible for the ethical climate that they established or tolerated.

A great deal remains to be learned and understood about the complex phenomenon of military leadership. The significance of good leadership at all levels of a military organization remains clear, however, and leaders can benefit from reflecting on both what is known and what is yet to be known about effective leadership.

KEVIN S. DONOHUE
LEONARD WONG
STEVEN M. JONES

SEE ALSO: Command; Generalship.

Bibliography

Bass, B. M. 1990. *Bass and Stogdill's leadership handbook*. New York: Free Press.

Gal, R. 1986. Unit morale: From a theoretical puzzle to an empirical illustration: An Israeli example. *Journal of Applied Social Psychology* 16:549–64.

Fitton, R. A., ed. 1990. *Leadership: Quotations from the military tradition*. Boulder, Colo.: Westview Press.

Hunt, J. G., and J. D. Blair, eds. 1985. *Leadership on the future battlefield*. McLean, Va.: Pergamon-Brassey's.

Matthews, L. J., and D. E. Brown, eds. 1989. *The challenge of military leadership.* McLean, Va.: Pergamon-Brassey's.

Taylor, R. W., and W. E. Rosenbach, eds. 1984. *Military leadership: In pursuit of excellence.* Boulder, Colo.: Westview Press.

U.S. Department of the Army, 1990. *Field manual 22-100: Military leadership.* Washington, D.C.: Government Printing Office.

U.S. Military Academy, Department of Behavioral Sciences and Leadership. 1988. *Leadership in organizations.* Garden City Park, N.Y.: Avery Press.

Yukl, G. 1989. *Leadership in organizations.* Englewood Cliffs, N.J.: Prentice Hall.

LIMITED WAR

Although the literature on limited war was extensive in the 1950s and 1960s, this does not mean that: (1) no limited wars had been fought before that; (2) theories on limited war were developed in those two decades only; (3) it has been possible to define unequivocally the strategic value of limited war theories, or even that (4) a clear and universally accepted definition of limited war has been found. Usually, however, *limited war* is defined as a war in which neither side seeks the total annihilation of the opponent. Since 1945 this has meant war short of nuclear war.

It is significant that modern limited war theory was developed mainly by British and American scholars. And it is equally significant that each limited war fought by U.S. forces has heavily influenced the evolution of limited war theory. This was true for the Korean War as well as for the Vietnam War. In both cases the United States went to war with a war theory not suitable for the kind of warfare it was going to wage. Hence, that theory had to be developed in the aftermath of those painful experiences. Neither the Korean War nor the Vietnam War were the first or last limited wars fought in the twentieth century. But they were the first wars in the nuclear age fought by a superpower without using nuclear weapons. It has yet to be seen if the Soviet Union will develop a limited war theory of its own after its experience in Afghanistan.

While limited war theory has been greatly elaborated upon during the 1950s, 1960s, and 1970s, ideas about limited war have been included in thoughts about the nature of war throughout recorded history. Fortunately, most wars have been limited in one way or another. The total destruction of Carthage by the Romans is a unique event in history.

Limited wars must not end with the annihilation of the loser; the victor must settle for more limited objectives. As outlined by all theoreticians of limited war, this limitation must be deliberate and consequently must lead to the limitation of means, not only in favor of the loser, but also to achieve an optimum peace at the least possible cost. Limitation in warfare can therefore be viewed as the proof of wisdom in statesmanship and strategic planning. As the Chinese military thinker Sun Tzu said about 500 B.C.: "Generally, in war the best policy is to take a state intact, to ruin it is inferior to this. To capture the enemy's army is better than to destroy it. . . . To subdue the enemy without fighting is the acme of skill." Or, as Sir Basil H. Liddell Hart wrote in 1925 (*The Future of War*): "The aim of a nation in war is, therefore, to subdue the enemy's will to resist, with the least possible human and economic loss to oneself." Warfare during the period between these two historical statements was limited in most cases, but not always deliberately so. Limitation in aims, and more often in means, occurred merely because of a lack of power or technical abilities to achieve the total destruction of the enemy. The Crusades and the Thirty Years' War serve as examples.

Because limitation was not deliberate, and was not chosen as a result of political decision making, there was little development of limited war concepts during those centuries. Only in the eighteenth century were concepts of limited war developed—motivated primarily by the fear of ruining the costly and valuable professional armies of the time.

At the beginning of the nineteenth century, the development of mass armies during the French Revolutionary–Napoleonic wars led to a decline in thinking about limited war. Clausewitz's statement that "war is an act of violence and there is no limitation in using it" was meant to emphasize the necessity for political control and congruence of means and ends in the reality of the political-military process of a war. He showed, in fact, that there is a wide range of limitations on the theoretically unlimited violence of war. This period marks the beginning of the age of total war, leading to the American Civil War and to World Wars I and II. Only a few military thinkers, for example, the Austrian archduke Charles in the nineteenth century and Sir Basil Liddell Hart in the period between the two world wars, tried to argue against *guerre à l'outrance*. However, to many war leaders of the nineteenth and twentieth centuries, the prospect of total victory seemed to be attractive enough to risk total defeat by committing all the resources of the nation in war. Finally, at the end of World War II, the nuclear bomb (the "ultimate weapon," the "weapon to end all wars") seemed to be the solution. The risk of total annihilation should deter all wars and bring peace forever.

Reality destroyed this overly optimistic view within a few years after World War II. Civil and revolutionary wars in China, Indonesia, Greece, the Philippines, Indochina, Nigeria, Malaya; the Kashmir Dispute; the first Arab-Israeli War (1947–49); and eventually the Korean War clearly showed the impossibility of deterring all wars by threatening use of the nuclear bomb. It even proved impossible when a nation in possession of the nuclear bomb was directly involved. This fact, together with the loss of a nuclear monopoly by the United States upon the introduction of nuclear weapons into the Soviet inventory, implying that nuclear deterrence might lead to mutual annihilation, prepared the way for modern limited war theory. A number of military thinkers before the Korean War had foreseen the implicit risks of relying on nuclear weapons to deter or to end a war. Among these was Sir Basil Liddell Hart, who as early as March 1946 expressed his hope that "international agreement will recognize the great destructive power of new weapons and lay down rules for limiting their use." Similar thoughts about the limitation of warfare were aired by a number of strategists such as Brodie, Kissinger, Osgood, and Halperin. Most of them had two main concerns: how to avoid the escalation of a local conventional war into an all-out nuclear war between the two superpowers and how to contain the expansion of communism. Different ideas on how to solve these two interrelated problems were the basis for the theory of limited war, which is more a set of ideas than a single formulated theory.

Meaning of Limited War

The basis for the modern limited war theory is the maxim expressed by Clausewitz that war is not an end in itself, but an instrument of policy. Since a policy leading to mutual destruction is inconceivable, wars in the nuclear age must be limited, at least when nuclear powers are involved or might become involved. In general, there are three fields of limitation: limitation of objectives, limitation of means, and limitation of scope.

LIMITATION OF OBJECTIVES

Limitation of objectives is the first and most important feature of limited war. Objectives form the basis for national policy and must be supported by the national will and the resources of the nation. Only if the objectives are limited can the war itself be kept limited. The limitation of objectives must be deliberate; it must guide, as well as be guided by, policy and not by the mere inability to seek unlimited objectives.

The Second World War was an unlimited war because it was fought for an unlimited objective (i.e., unconditional surrender of the Third Reich and Japan). Vietnam was a limited war because the United States had limited objectives: to repulse the North Vietnamese aggression and to foster the survival of South Vietnam. In practice, limiting objectives means a willingness to settle for a negotiated peace and to accept a compromise, an outcome only partly satisfactory. Clausewitz's classic definition that the object of war is to impose one's will upon the enemy must be constrained. The object of a limited war must be a better peace (Liddell Hart 1967).

LIMITATION OF MEANS

Directly connected with the limitation of objectives, and generally the most obvious limitation, is the limitation of means. While limitation of objectives might not be apparent, or might not be believable to the adversary, restraints in using force are easy to recognize and to prove. Again, restraints must be deliberate and not motivated only by the lack of means. They must also be massive. A small margin of limitation is not enough to make a war limited. World War II serves as an example. Despite the fact that chemical weapons, while available to both sides, were not used, one can hardly call this war limited. Since all the resources and all the forces of the nations involved were brought to bear, the nonuse of one single kind of weaponry did not make any difference.

Limitation of means has two aspects: one political-economic, the other military-technological. If a nation at war is dedicating all political and economic efforts to the single purpose of fighting (and winning) the war, one can hardly speak of a limitation of means. Limitation of means in this respect only occurs if the state is able to maintain its normal political and economic activities—at least to some extent. The Falklands/Malvinas campaign is a case in point.

The military-technological aspect of the limitation of means is more difficult to define. The question whether the term *limited war* can be used for a war with nuclear weapons has been discussed at great length. In his first book on the subject, *Nuclear Weapons and Foreign Policy* (1957), Kissinger presented the case for a limited nuclear war strategy. Others have rejected this idea. Nonetheless, there is as yet no consensus as to the extent (weapons yields or selection of targets) to which the use of nuclear weapons can be "allowed" within a limited war. Even a concept for a limited strategic war, with the possible use of strategic nuclear weapons against military and selected civil targets was conceived. The only limitation suggested in this case was to avoid massive strategic bombing of cities with nuclear weapons. This is the basis for the only definition of limited war on which all theorists are agreed: Limited war is a war short of strategic war with bombing of cities. The majority of scholars, however, have also agreed that a limited war must not include any strategic nuclear exchanges between the United States and the Soviet Union. This provision is one of the rationales for the strategy of flexible response adopted by the North Atlantic Treaty Organization (NATO). Below this threshold there is a second distinct borderline, perhaps the most significant distinction between limited and total war: the use or nonuse of any nuclear weapons. On the one hand, it has been widely argued that this might be the most important constraint in keeping a war limited. On the other hand, this position has been challenged with the argument that the effects of properly targeted small-yield nuclear weapons do not exceed the effects of conventional weapons; therefore, their use would not make any difference. The difference, according to this argument, lies in the targeting policy. The basic criterion would be to not target civilian assets or targets on the home territory of a nuclear power.

LIMITATION OF SCOPE

Limitation of the geographic scope has always occurred in warfare and will probably occur in the future. While both world wars were fought worldwide, they were not waged everywhere. If the term *geographically limited war* is to make sense, the war must be restricted to only a part of the territories of the belligerents. Again, this limitation should be deliberate and massive, as it was in the Falklands/Malvinas War.

The second possibility for a limitation of scope is the number of states involved in a war. Thus, the only really unlimited war would be a real world war, but neither of the world wars fought so far, nor any conceivable in the future, has included all nations.

This consideration has led to the suggestion that the term *local war* should be used for wars in a limited area or with a limited number of belligerents, not including one of the superpowers. This might make sense from the point of view of a superpower, but it seems that the rules for, and the problems of, limited warfare also apply to most local wars.

There are no generally accepted delineations among the kinds of wars discussed above. Most likely there are no clear-cut boundaries either, and thus the nature of these wars might change during the course of a war. Further clarification of this issue could be one of the future tasks of limited war theory.

Problems of Limited Warfare

The basic and most important problem of limited warfare is keeping the war within the limits envisaged. This normally cannot be done by unilateral declaration or behavior. Furthermore, sovereign states sometimes find it difficult to settle for limited objectives in a war; to fight with limited means; and to adhere to these limitations subject to the pressures of public opinion, unexpected enemy moves, and an unfavorable course of the war. The momentum of the war itself might endanger the self-imposed bounds.

Obviously, there is an absolute requirement for communication or agreement between the adversaries, a clear and understandable explanation of purposes and objectives to the public, and tight political control of the military side of the war.

Communication between the belligerents can be open or tacit. Its purpose is—explicitly or implicitly—to come to an agreement on limits and rules of conflict. As Thomas Schelling (1963) has suggested, a kind of "bargaining" might take place. One side may declare limits or indicate by its behavior that it would not go beyond certain limits (e.g., by not using all means at hand or by leaving some sanctuaries to the forces of the adversary). The enemy, when accepting these limits, may reciprocate by open agreement or abstentions on his part. In case of disagreement, the enemy may answer by letting the war become more violent and less restrained. This kind of mutual, deliberate escalation can be regarded as "tacit bargaining" and may go on until a level of warfare has been reached that both sides regard as an equilibrium between the "costs" and the possible benefits of the war.

The problem is that both sides must understand the messages of their adversaries and must have the desire to observe the "rules." Otherwise, escalation might easily get out of control and lead to disaster. As Schelling (1963) pointed out, competitive escalation in a war has some similarities with the "chicken" game played by teenagers in the United States. In this game two cars are driven toward each other at top speed, both astride the centerline of the road. The first driver to pull over "chickens out" and loses the game. Obviously in this game, as well as in an escalation process, success is with the player willing to run higher risks. Dangerous and apparently insane as this behavior is, Schelling has correctly stressed its essential rationality, since one's objectives might be achieved in this way.

Successful escalation (i.e., an escalation that leads to an accepted level of conflict short of an intolerable level of war) is only conceivable if the objectives are not intolerable either. This again demonstrates the close interrelation between objectives and means in limited war.

Limiting the means between adversaries of comparable strength is only possible if limited objectives are pursued. Goals short of victory are not easily explained to the public. They are a kind of negative goal (e.g., not to lose a country to communism or to defend freedom). Hence these objectives are often put into question. Doubts may arise as to whether or not the objectives are worth fighting a war for or allocating the resources and means necessary for that kind of war. In a limited war, both political and public interest are not necessarily focused on the war at all times. Therefore, ongoing international relations as well as domestic politics have considerable bearing on its conduct. As happened in the Vietnam War, this influence might lead to the complete abandonment of the initial objectives of the war.

Yet the decision-making process during the war may be swayed in the other direction, to abandon limited objectives and to increase the violence and the pace of the war. As history suggests, any society has a certain level of tolerance it can accept in a war. Beyond that level, a society is tempted to risk everything in order to gain total victory or to avoid total defeat. This threshold is different for each society and for each war. It is influenced by ideology and religion, by the internal structure of the society, and by the actual course of the war.

The notion that it might be possible to gain much more with just a little more effort may cause the incentive to override any restrictions. This may also be caused by the opposite perception. A belligerent who believes that he has been driven back against a wall might try to cope with his problem by escalating the war into an all-out war. Hence, both approaches need to be avoided. Neither total victory nor total defeat should be perceived as possible by any of the opponents. This requires continual monitoring and reassessment of the status of the war, and a continual effort to keep the delicate balance of justifiable limited objectives and means, both in the eyes of one's own public and in the perception of the enemy.

The same kind of monitoring and reassessment is necessary to prevent the war from gaining too much momentum. As Clemenceau said: "War is too serious to leave to the generals." An example commonly cited is the Korean War and the argument between President Truman and General MacArthur ("There is no substitute for victory.") over the future course of the war that eventually led to MacArthur's dismissal. But it is not always the generals who press for unlimited objectives. Halperin (1963) cited a Republican minority report to the U.S. Congress issued after the MacArthur hearings: "Our policy must be to win. Our strategy must be devised to bring about decisive victory."

Another problem in limited warfare is caused by third-party involvement. While it might be easy to limit objectives, means, or scope as long as the war is only between two opponents, things become more complex with each additional adversary that gets involved in the war. This not only automatically enlarges the scope of the war, it could heavily influence efforts to keep objectives and means limited. Third-party involvement may be directly military, or it could be in the form of political, economic, or logistic support. In any case, the objectives of the third party must be taken into account and will influence the process of decision making. The more important the involvement of the third power, the more influence it will have on the real decisions (its influence may become greater than that of the original belligerents), thus possibly leading to a slow erosion and finally elimination of limitation in the war. Coalition warfare, difficult enough in unlimited wars, demands the utmost of statesmanship in limited wars.

Third-party involvement may work in the other direction as well. As McClintock (1967) observed, "Another characteristic of twentieth-century limited war is the fact that international organization has played an important role, either in settling these armed conflicts or as serving as a useful palliative and sally port of belligerents in need of saving face." More than that, third parties (international organizations or states) may, through deeds and through avoidance, provide for the limitation of the war. Not delivering weapons is one way to moderate a war. Another is to mediate between the two adversaries. As O'Brien (1981) described for the 1973 October War, it can even be in the interest of both superpowers to limit a conflict and therefore to work together in the process of moderation and limitation.

Criticism of Limited War

As with any theory in the realm of social science, limited war theory has attracted a flood of criticism that questions the usefulness of the theory as a whole and brings to light perceived flaws in the theory.

The Soviet Union always considered *local wars*—its term for wars in which it was not directly involved—as a kind of imperialistic aggression. It even regarded (as G. D. Arbatov put it in 1974) "the idea to introduce and accept rules, courses of action and artificial limitations as illusionary and impracticable." Especially considering a war between NATO and the Warsaw Pact, Soviet military theory for some time flatly denied the feasibility of a limitation of war. According to Arbatov: "It is hardly [*sic*] to conceive, that a nuclear war, once unleashed, can be kept within certain bounds and it would not escalate into an all-out war." From this point of view, war between the two blocs, between socialism and capitalism, must lead to the final victory of the first. It is interesting to observe that, by 1989, the originally formulated position that such a war is unavoidable due to the class nature of the conflict between the two systems was no longer stressed by Soviet writers. Instead, the newly expressed political position was that war was no longer a means of politics. This political position has not yet been transferred to the technical side of military doctrine. Yet, Gorbachev's idea of "reasonable sufficiency" of military forces, sufficient for the defense and incapable of launching decisive offensives, may form the future nucleus for a new doctrine of limited war for the new states that once formed the Soviet Union.

The second major criticism of limited war theory as a whole has come from Western analysts. They have claimed that a limited war strategy might undermine the strategy of deterrence pursued by the two superpowers. They suggested that only the prospects of global nuclear destruction prevented the outbreak of a war between the two blocs for at least four decades. If, based on a limited war theory, a war could be considered as not inevitably leading to a nuclear war, the reluctance to wage war might decrease and thus weaken the strategy of deterrence. Under a limited war theory, this argument continues, war could also again be seen as a viable means of politics. It could be regarded as a usable technique for achieving political objectives, to be used whenever deemed appropriate and controllable in a way so as to preclude escalation to total war. Therefore, the probability of wars would increase.

It was Robert McNamara who, in the 1960s, while defending his strategy of flexible response, rejected these arguments by emphasizing that "one cannot fashion a credible deterrent out of an incredible action." He argued that a deterrent threat must be a rational instrument of policy, implying that the same must be true for the war theory forming the fundament of the deterrent threat. Otherwise, deterrence would not be credible. Except in very ominous circumstances, massive nuclear retaliation would be an incredible response and hence a poor deterrent; whereas limited war as a credible response would be much more of a deterrent in most of the conflict scenarios conceivable. Therefore, a limited war strategy would complement the strategy of nuclear deterrent and enhance overall deterrence.

Since McNamara's tenure as U.S. secretary of defense (1961–68), flexible response has been the cornerstone of U.S. and NATO strategy. But still the relation between nuclear deterrence and the capability to fight and control a limited war leaves more than enough space for strategic thinkers and policy makers. Views as expressed in the report of the Commission on Integrated Long-Term Strategy, *Discriminate Deterrence,* may mark a new beginning of limited war thinking, helping to implement a strategy for a future multipolar world. In addition to that, the process of arms control, in the nuclear as well as in the conventional realm, may cause further adjustments of limited war theory.

The third fundamental argument against limited war theory is that it was only developed to implement U.S. policy and that it is not applicable to any conflict scenario between other states, with the possible exception of war scenarios between nations possessing nuclear weapons and nonnuclear countries. This argument is difficult to reject, because limited war theory was evolved by American (plus a few British and French) strategists. The use of limited military means to achieve limited goals by the United Kingdom in the Falklands/Malvinas War and by France in the Chad War seems to prove this point.

On the other hand, the Gulf War between Iraq and Iran could be viewed as proof of the usefulness of limited war theory for wars between less powerful states. It might be protested that a war with millions of dead is not a "limited" one. But the war was started for limited objectives, it was limited in scope, and there were some restraints in the use of force despite the fact that chemical weapons were used by one side and some bombing of civilian targets ("war of the cities") occurred. The increase and decrease in the level of violence, which could be observed several times during the war, could be seen as deliberate escalation and deescalation in order to settle, through tacit bargaining, for acceptable conditions to terminate the war. Of course, it could be argued that some of the limits, especially in the level of violence, were not deliberate, but were merely dictated by the availability of military means. As of early 1991, the available information was inadequate to prove this point, but it was evident that the opponents seem to have achieved a peace settlement without having reached a single objective of the war and without the total defeat of either of them—a typical feature of a limited war.

The group of arguments against more practical aspects of the limited war theory includes the question on how to control a limited war. In the 1960s, it was argued that the whole structure of reasoning implied a level of rationality on the part of decision makers that was quite unrealistic. Because statesmen were liable to human weakness too, it was highly dangerous to assume that they could conduct a war as rationally and coolly as they could play a game of chess.

It is true that decision making is not always a matter of complete, strictly target-oriented rationality. As Graham T. Allison outlined in his book *Essence of Decision* on the Cuban Missile Crisis, decision making resembles a bargaining process heavily influenced by governmental politics and the output of bureaucratic organizational actions. But even when accepting this, no critic of political decision making would deny the usefulness or even the necessity of a rational framework—like the limited war theory—that influences the decision makers or other "players" in the process. Furthermore, historical examples from Korea to the Falklands/Malvinas provide evidence of the practicality of controlling the level of violence in a war and keeping it limited—presupposing a political decision to do so.

Some of the arguments against the merits of limited war theory are connected with the problem of limitation of means. One may argue that it depends on the point of view as to whether the means of warfare used are considered limited or not. In the Vietnam War, the limited use of force by the United States might have been considered unlimited by the North Vietnamese, who, from their side, used all military means at their disposal and did not in any way restrict the use of force, which was still, by the yardstick of a superpower, a limitation of means.

This brings about two more points of criticism: the problem of asymmetry of means (or objectives) of the two adversaries and the case of using limited means to attain unlimited objectives.

Again, the Vietnam War serves as an example. Both sides pursued different kinds of goals and used means that were considered limited by one side only. On the one hand, the U.S./South Vietnam side aimed at regaining the *status quo ante* and at repelling the North Vietnamese attack—a clearly limited objective. On the other hand, North Vietnam longed for the reunification of Vietnam under its terms, meaning the extinction of South Vietnam as a sovereign state—a total objective.

Asymmetry of means in a limited war is especially crucial in a war between states of different power. While the more powerful side could consider the war limited because it is not forced to use all forces at its disposal, the other, less powerful side, may be pressed to use virtually all of its military inventory and national resources. The limited war of one side can be a total war for the other side. One side may fight for limited objectives, such as limited territorial gains, whereas the other side may be forced to fight for sheer survival.

The last argument to be discussed is whether or not a war with limitations that result only from the nonavailability of means and from geographical restrictions can be called limited and whether or not the limited war theory can be applied. In other words, is a war limited when the limitations of means and scope are not deliberate and the objectives are unlimited, at least by implication?

The first Arab-Israeli War (1948–49) was limited in all aspects except for the objectives; but the limitations did not occur as a matter of policy, they were dictated by circumstances. The objectives were rather unlimited, with both sides wrestling for total supremacy in Palestine. The means were limited because no more were at hand, at least on the side of the Israelis, who had mobilized their complete society and economy. One other typical feature of a limited war did not occur—the war was not terminated by settling for a compromise between the opponents; rather, the war ended under pressure by third parties.

Obviously, the problem in this case is again connected with the point of view. Seen from "outside," especially from the standpoint of a great power, a war might seem limited. Seen from "inside," the same war might seem unlimited, using up all available means and pushing the nation involved to the brink of extinction.

Conclusion

In modern war theory, limited war is seen as a political process conducted with military means. The aim of this process is not to win at any cost but rather not to lose and to fight in such a way that the enemy will not escalate the level of violence too far and will settle for a compromise peace.

Limited war, as opposed to total war, must be conducted by an adherence to self-imposed, deliberate, and massive limitations, especially of objectives and means. As of today, no one had found a singular and simple answer to delineate the borderline between limited and unlimited means. Because of the problems involved in a nuclear escalation process, most scholars agree that a limited war must not be fought with nuclear weapons.

Nevertheless, limited wars can take on different forms that cover a broad spectrum of conflicts with or without direct or indirect involvement of a superpower. At one extreme of this spectrum are unlimited or total wars. On the other end can be found a congeries of conflicts—the realm of subconventional war and low-intensity conflicts.

The limited war theory has its bearing on strategy, especially the strategy of nuclear deterrence. It has been formulated to enhance deterrence, and it remains to be seen how the theory of limited war will influence the future interrelated processes of arms control and strategy formulation and how it will, in turn, be influenced by those.

The fact that most wars in human history have been limited, be it because of the prevailing circumstances or of the wisdom of statesmen and generals, has secured the survival of mankind so far. In the nuclear age, limitation of wars is more necessary than ever. If only because limiting war is the only way to avoid a nuclear Armageddon should war become unavoidable, limited war strategies must be devised and adapted to the political development of the world. Limited war is much worse than peace but much better than nuclear annihilation.

HEINZ KOZAK

SEE ALSO: Conventional War; Unconventional War.

Bibliography

Allison, G. T. 1971. *Essence of decision: Explaining the Cuban Missile Crisis*. Glenview, Ill.: Scott, Foresman.

Brodie, B. 1959. *Strategy in the missile age*. Princeton, N.J.: Princeton Univ. Press.

Deitchman, S. J. 1966. *Limited war and American defense policy*. Cambridge, Mass.: Massachusetts Institute of Technology Press.

Halperin, M. E. 1963. *Limited war in the nuclear age*. New York: John Wiley and Sons.

Howard, M., ed. 1979. *Restraints on war, studies in the limitation of armed conflict*. Oxford: Oxford Univ. Press.

Kahn, H. 1965. *On escalation*. London: Pall Mall Press.

Kissinger, H. A. 1957. *Nuclear weapons and foreign policy*. New York: Harper.

Knorr, K., and T. Read., eds. 1962. *Limited strategic war*. New York: Praeger.

Liddell Hart, B. H. 1967. *Strategy*. 2d ed. New York: Signet.

McClintock, R. 1967. *The meaning of limited war*. Boston: Houghton Mifflin.

O'Brien, W. V. 1981. *The conduct of just and limited war*. New York: Praeger.

Osgood, R. E. 1979. *Limited war revisited*. Boulder, Colo.: Westview Press.

Schelling, T. C. 1963. *The strategy of conflict*. Oxford: Oxford Univ. Press.

LOGISTICS: A GENERAL SURVEY

Armed forces around the world use a number of definitions of the term *military logistics* that differ in presentation of content as well as mode of expression. As an introduction to this general survey of logistics, an abridged description is herewith offered: Military logistics is the business—and big business at that—of planning, preparing, and providing materiel support for forces, thus enabling them to live and move, train in peacetime, mobilize and deploy in an emergency, and fight in war or keep the peace.

The military term *materiel* is a key word in this and other definitions. It is used to describe the vast range and quantities of equipments and commodities in the inventories of armed forces—inventories that have increased in length and complexity commensurate with all the impressive advances in military technology of recent years. They include items of materiel ranging from capital equipments such as ships, aircraft, tanks, and all types of vehicles and weapon systems through replacement assemblies and spare parts, to missiles and munitions, explosives and fuel, food and water, constructional stores, medical supplies, clothing and personnel equipment, maps, and other necessaries. To aid identification and management, military materiel is normally grouped into categories or classes of supply.

Logistics has two primary tasks, and both emphasize the central theme of materiel support. The first involves the development and production, the procurement and storage, the distribution, and eventually perhaps the disposal of the equipments and commodities used by modern military forces. The second task concerns the provision of an extensive variety of logistics services, listed in Figure 1. Each service has operational and nonoperational functions that may differ in situations of war or peace. For example: the supply function may vary from replenishing the ammunition stocks of fighting troops engaged in battle to replacing furniture in barracks; constructional engineering tasks may vary from building a fuel tank farm in a field location just behind the fighting troops and then connecting it to a fuel pipeline to maintaining accommodations in peacetime military garrisons.

One of the principal military functions included in Figure 1 is *support*. Although logistics is a main support function, as are military administration and

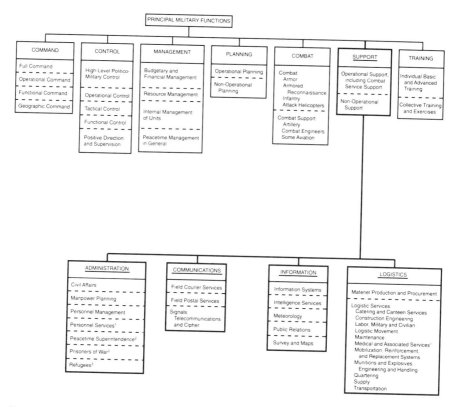

Notes:
[1] Medical and Associated Services (Dental, Nursing, Paramedical, etc.) are Personnel Services and Logistic Services, in that the Operational Casualty and Treatment System in exercises and in war is classified as Logistics
[2] Nonoperational service only
[3] Operational services only

Figure 1. Principal military functions.

the provision of communications and information, there is a problem of military terminology. Specifically, armed forces tend to classify their functions differently, and some regard logistics as an integral part of military administration. This article, in common with most of today's practice, treats military logistics and military administration separately, thus recognizing the continuous and sustained growth in popularity of the term *logistics* and its eminent importance as a main support function. This treatment in no way depreciates the value of military administration, which relates principally to people, while logistics mainly concerns materiel.

Operational logistics sustains forces engaged in combat, counterinsurgency, internal security, peacekeeping and disaster-relief operations, or training exercises. That part of operational logistics that directly supports and is in close contact with the fighting is often described as combat service support. Nonoperational logistics, on the other hand, covers a multiplicity of support tasks that are all part of the domestic routine of forces living and working in peacetime garrisons and barracks, at home or overseas.

Another way of describing operational logistics is to differentiate between levels or lines of support as outlined in Table 1.

By linking these levels of support by lines of communication, long distances can be spanned from home bases to troops deployed in distant theaters or areas of operations. The practical framework suggested in Table 1 can be used flexibly to provide the most suitable and most effective logistic structure to fit the circumstances. For example, fighting units have organic supply, maintenance, and medical support elements and, in certain circumstances, may receive support direct from home or overseas bases without it being necessary to introduce the intermediate levels. There are other permutations.

The terms *field* and *base logistics* are also quite commonly used by the

TABLE 1. *Levels or Lines of Support*

LEVELS	LINES	EXPLANATION	ALTERNATIVE DESCRIPTION
Immediate logistic support	First line	Support integral or organic to user/consumer units	Unit support
Primary logistic support	Second line	Direct support given to user/consumer units by primary logistic support units that are normally mobile and in field locations	Direct or field support
Secondary logistic support	Third line	Support given to primary by secondary logistic support units that are sometimes mobile and usually in field locations	General support
Tertiary logistic support	Fourth line	Support given to secondary by tertiary logistic support units and installations from invariably static, permanent locations	Base support

military. Field logistics encompasses the first three levels listed in Table 1, whereby materiel and services are provided in the field: from temporarily acquired or erected infrastructure, from hastily built or converted shelter, or, literally, from fields or forests. In an operational or combat environment, camouflage and concealment, local defense, and security can be as important as the technical provision of logistic support. Base logistics, as the term suggests, is provided from home bases, from main bases in overseas theaters, or from advanced bases in overseas areas of operations. It is usually, but not always, provided from permanent accommodation in a secure environment. Field logistics involves mobile, as well as static, stocks and service support, whereas base logistics invariably features large, static installations. These and other terms are illustratively used in some hypothetical operational scenarios presented later in this article.

Another way of describing logistics is to differentiate between the producer, or wholesaler, and the user or consumer, both linked by the supplier or retailer. To elaborate: to the defense producer, the military supplier is the intermediary who calculates materiel requirements, who procures and holds stocks in base depots or field storage, and who distributes the user's needs either automatically or on demand. To the military user, the supplier and the producer together satisfy his legitimate needs at the right time, in the right place, and in the proper quality and correct quantity.

Historical Development

The English word *logistics* has been in American military use for well over 100 years and has been gradually adopted by most other English-speaking defense communities and armed forces. More recently, the term has also become popular in civilian commerce and industry. It derives from the Greek adjective *logistikos*, meaning skilled in calculating. (Throughout history, the tasks of equipping, supplying, and moving armies have involved arithmetical calculation, some of considerable complexity. Napoleon is reputed to have described these calculating skills as "not unworthy of a Newton or a Leibniz.") In Roman and Byzantine times, the *logista* was an official who employed this skill as part of his vocation. Moving forward through history to Louis XIV's time, the French Army introduced the appointment of *maréchal-général des logis*, who was responsible for quartering troops. (The French verb *loger* means to billet or lodge, and the adjective *logistique*, when used in the military context, originally described the quartering service.)

In its broader and more modern sense, the term *logistics* first gained prominence in Jomini's theory of war. This was published in 1838, after the author had seen service with Napoleon. In expounding the trinity or interdependence of strategy, tactics, and logistics, Jomini described logistics as the means and the arrangements that enable strategy and tactics to be put into effect. His contemporary, Clausewitz, stressed that a wise commander, even if the resources of the province are quite sufficient, will not neglect to form magazines behind him as a provision against unforeseen events, so as to be able more readily to concentrate his strength at certain points. Both statements remain true today, although the scope and magnitude of modern military logistics have greatly expanded.

Unlike Jomini, who considered logistics to be of equivalent importance to strategy and tactics, Clausewitz regarded logistics as having a subservient role to the other two. This difference of emphasis is interesting because it still prevails in certain cases. In some armed forces, there is a definite acceptance by commanders, staffs, and units of the interdependence and interactivity of strategy, tactics, and logistics, to the point that all three have for long been equivalently represented on the general staff—the operational planning staff present at all levels of headquarters in military forces. C. Barnett describes the British machinations of the late nineteenth century: whether or not to adopt and employ the "continental" general staff structure and system that has been, or shortly would be, introduced in the main European armies and the U.S. Army at that time (*Britain and Her Army: 1509–1907* [London: Allen Lane, 1970], pp. 310, 336). In the end, the "continental" version was rejected; the British Army developed its own staff structure and system, but recently has partially introduced a general staff along the lines of the "evolved continental" model. B. von Schellendorf outlines the "continental" structure employed at that time (*The Duties of the General Staff* [London: His Majesty's Stationery Office, 1905]; see also Dupuy 1977).

In other armed forces, logistics has been separated with no similar effective integration of logistics within the general staff at every level of the force structure. To illustrate this difference, the Prussian and, later, the German Army incorporated the *quartiermeister-general* and his supply, transportation, and quartering staffs as part and branch of the *grosgeneralstab*, from the elder von Moltke's time onward, whereas the British Army's quartermaster-general is not part of the general staff—he reports directly and independently to a government minister—and there is no single chief of staff at each organizational level who directs and coordinates all aspects of operational planning on behalf of his commander.

Attitudes, like those of Jomini and Clausewitz, are hard to change. Tradition, rather than logical practicality, can govern military organization and method, for good and bad reasons, and disparities of attitude and approach toward logistics are reflected in other ways. For instance, authoritative published works on military logistics remain few and far between. Eccles (1959, 1965); Huston (1966); Thorpe (1986), including Falk's introduction; and van Creveld (1977) provide excellent commentaries on logistics, although some are now a little dated. In particular, Falk gives a brief, handy, abridged summary of the historical evolution of logistics.

The deficiency of publications moved Fuller, before the Second World War, to observe: "Surely one of the strangest things in military history is the complete silence about the problems of supplies [logistics]. In ten thousand books written on war not one is to be found on the subject, yet it forms the basis on which rests the whole structure of war: it is the very foundation of tactics and strategy" (G. C. Shaw, *Supply in Modern War* [London: Faber and Faber,

1938], p. 9; preface by J. F. C. Fuller). Jomini would certainly have agreed wholeheartedly with Fuller's concluding statement. They and others appreciated and recognized that the practical art of moving armies and keeping them supplied comprises "90 percent of the business of war" (A. C. P. Wavell, *Speaking Generally* [London, 1946], pp. 78–79). In another instance, Wavell's experiences during World War II led him to conclude:

> The more I have seen of war, the more I realise how it all depends on administration and transportation (what our American allies call logistics). It takes little skill or imagination to see where you would like your army and when; it takes much knowledge and hard work to know where you can place your forces and whether you can maintain them there. A real knowledge of supply and movement factors must be the basis of every leader's plan: only then can he know how and when to take risks with these factors; and battles and wars are won by taking risks. (*Ibid.*)

Since World War II, several notable works have emphasized the importance of logistics. One of them, by van Creveld (1977, p. 231), contains the assertion that, because there is a continuing dearth of published, authoritative logistical material, most available military history tends to place the cart before the horse. When reviewing van Creveld's work, Michael Howard illuminates deficiencies in a penetrating style all of his own:

> The traditional and disastrous distinction between "teeth" and "tail" arms, between executive and engineering branches, between flying and technical officers which has done so much to destroy the efficiency of our [British] armed forces in the twentieth century extends to writings about war as well. Military historians devote as little attention as they decently can to logistical matters before going on to describe the splendours and miseries of battle and generalship that make up the core of the drama. (*Sunday Times*, London, 19 Feb. 1978)

Historical commentary on strategy, tactics, and command may well be devalued to a considerable extent because of a lack of essential logistical dimensions. Yet, we must be cautious of publications that deal with logistics in an isolated manner. Military history should accurately and objectively record that the conduct of wars, campaigns, and battles is a *combined* effort. Strategists and tacticians, commanders and logisticians, soldiers and civilians, all share the trials and tribulations when working together to achieve success in war, just as all military forces and units—whatever their function—cooperate and collaborate to accomplish their missions and tasks to achieve victory. If operations are viable and feasible, because their logistic support is ready and sufficient, then less needs to be written of logistics than if operational risks—premeditated risks—have to be taken because of logistical constraints or inadequacies. When logistics has a profound influence on military policies, plans, and priorities, or when logistics moderates or restricts operations, then these facts and their associated circumstances are notable. Perhaps these notable facts and circumstances are too infrequently recorded in adequate detail. If this is so, then the cart may well have been placed before the horse, as van Creveld (1977) claims.

When reviewing the past and anticipating the future, it is worth remembering that logistics is a principal means of creating and sustaining combat power. It can be a key determinant of operational success or failure as is suggested here:

> Well planned and well executed logistics will provide the key to victory in battle, and plays a key part in combat readiness in war. The obverse is true. Neglected logistics can quickly reduce what may appear to be a potent military force to a rag-bag of sick, dispirited men, trained as fighters, but unable to move, shoot or communicate. It is a certain prescription for defeat, disastrous morale, and lack of confidence in their commanders, supporting staffs, and services, and, ultimately and maybe very quickly, in their weapons, equipment and ability to fight. (Alexander 1986 p. 43)

For centuries in the past, fighting men foraged and pillaged for food; they requisitioned quarters and commandeered the means of movement. Logistics, or its equivalent then, was considered to be a way of waging punitive war as well as a means of supporting war. Lands were laid to waste, bare of resources, and their people starved. Some armed forces still employ these methods very much as part of their operational doctrine today.

In early times, individuals or small bands of combatants seldom strayed far from sources of potable water, daily provisions, or other essentials. Early warriors were admirably self-reliant, self-contained, and self-sufficient, much more than most soldiers are today. However, as these small bands grew larger in size, when they proliferated in number, and when in ancient and medieval times they began to take the shape of modern fighting units and modern fighting formations, their operational aspirations became more ambitious and their combat capabilities more powerful. Thus, their need for sustained and responsive logistics also grew. This newfound capacity to rove and fight farther afield produced the requirement for specialized logistics, dedicated to the support of combat.

When conditions allowed, military forces continued to live off the land, often at the local population's and the enemy's expense. But it was the gradual, progressive introduction of an increasing variety of more sophisticated weaponry, transport, and equipment that demanded a proportional and parallel increase in the quantity and the quality of logistic support. During the last century and a half, the advent first of railways, steamships, telegraphs, and telephones, then wheeled and tracked motor vehicles, a miscellany of maritime and aerial craft, and a diversity of powerful and lethal forms of generating energy has given nations and their armed forces the capacity to wage war much more vigorously and destructively. With the dramatic development of the technology of warfare, logistics has become recognized as a key military function and a key organizational component of modern armed forces.

Timely, effective logistic support has always depended upon the ability of commanders and their staffs, their units, and their logisticians to anticipate requirements. The techniques of forecasting and calculating have been more successfully applied when logisticians have been able to work in close contact with those they support and when they have been able to keep themselves briefed on the probable course of combat, abreast of operations, and party to changes of plan and priorities. Early logisticians were usually attached to the military tactical headquarters on the field of battle or were grouped together as a supporting echelon as close as practicable to the fighting. In either case, they were firmly under the commander's direction and in easy communication with his subordinates. Logisticians also had to cooperate closely with the authorities of the state wherein they were operating or through which they were passing, from whom they acquired provisions, fodder, and other necessities. Sometimes their procurement methods were brutal and arbitrary; often payment or compensation was by no means automatic.

Whatever the composition of the military force, and whatever its operational doctrine and methods, logisticians and logistic support echelons had the weighty, continuous, unavoidable responsibility of anticipating and providing the everyday needs of those whom it was their duty to sustain. Whether troops were under siege, whether they were conducting siege operations or were on the march, whether they were attacking or defending, advancing or retreating, their requirements had to be met. Any failure to do so had obvious repercussions. Force requirements were pre-stocked in field dumps along the route, held in static or rolling magazines (van Creveld describes the rise of the magazine system [1977, pp. 17–26]), or carried in wagon columns behind the fighting troops. Thus, the ancient, professional business of military logistics evolved and developed into the modern complex of supporting services, facilities, and systems that forces have come to know, expect, and appreciate. In principle and in concept, logistics has changed little. Yet, in keeping with the growth of modern military forces and the complexity of modern technology, the function has grown enormously in scope and magnitude.

The introduction of standing armies and, in some cases, their stationing abroad meant that logistics had to be a substantial, active function in peacetime, as well as in wartime. The domestic needs of garrisoned troops had to be met, units had to be kept equipped for their war roles, and formations had to remain operationally ready. Furthermore, logistic plans had to be made and implemented for the swift, smooth mobilization of reserves to reinforce standing armies. Stockpiles of materiel had to be quickly activated, and national economies and industries placed on a war footing. Moreover, logistic planning and the rapid buildup of logistic support played an increasingly crucial part in the concentration and deployment of the total force. Once an emergency was declared or operations of war started, then logistical reinforcement and replenishment, replacement and refurbishment, came into their own. Whenever and wherever troops were engaged in armed conflict, it was necessary to sustain them at a specified level of combat intensity for a prescribed duration. Also, allowances had to be made for changes of plan and other unforeseen eventualities. Again, in principle and in concept, little has changed. Flexible response has for long been a familiar logistical characteristic.

Logistics has therefore become the challenging military vocation it is today: a professional occupation demanding special training, qualification, and expertise. Logisticians of all ranks require a high degree of conscientiousness, dedication, diligence, and skill. It is possibly their consistent, persistent attention to detail that creates a type of backstage, engine-room mentality and, because of this, conveys a somewhat unglamorous image to other soldiers. Yet, it is their duty to be ever present and to advise commanders, staffs, and units when operations can be supported or when logistic shortages require an adjustment to plans or priorities. It is also their duty to advise when operations are not sustainable or are not viable for logistical reasons; this is not to be misinterpreted as some gloomy preoccupation with obstructing operational intentions, for logisticians must be essentially "can-do" advisers. Logisticians may see themselves principally as resourceful perfectionists, but they also have to be practical realists. They must be prepared to accept that sometimes taking risks with logistics is prudent, as well as necessary. It is easier for them to accept this when they know their advice is invited and welcomed, evaluated, and heeded. Close, confident working relationships with their commanders, general staff planners, and the units dependent on their support encourage logisticians to give of their best.

Their best is undoubtedly needed, because advances in military technology, especially weapons systems, have created operational capabilities of voracious logistical appetite. This has paradoxical implications. As combat forces have become increasingly dependent upon a continuous connection with their logistic support, so their operational mobility can be inherently degraded, in spite of the constant efforts of operational commanders and planners to find ways around this restricting trend. As logistics now contributes ever more significantly to the development of operational strategies, doctrines, and concepts, and to the conduct of modern warfare, so the financial costs of providing sufficient logistics unerringly escalate. Moreover, the operational costs of *not* providing enough escalate as well.

The potentially huge logistic bill that nations and alliances may have had to face may well have played a part in deterring general total nuclear war and also encouraged force reductions in central Europe. Military powers will have to continue to invest heavily in logistics in order to retain an operationally viable and credible limited-localized war capability: a combat capability that effectively deters or defeats the maverick opportunist or adventurer who threatens peace, democracy, and foreign territorial integrity; and a logistic capability that effectively creates a force and sustains operations in difficult physical conditions and, for some, far from the home base, as in the recent Gulf War.

Therefore, military logistics remains vital, and Rommel explained why, in the context of his own desert campaign:

> The first essential condition for an army to be able to stand the strain of battle is an adequate stock of weapons, petrol and ammunition. In fact, the battle is fought and decided by the quartermasters before the shooting begins. The bravest men can do nothing without guns, the guns nothing

without ammunition; and neither guns nor ammunition are of much use in mobile warfare unless there are vehicles with sufficient petrol to haul them around. Maintenance must also approximate quantity and quality to that of the enemy. (B. H. Liddell Hart, ed., *The Rommel Papers* [New York, 1953], p. 328)

It is with the knowledge that logistics will continue to have a crucial role in future military operations that the discussion now turns to logistic principles—principles that can usefully assist with planning and implementing future support.

Principles

There is no set of commonly accepted global logistic principles. They differ, just as the principles of war differ, from one nation's armed forces to another's. Variations stem from doctrines, procedures, and, of course, from terminology and language. In any case, long-established principles should be periodically reviewed to ensure their currency and for the reasons Huston stated:

> No one aspect of the Army's logistical experience can be singled out as most valuable in providing guidelines for the future, for the future is, as always, uncertain. One thing can be forecast with assurance—the continuation of change. But it may also be assumed that, however far-reaching the changes, there must always be links with the past. Any general conclusion drawn from history as a whole must include the principle of change and the principle of continuity. (Huston 1966, pp. 689–90)

All history—not only military history—entails the study of past events, their relationship with the present, and their relevance as lessons for the future. Principles are constructed in similar fashion and serve the same purpose. Those concerned with continuity and change, for instance, apply equally to all military functions, not just to logistics. While there is no room in any respect for inertia, there is, as in all enterprises, a need for stability mixed with dynamism. With this in mind, a review of the literature suggests some threads of commonality among established logistic principles, as well as some requirements for updating. Six principles are proposed and each will be examined in turn:

1. unity of purpose
2. preparedness
3. viability
4. economy
5. responsiveness
6. resourcefulness.

Every logistic principle must support and correlate with the principles of war adopted by armed forces, taking those followed by the American and British as a baseline. Also, in selecting logistic principles, the interdependence and interactivity of logistics with strategy, tactics, and operational command must be taken into account. Logistic principles are, after all, but guidelines to help plan and provide combat power at critical times and places, in forms most conducive to operational success. They are neither theoretical abstractions nor rules for rigid compliance. They should help to teach and test, check and improve, monitor and evaluate concepts, such as military logistics. Not only are principles strongly governed by circumstances, they can also be contradictory. For example, the suggested logistic principle of viability presupposes sufficiency, yet the need for economy, implicit in another principle, indicates that sufficiency may not always be attainable. The American slogan "first with the most" may therefore have to be amended to "first with the best available."

There also may be some overlap, duplication, and repetition among a set of six principles, such as those suggested here. In addition, certain characteristics or *constants* would seem to apply to all or most of the six proposed principles. These constants are summarized in Table 2.

Having discussed the usefulness of principles and having established eight constants that commonly apply, we can now examine each of the six principles proposed.

Unity of Purpose

The main logistic services are listed in Figure 1. Although each is a separate service, together they form a cohesive part of the corporate logistic organization and effort. All should be integrated—that is, combined and coordinated—under appropriate command or control, at every level within a nation's military force structure, both in peace and war. Together, these services deliver to military forces the means of livelihood and functional capacity and, when necessary, the materiel and services to support combat operations.

At the higher levels of military organization—in ministries or departments of defense and in superior military headquarters—the corporate integration of logistic services and the corporate delivery of logistic support require unity of politico-military control, unity of civil-military management, and unity of military direction. The goal is corporately agreed-upon policies, plans, and priorities, with logistic and strategic objectives firmly set and pursued, regularly monitored, and objectively evaluated.

TABLE 2. *Eight Constants*

Information	This concerns the prompt, accurate provision of logistic intelligence drawn from the wealth of raw data that modern information systems generate, particularly computer systems.
Timeliness	This is key to any activity and to the application of all six logistic principles suggested.
Continuity Momentum Endurance Resilience	Cumulatively, these concern the *staying power* necessary in logistic support, as well as in most other military activities and actions.
Flexibility	This implies the capacity readily to accept and cope with change, without sacrificing stability.
Simplicity	This reflects in the ability to be clear, concise, and uncomplicated without impairing comprehension, efficiency, or attention to essential detail.

At lower levels—in force, formation, and tactical headquarters—a similar degree of integration of operational effort and activities is necessary: unity of command of a particular region or sector of operations, unity of operational planning, and unity of assigned missions and tasks. All enable strategic and tactical objectives to be achieved with the logistic resources available.

The tendency, at any organizational level, to give a commander or a chief of staff some lesser responsibility for the logistic support of forces—lesser, for instance, than he has for strategic and tactical matters—should be avoided. Full powers of command and comprehensive operational planning contribute valuably to the quest for unity of purpose within forces and formations and facilitate the guidance and conduct of logistic support.

Any tendency logisticians may have—when undertaking support tasks—to promote separate, vested interests in preference to common, corporate interests must be resisted and discouraged. Through firm leadership, good training, and varied military employment, logisticians should find it easier to view the broad perspective of military requirements, rather than restrict themselves solely to logistical routine and detail of equal importance. Logisticians must not hide, or be hidden, in watertight compartments. If they are, then unity of purpose may well be jeopardized; whether they work in a single service, joint service, or multinational environment; whether they are civilian producers or military providers; whether the situation is operational or nonoperational; whether it is peace or wartime. Overcompartmentalization and internal rivalry are best eschewed.

Logisticians should maintain profitable producer-user links, acting as the military intermediary between those who design and develop, produce, or procure materiel and those who use the provided equipment and commodities. The close working relationships of logisticians with commanders, staffs, dependent units, and producers of materiel should extend to all areas of their work. Mutual understanding and confidence, fruitful cooperation, and enterprising teamwork engender and strengthen unity of purpose in general, not just in logistical affairs.

PREPAREDNESS

If corporate operational planning involves logistics, what is planning? In this context, it may be described as a continuous process of matching military aspirations with intentions, commitments with capabilities, requirements with resources, availabilities with constraints. Plans seek to optimize economic, industrial, and logistic capacity, actual operational readiness, and potential combat effectiveness. However, as planning is principally a prediction, and since neither foresight nor military judgment is infallible, so logistic plans should include a safety margin for unforeseen and unforeseeable eventualities. They are bound to arise both in peacetime emergencies or in war.

By predicting likely contingencies and by anticipating the expected course of operations, general staff planners and their logistic advisers together endeavor to forecast force requirements. They may devise an operational structure of in-being, in-place forces and first add regular (permanent) and reserve (mobilizable) reinforcements, then battle replacements. Equipped, trained reinforcements may then be needed to complete formation orders of battle or unit establishments. Replacements of similar readiness may also be required to make up for equipment losses due to breakdown and, once war starts, due to battle damage. Through foresight, military judgment, and persevering, painstaking staff work, through reliable estimates of casualty and consumption rates, so the logistic plan begins to materialize. Like all plans, it requires constant updating.

Operational plans are best made, reviewed, and revised under the direction of one chief of staff at each structural level within a military force. He tasks and coordinates general staff and logistic planners and acts on behalf of the government minister or military commander to whom he reports. He ensures that all considerations and requirements—logistics included—are competently, cohesively, and completely assessed. Logistic preparedness is a product of this universal, continuous planning process.

Ensured preparedness greatly eases the necessary expansion of forces and logistic infrastructure if mobilization is necessary. There should be no fundamental alteration of logistic support organizations and systems during transition to war. A well-planned, well-regulated, smooth transition significantly assists forces to convert from their peacetime operational readiness status to a combat effectiveness status. In the event that some logistical adjustments are necessary, they are best undertaken swiftly and decisively. Adjustments caused by lack of foresight, lack of planning, or lack of preparedness are avoidable and could delay or dislocate operations or the support of operations. *Semper paratus* prevails.

VIABILITY

Before a force is committed to combat, that force must itself be viable and its operations feasible and sustainable. To aid viability (Russian: *zhivuchest*), force structures contain an appropriate mix and balance of constituent components and an appropriate ratio of combat to logistic elements. The mix, balance, and ratio may vary by type of operations, physical environment, and other considerations. For instance, at the end of World War II, the ratio of combat troops to logistic troops stood at 1:5 in certain American formations. It is difficult, however, to be precise about these parameters and measurements—is a forward repair team a combat or a support element? Nevertheless, precision is necessary as a contribution toward producing credible logistics.

When armed forces lack logistic credibility, both support and confidence will suffer. Given the absence of this credibility, adversaries may well be encouraged to embark upon some military opportunism or adventurism that they might not otherwise have contemplated. When armed forces are deprived of feasible, credible, logistic sufficiency, they do not have the resources to succeed. In short, operationally viable forces require sustainable logistic support.

Logistic sustainability does not alone guarantee operational viability. Other factors include: sound strategies and tactics; effective planning and force structure; good equipment; experienced command and inspiring leadership; proper training and readiness; a powerful combat capability with adequate reinforcement and replacement capacity; high morale and belief in a cause. However, logistic sustainability is a vital ingredient of successful military operations. It is achieved by combining resource sufficiency and forward impetus so that continuous, mainly rear-to-front support constantly—and, whenever possible, automatically—satisfies operational requirements, without operational commanders, formations, and units having to look frequently over their shoulders. Viable, sustainable logistic support enables commanders and their forces to achieve strategic and tactical objectives and to accomplish their operational missions and tasks and gives them the freedom of action to wrest the initiative, exploit success, and avert disaster.

Logistically viable forces are likely to be balanced, collective groupings of combined-arms-services teams. These teams are capable of conducting and supporting combat at a specific level of intensity for a prescribed period of operations—and for a part of the time without resupply, because viability assumes a degree of self-sufficiency. Logistic sustainability follows from this. It is measured and provided using three quotients: *days* of combat; *rates* of battle attrition and casualties, expenditure, and consumption; and *estimates* of replacement equipments and replenishment commodities. Logistic sufficiency is, therefore, the matching of estimated or determined requirements with the resources available. Resources include those provided from the rear by logistic organizations and systems and those held by the fighting formations and units themselves. Self-sufficiency ensures operational flexibility and ensures against breaks in, or disconnections with, rear support.

Logistic viability is more effectively ensured under operational conditions when support facilities are adequately dispersed and protected, whether the facilities are production plants or base installations, field support units or stockpiles of operational reserves. These potential targets, like lines of communication, are vulnerable to enemy attack. They are also liable to congestion and disruption. Dispersion and protection prolong their viability as logistic assets without running counter to certain principles of war, namely concentration and economy of effort. As in all things, moderation should prevail. Modern communication and information systems now considerably assist the control, management, and deployment of dispersed resources in time and space. Security—another principle of war—has to be optimized in operational areas that increasingly tend to have no clearly delineated, convenient front lines. Therefore, neither security nor logistic viability should be unacceptably reduced by creating a multiplicity of logistic bases, support areas, and lines of communication. Too much dispersion may degrade the logistic sufficiency and sustainability of a force at a given time and in a given area. Too little dispersion and too little protection may lose that force valuable, irreplaceable assets, making it logistically and operationally unviable.

ECONOMY

The well-established principle of logistic economy is open to misunderstanding and hints at rationing. To enforce economies does not imply a deliberate reduction of resources to such an extent that logistic support is no longer viable, sufficient, or sustainable. Just as effectiveness is a product of efficiency and economy working in tandem, so the constant drive for logistic effectiveness involves correction of inefficiencies and elimination of any unnecessary overlap or duplication of responsibilities and waste of precious resources. Logistic economy therefore means using resources—services, facilities, and stocks—most productively and sparingly. Ensuring that resources are effectively used by military forces may ameliorate the adverse effects of materiel and service constraints—often externally and suddenly imposed on forces. Logistic economy also means striking a judicious balance between over- and underinsurance: by providing not too little, not too much, but just enough resources. It additionally means striking a judicious balance between role-effectiveness and cost-effectiveness by economizing without unduly restricting the performance of a combat or support task.

Designing and producing military equipment of optimum reliability, maintainability, and endurance can reduce equipment downtime, which is the period that equipment is inoperable and therefore not available for use, and can also improve user confidence in equipment performance. Regular inspection and preventive maintenance also enhance equipment serviceability. Should equipment become defective or battle damaged, a forward repair capability optimizes battleworthiness and serviceability. Should equipments have to be evacuated to supporting rear maintenance facilities, skilled attention can reduce battle casualty replacement requirements. All these measures help to promote role-effectiveness and cost-effectiveness.

Logistic economy is also gained by long production runs of military equipment to reduce unit costs or by using suitable civilian models to save expensive procurement of special-to-military versions, when the latter are not really essential. In addition, cosmetic modifications, made during production or during the in-service life of equipment, are not always cost-effective, whereas functional modifications are role-effective. Furthermore, prolonging the in-service life of equipment may postpone its expensive replacement. On the other hand, delaying replacement may inflate future maintenance costs. The timely introduction of a new equipment, complete with an initial scaling of assemblies and spare parts, may well be more role-effective and more cost-effective.

Logistic economy is further gained by selecting the right equipments for development and purchase, by specifying the correct degree of sophistication and ruggedness, and by choosing the best manufacturer. Informed decisions have to be made between: multirole and single-purpose models; proven design and the latest technology; a well-established, highly specialized, comparatively narrow production base and a more speculative, more competitive, broader base; long lead times and off-the-shelf, supply-in-time procurement; and between repairable and discardable items. Moreover, equipment standardization and production specialization are likely to be logistically, as well as operationally, beneficial to both national and multinational forces.

Logistic economy is additionally gained by rationalizing and improving in-service support. Large logistic bases and installations can absorb extravagant resources purely for their own upkeep, when cheaper alternatives will suffice. Greater use of civilians and contractors in peacetime may well free military assets for other purposes, provided operational readiness is not penalized. Transport aircraft can be a quicker, more flexible means of logistic movement. However, if these aircraft consume too large a proportion of their fuel cargo in flight, a slower, less flexible, more economical form of transportation may be preferred. Operational stocks and war reserves held for a protracted period within the supply system may in practice inaccurately reflect updated, estimated, or actual requirements. The peacetime scale of equipment engineering and maintenance often exceeds the needs of war. More interoperability, mutual support, and cross servicing may be economically achievable within military alliances.

Appropriate joint service and international integration is logistically economical and efficient and may also be operationally effective. Centrally agreed-upon equipment policies and programs, centrally directed and coordinated producer logistics, and centrally established resource management can benefit nations and military alliances. Single-service major-user management of specific ranges of materiel items in common inventories and the rationalization of base logistic support can reduce overheads. Controlled competition between defense manufacturers for declining orders, and between armed forces for constrained resources, can also be advantageous. The escalating logistic bill compels the military to consider every effective measure to integrate logistics as a means of achieving prudent, practical economies.

RESPONSIVENESS

In an effectively responsive supply system, logistic support installations and echelons *push* predictable requirements forward in prescribed daily quantities, mostly automatically; and dependent units *pull* their unpredictable needs from the rear by demanding specified items. In an effectively responsive maintenance system, mobile specialist teams perform forward repair, if practicable. When tasks are beyond their capability or of lesser priority, repairable equipments are back loaded to workshops where defects or damage are rectified and the equipments returned to units. In an effectively responsive personnel casualty evacuation and treatment system, skilled first aid and medical attention are administered to the wounded as soon as practicable. If forward treatment is not appropriate or available, casualties are evacuated by waiting ambulance transport to field and general hospitals, and, when fully recovered, personnel normally return to their units. Other logistic support systems are similarly responsive to operational requirements and equally sensitive to combat priorities.

Responsive logistic services and facilities anticipate changes—they do not only react when changes have occurred. By increasing support in one sector and reducing support in another, adjustments are flexibly made to meet changing operational and tactical requirements. Thus, adjustments respond to a commander's developing plans and priorities. If it is necessary to introduce centralized control of logistic support—in a particular sector, at a specific level within a force, or for a stated period of time—this is effected in the interests of improving flexible response and not to undermine or fetter an operational commander's overall authority and responsibility.

Experience shows that operational plans made in peace need to be constantly reviewed, and those made in war require to be continuously revised. Indeed, peacetime plans seldom fit the real circumstances or meet the actual requirements of war. Responsive logisticians may anticipate and adjust, but they must also allow for unforeseen events and requirements. For logisticians to be responsive is commendable; for them to be able to maintain responsiveness over the period of a war, campaign, or battle is excellent. Both objectives call for unrelenting dedication to duty and attention to detail. The challenges and lack of rest logisticians and their units experience during peacetime exercises are but a glimpse at their task in war.

RESOURCEFULNESS

If the suggested principles of viability and economy appear to be somewhat contradictory, those of responsiveness and resourcefulness are surely complementary.

Logisticians, as well as all soldiers, may not respond effectively to the dangers and difficulties of war unless they are resourceful. The most versatile draw retrospectively on past experiences to deal as competently as they can with unexpected challenges. They may have to refurbish embattled formations or units in the best way practicable, enabling these forces to resume operations. They may have to cannibalize a battle-damaged tank, enabling another to be repaired to battle-worthiness standards, or modify equipment so that it can, perhaps at short notice, adequately perform an operational role different from that for which it was designed. Forces may have to live off the land, use local resources, or depend on other unconventional forms of supply.

Resourcefulness derives from practical aptitude and demands a positive attitude of mind. Imagination and ingenuity help the resourceful innovator to keep the initiative in times of crisis. However, developing the right aptitudes and attitudes in peacetime is a problem; therefore, resourcefulness in war often has to be instantaneously intuitive.

Some argue that, because advanced technology breeds specialists, soldiers who are not specialists are no longer as self-reliant and self-contained as they once were. Armies that traditionally emphasized *equipping the man* are now preoccupied with *manning equipment*. When the equipment breaks down, the unresourceful nonspecialist may blame technology and seek a replacement. An example often quoted concerns the division of responsibility and labor between tank crews and maintenance specialists. In peacetime, crew training may be limited to regular servicing and minor adjustments with specialists attending to repairs. In war, when specialists may not be available to help, it may be a matter of life and death for crews to make do and mend and keep their tanks in action. Practical preparation of nonspecialists is thus likely to improve their resourcefulness in a crisis, just as first aid training has saved the lives of countless wounded soldiers in battle.

Resourcefulness is not only an individual gift; resourceful logistics can be collectively acquired. For instance, logistically self-sufficient units and formations, combined-arms-services teams, possess integral self-reliance and self-containment. Potentially, they are more resourceful and less dependent upon specialized rear-area support. Working together, commanders, the general staff, and logisticians have ample scope and an undeniable need to plan and encourage resourceful support of military operations.

SUMMARY OF PRINCIPLES

Table 3 summarizes the six suggested principles of logistics. The key words might usefully be read in conjunction with the constants, listed in Table 2. These principles relate to the four hypothetical, illustrative scenarios that follow.

Scenario A

Some key considerations are outlined in this general survey of logistics.

SCALE AND SCOPE

This first scenario depicts very large multinational, conventional forces backed by nuclear, chemical, and biological weapons. It envisages operations on a major scale, conducted by combined forces in a number of theaters and areas of operations. It envisages central, allied operational command of balanced, collective forces: a mix of national contingents using common tactical and lo-

TABLE 3. *Summary of Suggested Logistic Principles*

Unity of purpose	Corporate effort
	Functional interdependence and integration
	Mutual understanding and confidence
	Cooperation and teamwork
Preparedness	Foresight and military judgment
	Determination of requirements
	Coordination of planning and plans
	Operational readiness
Viability	Feasibility and credibility
	Sufficiency
	Sustainability
	Dispersion and protection
Economy	Elimination of inefficiency and waste
	Role-effectiveness versus cost-effectiveness
	Rationalization, standardization, and specialization
	Integrated support
Responsiveness	Forward impetus and momentum
	Local, centralized control of resources
	Proactive, as well as reactive, support
	Dedication to duty
Resourcefulness	Versatility
	Improvisation and innovation
	Self-reliance, self-containment, and self-sufficiency
	Development of aptitudes and attitudes

gistical doctrines, concepts, and operating procedures. It also envisages integrated logistics of full scope and magnitude to support the forces deployed and the operations to be undertaken.

As far as land forces and joint land/air operations are concerned, allied commanders at corps level and above and national commanders at divisional level and below have full authority over assigned logistics and are fully responsible for the effective logistic support of their force, formation, or unit. Logistic integration and the reasonable degree of equipment standardization already achieved have enhanced the prospects of interoperability, mutual support, and cross servicing among the national contingents that make up the combined force. Single channels of command and comprehensive operational planning, local logistic control, and compatible management information systems have also enhanced capabilities at all structural levels to determine operational requirements, to take quick account of changed operational priorities, and to monitor and regulate day-to-day, hour-by-hour logistic support.

The plan provides for operational stocks of materiel in place in theaters and areas of operations. They are sufficient to sustain intense, conventional combat for a prescribed period of time. The plan also provides for stockpiles of war reserves either in place or available in logistic bases. It additionally provides for logistic resupply from home or other bases to replenish materiel usage, to replace materiel wastage, and to prolong conventional or nuclear operations. The planned system is outlined in Figure 2.

SYNCHRONIZATION AND COORDINATION

Intelligence indicators, alert measures, and the synchronized mobilization of multinational reserve forces all signal the start of transition to war. Existing in-place forces move to their operational sectors or battle positions, and they are joined by out-of-area, regular reinforcements. Concurrently, logistic support is activated and the initial out loading of stocks begins. These and the deployment of mobilized reserve elements add to the complexity and vitality of a massive movement operation, the plan for which has been agreed upon and rehearsed in peacetime. The movement plan incorporates all sea, air, and overland dispatch to, from, or within a theater of operations such as the one hypothetically illustrated in Figure 2. It also incorporates allied and host nation transportation and movement control facilities. The implementation of the plan is synchronized and coordinated by allied commanders.

REPLENISHMENT AND RESUPPLY

Initially, operations depend on in-theater or in-area stocks that are out loaded from depots and deployed in close support of forces. War reserves of materiel are designed to cover requirements for additional tasks and abnormally high expenditure, consumption, or casualty rates after war begins. In addition, strategic stocks of raw materials and components held in peacetime enable the defense industries of allies taking part in the operations to step up production so that resupply can begin as soon as practicable. The replenishment and

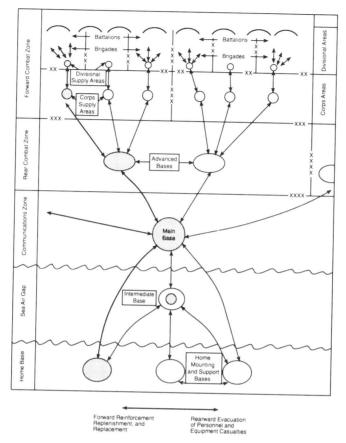

Figure 2. Scenario A: A developed theater of operations.

resupply systems are then complete and continue to operate for as long as possible.

Host Nation Support

The state or states forming the theaters and areas of operations have agreed to provide specific host nation support to allies contributing forces. This support is incorporated within the logistic buildup and deployment planning and, following implementation of the plans, continues for as long as possible.

Full Logistic System

Reference back to Figure 1, Table 2, and Figure 2, respectively, will recall the range of logistic functions and services available, the levels or lines of support, and the framework for an illustrative theater of operations. The full logistic system spans the facilities and distances from forward troops to home production plants, for as long as the lines of communication remain open. If the system fails at any point, friendly forces have to make do with the logistic resources they already possess, conserve them, and protect them from enemy attack.

SELF-SUFFICIENCY

Fighting formations and units are reasonably self-sufficient. They can operate, if the need arises, for several days without supply replenishment. They have facilities for repairing equipment and treating personnel casualties. Equipment and personnel decontamination and specialized medical support may be required should nuclear, chemical, or biological weapons be used. They have limited resources for dealing with massed casualties and have neither suitable nor sufficient road transportation to travel far for resupply.

Scenario B

The second hypothetical scenario illustrates a very much smaller scale of military deployment to assist the defense of a state that is under the threat of invasion by a hostile, well-armed neighbor. It outlines the operational setting, again concentrating on logistics. The commentary is written from the perspective of the supporting ally, who has strong forces and a developed operational capability.

A small, oil-rich state suddenly faces a threat of armed aggression from the north. It is an arid, desert, and quite primitive country with good roads, reasonable tracks, a developed port complex, and a prestigious international airport with facilities for strategic transport aircraft. There is another airfield near the principal oil field town in the center of the state. This airfield is capable of receiving and servicing medium-range tactical transport aircraft, helicopters, and fighters. A major surface oil pipeline connects the installations around the town with the port at the capital on the coast, where there is also a large refinery. The pipeline conveys crude oil to the port and delivers refined fuel to storage facilities at the town's airfield and the capital's international airport. The capital has modern infrastructure, including a modern, underutilized general hospital, and excellent port facilities run by the oil company (see Fig. 3).

The state is within strategic transport aircraft range of the supporting ally's home bases and a week's fast sailing from its home ports. A contingency plan for reinforcement and defense exists, and, after a rapid review and some revision of that plan, both allies agree to the following main tasks:

1. Indigenous land forces are to deploy as shown in Figure 3. The separate royal guard is to continue to protect vulnerable points, including the capital, port and international airport, as well as key dignitaries.
2. Indigenous naval and air forces, without reinforcements, are, respectively, to continue to protect coastal waters and the harbor from their base in the port and to provide tactical air reconnaissance, offensive air support, medium-range transport aircraft, and logistic helicopters from their bases at the international airport and the inland airfield.
3. The supporting ally's reinforcement land forces are to deploy near to the northern frontier and, initially, to conduct aggressive patrolling.
4. The supporting ally is to supplement and strengthen the state's operational command and planning capabilities.

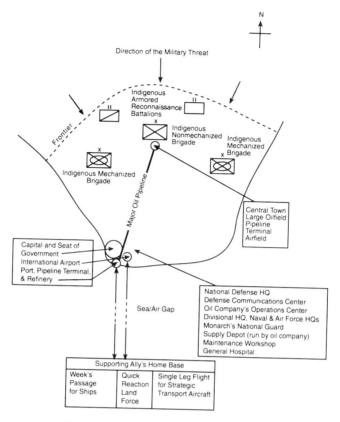

Figure 3. Scenario B: Opening situation.

5. The supporting ally is to provide logistic support for all indigenous and reinforcement land forces, less the self-contained royal guard. Some support is available from existing facilities and from local resources. The remainder is to be transported to the state by sea and air.

6. The supporting ally is to mount strategic air reconnaissance and early warning sorties and build up intelligence activities in the area.

The indigenous and reinforcement land forces are similarly organized. They use common main battle equipments, operating procedures, and terminology. The supporting ally's language is spoken extensively by the educated military and local population. The major oil company is jointly owned by the small state and the supporting ally, and the majority of its senior management and technical staff comprises seconded nationals or expatriates from the supporting ally. In addition, a number of the supporting ally's officers and technicians fill key appointments in the indigenous naval and air forces. The state's navy and air force are small but powerful. They are well trained and equipped, with sufficient logistic support. Further military details follow.

The national defense headquarters is located with other government departments in the capital. The commander in chief, a member of the royal family, has a small, efficient joint staff and a large, inexperienced civilian complement to assist him. He commands all forces, including the royal guard. Indigenous land forces, as well as the royal guard, are trained only for internal security duties. The national defense headquarters has a good communications center, network, and facilities. The oil company runs a small operations center that regulates its own large transport fleet, the pipeline, the refinery, and port facilities. It is located at the company's head office adjacent to national defense headquarters and has room for expansion.

A small divisional headquarters commands the indigenous land forces, but not the royal guard. It is currently sited with the national defense headquarters. The divisional commander is experienced and competent, but his general staff is inadequately trained and he has no logistic advisers. His division is undergoing intensive training at present and consists of:

- two mechanized infantry brigades comprising one tank and two mechanized infantry battalions, one artillery battery, and signal and logistic support companies;
- one nonmechanized infantry brigade of three rifle battalions, one artillery battery, signal and logistic support companies, and a troop-carrying transport battalion; and
- two armored reconnaissance battalions equipped with tracked vehicles and helicopters, and some organic support.

The logistic support organic to these formations and units needs no reinforcement, only training and specialist advice and assistance. To date, they have received support direct from static installations in the port area because no dedicated divisional-level logistic support exists. The supply depot provides a composite materiel service and is run by the oil company on an agency basis. The well-equipped maintenance workshop nearby is run by military expatriates. The general hospital admits military and civilian patients. The oil company can provide a substantial number of tanker trucks and other transport vehicles. Fuel, food, potable water, and labor are adequately available in the capital and central oil field town. The logistic assessment indicates the following main indigenous deficiencies: inadequate logistic command and planning capabilities, organization, systems, and training; no divisional logistic support; an inadequate military supply depot and no local resources team; no movement planning and control facilities.

The indigenous navy and air force can handle the reception and turnaround of military shipping and strategic transport aircraft.

Following the supporting ally's assessment of all operational and support requirements, it undertakes to provide:

1. a deputy commander in chief to be based at the national defense headquarters with the following main responsibilities: to act as chief of staff; to direct and coordinate the joint staff on behalf of the commander in chief; to task the defense communications center, network, and facilities; to establish a defense movement control center within the oil company's existing operations

center and to be responsible for its tasking and performance; to reinforce the joint logistic planning staff; and to set up and chair a logistic management committee with the oil company's managing director and key military officers and civilian officials as members

2. an increment for divisional headquarters comprising a deputy commander; a chief of staff; several general staff officers, including a complete G4 branch to undertake operational logistic planning; and certain specialist logistic advisers and their staffs

3. two reinforcement armored brigades with organic armored reconnaissance, combat, combat support, and combat service support units

4. a reinforcement logistic support force consisting of a headquarters, three battalions, a local resources team, and staff for the new defense movement control center

5. logistic support for all land forces, other than resources available locally

6. an operational reserve in the supporting ally's home base, should it be needed

Four additional operational planning arrangements are among those agreed upon for immediate implementation:

1. Reinforcements for the joint defense headquarters, the divisional headquarters, the local resources team, the staff for the defense movement control center, and key advanced parties are to arrive as soon as possible to start planning.

2. The national defense headquarters is to undertake in-area joint logistic planning of all support provided by an advanced base to be established around the capital, the port, and the international airport. The J4 branch is to be responsible for joint logistic planning, including joint movement planning.

3. Divisional headquarters is to undertake in-area land force and land/air operational planning, with its G4 branch dealing with logistic support and logistic training within the complete formation.

4. The supporting ally is to undertake all planning required to move reinforcements to the state and to sustain in-area operations by air and sea.

Once the initial reinforcements have arrived and planning has started, several additional decisions are made. Divisional headquarters is to move immediately to the central oil field town. It will locate at the airfield and establish a forward base there. It will extend its command to include the two reinforcement armored brigades, divisional troops, and the forward base. Air force headquarters is to provide a detachment of air staff for incorporation within divisional headquarters to assist with the planning and control of land/air operations and air logistic support. Air force headquarters is also to provide aero-medical casualty evacuation teams positioned in the forward and advanced bases.

The commander of the reinforcement logistic support force is to set up his headquarters in the advanced base, which he will command. He will deploy his force as follows:

1. A multifunctional logistic battalion is to be located in the *forward* base and will consist of

- a maintenance company with a field workshop and supply platoon
- a medical support company with a field hospital, ambulance platoon, and supply section
- several constructional engineering teams with requisite plant and equipment
- an administrative company with labor and local defense elements.

2. A supply battalion is to be located in the forward base and will be composed of

- an equipment and vehicle company with integral stock management, stock maintenance, handling, and transportation facilities
- two commodity companies, each with the facilities as above
- an ordnance engineering platoon
- catering and canteen services
- a map supply section
- an administrative company as in paragraph 1.

3. A supply battalion is to be located in the *advanced* base and will comprise elements similar to those listed in paragraph 2, plus a local resources supply platoon and a reserve of road transport to supplement the oil company's vehicle fleet. In addition, individual logistic reinforcements are provided to supplement the existing maintenance workshop and existing general hospital staffs.

4. Reinforcements are to be provided to run the newly established defense movement control center, including detachments to be positioned in the forward base, at the advance base headquarters, in the port, and at the international airport.

Having outlined the initial plan for in-area operations and support we should now return to the supporting ally's home base, where the main reinforcement process and the logistic buildup is about to begin.

PHASE 1—FINAL PREPARATIONS

The supporting ally's quick reaction force is ready for deployment at short notice. It consists of two component parts: air-portable elements and heavier elements that have to be transported by sea. The air-portable elements already have light scales of equipment and their immediate logistic support stocks. Additional items appropriate to desert operations are issued, such as special camouflage equipment and paint.

When the composition of the reinforcements is decided, the movement plan is made. The formations and units of the quick reaction force involved in the operation are returned from leave and placed on movement alert. The movement plan is implemented and the order given by the commander of the quick reaction force (deputy commander in chief designate) to move from peacetime locations to staging areas at home air bases and seaports. Final checks and adjustments are made to the movement plan and detailed instructions issued. The airlift and sealift of reinforcements commence.

PHASE 2—AIRLIFT

Air-portable elements are flown from one or more home air bases to the international airport of the state being reinforced. The movement plan allocates elements to sorties and provides loading instructions and manifests.

The strategic transport airlift requires overflying rights and air traffic control clearance, with emergency provision for landing and refueling en route. The aircraft return to home bases for additional passengers or cargo.

PHASE 3—SEALIFT

Troops, weapons, vehicles, equipment, and bulk stocks are embarked at one or more home ports. Sealift begins simultaneously with the start of the airlift. Transportation of these heavier elements is by naval logistic ships, auxiliary vessels, and civilian freighters. They disembark at the port of the state being reinforced.

Sailing time is one week for the fastest ships. The movement plan allows for a staggered arrival, which is convenient for the receiving port.

PHASE 4—BUILDUP

The national defense headquarters's in-area movement plan provides reception arrangements for reinforcements arriving by air and sea. Some are immediately flown or moved by road to the forward base, their operational deployment areas, or other employment locations. Others staying in the advanced base are moved by road to a transit area and then to their employment locations.

Urgent logistic requirements arrive by air, but the main buildup of operational stocks and war reserves follows by sea. In-area deployment to stockholding depots, units, or echelons is mainly undertaken by road. The logistic annexes of the divisional and joint operational plans respectively prescribe stocks to be held at all levels within the force.

Figure 4 illustrates the situation in the area of operations when all four reinforcement phases are complete. The following details of logistic support explain the services and systems provided:

1. In-area supply is normally by road from the supply depot in the advance base, via the forward base and brigade supply areas, and then to combat units. Air supply is used for urgent, air-portable requirements or when road transportation is impracticable. As well as the multipurpose helicopter, air supply involves medium-range transport aircraft operating into and out of the forward base. For example, at the airhead there, cargoes are loaded onto aircraft for air-dropping by parachute or free-fall delivery to units.
2. Forward repair is supplemented by the small field workshop in the forward base and the larger maintenance workshop in the advanced base.
3. Sick and wounded are treated forward and, if necessary, evacuated by road or air ambulance to the small field hospital in the forward base and the larger general hospital in the advanced base.
4. Constructional engineering tasks are undertaken by military teams in forward areas and range from building temporary accommodations to digging

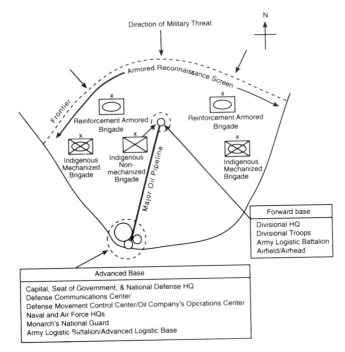

Figure 4. Scenario B: Reinforced situation.

wells. Tasks in the forward and advanced bases are carried out by civilian contractors. Adequate materials are available locally.

5. The oil company provides fuel from its pipeline and refinery. Some stocks of petrol, diesel, and lubricating oils are held in cans, but the main means of supplying fuel to brigades and units is by tanker truck. Food and certain other commodities are also available locally. Forward troops receive fresh and refrigerated rations regularly. Maps, mail, newspapers, and canteen supplies reach them through the normal supply system. Civilian labor is plentiful.

6. An additional task is to train indigenous logistic support personnel and units. The reinforcement operations, the strong defensive posture, the active and aggressive patrolling along the frontier areas, and the logistic buildup all serve to deter an attack. After six months, the reinforcement forces return to their home bases, leaving behind a logistic training team and certain logistic stocks. The supporting ally updates the contingency plan based on the experience gained.

Scenario C

Whereas the previous scenario describes a military emergency when reinforcement forces are invited to intervene and where local resources are plentiful, the next presents a different situation. Foreign insurgents have infiltrated a state and have forced the legal government to flee to a friendly neighboring country.

The intruders have now set up a puppet administration in the capital and are conducting a campaign to gain the support of the local population by brutal coercion. In this scenario, the supporting ally receives the request to intervene, from a government in exile, in a country that has precious little local resources to offer a military force and where certain elements of the population are hostile to or unsupportive of military intervention. However, the request has been made, not only to intervene, but also to defeat the insurgents, drive them out of the state, restore the rightful government, and reestablish law and order. The supporting ally agrees to assist and to mount an operation as soon as practicable.

The country is jungle covered (see Fig. 5). It has only primitive communications between an unwelcoming hinterland and the small coastal capital. There are jungle tracks linking riverside villages with hunting, farming, and logging areas, but, until the insurgents arrived, the two main rivers were the main arteries for trade and contact. Now riverboat trade has ceased. The local paramilitary police force is loyal to the legal government and is doing its best to remain in close touch with the hinterland tribespeople and the capital's business community. It is also in contact with exiled government ministers and

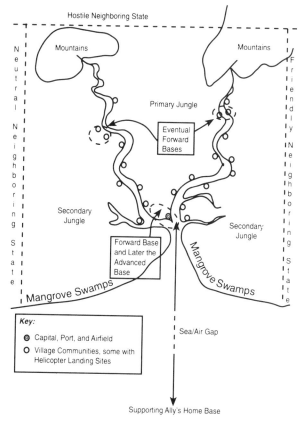

Figure 5. Scenario C.

officials, providing all the intelligence it can on the local situation. The police force has managed to hide the riverboat company's craft in creeks where the two main rivers join at the capital and port. It appears that most of the inland villagers either have fled to the jungle or are subjugated. The insurgents have set up several operating bases in the jungle and regularly visit villages to acquire food, medical supplies, and information. The puppet administration is evidently endeavoring to impose a 24-hour curfew in the capital, without much success. The military intervention is clearly also a *hearts and minds* operation.

The capital's port area has a single jetty with facilities to unload one reasonably sized freighter and a deepwater harbor where ships may anchor while their cargoes are unloaded by lighters onto the quayside. There is one airfield on the outskirts of the capital, with an all-weather strip and facilities suitable for medium-range tactical transport aircraft. The paramilitary police force had some helicopters until the president, ministers, senior officials, and their families fled in them. Several of the main villages on both rivers have helicopter landing sites, with several other landing sites within jungle areas.

The supporting ally has a large overseas base in the region, within medium tactical transport aircraft range of the capital's airfield and two days' sailing time for ships to reach its port. The operation is planned and mounted along lines similar to those described in Scenario B. The following commentary outlines the main events, again concentrating on logistics.

PHASE 1—INTERVENTION

Two parachute battalions drop on the airfield, secure it, and establish an operating base. They quickly make contact with the local paramilitary police force; secure the port, harbor, and riverboats; then secure vital points in the capital and capture the insurgent leaders. The battalions have sufficient logistic support to last 72 hours; however, their operation has been so successful that it enables the transport aircraft to fly in without delay.

The remainder of the air-portable elements of a parachute brigade are air landed. They establish a forward base around the airfield, with brigade headquarters, the third parachute battalion, combat support and combat service support units, and initial logistic support stocks located there.

Air-portable elements of a nonmechanized infantry brigade are flown in and relieve the parachute brigade in the capital and forward base. The parachute brigade regroups as a mobile, operational reserve. The main airlifted logistic buildup begins.

Logistic helicopters, the advanced parties of divisional headquarters, and key support units arrive in the forward base.

The local paramilitary police force reestablishes its authority in the capital and imposes strict curfews there, in the port and harbor areas, and in the lower reaches of the two main rivers.

The legal government returns and the president appoints the supporting ally's divisional commander as director of operations. The divisional commander establishes an operations and security committee with military, police, and government representation that also coordinates logistics.

PHASE 2—EXPLOITATION

The parachute brigade captures and secures the main villages upriver and opens several helicopter landing sites. It leaves one parachute battalion in the forward base as a mobile, operational reserve. It also opens and stocks some battalion bases in the best village locations.

The local police and tribespeople help to build defensible perimeters around the main villages and helicopter landing sites.

The infantry brigade, transported by rivercraft and helicopter, systematically and progressively clears both main rivers and links up with the parachuted forces. It leaves one infantry battalion in the capital to support the police. Logistic stocks are then ferried forward by river as well as by air.

The sea tail arrives in the harbor and port. Divisional headquarters, divisional troops, and the two brigades are now complete with their heavier elements. The logistic buildup is accelerated.

Combat and constructional engineers improve all the main facilities in the area of the capital, build harbor and river defenses, and improve existing and develop new up-country bases.

A second nonmechanized infantry brigade arrives by air and sea. The force is complete and the logistic buildup continues.

PHASE 3—CONSOLIDATION

Having regrouped and reorganized his force, the divisional commander/director of operations allots each infantry brigade a main river sector to clear and secure, with one infantry battalion remaining in the capital. He orders the parachute brigade to mount deep penetration patrols into the jungle and mountainous areas along the border with the state that sent in the insurgents. One parachute battalion remains as the mobile force reserve.

A brigade base is established in both river sectors, and an all-weather airstrip is built in each. These bases now become forward bases with enough logistic support and stocks for the two infantry brigades to be assured of reasonable self-sufficiency.

The original forward base around the capital now becomes the advanced base for the operations, and divisional headquarters, divisional troops, and the mobile force reserve are also sited there.

The local police and local guides provide invaluable assistance, tactically and logistically, to the conduct of operations in the hinterland. Gradually, well-controlled and -coordinated insurgent-free areas are being extended outward from firm, secure operational and logistic bases. These bases are established at patrol/platoon, company, battalion, and brigade levels.

Logistic replenishment of forward bases continues, the in-area buildup of stocks is now complete, and resupply from the supporting ally's overseas base maintains in-area operational stocks and war reserves.

Business is again starting to flourish in the capital. River trading resumes, the military force provides some logistic assistance for the hinterland tribespeople, the paramilitary police force is expanded and trained, the operations and security committee is working well, and life for a growing portion of the local population is returning to normal.

Without repeating relevant details for Scenario B, this commentary is concluded with some further logistical elaboration. Jungle operations present some severe challenges. Combat and combat support units operate mainly on foot, carrying light equipment and their immediate logistic stocks. Their heavier equipment and larger support stocks have to be transported over the jungle by air and moved into jungle clearings whenever practicable by helicopters. If no air transport is available, loads have to be carried by river craft or by troops, porters, or pack animals along jungle tracks, often over difficult terrain and in bad weather. The constantly hot, humid climate can also cause health and hygiene problems. The sick invariably outnumber the wounded in this type of operation. Acclimatization and many other preventive health and hygiene measures are vital, as in most extreme climates. Skilled first aid is also vital, as in all combat operations. Casualty evacuation can be difficult and hazardous—by air, by river, or on foot—in the quest to move the seriously ill and wounded to the nearest doctor or, if necessary, farther back to a field or general hospital.

The all-pervading dampness encountered in jungle conditions can result in inoperable equipment. The relatively small number of maintenance specialists, combined with movement problems, may well inhibit forward repair and equipment evacuation. As operations of this type critically depend on each item of equipment, wherever it is deployed, logistic support must effectively and by priority overcome these problems. Likewise, there are rarely enough sappers for the wide variety of constructional engineering tasks they are expected to complete in an area of operations such as the one depicted here. These tasks are, of course, additional to normal combat engineer missions. Improved shelter, tracks, bridges over rivers, and water supplies can lift morale considerably. Mail, news, and canteen supplies are also substantial comforts, especially for troops operating in small groups in an alien jungle environment, and items such as these are likely to be moved forward as part of the normal supply system—however tenuous the system.

Daily replenishment is the aim and is achieved whenever and wherever practicable. If bad weather, the unavailability of helicopters, or the inaccessibility of troop locations makes air supply impracticable, then jungle bases hold a small reserve of stocks. Otherwise, a simple operating procedure enables each patrol or unit to obtain daily replenishment according to a standard, agreed-upon list of commodities. Each commodity on the standard list has a simple code, used when it is necessary to add or subtract items, that is quickly transmitted by radio. This system of management by exception is efficient and economical and minimizes radio traffic. Daily supply packs are made up to standard or variable requirements in rear bases and airdropped, air landed, or moved by surface means. Daily supply is the system predominantly in use in this scenario. Air support is, however, the key to its full effectiveness and success. Without transport aircraft and helicopters, the delivery of daily supply packs can cause severe logistic problems. Air logistic support is a joint land/air operation that is best planned, coordinated, and controlled by the divisional commander in this scenario, with authority for local tasking of certain logistic helicopters also vested in brigade headquarters.

Scenario D

The three preceding scenarios have dealt with logistics in general war, a threatened limited-localized war of much lesser scale, and counterinsurgency operations. The last scenario illustrates support of an internal security situation when military forces come to the aid of a civil power in a remote island state. The island is heavily populated and largely undeveloped, with mineral resources of critical strategic and commercial importance to the supporting ally. The latter has a vital telecommunications, radio intercept, and satellite tracking installation on the island's single, high mountain not far from the capital. In addition, the supporting ally has enjoyed sole mining and export rights of the mineral resources, and a considerable number of its nationals manage the mines and mining services on the island. Apart from these nationals and a privileged minority of the local population, most islanders are uneducated, have a low quality of life, lack basic amenities, and are overtly discontented (see Fig. 6)

In an effort to increase its income and improve the lot of the ordinary people, the island's government negotiates and signs a deal that will enable other countries to dump large quantities of highly toxic waste in unused mine workings. This signals widespread dissidence, sabotage, and terrorism. The internal security situation is fast deteriorating and there are bomb fatalities occurring in commercial, retail, and higher-class residential areas. Strikes disrupt the mining industry and all public services, and the one port and the one airport are closed. The island's government revokes the toxic waste dumping agreement, imposes curfews, and threatens to declare martial law. The local police force is stretched to the breaking point.

The supporting ally anticipated trouble and has recently reviewed and revised its contingency plan for protecting its nationals, both resident and working on the island; protecting its mining interests and other vital installations; and evacuating its nationals should the need arise. It has no overseas base within operating distance of the island state, so has positioned a joint amphibious task force nearby, exercising and monitoring events closely. The supporting ally agrees to mount an internal security operation from the joint amphibious task force in order to help restore law, order, and normality on the island.

The task force consists of an aircraft carrier, maritime protection vessels, logistic ships, and a hospital ship. It carries afloat marines and infantry trained and equipped for riot control and other internal security duties, some Special Forces and intelligence elements, several explosive ordnance disposal (bomb disposal) teams, as well as appropriate logistic support for a force deployed on the island. The following description concentrates on the main military actions and particularly focuses on logistics.

The rear admiral commanding the joint task force has direct working links

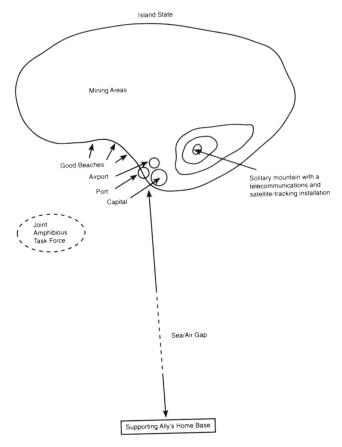

Figure 6. Scenario D.

with the island state's government and with his home base. He has responsibility for planning and conducting the internal security operations on the island and their support from his task force. He completes his exercise and moves his force nearer to the island.

Naval helicopters transport marines, infantry, and their immediate logistic support to an operating and logistic base established at the airport. The land-based element quickly builds up and deploys to selected vital or vulnerable points, commanded by a brigadier general who sets up his headquarters at the airport base. He remains responsible for land-based operations and support to the admiral and has priority call on sea-based reinforcements, logistic support, and helicopters. The land-based commander also provides direct liaison with the island's police force and public authorities. He gradually widens the scope and capacity of his internal security operations, builds up his land-based logistics, and progressively establishes a network of smaller operating and logistic bases.

Meanwhile, island nationals of the supporting ally, together with threatened local civilians, are moved into refuge areas for protection. Some are moved into transit areas to await transport to the airport or to the naval task force. The land-based military forces help the police and the managers of public services, communications, and utilities to get essential facilities working again as quickly as possible.

The port, however, remains closed and is the center of militant political and trade union activity. It is badly damaged, and its sea and land access is obstructed. The joint amphibious task force has logistic ships capable of beaching and discharging their roll-on/roll-off cargoes over the good beaches indicated in Figure 6. From early in the operations, logistic ships have been unloading reinforcements, the heavier equipments, and bulk logistic stocks to strengthen the land-based forces. This means of entry substantially supplements the air bridge from task force to island and allows helicopters to be used for tactical purposes and for transporting urgent logistic requirements from ship to shore or on over-island sorties. Helicopters returning to their land or afloat bases carry personnel casualties for treatment on the hospital ship or vital air-portable equipments for task force repair. Non-air-portable repairable equipment is evacuated from the island across the beaches and onto logistic ships.

The strike is broken at the airport and the facilities there start receiving strategic transport aircraft flown from the supporting ally's home base, staging and refueling in flight en route. High-priority air-portable reinforcements and logistic requirements are thereby transported to the island. Families are evacuated on returning flights.

When the land-based force is complete, the land force commander becomes directly responsible to the state's government for internal security operations. The admiral and the residue of his joint amphibious task force remain in island waters as a reserve, with a large proportion of the naval helicopters disembarked and land based under the operational control of the land force commander.

Eventually, the port is repaired and opened, the sea bridge links the island with the supporting ally's home base, and the logistic buildup is completed. The amphibious task force, less its land-based elements, then withdraws. When the situation on the island returns to normal, the land force thins out and a smaller internal security garrison of principally infantry and support elements remains for a few months. The garrison retains sufficient specialized logistic personnel and facilities to meet its operational requirements; it obtains, by then, most of its domestic needs from island sources. Apart from a contingency reserve of military materiel kept on the island for use by any reinforcements— should they be requested and airlifted there in the future—all other surplus logistic resources are returned to the supporting ally's home base by sea.

In this scenario as in others, the helicopter proves its worth tactically and logistically. In its logistical role, the helicopter carries internal or external cargo. Its crew is adept at reaching isolated locations to land or winch down loads. Ground- or ship-based supporting teams are specially trained to prepare loads and to task logistic helicopters. Weather, limited flying hours, serviceability, and availability all govern helicopter operations, but, with sound servicing and handling, the helicopter introduces invaluable flexibility and speed of reaction to operational environments.

There have been other significant improvements in the field of logistic movement. Bulk stocks of commodities are placed on pallets, in special containers, or on a combination of pallets loaded into containers for transportation by sea, air, rail, road, or inland waterway. For example, a single pallet may contain a number of complete artillery rounds—shell, propellant charge, fuze, and primer; pallets and containers may carry multi-item or single-item stocks for a particular purpose, mission, or user; the loading, unloading, or transloading of pallets or containers is considerably assisted by roller-conveyors mounted on the floor of the mode of conveyance—hold of a ship or floor of an aircraft, railway wagon, or road vehicle. Pallets and containers require specialized handling equipment and skilled operators. Provided these are available, substantial savings in time and manual effort are made by utilizing these and similar logistic movement means most effectively.

The computer, telecommunications, and such specific aids as telefacsimile have revolutionized the methods of monitoring, regulating, and controlling logistics. Management information systems of impressive and ever-increasing usefulness help commanders, planners, logisticians, and users to make the best operational use of available logistic resources. Rapidly advancing technology is having as much impact on logistic doctrine, concepts, procedures, and techniques as any other facet of military activity. This is so, whether we are examining the logistic support of global total nuclear war (Scenario A) or some form of armed conflict of lesser magnitude and intensity (such as Scenarios B–D); whether we are examining the logistic support of land or air forces, maritime logistics, or a combination of operational environments.

Conclusion

The challenges of *pure* logistics (forecasting and determining requirements) and *applied* logistics (planning, preparing, and providing support) remain as difficult today as in the past. Tailoring support to sustain a small, quick-reaction force is just as challenging and vital in the context of a particular operation as the accumulation of huge stockpiles of resources during a protracted period of cold war. It is possible that the days of vast, permanent, expensive, base logistic installations are numbered as greater dependence is judiciously placed upon the swifter means of logistic movement, "just-in-time" supply practices, and the management information systems now available. The days of "shoestring" logistics featuring rationed resources and financial stringencies are never likely to be numbered. The resources devoted to military support are always likely to be less than most conscientious logisticians relish.

Sound military judgment will continue to be crucially applied when deciding the *extent* of viable, yet affordable, logistic support needed to sustain military operations or foreseen contingencies. Sound logistic experience and expertise will continue to be crucially applied when deciding the *organization* and *methods* required to achieve effective operational readiness and effective combat service support. The principle of continuity provides a stable platform from which to provide operational logistics, while the principle of change underlines the constructive part that imaginative, innovative, new ideas should play in determining the most effective form of logistic support for the future.

Before the Second World War, when experimentation and preparedness were lacking, the military inclination to remain the same, despite the pressing need for change, drew this pithy comment from Liddell Hart: "There's only one thing more difficult than getting a new idea into a military mind, and that's getting an old one out" (J. C. T. Downey, *Management in the Armed Forces: An Anatomy of the Military Profession* [London: McGraw-Hill, 1977], p. 19). Now that the change from globalized cold war places renewed emphasis on the potential continuity of localized hot wars and now that the quest to reduce the overbearing logistic bill for standing forces stresses the desirability of seeking new support concepts without jeopardizing the essential need for resourceful logistics responsive to all military calls, so there should be an inquisitive demand for fresh ideas and some experimentation. Military commitments and requirements are compelling certain nations to review their defense policies, priorities, programs, and capabilities, given declining military budgets.

In conclusion, this general survey of logistics offers some reminders of the past that would seem relevant to the future. They may help in the review and revision of military support functions so that logistics remains appropriately geared to possible future developments.

SOME CONCLUDING REMINDERS

Huston (1966) makes this claim in his masterful work on logistics, *The Sinews of War:* "Logic would suggest—and military planners would prefer to believe— that logistic plans stem from strategic plans" (p. 424). He then proceeds to remind us of the succession of instances during World War II when high-level strategic decisions were based on logistical limitations, more than on any other consideration—hence the need to assess all factors and blend all considerations when making operational plans and command decisions and when making all preparations and meeting all requirements for support.

Van Creveld (1977) reminds us in his more recent, major work, *Supplying War:* "The aim of military organization is not to make do with the smallest number of supporting troops, but to produce the greatest possible fighting power" (p. 225). Hence the need to replace a fanciful preoccupation with "teeth-to-tail" ratios—of minimal descriptive and functional value—with force structures that create and maintain a mix, balance, and ratio of combat and support elements in meaningful, effective harmony.

Logistical lessons from past campaigns should be objectively recorded and descriptively presented; and, if they remain relevant to the future, they should be carefully taught and assiduously learned. Only by satisfying all these requirements will we be sure that evaluated lessons from the past are employed appropriately in the future and are not neglected or overlooked.

We are reminded to avoid the mistake of automatically attributing the logistic performance of combat and support forces during peacetime training to the way they may acquit themselves in a real war. Only if major peacetime exercises realistically test their logistic performance may we draw valid conclusions about operational readiness and combat effectiveness.

Military commanders and senior operational planners—who may lack all-around operational experience, through no fault of their own—need to receive sound logistical advice. Only by obtaining the best advice are they able to make informed military judgments and effective decisions. Advice on logistics also has to be relayed to, and understood by, involved politicians in many situations of military emergency or war.

We must be wary of lax, complacent, and unimaginative logisticians who may well offer "broad-brush" generalities as solutions or sanction waste and other inefficiencies in order to keep an uncontentious, low profile during their some-times undistinguished and long professional careers. Only if logisticians are prepared to be demonstrably single minded and to "rock the boat" when con-ditions warrant will deficiencies be corrected and improvements made.

Arbitrary cuts in peacetime may well expose yawning gaps in logistic support in an emergency or war. It will invariably be too late and too difficult to rectify deficiencies when the chips are down.

Finally, we are reminded that the continuity of change is a constant phe-nomenon of military logistics, as of any worthy enterprise, and this serves to emphasize the importance of planning and managing change now and in the future.

J. H. SKINNER

SEE ALSO: Combat Service Support; Consumption Rates, Battlefield; Mainte-nance; Reinforcements.

Bibliography

Alexander, G. M. 1986. Military logistics. *Journal of Defense and Diplomacy* 4(6).
Beaumont, R. A. 1985. Beyond teeth and tail: The need for new logistical analogies. *Military Review* 1985 (March).
Brown, K. N. 1987. *Strategics: The logistics-strategy link.* Washington, D.C.: National Defense Univ. Press.
Dupuy, T. N. 1977. *A genius for war: The German army and the general staff: 1807–1945.* Englewood Cliffs, N.J.: Prentice Hall.
Eccles, W. E. 1959. *Logistics in the national defense.* Harrisburg, Pa.: Stackpole.
———. 1965. *Military concepts and philosophy.* New Brunswick, N. J.: Rutgers Univ. Press.
Freedman, L. 1986. Logistics and mobility in modern warfare. *Armed Forces* 1986 (February).
Huston, J. A. 1966. *The sinews of war: Army logistics 1775–1953.* Army Historical Series. Washington, D.C.: Office of the Chief of Military History, United States Army.
International Institute for Strategic Studies (IISS). 1969. *Military logistic systems in NATO: The goal of integration—Part 1: Economic aspects.* London: IISS.
———. 1970. *Military logistic systems in NATO: The goal of integration—Part 2: Military aspects.* London: IISS.
Kelley, R. C. 1977. Applying logistic principles. *Military Review* 1977 (September).
Kennon, J. E. C. 1983. Logistics and the Royal Navy. *Journal of the Australian Naval Institute* 1983 (February).

Meixner, D. 1895. *Historischer Rückblick auf die Verpflegung der Armeen in Felde.* 2 volumes. Vienna.

North Atlantic Treaty Organization. 1989. *NATO logistic handbook.* Brussels: NATO.

Peilow, B. F. 1987. Should logistics replace administration as a principle of war? *Naval Review* 1987 (July).

Reed, J. 1988. A look at current and future logistic systems. *Armada International* 1985 (July).

Thorpe, G. C. 1986. *Pure logistics: The science of war preparation.* Washington, D.C.: National Defense Univ. Press.

van Creveld, M. 1977. *Supplying war: Logistics from Wallenstein to Patton.* Cambridge, UK: Cambridge Univ. Press.

LOW-INTENSITY CONFLICT: THE MILITARY DIMENSION

The term *low-intensity operations* was introduced in the 1960s, and from it, the term *low-intensity conflict* (LIC) emerged in the 1980s. It refers to a situation between peace (when no arms are used) and the full-scale use of weapons in conventional war.

During such a situation there is extensive diplomatic, economic, and psychological activity, but its primary feature is the covert or overt use of military force short of war. The military may have noncombat missions, such as training assistance, advisory assistance, or peacekeeping, but the missions may also be combat oriented, such as in counterinsurgencies, reprisals, or limited contingencies that call for so-called "special operations."

Because low-intensity conflict is not a uniform phenomenon but rather a series of dissimilar incidents, the part that military power can or should play in connection with those incidents cannot be precisely defined. As the forces that created a low-intensity conflict situation become more violent and confrontational, the opportunities for military involvement become clearer. These may appear in categories that include: insurgency, counterinsurgency, peacekeeping, and contingencies calling for "special operations."

Low-intensity conflict can involve activities ranging from diplomatic, economic, and psychological through subversion, insurgency, and guerrilla warfare. Clandestine and covert actions to seize or to release hostages may take place, and acts of terrorism—used as psychological weapons—may be carried out. Special operations forces may be used in any or all of these roles and in such capacities can contribute either to the success of insurgents or to that of the forces mobilized to fight insurgency.

Insurgency

Resistance to the governing structure of a country becomes most critical when dissidence and subversion produce active insurgency. While still technically within a low-intensity conflict context, insurgent movements may spawn guerrilla forces that add a substantial military dimension to the struggle. If guerrilla formations develop to proportions that permit them to engage conventional military units on equal terms, the insurgency may move from the low-intensity conflict arena to that of conventional warfare. Guerrilla warfare is a product of those forces that have combined to oppose the targeted government on every level at which it is seen to be vulnerable: psychological, political, economic, or military.

Both the political and military leaders of a nation threatened by insurgency must analyze and understand its root causes. If the targeted government becomes aware of and is sensitive to the rumblings of discontent among its population prior to open antigovernment violence, that government may reduce the threat through political, social, and economic reforms. Without a dynamic information campaign to convince the public that the contemplated reforms are real and imminent, however, the effect of even extensive ultimate reforms upon the incipient insurgency may be negligible.

Although a government may genuinely seek answers to problems known to spawn dissidence, subversion, and insurgency, corrective measures that are theoretically possible may not be feasible. Deep-seated racial, ethnic, religious, and social differences, which have resulted in conflict and turmoil for centuries, often defy correction even if patience, logic, and law are invoked hand-in-hand over protracted periods. Crushing economic woes of a one- or two-commodity country can sometimes be alleviated only by major changes in the foreign policies and trading patterns of several other countries. Those countries may be unwilling to modify their national lifestyles in order to relieve the internal stresses of the afflicted country and thereby to save it from internal upheaval.

Histories of major insurgent movements indicate that dissatisfaction with entrenched regimes is frequently so deep and fundamental that no concessions short of abdication will satisfy the insurgent leadership. If hostility toward the government, as expressed by dissident subversive propaganda, is shared by any considerable element of the population, efforts to suppress the insurgency are not likely to be successful.

Social and political systems that permit free dissent provide a much less favorable climate for subversion and insurgency than those in which voiced opposition is likely to be punished. On the other hand, some totalitarian systems have developed the mechanics of repression into a fine art. These may prove adequate for indefinitely holding in check even widespread potential for insurgency. Such repressive systems are often brittle, however, and subject to catastrophic disintegration. As was demonstrated in Eastern Europe in 1989, the majority who have been held vassal to the few may decide to endure the risk, pain, and trauma of breaking their chains.

Counterinsurgency

Counterinsurgency is a term applied to political, economic, social, military, and paramilitary measures that indigenous governments and associates use to forestall or defeat revolutionary war. It applies also to similar measures that occu-

pying powers use to prevent or defeat resistance movements. The role of military power in defeating an insurgency may range from substantial to supporting or even to peripheral. Counterinsurgency measures call for the use of almost every resource available to the government that is the target of the insurgency, including:
1. intelligence and counterintelligence
2. psychological operations
3. police
4. military forces
5. diplomacy.

Subversion

Successful counterinsurgency planning requires in-depth information about the subversive infrastructure. This infrastructure provides the insurgency with inspiration, intelligence, recruits, training, planning, and logistics. Neutralization of the subversive infrastructure by the counterintelligence systems of the government will normally receive a high priority. The cellular structure of a well-implanted resistance movement, however, makes it difficult to neutralize; vigorous government efforts may net minor and local successes without seriously damaging the overall underground movement.

A desperate government may try to inhibit the growth of subversion with repressive measures against the general population; the aim being to make cooperation with the resistance movement more hazardous. Such measures have achieved mixed results historically and generally create more dissidence than they suppress.

Psychological Programs

In free and open societies, psychological operations against domestic audiences range from difficult to impossible. In societies where free press and freedom of speech are looked upon as part of the fabric of the nation, government attempts to develop information programs, either for or against movements with strong political overtones, are not feasible.

Police-Military Cooperation

A well-trained, disciplined police force can be the first line of defense against civil disorder. If it works meticulously within the framework of the law and demonstrates attitudes that are viewed as fair and impartial, it can sometimes prevent escalation of minor incidents into major confrontations. Good police intelligence systems normally acquire intimate knowledge of the personalities, rumors, and activities in crowded urban ghettos, where living conditions may be one of the factors that gives rise to and nurtures subversion. If an insurgency grows to proportions that are beyond the capabilities of the police, military assistance may be called upon. A smooth transition from police authority to that of a militia or the regular armed forces can be facilitated by provisions of law, enacted and tested prior to their invocation in an actual emergency. The lack of such a smooth transition procedure in China in 1989 set the stage for the Tiananmen Square incident in Beijing.

Conventional military forces are not normally well suited to engage in counterinsurgency operations without substantial modifications. Changes in orientation, training, personnel selection procedures, organization, and equipment are dictated by the requirements of missions against an enemy whose tactics are unorthodox and whose targets frequently are less purely military than they are psychological and political. Coordination of military counterinsurgency activities with those of police and other nonmilitary governmental agencies requires mutually accepted and practiced operating procedures that may vary considerably from standard military models.

Military Counterguerrilla and Antiguerrilla Operations

Destruction of guerrilla movements through the complex formulas applicable to counterinsurgency can differ substantially from antiguerrilla tactics used by military forces in the field under wartime conditions. In the first instance, to supplement and complement tactical operations against guerrillas, popular support for the guerrilla movement must be eroded through carefully planned and executed civic actions, propaganda campaigns, and governmental reforms. In the last case, troop commanders may hold the civilian population responsible for guerrilla attacks and take drastic measures in reprisal. The long-term and lasting benefits that stem from viewing guerrilla movements as part of a political and social phenomenon that cannot be addressed solely through the use of military strength may be considered of secondary importance by a troop commander who sees his primary mission as one best accomplished through fire and movement.

Tactical operations by conventional military forces against guerrillas call for

1. mobility comparable to or greater than that of the guerrillas,
2. small-unit leadership of exceptionally high quality,
3. intelligence not always available through purely military collection systems, and
4. the ability to live in the field with minimal resupply for protracted periods.

Military Civic Action

Urgently needed civic assistance programs using conventional military forces, skills, equipment, and supplies tend to project the image of a benevolent government and to challenge subversive propaganda. But extensive use of military personnel for activities that normally lie within the civilian sector can also serve to create friction with labor unions and elsewhere within the economy. This in turn can give certain elements within the indigenous society perceived excuses for antigovernment attitudes. Military forces in civic action roles are most effective when their presence, guidance, and material support serve to inspire the local populace to address and solve their own problems. In matters of counterinsurgency, the actions and attitudes of the police and the military are generally seen by the indigenous population as reflecting those of the government whose orders are being implemented. Thus, in confronting an actual or incipient insurgency, the message sent to the people through the security forces is vital.

Population and Resource Control

In addition to their intelligence and counterintelligence capabilities, the police and military establishments are major instruments through which population and resource control may be exercised. Inhibition of freedom to travel—through such means as requirements for special passes, movable roadblocks, checkpoints, and curfews—assists security forces in making the environment more inhospitable for insurgents. Rationing of items needed to carry on normal living and business activity may aid in cutting the flow of public assistance to underground organizations and force them to surface in search of supplies. Both population and resource control can become counterproductive from a psychological point of view if they are viewed as illegal or arbitrary or if they are designed so that they harass the innocent while seeking the guilty. If martial law is put into effect as a counterinsurgency measure, its impact on the general public can be lightened by repeated government explanations of the reasons why certain civil liberties are being denied temporarily and promises that they will be restored as soon as national security is no longer in jeopardy. The success of population and resource control as a counterinsurgency measure depends on the selection and training of the security forces and their sensitivity in dealing with people under conditions of stress.

Insurgency and Counterinsurgency—Role of Foreign Assistance

Insurgency movements, both in the underground stage and later as active, organized guerrilla forces, may seek and receive assistance from foreign sources. In such cases the external counterinsurgency strategy of the targeted government will include not only physical interdiction measures but also vigorous diplomatic initiatives. The latter may urge censure and economic penalties against the foreign supporters of the indigenous insurgency while soliciting international approval, funds, military equipment, and supplies for its own counterinsurgency campaigns.

The impact of foreign assistance upon an indigenous counterinsurgency effort is a function of several important factors. Among these is the extent to which foreign aid and advice are the products of in-depth understanding of the history, political aims, anthropology, and mores of the recipient country.

It is unlikely that the strategy, tactics, organizational concepts, and equipment reflected in the skills and philosophical orientations of the foreign military forces will be appropriate for the highly specialized counterinsurgency needs of the recipient country. Motivation for foreign sources to provide assistance for governments confronted with incipient or actual insurgency generally falls within categories that can be described as strategic, economic, traditional, or idealistic.

The internal stability of a potential client nation may attract a patron nation's aid to ensure the patron's own security. Continued access to world markets and to strategic raw materials important both to national defense and to economic vitality may even suggest counterinsurgency assistance to governments whose ruling philosophies are only marginally compatible with those of the aid donor. Politically active ethnic groups within the societies of potential sources of foreign counterinsurgency assistance can either facilitate or negate the flow of aid to governments that have requested it. Idealistic or unrealistic parameters limiting the amount or the manner in which counterinsurgency assistance is used may stem from the foreign providers' attempts to project their own political and social systems as models for the government under attack.

In rare cases, the strategic aims and political objectives of the indigenous government under insurgent pressure coincide with those of the foreign sources of assistance. Most often, however, foreign counterinsurgency "advisers" are accepted primarily as conduits through which supplies, equipment, and funds may be acquired. Pressures from foreign aid donors aimed at influencing the political end products of indigenous counterinsurgency efforts succeed or fail in direct proportion to the sophistication and dexterity of the diplomatic efforts through which they are applied.

A domestic insurgency represents a condition that only the indigenous people themselves can solve satisfactorily. Outside help may be solicited and may be instrumental in enabling the indigenous government to remain in power; but the conditions placed upon provision of assistance from foreign sources may serve to produce a hybrid product unsuited to either the political or the social fabric of the recipient country. If foreign assistance to a beleaguered indigenous government is the decisive factor in defeating an insurgency, it may demonstrate that the base for the insurgency among the people was neither wide nor deep.

Historical Examples of Counterinsurgency

Examination of the counterinsurgency successes achieved by the British in Malaya (1948–57); the government of the Philippines under President Magsaysay (1946–54); and in Greece (1945–49) provides source material from which a number of common characteristics can be extracted. The British success in Malaya was chiefly due to easy ethnic identification of the insurgents (Chinese) and well-executed programs that isolated the guerrillas from the indigenous population. Magsaysay's victory was characterized by brilliant civic action and propaganda programs. Generally the success of the counterinsurgents in Greece has been attributed to the fact that the guerrillas' access to external support was effectively severed.

On the other hand, the failures of counterinsurgency measures in Cuba (1953–59); in South Vietnam (1959–65); and in Portuguese Africa and Zimbabwe (Rhodesia) during the same periods illustrate some characteristics of unsuccessful counterinsurgencies. The inability of the Batista regime to deal with Fidel Castro's insurgent movement had much to do with the blatant corruption of the government and lack of inspirational leaders working against the guerrillas. South Vietnamese forces failed to defeat the Vietcong because of political turmoil, superb Communist guerrilla organization, and mediocre government leadership. Both the Portuguese government in Angola and Mozambique, as well as the government in Rhodesia, lacked popular support and were therefore doomed.

Military Aspects of LIC

The role military forces play in low-intensity conflict situations may be quite minor. Most likely, more insurgencies have been quelled by rapid, effective political action than by military repression. On the other hand, external military assistance to an insurgent movement may be limited and, in some cases, counterproductive if that aid is seen as intrusive by the indigenous population. Intelligent, responsive, political measures, however, coupled with rapid, pervasive military operations may combine to defeat the best of insurgent movements. Although subversion and psychological programs are not necessarily military in nature, they may have military aspects. Military civic action and population and resource control efforts are likely to involve military forces and can be critical to the success of a counterinsurgency campaign.

The ongoing insurgent and counterinsurgent efforts in Afghanistan, Ethiopia, El Salvador, Cambodia, and Angola readily illustrate the persistence of LIC and the roles of military forces in these conflicts.

WILLIAM P. YARBOROUGH

SEE ALSO: Psychological Warfare; Special Operations Forces; Unconventional War.

Bibliography

Alexander, Y., ed. 1979. *Terrorism: An international journal* 3 (1 and 2). New York: Crane Russak.

Bacevich, A. J., J. D. Hallums, R. H. White, and T. F. Young. 1988. *American military policy in small wars: The case of El Salvador.* Institute for Foreign Policy Analysis. Cambridge, Mass., and McLean, Va.: Pergamon-Brassey's.

Collins, J. M. 1987. *Green Berets, Seals, and Spetsnaz.* McLean, Va.: Pergamon-Brassey's.

Kitson, F. 1971. *Low intensity operations.* Harrisburg, Pa.: Stackpole Books.

Levytsky, B. 1972. *The uses of terror.* New York: Coward, McCann and Geoghegan.

Molnar, A. R., et al. 1965. *Human factors considerations of undergrounds in insurgencies.* Washington, D.C.: American Univ.

Navarre, H. 1956. *Agonie de l'Indochiné.* Paris: Librairie Plon.

Sully, F. 1968. *The age of the guerrilla.* New York: Parents Magazine Press.

M

MACHINE GUN

In today's modern armies, machine guns constitute the main direct firepower of infantry troops against dismounted forces, lightly armored vehicles, and aircraft. Their use, however, is not restricted to infantry formations, and they appear in other combat units, in aircraft, aboard ships and patrol boats, as well as in combat support and combat service support units. They are classified by mission and physical characteristics into four general categories: light, general purpose, medium, and heavy.

Historical Background

Rapid-firing and multiple-firing weapons, precursors to the modern, fully automatic machine gun, were considered as early as the fifteenth century, when nations sought ways to increase their military's ability to inflict losses upon an enemy without increasing the overall number of gunpowder weapons.

Among the first successful designers of rapid-fire weapons was London lawyer James Puckel (1667–1724), who invented a single-barrel gun with manually operated revolving cylinders; this gun was reportedly capable of firing "63 times in seven minutes." Although the British Board of Ordnance declined to accept the weapon into service after a demonstration in 1717, Puckel was issued a patent (1718). The only record of service of the weapon comes from an account of an abortive expedition against the French in Saint Lucia and Saint Vincent in 1727.

In 1851, Belgian captain T. H. J. Fafchamps invented the *mitrailleuse*, a multiple-firing weapon with 37 rifled barrels encased in a wrought-iron tube. An iron plate with matching holes was used for loading and sealing the chambers, and a hand crank fired the weapon. In one minute, a practiced team could fire as many as 12 bursts, or 444 rounds. The *mitrailleuse* was accepted for French service in 1867 but lasted only a year because of repeated mechanical failures and because it was used in batteries—its proper tactical use among infantry was never exploited. The name continues in French use to describe a machine gun regardless of type.

The most successful rapid-fire weapon of the mid-nineteenth century was the handiwork of Dr. Richard Jordan Gatling (1818–1903), a South Carolina inventor less remembered for his agricultural inventions than his 200-shots-per-minute Gatling gun. Patented in November 1862, the gun fired cartridges sequentially from six musket-caliber barrels that were rotated by a hand crank, which also fired the weapon. Feeding ammunition was accomplished by gravity-feed mechanisms developed by James G. Accles in 1865 and by L. F. Bruce in 1881 and by a positive-feed magazine developed by Accles in 1893.

After numerous modifications, the United States Army ordered 100 of the weapons in 1866, and within twenty years, Gatling's "labor-saving device for warfare" saw service in nearly all the militaries that could afford it and in most regions of the world. The concept of the Gatling gun survives today in the form of electric-powered, multibarreled "miniguns"—machine guns used on aircraft and also for air defense.

Gatling's rapid-fire gun, however, did not meet the definition of fully automatic fire, which may be stated as: that process of feeding, firing, and ejecting carried out by the mechanism of the weapon, after a primary manual, electrical, or pneumatic cocking, as long as the trigger is held to the rear and there is still ammunition in the belt, feed-strip, or magazine. The same process describes semiautomatic fire, except that the trigger is pulled only once per shot and must be released between shots.

Hiram Maxim: Father of the Machine Gun

Intrigued by the challenge of designing a fully automatic gun, Hiram Stevens Maxim (1840–1916), an American who later became a naturalized British citizen, set about designing such a weapon in England in 1881. Between 1883 and 1885, Maxim patented most of the processes that would be used to deliver automatic fire on the battlefield. These processes relate to the method by which the energy developed from the expanding gases of exploding gunpowder is used in the operating cycle, either (1) the backward thrust of the recoiling mass, which is called recoil activation, or (2) the pressure generated by progressively burning powder in the barrel, called gas operation.

Maxim used the principle of the short recoil system, in which the barrel and breechblock return together a short distance until residual chamber pressure is low enough and the bolt can be opened without fracturing the cartridge case. The barrel then stops and the breechblock continues to the rear, its hooked lugs extracting and ejecting the spent case, then returning forward by the action of a recoil-compressed spiral spring. On its return, the firing mechanism cocks, the next cartridge is seated into the chamber, the barrel is shoved forward, and firing reoccurs. This cycle continues as long as the machine gun's trigger remains depressed.

The London press described Maxim's machine gun in 1884. A report read: "Hiram Maxim . . . has made an automatic machine-gun with a single barrel, using the standard calibre .45 rifle cartridge, that will load and fire itself by energy derived from recoil at a rate of over 600 rounds a minute." Maxim's name became synonymous with the machine gun he created, and by the time of his death in 1916 every major power had adopted the weapon, although some would replace it with other systems.

The tactical advantage offered by the Maxim was that it could be fired from the prone position, and the gun was small enough to be concealed. This increased the survival of crews and also led to more varied employment possibilities.

Developments in Ammunition

The success of the machine guns developed by Maxim and his contemporaries (Hotchkiss, Browning, and Lewis are three) would not have been possible without technological advances in metallurgy and chemistry. These combined to create the percussion ignition, center-fire metallic cartridge (developed by Col. Edward M. Boxer in 1866), and smokeless gunpowder (developed by Paul Vieille in 1886 and by Alfred Nobel in 1891). The fixed, or metallic, cartridge combined primer, propellant, and bullet in a stable case that was weatherproof and strong enough to withstand rugged, rapid handling by machine guns, as well as other weapons.

Before the advent of smokeless powder, firing positions could easily be identified as weapons discharged, enveloping the firer in a cloud of smoke. As battles continued, the smoke could be so dense as to obscure the battlefield, increasing the confusion of attacker and defender alike. Smokeless powder also had to be relatively slow burning, so as not to damage or destroy the weapon by blowing up in the firing chamber before expanding gases forced the bullet from the barrel.

With certain refinements, the ammunition used by machine guns today retain these characteristics.

Contemporary Description, Operation, and Use

LIGHT MACHINE GUNS

Light machine guns are found primarily in infantry squads and are served by a crew of two. These weapons are supported by a sturdy bipod to aid in accurate firing and usually weigh about twice as much as a rifle of the same caliber. As opposed to rifles, light machine guns have heavier, removable barrels that permit replacement when one becomes too hot from firing. Another distinguishing feature of light machine guns is that they are usually designed to use the same ammunition as the rifles in the squad.

Although capable of operating independently, light machine gun teams are usually protected by other squad members. When engaging a target, as the gunner fires, the assistant gunner will call corrections to the strike of the rounds and also assist with feeding or reloading ammunition.

The Finnish M78 Valmet, based on Finland's M76 assault rifle, is a good example of a light machine gun that is ideal for use by infantry squads in areas where they must operate dismounted. The M78 fires a 7.62mm cartridge, the length of which can vary from 39 to 51 millimeters (1.6 to 2 in.), from either a 15- or 30-round box, or a 75-round drum, making it a quite flexible weapon. The gun has a heavier and longer barrel than the M76 rifle and is fitted with a bipod and a carrying handle. It weighs 4.7 kilograms (10.3 lb.) empty and 5.9

kilograms (13 lb.) with a loaded 30-round box. It is gas operated, has a selective fire switch, and a cyclic rate of fire of 650 rounds per minute. A version of the Valmet light machine gun fires a lighter, 5.56mm × 45mm cartridge.

GENERAL-PURPOSE MACHINE GUNS

The general-purpose machine gun is a classification that came out of World War II as a development of the medium machine gun that had been in use since World War I. Combat experience showed that more effective fire could be produced by a lighter and handier machine gun. Such a weapon can be carried in a squad or section and used in the same way as a light machine gun, or it can be mounted on a tripod, fitted with an optical sight, and used as a medium support gun. It can also be mounted in tanks, armored cars, armored personnel carriers, aircraft, and patrol boats.

General-purpose machine guns are gas operated, featuring an adjustable gas intake from a point in the barrel. The gas regulator provides firing reliability independent of ambient conditions. Barrels are highly wear-resistant, air cooled, and capable of being changed in a few seconds. The front sight consists of a blade or cylinder fitted near the muzzle of the barrel, and the rear sight is a light, folding frame with spring-loaded thumb catches for setting the range slide.

Ammunition used in general-purpose machine guns varies in caliber and length, a typical round being 7.62mm × 51mm of the type used in the U.S. Army's M60 machine gun. Cartridges are contained in disintegrating link belts or articulated belts, with 50 to 250 rounds per box container. Many types of ammunition are used, including ball, tracer, armor piercing, incendiary, and armor-piercing incendiary. There are also blank, star, and drill cartridges.

General-purpose machine guns are available in an infantry model designed for use in mobile action, fired from the hip or using a bipod. They can also be mounted on tripods for defensive operations, on external cradles, and in swivel antiaircraft mounts. There are turret and coaxial models for use in armored vehicles and twin mountings for helicopter and armed aircraft employment.

The weight of the general-purpose machine gun with butt and bipod can be as much as 11 kilograms (24 lb.) and can increase to 24 kilograms (52 lb.) with the addition of tripod and heavier barrel. The effective range of these weapons varies from 500 meters (1,650 ft.) to over 2,000 meters (6,600 ft.) depending on the means used to stabilize the weapon during firing. Rates of fire depend on the design of the particular machine gun and can vary from 550 to over 1,000 rounds a minute.

There has been some criticism of the concept of arming the infantry squad with the general-purpose machine gun in lieu of the light machine gun because of the added weight and the lesser effect compared with that of medium machine guns. In the future, the trend may be to have a light machine gun at the squad level, with the general-purpose gun being retained as a support weapon.

The most effective tactical use is made of general-purpose machine guns when they are used in pairs or more, their fires integrated with other weapons of a rifle platoon or company. This is done on the defense by planning interlocking, primary direction of fire of machine guns and rifles, while covering dead (unobserved) space to the front with fragmentation grenades, claymore antipersonnel command-detonated mines, grenade launchers, and indirect-fire mortars and artillery. Because of the value of the weapon in area denial and inflicting casualties, defensive operations also require that the machine gun be manned continuously for security and be used only when the defenses are seriously threatened and not against enemy reconnaissance probes.

In offensive tactics, general-purpose machine guns will often be used to provide supporting fire for assaulting troops as part of a platoon or company attack. Selection of terrain for the supporting position is critical since at some point in the attack the assault elements will advance beyond the location selected for supporting machine guns. A typical support-fire technique is to fire from a position behind and to one side of the line of advance, walking the strike of the rounds ahead of the assault force. Similarly, if terrain permits, supporting fire may be directed over the heads of troops as they advance toward an objective on higher ground. An alternative offensive tactic is to have teams of general-purpose machine guns accompany the assault force to the objective, employing the weapon as a light machine gun. In this way, each squad may retain control over the firepower of the weapon.

In addition to direct involvement in ground combat actions, general-purpose machine guns are also used as air defense weapons. An example of such use is the German 7.62mm MG3, a successor to the well-regarded 7.92mm MG42 used in World War II, mounted in pairs on a twin pedestal.

The M60 machine gun previously cited, which came into service in the U.S. Army during the late 1950s, is typical of many general-purpose machine guns. The primary squad weapon of U.S. and allied forces in the Vietnam War, the M60 is gas-operated, with the barrel drilled radially downward 20 centimeters (8 in.) from the muzzle. After a bullet has passed this point, a small amount of propellant gas is forced through the vent where it enters the gas cylinder and forces an enclosed piston to drive back the operating rod. This short-stroke action carries the bolt back and imparts enough energy to complete the cycle of operation.

The M60 is a full automatic weapon only and has a cyclic rate of fire of 550 rounds a minute, which is slow enough for an accomplished firer to squeeze off a single round (Fig. 1). Its feed system is designed for the disintegrating link–type ammunition and was originally based on the German MG42 feed system used during World War II and subsequently modified. The M60 features a removable barrel assembly that also contains the gas cylinder plug and attached bipod legs, which makes for an awkward, two-man effort to remove a hot barrel.

Another type of machine gun that fits the general-purpose classification is the multibarrel machine gun, or minigun, of the type specifically designed for U.S. forces in Vietnam. The 7.62mm M134 Minigun uses a Gatling-type action and is based on the 20mm Vulcan air defense weapon. The M134 uses Gatling's concept with six rotating barrels fitted to a gun housing that contains a rotor assembly and bolt assembly. Six bolts are matched to the barrels, and, when loaded, the weapon fires through the bolt-barrel match at the twelve-o'clock

Figure 1. Two combat-ready Marines, an M60A1 machine gunner and his assistant, practice firing their weapon. (SOURCE: U.S. Marine Corps)

position. Fully automatic firing is provided by a 28-volt electric motor, and the M134 can fire at a rate of 6,000 rounds a minute.

When mounted in an aircraft, such as the AH1-Series Cobra helicopter, the M134 has proven effective as a close-air-support weapon against dismounted infantry, lightly armored vehicles, and patrol boats. Subsequent models have been designed for use on ground vehicles and watercraft and can be employed in both a ground support and air defense role.

MEDIUM MACHINE GUNS

Medium machine guns were first used in World War I, in pairs or larger numbers, as a support weapon to provide a heavy volume of fire for long periods. Most of the early medium machine guns were variants of Maxim's design or the similar Browning, the exception being the Hotchkiss. These water-cooled, belt-fed weapons were usually manned by a crew of three to four and used the same ammunition as that fired from rifles, although some cartridges were specially made for longer-range fires. The use of medium machine guns declined after the Korean War, as it was felt that more effective fire could be provided by guns mounted on light armored vehicles and by general-purpose machine guns.

HEAVY MACHINE GUNS

The heavy machine gun is one that fires a round of ammunition larger than the standard rifle cartridge and less than 20mm in caliber. The most popular caliber for many years has been the 12.7mm in service since World War I. Subsequently, 14.5mm machine guns were developed to provide a gun with greater hitting power. Most heavy machine guns are mounted in armored vehicles, although there are still some fitted to ground mounts. Others are retained in a variety of mounts as light antiaircraft weapons.

12.7MM HEAVY MACHINE GUNS

The 12.7mm heavy machine gun is gas operated and fully locked, with an adjustable gas intake from a point in the barrel. The barrel is highly wear-resistant, air cooled, and equipped with a quick-change barrel, although some models have a fixed barrel. The feed mechanism differs from type to type; some models use a large circular drum and feed from the left, while others have a flat rectangular feed cover and can be readily adapted to feed from either side.

There are a variety of two-wheeled mounts that can be moved by manpower, pack animals, or motor. A shield is sometimes provided when the configuration is for use against ground targets, and the mount can be converted for antiaircraft use.

Typical weights are about 36 kilograms (79.2 lb.) for the gun and something under 13 kilograms (28.6 lb.) for the barrel. Rates of fire are about 575 rounds per minute with an effective range of about 2,000 meters (6,600 ft.).

14.5MM HEAVY MACHINE GUNS

The 14.5mm guns are short-recoil operated with gas assistance from a muzzle booster. This type of gun was designed after World War II with a view to simplicity of manufacture. The body consists of a simple metal cylinder to which the various attachments are riveted or welded. The gun is solid in construction and all components are robust. Apart from the ejection opening, it is well sealed against dust and dirt. The barrel can be changed. Designed initially as an antiaircraft gun, the 14.5mm has also been successfully employed as an armored fighting vehicle machine gun.

The 14.5mm heavy machine gun generally weighs about 49 kilograms (107.8 lb.), has a cyclic rate of fire of about 600 rounds a minute, and ranges similar to 12.7mm guns. These weapons can be mounted on towed carriage mountings for combinations of one, two, or four guns. Twin- and four-gun assemblies are in wide use.

The 14.5mm KPV heavy machine gun, produced by the Soviet Union shortly after World War II, is an example of these heavier automatic guns. Designed expressly to fire the high-velocity antitank round used in the PTRD41 antitank rifle in an air defense role, the weapon is simple and easily manufactured. Subsequently, the Soviet military found the weapon suitable for mounting on armored fighting vehicles for use in ground combat. Its total weight approaches 69 kilograms (151.8 lb.), and it can be found in the republics of the former Soviet Union, other Soviet-influenced countries, and China. This heavy machine gun was used extensively by North Vietnam during the Vietnam War.

Summary

The evolution of the machine gun bears witness to the great advances in weapons-related technology, and although today's weapons are mature systems, robust and reliable, the evolutionary process is unlikely to cease. New advances in munitions, propellants, lightweight composite materials, electronics, and machine tooling promise to improve the lethality of machine guns even further.

Light machine guns will see increasing use in infantry squads, providing them with greater firepower than previously and more useful in terrain restrictive to the use of heavier guns. General-purpose machine guns are likely to continue in their diverse roles, providing support for infantry as well as protection against aircraft. Increased use of high-rate-of-fire general-purpose miniguns against air and ground targets will also occur. The distinction between heavy machine guns and machine cannons of over 20mm will blur as high-explosive rounds of less than 20mm are added to the firing capabilities of 12.7mm and 14.5mm guns.

From the ship-defense weapon envisioned by James Puckel in the early eighteenth century to the thousands-of-rounds-a-minute miniguns used in a general-purpose role today, rapid-fire and fully automatic guns demonstrate the quest of the world's militaries to improve the lethal effectiveness of their fighting forces. The machine gun, which proved its terrible potential in World War I, forced changes in tactical thought and deployments on the battlefield. Although it may never have a similar impact in another war, the machine gun will remain the infantry's most effective direct-fire weapon against other infantry.

SAMIR H. SHALABY

SEE ALSO: Ammunition; Automatic Weapon; Technology and Warfare.

Bibliography

Dupuy, T. N. 1984. *The evolution of weapons and warfare.* Fairfax, Va.: HERO Books.
Jane's infantry weapons, 1983–84. 1983. New York: Jane's.
Reid, W. 1976. *Arms through the ages.* New York: Harper and Row.

MAINTENANCE

The term *maintenance* has three distinctly separate military meanings and applications.

The first describes all supply and repair action taken to keep a force in condition to carry out its mission. In this sense, it has largely been supplanted by the term *logistics*, with supply and repair being two principal functions of logistic support in peace and in war.

Maintenance also describes the routine, recurring work required to keep a facility—plant, building, structure, ground facility, utility system, or other property—in such condition that it may be continuously utilized, at its original or designed capacity and efficiency, for its intended purpose.

The third meaning is the subject of this article. Here the term *maintenance* describes all the action taken to retain materiel in, or restore it to, a specified condition. This includes inspection, testing, servicing, classification as to serviceability, modification, repair, recovery, rebuilding, and reclamation. Here attention is confined to the application of this term to land forces.

A maintenance service, or equivalent military organization, is responsible for ensuring the operational fitness of army equipment. Consideration is given to achieving this aim from an early stage in the development of materiel.

Equipment engineering (maintenance) input is as vital during the design, development, and production phases as is the support provided during the service life of the equipment. Reliability, accessibility, maintainability, durability, and other important characteristics are "designed into" each piece of equipment with full regard to its maintenance as well as its operational performance. Information—much of it technical—is collated so that maintenance specifications, schedules, illustrated parts' lists, and publications are prepared prior to an equipment's acceptance and introduction into service. Similar arrangements are made to ensure that initial scales (lists and quantities) of assemblies, components, and spare parts are calculated so that stocks are available immediately when an equipment enters service. These scales will be refined through usage experience during an equipment's service life, quantities will be altered, and supporting stocks will be adjusted.

While in service, equipment is regularly and systematically inspected, tested, and classified as to serviceability. Defects are investigated and rectified through normal repair, the introduction of permanent modifications, or the development of new techniques and tools. Major overhaul and refurbishment may be necessary during service life and undertaken according to a planned program or when otherwise required.

Maintenance capabilities are classified according to the complexity and the amount of time the repair takes and also the level or echelon at which they are carried out.

The crews of vehicles or weapons may be trained to make minor adjustments and replace certain components. For instance, within the battalion, maintenance tradesmen, artisans, or technicians will undertake what are termed *unit* or *first-line* repairs, because they are carried out within the unit and are the first line of maintenance support. Some armies call this *organic* or *organizational* repair—terms obviously vary and can be difficult to translate from one language to another.

Complex tasks taking more time are generally undertaken by the mobile maintenance workshop that supports battalions, usually close at hand, to which equipment is back loaded. In most armies, the terms *field* and *second-line* repairs are used for these.

Certain more specialized workshop facilities that carry out *intermediate* repairs may be available at a *third line*. The complete rebuilding of equipment or assemblies, called *fourth line*, is classified as a *base* repair and is located even farther to the rear, requiring additional back loading. Some armies term this latter category *depot* repair. Base or depot maintenance workshops are highly specialized technically and are normally located in a rear support area.

When a piece of equipment breaks down or is damaged, the cause is diagnosed and recorded (Fig. 1), and then a condition code is specified. Apart from the code that describes the item as "serviceable," others indicate that:

Figure 1. Airborne forces—captain and equipment engineers inspect damaged assembly. (SOURCE: British Army [Royal Electrical and Mechanical Engineers])

1. No repair is needed at that time, but the fault should be kept under observation.
2. It can be returned to serviceability by the crew, if applicable.
3. It requires unit repair by maintenance tradesmen, artisans, or technicians immediately available within the battalion.
4. It needs field repair at the supporting workshop.
5. It must have more specialized attention.
6. It is beyond local or economic repair.

A battalion will normally have an integral or organic maintenance platoon, with a nucleus and detached company sections undertaking unit repair as first-line support.

A regiment (brigade) may have its own maintenance company and a division its own maintenance battalion, each capable of deploying mobile workshops that carry out field or second-line repairs and provide recovery and back-loading facilities. They support battalions and all other units in the field formations and are located in a forward area of the combat zone.

Quite often field or second-line maintenance resources will be retained at divisional level and not specifically allocated to regiments (brigades). Centralization of effort and control may improve efficiency, economy, flexibility, protection, and survivability, as well as provide a reserve capability for unforeseen needs. The allotment of resources to regiments (brigades) is an alternative and will also have advantages. The structure and procedures vary among armies, and the solution adopted depends on the operational situation and logistic doctrine.

Another variation may involve the field or second-line maintenance workshop detaching well-equipped, highly mobile, forward repair teams to rectify a breakdown "on site" in battalion operational areas. This capability may be restricted to prioritized, main battle equipments and may be limited to assembly exchange. Repair is carried out as close to the point where the equipment has broken down as is tactically prudent and technically feasible; each forward repair team will have some recovery capacity. The merits of this system are twofold: equipment that is operationally vital is restored to battleworthiness and functional efficiency as speedily as is practicable, and its back loading to the main field workshop is avoided. Forward repair teams, therefore, are a way of providing crucially important second-line maintenance at first-line level.

Yet another variation may be to split the main field workshop—that is, its resources less the forward repair teams—between two separate, operational locations on the battlefield. To do so may position support facilities nearer to customers, further enhancing concealment and survivability and enabling the two elements to "leapfrog" during a major move. On the other hand, this physical separation may unduly dissipate skilled and specialized resources, encumber control, and complicate the supply of assemblies, components, and spare parts. The choice, again, will be a tactical and technical decision.

At third line may be found specialized maintenance facilities that are needed to support fighting formations but, by their nature, are better deployed farther to the rear; these are often static rather than mobile. Complicated electronic repairs may fall into this category, as well as helicopter maintenance.

The timely, constant, and comprehensive supply of assemblies, components, spare parts, and consumable materials (from welding rods to nuts and bolts) is vital to the maintenance activity. Equipment that is classified beyond repair, or beyond the capabilities of repair and recovery at that time, may be "cannibalized," but this can only supplement and not replace effective supply support. The provision of tools and maintenance equipment is also vital.

Vehicle and weapon crews, like most equipment users, have a ready-to-hand stock of minor components, piece parts, and consumables. The battalion's maintenance platoon, or its equivalent in other units, will carry a mobile holding of supplies needed for unit repair at first line. Forward repair teams will take with them a small quantity and restricted range of major assemblies and the wherewithal to effect assembly exchange. Maintenance battalions or companies providing field repairs in divisions and regiments (brigades) will require a mobile second-line stock of supplies of a wide range and of a substantial quantity. The size or degree of specialization of static stocks will vary at third and fourth lines; a base maintenance workshop, for example, may be supported by its own supply depot.

Stocks on hand at each echelon seldom meet every demand—in fact, scales (lists and quantities) reflect frequency of demand for particular items—and stocks used have to be replenished. The supporting supply system provides operationally urgent or routine requirements based on priority of need and target delivery times.

In some armies, the maintenance service provisions, stores, and supplies its own requirements of assemblies, components, spare parts, consumables, tools, and specialist equipment. In others, a separate supply service meets the needs of the army as a whole as well as the maintenance function. Some organize supply and maintenance on a "user" basis with the artillery, for instance, having its own resources. Yet others work a combination of these systems. There is no standard pattern; the system practiced will generally have grown up by custom and tradition, and each will have advantages and disadvantages.

The maintenance plan aims to ensure the operational fitness of equipment. It forms the basis for providing the maintenance resources required to ensure that equipment operates effectively in peace, during training, and in war.

Maintenance planning depends fundamentally upon estimated equipment casualty rates. These are calculated and established by taking a wide range of usage measurements and the full range of army materiel into account. For example, some rates are based on average daily mileage of tracked and wheeled vehicles, on the flying hours of army fixed-wing aircraft and helicopters, or on the number of rounds fired with specific charges by guns. The aim is to use the rates as an aid to forecasting equipment failure as well as an estimate of expenditure or consumption of supplies in both peace and war. Maintenance planning also depends fundamentally on the estimates of battle attrition in war. This will help to forecast the extent, nature, and frequency of battle damage sustained by individual equipment in combat or support environments.

Estimates of equipment failure and battle attrition rates enable maintenance resources to be forecasted, justified, provided, allocated, and deployed, together with requisite supply stocks. However, the calculation of these rates may well prove to be a difficult process requiring skillful research, sound military judgment, and practical evaluation, as well as computerized assistance. Forecasts necessarily have to be based on the next war, not the last one, and are difficult to apply to the battlefield universally—spatially, temporally, longitudinally, or laterally. Therefore, maintenance planning, like supply and other logistic planning, must retain the ability to revise the rates quickly based on actual combat experience at the particular time fighting occurs so as to allow a margin for error and to keep some maintenance resources in reserve.

Preventive maintenance features prominently and significantly in any maintenance plan: regular inspection, functional testing, and scheduled or unscheduled servicing of a multiplicity of materiel. Detailed records help with the continuous and analytical assessment of workload activities, trends, training needs, development of skills, tools, equipment, techniques and procedures, and assemblies and spares requirements, and with the allocation and control of all resources. Equipment serviceability statements indicate to the tactical, logistical, and maintenance commanders and their staffs the running operational status and readiness of important parts of a force's inventory. If testing is satisfactory, then performance on ranges and field exercises is another indicator of equipment fitness for role. The state of equipment in a given unit is also a measure of supporting maintenance capability and competence.

When a force is committed to operations short of "general" war—that is, to a "limited" war—its composition in terms of combat, combat support, and combat service support elements can vary considerably, even within a single regiment (brigade) or a division. The scale of equipment taken with the force can also vary considerably: troops may be equipped to light, normal, or heavy scales and may rely on specific forms of transport or may move mainly on foot. How the type of combat, terrain, and climate is likely to modify estimated equipment casualty and attrition rates and whether quiet, normal, or intensive rates of equipment utilization are expected are other important factors. All these considerations will be taken into account when developing a maintenance plan for supporting the particular force involved.

The requirement for maintenance resources will be tailor-made to the force and to a set of parameters such as those mentioned. Obviously, resources will differ for operations in jungle, desert, mountainous, steppe, tropical, temperate, and very cold environments. Once needs have been assessed and resources decided, maintenance facilities will be phased into the area of operations and deployed to conform with the overall tactical and logistic plans. If, after arrival and during the course of the conflict, some maintenance resources are clearly in excess, they will be returned to base; if deficiencies appear in type or quantity, reinforcements will be dispatched; and if attrition demands replacements, these will also be provided.

In a general war, the full panoply of maintenance support is likely to be needed, less those elements strictly geared to peacetime requirements that will probably switch to different operational roles. Repair, recovery, back loading of equipment casualties, and route clearance are the principal maintenance tasks to be undertaken in this scenario.

Before battle is joined, units expect to have time to deploy from their peacetime barracks—either inside or outside the envisaged theater of operations—to their battle positions. During deployment, some equipment will break down, otherwise fail, or be accidentally damaged. Maintenance support has to be positioned in the operational areas of field formations early and in sufficient strength to deal with casualties sustained during deployment so that maximum equipment is held at the appropriate battleworthiness status. Many of these remedial tasks are likely to be outside the capability of unit or first-line repair resources and will require field or second-line maintenance attention.

The fluidity and lethality of conventional conflict—leaving aside the catastrophic effects of nuclear strikes—are likely to take a heavy toll on equipment in general war. High casualty and attrition rates will complement high utilization, expenditure, and consumption rates. This will be the case particularly for main battle equipments: armored fighting vehicles, infantry combat vehicles, attack helicopters, weapon systems of all types, surveillance and detection devices, combat engineer equipment, certain communications systems, and some logistic support vehicles and equipment.

There will have to be strict prioritization of maintenance tasks, well-controlled allocation, and husbandry of maintenance resources so that they are available for critical tasks; also needed are flexible cross servicing among maintenance elements to enable the timely reallocation and switching of resources to deal with higher priority tasks in adjacent areas of the battlefield. The rapid recovery of equipment casualties, their repair to battleworthiness standards, and their prompt return to their operational roles will have a decisive influence on the conduct and outcome of the battle.

Some contend that in a full-scale general war, there will be insufficient time to repair equipment casualties. They may be right, but recent intensive combat experience has shown that for every tank destroyed, three are damaged and repairable. As far as other main battle equipments are concerned, the contrast is even greater: for each one destroyed, ten are damaged but are repairable. Therefore, maintenance must remain a key part of combat service support, must continue to have the technical resources to respond as effectively and for as long as possible to the needs of forces and their materiel, and must endeavor to help sustain operations in the most difficult circumstances envisaged. Training for this particular role is particularly challenging in peacetime.

Not only will repair and recovery be vital, but also the back loading of equipment casualties to farther rearward, better protected, and more specialized maintenance facilities. In recent conflicts with their Arab neighbors, the Israeli armed forces operated an impressive back-loading system and quickly returned a high proportion of fit tanks to combat; in their case, efficient back-loading systems and special tank workshops were key factors in their operational success. Tracked or wheeled vehicle casualties may be towed back, drawn on suspended hoist, or carried on other transport. The establishment of equipment collecting and back-loading points—strategically and logistically well placed, with good communications and control—will assist with the timely back loading of all useful, repairable, high-priority materiel. Evacuation may well be undertaken mainly during the hours of darkness and by road, though certain armies plan to make much use of railways for as long as this form of transport operates. The importance of the maintenance task to remove "hulks" and keep routes clear of damaged, broken-down equipment for all forces and activities requires no additional emphasis.

Only if equipment casualties are beyond repair should they be abandoned; later, resources may become available to enable their restoration and return to battle. Only if repairable equipment casualties are in danger of being overrun and captured by the enemy should they be destroyed.

The maintenance role, therefore, remains crucial in general war as in other forms of conflict. The magnitude of the task, and the obscurities the fog of war will create, will not make it easy for maintenance troops and their commanders. They will have to draw extensively upon their resources of ingenuity, improvisation, and endurance in conditions difficult to simulate on training exercises.

J. H. SKINNER

SEE ALSO: Consumption Rates, Battlefield; Logistics: A General Survey.

Bibliography

Berman, M. B. 1988. *Evaluating the combat payoff of alternative logistics structures for high-technology subsystems.* Santa Monica, Calif.: Rand Corporation.

Federal Republic of Germany. 1972. Kommission zur Überprüfung der Materialerhaltung für Rad- und Kettenfahrzeuge einschliesslich des Ersatzteilwesens. *Rationalisierung der Materialerhaltung für Rad- und Kettenfahrzeuge.* Bonn: Bundesministerium der Verteidigung, Org. 4.

Integrated Logistic Support Symposium. 1969. *Proceedings.* Chambersburg, Pa.: USAMC Maintenance and Engineering Office.

Rybakov, K. V. 1971. *Zapravka qusenichnykh i kolesnykh mashin.* N.p.

Tripp, R. S., M. B. Berman, and C. L. Tsai. 1990. *The concept of operations for a U.S. Army combat-oriented logistics execution system with VISION (visibility of support options).* Santa Monica, Calif.: RAND Corporation.

U.S. Department of the Army. 1958. *PM: Preventive maintenance guide for commanders.* Washington, D.C.: Government Printing Office.

MANEUVER

Maneuver is one of the two basic components of combat; the other is firepower. In some usage, maneuver is simply another word for the movement of forces. More often, it is used to mean relational movement—for example, movement relative to an opponent's position, as in Napoleon's *manoeuvre sur les derrières.* In the term *maneuver warfare,* the word *maneuver* refers to an entire style of war, most often associated in this century with the German army. In modern usage, maneuver warfare theory has come to define maneuver in terms of time rather than position.

Maneuver as Movement

The use of the word *maneuver* as nothing more than a synonym for *movement* is seen in the common American use of the phrase *tactics of fire and maneuver* to describe an open-order advance by alternate rushes. No movement relative to an enemy, such as movement around his flank or into his rear, is implied. The simple movement of the rushing element is the *maneuver.* Such usage is also encountered in discussions or briefings, as in a battalion commander saying, "I maneuvered my unit to this road junction." He means only that he moved the unit; no movement relative to the enemy is to be understood.

This use of the word *maneuver* can be thought of as colloquial. While not incorrect, it is imprecise.

Maneuver as Movement Relative to an Enemy's Position

The sense in which the word *maneuver* is most often used, and is reflected in the definition offered in the U.S. Army's *Field Manual (FM) 100-5: Operations*, is "the movement of forces in relation to the enemy to secure or retain positional advantage." In this sense, *maneuver* means an attack on either or both of an enemy's flanks, movement into his rear to disrupt his supporting elements, or encirclement. Because such action is relational to the enemy, it may involve his movement more than one's own. *FM 100-5* says: "The effects of maneuver (obtaining an advantageous position) may also be achieved without movement by allowing the enemy himself to move into a disadvantageous position, as in an ambush or with stay-behind forces." This suggests that the essence of maneuver—in the classic usage of the term—is not movement per se but the achievement of positional advantage.

In this sense, maneuver has been one of the most powerful tools in warfare since the beginning of recorded history. Because of basic human psychology, a force that is hit where it is weak, where it does not expect to be hit, or in such a manner as to leave it cut off from its supplies, reinforcements, or line of retreat tends to panic and disintegrate. The principal effect of maneuver is thus more mental than physical—and therefore more powerful than simple physical attrition.

Maneuver played a major role in classical warfare, where decisive battles were usually battles of maneuver. At the Battle of Marathon in 490 B.C., the Greeks achieved a decisive victory by maneuvering against both flanks of the Persian force—a double envelopment. While most battles between phalanxes tended to be indecisive, the Thebans won decisively at Leuctra in 371 B.C. by attacking first on their left with the bulk of their force, pushing back the Spartan right, then turning and rolling up the Spartans from the right. This maneuver is often known as the oblique attack. The Theban leader Epaminondas may have been the first commander to employ an unequal distribution of forces to provide a basis for maneuver.

Perhaps the most decisive classical battle, one that influenced much subsequent military thought, was Cannae in 216 B.C. It was a battle of maneuver in which the Carthaginians under Hannibal drew the Roman center forward, then attacked around both flanks to encircle the Roman force. The Roman army was annihilated. Later, the Romans won the Second Punic War with a strategic maneuver in which the Roman commander Scipio Africanus invaded Carthaginian North Africa, forcing Hannibal to evacuate Italy to come to the defense of his homeland.

In Europe, maneuver went into eclipse with the fall of the Roman Empire. Medieval and early modern warfare tended to be straight-on slogging matches at the tactical level, with little or no thought given to the operational level. In contrast, in Asia, the Mongols were masters of strategic maneuver, moving in widely separated columns that concentrated unexpectedly at an enemy's most vulnerable point.

By the end of the seventeenth century, maneuver had again become a major part of European warfare. At the operational level, maneuver was often intended to separate an opposing army from its magazines, on which it depended for its supplies; an army thus cut off usually withdraws. *Tactical* maneuver is illustrated by the battle of Leuthen between the Austrians and the Prussians in 1757. The Prussians attacked in oblique order from the right, breaking the Austrians' line and forcing them to withdraw.

Napoleon placed heavy emphasis on maneuver, at least in his early battles and campaigns. French revolutionary armies were better adapted to rapid operational and tactical maneuver than were the professional armies of the European monarchies. Napoleon's were the first armies to be divided into divisions, which facilitated maintaining control while maneuvering; they freed themselves from dependence on magazines by living off the land; they raised the march step from 70 to 120 paces per minute; and they made extensive tactical use of light infantry operating in loose formations and of fast-moving columns.

Napoleon was famous for the *manoeuvre sur les derrières*, in which he employed a small portion of his force to capture his opponent's attention while swinging his main body behind the enemy, cutting his communications. Alternatively, he would overwhelm the enemy's center, again moving into his rear and cutting him off.

Speed, surprise, and shock were central components of Napoleonic maneuver at both the tactical and operational levels. It may be said that Napoleon introduced *tempo* into modern European warfare, presaging twentieth-century maneuver warfare.

In his later years, as emperor, Napoleon relied less on maneuver and more on brute force at the tactical level; Waterloo provides a good example. The postwar Napoleonic heritage caught more of his later tactics than the earlier, fluid tactics that emphasized maneuver.

But by the middle of the nineteenth century, the introduction of the rifled musket made brute force offensive tactics increasingly costly in casualties. The Prussian general Helmuth von Moltke (the Elder) responded by reemphasizing maneuver in the *Kesselschlacht*, where the object was to encircle the enemy, forcing him to assault into rifle fire in order to break out. A plan by Graf Alfred von Schlieffen early in the twentieth century expanded the *Kesselschlacht* concept to the operational level, calling for a massive encirclement of the French armies by the German right.

The death knell for maneuver on the modern battlefield seemed to sound with the failure of the Schlieffen plan in 1914. The battlefield had become one continuous field with no open flanks around which to maneuver, while the tactical strength of the defense seemed to preclude penetration. Firepower was dominant over maneuver.

Maneuver Warfare

In 1917 and 1918, maneuver reappeared on the western front in the form of new and radically different German tactics. On the defense, instead of densely manning forward trench lines and attempting to hold every inch of ground, the Germans allowed the Allied attacker to penetrate through a thinly held forward outpost line. As the Allied forces penetrated deeper, they encountered a growing density of machine-gun positions, prepared for 360-degree defense, and small groups of riflemen fighting from shell holes. This firepower disorganized the attacker and absorbed his momentum. When the German commander judged that the attack had begun to disintegrate, he launched a powerful counterattack designed to encircle the attacking force and restore the original defensive line. These "elastic defense" tactics relied heavily on maneuver, not only in looking to the encircling counterattack to achieve the decision, but also in using the attacker's momentum against him. In practice, they proved devastatingly effective.

On the offense, the new tactics brought maneuver down to the squad (*Stosstrupp*) level. Instead of attacking in waves, assault troops organized in combined-arms squads (light machine gun and trench mortar) attempted to infiltrate through weak points in the Allied defenses. Squads maneuvered independently, with corporals making tactical decisions. The attack had an unlimited objective; forward movement was to be sustained as far as possible. Enemy strong points were bypassed—a use of maneuver —and reserves were funneled in behind the most successful penetrations in order to expand them. Firepower was used to support maneuver by suppressing the defenders while the attackers moved behind them, and wherever possible positions were taken from the flank or rear (*Durchbruch und Aufrollen*).

The 1918 German offensive used these tactics, and they solved the tactical riddle of trench warfare. Massive breakthroughs were attained, and the Germans again advanced to the Marne. The tactical successes, however, could not be converted into victories at the operational level. The most important reason was again a factor of maneuver: a differential in operational mobility. The Germans had to advance on foot, with horse-drawn artillery and supplies, while the Allies shifted operational reserves by rail to build new defenses behind collapsing sectors of their line. Pitting rail against foot mobility, the Allies were able to outmaneuver the Germans on the operational level.

In World War II, the Germans solved the problem of operational mobility. The answer was the Panzer division: mechanized forces that could move forward faster than a rail-mobile defender, such as France in 1940, could shift laterally. The blitzkrieg combined the tactics of 1918—offensive and defensive—with the operational mobility afforded by mechanization. It is important to note, however, that as the German general Hermann Balck stated, blitzkrieg was conceptually complete by 1918; only the operational means were lacking. Similarly, the German tank tactics of World War II were identical to the infantry tactics of 1918.

This revolution in tactics and operations was largely missed by the Western Allies. While German and Soviet tactics were dominated by maneuver, British and American tactics remained refinements of the Allied tactics of World War I, relying primarily on massive firepower and materiel superiority. At the operational level, the Western Allies had some commanders who used maneuver, most prominently Gen. George S. Patton, but most Allied campaigns were frontal, linear, and slow paced.

In the 1980s, however, the German way of war has been discovered in both the United States and the United Kingdom, where it is often referred to as *maneuver warfare*, in contrast to *attrition warfare*. Maneuver warfare is now official doctrine in the U.S. Marine Corps, and its substance (although not the term) is the basis for the current edition of the army's *FM 100-5*.

Used in the term *maneuver warfare*, maneuver means substantially more than seeking positional advantage. It describes a style of warfare, a way of thinking about both tactics and operations. In maneuver warfare, the objective is the enemy's collapse as a cohesive, functioning force, not his incremental destruction through the application of firepower. The larger the force that can be collapsed as a whole, the better. Operational art dominates over tactics, and at the tactical level, the goal is to avoid battle as much as possible while attaining operational objectives. High tempo is itself a weapon.

Maneuver warfare regards both tactics and operations as highly situational. Therefore, it does not define itself in formulas or recipes telling the practitioner what to do. Rather, maneuver warfare is defined in terms of a few central concepts, derived from past German practice, of which five are of main importance at the tactical level:

1. *Mission tactics* (*Auftragstaktik*): In order to maintain high tempo and to take advantage of fleeting opportunities for decisive maneuver, the authority to make decisions must be decentralized. At the same time, unity of effort must be maintained. These two requirements are reconciled primarily through mission tactics, in which orders tell the subordinate what is to be accomplished while leaving him maximum latitude in deciding how to accomplish it. In effect, he is given a goal, and it is left to him to attain it. This is done at all levels of command. As part of mission orders, the subordinate is expected to show a high level of initiative. In turn, errors resulting from mistaken initiative are treated lightly.

2. *Focus of effort* (*Schwerpunkt*): In each situation, a commander decides what he will do to achieve a decision and what unit he will do it with. That unit is then designated the focus of effort. It receives all possible support: artillery and other supporting arms, reinforcements, reserves, supplies, and so on. To the greatest extent possible, the available combat power is concentrated to back its effort. This often means risks must be taken elsewhere. The object is to be superior at the point of decision, even if the force as a whole is inferior. As the situation changes, the focus of effort may be shifted, but at all times combat power is concentrated in its support.

3. *Throwing strength against weakness, not against strength* (*Lücken und Flächentaktik*, or tactics of surfaces and gaps): In the attack, a force practicing maneuver warfare does not attempt to advance a line; maneuver warfare is nonlinear. Rather, the force attempts to penetrate where the enemy is weakest and to avoid his strong points. Once in his rear, the strong points can be attacked from the flank or rear while the advance simultaneously continues into

his depth. The logic of strength against weakness is carried over into the defense as well, where the counterattack is launched when the enemy is deemed weakest. At the operational level, the Germans' advance through the Ardennes in the 1940 campaign is a good example of throwing strength against weakness rather than against strength. Because the French had committed their reserve in Belgium, the German action had the nature of a counterattack.

4. *The objective:* In maneuver warfare, the objective is defined in terms of the enemy, not terrain. Combined with mission orders, this leaves the subordinate free to use terrain as he sees fit. Generally, maps used in maneuver warfare do not have "goose eggs" symbolizing terrain objectives, nor do they have many, if any, lines. Instead, actions are shown as thrust vectors, indicating what is to be done to the objective (i.e., the enemy force).

5. *The reserve:* The reserve is given high importance in maneuver warfare and is the unit that often brings the decision. It is generally stronger than in attrition warfare, and it often comprises the best units and commander. The weaker the total force, the larger the percentage of the force that is generally kept in reserve. Strong reserves are as important at the operational level as they are at the tactical level.

These concepts are all intended to produce a force that is highly agile, fluid, and flexible. Maneuver theory sees warfare as dominated by unpredictability, uncertainty, and rapid change. Tactics are highly opportunistic, the operational level somewhat less so; but at both levels, a high premium is placed on doing the unexpected. Fog and friction are seen as normal, and the goal is to operate within them, magnifying them for the opponent. Command and control are replaced by leadership and monitoring, and implicit communication, based on a shared way of thinking, is stressed over explicit communication through "systems."

Maneuver Defined in Terms of Time Rather Than Place

In recent years, maneuver warfare theory has come to place its main emphasis on time rather than place. Traditionally, maneuver was defined as relational movement seen in terms of place; Sir Basil Liddell Hart's "indirect approach" is an example. Recent theoretical work, particularly that of retired air force colonel John Boyd, has instead emphasized relational movement in time or tempo.

Colonel Boyd's work began with the study of air-to-air combat. He noted that in the Korean War, where U.S. aviators achieved a 10:1 kill ratio over their North Korean opponents, the principal U.S. fighter, the F-86, was inferior to the North Korean MiG-15 in several traditionally key respects, including climb, acceleration, and sustained turn rate. The F-86, however, had two advantages that proved decisive: better outward visibility and quicker response to the controls. In other words, the U.S. pilot could see more easily and quickly what was going on and his aircraft could respond more quickly to a change in the situation. To use these superiorities, the Americans developed tactics that stressed a series of different actions. Each time the action changed, the Americans gained a time advantage that they could convert into positional advantage. Further, as the North Korean pilot realized he was losing in each successive action or maneuver, a psychological dimension became a factor: he tended to panic.

Colonel Boyd proceeded to examine the history of ground combat from the perspective gained from his study of air combat. He found that in many decisive battles, something similar had happened. One side took an action or a series of actions to which the other side could not quickly respond, and the side with the slower response was defeated. In effect, the slower side was outmaneuvered in time.

Generalizing, Colonel Boyd developed a theory that lies at the heart of current U.S. understanding of maneuver warfare. The theory states that conflict can be seen as time-competitive cycles of observation, orientation, decision, and action (OODA). Each party begins by observing. On the basis of the observation, each forms a mental picture of the situation—orientation. On the basis of this orientation, each makes a decision, then acts. Assuming the action has changed the situation, each again observes, starting the cycle anew. These cycles are often referred to as "Boyd cycles" or "OODA Loops."

The party that consistently goes through the cycles faster than its opponent gains a large, often a decisive, advantage. By the time the slower side acts, the faster party is already doing something different from what had been observed and the action of the slower side is irrelevant. With each cycle, the slower party falls farther and farther behind—that is, the time margin by which its action is inappropriate grows. Its situation is not just bad, nor is it simply deteriorating; it is deteriorating at an ever-accelerating pace. At some point, the slower party realizes what is happening, and it is then that it tends to panic or grow passive. It may be for the most part physically intact, but it has been defeated. A good example of this process is, again, the German campaign against France in 1940. Many of the actions the French took were correct, but they were always too late.

The Boyd theory defines what is meant by tempo: it is not just speed, it is relational speed. And it in turn defines what is meant by maneuver in modern maneuver warfare theory.

WILLIAM S. LIND

SEE ALSO: Blitzkrieg; Envelopment; Principles of War; Tactics.

Bibliography

Liddell Hart, B. H. 1974. *Strategy*. New York: Signet Books.
Lind, W. S. 1985. *Maneuver warfare handbook*. Boulder, Colo.: Westview Press.
Lupfer, T. 1981. *The dynamics of doctrine: The changes in German tactical doctrine during the First World War*. Ft. Leavenworth, Kans.: Combat Studies Institute.
Simpkin, R. E. 1985. *Race to the swift*. London: Brassey's.

MAPS, CHARTS, AND SYMBOLS, MILITARY

Maps and charts are graphic representations, normally on a plane (flat) surface, that depict natural or artificial features of part or all of the earth. They are prepared at an established scale, and map features are positioned relative to a coordinate reference system. Man-made and natural features are represented by symbols, lines, colors, and forms.

To enhance the ability of map users to recognize features portrayed, such features are represented by conventional signs and symbols. Most symbols are exaggerated in size on maps beyond the point of what they actually represent. For example, on a 1:250,000-scale map, the symbol for any building occupies an area of some 500 square feet on the ground, while a road symbol, if in actual scale, would be over 500 feet wide.

Maps provide information on the existence of, location of, and distance between ground features (e.g., populated areas and routes of travel and communication). Maps also indicate variations in terrain; extent of vegetation; presence of streams, lakes, and oceans; and heights of natural terrain features. The proper use of maps by military personnel enables troops and materiel to be transported, stored, and placed into operation at prescribed places and times.

Classes of Maps by Type

Topographic maps portray terrain features as well as the horizontal positions of the features represented. Vertical positions, termed "relief," usually are represented by contour lines.

Photomaps are first-instance or reproductions of aerial or satellite photographs on which grid lines, place names, route numbers, approximate scale, and other data have been superimposed.

Joint operations graphics are a series of 1:250,000-scale military maps designed for joint ground and air operations. These maps are published in air and ground versions with identical topographical data on each. Ground versions have elevations and contours in meters, air versions in feet. The air versions also have symbols that identify aids and obstructions to air navigation.

Photomosaics are assemblies of aerial photographs that are published when time does not permit compilation of a more accurate map. Accuracy of such maps depends on the methods employed in their preparation.

Military city maps are topographic maps, usually with a scale of 1:12,500 or 1:25,000, of cities that show important buildings, streets and their names, and other urban data of military significance.

Special maps are prepared for special purposes, such as trafficability, communications, or assaults. These maps usually are overprints of standard topographic maps with data not normally found on standard maps.

Classes of Maps by Use

Administrative maps are used to graphically record information pertaining to administrative matters, such as supply and evacuation installations, personnel and medical installations, straggler and prisoner-of-war collection points, service and maintenance areas, main supply routes, traffic circulation, and similar data.

Battle maps show ground features in sufficient detail for use by all combat forces, usually on a scale of 1:25,000 or 1:50,000.

Controlled maps have precise, or registered, horizontal and vertical ground control as their basis.

General maps have a small scale and are used for general planning purposes.

Line route maps, or map overlays, are used for signal communications operations and show actual routes and types of construction of wire circuits in the field. They also show the locations of telegraph stations and switchboards.

Map charts are representations of sea-land areas. They have the characteristics of a map to represent the land area and the characteristics of a chart to represent the sea area, with special characteristics added to make the map chart useful in military operations, usually amphibious operations.

Operation maps show locations and strengths of friendly forces involved in a given operation. They also may indicate predicted movements and locations of enemy forces.

Situation maps show the tactical, operational, or administrative situation at a given time.

Strategic maps have a medium or smaller scale and are used for planning operations such as troop movements, concentrations, and logistics operations.

Tactical maps have a large scale and are used for tactical and administrative purposes.

Traffic circulation maps show traffic routes and measures for traffic regulation. They indicate the roads for specific classes of traffic, the locations of traffic control stations, and the directions in which traffic may move. They are also called circulation maps.

Weather maps show prevailing or predicted weather conditions over a large area. They are usually based on weather observations taken at the same time at a number of stations.

Classes of Maps by Scale

Map scale is expressed as the ratio of representational map distance to true ground distance (Fig. 1). Confusion can arise when the terms *small scale*, *medium scale*, and *large scale* are read in conjunction with the quantitative scale. Map scale classes and their general uses are:

Small-scale maps. These are maps of 1:600,000 and smaller scale that are used for general planning and for strategic studies. The standard small scale in the U.S. armed forces is 1:1,000,000.

Medium-scale maps. Maps at scales larger than 1:600,000, but smaller than 1:75,000, are used for planning operations such as troop movements and concentrations and logistics operations. The standard U.S. medium scale is 1:250,000.

Large-scale maps. Such maps are used to meet the tactical, technical, and

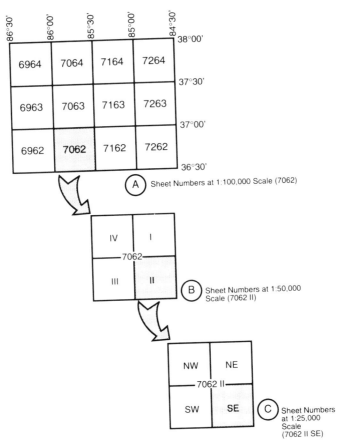

Figure 1. Map identification—1:100,000, 1:50,000, and 1:25,000 scales.

administrative requirements of field units. The standard U.S. large scale is 1:50,000.

Topographic Map Colors

Most military maps used in ground operations are topographic maps that differentiate among various types of terrain features through the use of different colors. This also may render the map a more nearly natural representation of the terrain. Colors usually found on North Atlantic Treaty Organization (NATO) maps are:

- black—the majority of man-made or cultural features
- blue—water features such as lakes, rivers, and swamps
- green—vegetation such as woods, orchards, and vineyards
- brown—all relief features such as contours
- red—main roads, built-up areas, and special features.

Other colors are used to show special information on military maps. The meaning of these colors is, as a rule, indicated in the marginal information of the map. An example of such a color is purple, used in aeronautical symbols and related information on joint operations graphics.

Marginal Information

The marginal information found on almost all military maps can be considered a "user's guide" to the map in question. Within NATO most military maps are relatively standardized in their depictions of information, although there are exceptions. These exceptions are pronounced when maps from outside NATO are encountered. Nonetheless, almost all maps, regardless of their country of origin, have marginal information that informs the user of the map's peculiarities; therefore, marginal information on any map should be examined prior to map use. Most Western maps have similar types of marginal information. Some of the more important data elements to be found in marginal information are:

Sheet name. The name of the map sheet is usually found in two places on most military maps: the center of the upper right margin and in the lower right corner. Map sheets are usually named after their most prominent cultural or geographic feature. Usually the name of the largest city or town on the map is used.

Sheet number. The sheet number is usually found in the upper right corner and is used as a reference number for the map sheet. For small-scale maps (1:1,000,000 and larger) sheet numbers are based on an arbitrary system that facilitates the orientation of larger-scale maps.

Series name and scale. These data are normally found in the upper left margin of the map. A margin series usually comprises a group of similar maps with the same scale and format. The series name may also be a group of maps serving a common purpose, such as military city maps. The name of the series is that of the most prominent area.

Series number. This number normally appears in the upper right and lower left margins and is a comprehensive reference expressed either as a four-digit number (e.g., 1215) or as a letter followed by a three- or four-digit number (e.g., M221; R6221).

Edition number. The edition number, usually found in the upper margin and in the lower left margin, gives the age of the map relative to other editions of the same map and the agency responsible for its production. The highest number represents the most recent edition of the map. For example, EDITION 2-DMA indicates the second edition of a map prepared by the United States Defense Mapping Agency. The higher edition number usually supersedes previous editions of the same map.

Bar scales. These scales are usually found in the lower center margin and are used to convert map distance to ground distance. There are usually three or more bar scales, each with a different unit of measure.

Adjoining sheets diagram. Most military maps at standard scales contain a diagram that illustrates the adjoining sheets. On small-scale maps (1:100,000 and larger) the diagram is termed the *Index to Adjoining Sheets* and consists of as many rectangles as required to surround the sheet under consideration. All represented sheets are identified with numbers. Sheets of an adjoining series, which have the same scale, are represented by dashed lines whether they are published or merely planned. On maps of 1:50,000 scale, the sheet number and series number of the 1:250,000-scale map of the area are also shown below the Index to Adjoining Sheets.

Legend. The legend is located in the lower left margin of the map. It identifies and illustrates the topographic symbols used to depict the most common features on the map. Symbols are not always the same, hence the legend is critical to avoid errors in use.

Declination diagram. In large-scale maps, this diagram is located in the lower margin. It indicates the angular relationships of true north, magnetic north, and grid north. This diagram is crucial to using the map, as the map must always be aligned with the earth's surface prior to use by orienting it on the correct north-south ground alignment through the use of a compass. On maps of 1:250,000 scale this information is stated in a note in the lower margin.

Contour interval. This information appears in the center of the lower margin and states the vertical distance between adjacent contour lines on the map. It

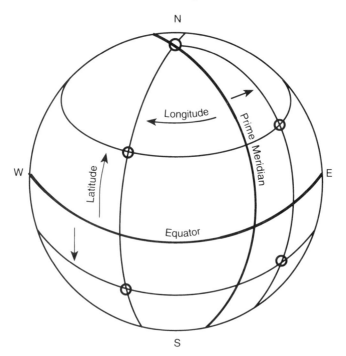

Figure 2. Longitude and latitude.

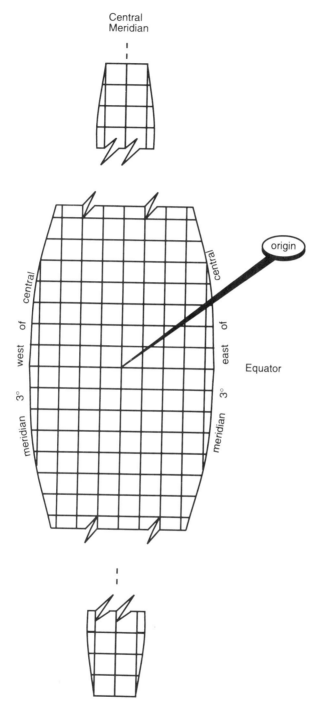

Figure 3. Representative UTM grid zone.

is an important datum, as it allows the user a ready means of computing his elevation.

The foregoing items of marginal information are only the most important ones; there are many data in the margins of military maps that the user must consider. A more detailed coverage of marginal information may be found in military map reading manuals, such as the U.S. Army's *Field Manual 21–26*.

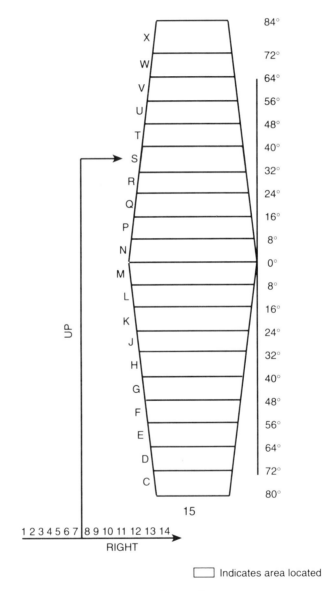

Figure 4. Grid zone designation.

Map Grids

To use a map to determine one's position, a precise location system is required. Such a system should:

- require no knowledge of the geographic area in question,
- be applicable to large areas,
- require no landmarks,
- be applicable to all map scales, and
- be simple to understand and use.

The traditional geographic coordinate system based on meridians of longitude and parallels of latitude has long been used for navigation at sea and in small-scale maps (Fig. 2). Both latitude and longitude represent a circle drawn

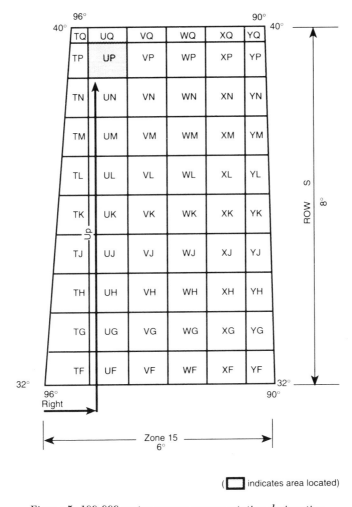

(☐ indicates area located)

Figure 5. 100,000-meter square representative designation.

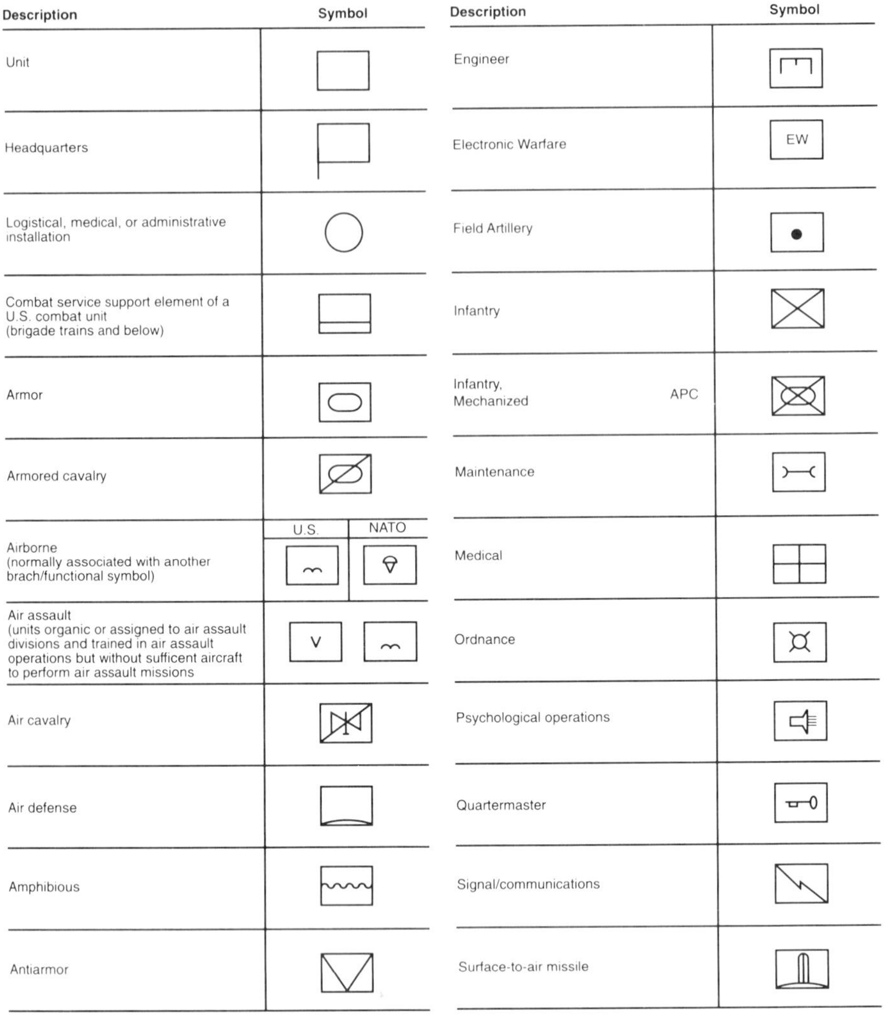

Description	Symbol	Description	Symbol
Unit		Engineer	
Headquarters		Electronic Warfare	EW
Logistical, medical, or administrative installation		Field Artillery	•
Combat service support element of a U.S. combat unit (brigade trains and below)		Infantry	
Armor		Infantry, Mechanized · APC	
Armored cavalry		Maintenance	
Airborne (normally associated with another brach/functional symbol)	U.S. / NATO	Medical	
Air assault (units organic or assigned to air assault divisions and trained in air assault operations but without sufficent aircraft to perform air assault missions)	V / ~	Ordnance	
Air cavalry		Psychological operations	
Air defense		Quartermaster	
Amphibious		Signal/communications	
Antiarmor		Surface-to-air missile	

Figure 6. Basic military symbols.

around the earth; geographic coordinates are expressed in angular measurement. Each circle is divided into 360 degrees, each degree into 60 minutes, and each minute into seconds. Longitude is measured east or west from the prime meridian at Greenwich, England; latitude is measured north or south from the earth's equator. It should be noted that many nations outside NATO do not use the Greenwich meridian as standard. While longitude and latitude are satisfactory for naval operations, there are two disadvantages to using this system for ground operations. First, latitude and longitude are curved lines, and second, the smallest subdivision of either is the second, which is accurate to only 24 meters (75 ft.). The curvature of the lines of longitude and latitude also cause quadrangles formed by the intersection of the parallels to be different sizes and shapes, which complicates measuring directions and locating points. Further,

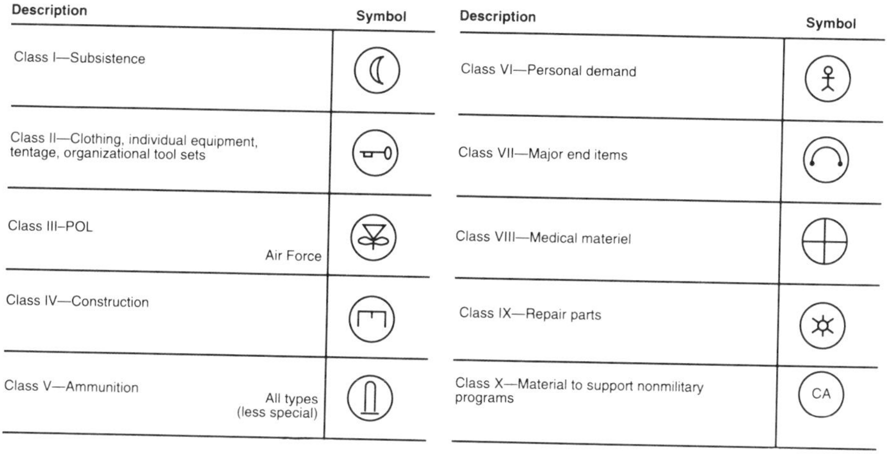

Description	Symbol	Description	Symbol
Class I—Subsistence		Class VI—Personal demand	
Class II—Clothing, individual equipment, tentage, organizational tool sets		Class VII—Major end items	
Class III–POL Air Force		Class VIII—Medical materiel	
Class IV—Construction		Class IX—Repair parts	
Class V—Ammunition All types (less special)		Class X—Material to support nonmilitary programs	

Figure 7. Logistics role indicators.

24-meter (75-ft.) accuracy is not sufficiently precise for all military ground operations. Military grids overcome these problems, although longitude and latitude usually are also indicated on military maps.

Military grids are no more than a rectangular grid superimposed on the transverse Mercator projection normally used in military maps. The universal transverse Mercator (UTM) grid covers the earth between 84 degrees north and 80 degrees south latitude (Fig. 3). As its name implies, it is superimposed over the transverse Mercator projection. The earth has 60 UTM zones and the grid is identical in each. Base values in meters are assigned to the central meridian and to the equator, and the grid lines are fixed in parallel to these base lines. Each grid line is given a value indicating its distance from the origin. Each grid zone between 84 degrees north and 80 degrees south is 6 × 8 or 6 × 12 degrees of latitude and longitude in size, is given a designation (Fig. 4), and is further subdivided into 100,000-meter squares. Each 100,000-meter square is identified by a pair of letters that is unique within the area covered by the grid zone designation (Fig. 5). The identification of the 100,000-meter square identification letters usually is shown in the marginal information on most NATO military maps. This system ensures that no two locations can be located at the same point on the earth. Military maps are broken down from 100,000-meter squares through 1:50,000- and 1:25,000-scale sheets (see Fig. 1).

The regularly spaced grid lines that appear on all large-scale military maps are divisions of the 100,000-meter square and are spaced at 1,000- or 10,000-meter intervals. Each grid line has a specific designation that can be used to pinpoint one's location. Most Western grid references are read from left to right, then up.

Military Symbols

Military symbols are graphic aids used on maps to identify items of operational interest. The keys to good military symbols are simplicity, uniformity, and

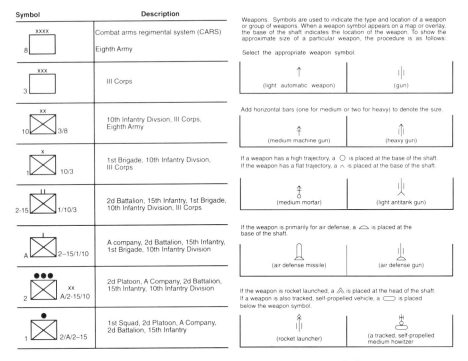

Figure 8. Representative fields for military symbols.
Figure 9. Representative equipment symbols.

clarity. Symbols are used to depict both friendly and enemy units, weapons, equipment, and activities. Within NATO, military symbols are governed by a standardization agreement (STANAG 2019) that generally defines the usage of symbols throughout the alliance, although there are variations.

Military symbols provide an easily recognizable means to express an operational plan, concept, or situation on a map. Under ideal conditions, colors are used to distinguish among friendly, enemy, and other symbols. The colors used within NATO are:

- black or blue—Friendly units, weapons, activities, and ground environment symbols not encompassed by other colors;
- red—Enemy units, weapons, and activities;
- yellow—Chemical, radiological, or biological areas, whether friendly or enemy; and
- green—Man-made obstacles, whether friendly or enemy.

Within NATO, fields around the basic symbol are used to display specific data regarding the symbol in question. The use of fields is necessary to clarify the status of the unit, weapon, or equipment depicted by the basic symbol.

Military symbols consist of a basic designator that indicates the type of organization represented, an interservice symbol, a size symbol, a unit role symbol, an equipment indicator, and various fields surrounding the basic symbol to

U.S. Description	STANAG 2019 Description	Symbol
Squad/crew	Smallest unit/UK section	
Section unit larger than a squad but smaller than a platoon	Unit larger than a U.S. squad/UK section but smaller than a platoon equivalent	
Platoon or detachment	Platoon/troop equivalent	
Company, battery, or troop	Company/battery/squadron equivalent	
Battalion or squadron	Battalion equivalent	
Group or regiment	Regiment/group equivalent	
Brigade	Brigade equivalent	
Division	Division	
Corps	Corps	
Army	Army	

Figure 10. Unit size designations.

further clarify and specify its identity. Representative NATO/U.S. military symbols are presented in Figures 6 through 10.

CHARLES Q. CUTSHAW

SEE ALSO: Geography, Military; Meteorology, Military; Theater of War.

Bibliography

Pombrik, I. D., and A. N. Shevchenko. 1985. *Karta ofitsera* (The officer's map). Moscow: Military Publishing House.

U.S. Army. n.d. *Field manual 21–26: Map reading.* Washington, D.C.: Headquarters, Department of the Army.

U.S. Defense Intelligence Agency (DIA). 1978. DDB-2680-41-78. *Handbook of Soviet armed forces military symbols.* Washington, D.C.: Defense Intelligence Agency.

MECHANIZED WARFARE

According to an authoritative definition, to mechanize a military force is "to equip [it] with armed and armored motor vehicles." While Leonardo da Vinci may have been the first to design an armed and armored vehicle, his was without a motor in the modern sense; therefore, the story of mechanized warfare may be said to begin with the Industrial Revolution. For it was the products of that revolution that first appeared as "armed and armored motor vehicles," tanks, in battle in World War I.

Success in warfare comes from operational concepts—the set of schemes that, at tactical and operational levels, describes how battles are to be fought and campaigns conducted. Technology simply provides the means whereby existing concepts may be executed more effectively or revised concepts introduced. Such is the case with mechanization. For example, Karl von Clausewitz's doctrine of massing at the decisive point in battle, basically an operational concept, is considerably facilitated by mechanization—a technology that enabled masses of troops and firepower to be brought to bear more quickly than before mechanization. Through mechanization, battles acquired a degree of tactical and operational mobility commanders had never enjoyed before. Later, mobility enabled blitzkrieg and mobile defense to become the dominant operational concepts of World War II, even though the operational utility of those concepts had been more than adequately demonstrated before mechanization— for example, by Napoleon in the Ulm campaign of 1805 and by the "foot cavalry" that marched with Stonewall Jackson in that busy summer of 1862 in the Shenandoah Valley of Virginia. It is important to understand the mechanization story in terms of the operational concepts that underlie the mechanization process in all armies.

Mechanization

The first armed and armored motor vehicle was the tank, which was introduced in World War I for the specific purpose of overcoming obstacles to maneuver by foot infantry—physical obstacles such as trenches, firepower obstacles such as the fires of artillery and machine guns. In that role, the tank moved at an infantry rate of march. In fact, in one very early battle in which the U.S. Army employed tanks, the tank unit commander, Col. George S. Patton, Jr., actually marched along on foot with the tanks as they attacked; he was wounded in that action—a reminder of one reason the tanks were there in the first place. It was possibly the missed opportunity to exploit the tactical breakthrough with tanks at Cambrai on 20 November 1917, and the realization of what might have been had the Allied forces been ready to exploit the breakthrough, that caused some officers to see tank-equipped forces as a modern equivalent of heavy cavalry and not just as protected firepower support for infantry. And so was born the idea of independent mechanized forces as a decisive arm in battle. It is the development of that idea that one inevitably follows in tracing the evolution of mechanized operations.

In the paragraphs that follow, the word *mechanized* will be used as defined—that is, "armed and armored vehicles." The term *armor* will be used to mean the combined-arms team of tanks, infantry, artillery, engineers, signal, and other supporting arms, combined in proportions dictated by mission, enemy, terrain, and weather in the operational area but with tanks as the primary combat element. *Armored* and *armor*, at least in regard to organizations, are synonyms.

ARMORED FORCES

The concept of an armored force as the dominant arm of a mixed military force of tanks, infantry, and artillery likely first came to being in both Great Britain and Germany at roughly the same time. In the former, mixed battalions of tanks and motorized (truck-mobile) infantry carried out tactical exercises (trials) in 1921 and 1922 as part of a temporarily assembled Experimental Brigade. Then, in 1923, the Royal Tank Corps was established. An Experimental Mechanized Force conducted tactical exercises in 1927 and 1928. Biases over what had been learned were so deeply rooted that the idea of a mixed armored force built around tanks was set aside; for British forces, it would not become a factor again until World War II. What did survive the trials on Salisbury Plain, however, was the perception and the pen of the British military writer, Capt. Basil H. Liddell Hart. As a young officer in World War I, Liddell Hart was shocked by the waste of massed infantry against massed artillery and machine guns, and he became convinced that if war must be fought, mechanization seemed a much less manpower-intensive way of successfully combining fire and maneuver. So, as his army and his country turned away from large-scale mechanization, Liddell Hart began to write about warfare of the future based on his growing conviction that mechanization could in substantial measure avoid, or at least reduce, the awesome bloodshed of World War I.

The second country, Germany, was prohibited by the Versailles Treaty from having most types of armored vehicles. Nevertheless, officers were studying and experimenting, as best they could, with mechanization, rapid tactical troop movement, and close cooperation between mechanized formations and armed aircraft to facilitate rapid operational-level maneuver.

So, in one country, Great Britain, soldiers were concentrating on the capabilities of tanks, whether they should be "light" or "heavy," and how best to organize and operate combined arms units. In the other, Germany, the Wehrmacht thinkers, largely unencumbered by technical and organizational details, carefully examined how best to combine ground and air mobility at tactical and operational levels to achieve quick decisive victory.

The Germans seized an additional important initiative around 1925 by entering into an agreement with the Soviets to set up and operate a tank factory and a school to teach mechanized warfare in the Soviet Union. Further, they conducted field experiments with Soviet forces to validate their ideas. From this experience, they emerged with a fairly well laid out set of operational concepts—doctrine, tactics and techniques, organization, and equipment needs. Several if not many of the Wehrmacht's most outstanding field commanders reflected the profound intellectual effects of this period of development and growth; noteworthy among them were Heinz Guderian, Hasso von Manteuffel, and Erwin Rommel.

For the Soviets, the major outcome of the German experience in the Soviet Union was the organization of large Soviet army formations known as Motor Mechanized Corps and the design, production, and fielding of the T34/76 tank—lineal antecedent of every Soviet tank up to, at least, the T80/125 model.

From the debut of the tank on World War I battlefields to the beginning of German military operations in Europe in World War II, milestones in armor force development were the Spanish Civil War (1936–39) and Soviet-Japanese hostilities along the border of Japanese-occupied Manchuria (1939). Of the latter, very little is known in the West; about the former, a great deal is known.

The armies of several nations drew some mistaken conclusions from events of the war in Spain. These nations concluded that operations in Spain confirmed that tanks—even heavily armored infantry support tanks—would very quickly fall prey to infantry antitank weapons. Therefore, it would not be operationally possible to maneuver major formations at a rate greater than that of advancing (on foot) infantry because to do so would expose the tanks to antitank weapons without infantry support.

The Soviet general staff was persuaded by the campaigns in Spain that they had previously pursued a wrong course. So, virtually on the eve of World War II, they disbanded their Motor Mechanized Corps—then about divisional size. Coincidentally, there was a purge of Soviet officers, which included many of those who were looked on as apostles of mobile warfare. Despite this fact, Gen. Georgi Zhukov, in the Battle of Khalkin Gol (Nomonhan) against the Japanese in Outer Mongolia in mid-August 1939, demonstrated that armor—the combined-arms team of tanks, infantry, and artillery—was a powerful battle-winning arm. The influence of this battle on Soviet political leadership, only a few days before the outbreak of World War II in Europe, is still not entirely clear. It does not seem to have affected the Soviet decision, made at that very time, to enter into a nonaggression pact with Germany. It may also have alerted the general staff to the folly of their decision to disband the Motor Mechanized Corps. Certainly the German campaigns in Poland (1939) and France (1940) were manifest evidence of the power of mechanized combined-arms forces; so while Khalkin Gol may have been a precursor, it was by no means the only such evidence. In any event, with the successful German campaigns in Europe as evidence, the Soviets, in a dramatic turnabout, quickly re-created large mechanized formations consistent with the concepts they had earlier learned from the Germans.

While German thinking about mechanized warfare had been initially uncluttered by concerns over equipment and organizational design because of Versailles Treaty limitations, once the decision to abrogate the treaty had been taken (1936), equipment design and organization problems came to the fore, and the Germans confronted the first of several persistent problems in mechanization: what should be the proportion of tanks and infantry; what and how much indirect-fire support is necessary for battles whose successful outcome hinges on quick maneuver in violent direct-fire battles? These are central problems in the mechanization equation. In the armies of many countries, they have not been resolved to this day.

The war establishment organization of circa 1939 Wehrmacht panzer (tank) divisions called for more tank units than infantry units at battalion and company levels, at a ratio of roughly four to three. By contrast, so-called light divisions had a more balanced organization in wartime, even though their nonwar tables of organization called for four infantry battalions and one tank battalion. This was more likely a reflection of the ability to equip tank units, given the state of mechanization at the time, than it was of a clear operational, hence organizational, concept. There were, in addition, independent tank brigades; it was intended that these should be used as necessary to "heavy up" light divisions or pure infantry divisions. After the Polish campaign, most of the tank battalions in these brigades were assigned to the light divisions they had previously supported, thus giving the light divisions relatively balanced ratios of tank and infantry units.

Operationally, it may well be that the failure of Guderian's panzer divisions to completely encircle the British forces at Dunkirk was more a function of the imbalance of tanks and infantry than anything else. For by the time the channel coast was within reach, the panzer divisions' infantry had been depleted to the point that the corps was not able to push infantry across the low ground in sufficient numbers to capture Dunkirk. It was a lesson not lost, for the 1941 German panzer divisions featured a much higher proportion of infantry than had their 1939 predecessors.

The second great dilemma with mechanized forces is that of logistics support. All armies, even the most robust, have faced this problem since the beginning of mechanization. To the Germans it came early in the campaigns of Rommel's Afrika Korps in North Africa. Since the Afrika Korps was the nemesis of both British and U.S. forces in North Africa, its operations have been widely studied and analyzed in the West. In perspective, however, it was a relatively small force—no more than 10 percent of the Wehrmacht's armor and mechanized forces. Even so, Rommel nearly ran through the British to the Suez Canal and beyond to the oil-rich Middle East. Had he done so, especially before the Allied landings in Northwest Africa, the war would surely have taken a quite different turn. That he did not do so is a reflection of gross logistical difficulties built up after months of highly mobile operations. To illustrate: when the Afrika Korps went in on its final attacks against the British in the Western Desert, before the British victory at El Alamein (October–November 1942), more than 80 percent of its equipment had been taken from the enemy; yet day after day Afrika Korps vehicle and maintenance crews were able to field sufficient fighting strength to permit the battle to continue. Eventually this makeshift logistics system and the relatively high replacement equipment losses to British air and naval action against the German Mediterranean convoys combined to hobble the Afrika Korps. The marvel is that Rommel was able to do as much as he did with so little for so long and that his forces came close to decisive victory despite their relatively small size and obviously inadequate logistical support.

In the United States, mechanization enjoyed slow beginnings. Perhaps no more than a handful of U.S. Army officers had experience with tanks in World War I, and the dominant persuasion of U.S. Army leadership in the period following World War I was that infantry was still the primary force in battle. Nonetheless, an experimental armored force, the 7th Mechanized Brigade, was assembled at Fort Knox, Kentucky, in the early 1930s and began to explore mechanization. Equipment was scarce. While this was largely a reflection of lean budgets during the Great Depression, it also reflected the infantry mindset of U.S. Army leaders and U.S. isolation from the most likely arenas of conflict. Then Army chief of staff Douglas MacArthur perhaps best reflected all this when he testified before the U.S. Congress in the early 1930s to the effect that the United States should not buy too many tanks, because they became obsolete so quickly. Inferred, of course, was the notion that mobilization—the systemic product of the Industrial Revolution—would enable training centers (military manpower factories) and tank and aircraft plants (military equipment factories) to spring into being and quickly produce integrated masses of men and equipment. These would then go off to war, fight, and win largely by simply overwhelming the enemy with numbers.

Confronted by this systemic bias, it was difficult, if not impossible, to achieve substantial mechanization of U.S. forces in time of peace. So it was that U.S. Army mechanization languished in the years between the world wars. In the Kentucky hills along the Ohio River valley, U.S. Army cavalrymen, led by Brig. Gen. Daniel Van Voorhies, struggled to bring out of their nominally funded experiments the lessons that would enable sound operational concepts—doctrine, tactics, and techniques for mechanized operations—to be drawn up. However, so strong was the infantry bias, and so limited the mechanization investment in these years, that most of the imaginative cavalrymen who had led U.S. tank units in World War I went back to the cavalry. According to institutional wisdom, tanks and mechanization were only for support of dismounted infantry, anyway; besides, cavalry and horses were more fun. In the years when his peers were struggling through Kentucky brambles with their embryonic mechanized force, Col. George S. Patton, Jr., perhaps the leading U.S. Tank Corps personality in World War I, was enjoying cavalry life in command of the 3d U.S. Cavalry Regiment at Fort Myer, Virginia.

On the eve of World War II, the armored forces of the U.S. Army found themselves with only tentative operational concepts, limited tactical experience in field trials, no operational-level experience at all, even in war games, and a handful of tanks assigned to general headquarters (GHQ) tank battalions.

Indeed, even the tanks would not have been present had it not been for the persistent efforts of (later) Maj. Gen. Adna R. Chaffee who, as a War Department staff officer, was successful in ensuring modest funding for building tanks. This was accomplished despite the vociferous opposition of the chief of cavalry.

President Franklin D. Roosevelt ordered partial mobilization in 1940, and after the Japanese attack at Pearl Harbor, 7 December 1941, the expanded and intensified mobilization system quickly began to produce soldiers and equipment in numbers. An armored force was organized at Fort Knox under Major

General Chaffee, and in great haste the United States set about to make up for lost time. Tactics and techniques were put together in tentative form, subjected to field trials in organizations as large as a corps, changed and amended as appropriate, then committed to battle, first in 1943 in North Africa.

Mechanization in World War II

Blitzkrieg—lightning war—a term made famous by media accounts of German training and early operations in World War II, was the serendipitous combining of considerable thinking by the Germans about mobility in war, tank and motorized forces, and a stable of remarkably talented field commanders. In blitzkrieg, mechanized and motorized formations moving at a rate at least four times that of dismounted infantry were sure guarantors of tactical and operational success. However, throughout the war, whether in Western Europe, North Africa, or Russia, the Panzertruppen almost always were at or beyond the limits of their logistical capabilities. From the German point of view, early and striking blitzkrieg successes in the west must be laid alongside three and a half years of strategic defense—actually offensive defense in the east and later a somewhat shorter period of similar activity in the west. The role of mechanized forces in these strategic offensive-defensive operations was incomparably tougher than was the case in the blitzkrieg days. This was because, in defensive operations, the initiative was yielded to the enemy, first at the strategic and then the operational level. The single factor that made blitzkrieg so effective was that it seized the initiative at all levels, from highest to lowest. The history of war instructs that more often than not victory in battle goes to the side that, at some point, seizes the initiative and sustains it to the end. Particularly, this is the case if surprise can also be achieved.

It is instructive to examine why, despite considerable numerical superiority, the Soviets were not able to defeat the Wehrmacht in the east much sooner than they did. The answer is most likely in the mix of tanks and infantry and in the Soviets' inability to take and hold the initiative. For most of the war, the Soviets had no mobile infantry—mechanized or truck mounted. Soviet tanks were, technically at least, as good or better than German tanks, and as the war continued, Soviet tank units came to be fairly well commanded. Yet, whether at tactical or operational levels, tanks alone could not succeed without infantry. Typically, in a corps- or divisional-level battle, Soviet tanks would break through a thin belt of German infantry and penetrate fairly deeply. Without infantry, they quickly fell prey to German antitank guns, reserves, or both. Then the tanks, having become separated from their supporting infantry near the forward line of troops, were helpless. German artillery then immobilized the unprotected infantry. It was a pattern repeated many times. The Soviets were among the first after World War II to field fighting vehicles for infantry; the lessons of World War II were obviously not lost. Soviet tanks improved in quality, with the T34/76 being succeeded by the surprisingly effective T34/85 as the mainstay of Soviet tank formations. The Soviet tractor industry produced good-quality, effective, tank cannons—largely derivatives of the Soviets' excellent field artillery—and the two came together to produce large numbers of very effective tanks. It is fair to say that operational mobility—at division and corps level—not only brought the Germans success in blitzkrieg operations but also succeeded in offensive-defensive operations in keeping the Soviet Army out of Germany proper for nearly four years.

In the west, where they saw themselves on a strategic defensive, German forces were also overwhelmed by numbers. The late U.S. start in mechanization was reflected in many ways during the war. Operationally, most U.S. commanders—with a few exceptions, like Patton—had not reflected sufficiently on concepts of mobile action. Early tanks were found to be undergunned. However, tank destroyers—open-turreted gun motor carriages with larger guns—were also fielded and the larger guns—76mm and 90mm—were moved to tanks. Infantry was motorized in some but not all infantry divisions; in armored divisions, infantry was mounted in half-tracks with light, bulletproof armor. Artillery in armored divisions was self-propelled but mounted on open-topped carriages.

Having pioneered in thinking about and experimenting with armor operations, the British entered the war reflecting the relative hiatus in mechanized developments that had set in following the Experimental Force trials on Salisbury Plain. In equipment, organization, and operational concepts, however, they were well ahead of their U.S. allies. British armor unit commanders proved themselves competent in the North African campaigns, although it was not until large amounts of U.S.-made equipment arrived and British equipment holdings became substantially greater than those of the Afrika Korps that conclusive successes were achieved. The British, however, suffered from underpowered armored vehicles, especially tanks. Traditionally, British tanks have featured better guns (firepower) but less motor power (mobility), and British operational concepts have concentrated more on battle attrition than on fast-moving mobile operations.

The state of military mechanization to the end of World War II found the world's larger armies each with a mechanized army inside a much larger "dismounted" army. These mechanized armies were not truly mechanized, in that they were not fully armored and armed. Infantry lacked mounted weapons, except for machine guns, and infantry carriers were at best lightly armored and without overhead cover. Artillery was towed or self-propelled but in the latter case lacked overhead cover. All these were grist for postwar developments.

Mechanization after World War II

MECHANIZATION, NATO, AND NUCLEAR WEAPONS

Following World War II, all surviving armies set to work on doctrinal, organizational, and equipment changes and improvements derived from their experience in and observations of the war just finished. In the West, it is fair to say that for the most part these changes primarily reflected perceptions about operations of the German Wehrmacht. The striking performance of the panzer divisions in the early days in the West and in Russia and the equally striking effectiveness of German mobile defensive operations, especially in the Soviet Union during the last years of the war, formed the basis for most of what was codified.

The offense remained the dominant form of combat, even for forces in strategic or operational defensive posture. Mobile strike forces arrayed deep in defensive zones would mass quickly to conduct offensive operations against deep penetrating armor formations, which would have been stripped of their supporting infantry as they broke through the infantry-heavy forward defensive zone. The Soviets codified their experience into an offensive operational concept featuring mass, momentum, and continuous land combat—mass meaning numbers concentrated in a small area, momentum meaning the product to be achieved by combining mass and velocity, and continuous land combat meaning the offensive employment of successive echelons at a rate that in the end would simply overwhelm the defender. Other than in the offensive zone, forces would be deployed for defense, in considerable depth, featuring infantry, well dug-in forward and heavy mobile armor reserves. To execute this concept there were, and are, tank divisions with mechanized infantry and motorized rifle divisions—mechanized infantry with tank support. Artillery, at first largely towed, underwent extensive modernization in the 1970s and 1980s. There were two aspects to this modernization. The weapons not only became self-propelled, they also became nuclear capable, able to provide artillery support for mechanized forces under all possible circumstances. The first-line units of Soviet forces were fully mechanized combined-arms forces—tanks, infantry, artillery and supporting air defense, engineer, signals, and other organizations. Theirs was a truly mechanized army, embracing in a uniquely Russian way the operational concepts first seized on so long ago by the early advocates of mobile warfare—Mikhail Tukhachevsky, Guderian, J. F. C. Fuller, Liddell Hart, Van Voorhies, and Patton.

In Western Europe and the United States, as this doctrinal evolution unfolded, it quickly became apparent that the growing conventional strength of the Soviet Union was a most vexing problem. For inherent in the changing force balance was the unpleasant truth that no longer could the Allies be guaranteed numerical superiority. So as the North Atlantic Treaty Organization (NATO) was being set up in the early 1950s, Gen. Dwight Eisenhower, as SACEUR, set forth the need for 96 divisions and 9,000 tactical fighters to defend NATO. Rejected by member countries unable or unwilling to provide these staggering resources, Eisenhower, when president, finally settled for 26 divisions—12 of them to be West German—1,400 fighter aircraft, and 15,000 theater and tactical nuclear weapons. Of the latter, about 7,000 were deployed, and 4,000 remained as of early 1990. Technology in the form of nuclear weapons was to make up for the disparity in numbers.

The U.S. Army had disbanded nearly all its armored divisions at the close of World War II. At NATO's inception, the United States re-created its armored forces, deploying several infantry and armored divisions to Western Europe. The remainder were stationed within the continental United States for deployment to reinforce the Europe-deployed force or elsewhere as required. When the North Koreans invaded South Korea in June 1950, U.S. Army divisions stationed in Japan deployed to Korea. Tank battalions were deployed from the United States to provide tank support for foot or truck-mounted infantry. But no mechanized units larger than tank battalions were employed by U.S. forces in Korea.

In the beginning, and for some time after, the United States, and so NATO, controlled an overwhelming strategic nuclear capability. From the mid-1960s, Soviet nuclear capabilities grew to the point that by the 1970s the United States no longer had the capability to reduce a Soviet counterstrike to reasonably tolerable levels. It was an early perception of this developing reality that led the administration of President John F. Kennedy to abandon the strategy of massive nuclear retaliation and to embrace the flexible response doctrine in its stead.

For a time, the Soviets apparently believed that war between NATO and the Warsaw Pact would be nuclear—it would begin and end that way. With time, the awesome totality of a nuclear conflict at tactical, operational, and strategic levels apparently overwhelmed the Soviets' ability to think logically about the matter. At that point their attention turned once again to operational concepts for the conventional battle—mechanized forces.

From about 1966, when they concluded they had achieved nuclear "parity," the Soviets embraced the notion that they could and should try to win at the theater level, avoiding the use of nuclear weapons. Their conventional weapons developments in five-year plans for 25 years clearly focused on the development and deployment of impressive capabilities in tanks, infantry fighting vehicles, artillery, air defense, radio-electronic combat, combat helicopters, ballistic missiles, and fixed-wing airpower. All of these means were designed to make mass, momentum, and continuous land combat a viable operational concept for conventional operations at the theater (operational) level of war.

The deployment in the early 1970s of large numbers of antitank guided missiles (ATGM) by NATO forces—weapons designated by acronyms such as TOW, HOT, Dragon, Milan—and the adoption in the West of an operational concept called Active Defense in 1976 gave pause to Soviet conventional force development. NATO, recognizing the considerable lack of operational depth in its geography, adopted a theater-level posture called Forward Defense. This concept recognized that in NATO's area, especially in the central region, there was insufficient maneuver room to conduct large-scale mobile defensive operations like those of the Wehrmacht in World War II and on which the mobile defense doctrine of Western armies was based. Active Defense simply recognized the advantages to be had by employing long-range, high-hit probability, antitank guided missiles in depth in the Forward Defense. In effect, it expanded the close battle space—the space at the forward line of troops—by virtually doubling the effective range of direct-fire systems employed there. To the Soviets, it meant that Soviet ability to break through NATO's antitank defenses without risking substantial loss and possible defeat was uncertain at best, doubtful at worst. NATO was again calling on technology to resolve the difficult problem of how to defend successfully against overwhelming numbers.

In response, the Soviets set about to solve the technical riddle of the shaped-charge warheads used on antitank guided missiles.

By the mid-1970s, the Soviets began to field a technological solution to the antitank guided missile problem—composite or laminate armors that were more than a match for early model ATGM warheads. While tank fleets with this advanced level of protection were growing apace—production running 3,000 to 4,000 units per year—Soviet technology provided the means for even better protection in the form of what is popularly called reactive armor. This consists of an array of appliqué boxes covering the tank's armor and containing specially designed explosives that detonate on impact, destroying the integrity of the incoming ATGM shaped-charge jet. Such armor was first fielded by the Israeli Defense Force (IDF) in the late seventies and early eighties. It went to war in the 1982 Operation Peace for Galilee mounted on IDF tanks and other more lightly protected armored vehicles. Some of these boxes fell into Syrian, and so into Soviet, hands. Beginning about 1986, similar, improved boxes began to appear on tank fleets in Group Soviet Forces Germany. Meanwhile, improved models were available in Israel.

Tanks with reactive armor on top of built-in composite or laminate armor would quite likely defeat the warheads of all deployed ATGMs in the world today and are a very attractive solution to what, for the Soviets, had been a most vexing problem—how to get through the deepening belts of antitank guided missile systems deployed forward in NATO without suffering inordinate losses in Soviet tanks.

The Soviets obviously believed that they had the means to achieve quick, decisive victory at the theater level of war with such thoroughness and dispatch that the West would not be able to make the nuclear decision before the Soviets were already consolidating their theater-level gains. With these competing technical developments in being and as the laboratories set about to resolve the next chapter in the armor-antiarmor saga, NATO's doctrine developers were at work to complete a more robust version of Forward (Active) Defense, one that would truly take on the twin problems of how to cope with numbers—mass in the close-in battle—while at the same time preventing mass and velocity (movement) from building momentum and preventing follow-on echelons from closing in quickly to overwhelm forward defenders. In the U.S. Army, this early 1980s doctrine is known as Air-land Battle. Its most important ideas are: deep attack against the follow-on echelons and the close-in battle are inseparable; seizing and holding the initiative through maneuver of forces and fires are essential to success; the objective of the battle is to win—not just to avoid defeat. Successfully conducted, the Air-land Battle can, with conventional means alone, considerably postpone the time at which the defender must consider the first use of nuclear weapons, thus raising dramatically the nuclear threshold.

Thus stood matters between NATO and the Warsaw Pact in regard to doctrine, forces and organizations, equipment, and the entire panoply of military capabilities at the end of the 1980s. In the Soviet Union, internal reforms started by Mikhail Gorbachev during his years as general secretary of the

Communist Party created the dramatic spectrum of government, economic, social, and finally military changes that began the 1990s. The Warsaw Pact is no more; Soviet forces will soon be gone from Eastern Europe, remaining there now only because there is no place for them to go in the former Soviet Union. The Russian republic has become the dominant member of a coalition of republics whose political, economic, social, and military futures have yet to be shaped. In place of the enormous conventional forces threat traditionally posed by Warsaw Pact forces, there remains a residual set of risks and uncertainties reflecting emerging policies of governments long dominated by dictators and Marxist economic centrism. Dominating residual military capabilities in the former Soviet Union's republics is, of course, the intercontinental ballistic missile/nuclear threat. The fairly clearly defined parameters of the long-standing deterrent standoff between the West and the Soviet Union no longer exist.

Meanwhile, as the Soviet threat—primarily the threat to NATO Europe—diffuses, world attention has been captured by events in the Middle East. As will be seen subsequently, doctrine (tactical and operational), organizations and forces, equipment, and training systems, all developed primarily for operations against the Warsaw Pact, have fought and won a substantial and dramatic victory against Iraqi forces armed with Soviet equipment, trained in Soviet tactics, and deployed in numerically superior force structures against the United States and allied coalition forces in the 1991 Gulf War. That victory is ample demonstration of the battle worthiness of Air-land Battle doctrine—the culmination of mechanization of warfare.

MECHANIZED OPERATIONS IN VIETNAM

Although large-scale armor and mechanized operations were not characteristic of U.S. Army operations in Vietnam, the story of the Vietnamese experience highlights many recurring dilemmas in mechanization and some new concepts of mobility.

After World War II, the French returned to Indochina and set up a colonial administration. Accompanying French military forces included armor units—tanks and "mechanized" infantry, although the latter were either truck- or half-track-mounted mobile infantry rather than truly "armed and armored" infantry. These armored units remained for nearly ten years, departing in 1956 when the last French units left Indochina. French experience, and that of their Vietnamese allies, determined concepts for employment of armor units of the South Vietnamese army. This experience also influenced the thinking of many U.S. military commanders concerning the feasibility of employing armor units in Vietnam.

The U.S. Army of the late 1950s and early 1960s, in fact, had little information regarding the use of armor in Vietnam. What little did exist came from scarce French army battle reports and from some information regarding the numbers and types of U.S. equipment that had been made available to the French and that they in turn had deployed to and employed in Vietnam. That equipment was of World War II vintage; it consisted of light tanks, half-tracks, and scout cars. By 1954, the French had deployed to Vietnam a vehicle fleet of about 450 tanks and tank destroyers and nearly 2,000 scout cars, half-tracks, and amphibious tractors. While those numbers seem substantial, the equipment was scattered over an area of nearly 230,000 square miles. By comparison, the U.S. Army deployed to Vietnam, and had in operation at the height of the fighting in 1969, nearly 600 tanks and 2,000 other armored vehicles operating over an area less than a third that size.

Of the U.S.-made equipment used by the French in Vietnam, all had been manufactured before 1945. Generally, armored vehicles were in poor repair and not fit for fast-moving mobile operations in a country where movement was difficult to begin with. Largely because of the poor mechanical condition of these vehicles, armor operations were a perpetual logistical nightmare. So, armor units were fragmented, set up in many small static positions, and at best used in support of infantry, at whatever marching pace the terrain may have permitted. The mix of armored vehicles and infantry always favored infantry by a substantial margin. All these facts and supporting evidence were duly reported by the French in some very candid after-action reports. Indeed, after the deployment of U.S. advisers following the French departure, observer reports contained the same kinds of information. Heavily classified and largely contained within the files of the U.S. Department of State, these reports were not disseminated in the Department of Defense. Thus there was a dearth of available information on which to base U.S. Army estimates about military operations in Vietnam. Indeed, most of what was known was derived not from military after-action reports, but from material written by civilian observers. Perhaps foremost among these was Bernard B. Fall, whose book *Street Without Joy* devotes one chapter to the six-month history of the destruction of a French mobile force—Groupement Mobile 100. The tragic tale of Groupement Mobile 100's demise seemed to many to symbolize the fate that awaited any armored or mechanized force trying to fight in the jungle. In truth, Groupement Mobile 100 was not really an armor unit. It was a truck-mounted task force of four battalions of infantry. Numbering about 2,600 troops, it was reinforced by one light artillery battalion and ten light tanks. The Groupement moved on roads and deployed to fight on foot. This made it extremely vulnerable to the simplest kind of ambush, and a series of such encounters finally destroyed it. The fate of this unfortunate force became the source of much adverse comment on French armor operations in Vietnam; it completely obscured many French and Vietnamese successes with armored forces. Later, U.S. commanders would repeat many of the mistakes reported on by the French and learn for themselves many lessons the French had drawn about armor operations in Indochina.

As World War II closed, the U.S. Army included sixteen armored divisions and many smaller battalion-size armor units, largely tank battalions for support of foot- or truck-mobile infantry divisions. The divisions of this armored force consisted of integrated combined-arms teams of tanks, half-track mobile infantry, and armored artillery. In the doctrine for employment of these units, there were no recognized limitations because of terrain, geography, or levels of combat intensity. Under the doctrine, forces were to be tailored for the mission, the threat, terrain and weather, and availability of friendly troops. It was believed that there was sufficient flexibility in the organization itself to permit adjustment to almost any set of circumstances. However, U.S. armored divisions were employed only in the European and North African theaters of operations in World War II. In the Pacific, armored battalions were deployed to support foot-mobile infantry, as was also the case in the later war in Korea. It was widely accepted that in jungle areas especially, but in operations in the Pacific Ocean areas in general, there was no opportunity for large-scale independent mobile combined-arms operations such as those of the World War II armored divisions. Force planners for Vietnam therefore concluded there was no place for armor units there—especially tanks. So it was that most U.S. Army divisions deploying to Vietnam initially left behind their organic tank and armored cavalry units.

Meanwhile, the South Vietnamese army's armored force was expanding under the tutelage of U.S. Army armor advisers. In the beginning, and for some time thereafter, tactics reflected French employment doctrine, as well as pressures to minimize casualties and equipment losses. Defense in static position, convoy escort, clearing roads, mobile relief force—all were typical missions. With the advent of post–World War II equipment—principally the U.S.-made M113 armored personnel carrier—small-unit mobile operations became possible, and success in several operations, primarily in the Mekong Delta, marked a turning point in U.S. and Vietnamese attitudes toward mobile operations. Now they were considered possible, even desirable, and the equipment held up. Over time, all this led to an increased capability and spirit of aggressiveness on the part of the Vietnamese tank, cavalry, and mounted infantry soldiers. Some of the most remarkable actions of the North Vietnamese 1968 Tet offensive and the North Vietnamese use of tanks in the 1972 offensive were those of the Vietnamese Armor Command. On the U.S. Army side, it was not until 1967, when a task force of officers was appointed to evaluate operations of tank and other armored units, that the extent of U.S. misperceptions about armor operations was finally set forth. It was found that operations by armor units had been conducted in every region of Vietnam; the severest restrictions on mobility were experienced in the Mekong Delta rice-growing areas and in the heavily forested areas of the Central Highlands. In coastal plains, piedmont, and the plateaus of the Central Highlands, armored vehicles were able to move with ease about 80 percent of the time, and indeed these areas had been traversed by French and Vietnamese armor units before the arrival of U.S. forces.

Vietnam's summer or southwest monsoon blows onshore, out of the Indian Ocean, from June through September, bringing the wet season to the Mekong Delta, the piedmont, and most of the highlands and plateaus of central South Vietnam. The northeast part of the country has its monsoon from November through February, when onshore northeast winds shed moisture over the northern third of the country. Even with these conditions further limiting mobility during the peak of the monsoons, the study group concluded that tanks could move about in mobile operations in more than 60 percent of the country during the dry season and more than 45 percent of the country during the wet season. The extremely versatile M113 armored personnel carrier in several configurations—troop carrier, cavalry assault vehicle, mortar carrier—could move in about 65 percent of the country year-round.

By the time these conclusions were made known (1967), the major force decisions had been made, and with some minor changes, the U.S. armor unit troop basis remained—constrained to the end by dependence on foot, truck, armored personnel carrier, or airmobile infantry, the latter being only foot-mobile when dismounted. There were no large-scale, division-level mounted mobile operations. In the Cambodian invasion of May 1970, however, a three-brigade task force led by a U.S. armored cavalry regiment staged the largest and most successful U.S. forces mobile operation of the war. In a fast-moving, hotly contested series of battles against three North Vietnamese divisions reinforced by three antiaircraft regiments, the 11th Armored Cavalry Regiment, in about five critical days, attacked into Cambodia for a distance of nearly 100 kilometers (60 mi.) and reached, along an extensive line, the limits of advance authorized by President Richard Nixon. It was the first, and indeed the only, mobile armored forces operation of large size during the war, until the North Vietnamese army attacked southward with considerable tank strength in the last days of the war.

Recognizing the need for mobility so dramatically demonstrated by tortuous foot-mobile operations in the jungle areas of the central and southwest Pacific in World War II, imaginative U.S. officers developed, in the early 1960s, new concepts in force mobility using the newly developed capability of the helicopter. Following some exciting field trials with heliborne infantry, it was concluded that airmobile infantry answered the needs for mobility so urgently felt in jungle operations of World War II.

While to some extent their perception was correct, it quickly became apparent that heliborne infantry also enjoyed some singular disadvantages. Foremost among these was the need for sure knowledge of the terrain and enemy by troops and leaders who had deployed quickly by helicopter to areas in which they had not operated recently, if at all. In addition, once on the ground, airmobile infantry is foot-mobile; in all too many cases, the enemy proved to be more mobile tactically simply because he had been there longer and knew the terrain intimately. Availability of firepower—artillery—to support the heliborne infantry is critical. All too often, overzealous heliborne commanders deployed troops near or beyond the limits of immediately available indirect fire and into situations in which the enemy had all his fire support available. Thus disadvantaged, heliborne forces inevitably suffered inordinate losses. Finally, as with all mobile operations, logistical support of deployed heliborne forces presents a problem. Just as the troops themselves were transported by helicopter, so were all their consumables, from rations to ammunition.

The U.S. Army's involvement in Vietnam highlights once again the persistent dilemmas of mechanization: the mix of units necessary for truly mobile warfare; the problem of bringing infantry to battle behind armor protection; and logistics support for armor units whether or not engaged in high-speed mobile operations. These dilemmas were aggravated, in this circumstance, by the mythology about jungle warfare, especially against what was for too long considered to be an "insurgent," "irregular" enemy that all too soon turned out to be a tough, highly motivated, well-led, regular military force—the North Vietnamese army.

MECHANIZED OPERATIONS IN THE MIDDLE EAST

By the time the state of Israel was proclaimed, it was quite clear to the leaders of the Jewish underground that as a nation they faced the likelihood of an all-out war against Arab armies that outnumbered them and were well equipped with fairly modern weapons, including armor—tanks, armored cars, half-tracks. Therefore, if the new nation was to survive, let alone grow and flourish, similar weapons in considerable numbers had to be available to the Israeli defenders. Their worst fears were realized when, following independence on 14 May 1948, Arab armies invaded from all sides. Egyptian armor and infantry columns attacked along the coastal road through Gaza, headed for Beersheba and Jerusalem. Syrian tank and infantry columns attacked into Galilee across the Golan Heights. The Iraqis and the Transjordanian Arab Legion attacked west across the Jordan River toward the Mediterranean coast.

The Israeli Defense Force (IDF) entered the 1948 War of Independence with nine underequipped territorial infantry brigades. In equipment, they were in no way ready to cope with modern forces featuring tanks, armored cars, and truck- or half-track-mobile infantry on equal terms. Nonetheless, with considerable ingenuity—genius in the use of what equipment they did have— and by means of superlative leadership they were able to beat off their attackers and survive. In many battles, the Israelis used mobility as a means of overcoming superior numbers and better equipment in the hands of their foes—a lesson not lost as they looked to the future. The campaign in Galilee and later in the Negev Desert demonstrated the IDF's growing ability to exploit tactical advantage by moving swiftly to achieve operational advantage. In at least one case this led to a strategic advantage—the long outflanking sweep into the northern Sinai that brought the War of Independence to a close.

The Israelis set about after the 1949 armistice to reorganize and refit their forces for other battles surely to follow. Due to the size of the population and the embryonic economy, it was necessary to invoke conscription and establish a reserve army as the mainstay of the military establishment. Twelve brigades existed at war's end. Nine became reserve units; the remaining three were organized into one armored and two infantry brigades. This arrangement largely reflected a lack of sufficient equipment to outfit more than the one armored brigade. They then set about in earnest to study armor operations and to procure for their forces sufficient tanks and other armored vehicles to equip more armored units. In the beginning, the French Cavalry School provided doctrinal education for officers; in addition, the French provided a considerable number of armored vehicles. There also began at this time a remarkable system of adapting the equipment of other nations to unique IDF needs. It is a technique of improvisation that has survived to this day, only diminishing as the

IDF has acquired its own tank—the Merkava—in sufficient numbers to obviate the need for piecing and patching tanks from other armies.

Equipment unreliability and the difficulties of working out doctrine—tactics and techniques—plagued the Israeli Armored Corps in the years between the War of Independence and the Sinai campaign of 1956. Many, if not most, senior leaders were, by 1956, still convinced that armor in support of infantry was the only feasible operational technique. Then the sudden and unexpected successes of the Armored Corps in the 1956 Sinai campaign converted, among others, Chief of Staff Moshe Dayan to believe in the potential of high-speed mobile operations with armored forces. Thus it was that, following the Sinai campaign, the IDF set about to remake an infantry army with tank support into a mechanized army. Several new armor brigades were formed, some based around tank units, others around half-track-mobile infantry.

In the decade following the Sinai campaign, the Israeli Armored Corps increased in strength, in equipment resources, and in command ability, largely under the remarkable leadership of Maj. Gen. Israel Tal. In the Six-Day War of 1967, it proved its mobile armored mettle against the Egyptians, Jordanians, and Syrians. The experiences of 1956 and 1967 convinced Israel's armor leaders of the superiority of tank forces in lightninglike operations. So impressed was the leadership with the potential for success tanks alone provided, it was concluded that infantry, in an IDF primarily made up of less-well-trained reservists, was not compatible with the requirements of mobile battle. Because of the cost of buying or building armored vehicles for the infantry and the overriding need for funds to build tanks, mechanization of infantry largely went begging.

There was, however, a larger issue than budget. The IDF's armor leaders recognized the need to mechanize whatever infantry they were to have with armored personnel carriers, if not with mechanized infantry fighting vehicles. The most readily available vehicle was the U.S.-made M113 armored personnel carrier, which, despite the fact that it provided only a modicum of overhead protection for embarked infantry, required that infantry dismount in order to fight and to remount in order to move. In addition, because the carriers were far less armored than even the tanks of that day, there was no way for the infantry to attack along the same axis and in concert with the tanks—they simply could not survive at the same level of protection as the tanks. This meant that infantry had to stand off, just at the time they were needed most. It also meant that enemy gunners, seeking to separate tanks from their supporting infantry, so as to get at the tanks with antitank weapons, would immediately target the infantry with artillery. It is the persistent problem of how to bring infantry to battle under sufficient armor to allow them to survive at the same rate as tanks.

In October 1973, Egypt, Syria, and other Arab states attacked Israel once again. The Israeli Armored Corps at first suffered from lack of infantry with the assaulting tanks, a problem corrected in later battles, and demonstrated once again the value of mobility in battle.

Soon laid out for all to see were the lessons of the October War: the staggering density of the battlefield at critical points; the presence on both sides of large numbers of modern weapons systems, mostly armored or mechanized; the increased criticality of command control; the increased likelihood of interrupted command control due to large numbers of sophisticated electronic warfare means; the inability of any single weapons system to prevail, reaffirming the essentiality of combined-arms combat; the outcome of battle reflecting, more often than not, factors other than numbers. In addition, it was starkly obvious that large-scale destruction in a short time was a most likely outcome of first battles in modern war, especially if surprise is an operative factor. Even as this drama was unfolding, the Israelis were hard at work under the scrutiny of Major General Tal, by now in charge of tank design and development, seeking a solution to their twin problems with a tank uniquely designed for the IDF and infantry under armor. The answer was the Merkava—Israel's "native" tank. With a front-mounted power train, a small turret ring, and trunnions mounted high in the turret, Merkava presents a nominal silhouette when hull down in the Sinai dunes or Golan boulders. In addition, doors opening rearward from a large rear stowage compartment leave room for an infantry squad or orders group, or for medical evacuation under fire—all under the same level of protection afforded by the tank itself. By 1990, the Merkava was in its third serial of production and was probably the most survivable tank in the world. Certainly it was the best designed from a standpoint of the survivability of the crew, vital tank components, and its capability to provide an acceptable way to get infantry to and from battle under armor. It was clearly the best solution any army had found to date.

Mechanization—The Future

The combined-arms team of armor tanks, mechanized infantry, artillery, and all supporting arms remains the pivotal force in conventional warfare. This is certainly the case in Korea, where large forces in high states of readiness face one another across international boundaries. Further, it is the case in the Middle East and in other areas of the Third World to which the world's largest arms producers have provided significant amounts of modern military equipment.

A perspective about the Third World is useful. In order to view the Middle East as a theater of operations in perspective, it is instructive to span the 30-odd years from the Sinai campaign of 1956 to the present. In the 1950s, the major armies of the region—Egyptian, Syrian, Iraqi, and Jordanian aligned against the Israelis—had combined inventories of about 1,500 first-line tanks and no more than about 500 first-line fighter aircraft. By 1990, those numbers were closer to 15,000 tanks and 5,000 first-line fighter aircraft. In numbers and in the mix of equipment present to be employed in battle, the Middle East is a theater in which armed conflict can be expected to be mobile mechanized warfare with first-line modern equipment, as dramatically demonstrated in the 1991 Gulf War.

Mechanization is also spreading into other parts of the Third World. In the mid-1980s, a study group in the United States, having examined the equipment

Figure 1. The U.S. Army's Abrams tank in the Iraqi desert during Operation Desert Storm, February 1991. The Abrams's awesome mobile protected firepower was a principal contributor to the victory achieved by the allied coalition in operations to free Kuwait from its Iraqi invaders. (SOURCE: Courtesy of U.S. Army Armor Center, Fort Knox)

holdings of several dozen nations of the world, found that in no less than 50 were there significant numbers of fairly modern tanks, infantry fighting vehicles, personnel carriers, artillery, and even combat helicopters. And so the belief, still held by some, especially in the United States, that somehow light infantry—foot, wheeled vehicle, or airmobile—can be inserted, survive, and accomplish a combat mission in the so-called Third World is more and more a myth. If the light infantry is to be the insertion force, then it must be equipped with weapons and protective measures that will enable it to fight successfully and survive against the threat it can expect to find. In no army has this been done—save possibly the Soviet airborne forces with their paradrop-capable armored vehicles and other equipment for operations against NATO rear areas.

Operationally, as well as tactically, conventional force warfare—mechanized battles of the future—will be set in the context of operational concepts that seek to take advantage of increased mobility in offensive and defensive operations to achieve rapid decisive success, bringing to military operations the opportunity for resolution of political conflict quickly and the advantage of the most imaginative, and so successful, of the mobile mechanized combatants. Nowhere is there more dramatic evidence of this than in coalition operations against Iraq's considerable modern mechanized forces in operations in Kuwait and southern Iraq in the early months of 1991 (see Fig. 1).

DONN A. STARRY

SEE ALSO: Air-land Battle; Armor; Blitzkrieg; Combined Arms; Land Warfare; Tank.

Bibliography

Brownlow, D. G. 1975. *Panzer baron: The military exploits of Baron Hasso von Manteuffel*. North Quincy, Mass.: Christopher Publishing House.
Dayan, M. 1965. *Diary of the Sinai campaign*. New York: Harper and Row.
Eshel, D. 1989. *Chariots of the desert: The story of the Israeli armoured corps*. London: Brassey's.
Guderian, H. 1952. *Panzer leader*. New York: E. P. Dutton.
Harmon, E. N. 1970. *Combat commander: Autobiography of a soldier*. Englewood Cliffs, N.J.: Prentice-Hall.
Herzog, C. 1975. *The war of atonement: October, 1973*. Boston: Little, Brown.
———. 1982. *The Arab-Israeli wars: War and peace in the Middle East. From the war of independence through Lebanon*. New York: Random House.
Horrocks, B. 1977. *Corps commander*. New York: Charles Scribner's.
Kahalani, A. 1984. *The heights of courage: A tank leader's war on the Golan*. Westport, Conn.: Greenwood Press.
Patton, G. S., Jr. 1947. *War as I knew it*. Boston: Houghton Mifflin Company.
Pitt, B. 1980. *The crucible of war: Western desert 1941*. London: Jonathan Cape.
———. 1982. *The crucible of war: Year of Alamein, 1942*. London: Jonathan Cape.
Robinett, P. McD. 1958. *Armor command*. Washington, D.C.: McGregor and Werner.
Rommel, E. 1953. *The Rommel papers*, ed. B. H. Liddell Hart. New York: Harcourt, Brace.
Simpkin, R. E. 1979. *Tank warfare: An analysis of Soviet and NATO tank philosophy*. London: Brassey's.
———. 1980. *Mechanized infantry*. London: Brassey's.
Slim, W. 1956. *Defeat into victory*. London: Cassell.
von Manstein, E. 1955. *Lost victories*. Chicago: Henry Regnery.
von Mellenthin, F. W. 1955. *Panzer battles: A study of the employment of armor in the Second World War*. Norman: Univ. of Oklahoma Press.

METEOROLOGY, MILITARY

Meteorology, as defined by Webster, is "the science of the atmosphere, especially with respect to weather and climate." It involves the study of phenomena that are not only in the air, but also on the surface of the earth, such as fog, dew, water, ice, wind, pressure, temperature, humidity, sunshine, and the like. Meteorology is especially concerned with the prediction of future weather and climatological studies.

Military meteorology is that meteorological information of particular interest to armed forces. It affects every aspect of military operations and is tailored to meet the specific needs of military commanders.

History

Meteorology as a discipline began at least as far back as early Greek civilization. In the third century B.C., Aristotle wrote *Meteorologica*, perhaps the best known early attempt to study, organize, and present meteorological data. His pupil, Theophrastus, observed and cataloged more than 200 weather phenomena, which he described in his *Book of Signs* (perhaps the first listing of weather indicators). By the first century B.C., the Greeks in Athens had established a weather observatory called the "Tower of Winds."

Meteorology as science, however, could not occur until observations could be made with precision. Not until the invention of the thermometer and the barometer in the late eighteenth century did this become possible. Even then, progress was slow until the invention of the telegraph in the mid-nineteenth century made it possible to rapidly send weather observations to a central location where they could be collected, analyzed, and plotted on maps to provide a rough picture of the weather over a large area. This made it possible to obtain a general idea of the movement of storms.

In America in 1743, Benjamin Franklin, who had already established the connection between lightning and electricity, correctly observed that storms were moving weather systems. In 1816, the first known weather map was drawn by Heinrich W. Brandes of Germany. He discovered that storms were moving low-pressure systems that were easily identified and tracked on weather maps.

Early efforts to establish weather reporting networks often followed the occurrence of some weather disaster. For example, in 1854, after a violent storm near Balaklava caught the allied fleet by surprise and caused great damage, the French government decreed that weather reports would be collected and sent to a central location. In America during 1868 and 1869, severe storms on the Great Lakes caused loss of life and extensive damage to shipping. This resulted in the establishment of a weather reporting network by the United States government, principally to warn against storms. This network was a responsibility of the U.S. Army Signal Corps and was the forerunner of the national weather service.

The science of meteorology took a great leap forward in 1922 when the Norwegian, V. Bjerknes, published the Polar-Front theory. This theory, still in use today, permits the scientific analysis of air masses and fronts and the tracking of storms. Later, Petterson developed formulas to mathematically calculate the movement of weather fronts, and Rossby developed diagrams to portray the structure of the upper atmosphere.

Meteorology, as a practice, began with the establishment of national weather services. Since weather affects nearly everything man does (his comings and goings, his work, his play, his health, and his disposition), the practical goal of the science of meteorology is to provide a service (i.e., to make an accurate prediction of the weather as far into the future as possible). A forecast of the weather for a given time and place is not only convenient to man in his every-day life, it is worth millions of dollars to the farmer, the fisherman, and the businessman, and it may be the decisive factor in the success or failure of a military operation.

The ultimate goal of the science of meteorology is to provide a weather service for a large and varied group of consumers. Because each group has different needs, meteorology is subdivided into specialties such as aviation, tropical, and military.

A national weather organization provides weather service to the general public and satisfies the needs of most consumers. Some consumers, however, for whom the weather is critical or whose need is unique, have set up special weather services to cater to their special needs. For example, most television stations and airlines have their own weather advisers, and the military generally has its own weather service.

National weather services throughout the world today use standardized procedures and processes. They are monitored by the World Meteorological Organization of the United Nations and share weather data and information freely, except in time of war.

A weather forecast requires thousands of surface and upper air measurements (mainly pressure, temperature, moisture, wind speed and direction, cloud type and amount, and precipitation) at specified times from around the world. These reports are transmitted to weather centers throughout the world, checked for error, and plotted on weather maps. Lines are drawn (manually or by computer) connecting points of equal pressure (isobars), equal temperatures (isotherms), equal moisture (moist tongues), and wind direction (streamlines) for the surface and for several levels in the upper atmosphere. With these distribution patterns of conditions in the atmosphere for some time in the past, the forecaster attempts (manually or by computer) to determine patterns that will occur in the future and to predict the weather that will occur with those future patterns.

Limitations of the Science of Meteorology

Meteorology is a very complicated science; it involves many other branches of sciences, including higher mathematics, thermodynamics, chemistry, mechanics, radiation theory, physics of fluids, transfer of energy, laws of motion, oceanography, and so forth. It is extremely difficult to write equations that can be solved by computers without making assumptions and ignoring small variables, which may have large effects on the answer.

Further difficulties in producing an accurate forecast are caused by the lack of sufficient weather observations (a minimum of one per square mile is needed), inaccurate observations, the impossibility of having an up-to-the-minute global picture of the "state" of the atmosphere, and the thousands of variations and perturbations in the atmosphere caused by constant movement of the air over geographic features (e.g., mountains, rivers, lakes, oceans, forests, cities, fires, deserts, glaciers, snowpacks, etc.) and by constant variations in clouds, sunshine, water vapor, and carbon dioxide. Small, often unnoticed, changes in the state of the atmosphere can produce major effects. The innumerable changes constantly occurring in the atmosphere approach the randomness of chaos. According to the "Chaos Theory" a butterfly flapping its wings in Peking might cause a snow storm in Washington three weeks later.

Radar and satellites, which can give a continuous picture of cloud cover for large areas of the earth's surface, are a great aid to the forecaster, especially in predicting the movements of large storms, hurricanes, and tornadoes. Despite the research and the modern scientific equipment, meteorology remains an inexact science; and the forecaster is hard-pressed to make an accurate "rain" or "no rain," "snow" or "no snow" forecast for a given location for more than 24 hours in advance. Forecasters still rely to some extent on intuition (i.e., on having a "feel" for the weather).

Effects of Weather on Military Operations

Although meteorology is not an exact science, there are two absolutes: (1) it is always present, and (2) it always changes. It is these changes that affect man and everything he does, including warfare.

Every phase of warfare is affected by weather. Military commanders through the ages have recognized this and have tried to pick propitious times for their operations. Before there were meteorologists, commanders consulted the gods, priests, oracles, and astrologers. For example, the Romans sacrificed a goat and had priests read the signs before their assault on Masada.

The weather affects every aspect of military operations, both tactical and strategic. It affects planning, logistics, transportation, communications, equipment, ballistics, and troop efficiency and morale.

Extremes of heat, cold, and humidity create problems with equipment as well as with troop morale and efficiency. Ballistics are affected by wind, temperature, and humidity. High winds, especially those associated with fast-moving cold fronts, thunderstorms, tornadoes, hurricanes, and typhoons, are detrimental to all forms of transportation, notably sea and air, and to paradrop operations. Rain can create mud, which hinders ground transportation of troops and supplies. Snow and ice make all forms of movement more difficult. Clouds, especially low clouds and fog, make airdrops and bombing operations more difficult and practically prohibit strafing of enemy positions and close air support of friendly troops. Fog creates problems for troop movement, reconnaissance, and aircraft and ship operations.

In the nineteenth century, Prussian general Karl von Clausewitz in his classic book, *On War*, recognized that weather injected an element of chance into the best-laid military plans. He wrote, "Fog prevents the enemy from being discovered in time, a gun from firing at the right moment, a report from reaching the general," while rain "prevents one battalion from arriving at all, and another from arriving at the right time because it had to march perhaps eight hours instead of three. . . ."

History is replete with examples of the effect of weather on military operations. In some instances, different weather patterns might have changed the course of history. For example, unfavorable winds delayed the launch of William the Conqueror's fleet in the invasion of England in 1066; a storm (typhoon), ever after called the Kamikaze or Divine Wind, resulted in the defeat of Kublai Khan's invasion of Japan in the thirteenth century. Unusually warm weather in Holland in the winter of 1672–73, after the Dutch had flooded much of their land, prevented the ice from getting thick enough to support Louis XIV's cavalry, so the invasion was called off.

Cold, ice, and snow can be a help or a hindrance to the military commander. Hannibal evidently took into account the alpine snows when he planned his march on Rome, but Napoleon failed to allow for the Russian snows when he marched on Moscow, and the Germans failed to allow for the severity of the Russian winter in their siege of Stalingrad. On the other hand, an unusually cold winter allowed the Russians to supply the city of Leningrad by truck over frozen lakes.

A good example of the importance of weather in military operations was Operation Overlord, the allied invasion of France. It was recognized early in the planning that weather might be a critical factor, and the weatherman became a key member of the planning team. The Allied High Command asked the meteorologists to predict the best weather for the invasion compatible with certain tide and moon conditions in the months of June, July, and August. After much study of weather reports, maps, and climatology, the consensus was 5 June. However, the weather was so bad that the invasion was postponed until 6 June. Even then, there were high winds, low visibility, and rough seas that created problems for the invasion; but it caught the Germans, who thought no one would attempt an invasion in such weather, by surprise. The weather became worse later on, and had an invasion been attempted then, it might well have failed.

Weather also played an important part in the Pacific during World War II. For instance, the Japanese were able to take advantage of a fast-moving cold front to shield the advance of their fleet toward Pearl Harbor. They also used cloud cover to hide the movement of their fleet during the battle of Midway. Severe cold fronts, moving south from Japan, greatly hindered the operation of U.S. fighter strikes from Iwo Jima to Japan. After the loss of a number of aircraft in these fronts, the strikes were halted until weather reconnaissance could be established along the fighter routes.

Weather reconnaissance, the gathering of weather information from special aircraft flights, played an important role in military operations during World War II. In the early days of the war this was mostly target reconnaissance to provide information for fighter and bomber strikes. It also provided valuable weather information along the North Atlantic ferry route, but it really proved its greatest value in the Western Pacific. From the beginning of operations in the Pacific, the U.S. Air Force weather experts had argued for the use of special weather reconnaissance aircraft because of the difficulty of making forecasts for such a large area with so few weather reports. It was not until a severe typhoon sank two destroyers and badly damaged an aircraft carrier that the formation of a specially trained and equipped B-24 weather reconnaissance squadron was authorized. This was the first long-range weather reconnaissance squadron to be manned, equipped, and trained for the sole purpose of gathering weather data, and it proved invaluable in providing weather reports over ocean areas and in locating and tracking typhoons and tropical storms. It was also used to provide route and target weather reconnaissance for fighter strikes against the Japanese home islands.

This service proved so valuable that after the war several other weather reconnaissance squadrons were organized and used not only in the Pacific, but also in the Atlantic to track tropical storms and hurricanes.

Another good example of the effect of weather on military operations occurred during the Berlin Airlift, which was probably the greatest air supply operation the world has ever seen. Weather was the greatest single threat to the operation. The book, *A Special Study of Operation Vittles*, has this to say about the effect of weather on the airlift: "Weather, the bane of all aircraft operations, furnishes the greatest single threat to the success of Operation Vittles. For the weather in this area is not only notoriously bad but also subject to rapid changes."

Most of the factors for a successful airlift, such as supply, maintenance, personnel, communications, and flight and control procedures, could be controlled, but not the weather. It soon became apparent that predicting takeoff and landing minimums with 60-meter (200-ft.) ceilings and 0.8-kilometer (0.5-mi.) visibility was beyond the state of the art of forecasting. So the Berlin Airlift operated on observed weather and the observations were made constantly at the takeoff and landing points (i.e., the runways). This was the birth of runway observations and it triggered the development of special automatic, electronic observing equipment such as the ceilometer (to measure cloud heights continuously) and the transmissometer (to measure visibility continuously). Even so, cloud height and visibility could vary from one end of the runway to the other and could change within minutes. Therefore, with respect to the weather: if the aircraft had takeoff minimums at the load bases, they went; if they could not land because of the weather in Berlin, they returned fully loaded. This, of course, was wasteful of manpower, fuel, time, and money, but it ensured that the maximum tonnage was delivered to Berlin. Thus, although the Berlin Airlift was not an economical operation, it was a success and caused the Russians to lift the blockade.

Organization of Military Weather Services

Weather information is so important to military operations that, in time of war, weather observations are often transmitted in secret codes to deny them to the enemy.

The military commander needs a wide range of meteorological information for his operations, not only current observations (temperature, wind, precipitation, etc.) and forecasts for short-range planning, but climatological data to give him averages and extremes of weather phenomena for long-range planning. He needs to know the stormy seasons, the dry seasons, and the monsoon seasons, the seasons of heat and cold and rainfall, in order to plan for worst-case scenarios.

Why would any commander ignore or overlook such vital information? Sometimes due to ignorance, but often due to frustration. It is easier to pin down such details as logistics, troop strength, terrain, and tactics, which remain relatively stable, than to pin down the weather, which changes from day to day, even hour to hour, and which the forecaster cannot predict with certainty. Still, the successful commander must apply this sometimes inaccurate information to his planning and operations.

To provide this important information, the armed forces of most countries have established special military meteorological organizations to provide weather information and advice to the commander. Much of this advice is based on the same weather data available from the national weather services, but it is supplemented by special data available only to the military (e.g., reports from combat zones, enemy territory, remote areas, weather reconnaissance flights, etc.) and it is specially tailored for particular military operations, which are usually highly secret. This special tailoring can best be done by military personnel who are well acquainted with military requirements and operations. Also in time of war, it is necessary that such personnel be in the military service so that they can be ordered into the field with land, sea, and air forces under combat conditions. Often weather personnel are in the vanguard of an operation, going ashore as soon as a beachhead is established or operating behind enemy lines. The first U.S. officer killed by enemy action in World War II was a uniformed weatherman.

In the military services, meteorological information is gathered by extensive networks, processed, and presented (usually by a staff weather officer) in the form of weather reports, forecasts, and climatological studies to the commander for his use in planning and operations.

Military weather services are generally organized along military lines into wings, groups, squadrons, detachments, or comparable units paralleling the organizations of which they are a part. Nearly all military weather organizations consist of observing stations, forecasting stations, weather centrals (centers), and staff weather units. They provide weather service to military commands from the highest headquarters down to field units. Each major commander usually has a staff weather officer to keep him abreast of weather conditions. Daily command briefings usually contain a weather briefing on current and forecast weather.

The Air Weather Service of the U.S. Air Force, which provides weather service to the U.S. Army and the U.S. Air Force, is perhaps the largest military weather organization in the world. It has a command (administrative) headquarters, a global weather central, two overseas weather centers, and seven wings to serve major commands, each with subordinate squadrons and many detachments located on air bases and with military units throughout the world. It also has mobile weather units (which can be deployed with troops in the field), weather reconnaissance units, and paradrop units. The U.S. Navy has its own Naval Weather Service to provide weather information to its bases, units, and ships at sea.

Future Developments

It is easy to see why the military commander is impatient with and frustrated by his weather adviser, who often cannot tell if it will be raining or snowing or clear three days from now. It is also easy to see why the meteorologist is frustrated by having to tailor his forecast to operational conditions (e.g., tides, phase of the moon, time of year or month or day, state of readiness, etc.). Most of the time the forecaster is not brought into the planning procedures early enough and his problem is to try to fit the weather into an action which has already been chosen because of other parameters.

Meteorology (weather) has always played a part in military operations, sometimes a critical part. While the still-inexact science of meteorology cannot be fully relied upon by the military commander, neither can it be ignored, except at the risk of failure or perhaps disaster.

Progress has been made since the day when the caveman sniffed the wind. Computers and satellites will further improve, and perhaps an exact equation for future weather can be written, but the realm of meteorology is so vast and so changeable that the problem of its best use by the military will probably always be with us.

Today, weather is a critical factor in the launch of space shuttles and satellites, and even if warfare moves into space, there will be meteors and particles and radiation to contend with, and the future commander will probably continue to be frustrated because his meteorological adviser will not be able to give him an exact answer. The ultimate military weapon would be complete control of the weather.

Nicholas H. Chavasse

See Also: Desert Warfare; Geography, Military.

Bibliography

Aviation Operations Magazine. 1949. A special study of Operation Vittles.

Battan, L. 1984. *Fundamentals of meteorology*. Englewood Cliffs, N.J.: Prentice-Hall.

Byers, H. 1974. *General meteorology*. 4th ed. New York: McGraw-Hill.

Cole, F. 1970. *Introduction to meteorology*. New York: Wiley.

Hughes, P. 1970. *A century of weather service*. New York: Gordon and Breach.

Lutgens, F., and E. Tarbuck. 1989. *The atmosphere*. Englewood Cliffs, N.J.: Prentice-Hall.

Thompson, P., and R. O'Brien. 1965. *Weather life science library*. New York: Time.

McGraw-Hill encyclopedia of science and technology. 1982. 5th ed. New York: McGraw-Hill.

Smith, D. G., 1982. *The Cambridge encyclopedia of earth sciences*. New York: Cambridge Univ. Press.

MILITARY

The term *military* refers to those institutions of managed lethal violence that are legitimized by state control. The broad definition includes all the organized groups, regular and irregular, national and tribal, that use violence for political or social ends. A more narrow definition may distinguish among armies, navies, air forces, marines, and, in some cases, special forces, missile units, and other branches. Police, internal security forces, and intelligence agencies are usually excluded from the definition, although these may have attributes of military organization.

Military systems have existed at least since classical times, but the modern military is generally traced to the rise of west European nation-states in the sixteenth and seventeenth centuries. But from the beginning a distinction was made between officers, usually members of the nobility, and other ranks, typically drawn from the lower strata of the society. There also appeared early on a mid-level group of noncommissioned officers (NCOs) who directly supervised the lower ranks. This tripartite division of commissioned officers, NCOs, and enlisted personnel still characterizes almost all military organizations. Not only do uniforms separate military members from the civilian population, but insignia distinguish the ranks from each other within the military.

In the nineteenth century, the military became professionalized. Rank and authority derived from ascribed status gradually gave way to that based on competence and education. Military academies and schools arose, ranging from officer commissioning programs to colleges of advanced studies in warfare and strategy for senior officers. This era also saw the formalization of military law with a separate judicial, punishment, and incarceration system. A highly structured and disciplined organization continues to be a defining characteristic of the military.

Many of these military patterns of hierarchy, professionalization, and unique lifestyle spread from the west European heartland to the United States and other parts of Europe. These patterns were then adopted by the newly independent states in Latin America, by Japan and China, and, finally, by the successor states of defunct empires in Asia, Africa, and Oceania. By the mid-twentieth century, a military system was seen as a virtual prerequisite for national independence.

Military recruitment and formal organization vary in several ways. Recruitment depends on either volunteers or conscription. Military forces are usually composed of both active-duty units and reserve or militia components. Some military systems, however, consist solely of active-duty professional officers, NCOs, and lower-rank enlisted volunteers. Others consist of a small professional core with a large militia. Most military systems are mixed, with varying ratios of professional and nonprofessional members and varying components of active and reserve units. Despite these variations, a common imperative in all militaries is to maintain a corporate institutional sense of the membership while seeking to instill a moral commitment from the individual.

Although a long-standing institution, the military confronts special tensions in the contemporary world. For example, in less-developed countries, the tendency for the military to intervene in matters of civil order poses problems for democratic politics. In advanced democratic nations, the role of the military is subject to political influences as basic as budgetary control. In many nations, the very purpose of the military as defender of the homeland from external aggression is brought into question by pacifist groups, as well as by changes in the international strategic picture.

As the twentieth century closes, the military may assume new missions—for example, peacekeeping, multinational interventions, antidrug trafficking, and environmental protection. In basic respects, however, the military in the foreseeable future will resemble the social organization that initially appeared with the rise of the nation-state.

CHARLES C. MOSKOS

SEE ALSO: Education, Military.

Bibliography

Andrezejewski, S. 1954. *Military organization and society.* London: Routledge.

Edmonds, M. 1988. *Armed services and society.* Leicester, U.K.: Leicester University Press.

Huntington, S. 1957. *The soldier and the state.* Cambridge, Mass.: Harvard University Press.

Janowitz, M., ed. 1964. *The new military.* New York: Russell Sage Foundation.

Moskos, C., and F. Wood, eds. 1988. *The military.* London: Pergamon-Brassey's.

MILITARY POLICE

Military police are a combat support element of modern armed forces designed to accomplish specialized missions in support of the combined-arms team. Military police originated from the need to ensure that stragglers on the battlefield were put under military control and returned to the battle and that prisoners were taken into custody. The German term for military police, *Feldjaeger* (literally, field hunter), expresses the original role of these troops. Before World War I, the U.S. Army relied on officers appointed as provost marshals and troops detailed temporarily to perform as military police (MP). For World War I, the U.S. Army established military police units, but Congress blocked a permanent active military police corps after the war, although MP units were authorized for the army reserve. With involvement in World War II imminent, the U.S. Army established the military police corps on a permanent basis on 26 September 1941.

Military Police Missions

In the U.S. Army, the military police are responsible for four major missions: battlefield circulation control, area security, enemy prisoner-of-war (EPW) operations, and law and order. The U.S. Air Force and Navy also have military and civilian personnel for the area security and law and order missions.

Battlefield circulation control facilitates the movement of military units and supplies by performing route reconnaissance, controlling stragglers and refugees, and expediting traffic. Complex movements, such as the flanking maneuver of U.S. and coalition forces for Operation Desert Storm in February 1991, require close coordination of military convoys to ensure that units arrive on time where they are needed. The movement plan is based on route reconnaissance performed by the MP units.

MP detachments operate traffic control points on the main supply routes to direct convoys and individual vehicles to their proper destinations. MP teams patrol the roads, enforce traffic and security regulations, and erect signs marking routes in the theater of operations. Stragglers and military personnel absent without official leave (AWOL) are collected at the traffic control points for return to their units. MPs also assist civil affairs units, preventing civilian refugees from hindering military movements by diverting them to secondary routes and assisting their movement out of the area of operations.

Area security is a major function of military police in the theater of operations. MP tactical support units in the U.S. Army are highly mobile and heavily armed with numerous automatic weapons. They are well suited to provide motorized patrols to protect convoys, act as response forces for counter-ambush operations, and secure designated critical assets, such as bridges, depots, ammunition supply points, and headquarters. When required, they fight, and they are trained and equipped to deal effectively with light forces and guerrillas. Military police and security police also provide physical security to military installations and other key facilities in the rear areas and within the United States; they protect against unlawful trespass and criminal or terrorist attack by providing guards, mobile patrols, and surveillance of key facilities and gates and other means of exit or entry.

EPW operations are a major responsibility of the Military Police Corps of the U.S. Army. (Prisoners of war [POWs] are termed enemy prisoners of war [EPWs] by the U.S. Army to distinguish them from U.S. personnel captured by the opposing side.) Most EPWs are captured by combat units, who are instructed to turn them over to military police personnel as soon as possible. MP units assigned to the divisions and corps gather prisoners at holding areas, where trained EPW units collect them and move them to EPW camps. Upon entry to the EPW camps, prisoners are processed in accordance with the Geneva Convention. They are fed, treated, given a physical examination, provided clothing and a blanket, fingerprinted, issued an ID card, and assigned an Internee Serial Number (ISN). The ISN and identity of each EPW are reported to the International Committee of the Red Cross, which has general oversight of prisoner matters. The United States takes pride in treating its prisoners well and making a careful accounting of each prisoner to the Red Cross to facilitate repatriation or other disposition in accordance with international law. During Operation Desert Storm, the U.S. Army MP units of the 800th MP Brigade,

U.S. Army Reserve, processed and secured nearly 70,000 Iraqi prisoners, most of whom were repatriated to Iraq.

The law and order mission of the military police involves law enforcement, criminal investigation, military prison confinement, and counterterrorism. Law enforcement ranges from writing tickets for traffic violations on military bases to apprehending military personnel whose conduct is illegal. Criminal investigation to identify persons who violate military law or civil law on military installations is accomplished by specialized units in the army, navy, air force, and Office of the Defense Inspector General. Military investigators present evidence to the Judge Advocate General staff officers of military commands, who decide whether to recommend a pretrial investigation as a prelude to court-martial. MP units secure prisoners convicted of felonies or held in custody while awaiting court-martial and also defend against terrorist attacks on military installations or activities; this includes providing protection for key individuals and negotiating the release of hostages.

Military Police Force Structure

Military police exist at every level in modern armies from the division to major commands. In the U.S. Army, each division has an MP company, and each corps, an MP brigade with several battalions. There is usually another MP brigade to support the theater army and another brigade for EPW operations. A separate criminal investigation unit typically operates directly under the theater or theater army commander. Commanders of divisions and larger organizations have a staff provost marshal to advise on military police matters and to exercise staff supervision of MP units assigned to or supporting the organization. The British army also has military police units who perform the entire range of police missions. German *Feldjaeger* units emphasize battlefield circulation control and law and order. The Italian armed forces include the *carabinieri*, which act as a military police and internal security force. The French *gendarmerie* is a paramilitary police force with area security and law and order missions. The Soviet armed forces used tactical military police units (*command troops*) for battlefield circulation control missions; separate state security forces (MVD or KGB) performed the other military police missions. These major nations set the general patterns followed by the other armed forces of the world to accomplish the military police missions.

JOHN R. BRINKERHOFF

SEE ALSO: Organization, Army.

Bibliography

U.S. Department of the Army. 1986. *Military police corps regimental history.* Fort McClellan, Ala.: U.S. Army Military Police School.
———. 1988. *Field manual 19-1: Military police support for the air-land battle.* Washington, D.C.: Department of the Army.

MINE WARFARE, LAND

Land mine warfare is an element of military engineering within the scope of land warfare. In its modern sense the term encompasses the planning and laying, the operational use, and the breaching and clearing of minefields. Originally, mine warfare meant the preparation and loading of demolition sites or chambers in the ground, brickwork, or rock in order to destroy the enemy's military installations.

In terms of etymology, the French word *mine* derived from the Latin *mina* (a vein of ore), which in a figurative sense also meant *tunnel, gallery,* or *pit* (to mine = to drive a tunnel). In a military context it meant gunpowder chambers (i.e., demolitions during sieges). The term was later applied to explosive devices that were put on the ground or buried and were designed to block terrain sectors.

Military Mining

Military mining is an offensive form of engineer support against enemy forces defending from field-type or structurally prepared fortifications. The means used to that end is called an "underground mine." It is employed at a particular time against specified targets.

Underground mining has been a facet of siege warfare since ancient times. Before the advent of gunpowder, miners would excavate tunnels under fortifications. The tunnels would terminate in larger cavities with wooden beam supports, and when the supports were burned, the fortification would collapse into the cavity.

Since the invention of gunpowder underground mines with explosive charges have been used, mainly to attack fortresses. They were last employed in World War I trench warfare. Superseded by modern developments in weapons technology, this type of mine warfare has merely historical importance.

DESCRIPTION AND EFFECTS OF UNDERGROUND MINES

Underground mines consisted of a tunnel, which was driven close to or under the perimeter of enemy fortifications, with a demolition chamber at its end, a firing circuit, and the firing point. The location of the mine, the desired effect of the demolition, and the time to fire the demolition were parts of a plan to seize a fortified place. Depending on the effect of the demolition, the mine could make a breach in the lines of fortifications, destroy obstacles and barriers, or even inflict casualties on the enemy and render his weapons useless. Moreover, the demolition often came as a surprise to the defending forces, causing panic and confusion.

DEVELOPMENT AND TYPES OF MILITARY MINING

At the beginning of the sixteenth century, the Turkish army successfully used underground mines when attacking fortresses, and their method of military mining spread all over Europe. In his famous work on siege warfare (published in

1700) Sébastien Le Prestre de Vauban (French marshal, 1630–1707) laid down principles of military mining that remained valid well into the nineteenth century. Mining was begun as soon as the sappers had completed the last parallel in front of the glacis of a fortress or fortified town. Before starting to work on the trench the glacis was searched for buried *fladderminen* (antipersonnel mines). While working in the tunnels, attention had to be paid at all times to listening tunnels and countermines of the defender. The attackers tried to deceive the listening posts by constructing phony galleries, in which the workers produced a lot of noise (noise gallery); defenders used countermines to collapse mines. The number and locations of demolition chambers were dictated by the type of fortification. According to Vauban's tables, explosive charges for mining could range from a few ounces to 26,690 pounds. The purpose of demolitions was not only to cause destruction, but also—with the rocks and soil ejected and rolling down—to form a breaching ramp that the assault troops could use.

These mining works, which also included the bracing of tunnels and chambers, the calculating and tamping of charges, and the preparing of firing circuits (powder trains) were very time consuming. Military mining during a siege could last 30 days or more. Furthermore, specialists were required for the job. At first, pitmen (coal miners) were hired, and it was not until standing armies were raised in absolutist times that mining units were formed (in France in 1673; in Austria in 1683). Their work demanded courage and special caution. Lack of oxygen and possible flooding made their job difficult. Eighteen miners and 36 unskilled workmen employed in three eight-hour shifts were needed to construct an assault mine.

Vauban's formulas for military mining could no longer be applied to siege operations against fortresses that had been built in accordance with the neo-Prussian method of fortification in the nineteenth century. But it was not until 1860 that the Swiss military theorist Rüstow made a summary of all the efforts up to that time, trying to reform this type of warfare, in his *Doctrine on Modern Siege Warfare*, creating a new theory on mining that was based on the lessons learned in the Turkish Wars (1823) by the Russian army and during the siege of Sevastopol in the Crimean War (1853–56) by the French and English. According to the new method, mine demolitions were used not only to make breaches, but also as an integral part of the approach in front of the glacis. The latest technology in civilian mining, more efficient munitions, galvanic ignition, and ventilators was used in the tunnels. Rüstow paid much attention to the ingenious system of structurally prepared listening galleries and countermines, which were also used against sappers and assault troops. Classical military mining came to an end in the Franco-Prussian War (1870–71).

In World War I, military mining—under different conditions—played a decisive role for the last time in the Dolomites and on the western front. On 7 June 1917 British engineers fired nineteen mines with 430 tons of Ammonal at a depth of 40 meters (44 yd.) at the Wytschaete Salient south of Ypres, destroying three German battalions. On 13 March 1918 Austrian engineers blew up part of Mount Pasubio, which was occupied by the Italians, using 50,000 kilograms (55 tons) of explosives and killing 485 men. Whereas the objective of demolitions in the mountains was mainly to free summits or mountain flanks from enemy forces with a single blow, the demolitions at the western front were designed to destroy large sectors of barriers and trench systems, to inflict high losses of men and materiel on the enemy, and to create wide breaches.

The demolitions on the western front were foreshadowed by the mine exploded by Federal troops under the Confederate earthwork at Elliott's Salient at Petersburg, Virginia, on 30 July 1864. The mine was charged with 8,000 pounds of powder and produced a crater 9 meters (30 ft.) deep, 18 meters (60 ft.) wide, and 52 meters (170 ft.) long. The subsequent Federal assault, however, was unable to exploit the temporary advantage gained by the explosion and the surprise.

Land Mine Operations

By nature, land mine operations are a defensive type of engineer support against attacking enemy forces. The means used for that purpose is the aboveground land mine. Its effectiveness can be either limited or unlimited in time; it acts against all types of forces and assets without distinguishing between friendly and enemy forces. The purpose of land mine operations is to block terrain sectors to enhance defensive operations.

DESCRIPTION AND EFFECTS OF ABOVE-GROUND MINES

Land mines are transportable, prefabricated explosive devices with fuzes. They are placed in hidden positions in the terrain and actuated by the target, which may be infantrymen or vehicles, with the mines being either "Mobility-kill" or "K-kill" mines.

DEVELOPMENT AND TYPES OF MINE OPERATIONS

In his book *Der vollkommene Deutsche Soldat* (The Perfect German Soldier; 1726) the German military historian H. Frieherr von Flemming described how to use a *Fladdermine*. It consisted of one or more pounds of explosive buried at a small depth in the glacis of a fortress and actuated by somebody stepping on it or touching a wire strung out at a low height above the ground. This type of mine evolved into the *Tretmine* (step-on-type mine), which went into industrial production before World War I and gained considerable importance in trench warfare during the war. Against infantry, shrapnel mines were used; they were anchored in the ground by a chain and, when activated, were thrown to a height of about 1 meter (1 yd.) and detonated. Toward the end of the war the first antitank mines were developed. These were scattered at random to reinforce wire obstacles and antitank ditches in front of the trench lines.

In World War II, large quantities of antipersonnel and antitank mines (Teller mines) were laid in patterns at all fronts. Laying large minefields with several thousand mines became one of the principal tasks of the engineers of all belligerents (loss rate of armored vehicles to mines was 17 percent). In the Arab-Israeli wars, the Vietnam War (loss rate: 70 percent), the Falklands/Malvinas War, and the (Iran-Iraq) Gulf War, mine operations also played an important role as part of barrier operations.

During the past 80 years a large number of different types of mines have been developed and used in combat (e.g., blast mines, fragmentation mines, shaped-charge mines, mines forming projectiles, and mines with anti-handling devices).

Breaching minefields by clearing lanes is possible, although risky. On the other hand, clearing minefields consisting of mines with unlimited laid life is still an unresolved problem. Large areas in North Africa (since World War II), on the Sinai Peninsula, and in the Falklands/Malvinas are still off-limits to any type of traffic.

MODERN MINE OPERATIONS

Conventional mines (first-generation mines) have an unlimited laid life (i.e., they remain effective until rendered useless from wear or decomposition). Modern (second-generation) mines have superseded conventional mines. They have fuzes with a laid life that cannot be changed or that can be preselected; in every case the laid life will be limited, ranging from several hours to several weeks. Upon termination of the laid life the mines will self-destruct or be neutralized automatically. There are some types of state-of-the-art mines that can be switched off prior to laid-life termination.

Regarding their mode of operation, mines are categorized as "antipersonnel mines" and "antitank mines." Antipersonnel mines act by creating a blast wave upon detonation (blast mines) or by propelling pieces of metal in all directions (fragmentation mines). Antitank mines create a blast wave that acts against the wheels and tracks of vehicles or, when based on the shaped-charge principle, have a full-width attack capability. For activating mines, pressure and tilt-rod fuzes, trip wire–actuated firing devices, and various sensors are used.

Depending on their mode of employment, mines are categorized as "placed," "scatterable," or "off-route" mines. Placed mines are laid by hand or mechanically, either surface laid (on the ground) or buried. Scatterable mines are dispensed through the air by means of ejection devices; off-route mines are placed manually in hidden positions. The off-route mine's projectile acts only in one predetermined direction. Modern mines may be equipped with an antishock device to prevent their being activated by artillery fire or blast waves. Moreover, they are provided with anti-handling devices. They will detonate if someone tries to change their position.

Mines can be placed by hand or by other means. Devices in use in the 1980s included mine chutes hooked up to mine transporters, plowshare-type laying devices (for burying mines), as well as mine launchers, which emplace mines at short distances from magazines by means of ejection charges. Mines can be thrown from helicopters, and artillery rounds can be used to emplace mines at great distances.

With modern mines and methods, a variety of obstacles can be placed in any type of terrain. They can act against armored and nonarmored vehicles, against infantry, or against both vehicles and infantry. They are a suitable means for stopping and containing enemy forces or for channeling them into particular terrain sectors where they can be destroyed by the fire of friendly forces.

Moreover, minefields help defenders hold terrain, gain time, save manpower, and inflict casualties on the enemy. Minefields rarely consist of one or only a few mines. Normally, large minefields up to several kilometers wide and several hundred meters deep are laid in accordance with procedures varying from nation to nation. Minefields consist of several rows of mines laid at predetermined spacings or of mine strips containing clusters of several mines laid at predetermined spacings. The spacing between mines may be measured, determined by means of mine cords provided with markings, or may be programmed in the laying device.

In small minefields the mines are laid in a random pattern. In minefields placed by artillery or aircraft the positions of the individual mines cannot be predetermined. The number of mines to be laid depends on the required obstacle effectiveness, which is expressed by the mine density (number of mines per meter of frontal width). First-generation mines, which act only against wheels and tracks, require a high density (one to four mines per meter), whereas density is low with second-generation mines (about one mine every 2 meters). The location and extent of a minefield will depend on the intention of the tactical commander at the front.

It is a responsibility of engineers to plan and employ minefields. Laying minefields with first-generation mines required a lot of manpower (engineer forces at platoon or company strength) and was very time consuming. Minefields consisting of second-generation mines can be emplaced quickly with little manpower required due to modern means of employment. As of the 1980s, minefields could even be laid in a combat environment to increase barrier density, to protect exposed flanks, and to interdict penetrated enemy forces. Minefields consisting of mines whose laid life can be preselected provide the tactical commander with the opportunity to block particular terrain sectors for a limited period of time and to reuse the mines for the movements of friendly forces (e.g., for counterattacks) after laid life has terminated. Minefields could also be laid during offensive operations, mainly to protect exposed flanks.

The engineer commander advises the tactical commander on barrier planning. Mine operations supplement the main elements of combat: fire and maneuver. They provide engineer forces and assets to lay minefields, reconnoiter and place minefields, provide operational use of minefields, reconnoiter and fight for enemy minefields, and provide information on minefields as well as record minefields.

For special barrier tasks the engineer commander will form barrier reserve forces or mobile barrier detachments for emplacing minefields rapidly and will support combat-effective barrier task forces with engineer forces.

Armies with a defensive organizational structure will always have a strong barrier operations element, as opposed to armies with an offensive structure, which will rely mainly on forces capable of breaching obstacles—and minefields in particular—rapidly and along a wide front.

Mine-clearing assets are engineer equipment suitable for creating passages (lanes and paths) through minefields. Frequently, these assets also can be used to facilitate and expedite the clearing of entire minefields. For detecting mines, mine probes, handheld detectors, and special engineer vehicles equipped with sensors are used. For breaching, one or several mine-clearing cords (line charges, Giant Vipers), which are towed across a minefield by a rocket, are used. Clearing equipment can also be mounted on tanks. Mines are hurled out of the tank's way by steel flails attached to rotating cylinders, are detonated by rollers consisting of steel disks, or dug out of the ground with mine plows. The use of mine-detection parties and mine-clearing assets in a combat environment is made difficult by covering and defending minefields by fire.

TRENDS AND DEVELOPMENTS

The new computer-aided technologies will be used for developing new mine-field systems. New mines will be developed that act against armored vehicles not only from the bottom but also against the sides and from the top (homing mines). In addition, mines will be developed to attack helicopters and low-flying aircraft. The first step in this direction is the off-route mine. In the future a mine's radius of damage will not correspond with the width of a vehicle, but rather with the size of the area to be blocked. A few "area-covering mines" will suffice to form an "area obstacle system." These third-generation mines will be able to acquire, identify, and destroy targets automatically. For this purpose they will be equipped with "smart" sensor devices (e.g., acoustic, seismic, magnetic, or identification-friend-or-foe sensors). In the future, mine operations will become a third component of battle, equal in importance to the elements of fire and maneuver. Careful coordination of barrier planning with the movements of friendly forces and fire-support plans is required to that end. Apart from the engineers, who plan their minefields as dictated by the terrain and—in a combat environment—by the situation, the artillery will gain importance due to its ability to fire mine rounds at large distances to lay target-oriented minefields deep into enemy terrain. These minefield systems will have a programmed laid life and a remote-control system to be used at will.

Rapidly changing combat situations require immediate collection, transmission, and processing of barrier data. For this purpose computer-aided information systems will be developed and integrated into computerized command post technology. Moreover, theoretical models of remote-control mine detectors and clearing assets have already been developed, which are to be used to breach minefields rapidly and safely.

ULRICH KREUZFELD

SEE ALSO: Engineering, Military; Fortification; Land Warfare; Siege.

Bibliography

Flemming, H. F. 1726. *Der vollkommene deutsche Soldat*. Leipzig: n.p.
Militärgeschichtliches Institut der DDR, ed. 1983. *Wörterbuch zur deutschen Militär-geschichte*. Berlin: Deutscher Militärvertrag.
Polap, E. 1987. Die Anwendung von Minen im Belagerungskrieg. *Schriftenreihe Festungsforschung* 6:179–205. Marburg: Marbuchverlag GmbH.
Powell, W. H. 1887. The battle of the Petersburg crater. In *Battles & leaders of the civil war*, eds. R. U. Johnson and C. C. Buel. Vol. 4. New York: Century.

Rüstow, W. 1860. *Die Lehre vom neueren Festungskrieg.* Leipzig: Forst'nersche Buch-handlung.

Schaumann, W. 1978. *Schauplätze des Gebirgskrieges.* Cortina d'Ampezzo: Foto Ghedina.

MISSILE, ANTITANK GUIDED

Antitank guided missiles (ATGMs) are a crucially important part of the arsenals of all modern armies and provide infantry troops with an effective, flexible means to defeat opposing armor. The newest class of antitank systems, ATGMs have only been in use for less than three decades. Completely dependent upon electronics technology for guidance, these systems have matured in parallel with technological advances. Substantial improvements in electronics minia-turization, fiber optics, and computational components promise to increase further the battlefield lethality and tactical flexibility of ATGMs.

From the outset of World War II, when the efficacy of modern armor was clearly demonstrated in battle, militaries have sought to improve armor-defeating weapons. As the quality and capability of armor protection increased, so did the caliber and size of antiarmor guns (which dominated medium and heavy antitank weapons during World War II), until it became apparent that their size and weight would soon become restrictive to efficient and effective use in battle. Weapons manufacturers, scientists, and military procurement officers began turning their attention to rocket-powered munitions that could be guided with the aid of electronics and improved sight devices.

Among the first ATGMs were the ENTAC (France) and the Cobra (Federal Republic of Germany) systems. Designed and fielded in the late 1950s to early 1960s, these wire-guided weapons were manual-control line-of-sight (MCLOS) systems. Effective to ranges of around 2,000 meters (6,600 ft.), MCLOS-type ATGMs were literally small aircraft with fins that more resembled wings, and the gunner controlled their flight much as a pilot would fly an airplane. A joystick apparatus and optical magnification sight permitted the gunner to keep the missile in sight until it reached its target and to control the missile's direc-tion through wires that played out during flight.

The MCLOS-type antitank guided missiles proved difficult for most soldiers to use—to fire, fly, and accurately strike an intended target. Almost immedi-ately, weapons designers sought to improve ATGMs through automation. This spawned a second-generation ATGM, the semiautomatic-control line-of-sight (SACLOS) system. SACLOS-type weapons used computer technology to bring the missile from the point of firing into the line of sight of the gunner. As long as the gunner holds the center of the sight picture on the target, the ATGM will fly true. SACLOS systems, of which the U.S. Army's TOW (discussed below) is perhaps the archtypical example, were a vast improvement over MCLOS weapons.

Advances in missile guidance technology promise to soon provide a third generation of ATGMs that will be fully, or near-fully, automatic. Through combinations of fiber optics, miniaturized television cameras, lasers, and artificial intelligence programming, ATGMs on tomorrow's battlefield will perform with greater flexibility, survivability, and lethal effect.

In the following, a number of the most significant ATGM systems are described, including some currently under development.

Missiles in Service and under Development

RED ARROW 8 (HJ-8) ANTITANK MISSILE (PEOPLE'S REPUBLIC OF CHINA)

The Hong Jian (Red Arrow) 8 ATGM, first revealed in the early 1980s, is a second-generation system designed by China's North Industries Corporation to engage tanks and armored cars. In addition, it can be used against fortifications and other battlefield targets.

Red Arrow 8 is a tube-launched, optically tracked, wire-command link and semiautomatic infrared-guided missile (TOW). The operator has only to keep the crosshairs of his sight on the target until the missile impacts. The missile weighs 11.2 kilograms (24.6 lbs.) and is fitted with a 120-millimeter (4.8-in.) HEAT (high-explosive antitank) warhead. It can penetrate 800 millimeters (32 in.) (static) and has a hit probability for a single missile of approximately 90 percent. Rate of fire is two to three rounds a minute. The missile is launched from a circular tube; four wraparound fins unfold as the missile leaves the tube. Its effective range is from 100 to 3,000 meters (330 to 9,900 ft.).

At least four versions of the Red Arrow 8 system have been revealed: mounted in the rear of a cross-country truck, tripod mounted, turret mounted with four missiles in a ready-to-launch position atop a Type YW 531 full-tracked armored personnel carrier (APC), and mounted on a pedestal in a 4×4 cross-country vehicle.

AT-2 SWATTER ANTITANK MISSILE (USSR)

Swatter is the North Atlantic Treaty Organization (NATO) code name for the missile the Soviets called the PUR-62 Falanga. Of similar size to its predecessor, the AT-1 Snapper, but 29.4 kilograms (64.7 lb.) heavier, this is apparently a more advanced missile (probably in the class of the French SS-11) and certainly one with a different configuration. Control is by means of ailerons on the missile's rear-mounted cruciform wings.

The standard mount on the BRDM-1 armed amphibious vehicle carries four missiles mounted on rails. Radio-command to line-of-sight guidance is employed; the command link has three frequencies to protect against electronic countermeasures. It may also have separate terminal homing (probably infrared) along with radio guidance that suits the Swatter for airborne roles such as armament on the Mi-24 Hind attack helicopter.

When deployed on the ground, Swatter does not arm until it is 500 meters (1,650 ft.) from the launch site. The Swatter launcher, as originally deployed on the BRDM-1, has a lateral traverse of 45 degrees. The most common version is that of four missiles in ready-to-launch position on the BRDM-1. In 1983, the improved BRDM-2 4 × 4 amphibious armored vehicle was identified mounting the Swatter with a quadruple launcher.

The Swatter uses solid-propellant and radio-command to line-of-sight guidance, possibly including terminal homing, to reach a range of 500 to 3,000 meters (1,650 to 9,900 ft.). The HEAT warhead can penetrate up to 500 millimeters (20 in.).

AT-3 SAGGER ANTITANK MISSILE (USSR)

The Soviet PUR-64 Malyutka missile (NATO designation: Sagger) is more compact than the AT-1 Snapper or the AT-2 Swatter. The AT-3 (Fig. 1) was first observed mounted on the BRDM-1 four-by-four amphibious scout car in 1965. This version has six missiles under armor protection. When action is imminent, the missiles and their overhead armor protection are raised above the top of the vehicle. This model has been phased out of active service and replaced by the BRDM-2, which has an elevating arm that carries six Sagger missiles, also under armor protection and raised only when required for use. In addition to the six missiles in the ready-to-launch position, an additional eight missiles are

Figure 1. A Soviet AT-3 Sagger antitank guided missile.
(SOURCE: U.S. Department of Defense)

carried in reserve. The Sagger has also been used in the air-launched mode from Mi-24 Hind helicopters.

There is also a manpack version known as the "suitcase" Sagger. It is carried in a fiberglass case with the warhead separated from the rest of the missile. The lid of the case incorporates a rail, allowing it to be used as a launcher. A separate control unit includes a periscopic sight, control stick, switches for missile selection, and batteries.

Sagger is fired from a remote position, which allows the operator to be 15 meters (49.5 ft.) from the launcher. A three-man firing team is normally employed, with a total of four missiles per team. Either one or two men may serve as missile controllers, each with a sight and control unit and two missiles, while the third man deploys ahead, armed with an RPG-7, to provide close-in protection. The Sagger is considered to have an effective engagement range of between 1,000 and 3,000 meters (3,300 and 9,900 ft.). Such a team could be deployed with four missiles checked out and ready to fire in 12 to 15 minutes.

Client states of the former Soviet Union on occasion devise their own methods of mounting and deploying weapons of Soviet origin. The Yugoslav M-980 mechanized infantry combat vehicle has mounted two Sagger-type ATGMs in the ready-to-launch position, as has the more recent and very similar BVP M80A mechanized infantry combat vehicle. China's North Industries Corporation also produces a missile system similar to the Sagger (Red Arrow 73), which is installed on the Chinese version of the BMP-1, the Wz 501.

The Sagger uses wire-guided command to line-of-sight guidance with optical tracking. It has a two-stage solid-propellant motor and a hollow-charge warhead that can penetrate 400 millimeters (16 in.). The missile has a launch weight of 11.3 kilograms (24.9 lb.) and a range of 500 to 3,000 meters (1,650 to 9,900 ft.).

AT-4 Spigot Antitank Missile (USSR)

This designation was at first provisionally assigned to a man-portable, tripod-mounted version of the AT-5 Spandrel antitank missile, called Fagot by the Soviets. As employed by infantry, a Spigot section comprised three men who carried four rounds plus the sight and mount. Although the Spigot and Spandrel are similar, the AT-5 Spandrel is larger.

The Spigot sight appears to use separate optical paths to track the target (under control of the gunner) and the missile, with corrections to the missile's trajectory being transmitted automatically as a result of the gunner's tracking the target. Along with this semiautomatic command to line-of-sight guidance with optical tracking, the missile has a solid-propellant two-stage rocket motor and a HEAT warhead that can penetrate 500 millimeters (20 in.). The launcher weighs an estimated 10 to 12 kilograms (22 to 26.4 lb.). Range is 2,000 to 2,500 meters (6,600 to 8,250 ft.).

AT-5 Spandrel Antitank Missile (USSR)

The AT-5 Spandrel is deployed on the Soviet BRDM-2 armored fighting vehicle (AFV). It has five tubular launchers mounted on the turret, an arrangement resembling those of the HOT and Milan antitank missiles, and probably carries ten missiles. The BRDM-2 has a hatch in the roof immediately behind the missile launcher, presumably used for reloading. A rotating optical sighting and tracking head is mounted on the roof of the BRDM-2. The shape of the missile launch tubes has led to speculation that a gas generator is used to eject the missile before the propulsion motor ignites. The Spandrel is also fitted as standard on the BMP-2 mechanized infantry fighting vehicle (IFV), which also mounts a 30mm cannon.

The AT-5 uses command to line-of-sight guidance with optical tracking. It has a solid-propellant propulsion system and a HEAT warhead that can penetrate 500 millimeters (20 in.). Its range is an estimated 4,000 meters (13,200 ft.).

AT-6 SPIRAL ANTITANK MISSILE (USSR)

The Spiral was first deployed by the Soviet Union in the early 1980s on the Mi-24 Hind D helicopter and was also in service with the armed forces of East Germany and Poland. The missile is believed to have a maximum range of about 8,000 meters (26,400 ft.), a HEAT warhead weighing about 10 kilograms (22 lbs.), and a radio-command guidance system, although some sources suggest it is infrared guided.

AT-7 SAXHORN ANTITANK MISSILE (USSR)

This man-portable system, designated Metis by the Soviets, is believed to be their equivalent of the U.S. Dragon antitank assault weapon. It seems to have a range of about 1,000 meters (3,300 ft.).

AT-8 SONGSTER ANTITANK MISSILE (USSR)

The Kobra (Soviet designation) missile is launched from the 125mm gun installed in the T-64B and T-80 main battle tanks. It is believed that there are two versions: one antitank and fitted with a HEAT warhead, the other anti-helicopter and carrying a high-explosive fragmentation warhead. Both are loaded through the breech. The missile uses laser- or radio-command guidance and has a maximum range of 4,000 to 5,000 meters (13,200 to 16,500 ft.). It is believed to weigh 25 kilograms (55 lb.).

SWINGFIRE ANTITANK MISSILE (UNITED KINGDOM)

Swingfire is a British long-range command-controlled antitank weapon system capable of engaging and destroying the heaviest armored and soft-skinned vehicles in service. The missile is wire commanded by an operator's joystick control; change in heading is achieved through thrust vector control. The system's missile control equipment can be installed either in a vehicle (as in the AFV variant) or on the launcher pallet. The missiles come prepacked in sealed launcher boxes. Propulsion is provided by a two-stage boost and sustainer solid-propellant motor. The warhead uses a hollow charge and is considered powerful enough to defeat all known combinations of armor. Range is from less than 150 meters (495 ft.) at direct fire (300 meters [980 ft.] with maximum separation) to a maximum of 4,000 meters (13,200 ft.). Special features include ease of concealment and immunity to electronic countermeasures (ECM).

DRAGON ANTITANK ASSAULT WEAPON (FGM-77 A/FTM-77A) (UNITED STATES)

Dragon, developed by McDonnell Douglas for the U.S. Army and Marine Corps, employs a command to line-of-sight guidance system and consists of three main parts: a tracker, a recoilless launcher, and the missile. The tracker includes a telescope for use by the gunner in sighting the target, a sensor device, and an electronics package. The tracker is reusable and is temporarily attached to the launcher, which is discarded after firing. The gunner never sees the missile after firing.

The missile is ejected from the firing tube by a gas generator using a recoilless technique. When it emerges, fins flip open and the missile starts to roll. Thereafter, propulsion and control forces are provided by 60 small sustainers that fire in pairs on demand from the tracker. In operation, the gunner sights the target through the telescopic sight, then launches the missile. The tracker senses the missile's position relative to the gunner's line of sight to the target and sends command signals over wire to the missile. As commands are continually received, the missile's side thrusters apply corrective control forces. The thrusters are fired at appropriate roll angles so that the missile is automatically guided throughout its flight.

The missile has a shaped-charge warhead and, for the Dragon I and Dragon II versions, a range of 60 to 1,000 meters (198 to 3,300 ft.). Dragon III has a maximum range of 1,500 meters (4,950 ft.).

MILAN ANTITANK MISSILE (FRENCH DESIGNED)

Milan is a wire-guided man-portable antitank missile system. The current second-generation system, Milan 2, incorporates a semiautomatic guidance technique. The gunner need only keep the crosshairs of the guidance unit on the target until it is hit. The system consists of a missile in a container and a launcher. The container, which also serves as a launching tube, is mounted on the launch-and-control unit. This in turn can be either mounted on a tripod to be fired from a ground position or mounted on a pivot for firing from a vehicle. Milan also has a night-firing capability with the MIRA thermal-imaging device. Target detection is possible at a range of over 3 kilometers (1.8 mi.), permitting the missile to take full advantage of the system's extreme range. To contend with improved tank armor, the three nations collaborating in Milan and MIRA production (France, West Germany, and the United Kingdom) have evolved an improved warhead (the K115) that has an increased diameter of 115 millimeters (4.6 in.)—as compared with the 103 millimeters (4.1 in.) of the standard item.

Upon launch the missile is ejected from its container by a gas-driven piston, and the launch tube itself is disconnected from the launch unit and discarded to the rear. When the missile emerges from the tube, its wings flick open, imparting a slow spin to the missile, which coasts forward until, at a sufficient distance from the launcher to avoid harm to the gunner, the warhead is armed. An infrared TCA guidance system is built into the launcher/sight unit.

The Milan uses semiautomatic-command wire guidance (SACLOS) featuring optical tracking of the target only. Infrared tracking of the missile and control by vectoring thrust of the sustainer efflux are automatic. Propulsion is provided by a solid-propellant boost and sustainer motor. The hollow-charge warhead can achieve penetration against a solid target at a maximum lethal range of 850 to 1,000 millimeters (34 to 40 in.). Range is 25 to 2,000 meters (82.5 to 6,600 ft.), with a time of flight to maximum range of 12.5 seconds.

SS-11 BATTLEFIELD MISSILE (FRANCE)

The SS-11 is a line-of-sight wire-guided battlefield missile intended for firing from land vehicles, naval vessels, and slow-moving aircraft. Normally it is fired from a launching ramp, but it may also be used with a simplified ground launcher. The designation SS-11 applies to the surface-to-surface version; the similar air-to-surface version is known as the AS-11.

The operator acquires the target by means of a magnifying optical device. As soon as the missile enters his field of vision after launch, the operator commands it to his line of sight with a joystick. Tracker flares are installed on the rear of the missile to help the gunner track it. When the missile is installed in a helicopter or ship, the simple sighting device used for land vehicles is replaced by a special stabilized sight.

The missile is driven by a two-stage solid-propellant rocket motor and can be fitted with various warheads. It has a range of 500 to 3,000 meters (1,650 to 9,900 ft.) and a minimum turning radius of one kilometer (0.6 mi.). Using a 140AC warhead, the SS-11 can achieve a minimum armor penetration of 600 millimeters (24 in.).

Since 1962, the SS-11B1 version, using transistorized firing equipment, has been produced with a variety of warheads, including an inert type for practice. Among them are the Type 140AC antitank warhead; the Type 140AP02 explosive semi-perforating antipersonnel warhead carrying 2.6 kilograms (5.7 lb.) of explosives and capable of penetrating an armored steel plate 1 centimeter (0.4 in.) thick at a range of 3,000 meters (9,900 ft.), then exploding some 2 meters (6.6 ft.) beyond the point of impact; and the Type 140AP59 high-fragmentation antipersonnel type equipped with a contact fuze.

A variant of the SS-11 has been produced and supplied to French, West German, and Saudi Arabian forces under the name Harpon.

HOT ANTITANK MISSILE (JOINT FRENCH-GERMAN)

HOT (*Haut subsonique Optiquement teleguide Tire d'un tube*) is a heavy antitank weapon developed by Aérospatiale and Messerschmitt-Bölkow-Blohm. The missile is a tube-launched, wire-guided munition using low-speed spin stabilization. Planned as a replacement for the SS-11 missile, it has a mission profile corresponding to a NATO requirement for a missile to operate primarily from vehicles (armored or unarmored) and helicopters. When the missile is launched, infrared radiation from its tracer flares allows a precision goniometer associated with the optical sight to measure the deviation from its reference axis, which is parallel to the optical axis. Any deviation of the missile from the optical axis generates an angular error signal that can be combined with an estimate of range (based on the known flight characteristics of the missile) to provide a measure of the linear departure of the missile from the line of sight. This measurement is then used to generate command correction signals to the missile, whose flight is controlled by means of a jet vane system. Once the target has been visually acquired, all the operator has to do is aim carefully at the target, launch the missile, and steadily maintain his aim during the missile's flight.

The varieties of vehicle types, both land and airborne, to which the HOT system has been adapted is extensive and includes the M113 services APC with two tubes and eleven rounds stored inside; the AMX 10P APC with four tubes; the Panhard VCR APC with four tubes and fourteen rounds inside; the VAB APC with four tubes and eight rounds inside; and the Rakentejagdpanzer 3 with one tube and eight rounds inside. Among helicopters, the system has been mounted in the B0-105M PAH 1 with six tubes; the Gazelle SA-341/SA 342L with four or six tubes; the Alouette III (in trials only); the Dauphin SA-361H with eight tubes; and the Lynx, also with eight tubes. The HOT has also been fitted to light unarmored vehicles (Land Rover 110 and Peugeot P4) with a single mount.

The HOT thus constitutes a long-range, wire-guided antitank weapon that uses command to line-of-sight guidance incorporating optical aiming with automatic infrared tracking (SACLOS). It uses a solid-propellant booster and sustainer for propulsion and mounts a 136mm hollow-charge warhead (HOT 2 has a 150mm warhead). The system has a range of from 75 meters (247.5 ft.) to more than 4 kilometers (2.4 mi.). Time of flight to maximum range is 17.3 seconds. It can penetrate more than 800 millimeters (32 in.) of solid armor in the HOT 1 version (the HOT 2 can penetrate more than 1,300 millimeters [52 in.]) and is also effective against composite armor.

TOW Antitank Missile (BGM-71) (United States)

Fielded in 1972, the TOW (tube-launched, optically tracked, wire-guided) missile is itself contained in a sealed storage and transport container that becomes a launch tube extension when placed in the launcher breech. After the breech locks, all electronic contacts to the missile are automatically closed and the TOW is ready to fire.

The missile contains two solid-propellant motors. The launch motor ejects the missile from the launch tube and is burned out by the time the missile has left the tube. Only after the missile has flown several meters does the flight motor ignite; thus, no protection is necessary for the gunner against hot exhaust gas and propellant particles. The flight motor is mounted in the center of the missile with its two exhaust nozzles mounted on either side, an arrangement that avoids interference with the guidance wires, which are placed at the tail of the fuselage. Steering commands are transmitted by two wires that uncoil from separate spools. Short cruciform wings in the center of the missile and cruciform rudder surfaces all unfold after leaving the launch tube. Missile maneuvering is achieved entirely aerodynamically—that is, without the use of jet vanes—so that TOW maintains good maneuverability throughout its flight. An electronics unit is mounted between the flight motor and the armor-piercing warhead.

After the missile leaves its launch tube, a light source in the tail comes on so that the optical sensor on the launcher, which is bore sighted with the gunner's telescope, can track the missile along its flight path.

TOW can be installed in most vehicles capable of cross-country travel. Within the U.S. Army it is mounted on jeeps, the high-mobility multipurpose wheeled vehicle (HMMWV), and the AH-1S helicopter. Armored vehicles using TOW include the M901 improved TOW vehicle (ITV), which has an armored weapon station featuring two launchers, a daylight sight, and the AN/TAS-4 night target-acquisition sight. The M-2/M-3 Bradley fighting vehicle also has a twin-tube retractable installation on the side of its turret, the tubes being retracted during loading and traveling. The M-2 infantry fighting vehicle carries five reload rounds; the M-3 cavalry fighting vehicle has ten reloads.

TOW is considered a heavy antitank guided-weapon system. It relies on automatic missile tracking and command guidance from an optical target tracker, using wire-guidance control of gas-operated aerodynamic surfaces. The warhead is a HEAT shaped charge. The system has a minimum range of 65 meters (214.5 ft.) and a maximum range of 3,750 meters (12,375 ft.). Its crew of four can achieve a rate of fire of three launches in 90 seconds.

The first phase of development of an upgraded TOW involved an improved warhead with a diameter of 127 millimeters (5 in.) that was intended to increase armor penetration. Of the same size and weight as the standard TOW warhead, it features an improved design. This version was called the improved TOW (ITOW) and featured an extensible nose probe to provide optimum standoff detonation distance so as to gain maximum effect from the hollow-charge warhead.

The second phase of development produced TOW 2, which incorporates a heavier warhead of still greater penetration performance and with a diameter of 152 millimeters (6 in.). This occupies the full diameter of the missile body. In this version the missile's guidance system has also been improved by use of a subsystem in which the analog computer is replaced by dual digital microprocessors to give greater flexibility in guidance programming as well as higher accuracy. To compensate for this added weight, the missile motor has an improved propellant that provides a 30 percent higher impulse. The TAS-4 sight has also been modified to function as a total independent guidance loop, and a high-intensity thermal beacon has been added to the end of the missile.

An improved version of TOW 2, the TOW 2A, has a tandem warhead designed to defeat reactive armor, with a small warhead added in the missile probe.

HELLFIRE MODULAR MISSILE (UNITED STATES)

The Hellfire modular antiarmor weapon, originally developed for use from ground attack helicopters in the antitank role, has also been fired in the ground-launched mode during U.S. Army tests. The ground vehicle used was a 1-ton pickup truck on which twin Hellfire launcher rails were pedestal mounted together with the fire control equipment. Modifications to the vehicle were minimal and consisted simply of installing the launcher pedestal, its azimuth and elevation controls, storage racks for six missiles, and a special firing panel.

As originally operated in the air-launched mode, Hellfire used a laser seeker to home onto reflected energy from either an airborne or a ground laser target designator, but combined infrared/radio frequency (IR/RF) and imaging infrared seekers are being developed for the system and will give the missile a wide range of delivery modes, including engagement from defilade. The missile has a range of 7,000 meters (23,100 ft.) and uses tandem twin shaped-charge warheads. The air-launched version is in production and in service with the U.S. Army. An antishipping version has been tested, and the ground-launched version is also available.

KAM-9 (TYPE 79) BATTLEFIELD MISSILE (JAPAN)

This system (also known as the Type 79 Jyu-MAT, or heavy missile, antitank) is an extended-range SACLOS antitank weapon. It can be used against both armored vehicles on land and armored watercraft. The missile is launched from a tubular container that is also used for transport and storage. A solid-propellant launch motor ejects the missile from the container to a safe distance from the operator, after which the flight motor ignites and accelerates the missile to its cruising speed of 200 meters (660 ft.) per second in a few seconds.

The Type 79 has been designed as a defensive weapon to engage the landing craft of an amphibious assault force, as well as to be employed against tank targets. A special warhead was designed to accommodate this dual role. It is basically a HEAT round incorporating an enhanced fragmentation effect. Two types of fuzes are employed: a contact fuze with a piezoelectric element for the antitank role and a variable delay fuze for the antiship mission.

Prior to firing, the missile container is placed on the launcher, which comprises the firing control device, missile checkout, tracking mechanism, and built-in sight unit. The optical sighting device is designed to be operated by one man. During the missile's flight the operator simply keeps the optical sight trained on the target. Sensors then translate course deviations to electrical signals that are fed into a computer. The computer then calculates necessary course corrections and feeds them into the missile through its guidance cable. Instead of the usual flare for infrared missile tracking, a xenon lamp is used as the infrared source for the Type 79. The lamp is powered by a thermal battery, which also provides electrical power for the missile guidance system. The launching system also features two operational modes: direct and separate firing.

A complete Type 79 firing unit consists of two launcher units, a sight unit, a control/guidance electronics unit, and a connecting cable reel. Each launcher is normally mounted on a tripod and one of them also carries the sight. The second launcher may be sited up to 50 meters (165 ft.) away from the sight; it is remotely operated by a connecting cable. This remote capability, coupled with the use of smokeless rocket motors, offers the operating crew good protection from enemy counterfire and provides enhanced operational flexibility. The missile has a maximum range of 4,000 meters (13,200 ft.).

RBS 56 BILL ANTITANK MISSILE (SWEDEN)

Bofors has developed a light antitank missile, designated RBS 56 and called Bill, for the Swedish army. Development was carried out in close cooperation with the Swedish army.

The RBS 56 is a wire-guided command to line-of-sight weapon with an effective range capability from 150 to 2,000 meters (495 to 6,600 ft.). It is fired from a container/launcher tube that can be either tripod or vehicle mounted. A sight that provides for both day and night operation is carried separately and attached to the container tube before launching. The manufacturer states that preparations for launching can be completed in 20 seconds. Propulsion is provided by a solid-propellant rocket motor that exhausts through nozzles located around the circumference of the missile body to the rear of the sustainer motor, which is housed in the nose section. Cruciform wings and control surfaces, located in the tail section (where there is also a tracking signal transmitter), flip out after launch.

The missile carries a shaped-charge HEAT warhead normally detonated by a delayed proximity fuze. The missile trajectory is automatically maintained at a height of approximately 1 meter (3.3 ft.) above the gunner's line of sight to the target; this is said to result in a higher kill probability in that the chances of striking the less heavily armored upper surfaces of a tank are increased while the angle of approach of the warhead means that it is less likely to strike a sloping surface at a shallow, glancing angle, thereby enhancing penetration characteristics. The angle of attack also ensures that, even when sloping surfaces are encountered, the thickness of armor to be penetrated is effectively lessened.

The system has a combat range of 150 to 2,000 meters (495 to 6,600 ft.) against stationary targets and 300 to 2,000 meters (990 to 6,600 ft.) against moving targets with a crossing speed of 10 meters (33 ft.) per second. Flight time to maximum range is 11 seconds.

MSS 1.1/MAF ANTITANK MISSILE (ITALY)

The MSS 1.1 is based on the Italian OTO Melara laser-guided antitank guided weapon. It is a man-portable system that can also be installed on light vehicles such as jeeps. Although its primary role is antitank, it has a secondary role against battlefield fortifications and hovering helicopters.

The complete system consists of the missile in its container, which also acts as the launcher, and a firing post that includes an adjustable tripod, projector, and sighting system. The missile has a two-stage solid-propellant rocket motor. The first stage completes its burn inside the launcher, providing sufficient power to get the missile out of the launcher. Then, at a safe distance from the operator, the second stage ignites and boosts the missile to its maximum speed. In good weather and light conditions an optical sight is employed, while a thermal imaging sight permits night operation.

This 130-millimeter (52-in.) missile weighs 14.5 kilograms (31.9 lbs.). It uses a HEAT warhead and has a maximum all-weather range of 2,000 meters (6,600 ft.), increased in fair weather to 3,000 meters (9,900 ft.); minimum range is 70 meters (231 ft.). Time of flight to the longest range is 16 seconds. At ranges of over 400 meters (1,320 ft.) the missile has a hit probability of 95 percent. Reaction time from initial target acquisition is 2 seconds.

MAPATS ANTITANK MISSILE (ISRAEL)

The systems division of Israel Military Industries, faced with a requirement for a new antitank missile capable of challenging existing and anticipated generations of new armor, developed a weapons system designated MAPATS. The MAPATS employs missile body and control surface arrangements similar to those of the TOW, but it uses an entirely different guidance technique and is thus more than merely an improved version of TOW.

The MAPATS system consists of an infrared beam–riding missile and a launcher/sight unit. It is fired from a crew-transportable launcher. The missile's fiberglass container forms part of the launcher system. Upon launch, the missile follows a laser-generated beam that is pointed at the target by the gunner. The system is said to be immune to jamming and completely automatic. The gunner has only to maintain the crosshairs on the target until the missile hits.

The main components of the launcher unit are the beam generator, a tripod, a traversing unit, the launch tube, and an electronics unit including batteries. The combined weight is less than 70 kilograms (154 lb.). The missile can be installed on a jeep, an M113 APC, or on a variety of other armored vehicles, including tanks.

The missile mounts a hollow-charge warhead weighing 3.6 kilograms (7.9 lb.) that can penetrate 800 millimeters (32 in.). It has a minimum range of 65 meters (214.5 ft.) and a maximum range of 4,500 meters (14,850 ft.). Missile flight time to maximum range is 23.5 seconds.

Antitank Guided Missile Developments

ADVANCED ANTITANK MISSILE SYSTEM—MEDIUM (AAWS-M) (UNITED STATES)

This system is intended to be a one-man portable weapon employed at infantry platoon level to defeat existing and anticipated tanks under conditions of day or night, including smoke and dust. It is designed to replace the Dragon and will have superior lethality and range, as well as a shorter time of flight. The operator will also be less vulnerable, and the launch signature will be less than that of the Dragon.

Three guidance technologies are under consideration. Ford's system is a shoulder-mounted missile, called Topkick, in which the operator directs the flight of the missile by sighting directly on the target. The missile is then guided by a low-intensity laser beam emitted by the projectile and the operator's line of sight. The system will engage the target by the top-attack method, using two fuzed warheads.

The Hughes system consists of a missile, with a medium-wave infrared staring focal plane array seeker, in a disposable launch tube accompanied by a reusable command and launch unit.

Texas Instruments is proposing a fire-and-forget system using an infrared seeker. The missile would feature two attack modes: top attack for use against armor and direct attack for use against helicopters and fortifications.

ADVANCED ANTITANK MISSILE SYSTEM—HEAVY (AAWS-H) (UNITED STATES)

The U.S. Army planned to inaugurate in fiscal year 1988 a program for development of the AAWS-H, actually compromising three weapons systems: one, a TOW replacement; another, a kinetic-energy kill (KEK) weapon; the third, a FOG-M with fiber-optic guidance. The TOW replacement is designated the advanced missile system—heavy (AMS-H). The KEK system is based on the LTV high-velocity missile (HVM); its missile will be a beam rider traveling at 1,500 meters (4,950 ft.) per second. The electro-optical suite would include a thermal imager.

TRIGAT PROGRAM (JOINT BRITISH-FRENCH-GERMAN)

The British, French, and German governments have decided to collaborate on development of two antitank missiles to meet their national requirements. These are versions of the so-called third-generation antitank (TRIGAT) missile, also known as PARS-3, ATGW3, and AC3G.

Two basic versions of the missile will be developed: a medium-range system (ATGW3-MR) to replace Milan and a long-range system (ATGW3-LR) to replace HOT, Swingfire, and TOW. The ATGW3-MR will be an infantry-portable system weighing about 16 kilograms (35.2 lb.) and designed to attack targets at ranges of up to 2 kilometers (1.2 mi.). It will feature an optical beam–riding missile.

The long-range missile (ATGW3-LR) will be constructed largely of plastic and will involve a conventional cruciform layout with folding wings and fins. It will be a diving attack missile designed to engage targets at ranges of about 5 kilometers (3 mi.) and using an as yet unspecified but very advanced warhead reported to be of the forward-facing tandem design. The missile will also feature an imaging infrared homing seeker for automatic target tracking. It will be capable of salvo fire against multiple targets. Both helicopter-launched and ground-launched versions are planned.

Conclusion

ATGMs provide infantry troops their best defense against enemy tanks and armored fighting vehicles. The continuing improvements in range, accuracy, and lethality provide a weapon that can be employed with great flexibility to support a variety of combat missions. Thus, there can be no doubt that active research and development will continue to characterize the field of antitank guided missiles.

Just how effective ATGMs will continue to be against tanks remains to be seen. But their effectiveness has been on the upswing since their inception, and it is likely to continue. As these relatively cost-effective weapons proliferate in the world's militaries, it is well to consider that they may constitute a new "killing power" for the infantry, a capability that could alter the shape of tomorrow's battlefields.

ALAA EL DIN ABDEL MEGUID DARWISH

SEE ALSO: Armor; Gun, Antitank; Rocket, Antiarmor; Tank.

Bibliography

Lee, R. G., et al. 1988. *Guided weapons*. Vol. 1 of *Land warfare: Brassey's new battlefield weapons systems and technology series*. London: Brassey's.
Jane's weapon systems, 1988–1989. 1988. London: Jane's.

ADDITIONAL SOURCES: *Armada International; Military Technology*.

MISSILE, SURFACE-TO-AIR (SAM)

The category of surface-to-air missiles (SAMs) includes all guided missiles launched from the surface of the earth whose primary function is to destroy a target in the air. Near the end of World War II the Allies attacked Germany with a great number of bombers flying at such high altitudes that the German antiaircraft guns were unable to engage them. Late in the conflict, in 1945, the Germans began production of antiaircraft missiles such as Wasserfall, Enzian, and Rheintochter, but the war ended before they could complete the project, with only a few such missiles having been produced. It was the Allies who got the benefit of that work following the war.

Soon many countries began development of modern air forces through manufacture of jet engines that produced speeds in the supersonic range and highly maneuverable aircraft capable of operation at high altitudes. These developments further complicated the problem for antiaircraft guns because of the long flight time of projectiles aimed at enemy aircraft, consequent loss of velocity, and lack of any means of making corrections to the projectile's flight path subsequent to firing. These deficiencies stimulated development of surface-to-air missiles as the next generation of antiaircraft weaponry.

SAMs are designed to destroy both piloted and pilotless enemy air attack means and to protect a wide variety of targets, from administrative and political centers to naval and air bases, troop concentrations, and rear-area installations. The first generation of SAMs appeared during the 1950s in the form of the Nike Ajax in the United States, the SA-1 Guild and SA-2 Guideline in the USSR, and the Thunderbird in the United Kingdom. These missiles were effective against aircraft flying at high speeds and altitudes.

Main Combat Properties

1. *Highly effective fire for destroying aerial targets:* This capability is achieved in three ways. Controlling the missile during its flight to the target minimizes the chance of a miss due to maneuvers by the enemy aircraft.

Because of the high speed and maneuvering capability of air targets, some elements of the missile guidance system must be able to sense the target and measure continuously the position of the missile with respect to the target. Powerful missile warheads, producing thousands of fragments capable of penetrating the target, are another important SAM attribute. And finally the high probability of a hit, due to the accuracy of the missile guidance system, ensures that the missile can be exploded on or very near the target.

2. *All-weather capability:* SAMs can engage aerial targets under any weather conditions, at any time of the day or night, and in any season of the year.

3. *Long range of engagement:* The capability for long-range engagement of the target enables SAMs to effectively defend large target areas such as administrative and political centers and industrial areas. This capability is achieved through the use of surveillance and guidance radars, which can detect and track targets at extended ranges, and by the use of powerful boosters in the missiles so that they can reach speeds exceeding those of their targets.

4. *Versatility in altitude of engagement:* SAMs can engage targets at ranges throughout the target envelope, from high altitude to very low level.

Types of SAMs in Modern Air Defense

Developing technology applicable to air attack systems has led to active research and development programs in SAMs. Designers have emphasized technical capabilities that enable SAMs to engage targets operating at supersonic speeds and from very low level (below 150 meters [500 ft.]) to very high level (above 15,000 meters [50,000 ft.]), targets whose reflecting surface is extremely small, maneuvering targets, targets at short or long ranges, and targets employing electronic countermeasures. To achieve these differing capabilities, air defense planners have developed a variety of SAMs: man-portable antiaircraft missiles, missiles for air defense systems providing close-in protection, missiles for tactical air defense systems, and missiles for long-range air defense systems.

MAN-PORTABLE AND LIGHTWEIGHT MOBILE ANTIAIRCRAFT MISSILES

These man-portable air defense systems (MANPADS) are designed to engage enemy aerial targets, including helicopters, flying at low altitudes. They can thus provide immediate close-in protection for combat troops in forward battle areas, for airborne and seaborne troops, and for such sites as airfields, air defense positions, and critical terrain and transportation network points. Such weapons are typically found in infantry, armor, and artillery battalions.

These missiles are characterized by ease of concealment, which enables the firer to gain surprise in engagement with enemy aircraft; light weight, so that they can be carried by individual soldiers and fired from the shoulder; and ease of employment from vehicles and surface ships for immediate protection.

First-generation systems encountered some problems. One of these was the matter of identification friend or foe (IFF). Given the speeds at which target aircraft flew, it was difficult to correctly identify an incoming aircraft as hostile or friendly in time to effectively launch a missile should the aircraft be determined to be hostile. To overcome this problem, launchers are mounted on pedestals or tripods that can also carry an IFF transponder. Other problems include tracking a target flying at high speed, engaging approaching aircraft in a head-on mode, and dealing with an enemy helicopter that pops up from the rear. Most of these difficulties have been overcome to some extent. Portable air defense missiles have been used to some effect in recent campaigns, notably in the Falklands/Malvinas, where the Argentinians used the U.K.-produced Shorts "Blowpipe," and in Afghanistan, where the mujaheddin guerrillas used the U.S.-manufactured Stinger with devastating efficiency.

U.S. Army Redeye man-portable. The Redeye entered service in 1966, eight years after development began. It is employed in the forward battle area to protect combat troops against low-level attack. Weighing 13 kilograms, it is designed to engage receding air targets flying at subsonic speeds. The system has a range of 2,000 to 3,500 meters (6,500 to 11,500 ft.). The target is tracked through an optical sight. After launching, the missile guides itself by homing on the heat energy radiated by the enemy aircraft's engine. This system is still employed in some countries.

U.S. Stinger man-portable. Previously known as Redeye-2, this missile entered service in 1979. It can engage approaching as well as receding targets and also oblique targets before they reach the crossing point. An IFF feature is incorporated in the aiming unit. The missile, which weighs 15.1 kilograms, is resistant to jamming and is not affected by such heat distractors as flame balls. It can reach a speed of Mach 2.2, thus enabling it to engage high-speed targets, and has a range of 3,000 to 5,000 meters (9,850 to 16,400 ft.). Stinger uses a passive infrared (IR) homing seeker that makes it a fire-and-forget weapon. A laser guidance system can also be used where the operator tracks the target through a lightweight stabilized sight that aligns the laser beam for target intercept by the missile.

Soviet Strela-2 man-portable (NATO designation: SA-7 Grail). This missile is designed to engage very low altitude receding air targets whose speeds do not exceed 800 kilometers per hour (km/h [500 mph]) (a modified type, the Strela-2M, can engage targets moving at speeds up to 950 km/h [590 mph]). The Strela cannot engage approaching targets. It is a shoulder-launched weapon that can be fired from a variety of stationary positions as well as from armored fighting vehicles on the move. It employs an infrared homing guidance system.

Soviet SA-9 (Gaskin). This missile is considered an improved version of the SA-7 heat-seeking Strela SAM. It consists of a quadruple launcher and a B-76 Gun Dish fire control radar mounted in front of the missile turret to provide detection and tracking. The method of target acquisition is presumed to be visual with subsequent aiming of the weapon by optical systems. When used as part of a larger air defense system, the SA-9 can be linked to search radars to assist in target acquisition. The system is mounted on a BRDM-2 amphibious reconnaissance vehicle. A full load consists of eight SA-9 missiles, each with a high-explosive fragmentation warhead larger than that of the SA-7, thus providing one reload for each of the four launchers. The missile's maximum range is 7 kilometers (4.3 mi.). It can engage targets from a minimum altitude of 20 meters (65 ft.) to a maximum of 4,000 meters (13,125 ft.), has a higher missile speed than the SA-7 due to an improved motor, and is capable of employment under conditions of darkness and in all weather. Infrared homing guidance is employed. This missile was first deployed by Soviet forces in 1968 to provide immediate protection for forward formations, especially armored elements, against very low level air attack.

Soviet SA-13 Strela-10 (Gopher). This missile is an improved version of the SA-9, engineered to resist infrared countermeasures. It was introduced into service with Soviet antiaircraft batteries of motorized infantry and tank regiments in the late 1970s. It has a maximum slant range engagement capability of 7.5 kilometers (4.6 mi.) and can intercept targets at 10 meters' (30 ft.) altitude and 3.5 kilometers (2.2 mi.). Four ready-to-fire missiles in canisters are mounted on a tracked vehicle, which can then provide protection for mobile armored units. This self-propelled system thus has a mobility advantage over the older wheeled SA-9. The system uses infrared homing guidance.

British Blowpipe. This is a lightweight system characterized by simplicity of operation, instant readiness, and rapid employability from vehicles, small ships, or hovercraft. It is fitted with a fully integrated IFF system to prevent firing against friendly aircraft. The guidance system is based on optical tracking of both missile and target and CLOS (command-to-line-of-sight) radio command. The warhead is a 2.2-kilogram dual-purpose blast shaped-charge warhead. This missile, which first entered service with the British army in 1977, is still in production and is used by eleven countries. During the Falklands/Malvinas War it was employed by both sides, and it was also reportedly used in Afghanistan. The missile has a maximum speed of Mach 1.5 and a maximum range of over 3,000 meters (2 mi.). Its maximum effective altitude is 2,000 meters (6,500 ft.). The system's major drawback is excessive weight. At 20.7 kg it is considered too heavy for the task at hand.

British Javelin man-portable. This missile, using a semiautomatic-command line-of-sight (SACLOS) guidance system, is capable of destroying high-speed ground attack aircraft or standoff helicopters at ranges greater than 4 kilometers (2.5 mi.). It is equally effective against crossing or receding aerial targets and provides quick reaction defense against the low-level air threat. The system is lightweight and is available in a multiple-launcher version consisting of three missiles and an aiming unit for dismounted or vehicle application. Since the Javelin first entered service with the British army and the Royal Marines at the end of 1984 a number of significant improvements have been made, including a higher impulse motor that provides a moderate increase in velocity and 1.5 to 2 kilometers (0.9 to 1.2 mi.) additional range; a new blast/fragmentation warhead and a modified fuze; and a guidance system employing SACLOS such that the missile does not have to be directly steered to the target by means of a joystick and radio guidance signals. The effectiveness of the missile will be further enhanced by introduction of the Thorn EMI Air Defense Alerting Device (ADAD), an improved optronic-infrared system.

Swedish RBS-70 low-level system. The RBS-70 is designed to engage helicopters and aircraft flying at very low altitudes. It employs a laser-riding guidance system that cannot be jammed by electronic countermeasures (ECM). The system is simple in terms of training, handling, and employment; is easy to deploy and rapidly prepare for combat action; can effectively be concealed on the terrain and is difficult to locate from the air; and has a high kill probability against both attacking aircraft and helicopters, even on directly approaching courses. The missile's range is about 5,000 meters (3 mi.).

The firing unit is normally operated by one man, although if several missiles are likely to be fired in rapid succession the services of a loader are needed. The weight of the total firing unit, arranged in three manpacks, is 80 kilograms. The missile body houses a receiver, which senses deviation from the laser line of sight, and a small computer unit that converts the deviation signals into guidance pulses so as to automatically maintain the missile on the laser beam. Both impact and proximity fuzes are fitted in the missile's nose; the proximity fuze employs laser technology. IFF equipment is supported on the mount. The missile is launched by means of a start and booster motor. Once clear of the launch tube, a sustainer motor takes over and powers the missile to its target.

An updated version, designated the RBS-70+, features a new beam receiver that increases the missile's engagement envelope by 30 to 50 percent. Another version, the RBS-70M Nightrider, is scheduled to enter service with the Swedish army in 1993. It will be fitted with an optronics package that includes a thermal imager for use in bad weather and under poor light conditions. This version will also feature a large fragmentation warhead and a more powerful sustainer motor that will extend the missile's range to 6 kilometers (3.7 mi.). The basic RBS-70 and RBS-70+ systems can be used in conjunction with the Ericsson GIRAFFE G/H band search radar.

French Matra Mistral. This missile weighs 20 kilograms and has a 3-kilogram warhead that consists of an explosive charge, impact and proximity fuzes, and a large number of tungsten balls. The proximity fuze has a sharp sensitivity cutoff to avoid premature detonation due to trees or the surface of the sea. The missile's passive IR homing head has a multielement sensor with a digitized signal processing unit, which offers excellent protection against all known IR countermeasures. The Mistral can be used to engage aircraft flying at up to Mach 1.2 at altitudes of as much as 3,000 meters (10,000 ft.). The so-called canard configuration of the missile provides very good maneuverability, enabling it to remain locked onto a target even in an 8-g turn. An IFF system and a thermal imaging sight are available for use with this system.

British Shorts Starstreak. This missile is an evolutionary development of Javelin, which will complement that system. The high-velocity (Mach 4) missile contains three beam-riding darts made of "dense metal" that can be guided individually to their targets. Upon firing, the missile is propelled out of its launch tube by a first-stage motor. At a safe distance a main motor boosts the missile to its maximum velocity in less than 300 meters (980 ft.). When the main motor burns out, the three darts separate from the missile carrier and are guided to their targets. The darts are thought to have a HEAT-type warhead that, with their residual high velocity, combines to produce a kinetic/chemical energy effect when they score a direct hit.

Upgraded MANPADS. There are a number of weapons systems under development that promise improvement in the field of man-portable missile systems. The trend is toward a dual-role capability so as to provide protection for units that may face ground as well as aerial threats. Employing a laser guidance system, the new missile, called Saber, is designed to be shoulder launched by a single operator.

There is also a trend toward upgrading MANPADS to vehicle-mounted multi-round configurations and to incorporating night-vision devices to provide around-the-clock capability. Examples include the U.S. Army Missile Command's SETTER system, which features a mount with two pods, each containing two Stinger missiles, together with a passive sensing day/night-vision system. There are also two self-propelled versions of the Stinger under development in the United States, and Boeing Aerospace has produced the Avenger based on the HMMWV vehicle.

Bofors RBS-90 (formerly the RBS-70M Nightrider). Bofors RBS-90 comprises a fire unit and two all-terrain vehicles. One vehicle contains local surveillance radar, while the other accommodates the mechanically driven two-round launcher incorporating a bore-sighted thermal imager, a laser range finder, and a daylight TV camera. The trend in such systems is toward high- or hyper-velocity missiles so as to counter late-unmasking targets.

SHORT-RANGE AIR DEFENSE MISSILE SYSTEMS

In contemporary warfare, low-level attacks are expected not only in the front but in rear areas as well. The low-level intruder remains one of the most difficult threats to counter. A gap opens between the coverage provided by medium/high-altitude systems and the network systems of man-portable anti-aircraft missiles and guns. This gap needs to be effectively closed by a specialized SAM system of short-range air defense missiles.

Efficient defense—of troops deployed on the battlefield and of important strategic sites—against the low-level threat requires short-range air defense systems with the following characteristics: rapid reaction time in engaging attacking aircraft that approach at high speed and very low altitude; ground mobility that provides high maneuverability so that troops can be protected during combat operations; air portability so missiles can quickly be moved to restore protection against air attacks from any direction or to reinforce protection in a new direction; ability to produce sufficient firepower to ensure the high kill probability needed to counter multiple and simultaneous attacks at very low altitudes. Achieving a high degree of kill probability involves accurate tracking of the aerial target; efficient guidance to achieve missile accuracy; high missile speed and maneuverability; controlled detonation of the warhead; warhead power; and the ability to fire several missiles simultaneously. To fill the gap in the air defense network, the missile's range must extend out to 5 to 10 kilometers (3 to 6 mi.) and provide coverage from very low levels up to medium altitudes. The missile system must also have an all-weather capability, the ability to avoid jamming even when operating under severe ECM conditions, and an integrated configuration in which fire control units and multiple missiles are mounted on one launching platform to facilitate concealment of the deployed system.

Most of the countries producing antiaircraft missiles have concentrated their efforts on developing air defense systems that are capable of dealing with enemy aircraft flying at low and very low altitudes, taking into account the desirable characteristics described above. The new versions of short-range air defense systems (or SHORADS) entering the service of various armed forces, both East and West, and the systems currently under development are designed to be integrated into an air defense system. Among current systems of interest are the following.

Soviet SA-8 Strela-3 (Gecko). This division-level air defense weapon of Soviet ground forces is designed for employment against low- and very low level aerial attack. The system consists of a quadruple launcher and associated fire control equipment mounted on a rotating turret carried by a three-axle, six-wheeled amphibious vehicle. The fire control system includes a surveillance radar (with an estimated range of about 29 kilometers [18 mi.]; it can be folded down behind the launcher so the entire weapons system can be airlifted by transport aircraft); a pulse-type tracking radar with an estimated range of 19 to 24 kilometers (12 to 15 mi.); an optical target tracker–telescope sight; and a television camera used for optical guidance of the missile when the tracking radar and command link are jammed by heavy electronic countermeasures.

The quadruple launching unit includes four missiles on the launchers and eight reload rounds. In a military parade subsequent to deployment of the Gecko system a new version appeared. It featured two triple launchers instead of the two doubles on the original model, thereby substantially increasing the system's ready-to-fire capability.

The command guidance system operates by proportional navigation and infrared terminal homing. Simultaneous firing of two missiles, with separate guidance for each, can be achieved, thus permitting engagement of two separate targets at the same time.

The system's maximum range is an estimated 12 kilometers (7.5 mi.), with missile speed in the Mach 2 range. The high-explosive warhead weighs some 40 kilograms.

British Rapier low-level system. This lightweight and highly mobile SAM system has the quick reaction time to be effective against rapidly maneuvering low-flying targets and also against such slower aerial targets as helicopters, which may suddenly appear at short range over screening terrain. The system is deployed for airfield protection with NATO forces in Britain and Germany.

The launch unit is mounted on a specially designed trailer carrying four missiles loaded and ready to fire, the surveillance radar, an automatic IFF system, a computer for target data evaluation, and a command transmitter. When the surveillance radar detects a potential target, the IFF automatically interrogates it to determine whether it is friendly or hostile. If the target is hostile, the tracker operator is alerted and the radar data is used to direct the tracker toward the target so that the operator will be able to pick it up in his optical sight.

The system includes two optical systems: target-tracking optics used by the operator to track the target and missile-tracking optics used to present the missile's flare image to the television system that monitors missile position. When brought into action the optical tracker is mounted on a tripod and connected to the launcher by cable. A radar tracker is used for night engagement or in conditions of poor visibility; it tracks both target and missile, then feeds displacement data on each to the guidance computer.

Each Rapier missile is treated as a round of ammunition, requiring no test or assembly before use. Two men can quickly and easily load a missile onto the launcher. The missile can attain a velocity of Mach 2 and has a range of 6.5 kilometers (4 mi.). The high-explosive warhead has an impact fuze. Guidance is command to line-of-sight.

A self-propelled variant of the Rapier system is mounted on the U.S.-designed M548 tracked carrier so as to provide mobility and an amphibious capability. The system can also be air transported.

The Rapier 2000, an upgraded version due to enter service in the early 1990s, will carry eight rounds. It will mount a new optronic tracker, also used in a scanning mode for surveillance, that is operated from a remote console. This system has been improved in almost every respect in order to meet such threats as heavily armored helicopters flying pop-up maneuvers, high-powered jammers, small targets such as remotely piloted vehicles (RPVs), and cruise missiles.

Rapier 2000 consists of three main elements, each mounted on a trailer: the launcher, surmounted by the optronic tracker; a surveillance and target-acquisition radar; and tracking radar. Rapier 2000 will fire the new MK2 missile, which is being developed in two versions: the MK2A, carrying a fragmentation warhead detonated by an "intelligent" proximity fuze for use against small targets such as RPVs; and the MK2B, which carries an impact-fuzed hollow-charge warhead for destruction of armored targets. Both rounds will be powered by a Thermopylae rocket motor burning high-energy propellant, which will extend the system's maximum range to 8 kilometers (5 mi.).

French Crotale System. This is an all-weather low-altitude system designed for protection of fixed and mobile ground forces and ships against multiple and simultaneous attacks from low- and very low level high-speed aircraft. It consists of two main units: an acquisition unit and a firing unit. The acquisition unit controls and coordinates up to three firing units. It is equipped with a pulse Doppler surveillance and acquisition radar with moving target indicator, capable of detecting targets flying at speeds up to 1,430 km/h (890 mph), altitudes up to 3,000 meters (9,800 ft.), and ranges out to 18 kilometers (11 mi.); an IFF system; and a data-processing system providing for simultaneous display of 30 targets and tracking of the 12 most menacing.

The firing unit consists of a turret with quadruple missile launchers aligned with and directed by the tracking radar and of a monopulse tracking radar capable of locking onto one target and simultaneous guidance of two missiles to the same target. Its maximum range is 17 kilometers (10.5 mi.). Also included are a television system designed to perform automatic tracking and missile guidance in clear weather or in case of electronic jamming; an infrared localizer to guide the missile on the firing axis after launching; and a digital computer that performs multiple tasks: calculation of possible interception, formulation of remote-control orders for guidance, formulation of orders to arm the fuze when the missile nears its target, and ordering the missile to destroy itself in flight when necessary.

The units of this system are mounted on self-propelled cross-country vehicles that can be fitted with sand tires. All vehicles are also equipped with an intervehicle link network for transmitting orders and data by cable and/or through radio communications using VHF radio links. The system is also air transportable, enabling it to continue to provide air defense for troops on the move. It can engage targets at speeds up to Mach 1.2 and altitudes from 50 meters (160 ft.) to 3,000 meters (9,850 ft.). It also features a very short reaction time, six seconds from first detection of a target to missile launch, the result of the highly automated system. Engagement range varies from 500 meters (1,600 ft.) minimum to 8.5 kilometers (5.3 mi.) maximum. Hit probability for a single missile is 0.7. The system has great resistance to electronic countermeasures due to its antijamming circuit protection, multiple frequencies, and television target-tracking and missile guidance. The high-explosive warhead is detonated by an infrared proximity fuze and has a lethal radius of more than 8 meters (25 ft.). The cable-link communications of the original Crotale have also been replaced with a microwave system for automatic data transmission and interchange of position coordinates among system elements, enhancing the capacity to assign targets to the most suitable launch sites.

Another version, known as Shahine, is an improved Crotale, having extended range (over 10 kilometers [6.2 mi.]), a modified guidance system, and a different engine and missile fuze. The Shahine is mounted in a tracked vehicle as opposed to the wheeled-vehicle mount of Crotale. Six ready-to-fire missiles, three on each side of the centrally mounted electronics, are mounted in a separate turret concentric with the radar turret, which provides for independent optical target reconnaissance. With a larger radar dish than available on comparable systems, the Shahine can track up to twelve targets simultaneously and with a greater discrimination capability. Target data is displayed on a plan position indicator that identifies the level of threat, number of targets, and bearing of fire units. The fire control radar operates in the K-band on three channels and can engage targets with up to two missiles simultaneously.

U.S. Chaparral system. This is a forward-area missile system developed to meet U.S. Army requirements for low-altitude air defense. The missiles are carried on and fired from a turret mounting four launch rails. Additional missiles (eight reloads) are stored on a pallet for ready access. The operator, located in the turret mount, aims the missile using an optical sight. Once locked onto the target and fired, the missile automatically guides itself to the target's heat source. Guidance is thus initially optical aiming, then IR homing to the target's heat emitter. Maximum range is about 4.8 kilometers (3 mi.) and maximum altitude about 2,500 meters (8,200 ft.). The missile, with a high-explosive warhead, uses a solid-propellant rocket motor to attain a flight speed of about Mach 2.5.

The system is being improved and retained in service. Among the improvements are a thermal imaging sight on the launcher to provide a night and inclement-weather capability; a smokeless motor to reduce the battlefield signature; an IFF system; ability to attack aircraft from a head-on aspect or from the side; and an anti-glint canopy for the missile launch vehicle to improve battlefield survivability of the overall system.

Euromissile Roland system. This system is the product of a joint Franco-German development program begun in 1964. It is designed for defense of vital objectives against aerial attack by targets flying at low and very low altitudes and supersonic speeds. Roland I is a clear-weather version selected by the French armed forces. It uses optical tracking and infrared missile guidance and can be employed only in daylight and good visibility. Roland II is an all-weather version selected by the German army to provide protection for armored units on the move. To meet this requirement, the equipment has been completely stabilized to permit continuous target acquisition and tracking, thus requiring the missile carrier to halt only at the moment of launch. This version incorporates both optical and radar tracking and guidance systems. It can be employed day or night and in inclement weather. It can be operated in either the optical or radar mode; changeover from one mode to the other is possible at any time, even after the missile has been launched and during the missile guidance phase of an engagement.

All Roland system components are installed in a single vehicle that constitutes an autonomous fire unit, thus permitting a target to be acquired while the missile carrier is on the move. The missile can be adapted, without major redesign, to any type of platform that provides sufficient space; the system lends itself to shipboard installation on most ships, even those of low tonnage. It thus acquires mobility comparable to that of the units it is intended to protect. The German army mounts the Roland system on the chassis of the Marder armored infantry combat vehicle, while the French mount their system on the hull of an AMX-30 tank. The U.S. Army has mounted its version on a special 5-ton 6 × 6 M812A1 truck for air-base defense.

The Roland missile is designed as a round of ammunition, thus simplifying storage and contributing to the weapon's high rate of fire. There are two launchers, each carrying one missile; in the hull are also two magazines holding four missiles each. Automatic reloading from the magazines takes place in several seconds, also contributing to a high rate of fire. The multiple-effect hollow-charge warhead has a lethal radius of more than 6 meters (20 ft.) and includes safety devices for arming and neutralizing the warhead. Two types of fuzes are used. A radio proximity fuze, specially developed for use against low-flying aircraft, initiates detonation of the warhead as the missile approaches its target. When engaging very low-flying targets, the proximity fuze can be disarmed to preclude possible detonation caused by ground effects; in such cases an impact fuze is substituted. The missile's solid-propellant motor enables it to maintain a velocity of about Mach 1.6 for a maximum flight time of thirteen seconds.

The Roland system has a maximum effective range of 6,000 kilometers (3.7 mi.) and a minimum range of 500 meters (1,600 ft.). Targets flying at up to Mach 1.3 can be intercepted. Hit probability is 50 to 85 percent, depending on the speed and course of the attacking aircraft; it is achieved by the combination of a highly accurate guidance system and use of the multiple-effect hollow-charge warhead initiated by an electromagnetic proximity fuze or an impact fuze. Roland I is guided by a CLOS system using optical aiming and automatic infrared tracking. For Roland II automatic radar aiming is provided. Acquisition of low-flying targets is achieved by a pulse-Doppler radar with elimination of fixed echoes. The system is highly resistant to electronic countermeasures.

A recently introduced version of Roland II features several improvements. The maximum range has been increased to 8,000 meters (5 mi.). The rocket booster motor now gives the missile a maximum velocity of 620 meters per second (m/sec. [2,000 ft./sec.]) in approximately two seconds as compared to 500 m/sec. (1,640 ft./sec.) achieved by earlier versions. The sustainer motor also keeps the missile at a higher speed so that it requires only fifteen seconds to cover the distance to its maximum range. The higher cruise speed also provides increased maneuverability. The warhead on Roland II is larger (9.1 kilogram versus 6.5 kilograms) and the missile is fitted with both a proximity and an impact fuze. The improved missile can be fired from either Roland I or Roland II launchers. To further increase the weapons system's effectiveness in the face of saturation attacks, Euromissile has proposed a "double-banked" Roland turret fitted with four ready-use missiles, two on either side. This would provide four missiles ready for immediate use, enabling the unit to engage a formation of four attacking aircraft.

TACTICAL AIR DEFENSE MISSILE SYSTEMS

These missiles are designed to destroy both piloted and pilotless air attacks. They are employed mainly to provide immediate protection for troop concentrations, both in assembly areas and during the course of operations, as well as for defense of vital objectives, industrial areas, administrative and political centers, and naval and air bases. Some missiles of this type are organized in army-level air defense units to augment divisional air defense capabilities. Other types of longer range are organized in front- or theater-level air defense to provide, to the greatest extent possible, unbroken detection and engagement envelopes extending laterally across the entire front or theater and forward of the forward edge of the battle area (FEBA) over enemy territory. The following SAM systems have been developed and are still in service.

HAWK (MIM-23) system. HAWK is an acronym for "home-all-the-way-killer," a missile first developed in the 1950s, which became operational in 1960. The missile has a maximum range of 35 kilometers (22 mi.) and is designed primarily to engage low-level supersonic targets at altitudes ranging from 30 meters (100 ft.) to 11,000 meters (36,000 ft.). It features a two-stage solid-propellant propulsion system; a semi-active homing device; and a conventional high-explosive warhead of the blast fragmentation type. The system is both mobile and transportable, including by airlift.

When a target is detected by the HAWK's acquisition radar, its position is relayed to illuminator radars, which in turn illuminate the target with electromagnetic energy that is reflected back to the missile's radar guidance system. HAWK then tracks the target by following this reflected energy.

The improved HAWK (MIM-23B) has a better guidance system, a larger warhead, an improved motor, and semiautomatic ground systems. The existing improved continuous-wave acquisition radar has been modified to provide single-scan target detection, particularly against maneuvering aircraft. The illumination radar has been fitted with a microcomputer to provide automatic search, discrimination between formation targets, and the capability of controlling missiles in flight so that they home in on the remaining targets during a multiple attack.

A frequency-agile digital continuous-wave acquisition radar with solid-state transmitter has been introduced to improve autonomous detection and provide track information of sufficient accuracy for weapon control. This 3-D radar can detect targets at all altitudes that can be engaged by the HAWK, even during heavy jamming, and also reduces the system's vulnerability to anti-radiation missiles.

In a variation called Sparrow HAWK, nine Sparrow missiles are mounted on a modified HAWK.

U.S. MIM-104 Patriot system. This is a surface-to-air medium-range missile system for area and point antiaircraft and antimissile defense. It is designed to counter both high-speed aircraft and missiles. With its improved ECM capability, it was designed as the replacement for HAWK and Nike Hercules in front- or theater-level air defense. The first operational units were formed in 1986.

The guidance concept adopted in Patriot is actually a combination of three different principles: preset, command, and TVM (track via missile) proper, the three techniques used in successive phases of the missile's trajectory. Immediately after launch, preset navigation based on a self-contained package stabilizes the missile and steers it into a coarse initial turn. This phase is short in both time and space; it ends when the radar acquires the missile in flight and starts to track both it and the target. A computer correlates the positions of missile and target, computes the most efficient trajectory to interception, and guides the missile onto that trajectory by means of coded signals sent via the same beam by which the main antenna is tracking the missile. In many cases this trajectory will take the shape of a climb to high altitude followed by a final dive onto the target.

With a Patriot system in operation, there may be up to five beams in the air: three beams of the main antenna—surveillance and detection, target track and illumination, and missile track and command uplink; the reflected beam from the target to the missile; and the TVM down-link beam. The missile's very high accuracy is mainly due to an innovative TVM that combines the advantages of command guidance with SARH (semi-active radar homing). The key points of its design and operational concept are enhanced mobility, multiple target-acquisition capability, very short reaction time, high single-missile kill probability, flight speed of about Mach 3, range of about 60 kilometers (37 mi.), warhead options of nuclear or conventional blast/fragmentation, and a four-missile load on the launcher. The key element in the system is a phased-array radar, which performs all the functions of surveillance, acquisition, and track/engage and missile guidance.

Soviet SA-2 V75 Dvina (Guideline). This missile (Fig. 1), first introduced into service in 1958, provides area defense against medium- to high-altitude threats. Its maximum altitude of target engagement is 18 kilometers (59,000 ft.), with a maximum slant range of 50 kilometers (31 mi.). The missile has command guidance. It is now reaching obsolescence but is still in service in some countries that are introducing improvements to the system. Its eventual replacement will probably be the SA-10.

Soviet SA-3 S-125 Pechora (Goa). This missile, designed to complement the SA-2, is used to engage aircraft at low and medium altitudes for front-level air defense. Maximum altitude of target engagement is 15 kilometers (49,000 ft.), with a maximum of 50 meters (165 ft.). Maximum slant range is 22 kilometers

Figure 1. The Soviet SA-2 (Guideline) missile. (SOURCE: U.S. Army)

(13.6 mi.). Semi-active radar guidance is used. The system is vulnerable to modern countermeasures.

Soviet SA-6 9M9 (Gainful). This mobile three-missile system is designed for the protection of mobile divisions against low- and medium-altitude air attack. It is mounted on a modified PT-76 tank chassis and is also air transportable. Its maximum altitude of target engagement is 12 kilometers (39,400 ft.), with a maximum low-altitude range of 30 kilometers (18.6 mi.), and a minimum effective altitude of 60 meters (200 ft.). Guidance is provided by a combination of command link and semi-active homing. Optical tracking of the missile appears possible for low-level operation or under ECM conditions. A radius of 4 kilometers (2.5 mi.) is assumed for the inner "dead" zone. The missile attains a speed of Mach 2.8 and carries an HE-fragmentation warhead with a total weight of about 80 kilograms. It normally has both impact and proximity fuzes.

Soviet SA-10. This missile, introduced in 1980, has a range of 100 kilometers (62 mi.) and altitude coverage of 1,000 to 30,500 meters (3,280 to 100,000 ft.). It uses solid-propellant and active terminal radar guidance. Maximum speed is Mach 6, and it has a 100-kilogram proximity-fuzed HE-fragmentation warhead. Its role appears broadly similar to that of the U.S. Patriot.

Soviet SA-11. This system comprises four missiles mounted on a large box-like launcher on a tracked chassis. Its range is estimated at 27 kilometers (16.7 mi.), with a maximum altitude of 13.7 kilometers (45,000 ft.). A large 3-D radar mounted on its own tracked chassis is associated with the SA-11, which uses radar guidance. The SA-11 was introduced to replace the SA-6.

LONG-RANGE AIR DEFENSE MISSILE SYSTEMS

U.S. Nike Hercules (MIM-14B). The Nike Hercules, a second-generation missile, introduced in 1958, features enhanced destructive capability and performance over the MIM-3 Nike Ajax. It has proven successful against high-performance aircraft at a variety of altitudes and has also successfully intercepted short-range ballistic missiles. Propulsion is provided by a two-stage solid-propellant rocket motor that achieves supersonic speeds and a range of more than 140 kilometers (85 mi.). Maximum altitude of engagement is over 45 kilometers (147,000 ft.). The missile uses command guidance and can carry either a nuclear or a high-explosive warhead.

Major improvements were made to this system in 1961, when new radars and modifications were added to extend its operational lifetime. These modernizations were designed to make the missile more maneuverable and to improve its ability to withstand ECM.

Soviet SA-4 (Ganef). This high-altitude, long-range surface-to-air missile is highly mobile; it is mounted in a self-propelled tracked vehicle that carries two missiles mounted on an SP ramp derived from the PT-76 tank. The ramp is also used as the launcher, which permits the missiles to be put into action very quickly. The system is used for the long-range protection of battle zones and important installations. It is considered an area-defense SAM system in service with the army to provide high-altitude protection of its forward elements. The concept of employment calls for the lead SA-4 battery to be deployed some 30 kilometers (18 mi.) behind the forward edge of the battle area, with the other batteries moving up in a belt about 15 kilometers (9 mi.) behind.

The missile has a maximum velocity of Mach 2.5, an effective range of about 70 kilometers (43 mi.), and a maximum altitude of 24 kilometers (78,700 ft.). It has an HE warhead, command guidance, and semi-active homing. The propulsion system is a ramjet sustainer with four solid-fuel boosters to provide initial thrust. This system is still in service, although a likely follow-on is the SA-12A Gladiator high-altitude SAM, which uses a phased-array radar capable of handling multiple targets.

Soviet SA-5 S-2OO Volga (Gammon). This missile, previously known as the Griffon and then for a time as the Tallin system, is designed to engage aircraft flying at extremely high altitudes and for the interception of not excessively complex missiles. It is normally transported on a single-axle, semitrailer towed by a tractor. The missile features a two-stage motor, a warhead that can be either nuclear or conventional high explosive, and a proximity fuze. It employs active radar guidance.

Most reliable sources feel that the missile should have a range of at least 180 kilometers (110 mi.; perhaps as much as 300 km [186 mi.]) and a ceiling of 29,000 meters (95,000 ft.). This very heavy missile system is still operationally viable against aircraft and missiles. It participates with antiballistic missile ABM-1 Galosh to form part of Moscow's defenses. SA-5 sites are still spread throughout the former Soviet Union for protection of strategically important areas.

British Bloodhound MK2. This system went into service with the RAF in 1964. Bloodhound-equipped RAF units are currently deployed in West Germany as part of the NATO air defense of Western Europe. The missile relies on semi-active homing for guidance; a receiver in its nose detects and follows radiation reflected by the target when it is illuminated by a target-illuminating radar (TIR). Launch control by computer is accomplished using data from the TIR. The missile has a range of more than 80 kilometers (50 mi.) and uses an HE warhead with a proximity fuze. The system is air transportable.

STRATEGIC AIR DEFENSE MISSILES

Both the United States and the former Soviet Union have developed antiballistic missile (ABM) systems that provide a limited defense in depth against incoming ballistic or fractional-orbit bombardment missiles.

U.S. Safeguard system. This consisted of the long-range Spartan interceptor missile with a nuclear warhead (range about 650 km [400 mi.]) and the short-range Sprint interceptor missile with a nuclear warhead designed to destroy warheads that have penetrated the upper layer of defense and reached the atmosphere. The system was sited in North Dakota to protect ICBM fields, but it was dismantled in 1976 because of doubts about its effectiveness.

Soviet ABM-1 (Galosh) system. Russia retains this system, which carries a multi-megaton warhead suitable for exo-atmospheric missile interception (with a range of 300 km [185 mi.]) to provide for the defense of Moscow. Since the early 1980s the system has been expanded to include the full 100 launchers allowed under limits of the 1972 ABM Treaty. The first new silo launchers for the SH-08 endo-atmospheric missiles, armed with a low-yield nuclear warhead, became operational in 1985, complementing the remaining force of Galosh ABM-1B exo-atmospheric missiles. The Galosh missiles may be replaced by a combination of the SH-04 exo-atmospheric and the SH-08 endo-atmospheric missiles. Thus a new Moscow ABM system, with 100 silo-based endo- and exo-atmospheric nuclear-armed interceptors, will be fully operational when the SH-08 enters service. It is believed that the ABM silo launchers will have the capability of one reload and refire per silo, although the reload/refire time is unclear. (The ABM Treaty prohibits automatic or semiautomatic or other similar systems for rapid reload of the permitted launchers.) Some air defense missiles also have an ABM capability, particularly the SA-12, which has been tested against tactical ballistic missile reentry vehicles.

Effect of Stealth Technology

The term *stealth* refers to a number of technologies that have been in development for more than two decades. They involve the use of radar-absorbing materials and of designs that scatter radar waves by contouring aircraft to eliminate the flat planes and sharp corners that reflect radar waves.

It is probable that future air targets, particularly bombers, reconnaissance, and fighter aircraft, will incorporate stealth technology. They will thus be less susceptible to detection and tracking by air defense surveillance and fire control radars, whether airborne or ground based. Stealth thus constitutes one important aspect of the revolution in aerial warfare.

Effect of Electronic Countermeasures (ECM)

All systems based on radar are susceptible to jamming and deception by electronic countermeasures as well as being vulnerable to attack once their position is known. ECM can involve active jamming by electronic means or passive jamming by the use of chaff, which appears as false targets. Jamming continues to be a complementary means of attack on radios and radars. Deception devices are also used as ECM. Obvious targets for attack by electronic warfare include surveillance, target-acquisition and tracking systems, and missile guidance systems.

The most common method of dealing with ECM is to build into the radar itself various forms of anti-interception devices. The best known is termed *frequency agility.* This is a method of continuously varying the emitted radar frequency so that an enemy intercept receiver and its associated jammer would find it extremely difficult to lock onto the transmission. The trend in the design of air defense systems is to seek to improve their resistance to jamming and other forms of ECM.

Future Trends

Dual-role Missile

ADATS (Air Defense Antitank System) was designed to fill a dual antiair and antiarmor role. In the air defense role, targets are assumed to include fixed-wing aircraft operating at very low level and helicopters using nap-of-the-earth tactics, all in conjunction with heavy ECM jamming. The use of a pulse-Doppler radar with a detection range in excess of 20 kilometers (12 mi.), electro-optical tracking, and laser beam–riding guidance in conjunction with a Mach 3+ missile and a guidance loop that is highly ECM-resistant is claimed to provide the short reaction time necessary to meet the mission requirements.

Combining Missiles and Guns

The new threat facing army ground forces is composed primarily of armored helicopter gunships using hovering standoff fire tactics to employ antitank guided missiles. The effectiveness of these weapons can be further augmented through the use of the terrain in nap-of-the-earth flight and pop-up firing tactics. The U.S. field army air defense system based on the Vulcan/Chaparral mix was scheduled to be supplanted by the Sgt. York version of the DIVAD (division air defense) gun system, but the latter was canceled in 1985 when it was judged ineffective in meeting the military threat of the Soviet helicopter M-24 HIND-E armed with the AT-6 Spiral antitank guided missile, a weapon with a range of 6 kilometers (3.7 mi.) or more. At that time it was stated that the best air defense system would be one consisting of a mix of guns and missiles.

Forward Area Air Defense System (FAADS)

The elements of a new integrated U.S. program for forward air defense are a pedestal-mounted Stinger program, designed to build a less sophisticated weapon than the DIVAD, and a fiber-optic guided missile (FOG-M) as the non-line-of-sight segment of FAADS. This missile carries a TV camera in its nose (to be replaced later by a staring focal-plane array) and transmits a video picture to the operator. FOG-M is launched "blind" vertically and transmits an image of the target to the operator, who then guides the missile to impact. The speed of the missile, which is limited to 150 to 200 meters per second (500 to 650 ft./sec.) so as to provide acceptable picture clarity, makes it primarily an anti-helicopter and antitank device.

Single Dual-role (Antiaircraft/Antimissile)

Current trends are toward merging medium surface-to-air missiles (MSAM) and antitactical missiles (ATM) into a single dual-role system. The future MSAM should be able to engage cruise missiles in addition to its primary antiaircraft role, but its capabilities against ballistic missiles would be restricted to self-defense. The French SA-90 (SAMP) system is a project intended as an antiaircraft system with the added feature of a respectable capability against tactical missiles. France is suggesting the ASTER-30 missile as a possible element for both MSAM and ATM programs.

Conclusion

As the foregoing descriptions of systems make clear, the entire field of surface-to-air missiles is in a state of rapid flux, with both the threat to be countered and the means of dealing with it changing rapidly and often. The illustrative weapon systems discussed in this essay may be viewed as representative of the spectrum of approaches to the problem developed during the 1980s and fielded in the early 1990s. Clearly they will be supplanted by subsequent generations of more capable systems as tactics, technology, and the nature of the threat continue to evolve.

KHEIDR K. EL DAHRAWY

Bibliography

Berman, R. 1983. *Rockets and missiles of World War III*. New York: Exeter Books.
Chant, C. 1989. *Air defense systems and weapons: World AAA and SAM systems in the 1990s*. London: Brassey's.
Friedman, R. S., et al. 1985. *Advanced technology warfare*. New York: Crown.
Jane's weapons systems, 1987–1988. 1987. London: Jane's.

ADDITIONAL SOURCES: *Aviation Week and Space Technology; International Defense Review; Military Technology; NATO's Sixteen Nations*.

MORALE

Morale is a widely used term referring to the enthusiasm and persistence with which soldiers, sailors, or airmen engage in the assigned missions of their unit. Often used as if it were an attribute characteristic of a group rather than an individual because of the central role of the unit's mission and goals, it has been called by some the most important single factor in war.

A military unit with high morale performs consistently at high efficiency, carrying out its assigned tasks promptly and effectively, each member contributing his share willingly and assuming that his fellows will do their part as well. Mutual help and encouragement are routine, and success is expected. Exemplary work is singled out for praise, and slackers are scorned. Members are proud of themselves and their unit, develop a strong identification with the unit and its reputation, and take great pleasure in displaying symbols of their affiliation (Shibutani 1978).

Related Concepts

The importance of group solidarity for effective military performance has been recognized for centuries, and military writers have often used the terms *cohesion* or *esprit de corps* as synonyms for morale. In the twentieth century the term *morale* has been drafted for use in nonmilitary contexts, where it has often been used to mean job satisfaction. Consultants to other industrial and commercial organizations have relied on the terms *job satisfaction* and *organizational commitment* to serve morale-like roles.

Cohesion is the bonding of soldiers to each other and their leaders in such a way as to sustain their will and commitment to each other and their unit despite the stress of combat. This personal loyalty, very close to what mental health professionals now call "social support," is often supplemented by a more impersonal bond between the soldier and a secondary group or institution (like a regiment or a large ship) larger than the face-to-face work group but smaller than the nation or even the service. This soldier-institution bond we call esprit de corps.

Job satisfaction is often a major constituent of morale when the term is applied to civilian industry or business, although it applies only in a very limited way to men in combat. In fact what many civilian organizations refer to as "organizational commitment" (Mowday, Porter, and Steers 1982) is probably closer to what military organizations mean by morale. It is more global than job satisfaction, is more stable in the face of day-to-day work experiences, and develops and dissipates more slowly. Like morale, organizational commitment has personal, work group, and organizational determinants.

Determinants of Morale

The founder of the U.S. Army's Morale Branch began his task with the assumption that everything in the environment of the soldier, and the state of mind of every person with whom he comes in contact, affects his morale. Although this daunting assessment is probably correct, it is also true that the most important factors in morale fall under three headings: personal, unit, and institutional.

PERSONAL FACTORS

Personal factors include both biological and psychological needs. Good health, good food, adequate rest and sleep, clean dry clothes, washing facilities, and protection from the elements are examples of the former and are regularly cited as causes of high morale (Manning 1991). The basis for these assertions is the very obvious rise in spirits produced by an occasional hot meal, warm bath, or undisturbed sleep. Most firsthand accounts of combat (Holmes 1985) make it clear that, almost by definition, these needs can be met only sporadically. The answer to this seeming paradox is not simply that all combat soldiers suffer from chronically low morale but what Stouffer and his colleagues (1949) called the concept of "relative deprivation." Servicemen expect to work hard in uncomfortable, hazardous environments where amenities are few. It is not so much the absolute level of physical discomfort that controls their morale as the relation of their discomfort to that of those around them or that which they have been led to expect is reasonable under the circumstances. Morale soars when the serviceman is provided with physical comforts that exceed his expectations and plunge when he gets less than he feels is his fair share of whatever is available or possible.

Still at the personal level, there are a number of psychological needs whose fulfillment plays a major role in morale, above and beyond physical factors. Post–World War II, pre-Vietnam social science was nearly unanimous in denigrating patriotism, or equally grand and glorious causes, as sources of motivation for the combat soldier. Disillusioned soldier-writers like Robert Graves and Siegfried Sassoon, as well as social scientists, thought ideology much overrated as an incentive to actual fighting (although not denying its effectiveness at inducing young men to join the armed forces). America's Vietnam experience and Iran's apparently enthusiastic persistence in its devastating war against Iraq suggest that this rejection of "Grand Causes" as important determinants of morale may have been premature or overstated. It would instead seem that at least a general acceptance of the worth of the social system for which the serviceman is fighting and a clear goal, whether abstract like religion or nationalism or concrete like Berlin or Tokyo or even taking the next ridgeline, are an essential component of high morale.

Just as important as a goal is a role: seeing oneself as a valued member of the fighting force with an important role to play in the unit's mission. Holmes (1985) provides an apt quote from a fellow Briton: "Many a man behaves as a hero or coward, according as how [sic] he is expected to behave." In civilian life suggested cures for low worker commitment include increasing job "scope" or eliminating "role conflict," or "role ambiguity."

Naturally the service member must see his or her goals as attainable and the roles as ones that can be carried out, requirements that emphasize the importance of both solid training (the service member must be given the appropriate skills to make a valuable contribution) and self-confidence (the service member must be provided evidence that his skills are in fact adequate—through successful training exercises).

UNIT FACTORS

By far the most important single determinant of a soldier's morale—of his willingness to close with and fight the enemy—is his relationship with those around him in his primary face-to-face work group (Glass 1973). A sense of mutual trust, confidence, and esteem among the servicemen and between them and their leaders serves as an effective buffer against the morale-sapping stresses of combat. These feelings, which are called "unit cohesion" in military settings and "social support" by mental health professionals, arise from shared experiences. In past generations, armed forces took advantage of preservice shared experiences by manning units (army regiments most prominently) with men of similar ethnic class and regional origins (and perhaps schooling in the case of the officer corps). Shifting demographics, increased mobility in the general population, and deliberate attempts to avoid inequities in risk and suffering have seriously weakened this cohesion-building strategy and made shared experiences while in the service the real glue that holds the fighting unit together.

Combat experience itself has long been recognized as the primary bonding force in the unit. Stephen Crane's *Red Badge of Courage*, for example, refers to the "mysterious fraternity born out of smoke and the danger of death." The vastly increased accuracy and lethality of today's weapons have made modern forces wary of leaving the task of creating cohesion entirely to the enemy. The U.S. Army, for example, has begun to change its industrial-model individual replacement system to one that focuses on keeping groups of soldiers together for extended periods of time. This in fact is the first requirement for building cohesion—the more time people are together, the greater the chance they will discover, invent, and experience commonalities. The more people involved, the more varied the settings, and the longer the group remains stable, the more its members will have in common and the higher the unit's cohesion will be. Three other requirements for high cohesion put some limits on this sweeping generalization. First, the effectiveness of a shared experience is generally proportional to the extent to which it is unique to the unit. That is, being in the army is common to all soldiers, but it is nowhere near as effective in bonding the soldiers of 2d Platoon of Alpha Company, 33d Infantry, as their unique experience of, for example, holding a mountain pass in the bitter cold during Exercise Bold Stroke or even winning the battalion basketball championship. Both of these examples also illustrate two additional requirements for high cohesion: the unit must derive some feeling of success or accomplishment from its shared experiences; and, the greater the requirement for interdependent activity, the greater the resulting cohesion (a successful basketball team requires considerable interdependence among its members; a good track and field team, little, if any).

The net result in a highly cohesive unit is that its individual members feel they are firmly embedded in a network of mutual obligation. They are confident that, in times of difficulty, they have others available who *can* help (i.e., have the ability and training) and *will* help them to stay alive and do their jobs.

ORGANIZATIONAL FACTORS

Leaders, even more than peers, must generate this confidence that they can and will help each unit member survive and succeed. Their subordinates must see not only that their leaders will not expend their lives through incompetence, but also that they will not waste them through indifference. Leaders of high-morale units do this in a variety of ways, including medals and other explicit acknowledgments of abilities and accomplishments, that reassure the soldier, sailor, or airman that he is a valued individual whose life will not be thoughtlessly expended. Paradoxically, firm discipline also provides this assurance, as long as it is seen as evenhanded, for we do not generally impose rules and standards on those about whom we care little. A third way in which leaders bolster morale and demonstrate that they care is by providing clear and meaningful unit missions—by seeing that the efforts of the unit and the risks they incur are for something undeniably worthwhile. For this reason, time spent explaining the *why* of a mission as well as the *what* often pays off in higher morale and stronger determination to succeed.

Leaders are also the links integrating their units into the larger organization and inculcating the values and goals of that parent organization into the small unit. The degree to which they succeed in this determines the extent to which their small units display esprit de corps. High levels of esprit mean that soldiers' loyalties go beyond their fellow unit members and immediate leaders—an important step if morale is to be maintained in combat, where casualties will inevitably undo a will to fight that is based on purely personal loyalties. Large military forces have often attempted to help their leaders in this task of establishing institutional bonding by providing a secondary group that is large enough to survive a bitter fight but not so large that the service member feels he or she is just another number. For navies this is most often a ship or a formation of ships. For the combat-arms soldier it is most often a regiment. Significant features of such secondary groups are distinctive names, colors, dress, territorial affiliation and recruitment, museums, bands, honorary ranks, veterans' associations, and publications. Replacements for casualties in the small units (e.g., the rifle companies) of such a system come from within the secondary group (the regiment), which ensures that they arrive already sharing a significant body of distinctive experiences with those they are joining. An additional effect is, ultimately, to link each soldier, sailor, or airman's self-esteem to the reputation and expectations of the secondary group.

Consequences of Morale Level

Military leaders have long seen high morale not only as a characteristic of successful fighting troops, but as a major cause of that success. Indeed, it might be said that the concept of morale was invented precisely because of the consistent inability to predict military victory purely on the basis of the relative size and composition of opposing forces. Xenophon had discovered and recorded in 400 B.C. that "not numbers or strength bring victory in war; but whichever army goes into battle stronger in soul, their enemies generally cannot withstand them" (Richardson 1978). Napoleon said much the same in opining that "in the end the spirit will always conquer the sword"; Tolstoy, in *War and Peace*, offered that "in warfare the force of armies is the product of the mass multiplied by something else, an unknown X . . . [which] is the spirit of the army, the greater or less desire to fight and to face dangers. . . ." Historians of the twentieth century, psychiatrists struggling with "shell shock," "battle fatigue," and "posttraumatic stress syndrome," and social scientists struggling to measure the "unmeasurable" in the midst of World War II have all provided ample testimony to the essential truth of these assertions as well as helped to codify the variables of which morale is a function. Modern technology has, if anything, given a greater role to morale factors, for greater lethality, range, and accuracy have put devastating firepower within the reach of the most backward of combatants and made dispersion on the battlefield a necessity for mighty powers as well as for insurgents in developing countries.

FREDERICK M. MANNING

SEE ALSO: Reinforcements.

Bibliography

Baynes, J. C. 1967. *Morale*. New York: Praeger.

George, A. L. 1971. Primary groups, organization, and military performance. In *Handbook of military institutions*, ed. R. W. Little, pp. 293–318. Beverly Hills, Calif.: Sage.

Glass, A. J. 1973. Lessons learned. In *Neuropsychiatry in World War II, zone of the interior*, ed. R. L. Bernucci and A. J. Glass, pp. 735–59. Washington, D.C.: Office of the Surgeon General, Department of the Army.

Holmes, R. 1985. *Acts of war*. New York: Free Press.

Kellett, N. A. 1982. *Combat motivation*. Boston: Kluwer Nijhoff.

Manning, F. J. 1991. Morale, cohesion & esprit. In *Handbook of military psychology*, ed. R. Gal and A. D. Mangelsdorff. New York: Wiley.

Mowday, R. T., L. W. Porter, and R. M. Steers. 1982. *Employee-organization linkages*. New York: Academic Press.

Richardson, F. M. 1978. *Fighting spirit*. London: Leo Cooper.

Shibutani, T. I. 1978. *The derelicts of Company K: A sociological study of demoralization*. Berkeley, Calif.: Univ. of California Press.

Stouffer, S. A., A. A. Lumsdaine, M. H. Lumsdaine, R. M. Williams, M. B. Smith, I. L. Janis, S. A. Star, and L. S. Cottrell. 1949. *The American soldier*. Princeton, N.J.: Princeton Univ. Press.

MORTAR

Mortars are short-range, high-trajectory weapons—usually muzzle loaders and ordinarily small, easily transportable infantry weapons—that are used to lob shells in support of frontline troops, usually by means of indirect-fire techniques. Available on short notice to answer the urgent and varied needs of units, they are indispensable for the attack of point targets, as well as for distributing fire over wide areas.

For many years mortars have been primarily ground-emplaced weapons, but the increasing mechanization of armies, along with the appearance of tactical nuclear weapons, has made it necessary to mount mortars on vehicles so that they can keep up with the fighting troops to which they are attached. Both the U.S. and German armies mounted mortars on half-track armored carriers during World War II.

Mortars have significant advantages in comparison with other artillery weapons, including simplicity and cheapness; high trajectory; high rates of fire; mobility, particularly in difficult terrain; low chamber pressure; negligible barrel wear; small dimensions, leading to ease of concealment; ammunition with excellent antipersonnel characteristics; and a low equipment-to-shell weight ratio. Mortars have been in use since at least the fifteenth century. They may be either rifled or smoothbored and either muzzle or breech loaded.

General Characteristics

Mortars are usually divided into three classes—light, medium, and heavy. The general characteristics of conventional mortars are as shown in Table 1; but special adaptations, such as the use of rocket-assisted rounds, can have dramatic impact on such things as maximum range.

Mortar Construction

The great majority of mortars have only four main parts: the barrel, the base plate, the mounting, and the sight.

The *barrel* consists of a steel tube with one end closed by a breech piece, which is screwed on or into the barrel. To prevent the escape of gases, a copper washer is inserted as an obturating ring to produce a seal. With few exceptions, the interior of the bore is smooth. The exterior surface is also generally plain, although a few mortars incorporate radial fins to assist in cooling. The firing mechanism is located in the breech piece. In many mortars a safety device allows for retraction of the firing pin, a highly desirable feature. In most light and medium mortars, the misfire drill necessitates lifting the base end of the barrel to cause the shell to drop out of the muzzle into the hands of a waiting crew member.

When a mortar is fired the downward force of the explosion is distributed over an optimum flotation area by means of the *base plate*. This reduces ground pressure, so that the mortar does not sink into the earth when fired. There are square and rectangular base plates, but the most popular today are circular plates that, if properly bedded in, facilitate 360-degree traverse of the mortar. All base plates are ribbed to provide strength, prevent buckling, and ensure against slipping.

The mortar *mounting* normally consists of a bipod, although a few tripods are in service. The mounting supports the upper portion of the barrel and carries the elevating and traversing gears. The latter consists of one or two cylinders, usually containing springs; in some heavier mortars a hydraulic system may be employed. The bipod also contains the cross-leveling gear, which allows the sights to be placed upright regardless of the slope of the ground on which the mortar is emplaced.

To produce the indirect fire that is the mortar's main function, the *sight* must be laid on some selected aiming point. The aiming point can be some prominent and easily recognized feature, or it can be an aiming post put out for that purpose. When the correct angle between the line to the target and the line to

TABLE 1. *Characteristics of Conventional Mortars*

MORTAR TYPE	CALIBER	TOTAL WEIGHT	SHELL WEIGHT	MAX. RANGE
Light	60mm or less	15–24 kg	0.4–1.5 kg	500–2,000 m
Medium	60–100mm	25–90 kg	1.6–6.8 kg	2,000–6,000 m
Heavy	>100mm	>91 kg	>6.8 kg	5,000–9,000 m

the aiming post has been established and then set on the sight, the barrel of the mortar will be pointing in the direction of the target. This permits fire to be placed close to the target; and any subsequent corrections are then made in the line of fire. Target data may be recorded with reference either to aiming point deflection or to the zero line established by a special sight mechanism. It should be noted, however, that since meteorological data are not available at the mortar position, and since true north thus can never be deduced or stored, data are never recorded in terms of azimuth. The actual sighting device that is aligned on the aiming post may be a collimator or a telescope.

Light Mortar

Mortars with a caliber of 50 to 60mm are part of the panoply of weapons at platoon or company level but, at least in large modern armies, usually only for specific tasks such as battlefield illumination and the support of commando-type units. Nevertheless many countries are producing light mortars of different types and characteristics to meet the varying requirements of modern military forces (Table 2). The following paragraph describes the three main types.

The standard light mortar has a circular base, a bipod mounting, a barrel clamp fitted with a recoil absorber, and an optical dial sight. The long-range version, similar to the standard mortar, has a longer barrel that permits the shell to gain velocity in the tube, thus extending the range. The commando-type light mortar has a lightweight barrel and a very small base plate. It is intended to be carried and fired by one man. There is no bipod, the barrel being supported at the requisite angle of fire by the firer's hand. This mortar typically has both a carrying handle and a sling. The table shows the varying characteristics of these three types of light mortars.

Medium Mortar

Most medium mortars now in service at the company level are of 81mm and 82mm caliber (Fig. 1); the only major exception is the U.S. 107mm weapon. Because of their light weight and flexibility, these mortars are considered one of the most important means available to an infantry company for applying indirect fire on short notice. Mortars are able to move with the supported unit and still be ready to respond promptly to any fire mission in support of advance infantry echelons.

TABLE 2. *Characteristics of Light Mortars*

CHARACTERISTIC	STANDARD	LONG-RANGE	COMMANDO
Caliber	60 mm	60 mm	60 mm
Barrel length	740 mm	1,000 mm	650 mm
Base plate diameter	350 mm	350 mm	150 mm
Firing weight	15.2 kg	16.1 kg	5.4 kg
Barrel weight	3.5 kg	4.6 kg	3.2 kg
Base plate weight	4.0 kg	4.0 kg	0.8 kg
Maximum range	3,400 m	4,300 m	1,600 m
Rate of fire (rds/min)	30	25	25

Figure 1. An 81mm mortar. (SOURCE: U.S. Army photograph)

The medium mortar can be transported by land vehicle, helicopter, pack animal, or man pack. When man packed it is carried by three soldiers, and it is robust enough to be dropped by parachute. Many efforts have been made to reduce the weight of medium mortars through the use of such lightweight metals as titanium, while at the same time increasing the range and lethality of their projectiles. Table 3 shows the principal characteristics of the various medium mortars.

Heavy Mortar

Heavy mortars of 120mm caliber are now in service in many armies at battalion and regimental level. Mortars of larger size, such as the 160mm weapon, are used as divisional mortars. The 120mm mortar is distinguished by its range and firepower. On the debit side, it is much heavier than the medium mortar and has proven very vulnerable to counter-battery fire.

TABLE 3. *Characteristics of Medium Mortars*

CHARACTERISTIC	81MM	82MM	107MM
Weight	Up to 61.5 kg	56 kg	Up to 87.4 kg
Barrel length	1,310 mm	1,220 mm	1,524 mm
Maximum range	4,100 m	3,000 m	6,800 m
Minimum range	85 m	100 m	770 m
Rate of fire (rds/min)	20	15–20	18
Crew	5	5	5

The 160mm mortar is the heaviest used by infantry divisions. Because of its long barrel, the 160mm is a breech-loading weapon. The barrel is pivoted for loading about trunnions placed near the center point. The weapon is towed by the muzzle, using either an armored personnel carrier or a heavy truck. Table 4 shows the characteristics of two types of heavy mortar.

Mounting Mortars on Vehicles

Medium and heavy mortars are mounted on tracked or wheeled light armored vehicles, along with the fire control equipment needed to employ these weapons. Such an arrangement enables the mortars to keep up with the infantry troops to which they are attached and to go into action quickly when needed.

To mount medium and heavy mortars without structural modification to the carrier vehicle, a hydropneumatic recoil mechanism is fitted above the mortar's barrel. This device has a long travel, which reduces the force that the firing of each round transmits to the vehicle's structure. The consequent large reduction in recoil eliminates the need for firing a preliminary series of bedding-in rounds that are necessary when the mortar is fired from the ground. Laying of the mortar is thus made easier and the time needed to go into action reduced.

A balance mechanism is also incorporated in the mortar's mounting; this is used by the crew to adjust the pivot to a fixed vertical position. The mortar can therefore be fired normally, regardless of the terrain and without regard to whether the carrier vehicle is on a forward, rear, or side slope. At the rear, the vehicle's floor forms the mortar's base plate. The mortar is simply suspended from the carrier vehicle by cable shock absorbers.

The crew can place the mortar in traveling position by tilting it forward toward the vehicle's floor, then closing the cradle's protective shutters. This also reduces the silhouette of the vehicle and lowers its center of gravity. The carrier vehicle can carry 60 or more rounds, giving the mounted weapons system the firepower required by troops operating far from their bases. These carrier vehicles can be transported by helicopters over short distances by use of a sling or by transport aircraft over longer distances. The standard mortar crew for mortars mounted in carriers may be reduced to four men instead of the six or seven required by dismounted weapons.

Ammunition

Mortar shells are classified in three main categories: explosive, smoke screening, and illuminating rounds. The shell consists of three main parts: the fuze,

TABLE 4. *Characteristics of Heavy Mortars*

CHARACTERISTIC	120MM	160MM
Weight (in firing position)	274.8 kg	1,300 kg
Barrel length	1,854 mm	4,500 mm
Rate of fire (rds/min)	12–15	2–3
Maximum range	5,700 m	Up to 9,000 m
Minimum range	640 m	750 m
Crew	6	7

TABLE 5. *Characteristics of Common Mortar Rounds*

60MM ROUNDS	EXPLOSIVE	SMOKE	ILLUMINATING
Total weight	1.37 kg	1.83 kg	1.88 kg
Weight of TNT	150 g	—	—
Weight of WP	—	350 g	—
Lethal radius of burst	13.5 m	—	—
Maximum range	1,800 m	1,470 m	1,000 m
Illuminating time	—	—	25–30 sec
81MM ROUNDS			
Total weight	3.25 kg	5.8 kg	4.6 kg
Weight of TNT	500 g	—	—
Weight of WP	—	1.86 kg	—
Lethal radius of burst	21 m	—	—
Maximum range	3,200 m	2,130 m	2,100 m
Illuminating time	—	—	50–60 sec
120MM ROUNDS			
Total weight	16.4 kg	12.6–13.3 kg	12.8–13.3 kg
Maximum range	6,010 m	6,000 m	6,300 m

the steel shell body (incorporating a charge that varies according to the kind of shell), and the fin assembly. The primary characteristics of the various types of 60mm, 81mm, and 120mm mortar rounds are presented in Table 5. The 160mm mortar fragmentation shell weighs 40 kilograms, has a bursting charge of 7.36 kilograms of TNT, and uses a point-detonating fuze.

Future Mortars

Any dramatic change in mortars in the foreseeable future is unlikely. Progress will probably be made, however, in terms of lighter and handier equipment employing new metals and materials. Other areas of potential development are improvement in the aerodynamic properties of mortar projectiles; functioning of the ejection fuze and the ejection process; dispersion and stabilization of submunitions and operation of their fuzes; and optimization of anti-armor and antipersonnel effects. Fire control will be developed by using electronics on a wide scale, which will enable mortars to engage a variety of targets with the need for few, if any, ranging rounds.

SAMIR HASSAN SHALABY

SEE ALSO: Ammunition; Artillery; Artillery, Tube; Firepower.

Bibliography

Bidwell, S., ed. 1981. *Brassey's artillery of the world*. 2d ed. London: Brassey's.
Jane's infantry weapons, 1987–88. 1987. London: Jane's.
Miller, D., and C. J. Foss. 1987. *Modern land combat*. New York: Portland House.

MUNITIONS AND EXPLOSIVES TECHNOLOGY APPLICATIONS

How conventional high explosives function and the principles relating to their operation are important considerations for militaries everywhere. This article presents definitions of a range of high-explosive charges used in various munitions and examines their relative effectiveness against targets. While the effect of different charge types on a target may vary in terms of penetration, when they are compared by caliber of munition, their efficiencies, in terms of crater volume, are quite similar. This is somewhat surprising and shows that, regardless of the way a charge is shaped, similar energies per unit mass are dissipated on detonation.

There are a large variety of designs for munitions that comprise projectiles and missile warheads. Thus, it is helpful to group these into a few basic types with respect to their particular design and application of explosives technology (see Fig. 1). This facilitates study of their principles of operation and examination of typical applications against targets. In practice, however, a mix of these different operational mechanisms will usually be employed.

Energy Carriers

The term *charge* is important and conveys the idea of the explosive as a "carrier of energy." The energy content of a high-explosive charge—the gas volume generated by the chemical reaction per unit of mass—is equivalent to that of a corresponding propellant charge. The significant difference between detonation at a target and combustion in a weapon's firing chamber is that the explosive charge releases energy much faster (by a factor of 10^6). This results in far higher kilo-joules per second, or generation of gas volume in liters per second,

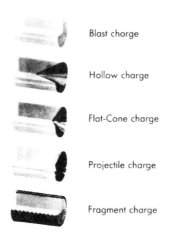

Blast charge

Hollow charge

Flat-Cone charge

Projectile charge

Fragment charge

Figure 1.Basic types of conventional high-explosive charges.
(SOURCE: Messerschmitt-Bölkow-Blohm GmbH)

respectively. This quick release of energy by conventional high-explosive charges is the reason for their specific characteristics.

As detonation occurs, the unreacted material in the explosive charge has an initial density p_0, an initial temperature T_0, and an initial ambient pressure p_0, within the detonation zone L (see Fig. 2). As detonation progresses, the detonation zone is rapidly subjected to increased density p_n, elevated temperature T_n, and significantly elevated pressure p_n. During this process, the detonation front travels with a detonation velocity D, and the explosive products move with their material velocity u, both in the direction of shock waves produced by detonation. The energy released in the detonation zone determines detonation velocity and occurs between 0.01 µs and 1 µs (µs = microsecond = 0.000001 second).

Considering the high pressure and temperatures of a high-explosive detonation, and the submicrosecond speed in which they are generated, the precise reaction process is unknown.

BLAST CHARGE

Blast charges are cylindrical, designed to fill evenly the space designed for them in warheads and projectiles. The blast that can be produced against a target is extremely powerful. For example, 1 kilogram of high explosive yields about 1,000 liters of gas (at standard temperature and pressure, STP) in 10 µs and reaches a temperature of several thousand degrees Kelvin. When this gas volume is restricted to the confined space of the casing of the undetonated explosive, an initial pressure of approximately 30,000 bars occurs. The gas then immediately expands, rupturing or disintegrating the casing, and pushes the surrounding air (or other medium) like a piston. This causes a shock wave to

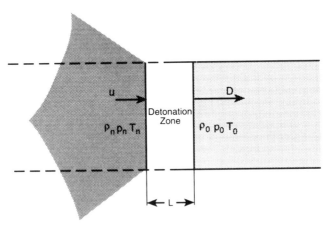

Figure 2. A schematic representation of the relations during detonation. At the shock front, the pressure p, density p, and temperature T have initial undisturbed values p_0, p_0, and T_0, respectively. The detonation zone is of constant thickness. Beyond this zone, p, p, and T are significantly increased. (SOURCE: Messerschmitt-Bölkow-Blohm GmbH)

form with a very rapid rise time and a period of overpressure. The overpressure is followed by a partial vacuum period and results in a positive impulse of blast wave, followed by a negative impulse.

The destructive power of the blast wave is caused either by the pressure amplitude or the impulses, depending on the type of target and configuration. If the resonant period of the target is much longer than the interaction time of the positive shock wave, only the impulse causes damage. If the target resonant period is shorter than the pulse, the pressure amplitude is important. Figure 3a shows typical response curves as the blast wave characteristics vary among high peak pressure, low impulse and low peak pressure, and high impulse. The three individual hyperbolas correspond to particular levels of target damage.

With the amount of high explosive usually used in missiles and warheads, the true situation is commonly midway between the extremes. In practice, the distance-to-charge relation (Fig. 3b) follows the "square root law for charges" (i.e., with a tenfold increase in distance a hundredfold increase in charge is required to obtain the same destructive effect). In the case of relatively small distances to a target with large dimensions, the distance cannot be measured to the center of mass, but to a suitable reference line or area.

Greater destructive effect can be obtained from the shock wave if there is direct contact with the target, although it is primarily in the localized area of impact. This is because there is no attenuation of the effect of the shock wave by an air gap. In other words, considerable destruction can be obtained with a relatively small amount of high explosive if the charge is placed in direct contact with the target.

SHAPED CHARGE

Sometimes called a hollow charge, shaped charges are hollowed out conically at the front; some are lined with conically shaped metal (e.g., 2-mm-thick copper sheets). Upon impact and detonation of an unlined shaped charge, the conical cavity focuses part of the blast against the target, resulting in greater penetration effect than a comparable blast charge despite the lower weight and somewhat greater distance from the center of mass to the target. Figure 4 shows a decreasing hole diameter and increasing penetration when the charge is concentrated by use of a liner along the charge axis.

Another interesting comparison is the length of time that a shaped charge interacts with a target, which is about 40 times longer than that of a blast charge. A shaped charge 100 millimeters in diameter placed against armor plate will penetrate 600 millimeters in 400 μs. In contrast, a blast charge of the same diameter will interact with the target for only 10 μs and achieve far less penetration.

The "concentration" effect and the increase of the "charge-target interaction time" are the two main phenomena that increase the efficiency of a shaped charge.

If there is some spacing, or standoff, of the shaped charge from the target, the penetration depth can increase up to seven calibers (Fig. 5). This additional,

Blast Effect

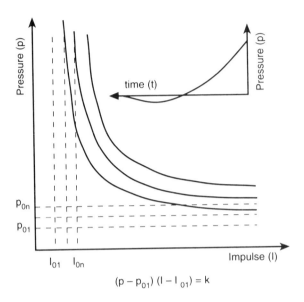

$$(p - p_{01})(I - I_{01}) = k$$

a.

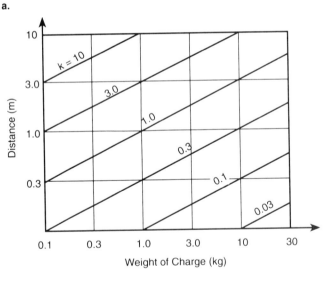

$$D = k \sqrt{W}$$

Figure 3. Part a. is a schematic representation of the pressure and impulse load of a target structure caused by the blast wave of a conventional high-explosive charge. Part b. is a representation of the "square root law for high-explosive charges" with different K-factors as a parameter. (SOURCE: Messerschmitt-Bölkow-Blohm GmbH)

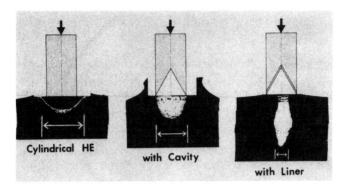

Figure 4. A comparison among a cylindrical high-explosive charge, a high-explosive charge with a cone-shaped cavity without a liner, and a high-explosive charge with a 2-mm-thick, 60° cone-shaped copper liner in the cavity. (SOURCE: Messerschmitt-Bölkow-Blohm GmbH)

initially unexpected phenomenon shows that an "energy carrier" is generated during detonation and that it can affect the target in an optimal way.

This energy carrier, the jet of the shaped charge, is formed from the liner during the initial stage of detonation. Not to be confused with plasma jets, the jet of a shaped charge is in fact a very high speed extruded length of metal with a very high velocity at temperatures no greater than a few hundred degrees Celsius. Acceleration of the liner and formation of the jet and the metal slug along the line of collapse can best be recorded with a flash radiograph (Fig. 6).

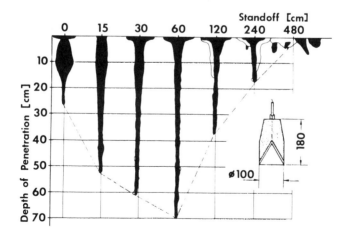

Figure 5. The typical standoff curve of a hollow charge. Initially the depth of the hole increases between the hollow charge and the target up to seven calibers because of the jet elongation effect. For greater standoff the depth of the hole decreases because of the deviation of the jet particles from the axis. (SOURCE: Messerschmitt-Bölkow-Blohm GmbH)

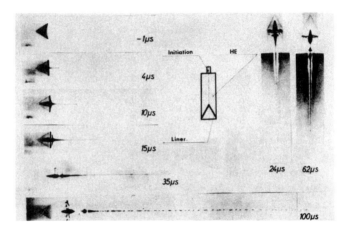

Figure 6. Flash radiographs of hollow charges at various times after detonation showing the jet formation of the liner, the jet elongation up to the particulated jet, and their capacity to penetrate targets. (SOURCE: Messerschmitt-Bölkow-Blohm GmbH)

These radiographs reveal the features of the specific efficiency of a hollow charge as:

• concentration of action along the charge axis through the jet,
• long interaction time through the long jet, and
• increased effect at a greater distance, since a longer jet is only formed at a greater distance

The continuous elongation of the jet is limited. After about 150 μs, a jet from a 100-millimeter shaped charge breaks up axially into particles; thus a so-called particulated jet is formed. The initial homogeneous jet, as well as the particulated jet, exhibit highly efficient penetration and perforation capabilities because of the enormously high pressure applied to any kind of target material. As a first approximation in computing penetration, the material strengths of the target can be neglected and hydrodynamic equations used to compute results that agree very well with practical experience.

Mechanical inertial forces dominate the penetration process and not thermally driven mechanisms similar to welding and flame cutting. The higher temperatures around the crater after shaped-charge penetration are consequences of deformation. The penetration process depends on purely mechanical displacement due to the high pressure generated during the interaction.

FLAT-CONE CHARGE

Similar in design appearance to shaped charges, flat-cone charges have a larger angle at the cone tip, about 140°, and operate on different physical principles. Whereas the liner in a shaped charge is accelerated along the line of collapse and forms a high-velocity jet and a relatively low-velocity slug, the liner in a flat-cone charge becomes inverted as a whole with a lower velocity, but with a higher mass and larger diameter. Accordingly, the holes created in a target by the shorter, but thicker, jets are not as deep; instead they have larger diameters.

Flash radiographs show the formation of the jet from a copper liner (Fig. 7). Mathematical expressions to explain flat-cone charge principles cannot be based on the well-known hydrodynamic equations of Birkhoff, MacDougall, Pugh, and Taylor (1948) and Pugh, Eichelberger, and Rostoker (1952). Rather, the liner must be sectioned into toroidal zones, and the accelerations, velocities, and directions of each of these toroidal zones must be calculated, taking into account the material flow strength if high accuracy is desired.

PROJECTILE CHARGE

The jets of shaped and flat-cone charges have an optimum penetrating effect when there is at least some, although relatively small, standoff from a target upon detonation. At greater standoff ranges the jets, while retaining some penetrating capability, tend to break up or particulate axially. Projectile charges, on the other hand, are designed to keep the resulting explosive-formed projectile (EFP) intact after detonation. By adjusting the impulses acting on the toroidal zones created by the explosion so that the tensile elongation of the liner does not exceed its rupture point, an integral mass, called earlier a self-forging fragment (SFF), now an EFP, is formed.

If the impulses acting on the toroidal zones are more elaborately controlled, fin-stabilized flying projectiles can be formed. These EFPs can be accurately aimed over a considerable distance between charge and target (Fig. 8).

The initial conditions and subsequent processes necessary for the proper formation of an EFP can be described quickly and easily, but among all of the charges discussed, this type is the most difficult to realize in practice.

FRAGMENT CHARGE

During the detonation of any metal-encased explosive charge, the casing is distended by the expanding gases and is accelerated to high velocities. Al-

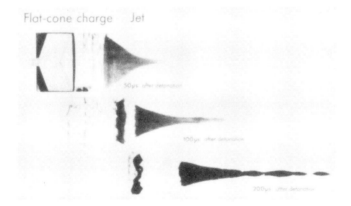

Figure 7. Flash radiographs show the jet formed by the inversion of the flat liner of a flat-cone charge. (SOURCE: Messerschmitt-Bölkow-Blohm GmbH)

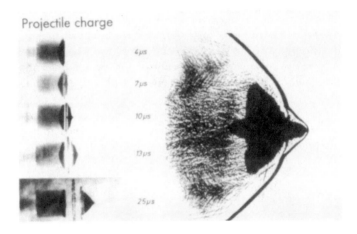

Figure 8. Flash radiographs of the formation of EFPs and a shadowgraph of a flying projectile. (SOURCE: Messerschmitt-Bölkow-Blohm GmbH)

though numerous natural fragments are formed by radial expansion, the fragments can be determined beforehand by special treatment of the casing. For example, grooves or zones of embrittlement in the casing will produce more uniform fragmentation, which can be controlled within certain limits. Depending on the target properties and the design of the warhead, the number, distribution, and size of fragments can be adjusted for optimal effect.

Comparison

In summary, the five fundamental charge types for munitions and their specific energy transfer mechanisms against targets are:

- blast charge with shock wave
- shaped charge with very long, but thin, jet
- flat-cone charge with a shorter, but thicker, jet
- projectile charge with the explosive-formed projectile over very long standoff range
- fragment charge with radial expansion to high velocities.

Shaped, flat-cone, and projectile charges exhibit their own specific penetration and perforation power with respect to standoff. The shaped charge, especially in close contact with the target, exhibits very high penetration depth. While their optimum standoff distance is somewhat greater than for shaped charges, flat-cone charges show less penetration and larger hole diameters. Projectile charges can deliver concentrated energy at great distances between charge and target. This also applies to fragment and blast charges, which cover a larger area than shaped, flat-cone, and projectile charges, which usually only produce an effect in one direction.

When the penetration depth and corresponding diameter of holes are com-

Types	Distance (in D_{Ch})	Crater		$\sum\limits_{i}^{n}$ Volume (in D_{Ch}^3)
		Depth (in D_{Ch})	Width (in D_{Ch})	
Blast charge	0	0.2 – 0.4	0.8 – 1.0	$\dfrac{0.9^2 \times \pi}{4}$ × 0.3 = 0.19
Shaped charge	1.5 – 6	5 – 8	0.1 – 0.3	$\dfrac{0.2^2 \times \pi}{4}$ × 6.0 = 0.19
Flat-cone charge	3 – 8	2 – 3	0.25 – 0.40	$\dfrac{0.3^2 \times \pi}{4}$ × 2.7 = 0.19
Projectile charge	1 –10^3	0.6 – 1.2	0.4 – 0.6	$\dfrac{0.5^2 \times \pi}{4}$ × 1.0 = 0.19
Fragment charge	1 – 10^3	0.05 – 0.10	0.05 – 0.15	$\dfrac{0.10^2 \times \pi}{4}$ × 0.08 × 300 = 0.19

Figure 9. A comparison of the conventional high-explosive charges with respect to standoffs, charge diameter, penetration depths, and crater diameter (width) and the volumes of the holes computed from depth and diameter values. All values are expressed in charge diameters. (SOURCE: Messerschmitt-Bölkow-Blohm GmbH)

pared for the different charges (Fig. 9), it is evident that damage to a target increases approximately as a square function of the hole diameter. When this operation efficiency is correlated to the hole volume, it shows that all types of charges generate about the same hole volume—0.19 cubic charge calibers, or D_c^3—including fragment charges (in which case the separate hole volumes are summed). While this is somewhat surprising, it is in no way a new energy constant. Rather, it indicates that from a definite supply of energy in the high-explosive charge, only a certain fraction—the deformation energy in the target—can be realized.

This seemingly trivial physical statement is not always obvious in practice. This observation clearly indicates, however, that the desire of militaries to double the diameter of the crater with the same charge weight and charge diameter in the course of further research and development cannot be achieved, since this would imply a fourfold increase in the energy content of the explosive.

MANFRED HELD

SEE ALSO: Missile, Antitank Guided; Precision-guided Munitions.

Bibliography

Birkhoff, G., D. P. MacDougall, E. M. Pugh, and G. Taylor. 1948. Explosives with lined cavities. *Journal of Applied Physics* 19:565–82.
Pugh, E. M., R. J. Eichelberger, and N. Rostoker. 1952. Theory of jet formation by charges with lined conical cavities. *Journal of Applied Physics* 23:532–36.

N

NIGHT VISION TECHNOLOGY APPLICATIONS

Today's technology allows all elements of armed forces to operate effectively at night—so much so that a well-equipped and well-trained force, using modern night vision equipment, has the potential to overwhelm an enemy force not so prepared.

Night vision equipment does not, however, present visual information of the same type or in the same form as that gathered in the daytime by the human eye. For this reason, a well-equipped but poorly trained force, venturing forth at night in the false security of modern technology, is courting disaster.

This article outlines the types and uses of equipment in the field today and speculates on what may come in the future.

The Discipline of Night Fighting Equipment

In general, night vision equipment gathers radiant energy (photons) from the electromagnetic (EM) spectrum, converts it into an electrical signal, inadvertently destroys some of the information, and presents what remains to a human observer or to the evolving "intelligent" machines. The equipment must be sufficiently inexpensive to be issued in high volume, rugged enough to withstand the abuse of the battlefield, able to function without repair for a reasonable time, and be repairable by military support systems.

Imaging systems perform well when they sense the observable characteristics of objects of military significance with sufficient resolution and field of view to make accurate situation assessments possible and allow an effective course of action to be pursued. Practical limitations are met in resolution, since the sensing medium cannot be made continuously finer, and in field of view, since the extent of the sensing medium cannot increase without limit. In addition, the ability to gather photons and convert them into electrons has limits in conversion efficiencies, EM spectral sensitivity, and the inability to collect photons in ever-increasing numbers due to atmospheric effects and the physical size and weight of optics and antennae.

Finally, the system must work in real time so that photon collection, conversion, processing, and subsequent presentation are accomplished over the entire field of view no less than about 30 times per second.

Technology

Human capability to operate at night can be augmented by providing hardware that performs the generic function shown in Figure 1. The transducer converts photons into electrons, which can be more readily manipulated. The processor runs the gamut from simple electron acceleration to the more complex process of encoding the position and time of entry and using this inferred information to inaugurate other processes. The latter process allows the information to be preserved and presented in a more useful form than is possible by merely "energizing" the information-bearing electron and passing it through the system in real time. The presentation medium, in turn, varies from a phosphor, which receives the accelerated electron and glows more brightly (emits many more photons) than the incident photon, to an ergonomic display, which presents the essential information in a preprocessed manner designed to allow the user to enhance mission effectiveness.

The information necessary to operate at night can be inferred from the relative position of reflected and emitted photons and their spectral and temporal properties. Figure 1 encompasses the human eye/brain combination, which is highly effective in the functions for which it evolved but is limited in angular resolution and in spectral and temporal response when functioning at very low light levels.

The military hardware that augments human capability falls into two major categories, active and passive, and is further characterized by the spectral region addressed by the photo/electron transducer.

Active Systems

Active systems generate the photons reflected from the scene and that are sensed by the transducer. This class includes the use of visible light (fires, flares, and searchlights) and of radiation from other spectral regions, which run the gamut of the electromagnetic spectrum from infrared-filtered searchlights through radars (including millimeter wave and laser radars). The effective utility of an active system is strongly dependent on the intervening atmosphere between system and scene.

The natural atmosphere allows only limited "atmospheric windows"— spectral regions of opportunity that allow EM radiation to penetrate without being scattered or absorbed. Even in these windows there can be heavy signal losses such as, for example, the glare associated with car headlights in even slightly inclement weather. Also, man-made obscurants are more effective against active systems, since they must make a double pass between the observing position and the target. High-energy photons (moving in the blue

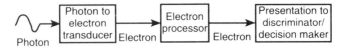

Figure 1. Function of night vision equipment.

direction away from the visible) have little practical application because of their inability to penetrate the atmosphere.

World War II witnessed the first use of radar and filtered searchlights, which were highly effective, in part because they were new. The disadvantage of active systems is the vulnerability attendant to generation of the signal. Receiving sensors, of the type used by an active system to interrogate the returning signal, can be employed by the enemy to track the radiation back to its source. This places a premium on passive systems.

PASSIVE SYSTEMS

Fielded passive systems are of two types: image intensifiers and thermal imagers.

Image intensifiers. An image intensifier uses the available radiation from the night sky generated by the moon, when present, and by the stars. The transducer is a photocathode made by evaporating metals to form a thin film.

An objective lens forms an image of the scene on the photocathode. Electrons are emitted into an evacuated area at the position where the photons strike and at a rate proportional to the intensity of the picture elements in the scene. The current electron processor is a microchannel plate (MCP). This electro-optical amplifier, composed of several million fused glass tubes, has the capacity to emit 10^5 to 10^8 electrons from each tube per single entering electron. This bundle of electrons is then accelerated by an applied field to an energy sufficient to light the phosphor.

Because an objective lens presents an inverted image, and since the electro-optics do not right the image, a fiber-optic twist is required behind the phosphor to restore the image to an upright position. The phosphor and fiber-optic twist represent the presentation element of Figure 1. The discriminator/decision maker is the human observer.

The first generation of image intensifiers, fielded by the United States in the late 1960s, did not have an MCP but used three stages of tubes coupled together by fiber optics. The initial development of fiber optics was carried out for this purpose.

A third generation of image intensifiers has been developed and deployed. It is similar to the second generation but has an improved photocathode, which collects more of the photons in the near-infrared region.

Thermal imagers. Thermal imagers sense emitted photons from objects in the scene. The atmospheric windows available are from 3 to 5 microns and from 8 to 14 microns. The latter region has proved more useful, since the objects of greatest interest emit more photons in this region. The transducer used is a solid-state material that changes an internal electrical property (voltage or conductance) with the incidence of signal photons.

The thermal imager differs from the intensifier in that signal photons are not emitted into a vacuum and guided with electron optics into the electron processor, but rather each discrete sensing element is connected to its dedicated amplifier, which in turn feeds a display element.

It is difficult to build a transducer with a very large number of very small elements and connect each to its individual amplifier. The approach that led to a practical device is shown in Figure 2.

A linear array of detector elements is scanned across the scene, creating two-dimensional coverage by allowing each element to time-share across a line of the scene. If the scanning mirror is used on both sides, synchronizing with the display elements is simplified. Each display element is connected to its sensing elements through an amplifier and glows with an intensity proportional to the amount of converted scene radiation. The display elements can be viewed directly by the eye or remotely by a video system.

The resolution of such a system is determined by the angle subtended by a single detector element. The smaller the element, the higher the potential resolution, but since system sensitivity is dependent on the total amount of detector material in the focal plane, the smaller the element the less sensitive is the system for the same number of elements. An ideal system would have a very large number of very small detectors. The practicality of building such a system decreases with detector size and with an increase in the number of elements. Current fielded technology has detectors in the hundreds, and the obvious course of future development is toward focal planes with thousands or tens of thousands of detectors.

System Performance and Utility

IMAGE INTENSIFIER CAPABILITY

Image intensifier technology is based on a photocathode with very low emission of electrons resulting from thermal energy. World War II near-infrared tech-

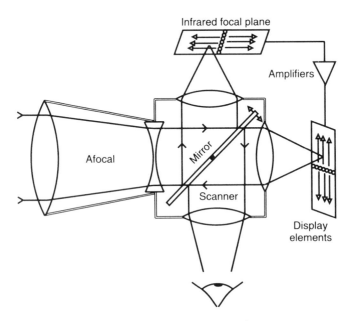

Figure 2. Thermal imager transducer.

nology required the use of a filtered searchlight in order to raise the photo current signal level of incoming photons above the level of those electrons being generated by heat energy.

Since the generation of filtered light represents a serious breach of security when opposing forces possess the ability to convert infrared radiation into visible energy, the need for passive operation required either cooling the photocathode, which was logistically too difficult, or developing a better photocathode. When developed, this photocathode permitted operation under starlight conditions (hence its name, "Starlight Scope").

It was introduced by U.S. forces into Vietnam in the mid-1960s and was widely copied by other countries. This first-generation technology was composed of three stages, but without an MCP electro-optical amplifier and without the fiber-optic twist. These stages were coupled with fiber-optic faceplates, the first application of fiber-optic technology, which had been developed for this purpose. The intensifier sights were mounted on rifles and crew-served weapons. The range of the devices was well suited to the range of the weapons.

The performance of image-intensifying devices is determined at high light levels (full moon) by the resolution limit imposed by the optical system, but at low light levels (starlight and lower) by the sensitivity of the photocathode. No increase in light amplification can overcome the lack of signal photons at low light levels, since a single captured photon contains only one piece of information, no matter how bright it can be made. For this reason the practical limitation on the range performance of image intensifiers is about that of the effective range of a rifle.

The impetus for the second generation was the need to develop a smaller tube for head-mounted applications. The night vision goggle was thus developed and fielded in large quantities. This head-mounted device allows general navigation and maintenance functions to be performed at night. It should not be assumed that equivalent performance to day vision is achieved, however, since the field of view is restricted to about one-third of human vision and the amount of available information, because of a paucity of photons, is noticeably limited. In addition, the spectral response of the photocathode makes foliage take on a "cotton candy" appearance. There is no color vision, and the darker areas are unfathomable, containing shadows, holes, or possibly a hostile tank.

The application of this technology is mainly for relatively short-range operations of infantry forces, including night navigation, maintenance, and fire control for small arms and crew-served weapons. An interesting exception is the use of night vision goggles to conduct night navigation of fixed-wing aircraft and nighttime nap-of-the-earth helicopter flight.

CAPABILITIES OF THERMAL IMAGERS

Self-emitted EM radiation from objects is a function of their temperature. Humans have a temperature of about 300 degrees Kelvin and emit radiation that peaks in the middle of an available atmospheric window at a wavelength of about 10 microns. Other living organisms also peak in this region, as do vehicles that transport humans. Thus, far-infrared devices (known as FLIRs, for forward-looking infrared, or thermal imagers) that operate in this window constitute the majority of fielded thermal systems.

The resolution of thermal imagers is inherently less than that of image intensifiers, owing to a smaller number of available sensing elements and the optical diffraction limit. Nevertheless, the improved signal strength coming from the target and the lack of dependence on available light levels allow the thermal imager to be more dependable and provide an extension of range performance over the image intensifiers by about two or three times. Also, since targets are brighter than their backgrounds, the thermal imager is better for finding targets, because targets are more conspicuous in the thermal image. Of great military significance is the thermal imager's use of radiation in a spectrum that inherently penetrates atmospheric conditions that defeat the visible spectrum. The result is that thermal imaging systems are the choice for armor and anti-armor weapon sights for night operations and for the majority of other long-range applications.

CAPABILITIES OF OTHER TECHNOLOGIES

It is always possible to make improvements in the performance of fielded systems; the question is whether the resource allocation is worth the improvement. The changes are of two types: evolutionary, in which the fielded technology is upgraded in incremental steps, and revolutionary, in which a new approach is embraced, with consequent large perturbations in the weapons platform and large additional expense.

The discipline of research and development programs must both generate technologies worthy of revolutionary change and determine at what point sufficient progress has been made to warrant expenditures for integration of a new technology approach. In the context of this article there are two other technology approaches that may be incorporated into weapons systems in the coming years: laser radars and millimeter wave radars.

Laser radars. Laser radars are simply thermal imagers with a laser illuminator, gated to take in only a narrow portion of the downrange scene. They have been in development for more than ten years and have proved more difficult to integrate and more expensive than thermal imaging devices.

They have the advantage of greater range performance because of the added signal due to the generated radiation and tend to eliminate the backscatter through gating. Also they are more covert than other illuminators because of the focusing of the beam and the relatively short time the beam is on. To date, however, their added improvement in performance has not been considered adequate to warrant the additional expense.

Millimeter wave radars. Currently fielded radars do not image. This is because diffraction phenomena dictate that resolution possibilities are determined by the ratio of aperture size (antenna) to wavelength. At the wavelengths used for World War II radars, antennas would have to be thousands of feet in diameter to make a usable image.

The impetus for millimeter wave radar is the possibility of obtaining usable resolution with antennas in the one-foot range. This technology is evolving quite rapidly and has the appeal of greater weather penetration than those working in the near and far infrared, while still retaining reasonably high resolution.

While active, these systems are more covert than microwave radars, because they use special beam-forming techniques. It remains to be seen whether they can stand alone and whether their complexity is offset by improved performance over current systems. This technology is a leading candidate as an element in a multisensor system. That would entail, however, still greater complexity and cost.

Training and Doctrine

Technology is of no use unless properly employed. The history of war holds many examples of winners who better understood how to exploit technology advantages than did their opponents.

Night vision technology has special disciplines, since society is intolerant of night training; the equipment is fundamentally disorienting in that it provides sensory information in a different and less satisfying form than human vision; and the concepts of exploiting the advantages of increased night mobility and effectiveness are inherently foreign to our military tacticians. Without well-thought-out doctrine and effective training, the advantages of night operations are not evident and the motivation to think and train for them are thus lacking.

There must first be a commitment on the part of a military force to operate at night. Then an iterative process must take place to train troops and assess their effectiveness. The arrived-at assessment must next be reviewed on the basis of interoperability of the combined-arms team, then doctrine must be based on the relative capability of forces operating at night and in the daylight. There is no point in investing in the hardware if it is not to be effectively employed.

It is essential to grasp the concept that, if forces are more effective at night than are opposing enemy forces, then these forces should choose to fight exclusively at night, if possible. If that condition is expected, then it follows that the majority of training for such forces should take place at night; that military bases should operate at night and sleep in the day; and that the needs of the night forces should dominate those of the day forces. That this is nowhere true today does not mean that an analysis and conscious decision have been made to abandon a night operations initiative. Rather it means that awareness of the potential has not been adequately achieved, that the implications are too bothersome, or that the proper conclusions have not been drawn.

Future Trends in Application of Night Vision Technology

DIMINISHING RETURNS FOR PHOTON COUNTERS

The history of night vision technology has been dominated by photon counters. Devices that could better convert photons to electrons, those more efficient in regions where information was greatest, were superior to their predecessors and were exploited to develop and field improved equipment. The photon counters have become so good that improvement in collecting signal photons has reached a point of strongly diminished returns. This has come about for two reasons. The first is that fielded equipment has met a large majority of the necessary applications, and further possibilities to improve mission effectiveness by generating devices that see better and farther at night are limited. Second, and more significant, the opportunity to see better and farther at night is limited by the extinction coefficient of the atmosphere. The amount of signal that can pass through the atmosphere falls off exponentially with range. This means that exponential improvements in sensitivity are required to improve range performance. Performance improvements in range are thus not worth the contortions necessary to get them.

DERIVED EXPLOITABLE TECHNOLOGY

Beginning in the late 1960s, when it was noticed that targets were brighter in the FLIR image than were the backgrounds, and that a thresholding technique might allow an alarm to sound upon the entry of a target, there have been continually intensifying efforts to process the signal from night vision devices to allow some form of machine autonomy. That activity is beyond the scope of this article.

It is safe to assume, however, that future advances in the applications of night vision technology will come from the use of multiple sensors whose signal is preprocessed and combined by computers. The potential application for this technology is enormous. The areas of use will run the gamut from assistance for manned systems to totally autonomous operation.

The sensor/processor combination will lead to automated systems that assist in or control the assessment of the battlefield and that assign resources to manage the battle. Weapons platforms will become autonomous, with the ability to navigate to target areas, decide what and when to fight, determine alternate courses of action, and be recoverable so that they can fight again another day.

Weapons will be able to determine points of attack in flight and kill with unerring accuracy.

The ultimate procurement and application question will be not performance but cost and whether men are more expendable than electronics.

LAWRENCE J. ACCHIONE

SEE ALSO: Artillery; Surveillance and Target Acquisition Equipment.

Bibliography

Bergmann, R. J., and L. P. Obert. 1980. *Propagation modeling and applications for electro-optical systems.* Fort Belvoir, Va.: Night Vision and Electro-Optics Laboratory. October.

Daly, J., F. Shields, et al. 1977. *Report of the ad hoc study group on commonality of thermal-imaging systems.* Fort Belvoir, Va.: U.S. Army Night Vision Laboratory. June.

Lloyd, J. M. 1975. *Thermal imaging systems.* New York: Plenum Press.

Milham, M. 1976. *A catalog of optical extinction data for various aerosols/smokes.* Aberdeen Proving Ground, Md.: Edgewood Arsenal. June.

Ratches, J. A., et al. 1975. *Night vision laboratory static performance model for thermal viewing systems.* Fort Monmouth, N.J.: ECOM.

NONCOMMISSIONED OFFICER

Noncommissioned officers are enlisted personnel designated as leaders or, particularly in this century, senior technicians. In armies and air forces, the principal noncommissioned officer rank is sergeant. There are a variety of sergeants, such as staff sergeant, gunnery sergeant, technical sergeant, first sergeant, and master sergeant. Junior or apprentice noncommissioned officers may be called corporals or lance corporals. In the United States, noncommissioned officers form the top six of the nine enlisted pay grades. The two highest noncommissioned officer grades were added after the Korean War and form a distinct senior level of enlisted leaders. No more than 3 percent of the enlisted members of a U.S. armed force may be serving in these two top grades at any time. Among the ranks in these top two grades are the sergeant majors, chief master sergeants, and master chief petty officers. In navies, noncommissioned officers are called petty officers. The lowest grade noncommissioned officer in a navy is a petty officer third class. After promotion to second class and then to first class petty officer, the next higher rank is chief petty officer. Chief petty officers are the highest ranking noncommissioned officers in navies. The most senior chief petty officers, equivalent to command sergeant majors, are the command master chief petty officer and the master chief petty officer.

The authors of the classic study of members of the United States Army conducted during World War II described the function of the noncommissioned officer as being "to bridge the gap between officers and men" (Stouffer et al. 1949). This critical—and often undervalued—role of first-line supervision has also been recognized in the study of the management of large civilian organizations (De Man 1929). Just as concern with the role and effectiveness of first-line supervision was a product of the Industrial Revolution, the importance of the noncommissioned officer stems from the historical transition from permanent warriors and temporary armies to permanent standing armies (Vagts 1959). Similarly in the naval service, the time passed in the early nineteenth century when adequate wartime manning in the enlisted ranks could be ensured through the combination of impressment and the utilization of merchant seamen. A system of long-term enlisted service was required. This system, augmented in England by the Royal Naval Reserve, began to provide a way of ensuring competence at sea in wartime (Lewis 1959).

Despite the importance of noncommissioned officers in the modern military organization, students of military organization—who have devoted extensive research to the recruitment, attitudes, and performance of commissioned officers—have paid surprisingly little attention to noncommissioned officers as a group. For example, a bibliography of some 1,500 studies of military organization includes two complete categories of references to military officers, with not a single reference to a study focused primarily on noncommissioned officers (Lang 1972). In part this may be because noncommissioned officers have not been regarded as military professionals. Professionalism is associated with lifetime pursuit; noncommissioned officers remain enlisted members whose service has generally been limited by the length of an enlistment, with no commitment to lifetime service. Variations on this practice are emerging. In the Federal Republic of Germany's *Bundeswehr*, one who makes the rank of sergeant may apply to become a professional. This involves an entitlement to stay until age 53 and receive retirement pay. It is more typical in contemporary Western military organizations for those members who reenlist for a second term of service to become career members in fact if not in regulation.

In some historical periods and nations, it was the warrant officer who served as the "man-in-the-middle" between commissioned officers and men. In modern military organizations, however, the role of the warrant officer has become increasingly that of the technical expert whose specialty is not conducive to promotion to the highest officer ranks. Thus, the bridge between officers and enlisted members has been increasingly that of the noncommissioned officer.

With the further mechanization and specialization of military tasks, similar forces have affected the role of the noncommissioned officer. Over the last century, noncommissioned officers have expanded as a percentage of the enlisted force (Lang 1972, 92ff.). From comprising a small percentage of the total enlisted force at the end of the nineteenth century, the requirement for noncommissioned officers has expanded until they comprise well over half of the enlisted force. This was also the case in the sea service. In the U.S. Navy, there was no insignia to distinguish petty officers from the rest of the crew until the late 1840s, and it was not until the 1880s that a clear military (as opposed to technical) authority began to appear (Downs 1986).

In large part this expansion was due to the increasing specialization and complexity of military organizations. As early as the seventeenth century, obstacles to the movement of lance corporals and sergeants into the commissioned ranks were in place. Today, these obstacles have generally been reduced for junior noncommissioned officers who are able to obtain the necessary credentials for commissioning. In the case of senior noncommissioned officers, however, there remains only a slight opportunity for a commission.

The requirement for enlisted members who are specialists in such occupations as communications, air traffic control, finance, personnel administration, supply, medical technology, and so on has spawned proposals for dual-track systems that differentiate between technicians on the one hand and combat leaders and military trainers on the other. This will probably continue to be an issue.

As with the warrant officer, the noncommissioned officer often fills a position that is primarily technical as contrasted with line supervision. In some military organizations, enlisted members may have two tracks for promotion—one for technical specialties and one for direct-line supervision. Whatever adjustments are made to accommodate these two requirements, the role of the noncommissioned officer will continue to be central to military efficiency and effectiveness.

FRANCIS M. RUSH, JR.

SEE ALSO: Officer; Warrant Officer.

Bibliography

De Man, H. 1929. *Joy in work*. London: Eden and Cedar Paul.

Downs, J. 1986. Prime hand to petty officer: The evolution of the navy noncommissioned officer. In *Life in the rank and file*, ed. D. Segal and H. Sinako. Washington, D.C.: Pergamon-Brassey's.

Lang, K. 1972. *Military institutions and the sociology of war*. Beverly Hills: Sage.

Lewis, M. 1959. *The history of the British navy*. Fair Lawn: Essential Books.

Moskos, C. 1970. *The American enlisted man*. New York: Russell Sage Foundation.

Stouffer, S., et al. 1949. *The American soldier*. Vol. 1. Princeton, N.J.: Princeton Univ. Press.

Teitler, G. 1977. *The genesis of the professional officers' corps*. Beverly Hills: Sage.

Vagts, A. 1937. *A history of militarism*. New York: W. W. Norton.

O

OFFENSE

The offensive, or offense, is the decisive military operation. (The terms *offensive*, as it pertains to military operations, and *offense*, a commonly accepted principle of war, are used interchangeably throughout this article.) The offense is designed for the destruction of enemy forces and the seizure of important land areas in order to achieve the political objectives of the conflict. Offense pursues positive goals; the objectives of defense are negative (i.e., to repel the enemy and wait until the objective can become positive). The term *offensive* has a general meaning and specifically refers to strategic and operational activities. At lower levels it is called *attack*, and at the lowest level it is called *assault*. The terms *attack* and *assault* are also applicable to actions where fire is involved (like follow on forces attack [FOFA] and assault breaker). When a defensive phase precedes the offensive, the latter is called a *counteroffensive*. A preemptive attack is an attack made in anticipation of an enemy attack within the offensive or counteroffensive.

Offensive includes the preparatory maneuvers, the proper attack against the enemy forces that are either defending themselves or undertaking a counter-offensive, and the exploitation of success. These three phases are present at all levels—strategic, tactical, and operational.

The terms *offensive, attack,* and *assault*, when referring to air or naval operations independent of land operations, have a different meaning. The counter-air offensive aims to destroy the enemy's air defense capability and to gain air superiority. The naval offensive is designed to destroy the enemy's naval forces, gain sea control, and restore the free use of maritime lines of communication. Maritime offensive operations can also be conducted against enemy maritime traffic (sea denial) or be used to project maritime power ashore by means of amphibious assaults, air raids, or ship weapons. Offensive operations can be conducted in space to destroy satellites (ASAT—i.e., antisatellite operations). The objective of an offensive in electronic warfare, as viewed by the commander, is to jam or prevent the use of enemy electronic means or to locate their positions by the use of electronic countermeasures or signal intelligence.

Finally, offensive operations can be conducted through psychological warfare to sap the enemy's morale.

History of Strategic Thought

The relative superiority of attack versus defense is commonplace in military literature. At tactical and operational levels, this assertion is justified by the fact that the attack seems to ensure initiative and decisive victory, but this is debatable at the strategic level.

According to Karl von Clausewitz, attack (*angriff*) and defense are two different forms of war, each with specific opportunities and bonds, without any reciprocal "polarity." In principle, defense, starting with denial and delay (*abwarten*) and culminating in counterattack (*ruckstoss*), is superior to attack in that defensive posture enhances the strength of the defender. Clausewitz made clear the positive and negative relationship of attack and defense. Indeed, defense may result in raising the political status of the war, forcing the attacker to exceed the limits he has tried to impose on the war.

Until the eighteenth century, war was intrinsically limited by political, economic, geographic, and technical obstacles. These obstacles were overcome in the nineteenth century, however, thus forcing strategic thought to face the problem of keeping war limited by using only military means.

The doctrine of strategic offense and war of rapid decision was basically a German doctrine. German strategy that aimed at parity in Europe and later at a "world condominium" with the British Empire required maintaining a capability so that a limited, as well as a short, war would be possible and successful for the attacker. Significantly, such a doctrine in the early twentieth century influenced other powers with strategic aims comparable to those of Germany. These included the Soviet Union, Fascist Italy, and Imperial Japan. However, for the Western powers, the chief problem was to defend their empires and prevent war; thus, the influence of German strategic thinking was limited to its operational and tactical aspects.

It is important to note that in both Imperial Japan and the USSR, as in contemporary national liberation and revolution strategies, the militaristic doctrine of rapid and decisive war was counterbalanced and often overcome by the opposite political theory of "long-lasting" war, which advocated a strategy of exhaustion, defensive-offensive posture, and indirect strategies. Such an option was justified by the assumption that Western societies could not be mobilized and would suffer losses to the same degree that socialist or underdeveloped societies might.

In Germany during the post-Napoleonic era, the idea of a short and decisive war was revived after the Prussian victory of Sadowa (1866). Shortly after the 1870–71 Franco-Prussian War, however, the German chief of staff, Gen. Helmuth von Moltke (the Elder), became convinced that the French army's improved capabilities and the possibility of a war on two fronts against both France and Russia would inhibit a strategic offensive in the west. Thus, in 1877, the German strategic concept was to plan a defensive-offensive posture in the west and a combined Austro-German offensive in the east.

The concept of a strategic offensive in the west reappeared, however, in 1888, when Moltke's successor, Gen. Alfred von Waldersee, planned a decisive

counteroffensive against France and advocated preemptive war. Simultaneously, he unsuccessfully opposed Adm. Alfred von Tirpitz's naval program,
which he feared might reinforce the British antagonism and divert resources
from the army.

Late-nineteenth-century developments in mobilization, firepower, supply,
and command and control suggested to Waldersee's successor, Gen. Alfred von
Schlieffen, the possibility of defeating France quickly in a unique and decisive
offensive battle, a large-scale Cannae. About seven-eighths of Germany's western forces were to be concentrated on the right wing, marching as a Napoleonic
bataillon carré through Belgium and northern France, enveloping the enemy's
flank with a maneuver preplanned in detail (*manoeuvre à priori*) similar to a
revolving door anchored at Metz, as described by Sir Basil Liddell Hart (1934,
pp. 68–69), thus enveloping and destroying the French army in a great and
decisive battle of annihilation or encirclement, the *vernichtungs* or *kesselschlacht*.

In the postwar period, Liddell Hart was the Schlieffen plan's main critic,
holding it (because of its failure) responsible for World War I massacres and for
what he judged to be the Clausewitzian misinterpretation of Napoleon's pre-
dicaments. Other scholars (Ritter 1956; Wallach 1967) considered the Schlieffen plan as the "beginning of the German and European misfortunes," even if
they acquitted Clausewitz and Moltke (the Elder) of the later militaristic de-
generation of German strategic thought. Liddell Hart and Ritter insisted that
underestimation of the logistical and technical difficulties were the principal
reasons for the 1914 German failure.

Although Schlieffen was strongly criticized in the 1880s by many German
generals—including von Schlichting, von Bernhardi, von Bülow, and von der
Goltz—opposing offense at all costs and maneuver a priori, none opposed him
in the decisive prewar decade.

The military historian Delbrück, developing the Clausewitzian theory of
intrinsic superiority of defense versus offense, restored the relative merits of
the strategy of attrition (*Ermattungsstrategie*) versus that of annihilation (*Niederwerfungsstrategie*) and used Frederick the Great and Pericles as two master
examples of the former. On this subject he sustained a twenty-year dispute with
a serving officer who considered it an insult to national military tradition. But
Delbrück thought that only *Niederwerfungsstrategie* was suitable for Germany
in existing prewar conditions. But after 1916, Delbrück advocated a defensive-
offensive posture in the west, with the possibility of a separate peace in order
to allow decisive offense in the east. He also criticized Erich Ludendorff's last
offensive in 1918 but never extended his criticism to the 1914 war plan. In 1919
Gen. Wilhelm Groener offered the opinion that the German defeat was caused
by the deviation of General Moltke the Younger from the basic concept of
Schlieffen's plan.

Between World Wars I and II, military reformers in all countries thought
that decisive war and strategic offense might be restored by airpower, mechanization, and industrial mobilization. Small, professional, mobile armies, combat ready and deployed in peacetime, should replace the obsolete large armies

and military mobilization that had led to trench warfare in World War I. However, not only the professional conservatism of military staffs but also innumerable technical and practical difficulties undermined such an attractive picture.

The 1939 Polish campaign differed fundamentally from the 1914 *Kesselschlacht* not only by 1918-type penetration and encirclement tactics, but also by the improved supply capability and mobility of the German right wing, although they were still largely based on horse-drawn supply trains and an all-conscript foot infantry. Airpower and motorized forces played a subsidiary role, making it impossible for the enemy to concentrate his forces on the southern flank.

Allied commanders in France were not wrong, in 1940, to expect a German "revolving-door" offensive across the same battlefields of World War I. Initially, this was exactly what the German staff planned to do, concentrate all mobile forces on the right wing. It was only later that Gen. Erich von Manstein, supported in a decisive way by Hitler, caused a change in the staff's approach. He moved the Panzergruppe Kleist (tank army) through the Ardennes, breaking down the Allied front (the Yellow Plan), then encircled the Allied left wing (the Red Plan).

Such a risky strategy succeeded due to Allied mistakes, such as the poor disposition of reserves and exaggerated accounts of German air and tank superiority, and to the masterly German operational combination of technical elements in what was called "lightning war" (blitzkrieg), a term that was neither official nor German.

According to some, the blitzkrieg operational principle was derived from the 1918 infiltration tactics of the World War I German assault infantry (*Stosstruppen*), not from the 1917 Allied tank raid at Cambrai or from the ideas the British military reformers (such as Fuller and Liddell Hart) maintained. Unlike traditional offensive operations, the lightning attack without artillery preparation should be directed against weaker points, bypassing strongholds. Ground-attack aircraft would provide continual fire support to mobile forces. Deep penetration by separate columns would exploit civilian roads and fuel supplies. Improved command and control systems would allow field commanders to coordinate dispersed units.

It was the continuing British resistance, following the French defeat, that strategically decided the war. As shown by A. Hillgruber, Hitler's 1938–40 "artichoke" strategy collapsed in the summer of 1940, forcing him into a desperate attempt at "world lightning war" (*Weltblitzkrieg*) in order to limit war at least in time if not in space and scope (Hillgruber 1965). Despite the German successes at the operational level, lightning attack operations proved inadequate to conquer the USSR, if not to defeat its first-line army. Thus, Germany was in the same situation as it had been in September 1914, having to face a siege war it could never win because of superior Allied resources.

The Japanese viewed the offensive differently. According to J. Esmein, Japanese strategic "intents" never considered the offensive as a way to decide war, even if it had been recommended, unsuccessfully, by the chief of staff, Uehara

(Esmein 1983). Also, at the operational level, the traditional "offensive" attitude of the army was counterbalanced by a "defensive" navy. The Pearl Harbor surprise and the hazardous attack at Midway were in contrast with the Japanese Imperial Navy's traditions. The fundamental choice of Japanese strategy was not between offense and defense, but between continental expansion at the expense of China and the USSR, as Tanaka theorized, or Asiatic liberation, as Ishiwara advocated in vain, preaching a long-term Asiatic crusade against the United States as Japan's ultimate mission.

At the beginning of the nuclear era, it appeared that nuclear weapons would be the principal strategic offensive means to win a war quickly, thus preventing an unlimited war. However, since the 1960s, both Soviet and Western military thinking have investigated conventional opportunities for decisive offensive operations in the nuclear era. Western analysts feared strategic scenarios that allowed the USSR to conquer Western Europe with conventional forces alone or to destroy the U.S. deterrent with a preemptive strike. Decisive technological progress in both nuclear and conventional weapons and command, control, communications, and intelligence (C^3I) systems in the 1970s restored the possibility of limited nuclear war.

Unlike Western strategy, which bases deterrence on offensive nuclear and defensive conventional forces, Soviet strategy emphasized offense at both levels, refusing to separate nuclear from conventional warfare. Soviet operational planning was based on a surprise nuclear attack, followed by conventional penetrations on a wide front, with the aim of disrupting and destroying the Western forces, taking key positions, occupying territory, and preventing invasion. This is more like the blitzkrieg than the pincer envelopments of the Great Patriotic War (World War II). Soviet military science never gave up the idea of victory (*pobieda*), which only in recent times has returned to Western military doctrine.

Attrition Offensive and Annihilation Offensive

There are two main types of offensive: attrition and annihilation. Attrition aims to weaken the enemy and is based on superiority of forces and weapons. Its goal is the direct annihilation of the enemy. Annihilation aims to destroy the enemy by hitting him with surprise and maneuver, thus neutralizing the majority of the enemy forces. It is based on attacking sensitive points in the enemy system in order to penetrate his defenses, disrupt unit cohesion, and then annihilate or capture the forces that have been surrounded or bypassed.

The attrition offensive consists of exerting uniform pressure against enemy positions. Its success is the result of the sum of each success achieved at lower levels. Such an offensive is normally frontal and directed against the enemy's main forces. Friendly forces are deployed mostly in width to fully exploit their superiority on the front of the defense system. In this type of offensive, fire across the entire front system is of paramount importance and requires enormously superior forces. It is less risky than other types of military operations but more exacting in terms of time and materiel. The attrition offensive gives the enemy more opportunity to disengage and conduct defensive actions in depth.

On the other hand, the annihilation offensive involves the concentration of the majority of forces at critical points of the enemy's system. It requires that some risks be taken elsewhere, demands speed of progress to prevent the enemy from recovering, and implies that the initial deployment of friendly forces be extended more in depth. The annihilation offensive is aimed at the flanks and the rear of the enemy—if necessary after a quick breakthrough of the front. Maneuver, speed, surprise, and firepower in depth are important. These actions can be conducted with numerically inferior forces because their power is multiplied when forces are concentrated at the critical points of the enemy system. This is obtained by exploiting not only material, but also psychological and morale effects that prevent the enemy from reacting.

A typical example of an attrition offensive is the steamroller offensive such as that at Verdun, while the annihilation offensive is typified by the blitzkrieg, the deep offensive conceived by Mikhail N. Tukhachevsky, such as the German invasion of the West in 1940. The so-called indirect approach theory of Liddell Hart is a special case of annihilation strategy.

Comparing the enemy forces to a system, the attrition offensive is applied to its boundaries, which will be increasingly compressed, while the annihilation offensive seeks to penetrate the interior of this system and destroy its cohesion. Aspects of attrition and annihilation may coexist in the same offensive operation and may be combined. The breakthrough of the enemy front to penetrate in depth and strike the flanks and the rear (and to destroy the enemy forces that have been deployed in depth) can be preceded by preemptive fires (air strikes and/or artillery).

The infiltration techniques adopted by the German infantry at the end of World War I were necessitated by the high technical-organizational standard achieved by the defense. Through penetration, the defending enemy forces are surrounded and forced to counterattack in order to break out of the encirclement, thus facilitating their annihilation. Attrition paves the way for fast penetrations in depth and annihilation of the enemy forces. In both cases, offensive operations seek to end the fighting in the shortest period of time and in the least depth, both to maintain initiative and surprise and to destroy the enemy forward forces, thereby preventing them from withdrawing and regrouping to form a defense in depth. Conversely, defense makes use of space and time as factors enhancing the combat power of one's own forces, avoiding their destruction, weakening the enemy, and extending him away from his bases. The defender thus waits for the force balance to turn in his favor, allowing him to take the offensive. The use of time and space in the defense is substantially different from their use in the offensive.

With the development of nuclear missiles, the offensive has acquired a technical superiority over defense. As a consequence, the offensive can be countered only by similar means of operations. This happened, in a less obvious way, in naval and air force combat at the tactical and operational levels where defense is structurally impossible and the occupation of air- and sea space is meaningless.

Offensive Phases

Offensive operations include three various phases that partially overlap: preparation, conduct of the attack, and exploitation of success.

Preparation encompasses all those activities and preparatory maneuvers for the attack that are intended to obtain mass and surprise. It includes planning for the attack, air and land reconnaissance of enemy defenses, diversionary attacks to render the main thrust sectors vulnerable, and relocation of friendly forces to assembly areas and attack positions near the line of departure. The preparation phase also includes air and land fire strikes to impair the enemy system, prevent the maneuver of enemy forces, and facilitate the penetration of enemy defenses.

The second phase of offensive operations, the conduct of an attack, requires a combination of fire and movement to make contact with enemy forces and to launch the attack. An attack can be conducted many times along the axis of advance to destroy or disrupt enemy forces in depth. It ends with consolidation of captured positions that can be used against possible enemy counterattacks. Consolidation, a temporary defensive posture, involves, in part, the arrival/ commitment of reserve forces with which to continue the penetration and exploit the success in depth.

Finally, exploitation of success involves penetration in increasing depth to objectives coinciding with key points of the enemy system until decisive results are obtained—whether by encirclement or destruction of the enemy forces bypassed. Timely utilization of reserves is essential for the final success and to prevent the enemy from withdrawing or counterattacking the penetration and taking advantage of the vulnerability of its flanks. Commanders must give priority to penetration in depth, which is conducted in successive stages to destroy the enemy units encircled. Dispersion of resources is to be avoided.

The outcome of exploitation of success depends heavily on logistic sustainability of the friendly forces penetrating in depth and on the capability of those forces to disrupt the enemy's logistic system. Exploitation of success ends with the consolidation of final objectives, or of any captured position, before the attacking forces lose their offensive capability and become exposed to risk of destruction by the defender's counterattacks.

Principles of the Offense

The offense is a commonly accepted principle of military doctrine. As such, it is very similar to the principle of initiative and with it the freedom of action. Offensive operations stress the need to prevail over the enemy and to exploit opportunities with aggressiveness. Accordingly, offensive operations are governed by principles.

Prerequisites for an offensive are: initiative and speed of maneuver, penetration, and exploitation of success to deny the enemy time to react. The additional principles that an offensive must follow, discussed in the following paragraphs, are those of mass and, consequently, economy of force, maneuver, unity of command, surprise, and security.

The principle of mass takes different forms in the attrition and annihilation offensives. In the former, it requires concentration of firepower and forces against the enemy in order to engage him in his forward positions and destroy him to prevent his withdrawal and a further defense in the rear positions. The annihilation offensive, as stated earlier, is not designed to destroy the enemy forces progressively, but rather to strike critical points of the enemy system, disrupt its cohesion, and penetrate in depth, disposing of enemy forces encircled in the forward positions later. In terms of numbers, it is a specialized or concentrated mass rather than a large one. The annihilation offensive must seek to acquire local predominance and is based on surprise, speed, and flexibility to minimize frontal engagements. The annihilation of enemy forces opposing the main thrust is only a means, not an end, as in the attrition offensive. Speed is the decisive factor to prevent the enemy from reacting, from protecting his own vulnerabilities by means of withdrawal. The theoretical value of mass is given by Lanchester's quadratic (square) law, which demonstrates that in a frontal engagement the losses of one of the contenders are in inverse proportion to the square of the quantity of his troops and in direct proportion to the enemy forces. Speed and surprise are multiplying factors of mass since they not only affect the material dimensions of the enemy system but also have mental and psychological consequences on its cohesion.

Linked with the principle of mass are those of economy of force, maneuver, and unity of command.

Economy of force means that to concentrate combat power behind the main effort, a commander must allocate minimum essential power to secondary efforts, even if he has to accept some risks.

Maneuver allows both the concentration of power in those sectors where an attack is to be mounted and realization of the opportunity to conduct a surprise attack, that is, to hit enemy vulnerabilities (which can be caused through diversionary maneuvers and deception) and rapidly penetrate in depth, after the mass has achieved a breakthrough, in order to prevent enemy reactions. Maneuver requires concentration of power not only in space but also in time so as to maintain in depth the power necessary to give an attack progressive momentum. To this end, adequate measures must be taken both to reinforce the forward effort and exploit favorable situations. The attack can proceed while a sufficient mass is maintained. However, once the reserves are expended, the attack is vulnerable to counteroffensive reaction by the defender. Maneuver alone cannot gain success, as it also requires successive allocation of power in order to destroy the opposing enemy forces. Maneuver nevertheless is the basis for success. In a counteroffensive the commander's fundamental decision is when to commence action to prevent the enemy from consolidating.

Unity of command is necessary to coordinate the various actions associated with the main and supporting attacks, to exploit mass and surprise, and to obtain the best results through the synergy of the elements of forces available.

Surprise is a multiplying factor of power and mass. It consists of attacking the enemy at an unexpected moment and place, in an unexpected way, and before he can effectively react. Concurrent with surprise are speed, secrecy, deception, concurrent diversionary actions, exploitation of adverse weather and terrain, use of new weapons systems, adoption of unusual tactics, or employment of unexpected strength. For surprise to be completely successful, a speedy progression and strength of forces sufficient to achieve the final objectives are required.

Security is conceptually the opposite of the principle of surprise. This does not mean that it is without risk. The more a successful attack is based on maneuver and surprise, the higher are the risks. Security requires a reasonable appreciation of the enemy's capabilities and above all his reaction time. It requires prearrangement of ad hoc measures that can be implemented with a proper redeployment of reserves designed to reinforce the attack, coupled with effective surveillance and reconnaissance. In this case, the best security lies in a speedy advance so as not to allow the enemy any time for reaction. In general, the more risks that are accepted (within reason), the greater is the success. There are comparatively few risks (assuming the superiority of forces) in an offensive based on the attrition of the enemy; they are enormous in an offensive based on maneuver and surprise. With the progression of penetration, the thrust of the attack slows down, partly due to the need to assign an ever-increasing proportion of forces to security duties. Exhaustion of offensive capability happens when mass cannot be maintained and its forces are assigned to security duties to prevent possible counteroffensives by the defender.

Offensive and Defensive Weapons and Negotiations on Conventional Stability

It has never been possible to clearly define whether a weapon or a weapons system is offensive or defensive. For example, the armor of a fully protected knight gave him both an offensive and defensive capability. The construction of forts along frontiers not only gave protection to the borders but created operational bases suitable for operations into enemy territory. Armor allows tanks to penetrate enemy defenses with a certain degree of protection. Light infantry units equipped with antitank and anti-helicopter weapons, although not particularly suitable for offensive actions in open terrain, can replace mechanized and armored units, which in turn can be employed in offensive operations. In some cases, especially in difficult terrain, light infantry can be employed in the attack. Maritime mine warfare can be pursued with either defensive or offensive goals. The appearance of multirole weapons systems in air, maritime, and land operations has made the distinction between an offensive and a defensive weapon more difficult. Tanks are essential for the defense to cut off penetrations. A ship can be used to defend a coastal area or a merchant convoy and to attack enemy warships, merchant ships, or coasts. The point is that "the offensive or defensive nature of a weapon depends on the observer's point of view: if it is in front, it is offensive; if it is behind, it is defensive." In principle, it is impossible to infer the offensive or defensive nature of a weapon from its technical data because offense and defense are a combination of defensive and offensive operations.

The offensive or defensive character of a weapon is determined by its use. Some weapons are better suited for offense, others for defense. This defensive or offensive character, however, is not related to the weapon itself but to the general structures, its possible roles in these structures, and above all the tasks assigned ad hoc. For example, the offensive or defensive nature of a tank depends on its quantity and organic position as well. A reasonably limited quantity of tanks can represent an essential element of a defensive structure as they may be used to launch a counterattack, which may be essential to hold the defense positions. A concentration of a large number of tanks in armored units gives it an offensive character.

Tanks, artillery, attack helicopters, and mobile antiaircraft and bridging units are systems more suitable for offensive operations. Less suitable are permanent fortifications, mines, antitank weapons, and fixed or semi-mobile antiaircraft weapons. The problem is assessing the operational outcome or technical performance of available weapons. The problem is not one of theory. In arms control negotiations, it is essential to identify the force structure that allows the realization of stability.

The problem, in military terms, is difficult not only because of qualitative factors that cannot be assessed in an unequivocal way, but also because of aspects that cannot be quantified such as morale, leadership, and reaction time of the political-military decision-making system.

The distinction between offensive and defensive weapons and force structure—or the preeminence of offense over defense (or vice versa)—and the way to correct it is considered of paramount importance in arms control negotiations where security is viewed as mutual rather than unilateral. The possibility of establishing reasonably stable structures derives not so much from a force balance as from the possible distinction between offensive arms or structures and defensive arms or structures. In other words, mutual security should be ensured by the predominance of defense over attack and, failing this, by adoption of measures necessary to redress the imbalance between defense and attack to favor the former. In the absence of these conditions it is impossible to identify intrinsically stable structures and approach the problem of arms control unequivocally.

In sum, the qualification of a weapon or a structure as "offensive" or "defensive" depends on the general context in which they might be employed and implies that the various technical inputs be changed into operational outputs.

General Types of Offensive Operations

SURPRISE ATTACK

A surprise attack is one where warning time is so short that it does not allow the enemy time to organize a defense. A surprise attack can never be ruled out, although modern surveillance systems make the likelihood of such an attack low, especially at the strategic level. It exists only if sufficient combat power by one side allows it to obtain established objectives.

The problem of a surprise strategic attack has become a very important factor in arms control negotiations. Ruling out the possibility of a surprise attack involves the adoption of operational measures such as confidence- and security-building measures (CSBMs) and structural measures such as redressing imbalances and the reduction and restructuring of forces or the withdrawal of troops from borders.

PREEMPTIVE ATTACK

A preemptive attack is an operation, undertaken before an imminent enemy attack. It is designed to disrupt the enemy system, inflict losses, and seize the initiative; it can be launched by a defender when the attacker is preparing an offensive.

HASTY ATTACK OR ATTACK AGAINST POORLY ORGANIZED POSITIONS

A hasty attack is launched when the enemy is unexpectedly met face-to-face or when a favorable opportunity must be exploited. In the phases following an attack, it is typical to maintain the momentum of a penetration so as to deny the enemy the initiative, to prevent his residual forces from withdrawing to positions in depth and avoiding encirclement or annihilation, or to prevent him from moving his reserves forward to fill the breach or launch a counterattack.

A hasty attack requires little planning and is launched against an unorganized or moving enemy. This type of attack is normal at the lower tactical levels.

DELIBERATE ATTACK OR ATTACK AGAINST STRONG DEFENSIVE POSITIONS

This is a methodical offensive action that concentrates combat power successively (forces and firepower) to gain local superiority and overcome the enemy. A deliberate attack develops through main and subsidiary efforts. It is preceded by recognition and reconnaissance of the enemy system in order to define the attack plan and to weaken the enemy through firepower. It can also include preliminary combat actions that are designed to destroy advance enemy positions or to take some of them, both to facilitate successive attacks and to deceive the enemy as to the real intentions of the attacker.

A deliberate attack is normally directed against a strongly organized enemy defense. After the preliminary phases, its planning must be adapted to the new situation. At a higher level, it can generate hasty attacks at the lower tactical levels.

ADVANCE TO CONTACT

This type of operation is designed to seek and maintain contact with the main enemy force and to create the most favorable conditions for an attack. It is based on maximum speed so that the enemy is allowed minimum time to strengthen his defense. Advance to contact includes observation and reconnaissance and, if necessary and deemed appropriate, can also include strikes against the enemy's covering forces to destroy them.

The advance to contact formation normally includes, in addition to the main body, the advance guard, flanking guards, and, possibly, a rear guard for protection.

RECONNAISSANCE IN FORCE

This is an offensive action before the attack that is undertaken to obtain information about the enemy's location, capability, and reaction. Normally, it is conducted against a limited objective.

EXPLOITATION OF SUCCESS

This is an offensive operation that follows the attack. It must take place immediately and is designed to carry success into the depth of the enemy's system once his defensive positions are disrupted.

At the lower tactical level it is aimed at expanding the effects of a successful attack and denying the enemy time for counter-maneuver. Exploitation of success requires a timely and firm commitment of reserves.

PURSUIT

It is through pursuit, the final stage of an attack, that the enemy forces in the advance positions that escaped encirclement are prevented from organizing further defenses and launching counterattacks. Pursuit must be conducted with maximum possible momentum, maintaining a sufficient mass through the utilization of all available resources and projecting logistic support, which is what determines its success.

Specific Types of Offensive Operations

RAID

A raid is an offensive operation, usually on a small scale, that is undertaken to destroy installations and elements of the enemy system (especially C^3I), capture prisoners, secure information, inflict damage (in particular to the supporting elements), oblige the enemy to disperse his forces in security tasks, and delay the arrival of reserves or supplies. A raid involves a penetration of hostile territory by land-, air-, or seaborne groups and is characterized by surprise, swiftness, and quick withdrawal. A raid can be carried out by forces both in the offensive and the defensive postures.

ASSAULT

An assault is the final phase of an attack, when units in contact with the enemy's advance defense positions make a decisive effort to destroy them. It requires superior forces and weapons, especially if it is a frontal assault.

MEETING ENGAGEMENTS

Typical meeting engagements are those that occur at the beginning of a war or between the attacking forces penetrating in depth and the defense forces advancing to counterattack. These are hasty attacks whose success depends largely on the speed of reaction and on the capability to seize the initiative.

COUNTERATTACK

This is an attack conducted by a defending force against an enemy attacking force for the specific purpose of regaining lost ground, destroying enemy penetrating forces, or gaining the time necessary to reorganize defensive positions in depth. A counterattack allows the defender to increase the opportunities to use his initiative, reducing those of the attacker and preventing the achievement of the attacker's objective of destroying enemy forces or seizing key terrain.

DIVERSIONARY ATTACK (FEINT)

A diversionary attack is designed to draw the enemy's attention away from the main attack. Minimal forces are employed to deceive the enemy. A diversionary attack aims to identify vulnerable points in the enemy system that the main attack can exploit. It is usually conducted by a smaller force than that conducting the main attack, on a wider front, with forces extended in depth, and with few reserves.

DEMONSTRATION

When an attacking force makes contact with the enemy system but does not engage the enemy, it is called a *demonstration*.

HOLDING ATTACK (SECONDARY ATTACK)

A holding attack is a form of diversionary attack conducted against the front of the enemy forces to facilitate the success of the main effort that takes place in adjoining areas. Its purpose is to divert the enemy's attention from the sector of the principal attack and induce him to commit his reserves prematurely. A holding attack can also be designed to hold the enemy forces in their frontal positions, thus preventing them from disengaging and escaping envelopment. It is the most common type of attack subsidiary to, or in support of, the main effort.

In short, a holding attack is a measure that on the one hand facilitates a concentration of a mass superior to that of the defense at the points where the attack is launched and, on the other, allows surprise and maintenance of the initiative.

Maritime Offensive

The main goal of maritime military power is to achieve navigation of the seas to one's own advantage and to the detriment of the enemy. This means free use of sea lanes, both to maintain one's war effort and to bring the offense to the enemy territory. To achieve this goal, two main strategies have been developed throughout the course of history: one, "battle" strategy, aimed at the annihilation of the enemy forces; two, "blockade" strategy, focused on the paralysis or confinement of enemy forces.

These strategies, however, can be pursued only when the naval force balance is favorable. In reaction to this, the weaker navies have developed and perfected other suitable strategies—for example, *guerre de course*, of which privateering was a major form in the seventeenth and eighteenth centuries, and submarine warfare against maritime traffic, its modern version.

All of the above strategies are offensive because at sea defensive operations, even tactical, seem doomed to failure or are less profitable. The absence of the terrain factor—with the exception of some particular cases—deprives defense at sea of its principal strong point, while the offensive continues to enjoy the advantages of mass, initiative, and surprise. The enormous production of resources and the possible scenarios of a modern war make a survey of maritime operations more complex and less clearly defined.

The distinction between offensive and defensive can be easier—but this is only a simplification—when naval air operations are specifically linked with land (the defense of one's own and an attack against someone else's territory). In this case, *defensive* operations (although in some cases tactical offensive proceedings are involved) are those designed to protect the national territory and maritime frontiers from sea-launched attacks. *Offensive* operations, on the other hand, are those directed against someone else's territory.

Defensive operations include all those operations that modern terminology defines as "power projection" into enemy territory (e.g., landing of forces by means of amphibious assault, coast bombardment, and air and missile attack). Offensive operations include coastal patrolling, mine barrage of possible lanes of approach to friendly internal or territorial waters, defensive mining, interception and neutralization of forces directed toward friendly territory, and running of a blockade.

Naval air operations related to an attack against enemy territory or the defense of friendly territory represent only one aspect of maritime warfare. The sea is a large line of communication, and as such, its use is essential in the strategy of maritime nations. In this context, naval air operations are intended both to keep secure friendly maritime lines of communication and to deny the enemy free use of his own. These goals can be attained both through offensive and defensive operations. Those operations against lines of communication have an offensive connotation even when conducted through static means (barrages, minefields, etc.). Conversely, the defense of lines of communication can be considered, in terms of operations, either defensive or offensive according to the situation.

In general, operations that give direct protection to naval formations or maritime traffic and those that interdict obligatory maritime routes (barrages) are defensive in nature, while those designed for the control of maritime areas of interest (which must indirectly give security to friendly lines of communication), by searching and neutralizing the enemy forces in these areas, are offensive in nature.

With the exception of those cases in which a particular oceanographic situation can be exploited, defensive strategies at sea are rather ineffective and are adopted only when more adequate measures are not practicable. An example is the protection of traffic, especially against the submarine threat, which requires an enormous amount of resources to establish an effective screen. In World War II, the battle of the Atlantic was won by the Allies when new systems (antisubmarine aircraft) were put into service and where, to improve direct protection of convoys, long-range search-and-destroy offensive operations against Axis submarines became possible.

The range and kill capability of modern weapons have given the attacker additional advantages. The first to attack can gain an advantage that often may be decisive. For this reason, even the most strictly defensive tactics require that defense be conducted with an adequate depth in space in order to oppose the offense as soon and as far as possible from the protected objectives.

Air Force Offensives

Air operations also have both offensive and defensive characteristics and aims. Offensive operations are considered to be those conducted to search for, and attack, the enemy, choosing the right moment and place. The same operations can be defensive in nature when conducted to preempt enemy initiatives.

Offensive air operations can be a combination of offensive and defensive air missions. Likewise, defensive air operations can be a part of an operation that is offensive on the whole. Since offensive and defensive air operations often have to rely on the same resources and are often conducted in the same airspace and at the same time, they cannot be considered separately. A "counter–air" offensive is a typical offensive operation designed to attain air superiority, which is often a prerequisite for air support of land, air, and maritime forces. Its goal is the annihilation of enemy air bases, antiaircraft defenses, and the airplanes on the ground.

The mass employment of aircraft during World War I gave birth to the "air dominance" doctrine—that is, a strategically offensive deployment of the air force to destroy the resistance and war support capability of enemy populations—that was promoted by Douhet, Trenchard, and Mitchell. A successful result of that conflict could have been possible with massive air attacks against civil and military objectives. The doctrine of "air dominance" was the basis of the massive bombardments during World War II. However, its implementation was a failure. After the war, the doctrine was viewed by NATO as the "dagger and shield"—where the dagger represented the air forces and the shield the land forces—to exploit the major element of its strength in the 1950s. Nuclear weapons gave the doctrine of "air dominance" the technical power required for success. In NATO's nuclear strategy, this doctrine is still present in the planning of decisive first and second strikes.

CARLO JEAN

SEE ALSO: Blitzkrieg; Defense; Principles of War; Strategy; Tactics.

Bibliography

Aron, R. 1976. *Penser la guerre. Clausewitz.* Paris: Gallimard.
Esmein, J. 1983. *Un demi plus.* Paris: Fondation pour les études de défense nationale.
Hillgruber, A. 1982. *Hitler's strategie. Politik und Kriegsführung 1940–1941.* München: Bernard und Graefe Verlag.
Leebaert, D., ed. 1981. *Soviet military thinking.* London: Allen and Unwin.

Liddell Hart, B. H. 1934. *A history of the world war 1914–18.* London: Faber and Faber.

Mette, S. 1938. *Vom Geist deutscher Feldherren. Genie und Technik 1888–1918.* Zurich: Scientia.

Paret, P., ed. 1986. *Makers of modern strategy from Machiavelli to the nuclear age.* Princeton, N.J.: Princeton Univ. Press.

Ritter, G. 1956. *Schlieffenplan. Kritik eines Mythos.* München: Oldenburg.

Rusconi, G. E. 1987. *Rischio 1914. Come si decide una guerra.* Bologna: Il Mulino.

Vigor, P. H. 1983. *The Soviet theory of blitzkrieg.* London: Macmillan.

Wallach, J. L. 1967. *Das Dogma der Vernichtungsschlacht. Die Lehren von Clausewitz und Schlieffen und ihre Wirkungen in zwei Weltkriegen.* Frankfurt am Main: Bernard und Graefe.

OFFICER

The term *officer* can be used in many ways. There are two major approaches to understanding its use in the context of military organizations. One approach is functional and focuses primarily on the officer as a leader of forces in armed combat. This approach dates from the beginning of recorded history. It relegates the officer's ancillary technical and administrative functions to a minor role. Where officership is viewed in terms of the leadership of military forces in the conduct of military operations, or as the capacities and skills associated with such leadership, the possession of military office such as a commission is not a prerequisite (Keegan 1987).

The second approach is organizational and focuses on the role of the officer within the bureaucratic authority structure of the modern nation-state. Indeed, the first use of the term *officer* to refer to a person occupying a position of authority in the army, navy, or mercantile marine, particularly a person holding a commission, dates back only to 1565 (*Oxford Universal Dictionary* 1955). The focus on the possession of military office and on the qualifications for such office is, in many respects, complementary to the functional approach. Combat leadership and effective generalship remain important factors. However, the size of modern military organizations, their technological and administrative complexity, and their position within the nation-state form and bound the status of the contemporary military officer (Fig. 1).

Prior to 1800, military office was typically a part-time pursuit rather than a full-time profession, and officership was directly related to social position. By the end of the nineteenth century, however, a corps of full-time professional officers existed in most major countries (Huntington 1957).

The emergence of an organized corps of officers recruited on the basis of education and skill rather than social origins, serving on a full-time basis rather than only during periods of conflict, and regarding military service as a profession rather than a part-time vocation is an outcome of two historical processes. One is the centralization of state authority; the second is the Industrial Revolution and the associated division of labor (Abrahamsson 1972).

Figure 1. An example of an officer: Gen. Colin Powell, former chairman of the U.S. Joint Chiefs of Staff. (SOURCE: U.S. Department of Defense)

The centralization of state authority resulted in a military organization recruited nationally rather than internationally. It also led to an officer who was recruited, initially in part and later almost entirely, from middle-class subjects of the state. This replaced an officer corps of nobles who could serve numerous masters sequentially.

Technological and logistical innovations in the art of war associated with the Industrial Revolution brought with them a demand for more complex military skills and techniques, an associated proliferation in the division of labor in military organizations, and an increased requirement for coordination and integration of military activities. Professional military schools, which were started in France, England, and Prussia late in the eighteenth century and exported to the United States (West Point, est. 1802), reflected these changes. They both responded to and furthered the transition from an aristocratic to a professional officer corps.

The problems associated with the capability to lead and direct the equipment and employment of huge armies and navies with increasingly complex and diverse activities were paralleled by similar developments in industrial organization. Subordination and discipline are equally important to the successful operation of both modern economic enterprise and contemporary armed forces.

The Industrial Revolution brought with it the requirement for workers to exercise judgment in the performance of their tasks. As the traditional authority system that was dependent on face-to-face relations became less relevant, methods of harnessing this discretion in support of organizational goals became increasingly important (Bendix 1956). Similarly, in military organizations, "as more and more impact has gone into the hitting power of weapons, necessitating ever-widening deployments in the forces of battle, the quality of the initiative in the individual has become the most praised of the military virtues" (Marshall 1947, p. 22).

Thus, officership in the military profession today differs in many important respects from officership as it existed in the military of the late eighteenth century. The transition from officership based on ascribed status and traditional authority to officership as a full-time profession with selection on the basis of achievement rather than social origin paralleled a similar transition from traditional authority to bureaucratic leadership and management in industry.

The pace and details of this transition varied from nation to nation. For the first three-quarters of the nineteenth century, for example, the purchase system, whereby an individual first bought his commission and then paid for each subsequent step in rank, remained in place in the British army (Woodham-Smith 1953, pp. 21–25). Even after the institution of new procedures (the purchase system was virtually abolished in 1870), the majority of British officers were amateurs, expecting up to six months of leave a year and oriented primarily to such civil concerns as estate management (Harries-Jenkins 1973).

Garnier's (1977) empirical data on British army officer selection outcomes indicate that particularistic criteria related to social class are still important in the selection of British army officers despite the technological sophistication of that army. The continuation of a strong relationship between social class and officer selection does not, however, minimize the significance of the more general transformation from particularistic to universalistic (ascription to achievement) selection criteria. In part this is a matter of degree. The relatively high proportion of British army officers with upper-class social origins today is not the same as the situation in the 1830s, when more than half of all German, British, and Swedish officers were of noble background.

More important is the fact that the contemporary officer's job remains a full-time pursuit rather than an occasional one. Advancement and continued service are now primarily dependent upon meeting specified standards of performance. Moreover, the officer's authority derives from the office itself and is no longer simply another aspect of the authority associated with the status of the officer in the society at large. The officer's authority over other military members is strictly limited by military law, and the authority to act on behalf of the state is similarly circumscribed by delegated organizational authority in place of personal authority.

Although the extent to which these practices are institutionalized in any country varies, appointment age, the maximum age, and years of service permitted for officers in specified grades are nearly always established. In the United States these rules have been translated into detailed federal law covering nearly every aspect of the appointment, promotion, separation, and retirement of officers, including officers of the national guard and reserve whose service is not full-time. Although the specific authority for such rules varies from nation to nation, the results are similar, and the position and authority of the contemporary officer are dependent upon these rules.

FRANCIS M. RUSH, JR.

SEE ALSO: Enlisted Personnel; Noncommissioned Officer; Rank and Insignia of Rank; Warrant Officer.

Bibliography

Abrahamsson, B. 1972. *Military professionalization and political power*. Beverly Hills, Calif.: Sage.

Bendix, R. 1956. *Work and authority in industry*. New York: Wiley.

Garnier, M. 1977. Technology, organizational culture, and recruitment in the British military academy. In *World perspectives in the sociology of the military*, ed. G. Kourvetaris and B. Dobratz. New Brunswick, N.J.: Transaction Books.

Harries-Jenkins, G. 1973. The Victorian military and the social order. *Journal of Political and Military Sociology* 1:279–89.

Huntington, S. 1957. *The soldier and the state*. Cambridge, Mass.: Harvard Univ. Press.

Janowitz, M. 1974. *Sociology and the military establishment*. Beverly Hills, Calif.: Sage.

Keegan, J. 1987. *The mask of command*. New York: Viking.

Lang, K. 1972. *Military institutions and the sociology of war*. Beverly Hills, Calif.: Sage.

Lewis, M. 1948. *England's sea-officers*. London: Allen & Unwin.

Marshall, S. 1947. *Men against fire*. New York: William Morrow.

Teitler, G. 1977. *The genesis of the professional officers' corps*. Beverly Hills, Calif.: Sage.

Van Doorn, J. 1969. *Military profession and military regimes*. The Hague: Mouton.

Woodham-Smith, C. 1953. *The reason why*. New York: McGraw-Hill.

ORDNANCE CORPS

Usage of the term *ordnance* is not uniform. One definition, "great guns such as cannon or artillery," is indicated in the context of its historical background. In later usage, however, ordnance embraces all kinds of military weapons, munitions, missiles, and agents and the related apparatuses necessary to activate or discharge them.

The ordnance corps is the branch of an army that procures, stores, and issues weapons and munitions, in some cases including military vehicles. In accordance with its Anglo-Saxon roots, an ordnance corps is usually established in those armies that in principle can be traced back to the British or U.S. armies. The range of ordnance corps responsibilities differs from army to army. For example, maintenance tasks are included as part of ordnance in the U.S. Army but not in that of the United Kingdom.

The kinds of duties performed by an army's ordnance corps are principally related to the functional area of logistics. In civilian usage, the term *logistics* originally had a relatively narrow meaning and application, such as production logistics or consumer logistics. Militarily, the meaning of *logistics* has generally been rather broad; it is probably best defined as "the creation and sustained support of weapons and armed forces so that they can be tactically employed in order to attain strategic objectives."

Throughout the history of armies, the influence of logistics on the successful outcome of battles has been significant, but it was only in the nineteenth century that a systematic analysis was made of the problems involved in the setting up of armies. Jomini was one of the first to make a distinction among strategy, tactics, and logistics. However, today's logistic problems distinguish themselves from those of the past because of the far greater technological complexity of weapons systems and the greatly increased consumption rates of supplies of all kinds on the modern battlefield. Fighting a modern battle depends to a large extent on the ability to provide continual logistic support to combat forces.

Royal Army Ordnance Corps

ORIGINS

The English ordnance department antedates the British standing army, of which it has since become a part (1857). "The Master of Ordnance, later known as Master General, dates back to the 15th century, the first officially recorded holder of the appointment being Nicholas Merburg in the year 1414. *His function was the supply of war materiel* which is still the primary duty of the RAOC [Royal Army Ordnance Corps]" (Fernyhough 1980).

The master general of ordnance held an important political post. He was the adviser to the king and Parliament on military matters. In the early days selection was not confined to soldiers; masters general of ordnance became cabinet ministers and were independent of the army or navy. In this context it should be noted that only an administrative body directly constituted by the government was able to equip the artillery and the engineers with their task-specific material. Obviously, requirements for cannon and gunpowder could not be satisfied by local resources as could the needs of infantry and cavalry.

Few people, and hardly any soldiers at all, were educated in the technology and economics of this matter. The consequence was that, for many centuries, only the civilian element of the government was qualified to deal with such problems.

The office of ordnance played an important part in the development of the British Empire over nearly three centuries. Its main responsibilities were setting up forts and barracks at every new outpost, providing accommodation for the troops and civil government, and caring for Crown lands. In 1683 the five principal officers (lieutenant general, surveyor general, clerk of the ordnance, storekeeper general, and clerk of delivery) formed a board of management, the Board of Ordnance. Chairman of the board was the master general; decisions were taken by vote.

In those days the army consisted of cavalry and infantry. There was little need for a standing army in Britain, but it was gradually realized that an army at home was needed to maintain British garrisons abroad. The task of the Board of Ordnance was to provide war materiel for garrisons overseas and to supply engineer and artillery units. For a long time, the Corps of Royal Engineers included only officers; the artisans were civilians.

The technical corps continued under the control of the master general of ordnance for many years. The Board of Ordnance saw to their clothing and equipment and therefore they were better cared for than the rest of the army. The officers were separately selected and trained in the Royal Military Academy, Woolwich, while the cavalry and infantry officer cadets went to the Royal Military College at Sandhurst.

The Board of Ordnance clothed and equipped its soldiers by means of centralized contracts. After inspection at the Tower, supplies were distributed through the ordnance corps.

The situation in the army (cavalry and infantry) was very different. Regiments were raised by a form of contract between the king and some nobleman who became colonel. A regiment was treated as the personal property of the colonel, who at first clothed it entirely as he pleased.

At that time several departments dealt with army matters. They were not organized under a coordinating head and had no clearly defined responsibilities. These departments and officials included the secretary of state for war and colonies, the secretary at war, the commander in chief, and the paymaster general. In addition to these, the board of general officers supervised the clothing and regimental equipment of the cavalry and infantry. The Board of Ordnance, under the master general, commanded and equipped the artillery and engineers and supplied the whole army in the field with arms, ammunition, greatcoats, and camp equipment. The commissariat supplied forage and fuel overseas but not at home. Finally, there was a combined army and ordnance medical service under three masters: the secretary at war, commander in chief, and Board of Ordnance. Its staff consisted of doctors and purveyors (hospital quartermasters).

1855 TO 1904

The Crimean War in 1854 dramatically demonstrated the inherent problems of the fragmented responsibility. Logistics played a far greater role in the Crimea than it had in the Peninsula War or in Flanders, and the resources and experience to mount a coherent, successful operation were lacking.

The main reforms that followed in 1855 can be summarized as follows. There was no longer a secretary at war, nor were "war" and "colonies" mixed in one department. A secretary of state for war was responsible for all civil work connected with the army. The Board of Ordnance became part of the War Office and the office of master general was abolished. All civil duties were switched to the secretary of state; military units were placed under the commander in chief. The board of general officers was abolished; soldiers' clothing and appointments were provided by the state. The commissariat was transferred from the treasury to the secretary of state, and a permanent military transport corps was created.

Although the structure of army administration was now simplified, unified control was still lacking. Previously there had been two armies, each supplied and administered separately. Now there was one army with two heads: the secretary of state for war—a civilian and a politician—was responsible for supply and finance; the commander in chief was responsible for military efficiency but not for economy.

When the War Office accepted responsibility for equipping the entire army, the amateurish methods of supply used during the Crimean War changed to a carefully worked-out system. Procedures were instituted to control the stocks of equipment; a military store officer had to open an account for every unit he equipped. Next it became accepted that any officer of the military store department could be called upon to accompany troops in time of war. A staff of clerks, artificers, and laborers was to be provided to accompany the force.

In 1865 the military store staff corps was formed; it later became the Army Ordnance Corps (AOC). The original personnel of the corps numbered 200 and increased to nearly 400 by 1869.

Noncombatant status was anomalous. The ordnance officer was considered a highly trained and well-paid specialist, but he was isolated from the rest of the army. The supply of arms and equipment became a more and more important factor in the success or failure of military operations, but this aspect of logistics tended to be overlooked due to the isolation of the service directly responsible for it.

1904 TO 1918

The next milestone in the history of the ordnance corps occurred in 1904 when a committee under Lord Esher advocated further reorganization in the structure of army control. Under its proposals, which were accepted, the dual control of the army ceased and the Army Council was formed. It survives today, now known as the Army Board of the Ministry of Defence.

The military members of the Army Council in 1904 were the chief of the imperial staff (CIGS), the adjutant general (AG) for personnel, and the quartermaster general (QMG) for materiel. The ordnance services, now called the Army Ordnance Department (AOD), were placed entirely under the QMG.

The World War of 1914–18 showed the deficiencies of the organization and installations. At the start of the war Britain's army was small, but it was the most highly trained and best equipped in Europe. It was virtually destroyed in the first year of the war, and no attempt was made to keep a portion of this valuable manpower as a cadre for the army that was ultimately to be created.

The need for an adequate supply system was felt almost at once. The fighting at Mons and Le Cateau called for extensive and urgent replenishment, but no adequate system existed. Despite the logistic experiences of the South

African War (1899–1902), the true significance of supply was not yet recognized. Practice was that when its equipment or supplies ran short, a division was withdrawn from the line, even during heavy fighting, to be reequipped. But this did not work. Military leaders realized that an efficient supply system was essential and that ordnance must participate in the logistic planning for a campaign. The British army that began in 1914 in France with one ammunition train and a few hundred tons of reserve had, in October 1918, eight great depots of 336,000 tons of ammunition and more than 120 ammunition railheads, giving final delivery to the enemy of more than 9,000 tons of shot and shell a day.

1918 TO 1945

In November 1918 the AOD and AOC were combined into the Royal Army Ordnance Corps, illustrating the increasing value of the ordnance services and giving recognition of their achievements in the war by the grant of the title "Royal." The Duke of York became the first RAOC colonel in chief; he succeeded to the throne as King George VI in 1936.

From then on, the RAOC was recognized as an important element in the efficiency of a modern army. Prior to the world depression in 1929, two important decisions were made: (1) the corps in 1927 was transferred from the QMG to the master general of ordnance (MGO), and branches of the Ordnance Directorate at the War Office were redesignated MGO7, 8, and 9; and (2) in the late 1920s responsibility for the supply, storage, and repair of all vehicles was transferred to the RAOC.

Many efforts at forming an up-to-date army ceased with the 1929 depression. By the end of the depression it was apparent that any British army of the future must be mechanized and that an efficient organization for the supply of vehicles and spares was necessary.

At the outbreak of World War II in September 1939, the RAOC was understaffed and overcivilianized. The small military staff was fully engaged in peacetime duties, and the ordnance services had neither the capacity nor the training for war. The corps's noncombatant status isolated it from the rest of the army (up to 1941), it was not in a position to influence logistic concepts, and it was rarely consulted.

The RAOC started with a few hundred officers and a few thousand men of the regular and territorial armies; during the course of only four years it developed into a highly efficient organization of 8,000 officers and 130,000 men.

The corps provided logistic support that had several main features. It maintained a controlling headquarters at the War Office, the Ordnance Directorate. The corps also created a United Kingdom base for the supply of all items of ordnance concern to all theaters and developed a comprehensive field force organization that provided a reliable and flexible system for the maintenance of a field army. In addition, the corps created a workshop organization for the repair, recovery, and manufacture of equipment at the base and in the field (this was the basis for the creation of REME in 1942). Finally, it formed a highly trained technical ammunition branch that inspected, conditioned, and repaired British ammunition and dealt with captured and unexploded enemy ammunition.

The focal points of all RAOC activity were the Ordnance Directorate at the War Office and the complex of central depots in the United Kingdom from which supplies were sent to all operational locations. Here, also, the war organization was well devised and all technical training planned, first under the supervision of Gen. Sir Basil Hill and then under Gen. Sir Leslie Williams (1941–46).

In the course of the war, the corps did active work in many parts of the world, including France (1939–40), Norway, North Africa, the Middle East, Sicily, Italy, and northwestern Europe (1944–45).

The Western Desert. Fighting in the Western Desert of North Africa provided the RAOC with the experience necessary to build a highly efficient supply and repair system. The field force organization formed as a result of these campaigns proved ideal for all later operations in the war, notably in Italy and northwestern Europe.

The permanent need of the army was for quick replenishment of food, water, petrol, and ammunition. These stores had to be held centrally at the base, with a quick system for getting demands from and stores forward to a unit. These requirements were met as soon as air freight became available. This supply problem will always be present in modern war.

U.S. Army Ordnance Corps

ORIGINS

The U.S. Army Ordnance Corps followed the historical example set by European countries in the Middle Ages, especially England as described above.

The traditions of U.S. Army ordnance began with the first days of the American Revolution. In 1775 the Continental Congress authorized General Washington to appoint an official as commissary general of the artillery stores, responsible for the procurement of arms and ammunition. Mr. E. Cheever was elected for this new position and he worked in close cooperation with Maj. Gen. Henry Knox, Washington's artillery chief. (In this function Knox considered himself comparable with the master general of ordnance in the British army.)

Congress established the Board of War and Ordnance in 1776. Its main responsibility was to arrange for the storage and maintenance of powder, artillery, muskets, and other materiel. The first ordnance depot was set up at Carlisle, Pennsylvania, in 1777.

1812 TO 1918

The Ordnance Department was founded by an act of Congress on 14 May 1812. The head of this new organization was the commissary general of ordnance, who was directly responsible to the president of the United States. The commissary general of ordnance was responsible for arms and ammunition procurement, for monitoring government armories and storage depots, and for recruiting and training ordnance artificers to be attached to regiments, corps, and garrisons.

The flaming bomb became the official emblem of U.S. Army ordnance in May 1833—the oldest military insignia of the U.S. Army. Prior to its selection by the Ordnance Department it was the insignia of the British Grenadier Guards, the Royal Engineers, and the Royal Horse Artillery.

Some statistics point out the magnitude of ordnance responsibility at that time. During the Civil War (1861–65), the Ordnance Department had to handle 90 million pounds of lead, 13 million pounds of artillery shells, and 26 million pounds of powder, as well as large quantities of other ordnance materiel, to be provided to the Union Army.

During the war with Spain in 1898, the U.S. Army had to learn one first important lesson, namely, how to equip and sustain a largely volunteer force. When U.S. troops were sent to the Philippines, the Ordnance Department had to solve the problems involved in transporting and sustaining an army thousands of miles from home. Both proved to be valuable experiences in light of the expanding twentieth-century role of ordnance in providing complete support to frontline troops.

During World War I, it was not surprising that the department expanded—from fewer than 100 officers, several enlisted men, and a small number of civilian employees to a force of 5,900 officers, 62,000 enlisted men, and about 75,000 civilians.

At that time commercial industries were not prepared to manufacture the highly technical and noncommercial materiel required by the army. It was necessary for the department to design and manufacture special machinery and tools for making new types of cannon ammunition, tanks, and other noncommercial articles.

Moreover, existing stocks of machine guns proved unsatisfactory for use in combat. Therefore, John M. Browning, an arms maker who developed light and heavy machine guns, was given the opportunity to produce these kinds of weapons in numbers in cooperation with the Ordnance Department.

The production of ordnance items grew to a total of 3,000 artillery pieces, 54 railway guns and howitzers, more than 50,000 trucks, 80 tanks, and more than 125,000 machine guns in the years 1917 and 1918.

1918 TO THE PRESENT

It is understandable that, as the size of the army decreased between World War I and World War II, so did ordnance responsibilities. The great challenge posed by the unavoidable participation of the United States in World War II placed the Ordnance Department in an awkward position, because it was necessary to boost production capacity to an extraordinary extent. Wartime ordnance procurement increased to a level of US$34 billion, nearly half the total of all previous army procurement.

In 1950 the Ordnance Department became the Ordnance Corps upon the enactment of the Army Organization Act. The office of chief of ordnance ceased to exist following a major army reorganization in 1962, although Ordnance

Corps personnel continued to perform their various tasks. In October 1985 the Ordnance Department was reestablished to assist the chief of ordnance/ commandant of the U.S. Ordnance Center and School (USAOC&S) at Aberdeen Proving Ground, Maryland, which in 1981 was given authority for military personnel in ordnance.

Organization and Roles of Ordnance Establishments

In modern military understanding the ordnance corps is a main part of the logistic services, unless it is organized as a separate branch in the structure of an army. The following descriptions of organization and roles, primarily in the British and the U.S. armies, will point out what is in line with that organization and where there are deviations.

GREAT BRITAIN

Regular army. The RAOC is responsible for the supply of all items of materiel needed in the army (except engineer supplies, construction materiel, and medical items); for the inspection and repair of certain items of materiel; and for the provision of ancillary services. The items of materiel for which the RAOC is responsible may be classified in four categories: (1) combat supplies, consisting of ammunition (including mines and explosives), rations, and petroleum, oil, and lubricant (POL); (2) ordnance stores, including spares and assemblies for vehicles, equipment, and army aircraft, clothing and items of personal equipment, general stores, and technical and warlike stores; (3) vehicles; and (4) guided weapons, for example, infantry antitank systems, provided through the normal ammunition supply chain.

The RAOC is responsible for the inspection, modification, and repair of ammunition, explosives, clothing, and certain general stores (furniture, tentage, textiles, etc.) and for the quality surveillance of rations and POL. The RAOC is also responsible for certain ancillary services including printing, laundry, bathing, industrial gas supply, fire prevention and protection, local purchase and contracts, and clerks and for explosive ordnance disposal (EOD), which includes the disposal of all stray land service ammunition and the neutralization of improvised explosive devices (IED). The RAOC is represented at all formation headquarters in a theater of operations.

The director general of ordnance services (DGOS) is the head of the RAOC in the Logistic Executive (Army). He is assisted by the director of supply operations (Army) (DSupOps[A]), who is responsible for stock holding, central supply, and the central ordnance depots of the United Kingdom Land Forces (UKLF).

Territorial army (TA). The roles of the TA have evolved into a triad: to complete the order of battle of British forces committed to NATO, principally with I (BR) Corps; to assist in maintaining a secure UK base; and to provide a framework for any further expansion of the nation's reserves in a time of crisis.

There are three categories of TA. Group A consists of formed independent and specialist TA units (including RAOC). Group B includes the University

Officer Training Corps (UOTCs), 4,000 strong, and certain specialist pools. Group C is the Home Service Force (HSF), made up of 4,300 ex-regular and TA soldiers.

The TA may be called up by the government in the following situations: when warlike operations are in preparation or progress (the higher liability); when national danger is imminent or an emergency has arisen (the lower liability); and in defense of the United Kingdom against actual or anticipated attack.

Independent units make up 82 percent of the TA. Each unit is based on its own training center and has its own regular army permanent staff. Another 15 percent of the TA is in specialist units. A specialist unit has no premises or regular permanent staff of its own and draws its volunteers from throughout the entire country.

The established strength of RAOC TA is 27 percent of the corps. Two-thirds of them go to the British Army of the Rhine (BAOR) on mobilization, and the RAOC mobilized order of battle is 30 percent TA. There are 15 RAOC Independent TA units located throughout the country with a total established strength of 1,055. The RAOC Specialist TA is commanded in peacetime by HQ RAOC TA.

Ministry of Defense (MOD). The MOD consists of five elements under the political direction of the secretary of state for defense.

Central staffs are responsible for defense policy and overall planning. The three service departments (navy, army, and air force) are responsible for management of their respective services in terms of operational requirements, organization, training, personnel, and logistics. The procurement executive (PE) is responsible for the procurement of equipment for all three services, from research through production.

The PE, headed by the chief of defense procurement, comprises the central divisions responsible for procurement policy and general management of the PE and the three systems controllerates that deal with land, sea, and air environments: controller of the navy, for sea system equipment; master general of ordnance, for land system equipment; and controller aircraft, for air system equipment.

Royal Ordnance Factories (ROFs). The ROFs are a manufacturing organization employing more than 20,000 people and comprising eleven factories that produce defense equipment. There are also two agency factories managed by industry. The U.K. armed forces are the major customer, but a substantial proportion of production is generated by overseas sales. The ROFs are mainly concerned with the manufacture of finished products, particularly guns, heavy armored fighting vehicles, engineering support, vehicles and equipment, ammunition, bombs, and guided weapons. They also manufacture subassemblies and components for sale as required.

U.S. ARMY ORDNANCE CORPS

The ordnance corps is responsible for the supply of repair parts and maintenance of ordnance-type equipment. The area of munitions materiel includes monitoring, inspection, stock control, and security. The area of explosive ordnance disposal (EOD) deals with locating, identifying, rendering safe, handling, removing, salvaging, and disposing of all kinds of munitions.

The items of materiel for which the ordnance corps is responsible may be classified in four major categories: (1) conventional tank and ground mobility equipment (related to Tank/Automotive Materiel Management); (2) guided missiles and free-flight rockets (related to Missile Materiel Management); (3) nuclear, conventional, and chemical munitions and warheads (related to Munitions Materiel Management); and (4) U.S. and foreign unexploded conventional, chemical, and nuclear munitions (related to EOD).

In 1986 the ordnance corps was brought in line with the army's regimental system. Key points were the establishment of the position of chief of ordnance, organization of the corps under the whole-branch concept (one branch, one regiment), and establishment of the office of chief of ordnance as the regimental headquarters for the ordnance corps. Aberdeen Proving Ground, Maryland, was established as the "Home of Ordnance Corps," and enlisted soldiers with ordnance training were assigned to combat arms regiments.

GERMANY

The British and U.S. armies are the main military organizations that have a separate ordnance corps. Armies of countries that were founded with major assistance from these two states, such as the armies of India and Japan, often created branches that were quite similar. Other countries concentrate all logistic tasks, including ordnance tasks, in one branch only. In most cases the ordnance functions are carried out by a special subbranch called the "Logistic Corps/Troops" or some group with a similar title. The German army is a good example.

Army logistic troops. The logistic troops of the German army ensure the materiel readiness of the army and support the medical service; they provide other users (such as the air force and navy) with materiel, for which the army is responsible; and they support allied forces within the framework of agreements established for a state of defense.

The basis for the accomplishment of this logistic mission is the employment of fully mobile, relocatable logistic troops and fixed logistic installations on the one hand, and utilization of civilian installations and services on the other.

Organization (regular army). The logistic troops are organized into supply support troops and maintenance troops; the medical troops form an organic branch. Supply support troops are responsible for the provision, storage, handling, and transportation of supplies. Maintenance troops have to ensure the evacuation and maintenance of disabled army materiel.

In addition to these logistics and medical troops, the army has so-called "units with a logistic mission" at its disposal. Pipeline engineers and the transportation elements of army aviation units fall into this category.

Every level of command in the regular army has its own logistic troops and organic support services for the accomplishment of its logistic missions. Essentially a corps has the logistic troops required for the support of the corps's troops as well as depots for the storage of the corps's stocks.

Each division has a supply battalion and a maintenance battalion at its disposal. The supply battalion of the division is organized as follows: headquarters and service company, supply company, supply company for materiel, supply company for bulk supplies, and transportation company. The division maintenance battalion includes the headquarters and service company, the maintenance company, the maintenance company for electronic equipment, and the maintenance and evacuation company. A brigade has one supply company and one maintenance company. Battalions and separate units have their own organic support services, which are organized as supply and maintenance subunits.

The preceding descriptions of the ordnance services of the United States, the United Kingdom, and Germany present the overall historical development and areas of responsibility of ordnance troops generally. The role of ordnance troops in supplying, maintaining, and repairing equipment is vital to military operations. The increasing complexity and sophistication of the modern equipment will undoubtedly place greater burdens on ordnance troops in the future, and they must be prepared to meet the challenge and keep their army's equipment functioning smoothly.

GÜNTER PAULEIT

SEE ALSO: Combat Service Support; Consumption Rates, Battlefield; Engineering, Military; Logistics: A General Survey; Maintenance; Transportation Corps.

Bibliography

Crocker, L. P. 1988. *The army officer's guide*. Harrisburg, Pa.: Stackpole Books.
Dijkstra, C. J. 1983. *Logistical support*. Paris: Assembly of Western European Union Collective.
Fernyhough, A. E. 1980. *A short history of the RAOC*. Andover, Mass.
Jomini, Antoine-Henri. 1836. *Précis de l'art de la guerre*. Paris.
———. 1881. *Abriss der Kriegskunst*. Berlin: Richard Wilhelmi.
Quick, J. 1973. *Dictionary of weapons and military terms*. New York: McGraw-Hill.
Sterling, P. D. 1987. *Serving the line with excellence: The development of the U.S. Army Ordnance Corps*. Aberdeen, Md.: U.S. Army Ordnance Center and School, Aberdeen Proving Ground.

ORGANIZATION, ARMY

All modern armies are organized similarly. All include the same basic functions necessary to conduct land combat with modern weapons. The proportions of these functions vary according to national preference and somewhat according to the weapons and equipment available, but all are present in the large combined-arms organizations. Armies are designed to operate and fight on land and are organized hierarchically in relatively fixed patterns from small units to large organizations. The functions of land combat are repeated at each level in the hierarchy, although smaller organizations may not include a separate unit for each function. Armies also tend to integrate their support units with their combat units at each level of the organizational hierarchy. When operating in the field, armies—unlike navies and air forces, which are tied to specific bases—bring their bases with them.

The evolution of army organization has been a process of creating and differentiating the functions of land combat. In early warfare, armies tended to have a single function—infantry combat. Over the course of history, new functions arose as technology evolved; the modern army is a complex and intricate organization requiring a high degree of management and leadership to do its work.

Basic Functions of Land Combat

The *command* function, sometimes called command and control, includes the decision, planning, direction, and feedback mechanisms that manage an army at each level in the hierarchy. At the lower levels, command is accomplished by an individual, sometimes with a deputy or assistant. At the battalion level and higher, commanders have staffs to help them accomplish the command function.

The *maneuver* function uses movement and firepower to seize or defend terrain features, destroy enemy forces, and weaken the will of the enemy to fight. Maneuver is accomplished by infantry or armored units, which alternately move and fire to accomplish military missions. Infantry usually fights on foot even though the troops may ride to the battlefield on horses, trucks, or armored personnel carriers. Mechanized infantry may fight while mounted in fighting vehicles. The infantry's role is to close with and destroy the enemy. Armor achieves shock power with its tanks and can penetrate enemy positions. Generally, the best results are achieved when infantry and armor work together in a combined-arms team. The infantry protects the tanks from close-in fires, and the tanks protect the infantry from longer-range fires. Infantry units include considerable firepower capability at each level, and armor units have the firepower of their tanks as well as other fire support. A primary characteristic of modern armies is the integration of fire and maneuver, in which some elements provide a base of fire to facilitate the maneuver of other elements. Tactical missions are accomplished by a carefully concerted alternation of fire and maneuver by all elements in the hierarchy of army organization.

The *reconnaissance* or scouting function consists of finding the enemy, preventing surprise, and sometimes delaying or harassing enemy attackers. Reconnaissance elements are not intended for sustained combat, although they have the capability to fight. The reconnaissance function formerly was performed by foot skirmishers or light cavalry, but in modern armies it is accomplished by personnel in light tanks, high-speed vehicles, helicopters, or aircraft.

The *fire support* function is to destroy, damage, or deter the enemy by bringing fires to bear on his troops, support, or lines of communication. Fire support is performed by rifles, machine guns, mortars, howitzers, rockets, missiles, armed helicopters, and combat aircraft. It is provided by fire support elements in infantry and armor units and by field artillery units, combat aviation units, naval guns and missiles, and air forces. Fire support provides protection for the maneuver elements by firing on enemy forces. One specialized part of the fire support function provides antiarmor weapons to destroy or damage opposing tanks and light armored vehicles.

The *air defense* function is to destroy, damage, or deter enemy helicopters, aircraft, and missiles. Air defense is performed by ground elements or aircraft armed with missiles and automatic guns designed specifically for this function. It is provided at each level of the hierarchy in armies and is obtained also from naval and air forces.

The *combat engineer*, or pioneer, function is to assist the movement of the friendly forces and impede the movement of the enemy forces. The former is accomplished by building roads, airfields, bridges, and rafts and clearing obstacles; the latter is accomplished by damaging roads and airfields, destroying bridges, and constructing obstacles. Combat engineer elements may also build structures and utilities needed for military or related civil use, although engineer construction units are provided to do most of that kind of work.

The *communications*, or signal, function is to transmit messages among the elements of the army and other supporting services. It is accomplished by special sections within headquarters units and at the higher levels of the hierarchy by signal units.

Administration, or combat service support, includes several subfunctions pertaining to the operations of the army in all aspects other than combat itself. Administration includes supply, maintenance, transportation, medical care, personnel management, and subsistence. There are administration elements at every level in the hierarchy starting with the company.

The *aviation* function includes operation of light aircraft and helicopters in support of the army. The aviation function is characterized by the use of aircraft to accomplish tasks of other functions: moving troops on the battlefield as part of the maneuver function; providing aerial reconnaissance; using armed helicopters for fire support; moving supplies, equipment, and wounded personnel; and allowing commanders to view the battlefield from above. Initially, the aviation function also included aerial combat, bombing, and close air support by high-performance aircraft, but most nations now perform these functions in air forces separate from their armies.

All of these functions except aviation are performed at each level in the hierarchy of army organization. As organizations become larger, these basic functions are accomplished by specifically designed and designated elements. The fundamental schema of army organization consists essentially of performing these same functions in an integrated and purposeful manner at each level in the hierarchy.

The historical evolution of army organization was achieved by adding new functional elements as compelled by the introduction of new technology. Initially, armies consisted entirely of two functions, command and maneuver; the maneuver elements were foot infantry, and the commanders led in person and even fought in battle. The introduction of horses and wheeled vehicles added heavy cavalry (armor) to the maneuver function and light cavalry to the reconnaissance function. The introduction of standoff weapons, such as slings, bows, and finally guns, caused the fire support function to be differentiated in the form of a special corps—artillery. During the Middle Ages, the engineer function achieved independent status to build fortifications and manage the sieges to destroy them. The communications function was important from the earliest days but gained specific recognition with the introduction of heliographs, telegraphs, telephones, and radios. The essential function of feeding and paying the troops and providing weapons and munitions has always been a necessary part of an army, but as weapons grew more complicated and armies larger it became necessary to create specialized units to perform the administration function. The aviation function arrived with the introduction in World War I of workable aircraft and has evolved, despite the formation of separate air forces, into an important function for most modern armies. Similarly, the command function has evolved from a single general giving instructions by voice to an elaborate network of commanders at various levels, supported by staffs and numerous components, to achieve successful control of all of the other elements of the modern army.

The Hierarchy of Army Organization

Although the names, strengths, and specific roles vary somewhat, all modern armies include the same basic elements in the hierarchy of army organization. Starting from smallest to largest, these are the squad, section, platoon, company, battalion, brigade, division, and army corps.

A *squad* consists of a squad leader (normally a sergeant) and seven to fourteen other soldiers. The squad is used in all branches of an army and is the smallest military organization. Originally, the size of a squad was determined by the ability of a single leader to command by voice, and it was employed as a single entity. However, the increased dispersion necessary to offset the increased lethality of modern weapons required the squad itself to be organized into teams.

The rifle squad is the basic element of infantry combat. There is great variety among rifle squads, but most modern rifle squads consist of a squad leader and two identical fire teams, each having a light machine gun as its principal weapon. Each fire team includes a leader, a machine gunner, and four to six riflemen, whose principal missions are to carry ammunition and protect the machine gunner. The fire teams alternate as maneuver or base-of-fire elements; that is, one fire team moves while the other team covers the movement with fire. Flexible interaction of fire and maneuver is the fundamental method of land combat at all levels.

A *section* is an organization larger than a squad and smaller than a platoon used within headquarters and in support organizations. It is led by a noncommissioned officer (NCO) and varies in strength from 10 to 40 personnel. In some armies, a section is also a combat element consisting of two or three squads.

A *platoon* consists of three or four squads and is led by a lieutenant or captain platoon leader assisted by a senior NCO—the platoon sergeant. The platoon is used in all branches of an army and has subelements for the maneuver, fire support, and command functions.

A generic rifle platoon includes three rifle squads as maneuver elements, a weapons squad as a fire support element, and a command section. Each rifle squad is a maneuver element for the platoon, although each contains both fire and maneuver capability internally. The weapons squad provides additional fire support with heavy machine guns to augment the fires of the light machine guns in the rifle squads. The command element consists of the platoon leader, the platoon sergeant, and a radio operator representing the communications function.

A generic tank platoon consists of four or five tanks with their crews and is commanded by a platoon leader in a tank. Each tank is a self-contained mobile fighting vehicle armed with a large flat-trajectory main gun, machine guns, and sometimes missiles. A tank platoon may fight in teams of two tanks, alternating fire and maneuver as directed by the platoon leader.

A *company* is a unit of 100 to 250 personnel consisting of several platoons and other elements. It is commanded by a captain, usually, although majors command companies in some armies. The functions of administration and air defense are introduced at the company level. Administration is performed by a first sergeant as senior NCO, a company clerk, a supply section, a maintenance section (depending on how much equipment the company has), and sometimes a mess section—all within a headquarters platoon. Command is accomplished by the company commander, the first sergeant, and several communications specialists.

A generic rifle company consists of three rifle platoons as maneuver elements, a weapons platoon to provide fire support, a headquarters platoon for administration, and a headquarters for command. A typical weapons platoon provides two new forms of fire support: high-angle fire using light (60mm or 81mm) mortars and flat-trajectory light antitank fire with light antitank guns or missiles. The headquarters platoon contains small elements for personnel and supply. In the U.S. Army, the mess and maintenance functions for infantry units have been centralized at the battalion level.

A generic tank company consists of three tank platoons as maneuver elements and a company headquarters, which includes personnel and supply sections. Because of the heavy maintenance load for the tanks, company headquarters may also have a maintenance section.

A *battalion* is a unit of 400 to 1,200 personnel consisting of several companies and other elements. It is commanded by a lieutenant colonel and is the smallest organization with a staff to assist the commander. Most staffs are organized to provide principal staff officers for personnel, intelligence, operations, and logistics, although some nations combine intelligence and operations into a single operations staff element and personnel and logistics into a single administrative staff element. The battalion is the basic unit for combat and combat support branches.

A generic infantry battalion is shown in Figure 1. It consists of three or four rifle companies as maneuver elements, a combat support company, a headquarters company, and a headquarters. The combat support company provides new weapons and equipment to augment those in the rifle companies, including a mortar platoon with medium mortars (107mm), tactical radar equipment, and an antiarmor platoon with heavy antitank missiles. The reconnaissance function is performed by a scout platoon in the combat support company. The air defense function may be introduced at this level by including in the combat support company a section armed with shoulder-fired air defense missiles. A separate engineer section or platoon is sometimes provided as well. The headquarters and combat support companies may be combined into a single unit. The headquarters company includes mess, maintenance, and signal sections and sometimes a transportation section as well. The headquarters includes the command, staff, and the personnel in the sections supporting the staff. An infantry battalion is a reasonably self-sufficient unit with explicit representation of six or seven of the nine functions of land combat.

A generic tank battalion is shown in Figure 2. It consists of four tank companies as maneuver elements, a headquarters, and a headquarters company. The headquarters company includes a medium mortar platoon for fire support and a scout platoon for the reconnaissance function, as well as a maintenance platoon and a support platoon to carry the battalion's basic load of ammunition and fuel. The combat engineer function is accomplished by an armored vehicle–launched bridge.

A *brigade* is an organization of units with an aggregate strength of 2,000 to 8,000 personnel commanded by a brigadier general or colonel. A brigade is used to form combat, combat support, and combat service support units into functional or integrated combinations. Brigade headquarters are used to command engineer, transportation, signal, and artillery battalions in single-function organizations. They are also used to command combat service support battalions of different types—supply, maintenance, medical—in multifunction organizations. A group headquarters commanded by a colonel also may be used to command several battalions or companies and may be major subordinate elements of brigades. A *regiment* has about the same strength as a brigade but is a fixed organization with a definite internal composition, while a brigade is a

Figure 1. Organization of an infantry battalion.

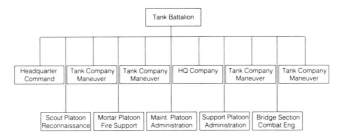

Figure 2. Organization of a tank battalion.

flexible organization with an internal composition tailored to the specific combat environment. In the U.S. Army, the only regimental organization still in
use is an armored cavalry regiment fulfilling the reconnaissance function for
army corps. In some armies, the term *regiment* is used for smaller units comparable to battalions in the U.S. and NATO armies.

Combat brigades are combined-arms organizations in that they integrate
infantry, armor, artillery, and cavalry units under a single commander for
combat. A combat brigade may be organic to a combat division or may be a
separate organization. An organic combat brigade is a tactical headquarters
commanded by a colonel to which combat battalions and combat support units
are attached or placed in direct support. Separate combat brigades are usually
commanded by a brigadier general and are assigned its subordinate units on a
permanent basis.

A generic separate combat brigade includes two to five infantry or tank
battalions as maneuver elements, an artillery battalion for fire support, a cavalry troop (company) for reconnaissance, a combat engineer company, and a
support battalion that includes the service support units. Brigades may be
tailored for their intended missions, and an air defense battery or aviation
company or battalion could be assigned as well. A separate brigade is a formidable combat force, and some nations use the separate brigade as their primary
combat organization.

A *division* (Fig. 3) is a combined-arms organization with 7,000 to 22,000
military personnel commanded by a major general. It includes three combat

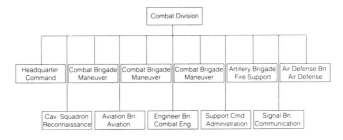

Figure 3. Organization of a combat division.

brigades as maneuver elements, an artillery brigade of three to five artillery battalions, a cavalry squadron with three or four cavalry troops (some of which may be air cavalry), a separate air defense battalion, a separate signal battalion, a support command with three or four service support battalions, and frequently an aviation battalion. The division artillery brigade commonly consists of a direct support battalion with light or medium (105mm, 152mm, or 155mm) howitzers for each brigade and one or two other battalions, including heavy (203mm or 240mm) howitzers or multiple-launch rocket launchers for general support of the division. Each of the nine basic functions of land combat is represented explicitly in a combat division.

In many armies, including the U.S. Army, the brigades organic to a division are tactical headquarters to which infantry and tank battalions are attached for a particular battle or campaign, while the rest of the brigade units—artillery battalion, engineer company, and combat service support elements—remain assigned to their own divisional units and placed in support of the brigade. This organizational concept allows a division commander to tailor his subordinate brigades to the combat situation and his mission. Other nations (Soviet Union, United Kingdom), treat the major subordinate elements of a division as regiments or relatively fixed organizations. Whether a division is flexible or fixed in theory, division commanders tend to organize their divisions for combat as they perceive necessary to accomplish their missions.

There are many different types of combat divisions, depending on the nature and mix of the included infantry and tank maneuver battalions. Infantry divisions have from seven to ten foot-infantry battalions and one or two tank or mechanized infantry battalions. Light infantry divisions include nine or ten light infantry battalions designed for rapid strategic movement and trained for low-intensity conflict. Airborne infantry divisions are designed to conduct parachute assaults, so the nine infantry battalions and other division units (including sometimes a light tank battalion) are designed for this role, and all division personnel are qualified parachutists. The U.S. Army has an air assault division with nine light infantry battalions manned by soldiers specially trained in helicopter operations. Armored divisions and mechanized infantry divisions are composed of a mix of 10 to 12 tank battalions and mechanized infantry battalions equipped with armored personnel carriers or infantry fighting vehicles. Tank battalions outnumber mechanized infantry battalions in armored divisions, while the converse is true in mechanized infantry divisions. In each of these divisions, the reconnaissance, artillery, engineer, and other units of the division base are equipped and trained to be compatible with the maneuver battalions. In an armored division, the artillery is all self-propelled on tracked vehicles, and the engineers ride in armored engineer vehicles. In a light infantry division, the artillery is light and towed by light vehicles, and the engineers have light trucks.

An *army corps* is the largest combined-arms organization currently used as a standard army formation. It has a strength of 50,000 to 300,000 troops and is commanded by a lieutenant general. An army corps may consist of two to seven divisions and supporting units. A generic army corps is shown in Figure 4. It

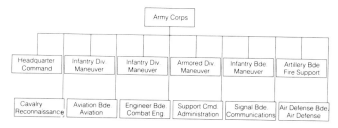

Figure 4. Organization of an army corps.

includes three divisions (two infantry and one armored), a separate combat brigade for augmenting a division or accomplishing a tactical mission, a corps artillery brigade with 10 to 15 artillery battalions organized into three or four artillery groups, an armored or air cavalry regiment with three or four cavalry squadrons, a corps support command with several area or functional commands, and brigades for the engineer, signal, air defense, and aviation functions.

The headquarters' staffs for both division and corps are organized into more staff sections than are found at the division or brigade headquarters. In addition to staff sections for personnel, intelligence, operations, and logistics, there may be separate staff sections for planning, civil-military affairs, communications, and other special activities deemed important enough to warrant an additional principal staff officer.

Army echelons above corps are organized for specific theaters and situations, but all include common elements for specific collateral functions of land combat. Field armies, consisting of two or more corps with an array of supporting organizations and commanded by a full general, exist in the armies of the larger nations, but usually they are tailored for a specific mission. In the 1991 Gulf War, Third U.S. Army Headquarters commanded VII Corps and XVIII Airborne Corps as the army component of the unified theater command for the Persian Gulf. (The U.S. Army also maintains several "CONUS Armies," which are administrative headquarters responsible for specific regions of the United States and are not intended to serve as field armies.) The Soviet Union used the term *army* to mean a corps and *front* to mean field army. In World War II the Allies, Germans, and Soviets formed army groups consisting of several field armies.

The collateral functions of land combat that are provided for in the echelons above corps include intelligence, military police, chemical, logistics, personnel replacement, and special operations. Intelligence units exist at battalion and higher levels in the form of staff sections. There are also intelligence units devoted to the collection and interpretation of intelligence. Some of these units exist at the division and corps level, but often they are organized into a single theater-wide intelligence command. The military police function also exists in the divisions and corps; there is a military police company in each U.S. division and one or more battalions in an army corps to provide law and order, area security, and battlefield circulation control. That part of the military police function involved with prisoners of war and criminal investigation often is organized into a single command under the army commander for a theater. Chemical units also are provided at every level, and there is a chemical company for each division, but the control of chemical assets, including smoke generator units, often is held at the theater or theater army level. The personnel replacement function normally is performed by a replacement command under the theater army commander.

Special operations forces include special forces, rangers, special operations aviation, civil affairs, and psychological operations units. These special operations forces usually are formed into a single command for theater-wide operations under the theater commander. In the war with Iraq, the United States assigned or attached civil affairs units to the corps and divisions, retained control of psychological operations at the theater level while placing units in support of the corps and divisions, and conducted Special Forces and ranger operations under a special operations command for the theater.

Finally, the echelons above corps include logistical commands to operate ports, railways, pipelines, highway transportation systems, supply depots, maintenance facilities, and other activities to support the operations of the corps. These logistical commands are organized either on an area basis with units of different functions or on a single-function basis for the entire theater. The exact variety and organization of the units operating at the echelons above corps depends on circumstances and national doctrine.

The organization of armies as national institutions tends to vary widely, but some common elements exist. The army headquarters is headed by a senior military officer who usually reports to a civilian minister of war or defense. The army is usually part of a unified military organization with the naval and air forces. The staffs at army headquarters are concerned with the normal staff functions for the army in the field and in addition have to deal with budgeting, public relations, and political issues. Armies commonly have major commands for the following functions: centralized personnel management, development and procurement of weapons and equipment, wholesale logistics (supply and maintenance), training and education, doctrinal development, and health care. In addition, there may be organizations devoted to computers and electronics, munitions, industrial production, political affairs and propaganda, and testing of weapons and equipment. The exact organization and delineation of responsibilities varies widely according to national preference and the size of the army.

Armies are usually separated into two or more components according to readiness standards. The active component consists of units with equipment manned by full-time personnel. There is a wide variety of reserve component schemes, but they all involve only a few full-time personnel augmented in some cases by part-time reservists who train regularly and in other cases by reservists who will report to their units only upon mobilization. Most armies keep some of their units in a reserve component with the same organizational tables, tactical doctrine, and training standards as the active component, although with reduced readiness and cost.

It is likely that the historical trend toward greater complexity and specialization in army organization will continue. Once considered a low-tech organization compared with air forces and navies, armies are now using large amounts of sophisticated high-technology equipment and will use more in the future. Consequently, the proportion of the strength of an army that engages directly in combat will continue to shrink. Since the earliest days, when every member of an army fought on the battlefield, the evolution of army organization has increased the proportion of support troops to combat troops until now only a few riflemen, machine gunners, and tank crews actually operate on the front lines.

This increase in support, however, has also resulted in a greater increase in the overall combat power of armies, so these fewer combat soldiers can deliver greater amounts of lethal munitions faster and more accurately than ever before. Because of the need to counter this increased lethality, armies will continue to move toward greater dispersion in tactical formations. Airpower and longer-range weapons mean that armies must disperse in depth as well as laterally. The combat area is getting deeper and more difficult to distinguish from the rear areas, if indeed there are any rear areas remaining.

Finally, as armies are becoming more technical, more specialized internally, and more lethal, they are becoming smaller. During World War II, the U.S. Army had 8 million military personnel, the German army numbered 4.5 million, and the Red Army about 7 million. Even during the height of the Cold War, the two major opposing coalitions were planning armies with at most 4 million or 5 million on each side. Currently, armies of the NATO nations are being reduced in size as the threat of a major conventional war diminishes. The trend among industrialized nations is for smaller armies that are well trained and equipped with modern, sophisticated weapons. The United States is planning an army of slightly more than 500,000 active and 600,000 selected reserve personnel for the mid-1990s. However, China, Vietnam, North Korea, India, and perhaps the Commonwealth of Independent States and Iraq are likely to have active armies more than 1 million strong for the foreseeable future. Despite reductions in size and the introduction of modern weapons, the fundamentals of army organization will tend to remain very much the same as they have been since Napoleon and Wellington collaborated unwittingly to combine respectively shock and firepower with linear tactics during the early years of the nineteenth century.

JOHN R. BRINKERHOFF

SEE ALSO: Force Structure; Military Police; Reserve Components; Staff.

Bibliography

International Institute for Strategic Studies. 1990. *The military balance, 1990–1991.* London: Brassey's.

Isby, D. C., and C. Kamps. 1985. *Armies of NATO's central front.* London: Jane's.

Keegan, J. 1983. *World armies.* Detroit, Mich.: Gale Research.

Scott, H. F., and W. F. Scott. 1984. *The armed forces of the USSR.* London: Arms and Armour Press.

Thomer, E. 1984. *Die Bundeswehr Heute.* Herford und Bonn: E. S. Mittler und Sohn.

U.S. Department of the Army. 1987. *Staff officers field manual 101-10-1/1: Organizational, technical, and logistical data.* Vols. 1 and 2. Washington, D.C.: Government Printing Office.

P

PERSONNEL

Personnel is a management function of great importance to armed forces because military operations are manpower as well as capital intensive. Armed forces are large organizations that number in the thousands, even for small nations, and have strengths of several million for large nations.

Personnel management is concerned with the individual service member or employee. The personnel function is the supply side counterpart to the manpower function, which establishes the demand for people. The manpower function is concerned with work to be done and establishes the authorized positions, or spaces, needed in military organizations. The personnel function deals with people to fill authorized positions.

The objective of the personnel system in an armed force—or indeed in any organization—is to provide the right number of people with the desired experience and necessary skills to get the work done properly. In armed forces, this means filling each authorized position with an individual having the skills, experience, and ability specified in the position's description. This is a difficult task because of the changing nature of the manpower program and the necessity to develop military-related skills internally over a long period of time.

Personnel Systems

BASIC PERSONNEL FUNCTIONS

Personnel functions are designed to provide management of individuals in the workforce from the moment of entering to the moment of leaving. There are six basic personnel functions:

- *Hiring* is the process of inducing or, for some military systems, compelling people to join the workforce. It includes the recruitment of volunteers, the conscription of draftees, and the classification and assignment of those being accessed.
- *Training* is the process of qualifying the individual to perform the job for which he or she was recruited.
- *Compensation* is the process of rewarding the individual for work done.

- *Career development* is the process of educating the individual and making changes in jobs to provide the basis for promotion and to meet organizational needs. It includes retention of qualified personnel and selection for key assignments.
- *Promotion* is the process of advancing the individual to positions of greater responsibility and increased reward.
- *Separation* is the process of removing the individual from the workforce. It includes identification and removal of those who are judged to be unsatisfactory performers or disciplinary problems. In military personnel systems, separation also includes eliminating those who fail to meet standards for promotion. Retirement is a special form of separation in which individuals are removed from the active workforce after full careers of satisfactory performance and provided a pension.

MILITARY VERSUS CIVILIAN PERSONNEL SYSTEMS

Almost all armed forces include a significant number and proportion of civilian employees. Therefore, it is common for an armed force to have two separate personnel systems: one for military personnel and one for civilians.

The basic approaches to personnel management are quite different between military personnel and civilian employees. The major differences are summarized in Table 1.

Military Personnel Systems

GENERAL CHARACTERISTICS

Military personnel systems are designed to obtain new members as young people at the lowest grades and train and develop them throughout the course of their careers. All facets of personnel management are usually controlled on a centralized basis by the headquarters of the service. Except for the lowest grades of private, seaman, and airman, even promotions to higher enlisted grades are handled on a centralized basis. Military personnel systems tend to be standardized but complex. They have to be far-sighted in order to provide the right number and kind of people for a force structure that may not exist until 25 years in the future. In addition, military personnel systems have to cope with rapid growth and rapid decreases in strength, according to the political situation of the moment.

TABLE 1. *Comparison of Military and Civilian Personnel Systems*

	MILITARY MEMBERS	CIVILIAN EMPLOYEES
Basis for grade	Person	Position
Accession	Centralized	Decentralized
Level of accession	At entry level	At any level
Promotion	Centralized	Decentralized

Grade. All military personnel systems associate the grade with the person rather than with the job. When a person is a private, sergeant, captain, or colonel, he is that grade in all jobs. Indeed, one function of the military personnel system is to put a person with the proper grade in each job. It is possible that military personnel may serve in jobs requiring higher or lower grades; however, this is a special case or a temporary assignment. Equating the grade with the person makes it easier to assign people to jobs, but in some cases it becomes more difficult because of the necessity of moving people from their present jobs simply because they do well and are promoted.

Initial entry. Military personnel systems bring young people in as new recruits at the lowest ranks. Training is necessary because there are no equivalent jobs in civilian life for infantrymen, fighter pilots, or submarine crewmen. Most military jobs require skills that have to be learned and practiced in military service in order for individuals to gain the experience and skill necessary to do the job correctly in combat. Although there are many jobs in military units that use civilian skills, all members of a military unit must be able to engage in combat and have a deep understanding of the military environment. Thus, almost all military personnel enter at the lowest grade and progress through the ranks over a period of service. Professional people, such as doctors, chaplains, and lawyers, are allowed to enter directly into military service as commissioned officers. A few persons with critical civilian skills, such as welders or medical technicians, may be allowed to enter the enlisted force at a mid-level grade (e.g., sergeant). But the general rule is to enter at the lowest grade and work one's way up in the organization.

Long lead times. Military personnel managers face a major challenge because of the long lead times involved in converting young civilians into skilled soldiers, sailors, or airmen. It takes several years to convert raw recruits into junior combat leaders or highly skilled technicians and as many as 20 to 25 years to convert new second lieutenants into highly skilled and experienced senior officers. Forecasting the size and shape of the armed forces 20 years into the future is a problem. Because of rapid technological and political change, the armed forces of any nation will be quite different in 20 years and will require a different mix of skills than could be planned for today. It is likely that important skills will be required in 20 years that do not even exist today.

Changing rules. The military personnel manager faces many changes that complicate planning and execution. The number of people in an armed force may fluctuate quite rapidly as the political situation changes and as budgets are cut or increased. It is possible that a set of personnel policies designed to promote moderate growth over a period of 15 years can be reversed overnight by a decision to reduce strength drastically. Because a reduction in personnel leads to short-term savings quickly, cutting strength is a favorite ploy of budget cutters. Rapid reductions in personnel strength, however, usually lead to long-term dysfunctions and cause tremendous problems for military personnel managers.

Major issues for military personnel managers. Major issues that face a military personnel manager in the modern era include recruiting, retention, youth and vigor, skill development, rapid expansion, reduction in force, and separation. These issues are covered in detail in the following paragraphs. Six tools available to the military personnel manager are conscription, compensation, training and education, promotion, reassignment and rotation, and retirement.

RECRUITING

Recruiting is the process of inducing young people to join the armed forces as enlisted recruits or junior officers. Those nations with entirely volunteer forces rely extensively and exclusively on recruiting programs to obtain the accessions to maintain their desired military personnel strengths.

Although most attention is paid to recruiting enlisted personnel (which is a major problem), the task of persuading young people to sign up for officer training programs, such as officer training schools, the military academies, and Reserve Officer Training Corps (ROTC), is also important. Recruiting officer specialists, such as nurses, doctors, chaplains, and attorneys, also requires a major effort.

Recruiters. The key to a recruiting system is the recruiter—a member of the military whose full-time duty is to induce people with the appropriate qualifications to enlist in the armed forces. Military recruiters are specially selected and specially trained to be salespeople for their respective armed forces. They have to be particularly trustworthy and of the highest character, for they work in a dispersed mode in recruiting offices located normally in the civilian community away from military installations.

Before World War I recruiting was a responsibility of each military unit. The captains of each company and the colonels of each regiment had the duty of maintaining their strength. Recruiters were members of the unit detailed temporarily to recruiting duty. Often a recruiting party would be sent to neighboring villages and towns to attract a crowd, make a sales presentation, and sign up volunteers. As armies got larger and larger, this unit-based recruiting system failed to support the needed numbers and, more importantly, the requisite quality of recruits. Units began to compete with each other for the best recruits to the detriment of the overall force, often driving up the cost of incentives offered to those who enlisted. After World War I, almost all armed forces established a centralized organization to do its recruiting, although some of the recruiters may have been detailed from their unit duties to the recruiting organization.

Nations who obtained the bulk of their enlistees by means of conscription did not pay much attention to recruiting. Recruiting offices were used primarily to accept volunteers who wanted special training and to attract specialists, such as nurses, who could not be obtained by conscription. The attitude was to wait for the customers to come in, and there was little advertising or thought about how best to attract volunteers. If the monthly quotas of recruits were not filled with volunteers, additional registrants could be drafted.

This all changed dramatically for the United States in 1973 when the peacetime draft ended and it was necessary to induce young men and women to volunteer for military service. Suddenly, effective recruiting became a necessity. The recruiting organizations of the armed forces were given high priority in terms of funding and quality personnel. Research into how to recruit was funded, and the lessons learned were transformed into extensive training and indoctrination for the recruiters. Supported by advertising campaigns and financial and other incentives, the recruiting organizations managed generally to meet their requirements for new recruits. Although there were problems initially as the new emphasis on professional recruiting was put into effect, the final results show that professional recruiting could attract young men and women into the armed forces in significant numbers. The United States's experience was matched by that in the United Kingdom and other nations that relied exclusively on volunteer enlistees.

The ultimate success of the professional recruiting force has not been without some problems.

The greatest problem is in achieving a fine balance between incentives for recruiters to sign people up and quality controls to ensure that unqualified people are not being signed up. Part of the success of the recruiting program in the United States has been to create an environment to motivate the individual field recruiters to work hard and meet their goals. The recruiters are given distinctive badges and preferential treatment. They have also been given performance quotas from time to time. However, the effect of an assigned quota, upon which the recruiter's career advancement depends, has in some instances caused recruiters to do anything to meet the quota. Overemphasis on quotas created situations in which recruiters signed up unqualified people, made insupportable promises to prospects, and even falsified test results. While these incidents have been pursued and resolved when discovered, it was clear that too much emphasis on firm quotas was not a good strategy.

Currently recruiting organizations avoid the use of the term *quota*, but all assign goals to be achieved by their recruiters. Combined with constant vigilance to avoid fraud and positive reinforcement for the recruiters, the goal approach appears to achieve a workable balance between recruiter production and adherence to the accession standards.

Recruiting applies primarily to the initial enlistment of non-prior-service personnel. However, many armed forces accept prior-service personnel who wish to rejoin their service or to join another service after a period of time in civilian life. Signing up prior-service personnel is a function of the recruiting organizations, and great care is taken to review the previous military records of each applicant before he or she is permitted to join. The recruiting of prior-service personnel is primarily at the initiative of the enlistee.

Advertising. Those nations that rely on volunteers to fill out their ranks also engage in substantial advertising targeted on young men and women with the desired qualifications. This contrasts with the nations that use conscription to obtain most of their new recruits and that do not have to advertise.

Since the advent of the all-volunteer force in the United States in 1973, the armed forces have engaged in extensive advertising campaigns. These advertising campaigns are sponsored by the individual armed forces and the Office of the Secretary of Defense for all of the armed forces, including in many cases the reserve components of these armed forces. The advertising has been targeted primarily on male high school graduates with high aptitude scores, the group that the armed forces want to attract. Those males who have dropped out of high school or have lower test scores have a higher propensity to enlist than the more qualified people, and the advertising also catches them but not as the primary target. Women are included in the advertising campaigns but are not a primary target because they have tended to enlist in sufficient numbers to meet the requirements in any case.

The advertising campaigns have been backed up by extensive market research and customer surveys, as with any other product. Much work has been done to find out what young people want, what would induce them to join up, and how much it takes to get them to enlist. This information is used to set the themes for the advertising and to support the incentives offered to those who enlist. Three basic themes have been offered in the U.S. recruiting advertising: patriotism, elite adventure, and career enhancement.

The patriotic theme tells prospects that serving the country is a good thing and plays on loyalty to the nation. The patriotic theme was not successful initially as the Vietnam War wound down, but it has been used as a minor note in recent campaigns that stress other values.

The United States Marine Corps typified the elite adventure theme with its slogan that it wanted just A Few Good Men. This theme was designed to attract those who would wish to join a small elite force. The elite adventure theme is also used to attract prospects for particularly dangerous work, such as pilots or airborne soldiers.

The most effective theme overall for general use, however, has been the career enhancement theme. This kind of advertising tells the prospect how he or she will learn a skill in the armed forces that will be valuable later on in civilian life. This advertising emphasizes the civilian-related skills in the armed forces, such as electronics technicians, medical technicians, and automotive maintenance. The U.S. Army used the slogan Be All that You Can Be with great success to appeal to young men and women to better themselves by starting out in the army.

The themes and their relative emphases have varied over the years as the mood of young people and the economic and political environment has changed. However, these advertising campaigns have been a highly professional and effective element of the overall recruiting program for volunteer armed forces.

Bonuses. Among the financial incentives to induce people to enlist and re-enlist are bonuses. A bonus is an amount of money paid, generally in a cash lump sum, to the individual as payment for making a commitment. Enlistment bonuses are paid to individuals who join the service for the first time. Military personnel already in the armed forces who extend their enlistments or reenlist for additional terms of service may receive reenlistment bonuses.

Bonuses are a favorite tool of personnel managers because they can be applied selectively to solve particular problems. There is no need to pay everyone a bonus; it can be paid only to those people who take some action desired by the military service. In the U.S. Army, for example, bonuses are paid to persons who enlist in and agree to serve in the combat arms—infantry, armor, artillery—because these skills do not attract large numbers of high-quality recruits responding to promises of training for civilian skills. Bonuses are offered to doctors to attract them to military service and to make up for the fact that military pay for officers is substantially less than doctors can make in civilian practice. The science of bonuses is thought to be so precise that the armed forces change not only the skills for which bonuses are awarded, but also the amounts of the various bonuses in their efforts to attract just the right number of qualified recruits into the vacancies in skill groups. Bonuses have proven to be a powerful tool to manage the filling of vacancies for particular skills.

Educational benefits. Another kind of financial incentive is used to attract to military service those young men and women who aspire to a college education and seek financial aid to do it. Educational benefits offer the enlistee a sum of money, either outright or by matching the savings of the individual, to be used to pay college tuition and expenses after leaving military service. The most famous and most effective program of educational benefits was the GI Bill after World War II. The purpose of the original GI Bill was not to entice high-quality people into the armed forces, but to induce the personnel leaving the service to go to college to benefit not only themselves but the nation as well. More recent versions of the GI Bill are aimed at high school graduates and those with high test scores who might otherwise be able to find attractive employment in civilian life. Most educational benefits apply across the board to all enlistees, but some benefits have been applied to selected skill groups needing additional recruits.

One problem with educational benefits is that they increase the propensity of the recipient to leave military service to go to college. Thus, they may be effective as enlistment incentives, but are disincentives to reenlistment. This problem can be solved partially by regarding an end to active duty as just part of total military service and encouraging personnel to continue military service in a reserve component. That allows the individual to stay in the armed forces while taking advantage of his educational benefits.

Terms of enlistment: location, skill, school. Another element of recruiting programs in the volunteer environment is the ability of the individual recruiter to negotiate the terms of the enlistment contract with a high degree of flexibility. The recruiter can offer to the prospective enlistee a choice of initial station, a choice of the skill and schooling to be received, and even a choice of when the person will report for duty. This ability to set the terms of enlistment to satisfy individual preferences undoubtedly leads to many more volunteers than otherwise would be the case. It also leads to a complicated situation as the armed forces try to live up to the promises made and fit the constraints into an already complicated military personnel management system. Nevertheless, these nonfinancial incentives have proven to be very effective in the recruiting program. The same individual preferences are also used in reenlistment programs, both for nations with volunteer forces and nations with conscript forces. As long as the terms of the reenlistment contract meet the needs of the service, it is highly advantageous to give people their choices of conditions of service and very inexpensive compared to bonuses and educational incentives.

Quality versus quantity. A major problem with all armed forces is achieving the desired balance between the quantity of personnel to be accessed and the quality of those personnel. This applies both to the nations with conscript systems and to those with volunteer systems. Although conscription may appear to allow flexibility in selecting the people to be drafted, the reality is that there is little flexibility in most conscription systems because of the necessity to avoid undue inequity. Attempts to reject lower-quality people would be viewed, correctly, as unfair to those with higher qualifications. Thus, conscription systems tend to take all who meet the minimum qualifications rather than to take only those with higher qualifications. Because the annual class of conscripts usually is more than sufficient to meet the requirements, it is seldom necessary to take all of those who are eligible in a given year. Thus, the problem of selecting those who shall serve when not all can serve has to be faced. Generally, it is politically necessary to base selection for conscription on a random basis (using a lottery) rather than on the basis of qualifications, which could be viewed as class based. For these reasons, conscription systems tend to draft a large group annually and accept whatever quality distribution exists in that group.

In volunteer systems, however, it is possible—perhaps even essential—to be discriminating about the quality of those allowed to enlist. The problem is that those of lower quality have a higher propensity to enlist. It is much easier to attract a high school dropout with poor scores and poor prospects in civilian life than it is to attract a college graduate with high scores and a good civilian job.

Nations with conscription address the accessioning function somewhat differently. Having the ability to compel people to join the armed forces means that recruiting is much less important, but it is still used. Even with conscription, the armed forces set goals for their desired mix of first-term people (serving an initial period of 9 months to 3 years) and career personnel, who serve for longer periods (up to 20 to 25 years). Although the lower enlisted grades can be conscripted, it is necessary to have some people sign up for longer service and become career professionals. While long-service personnel can be obtained from conscripts who reenlist, many nations with conscription try also to recruit volunteers for long-term service directly from civilian life. Those who enlist voluntarily for long-term service receive preferential treatment, better training and schooling, good assignments, faster promotion, and in some cases higher pay. So the recruiting system is designed to attract a smaller number of relatively high-quality volunteers for long-term service.

RETENTION

All armed forces find it necessary to persuade some of the first-term conscripts or volunteers already on active duty to remain on active duty once their initial terms of enlistment have expired. The personnel managers of armed forces establish their desired mix of first-term and career members based on their tactics and weapons and on the political and economic environment. Experience shows that a military person who makes a decision to reenlist once has a high propensity to stay in for a full career. For all intents and purposes, a member who reenlists becomes a career professional.

The percentage of the enlisted force that is to consist of career members varies greatly. NATO nations with conscription try to achieve a high proportion of career members, around 50 percent. The United States and the United Kingdom seek to achieve about 25 percent career members for their volunteer forces. The former Soviet Union and the nations of Eastern Europe sought a career content of about 20 percent. So the challenge of persuading first-term members approaching the end of their service to reenlist applies to all armed forces.

Retention or reenlistment, unlike enlistment, is commonly the responsibility of the unit to which the individual belongs. Commanders are graded on how well they retain qualified personnel, and unit officers and noncommissioned officers are appointed to head unit retention programs. Special training is available to those responsible for unit retention, and much effort is made to persuade qualified members to stay in military service. Retention is even more selective than recruiting. The measures of quality used for retention, however, are based more on actual performance than on test scores or civilian education. Basically, the armed forces set minimum standards for reenlistment, and the units decide who among those leaving are eligible for reenlistment. Members with poor disciplinary records or who have not performed well are denied reenlistment.

A major tool available to the retention program is the reenlistment bonus. This financial incentive can be applied quite flexibly to induce members with particular skills, or who promise to undergo certain training, to stay in the service. Some bonuses are available only for skills specified by service headquarters. Others are available to all qualified persons who reenlist.

Retention involves not only keeping good people on active duty but also convincing those people who do leave active duty to join a reserve component unit and participate in reserve training. Most military personnel systems are structured so that a person who leaves active duty remains in military service and is available for wartime service for a specified period of time. The value of that individual is increased if he or she trains with a reserve unit. Admittedly, active unit commanders and retention specialists place first priority on keeping people on active duty, but they are beginning to realize that keeping people in reserve units is also important.

Youth and Vigor

One of the characteristics of a military personnel system is its emphasis on youth and vigor; combat is young persons' work. Military personnel systems are designed to keep people moving up or out, so that at every grade there are no holdovers who grow too old to perform well under demanding conditions. While age limitations and retirement ages differ among the nations, those of the United States are representative. In the U.S. armed forces, most enlisted people serve either 3 to 4 years or 20 to 24 years. Those who reenlist tend to serve until they can retire, and the minimum retirement age of 20 years is set specifically to encourage enlisted people to leave when they are in their late 30s or early 40s. Career officers may also retire with a minimum of 20 years' service, but they tend to stay somewhat longer, particularly if they are promoted to full colonel (navy captain) or to general or admiral. Both officers and enlisted personnel, however, must retire with 30 years of service unless granted a waiver for special reasons. All officers are required by law to retire after 35 years of service, again with provision for a few waivers. Thus, U.S. law and Department of Defense regulations discourage service for officers over the age of 55. This accent on youth works against developing members with a lot of technological or managerial experience. It also results in a great deal of turnover within the force structure. Officers—particularly senior officers—seldom stay on a single job long enough to learn it thoroughly; they must make the next move in their career before it is ended by retirement or separation.

Career Development

Because the armed forces tend to "grow their own," they have to expend considerable resources in continuous development of the abilities of their members. The inexorable pressures to move up or out forces military personnel to learn quickly, for there is not much time to simply learn by doing. Thus, armed forces tend to devote a great deal of their time in training and education of their members. This ranges from initial recruit (basic) training, to short one- to-two week courses on a wide variety of subjects to one- and two-year resident courses for officers at the war colleges. Not only is the training and education arranged, but there is great attention paid to the proper sequence of assignments for development of the service member to carry out the duties of higher graded positions.

The career development system applies particularly to officers, who are required in many personnel systems to have at least one technical or functional specialty in addition to a primary specialty of infantry, armor, artillery, engineering, transportation, or supply. Career development patterns are developed for each officer branch specifying the steps that a successful officer should take to increase chances for promotion. For officers with two major specialties, moving back and forth from one to the other, back and forth from duty with troops to staff duty and schooling, and from tours overseas to home tours becomes a complicated and difficult path.

In the U.S. armed forces, the already complicated officer career development systems were complicated further by the requirement added by Congress in 1987 that all officers had to serve a joint tour of duty on a staff or activity that involved more than one armed force (army, navy, air force, Marine Corps, Coast Guard) in order to be promoted to general or admiral. Since there are not enough joint-duty positions to allow all officers to serve a joint tour, this new complication means that the officer corps soon will be separated into those who can make general and those who cannot, no matter how hard they try.

The rules and constraints on modern officer career development coupled with a policy of up or out, make it almost impossible for an officer to do within the time available everything he or she is supposed to do in order to succeed. Indeed, studies of those who do get promoted to general or admiral show that these successful officers spend very little time on any one assignment, but they do touch all of their required bases in the career development system.

RAPID EXPANSION

One of the challenges facing military personnel systems is the possibility that it will be necessary to expand the number of service members significantly in a short period of time. This requires that some thought and effort be given to accessing and training additional people during mobilization. It also requires consideration be given to maintaining pools of trained personnel in some form of reserve service.

Those nations that rely exclusively on volunteers to fill their active and reserve units in peacetime usually have a standby mechanism to permit conscription in wartime. These nations realize that although they can attract sufficient military personnel on a voluntary basis during peacetime or even during a small war, they would be unable to attract enough volunteers to meet their requirements during a major war. The United States keeps its Selective Service System on a standby basis, ready to start a wartime draft upon order by the president and approval by Congress. Because the newly drafted personnel are not going to be sufficiently trained for combat in less than three to four months, these personnel are not available during the initial days of a mobilization or war. Initial reliance must be placed on persons who have already received military training.

It is customary for all military personnel systems to make some provision for rapid expansion by retaining the ability to recall some or all of those persons who leave active duty. In the United States, for example, all persons who enlist in the armed forces incur an eight-year military service obligation. Even if they serve only three years on active duty, they are retained in the Individual Ready Reserve for five additional years during which they may be recalled to active duty by presidential authority. These personnel may choose to serve in a reserve unit during that period, and they may reenlist in the reserve at the expiration of their military service obligation if they choose. In European nations, conscripts who serve their initial obligated tours of active duty are then transferred to various categories of individual reserves. The youngest people who have left active duty most recently are assigned to the reserve category that is subject to recall first and that may be required to undergo some annual refresher training. As the reservists get older, they transfer into lesser ready reserve categories.

Military retirees are another source of trained personnel. The United States plans to make extensive use of recalled retirees for a major mobilization. However, there is no evidence that other nations, even those who retire officers fairly early, have considered retirees to be recallable assets.

REDUCTIONS IN FORCE

Military personnel planners also must consider how to reduce their strengths sharply and suddenly when peace appears imminent or at hand, as happened in 1945 and 1991–92. The history of military personnel management shows sudden increases at the onset of a war followed by equally sudden decreases at the end of the war.

The classic method of managing sudden strength cuts has been to create two classes of military personnel. This particularly applies to officers, from whom long service is the norm. In this system, the regular officers are the hard core of peacetime officers at a generally low peacetime strength. Upon warning of an impending emergency, these regular officers would be augmented by large numbers of temporary, or reserve, officers either trained for the occasion or kept on tap for this possibility. Once the war is over, the reservists would leave active duty and go back to their civilian jobs, while the regulars would once again constitute the peacetime force.

The dual status system worked well for the United States from the Civil War through World War II. Regular officers were few in number, and large numbers of reserve and temporary officers were commissioned to fight the wars. After the wars ended, the reserve and temporary officers were separated, and the regular officers resumed the peacetime duty of preparation. The Korean War and the Cold War disrupted the classic dual status system in the United States. In order to wage the Korean War, the United States had to recall thousands of reserve officers who had just been separated. During the Cold War, the United States kept many of these reserve officers on active duty instead of letting them go after the end of the Korean War. This created a situation in which the regular officers were only a small proportion of active-duty officers and, although the distinction between regular and reserve ceased to have real significance, it continued to exist. At times during this period the armed forces had three promotion lists: one for regulars, another for reserves, and a third for temporary promotions for both kinds. Regular officers had both permanent (regular) rank and temporary rank. Regular officers also had tenure, for this was the original purpose for having this officer category. Confusion existed between reserve officers on long periods of active duty (career reservists) and reserve officers serving in reserve component units.

The situation in the U.S. armed forces got so complicated, that it was completely modified and simplified by the Defense Officer Personnel Management Act (DOPMA) of 1980. DOPMA established a single order of precedence list for all officers on active duty. Under DOPMA, almost all officers in the grades of lieutenant and captain are career reservists. The goal of DOPMA is to have an all-regular officer corps by the eleventh year of service. At the time of selection for promotion to major (10 to 14 years of service) all officers are considered also for membership in the regular armed forces. Thus, almost all officers in grades higher than major with service greater than 14 years are regular officers. Having created a system with DOPMA that was designed expressly for the substantial peacetime strengths needed for the Cold War, it remains to be seen how the U.S. armed forces will use that system to respond to a large decrease in active-duty officer strength.

Regardless of how a particular officer or enlisted management system is structured, it is impossible to add or cut strength rapidly without doing serious damage to the entire military personnel system. Solutions designed to achieve short-term results often cause severe damage to the long-term prospects, so that having the right numbers and grades of military personnel with the necessary skills 20 years in the future may be made very difficult by hasty or unprogrammed actions.

SEPARATION

In order to maintain the force at authorized levels overall and by grade and specialty, it is necessary to have a way to separate officers and enlisted personnel from the service. The separation process falls into three general categories: undesirable personnel, excess personnel, and overage personnel.

Personnel whose conduct or ability make their continued presence in the armed forces a disadvantage are separated for cause. Members found guilty of crimes may be separated or discharged as a part of their sentence. Members found to be unsuitable for military life for various reasons may be separated involuntarily. Members found to be physically unsuitable for military service may be separated for medical reasons. In each of these cases, the person being separated has served in less than a fully satisfactory manner, and the discharge reflects this. Persons separated as a result of a sentence by a military court are given dishonorable discharges or, for lesser crimes, a bad conduct discharge. These two types of discharges serve notice that the individual was a disciplinary problem. Persons separated for unsuitability are given a general discharge, which does not imply criminal conduct but is not a recommendation either. Persons who serve satisfactorily and are separated through no direct fault of their own are given honorable discharges. Persons discharged for medical reasons generally are given honorable discharges, but this depends on the circumstances. All military personnel systems have to have these mechanisms to eliminate those who do not belong in military service.

Armed forces also have to be able to eliminate from their ranks officers and enlisted men who have served well, but who are in excess to their needs. Ratings for performance of duty and estimates of future potential are used to establish general orders of merit, and those high on the list are retained, while those lower on the list are separated. The placement of the line between retention and separation depends on the circumstances. During an expansion, the line is placed low on the list, and most or all are retained. During a reduction phase, however, the line is placed high on the list, and persons who might be promoted during expansion are separated instead. The personnel separated in this manner are valuable assets, and efforts are made to retain them in the reserve components so that they may be available during an expansion phase. Personnel separated as being in excess to needs receive honorable discharges. If the person is eligible for retirement, that option is open as well, and he or she will be encouraged to retire or, if necessary, forced to retire. Military strength reductions during 1991 and 1992 were facilitated by extending voluntary separation incentives that offered either a lump sum payment or a fixed-term annuity to encourage personnel to leave voluntarily.

Finally, it is necessary to separate personnel who get too old to provide effective service. These persons usually are retired and paid an annuity. The compensation, promotion, and retirement systems are designed to make it attractive for military personnel to leave active duty at the times desired by the personnel managers. If this does not work, the laws force people to retire by imposing absolute length of service constraints.

Civilian Personnel Systems

GRADE

Unlike military personnel systems, civilian personnel systems in government and industry tend to associate the grade of the employee with the job itself. That is, the person enjoys the pay, perquisites, and power of the job only when he or she fills the job. This means that an employee has to be filling (encumbering) a GS-13 position in order to be a GS-13. In order to be promoted to GS-14, that employee has to transfer to a position requiring a GS-14.

The grade-*qua*-position approach both simplifies and complicates civilian personnel management. It is simpler not to have to worry about placing a person with a particular grade only into positions of that grade, and the manpower system that grades positions becomes very important. On the other hand, there are serious adverse effects for systematic career development because the only way people can advance is by obtaining another job. Theoretically it is possible to have one's job upgraded to get a promotion, but this is rare. Thus, lateral movement to a job of the same grade is done only by those employees who are dissatisfied with their present supervisors or jobs or who are willing to slow down their advancement in the short term to gain broader experience for a longer-term benefit. Most civilian employees spend a good deal of their time calculating how to get into higher graded positions. This policy also means that promotion for many employees is blocked until their supervisor either dies, retires, or moves to a higher graded job. There is no sense of overall development as is possible with military personnel, for all advancement depends on the next step.

An exception to the grade in the position policy for civilian employees has been made for the members of the Senior Executive Service (SES), whose grade is supposed to rest in them as individuals. Despite some initial difficulties with the concept of grade in the man, the SES is now working the way it was intended, and SES members are moved around from job to job as deemed best for the overall civil service and without having to worry about the grade of the position. In this respect, the members of the SES are like their military counterparts, who are generals and admirals.

Lateral entry. Civilian personnel systems, even in armed forces, favor bringing in people laterally from civilian life where they have already gained the skills needed to do their jobs. In government, however, the concept of the civilian personnel system as a lateral entry is not really true. While it is possible to join the civil service directly from civilian life at a middle or high grade, the usual practice is for a young person to enter at a lower grade and work up to higher graded positions. Accordingly, the civilian personnel systems for armed forces resemble in many respects, and suffer the same problems faced by, military personnel systems.

HIRING

Recruiting for civilian employees is called hiring. This function is performed in the United States on a completely decentralized basis. There are several hundred civilian personnel offices in the U.S. Department of Defense. These usually are located at a major military base or headquarters and provide all civilian personnel services for a designated geographical area. When a civilian job vacancy occurs, the military unit requests the civilian personnel officer to hire a person to fill the vacancy. In order to ensure that there is no political or illegal influence used in the hiring process, the civilian personnel officer either draws up a list of candidates from preapproved lists (for lower graded positions) or announces publicly that the vacancy exists and solicits candidates; individuals who want the job submit applications. Sometimes the candidates to fill vacancies are limited to present government employees or even present employees of a particular organization. Otherwise, the vacancy is thrown open to all candidates, even those who are not presently working for the government.

Once the candidates have submitted their applications, an individual or most often a board of senior employees selects those candidates who are qualified. Generally the selection board designates the top three candidates, the names of whom are sent to the supervisor of the vacant position. The supervisor has the privilege of selecting his or her choice from the three names submitted by the board. There are a wide variety of processes and procedures, but this is the normal procedure. Thus, the hiring process is long and tedious, fraught with difficulties and chances for litigation. The result is that it is common in the civilian service for vacancies to remain open for extended periods of time while the hiring process takes place.

Despite all of the precautions to ensure fair competition for vacancies, the general belief of the employees themselves is that a person who is filling the vacant position on an acting basis and/or is preferred by the supervisor has a distinct advantage in being selected.

RETENTION

Retention is also a problem for civilian personnel managers. Civilian employees may resign at any time; generally their employment contracts do not bind them to specific terms of service. In a few cases, however, in which the employee has received schooling or other government assistance, a civilian employee may have incurred a service obligation.

One reason why civilian employees remain in government service, aside from job satisfaction (which is quite high), is to earn a retirement annuity. Government workers are thought, traditionally, to be willing to trade low wages for job security and a good retirement plan. Government retirement benefits originally were generous to promote retention. The Civil Service Retirement System (CSRS) was designed to retain civilian employees for a full career of government service. Under this plan, an employee entering as a young person has to work until age 55 when, with 30 or more years of service, he or she can retire with an immediate annuity. It is also possible under CSRS to retire at age 60 with 20 years of service or at age 62 with at least 5 years of service. The effect of CSRS has been to keep people employed long enough to receive their retirement annuity.

In 1987 a new retirement system, the Federal Employees Retirement System (FERS) was introduced. FERS was designed by Congress and some civilian personnel managers to reduce the costs of retirement to the government by shifting part of the burden of saving to the employees. It also was designed explicitly to make it easier for employees to leave and rejoin the civil service without losing all of their retirement benefits, as is the case under the CSRS. To this extent, FERS weakens the incentives for civilian employees to remain for a full career of 30 years with the government. All employees of the federal government hired after 1 January 1988 are covered by FERS, and all other employees covered by CSRS were offered an opportunity to transfer to FERS during 1987. Only a very small proportion of those under CSRS elected to change to FERS. Retention of employees in civilian positions could become a larger problem than before, even in peacetime.

Retention of civilian employees in wartime is a potential problem and a matter of great concern to civilian personnel managers. This is particularly true for civilian employees in the combat theaters. Unlike military personnel who must remain on duty in the combat theaters, civilian employees can simply quit their jobs and leave the danger area. While many, perhaps most, civilian managers will stay on their jobs despite the danger, there is no assurance of this. Employment contracts requiring civilian employees to remain at their duty stations are generally considered to be unenforceable. During Operation Desert Shield and Operation Desert Storm in 1990–91, many Department of Defense civilian employees volunteered for service in the theater of operations and performed well. Despite this positive experience, the armed forces remain concerned about placing too much reliance on civilian employees in the combat theaters, particularly in critical jobs.

Another potentially major problem in retaining civilian employees during wartime is competition from private industry. As industrial mobilization proceeds and more and more war materiel is produced, wages for skilled workers in the defense industry will increase. Once wages in the private sector exceed those in government, it is possible that civilian employees will quit their government jobs to work for defense industry. This same factor will make it hard for the civilian personnel officers to hire replacements for those who resign or to hire additional civilian employees needed to accomplish wartime work within the armed forces.

CAREER DEVELOPMENT

The government provides opportunities for civilian employees to develop their careers, but these opportunities are neither as extensive nor as popular as with the military personnel. Because of the grade-in-position policy, civilian employees tend to be apprehensive about leaving their positions to go to school for long periods of time; their position may be filled while they are gone. Nevertheless, a determined effort by civilian personnel managers has made it more attractive for civilian employees to attend both short and long courses designed to promote managerial ability as well as technical skills.

SEPARATION

Civilian employees may be separated for cause, medical reasons, or upon voluntary retirement. Separating a civilian employee for cause is a long and difficult process. Civil service rules were established originally to give protection to civil servants against political abuse and the spoils system, in which civil servants were fired to make room for friends of the new political masters. These rules make it hard to separate an employee for cause. It takes weeks and months of careful documentation by a supervisor to make a case for separation that will be upheld by the personnel managers. Numerous safeguards are mandated to ensure that the employee is given the benefit of the doubt at all stages of the process. Despite recent legislation to make it easier to fire a civilian employee, it is still very hard to do, which leads many supervisors to learn to live with substandard employees rather than go through the process of separation for cause. Separation for medical reasons is straightforward enough, except for the problems of establishing disability, if any. Separation for retirement is at the option of the employee, and there are no age limitations on how long a civilian employee may work if he or she wants to. Most employees retire between 55 and 65, although some continue well beyond that age.

Other Forms of Personnel

CONTRACTORS

In addition to military personnel and civilian employees, many armed forces rely also on private contractors to provide a variety of goods and services. These contractors are in addition to those in the defense industry who manufacture the planes, ships, tanks, ammunition, and missiles needed to equip and sustain the armed forces. Contractors also operate aircraft maintenance facilities, provide guards for base security, mow the lawns and collect the garbage on bases, operate dining facilities, write training manuals, and perform doctrinal studies. In each of these kinds of activities, the contractors do work that otherwise would have to be done by a government employee, either military or civilian. Instead of hiring another soldier or civilian employee for their defense establishments, many nations (particularly the United States) hire private organizations.

In the United States, it has been government policy to use contractors to perform many functions that traditionally have been accomplished by government workers. The general policy is that a contractor will be used unless it can be proven that an in-house operation can do the same work less expensively. There is also a provision that contractors will not be used for purely military functions. The U.S. policy has led to widespread use of contractors in base operations. Some U.S. military bases, in fact, are operated exclusively by contractors. One reason for this heavy reliance on contractors is that Congress has placed numerical ceilings on both military personnel and civilian employees, while separately providing the funds to operate bases and conduct other essential work. With money, but insufficient authorized manpower positions, those responsible to get the work done have no choice but to hire private contractors.

This policy means that it is necessary to consider using contractors when determining the appropriate mix of personnel to do the work. The use of contractors for critical work in potential combat areas has caused some anxiety for military planners. Since contractor employees are not obligated to remain in a combat area, there is a question of whether it is prudent to rely on them for critical work in peacetime or in wartime. During Operation Desert Storm some contract employees refused to work and left the combat area during the ground combat phase of the war. Despite some misgivings, the reliance of the U.S. armed forces on contractors to perform work has increased substantially in recent years.

Host Nation Support

Another form of personnel support may be provided to the armed forces of a nation by citizens of the nation where those forces are fighting. When both nations are allies, this is called host nation support. Host nation support may take the form of hiring local civilians to provide support for the fighting forces, or it may mean that the host nation provides organized units to perform some of the support functions. The use of local trucks, railroads, security guards, or labor battalions provided by the host country is a welcome addition to the capability of the overall force. Preplanned host nation support allows the foreign force to tailor its own supporting forces to avoid duplicating capability that can be made available locally.

Summary

The personnel function is the most important aspect of organizing, training, supporting, and operating military forces, but, because of the constraints that affect the armed forces when they prepare for or engage in military operations, the personnel function has become very difficult and complicated. Present policies that encourage using a large proportion of civilian employees and contractors to get the work done complicate the personnel function for armed forces. Integrating these three kinds of personnel with intrinsically different approaches and management systems is a formidable task made possible only because the basic element of every personnel system—the human being—tends to behave the same way whether a contractor, civilian employee, or military member.

JOHN R. BRINKERHOFF

SEE ALSO: Education, Military; Enlisted Personnel; Officer; Reserve Components.

Bibliography

Coffey, K. J. 1978. *Manpower for military mobilization*. Washington, D.C.: American Enterprise Institute.

Defense Manpower Commission. 1976. *Defense manpower: The keystone of national security*. Washington, D.C.: Government Printing Office.

Eitelberg, M. J. 1988. *Manpower for military occupations*. Alexandria, Va.: Human Resources Research Organization.

Foster, G. D., A. N. Sabrosky, W. J. Taylor, eds. 1987. *The strategic dimension of military manpower*. Cambridge, Mass.: Ballinger.

French, W. L. 1982. *The personnel management process: Human resources administration and development*. Boston: Houghton Mifflin.

Goldich, R. L. 1981. *Military manpower policy and the all-volunteer force*. Washington, D.C.: Congressional Research Service.

Klingner, D. E. 1985. *Public personnel management: Contexts and strategies*. Englewood Cliffs, N.J.: Prentice Hall.

U.S. Office of Personnel Management. 1981. *Manager's handbook*. Washington, D.C.: Government Printing Office.

PLANNING, MILITARY

Planning has always been an important part of military endeavors. Planning can be done by an individual leader or by one or more subordinates working with, or in support of, the leader. In ancient times, a chieftain would often call his war council together to decide whether to wage war and if so, how. During the classical age of Greece, the leaders of city-states who were charged with waging war consulted not only the ruling elders or representatives of the citizenry, but also the oracles, in an attempt to divine the intentions of their enemies and obtain the sympathies of the gods.

History

As the complexity of warfare increased, so too did the requirements for detailed and sensible planning. In *De Re Militari*, written for the Roman emperor Valentinian II in A.D. 390, Vegetius emphasized the importance of planning for sufficient provisioning of the legions at the outset of a campaign; described the necessity of gaining intelligence about the enemy's intentions and insisted that strict counterintelligence measures be adopted; and prescribed detailed operational planning, even down to the amount of room occupied by a single soldier within a formation, to allow for extrapolative planning for the amount of maneuver room required for a legion in a given formation.

MIDDLE AGES

During the Middle Ages in Europe, due to the prevalence of the feudal system, planning took on new importance and unprecedented degrees of difficulty. Even the greatest of kings depended on their vassals to provide soldiers and materiel for war making, and frequently this caused considerable compromise during the course of military operations. The Crusades, the greatest military undertakings of the Middle Ages, were constantly hampered not only by bickering between lords and overlords, but also by conflict between allies (e.g., between Philip of France and Richard of England on the Third Crusade). This sort of problem ensured that none of the Crusades was executed as planned and resulted in disaster for many of the fighting participants.

The introduction of practical personal firearms for mass armies during the early sixteenth century gave rise to new planning requirements for military operations. In addition to planning for tactical maneuvers, coalition warfare, intelligence and security matters, and subsistence provisions, ammunition and gunpowder had to be procured and maintained in adequate quantities. Tactics could be decided by generals and their subordinates, food could be gained by local purchase or plunder, but muskets and gunpowder were not easy to make, nor was saltpeter easy to find. During this era, the role of the quartermaster became absolutely critical as a result of the increased importance of logistical planning. In many European armies, the post of quartermaster was one of the very few officer positions to which a non-noble could aspire; the dedication necessary to truly master this aspect of the profession of arms was such that few nobles cared to devote the time required.

In the century and a half that followed the Thirty Years' War, the revulsion felt by many for the results of war on a grand scale brought on the era of limited war. Conflicts such as the War of the League of Augsburg, the War of the Spanish Succession, and even the Seven Years' War, while bloody, were fought by professional national armies of limited size and were financed by royal treasuries. Unlike the preceding Wars of Religion in Europe, which were fought largely by mercenaries who were compensated by booty and plunder, during this era, planning had to include consideration for personnel procurement, compensation, and retention to ensure the existence of an adequate professional fighting force. On this important planning requirement, the marshal-general of France, Maurice de Saxe, remarked in his mid-eighteenth-century *Rêveries* that "it is better to have a small number of well-kept and well-disciplined troops than to have a great number that are neglected in these matters."

During this era of limited, cautiously executed conflicts, siege warfare became the norm of combat. The reduction of massive fortifications such as those of the famous French engineer Vauban became matters that were far beyond the ability of untutored noble commanders to plan for and execute without the advice of professional military engineers. Thus another field of military planning, that of military engineering, involving siege machinery, fortification construction, and provisioning for protracted static campaigning, became open to the skilled and knowledgeable commoner.

Napoleonic Era and the Prussian System of Planning

The reintroduction of mass national armies with the *levée en masse* of the French Revolution in 1793 brought military planning requirements to new levels of complexity. The French postrevolutionary practice of promoting officers without regard to their noble status influenced even the Prussians, who during the period 1808–14, under the leadership of Gerhard J. D. von Scharnhorst, developed their famous General Staff. This organization, made up of officers who had demonstrated particular talent and ability for the planning and management of the many requirements of campaign preparation, revolutionized military planning. Coupled with new recruitment and tactical techniques, the vastly improved efficiency of the Prussian planning and preparation for war that resulted from the efforts of the General Staff were responsible for the tremendous success of the Prussian army. Following the Napoleonic era, schools for the academic preparation of officers were developed; across Europe, the other great powers developed general staffs of their own.

The efficacy of the Prussian system was proven to the world during the period 1866–71, when Prussia soundly defeated Austria in the Seven Weeks' War (1866) and France in the Franco-Prussian War (1870–71). In both of these conflicts, extremely detailed planning for the mobilization, transportation, armament, and actual strategic and tactical deployment of the Prussian and allied German states' armies were carried out with great precision by the Prussian General Staff. Of the world's major military powers, only the United States lacked a general staff at the end of the nineteenth century; after the near fiasco of the Spanish-American War, even the United States adopted a system modeled on that of the Germans.

World Wars I and II

The introduction and subsequent rapid development of military airpower during and after World War I caused many of the major powers to form air forces that were branches separate from the army or navy; clearly, optimum performance of any of the services now demanded joint operations. This requirement gave rise to the formation, before and during the Second World War, of joint planning headquarters to effectively coordinate the extremely complicated activities of the increasingly diverse armed services. The Germans' *Oberkommando der Wehrmacht* (OKW) and the United States' Joint Chiefs of Staff were two such organizations formed to facilitate the coordinated planning of joint operations.

During World War II and immediately after, there was also the need for coalition warfare by the Allies on a historically unprecedented scale. The complexity of such operations demanded the formation of combined headquarters such as the Supreme Headquarters, Allied Expeditionary Forces (SHAEF), which planned the invasion of western Europe and the subsequent combined and joint operations in that theater. The execution of operations involving thousands of aircraft and more than 85 ground divisions, including troops from the United States, Great Britain, Canada, France, Poland, Belgium, and Holland, constituted a planning challenge not previously encountered in the history of warfare.

After the Second World War, another new challenge in military planning developed from the establishment of permanent military coalitions. Alliances such as the North Atlantic Treaty Organization (NATO) and the Southeast Asia Treaty Organization (SEATO) involved planning requirements that went beyond the difficulties of wartime exigency due to the constantly changing political situations of the affected regions.

Modern Planning—Components and Procedures

Military planning today reflects the complexity of modern warfare. Due to the requirements to plan not only for tactical and strategic maneuvers, but also for complicated personnel, intelligence, logistical, and even politico-military affairs, the modern planning process involves a stepwise procedure designed to account for the impact of the myriad considerations of modern military endeavor. The U.S. Army's system, as conducted by a general staff, is one example of such a planning sequence and is illustrative of procedures used by most modern armies of the 1990s.

Upon receiving a mission from higher headquarters, or upon the commander's perception of the need for the execution of a particular operation, a mission analysis (usually called an *Appreciation* in the British army and an *Estimate of the Situation* in the American army) is conducted by the commander's staff. This mission analysis involves the identification of tasks to be performed pursuant to mission accomplishment in the light of constraints and capabilities of friendly units. Both explicit and implied tasks are determined and analyzed for feasibility from the perspectives of each of the principal staff officers. The G-1 (personnel officer) analyzes the tasks from the perspective of strength, medical, and morale requirements; the G-2 (intelligence officer) conducts an analysis of the enemy's capabilities and anticipated actions; the G-3 (operations officer) supervises the entire analysis process in addition to identifying operational requirements; the G-4 (logistics officer) analyzes the requirements for all classes of supply, including rations, fuel, and ammunition; and the G-5 (civil-military operations officer) examines the impact of the civilian situation including the local economy, refugee control, potential for guerrilla activities, and so forth.

THE ROLE OF PERSONNEL IN PLANNING

When the mission analysis is complete, the commander and the G-3 build a *restated mission*, or the mission as it pertains to their unit. The commander then issues to his staff his planning guidance, which may include instructions for the use of special weapons (such as nuclear or chemical munitions), command and control requirements, deception plans, and even specific courses of action that the commander may wish to see developed.

Once in receipt of the restated mission and planning guidance, each staff section then prepares its estimate. These estimates expand on the considerations already brought to light during the mission analysis. The role of the chief of staff becomes critical to this process because he ensures that all staff sections continually exchange pertinent information and that disagreements are resolved without burdening the commander.

The G-1 continues mission analysis from the perspective of personnel availability and preparedness for the operation. The number of troops available, their medical condition, anticipated replacement flow, morale and unit cohesion, and other considerations are weighed and analyzed as the G-1's estimate is completed. When finished, the personnel estimate identifies certain courses of action that are feasible in the pursuit of mission accomplishment.

The intelligence estimate, continued by the G-2 from the mission analysis, carefully considers the impact of weather and terrain on both friendly and enemy forces. Probable enemy courses of action are identified from the latest reliable human, imagery, and electronic intelligence available, as are enemy vulnerabilities and strengths. Upon completion of the intelligence estimate, the G-2 is prepared to comment on the feasibility of the friendly courses of action developed by the other staff officers in the light of information about the enemy.

The logistic estimate, prepared by the G-4, includes consideration of the impact and availability of all classes of supply, the transportation requirements, and the sustainability of various courses of action. The latter requirement illustrates the necessity for the constant exchange of information facilitated by the chief of staff.

The civil-military operations estimate analyzes the impact of the courses of action under consideration on the local populace and vice versa. Refugee control, property damage, religious customs, local holidays, and the extent of enemy influence over the region's population all affect the G-5's estimate.

As the G-3 completes the operation estimate, usually under the supervision of the chief of staff, he develops several potential courses of action designed to accomplish the mission in various ways. In this process, he must be apprised periodically of the feasibility of such courses of action from the perspective of the other staff officers. For example, a course of action involving a unit's passage through a chemically contaminated area might not be feasible if the G-1 advises the G-3 that morale in the unit is particularly low due to heavy casualties sustained during previous similar operations. Another course of action, perhaps necessitating heavy artillery preparation, might not be considered if the G-4 advises the G-3 that the amount of ammunition available will be seriously depleted by such a course of action. The estimate not only considers the dictates of the ethical standards of warfare, but also gives careful consideration to the potential impact of probable enemy courses of action, usually through a war-gaming process that analyzes the effects of each considered friendly course of action against each probable enemy activity.

Implementation

When this process is completed, the estimate is submitted to the commander by the G-3 or chief of staff. The commander then selects a single course of action. It may be one of the courses presented by the staff, or it may be one with considerable modifications made by the commander himself. In any case, the selection of this course of action becomes the basis for the staff's preparation of the operation plan or order.

THE OPLAN AND THE OPORD

The operation plan (OPLAN) or operation order (OPORD) follows a set format that provides consistency and clarity. The only difference between the two is that because the OPLAN is used for the execution of an operation at an unknown time in the future, times are represented in terms of "H hour," or the time of the beginning of the operation. For example, a preparatory activity such as loading paratroopers into aircraft three hours before the commencement of an airborne assault on a drop zone would be designated as occurring at "H − 3"; the requirement to seize assault objectives no later than an hour after the drop would be designated as happening no later than "H + 1." Also, due to their less concrete, potential nature, OPLANs include a set of assumptions under which it is assumed that the operation will take place. For example, to use the airborne model again, an OPLAN detailing an airborne assault would list as one of its assumptions that at least local air superiority would exist if the operation were to take place.

In the U.S. Army, Paragraph 1 of an OPLAN/OPORD is the *Situation*. This paragraph details the impact of terrain, weather, and enemy forces on the operation to be conducted. If the information is too voluminous to state succinctly, much of it may be presented in an Intelligence Annex to the order/plan. This paragraph allows the subordinate intelligence staffs to conduct their own analyses and estimates upon receipt.

Paragraph 2 is the *Mission*. This is the restated mission derived from the mission analysis. Mission statements always include the who, what, when, where, and why of the operation to be conducted. For example, "100th Infantry Division (who) attacks (what) commencing 120700NOV44 (when) along the axis Baccarat—Bertrichamps—Raon l'Etape (where) to seize the high ground west north of the Meurthe River in zone. (why)" The information contained in this paragraph allows subordinate units to conduct their own mission analyses.

Paragraph 3 is entitled *Execution* and includes both a statement of the overall concept of the operation, which is descriptive in nature, and a delineation of the task responsibilities of each of the units directly subordinate to the issuing headquarters. This allows subordinate units to understand easily how they fit into the overall scenario and what their specific tasks are. This is especially important for the conduct of their mission analyses. The instructions for subunits given in this paragraph are directive in nature, but are specifically not overly restrictive. These instructions typically impart the who, what, when, and where of their requirements, but leave it to the initiative of subordinate commanders and staffs to determine the how. This paragraph is usually supplemented by an annex delineating responsibilities for fire support and by a map overlay portraying the geographical conduct of the operation through a set of universally understood symbols.

Also included in Paragraph 3 are *Coordinating Instructions*, which prescribe requirements for smooth conduct of the operation; these instructions also detail the activities to be carried out by all subordinate units, such as the rendering of reports when accomplishing given missions and so forth. This obviates the need to state the same requirements over and over again and thus make the order unnecessarily long and cumbersome.

Paragraph 4, *Service Support*, outlines the supply and transportation requirements for the operation. Typically, due to the extremely detailed nature of such requirements, much of the information is contained in a separate annex included at the end of the order.

Paragraph 5 is entitled *Command and Signal* and includes information concerning the succession of the chain of command, location of command posts, and pertinent signal data for the operation. The latter information is usually also located in a separate annex to keep the basic order uncluttered and clear.

In addition to these basic paragraphs and supplementary annexes, there are often other annexes included in an OPLAN/OPORD for clarity and precision. These might include Airborne or Air Assault annexes with exact timetables of departures and arrivals of aerial mobility assets; Engineer annexes describing the exact locations of obstacles such as minefields and destroyed bridges; and Civil-Military Operations annexes detailing the requirements for refugee control or the need for particular care to be taken in the course of conducting operations in the vicinity of certain religious shrines. Such information is placed in annexes to ensure that the basic tenets of the order remain clear and comprehensible in the five basic paragraphs. Given that many OPLANs/OPORDs will be received, analyzed, and implemented under the stress of battle, such emphasis on clarity and simplicity is as essential as the precision and detail that must accompany it.

Once an OPLAN/OPORD is completed, it is presented by the G-3 or the chief of staff to the commander, who amends and eventually approves it for transmission to subordinate units. Since these units will also need to conduct the same procedures upon receipt of the OPLAN/OPORD, a general rule for the timing of planning is to take no more than one-third of the time available before the commencement of the operation for the planning activities of the immediate headquarters and to leave the remainder to subordinate echelons.

Soviet-style planning procedures vary in some ways from this procedure, notably in the use of *norms*. Norms describe the ideal performance of given types of units in a particular situation and, as such, provide a mathematical prescription for action. As a result, the parameters of any particular situation can rapidly be mathematically analyzed and an approved response completed. This at once allows the rapid formulation of the various staff and commander's estimates, but also tends to restrict flexibility. Such a procedure is consistent with the Soviet-style armies' emphasis on rapid, decisive offensive action and the retention of initiative and maximum flexibility at the higher echelons of command.

Conclusion

As the complexity of warfare increases, so too will the demands for detailed, comprehensive military planning. In the West, planning demands the formulation of standard operating and communications procedures due to the coalition nature of their military structures. Such agreements must be constantly updated to ensure congruence with the latest technological and doctrinal developments within each member of the various Western alliances.

Undoubtedly, automated information management systems will continue to play an increasing role in the evolution of military planning; computers for word processing standardized OPLAN/OPORD documents are already in use at the battalion level in the U.S. Army, and facsimile transmitters are in use at the same echelon for the rapid and secure transmission of these orders. In the future, staff and command estimates may be assisted, on a much more sophisticated level, by an automated version of the Soviet-style normative method. As the pace quickens and the complexity of modern warfare increases, such measures will be necessary for the adequate and timely planning of military operations.

KEITH E. BONN

SEE ALSO: Coalition Warfare; Command; Command, Control, Communications, and Intelligence; Command Post; Generalship; Joint Operations; Span of Control: Military Organizations and Operations.

Bibliography

Phillips, T. R., ed. 1985. *The roots of strategy.* Harrisburg, Pa.: Stackpole Books.

Saxe, M. de. 1757. *Les rêveries ou mémoires sur l'art de la guerre.* Mannheim: Drieux.

U.S. Department of the Army. 1984. *Field manual 100-2-1: The Soviet army—Operations and tactics.* Washington, D.C.: Government Printing Office.

U.S. Department of the Army. 1984. *Field manual 101-5: Staff organization and operations.* Washington, D.C.: Government Printing Office.

PRECISION-GUIDED MUNITIONS (PGMs)

The history of weapons has seen a constant striving for improvements in the delivery accuracy of projectiles intended to defeat small targets at long range. Up to and including World War II sufficient accuracy was achievable only at short ranges (approximately 1 kilometer), even for direct-fire guns with sophisticated laying equipment; indirect-fire philosophy was based upon the neutralization of areas by concentration of fire. To destroy targets at anything other than modest range, soldiers relied on the expenditure of large numbers of munitions and the laws of probability. Similarly, attack from the air, even so-called precision attack, called for saturation to achieve its aim.

The precision attack of targets—land, sea, and air—was the motivation for the continuing development of guided weapons (GW). Since early attempts during World War II, particularly in Germany, there has been a steady expansion in the diversity and application of guidance techniques. These have not only benefitted from the explosion in technological capability, but also have in large measure been a driving force in that explosion.

Precision-guided munition (PGM) is a relatively recent term, one that describes part of the family of GW systems developed since the 1960s. The term is generally limited to those devices that are adaptations or extensions of conventional ammunition, launched by conventional means or from conventional carriers (guns, mortars, artillery rockets, aircraft), and used to attack specific targets or classes of targets; it does not include those GWs designed to perform nonconventional munition roles. It encompasses weapons originally termed *smart* (because they use techniques that improve the performance of *dumb* free-fall munitions, either by modification or addition) and some *intelligent* or *brilliant* munitions that can seek autonomously for targets once they have been delivered into the target area, provided they still can be regarded as enhancements.

Thus, a terminally guided autonomous indirect-fire artillery shell for the defeat of armor is unquestionably a PGM, whereas a long-range direct-fire antitank guided weapon (ATGW), possibly employing similar terminal guidance techniques but is rocket powered from a special-purpose launcher vehicle, is not; the latter does not enhance the capability of an existing conventional weapon. Similarly, a guided bomb, comprising a guidance and control attachment to a standard free-fall bomb, is a PGM, but an air-launched ground attack GW is not.

Precision-guided also needs to be clearly defined, because there is a growing class of enhanced munitions that involve the use of explosively formed projectile (EFP) warheads, and these are not strictly PGMs. Such warheads can defeat targets from a distance, typically 100 meters (325 ft.), by the kinetic-energy effect of a formed metal slug; the warhead can be armed by a fuzing system that detects the target with sufficient precision. These sensor-fuzed munitions (SFMs) are distinguished from PGMs (which are guided to hit the target to achieve, generally, a greater lethal effect) for the purpose of this chapter. In practice, the distinction is a fine one, and as will be seen, some of the improved conventional munitions under development offer both PGM and SFM alternatives.

Classes of PGMs

Within the above definition a number of classes of PGMs can be identified as they relate to the mode of operation and the type of conventional munition they enhance or replace. Figure 1 shows this broad range of weapons and lists examples that have been reported in the open literature; some of these have

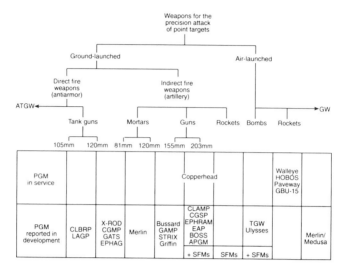

Figure 1. Classes of PGM.

been described in considerable depth, particularly those already in service and others in which advanced development proving is under way.

The weapons shown have all been developed for the attack of "point" targets on the ground, where precision is clearly required to achieve high hit probability. Such targets have included high-value defended targets, notably buildings, hardened emplacements, bridges, and vehicles, particularly armored vehicles. In the main, the high-value targets have been located well into enemy-held ground and have been attacked by interdiction aircraft, giving rise to one category of PGM, the smart/guided bomb, carrying very high destructive power. In attacking vehicles, the most effective lethal mechanism is a comparatively small warhead that is very accurate (circular error probable < 1 m), and this has led to another category associated mainly with the attack of armor by both direct- and indirect-fire weapons.

In the cases of air-launched and direct-fire ground-launched weaponry, GWs also play a major role, and in these categories a simple distinction can be made between GWs and PGMs, as already suggested in the introduction. In the case of indirect-fire weapons, however, guidance technologies have not previously been applied, since the initial weapon aiming cannot be carried out at the launch point. The development of autonomous guidance techniques has now enabled a terminal aim point to be established against remote targets (provided the weapon can be delivered accurately to the target area), and such methods form the basis for PGMs.

The three classes of PGMs (air-launched, ground-launched indirect-fire, and ground-launched direct-fire) can be usefully dealt with separately, since they have distinctive characteristics, and it is convenient to start with the air-launched, since they were the breeding ground for smart guidance techniques.

Weapons Applications

Air-launched PGMs

The war in Vietnam saw the introduction of the first really effective PGM, the Walleye TV-guided bomb, AGM-62; in this system a TV camera was fitted in the nose of the bomb, and the guidance system was locked on to a target image before the Walleye was released from the carrying aircraft. The bomb was subsequently controlled by aerodynamic tail controls to correct the bomb's ballistic trajectory.

The Walleye was used to good effect to provide precision attack against ground targets such as bridges, targets that had proved to be relatively resistant to saturation bombing attacks. Started in 1963, the weapon saw several improvements in warhead and guidance capabilities, in particular enabling the operator to improve the aim by intervening directly in the flight control. This intervention was made possible by a data link between the bomb and a TV display in the launcher aircraft. The Walleye, procured by the U.S. Navy, continued in production through the mid-1980s.

In parallel with the Walleye, the U.S. Air Force procured two guided-bomb systems: HOBOS, an improved TV-guided system, and the Paveway weapons family, utilizing laser semiactive guidance. With the latter system, targets are illuminated by a narrow-beam high-power laser (at 1.06 μ), either from observers on the ground or from aircraft-mounted stabilized projectors. The bomb is guided to the target by sensing and tracking the laser energy reflected from the target.

All of these systems are provided in the form of a kit used to adapt existing "iron bombs" of up to 3,000 pounds, and the latest version of Paveway is designed for low-level delivery missions to reduce aircraft vulnerability. Production numbers of Paveway of more than 25,000 are reported through the late 1980s, many for export to a total of seventeen countries.

Further improvements to guided bombs have included the adoption of imaging infrared (I^2R) seeker heads to provide an all-weather operating capability, using either "lock-on before launch" principles or delayed lock-on through the data link, as typified by GBU-15.

More recently, improvements to these systems have included the addition of propulsion to increase delivery standoff range or enhance maneuver capability; such developments, typified by the AGM-123 Skipper, really bridge the gap between PGMs, as defined above, and air-launched guided missiles. Many other countries have undertaken studies of similar weapons, and France and Israel have developed systems for service.

The main thrust for the development of guided bombs was the operational need for weapons that could be accurately guided against key targets that were immune to other forms of attack but critical to the outcome of action of ground forces, as typified by the Vietnam conflict. The technological state of the art was quite sufficient at that time to provide the necessary solutions and was consistent with techniques already maturing within the burgeoning GW industry.

In the air-launched category we can include one further example, a spin-off from recent developments of the Merlin 81mm mortar PGM, described later. The Merlin guidance/warhead package is fitted to the front of a standard 81mm air-to-ground rocket and air launched from helicopters on an elevated trajectory to engage armor formations at long standoff ranges. This Merlin/Medusa system is intended to be salvo launched, similar to the mortar-launched weapon.

GROUND-LAUNCHED INDIRECT FIRE

This category of weapons has provided a greater variety of techniques and applications of PGMs than any other, although the work on guided bombs provided much of the technological impetus.

Following the Vietnam period, attention turned in the 1970s to operations in Europe and the growing armor threat facing the NATO forces. Although the emphasis was still on the development and replacement of the current direct-fire weapons (long- and medium-range ATGW and tank gun systems), the great strength in depth of the Warsaw Pact armored forces suggested the need for NATO to improve the effectiveness of depth-fire systems, both for interdiction and for support to the forward battle area, traditionally provided by artillery. Armored targets are quite small and well dispersed, and the basic dispersion of conventional long-range artillery is such that its lethality against armored ar-rays, especially ones that are moving, is very low. Precision guidance for artillery was seen as crucial to the defeat of these forces, and a new drive commenced that has taken the concept of PGMs to an altogether higher level of sophistication. Indeed, the term *PGM* is frequently related solely to the attack of armor.

While the direct-fire ATGW systems employed complex guidance technologies, these were not in general appropriate to indirect-fire systems, where lines of sight to the target are not available at the weapons' launch site. Of those techniques used for the earlier smart weapons, only laser semi-active guidance was suitable, provided the target-designator equipment could be positioned close enough to the battle area. This situation, along with the design experience from the Vietnam era, provided a springboard for the evolution of a new class of weapons, starting with the Copperhead PGM.

Although successfully demonstrated, offering good performance, and in full service with the U.S. Army in Europe, the Copperhead was not taken up widely in NATO. This is possibly because of the operational shortcomings of laser semi-active guidance, notably the limited all-weather capability (especially in low clouds) and lack of autonomy for depth fire, rather than the technical performance of the weapon. Indeed, it is believed that work in Germany on the use of the same guidance method for a 120mm mortar bomb, Bussard, stopped for similar reasons. The Copperhead did, however, effectively demonstrate the maturity of technologies able to withstand the hostile gun-launch environment (around 10,000-g acceleration) and encouraged numerous further activities.

By the late 1970s the emphasis was on providing fully autonomous guidance for artillery-delivered systems. The state of the art for guidance sensors and miniaturized electronics pointed toward the feasibility of highly sophisticated processing algorithms being contained within the tight volume constraints of tube-launched munitions. Autonomous operation could be provided through I²R and millimeter-wave (mmW) radar techniques that would enable land targets to be automatically acquired and tracked within complex terrain scenes.

The conventional artillery delivery methods are rocket launchers, guns, and mortars, and conceptual autonomous PGMs have emerged in each of these categories. Such PGMs offer a particular benefit over other forms of guided weapons; they allow full use to be made of the primary weapon (the launcher), the manpower, and the logistic facilities already in place, amplifying the effectiveness and flexibility of these existing assets at relatively low cost. This re-emphasizes the idea of PGMs as extensions and adaptations of conventional weapons, as described in the opening paragraphs.

Following Copperhead, examples of the application of I²R and mmW technologies are as follows:

Rocket launch. The NATO multiple-launch rocket system (MLRS), initially designed to deliver bomblet and mine submunitions, has been extended in phase three to deliver the terminally guided warhead (TGW). Three terminally guided submunitions (TGSMs) are dispensed from each TGW in a salvo of rockets that overfly massed armor formations. The engagement, delivery, dispersion, and individual TGSM target-acquisition logics are designed so that a high level of attrition is achieved in each attack, against either stationary or moving target formations, making the weapon a highly effective interdiction weapon. Each TGSM carries an advanced mmW seeker able to distinguish targets against their backgrounds by use of radar pattern recognition techniques. Such a weapon does, of course, require the approximate location of armor formations to be known, so battlefield intelligence is a most important adjunct to its successful usage. MLRS-TGW is under development by the U.S./UK/French/German consortium MDTT.

A somewhat simpler rocket-delivered PGM is Ulysses, a UK/Italian private venture development utilizing a version of the 120mm terminally guided mortar bomb (TGMB), Griffin (see below), carried as the payload on the 122mm FIROS 30 artillery rocket. Although a single TGSM is carried on each rocket, the launcher vehicle carries 40 rockets (compared with 12 on the MLRS), so overall firepower is not radically degraded.

Gun launch. Much work has been carried out to develop an autonomous equivalent of the Copperhead for the 155mm howitzer. This size howitzer is the standard caliber for most Western armies, is deployed in large numbers, and has adequate range, rate of fire, and mobility for use in all the artillery roles— interdiction, counter-battery, and close support.

National programs have been conducted in the United States, United Kingdom, France, Germany, and Sweden, but the main activity now centers on another NATO program, the autonomous precision-guided munition (APGM) (see Fig. 2), currently in the feasibility stage.

The APGM also utilizes an mmW seeker, similar in complexity to that for

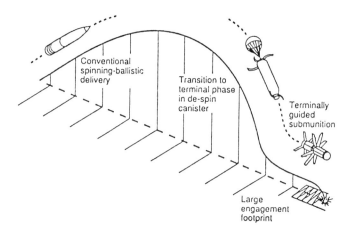

Figure 2. Flight sequence for the 155mm APGM. (SOURCE: Alliance Development Corp.)

MLRS-TGW, with high detection performance against moving and stationary targets and the highly accurate delivery of a heavy shaped-charge warhead system.

A principal difference between APGM and TGW is the operational role. Although APGM is intended to provide a potential for depth fire (interdiction) and counter-battery, its prime function will probably be as a close support weapon, in which fire is called for, and monitored by, forward artillery observers. Armor formations would be engaged, using salvo delivery from (for example) a pair of guns, with target-acquisition algorithms able to avoid multiple hits on individual targets.

In the APGM program, high priority is placed upon having a so-called conventional geometry shell configuration, which implies, among other features, a spinning ballistic flight. Unlike Copperhead, which is decoupled from the spiral rifling in the gun barrel, APGM spins at 300 hertz at launch and is accelerated at 16,000 g. This presents some considerable engineering difficulties in packaging and protecting the delicate components required in the seeker and electronics of the guidance system.

Mortar launch. After the aborted work on the laser semi-active Bussard, later work on TGMBs concentrated on an I^2R homing technique. It was proposed for a later version of Bussard, worked on in the United States on GAMP and terminated, and continues to be used on the Swedish STRIX system.

However, artillery systems normally involve high trajectories, typically on the order of half the delivery range, and the performance of I^2R seeker systems can be severely restricted by cloud cover. The high incidence of cloud cover in Europe has driven the need to realize effective mmW seeker designs for all artillery PGMs, mmW transmission being relatively unaffected by clouds or modest rainfall. Work on simple mmW seekers for TGMBs was spearheaded by British Aerospace (BAe) in the United Kingdom in connection with the Merlin 81mm TGMB (Hooton 1986).

The objective of the Merlin program is to provide the infantry with a low-cost capability against armored vehicles. This is achieved with a new round of ammunition, optimized for attacking vehicles at ranges up to 4 kilometers (2.5 mi.) but usable with the standard 81mm and 82mm mortars in worldwide service and employing normal mortar-fire drills and techniques.

The guidance system uses a simple, all-weather, and low-cost mmW seeker, primarily intended for the attack of moving targets (under the control of forward observers), but also having some capability against stationary vehicles. The requirement to contain the seeker and electronics within the small caliber and length of Merlin has stretched the technologies for microwave and electronic circuit miniaturization and for enabling components to withstand high g forces. Development of Merlin is well advanced, with all aspects of performance now demonstrated.

Merlin technology also is being used in a cooperative development for the 120mm TGMB, the Griffin. Thomson-Brandt Armement in France, MFA in Switzerland, and BPD in Italy are working with BAe to provide a system with a capability for attacking the most heavily armored battlefield targets from the top. The Griffin also will be a low-cost weapon, with high performance against the priority moving targets in the close support battle.

GROUND-LAUNCHED DIRECT FIRE

PGM activities have been related to improving the performance of tank guns at ranges where high ballistic accuracy falls off. Initial work was carried out in the United States on 105mm gun ammunition using both laser beam–riding guidance and laser semi-active guidance techniques. As early as 1959 development was started in the United States on Shillelagh, an antitank guided missile fired from a 152mm gun and accelerated to Mach 3.5 by rocket motor. The gun, mounted in the Sheridan armored vehicle, could also fire secondary ballistic rounds; this duality of purpose is the inverse of later weapons, and Shillelagh is not classed as a PGM. These were not pursued beyond the initial stages, other than with the adoption of the Copperhead technology for a 4.5-inch gun-launched projectile for the U.S. Navy. This is known as Deadeye and is currently in early production.

More recently, work has been carried out on 120mm tank guided ammunition. Notable are two weapons in early development in the United States:

X-ROD: A guided, in-flight rocket-boosted kinetic-energy (KE) penetration round for enhancing performance against armor at ranges beyond 1.5 to 2 kilometers (.9 to 1.2 mi.).

CGMP: A command-guided multipurpose projectile for engaging helicopters at ranges of up to 6 kilometers (3.7 mi.). This munition is likely to carry a general-purpose high-explosive (HE) warhead and be guided using line-of-sight (LOS) guidance techniques.

Similar work is at an early stage in the United Kingdom, France, and Germany (Fletcher 1988). One UK design, GATS (guided antitank shell), is reported to employ similar techniques to those of X-ROD and is designed to improve KE penetration of armor at all ranges and to offer an anti-helicopter capability.

Studies have been carried out in Germany on terminal homing weapons for the 120mm gun (code-named EPHAG), using either I²R or mmW techniques; the present status of this work is uncertain, but such autonomous weapons are likely to receive greater attention as technological constraints diminish.

Guidance and Control Technology

The term *precision guidance* implies that PGMs require an unusually accurate guidance capability package beyond that associated with other guided weapons. This is not necessarily so. The important requirement is that, in contrast with unguided conventional weapons, the effects of PGMs can be delivered with adequate accuracy; the actual requirements for accuracy vary with the class of weapon. Thus a guided bomb, based on, for example, a 1,000-pound iron bomb, requires only modest accuracy to defeat a hard target, probably a CEP of a few meters. On the other hand, an APGM or TGMB will need to hit the top of a tank with a CEP of less than 1 meter (3 ft.) to have the desired effect.

This is consistent with the general characteristics of these different weapons. A guided bomb is very heavy by most GW standards, and the lack of maneuverability will itself limit accuracy. On the other hand, an antiarmor PGM will be relatively agile and be able to utilize precise aim-point corrections during the closing stages of terminal homing.

Types of Guidance

For most PGMs we can dismiss the use of line-of-sight (LOS) guidance techniques, but in the case of the tank gun PGMs, LOS command guidance presents no major design or development hurdles. For the rest, homing guidance methods will be used, and these fall into the following classes:

- laser semi-active
- infrared
- passive radiometric
- active mmW radar.

Laser semi-active homing, although the most useful in ensuring the engagement of specific targets (rather than allowing the PGM to self-select the target), is operationally more limited for the reasons already stated. It is unlikely that new systems will evolve using this technique.

Infrared techniques are capable of high resolution of point targets and at longer wavelengths (8 to 12 μ) offer good all-weather performance below cloud cover. High-resolution imaging IR would be used for precision homing systems, but hot-spot detection methods also have a useful role in multiwavelength systems.

Passive radiometry, although offering some potential in terminal tracking, does not perform adequately under all likely ambient conditions.

Active radar, at millimetric wavelengths (mmW), is now a favored technique (Wilke 1986; Goodman 1989). At frequencies around 90 to 100 gigahertz, narrow beam widths can be obtained that give good resolution capability against small ground targets and good all-weather, through-cloud performance. Major advances over the last ten years in solid-state emitters, microwave circuitry, and radar signal processing methods have brought the technology to a level where reliable target-detection performance can be achieved at ranges consistent with PGM operation.

Combinations of these techniques are being considered for a variety of applications. For example, the SFMs previously referred to use a combination of IR hot-spot and very simple active mmW radar to detect tank targets and trigger the warhead. More sophisticated I^2R/mmW seekers are under study to improve the overall performance of PGM-type weapons, particularly to obtain greater flexibility in dealing with countermeasures and extreme climatic conditions.

GUIDANCE FUNCTIONS

An autonomous homing guidance system must be able to

- search for targets
- detect a target in its natural background
- recognize or identify the target as one of interest
- maintain track on a selected target throughout the whole of the homing phase
- establish an effective aim point for the munition to hit.

Both I^2R and radar seekers perform these tasks adequately (some better than others), and the choice largely rests upon in-flight and trajectory considerations. Active radar systems do, however, have another important advantage, that of a ranging capability. This enables a PGM to determine height above the ground, range to go, time to go, flight path attitude, and other factors, providing important navigational information that can be used to set up the terminal phase of the trajectory with greater accuracy.

ELECTRONIC PROCESSING

Although dependent upon the precise nature of each seeker, the processing requirements for I^2R and mmW are similar. I^2R involves a heavy processing load for image manipulation to extract target pattern information and to carry out a variety of tracking algorithms; mmW requires multichannel processing for range and angle tracking, but the target pattern recognition algorithms (even using full scattering matrix processing) are based upon multidimensional look-up tables and are simply implemented.

In either case the use of microprocessor-based systems and advances in miniaturization have led to the development of very small weapons' electronic assemblies able to withstand very high launch accelerations. For example, such an electronic assembly for the Merlin TGMB, which is contained within the 81mm-diameter projectile, carries out all the radar processing, autopilot, and control functions.

TERMINAL GUIDANCE STRATEGY

An important aspect of PGM operation, particularly for those in the indirect-fire category, is the strategy adopted for the autonomous search for targets and target selection. All the examples given, whether launched by mortar, gun, or rocket, are designed primarily for operation against groups of targets, and overall effectiveness is achieved by using multiple PGMs. Each PGM has an area on the ground over which it can search for targets, ideally matched by its maneuver capability; this is known as the "footprint" of the weapon. If each successive PGM were delivered to precisely the same point, every PGM would likely attack the same target at the same point in its own footprint, and the overall mission would be ineffective.

Fortunately, few delivery methods offer repeatability of this sort, and a salvo of PGMs will be dispersed according to the delivery accuracy. Even so, the seeker system has to be designed so that an optimum effect can be achieved for a salvo of PGMs against an array of targets, and points that have to be taken into account include the following:

- delivery system accuracy
- footprint size
- search scan pattern
- interval between PGMs
- target detection criteria (moving or static or both).

The design that is best for one target engagement scenario will not necessarily be best for another, and design compromises have to be made. Alternatively, projectiles might be programmed before launch to set up operating parameters best suited to a scenario. Modern microprocessor systems are well able to adjust the system configuration appropriately, and future PGMs are likely to offer this kind of operational flexibility.

Future Trends

Following the successful development of a wide range of guided bomb PGMs, the second-generation artillery-delivered PGMs are now being developed, primarily for the antiarmor (including counter-battery) role. These weapons are planned to enter service through the 1990s and into the next century and will provide a formidable defensive capability against massed armor.

Some further improvements in the technologies involved can be foreseen, for example, in the area of protection against countermeasures, offering product improvement opportunities; the development of even "smarter" techniques is difficult to foresee, since the need for further growth in the indirect-fire anti-armor capability is likely to be limited. An extension of existing PGM designs to new delivery systems is likely to be a more important trend. This raises an interesting question regarding the clear distinction drawn between PGMs and GWs proposed in the opening paragraphs. A PGM developed for an artillery rocket (e.g., MLRS-TGW) might be employed from an air-launched standoff carrier vehicle such as MSOW; it is no longer an extension of a conventional ammunition, but is it still a PGM?

The third category described, PGMs for direct-fire guns, has remained relatively dormant, mainly because the need for high accuracy beyond the normal fighting range of tanks has been questioned. The growing importance of the threat of armed helicopters to the tank forces could awaken greater interest in such weapons, and the present development of autonomous guidance techniques might provide the technical impetus. The tank gun environment is even more severe than that of the 155mm howitzer, but even so the transfer of technology is not expected to pose a major problem.

ROBERT F. JACKSON

SEE ALSO: Missile, Antitank Guided; Sensor Technology; Surveillance and Target Acquisition Equipment.

Bibliography

Evenkamp, R. 1988. New ammunition technologies for indirect fire. *Miltech* 7:43–49.
Fletcher, R. 1988. CAP study on guided projectiles. *Jane's Defence Weekly*, 9 July, p. 39.
Gethin, M. J. 1988. Alive and well: The oldest of air defence weapons. *Defence*, September, pp. 693–99.
Goodman, G. W., Jr. 1987. Millimeter wave radars make all-weather fire and forget possible. *Armed Forces Journal International*, September, pp. 77–80.
Hooton, T. 1986. More punch for the infantry: The intelligent mortar round. *Miltech* 3:46–52.
NATO's Sixteen Nations. 1982. Weapon systems series: Copperhead—A quantum jump. April/May, pp. 100–4.
Wilke, K. H. 1986. Microwave sensors for intelligent ammunitions. *Miltech* 5:32–42.

PRINCIPLES OF WAR

Principles of war are a collection of basic experience parameters, rules, or maxims of conventional warfare for the successful conduct of military operations. They are the result of a comprehensive scientific analysis of campaigns and wars.

Purpose

The principles of war are used for the training and education of military commanders and for the conduct of military operations. For officers, knowledge of the principles of war promotes military expertise regarding developments and effects on the battlefield. The principles of war are also a suitable standard of comparison for the evaluation and assessment of completed operations, plans for operations, and new concepts.

In war, principles of war serve as a basis for command and control decisions. Their application enhances the ability to meet the challenges of complex and unforeseeable battlefield events with simple but effective responses.

Form and Applications

Generally, principles of war are expressed in one of three ways: as a list of key terms (e.g., offensive); in a form of sentence (e.g., adjust your ends to the means); or as text, where an aspect of decisive significance for the winning of military operations (e.g., mobility in defensive operations) is emphasized and explained.

The application of principles of war is not uniform and often is directly related to the form of presentation. The views range from rigid adherence to principles of war in all situations to flexible use, which is influenced by the conditions specific to each case. The more succinct the form of representation, the more dogmatic the application. In a mission-type order environment the application of the principles of war is dependent upon the evaluation of the given situation by the military commander.

The possibilities and limits of a meaningful application of principles of war vary with the level of command. Although principles of war are applicable at the strategic, operational, and tactical levels of command, the priorities and applications may vary due to different targets and situations at the different levels of command. For example, a principle such as "to mass forces at the decisive place and time" on the strategic level may call for dispersion of forces at the tactical level; or the application of the principle "offensive" in order to seize, retain, and exploit the initiative on an operational level may require a static defense by units on the tactical level.

Authors and Areas of Application

Sun Tzu

The oldest statements on principles of war are ascribed to the military thinker and writer Sun Tzu (China, ca. 500 B.C.). He did not provide a list of principles of war; he proceeded from the assumption that the art of war does not have any fixed rules, that rules result only from the conditions of the concrete situation. Nonetheless, in *The Art of War*, he presented ten factors of decisive significance for victory or defeat in war, which are by their nature principles of war:

1. invincibility lies in the defense, the possibility of victory in the attack;
2. know the enemy and yourself;
3. strike only when the situation ensures victory;
4. strike the enemy where he is least prepared;
5. weigh the situation before moving;
6. be flexible;
7. recognize the hazards and the weather;
8. deceive the enemy;
9. surprise the enemy;
10. separate the enemy from his allies.

Karl von Clausewitz

Clausewitz recognized the usefulness of principles of war for the training and education of officers. But he also concluded that a capable and trained military leader must not adhere dogmatically to the principles of war; his military assessment should be determined by experience, intuition, and the conditions of the situation. An analysis of Clausewitz's *On War* reveals at least nine conclusions, which have the character of principles of war:

1. *Superiority of defense.* When Clausewitz had examined the art of defense and offense and their relationship at the tactical and strategic levels, he concluded that defense is a stronger form of war than attack. Clausewitz placed a high value on defense and felt that commanders should always consider the advantage of defensive actions to reach the military objective.

2. *Active defense.* Clausewitz visualized an active defense. Without this active element—more in tactics than in strategy—defense cannot exploit its advantages; to stay strictly defensive would mean to remain utterly passive. The defender must watch for opportunities to launch counterattacks to overcome and weaken the enemy whenever and wherever possible.

3. *Simplicity.* Simplicity as a requirement for planning and conducting actions on the battlefield is a matter of Clausewitz's own experience. In connection with friction he states, "Everything in war is very simple, but the simplest thing is difficult." Since war is the realm of uncertainty, and Clausewitz believed that three-quarters of the factors on which action in war is based are wrapped in a fog of greater or lesser uncertainty, all plans for operations must be very simple. Difficulties and complexity arise with and by the conduct itself.

4. *Offensive.* Although Clausewitz emphasized the relative strength of defensive combat more than that of offensive combat, he also emphasized that wars cannot be won by staying on the defensive. He pointed out that victory can be achieved only by taking the offensive.

5. *Concentration of forces.* Clausewitz frequently reminded his readers that numerical strength was an important ingredient for success in war. He stated that to ensure numerical superiority, a commander must keep his forces concentrated and avoid all temptations to detach elements from the main body except under the most urgent circumstances.

6. *Economy of force.* Clausewitz expressed this concept as the full employment of all elements of a command, with none allowed to remain idle. Although this is different from the meaning given to the concept by the U.S. Army (see below), there are some similarities, including Clausewitz's use of troops to occupy some of the enemy's forces and reduce his overall strength, and his view that economy of force is a corollary of concentration of force.

7. *Main effort.* Clausewitz mentioned the need for a main effort, or a strength, at the decisive place and time. When Clausewitz explained the advantage of the superiority of numbers of soldiers, he concluded that as many troops as possible should be brought into the engagement at the decisive point.

8. *Reserves.* Reserve forces and their use played a major role in Clausewitz's considerations. He taught that all the troops should not be brought into combat immediately; some should be held behind the front lines, far enough back to avoid envelopment of the total force by the enemy. Clausewitz felt that the commander should not give up the battle as long as he had sufficient reserves, and that their employment might determine the outcome of the battle.

9. *Surprise.* Clausewitz discussed the element of surprise as an independent principle both in tactics and strategy; he believed surprise to be a significant element in qualitative combat power. Surprising courses of action resulted in a

disconcerted enemy. The best way to achieve surprise was with the rapid use of forces.

UNITED STATES ARMY

Principles of war have been presented by Clausewitz, Jomini, Douhet, and others. Modern versions of the principles of war, as understood by British and American forces, are based upon a formulation by the British theorist J. F. C. Fuller in 1920.

The tradition of the U.S. Army's principles of war can be traced back to December 1921, when nine principles were listed in *War Department Training Regulation no. 10-5:* (1) objective, (2) offensive, (3) mass, (4) economy of force, (5) movement, (6) surprise, (7) security, (8) simplicity, and (9) cooperation.

The 1986 edition of the U.S. Army's *Field Manual 100-5* also lists nine principles of war. They have withstood the test of analysis, experimentation, and practice; and they are applicable on the strategic, operational, and tactical levels.

The nine principles of war and their imperative definitions are:

1. *Objective:* Direct every military operation toward a clearly defined, decisive, and attainable objective.
2. *Offensive:* Seize, retain, and exploit the initiative.
3. *Mass:* Concentrate combat power at the decisive place and time.
4. *Economy of force:* Allocate minimum essential combat power to secondary efforts.
5. *Maneuver:* Place the enemy in a position of disadvantage through the flexible application of combat power.
6. *Unity of command:* For every objective, ensure unity of effort under one responsible commander.
7. *Security:* Never permit the enemy to acquire an unexpected advantage.
8. *Surprise:* Strike the enemy at a time or place and in a manner for which he is unprepared.
9. *Simplicity:* Prepare clear, uncomplicated plans and clear, concise orders to ensure thorough understanding.

The U.S. Army emphasizes the value of the principles of war in training and in the conduct of warfare. The principles of war serve U.S. Army officers as checklists for planning and operations. For the war-gaming process they play a key role in the evaluation of each course of action and of the decision-making process.

ARMY OF THE FEDERAL REPUBLIC OF GERMANY

The German army's basic manual, *Heeresdienstvorschrift 100/100,* does not contain a list of principles of war. This is in accordance with traditional German doctrine since the era of Helmuth von Moltke in the nineteenth century. The command and control of forces is an art, a creative activity based on character, skill, and mental power.

The German army does not provide any rigid formulas or instructions on how individual operations should be conducted; but every commander must be guided by clear principles. Success is ensured only by giving commanders the freedom to judge and act within the scope of their missions, not by binding them strictly to principles of war. Only general principles are applied: active defense, fire and maneuver, building reserves, proper use of terrain, simplicity, surprise, and deception.

These general principles, which have the character of principles of war, provide the framework for training and peacetime exercises. They ensure a common understanding of tactical concepts and ideas for all officers and form the basis for the application of mission-type orders.

GERTMANN SUDE

SEE ALSO: Deception; Friction; Reserves.

Bibliography

Alger, J. J. 1982. *The quest for victory: The history of the principles of war.* Westport, Conn.: Greenwood Press.
Clausewitz, C. von. 1976. *On war.* Ed. and trans. M. Howard and P. Paret. Princeton, N.J.: Princeton Univ. Press.
Sun Tzu. 1963. *The art of war.* Trans. S. B. Griffith. Cambridge, Mass.: Oxford Univ. Press.
U.S. Department of the Army. 1986. *Field manual 100-5.* Washington, D.C.: Government Printing Office.

PSYCHOLOGICAL WARFARE

Not until after World War II had the discipline of psychological warfare progressed to the point that its several aspects were defined accurately. At that time, the U.S. Army defined *psychological warfare* as "the use of communications media and other psychological means, in a declared emergency or war, with the purpose of bringing psychological pressure to bear on the enemy and to influence favorably the attitudes of hostile groups and other target audiences in areas that are under enemy control. The primary goals are to weaken the enemy's will to engage in or to continue hostilities and to reduce his capacity for waging war." The North Atlantic Treaty Organization (NATO) provided a similar definition when it stated, "Psychological warfare is the dissemination of propaganda designed to undermine the enemy's will to resist, demoralize his forces and sustain the morale of our supporters." Finally, Sir Campbell Stuart defined *propaganda* as "the presentation of a case in such a way that others may be influenced."

Psychological warfare is waged through *psychological operations* (PSYOPs), which are planned peacetime or wartime psychological activities directed toward enemy, friendly, or neutral audiences, with the goal of creating attitudes and behavior that will facilitate achieving one's political or military objectives. They encompass those political, military, economic, ideological, and information activities that are designed to achieve a certain psychological effect. Each psychological operation has a PSYOP approach, a technique used to induce a desired reaction on the part of the target audience; each involves a PSYOP campaign, a series of planned propaganda and psychological actions undertaken to achieve a psychological objective or objectives; and each is judged against a PSYOP estimate, an analysis of the current situation from a psychological perspective. This estimate considers feasible courses of action, analyzes and compares them, and makes recommendations regarding key PSYOP factors that will affect the accomplishment of the overall mission.

Psychological operations include psychological action, psychological warfare, and psychological consolidation. *Psychological action* is defined as using psychological media and supporting activities in peace and war to reduce the enemy's actual or potential prestige in potentially hostile or neutral nations while increasing friendly influence and feelings in the same. *Psychological consolidation* involves actions intended to establish and maintain order and security for friendly forces in a combat zone and rear areas and to gain the support of the local population in the occupied territory. Planned activities in peace and war are directed at the civilian population in areas under friendly control to achieve behavior that supports the military objectives, facilitates military operations, and promotes maximum cooperation among the civilian population.

Psychological operations are conveyed over *psychological media*, the technical and nontechnical media that establish communications with a target audience. The operations are developed with consideration of the psychological situation, that is, the current emotional state, mental disposition, or other behavioral motivation of the audience. (This situation is founded primarily on national, political, social, economic, and psychological peculiarities but is subject to the influence of circumstances or events.) Once the situation is defined, a psychological theme—an idea or topic on which a psychological operation is based—is developed. Each operation is planned to achieve a psychological objective, which is a statement of measurable response expected from a target audience as a result of a psychological operation. The objective must accurately define the specific behavioral response or attitude change required; this, in turn, must support the PSYOP goals.

These definitions, developed after World War II, were based on the experiences of that war. Accordingly, it is of value to examine that conflict in order to understand the origins, scope, and intentions of psychological warfare.

Background

Attempts to influence military opponents by psychological or propagandistic means are as old as war itself. In his *Art of War*, the fifth-century Chinese military theorist Sun Tzu stressed the importance of manipulating human behavior in times of crisis and war. Despite many individual instances of psychological warfare throughout history, only in the twentieth century has it been developed and used systematically as an important new discipline for warfare.

During World War I, psychological warfare was used successfully by the

Triple Entente against the German Empire on a scale hitherto unknown. Its effectiveness demonstrated its importance in warfare. However, there was no detailed discussion on the subject until relatively recently; those researching the discipline must refer to analyses of its use during World War II.

World War II involved national commitments on a scale previously unknown. The war demanded maximum personal sacrifices not only by the soldiers at the front but also by the civilian population. Psychological operations were of paramount importance, and the term *home front*, central to the German domestic propaganda of the time, highlighted the psychological dimension of those targeted.

In a sense, psychological operations are the means by which the political leadership influences a nation. Giving primacy to politics had fatal consequences for German propaganda during the war, because the propaganda eventually was proven false. The credibility of specific propaganda should be an inalienable precondition of psychological operations. It should withstand scrutiny not only in the short and medium term, but also in the long term.

During World War II, British propagandists defined the terms *white, gray*, and *black propaganda*, which are generally accepted and still used today. White propaganda clearly identifies its origin—for example, a safe-conduct leaflet for soldiers that carries the stamp of enemy authorities or the signature of a prominent enemy general and openly asks for capitulation under honorable conditions. Such a leaflet was a World War I German invention that was used by all powers during World War II and subsequently in wars in the developing nations. When white propaganda is readily identified as enemy propaganda, it must overcome the suspicions and mistrust of its target groups if its message is to be accepted as credible.

Gray propaganda does not clearly identify the producer; it cannot be immediately traced. A classic example is the Anglo-American German-language newspaper, "News for the Troops," the best-known leaflet newspaper of World War II. It was produced by the British propagandist Sefton Delmer and a special staff. To mask its true source, the paper cited the Wehrmacht as its publisher. Despite this deception, the newspaper was recognized by the Germans as enemy propaganda because of its biased reporting (Daugherty 1958).

Black propaganda involves total deception. It is attributed to a counterfeit source and its true origins are hidden. A most impressive example of black propaganda is the so-called Mölders letter, forged by a member of Delmer's staff. This forgery was so convincing that large sections of the German population believed it had been written by Col. Werner Mölders and that it proved his Christian opposition to the Nazi regime (Howe 1982).

Examples from World War II

WAR ON THE AIRWAVES

Wartime broadcasting contained all three types of propaganda. Probably the most famous white propaganda was that transmitted by "Tokyo Rose" to Allied forces in the Pacific theater. Using black propaganda, both German and British broadcasters achieved remarkable results. This war of the airwaves became a major psychological warfare operation, with covert broadcasting stations playing a major role. Accompanying the invasion of France in 1940, the covert German stations "Radio Humanité" and "Voix de la Paix" had a sweeping impact with their French-language programs during the spectacular victories of the Wehrmacht. Their goal was to create a panic in the French population through atrocity propaganda in order to prompt an uncoordinated stampede that would disrupt the operational freedom of Western Allied units. French and British reports document that the chaos of moving refugees on French roads in May and June 1940 did, in fact, decisively disrupt Allied troop operations. These operations were the most successful of all German wartime broadcasting propaganda (Buchbender and Hauschild 1984).

After 1941 the covert German stations were able to achieve only occasional success. The German propaganda operation Southern Star, broadcast on station "Wanda" and directed at Anders-Corps Polish forces in exile between the spring of 1944 and April 1945, achieved its demoralizing aim for only a short period before it was identified as German propaganda. Its most effective aspect was that which informed the Poles of the constantly deteriorating situation in Poland as Stalinization occurred. The goal of the propaganda was to convey the truth in a psychologically skillful fashion. On 19 April 1944, for example, an Anders-Corps intelligence officer reported that although the information broadcast on station "Wanda" had been identified clearly by Polish soldiers as subversive propaganda, it nonetheless "put its finger on the open sore of reality." This broadcasting prompted considerable numbers of Poles to desert and to report to the German units in Italy in 1944 (Buchbender 1984).

In 1945 the British had at least 48 secret broadcasting stations with programs in 16 languages that were targeted against almost every audience. Among these, ten were aimed at specific German audiences such as convinced Christians, patriots, members of the NSDAP, and soldiers of the Wehrmacht or the Waffen-SS. The Germans corroborated the dimensions of this effort by the British, reporting in February 1944 that there were 55 secret enemy stations broadcasting. Three of the British secret stations were regarded as most dangerous: "Gustav Siegfried I," "German Short Wave Station Atlantic," and "Soldatensender Calais" (later called "Soldatensender West").

LOUDSPEAKERS

In addition to leaflets and radio broadcasts, the loudspeaker—clearly white propaganda—was also used by all combatants on the battlefield. Using it against encircled enemy formations, especially on the northern and central fronts, the Germans convinced thousands to desert during the first two years of the eastern campaign. The Soviets later achieved equally remarkable success against Wehrmacht units that had been cut off or separated, especially after the large-scale Allied offensive of the summer of 1944 had begun. U.S. and British use of loudspeakers after the Normandy landing was extremely effective, the greatest success being the capitulation of the Cherbourg fortress.

Effects of Psychological Operations

It is extremely difficult to determine precisely the effectiveness of psychological warfare during World War II because little information exists (U.S. Strategic Bombing Survey 1947). A comprehensive analysis has not been undertaken, since the necessary empirical material for such a survey is not available. It is especially difficult to determine the effects of radio propaganda, whether white or black. Although British broadcasting propaganda achieved limited successes in isolated cases, it did not achieve its goal—the physical collapse of the German civilian population. The Allied doctrine of unconditional surrender provided German counterpropaganda with a psychological advantage that permitted developing new methods of influencing the population (Fig. 1). Wars cannot be won by propaganda alone, particularly when the contingent psychological operations are burdened by shortsighted political concepts with heavy psycho-political content.

Psychological Warfare after 1945

Following World War II, both the West and the Soviet bloc devoted considerable efforts to developing psychological warfare. The Soviet Union perfected its concept of disinformation and its "active operations" pertaining to psychological warfare. Meanwhile, the United States devoted considerable resources to the discipline and developed psychological operations units. The prolonged Cold War inevitably led to an intensification of East-West propaganda that

WANTED

This gangster, who you see in his element in the picture, incites you by his example to participate in a form of warfare in which women, children and ordinary civilians shall take leading parts.

This absolutely criminal form of warfare which is forbidden by the

HAGUE CONVENTION

will be punished

according to military law

FOR INCITEMENT TO
MURDER

Save at least your families from the horrors of war!

Figure 1. German leaflet dropped by balloon on London and the southern counties in the summer of 1940 (front and back pages).

surpassed that of World War II in sophistication and effect. The two major alliances, NATO and the Warsaw Pact, developed military psychological operations units that would attempt to influence the enemy in wartime through broadcasting, leaflets, and loudspeakers.

Since 1945, there has been intensive use of psychological operations in the wars of the developing nations around the world. Broadcasting and leaflet propaganda have employed the means and methods used in World War II. During the Arab-Israeli, Korean, Vietnam, Afghanistan, Falklands/Malvinas, and Iran-Iraq wars, psychological warfare was an integral part of the overall concept of waging war. For example, during the Vietnam War, "Hanoi Hannah" used the same technique "Tokyo Rose" had used in World War II—interspersing popular music with propagandistic messages that were intended to lower morale. During Operation Desert Shield in 1990, an Iraqi female used a similar format in her propaganda broadcasts to U.S. troops deployed in Saudi Arabia. Above all, the employment of secret broadcasting stations has given a new dynamism to the psychological operations of official broadcasting propaganda. In 1988, some 250 secret stations in Southeast Asia, the Middle East, and Latin America were broadcasting disinformation programs. Just as war remains a means of politics, psychological warfare will continue to be used by those who wage war.

Target groups will continue to be deceived by skillful disinformation. However, the most potent opponent of the propagandist is not the enemy, but time. In the medium and long run—especially in the current electronic age—a media-related policy that dispenses with lies and deception, and instead uses truth as its weapon, will survive and succeed.

ORTWIN BUCHBENDER

SEE ALSO: Morale.

Bibliography

Buchbender, O. 1978. *Das tönende Erz: Deutsche Propaganda gegen die Rote Armee.* Stuttgart: Seewald.

Buchbender, O., and R. Hauschild. 1984. *Geheimsender gegen Frankreich: Die Täuschungsoperation "Radio Humanité," 1940.* Herford: Mittler.

Buchbender, O., and H. Schuh. 1978. *Flugblattpropaganda im Zweiten Weltkrieg: Dokumentation und Analyse.* Stuttgart: Seewald.

———. 1988. *Die Waffe, die auf die Seele zielt: Psychologische Kriegführung, 1939–1945.* Stuttgart: Motorbuch Verlag.

Carrol, W. 1948. *Persuade or perish.* Boston: Houghton Mifflin.

Daughterty, W. E., ed. 1958. *A psychological warfare casebook.* Baltimore, Md.: Johns Hopkins Univ. Press.

Delmer, S. 1962. *Black boomerang.* London: Martin Secker and Warburg.

———. 1962. *Trail sinister.* London: Martin Secker and Warburg.

Howe, E. 1982. *The black game: British subversive operations against the Germans during the Second World War.* London: Michael Joseph.

Kirchner, K. 1974–1988. *Flugblattpropaganda im Zweiten Weltkrieg.* 10 vols. Erlangen, Germany: Verlag D + C.

Lerner, D. 1949. *Sykewar: Psychological warfare against Germany, D-Day to VE-Day.* New York: George Stewart.

Rhodes, A. 1975. *Propaganda, the art of persuasion: An Allied and Axis visual record, 1933–1945.* London: Angus and Robertson.

Selesnjow, I. S. 1976. *Krieg und ideologischer Kampf.* Berlin-Ost: Militärverlag.

Stuart, C. 1921. *Secrets of Crewe House: The story of a famous campaign.* London: Hodder and Stoughton.

U.S. Department of Defense. 1979. *Field manual 33-1: Psychological operations.* Washington, D.C.: Headquarters, Department of the Army.

U.S. Strategic Bombing Survey. 1947. *The effects of strategic bombing on German morale.* 2 vols. Washington, D.C.: Government Printing Office.

Watson, P. 1978. *War on the mind: The military use and abuse of psychology.* London: Penguin Books.

Zeman, Z. 1978. *Selling the war: Art and persuasion in World War II.* London: Orbis.

R

RADAR TECHNOLOGY APPLICATIONS

Radar, an acronym for *radio detection and ranging*, is a system for detecting and locating objects that scatter back ("echo") electromagnetic waves in that part of the spectrum classified as "radio waves." In principle, any electromagnetic wave can be used for this purpose, but the radio wave portion of the spectrum has certain advantages, in particular the penetration of the earth's atmosphere to useful ranges in all weathers.

Because it can detect and accurately locate targets at long ranges in all weather conditions, radar has, for nearly fifty years, been the primary military above-water sensor. It retains that role to the present day and for the foreseeable future. In many battles during and since World War II the outcome has been determined by the effective use of radar.

History

There are a number of claims as to the origin of modern radar. A balanced assessment must be that, following some early experiments with radio interference effects that we would today classify as continuous wave radar, serious development began to occur in the 1930s, when the threat of war in Europe spurred simultaneous development in a number of European countries. In contrast, although U.S. engineers had achieved a form of radar detection as early as 1922, there was no official U.S. support for further work and radar development progressed initially more slowly in that country than in Europe.

In the United Kingdom, where it became clear that warning of air attack was likely to be vital to the country's survival, development was rapid in the years 1935 to 1939. Following demonstrations of aircraft detection in February 1935, production of radar warning stations proceeded with unstinting official support, and by the outbreak of World War II in 1939 Britain already had in place a chain of land-based air-defense radars covering the east coast, the "Chain Home" system.

The development of airborne radar became Britain's next priority in order to counter night air attack when the Chain Home radars could not put a defender into visual contact with an intruder. Air-to-surface-vessel radar was another imperative, responding to the U-boat threat to the Atlantic convoys that were essential to Britain's survival. The invention of the resonant cavity magnetron in England in 1940 was the single most important wartime radar development. Magnetron-equipped higher-frequency airborne radars were also developed, and radar was applied to offense as well as defense.

Naval radars were developed early in the war and played a decisive role in the war at sea. On the German side, prewar interest and support in radar were not continued during the early phases of the war. As a result, despite the fact that the world's first naval radar went to sea aboard the German *Graf Spee* in 1936, German radar development generally lagged behind that of the Western Allies during World War II.

Radar was also used by the British army to help direct searchlights and antiaircraft guns. According to some accounts, impressive increases in effectiveness were achieved (Swords 1986; Watson-Watt 1957).

As a result of rapid advances in radar technology during the war, by 1945 radar hardware technology design had evolved to a level of sophistication, in a period of only about ten years, comparable to many much older technologies. Since 1945 radar research has been less intense, reflecting both the transition from a war-driven development and the relative maturity of much of radar hardware design.

Today radar and its derivatives are widely used in all developed societies for such applications as road traffic speed measurement, air traffic control, and ship navigation, and they continue to play a major role in military weapons, surveillance, and navigation systems.

Principles

Essentially, a radar consists of a means of generating a suitable radio frequency wave, an antenna to launch it, an antenna to receive the scattered energy, and a means of detecting and measuring what is received. Often the same antenna is used to both transmit and receive signals and is switched back and forth from transmitter to receiver.

A basic radio wave consists of a "pure" or "unmodulated" sinusoidal wave. To be useful, the radar signal must have some form of modulation or coding impressed on it, as range is determined from the time taken for the radio wave to propagate to the target and back, and there must be some recognizable change to use as a time reference.

Most radars transmit a repetitive pulse modulation of the radar oscillator; that is, the radio wave is turned on for a short period, then off for a much longer period, before the cycle repeats. Very powerful pulses can be generated using thermionic devices (the resonant cavity magnetron in particular), so to some extent the use of pulse transmission by radars has been a matter of technological convenience.

With the modern development of solid-state devices that can generate continuous radio frequency waves, there is now reason to depart from pulse waveforms. "Long" pulses, within which the radio wave is modulated in frequency, are finding application.

A measure of how well a range-finding technique works is its ability to separate or resolve two closely spaced targets. Theory shows that good range resolution can be attained only if the bandwidth of the radar waveform is large, hence from this viewpoint it matters not whether this wide bandwidth is achieved by a short pulse modulating the radio frequency or by frequency modulation within a much longer pulse.

To locate an object, it is also necessary to find its bearing from the radar. This is achieved by the use of directional transmitting and receiving antennas. Such antennas may be considered as having "beams" within which the major part of the transmission is constrained or within which returned echoes are received. The angular resolution is inversely proportional to the size of the antenna—its so-called aperture—measured in units of wavelength. So directional antennas (i.e., with narrow beams) must be large compared to the wavelength of the radio wave—typically some tens of wavelength in size—in order to obtain useful directional properties.

In addition to locating a target, a radar can measure its velocity. The echo from a target with a component of velocity toward or away from the radar will undergo a shift in frequency—the Doppler effect—which allows this component of velocity to be determined. Alternatively, if the radar tracks the target continuously, the record of change of range allows radial velocity to be calculated.

The range at which a radar can detect a target is governed by many factors. One limit is imposed by background noise, whether inherent in the receiver itself or from some external source. Higher transmitter power can overcome noise, but because the radio waves have to propagate two ways (to the target and back), detection range only increases in general as the fourth root of transmitter power, so doubling the power only improves detection range by a factor of 19 percent.

Echoes are received not only from the target but also from other objects at the same range. In particular, radar echoes are received from rough land or sea. The cumulative effect of all these unwanted echoes, termed *clutter*, tends to obscure the target. The level of clutter varies in a complex manner with radar frequency; it can be reduced by using more directional transmitter or receiver antennas so that fewer unwanted echoes overlap with that from the target. Often the target velocity, as determined through the Doppler shift of the radar frequency, allows its echo to be separated from the clutter.

Applications

The primary applications for radar are summarized below:

- *Air surveillance:* Long-range early warning, air route/airport surveillance, target acquisition, and control of intercept
- *Space surveillance:* Exo-atmospheric surveillance of missiles and space objects
- *Surface search:* Sea, ground, and battlefield surveillance and reconnaissance
- *Weather:* Observation of precipitation and air movements
- *Weapons:* Tracking, guidance, and fire control

• *Remote sensing:* Sensing from satellites and aircraft
• *Navigation and instrumentation:* Aircraft Doppler navigation radars, police speed-measuring radars, satellite navigation systems.

The application drives the radar design. For example, a surveillance radar normally has its principal antenna dimension horizontal so that it realizes a "fan-beam" that is narrow in azimuth and broad in elevation. Such a radar gives location in range and azimuth only.

To locate targets in elevation as well, as is required for weapons guidance, a pair of orthogonal fan-beams may be used. Alternatively, the radar may utilize one or a cluster of "pencil beams." Tracking, guidance, and weapons fire control radars usually cover such narrow arcs in azimuth and elevation that they need to be cued by another radar.

Wave Frequency

A number of factors influence the choice of radar frequency. General characteristics and trends may be summarized as follows:

High Frequencies

Advantages	Disadvantages
Narrow beams with small antennas.	Increasing atmospheric and weather attenuation.
Significant scattering even from small targets.	Stealth technology is easier to implement.
Greater scope for employment of counters to jamming.	Clutter is likely to be more of a problem.

Low Frequencies

Advantages	Disadvantages
Long range (low attenuation).	Large antennas or broad beams are required.
Stealth technology is less effective.	Limited bandwidth restricts ability to incorporate some electronic counter-countermeasures.
Clutter may be less of a problem.	Echoes from small targets (i.e., less than a quarter of a wavelength in size) are weak and may not be detected.

The radar designer must weigh these advantages and disadvantages, and a number of subtleties that go beyond the scope of this article, to arrive at a suitable frequency of operation for a specific application. Two examples illustrate the trends: For long-range air search, frequencies below 1.5 gigahertz are used, whereas fighter aircraft radars operate in the 6 to 18 gigahertz range.

During World War II radar frequency bands were given letter designations to avoid disclosing precise frequencies against which countermeasures could be targeted. With minor changes, these designations are still in use today. The electronic warfare community has introduced an independent band designation scheme. Figure 1 shows both designations with typical applications.

Developments in Technology

Since World War II, development of radar has continued at an evolutionary rate. Although the principles of radar and basic radar system functions remain unchanged, there have been substantial advances in many areas. Current and future developments that will influence radar design are described below.

SOLID-STATE TECHNOLOGY

With the availability of cheap, reliable integrated circuits has come the opportunity to apply advanced signal processing techniques to the digitized output of radars. Implementation of spectral estimation in solid-state circuits has improved the ability of radar to detect and track targets in clutter, to resist deliberate countermeasures, and has allowed greater operational flexibility.

Solid-state technology has also been applied to radar transmitters. The gains have been not so much in the level of power radiated as in the quality of the signals and the reduction in size and weight of the components.

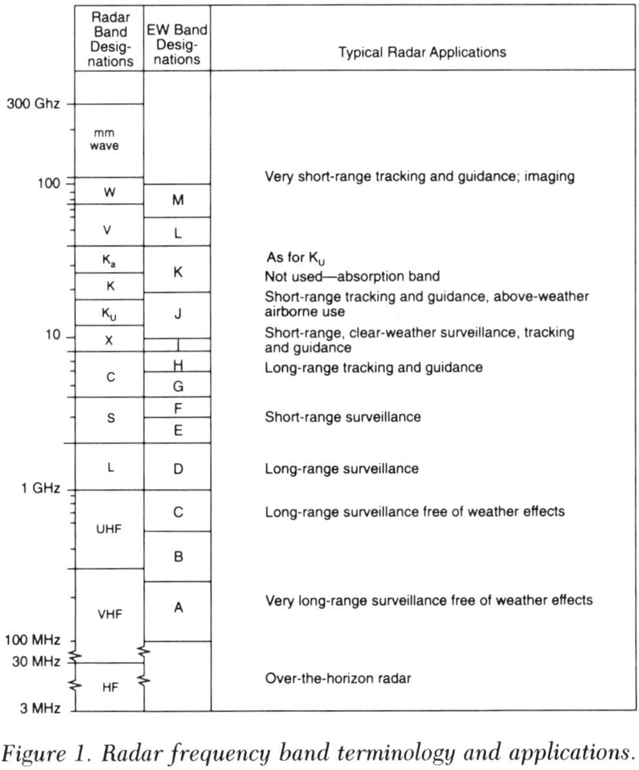

Radar Band Designations	EW Band Designations	Typical Radar Applications
mm wave		
W	M	Very short-range tracking and guidance; imaging
V	L	
K$_a$	K	As for K$_U$
K		Not used—absorption band
K$_U$	J	Short-range tracking and guidance, above-weather airborne use
X	I	Short-range, clear-weather surveillance, tracking and guidance
C	H	Long-range tracking and guidance
	G	
S	F	Short-range surveillance
	E	
L	D	Long-range surveillance
UHF	C	Long-range surveillance free of weather effects
	B	
VHF	A	Very long-range surveillance free of weather effects
HF		Over-the-horizon radar

(Frequency scale: 300 Ghz, 100, 10, 1 GHz, 100 MHz, 30 MHz, 3 MHz)

Figure 1. Radar frequency band terminology and applications.

ANTENNA TECHNOLOGY

Most radars use a shaped reflector antenna, fed from one or more horns. An alternative modern technology is a flat array of individually radiating elements whose excitation is preset. Such antennas require physical movement to steer the beam. A "phased array" is an antenna consisting of individual elements whose phases can be controlled in such a way that beams can be steered without physical movement. Close control can be exercised over emission in or reception from undesired directions, and beam steering is extremely rapid.

Phased arrays may be constructed using well-established microwave engineering techniques, but costs are very high because of the multiplicity of components. A current approach is the application of microwave monolithic integrated circuits (MMICs) to realize transceiver modules comprising only a few integrated circuits. Gallium-arsenide technology is seen as the key to this approach, but costs will still be high.

Whereas almost all array antennas realized to date are planar, small electronically controllable array elements present the possibility of conforming arrays to the shapes of, for example, aircraft. Such "conformal arrays" may well pay a penalty in terms of radar performance but will be attractive in terms of aerodynamics and weight.

Side-lobe cancellation, null steering, and adaptive array processing are each a mix of antenna and signal processing technologies allowing selective cancellation of interfering signals. A great deal of research has been carried out in this area, and it can be expected that new radar systems will increasingly incorporate capabilities for adaptive antenna pattern modification in response to interference and jamming.

SIGNAL PROCESSOR ARCHITECTURES

Advances in microelectronics have fueled development of new architectures to meet the high-throughput, high-precision requirements of radar signal processing. Techniques include pipeline processors (in which the same sequence of processes is applied in turn to the signal steam), parallel processors (with many processors, each performing the same operation on a different sample of the signal), and systolic processors (comprising an array of identical processing elements, each communicating only with adjacent elements).

SOFTWARE

There has been a trend toward computer control of radar functions, with less dedicated hardware and more flexibility achieved through the use of software. It has become apparent, however, that large software programs without good software engineering practice will be unreliable and difficult to maintain and adapt. Increased emphasis is being placed on structured, well-documented software written in high-level languages such as Jovial, Ada, and Coral.

INTERFACE WITH OPERATOR

Advances in radars have generated a vast amount of information—for example, the range, bearing, speed, track, and echoing strength of a target—

multidimensional data that are too burdensome for an operator to assimilate unaided. Many of the decisions formerly considered operator functions are now made in the radar's data-processing system (e.g., setting of detection thresholds, association of detections with tracks), and the operator may see only a high-level synthetic display. Advances and new approaches are continually being made in the way inputs are taken from and multidimensional data are presented to an operator. The interface with the pilot of a single-seat aircraft is particularly challenging; head-up type displays, synthesized voice communications, and speech recognition will continue to be developed.

TARGET IDENTIFICATION

A major area for development is that of robust target identification. Identification friend and foe (IFF) is one approach, but this cannot be relied on absolutely because it is subject to interception and deception. There is thus intense interest in techniques that recognize some target "signature" or allow some type of identifying radar image to be developed. A current example of the latter is the U.S. AN/APS-137/V inverse synthetic aperture radar (*Jane's Weapon Systems* 1988), which presents a two-dimensional target image to an operator.

SYSTEMS INTEGRATION

With the many modes of operation of which modern military radars are capable and with the extensive flexibility available, increased attention is being paid to integrating all the radar subsystems into a coherent whole and in turn integrating the radar itself, together with all the other weapons and sensors, into a total fighting unit. The full potential of an expensive radar cannot be realized if its component systems are poorly integrated.

Current and Emerging Systems

The preceding section has summarized some important technological developments that will influence new radar designs. There are also some developments in systems that warrant highlighting because of increasing or future military applications.

SYNTHETIC APERTURE RADAR (SAR)

Good radar angular resolution requires a large antenna. If the required size exceeds what can be reasonably constructed, the principles of synthetic aperture radar may be invoked: A radar that moves continuously along a controlled path and that has the sequence of radar returns accurately recorded and processed behaves in many ways as a radar with an extended aperture. Airborne and spaceborne SARs can attain resolutions between several meters and several tens of meters. Photograph-like images are produced. Modern multimode airborne radars incorporate an SAR or SAR-like mode, which allows development of a ground map from a standoff range. When SARs are coupled with technologies for storage of and association with map data, powerful new tools for navigation and planning of air-attack missions become available.

BISTATIC RADAR

Driven by a radar's vulnerability to physical and electronic attack, designers have experimented with radars in which the transmitter and receiver are separated. Such a bistatic radar has the advantage that the receiver can be quite covert. The transmitter antenna is still vulnerable to antiradiation missile attack, but it may be possible to locate it out of danger or provide adequate protection. A further advantage claimed for bistatic radar is that stealth techniques are less effective for large bistatic angles.

MULTIFUNCTION RADAR

The flexibility of phased arrays allows a single radar not only to engage multiple targets simultaneously but also to perform other radar functions, such as long-range search in a complex pattern according to the threat situation. A great deal of intelligence needs to be built into such a radar to allow adaptive control of dwell time and the tailoring of priorities in response to threats because the radar's time and power must be shared among its multiple functions. Examples of such radars are the UK multifunction electronic scanning adaptive radar (MESAR) under development and the U.S. Navy Aegis system deployed on Ticonderoga-class ships. Other radars must be retained as well, however, because the multifunction radar, which operates in a single frequency band, cannot satisfy all requirements.

OVER-THE-HORIZON RADAR (OTHR)

One of the most significant advances in radar in recent years has been the development of over-the-horizon radars. Conventional radars use relatively high-frequency radio waves (generally above 1 gigahertz) that travel essentially in straight lines; thus, their range is limited by the horizon.

The coverage of a radar can be extended considerably by using radio waves with a frequency below 30 megahertz, which can travel beyond the horizon either by so-called surface-wave propagation or by reflection from the ionosphere (ionized layers in the earth's atmosphere at heights of about 100 to 300 kilometers [62 to 186 mi.]). For surface-wave OTHR, ranges of several hundred kilometers can be achieved, regardless of the height of the target; using propagation via the ionosphere (the "sky wave"), the range can be several thousand kilometers, as illustrated in Figure 2.

Such impressive detection ranges, however, can be attained only at considerable cost and complexity. Because they operate at lower frequencies, OTHRs need very large antennas. Such a radar situated near Alice Springs in central Australia is 2.8 kilometers (1.7 mi.) long. The beam is aimed electronically, as described in the section on Antenna Technology above.

To realize sufficient sensitivity at the long ranges involved, transmitters tend to transmit continuously rather than in short pulses. OTHRs therefore are usually bistatic, with typically 100 kilometers (60 mi.) between transmitter and receiver sites. Doppler processing is essential to distinguish moving targets in the heavy clutter environment. To cope with the vagaries of the ionosphere,

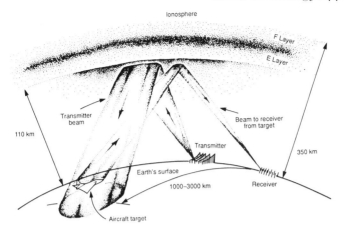

Figure 2. Principle of operation of over-the-horizon radar.

propagation conditions must be monitored continuously and the radar parameters adjusted accordingly.

New Airborne Early Warning Systems

A number of nations have recognized the advantage conferred in air combat by an airborne early warning and control system—an airborne radar with communications and control facilities. The U.S. Boeing AWACS and the Soviet Ilyushin-76 "Mainstay" are well-known examples of very capable systems. There is also interest in less costly but correspondingly less capable systems.

Future

Military requirements were responsible for the explosive growth in radar technology during World War II and continue to force the pace of development. Over the next decade there will be a proliferation of OTHRs and an increase in the number of space-based radars for both civil and military use. Inevitably, radar complexity and capability will be forced to increase further to counter developments in electronic countermeasures. Whatever the exact form developments take, there is no doubt that radar will continue to occupy a central role in many military systems for the foreseeable future.

H. A. d'Assumpçao
D. H. Sinnott

See Also: Surveillance and Target Acquisition Equipment.

Bibliography

Adam, J. A. 1988. Pinning defense hopes on Aegis. *IEEE Spectrum* 25(6):24–27.
Allison, D. K. 1981. *New eye for the Navy: The origin of radar at the Naval Research Laboratory.* NRL Report 8466. Washington, D.C.: Naval Research Laboratory.
American National Standards Institute. 1985. *Standard letter designations for radar frequency bands.* ANSI/IEEE Standard 521–1984.
Bowen, E. G. 1987. *Radar days.* Bristol: Adam Hilger.
Brookner, E. 1977. *Radar technology.* Norwood, Mass.: Artech House.

———. 1987. Radar trends to the year 2000. *Interavia* 5: 481–86.

Friedman, N. 1981. *Naval radar.* London: Conway Maritime Press.

Jane's weapon systems, 1987–88. 1987. London: Jane's.

Nathanson, F. E. 1969. *Radar design principles: Signal processing and the environment.* New York: McGraw-Hill.

Skolnik, M. I. 1985. Fifty years of radar. *Proceedings of the IEEE* 73:182–97.

Swords, S. S. 1986. *Technical history of the beginnings of radar.* Exeter, Devonshire: Short Run Press.

Watson-Watt, R. 1957. *Three steps to victory.* London: Odhams Press.

RANK AND INSIGNIA OF RANK

Rank in most armed forces is based on performance and time in service, although in some nations it is still very dependent on social status. Rank establishes superiority, and superiority within the same rank generally is determined by seniority. Rank also often reflects one's responsibility, to the extent that individuals of a given rank, such as colonel, are expected to be able to lead and command a certain number of individuals or administer a given number of commands. In wartime, rank often is strongly influenced by combat performance, and battlefield promotions of the most valiant or capable people may occur.

Today, one can observe two major distinctions in rank: (a) different ranks for officers and enlisted people and (b) unique ranks for navies.

Within both officer and enlisted ranks, larger groupings usually serve to differentiate inexperienced individuals from more seasoned, mature ones. In the U.S. Army, for example, junior ranks are intended to train individuals, to permit them to mature, and to provide them experience in leading smaller groups. In the officer corps, these are referred to as company ranks and are second and first lieutenant and captain, while in the enlisted ranks, they are the first three ranks. A second grouping contains experienced supervisors, with the training and maturity to lead and supervise significant numbers of people. Generally, these individuals are capable of taking and interpreting orders, formulating plans to fulfill their missions, conceptualizing orders so that their subordinates can fulfill the tasks necessary to complete parts of the mission, and judging whether a mission has indeed been accomplished. In the U.S. Army's enlisted ranks, these are the second three ranks, while in the officer corps, they are majors, lieutenant colonels, and colonels. The third grouping is best characterized as the executive leadership and is composed of people who lead large groups or several commands. Collectively, they are in charge of a nation's military and are usually that military's best and most experienced leaders. In the U.S. Army, these are the three most senior enlisted ranks; in the officer corps, they are referred to as flag officers, consisting of four ranks of generals.

Many nations' armed services also have warrant officers, most often drawn from the enlisted corps or recruited for special discrete officer tasks. They occupy a unique position between the enlisted and officer ranks. Depending upon the country, they may be considered senior enlisted personnel or in the lower officer ranks (see Table 1). In the U.S. military, warrant officers are treated as officers but are only promoted within the warrant officer grades and do not compete for promotion with other officer ranks.

Differing Ranks

ARMY AND MARINE CORPS

In the U.S. Army and U.S. Marine Corps, ranks are generally similar, both to each other and among different nations. "Lieutenant" and "captain" are junior officer ranks, "major" and "colonel" reflect mid-level ranks, and "general," the highest officer ranks. Likewise, in the enlisted corps, "private" and "corporal" reflect basic ranks, "sergeant" ranks are mid-level ranks, and embellished sergeant ranks, such as "first sergeant" or "sergeant major," reflect the senior ranks.

AIR FORCE

In nations such as the United States, where the air force was created out of the army, the army and air force ranks are identical. In other nations, air force ranks reflect the concept of airpower, such as flight lieutenant.

NAVY

Most of the world's navies have been influenced heavily by British tradition; hence, naval ranks tend to be different from other armed services. "Ensign" and "junior lieutenant" are often the two junior ranks; "lieutenant," "lieutenant commander," and "commander" are the middle ranks; and "captain," "commodore," and several ranks of admirals compose the senior ranks. This is confusing to other services, where lieutenants are generally very junior officers and captains are mid-level officers.

A navy's enlisted ranks can be equally confusing to those not in the naval service. The three junior ranks are often referred to as "seaman" ranks, the next three are "petty officer" ranks, and the senior ranks are several levels of "chiefs"—although there is a host of exceptions.

Insignia of Rank

There are many peculiarities among the rank insignias of the world's military organizations. The number and treatment of enlisted ranks vary from service to service and nation to nation, but a few generalities can be made about the officer ranks.

ARMY, AIR FORCE, AND MARINE CORPS

Army, air force, and Marine Corps officer insignia are often made of metal and are often worn on the shoulder epaulets of the jacket or the collar of the shirt. (One exception to this is in the NATO air forces, where ten of the nations' air forces wear their rank on the cuffs of their sleeves.) The metal insignia are usually of gold or silver, but can vary. Bars, stars, and oak leaves are very

TABLE 1. *Comparative Ranks for Enlisted Personnel/Warrant Officers: United States, United Kingdom, Former USSR*

UNITED STATES			UNITED KINGDOM			FORMER USSR		
Army	**Navy**	**Air Force**	**Army**	**Navy**	**Air Force**	**Army**	**Navy**	**Air Force**
Basic Private	Seaman Recruit	Basic Airman	Private Class 4	Junior Rating	Aircraftman	Ryadovoy (Private)	Matros (Seaman)	Ryadovoy (Private)
Private	Seaman Apprentice	Airman	Private Class 1–3	Able Rating	Leading Aircraftman	Efretyor (Private First Class)	Starshiy Matros (Senior Seaman)	Efretyor (Private First Class)
Private First Class	Seaman	'Airman First Class	Lance Corporal	(No Rating)	(No Rating)	Efretyor (Private First Class)	Starshiy Matros (Senior Seaman)	Efretyor (Private First Class)
Corporal	Petty Officer Third Class	Senior Airman/ Sergeant	Corporal	Leading Rating	Corporal	Mladshiy Serzhant (Junior sergeant)	Starshina 2d Stati (Petty Officer Second Class)	Mladshiy Serzhant (Junior Sergeant)
Sergeant	Petty Officer Second Class	Staff Sergeant	Sergeant	Petty Officer	Sergeant	Mladshiy Serzhant (Junior sergeant)	Starshina 2d Stati (Petty Officer Second Class)	Mladshiy Serzhant (Junior Sergeant)
Staff Sergeant	Petty Officer First Class	Technical Sergeant	Sergeant	Petty Officer	Sergeant	Serzhant (Sergeant)	Starshina 1st Stati (Petty Officer First Class)	Serzhant (Sergeant)
Sergeant First Class/ Master Sergeant	Chief Petty Officer	Master Sergeant	Staff Sergeant	Chief Petty Officer	Flight Sergeant	Serzhant (Sergeant)	Starshina 1st Stati (Petty Officer First Class)	Serzhant (Sergeant)
First Sergeant/ Sergeant-Major	Senior Chief Petty Officer/Master Chief Petty Officer	Senior Master Sergeant	Warrant Officer Class 2	(No Rating)	(No Rating)	Starshiy Sergeant (Senior Sergeant)	Glavnyy Starshina (Chief Petty Officer)	Starshiy Sergeant (Senior Sergeant)
Command Sergeant-Major/Sergeant-Major of the Army	Fleet Force Master Chief Petty Officer/ Master Chief Petty Officer of the Navy	Chief Master Sergeant/Chief Master Sergeant of the Air Force	Warrant Officer Class 1	Fleet Chief Petty Officer	Warrant Officer	Starshina (Sergeant Major)	Glavnyy Korabel'nyy Starshina (Chief Ship Petty Officer)	Starshina (Sergeant Major)
Warrant Officers			**Warrant Officers**			**Warrant Officers**		
Warrant Officer W-1	No Rank	No Rank	There are no equivalent warrant officer ranks in the British armed forces.			Praporshchik (Ensign)	Michman (Midshipman)	Praporshchik (Ensign)
Chief Warrant Officer W-2	Chief Warrant Officer W-2	No Rank				Starshiy Praporshchik (Senior Ensign)	Starshiy Michman (Senior Midshipman)	Starshiy Praporshchik (Senior Ensign)
Chief Warrant Officer W-3	Chief Warrant Officer W-3	No Rank				No Rank	No Rank	No Rank
Chief Warrant Officer W-4	Chief Warrant Officer W-4	No Rank				No Rank	No Rank	No Rank

Note: This chart illustrates the sequence of ranks for several military services. Although accurate, it is not recommended as a reference for protocol, rank, or authority equivalence.

popular, and some ranks in some air forces are propellers. Stars may represent the rank of general, and the larger or more pronounced an insignia, the more senior the rank. There are many exceptions to this, however: some nations award banks of stars to junior or mid-level ranks, and others provide relatively showy insignia for all of their military ranks.

The covers (hats) of more senior officer ranks often have gold or silver embellishments on their visors, whereas the visors of junior officers are plain. Additionally, the flag officer grades may have greater embellishments to distinguish them from the lower senior ranks.

NAVY

In the U.S. Navy, the sleeve is the location of insignia. While metal rank devices sometimes are worn on the collar of an officer's khaki work uniform, and insignia shoulder boards are worn on some uniforms (most often the two-piece white uniform with a white shirt), most naval officer ranks will appear on each sleeve of the jacket (blouse) a few inches above each cuff. These ranks appear as gold stripes of three widths: half stripes, stripes, and broad stripes. Non-flag ranks generally are indicated by combinations of stripes and half stripes, with the number of stripes increasing with rank. Some navies place a loop in the uppermost stripe. Broad stripes are reserved for admirals. The lowest of these ranks may be a single broad stripe, and succeedingly higher ranks are then indicated by additional regular stripes. Directly above the stripes there sometimes appears a symbol indicating the officer's profession. A star is often used to indicate officers of the line, while other symbols are used to denote the supply corps, medical corps, and so on.

Navy enlisted insignia are most often seen on the sleeve a few inches below the shoulder. There are many variations, but anchors may appear in these insignia to indicate naval service, and rank seniority is denoted by the number of stripes, stars, stripes and stars, or other combinations. A person's specialty or profession may also be denoted with an emblem. For example, in the U.S. Navy, a boatswain's mate is denoted by crossed anchors.

BRUCE W. WATSON

SEE ALSO: Noncommissioned Officer; Officer; Soldier; Warrant Officer.

Bibliography

Boatner, M. M. 1976. *Military customs and traditions.* Westport, Conn.: Greenwood Press.
Castano, J. B. 1975. *The naval officer's uniform guide.* Annapolis, Md.: U.S. Naval Institute Press.
Company of Military Historians. 1977. *Military uniforms in America.* Vol. 2, *Years of growth 1796–1851.* Novato, Calif.: Presidio Press.
Kerrigan, E. E. 1967. *American badges and insignia.* New York: Viking Press.
Tily, J. C. 1964. *The uniforms of the United States Navy.* New York: Thomas Yoseloff.

REINFORCEMENTS

There are two categories of reinforcements: individuals and units (formations). The individuals are fully trained, equipped, and fit to take their places in units in order to bring those units up to wartime strength when they have been maintained at a lower peacetime strength. There are also entire units and formations that reinforce in-place forces to complete the order of battle for planned operations. They may bring their equipment with them or draw it from pre-positioned stockpiles after arriving in the area or theater of operations.

Reinforcements in both categories may be from regular or reserve forces. They know their assigned war roles because they train with their "parent" units and formations during peacetime. Individuals, units, or formations that have an immediate part to play when battle starts must arrive during the transition-to-war phase; others, which have support roles, may allow more time to arrive. Much depends on the amount of warning given and the time required to travel from peacetime locations to the battle area, to draw and check equipment if necessary, to move forward (often on congested routes), and to deploy securely into operational positions. Regular reinforcements are normally at a higher state of readiness than reservists who must be mobilized, assembled, and medically checked prior to movement. The reservists' state of training and fitness for a role are also important considerations. All these factors are taken into account when assigning reinforcements to operational tasks.

Replacements are different from reinforcements; personnel and materiel replacements are required when units and formations incur losses during war. They do not have as high an arrival priority as reinforcements, although their provision is equally as important. The replacement system is described elsewhere in this encyclopedia.

Figure 1 illustrates an operational reinforcement system not specific to any one army or theater of operations.

Movement to the battle area or theater of operations is by air, sea, rail, road, or a combination of these means. Reinforcement units and formations that need to draw equipment from pre-positioned stockpiles, usually held in the communications or rear combat zones, are assisted by transport, specialist personnel who help them check and activate the equipment, and labor. Equipment required by a single unit is normally stored in one location.

Reinforcement individuals and formed units are received, accommodated, and administered by force and corps holding units, which also provide welfare and training facilities. Reinforcement formations usually have separate staging areas because of their size, the need for dispersion, and the additional protection this affords. They move as quickly as possible through the system to join their units or formations in the rear or forward combat zones.

Certain individuals and formed units are earmarked to provide crews for tanks, self-propelled guns, and other armored fighting vehicles. These and other main battle equipment are held in peacetime depots or in the units' own barracks, and kept serviceable to bring battalions, brigades, and divisions up to

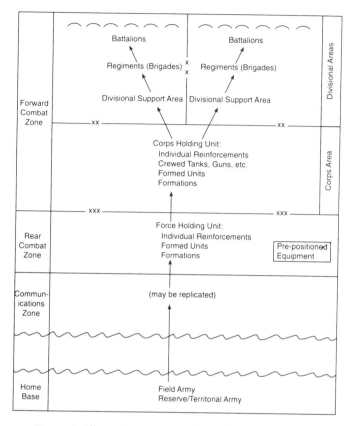

Figure 1. Illustrative operational reinforcement system.

full war-fighting strength. Reinforcement crews need a brief period of intensive training in their equipment immediately before joining their units and deploying with them to battle positions.

Reinforcements destined for divisions will pass through report points in the divisional support area and then to divisional troop units, regiments (brigades), or battalions. Within allied commands, such as those of NATO, reinforcement formations may be from armies of other nations. For example, a German division or brigade may join a corps of another nationality.

The system ensures that all reinforcements join their parent units and formations ready for preplanned operational roles. Headquarters staffs at each level monitor the progress of reinforcements through the system until they arrive at their prescribed destinations. Any priority shortages will be covered by reassignments so that units are at wartime strength and the order of battle is complete.

J. H. Skinner

See Also: Reserve Components.

Bibliography

Historical Evaluation and Research Organization (HERO). 1980. *German and Allied reserves in 1914*. Dunn Loring, Va.: Historical Evaluation and Research Organization.
Palmer, R. R., B. I. Wylie, and W. R. Keast. 1948. The procurement and training of ground combat troops. In *United States Army in World War II*. Washington, D.C.: Department of the Army.
Pigott, A. J. K., comp. 1949. *Manpower problems*. London: Her Majesty's Stationery Office.

RESERVE COMPONENTS

Nearly every modern nation maintains some kind of reserve structure as part of its armed forces. These reserves are designed to expand, augment, or otherwise support the existing standing army, navy, and air forces. Reserve components provide attractive benefits to a nation as a part of a total national security program by providing a larger total armed force at less cost than having the entire force on active, full-time status. Reserves retain a reservoir of trained and combat-capable personnel, thereby allowing rapid mobilization of a larger force and reducing training requirements after mobilization. Some nations have laws that require nearly every able-bodied male to receive military training and to be ready for mobilization during wartime.

This discussion of reserve components addresses the reserve components and structures in general, the reserve structure of the United States, the types of reserves maintained by European countries, and the total force policy in the United States.

Reserve Structure

The two general models for reserve components are militia and national.

MILITIA

The militia structure has its roots in medieval England and it was later translated to colonial America. Under this approach, all able-bodied male citizens owed the state—originally the Crown—military service as needed for security. Each individual maintained his own arms, mustered and trained under local lords, and, when required, answered a call to arms for defense of the realm. Only during the seventeenth century was the militia system replaced as England's second line of defense (after the navy) by a standing army raised through regular enlistments.

In colonial America, the militia system was essential for protection of isolated settlements in a hostile environment. Suspicious of a standing army, the colonists found the militia system well suited to the conditions in which they lived. Labor was scarce, and the settlements needed every available man to work. Local defense met the security needs of settlements where every man could answer the call on short notice. The enemy threat was often local also, consisting of native Americans within the immediate area.

The colonial militias were the basis for the resulting reserve components of the United States. From them emerged the national guard organizations of today. During the nineteenth and twentieth centuries, the militias proved less effective as the nature of the enemy changed and citizens became reluctant to respond to a call to arms for an expedition to remote or overseas locations such as Canada, Cuba, Mexico, and the Philippines.

The U.S. reserve components in the 1990s are principally units organized in local areas under the management and command of local reserve commanders. The U.S. reserve structure has two separate elements, each with its own chain of command: national guard units under control of state governors and reserve units under control of active military service organizations. In time of war, the national guard and reserve would be mobilized principally to fight as units integrated into active duty military organizations.

NATIONAL RESERVE

National reserves are the norm in Europe, including the former Warsaw Pact. These are the products principally of national or universal military service, in which nearly all able-bodied men enlist or are drafted into an active-duty military organization, receive basic and some advanced training, and serve for a short, fixed period of time such as nine months to two or three years. After active duty, all personnel remain on reserve rolls for a certain number of years or until reaching a specific age; during this time they receive periodic refresher training or duty.

A national reserve force is normally designed to maintain a large pool of previously trained personnel who can be rapidly mobilized to augment and fill out a standing armed force, which may be rather small in some nations. These reservists are completely under the control of the regular military chain of command and in most instances would fill vacancies in the regular structure rather than forming and fighting in their own units. They provide an expandable force structure capable of rapid mobilization.

In the final analysis, any reserve structure—whether of the militia or national model—must be evaluated on its ability to mobilize and fight in defense of national security. The flexibility of an armed force to mobilize its manpower rapidly to meet a sudden, serious threat to national security is critical in today's world. A large reserve force that is well trained and ready to be called up in a matter of days—not months—is a central part of this mobilization requirement.

U.S. Reserve Components

The reserve components of the U.S. armed forces consist of two national guard components (Army National Guard of the United States and Air National Guard of the United States) and five reserve components (U.S. Army Reserve, U.S. Naval Reserve, U.S. Marine Corps Reserve, U.S. Air Force Reserve, and U.S. Coast Guard Reserve). The national guard components are all organized into units; the reserves consist of both units and individuals.

The U.S. Coast Guard operates as a separate armed force during peacetime and reports to the Department of Transportation. During wartime, the Coast Guard is transferred to and becomes a part of the Department of the Navy. The U.S. Coast Guard Reserve, as a part of the Coast Guard, also trains and operates in peacetime as part of the Department of Transportation. Because its principal use is to augment the Coast Guard and therefore the navy during wartime, the Coast Guard Reserve is organized and managed much like the Naval Reserve but with a principal wartime mission of port security.

Duty in the armed forces of the United States has been voluntary since 1973, when the Vietnam-era draft ended. Upon a member's first enlistment, he or she by law must serve a total of eight years in a military service, whether enlisting in a regular component or in a reserve component. This total eight-year military service obligation (increased in 1984 from six years) can be served in three ways: all on active duty, some portion on active duty in accordance with the individual's enlistment agreement and the balance in a reserve component, or all in a reserve component.

The normal procedure is for an individual to serve four years or more on active duty in the regular army, navy, Marine Corps, air force, or Coast Guard, followed by the remaining time in the reserves. This reserve duty can either be in a reserve unit or as an individual reservist. Where possible, duty in a reserve unit is desired, as more training is available and higher readiness is the result. This choice is voluntary. Because of training opportunities and pay benefits, the reserve components have had little trouble attracting large numbers of prior-service veterans to train in units.

The all-volunteer armed force has been quite successful since its implementation, and the attractiveness of active-duty careers has resulted in high retention rates and a subsequent shortage of personnel leaving active duty to fill reserve component positions. As a result, the national guard and reserve also enlist and train non-prior-service personnel. In this case, all eight years of the military service obligation normally would be served in a reserve component.

Within the reserve components, all national guard and reserve personnel are assigned to one of three reserve component categories: the ready reserve, the standby reserve, or the retired reserve. All national guard members, as members of units, are in the ready reserve.

READY RESERVE

The ready reserve comprises military members of the national guard and reserve, organized in units or as individuals, liable for recall to active duty to augment the active components in time of war or national emergency. The president of the United States may order up to one million ready reservists to active duty involuntarily for up to 24 months upon the president's declaration of a national emergency. When Congress declares a state of war or national emergency, the president may order all ready reservists to active duty involuntarily for the duration of the war or emergency plus six months. The ready reserve itself consists of three subcategories: the selected reserve, the individual ready reserve, and the inactive national guard.

Selected reserve. The selected reserve consists of those units and individuals within the ready reserve designated by their respective services and approved by the Joint Chiefs of Staff as so essential to initial wartime missions that they have priority over all other reserves. All selected reservists must attend monthly training as well as two weeks of annual active duty.

The president of the United States may order up to 200,000 members of the selected reserve to active duty involuntarily for any operational mission, pending crisis, or emergency for 90 days without declaring a national emergency. Members and units of the selected reserve, because of the very nature of such an emergency mobilization possibility, must be prepared to report for duty within 24 hours of notification.

The selected reserve consists of units, trained individuals, and trainees. The selected reserve units are staffed and equipped to serve and/or train either as separate operational units or as augmentation subunits. Each selected reserve unit includes trained reserve members who participate in unit training activities on a part-time basis as well as a few full-time support personnel who have been ordered to active duty voluntarily for the purpose of organizing, administering, recruiting, instructing, or training the part-time members.

The trained individuals of the selected reserve are usually preassigned to mobilize with an active component unit upon mobilization. These individuals are called *individual mobilization augmentees*, and they train on a part-time basis with the active component unit or organization with which they will mobilize. A few full-time trained individuals perform similar functions as the full-time members in units.

Selected reserve trainees are those newly enlisted members without prior military service who are either in the process of receiving basic and initial skill training or awaiting orders to start such training. Some trainees receive training only in the summer between high school or college programs and require two summers to complete their required training. U.S. law prohibits deploying overseas on land any member of the armed forces until they receive a minimum of 12 weeks of basic training or its equivalent.

Individual ready reserve and inactive national guard. The individual ready reserve and inactive national guard consist of those ready reservists who are not in the selected reserve.

The individual ready reserve is a personnel pool consisting principally of individuals who have had military training, have served previously in the active component or in the selected reserve, and have some period of their military service obligation remaining. These personnel are required to complete their military service obligation (six years if they enlisted prior to 1984; eight years if they enlisted in 1984 or after) in either an active or reserve component. Special annual musters are required for members of the individual ready reserve to maintain current addresses and other information pertaining to their mobilization potential.

The inactive national guard consists of national guard personnel in an inactive status who are unable to train with their units. They remain attached to their units, however, and would mobilize with their units in an emergency. The inactive national guard is designed for members who temporarily cannot train with their units but expect to do so again within a certain time, usually one year.

STANDBY RESERVE

The standby reserve consists of personnel who maintain their military affiliation without being in the ready reserve. They generally have completed their military service obligation, are not required to perform training, and are not part of units. The standby reserve is an additional pool of trained individuals who could be mobilized if necessary to fill staffing needs in specific skills. The number of reservists in the standby reserve is decreasing, mainly as a result of Defense Department policy initiatives to emphasize accession and retention of personnel in the ready reserve. If, however, an individual has completed his military service obligation, does not wish to remain in the ready reserve, and is willing to retain a military affiliation in case of emergency, then he can be assigned to the standby reserve. Some members of the standby reserve in active status may receive training on a voluntary basis without pay.

In time of war or national emergency declared by Congress, the standby reserve may be mobilized involuntarily for the duration of the emergency plus six months. A member of the standby reserve may not, however, be ordered to active duty involuntarily until the secretary of the military department determines that not enough qualified reservists in the ready reserve or in the inactive national guard are available.

RETIRED RESERVE

The retired reserve comprises all reserve officers and enlisted personnel who receive retired pay on the basis of their active-duty or reserve service or who have qualified to receive pay upon reaching the age of 60.

All retired members who have completed at least twenty years of active duty (with either regular or reserve components or a combination thereof) may be ordered to active duty whenever required as determined by the secretary of the appropriate military department. A national emergency or act of war is not a precondition. The secretary may exercise this authority to accomplish whatever work is deemed important.

Other members who qualify for retirement resulting from active and reserve service, but have not accumulated twenty total years of active duty, may be ordered to active duty during a national emergency or an act of war declared by the U.S. Congress. As with the standby reserve, those retired reservists who do not have twenty years of active duty may not be mobilized until the service secretary determines that insufficient reservists are in an active status or in the inactive national guard.

All military retirees are categorized by the length of time after retirement and whether or not an individual has a disability that would preclude recall in a mobilization. Category I military retirees are within their first five years of retirement, under age 60, and not disabled. Category II retirees are retired more than five years, under age 60, and not disabled. Category III includes all others, including those who are disabled. All Category I and II retirees are considered mobilization assets and are counted as part of the total U.S. Department of Defense mobilization base. Category III retirees with selected skills, primarily medical personnel, are also considered mobilization assets on a case-by-case basis.

TRAINING OF U.S. RESERVE COMPONENTS

Significant training is provided for members of the national guard and reserve to ensure that trained and qualified units and members are available in time of war or national emergency. The secretaries of the army, navy, air force, and transportation (in the case of the Coast Guard) are responsible for making sure members of the national guard and reserve receive the necessary training. This required training is in accordance with mobilization assignments and required readiness levels and can be accomplished on a part-time (inactive status) or full-time (active-duty) basis.

Selected reserve training. All members of the selected reserve must participate in two days of training monthly, normally with their units on a selected weekend of the month. In addition to the monthly training, members must spend two weeks on active duty for training each year, again normally with their unit. This training ensures proficiency in individual skills as well as unit training and exercises. For selected units, the active-duty period is spent on exercises overseas, practicing missions that would be required during wartime.

In addition to proficiency training, all members must have the proper basic and skill training in their specialties. When prior-service personnel leaving active duty join a guard or reserve unit, they often already have a certain level of skill from their active-duty experience. Changing skills or acquiring additional skill training can be achieved either through on-the-job training in the units or through full-time, regular, active-duty service schools. A jet engine mechanic, for instance, could be sent to a regular service school for the eight or ten months required to provide the necessary skill training. The same opportunities exist for a tank mechanic or radar specialist.

When a non-prior-service member joins the national guard or reserve, which is the case in approximately half of the accessions, this new member must be provided with basic training and then skill training. Because many non-prior-service guard and reserve members are still in their last year or two of high school or attending college, this training may be accomplished over two summers before the member becomes fully proficient in the selected skill. Most new accessions, however, receive this initial entry training in one continuous period of active duty.

The same training opportunities are offered to members of the national guard and reserve as are offered to active-duty regular members of the services. Basic training, skill training, professional military education, and specialized training are available to every member of the reserve components. Guardsmen and reservists attend the service's staff and war colleges, pilot and navigator training, and other officer and enlisted professional training programs.

Training of the individual ready reserve. The individual ready reserve has access to the same training as members of the selected reserve, but they are not required to attend training. The only requirement is that these members keep their headquarters informed of their addresses, military status, and physical status. Once a year, they are selectively mustered to verify the above data.

In addition, they may participate voluntarily in training. Depending on the availability of training space, they may volunteer for short- or long-term schooling in their specialties or for additional professional military training through correspondence courses or by attending staff and war colleges. Many members of the individual ready reserve participate in training with a *volunteer training unit*. By continuing their voluntary participation, members of the individual ready reserve may qualify for retirement credits and be considered for promotion. They may also volunteer to join a unit in the selected reserve and thereby move from the individual ready reserve to the selected reserve.

PAY AND RETIREMENT CREDIT FOR MEMBERS OF THE U.S. RESERVE COMPONENTS

Members of the national guard and reserve receive pay commensurate with their rank or grade and level of participation in training activities. Every member receives "points" for participation, which represent credits for pay and retirement. For instance, 50 points must be acquired each year to get credit for a "good" year that is creditable toward retirement. Every member of the guard or reserve receives 15 points just for being in a reserve component. To this must be added 12 to 14 points for annual active-duty training (depending on the length of the training) and four points for each weekend (two days) of training received during the year. Thus, up to 77 points can be acquired by attending all training.

Pay is received for most training points on the basis of one day of active-duty base pay at the particular rank or grade of the individual for each point. Additional points can be received for correspondence courses, but these are not for pay. The total number of points that can be counted toward retirement credits is 60 each year. Points beyond that level are noted in the member's personnel record and considered for promotion purposes.

If a member cannot complete a "good" year with at least 50 points, he is removed from the selected reserve and assigned to the individual ready reserve.

Members of the individual ready reserve do not get paid for monthly training or correspondence courses. Should these members be authorized to receive two weeks of active duty during the year, they are paid as for the selected reserve. Members of the individual ready reserve can get credit for a "good" year toward retirement if they get the necessary 50 points through membership (15 points), active duty for training (12 to 14 points), voluntary training periods during the year, and correspondence courses.

A guardsman or reservist must have a total of 20 "good" years of service creditable toward retirement in order to receive any retired pay at age 60. The amount of retired pay is based on the number of points received as a member of the reserve components plus any active-duty time served before or during membership in the guard or reserves. Both the pay and the retirement credits provide a strong incentive for individuals to remain in the guard and reserve and to participate fully in these programs.

NATO Reserve Systems

Most NATO countries have reserve systems that are part of a national service obligation. Other than the United States, only Canada and the United Kingdom have completely volunteer armed forces. Iceland has no armed forces, and Luxembourg has no reserve forces. The forces of the other countries are a mixture of conscripts and volunteers with some kind of individual reserve system in which reservists either form a general pool or have a specific assignment upon mobilization. Norway has a mobilization army with 90 percent of its personnel in reserve status. These individuals generally have specific unit assignments for mobilization.

Most countries have either no organized reserve units or a few specialized units (e.g., Italian Alpine battalions) and manage their members as individuals planned for augmentation. The idea is for a quickly expandable armed force, for which individual reservists first provide fillers and then casualty replacements after the war has commenced. Some active-duty units split into two or three new "clone" units to accommodate the reservists as they are mobilized.

Some reservists have preplanned orders to join units they served with on active duty. Active-duty tours vary from a few months (9 in Denmark) to as much as 30 months (Greece). Although universal service may apply in general, not all serve in reality, and therefore all are not trained. For those serving, a military service obligation remains until a specified age or for a number of years. The age requirement varies from 35 to 46. Commissioned officers often have longer obligations than enlisted personnel and warrant officers. In the Federal Republic of Germany, members were obligated until age 60. Some reserve training was provided, but it was sporadic and often not accomplished even when required by law.

FEDERAL REPUBLIC OF GERMANY

During World War II the Germans demonstrated a phenomenal capacity to provide personnel to create, maintain, and refit the divisions of the *Wehrmacht*. The *Wehrkreis* system of military districts created more than 300 infantry divisions between 1934 and 1944. In 1944 alone, during the bleakest period before the beginning of the end, more than 54 divisions were created.

Seeking to avoid the excesses of Nazi Germany in World War II, the Federal Republic of Germany established constitutional constraints that in some respects inhibited the creation and maintenance of a professional military force capable of contributing effectively to NATO deterrence. One important aspect of this military force was the creation of a territorial army to support and supplement the combat missions of the regular army (*Bundesheer*). An effective organization of personnel pools provided fillers for understrength active units, staffed combat support units maintained at cadre strength, and provided replacement battalions to compensate for combat attrition.

Limitations placed on the *Bundesheer* force structure restrict active-duty peacetime corps-level units to 50 percent staffing, division-level units to 75 percent, and brigades and other tactical formations to 95 percent. The mobilization system and corresponding personnel pools compensate for the reduced peacetime authorizations.

The personnel pools are divided into the ready reserves, active unit fillers, and territorial army personnel. The first two categories provide trained personnel to bring active peacetime units up to full combat capability. The territorial army would utilize fewer capable reserve personnel in rear-area missions to free active personnel for forward defenses. This system allows the German army to increase rapidly from 300,000 personnel in peacetime to approximately 1 million in wartime.

To ensure a capability for forward defense missions, the *Bundesheer* created a standby readiness pool of trained personnel to replace new inductees and vacancies in units. This constitutes 20 to 25 percent of the total personnel of forward units. These personnel are drawn from the ready reserve pool, which forms the battalion-level reserves for forward-deployed units.

The territorial army relies on reserve personnel to fill out its wartime personnel requirements to a far greater extent than does the *Bundesheer*. One of the territorial army's prime missions is to mobilize and train replacement battalions to compensate for combat losses.

The Federal Republic of Germany's reserve system is based on the universal military obligation of all personnel who have been conscripted or have volunteered for active service. Conscripts are inducted for 15 to 18 months (depending on the needs of the service) and then have an obligation until age 32 for enlisted personnel, age 45 for noncommissioned officers, and age 60 for officers. Former regular soldiers are obligated until age 65.

Reserve personnel are divided into three classes: ready reservists, alert reservists, and replacement reservists.

The ready reserve has a strength of 30,000 and is composed of those conscripts who served 15 months of their 18-month active-service obligation. After this three-month-early release, they can be recalled within the following year to serve their remaining time. Only the best conscripts are selected for this status because their mission is to provide rapid deployment of in-place combat personnel for immediate combat duty in a crisis. They bring the frontline units up to wartime strength. In a practical sense, they are counted as a part of the active service that is on extended leave.

The alert reserve (approximately 800,000 personnel) is composed of those personnel not selected for the ready reserve as well as those ready reservists who have already served a year in that category. Personnel in the alert reserve serve for five years with a preselected mobilization assignment until about age 30. After this service, personnel are placed in the replacement reserve, which is called up only if needed. They would act as casualty replacements in time of war. Personnel remain in this category until they complete their military obligation.

Although the NATO reserve systems are significantly different from that of the United States, the traditional European conscription-based reserve system is very well suited to rapid mobilization. It has a proven capability to deliver large numbers of trained reservists to replacement depots and cadred units at high speed under desperate circumstances.

Russia and Eastern Europe

The demise in 1989 of the Warsaw Pact, which bound the nations of Eastern Europe into the military orbit of the Soviet Union, and the breakup in 1990 of the Soviet Union into its constituent republics initiated changes in those nations' military policies and reserve systems whose outcomes are still uncertain. Under the Warsaw Pact, Bulgaria, Czechoslovakia, the German Democratic Republic, Hungary, Poland, Romania, and the Soviet Union all had similar doctrine, organizations, tactics, military accession methods, and reserve systems. These policies and practices are changing as some nations convert from socialist systems to free-market systems and as they reduce the size of their armed forces. The systems that emerge will depend on how the previous practices can be modified to minimize serious problems.

The reserve systems of the Soviet Union and the other nations of the Warsaw Pact were based on the centuries-old reserve mobilization system of Russia. In past wars, Russia often had to mobilize all of its national resources to resist invasion or expand its borders, and the critical factor was building very large forces rapidly. From July to December 1914, for example, Russia mobilized over four million men to fight Germany and Austria-Hungary, although many were poorly equipped and poorly led and fed. During the first six months after being attacked by the Germans in World War II, the Soviets fielded 291 divisions and 94 brigades using this system.

The essential features of the Russian (Soviet) mobilization system are mass conscription of very large numbers of one-term enlisted personnel, minimally trained, narrowly focused, and subsequently discharged to obligated reserve call-up status, and receiving little or no refresher training during 5 to 25 years of total military obligation. The Soviet Universal Military Training Law of 1967 prescribed a universal system for all males. With the exception of a few women, volunteers were not allowed. Unless exempted, all men between the ages of 19 and 22 had to serve an initial tour of two to three years.

This form of conscription generates large numbers of recruits that have to be accommodated in the armed forces. Thus, this universal long-term conscription system required either very large standing armed forces, or the exemption of a large part of the annual cohort of military-age males, or both. As long as the socialist nations maintained large standing forces to counter a perceived NATO threat, it was possible to have nearly universal conscription, but as the armed forces are reduced, the proportion of each year's annual cohort that is actually conscripted becomes smaller and smaller until it is impossible to maintain the image that all will serve, and at this point a change to either a volunteer force or a short-term conscription system has to be made.

The long-term form of conscription also generated large numbers of personnel with two to three years of military training and experience to form a reserve for mobilization. Generally, the attention paid by the armed forces to these reservists was greater for those who had recently left active duty and were therefore presumed to be of greater immediate value when recalled. During the early years after leaving active duty, the reservists were required to participate frequently in training, generally while on short periods of active duty. As the reservists got older, their training was decreased until they reached the maximum age for reserve service, which was around 50 for enlisted personnel and up to age 65 for officers. In the early 1980s the Soviet army of 4 million active soldiers was backed up by 4 million reservists who had completed their active duty during the previous five years and another 20 million older reservists. Reserve enlisted personnel received little training, and the training they did perform sometimes consisted of nonmilitary activities, such as crop harvesting or construction work. Reserve officers, however, often received professional military training and participated in military activities.

Because of the large number of individual reservists available, the method for expanding the military forces was to use them as fillers to augment active component cadres in forming new units or bringing existing understrength units to full wartime readiness. Many active-duty units were deliberately maintained under strength with the intention of bringing them to full wartime strength by filling them with reservists. During the 1970s, only about 30 percent of Soviet divisions were maintained as Category I divisions at or above 90 percent of their authorized strength. The other 70 percent of the Soviet divisions were cadre units to be filled by mobilized reservists. Category II divisions were maintained at about half strength, and Category III divisions at less than half strength.

Mass conscription and mass reserves pertained primarily to armies in the Soviet Union and the other Warsaw Pact nations. The Soviet Strategic Rocket Forces were fully manned with a mixture of conscripts and long-service personnel and would not be augmented upon mobilization. Navies and air forces of these nations also rely less on augmentation by reservists than do the armies.

General mobilization in the Soviet Union entailed a complete buildup of all of the armed forces to their prescribed wartime strengths in personnel and equipment. The process included alerting and assembling reservists, assigning them to units, obtaining necessary equipment and supplies, and moving the units to an area of operations. Large-scale mobilization of Soviet reservists occurred three times during the Cold War: in 1968 for the invasion of Czechoslovakia; in 1979 for operations in Afghanistan; and in 1990 for the aborted invasion of Poland. These mobilizations were not always carried out well. Cockburn (1983) describes the mobilization for Afghanistan as a "disaster," particularly in the Soviet Carpathian Military District, where "large numbers of reservists . . . failed to answer the call" and "many could not . . . be located . . ." Many of those who did respond to that call-up were bivouacked in tents in the open during winter owing to a lack of permanent housing facilities. How mass mobilization of these reservists for a major conventional war in Europe would have worked, fortunately, was never tested.

As Belarus, Russia, Ukraine, and the other nations of Eastern Europe try to achieve a new form of political and military organization, they will also change their military policies and their reserve systems. The outcomes will be different for each nation because the single model provided by the Soviet Union for so many years no longer suffices. Russia announced in 1992 that it would reduce its armed forces from 4 million to about 1.5 million and try to move toward a volunteer type of force. The new nations of Belarus, Ukraine, Central Asia, and the Baltic have all announced plans to form their own armed forces, generally smaller than when they were republics of the Soviet Union and oriented toward self-defense, but the details of how this is to be done are not yet evident. Romania and Bulgaria have retained the policies of a socialist state, and the other nations of Eastern Europe are adopting military policies suitable for their individual needs as the ultimate political and economic realities of the future dictate. How these changes will affect the size and shape of the reserve systems remains to be seen. In perhaps the most extreme change of all, the German Democratic Republic—once the most militaristic of the socialist nations— merged into the Federal Republic of Germany.

German Democratic Republic

Until mid-1989 the German Democratic Republic (GDR) was thought to have had the best-led, best-equipped, and best-trained army in the Warsaw Pact's non-Soviet forces. The forces were kept in a state of continuous alert, which even Soviet troops did not achieve. Their military strength was buttressed by a program of societal militarization unlike that in other Warsaw Pact nations. In the GDR, adoption of Soviet political institutions and control mechanisms guaranteed solid Soviet political control but also revived the Prussian-German tradition of a powerful authoritarian state.

Although the GDR had a peacetime active armed force among the smallest in the Warsaw Pact, the military power of the state was highly respected. In addition to formidable groupings of regular armed forces, the GDR fielded several reserve, elite, and paramilitary formations that might have played important roles in a conflict. Peacetime active-duty figures, therefore, are misleading. The reserves had 400,000 personnel (65 percent of the army's total strength), with 330,000 in the ground forces.

All GDR reservists spent three months per year in refresher training until they had accumulated 24 months. An additional 250,000 men had a reserve commitment to age 50. Reservists were designated category I or II: category I reservists ranged from age 20 to 35, and category II reservists from age 36 to 50 (officers to age 60). In addition to the 24 months' reserve training, the army of the GDR conducted "reservist exercises" lasting up to eight days; those exercises were designed to develop speed, readiness, and clandestine capabilities within the reserve mobilization system.

The collapse of the Communist order in the GDR beginning in the autumn of 1989, the merger of the former East German and West German states in 1990–91, and continuing conventional force reductions talks and agreements affecting European nations have significantly altered the size, capability, and organization of the reserve component of the *Nationale Volksarmee* (NVA). In

January 1990 the NVA ceased calling up for active duty some 20,000 reservists annually. During the rapid dissolution of the GDR in 1989–90, a large exodus, including widespread emigration of East Germans, quickly depleted the GDR forces of some of their reserve manpower. By March 1990 the once-supposed 500,000 reservists between 21 and 26 years of age discharged from active service within five years (and in principal ready to have manned five mobilization divisions) had dwindled by at least one-third. The reunification of Germany in 1990–91 began the elimination of the old GDR reserve and mobilization system and the amalgamation of the GDR forces selectively into the new German armed forces.

Toward a U.S. Total Force

At the end of the Vietnam War, the American public became strongly opposed to continuation of the draft, which was viewed by many as unfair. This view was strengthened by the general unpopularity of the Vietnam conflict itself. President Nixon, as a part of winding down the Vietnam War and ensuring a continued strong national defense, established a commission to investigate the possibility of maintaining the armed forces on a volunteer basis.

The Gates Commission determined that, by raising compensation to near civilian-market levels, the United States—considering the civilian economy and the size of the youth cohorts at that time—could maintain a standing armed force of about 2 million personnel. This, however, was considered insufficient to protect national security. To make an all-volunteer force viable, therefore, increased reliance on the reserve forces was necessary.

Prior to the all-volunteer force, the reserve forces in the United States were just that—forces in reserve or the background, usually in subordinate roles and assigned secondary missions. They received relatively few resources for management, training, and readiness. The belief persisted from the days of the American Revolutionary War that the reserves were not reliable or capable. An extended period of time was considered necessary to train and equip reserve units properly after mobilization. This in fact had been the case with the majority of forces utilized in World Wars I and II, who were actually reservists—civilians called up, trained, and deployed. Selected guard and reserve units had been mobilized, however, for Korea, Vietnam, and minor crises, and some of these were committed with less delay than in the world wars.

Despite the great concern about placing increased reliance on the reserve components, no other alternative existed for ending the draft. Accordingly, Secretary of Defense James Schlesinger formally announced in 1973 a total force policy that established a full partnership between the regular components of the armed forces and the national guard and reserve. This partnership meant equivalent and consistent treatment of the total force in the areas of training, standards, and readiness. A concerted effort would be made to organize, train, equip, and employ both regular and reserve forces in the most effective overall manner.

The total force policy, along with subsequent expanded mission responsibilities, has placed very demanding requirements on the reserve components.

Although they remain civilian volunteers who serve during peacetime on a part-time basis, the reservists must still be ready for immediate mobilization and rapid deployment into combat. These citizen-soldiers have to achieve and maintain a high state of readiness characteristic of the regular components.

The U.S. Congress and the Department of Defense have both recognized and supported this increased role for the reserve components and its ramifications. As a result, the total force policy has transformed the U.S. armed forces into one of the world's most powerful military forces.

In 1982, Secretary of Defense Caspar Weinberger stated:

> We can no longer consider Reserve forces as merely forces in reserve. . . . Instead, they have to be an integral part of the Total Force, both within the United States and within NATO. They have to be, and in fact are, a blending of the professionalism of the full-time soldier with the professionalism of the citizen-soldier. Only in that way can we achieve the military strength that is necessary to defend our freedom.

The total force policy reinforces the American traditional belief that in a democracy the major responsibility for the nation's wartime defense must be assigned to the citizen-soldier. It also allows reduced funding for the regular, active-duty, standing armed forces required for national security. Consistent with the colonial model of the militia, the national guard and reserve are trained and led by reserve noncommissioned and commissioned officers, also citizen-soldiers.

The reality of the total force policy is that the United States cannot successfully mount and sustain a significant military operation without the guard and reserve. The total force policy provides a militarily sensible and practical response to the speed with which a military crisis can unfold in modern-day warfare. The reserve components must be maintained at combat-effectiveness and mobilization-readiness levels commensurate with the active forces they will be required to reinforce. Therefore, as a practical matter, they must be integrated as fully as possible in peacetime with the units with which they will operate in wartime.

Historically, reserves have often been described as the *fourth force*, supplementing the classical forces of land, sea, and air. In this role, they have been fully in reserve, called only when a nation has been in dire straits, and useful only after a long period of training. The U.S. total force policy represents a significant departure from the fourth-force thinking. The total force is a viable, integrated force that has increased operational value through training, condition, and availability. The reserve components are in full partnership with the regular components for the purpose of deterring war, providing defense, and waging war if necessary. They represent a serious intention of the nation and its military planners to make the reserves an effective force in increasing the nation's potential combat power.

DAVID A. SMITH

SEE ALSO: Personnel; Reserves.

Bibliography

Austin, L., ed. 1988. *The anthropo factor in warfare: Conscripts, volunteers, and reserves.* Washington, D.C.: National Defense Univ. Press.

Cockburn, A. 1983. *The threat.* New York: Random House.

Collins, J. M. 1978. *Imbalance of power.* San Rafael, Calif.: Presidio Press.

Merritt, H. L., and L. F. Carter, eds. 1985. *Mobilization and the national defense.* Washington, D.C.: National Defense Univ. Press.

Simon, J., ed. 1988. *NATO–Warsaw Pact, force mobilization.* Washington, D.C.: National Defense Univ. Press.

U.S. Department of Defense. 1987. Directive 1215.6, *Uniform reserve, training and retirement categories.* Washington, D.C.: Department of Defense.

U.S. Department of Defense, Office of the Assistant Secretary of Defense (Reserve Affairs). 1987. *Reserve components of the armed forces.* Washington, D.C.: Department of Defense.

———. 1988. *Reserve components of the United States armed forces.* DoD 1215.15-H. Washington, D.C.: Department of Defense.

Wilson, B. J., III, ed. 1985. *The guard and reserve in the total force.* Washington, D.C.: National Defense Univ. Press.

Woller, R. 1978. *Warsaw Pact reserve systems: A white paper.* Munich: Bernard und Graefe Verlag.

RESERVES

Reserves can be a decisive element in warfare. The provision of reserves in adequate strength, appropriate distribution, and employment according to the situation is part of the art of leadership, because reserves enable the commander to decisively influence the course of operations, battles, and campaigns.

Karl von Clausewitz (1780–1831), the best-known German military theorist, stated: "A reserve has two distinct purposes. One is to prolong and renew the action; the second, to counter unforeseen threats" (Clausewitz 1976). As simple as this may sound, it remains a difficult task. It requires the military commander to adjust to the nearly unlimited variety of combat situations, which in turn requires him to carefully assess all pertinent factors.

Clausewitz was the first to treat the theoretical aspects of reserves extensively. Before him and until the age of Napoleon, war was primarily the art of skillful maneuver to force the enemy to give up his positions without fighting.

Therefore, it is not surprising that the numerous books on "rules of war" written during the seventeenth and eighteenth centuries rarely mention reserves. It was not until the nineteenth century that manuals and textbooks included chapters on drill, tactics, and grand strategy and discussed reserves also. Henceforth military commanders attempted to penetrate the phenomena of war and the art of war by applying appropriate theories. Inevitably they were confronted with the significance of reserves.

Definitions of Reserves

In 1861, a British military dictionary defined reserves as "a select body of troops kept back to give support when needed, or to rally upon" (H. L. Scott 1861,

London). A more complete definition is found in the *Dictionary of Military Terms* (Dupuy et al. 1986):

> That portion of a force that is held out of combat in anticipation of its being used later to influence the outcome of a battle, engagement or operation. Such a reserve held out by an army is called the army reserve (or the army's reserve), that held out by a corps is the corps reserve, and so forth. (2) A military organization of people not on active duty but holding ratings or commissions and available to be called on active duty when needed. Members of a reserve may or may not attend regular training meetings and serve periodically for short periods of active duty. (3) A member of such an organization.

The Marxist view differs little. The *Brief Lexicon of Operational, Tactical and General Military Terms* (1958, Moscow) mentions two kinds of reserves:

1. sources of men and materiel that can be used in the course of war or an operation
2. a portion of the battle formation of the troops that is designed to be put into action at the decisive moment or to repel sudden strikes (attacks) of the enemy.

Concerning Communist forces, a distinction must be made between the terms *reserves* and *second echelon:*

- a typical second echelon is considerably stronger than a typical reserve
- the commander of an echelon knows the task he will have to perform whereas the commander of a reserve does not
- echelons are not available for employment or tasking by higher command levels while higher commands (e.g., a corps) may state conditions for the employment of a lower echelon's reserves (e.g., the reserve of a division).

The *Great Soviet Encyclopedia* (*Bolshaja Sovetskaja Enciclopedija* [1978, vol. 7, p. 92]) defines reserves in a similar way.

Reserves can be classified as combat reserves and noncombat reserves. The combat reserves can be further broken down into strategic, tactical, or operational reserves.

Combat Reserves: Strategic

TYPES OF STRATEGIC RESERVES

Reserves can be planned and organized. This applies in particular to strategic reserves and also to some of the combat forces kept in reserve at the operational level. It is useful to differentiate between the following ways of organizing reserves:

- to build up (i.e., to create reserves in addition to the forces already available)
- to form (i.e., to create reserves from the forces available in time of crisis)
- to acquire (i.e., to create a reserve by thinning out committed forces who are in contact with the enemy).

In many countries, most ground force reserves (both operational and tactical) are not on active peacetime duty; they must be mobilized in time of tension.

The situation is different with the fighting components of air forces and navies. Their high technological standards make it difficult and cost ineffective to store the hardware and to mobilize in time of tension. Therefore, few nations retain large naval and air force reserves like the U.S. National Guard and the former Soviet Category III divisions.

In addition, navies and air forces are most suitable for rapid deployment and redeployment, even at strategic distances (Douhet 1943, *Command of the Air*, New York; Mahan 1890, *The Influence of Seapower on History 1660–1783*, Boston). This is another reason for nations to keep the bulk of naval and air forces on active duty (i.e., to have the means available to respond quickly and effectively to emergencies).

Nevertheless, strategic air forces, land-, air-, and sea-based long-range missile units, as well as the strategic nuclear capability can also be regarded as types of strategic reserves.

The first requirement of a reserve is that it be freely movable. This applies almost always to air and naval forces; they can easily and rapidly be withdrawn, redeployed, and recommitted elsewhere. Such actions are more difficult and time consuming with ground forces. Therefore, at the strategic level, the supreme commander should retain a powerful ground force (corps or army) as his reserve, which may be made up of units mobilized or on active peacetime duty. These forces could be withheld from action while at the same time being a component of theater of war forces or of an army group, or they could be retained back in the home country (or, in alliances, in another country) to be committed as the strategic situation develops.

Planning and staging of reserves are strongly influenced by political considerations since they have a strong influence on such politico-military factors as forward defense and mobile strategic defense and/or the short-war or long-war options.

After initiation of hostilities, military necessities may dictate staging and commitment of strategic reserves. This happened in World War I when the German Alpine Corps, stationed in Romania, became the strategic reserve of the supreme command for the Austrian Army Group "Erzherzog Joseph."

During the Russian Civil War and during the Great Patriotic War of 1941–45, the Russians had great difficulty in establishing strategic reserves. There is general agreement in the East and West that such reserves are necessary, that they comprise the units available to the supreme command and to theater commanders, and that they comprise the manpower and economic reserves that enable a country to conduct a protracted war (Sokolovskii 1968, *Military Strategy*, pp. 209, 228).

PURPOSE AND TASKS

Reserves of combat forces are more dynamic than other types of reserves. A strategic reserve is an instrument of the supreme command. Its purpose is to decisively change the course of a campaign, or of an important battle, or any threatening crisis within the theater. For instance, in the North Atlantic Treaty Organization (NATO), the Supreme Allied Commander Europe (SACEUR) has a powerful reserve consisting of ground, air, naval, and marine forces provided by several nations (although primarily by the United States). Some of these are earmarked for specific subordinate commands to facilitate planning for transport, off-loading, processing, and employment. But they are still at the SACEUR's disposal, as shown by the units having several employment options to prepare for. Other units do not have such options (i.e., they are at the completely free disposal of the SACEUR).

According to Soviet doctrine, strategic reserves were to enable the supreme military commander to reinforce the main body, to bring second echelons (and operational reserves) up to strength, and to provide for new groupings of forces to achieve a decision at the main points of operations. In addition, they could be assigned the task to settle critical situations of strategic importance.

BUILDUP

In most cases, the buildup of strategic reserves takes place on a long-term procedural basis. Considerations, however, go far beyond provision of weapons systems, manpower, and military units. Strategic reserves must often travel long distances and, once committed, must be supported logistically, far from their home bases.

One of the means to facilitate planning is to "earmark" (i.e., to promise) during peacetime parts of the strategic reserve for wartime use by subordinate commanders. This allows planners to identify ships, ports, ammunition handling locations, fuel, roads, and railways as well as holding areas, radio frequencies, hospital beds, and so forth. On the other hand, although earmarking does not mean a firm commitment, it restricts the supreme commander's freedom of action, a fact that illustrates the heavy burden placed on modern armies by their large, cumbersome, and demanding size. In NATO, the SACEUR's strategic reserve consists of military units from several nations, but primarily from the United States. Several of the divisions (both active peacetime and national guard) and air wings have been earmarked for one of the major subordinate commands (i.e., Allied Forces Northern, Central, and Southern Europe or United Kingdom Air Defense). These lower commands are responsible for further planning for their "regional reserves."

There were fewer difficulties for the Warsaw Pact countries. According to Western assessment, the pact's high command in case of war would have retained a strategic reserve of some 10 to 15 divisions and an equivalent air capability. None of these assets would have faced the transportation problems faced by U.S. ground troops. A strong military airlift command would have assisted the deployment of the Warsaw Pact (or Soviet) strategic reserve, which consisted not only of army divisions, but also of special forces airborne units and air force wings.

Both the United States and the Soviet Union developed special structures for strategic reserves. Both had airborne divisions. The United States organized light divisions to ease the deployment problem. The Soviet Union could have used operational maneuver groups (OMG) on a strategic scale. But these were not reserves in the true meaning of the word. By their employment, a strategic effect was to be achieved, and their employment was foreseen once a gap had been made in NATO forces (not in order to create a gap).

STRENGTH AND COMPOSITION OF STRATEGIC RESERVES

The purpose of strategic reserves determines their strength and composition. Unlimited or limited freedom of action creates differences in strength and force structure. Size and force structure of strategic reserves are strongly influenced by the political purpose and by the nature of the strategic threat posed by the potential enemy. Also, a balance must be struck between quantity and quality.

Long-range nuclear delivery means, and, indeed, the entire nuclear capability, can be considered a reserve of the supreme political authority. Obviously, such capability is available only to a few states.

Conventional strategic reserves are of particular importance. Again, decisions in the political arena (e.g., arms control measures) influence their size and composition. Light forces pose relatively few transportation problems. Also, logistic support is relatively easy. On the other hand, such divisions have difficulty in open terrain and lack the offensive power of mechanized forces. Thus they may be in need of rapid reinforcement.

EMPLOYMENT OF STRATEGIC RESERVES

Strategic reserves must be concentrated so that rapid employment is possible. If necessary, they must be moved from their home stations closer to the theater where employment seems likely. This, however, may be difficult: the large distances often involved create long deployment times, at least for army and naval infantry formations. If deployment does not begin until after the outbreak of hostilities, they may arrive too late. If deployment is initiated during a preceding crisis, it may have a strong escalatory effect. Therefore, deployment of military formations during a political crisis must be finely tuned to the overall crisis management activities conducted by the supreme political authority. Their deployment should avoid escalation but should clearly demonstrate political determination and solidarity.

Combat Reserves: Operational

TYPES OF OPERATIONAL RESERVES

The operational level also requires reserves to preserve freedom of action and to counter unforeseen threats. "Army elements consisting of several divisions or army corps form . . . a special reserve made up of large complete formations, entire corps or divisions, which is placed at the sole disposal of the supreme commander" (Blume 1892, p. 161). This reflects a principle that became apparent with the organization of mass armies: "It is recommended to be economical with forces, to form strong reserves, including artillery reserves" (Freytag-Loringhoven, *Die Exerzierreglements für die Infanterie von 1812, 1847, 1888 und 1906*). This view is generally recognized. *Field Manual 100-5* of the U.S. Army (1985) notes: "Operational reserves contain . . . corps or divisions (or equivalents), held in reserve by the large unit commander." U.S. doctrine does not, however, provide for artillery reserves.

NATO commanders are short of operational (i.e., corps and/or army group) reserves. Most of the reserves come from the United States and must be transported to Europe in time of crisis (e.g., III [U.S.]) Corps reserve in the Federal Republic of Germany).

Official Soviet terminology mentioned only tactical reserves and strategic reserves, but a considerable portion of their strategic reserves were allocated to the operational level (i.e., front level up to theater command level). This resembles what has been said of Clausewitz's view: "While Clausewitz does not specifically address operational reserves, it is clear that his notion of the strategic level of war closely conforms to what is now regarded in our army as the operational level" (Eckert 1986, p. 144).

One of the main features of a reserve, to be freely disposable at any time, is always available to air assets. They can easily be retasked and, if necessary, withdrawn, redeployed elsewhere, and recommitted. Therefore, it has been unusual to keep an air reserve at the operational level, a tendency strongly compounded by the fact that aircraft not employed are a liability and can be destroyed on the ground. There was a strong tendency in the Warsaw Pact, however, to regard some of the fighter force employed in defense of the homeland as a reserve that, situation permitting, could also be committed to support large-scale offensives.

Purpose and Tasks of Operational Reserves

An operational reserve is designed to force a favorable outcome of the battle by conducting mobile operations at the *Schwerpunkt* in a campaign, battle, or action that assumes strategic proportions. Some examples are Leuthen (1757), Austerlitz (1805), Gettysburg (1863), the Allied counteroffensive in World War I (July–August 1918), and Operation Rochade of Army Group Don (1943). Excellent examples of masterly employment of operational reserves are provided by Napoleon's battles. Usually, the Imperial Guard was withheld as *masse de décision* or *masse de rupture.* Sometimes reinforced by other units, it decided the battle by envelopment or breakthrough (Chandler 1966, *The Campaigns of Napoleon*, p. 178, New York).

There is little difference between the views of Western armies and socialist armies about the purpose of operational reserves. "In defense, the greatest value of a reserve is its ability to provide the commander flexibility" (Eckert 1986, p. 5). Obviously, for this purpose reserves must be highly mobile.

In an offensive, operational reserves should support success, usually at the schwerpunkt. Should the commander desire to shift his main effort to another sector, however, employment of reserves is one of the chief means available.

Buildup of Operational Reserves

At the operational level (corps, army, army group) reserves must be formed. Until World War II the following principle was valid: "Army elements consisting of several divisions or army corps form . . . a special reserve made up of larger, complete formations, entire corps or divisions, which is placed at the sole disposal of the supreme commander" (Blume 1892, p. 161).

In both world wars, however, it was very difficult to establish sizable operational reserves. In addition, the attacker tended to commit them in order to reinforce success, whereas the defender usually was too hard pressed. The Germans, fighting on interior lines, more and more relied on shifting troops from France or Italy to the Russian front and vice versa. Often the defender had to acquire reserves by withdrawing units from less-threatened sectors (i.e., by thinning out the forces committed there).

Soviet writings emphasized the importance of reserves for all commanders, from the highest level down to company level. They often differentiated between "special" and "general" reserves at the operational level also. This division was almost classical and it used the terms used by Machiavelli when he spoke of a "well prepared reserve system" (Jähns 1889, *Geschichte der Kriegswissenschaften*, p. 467, München). Soviet writers seldom used the terms *acquire* or *form*. Evidently, they assumed that reserves were always available and that the commander had them at his disposal. Both old Russia and the modern Soviet Union had a sufficiently large population to validate this assumption, whereas the manpower base of Western nations is significantly smaller.

STRENGTH AND COMPOSITION OF OPERATIONAL RESERVES

The mobility and composition of reserves follow rules developed as a result of modern warfare. Until World War I, and possibly later, commanders acted according to intuition. "An army corps is well advised to designate always one of its combined arms brigades as reserve" (Freytag-Loringhoven, *Die Exerzierreglements für die Infanterie von 1812, 1847, 1888 und 1906*, p. 5). More and more, however, commanders realized that different enemy situations, terrain, and types of combat require different solutions to the reserve problem. During World War II, a Soviet corps of three divisions often tried to keep one in reserve. If possible, armies and army groups tended to have two or more divisions, often of different composition, in reserve. This often proved impossible, however, since the forces were not available.

Only reserves with high mobility are able to rapidly redress a dangerous situation or to exploit success rapidly. Therefore, in World War II mechanized or armored divisions were often used as reserves. Since World War II, almost all industrial armies have motorized and mechanized their ground forces; mechanized reserves no longer enjoy superior mobility over infantry divisions. In addition, refugees may block many of the deployment routes. Therefore, airmobile units are better suited as a reserve for the defender, whereas the attacker may prefer to continue to rely on mechanized reserves since airmobile reserves would not have enough punch and hitting power to support or reinforce an offensive. In addition, the attacker may be less encumbered by refugees blocking the roads.

The problem of providing sufficient reserves at the operational level is exacerbated by a peculiar feature: if every level of command, from the company or battalion upward, holds a certain percentage of its troops in reserve, the strength of the reserves will soon exceed that of troops actually committed to fighting the enemy. Therefore, preplanned and specific contingents to be held back as a reserve would be a disadvantage. Strength and composition of reserves, and especially of reserves at the operational level, must be closely geared to the situation, mission, terrain, and the available reserves at other levels of command.

According to Soviet doctrine, reserves had to be available. The operational reserve was under the command of the theater commander (*reservyy verkhnovo glavnokommanduyushchevo* [RVGK]) and consisted of divisions and armies; as far as artillery was concerned, of brigades. The RVGK reserves were to bring the committed divisions up to full strength again or reinforce them.

EMPLOYMENT OF OPERATIONAL RESERVES

Operational reserves have a key role during the main battle. The smaller the proportion of the force, which as a reserve contributed to the success achieved by its mere existence, the less a new enemy force can be successful. Clausewitz (1976) demanded the greatest "economy of force." He was aware of the problems involved in commanding mass armies and the indispensable mobile employment of reserves:

> Time and space are vast, the circumstances that have set events in motion so well known and so little subject to change, that the enemy's decisions will either be apparent early enough or can be discovered with certainty. . . . Moreover, even if a strategic reserve should exist, in this area of strategy its value will decrease the less specific its intended employment. (Clausewitz 1976)

In order to be effective, operational reserves must also always be close enough to the center of action. However, these forces must be available without representing a formed "a priori reserve" outside the main battle. "As a rule, then, loss of ground and lack of fresh reserves are the two main reasons for retreat." At another point Clausewitz says: "A beaten army cannot make a comeback the following day, merely by being reinforced with strong reserves."

The critical issue is ". . . how to develop a concept which achieves the necessary degree of operational flexibility within the political guidelines which would enable us to take the initiative ourselves at an early stage" (Eckert 1986, p. 1).

The requirement to provide new reserves when the old reserve has been committed sounds sensible, but in reality it is very difficult to fulfill. When the Red Army in 1941, not yet prepared for defense, was unable to form reserves, the initiative stayed with the German army. The latter, however, lost freedom of action and initiative when it was no longer able to cope adequately with the proper relation of time, space, and forces. Accordingly, only parts of the characteristic capabilities of the operational reserves became effective. The forces could no longer be echeloned in depth without overstretching the front areas. In addition, disastrous situations developed when armored units, acquired as operational reserves, were employed at the wrong time and in the wrong place (Niepold 1985, p. 255).

Operational reserves are often earmarked for a decisive counterattack, but it is difficult to employ the reserves adequately for this purpose (i.e., to allow an enemy penetration to develop while marshaling and concentrating friendly reserves for attack against the flanks or the rear of successive waves of attacking enemy forces). Theoretical and historical analysis supports this view. Terrain, tactical ability, strategic goals, luck, command structure, and command style often have thwarted such counterattacks. On the other hand, if properly planned and executed, it is the most effective use of operational reserves (Senger und Etterlin 1959, *Der Gegenschlag*, pp. 138–44, Neckargemünd).

Combat Reserves: Tactical

Types of Tactical Reserves

Tactical reserves are reserves of commanders from company level up to division level. Accordingly, they are available at intermediate and low command levels.

Soviet forces differentiated between reserves and second-echelon forces, both of which, according to doctrine, were to be available to all branches at all command levels (Suvorov 1986, p. 419; Vigor 1982, p. 73).

Purpose and Tasks of Tactical Reserves

Tactical reserves are used for different purposes and are assigned different tasks depending on the type of combat. On the tactical level also, the purpose of the reserves is closely related to freedom of action. In general, tactical reserves have the following tasks:

1. *in attack:* to shift the schwerpunkt swiftly, to sustain the attack, to exploit success, or to overcome critical situations
2. *in pursuit:* since complete freedom of action is available, reserves are not required and, if still available, should be committed in order to deny the enemy any respite
3. *in defense:* to contain a penetration and, if the situation permits, to launch counterattacks in order to restore the defense
4. *in a delaying action:* to conduct limited-objective counterattacks or to facilitate withdrawal of friendly forces.

Acquisition of Tactical Reserves

Acquisition of reserves at the strategic and operational levels is much more difficult than the acquisition of combat troop reserves. Provision of combat troop reserves can be ensured more easily in the tactical area because at this level distances are short and troops withdrawn or staged elsewhere have a fair chance of arriving in time at the place of decision.

Contrary to higher command levels, drawing reserves is a creative process, especially when the commanders do not follow the simple rule of putting a given percentage of their troops in reserve but assess the overall situation and then decide on numbers and kinds of troops.

In the nineteenth century and until World War I, the question of reserves was in danger of becoming merely a formal division of troops. In World War II, the drawing of reserves was based on the type of combat, the special qualifications of a unit, and the requirements of the mission. Today, this applies even more. The reserve must be qualified according to its strength and materiel to perform the task assigned to it (Osterhold 1963, p. 146).

In the Soviet army, it was the exception when reserves were "drawn." This applied at the tactical level also. From division level down to the battalions, reserves were already available in the units of the first strategic echelon. *Reserve* implied emergency and reinforcement in the meaning of adding. As already stated, in the "Soldiers Manual" of 1927: "The personnel of a unit will never be removed from combat; it can only be reinforced." There were two factors that supported the Soviet way of forming reserves:

- At all command levels, "reserve" and "echelon" merge, and in everyday routine these terms are sometimes used as synonyms (Vigor 1982, p. 74).
- From a tactical viewpoint, a unit echeloned in depth to the rear according to Western customs was a second tactical echelon in Soviet terminology.

STRENGTH AND COMPOSITION OF TACTICAL RESERVES

The strength and composition of tactical reserves are also determined by the overall purpose of reserves, that is, to assist in the preservation of freedom of action. A defending force often will have little freedom of action, certainly not until the attacker's schwerpunkt has been revealed and not unless reconnaissance has provided the defender with adequate information. In such a situation, maximum reserves are desirable, up to and even exceeding 50 percent of the combat troops available. On the other hand, during a successful offensive action, freedom of action is ensured. Therefore, a minimum of reserves is required, if at all. Often it is better to commit all reserves and to fight without reserves, in order to grant no respite to the enemy and to keep him on the run. If reserves were withdrawn or withheld, the enemy might gain the respite he needs to regroup, to commit whatever reserves he may still have, and even to launch a counterattack that deprives the attacker of the freedom of action he wanted to preserve through his reserve.

The terrain (open or covered with woods and villages) and the intended employment (counterattack or blocking enemy advance) affect the size and composition of a reserve, especially in the selection of infantry or armor units. Engineers and most of the combat support and service support units have freedom of action, but their personnel do not, and they may become worn out. Thus, a commander may decide to support his schwerpunkt with a logistic troop schwerpunkt.

The Soviet land forces established reserves in peacetime. They were chosen according to the demands for strong firepower for attack or defense. That is, at battalion level, these were mortar platoons; at regimental level, antitank batteries; and at division level, artillery (both tube and rocket). This component may also have consisted of combat troops or support troops. In general, the combat troops deployed "in the second line" (second echelon) could be regarded as reserves. From an operational point of view, these forces were even called a "dummy reserve" (Suvorov 1986, p. 424; Vigor 1982, p. 71).

At the tactical level, reserves represented about one-tenth of the forces provided as the second tactical echelon, which therefore was much stronger than a typical reserve. This illustrates that reserves were considered supplementary only and did not play a decisive role, which may be considered indicative of the tight, preplanned system of Soviet tactics. Also, this may be one of the reasons for the basically offensive-oriented interpretation of the Soviet armed forces.

The overall situation and the types of combat foreseen are additional factors for determining the composition of reserves. Often, the choice is limited and commanders must be satisfied with what is available. In defense, commanders will try to have strong armored reserves if the terrain is suitable. In attack, it will often be advisable to commit all reserves and to go on fighting without them in order to give the attack the greatest possible impetus. In this case, concentration of effort and forces will be the governing principle.

EMPLOYMENT OF TACTICAL RESERVES

The principles governing the employment of tactical reserves and of operational reserves are similar and interrelated. Time of employment and schwerpunkt are determining factors. Operational reserves, however, must always be employed with regard to strategy. The employment of tactical reserves is strongly influenced by the type of combat. In no case may the tactical level be encroached upon by the operational level. Extensive freedom of action of the tactical commander may help the operational level to better cope with the obscure general situation. Initiative, flexibility, and quick reaction at the tactical level, in accordance with *auftragstaktik*, will be valuable. At the operational level, flexibility is the key, which requires renouncing reserves established according to fixed rules and employed according to a preconceived notion.

At the operational and tactical levels, flexibility dominates. As Liddell Hart argued, an optimum of reserves implies concentration of one's own strength against the weakness of the enemy. This emphasizes the importance of reconnaissance. In attack, good reconnaissance may cause the commander to commit his reserve without reconstituting a new one in order to attack with the greatest momentum possible. In defense, the best way to use reserves is to trade them for initiative (Osterhold 1963, p. 151). Initiative is more important than all other tactical advantages and assets (e.g., the German breakthrough at Sedan in 1940 and MacArthur's amphibious operation at Inchon on 15 September 1950).

Reserves should not be committed in a piecemeal manner and should not be broken up; but the first requirement is to commit reserves successfully. Therefore, reserves of major units normally consist of armored forces, which should be employed in attack or counterattack roles. Only this employment will produce a decisive and effective advantage. For this purpose, a local schwerpunkt should be established in order to penetrate the enemy's defense and to deprive him of the initiative.

If several successive levels of command have reserves available, their employment must be coordinated and often combined. Otherwise the reserves of successive command levels, committed successively, would be defeated one by one. This was clearly one of the disadvantages of the Soviet echelon principle. Soviet commanders could redress a critical situation or could exploit success by committing their second echelon. Therefore, the threshold for employment of reserves could be much higher than it was for Western commanders.

Noncombat Troop Reserves

Commanders at all levels may decide to influence the battle not only with reserves of armor and infantry, but also with combat support troops such as artillery, antiaircraft, engineers, or even service support troops. It is unusual, however, to have reserves of artillery and antiaircraft assets because they always have freedom of action and can always be easily withdrawn and recommitted elsewhere. Commanders often find it useful, however, to have a reserve of those noncombat troops whose working capability is limited (e.g., engineers, maintenance troops).

Finally, at all times, commanders have kept reserves of logistic stocks, primarily of fuel and ammunition, but also of spare parts, transportation, and medical facilities, in order to support their schwerpunkt logistically.

DIETER BANGERT

SEE ALSO: Echelon; Reserve Components; Strategy; Tactics.

Bibliography

Baxter, W. P. 1986. *The Soviet way of warfare.* London: Brassey's.
Bauer, B. 1986. Luftbewegliche Kampftruppenreserve zu Stabilisierung einer operativen Krise (Air mobile combat troop reserve to stabilize an operational crisis). *Kampftruppen* (Combat troops) 3:103–5.
Blume, V. 1882. *Strategie* (On strategy). Berlin: Mittler & Sons.
Bolt, W., and D. Jablonskey. 1987. Tactics and the operational level of war. *Military Review* 2:2–19.
Clausewitz, K. von. 1976. *On war.* Ed. and trans. M. Howard and P. Paret. Princeton, N.J.: Princeton Univ. Press.
Eckert, G. M. 1986. *Operational reserves in AFCENT.* Fort Leavenworth, Kans.: School of Advanced Military Studies and U.S. Army Command and General Staff College.
Hanna, M. L. 1986. *Employment of reserves in the operational defense.* Fort Leavenworth, Kans.: School of Advanced Military Studies and U.S. Army Command and General Staff College.
Killebrew, R. 1985. NATO—Deterrence and light divisions. *Military Review* 5:5–12.
Niepold, G. 1985. *Mittlere Ostfront—Juni 1944* (Central eastern front—June 1944). Herford: Mittler.
Osterhold, W. 1963. *Taktik klipp und klar* (Tactics—Quite evident). Darmstadt: Wissen und Wehr.
Poirier, R. C., and A. Z. Conner. 1983. Soviet strategic reserves: The forgotten dimension. *Military Review* 11:28–40.
Rodmaker, O. J. 1983. War reserve. How it works. *Marine Corps Gazette* 67:52–7.

Royal United Services Institute for Defence Studies. 1987. The air mobile divisions. Operational reserves for NATO. *Journal of the Royal United Services Institute for Defence Studies* 1:23–30.

Suvorov, V. 1986. RVGK—Die Strategischen Reserven des sojetischen Oberkommandos (RVGK—The strategic reserves of the Soviet high command). *Internationale Wehrrevue*, vol. 4.

Uhle-Wettler, F. 1971. Grundsätze für Einsatz und Stärke von Reserven (Principles of employment and strength of reserves). *Truppenpraxis* 2:182–9.

Vigor, P. H. 1982. Soviet echeloning. *Military Review* 8:69–74.

———. 1983. *Soviet blitzkrieg theory*. London: Macmillan.

ROBOTICS, MILITARY (LAND SYSTEMS)

Many existing weapons platforms may be expected to change from fully manned to partly manned, to remote or tele-operated, and from there to more and more fully autonomous systems.

In the past, military mission needs and perceived opportunities drove most military robotics programs. To date, robotics and applicable artificial intelligence have been developed for existing vehicles, not new platforms.

Use of Robotics in Land Combat

Rapidly advancing improvements in electronics, computers, and communications hold the potential to revolutionize land warfare. Robotics and artificial intelligence can change conventional weaponry into intelligent robotic platforms that can search for, recognize, designate, and attack targets at ranges and in places too hazardous for manned vehicles. This shapes a simple design philosophy from which can evolve weapons that will support bolder tactical doctrines and pave the way for field operations supported by more lethal battlefield weapons. Pursuit of this goal requires identification and realistic estimates of functions that could be better or best performed by robotics.

Special study groups sponsored by the U.S. Department of Defense have identified and prioritized potential applications of robotics. It is not too surprising that each of the several groups has generated arrays of applications only slightly different from those developed by the others. Each group independently arrived at the same conclusion: the technology is in hand for the military to pick a few applications as starting points and to proceed. The prioritized lists developed by these groups resemble each other so closely that it appears a consensus exists about what robotics can do for modern ground warfare in the immediate future. The tasks are to take men out of dangerous positions, use existing platforms now, try to see (sense) as much as possible, avoid obstacles, report information, draw fire away from friendly forces, kill targets, tele-operate now, and introduce more and more autonomy over time.

In short, in order to formulate a robotics development and testing strategy, it is essential to know: (1) What are the technologies and applications that offer the most military value added? (2) What set of criteria would best balance military requirements and technological feasibility? (3) What funding strategy would best support evolving military robotics and artificial intelligence applications?

The task of augmenting the capabilities of the twenty-first-century field soldier with increased technology in reality emulates the nearly four decades of improvements achieved in the office and individual workplace. The age of man-operated machines is giving way to machine-assisted automation. Indeed, semiautonomous or man-in-the-loop applications of robotics and artificial intelligence are becoming commonplace in the commercial environment. It is only a matter of time before military planners fully recognize the potential for self-moving cognitive weaponry and vehicles.

In the next five to 15 years, more and more autonomy can be built into battlefield equipment. By the turn of the century, rapid sensing and speed in assimilating and interpreting what is seen or sensed will be possible by embedded computers utilizing very high speed integrated circuits and aided by advances in computer architecture and software. Accordingly, the broad categories of battlefield applications to emerge include autonomous weapons, vehicles with complete autonomy or remote-control functions (depending upon the desired mobility and mission) such as surveillance and target acquisition; robotics for logistic support, such as ammunition handling; and expert systems to support battlefield personnel and equipment.

To sum up, the potential contributions of robotics increase battlefield effectiveness through:

- reduced exposure of personnel to extreme danger in battle or to other dangerous duties such as rescue, decontamination, evacuation, and intelligence collection;
- personnel cost savings, either in operations or support, with a resulting reduction in life-cycle costs;
- reduced workload for skilled manpower categories (a simple reduction of personnel requirements is not sufficient if robotics increase the required skill levels, particularly those in short supply, such as intelligence analysts, electronic maintenance specialists, and missile maintenance specialists);
- improved decision making under tactical stress conditions, including the introduction of artificial intelligence assistance (but not usurpation of the commander's judgment ability), including collection, analysis and fusion, execution and elaboration of decisions, and dissemination; and
- new operational concepts, perhaps not previously feasible, requiring a discreet change in doctrine and tactics, though not necessarily new hardware.

The matrix of Table 1 provides a listing of applications, accompanied by the key technological developments, that must be addressed to achieve the mission area goals.

TABLE 1. *Land Combat Applications for Robotics*

ROBOTICS MISSION OR APPLICATION	TECHNOLOGY DEVELOPMENTS REQUIRED FOR APPLICATION	KEY TECHNOLOGIES, R&D REQUIRED	TIME FRAME FOR INITIAL LIMITED AUTONOMY
Reconnaissance	Mobility; self-defense; optical/IR sensors; position location; communications	AI for autonomy; materials; sensor integration; communications; power sources	1986–95
Tank robotics	AI intelligent display; automatic fire control; auto-loading; self-defense against ATGM, infantry; crew reduction; transportable (30 tons); self-diagnostics; lightweight armor	Onboard computers AI for display; IFF; lightweight materials for armor; fire-control sensor suite; meteorology; and miss indication	1995–2000
NBC recon robotics	Component modularity; commonality; NBC sensor suite; self-decontamination; position location; secure communications	Biotechnology; water- and airborne agent sensors; AI for 3-D profiling threat agent; low false-alarm remote detection, identification, and profiling; discrete, selective, small-size agent sensors	1995
Air defense robotics	Common chassis; search/track radar; fire control, modular reload; self-defense day/night, all-weather vision; high mobility	Zero defect IFF; secure, redundant non-jam communication; weapon lethality, accuracy	1995–2000
Robotic artillery/mortar	Vetronics; deployability; sensor suites; communications; fire control; self-defense; vulnerability reduction to EMP and RF jamming; self-guidance missiles; autonomous position determination	Auto-loading; sensing; terrain and target recognition; AI for fire control; modular rearming	1995
Ammunition handling	Vehicle integration; configuration of robotics to ammo pallets, bundles, etc.; transportability; power packs; low maintenance	Optical sensing; reconfiguration of onboard robotics	2000

Mine/obstacle clearance	Locate (position) self and enemy; mine detection; day/night, foul-weather operability in smoke, water, obstacles, and craters; mine clearance mechanisms; vehicle recovery; terrain recognition; mine neutralization; self-diagnostics	Minefield sensors; terrain recognition; self-location; LPI links	1995
Smoke deployment	Common vetronics; size and weight; high mobility; obstacle avoidance; position location; rapid refuel, rearm; survivability, transportability	Smoke deployment methods materials; micrometeorology; air-land battle environment; effectiveness of obscuration against sensors	2000
Helicopter robotics	Computer automation; sensor arrays; secure communication links; terrain recognition; self-location and status; day/night, all-weather operability	Sensor fusion; AI for pilot assistance; target selection and engagement; terrain following; fire control; wire/obstacle avoidance; sensor threat detection	1995–2000
Explosive ordnance disposal	Mobility; lightweight; low power requirements; fusion; remote sensors; manipulators; high strength; small size	All-weather sensor manipulation; low-weight power pack	1989–93
Perimeter security	Day/night, all-weather operability; secure communications; self-defense; mobility; rapid rearm	All-weather sensor; zero defect IFF; terrain recognition	1989–92

Key:
AI = artificial intelligence
ATGM = antitank guided missile
IFF = identification friend or foe
EMP = electromagnetic pulse
RF = radio frequency
LPI = low probability of intercept communications links
EO = electro-optical
NBC = nuclear, biological, chemical

Current Applications and Development Activities

At any given time, military needs must be satisfied with available technology. Much existing technology (e.g., vision, mechanics, sensors, and expert systems developed in the last 30 years) can be utilized effectively by modification to satisfy the applications identified in Table 1.

Applications are intended to take advantage of a unique set of emerging robotic technologies that can be described in terms of:

Performance. The ability to achieve mobility, manipulation, tracking/guidance, and weapon firing.

Detection. The sensor integration capability to perform reconnaissance functions.

Information transfer. An internal movement of needed data from the sensor to the central processor via fiber optics or to a remote terminal via appropriate data links.

Artificial intelligence. The processing of data according to a knowledge-based derived set of predetermined algorithms.

Self-reliance. The ability to assess (with semi- or complete autonomy from human interaction) the situation so as to reduce the susceptibility to enemy fire as well as to improve inherent system reliability.

What follows is a review of ongoing robotics efforts so as to provide a snapshot of the state of development.

DEVELOPMENT PROGRAMS

Autonomous land vehicle (ALV) project. The ALV project, begun in 1984, demonstrated that vehicles can move autonomously, albeit slowly, based on prestored maps of the test terrain. Two very important adjuncts to the ALV program have been developed. These vehicles were part of the advanced ground vehicle test (AGVT) bed (see below). Both vehicles were tele-operated (not autonomous) via line-of-sight microwave communications links.

ALV has successfully completed its planned programs of following a relatively straight unobstructed road, then following a roadway to a specified goal point several kilometers away at a speed of about 10 kilometers per hour (km/h [6 mph]). Later tests included higher speed, obstacle identification, and obstacle avoidance. Planned future development will include off-road, then on-and-off-road traversal of a "global" path. Top speeds of about 20 km/h (12 mph) are planned over paths of about 5 kilometers (3 mi.). The ALV program has spearheaded land combat system robotics development toward autonomous vehicle motion. The program has also demonstrated unequivocally that the goal of full autonomy will be achieved.

Advanced ground vehicle test (AGVT) bed. The AGVT program successfully demonstrated completion of a route reconnaissance mission using both a modified M113 tracked personnel carrier and a wheeled vehicle. Both were tele-operated and designed to move with limited autonomy using road-following algorithms developed in the ALV program. The wheeled vehicle was controlled from a mobile control van that communicated with and monitored (command and control) the robotic vehicle. The robotic vehicle was equipped with servo-controls, a tele-operation sensor (stereoscopic TV camera) reconnaissance mission module, inertial navigation unit, and vetronics—that is, an integrated vehicle electronic system. The servo-controls provided remote steering, braking, engine speed, and gear-shifting. The tele-operation sensors transmitted audio and visual information to the driver in the control van. A microwave system transmitted command and control information between the vehicle and control unit. Both vehicle demonstrations were successful. The wheeled vehicle, in fact, successfully covered its controlled and autonomous route at speeds of 32 km/h (20 mph) during a heavy snowfall.

Remote control center (RCC)–robotic combat vehicle (RCV). The RCC-RCV program involves a remote control system with communications links that are either covert or non-jammable. Multiple RCVs would be remote controlled through this communications link, with a limited capability for autonomous travel out of the line of sight of the RCC. The RCC would be a modified personnel carrier, while the RCV is a modified high-mobility, multipurpose wheeled vehicle. Sensor payloads include those configured for target acquisition, self-position location, and aiming and laser designation.

Advances in autonomous mobility from the ALV program will help to advance RCV mobility through computer enhancements. One such program is computer-aided remote driving (CARD). The CARD program can provide the RCV commander with the capability to manage multiple RCVs and/or communicate through a low-bandwidth communications system. CARD, through a stereo vision display located in the RCC, allows an RCV driver to pre-drive a path. This is accomplished by using a cursor to designate a three-dimensional path in a stereo display. The RCV will then follow the path through to completion.

Communications are critical. Thus, a low-bandwidth communications link between the RCC and the robotic vehicles is an operational imperative. The use of a fiber-optic cable is questionable in an operational environment. A non-line-of-sight operation, coupled with available bandwidth, when multiple systems are operating, necessitates the development of a low-bandwidth communications system. This is a priority area needing resolution before a robust system capable of performing combat missions is fielded.

Multi-RCV control will be accomplished by RCC crews managing and controlling up to four RCVs with only two operators and a commander.

Tele-operated mobile platform (TMP). The TMP is a small, lightweight vehicle designed for limited terrain traversal by the infantry. The platform can be a test bed for several mission packages, including antitank direct fire, fiber-optically guided missiles, laser designation, and NBC (nuclear, biological, chemical) scouting. The small size is really the only feature that distinguishes TMP from other proposed vehicles. The fiber-optic cable tether links video and audio sensors on board the vehicle with the tele-operator. A man-portable remote control console permits control of the vehicle and onboard sensor or weapons packages. Future plans for the vehicle include secure radio frequency (RF) communications and limited self-navigation capabilities.

Specifications for the vehicle call for a maximum speed of 30 km/h (18 mph), not to exceed 300 kilograms (660 lb.) overall weight, 40 percent grade ability at 8 km/h (4.8 mph), a 3-kilometer (1.8-mi.) communications link, and the capability of transporting and firing four antitank missiles. The platform camera should be capable of wide and narrow zoom viewing.

Commands from the operator are sent to the controller on board through the fiber-optic link (with a very high frequency [VHF] backup link). The controller decodes them and then initiates local control over the vehicle components. Electronic control provides the fiber-optic modem interface for receiving and transmitting data to and from the fiber-optic modem, programmable control for the weapons, and control of the camera zoom and focus. The tether control devices contain the basic automotive controls—steering, brakes, throttle, and head azimuth and elevation controls of the weapons.

MILITARY APPLICATIONS

Explosive ordnance disposal (EOD). EOD is of intense interest for base, air base, and shipboard use involving small, high-mobility platforms with accurate vision and remote manipulation; versatile, interchangeable end effectors; and multiple-mission capability (mine/bomb deactivating, mine/bomb clearing).

EOD robots can be mounted on tracked vehicles that are battery driven. A remotely operated manipulator has a limited capability to change its end tool for specific tasks involving munitions that range from homemade bombs to military explosive ordnance. The sensors that the remotely placed human operator relies upon include vision devices (TV) and microphones on the remote manipulator controls. Operator stress due to limited feedback information (vision, control, and other sensors) is one of the problems with existing robots.

Tele-operated vehicle (TOV). The U.S. Marine Corps tele-operated vehicle is another example of a land vehicle tele-operated using fiber optics. The platform is an off-the-shelf, high-mobility multipurpose wheeled vehicle. Stereo video and binaural acoustic sensors comprise the simple sensor suite. Sensors and driving actuators are tele-operated through a fiber-optic communications link. The vehicle can go about 80 km/h (48 mph) on the highway and about 35 km/h (21 mph) off the road with limited or no autonomy. TOV payloads include a laser designator, ground-launched Hellfire missiles, grenade launchers, and heavy machine guns. NBC reconnaissance and monitoring are planned.

Field material handling robotic technology (FMR-T). Field material handling robotic technology consists of a modified crane or front-end loader that will perform loading and unloading of palletized ammunition with a plus or minus 12-centimeter (4.8-in.) placement tolerance. Continuing research involves improved end-effector dexterity and development of strong, quick, lightweight actuators and lightweight arms with controls for flexing.

Minefield reconnaissance and detector system. In this system, the vehicle appears to be battery operated, with a tele-operator in the control vehicle, which is a modified half-ton truck that houses the equipment needed to monitor the robotic vehicle sensors, control the vehicle, and operate the minefield detectors. An RF communications link is planned.

Robotic breaching assault tank (ROBAT). A robotic breaching assault tank has been developed as a near-term countermine, counterobstacle vehicle. Basically, the vehicle is a modified U.S. M60 tank chassis outfitted with a roller, plow, and line charges. Markers outline the cleared path. The vehicle can be controlled by means of a line-of-sight radio frequency command link or a fiber-optic vehicle link, either from another vehicle or from a man-portable control unit.

Future plans for a product-improved version include night-vision and material- (ammunition-) handling capabilities, plus limited self-navigation progressing toward total autonomous operational capability.

MILITARY APPLICATIONS IN THE UNITED KINGDOM

A brief overview of UK military applications of robotics (unmanned vehicles) in service and research at the Royal Armament Research and Development Establishment (RARDE) follows.

- A controller has been tested indoors, using bar-coded markers for position location, and is being adapted for outdoor use in rough terrain. Other devices are being adapted for explosive ordnance disposal.
- Experimental vehicles include adaptation of a skid-steering vehicle to be driven remotely by steering wheel, tiller, or joystick. This baseline vehicle can be driven from any position in the vehicle with seat-of-the-pants feel and TV monitors, or from a remote van. Improvements contemplated include optimized controllers and control algorithms and sensor (vision) systems. Future options for use with TV monitors include a helmet-mounted display with semitransparent mirrors to provide a direct heads-up view. A head direction sensor and possibly another TV channel will permit stereo viewing.
- A tank is being outfitted with remote control for use as a moving target for smart munitions.
- An excavator (front-end loader) has been modified for remote control. Operated from a remote computer, it can be programmed to run sequences of operations for such duty as trench digging.
- Other vehicles include a modified wheeled vehicle and remote driving equipment and several experimental vehicle concepts.

Experimental vehicles have been conceived to assess mobility in wheeled and tracked vehicles. Some experiments in walking machines are ongoing. Ultrasonic sensors and a laser scanner have been used for obstacle avoidance and terrain gradients. A complete vehicle, called the "mobile autonomous intelligent device," has been completed. In trials, this vehicle has navigated paths outside a laboratory and returned to within 1 meter (about 1 yd.) of its start point. A laser, recently integrated, has identified obstacles and implemented replanning of the route, with all processing done on board.

The premier project at RARDE is the road vehicle autonomous (ROVA). This is a road- and track-following commercial van using passive vision for tracking the road edge versus a reference system to adjust position of the vehicle.

In conclusion, like that of the United States, the UK approach has been continual, favoring a gradual transition (perhaps even evolution) from tele-operated to semiautonomous to autonomous vehicles.

Summary

Industry has demonstrated the capability for quickly developing tele-operated (man-in-the-loop) military vehicles. However, research and development of fully autonomous military vehicles and equipment have proven to be very difficult and expensive. Autonomy must evolve over a longer period of time. Military planners and the industrial respondents to their requirements will have to continually address how much they can afford to push the state of the art for more autonomy.

FRANK D. VERDERAME

SEE ALSO: Technology and Warfare.

Bibliography

Abronson, R. 1984. Robots go to war. *Machine Design* 6 (December):72–79.
Asimov, I., and K. Frenkel. 1985. *Robots: Machines in man's image.* New York: Harmony Books.
Deken, J. 1986. *Silico sapiens: The fundamentals and future of robots.* New York: Bantam Books.
Fulsang, E. 1985. AI and autonomous military robots. *Unmanned Systems*, Spring, pp. 8–16.
———. 1985. Robots on the battlefield. *Defense Electronics*, October, pp. 77–82.
Harrison, H. 1962. *War with the robots.* New York: Pyramid Books.
Shaker, S. M., and A. R. Wise. 1988. *War without men: Robots on the future battlefield.* London: Pergamon-Brassey's.
Todd, D. 1983. *Walking machines: An introduction to legged robots.* New York: Chapman and Hall.

ROCKET, ANTIARMOR

Infantry doctrine and tactics of today's armies do not ignore the fact that, at some point, an opposing armored formation will have to be dealt with at close quarters. Accordingly, infantry soldiers are equipped with lightweight anti-armor weapons capable of stopping tanks at close range. With some exceptions, most of these weapons are portable rocket launchers capable of firing a tank-defeating warhead at effective ranges of 25 meters (80 ft.) to about 500 meters (1,600 ft.).

In some antiarmor rockets a fast-burning propelling charge is consumed before the warhead leaves the launcher, which is similar to the recoilless propulsion principle. Thus, the flight of the projectile follows a ballistic trajectory. Other weapons feature a slower-burning charge, designed to propel, or even accelerate, the rocket during flight. These warheads follow a flat trajectory, which can be an advantage in engaging moving targets or narrow openings in bunkers and blockhouses.

Antiarmor rockets came about during World War II as infantry soldiers demanded a weapon that could defeat or cripple armored vehicles, which had been greatly improved from those of World War I. Initial attempts by the British and the Italians focused on weapons that could shoot, or "throw," a mortar bomb. These early weapons—the British PIAT (Projector Infantry Antitank) and an Italian antitank grenade launcher—were not rocket-based systems and had the further disadvantage of being either cumbersome or generally ineffective.

It was the German antitank philosophy that led to a family of rockets given the generic name of Panzerfaust. The first of these was brought into service in late 1942 and, unlike the PIAT, could easily be used by one man. In the hands of a determined soldier these weapons were quite effective, and they continued to be improved throughout the war.

The U.S. answer to the Panzerfaust was the M1 rocket launcher, more affectionately known as the bazooka. When the British adopted the M1 they called it the 3.5-inch rocket launcher. It first saw service in Tunisia in 1943 and was effective out to a range of about 100 meters (328 ft.).

Since that time, the capabilities of modern tanks have been remarkably improved in terms of mobility, firepower, and shock action. Consequently, most armies have concentrated on acquiring improved antitank weapons; low-cost, portable antiarmor rockets have become the most popular and numerous. The following paragraphs discuss the range of currently available and developmental infantry antiarmor rocket weapons.

RPG-7 Antitank Weapons System (USSR)

The RPG-7 (rocket-propelled grenade) antitank weapon is one of the most effective systems in service. Its range covers the critical defensive zone out to 300 meters (984 ft.), a sector in which the employment of medium- and long-range weapons systems is impracticable from the tactical point of view. Among the RPG-7's outstanding characteristics are great destructive power, high accuracy, portability, ease and rapidity of deployment, and maintainability. It has demonstrated its operational reliability and effectiveness in almost all recent armored engagements.

The RPG-7 rocket includes a hollow-charge warhead with an electromechanical fuze; a sustainer that starts ignition at a distance from the launcher so as to ensure the gunner's safety; and a booster for ejecting the rocket at the proper muzzle velocity. No testing of the rocket is required before launching. The launcher is a shoulder-type dynamo-reactive recoilless gun. It consists of a barrel, which serves to direct the rocket projectile on its trajectory and which is connected to a diffuser for exit of ejection gases, and the firing mechanism, which both initiates firing and secures the launcher.

The overall system, ready for combat, weighs 8.5 kilograms; each round weighs 2.2 kilograms. Fuzing is of the electromechanical nose/base type with inertial arming. The weapon has an effective operating range of 350 meters (1,148 ft.) and a minimum range of 200 meters (656 ft.). It can penetrate 260 millimeters (10.2 in.) of armored steel and sustain a rate of fire of four to six rounds per minute. The system includes a 2.7-power telescope with a 13-degree field of view.

RPG-16 Portable Rocket Launcher (USSR)

This appears to be a product-improved version of the RPG-7, retaining most of the characteristics of that weapon. A bipod has been fitted to the front of the tube, probably to aid steadiness of aim when there is opportunity for its use. This version has a practical range of 500 to 800 meters (1,640 to 2,625 ft.) and can penetrate 375 millimeters (14.6 in) of armor. Its warhead is of the over-caliber type. Sights are optical, with an infrared (IR) night sight available.

RPG-18 Light Antiarmor Weapon (USSR)

This disposable weapon employs a small rocket and a shaped-charge warhead. The launcher is made of an extruded light-alloy tube; it telescopes when not in use. The two halves are fastened together by a bayonet catch that must be rotated to release the halves. The launcher is extended before firing. Its rear portion features a bell-shaped venturi. The sights are simple pop-up frames with markings for ranges of 50, 100, 150, and 200 meters (164, 328, 492, and 656 ft.). Since there is no shoulder stop, the firer must judge where to position his head and eye during firing. (A version of the RPG-18 has also been manufactured in other former Warsaw Pact countries, where it is known as the RPG-75.)

The RPG-18 has a 64mm round weighing 1.4 kilograms and capable of penetrating 375 millimeters (14.6 in.) of armor. The overall system weighs 2.7 kilograms. Combat range is considered to be 200 meters (656 ft.).

Type 56 40mm Antitank Grenade Launcher (People's Republic of China)

This copy of the Soviet RPG-2 launcher, with the same weight and dimensions as the original, fires the Chinese-designed and -produced Type 56 HEAT (high-explosive antitank) grenade with an 80mm warhead. This round has better penetration than the Soviet PG-2 HEAT round at normal angles of impact (265 millimeters [10.4 in.] versus 150 to 175 millimeters [5.9 to 6.9 in.]), although at 45 degrees of obliquity it may be a less efficient penetrator. Maximum effective range is 150 meters (492 ft.). A rate of fire of four to six rounds a minute can be sustained.

M-55 55mm Antitank Grenade Launcher (Finland)

This current light antitank weapon of the Finnish army is of more elaborate construction than many such man-portable launchers. Developed in Finland, it weighs 8.5 kilograms. The round, weighing 2.5 kilograms, can penetrate 200 millimeters (7.9 in.). The launcher has a rate of fire of three to five rounds per minute and is issued six per company in the motorized battalions.

AC 300 Jupiter Short-range Antitank Weapon (Euroac)

Jupiter is a short-range LAW (light antitank weapon) under development by Euroac, a joint subsidiary of Lunchaire and MBB (Messerschmitt-Bölkow-Blohm), and designed to defeat current and future main battle tanks. It features a discardable steel launcher with a reusable three-power optical sight and fires a 115mm shaped-charge warhead that is over-caliber to the 70mm launch tube. Some novel features have been incorporated into the design, which was adapted from the MBB Armbrust.

A gas generator in the center of the launch tube acts on two pistons. These pistons in turn eject the rocket and a counter-mass of plastic flakes, then form hermetic seals at both ends of the tube, ensuring a low launch signature with no smoke or flash and less than 135 decibels of noise. The rocket is ejected from the rocket tube at 180 meters (590 ft.) per second, stabilized by fins, then rocket assisted to a velocity of 275 meters per second (m/sec. [902 ft./sec.]). These techniques result in a weapon that is virtually signature free and capable of being fired from an enclosed space or within 80 centimeters (31 in.) of a rear wall. The warhead has standoff determined by a probe housed inside the warhead during transport and then extended 100 millimeters (3.9 in.) when the weapon is prepared for firing. The complete weapon weighs 12 kilograms. This system has an effective range of 300 meters (984 ft.) and penetration at 0 degrees of obliquity of more than 800 millimeters (31.5 in.) of armor.

ACL-STRIM Antitank Rocket Launcher (France)

This man-portable antitank weapon has been adopted by the French army, where it is known as the 89mm LRAC Model F.1. Designed primarily for infantry use, the ACL-STRIM is a lightweight system with an effective range of 400 meters (1,312 ft.). Its launching tube is made of glass and resin laminate and features a shoulder piece and foregrip that can be adjusted to fit the user.

The rocket comprises a warhead and a propulsion system. The shaped charge is contained in an aluminum-alloy casing streamlined by a plastic fairing. To the rear of this is the base fuze, which is set at safe in the transport position and is subsequently armed in flight by gases tapped off from the propulsion system. During transport the rocket is carried in a sealed container that in operation forms part of the launching tube and contains the electrical circuits that mate with the firing circuits in the launcher.

At normal (0 degrees of obliquity) incidence this rocket will penetrate 400 millimeters (15.7 in.) of armor; it is effective at incidence angles up to 75 degrees from normal. The system in firing position weighs 8.6 kilograms. Its combat range varies with the maximum ordinate (360 meters [1,180 ft.] at a maximum ordinate of 2.3 meters [7.5 ft.], for example), with a resultant effective range of 400 to 500 meters (1,312 to 1,640 ft.). At a range of 400 meters (1,312 ft.) the rocket's time of flight is just under two seconds. A number of different rounds are available for use with this system, including antitank, antipersonnel/light armored vehicle, smoke, incendiary, and practice. A sub-caliber device is also available for training use.

C-90 C Light Antitank Weapon (Spain)

This light, disposable system has been designed to provide the infantryman with a simple antitank weapon effective at ranges up to 250 meters (820 ft.) for moving targets and 400 meters (1,312 ft.) for stationary targets. A glass-reinforced plastic container-launcher holds the warhead and rocket motor while also supporting the firing mechanism, optical sight, and carrying strap.

The round consists of a 90mm shaped-charge warhead, capable of penetrating up to 470 millimeters (18.5 in.) of homogeneous armor; an instant fuze placed behind the warhead that makes it effective over its full caliber; a rocket motor; and a fin-stabilizing unit. An optical sight provides two-power magnification and a reticule appropriately marked for distance and lateral prediction. A permanent light source fitted inside the sight permits the gunner to see these markings even at night. The overall system weighs 3.9 kilograms.

Sabracan Antitank Weapon (France)

This French weapons system, jointly produced by Thomson-Brandt, features an expendable shock-resistant telescopic casing. After firing, the firing grip and sight are removed and the casing discarded. The grip and sight are then transferred to a fresh prepacked round. The 130mm firing tube is made of carbon fiber and Kevlar, providing light weight for such a large caliber.

The warhead is a 3.5-kilogram shaped charge that has been optimized for the defeat of composite armor. The rocket is launched at 210 m/sec. (689 ft./sec.), after which a sustainer motor is ignited, boosting the velocity to 275 m/sec. (902 ft./sec.). Eight fins provide stabilization. Armor penetration exceeds 800 millimeters (31.5 in.).

The overall system weighs 13.5 kilograms and has a range of 300 meters (984 ft.) when hand fired and 600 meters (1,968 ft.) when fired from a mount.

APILAS Light Antiarmor Weapon (France)

The APILAS (armor-piercing infantry light army system) is a product of the Matra Manurhin Defense Company of France. It is a disposable, man-portable launcher containing a 112mm projectile that carries a HEAT warhead propelled by a fast-burning rocket motor. The system has some interesting characteristics.

The rocket is supplied prepacked in an aramid-fiber launch tube with a retractable sight that is bore sighted in the factory and needs no field adjustment. A separate box containing three lithium batteries is clipped to the launcher. Firing requires three successive actions: rotation of a security switch for mechanical arming, pressure on an arming switch, and finally pressure on the trigger.

The rocket motor is of wound aramid-fiber construction with an aluminum venturi. The shaped-charged warhead is initiated by an electrical fuze system powered by a thermal battery that is armed by gas pressure released when the rocket is launched. A mechanical delayed-arming system guarantees the warhead to be unarmed out to 10 meters (32.8 ft.) from the launcher and fully armed from 25 meters (82 ft.) onward. The warhead has a long, tapered nose cone that permits normal functioning at incidence angles of up to 75 degrees, while the fuzing system ensures detonation even on graze contact of the warhead shoulder.

The complete weapon weighs 9 kilograms, almost half of which is the weight of the projectile. Its effective range is 330 meters (1,083 ft.), and time of flight is 1.2 seconds at that range. Penetration exceeds 700 millimeters (27.6 in.) of rolled homogeneous armor and more than 2,000 millimeters (78.7 in.) of reinforced concrete.

B-300 Light Antiarmor Weapon (Israel)

The B-300 is a man-portable, shoulder-fired, semi-disposable antiarmor system with an effective range of 400 meters (1,312 ft.). It can be carried, loaded, and fired by one man. The system breaks down into two major sections: the launcher, with a variety of sight options, which is reusable; and an 82mm projectile in a sealed container that is disposed of after firing. The projectile has eight penknife blade–shaped fins folded forward around the motor nozzle.

The launcher is provided with a built-in battlesight, although a stadia telescopic sight is also available. The latter is equipped with a special light for use in conditions of poor visibility. For night operation a starlight telescopic sight can be mounted on an adapter.

The system can penetrate in excess of 400 millimeters (15.7 in.) at a graze angle of 65 degrees. It takes only 20 seconds to put it into action. Ammunition comes packed in three-round backpacks (weighing a total of 15.5 kilograms) or six-round wooden boxes. In addition to the basic HEAT projectile, there are practice rounds with an impact marker for day or night use and dummy rounds with a noise cartridge for loading and firing practice.

Armbrust Short-range Antiarmor and Self-defense Weapon (Germany)

The German Armbrust, produced by MBB, has unique features that set it apart from most other short-range antiarmor weapons. It has no firing signature, emits neither smoke nor blast from the muzzle nor flash from the rear, is quieter than a pistol shot, can be fired from small enclosures or roofed foxholes without danger or discomfort to the firer, has no recoil, requires no maintenance, and weighs only 6.3 kilograms.

This system is particularly suited for combat under specialized conditions. Its characteristics provide Armbrust with wide applicability not attainable by any other short-range antiarmor weapon.

The antiarmor warhead can penetrate 300 millimeters (11.8 in.) of normal or spaced armor at 0 degrees of obliquity. In addition, it pierces such materials as stone and reinforced concrete. Armbrust is ideally suited to targeting an enemy vehicle at its weaker points. Thus a gunner can, for example, engage a vehicle from an upstairs window during fighting in towns without endangering himself directly. The gunner can also generate a higher rate of fire since there is no disclosure of the firing location to the target and hence less need to repeatedly displace and relocate for the safety of the firing party.

This system is man portable, shoulder fired, and expendable. It has a maximum range of about 1,500 meters (4,920 ft.) and an operational range against tanks and other armored vehicles of up to 300 meters (984 ft.). Time of flight to a target at the latter range is about 1.5 seconds. The weapon's main characteristics are low signature, no flash or blast, and low infrared detectability, along with a small rear danger area. Firing requires no additional appliances, testing, or maintenance. The launcher is thrown away once the weapon has been fired. The side-mounted reflex sight permits the firer to maintain a very low silhouette, which enhances concealment and safety. The gunner needs no ear protection, nor is there any cause to flinch when pulling the trigger, so that total concentration can be given to aiming. Armbrust may also be fitted with a laser target marker for night combat.

83mm Rocket Launcher 58/80 (Switzerland)

The Rocket Launcher 58/50 portable antitank weapons system was developed by the Swiss Federal Arms Factory Bern as a successor to the 83mm Rocket Launcher 58. It can fire every type of 83mm rocket ammunition in the Swiss army's inventory. The system weighs 8.5 kilograms and has an effective range of 200 meters (656 ft.) against moving targets and 300 meters (984 ft.) against stationary targets.

84mm RCL Carl-Gustav (Sweden)

There are two versions of this Swedish weapon: the 84mm RCL Carl-Gustav M2 and the more recently developed M3. The M2 weapon is a recoilless gun, intended primarily for use as an antitank weapon but suitable also for other assault roles. It can fire HEAT, HE, smoke, or flare ammunition and has a practical range, with HEAT rounds against moving or stationary targets, of 500 and 700 meters (1,640 and 2,297 ft.), respectively, and with HE rounds of 1,000 meters (3,280 ft.). Smoke can be fired up to 1,300 meters (4,265 ft.) and flare shells up to 2,300 meters (7,546 ft.). Cartridge cases are of light metal alloy with a plastic blow-out disk at the rear. The HE, smoke, and flare shells are spin stabilized. The 84mm FFV 551 HEAT round is rocket assisted and stabilized by fins that unfold as the round leaves the tube. This shell can penetrate 400 millimeters (157.5 in.) of armor, while a piezoelectric fuze system enables the weapon to function at up to 80-degree angles of incidence. The practical engagement range of this ammunition is 700 meters (2,297 ft.). A rate of fire of about six rounds per minute is easily achieved.

To meet the more sophisticated tank threat of the 1990s, the system will be upgraded with an oversize HEAT round designated FFV 597. It will be rocket assisted and spin stabilized, with a warhead designed to penetrate the front of compound-armor main battle tanks. It will be able to penetrate more than 900 millimeters (35.4 in.) of armor and have an effective range of 300 meters (984 ft.).

This weapon can be carried, loaded, and fired by one man, but a two-man team is standard, with one carrying and firing the gun and the other carrying ammunition and assisting in the loading operation. The gun is breech-loaded and cannot be fired until the venturi has been rotated back into position and locked after the round has been inserted.

The weapon is normally fired from the shoulder using either open or tele-scopic sights. The telescopic sight has two-power magnification, a 17-degree field of view, and a temperature correction device.

The M3 version is substantially lighter and somewhat smaller than the M2 without sacrificing performance characteristics. It can utilize all types of am-munition designed for the M2.

LAW 80 (Light Antiarmor Weapon) (United Kingdom)

The British LAW 80 is a one-shot, low-cost, disposable short-range antitank weapon; it was developed to replace existing weapons that are either light and ineffective or of a size that demands crew operation to achieve lethality. It provides a capability for the individual soldier to engage current and future main battle tanks at ranges out to 500 meters (1,640 ft.) from any aspect, including head-on, and achieve a high probability of target effect.

It is dangerous and time consuming for antitank crews to be forced to engage with a second weapon. To achieve the accuracy attained by LAW 80, a built-in 9mm spotting rifle is used. It contains five pre-loaded rounds, any number of which may be fired without revealing the position of the firer. This ammunition is ballistically matched to the main projectile and is equipped with a tracer with a flash head to record a hit on a hard target. The gunner can then at any time switch to and fire the main projectile.

The forward part of the LAW's projectile consists of the HEAT warhead and its fuzing unit, along with a double ogive nose switch that also provides the optimum standoff distance. The fuzing unit generates electrical energy to fire the warhead by means of piezo crystals and contains various safety devices to ensure that the warhead does not arm until safe separation from the firer is achieved. At the rear of the projectile the composite aluminum and filament-wound motor case has an extruded vane propellant. Four wraparound fins are mounted on the rear of the motor. These are spring loaded to erect at muzzle exit to provide stability and to spin the projectile as it travels to the target.

This system weighs 9 kilograms, has a maximum effective range of 500 meters (1,640 ft.), and can penetrate more than 650 millimeters (25.6 in.) of armor. It has a rear danger area of only about 20 meters (65.6 ft.).

Folgore Antitank Weapon (Italy)

Folgore is the name given to a light, recoilless, 80mm antitank rocket developed mainly to meet the requirements of the Italian army. It is a two-man system classified by its designer as a short-range weapon, having a maximum range of 1,000 meters (3,280 ft.) and a minimum range of 50 meters (164 ft.).

Folgore can be fired from either the shoulder or a tripod. In the tripod version two men perform the function of aimer and loader. The shoulder-fired version of the weapon is provided with a lighter optical device and fired by one man. The maximum effective range in this mode is reduced to 700 meters (2,297 ft.). The ammunition, which is the same for both versions, is composed of a rocket and a launching charge. The rocket is fin stabilized and has a hollow-charge warhead. There are also a number of designs for turret installation of this weapon for use in various armored vehicles.

Panzerfaust 3 (Germany)

The German Panzerfaust (Pzf 3) is a compact, lightweight, man-portable, shoulder-fired unguided weapons system providing effective engagement capabilities against current and future main battle tanks. It consists of a disposable cartridge with a 110mm warhead and a reusable firing and sighting device.

The Pzf 3 concept fulfills a number of basic tactical requirements: high kill probability against current and future main battle tanks, even when frontally engaged; the capability of being fired from enclosed spaces; and low cost, so that it can be distributed to all types of military formations. It also provides for potential growth, since it is possible to modify the warhead shape and caliber to meet different tactical requirements without affecting the configuration of the launch tube. At present a 60mm launcher fires a 110mm projectile. The overall system weighs 12 kilograms and has a range of 300 meters (984 ft.) against moving targets and 500 meters (1,640 ft.) against those that are stationary. Penetration capability exceeds 700 millimeters (27.3 in.).

The system's versatility is further illustrated by the fact that development of HEAT, multipurpose fragmentation, smoke, and illuminating warheads has been included in the project. Night combat capability is achieved through use of an infrared target marker fitted to the telescopic sight mount and used in conjunction with infrared goggles.

A further application that has been explored is adaptability of Pzf 3 to a LAW-mine configuration. In this application a single launcher is set up coupled to an automatic sensor, thus forming an unattended antitank mine that would be initiated automatically as a tank came into the sensor zone.

M72 LAW (Lightweight Multipurpose Assault Weapon) (United States)

The U.S. M72 is light, short when configured in the carrying mode, and expendable after firing. Its small size makes it easy to carry, while its low weight (3.2 kilograms) does not add appreciably to the existing considerable load of infantry soldiers. The M72's multipurpose capability is also unique in this class of antiarmor weapons systems. Its accuracy, safety, and reliability give the combat soldier a highly effective short-range assault weapon. On both operational grounds and considerations of cost-effectiveness this weapon is impressive, including its performance, acquisition cost, and training and logistics factors.

Instalza 88.9mm Rocket Launcher (Spain)

The 88.9mm rocket launcher is an antitank weapon that was designed to perform also as light artillery, firing antipersonnel rounds against unprotected troops. Featuring very little recoil, it can easily be used by one man and rapidly moved from point to point. The system can utilize three different types of ammunition: the CHM-81L antitank rocket, the MB-66 antitank and antipersonnel rocket, and the FIM-66 smoke rocket. With the CHM-81L the system has a maximum range of 600 meters (1,968 ft.) against fixed targets and 450 meters (1,476 ft.) against moving targets; comparable ranges for the MB-66 round are 1,000 and 300 meters (3,280 and 984 ft.), respectively. Overall weight of this system is 6 kilograms. It includes a two-power optical sight.

AT4 FFV Light Antitank Weapon (Sweden)

FFV has produced a lightweight, simple, and effective disposable weapon for use against armored vehicles. The AT4 consists of a launch tube fitted with a firing mechanism, sights, and accessories and containing a round with a propelling charge. A completely new warhead design gives a secondary behind-armor effect in the form of a high-pressure rise and flash, thus producing a blinding and incendiary effect in addition to armor penetration.

The low weight and easy handling of this antitank weapon system make it possible for any infantryman to carry it. The AT4 is thus used primarily to engage those armored vehicles most frequently encountered on the battlefield, such as armored personnel carriers and light tanks. The system weighs 6 kilograms, has a range of 300 meters (984 ft.), and can penetrate more than 450 millimeters (17.7 in.) of armor.

Mecar 3.5-inch Long-range Rocket (Belgium)

Mecar has consistently improved its range of ammunition and has produced a long-range round for the popular 3.5-inch rocket launcher still widely used throughout the world. In addition to increased range, the improved warhead has been reduced in weight at the same time that its penetration and effectiveness have been increased.

The round is in two parts, a booster and the main projectile. The booster provides the initial muzzle velocity, but burns out before the projectile leaves the muzzle. It also ignites a short-delay fuze that in turn ignites the main motor; this motor accelerates the projectile to a maximum velocity of 300 m/sec. (984 ft./sec.) by the time it is 210 meters (689 ft.) downrange. The result is a much flatter trajectory, particularly beyond the middle of the flight. A useful result of the improved trajectory is that, for 80 percent of firings at battle ranges, the only aiming mark needed is the one for 100 meters (328 ft.) on the optical reticule. This rocket has thus given the elderly 3.5-inch launcher a much-needed new lease on life and brought it into the same performance bracket as many more modern rocket systems. The system weighs 2.7 kilograms, has a range of 500 meters (1,640 ft.), and can penetrate 275 millimeters (10.8 in.) of armor.

Summary

As these descriptions make clear, the field of infantry antitank weaponry is currently characterized by a wide variety of technological innovations, featuring both product improvement and new departures. Given the overwhelming importance of antitank defense, the energy and investment devoted to attaining improved performance of this mission may be expected to continue unabated.

ALAA EL DIN ABDEL MEGUID DARWISH

SEE ALSO: Armor; Gun Technology Applications; Mechanized Warfare; Missile, Antitank Guided; Tank.

Bibliography

Alder, K. 1986. A brief survey of up-to-date anti-tank weapons and tactics. *Armada International* 3:14–26.
Jane's infantry weapons, 1987–88. 1987. London: Jane's.
Lee, R. G. 1985. 2d ed. *Introduction to battlefield weapons systems and technology.* London: Brassey's.
Reid, W. 1976. *Arms through the ages.* New York: Harper and Row.

ADDITIONAL SOURCES: *Military Technology; NATO's Sixteen Nations.*

RULES OF ENGAGEMENT

The term *rules of engagement* (ROE) defines how military forces should act or react to an adversary's action in peace and in time of crisis. ROE do not define how military forces "engage" an enemy, as the term suggests. They are designed to ensure continual political control of the armed forces to prevent overreaction and too rapid a reaction by one's own forces that could endanger crisis management (CM) activities conducted by the political authorities. ROE provide guidance to enable military commanders to take swift and appropriate actions.

An incident that best illustrates the aim of rules of engagement (i.e., to keep actions under control, to restrain uncontrolled escalation) occurred during the so-called Cod War of 1958–61. The Icelandic gunboat *Thor* fired some twelve shots to stop the British trawler *Arctic Viking*. The British destroyer *Contest*, intercepting, fired four rounds in return at the Icelandic boat, which finally broke off the engagement.

ROE are of special value in an alliance, the members of which could suffer from ill-considered actions of other states' military forces. This becomes even more important when member nations have put their forces under alliance command while keeping them under national political control. ROE are issued by political authority and should be continually adapted to the politico-military situation. They guide military actions in peacetime and in all stages of a crisis until war breaks out. In war they may be continued as constraints. With reference to the North Atlantic Treaty Organization (NATO), ROE would no longer apply for NATO forces upon implementation of the General Defense Plan (i.e., if war begins).

Principles of Rules of Engagement

It is clear that there are considerable constraints on the use of force. The United Nations Charter codifies the application of force: states must refrain "from the threat or use of force against the territorial integrity or political independence of any State." However, the Charter also says: "Nothing . . . shall impair the inherent right of individual or collective self-defence if an armed attack occurs. . . ." Within this framework, "refrain from threat or use of force" on the one side, and "the right of self-defence" on the other side, the ROE forms a fragile architecture of directives to find the proper balance between both principles.

Some general principles that govern the rules of engagement can be defined as follows: (1) actions must be in consonance with international law and the sovereign right to take action in self-defense; and (2) actions may not result in a more dangerous situation (i.e., avoid any provocation and unwarranted escalation). These general rules result in rather restrictive directives to military commanders. For instance:

- avoid combat actions, except in self-defense;
- simulated attacks are forbidden;
- firing of warning shots is forbidden; and
- intercepting aircraft is permissible only if sufficient indication is available that the aircraft is to commit hostile action or if it commits hostile acts.

The problems arising from acting under the rules of engagement are mainly to do with judging the intention of a suspicious subject and identifying an unknown object. Is the aircraft displayed on the screen hostile, civilian, or friendly? Is the aircraft flying suspicious routes or in distress and unaware of its position? What is that sonar contact at 5,000 yards up to? When will the buzzing aircraft release a missile or drop a bomb?

These examples illustrate the burden military commanders carry when engaging with a suspicious object, a burden that cannot be removed by any rules of engagement.

Summary

ROE are required for all three services. Land forces, as a minimum, require guidance as to how close military units may approach the border in peace and in time of tension before or after deployment to war stations. Air forces want, as a minimum, guidance on how to react with surface-to-air missiles and interceptors to enemy military or civil intruders. Naval forces need guidance on how close to approach enemy merchant or navy vessels and how to react to enemy harassment such as radio interference, aiming of weapons, locking-on of radar, and so forth.

Just as armed forces are political instruments, so too are rules of engagement the prerogative and responsibility of government.

This tool aims to balance the need for immediate reactions by the local commanders and the politicians' wish for remote control of all sensitive and critical developments.

Modern technology places a very high premium on surprise attack, especially on enemy airfields and ships; reaction time might be as low as minutes. Therefore, ROE must carefully balance the requirements imposed by crisis management and those imposed by the need to prevent one's own forces from being left in the position of defenseless victims without sufficient and timely, adequate reaction. Obviously, this requires politicians who have a wide and firm knowledge of all relevant aspects.

The aforementioned *Thor/Contest* incident shows how carefully the principles of necessity and adequate reactions were watched. The Icelandic gunboat *Thor*, as well as the British destroyer *Contest*, fired shots, but the shots were not lethal, neither in the character of the ammunition used nor in the direction of fire.

ROLF BERGMEIER

Bibliography

Hayes, B. C. 1989. *Naval rules of engagement: Management tools for crisis.* Santa Monica, Calif.: Rand/UCLA Center for the Study of Soviet International Behavior.

S

SECURITY CLASSIFICATION

Since World War II, almost every nation in the world has found it necessary to withhold from the public some information concerning its defense matters. This information is often called *national security information;* it is classified, often within a system that has several levels of classification, in order to protect it from unauthorized disclosure. The numbers of security levels may vary; the name at each level (secret, top secret, discreet, confidential, etc.) may also vary. Most systems are similar, however, in that they restrict the flow of information, they screen those who are allowed to see the information, and they provide security for the information. The following discussion examines the U.S. security classification system, much of which has been revealed through congressional investigations and public writings. The British, French, and NATO systems are similar. Although little is known of the former Soviet Union's system per se, it too had a multilevel security classification system.

Security classification is a categorization by which each document or item of national security information is assigned a level of security that provides adequate safety for the information it contains. The current U.S. security policy is codified in Executive Order 12356, "National Security Information," dated 2 April 1982. It defines national security information as classified information and states that such information shall be classified at one of the following three levels.

Top secret is assigned to information that requires the highest degree of protection, since its unauthorized disclosure could reasonably be expected to cause exceptionally grave damage to national security. Examples of "exceptionally grave damage" include armed hostilities against the United States or its allies; disrupting foreign relations that vitally affect national security; compromising vital defense plans or complex cryptologic and communications intelligence systems; revealing sensitive intelligence operations; and disclosing scientific or technological matters that are deemed vital to U.S. national security.

Secret is assigned to classified information that requires a substantial degree of protection, since its unauthorized disclosure could reasonably be expected to cause serious damage to national security. Examples of "serious damage" include disrupting foreign relations that significantly affect U.S. national security; significantly impairing a program or policy directly related to national security; revealing significant military plans or intelligence operations; and compromising significant scientific or technological developments relating to national security.

Finally, *confidential* is assigned to classified information that requires protection because its unauthorized disclosure could reasonably be expected to cause damage to national security. Restrictive markings concerning cryptologic materials, sensitive intelligence sources and methods, nuclear weapons information, and other caveats may be assigned to further limit the dissemination of material.

In addition to this classification system, there is information that is considered so sensitive that it must be protected in special channels. This type of information, often called *sensitive compartmented information*, is afforded particularly heavy physical security and is often given a code name. Those who see it must have a top secret clearance and in addition must undergo an intense security screening to receive clearance to view the information under that code name. Release of this information is on a strict "need-to-know" basis.

Classification Authority and Classifying Information

Under Executive Order 12356, the authority to classify information as top secret was granted to the president, agency heads, and officials designated by the president in the *Federal Register*. They, in turn, could delegate authority to their subordinates in writing, but the order emphasized that the number of delegated authorities was to be minimized. Similar stipulations were made for secret and confidential material.

The individual who prepares a piece of material usually assigns the security classification to the document. It is then classified under the authority of an individual who has either the authority or the delegated authority to classify such material.

Downgrading, Declassifying, and Sanitizing Information

Downgrading is the process of changing a security classification from a higher to a lower level. Declassification and downgrading instructions, notations that are required on a classified document, tell when the material may be downgraded to a lower classification and when it may be declassified. In many cases, an automatic downgrading system is used to downgrade and declassify material after established intervals of time. In the case of sensitive information that cannot be automatically declassified, a notation will indicate that the document is excluded or exempt from the system and must be reviewed before it is downgraded or declared unclassified.

A classification review of a document determines whether it can be downgraded or unclassified and can be made at any time after the document has been classified. *Declassification* is the result of a decision to declare official information unclassified on the basis that its disclosure is no longer detrimental to national security. It is then removed from the security classification system. Finally, there may be a situation in which a document is deemed to remain classified, but that portions of the document are of a lower classification or are unclassified. In this instance, the document may be *sanitized*, which means that certain classified portions are removed in order to allow for downgrading the document to a lower security level, or all classified matter is removed so that the resulting document can be declared unclassified. Most often sanitization is done to protect sensitive intelligence sources, methods, capabilities, analytical procedures, or privileged information, while allowing the document to be disseminated more widely.

Safeguarding Classified Documents

Classifying a document means that it must be afforded a degree of protection. The degree will vary in accordance with the level of classification, but generally speaking, classified documents are kept in a controlled area, a place that is sufficiently secure so that it will prevent unauthorized individuals from gaining access. Here a document is held in custody from the time it is created until it is destroyed or declassified. It is passed from one authorized person to another by means of an accountability system, in which the receiver signs for and provides a receipt to the provider of the material.

People are granted access to classified information after they have been screened through an investigation, often consisting of a National Agency Check (NAC) and a Background Investigation (BI). Based on the results of the investigation and the requirements of their job, they may be granted a *clearance*, which is a determination that a person is eligible for access to a specific level of classified information. An associated term, *access authorization*, is a formal act that is required to certify that a person who has been screened and approved for access to classified information is authorized to have such access. This act is normally a security briefing or indoctrination, in which the person is cautioned concerning the responsibilities of having such access, is told the meaning of the different classification levels, and is provided other information of a security and counterintelligence nature. The individual is then asked to sign a nondisclosure statement, agreeing not to divulge information to anyone who is not cleared for access or does not have a need to know the information. Similarly, an *access suspension* is the temporary removal of one's access to classified information because of a circumstance or incident that has involved the individual and that may have a bearing on his or her eligibility for access.

In addition to the requirement for a security clearance, an individual must have a *need to know*. This means that he is not authorized access to classified material solely by virtue of his rank, office, position, or level of security clearance. Rather, access is granted only when a valid need for the information exists. Verification of this need to know rests with the custodian of classified information.

When these requirements are met, the person is granted *access* to the necessary classified information. Access is the ability or opportunity: (1) to obtain knowledge of classified information; or (2) to be in a place where one would be expected to gain such knowledge; or (3) to sabotage or to interface with the national defense effort. A person does not have access merely by being in a place where classified information is kept, if security measures prevent him or her from gaining knowledge of the information or interfacing with the national defense effort.

In turn access is related to *disclosure*, which is the authorized release of classified information through approved channels. (This contrasts with a *compromise*, an unauthorized disclosure that exposes classified information or activities to people who are not cleared for access to it.)

As time passes, the information in a given document may become dated. This implies that (1) the information may become less sensitive, or (2) the document will no longer be needed even though it still is classified. In the former case, the document may be downgraded or even declassified in accordance with the procedures discussed above. In the latter case, when the material is no longer needed, it is inventoried and a notation is made on a certificate of destruction, which is the official record of the disposition of the material. The material is then actually destroyed, often by passing it through a shredder or by tearing it up. The remains are placed in a burn bag; burn bags are protected and continually inventoried until they are destroyed in an authorized burn, pulping, or other destruction facility.

SUSAN M. WATSON

Bibliography

Office of the President of the United States. 1982. *Executive order 12356, National security information*, April 2. Washington, D.C.

U.S. Congress. Senate. 1976. Final report of the Select Committee to Study Government Operations with Respect to Intelligence Activities. *Report 94–755. Book 1: Foreign and military intelligence.* Washington, D.C.: Government Printing Office.

U.S. Department of Defense, Defense Intelligence College. 1987. *Glossary of intelligence terms and definitions.* Washington, D.C.: Defense Intelligence College.

U.S. Department of Defense, Information Security Oversight Office. 1982. *Directive no. 1: National security information.* Reproduced in *Federal Register*, 25 June, pp. 27, 836–41.

U.S. Department of Defense, Joint Chiefs of Staff. 1986. *Department of Defense dictionary of military and related terms.* Washington, D.C.: Government Printing Office.

SENSOR TECHNOLOGY

The age of military sensors began in earnest during World War II with the advent of radar applications and the beginning of interest in infrared (IR) and television. Simultaneously, the age of electronic countermeasures (ECM) and electronic counter-countermeasures (ECCM) was born, and the development of other sensor technologies followed. In the quarter century following the war, radar and its applications to air defense systems advanced so far that some believed that the day of penetrating bombers and attack aircraft was over. The development of stealth technology and systems has now begun to shift the balance back in favor of the offense. Thus radar faces some major new challenges. Some of the new technologies and concepts are covered in this article.

Applications for radar have proliferated on the battlefield and at sea. Radars are used to search for and image ground targets. Electro-optical sensor technology, especially IR, has advanced rapidly since the war. This progress was driven by the need to see, to operate, and to fight at night, as well as by the opportunity to hit targets with heat-seeking guided weapons. Eventually, technology reached the point where targets could be imaged with IR from significant ranges and where forward-looking infrared (FLIR) on aircraft, tanks, and other platforms could be used for search purposes. Lasers have been used extensively for target ranging and designation and are beginning to see applications in surveillance and target acquisition, used in conjunction with other sensors.

This article is not intended to survey all the technology for advanced sensors but to cover some important requirements and advanced concepts. It will show that the range of possible uses of sensors in military applications is growing rapidly.

Battlefield Reconnaissance, Surveillance, and Target Acquisition

One of the more important, and potentially revolutionary, innovations in conventional high-intensity warfare has been the extension of antitank warfare capability from line-of-sight range to 100 kilometers (60 mi.) and more. For example, in the United States the Assault Breaker project was started in the mid-1970s to develop a missile system that could be surface-to-surface or air launched with smart submunitions, a target-acquisition and engagement radar system, and a correlation and fusion center that would combine radar information with information available from other battlefield and defense-wide sensors (Fig. 1). The concept was driven by the need to "close the loop" tightly between sensors and engagement weapons in order to assess the attacking formations and engage them promptly, with precision, and at long range. The Assault Breaker initiative included technology development and demonstration programs known as the Pavemover radar, the Beta correlation and fusion program, and the missile and its submunitions demonstration using adaptations of the Patriot missile and the Lance II missile.

As an example, to carry out effective attacks on deep targets such as tank companies, the attacker needs to detect, classify, and track in more or less real time. No single sensor can do that, but a combination of sensors can work quite well. Moving target indicator (MTI) radar can detect moving targets with a radar cross section on the order of a square meter but does not resolve the target well enough to classify it based on its radar backscatter features. Synthetic aperture radar (SAR) can, under some conditions, image targets of interest and help classify those targets, but it does not have the subclutter

105MM STAFF TANK ROUND CONCEPT

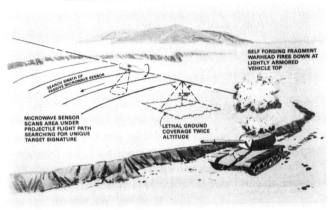

Figure 1. A missile with a multiple submunition warhead launched from either a standoff attack aircraft or a ground-based launcher is command guided to the target area by the surveillance aircraft. (SOURCE: U.S. Department of State)

visibility of MTI radar. Imaging IR sensors such as FLIR are important adjunct sensors that can image targets, day or night, but only at a limited range. They are helpful against targets using smoke but are less useful in clouds, heavy fog, and rain. Signal intercept sensors (SIGINT) provide valuable means of correlation with radar sensors to provide classification and assessment of target arrays. Communications intercept (COMINT) reports, combined with emitter locations from direction-finding or time-difference-of-arrival sensors and the radar detections and locations, can provide powerful means for detection and classification. A correlation and fusion center combines this information in a timely fashion and provides firing units with target reports, which consist of the description and location of the targets.

What is needed to complement a powerful airborne radar system with ground-based fusion centers is an organic reconnaissance, surveillance, and target-acquisition (RSTA) capability in the ground forces, probably at the corps, division, and battalion levels. These organic RSTA systems can be made survivable by employing signature reduction and signature control technologies in the system platforms and their sensors. Radar will be essential in any organic system that meets the needs of corps and division commanders. These future radars might be bistatic, with transmitters located in high-altitude "sanctuaries." In this way, the platforms carrying out the detection functions can be stealthy. A key technology that makes this concept possible is conformal antenna arrays, which will receive the radar signal transmitted by the friendly transmitter but will cancel the enemy's radar signals. Monolithic microwave integrated circuits (MMIC) are one of the technologies that may provide radar arrays with this characteristic.

A very different concept is more appropriate for organic RSTA at the battalion level. These systems should be small, simple, and easily deployed and operated by a battalion, requirements that can be met by unmanned air vehicles (UAVs). Various types of UAVs are candidates for this application: tethered ducted fans, rotary-wing vehicles, and fixed-wing aircraft. Small size and survivability of the platform are essential. Low-probability-of-intercept (LPI) radar will also be required, and electro-optical sensors will complement the radar sensors.

In summary, the successful detection, identification, and location of targets on the high-intensity battlefield require a correlation and fusion process for information from a family of sensors that detect moving targets, sitting targets, emitting targets, and communicating targets. MTI radar, SAR radar, SIGINT receivers, and COMINT systems are the key sensors required. The overall RSTA complex must include organic systems deployed with the maneuver elements of the ground forces as well as theater-wide systems and input from national systems. The systems required to provide targeting information well into the conflict period must be survivable. Low observable technology that can be applied to the sensor platforms and sensors and thus provide survivability is emerging and must be exploited.

Sensors for Reconnaissance-Strike Systems

RSTA sensors, which were discussed in the previous section, would be used, along with various strike systems, against targets that are more often moving than stationary. Those targets are more likely to be found in the open, on roads, or in open cross-country areas, rather than obscured by foliage or camouflage.

Other targets, however, are stationary most of the time, although they may occasionally move. These targets have high value to the opposing forces, and therefore, when stationary, they will be concealed as much as possible by trees and/or by camouflage. In attempting to target and attack them effectively, one cannot depend on their movements. Such targets on the tactical battlefield include, for example, tactical ballistic missiles, mobile command posts in rear-echelon follow-on forces, and other critical nodes such as air defense units and ground control intercept sites.

Strategic targets, for example, ground mobile intercontinental ballistic missiles (ICBMs), are also of interest. They too can be concealed by foliage and camouflage. These high-value systems might be locatable and engageable with reconnaissance-strike systems similar to the tactical systems.

This type of reconnaissance-strike system is extremely important both as a deterrent and as a weapons system. Such systems appear to be feasible with emerging and available technology for the sensors, sensor processing, and survivable vehicles to carry sensors and munitions. Off-board sensors to provide other necessary data are also available. The development and fielding of these reconnaissance-strike systems will be one of the next major advancements in weapons system technology.

Standoff radars or any low-incidence-angle target-acquisition sensors will not work against hidden, non-moving targets. To detect such targets requires sensors that can "see" targets beneath canopies and camouflage. Generally the search sensors must be directed downward to detect targets beneath trees and in small clearings or along narrow roads through the woods. Thus, side-looking or synthetic aperture radars are not useful in this application.

Sensors with three-dimensional imaging capability, or depth perception, are required; and multiple sensors are needed to achieve this. One effective combination uses active lasers to measure relative range to an accuracy of about 10 centimeters (4 in.). The range measurement is then combined pixel by pixel with Doppler-shift information from the same laser and then, also pixel by pixel, with the passive optical image obtained at the same and/or a different wavelength of the laser. These sensors might be in the visible, near-infrared, far-infrared, or multicolor range. There are advantages and disadvantages at each wavelength. Various spectral, temporal, and spatial characteristics of the multiple sensor output can be used to increase the detection and discrimination capability of such a set of sensors.

Reconnaissance sensors must be mounted on a platform that can survive while carrying out a cued search, flying over regions of interest that may be heavily defended by air defense systems. To survive, that platform must employ stealth technology and/or defense suppression. When high-value targets are detected, located, and classified, they should be attacked directly. In some scenarios, attack by a different system might be feasible, but direct attack from the same platform with unguided or (under certain conditions) smart submunitions would be preferred. Air vehicles carrying reconnaissance-strike systems could be manned or unmanned, but because survivability is a key requirement under high-threat conditions, autonomous unmanned vehicles will probably be the preferred choice. If an unmanned vehicle is used, it will have to be fully autonomous. It will have to navigate autonomously to the cued area, proceed through an intelligently determined search pattern, automatically detect and recognize targets of interest, and finally attack those targets. The development of such a capability has high priority and is now under way in the United States.

Air Combat/defense Sensors

In major conflicts, beyond-visual-range (BVR) attack strategies play a key role in air-to-air combat. For example, the backbone of NATO air defenses is the NATO airborne warning and control system (AWACS), combined with interceptors such as the Tornado and F-15, as well as air combat fighters such as the F-16. NATO air forces, with programmed systems, have the capability to employ a BVR strategy that can overcome a numerically superior force. The new advanced medium-range air-to-air missile (AMRAAM), combined with the Sparrow missile, is the key to getting sufficient platforms into long-range battle. This is not to imply that short-range combat and short-range air-to-air missiles are no longer relevant or important. Quite the contrary, the BVR strategy is designed to effectively whittle down the opposing force prior to the start of short-range air-to-air combat.

Technology is likely to degrade BVR capabilities in the mid-1990s and beyond for the following reasons:

- improvements in BVR intercept and missile capability by all major powers
- continued emphasis on and heavy gains in the area of active electronic countermeasures, which may in turn negate the detection advantage that current early warning and airborne intercept radars on the interceptors and fighters provide
- the possibility that air-to-air antiradiation missiles could be developed and effectively used at significant ranges against both early warning and intercept radars
- development of low-observable aircraft, which will seriously degrade the BVR capability of current and emerging systems.

In the future, the entire architecture for air-based defenses will be changed, as well as the systems employed within that architecture. Advanced surveillance and warning radars will be driven to frequencies lower than today's. Future airborne intercept radars on interceptors and fighters will have a passive as well as an active operational mode. A bistatic or multistatic radar system for fire control in air-to-air engagements will be required. Interceptor and fighter radars will operate in the receive-only mode, utilizing transmitters on high-altitude survivable platforms located in sanctuaries. If these multimode radars are to be employed, it will be necessary to mount them on advanced aircraft without increasing their radar cross section. So-called smart skin technologies employing MMIC or even wafer-scale integration of solid-state monolithic integrated circuits may make such an advanced and effective capability possible.

In this future environment, with a degraded BVR capability, greater emphasis must be placed on close combat capability that will permit air forces to fight and win an air battle at short ranges against a superior enemy. This will require three things: (1) more maneuverable combat aircraft; (2) aircraft fitted with sensors that allow them to detect and classify aircraft at almost any aspect angle; and (3) aircraft equipped with short-range air-to-air missiles that can engage targets at extremely large off-boresight angles.

As far as sensors are concerned, radar dishes in the nose of aircraft will not provide an adequate aperture. It will be necessary to use conformal-array radars situated in the wings, the forward fuselage, and the aft fuselage. Transmit-and-receive modules with solid-state integrated circuits, possibly with integration at the wafer scale, should make this possible. The question remains whether the yield of such devices can be increased enough and the cost reduced to a sufficiently low level that the sensors will cost less than the rest of the airplane.

Infrared search and track (IRST) sensors will probably play an important role in the future of airborne early warning aircraft, interceptors, and fighters. IR cannot be relied on in the absence of clear line of sight; but it can frequently provide a valuable sensor function, for example, in combination with radio-frequency (RF) sensors that lack great spatial resolution and to back up radar sensors in the face of active electronic countermeasures. Technology is now making possible medium-wave and long-wave IR monolithic focal-plane arrays with high sensitivity and high resolution. One of the key problems when IRST was first being tried was the difficulty in separating targets from background. High false-alarm rates resulted in the operators finally rejecting the system. Now much greater processing capability is possible on the aircraft, and there are new ways to distinguish the targets from the spatial background fluctuations.

Carrier Battle Group and Surface Action Group Defense Sensors

Carrier battle groups with air-delivered nuclear weapons are currently serious strategic threats. Carrier battle groups may be successfully attacked by long-range bombers with antiship missiles, surface ships with antiship missiles, and submarines with antiship missiles and torpedoes. The threat posed by such weapons is so severe that a large fraction of the great cost of the carrier battle group ships, aircraft, submarines, and weapons systems is required just to defend the battle group, not as part of its attacking force.

The air threat is posed by long-range bombers that now can launch antiship missiles from the horizon. Very heavy attacks can be launched with 50 or more attacking bombers, each carrying jammers and long-range standoff antiship missiles. Electronic jammers make it virtually impossible for airborne early warning aircraft to get sufficient detection and assessment at a range that allows the carrier-launched interceptors to be vectored into defensive positions early enough to be effective. If equipped with new technology, strategic bombers can increase dramatically the distance from which this threat can be posed.

In conjunction with bomber attack, submarines can attack by launching antiship missiles and/or torpedoes. Some of the missiles are now capable of very high speed at very low altitude (sea skimmers). These have seriously decreased the reaction time available for defensive missiles to be launched by surface ships in the carrier battle groups. Furthermore, the most recent submarines introduced for attack against carrier battle groups can stand off at extreme ranges, beyond the effective range of the carrier-based or destroyer-based antisubmarine warfare (ASW) aircraft, and attack the battle group with antiship missiles.

The key to better defense of carrier battle groups or surface action groups is to extend the range at which attacking bombers are detected and assessed so that aircraft interceptors can be employed in the deck-launched intercept (DLI) mode. This requires the effective range of assessment to be 1,300 to 1,600 kilometers (800 to 1,000 mi.) from the center of the carrier battle group. To achieve that performance, the radar sensors must be located in high-altitude aircraft or in space. So far, however, space-based radar is not able to provide sufficient performance against plausible future threats, but technology does permit the required solution with radars and IRST sets on high-altitude aircraft, which can be manned or unmanned.

With high-altitude, long-endurance aircraft sensors, the active carrier battle group and surface action group defenses could be further strengthened by the employment of a long-range "outer air battle" surface-to-air missile that would engage bombers prior to missile launch at about an 800-kilometer (500-mi.) range. Technology for such hypersonic surface-to-air missiles is being pursued.

A conformal-array radar suitable for high-speed missiles is currently being developed and has already had antenna elements tested at high Mach numbers using reentry vehicles. The radar employs solid-state microwave integrated circuits with thermal-protective materials that can survive the hypersonic thermal environment.

The submarine threat to carrier battle groups and surface action groups is increasing even faster than the bomber threat. New submarines are quieter, larger, and more difficult to kill. These submarines can stand farther off from the carrier battle group ASW defenses, are furnished with targeting information, and are connected to an effective command and control system.

As submarines become much quieter, worldwide ocean surveillance systems will no longer be able to perform effectively. Some other architectures, such as a barrier detection system combined with other forms of trailing and prosecution, will be necessary.

Technology is being developed that involves lasers carried by aircraft for detection of submerged submarines. This technique, and other non-acoustic submarine detection techniques, may sometime in the future permit carrier battle groups with organic systems, as well as land-based and submarine systems, to detect and localize submarines in the vicinity of carrier battle groups at ranges out to several hundred miles. Active surveillance and engagement systems that augment or replace passive systems will also be necessary.

Tactical Satellite and High-altitude Long-endurance Sensors

There is rapid growth of interest in lightweight (100 to 1,000 kilogram) satellite systems, some of which are sensors for tactical rather than strategic or intelligence applications. In the United States, this interest parallels the emergence and growth of a private or commercial launch industry. Military interests, of course, include communications, which may be the broadest application of lightweight satellites. Some battlefield sensors, such as electro-optical imaging systems, can be of severely limited usefulness in space because of the significant probability that the sky may not be clear and may continue not to be clear for a few days at a time. Combined with the urgent need for immediate data during periods of crisis and escalation to conflict, this may restrict electro-optical imaging for tactical applications to other regions of the world of high interest where the sky is more likely to be clear.

Space-based radar on lightweight tactical satellites is not likely to be feasible, since radars for operation at these long ranges are quite heavy given present and foreseen technologies. Imaging IR systems are more feasible in lightweight packages; but they would face weather problems and thereby lack of responsiveness, except perhaps for high-altitude aircraft and missiles.

For lightweight tactical satellite sensors, this leaves passive radio frequency detection and localization. Mapping various emitters on the battlefield may in fact be an interesting and valuable application for lightweight satellites.

Unmanned high-altitude long-endurance aircraft, with days and days of endurance at altitudes above 18,000 meters (60,000 ft.), represent a new dimension in capabilities. Performance lies somewhere between the patrol aircraft and a satellite in both endurance and altitude. The payload capability is much larger than the lightweight satellite, and since it can be deployed closer to targets of interest, good radar performance can be achieved. The platform is ideal for IR, electro-optical, and passive sensors such as SIGINT.

New Threats to Sensors

As sensors become more widespread and effective on the battlefield, new countermeasures, direct and indirect, will emerge. Since the early days of electro-optical active and passive sensors' employment, the possibility of laser countermeasures was recognized. Initial work was done in the 1970s to learn how to design into the sensors a hardened capability to survive laser counter-measures. Over the years, lightweight, tactical, medium-power lasers have proven feasible at most wavelengths of interest, ranging from visible to infra-red. Such systems can be used for counter-vision, damage of optical compo-nents, saturation and blooming of detectors, and permanent damage of sensors.

In addition to laser countermeasures, there is also the prospect of high-power microwave weapons. Such weapons may be feasible for certain applications against electronics equipment of all kinds, including sensors for surveillance, target acquisition, and strike.

Much remains to be understood in order to realize the full potential of counter-sensor weapons, as well as to be able to harden existing or new sensors against this threat.

Conclusions

In the last quarter-century there has been a virtual explosion in technologies and concepts for new sensors with important military functions. Improvements in radar technology, as well as the associated processing technology, have made it possible to routinely detect and raid-count aircraft over the horizon with high frequency (HF) radar; detect and maintain track on hundreds of enemy aircraft from surveillance aircraft at ranges out to the horizon limit of several hundred miles; use fighter and interceptor radars to detect and engage enemy aircraft while looking down against the ground clutter; image ground targets even in bad weather at ranges exceeding 160 kilometers (100 mi.); and, at sea, engage many antiship missiles simultaneously with radar-directed surface-to-air mis-siles at ranges measured in tens of kilometers.

It is possible now to routinely steer radar beams electronically, and attempts are being made to develop radars that can be assembled using small solid-state transmitter/receivers that can be mounted conformally in an aircraft's skin. These devices will permit multimode apertures for radar, passive or active, and ECM while maintaining the stealth of the aircraft.

As radars become more advanced, the demands on, and the threat to, them will become more severe. Radars will face reduced target cross section, more powerful and sophisticated ECM, antiradiation missiles, and other challenges.

Electro-optical sensors have provided night-vision and war-fighting capabilities to armed forces. The prospects for further proliferation of IR thermal sights are good due to the advent of uncooled pyroelectric detectors. IRST sets will become essential complements to radar because of the increasing radar threats described above.

Technology for improved IR sensor capabilities is advancing as a result of research on materials and focal-plane arrays. Combined with continued rapid growth in computational technology, this will lead to expanded applications on the battlefield and possibly on lightweight tactical satellites.

Multiple sensor techniques, including correlation and fusion, will continue to see growth in applications on the battlefield. Active-passive sensor suites with "depth perception," provided by their three-dimensional imaging capabilities, will provide the next major step forward in precision weapons. With these techniques, an autonomous reconnaissance-strike system on a UAV will make it possible to find and destroy high-value targets, such as mobile command posts, in the enemy's rear areas.

As a result of the increased capabilities and importance of sensors, the active and passive threats to them will increase. It will then be necessary to develop ways to protect sensors from various directed-energy weapons.

ROBERT MOORE

SEE ALSO: Deception; Electronic Warfare Technology Applications; Radar Technology Applications.

Bibliography

Dickson, P. 1976. *The electronic battlefield.* Bloomington, Ind.: Indiana Univ. Press.
Figgures, A. C., et al. 1990. *Surveillance and target acquisition systems.* London: Brassey's.
Hall, P. S., et al. 1990. *Radar.* London: Brassey's.
Kiely, D. G. 1988. *Naval electronic warfare.* London: Brassey's.
Price, A. 1977. *Instruments of darkness: The history of electronic warfare.* London: Macdonald and Jane's.

SIEGE

The term *siege* comprises all measures related to battle over a castle or fortified town, namely, those of the attacker, necessary for conquering the fortress, and those of the defender, to prevent such conquest.

General Background

In German-speaking countries, the word *Belagerung* (siege) draws attention to a particular characteristic of this procedure, that is, to the aggressor having set up his camp (*Lager*) in front of or around the fortress (Fig. 1).

The siege or defense of a fortress should always be considered and assessed in the light of military operations as a whole, not as an end in itself.

Apart from the besieging (attacking) forces and the defending forces in the fortress, a prerequisite for a successful siege requires both sides to have a field army available and capable of operation.

The attacking side must be able to protect its besieging forces, its siege operations, and its supply connections from the activities of the enemy field army. Otherwise the siege must be called off. For example, the Prussians had to stop the siege of Prague after their defeat at Kolin (18 June 1757) and of Olmütz after the Austrians intercepted a supply transport of 4,000 wagons at Domstadl (30 June 1758).

In war history, there is no known case of a defender, once encircled in a fortress, being able to compel the attacker to call off a siege alone and with his own resources. Defense of a fortress is always a battle to gain time. Frederick II writes in his *Instructions pour les généraux* in 1747: "The art of defending fortresses consists in deferring the moment of surrender. The entire knowledge of fortress governors and commanders is aimed at gaining time."

It was always up to the local defender to gain time until the field army could relieve the fortress. No matter how well a fortress was equipped with personnel, weapons, ammunition, and food supplies, if the siege lasted long enough, these supplies would eventually become exhausted. The Prussians, for example, had to capitulate in Danzig (26 May 1807) when ammunition had almost run out. A few days later the defense would have had to have ceased of its own accord.

The successful defense of fortresses as recorded in war history is always attributable to activities and events occurring outside the fortress (e.g., Vienna 1683, Prague 1757, Olmütz 1758). These need not necessarily be military activities; they could be political events such as a peace treaty (e.g., Kolberg and Graudenz in 1807) or other causes (e.g., Marienburg 1410). The French were forced to capitulate in Danzig in 1813, not only because of the rapid decrease in occupation forces, but finally because of the lack of food supplies.

The military methods for carrying out a siege or defending a fortress have changed over the centuries. These methods should be considered and assessed in connection with the technological possibilities of the respective period, not only as far as weapons techniques are concerned.

Historical Development

From ancient times to the middle of the fourteenth century, cold steel was used for battle. Long-range weapons of the period were restricted to purely mechanical apparatuses.

The subsequent period, to about the end of the fifteenth century, can be regarded as transitional. After the introduction of gunpowder into warfare, the first guns appeared during sieges, and the art of fortification changed to adapt to this new type of offensive.

The following period continued approximately to the end of the nineteenth century. In the last decades of this period, there was considerable development in gun and weapons technology. At first, however, this had little effect on the procedures and methods of siege. During this time increasing use was made of siege artillery and underground combat (mining) under fortresses was systematically developed.

In the twentieth century, attacks on long-standing fortifications such as Tsingtao (1914), Antwerp (1914), and Novo Georgievsk (1915) bore little resemblance to siege fighting of earlier days. The era of the classical ring of fortifications was over. As a result of the increased effective range of firearms, of much more effective artillery ammunition, and finally (at a later stage) of the possibility of aerial attack, permanent new fortifications consisted of detached installations, separated from each other according to the effective firing range of modern weapons.

Encirclement of these installations was practically impossible because of their greater surface area. In addition, land warfare in this century had, with its varied field positions, to a large extent adopted the forms of earlier fortress or siege fighting. Trench (or sap) warfare, once characteristic of a siege, was now commonplace on the battlefield. The only difference between siege warfare in this century and battles on the open field was that the defender fought not only from field fortifications but also from permanent installations of heavily reinforced concrete, which had generally been constructed in peacetime. Consequently the attacker needed particularly large contingents of heavy artillery and enormous quantities of ammunition to overcome these permanent installations (e.g., Verdun [1916] and Sevastopol [1942]).

Preparation for a Siege

BY THE DEFENDER

At all times prior to besiegement of his fortress, the defender had to ensure that:

- the fortress had an adequate garrison for its defense,
- the supplies necessary for defense (weapons, ammunition, food, and other stocks) were available in the fortress, and
- the structural installations (walls, ramparts, bulwarks, trenches, palisades, mines, etc.) were in a defensible state.

It was usually necessary to reinforce the available garrison with troops from the field army, while weapons and ammunition were generally stocked long in advance as a precaution. Attempts were made to bring additional food supplies into the fortress from the surroundings (with no consideration for the local population) until this was prevented by the attacking forces. Those people not essential for defense were often banished from the fortress in large numbers as "unnecessary eaters," in order to ease the food situation.

Apart from repair work on the actual fortifications, another structural form of preparation was the razing (i.e., in practice generally burning down) of all villages, buildings, gardens, woodlands, and so forth, within the so-called *reglementary* distance. This was intended to deprive the attacker of all cover for siege preparations within the range of the weapons in the fortress.

One of the first tasks of the besieger was to attempt to cut off the fortress from its connections with the interior, with its field army, and with its supply depots, or at least to hinder these connections as much as possible from the geographical, tactical, and technical standpoint.

Conduct of the Siege

Before the Introduction of Gunpowder

In ancient times and in the Middle Ages, fortified installations were built primarily of stone, usually with very high walls. The defenders used bows and arrows or crossbows, threw stones, or poured boiling liquids on the attackers. At that time siege apparatus was made entirely of wood, and the defenders attempted to set it on fire by using flaming projectiles (e.g., burning barrels or arrows). Close combat took place when the assailant reached the crest of the wall.

The besiegers used a large variety of siege machines for various purposes and of varying construction, either to breach walls or to climb them and close in on the defender. The long-range weapons included ballistas, catapults, trebuchets, mangonels, and others, which threw stones, baskets of stones, and even animal carcasses. Large mounted crossbows for spears up to 5 meters (16 ft.) long were also used.

In addition, battering rams were used for breaching walls or gates. These were strong beams with iron at the end that hung horizontally from chains and were rammed against the wall by eight to twelve men. Wall borers were used for the same purpose. These instruments and their crews, which had to stand directly at the base of the wall, were shielded from the volleys of the defender by wooden roofs.

The sappers advanced up to the base of the wall in the saps, or open trenches with wooden coverings. Then they broke stones out of the outer walls and dug through the inner rubble stones. Once the trench was complete and shored up, faggots were heaped under the wall. Burnable material (sometimes lard) was added to this to ensure that the supporting struts were destroyed by fire and the wall would collapse. A similar procedure was used in underground galleries, if the requisite highly qualified personnel were available. The use of gunpowder for mines first occurred in the sixteenth century.

In order to conduct such work on the wall, so-called penthouses or testudos were used. These were wheeled wooden protective roofs, which were moved forward with winches.

Enormous wooden siege towers were also built, from which the defender on the wall could be better bombarded by crossbowmen and archers. These towers could be used to engage in close combat on the walls, with the aid of attached drawbridges.

The protective roofs, penthouses, siege towers, and such were covered with fresh animal skins, sod, or even dung to protect them from the defender's incendiary projectiles.

Storming ladders, some of which could be extended like present-day fire ladders, were used to storm the crest of the wall.

AFTER THE INTRODUCTION OF GUNPOWDER

With the introduction of gunpowder, the first guns were used in sieges. These muskets fired stone shot of considerable weight over a distance of approximately 250 meters (820 ft.). During the siege of Tannenberg Castle in 1399, the second stone shot weighing about 150 kilograms penetrated the rubble wall, which was 2.875 meters (9.5 ft.) thick. After 40 shots the castle was ready for storming. However, it was only possible to fire about six shots daily. In 1414, the walls of Plaue Castle, 4.5 meters (15 ft.) thick, were unable to withstand similar fire for more than a few days. In German-speaking countries, such guns were known at the time as *Mauerbrecher* (wall breachers).

Inevitably, the construction of fortifications was adapted to resist this new means of combat. Fortresses built thereafter were predominantly surrounded by ramparts of heaped earth and possessed considerable artillery strength. In the eighteenth century, the Prussian engineer Lieutenant Colonel Le Febvre estimated that for the defense of a fully consolidated fortress with eight bastions, over the duration of two months, with a garrison of 6,000 men, 90 cannons (with 66,000 cannonballs), 48 mortars (with 27,000 bombs), 40,000 hand grenades, 116,851 kilograms (130 tons) of lead (for musket and case shot), and 208,929 kilograms (230 tons) of gunpowder (for rifles, small arms, and mines) would be required.

During that period, once an army had encircled a fortress, the first activity was to emplace the siege artillery. In the eighteenth century the field artillery of the field armies was usually limited to cannons with calibers between 7.5 and 12 centimeters (3 to 5 in.) and howitzers of 15 to 17 centimeters (6 to 7 in.). These guns were not adequate for destroying fortifications during a siege. Siege artillery therefore included mainly cannons of 12 to 15 centimeters (5 to 7 in.) and mortars between 17 and 35 centimeters (7 to 14 in.). In the seventeenth century siege artillery included even larger calibers.

To besiege a fortress of the above-mentioned size and equipment, Struensee, in his book *Anfangsgründe der Artillerie* (The Origins of Artillery) (Liegnitz and Leipzig 1788), calculated the necessary siege artillery (excluding the guns available in the field army) as 80 cannons and 80,000 cannonballs (673,062 kilograms [740 tons]), 20 howitzers with 10,000 grenades (approximately 185,000 kilograms [200 tons]), 20 mortars with 10,000 bombs (approximately 280,000 kilograms [300 tons]), 371,586 kilograms (approximately 410 tons) of gunpowder, plus entrenching tools and platforms for the guns. Although this siege artillery consisted of only 120 pieces of ordnance, it comprised 3,063 vehicles and 13,292 horses. Generally, farmers were obliged to carry out these transports with their own horses. The marching formation of such siege artillery could well be 6 to 10 kilometers (3.75 to 6.2 mi.) long or more. Consequently, heavy troop detachments from the field army were required to provide cover. Therefore, the Prussians took advantage as often as possible of the available waterways (e.g., Elbe and Oder rivers) in the eighteenth century for transporting their siege artillery.

Until the end of the eighteenth century, the artillery personnel for the siege artillery were provided by the artillerists from the field army. It was not until the beginning of the nineteenth century that the siege artillery was manned by its own personnel, personnel drawn chiefly from fortresses that were not being threatened at the time.

Once the siege artillery was brought up, the siege work began, under the direction of the engineer officers.

First, the point of attack on the fortress was determined. The sections of the fortifications protected by moats or river courses were usually considered unassailable. The substratum on the side selected for attack should facilitate the necessary extensive earthwork as far as possible. Attack against the curtains of the bulwark on the side where the entrance lay was usually impracticable because of fire from the bastions flanking the curtains. Consequently, attacks were directed against a particular bastion, while at the same time eliminating defense fire from the adjoining bastions.

On the attacking side, a trench (or first parallel) was dug parallel to the fortifications and approximately 500 meters (1640 ft.) from the glacis. This was usually done under cover of darkness and with strong infantry cover. This trench was about 1 meter (3 ft.) deep and 2 meters (6.5 ft.) wide, and relatively straight communications trenches led from it back behind the nearest natural cover.

The first batteries (firing positions for the siege artillery) were set up in this "first parallel" and were positioned in such a way that particular parts of the fortress could be subjected to constant fire. The object was to demolish as much of the ordnance of the fortress artillery as possible. This was difficult because the fortress ordnance, mounted on specially low fortress carriages, was well protected behind the breastwork of the ramparts. The cannon and howitzer batteries in the trenches were therefore positioned to enable them to sweep (enfilade) the face and flanks of these areas of the fortress.

As far as possible the batteries were cut into the ground (the base was equally as deep as the base of the trench), and the base of the embrasure for the barrel of the cannon or howitzer was level with the ground. In addition the batteries had a breastwork composed of earth heaped up to about 1.6 meters (5.25 ft.) above the ground. The height of the cover in front of the ordnance and their crews was therefore approximately 2.6 meters (8.5 ft.), high enough to ensure that no one was visible at a distance of 400 meters (1,300 ft.) from the top of a 10-meter (33-ft.) high fortress wall 15 meters (49 ft.) behind the breastwork. The embrasures for the gun barrels were then cut into this breastwork. Only the mortar pockets had no embrasure.

The earthwork for the batteries was carried out by workmen supplied by the infantry. Construction of the platforms and cutting of the embrasures were left to the artillerists. Each completed battery was armed at the earliest opportunity with two to eight (seldom more) guns. Sometimes guns of varying calibers and of different types were in the same battery.

During the entire siege, the batteries maintained constant fire against the targets designated to them. For example, during the besiegement of Schweidnitz (4 August–9 October 1762) the Prussians shot 146,308 cannonballs, grenades, bombs, case shot, stone baskets, and mirror grenades from 100 siege guns. It was assumed at this time that a barrel of a new siege gun was totally worn out after 2,000 shots. The Austrian defenders fired 125,453 shots or projectiles during this siege. The besiegers suffered 3,228 dead or wounded, the defense lost 3,033 men.

The first parallel was well manned with infantry, which was relieved daily, to provide protection for further work and for the batteries against attacks from the fortress garrison. The artillerymen in the batteries, who maintained continuous fire against certain parts of the fortress during daylight (and sometimes during the night), were also relieved daily.

Trenches led from the central part of the first parallel in zigzag courses toward the fortress. These trenches merged approximately 150 to 200 meters (490 to 650 ft.) in front of the glacis into the "second parallel," which was one-quarter to one-third the length of the first parallel. Batteries were also installed in the second parallel. A third parallel (also with batteries, chiefly for mortars) was constructed similarly. During the 1807 siege of Danzig, the third parallel was fewer than 100 meters (328 ft.) from the fortress (dry) moat.

Specially trained sappers advanced on the fortress from the second parallel through the trenches or saps, across terrain that was under constant fire from the fortress. In preparation for sap construction, a large number of gabions had to be made. These gabions were produced by driving several stakes 1.25 meters (4 ft.) in length in a circle of approximately 0.7 meters (2.3 ft.) diameter into the ground and weaving brushwood through them to a height of about 1 meter (3.3 ft.). Larger gabions were also built, about 2.5 meters (8.2 ft.) long and with a diameter of 1.25 meters (4 ft.). These were filled with brushwood or straw, if there were no woolpacks available, and afforded particularly good protection against rifle fire.

The engineer officer determined the main direction of the sap, which was always aimed at a particular point of the enemy fortifications. However, if the sap was built in a straight line, the enemy would be able to sweep along it with fire from the fortress, thus rendering work impossible. Therefore, the sap was cut in a zigzag formation so that it always ran at a relatively obtuse angle to the main direction. The individual parts of the sap in any one direction had to be short enough to prevent the enemy fire from reaching the soldiers in the sap.

A sapper who worked with his right shoulder toward the fortress placed an empty gabion to his right. About 0.6 meters (2 ft.) away from the gabion (so that it remained in position if the trench collapsed for any reason), he dug a small piece of trench approximately 0.6 meters (2 ft.) wide and 0.6 meters (2 ft.) deep and threw the earth into the gabion next to him. Then he positioned the next gabion in the same way. A second sapper behind him deepened and widened this trench to about 1.25 meters (4 ft.) and likewise threw the earth into the gabion or beyond it. Thus a 2-meter (6.5-ft.) high cover was created on the enemy side. The sappers rolled the large gabions filled with woolpacks or the like ahead of themselves as protection against enemy fire coming from the direction they were heading. Auxiliary workers brought the material required by the sappers and filled the spaces left between the gabions with sandbags.

When the sapper reached the planned turning point, he first installed more gabions in the same direction as before, in such a way as to form a convex curve toward the fortress. These curves at the turning points were known as "hooks." The sapper then returned to the turning point, removed three or four gabions from the previous breastwork, placed the rolling gabion in the gap and continued working, only this time with the gabions to his left, as he now had his left shoulder toward the fortress.

This type of sap, which had gabions on one side only, was called a "single sap." From the third parallel onward, "double saps" were constructed, with gabions on both sides. The most stable form was the "covered sap," which had filled gabions on both sides, was about 1.90 meters (6.2 ft.) wide and deep, and was covered with beams about 15 centimeters (6 in.) thick and then with faggots, brushwood, or earth. In the dark, or if the enemy fire was minimal, the engineer officer ordered "hurried saps" to be erected. For this, 200 to 300 workers, each with a gabion, lined up in the planned direction of the prospective trench and drove the gabions into the ground. These gabions were not filled with earth until later. Much time could be gained in this way during favorable circumstances, whereas the sappers would perhaps have needed days. The so-called half-sap also served to gain time. For this the sappers hastily positioned 10, 20, or 30 gabions, which were not filled with earth until later. This action was likewise only possible under cover of darkness or under reduced fire.

The defender attempted to hinder and destroy this work not only with fire, but also with sorties from the garrison. For the latter, soldiers were detached in large numbers as "workers," to destroy the besiegers' work and render the besiegers' guns (in the batteries) and ammunition unserviceable.

As soon as the besieger began to advance on the glacis, the miners started their underground work on both sides. The soldiers of the miners corps were recruited as often as possible from former mine workers who had the requisite experience for this task.

The miners defined explosions with black powder as follows:

- if they were more than 3 meters (9.8 ft.) underground, as "mine,"
- if they were less than 3 meters (9.8 ft.) underground, as "contact mine" (*fougasse*),
- if the target was an underground passage or other cavity, as *camouflet*, and
- if they were intended to destroy entire fortifications, with 2,500 kilograms powder or more, as "pressure balls" (*globes de compression*).

A cavity prepared for an explosion but not yet filled with powder was known as a blast hole (*fourneaux*).

In or behind the third parallel the besieging miners began to dig galleries, about 1.25 meters (4 ft.) high and 1 meter (3.25 ft.) wide, lined with wood. Once the miners had reached the selected site for the explosion, they dug out the blast hole perpendicular to the previous direction of the gallery. Into this the mine chamber, a dismantled wooden case was brought into position and then filled with black powder as instructed.

To ignite the mine, an ignition "sausage" was fed out of the mine chamber. This sausage was a tube made of linen and filled with granulated powder, leading back to the point of ignition (*Minenherd*). This ignition sausage was laid in a 6-centimeter (2.5-in) wide wooden duct, covered with a board, to protect it from moisture on the floor of the mine gallery or other damage. The gallery was finally tamped up with sod or earth, over a length of 6 to 10 meters (19 to 32 ft.). The miner ignited the granulated powder in the ignition sausage with an ignition sponge at the appointed time and then retreated quickly before the ignition sponge had burned down to the granulated powder. Immediately after the explosion, the besiegers prolonged their saps into the crater and reinforced them as above with gabions. Further mines were used in an attempt to make the palisades of the covered passage, the supporting walls of the counterscarp or the scarp, collapse, thus facilitating entry into the fortress.

This underground mine warfare required much time, especially as the miners in the garrison had the advantage over those of the besieger.

Galleries were usually erected as a precautionary measure while the fortress was under construction, or at the latest during preparations for defense against an approaching besieger, in order to ward off the besiegers' mines by exploding countermines.

For this a magistral gallery was constructed behind the retaining wall of the main rampart, as deep as the ground allowed. This gallery was 1.6 to 1.9 meters (5.2 to 6.2 ft.) high and 1.0 to 1.25 meters (3.2 to 4.1 ft.) wide. Under the covered passage, just behind the revetment of the counterscarp, a similar passage was built as the "first encircling gallery" (*galerie de première enveloppe*) and sometimes behind the glacis as well as the "encircling gallery" (*galerie d'enveloppe*). This gallery continued around all the parts of the fortress threatened by the besiegers' mines, and all the galleries were interlinked by *rameal* passages (*rameaux*).

The walls of all these galleries and passages had openings at specific intervals that were one stone wide in stone walls and sealed with a door when wooden structures were used. In the event of a siege, more galleries against possible enemy mines could be constructed from these points, depending on the tactical situation.

Generally, in the construction of the encircling gallery under the glacis, other passages (0.95 to 1.10 meters [3 to 3.6 ft.] high and 0.75 to 0.95 meters [2.5 to 3.0 ft] wide) were built over a distance of 55 to 75 meters (180 to 250 ft.) under the approaches. The ends of these galleries were provided with blast holes as a precaution. They were known as "listening galleries" where the fortress miners could go during a siege to determine whether and where the besieger was advancing with his attacking galleries.

All these galleries, however, could only be built on the assumption that no water was encountered at depths of 5 to 6 meters (16 to 20 ft.). The fortress was secure against mine attacks by the besieger if water was to be found at such levels.

The fortress miners used their galleries during the siege to extend their mine galleries toward the attacking galleries of the besieger, the object being to destroy the work carried out by the besieger with camouflets and gain time. Thus, the miners conducted duels with each other under the surface for weeks at a time.

The last resorts for the defender in preventing the besieger from scaling the main rampart, before close combat on the breastwork started, were the "assault beams" (*Sturmbalken*). These were round logs 5.5 to 7.5 meters (18 to 25 ft.) long and 30 centimeters (12 in.) in diameter, which hung horizontally in three rows, one above the other along the upper edge of the breastwork. Each one was fixed separately with ropes, behind the inner edge of the breastwork, in such a way that they could be released one by one with a blow from an axe, and crash down on the attacker. The besieger would try to destroy these assault beams with artillery fire before the assault.

These attack or siege procedures changed little until the introduction of rifled artillery in the second half of the nineteenth century. It was at this time that siege batteries began to be erected outside the parallels, at distances of up to 5,000 meters (3.1 mi.) from the targets.

The Twentieth Century

Since the commencement of the twentieth century; war in the open, with extensive trench systems, took on the character of earlier sap combat, which had only been customary against fortresses. The surface area of fortresses with detached forts had grown to such an extent that a classical siege by encircling the fortress was no longer possible.

During World War I enemy field positions were still undermined and subsequently blown up (as described above), but this method was no longer used against permanent fortifications. The only peculiarity of sieges (or, more precisely, of combat over fortresses) as compared with field combat was the particularly concentrated use of artillery, especially heavy and very heavy artillery. On 21 February 1916, 219 batteries with 850 guns were used over a 15-kilometer (4.3-mi.) front near Verdun, and for each day of fighting 187,320 rounds of ammunition were available. Of the 850 guns, 155 had a caliber between 211mm and 420mm. Another example of the use of very heavy artillery was the utilization of "Dora" (800mm) in 1942 at Sevastopol.

Since encirclement was no longer possible due to the increased surface area of fortresses, it was necessary to isolate fortresses with the aid of extensive artillery or air support. Apart from disrupting communications, these attempts had little effect.

The protracted, permanent linear defense installations of the twentieth century, which stretched over several hundred kilometers, could no longer be besieged. They either had to be circumvented (the Maginot line in 1940) or frontally attacked and penetrated at weaker points (West Wall 1944–45). They were not suitable for all-around defense in the rear of an advancing enemy, as fortresses had been until the end of the nineteenth century.

GERT BODE

SEE ALSO: Defense; Engineering, Military; Fortification; Mine Warfare, Land.

Bibliography

Bell, J. B. 1966. *Besieged: Seven cities under siege.* Philadelphia: Chilton Books.
Duffy, C. 1975. *Fire and stone: The science of fortress warfare, 1660–1860.* Newton Abbot, UK: David and Charles.
———. 1979, 1985. *Siege warfare.* 2 vols. London: Routledge and Kegan Paul.
Fall, B. B. 1966. *Hell in a very small place: The siege of Dien Bien Phu.* Philadelphia: Lippincott.
Kehrig, M. 1974. *Stalingrad—Analyse und Dokumentation einer Schlacht.* Stuttgart: Deutsche Verlags-Anstalt.
Pepper, S. 1986. *Firearms and fortifications: Military architecture and siege warfare in sixteenth century Siena.* Chicago: Univ. of Chicago Press.

SMALL ARMS

Small arms are generally thought of as weapons that are light enough to be used by an individual soldier rather than a team. Earlier in the history of man, such weapons as fighting knives, the long bow, and the crossbow were the small arms. Today's small arms, however, are designed to shoot a projectile, usually against targets within the firer's range of vision (although the target itself may be obscured from view). Today's small arms gunpowder weapons, in fact, date from the mid-fourteenth century.

The first "hand gonne" consisted merely of a small brass or iron tube secured to a wooden stock that shot lead balls. These hand cannons, first mentioned in literature in 1364, were used primarily as defensive weapons behind fortifications, although some generally ineffectual attempts were made to mount them on horseback along with their firers. A truly satisfactory handgun was not developed for another hundred years, when the Spanish adapted a trigger mechanism to a handgun, thus creating the harquebus or matchlock.

The Spanish introduced the harquebus to America, where it saw service for nearly a century and a half before being replaced by the better-designed flintlock. Typical of such matchlocks was the 4.5-kilogram (10-lb.), .72-caliber model that shot a .66-caliber ball, with the difference owing to the irregularities in the ball, which was difficult to produce to closer tolerances.

Early gunpowder-operated small arms improved slowly with the gradual advance of technology. In the first decades of the nineteenth century, for example, British soldiers still used the famous "Brown Bess" musket—a flintlock that had been accepted into service 160 years earlier. A muzzle-loading weapon, Brown Bess weighed 4.5 kilograms (10 lb.), took four minutes to reload after firing, and was consistently accurate only to distances of about 40 meters (132 ft.).

Early firearms had many significant impacts on the conduct of warfare, among which are: their shot could penetrate armor worn by man and horse; pistols could easily be carried by light cavalry, giving them additional offensive punch; and the average soldier could quickly learn how to use them. Of greatest import, however, was the evolution of tactical warfare, placing emphasis on the combined arms of artillery, light cavalry, and infantry. Within infantry formations, the technique of "fire and movement," introduced by the Marquis di Pescara in the 1520s, remains with infantry formations to this day.

At the Battle of Pavia in 1525, Francisco Pescara, the father of modern infantry, won for the Spanish crown the most decisive battle of the generation by shooting and maneuvering. Success at Pavia ensured Spanish control of Italy until the eighteenth century; it also clearly demonstrated the increasing importance of the new firing weapons.

The development of the bayonet in France at the end of the fourteenth century (which was plugged into the bore of a musket for use), and the subsequent invention of a socketed bayonet with offset blade, ended the use of the other primary infantry weapon of the day—the pike—since the capability of both weapons could now be preserved in a single piece. The British and Germans officially adopted the bayonet in 1697; the French, in 1703.

The single most important technological improvement to small arms—perhaps to larger-caliber arms as well—was the introduction of the cylindro-conoidal bullet. Invented in 1823 by British captain Norton of the 34th Regiment, the new bullet derives its popular name—minié ball—from French captain C. E. Minié, who adapted it for use in the 1840s. The minié ball greatly increased the range and accuracy of infantry firing weapons by taking full advantage of rifling (developed in Germany in the late 1400s), which upon firing imparts a stabilizing spin to the round.

Successful development of the new bullet depended upon advances in percussion cap technology, which came about in the first three decades of the nineteenth century, and its successful use in battle was facilitated by development of a satisfactory breech-loading mechanism. One such mechanism was perfected by the American Christian Sharps in 1859 and was widely used in rifles by both sides throughout the American Civil War.

The minié ball was first used in the Kaffir War of 1851 and the Crimean War of 1854–56. For most wars of the latter half of the century, the cylindro-conoidal bullet made the infantry more lethal than other combat arms, including the artillery. Riflemen could now fire accurately at ranges of 500 meters (1,650 ft.) and greater; skilled marksmen were used as snipers; and volley fire against attacking columns was murderous. This technological improvement in small arms changed tactics, making tactical defense superior over the offense until the end of World War I.

Today, small arms constitute the primary weaponry for individual infantry soldiers and special-purpose troops such as rangers, parachute troops, commandos, and reconnaissance forces. Small arms are also used by other branches of the armed forces as self-defense weapons.

While there has been substantial improvement in applied small-arms weapons technology since World War II, there has been little in the way of new principles for operation. Nearly all small arms operate on the recoil, blowback, or gas principle; the exceptions being experiments with certain rocket-propelled pistol ammunition and a recoilless gun (discussed later). The caliber of small arms varies, but the most popular are between 5.45mm (.215 inch) and 11.43mm (.45 inch). There are some larger caliber exceptions, notably the 40mm (1.57-inch) M79 and M203 grenade launchers used by American infantry soldiers (discussed later).

Small arms are difficult to classify along strict lines of mission, use, or type of munitions. They fall generally into four categories: handguns or pistols, which are further comprised of revolvers and self-loading pistols; assault weapons, which include submachine guns, machine pistols, and assault rifles; shoulder-fired weapons, most common of which are rifles; and special-purpose weapons, of which grenade launchers are an example. The remaining portions of this section discuss a critical selection of small arms in use in militaries around the world today.

Pistols

Pistols, or handguns, are small-caliber weapons used for self-defense by individuals in military, police, and civilian contexts. They exist in the form of pistol revolvers and self-loading pistols. Revolvers have been known since the beginning of the fifteenth century, but a successful weapon was not made until the early eighteenth century. Both single-action and double-action versions have been produced, although subsequent development has seen many small innovations but no new principles. Samuel Colt is credited with developing the first revolvers (U.S. patent 1936) to see widespread military use. Today, revolvers in the world's militaries have largely been replaced by self-loading pistols (Fig. 1).

REVOLVER

Revolvers may be single action, double action, or both. The single-action revolver, which is no longer widely produced, requires the firer to cock the hammer by hand between shots. A pull on the trigger releases the hammer, which is rotated forward by its compressed spring. The double-action revolver enables the firer in one long trigger pull to cock the hammer, rotate the cylinder, and release the hammer.

Revolvers fire cartridges that include the 0.357 magnum, 0.38 special, 0.38 Smith & Wesson, and 9mm parabellum. They are side loading and hold up to six rounds in the chamber. Barrels, which are up to 197 millimeters (7.9 in.) in length, are rifled with five or six grooves. Sights typically consist of a fixed-blade fore sight and a fixed-notch rear sight.

The .38 Special/.357 Magnum Sterling revolver is an example of a recent production side arm that is suitable for military use. It is the first new revolver

Figure 1. The 9mm Beretta (right) is the first new U.S. military handgun since the 1911 introduction of the .45-caliber pistol (left), and provides compatibility with the NATO allies. (SOURCE: U.S. Army Audiovisual Center)

to be produced in the United Kingdom in over 60 years and features two springs that support its single- or double-action operation. The benefit of such an arrangement is a smoother trigger pull and a more rapid, and accurate, placement of shots on a target. The weapon chambers six rounds, weighs just over 1 kilogram (2.2 lb.), and has an overall length of 24 centimeters (9.6 in.).

SELF-LOADING PISTOL

The self-loading, or automatic, pistol was made possible by developments in ammunition and the production of a strong self-contained case capable of withstanding the powder pressure and the stress of loading and extraction. These developments, combined with production of propellants able to burn away completely during the first few centimeters of bullet travel, made possible the modern automatic pistol that has been widely known since the last decade of the nineteenth century.

This type of weapon carries out all stages of operation except firing through the energy that originates from the powder charge. That energy can be used in either a blowback- or recoil-operated design. The blowback-operated pistol features a low-powered cartridge of parallel-sided shape that fires a light bullet at comparatively low velocity. This method of operation is commonly found in 0.22 rimfire pistols and may be encountered in pistols up to 0.380 (9mm short). The recoil-operated pistol uses a powerful cartridge that leads to a recoil operation that requires a locked breech at the moment of firing. This method of operation is commonly found in 9mm × 19 parabellum, 7.62mm × 25, and 0.45-caliber pistols. In both blowback- and recoil-operated pistols, the trigger must be released and then pulled for each shot fired. These two types of pistols are found in many versions. In addition, there may occasionally be found automatic pistols that fire successive rounds during one continued trigger pull. Such pistols have a serious drawback in that the pronounced muzzle accelerates upward as each successive round is fired, thus reducing hit probability.

Blowback-operated and recoil-operated pistols differ in a number of their characteristics. Both may be single or double action and self-loading. Blowback-operated pistols are capable of semiautomatic operation, have magazine capacities of up to eight rounds using a detachable box magazine, and use 9mm short, 7.65mm, or 0.32 automatic cartridge pistol (ACP) cartridges. They are typically lighter than their recoil-operated counterparts, which have short recoil, have magazine capacities of from seven to ten rounds, and use 9mm parabellum, 7.65mm parabellum, 0.45 (ACP), or 0.38 (super) cartridges.

The venerable U.S. .45 Model 1911A1 automatic, originally manufactured by Colt, is an excellent example of a recoil-operated, self-loading pistol. Still in service in many militaries around the globe, the Colt .45 is not truly automatic, requiring that the trigger be pulled to fire each shot. The pistol has a seven-round magazine, weighs nearly 1.5 kilograms (3.3 lb.) when loaded, and has an effective range of 50 meters (165 ft.). Many variants of the .45 have been produced.

With the development of self-loading pistols came efforts to field fully automatic versions of these side arms for use in infantry assaults. The German Luger, developed in World War I, was later modified to fire on full automatic as rounds were fed from a 32-round drum placed at the base of the handgrip. Although the Luger continued to be used through World War II as a side arm, the machine-pistol version proved unsatisfactory because of excessive barrel wear and overheating. Similar problems have plagued other attempts to develop effective fully automatic pistols, and their intended function is now performed by submachine guns and assault rifles.

There are very significant differences in operation and effectiveness between the two main types of pistols. Revolvers are simple in design and operation, require few applied safety measures, have no misfeed problems, and provide smooth trigger action; they are also limited in ammunition capacity, take a long time to reload, and have low muzzle velocity. In contrast, the automatic is complicated in design, requires applied safety measures, has to be cleared by hand when misfires occur, and typically has a less smooth trigger action than the revolver; however, automatics also feature greater ammunition capacity, rapid reloading, and high muzzle velocity.

Assault Weapons

Assault weapons include submachine guns and assault rifles.

Submachine Guns

Submachine guns are fully automatic weapons used for producing short-range firepower. They are light enough to be fired from the hip and are used by armed forces for close-in fighting and by guerrilla and irregular forces for special operations.

Submachine guns first came into use during World War I, but further development during the 1920s brought refinements and some degree of similarity to the design of the various weapons in this class. They reached their peak of use during World War II, when they were used in large numbers and by many countries. Subsequent development has concentrated on lowering the cost of manufacture and reducing size and weight.

In general, all submachine guns are lightweight, handy, and easy to carry; use low-powered ammunition with limited range and penetration; are magazine fed; are automatic fire, usually with accompanying provision for single-shot operation; and are cheap and simple to produce.

The main characteristics of submachine guns include their blowback operation and selective modes of fire. They typically fire 9mm × 19, 0.45 ACP, or 7.62mm × 25 ammunition from box magazines holding up to 40 rounds. Weight is in the range of just under 5 kilograms (11 lb.) loaded. Barrels feature four, six, or seven grooves; muzzle velocity is up to 350 meters (1,155 ft.) per second; the rate of fire can be as much as 1,315 rounds per minute; and effective range is up to 200 meters (660 ft.).

The 9mm Carl-Gustaf submachine gun of Swedish manufacture is a popular example of an automatic assault weapon. Originally the submachine gun used the Suomi 50-round box magazine, but in 1948 an excellent two-column magazine holding 36 rounds was introduced. The weapon was developed further by the United States; a silenced version was used by U.S. Special Forces in Southeast Asia. The weapon was also copied in Indonesia and is still being produced in Egypt under the name Port Said; it was widely used in the 1973 October War and in the 1991 Gulf War.

For some years, the general opinion has been that the days of the submachine gun were numbered and that short assault rifles such as the 5.56mm would take its place. But the basic characteristics provided by submachine guns are still needed—short-range knocking-down power with a bullet that has considerable spin and stability. Many efforts are still under way to develop submachine guns of 5.56mm, especially for use by security, police, and antiterrorist forces.

5.45mm to 5.56mm Assault Rifles

These light assault rifles are used by infantry operating without continuous logistical support or who are in mountainous or other difficult terrain. The light weight of the weapon and its ammunition permit the soldier to carry more ammunition without degrading his mobility. The weapon weighs about 3.8 kilograms (8.4 lb.); 200 rounds of ammunition weigh about the same as 50 rounds for a similar conventional weapon. There are also accuracy advantages deriving from the rifle's ability to fire single rounds, controlled three-round bursts, and continuous bursts with remarkable accuracy due to the near-total absence of recoil. The piston-actuated gas system allows for a choice of two power settings (for normal and adverse conditions) that are achieved by regulating the bleeding of the gas entering the cylinder. Thus a cyclic rate of fire of 750 rounds per minute can be maintained even under adverse firing conditions.

Feeding can be accomplished from a 20-, 30-, or 40-round magazine or from a 200-round container, thus sustaining a high rate of fire. The ball cartridge offers significant improvements in extended-range effectiveness, while the tracer cartridge extends the visibility of the round during daytime by as much as 50 percent over that of the standard tracer round for other calibers. Again, this type of rifle comes in versions having either fixed or folding stocks. Since the 5.56mm version is only about 99 centimeters (39.6 in.) in length (or 76 centimeters [30.4 in.] long with the stock folded), it is as easy to handle as a submachine gun.

Both 5.45mm and 5.56mm assault rifles are gas operated, have selective fire options, and lock by means of a rotating bolt. They typically have accessories providing for a bayonet, bipod, blank firing attachment, night sight, optical sight, and sling. The 5.45mm version is rifled with four grooves, has a cyclic rate of fire of 650 rounds per minute, and produces a muzzle velocity of up to 900 meters (2,970 ft.) per second. It weighs slightly less than the 5.56mm version, about 3.6 kilograms (7.9 lb.) compared with 3.8 kilograms (8.4 lb.). The 5.56mm version has a rifled barrel with six grooves, a cyclic rate of fire of 600 to 750 rounds per minute, and a muzzle velocity of up to 965 meters (3,184.5 ft.) per second. There is a complete range of ammunition for both 5.45mm and 5.56mm assault rifles, including ball, tracer, armor piercing, blank, drill, and grenade launching.

It seems that the standard assault rifle calibers for the remainder of this century are going to be the 5.45mm and 5.56mm. The only developments that may occur involve ammunition with increased efficiency, accuracy, and stability.

Shoulder-fired Rifles

Shoulder-fired rifles are considered the main weaponry of the individual soldier. Over the years, extreme changes in battlefield requirements have in turn brought about many changes and innovations in rifle design. During the period from 1870 to 1990, remarkable changes occurred, including the development of bolt-action magazine rifles firing powerful rounds of roughly 7.92mm. Such weapons continued in use through the end of World War II. There followed another round of innovation such that by 1960 most armies of the world were equipped with self-loading rifles supplied with ammunition from box magazines holding at least 20 rounds of 7.62mm. The various rifles of this kind have now been in service for a minimum of 15 years. The goal of increasing the maneuverability of individuals so they can better cope with the dramatically changing circumstances envisioned on a nuclear battlefield has led to yet another round of innovation and produced the latest family of 5.56mm and 5.45mm rifles. There is also a special category of sniping rifles.

General Characteristics of 7.92mm Rifles

Rifles in this category are semiautomatic. They were in production for at least the first 50 years of the twentieth century, and some continue in use with the armed forces, of certain countries, in some paramilitary and police forces, and in the hands of private individuals. Such rifles are characterized by a manual-bolt operation; lock by means of a rotating bolt; feed from a five-round internal or detachable box; and have a rifled barrel with four grooves, a muzzle velocity of up to 754 meters per second (2,488.2 ft./sec.), and an effective range of as much as 600 meters (1,980 ft.).

GENERAL CHARACTERISTICS OF 7.62MM RIFLES

This category, known as assault rifles, consists of two types. One has a fixed wooden stock and is generally used by infantrymen; the other has a folding stock and is used primarily by special forces and tank troops. Such rifles have selector levers permitting them to fire single shots or fully automatically. Some have the option of affixing night-vision devices to their sights. They are gas operated, use a rotating bolt for locking, feed from detachable box magazines holding up to 50 rounds, have rifled barrels with four grooves, produce a muzzle velocity of up to 960 m/sec. (3,168 ft./sec.), and have a cyclic rate of fire of as much as 650 rounds per minute and an effective range of 350 to 400 meters (1,155 to 1,320 ft.).

One of the more common rifles of its day was the NATO M-14 rifle, which fired a standardized 7.62mm cartridge from a 20-round magazine. Adopted in 1957 as the successor to the M-1 Garand rifle, the M-14 saw service by American troops in the early stages of the Vietnam War. The M-14's effective range of 460 meters (1,518 ft.) can be extended to 700 meters (2,310 ft.) with the use of a stabilizing bipod.

The Soviet 7.62mm AKM assault rifle is a 1959 upgrade of the AK-47 and typifies this kind of small arm. It has a selective fire mode of fully or semiautomatic, weighs over 3 kilograms (6.6 lb.), and fires rounds at a cyclic rate of 600 rounds per minute to an effective range of 300 meters (990 ft.).

Today, assault rifles are tending toward smaller calibers, with the Soviet AK-74 firing a 5.45mm round and the U.S. M-16 firing a 5.56mm round. Continuing developments in lightweight ammunition promise to further increase the firepower capacity of infantry troops who use these small arms.

SNIPING RIFLES

Sniping rifles are intended for use by military and security forces as precision weapons capable of engaging a target for a first-round hit at all ranges out to 400 meters (1,320 ft.) under favorable weather conditions or out to the range limits of the sights employed when fitted with a passive night-vision infantry weapon sight. Such rifles are also employed in marksman training and competition when fitted with aperture sights. Sniping rifles are made in 7.92mm and 7.62mm versions.

The 7.92mm sniping rifle is a semiautomatic weapon that features a receiver adapted to handle a 7.92mm cartridge, typically fed from a ten-round detachable box magazine. They are usually fitted with telescopic sights having about four-power magnification. The sight bracket is designed to accept a passive optical night sight. The main characteristics of such rifles are gas operation and self-loading, locking by means of a rotating bolt, a four-groove rifled barrel, muzzle velocity of about 720 meters (2,376 ft.) per second, and effective range up to 800 meters (2,640 ft.). They may weigh as much as 4.2 kilograms (9.2 lb.), excluding sight and magazine, which can add up to 0.9 kilograms (almost 2 lb.) more to the overall weight. The practical rate of fire is 30 rounds per minute.

The 7.62mm sniping rifle, while produced in a variety of models, falls primarily into two types. One is a bolt-action rifle with a four-round magazine; the other is a single-shot or semiautomatic weapon with a ten-round magazine. These rifles have proven extremely accurate, producing in the hands of a skilled marksman a 99 percent probability of a first-round hit at ranges out to 400 meters (1,320 ft.). The bolt-action version fires single shots and has a manual bolt, whereas the semiautomatic model is gas operated, has a short-stroke piston, and is self-loading.

There appears to be no significant development in the design of sniping rifles expected in the near future. The only development that may occur would involve advances in telescopic sights, such as using a passive infrared sight.

Special-purpose Small Arms

Light Machine Gun

Light machine guns are weapons utilized by infantry troops to provide a base of fire at the squad and section level. The ammunition used by such weapons is the same as that used by rifles. The importance of the light machine gun in infantry warfare dates from World War I. Since that time, there have been many developments in the machine gun to adapt it to the requirements of modern warfare.

Light machine guns come in many forms, but in general they have in common certain features not found in rifles: changeable barrels, enabling the firer to very quickly (within 20 to 30 seconds) remove a hot barrel and replace it with a cool one, then continue firing by releasing a simple latch or lock; robust bipods that assist in keeping the gun steady during burst firing; and belted ammunition. Typically, light machine guns weigh roughly twice as much as a rifle of the same caliber and can be managed by one person, but they are usually manned by a two-man team.

Grenade Launcher

Unlike most small arms, grenade launchers are usually single-shot, breech-loading weapons. There are some automatic recoil- or blowback-operated exceptions, but these are primarily crew-served weapons. The principal advantage of grenade launchers is that they provide infantry soldiers the ability to fire at point or area targets with an exploding round between the effective throwing range of hand grenades and the minimum safe distance for firing mortars and artillery. The arcing trajectory of the round, either high or low angle, also provides the ability to engage targets masked behind vegetation or folds in the terrain.

The 40mm M-79 grenade launcher, used extensively in the Vietnam War, gave American troops the capability to engage enemy point targets to 150 meters (495 ft.) and area targets to 350 meters (1,155 ft.). However, the United States Army developed the requirement to have grenade launcher capabilities combined with those of the M-16 rifle. The result was the M-203, which mounts a 40mm sliding-tube launcher underneath the barrel of the M-16 rifle. This weapon was fielded in 1970.

RECOILLESS GUN

An innovative series of recoilless guns, developed by the firm of Raikka in Finland, features three man-portable weapons that can be considered special-purpose small arms. The Raikka 81, 55, and 44 models (so designated because of their caliber) can engage armored or personnel targets effectively at ranges of between 200 meters (660 ft.) and 3 kilometers (1.8 mi.). While unlikely to become widely used, they provide an interesting variant to small-arms weapons.

Conclusion

Future small arms will undoubtedly feature greater flexibility in firing modes and the type of ammunition used. New "caseless" ammunition will serve to lighten soldier's loads or increase the amount of ammunition that can be carried. Developments in smaller caliber exploding rounds and smart weapons technology may combine to create new capabilities for the infantry. Regardless, the future of small arms is that they will continue to be used, primarily by foot soldiers, who will continue to fire and maneuver as they did in Pescara's time nearly 500 years ago.

SAMIR H. SHALABY

SEE ALSO: Ammunition; Automatic Weapon; Grenade; Machine Gun; Sniper.

Bibliography

Brodie, B., and F. Brodie. 1962. *From crossbow to H-bomb*. New York: Dell.
Ezell, E. C., ed. 1977. *Small arms of the world*. 11th ed. Harrisburg, Pa.: Stackpole Books.
Hogg, I. V. 1977. *The encyclopedia of infantry weapons of World War II*. New York: Crowell.
Jane's infantry weapons, 1984–1985. 1984. London: Jane's.
Reid, W. 1976. *Arms through the ages*. New York: Harper and Row.

SNIPER

A sniper is a specially equipped, highly trained expert rifle marksman skilled in camouflage, land navigation, field craft, and gathering information and is capable of delivering highly accurate, long-range fires to create casualties among selected enemy personnel. Originally, the term was used in the nineteenth-century British army to refer to an individual who successfully hunted the snipe, a small, fleeting game fowl in India that was a particularly difficult target.

The principal mission of the sniper is to support combat operations by inflicting casualties in a particular enemy formation in order to slow their movement, disrupt operations, create confusion, and undermine morale. Secondarily, the sniper gathers information on enemy locations and movements, terrain, obstacles, and other items that can facilitate the conduct of future military operations. The sniper is used in both defensive and offensive operations where precise long-range fires can support the accomplishment of the unit mission. They are also employed on combat patrols, ambushes, countersniper operations, in urban areas, and as part of stay-behind forces with the mission of delaying the movement of enemy formations.

The sniper engages targets beyond the effective range of the service rifle. A sniper is normally equipped with a high-powered, long-range rifle that can incorporate a telescopic sight for either day or night use. Snipers work and train in two-man teams fulfilling either sniper or observer functions.

In World War I, both the Germans and British used expert marksmen armed with special rifles and telescopes. In World War II, the Russians, as well as the Germans, integrated snipers into their tactical formations. More recently, the U.S. Army used snipers in Grenada, where expert marksmen were effective against enemy mortar crews at ranges up to 800 meters (approx. 0.5 mi.). The sniper will continue to play a role in future conflicts, particularly at night and in terrain where the sniper can take advantage of natural concealment.

JAMES D. BLUNDELL

SEE ALSO: Ground Reconnaissance; Infantry; Night Vision Technology Applications; Psychological Warfare; Small Arms; Special Operations; Special Operations Forces; Unconventional War; Urban Warfare.

Bibliography

Luttwak, E., and S. Koehl. 1991. *The dictionary of modern war*. New York: Harper Collins.
U.S. Department of the Army. 1989. *Sniper training and employment* (TC 23-14). Washington, D.C.: Dept. of the Army.

SOLDIER

The term *soldier* refers usually to an enlisted member of an army. In this sense it includes the noncommissioned officers, specialists, and the private soldiers who comprise the lower ranks. The word *soldier* also applies broadly to all of the members of an army, including officers (Fig. 1).

The term *soldier* originated in Roman days. The legionnaires of ancient Rome were paid with a gold coin called a *solidus*. From this origin we have the French *soldat* and the English *soldier*.

This word can also be used as a verb with two meanings. The straightforward usage of *to soldier* is to engage in a military action or campaign during war. The

Figure 1. A Chinese Nationalist soldier stands guard on Taiwan's shoreline, 1955. (SOURCE; U.S. Library of Congress)

other, derogatory, meaning of *to soldier* is to perform duties halfheartedly with no real intent to do good work. The latter meaning has fallen into disuse.

JOHN R. BRINKERHOFF

SEE ALSO: Enlisted Personnel.

SPACE, MILITARY ASPECTS OF

Since the earliest days of man-made orbiting satellites, both the United States and the former Soviet Union recognized and attempted to exploit the potential of space for military purposes. As other nations began to orbit payloads, military satellites were launched by and for Canada, China, France, Great Britain, Israel, and Japan; but the overwhelming utilization of space for military purposes is by the two major powers. They developed the infrastructure, invested the resources, and capitalized on the military potential from space systems for themselves and their allies. Since the dissolution of the Soviet Union, pieces of the Soviet space programs have been taken over by the republics of the Commonwealth of Independent States (CIS). It is still too early, however, to determine how the programs will be sorted out.

Despite visible and public pronouncements about their commitment to the "peaceful use of space," the United States and the former Soviet military establishments moved vigorously into this arena. Each a signatory to the 1967 Outer Space Treaty, which places limitations on military space activities, both countries evolved their space programs to the point where U.S. military space funding has eclipsed civil space funding since 1981 while more than 90 percent of the USSR's launches were categorized as being for military or military-related purposes. Each country spent about US$80 billion on military space in the past decade.

While, as of the early 1990s, neither country had deployed a space weapon capable of inflicting damage on earth, the Soviets, from 1966 to 1972, tested a fractional orbital bombardment system designed to carry nuclear warheads into the United States from the southern or unexpected route. U.S. emphasis on ballistic missile defense through its Strategic Defense Initiative (SDI) is believed by some to portend a weapons capability. Although not tested since 1982, the USSR continued to maintain the world's only operational antisatellite system—a ground-launched co-orbital interceptor. Conversely, the United States had a program during the 1980s to develop an air-launched miniature antisatellite vehicle carried by F-15 interceptor aircraft. This U.S. program never became operational.

The most prevalent military satellite systems have been for worldwide communications and remote sensing (surveillance, treaty monitoring, weather, and attack warning). These military functions use space as the ultimate high ground, over which opposing forces have fought since warfare began.

History

The Soviet Union's 4 October 1957 launch of Sputnik 1 from the Baikonur cosmodrome was the extrapolation of German A-4 military rocket research, which first had a successful launching in October 1942. The United States, which did not orbit its Explorer 1 satellite until January 1958, had nonetheless been examining the potential for military space beginning in the mid-forties with studies at the Rand Corporation in California. Rand had envisaged using space for communications, navigation, weather monitoring, and surveillance—and by 1960 the United States had military space efforts in each of these areas.

During the 1960s, space launch activity by each country was heavy, reflecting both enthusiasm for pursuing space spectaculars (with their corresponding psychological benefits) and frequent system failures resulting from applying immature technology to an inherently risky pursuit. By the 1970s both major powers had settled into a more mature pattern, which concentrated on effectively exploiting space for military purposes. The Soviets, having lost or dropped out of the race to place men on the moon, were determinedly augmenting terrestrial military systems with space systems—but not phasing out older capabilities. While both countries increased their reliance on space systems, it was believed that the United States was more dependent on space due to its technologically advanced, longer-lived systems and its predisposition to retire non-space systems once a satellite equivalent had been achieved. Both sides pursued investigation of space weaponry (the United States had a Johnson Island–based antisatellite missile system while the Soviets had a co-orbital interceptor), but the USSR appeared more aggressive.

By the 1980s, the enormous resource requirements associated with space systems were beginning to force greater sharing of civil assets by the military, increased attempts to reduce costs through advanced technology and system engineering, and outright inhibitions in being able to undertake all the missions that the military might have desired.

The Soviets put increasing emphasis on man in space, establishing world endurance records by cosmonauts onboard various configurations of their Salyut spacecraft. In the United States, despite a long heritage of military men serving as astronauts, the U.S. Defense Department was never able to find a compelling military need for man in space. The United States relied instead on automation technology to provide highly sophisticated and capable unmanned satellites.

Due to differences in design requirements, cost considerations, and technological capabilities, U.S. military satellites tend to be larger, more complex, and longer lived than equivalent Soviet systems. Abandoning the traditional military wariness of relying on civil services for basic support, the U.S. Department of Defense agreed, in the 1970s, to design future military payloads for launch exclusively on the space transportation system, usually called the shuttle, and allowed its expendable launch vehicle capability to decay. The error of that decision was demonstrated in the almost two-year hiatus in military launches brought about by the 1986 *Challenger* disaster (with its stand-down through late 1988) as well as several Titan and Atlas failures (possibly reflecting the deterioration of the industry). Not unexpectedly, the response was to breathe new life into the expendable launch vehicle programs (Titan IV, Delta II, Atlas II) and revise launch plans so that very few military payloads use the shuttle. Still, it has taken several years to orbit the backlog of grounded satellite systems.

By the end of the eighties the Soviets maintained about 150, and the U.S. military about 100, active satellites in orbit, with the Soviets routinely launching replenishments at a rate of about 100 per year and the United States less than 20. Ninety-five percent of Soviet space systems had military applications.

Both defense establishments worked hard to integrate space systems with the other elements of their military force structure through joint exercises, training, and doctrine development. Although the United States added some satellite interaction to its worldwide deployment exercises and some of its simulation and training scenarios, the Soviets demonstrated unprecedented integration with their twentieth antisatellite test in June 1982. The Kosmos 1379 shot was similar to previous missions, but this time it was tied to a larger exercise in which the Soviets launched two intercontinental ballistic missiles (ICBMs), two antiballistic missiles, one submarine-launched ballistic missile

(SLBM), and an SS-20 intermediate-range ballistic missile, plus an antisatellite weapon in a seven-hour period. Within hours, the Soviets launched two other satellite payloads (navigation and photo reconnaissance), possibly to simulate their ability to replenish systems negated by the United States in the wartime scenario they were conducting.

Organizations

U.S. organizational response to the military space mission evolved from an acquisition-dominated structure in the 1960s to one seeking an operational balance in the late 1980s. In 1958, the U.S. Congress responded to the shock of Sputnik with legislation creating the National Aeronautics and Space Administration (NASA) as the U.S. lead agency for space (but reserving the national security missions to the Defense Department) and urging the Defense Department to establish an Advanced Research Projects Agency as the focal point for all military space activity. The civilian agency absorbed the major army (Redstone Arsenal launch vehicles and Jet Propulsion Lab's [JPL] Explorer Satellite) and navy (Navy Research Laboratory [NRL], Project Vanguard) space capabilities, and the air force became the Defense Department's lead agency for space, with the research agency relegated to technology development.

In the early 1980s, U.S. commanders became more aware of the potential value of satellite systems to the war-fighting community and established a Joint Planning Staff for Space in the Office of the Joint Chiefs of Staff. By 1982, the air force had created an Air Force Space Command in Colorado Springs. The navy (1983) and army (1988) followed suit with similar units. A unified U.S. Space Command with its own commander in chief was activated in September 1985, with the mission of space control, space support, and aerospace defense.

In the Soviet Union all aspects of the military space program were dominated and controlled by the Communist Party of the Soviet Union, with the Military Industrial Commission responsible for system acquisition and program management. Cosplan, the State Committee on Planning, as well as the USSR Academy of Sciences and the State Committee on Science and Technology, probably also had major management input. Vladimir Chelomei, who developed the first Soviet air-launched cruise missile, is credited with creating first-generation military satellites and the SL-12 Proton space booster. Sergei Korolev is cited as the designer of the Sputnik and Vostok programs.

Operationally, three of the five components of the Soviet armed forces were involved in the military aspects of space. The Strategic Rocket Forces were responsible for space launches, satellite tracking, payload recovery, and logistical support. The air force managed the Soviet manned space programs, while the Troops of Air Defense provided antirocket and antispace defense. There were signs that the former Soviets, who defined a theater of operations as any self-contained geographical area of military, economic, and strategic significance coordinated under a single operational command, were preparing to establish a space theater of operations in the early nineties.

Missions and Systems

As early as 1965, the doctrinal *Soviet Dictionary of Basic Military Terms* outlined the USSR's view of its military space mission by stating that "mastery of space is an important prerequisite for achieving victory in war." Even earlier, U.S. president John F. Kennedy noted, "If the Soviets control space they control the earth, as in the past centuries the nations that controlled the seas dominated the continents."

Both sides recognized that superiority in space could help to offset military disadvantages brought about by other factors: for example, the United States could compensate for numerical inferiority by using space as a terrestrial force multiplier; the USSR could communicate with and achieve positive control over the vast territory through which its forces were to be deployed. By integrating space systems into their respective combined-arms operations, each side improved the effectiveness of its forces. Moreover, certain operations (e.g., long-haul communications, global weather, deep surveillance, and all-weather navigation) are performed better and more cost effectively from space than from land or sea.

Figure 1 depicts typical interrelationships between elements of military space systems. These systems require a launcher, the mission satellite, a command and control scheme (tracking, telemetry, and control) to task and direct the on-orbit satellite and to monitor its health and status, and a downlink to get mission information from the satellite to user ground stations (whether in the air, on land, or at sea). Various options exist for supplying each of these system elements. Cost, mission requirements, and technological capability considerations are combined in making the trade-offs that yield ultimate space system design.

There are five categories of missions for space systems: ballistic missile defense, support for space systems themselves; space system enhancement of terrestrial forces; application of weapons from space; and control of space.

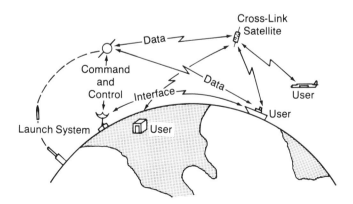

Figure 1. Typical military space systems' elements.

BALLISTIC MISSILE DEFENSE

Intercontinental ballistic missiles fly trajectories that propel them through space at altitudes higher than many low-flying satellites. Accordingly, the antiballistic missile activities of a nation become intertwined with its military space programs. The Soviet Galosh system ringing Moscow would achieve its kill in space if ever used. Soviet ground-based laser and directed-energy weapons developments could have antisatellite as well as antiballistic missile applications. Since the United States and the former USSR employ multiple independently targetable reentry vehicles (MIRVs) on their ICBMs, economy-of-force considerations make a space-based antiballistic missile system very attractive; that is, it is much easier to destroy ICBMs during boost phase when the MIRVs would still be a single target. This logic has been a major factor in U.S. SDI and the equivalent USSR Red Shield design architectures.

In the United States, the air force and army play major roles in ballistic missile defense with systems research and development focused in the Defense Department's Strategic Defense Initiative Organization and planning for operational employment conducted by the U.S. Space Command. In the former Soviet Union, the Troops of Air Defense included an antirocket defense component to support the Moscow antiballistic missile facilities.

SPACE SYSTEM SUPPORT

Providing support to the space systems themselves—from launch through on-orbit control to de-orbit—is critical to ensuring that the satellites will be able to perform their military missions when required.

Launch sites. The United States launches its military satellites from two major centers. Six space-launch complexes at Vandenberg Air Force Base, midway up the Southern California coast, are used to place satellites in polar orbit, flying south over the unpopulated Pacific Ocean. Located closer to the equator to take advantage of the earth's greater rotational speed at lower latitudes, six air force launch complexes at Cape Canaveral and two space shuttle complexes at the Kennedy Space Center in Florida are used for geosynchronous launches. Fly out is over the Atlantic Ocean, again avoiding populated areas for safety reasons. Smaller test and suborbital payloads have been launched from White Sands, New Mexico; Green River, Utah; Wallops Island, Virginia; and Poker Flats, Alaska.

In the former Soviet Union there are about 20 launch pads from two principal sites, Tyuratam—the old Baikonur—and Plesetsk. A lesser-used spaceport, Kapustin Yar on the Volga River, lies at about the same latitude as Tyuratam. These higher-latitude sites make it more difficult to achieve geosynchronous orbit over the equator; low-altitude circular or highly elliptical orbits consume much less fuel and allow increased payload capacity even if greater numbers of satellites are required to meet stated mission requirements. In the late 1980s, 75 percent of Soviet launches were to low-altitude orbits compared with about 25 percent for the United States.

Launch vehicles. Both nations built launch vehicles primarily by modifying former ballistic missiles. The Soviet SL-4 launch vehicle—workhorse of the fleet—can lift approximately 7,500 kilograms to low-earth orbit and accounted for almost 50 percent of Soviet launches in the late 1980s, even though it was a direct descendant of the booster that launched Sputnik. Other ballistic missile derivatives in use include the SL-6 (2,100 kilograms to deep space); the SL-8 (1,700 kilograms to low-earth orbit); the SL-11 (4,000 kilograms to low-earth orbit), which launches the Soviet antisatellite weapon, EORSAT and RORSAT; and the SL-14 (5,500 kilograms to low-earth orbit). Larger Soviet boosters, including the SL-12 (2,000 kilograms to deep space), the SL-13 (19,500 kilograms to low-earth orbit), and the newer SL-16 capable of economically placing more than 15,000 kilograms into low-earth orbit, round out a fleet that historically launches a satellite every three or four days. In mid-1987, the Soviets conducted the first flight test of an SL-X-17 heavy-lift launch vehicle. Named Energiya, the liquid hydrogen–powered SL-X-17 is believed to be able to place more than 100,000 kilograms into low-earth orbit, about on par with the U.S. phased-out Saturn V and almost four times the lift capability of the space shuttle. Unlike Saturn V, which was used only for NASA's Apollo and Skylab programs, the Energiya was to be employed by the Soviet military both as a heavy lifter and to carry the Buran Soviet shuttle (first successfully flown without a crew in 1988) into orbit.

The Soviets repeatedly demonstrated the ability to achieve multiple successful launches in short periods of time. During the Falklands/Malvinas conflict in 1982, the Soviets conducted 28 space launches in just 69 days. In June 1984, they launched three completely different spacecraft types on three different launch vehicles within 12 hours. Turnaround time for some launch systems is fewer than six hours on the same pad.

The U.S. military launch vehicle fleet had been allowed to dissipate prior to the 1986 shuttle disaster, but was rebuilt thereafter, again largely based on ballistic missile derivatives. The last Scout rocket placed two navy navigation payloads in orbit in 1988. The Delta, capable of lifting 3,500 kilograms into low-earth orbit, was derived from the Thor intermediate-range missile and by the late 1980s was being replaced by a new Delta II launch vehicle primarily to launch global positioning system (GPS) navigation satellites. Similarly, the Atlas, a variant of its namesake ICBM, and capable of orbiting 6,100 kilograms to low-earth orbit, was giving way to the Atlas II medium launch vehicle. Titan II missiles were taken out of service with the Strategic Air Command, refurbished, and used to launch small military payloads beginning in 1988. Earlier a Titan derivative, the Titan III, had become the workhorse of the military, launching payloads both to low-earth orbit and to geosynchronous orbits. The last operational version, the Titan-34D was capable of placing 15,000 kilograms into low-earth orbit—a capability similar to that of the Soviet SL-16.

In the late 1980s, contracts were let by the U.S. Air Force to procure Titan IV vehicles, sized to accommodate shuttle-class payloads. The redesigned shuttle program, with its increased costs, lower payload lift capability, and less frequent launch rate, will play a decreasing role in military space operations.

Preliminary research and development were also under way for design of an advanced launch system to develop a new family of vehicles, including economical heavy-lift launch capability. Several upper stages—additional propulsion units designed to move payloads from the initial orbit achieved by the basic launch vehicle to higher mission orbits—were in use by the military. Primary among these were the inertial upper stage and the Centaur. Defense Advanced Research Projects Agency (DARPA), under its Advanced Space Technology Program (ASTP), was funding development of a winged launch vehicle to be carried by a B-52 and capable of orbiting 270- to 400-kilogram payloads to low-earth orbit.

Tracking and control. Once launched, satellites, either manned or unmanned, require a fair amount of external input to maintain operational effectiveness. Although both the United States and the former Soviet Union seek to minimize the ground support of orbiting systems through advances in onboard data processing—leading to more autonomous operation with inherent reduction in support costs and increases in survivability potential—current technology still mandates substantial ground control. The United States employs an air force–managed satellite control network consisting of a Consolidated Satellite Operations Center in Colorado Springs, Colorado; a Consolidated Satellite Test Center in Sunnyvale, California; and a series of 12 remote tracking stations, most located overseas. Once a satellite is launched, it is checked out, initialized on orbit, and its health and status continuously monitored via the network. For some missions the actual satellite tasking and data retrieval are likewise accomplished by the network. Other missions use dedicated mission ground stations, some of which are land-, sea-, or airmobile, to command and read out satellites. As a part of its eastern and western test range support activities, the U.S. military also employs satellite-tracking aircraft and ships. The Automated Remote Tracking Station program was the latest upgrade to U.S. tracking and control capabilities.

The Soviets eschewed employment of ground stations outside their own territory, relying instead on a fleet of 12 oceangoing vessels deployed in both the Atlantic and Western Pacific. Generally named after Soviet cosmonauts (the *Yuri Gagarin* was the first ship in the group) the latest space event support ship was the *Marshal Nedelin*, completed in 1983 and homeported in Vladivostok. These ships augment seven major space tracking and control stations in the homeland.

The United States recovers all mission data from its military payloads electronically; the former Soviets continue to retrieve some data via parachute soft-landing over the USSR landmass.

De-orbit. At the end of useful mission life, satellites in low orbit fall to earth as their orbits decay. No longer able to maintain orbital speed and position due to depletion of the control gas that powers adjustment thrusters, a low-flying satellite will be overcome by atmospheric drag, begin to tumble, and plunge toward earth, generally burning up due to reentry heating. Nonfunctioning satellites at synchronous orbit remain where they expire unless consciously repositioned out of locations needed for replacement satellites.

The U.S. Space Command routinely tracks some 7,000 objects, 10 centimeters or larger, orbiting in space. Only 5 percent of these larger objects are operational spacecraft; the remainder is debris.

ENHANCEMENT OF TERRESTRIAL FORCES

Force enhancement is the support of terrestrial forces (on land, at sea, and in the air) by space systems. Included in this mission area are communications, navigation, weather, and surveillance.

Communications. The United States launched Signal Communications Orbiting Relay Equipment, its first military communications satellite, in December 1958. It transmitted taped messages for 13 days. Serious military satellite communications employment began with the 1966 launch of the Initial Defense Satellite Communications Program (IDSCP). Eventually growing to a constellation of 26 satellites, IDSCP provided, among other missions, a military control link between Washington, D.C., and South Vietnam.

Over 70 percent of U.S. worldwide military communications now travel via satellite. Using IDSCP as a basis, a series of geostationary satellites, designated NATO-1 through NATO-3C, were launched beginning in 1970. Designed to handle diplomatic and military traffic between the United States and 13 NATO countries, two NATO-4 satellites were being developed for launch in the early nineties.

The Defense Satellite Communications System (DSCS) has provided secure, worldwide, wideband, long-haul communications capability since 1971. The current phase, DSCS III, with an estimated ten-year operational lifetime, consists of four three-axis stabilized, nuclear-hardened satellites in synchronous orbit with two on-orbit spares. DSCS III has 61 receiving and 19 transmitting multiple-beam antennas capable of relaying 1,300 simultaneous two-way voice transmissions in the super high frequency (SHF) range. It augments DSCS II satellites still in service, has two ultra high frequency (UHF) back-up antennas, some encryption and antijam capability, and hosts a single channel transponder used by the National Command Authorities to relay the Emergency Action Message (EAM). An even newer generation, DSCS IIIC, was in development in the late 1980s. DSCS satellites are developed and procured by the air force, with the army procuring the receiving terminals.

A highly survivable EHF (extremely high frequency) band Military Strategic-Tactical and Relay (Milstar) system was in development for an early 1990s' deployment. It features special orbits, extensive hardening, advanced antijamming techniques (such as fast frequency hopping), and high-level encryption. Milstar will also be capable of communications with the US$2 billion worth of ultra high frequency terminals in the military's current inventory.

The U.S. Navy, employing Fleet Satellite Communications Systems as well as several leased systems, relies on satellites for up to 90 percent of its worldwide message traffic. First launched in 1978, this system became fully operational in 1981. Four active satellites provide worldwide coverage (from 70 degrees above and below the equator) among more than 2,000 ships, submarines, and aircraft (both air force and navy), as well as ground facilities, the Strategic Air Command, and the national command authority. These vehicles also carry an EAM package (known as AFSATCOM) and two in the series were modified to handle EHF communications as precursors to Milstar. Eight of these satellites were procured (one was lost in 1987 when its Atlas booster was destroyed during launch after being struck by lightning), and in late 1988 a contract was awarded for a follow-on satellite that will be compatible with existing navy ultra high frequency terminals, will have an SHF jam-resistant uplink, and will bridge the navy's requirements gap until Milstar support is received.

Between SCORE and Milstar, several other military communications satellites were developed for experimental or special communications missions. The Strategic Air Command uses a suborbital emergency rocket communications system to ensure delivery of the EAM, while the military as a whole shares time on NASA Civilian Tracking and Data Relay Satellites. Research was under way for a laser communications satellite system to communicate with submerged submarines.

The Soviets relied on communications satellites for about half of their military dispatches. With troop control as one of their uppermost requirements, almost half of their orbiting satellites perform command, control, and communications (C^3) missions. Driven by geographic considerations, the USSR pioneered the use of highly elliptical (400 km by 40,000 km [250 mi. by 25,000 mi.]), inclined (63-degree to 65-degree) orbits (known as Molniya orbits) to provide eight-hour-per-day satellite coverage over the high latitudes of the Soviet Union. The Molniya 1 constellation makes use of this orbit with eight satellites in orbital planes separated by 45 degrees. Each satellite in the network traces the same path over the earth each day at three-hour intervals. It carries at least one 40W transponder operating in the 1.0/0.8 gigahertz band.

In geosynchronous orbit, Raduga and Gorizont general-purpose communications satellites provide support to the military (as well as handling civilian telephone, telegraph, and television traffic) while three Kosmos data relay satellites comprise a satellite data relay network designed to support the manned Mir (Salyut) space station, which conducts military earth observation and other experiments transmitting encrypted data to the ground.

Two low-altitude systems, an "8 Ball" cluster of 40-kilogram satellites orbiting in circular 1,500-kilometer (930-mi.) orbits and a constellation of three 750-kilogram satellites circling the earth at 800 kilometers (500 mi.), are dedicated to military communications. Direct communications among ships, aircraft, bases, and forces in the field are provided by the "8 Ball" system operating in a store/dump mode at very- and ultra-high frequencies. A total of 24 satellites, all in the same orbital plane, satisfy network requirements and provide stations at the latitude of Moscow virtually uninterrupted coverage 17 hours each day. Longer-range military communications are achieved with the three heavier satellites operating in orbital planes spaced 120 degrees apart. These satellites receive information from low-power transmitters around the world, then store the data until it can be dumped to a receiving station on the ground. Their ground tracks repeat every 85 orbits for repetitive coverage. Both low-altitude systems have historically been replenished with three launches per year.

Navigation. A second major area of military force enhancement is satellite navigation. The first U.S. navigation satellite, Transit, was developed by the navy to provide Polaris missile submarines with position-fixing data accurate to 150 meters (500 ft.). Successfully launched in 1960, the simple, gravity-gradient stabilized polar satellites performed flawlessly and well beyond their anticipated useful lifetimes. Improved versions continue to provide worldwide navigation information to both civilian and military users (including the former Soviet navy) equipped with inexpensive receivers. Even greater positional accuracy is achieved with the navigation satellite timing and ranging (Navstar) global positioning system. A GPS terminal operator can receive a readout of his current position with a spherical error probability of less than 16 meters (50 ft.). Twenty-one operational GPS satellites in 20,000-kilometer (12,400-mi.) circular orbits (plus 3 on-orbit spares) will comprise the final constellation.

The satellites broadcast in two L-band frequencies, enabling passive use of the system (e.g., without signaling his presence to the enemy with a radio transmission). Key to each GPS satellite are the three built-in atomic clocks (accurate to one second in 36,000 years), which allow precise velocity measurements.

The former Soviets have been flying their own version of the U.S. Transit navigation system since 1967. The system consists of six satellites in orbital planes separated by 30 degrees of right ascension. The satellites orbit at 1,000 kilometers (620 mi.) with inclination angles of 83 degrees, allowing signals to be received worldwide. It uses the same Doppler technique as Transit and similar very high frequencies. The Soviet Global Navigation Satellite System is also similar in design to the U.S. GPS. It employs the same basic semi-synchronous orbits and similar frequency bands and is deployed in constellations of three or four satellites in each of three orbital planes (GPS uses six planes).

Meteorology. Both military services have been using space systems for weather observation—the third element of force enhancement—since the 1960s. The United States launched its first weather satellite in 1960 as part of a program that later evolved into the Defense Meteorological Support Program (DMSP). DMSP employs two satellites in 800-kilometer (500-mi.) sun-synchronous polar orbit, each carrying multiple sensors including line scan visible and microwave imagers, infrared moisture and temperature sounders, and various radiometers and spectrometers. Collected worldwide weather information is stored for readout and transfer to the U.S. Air Force Global Weather Center at Omaha, Nebraska; more local data can be immediately dumped to tactical stations (vans) as the satellites pass overhead. DMSP supports both strategic and tactical missions. Some of its information (especially warning of severe storms) is also passed to the civil community, and in this mission area the military makes extensive use of the civilian assets, the polar-orbiting Television Infrared Observation Satellite and the Geostationary Operational Environmental Satellite operated by the Department of Commerce's National Oceanic and Atmospheric Administration. Advanced requirements for environmental sensing, particularly the navy's desire for oceanographic information, led to several proposals for a naval remote ocean surveillance satellite, but resource constraints frustrated such a development for more than a decade.

The Soviet meteorological satellite, Meteor, began operation in 1965. Since 1969, two or three Meteor satellites have operated simultaneously through three primary receiving sites and over 50 ground stations. The ex-Soviet military takes full advantage of a civilian counterpart, Meteor 2, which carries advanced sensing equipment at a mean altitude of 950 kilometers (600 mi.) from which it can access one-fifth of the world during a single orbital pass.

A Meteor 3 network, consisting of three satellites in orbital planes separated by 120 degrees, was in development to replace the Meteor 2 system and to take over as the entry point for the Soviet military's exploitation of not only civil weather data, but also of the substantial Soviet civil earth resources and environmental monitoring programs.

Surveillance. Surveillance from space is the final element of force enhancement. The United States has used space systems to increase its land-based early warning capabilities and to help prevent surprise attacks since 1960, when the Missile Detection Alarm System, or Midas, was launched and followed a year later by the Samos satellites. Evolving through a long series of technical performance upgrades and survivability enhancements (and their corresponding classified program designators and name changes), today's early warning satellites provide North American Air Defense Command (NORAD) with near real-time warning and confirmation of launch events through synchronous infrared satellites, U.S. and overseas ground sites, and a series of mobile ground stations operated by the Air Force Space Command. The U.S. system worked well during the Persian Gulf War of 1991 in pinpointing quickly the launch sites of Iraqi Scud missiles. Likewise, the CIS employs a series of highly elliptical launch detection system satellites that augment their over-the-horizon radar warning of possible U.S. missile launch. Because of their semi-synchronous Molniya-like design, the system requires more satellites and achieves less complete coverage than its U.S. counterpart. The program has been plagued with development problems and does not appear to be capable of observing U.S. missile launches from submarines.

In mid-October 1963 the United States launched the first Vela satellite to monitor the Nuclear Test Ban Treaty. Six pairs of Vela spacecraft were launched prior to 1970. They went into 100,000-kilometer (62,000-mi.) orbits with 38-degree inclination, allowing placement on opposite sides of the earth. The Vela surveillance mission was gradually transitioned to subpayloads on (host) satellites. Later versions of the GPS were fitted with nuclear detection systems for both treaty monitoring and post-hostility bomb damage assessment.

President Johnson's 1967 offhand comment to the effect that the value of one satellite photo was worth the price of the entire space program was the only official acknowledgment that the United States employed such systems until President Carter's 1978 Cape Kennedy speech in which he cited the value of photoreconnaissance satellites for treaty monitoring and verification.

The former Soviets have a robust reconnaissance and surveillance satellite program. The first Soviet photoreconnaissance satellite (Kosmos 4) was launched in 1962 and similar systems have been on orbit ever since. Most satellites are short lived (less than two months) and return their exposed film by deorbiting the payload over the homeland. Five generations of photo satellites, including high-resolution (0.2 meters [8 in.]), wide area search, and near real-time data imagery systems, have been deployed. The Soviets also launched over 100 signal intelligence collection satellites since 1967. Several series of such payloads have evolved, and a mid-1980s U.S. military assessment noted that Soviet space-based electronic intelligence assets were being upgraded.

The military establishment of each side makes use of indigenous civil remote-sensing assets (Landsat in the United States, Priroda in Russia) in support of its surveillance and monitoring missions. Landsat, a civil remote-sensing satellite, provides multispectral data useful for mobility planning in support of ground and amphibious operations.

Unique to the former Soviet Union are two surveillance/targeting systems: the radar ocean reconnaissance satellites and the electronic intelligence ocean reconnaissance satellites. Both launched by the SL-11, they orbit at 65 degrees' inclination, permitting almost complete surveillance of all strategic waterways. Working in concert these satellites attempt to detect, identify, and track U.S. naval forces and to relay the collected information directly to Soviet naval and air elements for targeting purposes.

The U.S. Air Force and Navy have for over ten years attempted to begin development of a wide area all-weather surveillance system, a space-based radar. The system's expense, coupled with bureaucratic disagreement over mission requirements and program management, have slowed progress as of the early 1990s, but strong support from the commander in chief of U.S. Space Command may change this.

APPLICATION OF WEAPONS

Neither the United States nor the former USSR has developed the capability to deploy offensive weapons in space that could achieve kills on earth. The 1967 Outer Space Treaty bans nations from orbiting weapons of mass destruction. The United States argues that, at least theoretically, systems deployed in space could contribute to deterrence in peacetime and to more rapid conflict termination in war. Clearly, a deployed defensive antiballistic missile system as envisioned by the Strategic Defense Initiative Organization would represent substantial application of force toward ballistic missile trajectories near earth.

The former Soviets, combining extensive research in laser weaponry with projected heavy-lift launch capabilities that far outstrip observable and estimated launch requirements, may be pursuing a space weapon. Between 1966 and 1971, they conducted 18 tests of a fractional orbital bombardment system. Designed to be fired by F1 (Scrap) rockets into 160-kilometer (100-mi.) orbits, this system's nuclear warhead would travel three-quarters of the way around the world over the South Pole, then be slowed by retro-rockets so they reentered before achieving a complete orbit. Coming from the south, such a system would avoid the early warning radars that were designed to alert the United States of incoming attack. The United States eventually deployed large phased-array radars (Pave Paws) on its southern border and the Soviet launchers at Tyuratam were to be dismantled under terms of Article VII of the SALT II Treaty.

SPACE CONTROL

Space control, analogous to control of the sea lanes of communication or air superiority, involves the protection of U.S. and allied space assets from enemy threats and disruption while at the same time denying or negating the enemy's own space capability. U.S. policy had treated space as a benign environment until the end of the Nixon administration, when military policy makers formally recognized that space was no longer a sanctuary.

Space control requires two distinct capabilities for achievement: precise tracking, monitoring, and observation systems to provide accurate situational information, and a weapons mechanism.

Monitoring and observation. The United States monitors activity in space with a worldwide network of radar and optical sensors operated by the U.S. Air Force and Naval Space Commands for U.S. Space Command. These include four Ground-based Electro-optical Deep Space Surveillance systems, the Naval Space Surveillance radar fence across the lower United States, and several types of large conventional and phased-array radars. Plans to augment this coverage, either with a space-based system capable of sensing cold satellite bodies or onboard sensors flying on U.S. satellites to provide unambiguous warning of attack, have not materialized. The former Soviets monitor space with 11 Hen House phased-array radars as well as their Cat House and Dog House antiballistic missile radars and probably their space support ships. A broad array of optical ground sites are also available.

Space weapon. For a weapon to complement the observation systems, the former Soviets have an SL-11–launched co-orbital antisatellite interceptor that was first tested on 20 October 1968, was declared (by the U.S. Department of Defense) operational in 1971, and was last used (for the twentieth time) as part of a major Soviet missile test in June 1982. Of the 20 one- and two-revolution tests, with both radar- and infrared-seeking sensors, nine were judged successful.

Since the SL-11 is launched about five times per year in connection with other missions, some argue that the long elapsed period since the last antisatellite test is not significant. In March 1978, the Carter administration began a series of three negotiations aimed at, but unsuccessful in, achieving an antisatellite arms control agreement. The former Soviets could also employ the Galosh antiballistic missile system, ground-based lasers, and systems espoused under their radio electronic combat doctrine to the space control mission.

Motivated in part by the Soviet orbital bombardment system, the U.S. military began developing its own antisatellite weapon (Project Bold Orion), which held two flight demonstrations, launching missiles from a B-58 and a B-47 in 1959 and achieving a deliberate near miss on the Explorer 6 Satellite. Several other satellite interception projects were planned or begun but never tested (Saint, Bambi, Project Mudflap), and in the early 1960s the United States deployed nuclear-tipped Thor missiles on Johnson Island (Program 437) as a militarily operational antisatellite system. When the Soviets stopped testing their system, the United States dismantled Program 437 and stopped all antisatellite planning activity. It was at this point that the Soviets resumed testing. By 1975 the United States began development of a miniature kinetic kill vehicle to be launched on a Short-range Attack Missile (SRAM)/Altair missile by an F-15 executing a high-performance snap maneuver. The F-15 flew five successful or partially successful tests (including actually destroying the P78-1 Solwind satellite, a still functioning research craft very near the end of its useful life). In 1985, the U.S. Congress placed a ban on further such tests despite the fact that the test program had seven more live firings to go and two instrumented test vehicles had already been placed in orbit. By mid-1988, this program was cancelled. Subsequent ASAT development has been undertaken by the U.S. Army with a modestly funded ground-based interceptor program that has as a corollary objective the limiting of orbital debris that might accompany weapons employment.

Survivability

The 1991 Gulf War demonstrated the importance of space to military fighting forces. Because Iraq did not have the necessary countermeasures, the U.S.-led coalition was able to command and control widely dispersed forces, to accurately forecast weather, to sense enemy troop movement, to provide missile alert warning, to precisely navigate barren and featureless terrain, and to effectively communicate both in the field of operations and back home—all with dramatically successful effects.

In the 30 years since satellite systems were proven feasible, both the United States and the USSR developed military systems to exploit space for good advantage. Essentially parallel operational programs have continued to mature in both the East and the West, although diverging employment variations reflect differing technological competence, resource availability, and institutional concerns. A major determinant of the future value of space systems to military commanders and war planners will be the extent to which satellite systems are survivable in peacetime, crisis, and conflict.

Space survivability means that a space system will perform its mission at a needed level of capability, as long as required, within a specified level of conflict. Being unable to launch satellites into space is as much a survivability issue as is the problem of satellites being destroyed by antisatellite weaponry, blinded by laser, or jammed by electronic warfare or of having ground stations eliminated. A commander is unwilling to rely on a system he believes (rightly or wrongly) to be more vulnerable to enemy (or natural) negation actions than the terrestrial assets he currently employs. The inherent survivability of space assets over terrestrial systems is often overlooked and misunderstood.

The robust on-orbit constellations of satellites of the former Soviet Union and its expansive launch capability probably places it ahead on this issue in a conflict (vs. peacetime) environment. The United States has begun to emphasize assured mission capability as its enhanced survivability strategy and is working toward more vigorous launch-related capabilities, less vulnerable orbital assets, and increased ground and space mission redundancy.

DAVID MESSNER

Bibliography

Gray, C. 1982. *American military space policy.* Cambridge, Mass.: Abt Books.

Hobbs, D. 1986. *An illustrated guide to space warfare.* New York: Prentice-Hall.

Johnson, N. 1988. *The Soviet year in space 1987.* Colorado Springs, Colo.: Teledyne Brown Engineering.

Schichtle, C. 1983. *The national space program.* Washington, D.C.: National Defense Univ. Press.

Stares, P. 1985. *The militarization of space.* New York: Cornell Univ. Press.

———. 1987. *Space and national security.* Washington, D.C.: Brookings.

Turnill, R. 1987. *Jane's spaceflight directory.* New York: Jane's.

U.S. Department of Defense. 1987. *The Soviet space challenge.* Washington, D.C.: U.S. Department of Defense.

———. 1988. *Soviet military power.* Washington, D.C.: U.S. Department of Defense.

U.S. Senate. 1982. *Soviet space programs: 1976–1980.* Washington, D.C.: United States Senate.

SPAN OF CONTROL: MILITARY ORGANIZATIONS AND OPERATIONS

Span of control, echelons of command, and size of units are the three components of organizational structure. Span of control encompasses the number of subjects (personnel), objects (e.g., vehicles), or units that are controlled, managed, or led by one echelon of command and represents the structural width. The hierarchy is expressed by the number of command echelons within an organization and represents the structural depth. A decreasing span of control (smaller number of subordinates) results in a larger number of echelons (more organizational depth), in a requirement for more leaders, and in a larger number of headquarters; however, the size of each headquarters becomes smaller. Other effects are an improved controllability of subordinates (positive), a longer duration of communications, and an increased tendency to bureaucracy (both negative). No uniform statements can be made regarding different human behavior under various spans of control. Generally, a decreasing span of control reduces the freedom of decision making at individual echelons as well as their responsibility. Modern motivational research indicates that decreasing responsibility reduces motivation and consequently work productivity. Conversely, an increasing span of control (widening of the structure) means fewer echelons, leaders, and headquarters, which, however, become larger.

In a simplified example of Allied Forces Central Europe (AFCENT), we show first a deep structure with a large number of echelons and a small span of control (Fig. 1). Then, using the same base (1,800 companies and one AF-CENT), a wide structure is shown that has one-third fewer echelons and a correspondingly larger span of control (Fig. 2).

In the search for the optimal span of control, the span is reduced or extended until the associated advantages exceed the disadvantages.

Theory of Optimal Span of Control

The concept of optimal span of control has been—as have most elements of classical organizational theory—developed on the basis of experience with military forces as the oldest large organizations, according to Karl von Clausewitz and Ian Hamilton. There are two schools of thought: the theory of limited span of control and the theory of span of control determinants.

The first theory assumes that there are objective conditions. These are seen in a direct relation between leaders and subordinates. The number of leaders increases with the number of subordinates in a geometrical progression result-

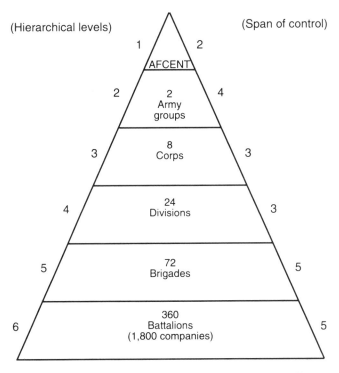

Figure 1. Deep structure (large number of echelons, small span of control; AFCENT = Allied Forces Central Europe).

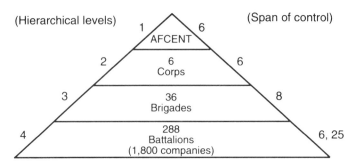

(Hierarchical levels)   (Span of control)

1 — AFCENT — 6

2 — 6 Corps — 6

3 — 36 Brigades — 8

4 — 288 Battalions (1,800 companies) — 6, 25

Figure 2. Wide structure (few echelons, large span of control; AFCENT = Allied Forces Central Europe).

ing in a number between three and six. The military field followed this concept from the beginning and, generally, used the smallest element as the basis. The Chinese concept (400 B.C.) subscribed to the five-based principle, and the French (Moritz von Sachsen [Marshal de Saxe], eighteenth century) used a constant four-based system. Rather than proposing an exact number, Clausewitz viewed the optimal span of control as being between three and eight and selected the number five as a compromise.

In contrast, modern organizational science developed the theory of span of control determinants that established restrictions or extensions of the limited span of control. This results in a multilayered system of determinants:

1. *Nature of tasks:* This includes, first, the degree of homogeneity of the tasks; second, their degree of difficulty; and third, the frequency of incidents.
2. *Geographic conditions:* The physical distance between leaders and subordinates, the significance of which is, however, strongly influenced by traffic conditions in general and the communications system in particular.
3. *Command and control system:* The leaders' freedom of decision making, leadership style, and headquarters' size have an impact on this.
4. *Quality of participating personnel:* This pertains to personnel capability and decision making. Very important in this context is the experience of participants, especially with respect to leadership.

For each determinant a distinction should be made among the technical potential, resources available, and the various costs. Consequently, deviations also occur within the structure of the same organization.

In various fields, numerous tests were made to determine, by appropriate scoring systems, mathematically optimal values for special tasks in certain areas. However, it always turns out that in a given organization different optima develop in different sections of the same level.

The peculiarities in determining the optimal span of control in the military field result, first, from the heterogeneous structure of military forces; second, from the constant personnel turnover; and finally, from the different infrastructure in peace and war. An important consideration in this context is the survivability of units, which requires not only a high degree of decentralization, dispersion, and mobility, but also "double" command and control levels (e.g., main and alternate command posts).

Development of Spans of Control and Hierarchies in the Military Field

A historical review shows three different approaches to military structures with different systems.

SYSTEMS WITH A UNIFORM CONCEPT

The first approach is the structure of Chinese forces (600–400 B.C.) with a constant five-based system (infantry) or a 10-based system (cavalry): *wu* (5 warriors), *ljang* (5 *wu* = 25 warriors), *dsu* (5 *ljang* = 125 warriors), *lu* (exception within the system: 4 *dsu* = 500 warriors), *ssi* (5 *lu* = 2,500 warriors), *djun* (5 *ssi* = 12,500 warriors).

A similar structure can be found in other Eastern armies (Mongols, Arabs, Turks, Russians) between the twelfth and sixteenth centuries with a decimal system (groups of 10, 100, 1,000, and 10,000), which also has an exception in the form of a "group of half a hundred" (five-based system downward, two-based system upward).

Macedonian armies were based an a wing system (phalanx). The basis was the *lochos* with sixteen warriors in depth that doubled in four successive steps (2, 4, 8, and 16 *lochoi*). The first "large" tactical unit was the *syntagma* (16 × 16 = 256 warriors). Four small wings were combined to form a "large phalanx" (16,384 warriors).

Finally, the medieval mercenary armies had a three-level structure with a 10-based system (Germany) or a 16-based system (Spain): section (10 and 16 men, respectively), troop (10 and 16 sections, respectively), and regiment (10 and 16 troops, respectively).

ROMAN SYSTEM

The Roman army organization originally used the 10-based system: the group of 100 (century) and the legion (10 centuries). Because of reducing the century to 30 warriors at the lowest and the demand for increasing legion strength (3,600), it was necessary to increase the number of centuries to 60 and to introduce an intermediate level by combining two centuries into a maniple and three maniples into a cohort (which was the actual tactical formation). The spans of control were 60, 2, 3, and 10.

EUROPEAN SYSTEM OF MODERN TIMES

The basis of modern armies was the mercenary system. The troop as the original group of 100 grew in the course of time to a maximum of 1,000 men. Then, in the seventeenth century, it was reduced to 300 and gradually received the designation "company." The company was the actual tactical unit. Only later were companies combined into regiments. The *Gevierthaufe*, a new intermediate level, emerged in the sixteenth century; later it became the battalion. Until the seventeenth century, there was no intermediate level between the regiment and the ad hoc formations of the *arrière-ban*. Intermediate levels were introduced in the following order: brigade (Gustavus Adolphus), division (French revolutionary armies), corps (Napoleon), and army (von Moltke the Elder). The army group (German army, 1916) and the "theater" followed. Before that, the "platoon" was introduced between company and section (mid-nineteenth century). This adds up to a twelve-level system.

Table 1 shows that, over the course of time, span of control has settled between three and five, and the different levels naturally necessitate different functions: the lowest level (up to platoon) concentrates primarily on training; the company is considered the basic form (disciplinary powers), while tactical units evolved to battalions and brigades. Major formations (division and higher) partially represent ad hoc combinations (e.g., the U.S. brigade).

The greatest differences in span of control can be seen in the company. Minor deviations also result when companies are combined into battalion-size units, in which case special organizational forms necessitate some changes to the general rule.

Organizational Size and Span of Control of the Company

The company is the oldest military unit; today, it is regarded as the basic organization for training, personnel services, and logistic support. The greatest similarities of companies within one branch exist in size and structure, but

TABLE 1. *Hierarchical Structures of Modern Forces (Twentieth Century)*

LEVEL	UNIT DESIGNATION	NUMBER OF SUBORDINATE UNITS	STRENGTH
12	Theater	2–3 army groups	
11	Army group	3–4 armies	800,000–1,200,000
10	Field army	2–5 corps	200,000–500,000
9	Corps	3–4 divisions	48,000–100,000
8	Division	2–3 brigades	12,000–25,000
7	Brigade	2–3 regiments	3,000–5,000
6	Regiment	3–4 battalions	1,600–4,000
5	Battalion	4–5 companies	400–800
4	Company	3–4 platoons	60–200
3	Platoon	3–4 sections	20–50
2	Section	3–4 squads	6–16
1	Squad		2–4

companies differ from branch to branch not only over the course of time but also in international comparisons.

As of 1988 the situation in the German Field Army (1988) was as follows. Company strength varies between 62 (armor) and 195 (supply); the ratio of noncommissioned officers (NCOs) to men is between 1:0.9 (signal) and 1:7.6 (transport), and officer density (soldiers per officer) ranges from 21 (armor) to 47 to 49 (transport/supply).

There have also been some marked changes over time. For example, personnel strength of German infantry companies has decreased from 3/20/230 (i.e., officers/NCOs/enlisted men) in the year 1914 to 3/21/178 in 1939 and then to 3/13/85 in 1988. Moreover, changes occurred during the short history of the German Bundeswehr. These changes have come about not just because of new weapons and equipment, but also because of different tactical tasks. Further, different degrees of centralization and decentralization have an impact. Finally, differences are also caused by partial transition to skeleton units. Peacetime and wartime strengths differ substantially, and the "informal" organizational size plays a special role in regard to wartime strength. This informal size results from "unofficial" weapons and equipment holdings, from soldiers taken over from other companies, and, finally, from illegally recruited volunteers.

Deviations can also be observed when making an international comparison of companies. Table 2, however, shows a marked similarity in officer density (soldiers per officer), which in most cases is 13. Deviations must be seen in context with the qualitative level of men and NCOs, the competence of company commanders, tactical aims, and the availability of organic logistic support elements.

TABLE 2. *Tank Company Strength in Selected Forces*

NATION	NUMBER OF BATTLE TANKS	PERSONNEL STRENGTH	OFFICERS	OFFICER DENSITY
Switzerland	10	123	5	25
Fed. Rep. of Germany	13	62	3	21
Austria	13	96	5	19
Yugoslavia, Hungary	13	52	4	13
United States	14	63	5	13
UK	14	90	7	13
Italy	16	84	4	21
Poland	16	64	5	13
France	17	90	7	13

Formations and Optimal Span of Control

In regard to the composition of formations, a distinction must be made between pool and task systems. The pool system is based on rigid assignments (battalion and partially also brigade) while the task system is assembled from basic elements using the modular system (corps level and higher).

Generally, the lowest element is the battalion, the largest tactical unit. In all countries, during peacetime, it consisted of four companies until the fifties. Over the past 30 years, the number of companies generally has increased to five or six; however, the size of the next higher unit (regiment, brigade) plays a role in this context.

The Austrian battalion has the smallest span of control (four companies) and the Finns, the largest (seven companies).

The classical central European sequence of battalion/regiment/brigade was given up during World War I with the elimination of the brigade level (two regiments). The regiment (generally with three battalions; the Austrian/Russian armies had four and the Spanish/Swedish armies had six battalions prior to World War I), as the largest classical "pure" unit, to a large extent disappeared after World War II in the North Atlantic Treaty Organization (NATO). It was replaced by the brigade as a mixed unit. Because of its various organic elements, the brigade possesses "autonomy." In addition, it can be complemented using the modular system. Some regiments, however, have been retained for the purpose of main effort operations (corps troops, artillery, army aviation). The regimental level still exists in militia-type armies (e.g., German and Austrian home defense regiments, Swiss regiments). The elimination of battalions (France) and corps (Warsaw Pact) by a corresponding transfer to the next higher level, though, constitutes only a change of name: the French regiment corresponds to the battalion and the Warsaw Pact army corresponded to the NATO corps. During the 1980s, the Soviet Union experimented with and temporarily constituted a few large, mobile corps within its ground forces, primarily for war in Europe. On the other hand, Hungary, for example, reorganized its ground forces on the basis of brigades.

In some countries the regiment has been retained as an organizational form, although the brigade principle has been introduced (Swedish and Swiss tank regiments, with one tank battalion and one mechanized infantry battalion).

Altogether, the number of echelons has decreased and the span of control has increased. This change is especially apparent in German forces. Before World War I, the German army consisted of 6 "army inspections," 23 army corps, 46 divisions, and 184 brigades. In contrast, SACEUR's (Supreme Allied Commander Europe) command includes 2 army groups, 8 corps, 12 German and 14 allied divisions (26), as well as 36 German and 25 allied brigades (61), all of which have nearly the same personnel strength at each unit level. This means that the forces today are led by only one-third of the original number of corps and brigade headquarters and by just a little more than one-half of the original number of division headquarters. It should be noted, however, that the headquarters' size has multiplied. Peacetime strength of a German infantry division in 1914 was about 12,500 men, in 1939 approximately 15,000 men, and in 1985 about 18,500 men.

The number of units assigned to a major formation (brigade or division and higher) already varies substantially in peacetime. In addition to the assigned "independent" units beginning at battalion level, there are other organic elements that, taken together, have in most cases the same strength as an assigned unit (e.g., corps troops with divisional strength, brigade troops with battalion strength, etc.).

Adaptations to changed structures are made by all forces throughout the world; however, considerable differences in the frequency of such major changes exist. There are two extremes: on one side the continuing reforms in the U.S. Army, the German Bundeswehr, and the Austrian army and on the other side the very long adherence to traditional structures (Warsaw Pact, Swiss, Asian armies). Now, various models of the German Field Army since the founding of the Bundeswehr should be mentioned: Army Structure 1 (1956–58), with a battle group structure (armored and infantry divisions); Army Structure 2 (1958–70), with the introduction of the brigade organization and a corresponding "devaluation" of the division (armored and mechanized infantry divisions); Army Structure 3 (1970–78), with partial transformation of mechanized infantry divisions into motorized rifle divisions (Jägerdivisionen); Army Structure 4 (1979–90), with an increase in the number of formations (five instead of four battalions) but unchanged total personnel strength (increasing span of control, decreasing battalion strength); and finally Army Structure 5 (beginning 1992), during which one-half of each tank and mechanized infantry battalion will be skeletonized.

Several theoretical concepts that have originated in the past years are likely to be discussed in the near future in view of an optimal span of control. In 1976 Jochen Löser recommended the elimination of the 12 Bundeswehr divisions and an increase of general commands (six instead of three) in order to achieve improved cooperation between the field army and territorial army. Three years later, Johannes Gerber questioned the necessity of one of the major formations (brigade, division, corps), this having been provoked not least by the very different span of control of the three German corps.

Earlier, J. Z. Duncker recommended the retention of only the battalion and army corps as separate units and, in addition, the formation of "ad hoc battle groups" commensurate with the situation. The American division is oriented toward this principle: the brigade is viewed only as a command and control instrument with ad hoc assignments of units.

Special Formation Structures

When forming units, three problems arise: the question of the largest "pure" formation, the smallest "mixed" formation, and the type of mixed formation to be created.

A "pure" unit is one consisting of soldiers from the same branch (e.g., infantry, artillery, or signal), irrespective of any specialists assigned from other branches, who in turn form an element within that unit. Pure units up to and including the regiment are not disputed; yet this does not rule out adding troops of one branch to a mixed formation (e.g., engineer company or signal platoon in an armored brigade). Only the artillery branch departs from this principle: the corps or army artillery is regularly of brigade size, and the former Warsaw Pact's army groups ("fronts") had at their disposal one artillery division (earlier, even one artillery corps) as a pure major formation.

The criterion for mixed formations is their viability, which finds its expression in combined-arms combat. Until the end of World War II, the smallest autonomous formation on the continent was the division (from this the term *divisionalization* was derived, which is used in organizational theory). Temporarily, the attempt was made to overcome the division's unwieldiness by relying more on improvisation than on planning. In NATO and in various neutral nations, the old Austrian and British brigade solution has prevailed, although differences in weaponry still exist.

The regiments of the Warsaw Pact armies were also mixed to some extent, but their composition and numbers of regimental troops made their independence doubtful. In the former Soviet Union's ground forces, the basic maneuvering unit was the army.

The motorized infantry division and armored division have evolved from the two classical division types—the infantry and the cavalry division. In addition, there is the mechanized infantry division and the airborne division. The various types of divisions differ primarily in the number of organic armored units (the armored division has two armored brigades and one mechanized infantry brigade, and the mechanized infantry division has one armored brigade and two mechanized infantry brigades). Personnel strength of divisions is about the same nationally. Internationally, there are differences between NATO and the former Warsaw Pact: the strength of a Warsaw Pact division was about three-quarters that of a NATO division because of differences in the number of organic logistic troops.

There are continual and ongoing discussions on two proposals: first, the demand for creating a "uniform division," and second, the concept of the ad hoc battle groups mentioned earlier.

OSWALD HAHN

SEE ALSO: Command, Control, Communications, and Intelligence; Echelon; Formation; Theater of War.

Bibliography

Gerber, J., and O. Hahn. 1980, 1983. *Betriebswirtschaftslehre und Streitkräfte*. 2 vols. Regensburg: Walhalla und Praetoria Verlag.

Gollwitzer, M. 1992. Die Hierarchie im Heer aus betriebswirtschaftlicher Sicht. Diss., Nürnberg.

Hahn, O. 1986. *Betriebsgrösse von Truppenteilen, Handbuch zur Ökonomie der Verteidigungspolitik*. Regensburg: Walhalla und Praetoria.

Hamilton, I. 1921. *The soul and body of an army.* London: Edward Arnold.
Müller, W. 1980. Leitungsspanne. In *Handwörterbuch der Organisation.* Stuttgart: Poeschel.

SPECIAL OPERATIONS

Special operations are military and paramilitary activities that usually involve relatively small units or teams of carefully selected and highly trained individuals. These units often use unorthodox tactics and equipment against targets that lie outside the parameters that usually govern the uses of conventional military forces. Special operations normally take place in hostile, denied, or politically sensitive areas that are beyond the operational capability of tactical weapons systems and conventional maneuver forces.

Special operations, normally classified as "high risk" unconventional military actions, are designed to confuse and damage the morale of the enemy. Because of the variables and uncertainties that are characteristic of special operations, their successful accomplishment should be looked upon as a bonus rather than as a requirement for the accomplishment of a major tactical or strategic plan. If they do succeed, such a bonus may be very substantial.

Special operations forces may be especially suited for seizure and temporary defense of key terrain features as part of an overall tactical scheme in which other forces will subsequently play the principal role. Because situations in which special operations might be considered appropriate may occur with little or no warning, training lead time may be short and certain essential elements of intelligence may be marginal or entirely lacking. To maximize resources, imaginative and innovative schemes aimed at disguising the identity, destination, and intentions of a special operations force are essential to the success of any time-sensitive mission. These schemes may include communications deception, feints toward nonexistent targets, and psychological measures to increase the impact of the outcome.

Command and Control

Special operations' missions are pursuant to the orders of the highest authority in government. Yet the dynamics of a situation that requires a special operations mission may change while the forces are en route. Therefore, once the operation has been set in motion, the authority that launched it should allow the commander of the forces involved to exercise his initiative and judgment. Rapidly changing and unforeseen events en route or at the site of the action may necessitate a course of action different from that specified in the approved plan.

Legal and Political Considerations

The approved plan for a special operations mission will always be extremely sensitive to legal, political, and logistic constraints. A change in these factors during deployment may be sufficient cause to abort the mission. For example, the clandestine and covert aspects of special operations may elicit substantial opposition from influential elements of free and open societies. Arguments to justify these actions may consume vital time, serving to compromise the overall security of the operation.

As soon as a special operation is under way, diplomatic posts in areas that are likely to be affected politically, militarily, psychologically, or otherwise should be prepared to respond to questions by the indigenous governments.

In view of the significant possibilities of failure, special operations must involve imaginative and sophisticated plans for "damage control." This is particularly important where both domestic and foreign political repercussions could constitute an impediment to the conduct of both military and diplomatic affairs.

Special operations' targets that have been deemed, at a very high governmental level, important enough to risk reputations, careers, and even the personal liberties of those involved in the major decisions have sometimes been launched without regard to the normal processes that might have given them legitimacy. Failure in such cases can bring consequences that reach far beyond the environment of the missed targets themselves.

Security—Logistics and Rehearsals

The logistical preparation for certain types of special operations may involve the acquisition of items not considered standard in the armed services or the regular security forces of a nation. The search for and procurement of these items for the use of special operations forces must be guided by strict adherence to counterintelligence plans that are designed to prevent knowledge or even speculation concerning their contemplated end use.

As surprise is a major consideration in the planning for special operations, rehearsals and briefings on specific locations, personalities, and tactical objectives vital to the accomplishment of the mission must be carried out with extraordinary attention given to counterintelligence. Precautions must be taken to ensure that all aspects of mission planning are protected from possible hostile intelligence collecting efforts or inadvertent disclosure on the part of the mission planners.

Wartime Operations

In wartime, special operations may be mounted against enemy rear areas for the purpose of taking prisoners, sabotage, or the collection of intelligence. One such mission may be the locating of and directing fire against concealed enemy targets both for direct action by special operations forces or in conjunction with indigenous guerrilla bands and their clandestine support mechanisms.

Interesting examples of various types of special operations undertaken in time of war abound. Among them are:

• the capture by German airborne troops of Fort Eben Emael at the junction of the Meuse River and the Albert Canal on the Belgian frontier on 10 May 1940;

- the rescue of Benito Mussolini by German airborne troops under Capt. Otto Skorzeny from Hotel Campo Imperatore at an altitude of about 1,770 meters (5,900 ft.) in the Apennine Mountains of Italy (12 September 1943);
- "Colossus," a sabotage mission carried out by British airborne troops against an aqueduct near Solverino in southern Italy on 10–11 February 1941;
- "Biting," a technical intelligence operation conducted by British airborne troops against a German radar installation at Bruneval near Le Havre, France, 27–28 February 1942;
- the 18 April 1942 surprise attack against targets in Japan by B-25 bombers of the United States Army Air Corps launched from the aircraft carrier *Hornet* and commanded by Lt. Col. James R. Doolittle;
- the airborne phase of Operation Torch, which called for the sabotage of Vichy French aircraft at La Senia and Tafaroui airdromes in Algeria by U.S. parachute troops flying in an unescorted formation from Land's End, England, on 6–7 November 1942; and
- Operation Kingpin, carried out by U.S. Special Forces on 21 November 1970 for the purpose of rescuing U.S. prisoners of war from Son Tay prison compound about 37 kilometers (23 mi.) from Hanoi, North Vietnam. Although the planning and execution of the operation were highly professional, failure of the mission was the result of inadequate intelligence. The rescue force reached its target only to find that the Americans had been moved to another location. The rescue force returned without loss of any of its own personnel.

Peacetime Operations

Special operations may be undertaken in peacetime to counter terrorism, to release hostages held by representatives of foreign factions or powers, to eliminate installations or activities seen to constitute major security threats, to effect reprisals for assaults against persons or interests of a sovereign state, or for psychological reasons.

In peacetime, special operations may involve use of aerial routes that are monitored and controlled by foreign governments. Therefore, among close allies, diplomatic rapport and agreements that would facilitate departure from normal regulatory rules may be sought.

One of the most successful peacetime special operations was that conducted by Israeli commandos to rescue hostages taken by Palestinian terrorists who had hijacked Air France Flight 139 on 27 June 1976 while en route from Tel Aviv to Paris. The aircraft and hostages were diverted to Entebbe, Uganda, where, on 4 July, shortly after midnight, an Israeli force under Lt. Col. Yonni Netanyahu, in an action that took only 53 minutes, rescued all of the hostages except three who were killed in the course of the action. Lieutenant Colonel Netanyahu was also killed.

"Eagle Claw," a hostage rescue mission conceived at the highest levels of the U.S. government and launched into Iran on 24–25 April 1980, failed because of a number of identifiable deficiencies that should be of great interest to serious students of special operations. As a result of the failure of "Eagle Claw," the

U.S. Congress insisted that the U.S. military establishment form a unified command under which all special operations forces would be gathered so as to ensure coordinated action in the conduct of future special operations.

Personnel Considerations

In both war and peace, the physical and psychological pressures to which special operations personnel are subjected can result in "burnout" on the part of individuals who remain too actively involved over protracted periods of time. If it becomes necessary to relieve and reassign such individuals it must be done without compromising information concerning targets, methods, problems, and capabilities.

Rewards and incentives for special operations personnel should be governed both by the requirement for security and by the often unorthodox values of the types of people who are attracted by such high-risk missions. Unfortunately, fame and recognition—normal rewards—may bring reprisals from those at home and abroad.

WILLIAM P. YARBOROUGH

SEE ALSO: Low-intensity Conflict: The Military Dimension; Special Operations Forces; Unconventional War.

Bibliography

Barnett, F. R., B. H. Tovar, and R. H. Shultz, eds. 1984. *Special operations in U.S. strategy.* Washington, D.C.: National Strategy Information Center.

Charters, D., and M. Tugwell, eds. 1989. *Armies in low-intensity conflict: A comparative analysis.* London: Brassey's.

Collins, J. M. 1987. *Green Berets, SEALs, and Spetsnaz: U.S. and Soviet special operations.* Washington, D.C.: Pergamon-Brassey's.

Geraghty, T. 1980. *Who dares wins: The story of the special air service, 1950–1980.* London: Arms and Armour Press.

Paddock, A. H., Jr. 1982. *U.S. Army special warfare—Its origins.* Washington, D.C.: National Defense Univ. Press.

Whittier, H. S. 1979. Soviet special operations/partisan warfare: Implications for today. *Military Review* 59(1):55–57.

SPECIAL (OPERATIONS) FORCES

Special operations forces (SOF) conduct special military operations within the context of waging unconventional warfare (UW). For the most part SOF receive basic military training and are constituted as regular military troops; after this they are organized, trained, and equipped for operations peculiar to UW. SOF are different from paramilitary forces, which SOF often operate with and in support of. Paramilitary forces are not regular military forces—this distinction is an important one.

Quick's *Dictionary of Weapons and Military Terms* defines SOF as "military personnel with cross-training in basic and specialized military skills, organized into small . . . detachments with the mission to train, organize, supply, direct, and control indigenous forces in guerrilla warfare and counterinsurgency operations and to conduct unconventional warfare operations."

While there is no single, internationally accepted definition of SOF, Quick's definition is consistent with most official sources. Even so, useful working definitions of SOF and special operations vary both among experts and generalists.

In the 1980s the Soviet view of U.S. Special Operations Forces was that the latter were increasing in size and scope of responsibility in furtherance of U.S. secret operations and "neoglobalism" (Yashin 1986). The Soviet armed forces called their SOF *spetsialnoye nazhacheniye* (abbreviated as *spetsnaz*), meaning special-purpose troops or troops of special designation. In the United States the Joint Chiefs of Staff (JCS) define SOF as those forces whose special training and resourcefulness for UW, counterterrorism, collective security, and psychological and civil actions operations allow versatility in supporting either conventional military operations or in conducting independent operations in cases where the use of conventional forces may be impractical or impolitic.

This latter situation, calling for political judgment, plays a key role in the policy, planning, financing, and employment practices governing SOF—the more so in peacetime than during open and obvious warfare. Fielding and employment of SOF are most appropriate along the edges or margins of armed conflict when a nation desires to refrain from compromising or openly displaying its national honor and prestige. SOFs, therefore, are seen as having a political usefulness apart from that of regular conventional military forces whose physical presence is obvious. Because SOF are purposely organized and trained to operate secretly (clandestinely and covertly) and not to attract notice, SOF are the force of choice in situations where risk of involvement (in particular, increasing involvement) and public attention are to be avoided. For example, as international affairs have become highly transparent, small commando contingents are much less visible than capital warships, brigades of regular soldiers, and equipment or wings of aircraft.

Special operations forces are among those often referred to as elite forces, which include airborne, certain marine, and commando forces. Elite forces usually are held out as contingency units under direct control of high commands at theater and national levels. The term *elite*, in this context, connotes unusual qualifications involving selection and assignment criteria based on a soldier's exceptional physical and mental abilities and potentials. Both in training and when committed into action, demands placed on SOF are such that only the most highly qualified personnel can be expected to be successful. Great physical stamina and agility combined with—and perhaps even more important—intellectual and intuitive skills, buttressed by self-discipline, willpower, and goal orientation, are often required by special military operations.

SOF personnel tend to opt early for career status in the armed forces and are recruited from among those seeking action without regard for the overt conditions of war or peace. Nevertheless, SOF eschew bravado and derring-do, instead emphasizing survival, the minimizing of casualties, and recommitment.

SOF attempt to avoid and sometimes disdain assignments to missions more effectively performed by regular, line military units. SOF are lightly armed and equipped, unmechanized, and organized in small operating teams roughly of squad or platoon size. Adding several such SOF units together to obtain a numerically larger unit in no way creates a force with the maneuver and firepower of larger line units such as battalions or brigades. To employ SOF in tasks other than those for which they are intended by training and organization risks their survival and may result in their being unavailable or understrength for their intended special operations.

Missions

SOF are fighting combat forces rather than combat support or service troops. Except when taking on a defensive posture during retrograde or when in a temporary protective posture, SOF maneuvers are offensive operations. The modus operandi of SOF is not to stand and fight but to hit and run. Not constituted to advance or withdraw in strength, SOF are created especially for commando operations and for other special operations such as counteracting insurgents, terrorists, and command, staff, and communications elements.

In the latter role, SOF in the 1970s and 1980s have been employed in what came to be called C^3 countermeasures (C^3CM) operations (C^3 means command, control, and communications). While the former Soviet Union may have "invented" C^3CM in its present form in the mid-1960s, and while Western writers on Soviet special operations emphasized the C^3CM mission of Soviet SOF, Soviet sources maintained the C^3CM mission only in historical terms, principally referring to World War II.

Though SOF train on native or friendly territory and could operate there as well in time of war, it is almost universally characteristic of SOF that they conduct conflict or combat operations on foreign territory and in foreign air- and sea space. This is almost always enemy territory or enemy-held territory, often rear areas. In so operating, intelligence collection and reconnaissance (i.e., finding, identifying, and describing targets for subsequent attack) are primary SOF missions. By operating unobtrusively in small groups, SOF are able to reconnoiter potential targets in a proximate, immediately observable way that is not within the capabilities of other reconnaissance means. Because any reconnaissance operation is a strong indicator of intention to attack, it is imperative that reconnaissance be as covert as possible—a technique in which SOF excel. A leading former Soviet source (Suvorov 1987) stated that reconnaissance was *the* primary mission of Soviet SOF. Indeed Soviet SOF was the only SOF organized directly subordinate to military intelligence authorities at operational, theater, and national levels. Even when involved in other missions, it is incumbent on SOF to collect and report time-sensitive intelligence information.

During the 1980s Western media reports suggested that Soviet SOF conducted peacetime training and intelligence collection operations in the territories of their potential wartime enemies, including U.S. territory in Alaska and at the U.S. Pacific Missile Test Range at Kwajalein Atoll. Artifacts of this Soviet activity, such as uniform items and even liquor containers, were cited as evidence of this Soviet clandestine action. While such peacetime SOF operations may be alarming, it is uncharacteristic of disciplined SOF, rigorously conditioned for survival and evasion, to leave behind recognizable traces of their presence.

In the 1980s some North Atlantic Treaty Organization (NATO) and other nations took quite seriously the threat of Warsaw Pact SOF operating on NATO national territories in time of war. The United States, United Kingdom, and other NATO countries conducted training exercises to improve their defenses against the former potential Warsaw Pact special operations. The United Kingdom was especially sensitive to such a threat, and it conducted a large, territorial army exercise called Brave Defender amid media reports that Soviet military intelligence, which tasked and controled *spetsnaz* units, had penetrated British protest groups. Given the several potential SOF targets in NATO territories and the fact that *spetsnaz* units operated extensively in Afghanistan throughout the Soviet-Afghan War, 1979–89 (a war chiefly characterized by insurgency), NATO's concern about defenses against SOF in a European war seemed well founded.

During World War II in Europe and in East and South Asia, SOF expanded significantly and developed extensively under such agencies as the American Office of Strategic Services (OSS) and the British Special Operations Executive (SOE). The Soviet Union made wide use of SOF both in Europe and in the Far East.

As a basis in history and in practice continuing to the present day, the primary mission of SOF is to cultivate, aid, and guide resistance, guerrilla, and insurgent groups of paramilitary forces. Small SOF teams of between three or four and a dozen troops are "inserted" into enemy or enemy-held territory by such means as parachuting, swimming, naval submarine transport, aircraft, motor vehicle, or on foot—sometimes over long distances—where these teams join with partisan groups to conduct armed sabotage, harassment, and psychological operations. *Resistance*, by Professor M. R. D. Foot, is a foremost history of such SOF operations in Europe during World War II. American special operations also were conducted in the China-Burma-India theater in World War II (Peers and Brelis 1963).

Out of this experience in what one author calls "war in the shadows" (Asprey 1975) grew an SOF capability not only to support resistance groups in dangerous, active ways but also the mission of countering resistant and insurgent operations. In American SOF this latter mission as a capability developed extensively and intensively during the Second Indochina (Vietnam) War (1964–75), a war in which American involvement began and expanded on the basis of SOF counterinsurgency and civil actions operations. During the First Indochina War (1949–54) the French did not use SOF until late in 1951, and then employed a large composite commando group of about 400 men who were not intended to be exfiltrated but who were instead left in place as guerrillas except for casualties (Fall 1964).

British SOF experience in counterinsurgency also became highly developed during the period after World War II by means of special operations conducted in Malaya, Borneo, the Arabian Peninsula, and indigenously in Northern Ireland (Geraghty 1980).

There are notable instances of SOF resistance and counterresistance operations in conflicts before World War II. Indeed, U.S. SOF can trace its origins to the American Revolutionary War. One of the most continually intriguing SOF operations concerns the raising and support of Arab resistance against Turkish occupiers during World War I, out of which grew the legendary exploits of Lawrence of Arabia, a British Near Eastern scholar and intelligence officer attached to Great Britain's Cairo-based Arab Bureau, which was a forward intelligence organization. In 1916, Thomas Edward Lawrence penetrated into western Arabia by crossing the Red Sea; there he organized and led armed Arab resistance that created considerable havoc along Turkish railroads and in their encampments. In its time, Lawrence's operation was a minuscule sideshow of the Great War and little reported, but afterward Lieutenant Colonel Lawrence wrote nearly a million words about his adventures, thus ensuring his place in a history much larger than that of SOF itself. Compelled to secrecy in their times and places, special operations become known only by historical and personal accounts produced 10 to 20 years after the operations were conducted.

During the 1970s and 1980s it became fashionable in NATO countries to add counterterrorism to the missions of SOF. Considerable enthusiasm, manifested by increased funding, equipping, and training, was shown for this new mission amid a measurably growing threat of terror as a political instrument. Nevertheless, misgivings arose concerning the assigning of counterterrorism missions to military SOF because terrorism, which has quasi-military characteristics, is essentially a criminal activity thought to be more appropriately assigned to police and investigation agencies, leaving SOF to concentrate on military operations that have a basis in law and morality different from that of crime. Still, the prospect that terrorists might come into possession of nuclear or chemical weapons lent credence to the employment of special military forces to combat terrorists in extreme cases. It can be seen, though, that counterterrorism as an SOF mission emphasizes the absence of clear and compelling definitional boundaries and less than sharply outlined concepts of operations that continue to characterize special military operations and SOF organizations.

At the present time the missions of the SOF of most countries include one or more of the following: inducement and support of resistance in conflict situations (some of which are not wars in the usual or traditional sense), intelligence collection and reconnaissance, certain rescue operations (principally amid conflict), certain C^3CM operations, so-called civil actions, and counterinsurgency, counterrevolutions, and counterterrorism.

Organization, Skills, Tactics

Though targets of SOF operations may be tactical or strategic, all special operations themselves are tactical in nature as they are conducted by small military teams, detachments, or companies often operating at great distances from home bases. For administrative and some operational command and control purposes, SOF units are usually organized in battalions, regiments, brigades, or groups. While the USSR was the only country whose SOF were organized subordinate to an intelligence agency (in the sense of military organization per se), the United States is the only country with an entire armed forces service having an inherent and recognized special operations capability and mission: the U.S. Marine Corps, which began reemphasizing its special operations mission and capability in 1984–85. This service mission is traced back in time to the early history of the United States and was documented in a 1940 U.S. Marine Corps field manual entitled *Small War Manual*, which contains a "special operations" section.

Special operations units are found in reserve and territorial formations of some countries. SOF are not limited to ground services. Air and naval services often contain SOF units; notable among the sea services are the U.S. Navy's SEALs (sea-air-land—see Fig. 1), the UK SBS (special boat squadron) of World War II, and the former Soviet naval *spetsnaz* brigades (said to be more active than the Soviet ground forces *spetsnaz* [Suvorov 1987]). In the early 1980s the U.S. Air Force established the 23d Air Force at Scott Air Force Base, Illinois, and later the First Special Operations Wing as its SOF organization.

Italy's SOF is the 9th Airborne Assault Battalion of the Folgore Airborne Brigade. Italy also mans a naval commando company, the Commando Raggruppamento Subacquei ed Incurosori. The United Kingdom maintains the Special Air Service (SAS) as its principal SOF; Australia also has an SAS regiment. Turkey has its Special Warfare Department whose NATO-unique mission is to organize and support native resistance groups inside Turkey in the event of armed foreign occupation. A commando brigade is the offensive SOF unit in Turkey's armed forces.

Some armed forces in Latin America contain SOF units, usually regular line units with additional special operations training and missions. Examples are the PRAL of El Salvador and Honduras's 2d Airborne Battalion and its counterterrorist Special Squadron.

France has no clearly identifiable SOF. It probably employs elements of the 9e Division d'Infanterie de Marine (Saint-Malo) or the 11e Division Parachutiste (Corsica) for special operations. From late 1951 to 1953 in the First Indochina War, the French SOF were the composite airborne commando group known as the GCMA (Groupement de Commandos Mixtes Aéroportés), later changed to GMI (Groupement Mixte d'Intervention), which in December 1953 took control of all·operations behind enemy lines whether or not airborne.

Canada's Special Service Force brigade is its SOF. Greece, Portugal, and Belgium operate paracommando brigades, regiments, or battalions. In 1987–88 former British SAS commandos under Col. Kenneth White were reported to be training Sri Lanka's Special Task Force in counterinsurgency and counterterrorist operations. Neutral countries usually do not have SOF in their military orders of battle. An exception is the Austrian GEK (Gendarmerieeinsatzkommando), which consists of three-man teams.

In April 1987 the United States established a unified joint command for an

*Figure 1. French commandos and U.S. Navy SEALs train to-
gether on a "spy-rigging" exercise.* (SOURCE: U.S. Department
of Defense)

all-service SOF called the U.S. Special Operations Command (USSOCOM)
under army general James J. Lindsay. In May 1990, General Lindsay retired
from active duty and was relieved by Gen. Carl Stiner. The bulk of USSOCOM
forces consist of eight U.S. Army regular and reserve special operations groups
and three Ranger battalions. The U.S. Navy's Special Warfare Groups were not

transferred to USSOCOM, and U.S. Marine special operations capabilities are not to be employed unless U.S. Army SOF are unavailable. In lieu of this, the U.S. Navy created, in April 1987, its own Naval Special Warfare Command with the purpose of coordinating with USSOCOM. At that time special operations were added as a new classification of basic army career skills—the fifteenth—to army personnel accounts.

Ability in foreign languages has always been essential to successful special operations. SOF personnel must also be expert in operating and maintaining their specialized, man-portable equipment and weapons. Parachuting, swimming, survival, emergency medical treatment, survival abilities, and the expert use of explosives are skills that must be mastered by SOF personnel. These personnel also must be proficient in training foreign military and paramilitary personnel and in promoting guerrilla campaigns in the midst of enemy forces.

The nature of traditional and abiding SOF tactics can be best represented by the coined term *anti-infrastructure* to denote generally SOF tactics in the offensive. SOF targets and those of the resistance groups that SOF support consist of enemy lines of communications enemy command and control facilities and posts, and enemy energy and power sources and transmission paths. Sabotage and subversion of all kinds against bridges, power plants, headquarters, supply and weapons storage sites and depots, food and water sources, and fabrication facilities are preferred tactics. "Train killing" is a favored SOF tactic. In World War II the OSS used inter alia a coal look-alike plastic explosive to disable locomotives—a much easier method than blowing up bridges and rail lines.

An excellent, firsthand account of SOF tactics is Seitz's book on partisan operations in Yugoslavia during World War II. Col. Aaron Bank, an American SOF officer during World War II and afterward, sums up SOF tactics as consisting of "unconventional warfare behind enemy lines—ambushes, raids, [destruction] of lines of communications . . . sabotage, [gathering] intelligence, inducing subversion and generally harassing the enemy. . . ." Bank warns, "Don't slug it out with the enemy; hit and run" (Bank 1986, pp. 91, 27).

Equipment

Besides handheld weapons and explosives, SOF use and maintain a variety of specialized equipment. Remotely monitored sensing devices, paravanes (depth-controlled devices used by warships to cut moorings of floating mines), swimmer delivery vehicles, and small radios (briefcase size or smaller) that permit low-probability-of-intercept transmissions are among sophisticated contemporary SOF equipment.

Miniature SOF submarines accommodating two to six men and quiet rotary and fixed-wing aircraft (including new tilt-roter aircraft) are used to infiltrate, exfiltrate, and resupply SOF in the field. Various sea animals (dolphins, sea lions, seals, and whales) are trained to assist seaborne SOF in finding and delivering explosives, in recovering devices, and in working cables under water.

Future Prospects

The role, size, and sophistication of SOF worldwide are growing in the late twentieth century. Total manpower is larger than at any time since World War II. Unconventional warfare is a renewed subject of political and military analyses and of many conferences and publications coming to the fore during the last decade. In 1989, USSOCOM became the first unified U.S. military command to be granted its own budget rather than being financed by its component services.

In 1984 a U.S. deputy undersecretary of defense testified before a committee of the U.S. Congress that "special operations forces are today the most heavily used of our military forces" and that SOF are "carrying the burden of contemporary conflict . . ." (McCartney 1984).

Proxy wars, terrorism, low-intensity conflict, and insurgent movements are projected by informed studies to dominate the conflict spectrum over the next decade or longer. The superpowers and their allies are now in the process of reducing conventional armaments and further reductions in nuclear weapons are almost certainly in the offing as of this writing. In combination, these factors leave unconventional warfare and special operations forces with future roles more important than in the past. In the not-too-distant future it is likely that public and government attention will center more certainly, at least in some cases, on special military operations and their forces than on conventional and nuclear forces for attempting to stabilize or resolve intractable security problems without resources to ordinary warfare.

JAMES T. WESTWOOD

SEE ALSO: Airborne Land Forces; Low-intensity Conflict: The Military Dimension; Special Operations; Unconventional War.

Bibliography

Adams, J. 1988. *Secret armies: Inside the American, Soviet, and European Special Forces.* New York: Atlantic Monthly Press.
Asprey, R. 1975. *War in the shadows.* Garden City, N.Y.: Doubleday.
Bank, A. 1986. *From OSS to Green Berets.* New York: Pocket Books.
Barnett, F., et al., eds. 1984. *Special operations in U.S. strategy.* Washington, D.C.: National Defense Univ. Press.
Berkowitz, M. 1989. Moscow's secret spy subs. *Washington Post,* 15 January 1989, p. C5.
Collins, J. 1987. *Green Berets, SEALS, and Spetsnaz.* Washington, D.C.: Pergamon-Brassey's.
Eshel, D. 1984. *Elite fighting units.* New York: Arco.
Fall, B. 1964. *Street without joy.* Harrisburg, Pa.: Stackpole.
Foot, M. 1977. *Resistance.* New York: McGraw-Hill.
Geraghty, A. 1980. *Inside the S.A.S.* New York: Ballantine Books.
Lawrence, T. 1927. *Revolt in the desert.* New York: Garden City.
McCartney, J. 1984. A revival of secret U.S. forces. *Philadelphia Inquirer,* 25 November, p. 1.
Paddock, A. 1982. *U.S. Army special warfare: Its origins.* Washington, D.C.: National Defense Univ. Press.

Peer, W., and D. Brelis. 1963. *Behind the Burma Road.* New York: Avon Books.

Quick, J. 1973. *Dictionary of weapons and military terms.* New York: McGraw-Hill.

Rosenthal, A. 1989. Tale of a Soviet cap and a missing recorder. *New York Times,* 12 January, p. 10.

Seitz, A. 1953. *Mikhailovic: Hoax or hero?* Columbus, Ohio: Leigh House.

Suvorov, V. 1987. *Spetsnaz: The inside story of the Soviet special forces.* New York: Norton.

Yashin, S. 1986. Uniting in a single fist. *Krasnaya Zvedya* (Red Star), 27 November, 2d ed., p. 3.

STAFF

The term *staff* describes a group of officers assigned to each headquarters within the military hierarchical structure that collectively assists the commander to discharge his vested responsibilities. Individually, staff officers, acting on behalf of their commander and according to their specified duties, help to plan, direct, control, coordinate, supervise, monitor, and evaluate operations during an emergency or in war; they also help to regulate peacetime training and domestic routine.

Every staff officer holds a particular post in the headquarters establishment (table of organization) in which he serves, and each post is categorized as a staff appointment. The designation of staff appointments may vary with the level of organization—defense ministry, higher military headquarters, field formation, or unit. Detailed designations may also vary among the armed services of the same nation and between the armed forces of different nationalities.

In general, however, staff structures incorporate the commander's personal staff; the general staff; specialist support staffs; a peacetime administrative staff; as well as allied or combined staffs and joint staffs.

It is usual for a military commander to have a small personal staff that principally consists of a military assistant and a military secretary. The military assistant deals with correspondence, organizes the program, and keeps the commander personally briefed. The military secretary processes personal-in-confidence reports on personnel and the wide range of private affairs relevant to military service that the commander must address. These two appointments may be filled by a warrant officer at brigade level, a captain at division, two majors at army corps, or two lieutenant colonels at army or army group levels.

In higher military headquarters and in larger formation headquarters, the commander may have a deputy and will invariably have a chief of staff; both of these subordinates may also have personal assistants. The rank of a deputy commander is normally one grade lower than that of the commander, and a chief of staff, two grades lower. Thus, if a division commander is a major general, his deputy is a brigadier general and his chief of staff, a colonel. Likewise, if the commander of an army corps is a lieutenant general, his deputy is a major general and his chief of staff is a brigadier general. In turn, the rank structure of the staff is determined by the rank of the chief of staff at each level.

For example, at army corps headquarters where the chief of staff is a brigadier general, the heads of staff branches may be colonels or lieutenant colonels.

A military commander's authority and responsibility determine the main structure, size, and composition of the staff. The commander may have an operational or a nonoperational role, or he may combine both. In every circumstance, however, he is likely to have a planning staff. An operational planning staff—known as the general staff in army organization—deals with the arrangements involved with its commander's exercise of command or control in an operational situation, whether the situation relates to war, peacekeeping operations, or some other military emergency. A nonoperational planning staff—sometimes known as the administrative staff—handles the commander's peacetime responsibilities, normally restricted to barracks living and domestic routine.

In land forces, branches of the general staff bear the prefix letter G and some armies use the prefix S to denote unit officers charged with staff duties. Staff branches in naval, air force, and joint headquarters have different prefixes: the letters N, A, and J, respectively. The following list outlines an example of army general staff organization:

G-1 Operational planning concerned with organization, manpower, and military administration; also general staff and headquarters coordination
G-2 Operational staff intelligence input to planning
G-3 Operational planning of combat and collective training, including an exercise planning staff
G-4 Operational logistic planning
G-5 Operational aspects of civil affairs and civil and military cooperation (CIMIC)

In addition, a commander takes operational advice from specialist support staffs: either functional staffs or individual specialist advisers. Again, their variety, size, and composition depend upon organizational level and operational tasks. A functional staff at division headquarters, for example, is likely to include a supporting commander and several specialist officers in such branches as artillery, aviation, combat engineers, communications, supply, and maintenance. Each combat support or combat service support staff plans and operates its own functional support within the formation; it also works closely with the general staff and other functional staffs to ensure that the commander receives comprehensive, timely, and pertinent operational advice and that the formation receives effective support. Functional staffs provide a similar service at nonoperational headquarters, where their work mainly concerns peacetime training and domestic routine. Individual specialist advisers also include a senior chaplain, lawyer, financier, operations analyst, computer expert, or public relations officer.

In certain operational circumstances, an army formation commander may have functional staffs or specialist advisers from the navy, air force, flanking forces, and host nation authorities. Operations may involve the provision of naval gunfire support or close air support, the move of units to or from a flanking formation, and the use of a variety of local resources and services. These supporting staffs are permanently or temporarily attached to particular formation headquarters, and thereby form an integral part of the staff, during peacetime exercises or wartime operations.

The personal and working relationship, at any force level, between the commander and his chief of staff must be soundly based upon mutual trust and confidence, although their personal qualities and characteristics may differ considerably. One is a leader and the other, an ever-present counselor, adviser, and coordinator. Their relationship should set an example for the whole staff of a headquarters to emulate. The continuity of such a relationship is also significant. A successful field commander in war may prefer to retain the same chief of staff from campaign to campaign—for example, the lasting relationship of Bernard Law Montgomery and Francis de Guingand during the Second World War. While a field commander frequently visits subordinates in battle, the chief of staff's place generally is at headquarters and his job is to "run the shop" on behalf of the commander, keeping the commander free of minutiae.

Whether the headquarters is in its peacetime barracks or in the field, whether it is mobile or static, whether it is small or large, the job of the chief of staff is to comprehensively direct, coordinate, supervise, monitor, and evaluate all staff work on behalf of his commander. It is the chief of staff who brings cohesion to the general staff, the separate functional staffs, and all specialist advisers. It is he who brings together all their efforts and keeps plans and orders updated. He relies on specialist support staffs to contribute information and advice to his initial planning framework. He guides the general staff to complete the draft plan for his finalization, prior to his presenting the plan for the commander's approval. The amount of personal intervention and overall control that a chief of staff has to apply to the staff *in toto* will depend as much on his personality and style as on the proficiency of the staff. Just as a good commander can extract near miracles from a mediocre force, so a good chief of staff can convert an average group of staff officers into a well-oiled military machine.

An operational commander may also have peacetime administrative responsibilities arranged on a geographic-garrison-barracks basis. His authority, as well as his responsibilities, in this regard may extend beyond his own operational formation to incorporate other units that are located in peacetime within his designated administrative area. This may apply to a nonoperational commander who has solely a peacetime administrative function. Whichever the case, an administrative staff deals at headquarters with such affairs as boards of inquiry, courts-martial, sports and welfare, accommodation and housing, family amenities, and the day-to-day domestic running of the headquarters. The deputy commander may take responsibility for these activities and then switch to his war role on peacetime training, formation exercises, and operations.

The staff of a headquarters as a whole receives clerical, communications, information, logistic, and administrative support services from its own resources. Together with guard and security elements, these forms of support services are militarily provided in operational headquarters. In nonoperational headquarters they may be largely civilianized.

Mention has been made so far of the staff in the context of a single service, army, setting. A combined staff comprises officers provided by two or more allied nations, and a joint staff consists of officers provided from more than one armed service (navy, army, air force) of the same nation. In either case, one officer is appointed to each post on the *integrated* staff establishment, irrespective of nationality or color of uniform. In practice, however, it is not always easy to achieve effective integration; this has proved to be so, for instance, in the larger North Atlantic Treaty Organization (NATO) headquarters. Particular nations or particular armed services may wish to widen their respective representation in certain staff departments because of their key or prestigious role, irrespective of the number of posts available or the quality of posts allocated to them. Effective multinational and joint service integration can, therefore, create difficulties especially when, in allied headquarters, many nationalities may compete. Some doubling up, however, improves general military training and language proficiency despite the extra costs involved.

Written and oral communications in a common working language using common staff procedures are essential to the efficiency and economy of international headquarters. Integration of organization and representation, language and procedures, and the methods by which multinational staffs function can cause problems. Firm leadership, sympathetic management, and wholehearted cooperation help to overcome the problems; this is likely to be a useful lesson for the future, which may well feature a wider variety of operations and the need for even more adaptable staff work.

J. H. SKINNER

SEE ALSO: Command; Command, Control, Communications, and Intelligence; Generalship; Joint Operations; Logistics: A General Survey; Officer; Span of Control: Military Organizations and Operations.

Bibliography

Halleck, H. W. [1846] 1971. *Elements of military art and science*. Reprint. Westport, Conn.: Greenwood Press.

Hittle, J. D. [1961] 1975. *The military staff, its history and development*. Reprint. Westport, Conn.: Greenwood Press.

U.S. Department of the Army, Headquarters. 1953. *Field manual 101-10: Staff officer's field manual: Organizational, technical, and logistical data*. Washington, D.C.: Government Printing Office.

———. 1977. *Field manual 100-5: Operations*. Washington, D.C.: Government Printing Office.

STRATEGY

Strategy generally denotes the design and implementation of a plan for the coordinated employment of resources with the aim of attaining assigned objectives. Strategy links the objectives with the means to achieve such objectives in peace and in war.

The word *strategy* is of Greek origin. It originally meant the art of military leadership, but later came to include statecraft, to the extent that it was military in nature. Karl von Clausewitz understood strategy to be the "use of engagements" in war. Traditionally, strategy has had something to do with the preparation for and execution of war. But with the increasing complexity of war materiel and of social life, it became necessary to include nonmilitary factors—such as political, economic, technological, social, psychological, and moral aspects—in the formulation and application of strategy. As a result, strategy is no longer merely a concept for warfare but an inherent element of statecraft—the idea of a grand strategy is foreseen.

British military writer Sir Basil Liddell Hart sought to get away from the traditional, narrowed focus of strategy on warfare, and in the 1950s, with the term *grand strategy*, he provided a broader, more comprehensive definition. In his view, it is the task of grand strategy to guide and coordinate all the resources of a nation or an alliance to achieve the war objective established by policy. To him, the policy for pursuing war differs from grand strategy only in that the policy establishes the war objectives while strategy points the way to achieving them.

A study of the writings of Clausewitz, Liddell Hart, André Beaufre, Henry Kissinger, Helmut Schmidt, and V. D. Sokolowski leads step-by-step to a broader understanding of strategy: strategy is, by these accounts, the "design" and the "guiding idea" for the attainment of political objectives. It is an instrument of policy, a method, and a means of action. For policy, it shows how political aims can be achieved. It directs political action toward the objective and promotes such action and makes it possible to seize the political initiative.

In modern times, the meaning of the term *strategy* has broadened and has led in part to a confusion of the term and to a loss of substance of its content. With increasing frequency, such terms as *economic strategy, sales strategy*, and *election strategy* are being used. Protecting oneself against illness may even be called good strategy. Investment consultants, insurance companies, industrial firms, and football coaches may be said to employ this or that strategy.

With societal development, the meaning of *strategy* has thus changed, particularly in Western civilization. Originally understood mainly in the sense of military strategy or national strategy, the term has found broad application in political, economic, and social spheres.

Use of the Term

Used alone, the term *strategy* has a general meaning: the design and implementation of a concept for the coordinated employment of resources to attain certain objectives. Only when modified by an adjective does the term assume a specific meaning. Some examples include:

- *Grand* strategy—designed to attain political objectives, including the assurance of external security and social development
- *Security policy* strategy—designed to attain security objectives
- *Foreign policy* strategy—designed to influence foreign states or international organizations in pursuit of foreign policy objectives
- *Economic* strategy—designed to attain economic objectives
- *Military* strategy—designed to attain, through the use of military assets, military and security objectives.

According to the *Dictionary of Military and Associated Terms* (U.S. Department of Defense 1987) strategy is "the art and science of developing and using political, economic, psychological, and military forces as necessary during peace and war, to afford the maximum support to policies, in order to increase the probabilities and favorable consequences of victory and to lessen the chances of defeat."

In this definition it becomes clear that strategy, which in the U.S. tradition has come to mean military strategy, has been broadened to mean a more comprehensive national strategy utilizing all the resources of the country in order to ensure security and protect national interests. In this sense, the official statement of the White House, *National Security Strategy of the United States* (Reagan 1988), reflects, in a broad approach, five key national interests that U.S. strategy seeks to ensure:

1. the survival of the United States as a free and independent nation, with its fundamental values intact and its institutions and people secure;
2. a healthy and growing U.S. economy to provide opportunity for individual prosperity and a resource base for national endeavors;
3. a stable and secure world, free of major threats to U.S. interests;
4. the growth of human freedom, democratic institutions, and free market economies throughout the world, linked by a fair and open international trading system; and
5. healthy and vigorous alliance relationships.

The primacy of policy determines the relationship between policy and strategy. Since policy assigns the various goals of a state, strategy as the method and means of achieving those goals remains subordinate.

The goals set by the highest political authorities of a country are reflected, in breadth and depth, in the development and application of a grand strategy. Typical examples of this kind of strategy are government declarations at the beginning of legislative periods, party platforms, and multiyear plans of socialist systems. A grand strategy supersedes individual specialized strategies. Just as individual goals in a certain policy area—for example, security policy—must accord with the overall interests of a country, the country's security policy strategy must be in agreement with its grand strategy.

Selected Strategic Thinkers

Karl von Clausewitz writes that strategy is the use of engagements for the object of the war, and he defines one political and two military levels of war. His famous conclusion about the political level states that "War is merely the continuation of policy by other means." In this way he puts the responsibility for war itself on the political plane; he defines it expressly as an instrument of policy, as an act of force "to compel our enemy to do our will"; hence, war becomes the "means" of the political level.

Clausewitz distinguishes between two military levels of war: strategic and tactical. "Tactics teaches the use of armed forces in the engagement; strategy, the use of engagements for the object of the war." The conduct of war is not a single act, but a "greater or lesser number of single acts, each complete in itself," which Clausewitz calls "engagements." These types of military action take place on the tactical level; fighting forces trained for combat are the "means" and victory is the desired "end." On the strategic level, the "end" of the tactical level (victories) becomes the "means." The "end" on the strategic level, Clausewitz believes, is concerned with the war itself, and, in a final stage, the "ends" may be those objectives that should lead directly to peace. In the sense of Clausewitz, peace is more likely to be an issue of the political level than of the strategic.

It is especially important to understand Clausewitz's idea about the relationship of the levels of war. Because in war one must see the overall picture and the connection of its parts, he concludes that every means "must influence even the ultimate purpose," which he considers to be "peace." He also claims that at every stage of this sequence of "means and ends" (see Table 1), a new judgment related only to that specific level has to be made; the standpoint is different, however, because the "means" and "ends" are not the same. Thus, as one victory on the tactical level does not ensure peace, the strategic level must not use the forces themselves but engagements in the conduct of the war. As shown in Table 1, Clausewitz does not apply "victory in war" as the "end" on the strategic level. In fact, he expressly denies that victory is the "end" on this level. He believes, instead, that strategic success is a series of victories on the tactical level and finally the whole exploitation of the military operations on the political level.

An analysis of Clausewitz's *On War* (1984) reveals several statements that show the difficulties in limiting issues to the strategic or tactical level. For example, Clausewitz

TABLE 1. *Interpretation of the "Means-End" Relationship in* On War

LEVEL	MEANS	END
Tactical	Forces	Victory in engagement
Strategic	Victories in engagements	Conduct of war
Political	War	Impose our will on the enemy; peace

- considers individual acts that can belong to both strategy and tactics because of space and time,
- expresses the difficulty of determining whether a corps in the reserve is a force on the strategic or the tactical level,
- cannot precisely delineate if the preparation and provision of quarters are a matter of strategy or of tactics,
- introduces the term *campaign* on the strategic level because he needs a military operation between "engagement" and "war" since the distance in time, space, and force is too great between the two.

One can justifiably argue that Clausewitz sometimes reached the conclusion that there should be a third military level between strategy and tactics, but he did not define a new one expressly below strategy. Therefore, with Clausewitz, strategy remains connected upward with policy and downward with tactics.

Basil H. Liddell Hart defines strategy as the art of allocating and employing military means in such a way that the ends of policy are achieved. He distinguishes strategy from grand strategy, which he understands to be a kind of policy of execution. He thus assigns the term *grand strategy* to the political aim and the terms *pure strategy* or *military strategy*, generally called only strategy by Liddell Hart, to the military aim.

From the study of history, Liddell Hart develops an edifice of strategic thought. He considers war not only in its military form but also under foreign policy and economic aspects, as well as with a view to its psychological effects. He thus opens the way for a comprehensive political view of war that at the beginning of the century, and especially during World War I, had fallen into oblivion. Liddell Hart distinguishes clearly between policy and strategy: policy determines the goal of acting and thus the purpose of strategy. The political goal is not only related to the war but also to the protection of the interests of a nation. According to Liddell Hart, nations do not conduct war for the sake of war but as a continuation of policy. The goals of war must therefore be so defined as to make possible a better state of peace than existed before the war. (Of course, goals may change during the course of a protracted war.) *Grand strategy* is practically synonymous with the policy determining the conduct of the war and differs from policy merely in that the latter sets the goal.

The purpose of strategy in the narrower sense is to deprive the opponent of his freedom of action. This is achieved when the opponent is so physically and psychologically paralyzed that he desists from pursuing his intentions any further. This can be accomplished in one of two ways: either by a favorable strategic situation or through battle. While the former is achieved by deception, by a maneuver, or by the application of strong psychological pressure but without direct violent conflict (i.e., by an indirect approach), the latter is achieved by the destruction of the opponent's forces, with maneuver and surprise the chief elements of the strategy. For a strategy to be successful it is necessary, first and foremost, according to Liddell Hart, that the objective and the means be properly assessed and coordinated. But a strategy will accomplish its purpose only if the plan for how to proceed remains flexible enough to allow for suitable alternatives to one's actions in the event of unforeseen enemy behavior and other unexpected developments.

To apply grand strategy means to be concerned not only with winning military victory but also with the conditions for the ensuing peace. The essential aim is to guide and coordinate all the resources of a nation or an alliance so as to attain the war objective established by policy. From this are derived the individual tasks: the provision of manpower and material reserves for the armed forces, the strengthening of a nation's fighting spirit, the distribution of resources in the armed forces and in the rest of society, and the employment of military means, with its associated financial, economic, political, and psychological effort. Like strategy, grand strategy comprises all the leadership actions directed at accomplishing the political purpose of the war.

André Beaufre believes that strategy is the art of the dialectics of wills that use force to resolve their conflict. As he understands it, dialectics is an antagonism resulting from the contrast of two wills. The essence of this strategy is the struggle for the freedom of action of each of the opponents.

Beaufre believes strategy is more than traditional generalship. To him, it is a method of thinking that has a shaping function, one that realizes the generally applicable thoughts brought forth by philosophy. But strategy is equally a functional area that comprises all the efforts of warfare, or of applying the physical means of power, to attain political objectives. Strategy thus becomes a planning procedure, the outcome of which is a concept or a practical guideline.

Strategy, according to Beaufre, must not be rigid; rather, every specific situation calls for a specific strategy through which the situation can be ascertained and evaluated and a plan of action worked out. In this way, strategy allows us to control events instead of being swept along by them. By using the term *strategy*, Beaufre associates the employment of power to achieve political objectives.

Strategy means, first, a political analysis, the examination of the political situation and its general direction so that the political will can be determined and prepared for—strategy as the means to achieve the political objectives. Moreover, according to Beaufre, strategy lays down the methods, as circumscribed by policy, by which the political purpose is to be achieved. The possibilities are many; they are characterized by the attributes "deterrent" or "active," which are again broken down into "direct" and "indirect," "total" or "limited," and "offensive" or "defensive." Beaufre also calls this manner of procedure strategy and thus characterizes its main features.

Strategy employs the means available to it so that the goal is achieved. This goal consists of bringing about a decision by producing in the opponent such a strong moral effect that he accepts the conditions offered him. Strategy aims at physical and psychological capitulation. In this sense, it involves primarily violent means, so that strategy is the means for the application of a violent policy, with the means of strategy comprising a spectrum that may range from the use of nuclear weapons to propaganda to a trade agreement—that is, political, military, economic, and psychological means stand in the foreground. Proceeding from the total form of war, strategy, to Beaufre, is also total. Its task is to map out the conduct of total war.

The goals of strategy are determined by policy. Policy also determines the measure of the means necessary and the methods to be applied. Beaufre thus codifies the primacy of policy over strategy.

Henry H. Kissinger, former U.S. secretary of state, defines strategy as the manner in which a society secures its future.

Kissinger's understanding of strategy is based on the idea that policy is the art of leadership of a statesman in looking after the interests of a nation in its external relations, and that policy pursues the aim of ensuring the security of that nation in a system of balanced forces. To Kissinger, strategy is a long-term concept that becomes the maxim for action in foreign policy. Strategy has a nationally oriented trait and encompasses, as does policy to which it is subordinate, the entire spectrum of political, economic, and military aspects in the sense of *grand strategy*.

But Kissinger also uses the term in its narrower sense, as the use of military power. The task of this kind of strategy is to coordinate military means, including nuclear weapons, in space and time in such a way that a political objective can be achieved—in peace, the security and stability of forces; in limited war, the continuing deterrence of nuclear war and the local superiority of friendly forces to maintain equilibrium. Thus understood, Kissinger also views war in part as a means of settling political conflict. War must be prevented in its total form by a deterrent military system and by a clear, also in part deterrence-oriented, political concept. In this sense, strategy comprises that area of policy in which the military instrument is used to ensure a country's security.

Kissinger links policy and strategy by the demand that a strategic doctrine must translate power into policy. Military or other means of power are to be provided in order to gain, by their mere existence or by their employment, freedom of action for policy. Strategy is thus a component part of policy.

Policy and strategy must be linked by the identity of wills; a disparity in the goals of the two is dangerous. Recognizing that policy provides the model, strategy, as a concept, either in its general form related to overall policy or its special form related to military policy, provides the procedure for gaining political freedom of action. Kissinger expresses at the same time that structurally and functionally policy has primacy.

Kissinger favors political decisions that prove that democracy is capable of mustering the moral force for action. A prerequisite for this is a strategy that, consistent with political genius, ensures freedom of political action, and to that end it offers a concept for the employment of means and methods in time and space.

Helmut Schmidt, former chancellor of the Federal Republic of Germany, states that strategy is something on a higher level, something more than the employment of armed forces, and is therefore "not a matter for generals but for governments, though it can assign tasks to generals. Political, economic, social and other factors contribute to the range and objective of a country's strategy."

In today's world, however, he considers national strategies to be anachronistic. As a consequence of economic and security policy interdependencies, no nation is able by its national forces alone to ensure its political and economic objectives and external security. Schmidt calls for a harmonization of the economic and security policies of the Western states. He calls such a strategy that transcends national frameworks a *grand strategy*. It constitutes a uniform, harmonized concept for foreign policy, economic policy, and classical military strategy—all of which operate in the same framework. Strategy (in the sense of a grand strategy) and policy are thus equated. Should the West be able to agree on a grand strategy, the national economies of the countries would be stabilized, the threat of war reduced, and peace preserved. The development and implementation of a Western grand strategy calls for intense diplomatic work and is conditional on the purposeful will of leadership in the countries concerned. It still remains necessary, according to Schmidt, to contain the expansionist grand strategy of the Soviet Union, but the efforts for defense must not impair the economic vitality of the countries. The greatest chance for democratic and industrialized Western nations to maintain their position in the world is in the economic area. Economics is thus the center of gravity of a grand strategy of the West.

V. D. Sokolowski, marshal of the Soviet Union, in his work *Soviet Military Strategy* (1975), stresses that the Marxist-Leninist view of strategy—just like policy and tactics—must orient itself toward the ultimate goal of socialist ideology: the attainment of world communism through revolution. Only in this goal—in which policy, strategy, and tactics are combined—does strategy receive its reason and its task. According to Sokolowski, in the political sense strategy is the coordination of resources, time, space, and methods into a guideline that becomes the maxim for political action. In the military sense strategy is a system of scientific findings about the laws of war and the conduct of armed struggle on behalf of certain class interests. Political and military strategy comprise all the elements of an overall concept for the pursuit of world revolution. Strategy (in Lenin's view more long term than tactics) thus belongs in the realm of policy; it is permeated by policy at all levels of society and in all phases of its evolution and implementation. Strategic objectives must therefore derive from policy or have already been determined by it.

With regard to military strategy, Sokolowski offers the following definition:

> Military strategy is a system of scientific knowledge dealing with the laws of war as an armed conflict in the name of definite class interests. Strategy—on the basis of military experience, military and political conditions, economic and moral potential of the country, new means of combat, and the views and potential of the probable enemy—studies the conditions and the nature of future war, the methods for its preparation and conduct, the services of the armed forces and the foundations for their strategic utilization, as well as foundations for the material and technical support and leadership of the war and the armed forces. At the same time, this is the area of the practical activity of the higher military and political

leadership, of the supreme command, and of the higher headquarters, that pertains to the art of preparing a country and the armed forces for war and conducting the war.

Since the development of weapons technology has had a basic influence on the nature of war and military strategy, the character of military strategy has also changed, according to Sokolowski.

In modern warfare, he believes, military strategy will become a strategy of strikes conducted with missiles and nuclear weapons, in combination with operations by all the services, with the objective of simultaneously attacking and destroying the economic capability and the armed forces of the enemy in the entire depth of his territory so as to achieve the war objectives within a short period of time.

"Alternative" Strategies

One of the results of the continuing evolution of conventional and nuclear weapons has been that, in the strategic community and in the most diverse groups of the open Western societies, intensive discussions are taking place about the right way to prevent war and preserve peace with freedom. Generally termed *alternative* strategies, these are notions, proposals, and concepts that are not in consonance with the valid strategy of the North Atlantic Treaty Organization (NATO). The principal motive for the development of alternative strategies is criticism of the principle of deterrence and the role of nuclear weapons.

Nuclear-free, chemical-free, and tank-free zones in Europe on either side of the border between NATO and the Warsaw Pact were discussed along with proposals for a so-called defensive defense or a nonprovocative defense. A first high point in the European debate on alternative strategies was the hearing held by the German Bundestag in late 1983 and early 1984.

Essentially, what the proponents of alternative strategies are seeking to achieve is a radical restructuring of the armed forces to eliminate offensive capabilities at all echelons and to make clear to an opponent that he is not being threatened.

So far, alternative strategies have not been able to assert themselves because they emphasize war-fighting options at the expense of war prevention, reduce the risk to the potential aggressor, sometimes offer only a semblance of security without really increasing stability in the East-West relationship, and put the defender in a static, reactive position, burdening him with the problems of the war and leaving the initiative to the aggressor.

GERTMANN SUDE

SEE ALSO: Principles of War; Tactics.

Bibliography

Beaufre, A. 1963. *Introduction à la stratégie.* Paris: Librairie Armand Colin.
———. 1964. *Dissuasion et stratégie.* Paris: Librairie Armand Colin.

Biehle, A., ed. 1986. *Alternative Strategien (Das Hearing im Verteidigungsausschuss des Deutschen Bundestages)*. Koblenz: Bernard/Graefe Verlag.

Clausewitz, C. von. 1984. *On war*. Ed. and trans. M. Howard and P. Paret. Princeton, N.J.: Princeton Univ. Press.

Close, 1983. *Time for action*. Oxford and New York: Oxford Univ. Press.

Dunn, K. A., and W. Staudenmaier, eds. 1985. *Alternative military strategies for the West*. London: Westview.

Kissinger, H. A. 1961. *The necessity for choice: Projects of American foreign policy*. New York: Harper.

———. 1979. *White House years*. Boston: Little, Brown.

Liddell Hart, B. H. 1942. *The way to win wars. Strategy of indirect approach*. London: Faber and Faber.

Luttwak, E. N. 1987. *Strategy—The logic of war and peace*. Cambridge, Mass.: Harvard Univ. Press.

Paret, P. ed. 1986. *Makers of modern strategy from Machiavelli to the nuclear age*. Princeton, N.J.: Princeton Univ. Press.

Reagan, R. 1988. *National strategy of the United States*. Washington, D.C.: Pergamon-Brassey's.

Schmidt, H. 1986. *A grand strategy for the West*. New Haven, Conn.: Yale Univ. Press.

Sokolowski, V. D. 1975. *Soviet military strategy*. Ed. and trans. H. F. Scott. New York: Crane, Russak.

U.S. Department of Defense, Joint Chiefs of Staff. 1987. *Dictionary of military and associated terms*. Washington, D.C.: Government Printing Office.

Weigley, R. F. 1977. *The American way of war*. Bloomington: Indiana Univ. Press.

SURVEILLANCE AND TARGET ACQUISITION EQUIPMENT

According to the Department of Defense's *Dictionary of Military and Associated Terms* (1987, Washington, D.C.), surveillance and target acquisition equipment is used to systematically observe certain areas, places, people, or equipment and then to detect, identify, and locate a target in sufficient detail to permit the effective employment of weapons. The equipment and systems used for surveillance and acquisition may be optical, infrared, laser, radar, or acoustic in nature. They differ according to operating frequency or band, source of radiation (transmitter), sensor (detector), scanning system, and means of amplification. The various types of systems are discussed below.

Optical Systems

HUMAN EYE

The human eye is the basic optical surveillance device. It can distinguish between colors and tones (the optical frequency spectrum ranges from 0.4 to 0.7 micrometers [μm]), has a moderate field of view (approximately 30 degrees in elevation and 40 degrees in azimuth), and can detect movement by peripheral vision out to nearly 180 degrees in azimuth. The eye also has a dynamic response range of about 10:1, which is far greater than any other single light-sensitive device.

TELESCOPES AND BINOCULARS

The range of the human eye can be extended with the use of telescopes and binoculars. The former are divided mainly into those that use mirrors and those that use lenses; these are further broken down on the basis of their second elements, positive (converging) or negative (diverging) power. Binoculars consist of two object glasses, two prisms, two graticules, two field lenses, and two eye lenses. They are usually described in terms of two numbers: the first indicating the magnification and the second, the diameter of the objective glass (in millimeters). The ideal military binocular used today is 7 × 42.

Infrared Systems

In 1800, Sir William Herschel found that the temperature of sunlight, dispersed into colors by a glass prism and recorded by a thermometer, increased from violet to red and then continued to increase, reaching a maximum in the dark region beyond the red and the visible spectrum. Thus the infrared (IR) region of the electromagnetic spectrum was discovered. For more than a hundred years, little use was made of IR energy, largely because of the lack of a suitable detector. Early in World War II, however, captured equipment revealed that the Germans were using IR for secret signaling between infantry groups, for surveillance of Russian tanks in the darkness, and for detection of Allied night bombers that had been able to confuse radars by using chaff. This marked the turning point in the practical application of IR to military problems.

An IR system is composed of five basic units: the source of radiant energy, an optical system (with suitable IR components), a detector of IR radiation, the transmission medium, and finally the output unit through which the data are made available to the operator or observer. The source may be installed on the observing equipment (such as a tank in the case of an active system) or it may be the emissions of the target itself (the case with passive systems). The optical unit of a military IR system serves to collect the radiation and focus it on the sensitive area of the detector. Sometimes this system incorporates a scanning device, and sometimes the beam is chopped just in front of the detector in order to provide an alternating current signal.

IR detectors, a very important element of the system, are closely related to the region of the IR radiation. Those used in the near-IR region closely parallel those used for the visible portion of the spectrum, such as IR vidicons and photomultipliers. Photoconductors are efficient detectors for the intermediate region of the IR spectrum, while the far-IR region can be detected only with a device that absorbs the radiation and changes one or more of its physical properties as a result of the increase in temperature. A large portion of the technical progress in recent years has been due to developments in the field of detectors.

The transmission medium is the atmosphere itself. At low altitudes—10 kilometers (6.2 miles) and below—IR radiation may be absorbed by water vapor and carbon dioxide, which may limit the operation of the system. For very high altitude observations, the deleterious effects of atmospheric absorption need hardly be considered. The output unit may incorporate sophisticated signal processing techniques (such as those used in radar and sonar systems), or the signal may be presented for visual observation in real time on a cathode ray tube.

IR DETECTORS

The detector forms the principal element in any IR surveillance system; the rest of the equipment is built around it. There are two fundamental types of IR detectors: thermal and photo. The electrical properties of both types are changed as a result of incident radiation.

In general, thermal detectors absorb radiation rather uniformly over the spectrum. They are the only detectors that can operate without cooling to wavelengths as long as 14 micrometers. The photon absorption in thermal detectors causes a rise in temperature and subsequently a change in the electrical properties of the detector. Two of the most common thermal detectors are thermocouples (which develop thermal voltage) and bolometers (which change electrical resistance as a result of heating).

In photodetectors, the IR radiation that is absorbed excites electrons of the detector material to the conducting state. Semiconductors are contemporary IR detectors with a response beyond 1.5 micrometers. For visible and near IR, photoemissive tubes are ordinarily used. Photodetectors include photoconductive, photovoltaic, and photoelectromagnetic detectors. The operation of the image tube (the essential component of the sniperscope and the snooperscope used in World War II) is based on photoemission. The essential element is its IR-sensitive photocathode. Radiation on the photocathode causes electrons to be emitted from the other side into the vacuum within the tube and are then focused on the phosphor viewing screen.

IR SURVEILLANCE SYSTEMS

The primary function of an IR surveillance system is to search for and then indicate the presence and location of IR-radiant targets within a prescribed field of view. A passive search system consists—in its elementary form—of a telescope with instantaneous field-of-view or resolution elements (steradians) that scan the total search field (in steradians) in a specified time, the frame time. Whenever a radiating target appears in the field of view, the detector produces an electrical signal that allows an azimuth-elevation description of the target.

There are three basic types of scanning for a search system: the scanning spot, the multiple-scanning spot, and the mosaic. In the first type, the field is repeatedly scanned by successively observing single elements until the total field of observation has been covered. In the second, the multiple-scanning spot, the field is divided into sections and each section is scanned by a detector channel the same way it was done by the scanning spot device. The third system, the mosaic, involves subdividing the field into smaller regions, each of which is observed by a single stationary detector element. This detector unit takes the form of a two-dimensional matrix of elements. The maximum range at which an IR radiating target can be detected depends on how well it can be distinguished from the noise appearing with the signal.

THERMAL IMAGING SYSTEMS

Thermal imaging systems are now used in fighter aircraft and helicopters in an application known as FLIR (forward-looking infrared). They are also used by ground troops (in tanks and armored personnel carriers), in air defense, and aboard ships. The system detects the differences in levels of IR radiation radiated by all objects above absolute zero in temperature. The hotter the object, the more radiation. A body at 700 degrees Celsius peaks in radiation at 3 micrometers (in the near-IR range), while the human body at 20 degrees Celsius emits most strongly at around 10 micrometers. Most of this IR radiation is absorbed by the atmosphere, but there are two transmission windows in the 3- to 5-micrometer and 8- to 13-micrometer bands. Detectors working in the 3- to 5-micrometer band are more suitable for detection of hot bodies such as jet engines and vehicle exhausts, while relatively cold targets such as people and cold vehicles can be detected in the 8- to 13-micrometer band.

Cadmium mercury telluride (CMT) is the most useful material for high-resolution thermal imaging because it is sensitive to a broad band of IR wavelengths (from 2 to 14 micrometers) and can detect very small differences in temperature. Because CMT is so sensitive to IR, it must be cooled to 77° Kelvin to eliminate thermal noise (the background heat that would generate a current in the detector, swamping the picture of the scene). Cooling is achieved by liquified nitrogen or by the use of a mini-cooler.

The lenses that collect and focus radiation on the scanner are made of germanium because glass is a poor transmission medium for IR radiation in the useful band. The scanner is a rotating polygonal mirror that scans across the target and reflects the image of the target onto the detection array. The ideal detector would be one consisting of a mosaic of elements. Attaining a resolution of 0.5 milliradians and a field of view of 20 degrees would require about a half million detector elements (or picture points), each with its own preamplifier. A typical cooled CMT detector would include 150 elements, each 50-micrometers square.

During scanning, the signal from each element is preamplified, delayed, and added to the signal in the following element. When the last element is reached, all the signals are added together, further amplified, and visually displayed. Each line on the display is made up of several hundred scans of the detector. With this type of detector, the preamplification, delay, and summation circuits are external, so leads from each of the elements have to come out of the detector. This produces complex and bulky circuitry. The answer to this problem is the use of SPRITE.

SPRITE THERMAL IMAGERS

SPRITE (signal processing in the element) detectors are a new concept replacing the detecting array and its external processing circuitry. In place of the many separate elements or wafers of CMT (each with its own output wire, preamplifier, and delay unit), there is on each a single, much longer strip with a single output wire and preamplifier leading to the visual display.

The purpose of having many separate elements in each detector, with associated delaying and summing circuits, is to generate enough signal for a good picture from the tiny amounts of IR given off by small, cool, and distant targets. At the same time, the picture must be kept coherent and a high signal-to-noise ratio must be maintained. This is achieved in the SPRITE detector by passing a bias current along the length of the detector and matching the scanning speed of the flapping mirror precisely with the bias current speed. The bias current carries the charges generated by the incident IR radiation along with it, ensuring that the charges generated by the same part of the outside scene remain together and reach the output together. The summation, time delay, and all but one of the preamplifiers required by conventional detectors are thus eliminated, making the SPRITE-based thermal imager simpler, cheaper, and more robust than conventional imagers.

Laser Systems

The word *laser* is the acronym for light amplification by stimulated emission of radiation. In 1960, Maiman succeeded in operating a pulsed ruby laser. In 1961, Javan introduced the first continuous wave (CW) helium-neon gas laser. Contemporary lasers emit electromagnetic radiation in the ultraviolet, visible, and infrared regions of the spectrum. Laser radiation is characterized by its high degree of temporal and spatial coherence. Laser output can be produced as a continuous beam (CW mode), as a train of pulses (multiple-pulse mode), or as a single giant pulse (Q-switching mode). Lasers have many civil as well as military applications. Among the latter are the laser range finder; surveillance and target acquisition; and target illumination, designation, and tracking.

LASER OPERATION

A laser consists of an amplifying, active atomic medium (solid crystal, gas, or liquid) contained within a cavity resonator. The resonator maintains an electromagnetic field configuration whose losses are replenished by the amplifying medium. A source of spontaneous radiation is used to excite (pump) the laser. The optical cavity resonator consists of a cylindrical region containing the active medium and two opposing plane parallel or curved reflectors at right angles to the cylindrical axis. The oscillations consist essentially of a standing wave generated by a plane wave bouncing back and forth between the two reflectors.

Pumping, achieved by external excitation, provides the energy that is needed to raise atoms or molecules of the active material to a more excited state. Laser action is initiated by photons that are emitted spontaneously after pumping is begun. These photons interact with the excited atoms of the active material as they pass through the cavity, causing them to lose energy by stimulated emission. (The difference between spontaneous and stimulated emission is that the latter is radiated from excited atoms in the presence of external radiation of the same frequency.) Each emitted photon produces a wave that grows in amplitude on successive interactions with the atoms of the active material. This wave is reflected back and forth by the cavity mirrors, stimulating more atoms and thus producing more amplification. If the gain by stimulated emission exceeds the losses that occur (by scattering and absorption in the active material and mirror reflection losses, for example), the lasing process continues.

The active medium may be solid, gas, or liquid. A helium-neon gas laser emits CW laser radiation principally at 0.6328 micrometers in a power output range from 1 to 20 megawatts (mW). A carbon dioxide laser emits in the 9- to 11-micrometer range, with the strongest line at 10.6 micrometers. Peak output power on the order of 200 kilowatts over a pulse length of 60 nanoseconds has been achieved with a CO_2 pulsed laser. CW radiation in excess of 1 kilowatt may be obtained from such lasers. Some solid-state lasers use ruby crystals lasing at 0.694 micrometers or neodymium glass lasing at 1.06 micrometers. Semiconductor injection lasers (such as gallium arsenide) emit power of several megawatts in a wavelength band between 0.84 and 0.9 micrometers.

The beam width of a laser is measured in milliradians. The output of a pulsed laser consists of a series of spikes. In order to make this output suitable for military applications, the output pulse must be controlled by changing the quality of the optical resonator, using a technique known as Q-switching. Thus, a switch is used to degrade the resonator quality for the duration of the pumping pulse. Restoration of the Q to its original value results in a single output pulse with peak intensity several orders of magnitude larger than in normal operation. The switching action may be accomplished by means of a rotating mirror or prism, with an electro-optical switch (as in a Kerr cell or Pockels cell), or by photochemical (saturable dye) methods. In Q-switching, laser radiation is emitted during pulse times on the order of several nanoseconds. Pulse duration on the order of picoseconds is achieved through mode locking, a technique in which the transmission of the electro-optical switch is modulated and synchronized to correspond with the photon round-trip time in the cavity.

Laser Range Finders

The laser range finder is composed of a Q-switched laser, an optical system (made up of transmitting and receiving telescopes, a splitter, and filters), a detector, and electronic circuitry. The laser output is coupled to a small transmitting telescope that decreases the cavity output divergence, thus increasing the range. Part of the output is fed, through the splitter, to a photodiode for synchronization of the range counter. When the laser beam is reflected by the target, some of the reflected radiation is collected by the receiver telescope and focused on the detector. The filter reduces background noise. The electronic circuitry amplifies the detector output, calculates the range, and displays it. Medium ranges of 4 to 10 kilometers (2.4 to 6.2 mi.) are achieved by a solid-state Q-switched laser (ruby or neodymium glass). Ranges on the order of 20 kilometers (12.4 mi.) or more are achieved by carbon dioxide Q-switched lasers.

LASER RADAR SYSTEMS

Laser radar systems are known as LADAR, the acronym for laser detection and ranging. The system operates in a way similar to radar, with the exception that the transmitter is a laser instead of a microwave. The laser transmits a pulse, then waits a finite time for the return reflected from a target. The time of return determines the range. A scan mechanism also allows angular coordinates to be determined. Laser-beam scanning, which may be done mechanically or electronically, is not a simple task, as the beam is very narrow. Electronic scanning is achieved by changing the refractive index of the scanning medium. Examples of such laser-beam steering are the Kerr cell, the Pockels cell, and electroacoustic deflection techniques. When electromechanical means are used, the narrow beam electronically sweeps back and forth over the required area as the transmitter rotates. From a system standpoint, it seems likely that a combination of electromechanical and electronic scanning best solves the problem of laser-beam scanning.

LASER DESIGNATORS

The principle of target designation is that the target is illuminated by a laser beam, then a detector in the nose of a bomb or artillery shell (a so-called smart weapon) homes in on the radiation reflected from the target. The laser's narrow beam ensures high resolution and accuracy of target designation. The laser transmitter and the detector may be in two different places (bistatic operation) or in the same place (as in airborne equipment).

Radar Systems

Radar is the acronym for radio detecting and ranging. First deployed shortly before World War II, it operates by radiating electromagnetic energy in a very wide band of the radio frequency (RF) spectrum. The radar wavelength extends from millimeters to several meters. Radars are classified according to transmitter waveform as pulse radar, which transmits a train of pulses at a certain recurrent frequency; CW radar, which transmits continuous waves; and FM-CW radar, which transmits CW modulated linearly in frequency. Radar is a combination transmit-receive type of equipment and thus must include a transmitter, modulator, receiver, duplexer, antenna, synchronizer, and displays.

SURVEILLANCE RADARS

Surveillance radars radiate electromagnetic waves in the form of a fan beam, narrow in azimuth (a few degrees) and wide in elevation (more than 20 degrees). As the antenna rotates, the fan beam scans the hemisphere around the radar site. The beam width must be adequate to cover the necessary height. During antenna rotation, the target range and azimuth are measured, although it is not possible to measure the height with a fan beam. For this, a special height-finding radar must be used. The antenna beam of height-finding radar is narrow in elevation but considerably wider in azimuth. Some surveillance radars measure all three coordinates (range, azimuth, and height). These systems, known as three-dimensional radars, use either a frequency-scanned or a phased-array antenna.

TRACKING RADARS

Weapons systems require continuous and accurate measurement of target coordinates. This is achieved by a tracking radar that measures the coordinates and tracks the target automatically. The tracker receives the approximate location of the target from a surveillance radar. Through the use of three servo loops (one for range and two for angular coordinates), the tracker follows the target in the three coordinates and automatically makes error corrections. Certain surveillance radars perform all the functions: detecting the target, measuring the coordinates, and tracking it. These are known as track-while-scan (TWS) radars.

SIDE-LOOKING AIRBORNE RADARS (SLAR)

One of the most advanced reconnaissance sensors available, SLAR is used for coastal and border surveillance, area mapping, route survey, and tactical reconnaissance. It utilizes radar's unique ability to "see" during both day and night, and under all weather conditions, to generate radar imagery of objects and terrain situated 90 degrees off the flight path of the aircraft. This enables the aircraft to maintain a standoff position yet still monitor activities at distances up to 100 kilometers (60 mi.)—the maximum range of the radar—from its flight line. Radar returns from the SLAR can be recorded aboard the same aircraft and either processed when it returns to base or data linked to a ground station up to several hundred kilometers away (determined by the range of the data link) for real-time readout and interpretation.

Acoustic Systems

SONAR

As radar waves cannot propagate in seawater because of excessive attenuation, acoustic waves are used for the detection of submarines and torpedoes and to communicate with underwater stations or vessels. The sonar used to detect, locate, and identify sea targets may be passive or active. The former listens for the sound of engines, while the latter transmits sound waves and receives reflections from intercepted targets.

RADIO ACOUSTIC SOUNDING (RAS)

In meteorological use, an upward-pointing sound projector is usually placed on the ground near a radar set that tracks the emitted sound pulses. Information on atmospheric temperature, humidity, winds, and other conditions are obtained by measuring both the usual velocity-induced Doppler shift and the change in Bragg-resonant frequency arising from variation in the local speed of the sound. The basis for RAS is that a coherent sound wave can have greatly enhanced backscatter for a radar signal that meets the Bragg resonance condition. Using RAS, it is also possible to detect stealth aircraft, either by monostatic or bistatic radar detection of both tonal and broadband sound fields that are emitted by a moving point source of sound (the source of tonals such as aircraft turbines).

Conclusion

The field of surveillance and target acquisition is one of the most technologically active and interesting. The wide range of technologies employed, the impact— current and potential—of collateral advances such as microminiaturization, and the critical nature of the military missions performed ensure that it will continue to be challenging and dynamic.

IBRAHIM AHMED SALEM

SEE ALSO: Electronic Warfare Technology Applications; Intelligence, Tactical; Night Vision Technology Applications; Radar Technology Applications; Sensor Technology.

Bibliography

Hudson, P. 1969. *IR system engineering.* New York: Wiley.

Levi, L. 1980. *Applied optics.* New York: Wiley.

Rogers, A., et al. 1983. *Surveillance and target acquisition systems.* London: Brassey's.

Ross, M. 1966. *Laser receivers, devices, techniques, systems.* New York: Wiley.

Smith, F., et al. 1975. *Optics.* New York: Wiley.

Smith, R., et al. 1957. *The detection and measurement of IR radiation.* London: Oxford Press.

Skolnik, M. 1970. *Radar handbook.* New York: McGraw-Hill.

Verdeyen, J. 1981. *Laser electronics.* Englewood Cliffs, N.J.: Prentice Hall.

T

TACTICS

Tactics is the art of fighting battles. While several other aspects of the military art (such as strategy, operational art, training, and technology) can influence the outcome of a battle, tactics is the battle itself and the essence of the military art. While many human endeavors use the expression "life-or-death struggle" figuratively, in battle it is meant literally. And this deadly aspect gives tactics a quality that can be easily overlooked in the warm comforts of academic analysis. The degree of risk under which participants in battle labor must be sympathetically understood when judging tactics.

The word *tactics* is derived from the Greek *taktos*, meaning "ordered" or "arranged." From an origin relating to the initial formations of forces for battle, the word *tactics* now encompasses the use of all means available to a commander throughout the battle, including the approach to battle, the arranging of forces, the integration of various units and weapons, and actions during battle.

The Nature of Battle

In battle, one group attempts to prevail over another. The existence of an independent adversary makes a battle a collective duel and creates the uncertainty that permeates its conduct. In battle, one group prevails over the other through a physical and psychological domination. The adversary is either destroyed, or he is convinced that he is going to be destroyed. In evaluating tactical effectiveness, one cannot easily separate the physical impact from the psychological one, for they interact with and reinforce each other. Extreme results in battle are seldom, if ever, achieved; complete destruction is uncommon, but a battle without bloodshed is not a battle at all. Therefore, in terms of destruction and risk, battles fall between the extremes of annihilation and bloodless maneuver. But while only some participants are killed or wounded in battle, the threat of physical destruction is present in the minds of *all* participants. What happens to a soldier mentally can be as important as what happens to him physically. The collective feeling of hopelessness can destroy a group's cohesion as effectively as can their actual physical destruction. Therefore, the

1021

psychological impact of an action must always be considered along with the physical impact.

Factors of Battle

The elements that influence a battle can be summarized as three basic factors:

- the quality of the forces engaged (the means)
- the conditions under which the battle is fought (the environment)
- the conduct of the battle itself.

THE MEANS

The means are the soldiers and equipment (and this includes weapons) that are employed in battle. It also includes the quality of the human resources—from the common soldier to the general—and how they are organized. The quality of forces is often the most difficult to define or measure. While all tribes and nationalities seem to cling to the belief that their own particular group possesses a monopoly on military virtue, the more prudent societies maintain military institutions to encourage and develop it.

The collective action of soldiers in battle is not the movement of an inanimate machine. Instead, a military organization is a collection of independent-minded and mobile humans who require the imposition of order over their actions to give their efforts coherence. How the organization harnesses and directs the human effort and how durable that organization is under adversity are important factors in tactical success.

The tools of the soldier are his weapons, ranging from crude implements to complex systems whose creation tests the limits of human ingenuity. The complexity and lethality of weapons have reached such a level that some observers feel that technology is now the overriding factor in battle. Success, therefore, is the aggregate effect of well-organized units that are consistently and effectively employing their weapons under leadership that exhibits sound judgment, with the added factor of chance permeating the entire endeavor. Historically, it has been rare in land warfare that one factor has rendered the others irrelevant.

ENVIRONMENT

Battles do not occur in abstract isolation. There is no standard "game board" that duplicates conditions. The means of battle and its environment contain so many variables that the application of force in battle—tactics—is rendered an art, not a science.

An obvious environmental factor is the land upon which the battle is fought. (A brief summary of tactics on sea and in the air is contained at the end of this article.) Terrain features can be both natural and man-made. Besides the variation of the ground, the weather—a factor beyond the human ability to accurately predict, let alone control—is a significant environmental factor. Both terrain and weather can have great impact on the effectiveness of a soldier and his weapons, and the tactician must always take this into account.

In a broader sense, the term *environment* also includes the factors that determine the context in which a battle is fought. Battles are not isolated endeavors; each occurs within situations determined by the higher levels of war. These levels are *strategy*, which is the art of applying and distributing military means to fulfill the ends of policy (or the highest level of military endeavor), and *operations*, the employment of military forces in a theater of war (the intermediate level between strategy and tactics). Decisions at the strategic and operational levels can profoundly affect the conditions of a battle, such as the location or the state of the forces involved. Skill at the higher levels is also essential after a battle, for the results of the battle must be integrated into the larger context of national war aims.

CONDUCT OF THE BATTLE

Strategic and operational conditions can greatly affect the chances for success in battle, but the importance of the tactician is that once battle is inevitable, whatever the condition of forces and terrain, he effectively employs his forces to achieve his goal. Tactics is, therefore, a level of war inferior in scope to strategy and operational art. Because battle is the culmination of military effort at all levels of war, however, the results of battle can override strategic or operational conditions. Tactical failure can ruin the strategic and operational advantages that preceded the battle, or success on the battlefield can retrieve an army from a desperate strategic or operational dilemma.

In the most basic sense, all tactical actions are a duality of aggression and protection. The tactician seeks to destroy enemy forces, while at the same time protecting his own forces. The tactician positions and directs his forces, attempting to use terrain to maximum advantage for either aggression or protection.

To judge a tactician's skill, one must understand his mission or his goal. The fundamental duality of aggression and protection extends to the basic tactical missions of attack—to initiate action—and defense—to deny or frustrate an adversary's action. (All tactical missions are derivatives of these basic concepts.) Attack and defense do not exist in pure forms—all tactical actions are a combination—one examines the overall purpose of the activity to define the mission as attack or defense.

Tactical movement is called *maneuver*. The tactician orients his forces on the enemy, and from this orientation the three basic forms of maneuver are derived. The first is directly against the enemy, the frontal attack. The second is against the enemy's flanks (sides) or rear. (When a force passes completely around a flank and attacks the rear, it is called an *envelopment*. When the force passes around both flanks to hit the rear, it is called a *double envelopment*.) The third basic form of maneuver is when the force moves to a new location, while not in direct contact with the enemy, to force the enemy to vacate his present position. In the offense, this is called a *turning movement*. In the defense, it is called a *feigned withdrawal*.

Since battle is the deadly focus of all military effort, the responsibility of the tactician is immense. He attempts to control an activity that tends toward chaos. At any level in the organization, the tactician must direct the forces under his control, coordinate his actions with other friendly forces, and report his actions to his superior headquarters. At the same time, the tactician is attempting to determine what his adversary is doing. Except under the most fortunate circumstances, the tactician has extremely imperfect knowledge of the intentions of the adversary. Therefore, the tactician directs his forces in anticipation of what the adversary could do, not what the adversary will do.

Once the battle has begun, control becomes increasingly difficult. The tactician can attempt to control action by means of a plan, or he can react to events as they occur. The nature of battle is unkind to both endeavors. The variables of battle are so numerous that plans can seldom cover all situations. Reacting to events is no easier; responding effectively to the chaos and uncertainty of battle requires qualities of judgment, organization, and communication that are supremely difficult to achieve, both in human and technological terms. Ultimately, the tactician and his organization must possess both the ability to anticipate events and the ability to react to events.

A portion of a force that is devoted to future events is called the *reserve*. It can be formed from units employed elsewhere in the battle (a lateral reserve) or from units intentionally removed from the battle (a subtracted reserve).

Change and Consistency in Tactics

Because the stakes in battle are the highest of any human endeavor, a natural inclination toward caution prevails. To operate under the extreme conditions of battle, military organizations require well-practiced procedures. This conditioned behavior, often the object of derision in caricatures of military life, is essential to achieve effective performance, both individually and collectively, in the midst of chaos and stress. Equipment, particularly in the industrial age, also requires standardization, not only for its production, but also for training in its use and for its maintenance.

No set of procedures, however, can ever entirely cover the variety of events in battle. Human and environmental variations create unique circumstances in every case. Tactics, therefore, becomes an art and, as such, demands creativity. The tactician is thus faced with the dilemma of taking means that rely heavily on method and applying them in situations that require adaptability. The tactician must balance the requirement for conditioned action (actions according to method) with the demand for creative action (adapting the methods to unique situations). The correct balance between conditioning and creativity is extremely difficult to achieve; given the risks of battle, most practitioners err on the side of overreliance on method. Tactical innovation, always risky, is often developed only in situations of great desperation.

Brief Survey of Tactics

The chronology of military history is divided into two parts: classical tactics (the period from the ancients to Napoleon) and tactics in the age of technological acceleration (from the early nineteenth century to the present day). The reason for this division is that during the period of classical tactics, the factors of human society that would affect the art of war (political, social, economic, and technological) did not change at an overwhelming rate. While changes obviously occurred, their impact was seldom so severe as to disrupt the continuity of tactics. There was sufficient inertia, particularly with regard to technological change, that the effects of change were dampened, and the tactician could absorb the conditions of his day into his art. With few exceptions, changes were gradually incorporated in tactics. The age of classical tactics was also a period when battles were limited in time (usually one day) and space (the scope of activity could be directed by one commander).

The period of technological acceleration is characterized by rapid and thorough changes that threaten the continuity of past experience. All of the factors of human society, and especially technology, have experienced profound and accelerated changes in the past 150 years. The tactician has been hard pressed to assess and absorb these changes as they relate to war. During this period there has also been a profound increase in the scale of the factors of time and space as they relate to battle. The physical space of a battle has greatly enlarged (see Table 1), and the duration of battles is now measured in days. The direction of battles has also changed, becoming more decentralized, for no single commander can comprehend or direct this enormous activity by himself. These changes have created considerable confusion in the art of tactics in our era.

Classical Tactics

From biblical accounts, from ancient epics such as *The Iliad*, and from archaeological excavations such as the terra-cotta soldiers at the tomb of Shi Huang Di in Xian, China, one can gain an understanding that, as man's existence became more ordered, so did his approach to war. In the Western world, the first detailed accounts of tactics began with the ancient Greeks. The armed forces of the Greek city-states developed into compact bodies (phalanxes) of heavily armed infantry (foot soldiers, called hoplites, armed with body armor, a shield, and a long spear or pike). The strength of these formations was in the collective discipline of the deep ranks of infantry, the protection of their armor, and the shock, both physical and psychological, they could deliver. The initial array of forces was the most significant way that a commander could influence the battle; once the battle was joined, control was extremely difficult. The Greek

TABLE 1. *Frontages and Depth*

	Napoleonic Wars	American Civil War	World War I	World War II
Average frontage of 100,000 men (in mi.)	5.7	6.4	11	38.4
Average depth of 100,000 men (in mi.)	1.4	1.6	13	45
Area occupied by 100,000 men (in sq. mi.)	8.05	10.3	140	1,727

Source: *Final Report on Historical Trends Related to Weapons Lethality*, 15 October 1964, Historical Evaluation and Research Organization, Washington, D.C.

system had largely evolved in isolation, by the slow process of trial and error, and was heavily influenced by the social organization of the city-state.

In 490 B.C., on the plains of Marathon (about 40 kilometers [24 mi.] northeast of Athens), an outnumbered Athenian army was attacked by a recently debarked Persian army. The Persians, having conquered a large area in Asia with their cavalry and archers, enjoyed a great reputation for military prowess. They were undertaking a strategically sound plan for the conquest of Athens. But once the two armies collided, the Greek phalanx prevailed, and the *tactically* superior force determined the outcome of the campaign.

Using the Greek phalanx as a base, the Macedonian overlords of Greece in the fourth century B.C., Philip and Alexander the Great, added cavalry and light infantry. Alexander, a rare combination of superb strategist and master tactician, took this force and, although outnumbered, conquered Persia. In battle, he used flexible formations to exploit weaknesses in his adversaries, and he controlled his army by leading from the front (which resulted in his being wounded several times).

Besides having a well-trained force with a balance of arms (heavy infantry, light infantry, cavalry, and engineers) that adapted well to different conditions, Alexander also knew how to concentrate force at the critical point. For example, at the battle of Gaugamela in 331 B.C. (Fig. 1), instead of advancing against the Persians in the usual line, the heavily outnumbered Alexander arranged his men in an echeloned formation with force concentrated on his right. Alexander's force penetrated the Persian line and began to roll up the Persians from the side. The Persians could not reorient to this unexpected penetration and fled in disorder. The massive Persian casualties occurred after the Persian army lost its cohesion and broke. Alexander's success was due not only to his tactical concept but, more importantly, to the ability of his army to execute that concept.

When Alexander died of malaria in 323 B.C., his empire was divided among his generals. But in the sense of expanding military power, his real heirs were the Romans, who developed the most successful military system in the ancient world. From an initial system copied from the Greek phalanx, the Romans developed smaller, more flexible infantry formations that could easily adapt to

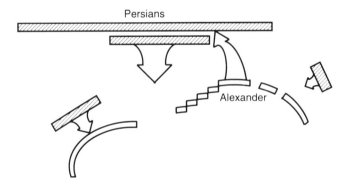

Figure 1. Battle of Gaugamela, 331 B.C.

different conditions. The genius of the Roman system was its division into smaller subordinate units with a practical chain of command and the use of soldiers in waves or echelons. Eventually, the third wave of soldiers, called the *triarii*, evolved into a reserve, a body the commander could use to influence the battle after it had begun.

The Romans faced a severe challenge in the latter part of the third century B.C., when the Carthaginian general Hannibal roamed throughout Italy for sixteen years. Hannibal was a great tactician, anticipating the actions of his enemy and using his forces to spring deadly tactical traps of such scale as to annihilate almost entire Roman armies (Fig. 2). Despite Hannibal's tactical skill, the Romans shrewdly applied pressure to other theaters of war and finally succeeded in forcing Hannibal back to Africa, where he was defeated by the great Roman tactician Scipio Africanus.

When Rome fell in the fifth century A.D., western Europe slipped into anarchy, and the level of organization and skill of military institutions fell into decline. Tactical skill, however, did exist outside of western Europe. The Arabs and the Byzantines possessed very effective military organizations. Perhaps the most successful practitioners of tactics of all time were the Mongols, who exploded out of their homelands in the thirteenth century under Genghis Khan and conquered vast areas of the globe. The Mongols' superb military organization evolved from their tough existence in the steppes of central Asia. Organized in compact units with a well-defined command structure, they were thoroughly drilled in well-timed maneuvers, often communicating with signal flags. The Mongols took the classic nomadic tactic of luring the enemy by feigned retreat until the enemy was strung out and disorganized, then counterattacking; they refined this tactic until it was nearly flawless. The Mongols also displayed great flexibility by adapting to siege warfare, as well as demonstrating an unfortunate alacrity for using terror.

Western Europe did not emerge from its level of tactical immaturity until the fifteenth century. The first evidence of tactical improvement was the emergence of disciplined infantry, begun by the Swiss and quickly imitated. The second factor was the gradual increase in the use of firearms. Gunpowder had been invented in China, but it was Europe that applied it most successfully to the art of war. Mixes of different weapons and tactical organizations were tried over the next 200 years, with Gustavus Adolphus of Sweden (seventeenth century) being the most important individual innovator. By the beginning of the eighteenth century, European armies had evolved into a combination of the basic arms of musket-bearing infantry, artillery, and cavalry. The missile weapon, either musket or cannon ball, was now dominant over the shock weapon, the spear or the pike. The latter weapons still existed in the form of the bayonet and the cavalry saber, but these were only effective when infantry units lost their cohesiveness. The tactician now had to apply the combination of the basic arms (infantry, cavalry, and artillery) according to the conditions of the battle, and the timing was becoming more important. Formations were not simply arrayed and put into motion for one great collision. As Alexander and Scipio had foreseen, waiting for the enemy to reveal a weakness and then

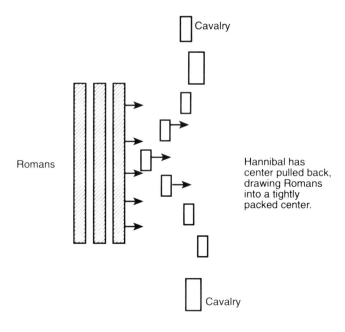

Cavalry

Romans

Hannibal has center pulled back, drawing Romans into a tightly packed center.

Cavalry

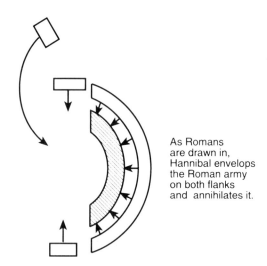

As Romans are drawn in, Hannibal envelops the Roman army on both flanks and annihilates it.

Figure 2. Battle of Cannae, 216 B.C.

striking at the critical moment had become an integral part of the art of tactics. The tactician now had to possess a sense of the progress of the battle (never an easy task) in order to influence events as the battle developed.

The incessant fighting in Europe provided ample opportunity for tacticians to develop. The French, during the reign of Louis XIV, developed modern administration to organize and sustain large armies. Commanders such as John Churchill, duke of Marlborough (British), and Eugene, prince of Savoy-Carignan (Austrian), displayed superb tactical ability. Probably the greatest tactician of the eighteenth century was the Prussian king Frederick the Great, who, although usually outnumbered, used his superbly trained and disciplined forces in bold maneuvers (Fig. 3) to keep his numerous foes from destroying Prussia.

The final refinement of the tactics of the musket, artillery, and cavalry occurred in the French Revolutionary–Napoleonic wars. Although Napoleon is often criticized as a tactician, this criticism is misdirected, intending instead to

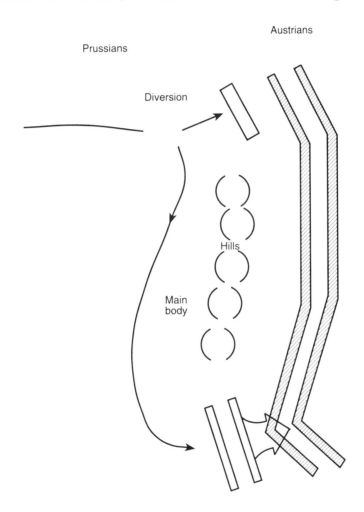

The masterpiece of maneuver: using terrain to mask his movements, Frederick fixes Austrian attention to its right, then hits the Austrian left, defeating a force over twice his size.

Figure 3. Battle of Leuthen, 1757.

criticize his failure to be a tactical innovator (which he was not). While Napoleon was not an inventor at the tactical level, he fully understood how to employ the means at his disposal. How he combined superb technical ability with uncanny strategic and political insights is often overlooked. Napoleon knew that his strategy often hinged on the outcome of battle. He had risked several "Waterloos" before 1815, and in most of those instances his tactical sense of timing, use of reserves, and perception of the critical point prevailed over his adversaries.

TACTICS IN THE AGE OF TECHNOLOGICAL ACCELERATION

With the advent of the conoidal bullet in the rifled musket (mid-1800s), the weapons of war, and therefore tactics, changed at an accelerated rate. The list of crucial technological developments has continued: improved explosives, the machine gun, indirect fire, chemical warfare, armored vehicles, electronic communications, aircraft, missiles, and nuclear weapons. The pace of technology has overtaken the ability of the tactician to assess changes and adapt to them.

The dilemma is that the tactician is seldom an inventor. His role is to use the means at his disposal to defeat his enemy. While his means (weapons) may change at a rapid rate, the ability of his organization to adapt to those changes is limited. Such crucial aspects as the conditioned behavior of his soldiers or the structure of his technical support will not change overnight to accommodate a new weapon. And not all technological innovations justify the enormous effort required to effect a change. One of the greatest problems in the era of accelerated change is to determine the degree to which a technological innovation requires a tactical change. Particularly in the area of land warfare, the impact of technological change can be very difficult to gauge.

The first brutal evidence that technology had ushered in a new era of tactical confusion was provided in the American Civil War. A host of generals trained and inspired on Napoleonic examples found themselves in a war where battles lasted days and extended over vast stretches of land. The large number of generals killed by rifle bullets indicated that tactical control was, of necessity, becoming decentralized. Generals, aided by growing staffs, moved large bodies of men. It was left to subordinates to direct specific engagements. Direct control of a battle, such as Wellington had exercised at Waterloo, was an anachronism.

Frontal assaults proved frustratingly futile, not only under the direction of mediocre generals (such as Ambrose Burnside at Fredericksburg), but also under the direction of the very capable ones (Robert E. Lee at Gettysburg and Ulysses S. Grant at Cold Harbor).

The pain of the tactical lessons of the American Civil War would be compounded by the inability of others to heed them. The development of the machine gun and indirect artillery fire with improved explosives in the late nineteenth century would reinforce the tactical developments of the Civil War, but the trends were largely overlooked. With the benefit of hindsight, the Franco-Prussian War (1870–71) can be seen as a struggle where the strategic lessons on mobilization overshadowed the tactical warnings.

The full price for failing to adapt tactics to accelerating technological changes was paid in World War I. Armies structured to employ masses of riflemen were destroyed as the full efforts of modern industry created a battleground whose lethality exceeded all expectations.

The war, especially on the western front, became a frustrating and gruesome exercise in trial and error. Several profound changes evolved:

1. The number of weapons became more diverse, and the employment of specific weapons became more specialized. Diversification of weapons extended down to the small-unit (battalion and company) level. The concept of the infantryman with the standard-issue rifle as the basic element of the army became obsolete.

2. Weapons were employed on such a scale that the environment itself could be altered (artillery craters hampered movement, chemicals contaminated areas).

3. The expenditure of the means in battle, both human and material, increased dramatically.

4. Because of the extension of the space of the battlefield, the organizational level where tactical artistry was required was now much lower than it had been in the age of classical tactics. The noncommissioned officer and the junior officer now had to adapt their resources to the environment and to the enemy; they could no longer rely on a drilled formula. Where colonels and higher had applied tactics in the classical age, now sergeants and lieutenants did it. This devolution of tactical responsibility was perhaps the most profound organizational change of the war.

5. Large formations became obsolete. Units moved in small groups, alternating between firing and movement. Armies no longer fought within visual sight of each other, and many units, particularly artillery, were completely out of visual range. Armies had to use terrain to protect themselves, and digging and fortification reached new levels of importance.

The major combatants all attempted to find solutions to the tactical deadlock by vastly increasing the scale of operations (especially increasing artillery fire), by developing new weapons (the British invented the tank), or by developing new tactics. There was no magic solution. With regard to tactics, the Germans demonstrated the most effective corporate ability to adapt to the new conditions.

Reacting to Britain's technique of massing artillery for assaults, the Germans developed a doctrine for elastic defense in depth, wherein scattered defensive forces tried to avoid the massive artillery, harassed the attackers, and delivered devastating counterattacks to restore the coherence of the defense. This doctrine proved highly successful in 1917. Using the same philosophical approach, in 1918, the Germans employed an offensive doctrine that utilized a sudden attack in depth to physically and psychologically dislocate the enemy while at the same time maintaining the momentum of the attack before the enemy could react. The German tactics incorporated the new conditions of the importance of small units, the diversification of weapons, the necessity for coordination of the different arms, and the decentralization of tactical execution.

The Germans failed to achieve victory because of strategic blunders and a lack of operational mobility. The Allies, especially the forces of the British Empire, were discovering and applying similar tactical principles in the offensives of the summer of 1918. But in the interwar years, the Germans continued to refine their tactical lessons of World War I, while the Allies either fastened on simple and rigid formulas (the French) or seemed to forget their successes of 1918 (the British).

In the 1920s and 1930s, the Germans applied the technological innovations of the armored vehicle and the aircraft to their solid foundation of tactical principles from World War I. The Germans then unleashed a new form of rapid war, popularly known as blitzkrieg, throughout Europe in the first years of World War II. The offensive gained the upper hand as the German forces penetrated deep into enemy territory. Success was not due to the existence of the tank per se, but in the Germans' ability to integrate different elements (tanks, motorized infantry, and tactical aircraft) into a very powerful whole (panzer divisions, corps, and armies). Unlike the static conditions of World War I, battles became fluid, and radio communications contributed to the ability of units to react to changing situations.

It is impossible to describe the variations of tactics that occurred in the greatest struggle in history. Increases in the lethality and range of weapons continued the trend of smaller units covering more area. As artillery had been integrated into the plans of maneuver in World War I, now tactical airpower was an integral part of the firepower of the large tactical units of World War II. While the scale of operations in terms of space continued to increase, the speed of movement and communications compressed the time of reaction. The cycle of actions and reactions became as intricate as the variety of weapons systems at the disposal of the tactician.

Perhaps the most cogent tactical lessons of World War II concerned the relationship between tactics and the higher levels of war (strategy and the operational art) and the relationship between the conduct of war and industrial production. While the tactical skill of the German and Japanese forces was impressive, once their forces lost the strategic initiative, their tactical skill could not prevent their ultimate defeat. On the eastern front, the Red Army, after having sustained terrible losses in the beginning of the war, slowly began to drive the Germans back. The Soviets have often been criticized for employing crude tactics, but their soldiers and weapons were very durable, and their generals displayed outstanding ability in creating favorable conditions at the theater, or operational, level with their skillful movement and concentration of field armies. This ability often rendered the German tactical skill far less effective.

In the other major land war—that between Japan and China—the Japanese could never deliver a fatal stroke to China even though the campaigns consumed a large portion of the Japanese army. The complicated struggle for China was not resolved until 1949, when the Chinese Communists under Mao Tse-tung triumphed over Nationalist forces led by Chiang Kai-shek. Mao developed theories of the relationship between armies and their social environment that would have considerable application in the guerrilla wars that followed World War II.

In the Pacific theater of World War II, hard-won naval supremacy gave U.S. forces great operational flexibility. U.S. forces either bypassed Japanese concentrations (a specialty of Douglas MacArthur) or concentrated massive firepower against Japanese positions and invaded with amphibious forces (much of the doctrine and equipment for amphibious warfare had been developed in the United States before the war). The key to the Americans' success was that they could choose where they would attack and isolate other Japanese forces. At the tactical level, these assaults were costly, but in the case of every major U.S. attack, the American forces prevailed.

While the campaigns in North Africa and Italy were secondary in relation to the total war effort, the second front opened up in Europe with the Normandy invasion (the largest amphibious assault in history). The American, British, Canadian, and French armies, with their major equipment supplied by the United States, relied heavily on tactical airpower as they drove the Germans back to the Reich. The development of effective antitank weapons had restored some power back to the defensive, and the Germans used fortifications and urban areas effectively in delaying the Allied drives. Still, the pressure finally overcame the German forces.

World War II ended with the massive invasion of Manchuria by the Soviet Union and the dropping of two atomic bombs on Japan by the United States. The former operation represented the culmination of the tactical and operational lessons of World War II; the latter was viewed as the advent of a new age of weapons that rendered the previous tactical lessons obsolete. Tactical activity after World War II was not devoted to the digestion of the wealth of acquired tactical experience, but to the restructuring of forces in light of the destructive power of nuclear weapons. To some observers, the existence of nuclear weapons rendered tactics irrelevant, for war would be decided in the strategic exchange of these weapons of mass destruction.

Tactics at Sea and in the Air

World War II ushered in an era where combat on land, at sea, and in the air would be frequently intermingled. It is necessary to examine some of the peculiarities of war in different elements. The division of weapons and organizations into the neatly defined elements of land, sea, and air runs the risk of being a false compartmentalization, for the division is never entirely neat and the parts are neither similar nor equal. Man is a land creature, but the sea and air are mediums of travel. In this regard, however, the sea and air are very different. With the benefits of ships, man can exist at sea for extended periods of time, whereas in the air, he can operate for only brief periods. (With the development of space stations, operations in space could assume many of the characteristics of operations at sea.) In order to operate in the air, man depends upon a very intricate machine that must spend considerable maintenance time at a base, either on the ground or at sea (aircraft carrier).

Whether embarking on extended operations at sea or the temporary operations in the air, one is completely dependent on an artificial creation, a ship or aircraft, to operate. This dependence has created a much greater sensitivity to technology in sea and air tactics than is the case in a land war, where the immediate impact of technology is often far more difficult to assess.

NAVAL WARFARE

The basic principles of tactics apply to war at sea: the tactician employs his means in a specific environment to impose his will on an active enemy, and he must protect his forces while he attempts to destroy those of his adversary. The environment and the means, however, are considerably different from those of land warfare. The oceans are avenues of transport, or lanes of communication. The sea cannot be held or occupied as can a piece of ground. What one achieves in naval warfare is the control of the sea as a means of transit. Command of the sea is command of a right of passage, not control of a specific territory. Once command of the sea is achieved, one can protect one's own seaborne commerce and attack the enemy's, protect oneself from seaborne invasion, and give support to military expeditions on land.

The basic unit of tactics at sea is the seagoing vessel, which becomes the platform for the weapons of naval war. Naval tactics depend upon how skillfully the participants can handle the vessel, as well as on how skillfully they can use the weapons. These skills are highly specialized. In the Napoleonic Wars, for example, the French could never raise a navy to successfully dispute command of the sea with the British, although the French very successfully raised mass armies. But there are several examples of peoples who have approached naval warfare with determination and who have raised fleets and had remarkable success: the Spartans, Romans, and Arabs.

TACTICS AT SEA

The object of naval strategy is to achieve command of the sea. Naval tactics is the arranging and maneuvering of naval vessels (which in the twentieth century include surface and undersea vessels as well as aircraft) to fight the enemy at sea. The basic importance of organization and leadership applies in naval warfare as it does in war on land, but the factor of technology has a greater impact on naval war. Because fighting is done on very specialized platforms (naval vessels) in an environment hostile to human existence, the impact of technology can be very sudden. For example, in the early eighth century, Constantinople was saved from an attacking Arab fleet by the use of Greek fire. In the late sixteenth century, the "tortoise ships" (ironclad galleys) of the Koreans won crucial victories over the invading Japanese fleets. In the modern era, the development of steam power and armor made wooden sailing ships obsolete. The building of big-gun battleships at the turn of the twentieth century had the same effect. The development of the submarine, aircraft, and missiles has profoundly changed naval warfare.

AIR WARFARE

Very soon after its invention, the airplane found significant uses in war. From its initial use in World War I to its extensive use in World War II, the roles of aircraft in war (both on land and at sea) have evolved into reconnaissance, transport, attack of tactical units on the ground or at sea, independent bombing, and fighting for control of the air. Of these roles, only the fight for control of the air (or air superiority) can relate to "air tactics" in the purest sense. In this instance such tactics are heavily dependent on the capabilities of the platform (the aircraft) and its weapons. In a manner very similar to naval warfare, this aspect of air warfare is extremely dependent on technological capabilities.

In other roles of aircraft in war (reconnaissance, transport, ground [or sea] attack), the air component is a part of the overall tactical situation. The helicopter, developed in the period following World War II, has become integrated into the ground forces of the major military powers, particularly in transport and ground attack.

All aircraft are only capable of operations of short duration; they are highly dependent upon the existence of secure bases for considerable maintenance; and they are very sensitive to weather conditions. Despite these limitations, aircraft have a speed and an ability to be concentrated that can have a devastating effect on forces on land or at sea. In World War II, the organizational technique of centralizing air assets and concentrating them on a mission basis—as opposed to distributing air assets to ground units on a routine basis—was developed. All tactical units must now consider as a matter of habit how they intend to defend against aircraft, either passively (avoiding detection) or actively (engaging aircraft with weapons).

Tactics in the 1990s

In the forty years since the end of World War II, tactics has entered an ambiguous age. Constraints on the use of nuclear weapons have diminished the profound impact on tactics that the new weapons originally heralded, but the modern tactician must still contend with the constant possibility of their use.

In the postwar era, conflicts have taken on numerous forms, from terrorist incidents to several guerrilla wars, to wars with large forces but engagements below the division (15,000-soldier) level (U.S. participation in Vietnam, Soviet participation in Afghanistan), and to wars that bear strong resemblance to the tactics of the world wars (the Korean War, the Arab-Israeli wars, the Gulf War).

Throughout the changes, the mission of the tactician has remained the same: arranging and directing his forces to impose his will on the enemy while protecting his own forces. Technology has created more lethal weapons, and recent efforts have been directed to increase the ability to survey the battlefield and to communicate. But the ultimate reliance on human judgment remains, whether in the foxhole, the bridge of a ship, or in the cockpit.

TIMOTHY T. LUPFER

SEE ALSO: Defense; Envelopment; Friction; Geography, Military; Maneuver; Meteorology, Military; Principles of War; Technology and Warfare.

Bibliography

Brodie, B., and F. Brodie. 1973. *From crossbow to H bomb.* Rev. ed. Bloomington, Ind.: Indiana Univ. Press.

Chandler, D. G. 1966. *The campaigns of Napoleon.* New York: Macmillan.

Clausewitz, C. von. 1976. *On war.* Ed. and trans. M. Howard and P. Paret. Princeton, N.J.: Princeton Univ. Press.

Corbett, J. [1911] 1972. *Some principles of maritime strategy.* Reprint. London: Conway Maritime Press.

Creasy, E. [1851] 1963. *Fifteen decisive battles of the world.* London: Dent and Sons.

Dupuy, R. E., and T. N. Dupuy. 1970. *Encyclopedia of military history.* New York: Harper and Row.

Ellis, J. 1980. *The sharp end.* New York: Scribner's.

English, J. A. 1981. *A perspective on infantry.* New York: Praeger.

Esposito, V., ed. 1959. *The West Point atlas of American wars.* New York: Praeger.

Falls, C., ed. 1964. *Great military battles.* New York: Macmillan.

Fioravanzo, G. 1979. *A history of naval tactical thought.* Trans. A. Holst. Annapolis, Md.: U.S. Naval Institute Press.

Fuller, J. F. C. 1956. *A military history of the Western world.* 3 vols. New York: Funk and Wagnalls.

Griess, T., ed. 1985–86. *West Point military history series.* Wayne, N.J.: Avery.

Griffith, P. 1981. *Forward into battle.* Sussex, UK: Antony Bird.

Higham, R. 1972. *Airpower.* New York: St. Martin's Press.

Keegan, J. 1977. *The face of battle.* New York: Random House.

Montross, L. 1960. *War through the ages.* 3d ed. New York: Harper and Row.

Oman, C. [1923] 1969. *The art of war in the middle ages.* 2 vol. Reprint. New York: Burt Franklin.

Preston, R., and S. F. Wise. 1970. *Men in arms.* 2d ed. New York: Praeger.

Ropp, T. 1962. *War in the modern world.* New York: Macmillan.

Sun Tzu. 1963. *The art of war.* Trans. S. B. Griffith. Cambridge, UK: Oxford Univ. Press.

Wynne, G. C. [1940] 1976. *If Germany attacks.* Reprint. Westport, Conn.: Greenwood Press.

TANK

A tank is a tracked fighting vehicle with heavy armor protection. There are two main kinds of tanks: battle tanks (the principal assault weapon of armored formations) and reconnaissance tanks. Tanks were first used by the British in World War I and gradually replaced horses in the cavalry corps until they became known as the "armored corps." The history of the tank is presented in the article entitled "Armor."

Tanks are designated light (25 tons or less), medium (25 to 50 tons), or heavy (more than 50 tons), according to weight and the weapons they carry. Main battle tanks usually weigh between 50 and 60 tons.

The tank's main armament is usually a gun of at least 105mm. Over the years, tanks have grown heavier and more powerful to accommodate increases in the caliber of the tank gun, its muzzle velocity, the ammunition stowage needed to increase battle endurance, the armor thickness, and the need for high mobility, agility, and maneuverability. Antitank weapons consequently have become both enormous and more effective. Enemy infantry, vehicles mounting antitank weapons, mines, antitank gunnery, and aerial antitank air-to-surface missiles all pose serious threats to tanks. To counteract these increasing threats, the tank's fire control and defensive systems, the armor, the engine, and the main gun all have been upgraded and made more complex. Moreover, the tank's dimensions—especially height—must be limited as much as possible so that the vehicle does not present an easy target. Thus, tank designers are faced with a complex and difficult set of trade-offs.

Basic Tank Design

ARMOR

The tank hull is the main infrastructure and supports the main weapon, consisting of the turret and the gun; the drive train, made up of the engine and transmission; the running train, including the drive sprockets, track, road wheels, idler wheels, and support wheels; the fuel tanks; and ammunition stowage compartments (see Figure 1).

The crew compartment typically is located inside the turret in front of the engine and transmission. The driver's station usually occupies the front compartment, although a recent prototype permitted the driver to steer the tank by remote control from a seat in the turret. The crew compartment is usually in the middle of the tank, while the engine compartment is in the rear or in some cases alongside the driver's station in the front.

The hull is protected by armor. The amount of protection depends on the thickness, angle of inclination, and type of armor used—usually superhardened or double-hardness steel laminate and composite materials. Generally rugged construction helps the tank withstand the shock of direct hits. Further protection is provided by skirt plates covering road wheels; an extremely flat slope for a heavily armored glacis; placement of the engine and transmission in the front of the vehicle; and spaced armor at vulnerable points around and above the turret and behind and on the sides of the fighting compartment.

Indirect protection is provided by other design features: a low silhouette; a compartmentalized interior that separates crew, ammunition, fuel, and engine; mobility and agility; reduced infrared, acoustic, and electromagnetic signatures; and rapid-reaction fire detection and fire extinguishing systems.

The tank turret contains the fighting compartment with its large-caliber gun (up to 125mm in some configurations) and one or two coaxial multipurpose machine guns. The turret protects the tank commander, gunner, loader, and most of the tank's vital fighting systems (gun, fire control, sighting and observation, auto-loader, and a portion of the ammunition). Turret designs have changed to counter recent improvements in antitank weaponry. These changes have reduced the above-hull target areas on the front and sides, but the turret still must protect the crew against both horizontal and vertical attacks. Top attacks are especially threatening to flat-roofed configurations; lower turrets and smaller, mushroom-shaped turrets with compact array armor may counter

Figure 1. U.S. 2d Armored Division M1 Abrams tanks in West Germany (1987) prepare to move out for exercises Reforger 87 and Certain Strike. (SOURCE: U.S. Army photo; Robert F. Dorr Archives)

this danger. Turret ballistic protection can be increased by adding armor plate composite ceramic modules to the gun mantle and turret sides. New "topless" or "turretless" tanks seat the crew in the hull; while this design provides greater protection to the crew, it eliminates the gun's independent traverse and denies the commander "top vision."

The main gun usually has unrestricted traverse in the horizontal plane and a vertical range of +20 degrees to −10 degrees. Gyrostabilizers permit the tank to engage targets while on the move and increase the probability of a first-round hit at long distances. In addition to the multipurpose coaxial machine gun, a small-caliber antiaircraft weapon may be mounted on the turret for air defense.

The ammunition reserve for the main gun is stored in the auto-loader and elsewhere in the turret, as well as in the hull. An air-conditioning system is connected to the turret or mounted to its rear.

ADD-ON ARMOR

Add-on armor extends the viable lifetime of existing tanks that otherwise would be vulnerable to new antiarmor weapons. Supplementary armor plates or arrays can improve a tank's ballistic protection without markedly degrading its dynamic or economical performance if weight increases are no more than about 7 to 8 percent. Greater increases in weight require a corresponding increase in engine power.

Blazer is a type of reactive armor that constitutes a new trend in armored fighting vehicle protection. It may be tailored for a certain type of tank and comprises a number of modular protective elements, each weighing about a ton and containing a special explosive compound, that are mounted with bolts welded to the hull or turret. When a shaped charge is initiated, the protective element explodes. The charge is not activated by small-arms fire, artillery fragments, or sympathetic detonation.

Toga armor is a kit of special armored steel plates assembled on aluminum or steel fixtures welded on the hull of an armored vehicle. The space between the original wall of the vehicle and the toga plates deflects bullets from their original trajectory and consumes a large part of their kinetic energy. Toga also reduces the "beyond-armor" residual effect of shaped charges. Toga armor can be used on floating vehicles if the gaps between the additional armor plates and the vehicle wall are filled with a special foam insert.

FIRE CONTROL SYSTEMS

The increased size of the modern battlefield and the growing demands of contemporary battle require tanks that can fire on the move and aim quickly and accurately to increase the probability of a first-round hit. The ability to detect the enemy in the dark helps tanks avoid his fire and gain the initiative. Thus, modern tanks are equipped with advanced fire control systems that include stabilizers, range finders, and night-vision devices.

A basic stabilization system uses two closed-loop servo systems: one operating about the elevation axis of the gun and the other, about the traverse axis of the turret. A gyroscope in each loop senses the angular velocities of the gun in elevation and azimuth and compensates for any difference between these velocities and those commanded by the gunner. This automatically maintains the gun at a fixed position, regardless of the tank's roll, pitch, or yaw.

Early stabilizers employed a single gyro to stabilize the gun in elevation only. This was later modified to add a second gyroscope to stabilize traverse. While these aided significantly in target acquisition and aiming, the tank still had to stop and small adjustments had to be made in order to increase the probability of a first-round hit to acceptable levels of accuracy.

Second-generation stabilizers incorporated two additional gyros, which responded to the angular velocities of the vehicle and provided anticipatory commands to the elevation and traverse drives. The stabilization of the gun was considerably improved, but the gunner still had to aim the gun by closing the overall weapon-target loop by means of visual feedback.

The use of director systems and coincidence firing and rate aids further improves accuracy and aim speed. Director systems are based on an independently stabilized gunner's sight with a gun slaved to it rather than driven directly. As a result, greater overall accuracy is achieved. Open-loop rate aiding provides supplementary sensors that measure translational disturbances normal to the gunner's line of sight. Digital fire control computers process the data and determine the necessary compensation.

Tracking moving targets from moving tanks becomes increasingly difficult as the speed of the tank increases. In auto-tracking, the gunner locates the target in a television display. The auto-tracker automatically follows the target and transmits target data to the fire control computer, which maintains the line of sight with high accuracy. Some auto-tracking systems claim to provide moving tanks with a hit probability very close to that of a stationary tank.

Laser range finders can measure the distance to a target within plus or minus 5 meters (16 ft.) and with a high degree of angular selectivity. A very short laser pulse is aimed at a target, and the time between pulse emission and the return of an echo signal is measured. Low frequency and low output power are used to measure the range to slow targets such as tanks. Such laser rangefinders, combined with direct systems and television and infrared cameras, and installed on a stabilized director, make efficient fire control systems with improved hit probability. "Snooperscopes" used by the U.S. Army in World War II made use of a curved photocathode tube to gather light, convert it to electrical energy, and direct the resultant electrons through an electrostatic focusing gate. When the amplified energy electrons hit a phosphor screen output window, an enhanced image became visible. Night-vision devices have become much more sophisticated since then. The most recent advances in night-vision technology use gallium arsenide to coat the inner surface of an output window, thus improving both white-light sensitivity and response to shifting into the infrared region. Even under extremely low light conditions, the current signal for the photocathode is increased. The result is that this latest equipment will function fully with no more than overcast starlight to work with, whereas the predecessor systems required at least a quarter moon to perform effectively.

Infrared devices provide night vision by passively detecting the heat radiation given off by targets and amplifying it to create an infrared "thermal" image. Light intensification devices increase the contrast and luminosity of a night scene to make it perceptible to the human eye. These night-vision devices use image intensification techniques to amplify the existing ambient light and utilize a light-frequency shift to make the final image more compatible with what the human eye can detect.

Tank Engines

As main battle tanks grow heavier and more complicated, they require more powerful engines. In addition to tank engines, or power packs, power train components are necessary to translate engine performance into mobility. The components include drive train, transmission, steering system, and brakes. Although not mobility related, the fire alarm and extinguishing subsystem is considered here for completeness.

DRIVE TRAIN

The drive train converts power from the engine into a tractive force to move the vehicle. It consists of track, road wheels, support rollers, roller wheels and track tension adjustment, suspension system, dampers, and hydropneumatic suspension. When a tracked vehicle is upgraded to meet new tactical demands and threats, its power plant must follow suit. Demands on the engine include light weight and compactness relative to the power generated, improved fuel economy, and improved torque characteristics.

The gas turbine engine seems superior to the diesel engine in meeting most of these requirements. Relative to a comparable diesel engine it is lighter in weight, smaller in size, and has better torque characteristics; it has highest torque at low speed, producing high acceleration and climbing ability at takeoff and in low gear, characteristics that match the ideal performance required of land combat vehicles. The gas turbine also loses less power due to takeoff by auxiliaries, even when it comes to cooling (which represents a considerable loss in diesel engines). Also, gas turbines do not lose power when ambient temperatures rise (up to +50 degrees Celsius, or +106 degrees Fahrenheit). Gas turbines are also easier to start (even in cold weather), need less than half the time required by diesel engines to warm up, and can do this without special warm-up equipment at temperatures down to −30 degrees Celsius (−22 degrees Fahrenheit).

Gas turbines consume more fuel than diesel engines, but they can operate on a wide variety of fuels—including gasoline, kerosene, and jet fuel—without substantial loss of power and without producing smoke. Gas turbine engines also generate less mechanical noise and vibration. The gas turbine also weighs about half as much as a diesel engine of equivalent power; however, there is no saving in space requirements (an even more important consideration than weight) because the gas turbine's high consumption of inducted air requires a large air filter and manifolds, and its higher fuel consumption requires larger fuel tanks. The gas turbine's fuel consumption at partial loads reduces the vehicle's cruising range, although a heat exchanger fed by exhaust gases may help to decrease this fuel consumption.

The gas turbine has earned a good reputation for reliability and durability. Compared with a diesel engine, it has about 30 percent fewer parts, one-third the number of bearings, and half the number of gears and seals, and it requires no oil or filter changes.

The gas turbine has great potential for increasing the combat readiness of a battalion of tanks. Only about one-third as many spare power plants would be required as compared to a diesel fleet, and removal and replacement of a gas turbine can be accomplished in an hour or less as opposed to the four hours required to pull and replace a diesel engine. However, the high manufacturing cost of gas turbines, due to the highly heat-resistant materials involved, continues to be a disadvantage, along with the high fuel consumption and the noise generated by air induction. These factors will keep the gas turbine from being adopted for the majority of military vehicles, where an efficiently supercharged diesel engine will continue to provide a satisfactory solution.

Multifuel engines are diesel engines that can also operate on other types of fuel, such as gasoline and kerosene. They are not in widespread service for military purposes, however, because they are less reliable with alternative fuels than most single-fuel engines.

Tactical requirements have raised the issue of increasing maximum range between refuelings. The fuel capacity of tanks is limited by the space available, especially in tracked vehicles. Gasoline has become almost unacceptable as a fuel for armored vehicles, due to its flammability. Diesel fuel is less highly combustible, and diesel engines are more economical than gasoline engines. Also, fuel consumption does not greatly increase under partial-load conditions, which are the usual mode of combat vehicle operation. Thus, for the same volume of fuel, the diesel engine provides a significant increase in cruising range compared with the gasoline engine. This may as much as double the range, especially during military operations, when reduced refueling problems and increased independence of individual vehicles are crucial—especially for patrol, reconnaissance, recovery, and internal security vehicles. These various advantages have led to "dieselization" of military vehicle fleets.

Turbochargers are superchargers driven by small gas turbines. A turbocharger includes a rotary compressor driven by a turbine that uses the main engine exhaust gases to increase the pressure of the induced air in the engine cylinders. This, in turn, increases the quantity (by weight) of that air. As more oxygen is admitted to the cylinders during their suction strokes, more fuel can be burnt; this increases both the efficiency and the power of the engine.

The technology of turbochargers has now been applied to medium- and high-powered engines, another factor encouraging dieselization. Besides the considerable increase in power (on the order of 15 to 30 percent) for the same engine capacity, fuel economy is improved by about 20 percent. Better emission control and cooler exhaust gases also result. Air coolers after supercharging help increase system efficiency and further improve fuel economy. Turbochargers with variable turbine nozzles have also greatly improved engine performance. Engine designers are now concentrating on improving superchargers to achieve maximum compactness of military vehicle engines. With recent advances in technology, the diesel engine now seems to have drawn equal with, or even surpassed, the gasoline engine in terms of reliability, durability, maintainability, and repairability.

Tanks have two track loops, each consisting of between 50 and 90 interconnected links. One track sometimes has one or two more links than the other as the result of the relative displacement of the idler or road wheels on each side. The track envelops the road wheels, which rest on the upper side of the track where it comes into contact with the ground. The upper links of the track encircle the outer circumference of both the idler wheel and the drive sprocket. In some cases the returning track also lies across the top of the road wheels; in other designs the road wheels are smaller and the track is held above them by a series of support wheels or rollers. The track is positively meshed with the drive sprocket by a double row of teeth.

Track links may use a single pin or double pin (end connectors with a rubber bushing). Track pads often are detachable, since they wear out more quickly than the links. Under certain combat conditions, it is useful to remove the pad and operate on just the metal track. During winter operations, snow grips can be fitted in place of the rubber track pads. Track life may be as much as 4,000 miles, while that of the pads seldom exceeds 1,000 miles. A wider track prevents the tank from sinking into soft soil (as does longer track), but steering can become difficult if the track is too wide.

The road wheels are usually steel with vulcanized rubber treads. They are positioned on both sides of the vehicle, fitted in the trailing position on axle arms attached to the torsion bars. Tanks usually have between five and seven road wheels. Spreading the weight of the tank over a total of 14 road wheels (seven on each side) improves the durability of the wheels, bearings, and torsion bars and permits the use of smaller-diameter wheels (which lowers the overall silhouette of the vehicle). Such weight spreading also produces more uniform soil pressure and improved agility and mobility. The last road wheel on each side is mounted on a leading rather than trailing arm, which helps minimize the height of the hull. Overlapping road wheels would distribute the load more uniformly, but more road wheels would be needed, so this solution has not been favored.

Support rollers support the upper part of the track. They are, in effect, small-diameter road wheels, usually three or four on a side, although three double-track support rollers often are used on each side.

The idler wheel maintains the tension of the track. Idler wheels are installed at the front of the vehicle, one on each side, when the drive sprocket is in the rear, or in the rear if the drive sprocket is at the front. The idler wheel is moved to change the tension of the track and achieve optimum grip and minimum drag. The adjustment is made by means of a hydraulic power cylinder or a mechanical crank or tension bar.

Currently, the conventional suspension system for both tanks and other tracked vehicles uses transverse torsion bars. High-hardness torsion bars connect the axle of the road wheels in their trailing position to the tank's hull on the opposite side. Usually single torsion bars are used, but double or tubular types may also be employed. In double bars, the main torsion bar is twisted to a predetermined angle, and the secondary torsion bar is "wound up" with a cam, giving a stiffer ride on both the main and secondary bars. In the tubular type, one torsion bar is inserted inside another and both are twisted simultaneously to a higher tension.

Dampers may be mounted internally for protection or externally for better dissipation of built-up heat. They usually are installed on the front and rear road wheels. Two to five dampers, depending on the number of road wheels, are used on each side of the vehicle, mainly on the farthest forward and aft wheels of the tank. Both rotary and telescopic dampers are used.

Hydropneumatic suspension has a nonlinear load deflection characteristic and permits damping at all wheel stations. A crank is attached to a pivot and rotated. This moves the main piston via the connecting rod, forcing oil through a controlled orifice plate damper and displacing a separator piston. This in turn compresses a nitrogen spring contained in the bottle end of the unit. Hydropneumatic suspension may be adjusted to change the maximum elevation and depression angles of the tank gun in accordance with the "reclining" and "kneeling" capabilities of the suspension. Adjustments in the maximum depression angle can have important tactical advantages when the tank is in a hull-down position on a reverse slope. The adjustable suspension can also help hold the chassis level when the tank is on a side slope. However, because of the technical risk associated with hydropneumatic suspension, including maintenance requirements and susceptibility to battle damage, most design engineers favor the conventional torsion bar approach.

TRANSMISSION

The threats of the modern battlefield pose a great challenge to the tank designer, particularly in the matter of the transmission. The main requirements of a tracked vehicle transmission derive from those of the vehicle itself: size; performance, with emphasis on maneuverability; reliability; and operating cost considerations, including fuel consumption.

The basic drive system includes the main clutch (usually a multidisc type); the gearbox; the transmission to the two drive sprockets, each through a multidisc side clutch; and a final drive (reducing unit). The tank is steered by disengaging the clutch on the side nearer to the direction of the turn (i.e., the left one for a left turn). Side or steering clutches are typically disengaged by means of two sticks located on either side of the driver. Disengaging the clutch diminishes the power transmitted to the track on that side, while the opposite track remains fully powered; this turns the tank in the direction desired. Full disengagement causes the inner track to brake, turning the tank in that direction at its minimum radius (which is equal to its track gauge, the distance between the center lines of its two tracks). A simultaneous full pull on both sticks stops the tank.

As steering systems developed, a two-speed planetary reduction unit in the final drive was adopted. In this arrangement, the steering sticks (or laterals) have positions for two track speeds. This gives the tank two radii of steering, each one corresponding to a certain speed of the planetary reduction. The reduction gear can be used to overcome a temporary resistance by simultaneously pulling both sticks to the first position; pulling them both to the second position stops the tank. These drive systems use a frictional starting clutch and a stepped gear unit, synchronized or power shiftable. They are not well suited for use in high-maneuverability, all-terrain vehicles, as they place very exacting demands on the driver while offering restricted maneuverability compared to other systems.

Electrical or hydrostatic mechanical systems can control the main engine to make use of the most favorable fuel curve or optimum power utilization characteristics. The hydrostatic variable speed gear, together with a mechanical path in parallel, can ensure the necessary torque multiplication. Infinitely variable low-range transmission systems consist of an infinitely variable hydrostatic transmission, a mechanical drive train, and an epicyclic unit. In the starting gear, the power input is passed to the output side via the hydrostatic system. Once the hydrostatic pump has fully opened, the system switches from the first clutch to the second, changing the power flow in the transmission. The transmission efficiency and usable transmission output remain low, although the input power is kept at a constant level.

Stepped gear units with torque convertors and lockup clutches (four-speed power-shift transmissions) driven by diesel engines do not provide constant power levels, but they do provide better efficiency. Despite low power utilization levels, the average power yield is greater. This is due to the idle power, which passes through the hydrostatic system.

Most modern armored vehicles are equipped with power-shift stepped gear units combined with upstream torque convertors. The power-shift transmission consists of a series of interlinked planetary gear sets, several multidisc clutches, and multiple disc brakes. The number of gears depends on the installed engine power as well as on the required characteristics of the individual vehicle (four to six gears are standard).

STEERING SYSTEMS

Differential-geared steering, used in light tracked vehicles, has a fixed steering gear ratio, which means that there is a fixed radius turn for a given speed and forward gear. Large-radii tanks can be steered by a skillful application of power and slippage of the clutch and brake, but that leads to excessive heat generation and wear, especially in vehicles above 20 tons, and is characterized by jerky movements.

In the electrohydraulic differential steering system, the driver controls the system with a tiller bar similar to motorcycle handlebars. The steering handlebar incorporates a twist-type throttle, a handle for the main brakes, and a hold button for the gears.

The handlebar can be raised or lowered to suit the driving position. An automatic gearbox allows the driver to select neutral, forward, or reverse. He may also choose the full range of six gears engaged automatically or may limit the choices to fourth gear top. An emergency lever enables the driver to mechanically select the second forward gear or low reverse in the event of electrical failure. Turning the handlebar left or right triggers a microswitch that activates a solenoid valve, putting full pressure from an engine-driven pump onto the hydraulic caliper disc steering brakes and turning the vehicle at a radius determined by the gear engaged.

Steering drives have progressed from clutch-and-brake steering to superimposed steering systems. The main drawback of the clutch-and-brake system, which was equipped with differential gear units, was the lack of accurate steering. Such systems were also difficult to operate, and they drained operating power when in use. The vehicle also could not be rotated about its vertical axis (pivot steering), an important requirement for the main battle tank.

Superimposed steering systems split the engine power between the vehicle and steering drives. The vehicle drive powers a central shaft located between two "summarizing gear units." These units are powered by the steering drive via a "zero shaft" and an odd number of intermediate gears. The speed of the vehicle drive is added to the steering drive speed, and the sum is passed on to the output shafts connected to the final drives. Because of the odd number of intermediate gears, the steering speed is greater on one side than on the other; the vehicle thus describes a curved path. When the "zero shaft" is held stationary, only the vehicle main drive powers the output shafts, and the vehicle travels in a straight line.

Fixed-radius steering systems allow for one, two, or three different turning circles predetermined by the steering drive, whereas stepless steering systems permit stepless directional variations ranging from straight ahead to the minimum turning radius of the vehicle (the system used for most wheeled vehicles). The steering drive consists of gear wheels and clutches permitting the "zero shaft" to be held stationary for straight-ahead travel and moved in one direction or another for turning. A hydrostatic control unit provides infinite-variation range, and there is a mechanical gearbox for the minimum radius and a summarizing epicyclic between the hydrostatic system, mechanical gearbox, and zero shaft. There remains, however, the drawback of that "step" and the consequent jerk on the steering.

The fully hydrostatic steering system is distinguished by its infinitely variable steering radii, just as in wheeled vehicles; reduced requirements for driver training; controlled steering; accurate cornering in correspondence to steering wheel position; pivot steering; and high efficiency over a wide range. The main drawbacks are its considerable size and weight, especially when used with high-powered vehicles.

In a power-split hydrostatic mechanical steering system, the steering drives require constant torque, as opposed to the constant output power needed for vehicle propulsion. This system is distinguished by its excellent efficiency because of the power split feature and by its reduced size and weight. The only disadvantage is the number of gear components required.

BRAKE SYSTEMS

A brake system must function as a service brake, a sustained-action brake (downhill brake), and a parking brake. Mechanical friction brakes may be either wet or dry. Wet brakes use an oil-cooled system located within the transmission. Dry friction brakes are mounted on the transmission or in the hull. Dry brakes are preferred in tanks, because abrasion particles from the brake lining cannot enter the oil and cause hydraulic malfunctions. Dry brake discs also fail less often than wet discs. Mounting mechanical friction brakes on the transmission, rather than in the hull, requires less space and combines the brake and its operating device into one unit, thereby facilitating design and maintenance work.

The mechanical friction brake functions as operating and parking brakes. For extended downhill travel, where a large quantity of heat is generated over a protracted period of time, an additional sustained-action brake is required. The sole form of sustained-action brake in tanks is the engine brake. The exhaust of the engine dissipates the heat generated during braking. However, the braking effect of the engine is frequently too weak or even nonexistent.

Hydraulic retarders are mounted on the transmission and take over the function of sustained-action brakes. The retarder is located upstream of the vehicle drive to keep it operating at high speed, regardless of the speed of the vehicle, and thus ensure low unit volume. The system does not wear, since heat is generated directly in the transmission fluid and can easily be dissipated by means of the cooling system. Where hydrostatic/hydrodynamic steering systems are used, the steering couplings can perform the additional functions of a retarder. This eliminates the need for a separate hydraulic retarder.

If an operating brake is to meet high deceleration requirements at maximum speeds and in short intervals, friction brakes alone will not suffice. A combination brake, comprising a heavy-duty retarder mounted on the control transmission shaft and a mechanical friction brake, will be needed. The non-wearing heavy-duty retarder performs 90 percent of the work involved in the friction brake. The response time of the retarder system is less than 0.2 seconds. The braking torque preset by the driver is applied via a system of valves and is shifted to the friction brakes as the retarder force decreases. This process requires no driver involvement. The retarder is also used as a sustained-action brake.

Such a combination braking system offers a number of benefits, including low unit volume and weight; low wear and therefore high dependability; improved heat dissipation via the transmission fluid; no abrasive particles in the transmission; and no overheating of the braking system.

Fire Alarm and Fire Extinguishing Systems

These systems are installed in main battle tanks to give the alarm in case of fire and to extinguish any fire automatically. The alarm operates when a threshold temperature has been reached, or when combustion products decrease the dispersion of light in the visible or invisible spectral range, thus functioning as an "optical" smoke alarm. It may also respond to either infrared or ultraviolet radiation within a flame, a reaction known as "radiation alarm." The radiation alarm has a short reaction and response time and is quite sensitive. To reduce the incidence of false alarms, an explosion suppression system has been designed for the crew compartment. It includes some four optical detectors and a control unit for the suppressing agent.

The simplest extinguishing system for the engine compartment consists of two thermal alarm devices, an activating switch, and the extinguishing agent bottle. More complicated systems may have fire warning wiring that is divided into two groups: one for automatic operation and the other for manual. A test circuit may also be provided for use in periodic checking of the system. The sensors are designed to detect a hollow-charge jet, hydrocarbon fire, or explosion and to generate an output signal in less than 2 milliseconds. The trigger signal is sent to the control electronics unit, which determines which sensor is being activated and sends a high current signal to the corresponding valves. The valves themselves are also quick reaction, which means that an explosion can be stifled before it builds up to full force. Opening a valve discharges the bottles containing Halon suppressant and dry nitrogen at about 50 bar. A suppressant concentration of more than 3 percent is necessary to extinguish most hydrocarbon fires, while greater than 6 percent is required to produce a completely inert atmosphere. CO_2 suppression bottles may also be used. The total time needed for such a system to completely suppress a fuel or oil explosion is between 80 and 120 milliseconds.

Trends in Tank Design

The increased threat and proliferation of antitank weapons and the advent of new antitank weapons carriers have engendered a wide range of reactions intended to maintain the viability of the tank: development of the auto-loader, reductions in volume under armor, ammunition positioning and handling, and increasing automation.

Although design factors and tactical requirements are sometimes contradictory, performance characteristics such as agility, mobility, and maneuverability cannot be sacrificed. Tank speed does not necessarily increase proportionally with power increases. In any event, agility is more important than increasing speed beyond about 70 kilometers per hour (km/h or 45 mph).

Current trends are fairly clear, especially those having to do with weight and power. Performance and configuration trends may be affected by technological development and innovative approaches to vehicle configuration. But changes in active protection systems and ways of integrating major components such as engines and transmissions are still limited due to costs. Likewise, matters such as fuel placement, ammunition stowage and handling, sighting equipment, reduction of frontal area and vehicle silhouette, selection and location of engines, and choice of the transmission and suspension systems must be carefully considered to optimize the tank's configuration, weight, and power and meet performance requirements and production cost goals.

Crew considerations are also affected by technological advances. The use of auto-loaders could render one crew member unnecessary, for example, and perhaps some maintenance could be carried out by specialized non-crew members. But there are certain irreducible limits imposed by the necessity for 24-hours-a-day operation under combat conditions. It takes a four-man crew, for example, to keep the tank on alert status around the clock using two-man shifts.

Even within established parameters of weight and external configuration, there are complex calculations to be made. Determining passive and active armor protection, as well as its design and the in-hull arrangement, is key. For example, separation of fuel and ammunition by means of internal armored bulkheads can improve crew survivability if the tank gets hit. A transversely mounted engine was once favored because it could save space behind the turret basket for ammunition stowage. Other arrangements have located such stowage in the turret itself, placed forward behind the heavy frontal armor. Locating ammunition near the hull floor offers added protection against incoming anti-tank missiles but makes it more vulnerable to the effects of antitank mines. Positioning ammunition outside and to the rear of the vehicle (e.g., on a mechanized reload pod) may enhance crew safety but makes the ammunition supply more vulnerable. Tank design is the art and science of dealing with an infinitude of such difficult trade-offs.

WEIGHT AND POWER

The maximum weight of the tank probably will level off between 40 and 68 tons, because bridges and transporters will not accommodate heavier vehicles. This relative fixed limit means that designers who want to improve armor protection (which usually means adding weight) must reduce interior volume.

A study of 34 tanks produced over the last two decades shows that half have a weight between 40 and 48 tons, a quarter weigh 50 to 60 tons, and the remaining quarter are in the range of 60 to 68 tons. Two-thirds have a power-to-weight ratio of 12 to 20 horsepower per ton, while the remaining third have a ratio in the 20- to 29-horsepower-per-ton range. However, some excellent tanks possess only average power in comparison to their weight, but nevertheless they show outstanding mobility, agility, and maneuverability as the result of other parameters such as specific ground pressure, transmission design, and steering characteristics.

So long as tanks are able to achieve a maximum speed of about 70 km/h (45 mph), there is little advantage to be gained from further increases in top speed; rapid takeoff and acceleration are more important. Tactical doctrine for armor employment suggests that tanks avoid destruction through a combination of active, passive, and reactive means. Heavy armor and suppression by fire are examples of the latter two, while a tank's agility is an active measure that could enable it to avoid some antitank weapons.

The trade-off between agility and protection is classic. Increasing the armor not only adds the weight of the armor itself, but also requires a more powerful (and heavier) engine and accessories. Even with increased engine capacity there is normally a loss of agility associated with such increases in weight and bulk. Similarly, larger guns and their associated ammunition, or additional fuel to increase range, add to the tank's overall weight and exact a penalty in terms of agility.

The trend in tank design over the past two decades has been to increase the average power-to-weight ratio by about 50 percent. Weight increases over the same period have been much less. Thus, while tanks have been getting heavier, they have also been getting even more agile, comparatively speaking.

MOUSTAFA ALY MORSY ALY

SEE ALSO: Armor; Armored Ground Vehicle; Armored Land Vehicle Technology Applications; Engine Technology, Ground Vehicle; Land Warfare; Mechanized Warfare; Missile, Antitank Guided; Night Vision Technology Applications.

Bibliography

Hilmes, R. 1987. *Main battle tanks: Developments in design since 1945.* Trans. R. Simpkin. London: Brassey's.
Jane's armour and artillery, 1983–1984. 1983. London: Jane's.

ADDITIONAL SOURCES: *International Defense Review; Military Technology.*

TECHNOLOGY AND WARFARE

Technology has played a major role in war since ancient times, changing the nature of warfare many times throughout history. Almost all technologies are used in war: weapons and other specific military equipment technologies, civilian technologies, and system technologies. These technologies have had a major impact on the way wars are fought, on force structure, and on doctrine and tactics. Beyond that, superiority in military technology has quite often led to political supremacy and domination, as in the case of European colonization.

On the other hand, war and the preparation for war in peacetime have had a pronounced impact on the advance of technology, in particular its rapid implementation under crisis conditions. There is thus a complex web of interactions between technology and the conduct of war.

Those interactions have become more intensive and rapid in the last 150 years, and even more so in the twentieth century, during which weapon innovation has become an organized and directed process. The process is based on many research and development (R&D) establishments all over the world, heavily supported by governments and industry. The purposeful, organized, and rapid military-technological innovative process of this century is quite different from that of previous periods in organization, methods, and the very close relations between the military and the scientific-industrial establishment.

Technological innovation is the prime engine of the technological arms race. This qualitative race, which may lead to radical changes in strategy, force structure, doctrine, and tactics, is now perhaps more important than the mere quantitative arms races of the past (and present). The potential of the military-technological innovative process to cause upheavals in existing military postures requires an understanding of the dynamics of this process and the roles of the various players.

Undoubtedly the future will bring more radical changes, such as the capacity for space war, an increasing threat to mobility arising from the diffusion of precision firepower, and others yet unknown.

Historical Perspective

Examples of the effect of technology on warfare include the use of stone weapons in prehistoric times; the invention of the wheel and war chariots; bronze and iron weapons; the longbow defeating armored, mounted medieval knights; artillery destroying feudal castles and extending war to rear areas; and the farther extension to the rear by aerial bombing and missiles in the twentieth century.

The character of the interaction between the evolution of technology and the evolution of society (including the evolution of warfare) has changed markedly through history. This changing interaction may be divided roughly into the following periods according to the pace and process of technological change:

1. until A.D. 1500, very slow random pace based mostly on accidental discoveries without any theoretical background
2. between 1500 and 1800, increasing pace, still based mostly on trial and error—very limited theoretical background
3. in the nineteenth century, rapid pace of change based more and more on increasing scientific and technological theory and infrastructure
4. in the twentieth century, worldwide organized and directed innovative processes based on formal R&D establishments using the most advanced knowledge base, with its rapid pace due to heavy support by governments and industry.

The purposeful, organized, and rapid weapon innovation process of the twentieth century is quite different from that of previous periods. This article will therefore concentrate on the interactions between technology and warfare in our era, including future trends.

Overall Relations Between Technology and War

There are three types of technologies used in war:

1. military technologies connected specifically with military artifacts
2. civilian technologies (e.g., transportation, communications, and medical) that are important in war
3. system technologies applied to the preparation for and conduct of war.

All influence and are influenced by war.

INFLUENCE OF WAR ON THE EVOLUTION OF TECHNOLOGY

The influence of war on the evolution of technology has been important in long wars that last for years and involve many campaigns (e.g., World War I and World War II). During a long war the development of military equipment is accelerated, although it may take years for development to be completed and for the resultant equipment to arrive on the battlefield in meaningful quantities. Also, such development is nearly always derived from basic scientific and technological work, often done many years before the war. The case of radar, which played a major role in the Battle of Britain in 1940, is typical. The first observations of radio reflection from aircraft were made at His Majesty's Signal School in 1923. Similar observations were made by the British Post Office in 1931. The British decision to proceed with full-scale development and construction of a net of radar stations to protect southeast England was made in 1935, only after the danger from a rearming Germany became clear.

New weapons that entered service in World War II, such as radar, proximity fuzes, jet aircraft, and missiles were based on technologies developed in the 1920s and 1930s. Some, like radar, had a major impact. Others, such as the German jet fighters, which entered service in small quantity in 1944, had a negligible influence in that war. Note that in the case of the German jet fighters, the decision to mount a large-scale effort was not made until after the beginning of the war. Thus, even a long war is, in most cases, not long enough for a completely new technological development to achieve a considerable impact on the battlefield.

One famous exception was the atomic bomb. A large number of technologies were developed from scratch in the course of the project. The success of this exception was made possible by the expenditure of tremendous resources, by using many parallel approaches to ensure success, and by the extremely low number of weapons required to produce a decisive impact on the outcome of the war.

INFLUENCE OF MILITARY DEVELOPMENT IN PEACETIME ON THE EVOLUTION OF TECHNOLOGY

Arms races have been commonplace in human experience for a long time. Since the Industrial Revolution, the qualitative, technological component of these races has increased steadily. Following World War II, the official doctrine of the West was to counter Soviet quantitative superiority with qualitative, technological superiority. The East, while not forsaking quantity, also joined this intensive technological arms race, which became a prominent feature of international relations in the late 1900s. This competition has also been a prominent factor in the rapid evolution of many post–World War II technologies such as solid-state electronics, jet transports, nuclear power stations, and satellites.

Is military development necessary for the evolution of technology and economic growth? Definitely not, as can be observed from the highly successful post–World War II economic development of the Federal Republic of Germany and Japan. Those countries, which were not allowed to build military equipment after that war, channeled all their resources, as well as very substantial resources provided by their recent conquerors, toward the achievement of their remarkable economic success. Thus, economic growth and the advance of technology may be facilitated in various ways.

INFLUENCE OF SHORT RECURRENT WARS ON THE EVOLUTION OF TECHNOLOGY

The Arab-Israeli conflict provides a good example of the impact of short recurrent wars. Israel, faced with a huge numerical disadvantage, had to choose quality and build a large scientific and industrial defense establishment to achieve a qualitative technological edge on the battlefield. That was made possible by the high quality of its manpower, both in the laboratories and on the battlefield, along with massive financial and technological assistance from governmental and private sources in Western countries. Recurrent wars every decade led to the rapid evolution of new, sometimes innovative, weapons systems and their first use in combat. The 1982 Lebanon War furnished quite a few examples, including surveillance by remotely piloted vehicles (RPVs) and reactive armor for tanks. Note, however, that almost no basic advances in military technology were made by Israel. The outcome of the pressures of short recurrent wars is in this respect quite similar to the case of a long war. Building on basic scientific and technological advances made before the war (in the case of World War II and the Vietnam War) or elsewhere (in the Israeli case), the pressing need leads to accelerated development and fielding of military equipment.

INFLUENCE OF TECHNOLOGICAL SURPRISE ON WAR

The influence of technology on the nature of warfare and on history was discussed briefly in the beginning of this article. Here the issue is: Can a technological advantage, cloaked in secrecy and applied by surprise, decide the results of a war? Again, it is necessary to differentiate between long wars and short wars. In a long war, with many campaigns over a large territory or even worldwide (e.g., World War II), one campaign is usually not decisive. Thus, the highly successful Japanese surprise at Pearl Harbor could not decide the outcome of World War II in the Pacific. On the other hand, in a geographically limited war, where a single campaign can be decisive, surprise by technological or other means (e.g., strategic or tactical) may determine the outcome. The almost total destruction of Arab air forces on the ground by the Israeli air force surprise attack at the very beginning of the 1967 war, for example, sealed the outcome of that war.

In order to achieve not just surprise but decisive advantage, by means of a secret technological advantage, it must be combined in sufficient quantity with other necessary equipment, force structure, doctrine, tactics, and meticulous, flexible mission planning, as was the case in the destruction of the Syrian ground-to-air missile array in the Bekaa Valley during the 1982 Lebanon War. Otherwise, the results will be disappointing, as in the case of the surprise appearance of 49 tanks on the Somme battlefield in 1916. The tanks were mechanically unreliable, and only nine returned from the battle under their own power. There was also practically no comprehension of suitable doctrine and tactics for their use in battle. As a result, their impact on that battle was negligible.

Technological-Military Innovation Process

Technological-military innovation involves two types of players acting in a two-sided environment, the military establishment and the relevant industrial-scientific establishment. The environment in which they operate includes the political and economic climate of a country and those of its adversaries. This discussion will first concentrate on the process itself and the role of the two players and then on the influence of the environment on the process.

WEAPONS SYSTEMS DEVELOPMENT AND BATTLEFIELD SYSTEMS EVOLUTION

It is important to stress that the introduction of a weapon or weapons system embodying a new technology is not an end in itself. It must become a part of and contribute to the success of a larger battlefield system (BFS) that is composed of personnel and weapons of various types integrated by suitable structure, doctrine, and tactics (e.g., a combined-arms team or an air defense system). In many cases, an improved weapon can be accommodated within an existing, unchanged battlefield system (as when a larger diameter tank gun is retrofitted). In many cases, however, a substantial change in fighting capabilities requires substantial battlefield system innovation, not just weapon innovation.

Weapon innovation differs from BFS innovation in the process of its evolution and in the locus of innovation. The evolution of a weapon or a weapons system occurs through successive generations. A weapons system has a finite life, during which it may be improved by various modifications. At some point, however, it inevitably becomes obsolete and is replaced in toto by a new-generation system. A BFS, on the other hand, is not built in one piece. It evolves gradually, mostly through incremental changes in equipment, personnel, structure, doctrine, and tactics.

As for the locus of innovation, radical weapon innovation is usually driven by technology push, led by the scientific-industrial establishment, often without an understanding of battlefield realities. Improvements in existing weapons, by contrast, are triggered most often by military need and usually follow the path of normal evolution.

BFS innovation, stimulated by new technology or other factors, is properly in the province of the military. But since such innovation is often disruptive and threatening to established military institutions, military personnel often have no incentive to advance it.

Successful technologically based military innovation requires the proper meshing of weapon and weapons system development with BFS evolution, a meshing of two different processes with two very different players.

BFS EVOLUTION

Problem of feedback. Evolution requires feedback on systems operations in the real world. Without such feedback, natural selection, the survival of the systems best suited for real-world conditions, cannot function properly. For most military systems, real feedback is not available in peacetime, despite all the simulations, field exercises, and other substitutes for combat used by military organizations. Hence, equipment selection in peacetime is often shaped by other forces. Political, bureaucratic, industrial, and scientific pressures, which often determine the selection of weapons in peacetime, by no means lead to survival of the weapons best suited for wartime. A case in point was the resistance of most air forces and some industries to the widespread application of unmanned aerial vehicles (UAVs).

Normal and radical evolution. Complex systems evolve in various ways, ranging from normal to radical. Normal evolution proceeds within the existing framework and results in incremental change. Radical evolution involves, in the long run, far-reaching changes resulting in a basically different system. In both cases the process of change is slow and gradual, but the outcomes are very different.

Normal evolution leads to improved performance of an existing BFS within the currently perceived battlefield scenario. Such a course may result in defeat when the battlefield scenario undergoes substantial changes. Radical evolution may lead, if successful, to large and qualitative expansion of present capabilities, including completely new capabilities within a new environment (an example is SDI, the Strategic Defense Initiative).

The opportunity for radical change is often opened by a new technology, as night-vision technology opened up the possibility of 24-hours-a-day battles. Obviously, the realization of such a possibility requires a great deal more than technology alone.

BFS evolution paths. The evolution of BFS may proceed via several paths:
1. improving present system performance, which is the fastest process
2. introducing new operating methods without a change in equipment
3. introduction of new equipment without structural change, or a hardware change—a common path for the introduction of new technology
4. system restructuring, including further changes in equipment—a very slow process
5. radical structural change without a change in equipment, usually in response to crisis conditions
6. combined radical change, involving radical hardware and software changes (this path is rare).

Normal evolution follows paths 1 through 4. Radical evolution proceeds via paths 5 and 6. New technology is involved in paths 3, 4, and 6.

Succeeding generations of a new technology may enter into weapons systems and BFS along different paths. First of all, the new technology is usually introduced in an independent item of equipment (e.g., night-vision goggles). Later generations will find their way into complex battlefield systems, at first within the existing structure (following the path of least resistance and of higher incentives to both producers and users). Only much later will the "new" (by now old) technology be combined with system restructuring. This multistage process, wherein force structure and tactics are adapted to make full use of the new technology, is slow and expensive and involves a long delay in the application of new technology to the battlefield. Also, without real feedback in peacetime, it does not always result in an effective new system.

Combined radical change is risky and rare. It involves larger technological and tactical uncertainties than those present in normal evolution. More important, it faces organizational resistance embodied in the present force structure and sometimes in the political system. Nevertheless, there have been some very successful changes of this type.

The introduction of the tank offers an excellent example of the different evolution paths that may be followed for the same weapons system by different countries during the same time period. Before World War II, Guderian in Germany combined the emerged technologies of his time—tanks, radio communications, and dive-bombers—into a new force structure and tactics to create the blitzkrieg innovation. The British and the French, on the other hand, although they had more tanks than the Germans, dispersed them as supporting weapons in their infantry divisions. This doctrinal choice was a major factor in their defeat in 1940.

Guderian did not invent the concept of the armored force. It had already been advocated by the British general Fuller in 1919. Small armored unit tactics were developed by the British in the 1920s. Guderian's success in the transition to the large-scale blitzkrieg concept was due to many factors, including: (1) the destruction of the old German army as a result of the Versailles peace treaty and (2) an active search for a solution to the 1914–18 stalemate so that the offensive doctrine of Nazi Germany could be implemented.

Another example of successful radical evolution is the Israeli navy's missile boat system. This novel system was created in one direct leap. The vessel, the Gabriel sea-to-sea missile, and other equipment, doctrine, and tactics were all developed in parallel. The decision to implement this risky approach was sealed by the destruction of the old destroyer system (the sinking of the *Eilat* in 1967). This demonstrated how a high-risk situation can force radical combined change under difficult conditions.

The Innovation Process: Properties and Prospects

The present state of technological-military innovation in most advanced countries may be summarized as follows:

1. A large worldwide R&D establishment is advancing the scientific and technological base on a broad front, creating a large menu of opportunities for new weapons and weapons systems.
2. Normal evolution produces, through a slow and lengthy process, new and improved weapons systems every year. These systems enhance performance within the present framework. Some are overtaken by the changing battlefield scenario and are never completed. This happened to the U.S. DIVAD (division air defense gun), which could not cope with an increasing helicopter threat.
3. The introduction and acceptance of radical innovations are rare and very slow. RPV technologies, for example, have been available for many years. Still, even after the successful application of RPVs by Israel in the 1982 Lebanon War, progress in adopting them in other countries has been slow.

Basic improvements in this process will probably require broadening and combining the weapons development process within the larger BFS evolution process. A great deal depends on the environment, which will be discussed later. Some possible changes in the process itself will be addressed now.

The proper meshing of equipment and BFS development depends on the opportunity or need for radical change. Where a new technology apparently offers such an opportunity, the new system concept should be explored in tactical experiments, even before the new equipment is built. Such experiments, leading to a decision to develop or reject a new tactical system concept, may often be performed with surrogate equipment. Using a manned aircraft as a surrogate for an RPV in a tactical experiment, for example, can yield valuable information on the preferred characteristics of the RPV system itself, as well as its relationship with other systems on the battlefield. Such experiments have been useful in the past, as when Guderian developed the blitzkrieg doctrine in field experiments using dummy tanks made of sheet iron set up on cars and trucks.

The first generation of a radically new system is almost never a dominant design, technically or operationally. It usually serves as an experimental generation, pointing the way to further evolution.

The split responsibility in most armies for training, combat development, requirements generation, and technical program management is not conducive to an overall system view or overall responsibility and accountability. It actually promotes normal, incremental, disjointed evolution. This problem is more serious in ground forces because of their complexity and diffused decision mechanisms.

The radical evolution of strategic forces after World War II, involving the development of completely new weapons, doctrine, and force structure, was accomplished by specific organizations designed to accomplish radical system change. Similar approaches may be necessary in the future to utilize technological opportunities for radical change.

Influence of the Environment

INTERNAL POLITICAL ENVIRONMENT

The political and economic environments of a country and its adversaries play a major role in the application of technology to military objectives. Political decision making is concerned not only with grand strategy, overall missions, and budget allocations, but also with such other considerations as general technological advance, economic growth, and employment. Investment in military technology is sometimes justified by projected spin-offs to the general economy. As mentioned before, direct investment in civilian R&D is probably a better way to promote economic growth not dependent on large military exports.

Policy makers, notably in the United States, are involved in detailed line-by-line management of the defense budget, often motivated by local considerations. Such scrutiny is not well suited to maintaining an overall system view. Economic considerations often push politicians to call for premature and even dangerous equipment standardization. In a world full of operational and technological risks, variety is often a very necessary insurance policy.

TECHNOLOGICAL ARMS RACE

The pace of military development and procurement is to a large extent determined by relationships with adversary countries. The technological arms race of the twentieth century has become more expensive every decade. Attempts to arrest the increasing cost of new weapons systems have been only marginally successful. The hopes for cheap, smart weapons in the future are also quite exaggerated, because military requirements are performance oriented, not cost oriented like many civilian products. Each generation of a specific military product is considerably different from the previous one. Therefore, unit cost increases as a result of increased product complexity and production diseconomies.

The technological arms race between the United States and the former Soviet Union became, by and large, an economic contest. Many development and procurement decisions were heavily influenced by the relative economic costs of actions and counteractions. Forcing the adversary to spend much more than one's own nation is a valid and important objective and is sometimes unconnected with preparations for a real war.

The ever more expensive race cannot be arrested at the technical level and cannot be sustained economically at higher and higher levels, even by superpowers. It can be arrested only by reduction in political conflict and by arms control. In recent years, the economic imperative imposed by the rising costs of the race was one of the main factors that led to the end of the Cold War and wholesale reductions in military forces.

Future Trends

SHORT AND LONG CYCLES IN THE LIFE OF WEAPONS SYSTEMS

Before discussing possible future trends, it is useful to discuss a few characteristics of weapons systems' life cycles. Perhaps the best-known phenomenon is that of the continual contest between systems, countersystems (or countermeasures), counter-countermeasures, and so on. Over a certain period, a system is preponderant; later a countersystem is invented or improved, and the balance tilts in its favor for a while. In the meantime, the original system is improved, and the balance tilts back. This pendulum of dampened oscillations creates a balance zone between system and countersystem, with neither becoming absolutely dominant (Fig. 1a). The contest between tanks and antitank weapons, which has continued for more than half a century, is a good illustration of this oscillating balance. From time to time the lethality of antitank weapons is improved, giving them an advantage for a while, only to be countered by improved armor a few years later.

This common wisdom must be qualified by two important points. First, the contest between sophisticated weapons systems is often characterized by large oscillations and temporary absolute dominance of one side or the other. The contest for superiority between aircraft and air defense is illustrative. In the 1967 Arab-Israeli War, Israeli aircraft enjoyed almost absolute superiority. By 1973 the Arabs had deployed a massive air defense complex, enabling them to inflict heavy losses on the Israeli air force and reduce its effectiveness drastically. In the 1982 Lebanon War, the Israeli air force destroyed almost all Syrian air defense batteries in the Bekaa Valley without sustaining any losses (Fig. 1b). This trend in favor of the air arm was demonstrated vividly again, albeit under very special conditions, in the 1991 Gulf War. In the future, air defense may again gain the upper hand.

Second, these oscillations, with a period of five to ten years, describe only the

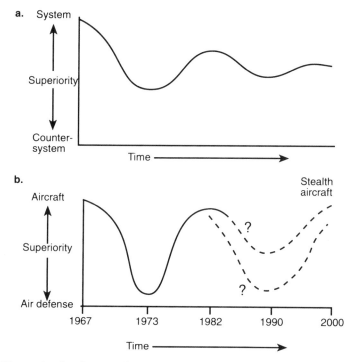

Figure 1. The changing balance between systems and countersystems.

short-term picture. Over a much longer period, half a century or more, we observe the decline of previously dominant systems and their replacement by completely different systems, which then play the major role. Battleships became dominant by the end of the nineteenth century, ruling the seas during World War I. By 1939, with the ascendance of aircraft and the deployment of aircraft carriers, battleships were already obsolete. For a time, this was hardly noticed. The truth was perceived suddenly in December 1941 when carrier-launched Japanese aircraft sank and damaged many American ships in Pearl Harbor and, shortly afterward, two major British ships off the coast of Malaya. Now, perhaps the day of aircraft carriers and other large ships is over. There have already been several ominous signs of the capabilities of antiship missiles: the sinking of the *Eilat* in 1967 by a Russian Styx sea-to-sea missile, the Falklands/Malvinas War, and the Persian Gulf confrontations between Iran and Iraq.

The long life-cycle waves are often obscured by short-period oscillations. While discussing future trends, it is difficult to discriminate between a down wave in a short-period oscillation and a permanent long-term decline. It is nevertheless necessary to try to point out cases where a long-wave decline may be approaching.

Trends in Combat Components

The first guided missiles were invented in Germany during World War II. Within a few years Germany had developed a wide variety, from small antitank guided missiles to large V-2 ballistic missiles. Since then the accuracy and lethality of precision firepower have improved steadily. Missiles are already dominant in naval and air warfare. On land, their progress has been much slower because of the inherent difficulties of the ground medium. Improving guidance methods, including automatic target acquisition, will solve problems of detection, discrimination, and target acquisition against the difficult land background. High-energy weapons may contribute to the direct-fire battle. But the greatest impact of precision firepower on land warfare may be in the extension of the current battle forward beyond the hill. Indirect precision fire can kill tanks out of sight, before they reach direct-fire positions.

Successful, even if partial, bypassing of terrain line-of-sight restrictions can lead to radical change in land warfare. Such a change is dependent on timely, highly responsive surveillance and target acquisition. The combination of behind-the-hill surveillance, target acquisition, and lethal indirect fire, both day and night, is going to increase the scope of the current land battle in both space and time.

In general, the ascendancy of precision firepower calls into question the viability of the major mobile platforms: ships, aircraft, and tanks. The problem of large ships has already been discussed. Indeed, it is not necessary to sink a ship; simply causing enough damage to take it out of action for a long time (as happened with the USS *Stark* in the Persian Gulf) will suffice. Hence, the future may belong to small, fast boats and submarines.

As for aircraft, their survivability problem may be solved by standoff weapons and, in the future, by massive and expensive transition to stealth aircraft (but the present estimated cost for one stealth bomber is US$450 million). Whether such solutions will be cost effective and permit full air participation in the air-land battle remains to be seen.

The problem of mobility on the land battlefield is even more serious. In the future, the vulnerability of tanks is going to increase considerably. The advent of top attack weapons creates a very difficult problem. Weight limitations make it practically impossible to protect completely against such weapons by covering all the soft top of the tank with heavy armor. Thus, tanks will perhaps become almost as vulnerable as light armored vehicles. Mobility will be threatened also by attack on the soft belly of the tank by new, smart, rapidly dispersed mines. Some observers contend that we are approaching the final decline of the heavy battle tank as the major mobile platform on land. Many welcome this prospect, seeing it as leading to superiority of the defense. Others fear a return to the bloody stalemate of World War I.

Electronic and electro-optical countermeasures will blunt to some extent the impact of missiles and combat intelligence. Because of the variety of communications, guidance, and sensor types, methods, and wavelengths, however, their overall effect will be limited. They thus do not offer a panacea for the mobility problem. Communications jamming, when successful, will complicate the problems of mobile warfare even further, making coordination among moving troops more difficult.

After the turn of the century, mobile survivability on land will probably depend more on mobility and agility than on heavy armor. Those are much easier to achieve with light armor or helicopters. The helicopter's freedom from terrain constraints enables it to employ fast-moving concealment tactics better than any land vehicle. Such properties have moved some observers to claim that the helicopter is going to become the next major fighting platform in land warfare, but these ideas are immature and do not yet form a coherent, accepted concept anywhere. The point is that, in order to prevent a World War I–type stalemate, it is necessary to seek actively new, radical solutions to the land warfare survivable mobility problem. Such an active search is not evident in present land forces programs.

Another long-term solution to the land warfare mobility problem might be the use of robots or unmanned vehicles (UVs). Unmanned aerial vehicles already exist as standoff weapons and RPVs. In all cases such vehicles must be survivable enough to perform their missions. Land UVs face the additional difficult problem of traveling over rough terrain and man-made barriers. Future land UVs might therefore be UAVs.

The application of computers improves the efficiency of many military tasks. Can they improve command and control effectiveness? It all depends on the way they are applied. One approach is to collect centrally more and more data from more and more sources about enemy and friendly dispositions. The data are fused, analyzed, and presented to the high-level decision makers. Orders and processed intelligence are then disseminated to the fighting units. Such tightly coupled, critical nodes, however, dependent on a supersystem, could easily collapse under the stress of war.

Effective command and control in the current battle requires that units be capable of dealing autonomously with most immediate contingencies affecting them. This calls for local self-contained BFSs loosely connected to higher levels. In computer language, it is the personal computer against the mainframe. The technology is already available to build almost any system desired. Specifications should evolve from the perceived logic of the battlefield, verified by early tactical experiments, and not from notions taken from the way banks control their branches.

TECHNOLOGY AND HUMAN PERFORMANCE

The increasing complexity of military equipment has often raised the question of whether it can be used effectively by regular troops. It is necessary to differentiate between single-purpose weapons and multipurpose weapons systems. The first, even if complex internally, can be used very effectively by technically untrained fighters, as was the Stinger portable surface-to-air missile in the hands of the Afghan guerrillas.

On the other hand, multipurpose systems possess high external complexity in that they may be used in many different battlefield scenarios and situations. The effective application of such systems requires much more sophistication. Understanding how the system works, how its parts interact, and what its real capabilities are under various conditions is necessary for achieving the full performance spectrum of the system. In these systems, such as aircraft, high-caliber personnel and long training are essential.

As external complexity increases, however (for example, when the amount of information from various sources that must be processed rapidly by the operator or pilot increases), even highly skilled personnel may be overwhelmed. Computerized decision aids and synthetic displays are used to alleviate this problem. Head-up displays in high-performance aircraft and other complex situation displays are examples. In the future, better displays and computerized expert systems that mimic the human expert, such as the so-called pilot's associate, may be of further help.

A note of caution is necessary. Such aids to the human operator are based on complex computer programs that cannot be tested completely and always retain some hidden errors. Moreover, preprogrammed decision laws and synthetic displays, by their very nature, ignore and suppress some information. In certain unanticipated and undesigned-for situations, the lack of this very information or the sudden appearance of a hidden error could cause catastrophic results. The 1988 shooting down by a U.S. warship of an Iranian civil airliner over the Persian Gulf is a vivid example of this danger.

Such caveats are even more relevant in the case of very complex systems that must operate very rapidly under extreme conditions, perhaps in a fully automatic mode (such as antiballistic missile defense systems).

TRENDS IN COMBAT DIMENSIONS

The scope, intensity, and pace of combat will increase with improved operational capabilities in the following dimensions:

1. *The deep three-dimensional battlefield:* Long-range surveillance, precision firepower, and airborne VTOL (vertical takeoff and landing) mobility result in a far deeper battlefield. Missiles will also be used against civilian populations in rear areas, as was done in the war of the cities in the Iran-Iraq War.

2. *The 24-hour battle:* The availability of continually improving night-vision sensors suggest the possibility of around-the-clock battle. It is quite difficult to implement but if successful would confer considerable advantage on the battlefield.

The optimal use of space and time is not achieved by spreading resources evenly over all ranges and hours. The debate within the North Atlantic Treaty Organization (NATO) about the meaning and preferred ranges for follow-on forces attack illustrates the necessity of choice.

SPACE WAR

The discussion to this point has dealt mostly with conventional warfare. A few comments will now be made about other types of war. The use of space for peaceful and military applications began in 1958 with the Soviet Sputnik, the first satellite. Since then the use of space for communications and intelligence gathering has become widespread and highly important. In the last few years the proposed SDI had focused attention on other major military missions that could perhaps be implemented in space.

Space is the only major new niche introduced since the invention of aircraft at the beginning of the century. Meaningful utilization of such a new niche would require a tremendous initial investment, dwarfing the Manhattan and Apollo projects. Also, no defense establishment can abandon old niches simply because a new one appears. Thus the growth of the space niche will mean a considerable increase in defense budgets, unless limited by arms control agreements.

From a technological evolution point of view, the idea of building a tightly coupled, strategic defense supersystem in one piece is not realistic, all the less so considering the multitude of large operational and technological uncertainties involved and the impossibility of real testing in peacetime. Some observers therefore claim that strategic defense is infeasible. In any case, evolution of strategic defense requires a slow and gradual approach aimed at achieving a collection of loosely coupled systems, each one capable by itself of performing effectively a worthwhile mission.

Large, tightly coupled systems, whether in C^3I (communications, command, control, and intelligence) or strategic defense, are sensitive to various disturbances and especially to wartime actions that often cause their rapid collapse.

NUCLEAR WAR

Future developments will emphasize technologies connected with arms control agreements: verification and violation detection. Still, the belief that technology can ensure 100 percent compliance is somewhat optimistic. As in electronic warfare, for every measure there is a countermeasure, not necessarily technological.

SUBCONVENTIONAL WAR

Terrorism and guerrilla warfare have been very common since World War II. It may be argued that they have become the leading form of real warfare in our era. Technology has been widely applied to covert operations and terrorism. Many special types of miniature equipment, both lethal and nonlethal, have been developed for these activities.

As for guerrilla warfare, the common wisdom has been that only simple and light weapons from the arsenal of large-scale conventional war are suitable (such as the RPG-7, a Soviet short-range, man-portable antitank rocket). Obviously, guerrilla fighters need weapons that are simple to operate, but not necessarily simple inside. To counter Soviet helicopters in Afghanistan, the complex but easy to use Stinger missile was required. Guerrillas fighting a modern army often need and obtain sophisticated weapons to counter their opponent. The development of special light equipment for light infantry in the advanced countries will increase the available menu for guerrilla operations.

Concluding Remarks

Technology will continue to affect pervasively all types and aspects of warfare, offering solutions and creating problems. Some important future issues are mobility in land warfare, the increasing use of space in warfare, the dangerous attraction to complex supersystems, the role of technology in arms control, and the deficient process of military-technological innovation.

ZEEV BONEN

SEE ALSO: Electronic Warfare Technology Applications; Radar Technology Applications.

Bibliography

Bonen, Z. 1981. Evolutionary behavior of complex sociotechnical systems. *Research Policy* 10:26–44.

———. 1984. The technological arms race—An economic dead end? In *Israeli security planning in the eighties*, ed. Z. Lanir, pp. 108–30. New York: Praeger.

Deitchman, S. J. 1983. *Military power and the advance of technology*. Boulder, Colo.: Westview Press.

Handel, M. I. 1986. Clausewitz in the age of technology. In *Clausewitz and modern strategy*, ed. M. I. Handel, pp. 51–94. London: Frank Cass.

———. 1987. Technological surprise in war. *Intelligence and National Security* 2:5–53.

Isenson, R. S. 1969. Project Hindsight: An empirical study of the sources of ideas utilized in operational weapon systems. In *Factors in the transfer of technology*, ed. W. H. Gruber and D. G. Marquis. Cambridge, Mass.: MIT Press.

Simpkin, R. E. 1985. *Race to the swift*. London: Brassey's.

Van Creveld, M. 1991. *Technology and war: From 2000 B.C. to present*. London: Brassey's.

THEATER OF WAR

The term *theater of war* takes its origin from classical Greek, where *theatron* meant an open-air place for the presentation of large spectacles. The Romans later adopted the word as *theatrum*; its meaning expanded to denote any place of action and, even more generally, the place where man lives and acts. One of the first collections of world maps, published by Abraham Ortelius at Antwerp in 1570, was titled *Theatrum Orbis Terrarum*, and from such use it was only a short step to *theatrum belli* (theater of war), a term used by Sweden's Gustavus Adolphus in the early seventeenth century. The French also used the term (*théâtre de la guerre*), and during the time of French cultural supremacy, in the late seventeenth and early eighteenth century, the term was accepted by many Europeans (English, theatre of war; German, *Kriegsschauplatz*; Italian, *teatro della guerra*; etc.).

Modern Use of the Term

Today "theater of war" denotes a large geographic region (i.e., land, sea, and airspace) in which major military activities are carried out by large bodies of troops, such as the Pacific and European theaters of war in World War II. In these theaters, campaigns are fought to fulfill the goals established by military strategy. Theaters of war often are subdivided into theaters of operations, areas in which major formations such as army groups, fleets, and (tactical) air forces fight according to the rules of operational art.

Subdivision of Theaters

For many reasons, a further subdivision of theaters is necessary. Delegation of responsibilities to lower commands is almost always related to a clearly defined geographic area where they execute their missions. Responsibility for rear-area security cannot be shouldered directly by the highest authority involved, but must be delegated to authorities closer to the events. Space must be allocated not only for troops and headquarters, but also for civilian use, including refugees. Users and responsibilities for lines of communication (e.g., roads, rivers, canals, railways, and ports) must be determined. Since military commanders must be invested with certain rights in relation to the civil population and their assets, especially in areas close to the front and on the battlefield, a geographical definition of the military commanders' various rights and prerogatives is indispensable. This is of special importance in coalition warfare when commanders of one nation may have to exert considerable powers that will affect civil and police authorities of another nation.

Theaters often are divided into a communications zone and a combat zone, the latter further subdivided into rear combat zone and forward combat zone (Fig. 1).

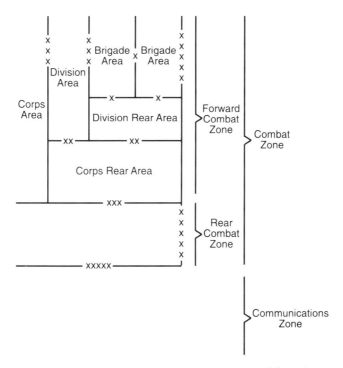

Figure 1. Subdivision of theater of war (ground forces).

Within the forward combat zone, commanders (e.g., corps commanders) are assigned certain areas. Each commander normally reserves the rear part of his area as the corps rear area, especially for service support troops and headquarters, but possibly also for reserves and combat support troops. In the rear area, allocation of space for troops and installations will often be effected by the chief logistics officer in cooperation with the chief operations officer and following the commander's general guidance. Often, the chief logistics officer will also organize rear-area security.

The area closer to the front is assigned to the next lower echelon (e.g., to divisions). Division areas are subdivided into division rear areas and brigade areas and finally into brigade rear areas and battalion areas.

The airspace is not subdivided into units comparable to the land forces' battalions or even companies, but into air force squadrons. Normally, only major formations such as the North Atlantic Treaty Organization's (NATO) Allied Tactical Air Forces (ATAFs) have a clearly defined geographic area assigned, where they operate their hundreds of combat aircraft and dozens of surface-to-air missiles (SAMs). Further subdivision of these large areas is effected not by boundaries, but by tasks, such as air defense, air attack, and so forth.

The oceans also are subdivided only into very large areas comprising thousands of square miles, such as NATO's EASTLANT and WESTLANT (eastern and western Atlantic) commands. Here again further subdivision is not effected through boundaries, but through task organization, with commands responsible for individual tasks such as submarine command and control, (naval) air warfare, and mine clearance. Special agreements between adjacent commands and standing operating procedures (SOPs) regulate command and control of forces that transit from one area into an adjacent one. They also regulate exchange of intelligence, weather data, and other information.

Boundaries

Boundaries separate the areas assigned to adjacent units and also separate forward areas from rear areas. Boundaries of areas assigned to naval forces and air forces normally are straight lines. This is also true for boundaries between major formations of land forces. However, in the combat zone, boundaries between adjacent land forces must follow terrain features that are easily identifiable even at times of low visibility and in the heat of battle (streams, trails, roads, etc.). Otherwise, local incidents may develop into grave tactical situations since responsibility for the correction of such incidents is unclear and may be accepted by neither side.

Boundaries of major formations are extended well into enemy territory to facilitate coordination of fire and reconnaissance as well as command, control, and employment of Special Forces working in the enemy hinterland. Boundaries of major air force formations such as ATAFs should be identical with the boundaries of corresponding ground force formations, such as army groups, to facilitate air-ground cooperation.

FRANZ UHLE-WETTLER

SEE ALSO: Command; Geography, Military; Logistics: A General Survey.

Bibliography

Eshel, D. 1989. *Central front Europe*. London: Brassey's.
Headquarters, Department of the Army. 1953. *Field manual 101-10: Staff officers' field manual: Organizational, technical, and logistical data*. Washington, D.C.: Government Printing Office.
———. 1977. *Field manual 100-5: Operations*. Washington, D.C.: Government Printing Office.
U.S. Army. 1978. *Soviet army operations*. Arlington, Va.: U.S. Army Intelligence and Threat Analysis Center.

THEORY OF COMBAT

A theory of combat is the embodiment of a set of fundamental principles governing or explaining military combat, whose purpose is to provide a basis for the formulation of doctrine and to assist military commanders and planners to engage successfully in combat at any level. Such a theory includes the following elements:

1. identifying the major elements of combat and the combat processes through which they operate and patterns in the interactions and relationships among them,
2. describing combat structures and patterns of interactions and relationships of variable factors that constantly shape or determine the outcome of combat, and
3. expressing in quantitative terms the patterns so identified and described.

Elements of a Theory of Combat

Military combat can be defined as a violent, planned form of physical interaction (fighting) between two hostile opponents where at least one party is an organized force (recognized by governmental or *de facto* authority) and one or both opposing parties hold one or more of the following objectives: to seize control of territory or people; to prevent the opponent from seizing and controlling territory or people; to protect one's own territory or people; to dominate, destroy, or incapacitate the opponent.

The above definition refers to interactions and levels of combat. This is a recognition of the fact that fighting between armed forces—while always having the characteristics noted above, such as fear and planned violence—manifests itself in different fashions from different perspectives. In commonly accepted military terminology, there is a *hierarchy of combat*, with war as its highest level, followed by campaign, battle, engagement, action, and duel.

Search for a Theory of Combat

Since the early days of civilization men have sought general rules about the nature of war that could help them prevail in future conflicts.

The oldest surviving military treatise is *The Art of War*, written by Sun Tzu in China about 500 B.C. Over the next 2,300 years, others tried to formulate a theoretical approach to warfare. Sextus Julius Frontinus wrote *On Military Affairs* and *Strategems* in the first century. Two centuries later, another Roman, Flavius Vegetius Renatus, wrote a book also entitled *On Military Affairs* (more generally known as *Military Institutions of the Romans*), which was often used as a reference by the military scholars of medieval Europe. There were several theoretical works on war by Byzantines: Mauricius's *Strategikon*, *The Tactica* of Leo the Wise, and others. In the century before Napoleon, there were such writings as *Reveries on the Art of War* by Count Maurice de Saxe and *Instructions to his Generals* by Frederick the Great of Prussia.

THE GREAT THEORISTS

Napoleon. Napoleon Bonaparte, more than any other, was responsible for stimulating the search for a theory, science, or collection of laws on war. Although he never committed his ideas on military theory to paper in a coherent, unified form, he did leave an extensive collection of empirical—as opposed to conceptual or theoretical—maxims. From these maxims, and from analyses of his performance on the battlefield, others have distilled the principal elements of his theoretical ideas. In his correspondence and recorded statements, as in his *Maxims*, Napoleon made it clear that his concepts and thinking on war had been derived basically from the study of the campaigns of earlier generals.

As noted, Napoleon never articulated his theory or theories of war, except for occasional passages in his letters—for instance the letter of 27 August 1808, written to try to teach his brother Joseph how to rule Spain, in which he implied that "the moral is to the physical as three is to one"—and the uneven litany of concepts to be found in his *Maxims*. It was necessary for his younger contemporaries, Antoine Henri Jomini and Karl von Clausewitz, to attempt to give these concepts the theoretical substance they deserved.

Jomini and Clausewitz. It is doubtful that Jomini and Clausewitz met during the short period when they were both in the service of the czar or later. During the 1820s each was very familiar with the writings of the other and, as somewhat jealous rivals, each was critical of the other's work.

Jomini tried to explain Napoleon's ideas on theory. But in his many writings, Jomini was never able to capture the philosophical aspects of Napoleon's thinking on war satisfactorily or to distill the essence of his theory. The result was a somewhat mixed bag of discussion, rules, aphorisms, and maxims.

Clausewitz was able to capture Napoleon's philosophy and to add to it some ideas of his own, but he also found himself baffled by the problems of distilling a theory out of this philosophy. Like the bible in theology, Clausewitz can be quoted to support both sides of almost any argument in military affairs or as a source for almost any sound or unsound concept that one might desire to document. Such quotations are usually out of context, or else the seeming contradictions result from the fact that he never had a chance to edit a final version of his master work.

Clausewitz is often quoted erroneously as ridiculing the idea that there could or should be any fixed set of principles of war. Although some of his words out of context could be so interpreted, he devotes several chapters of *On War* to a discussion of a theory of war and affirmed that there *are* principles. He lists, though not in sequential fashion, eight of the nine principles usually accepted by modern military scholars, but he admitted implicitly that the formulation of the theory would require an effort beyond that of *On War* or possibly beyond the limits of what could be accomplished in terms of the scientific method of his time. He did decry attempts to produce precise and mathematical rules for combat to be followed by generals on the battlefield. Yet Clausewitz did think mathematically and quantitatively, and from that thinking he provided the rudiments of the most substantial theory of combat so far produced.

Much has been made of the differences between Jomini and Clausewitz, but these differences were not great and were essentially philosophical rather than interpretive or practical. Both were stimulated to prolific writing on war by the example of Napoleon, and both drew essentially the same conclusions from their respective studies of that example. Both were convinced that Napoleon demonstrated that there is—or should be—a theory of war and that such a theory was based upon fundamental principles. They generally agreed on what those principles were: such things we now call mass, maneuver, objective, and surprise.

There were two principal differences. The first was in their approaches: Jomini was more doctrinaire; Clausewitz, more philosophical. Jomini tried to derive a framework of rules for battlefield success in war from his identification of principles used by Napoleon. Clausewitz, equally impressed by the principles, did not consider it possible for those principles to provide more than general guidance for a subsequent commander, who should adapt his understanding of the principles to his own "genius." There are many indications in the text of *On War* that Clausewitz believed that it might some day be possible to formulate a more comprehensive, more scientific body of theory in the form of laws and principles than he believed was possible in the 1820s. In his time, however, he was convinced that such a formulation was impossible, and thus he was very critical of Jomini's efforts to draw up rules for generalship.

The second difference was intellectual. Jomini was unquestionably a man of great analytical ability, highly intelligent, even brilliant. Clausewitz was an intellectual giant worthy of comparison not only with a Napoleon and a Scharnhorst, but also with the contemporary philosophers Kant and Hegel. Jomini studied, and understood very well, the warfare of his time. Clausewitz recognized the relationship of the warfare of his time with the behavioral, social, and political natures of man. Jomini identified the trees of war. Clausewitz not only knew the trees; he saw the forest.

Other theorists since Napoleon. Ten other theorists since Napoleon have influenced the course of the search for military theory. There is not likely to be complete agreement among military scholars as to which names should be included in such a list. It would, however, be difficult to ignore the contributions made by any of the following men.

Denis Hart Mahan was essentially a follower of Napoleon through Jomini. He was the first great American military theorist. He compiled maxims and rules that he thought were relevant to military theory in America, but he never tried (so far as is evident from available writings) to produce a theory.

Helmuth von Moltke was both an eminent historian and an eminent military thinker. He was also a superb organizer and director of combat. He did little, however, to advance military theory *per se*, other than in unrelated, although perceptive, comments such as that addressing the need to combine the tactical defensive with the strategic offensive. He was essentially a manifestation of the capabilities of an institution of genius; any number of his Prussian contemporaries could have done as well had they been in his place.

Charles J. J. J. Ardant du Picq was perhaps the most perceptive writer on the subject of moral forces (behavioral considerations) in war. His book *Battle Studies* (1921) is one of the best of a handful of truly great military classics. He was killed in battle in the Franco-Prussian War before his work could be incorporated into any kind of theoretical context, which was unfortunate for France.

Alfred Thayer Mahan was an American military theorist in the style of Jomini, of his own father (Denis Hart Mahan), and of Moltke. His focus was on naval warfare and theory. A profound and gifted thinker on military and naval affairs, he well understood the relevance of military history to the contemporary military problems of his time. He dominates the roster of naval theorists much as Clausewitz stands out over other theorists of land warfare. He recognized principles and analytically employed them but never attempted a scientific, analytical approach to military theory.

Count Alfred von Schlieffen served after Moltke's successor as chief of the German General Staff. He was another studious, profound thinker on war who never attempted to distill a theory of combat from his knowledge of military history and the warfare of his own time. The so-called Schlieffen plan has become a matter of controversy that has inhibited serious study of his military genius by writers or readers of the English language. Perhaps the best-known work in German was by a worthy successor, Groener (1927). As a soldier and a general, Schlieffen was probably superior to Moltke, but he never had an opportunity to command in battle or war.

Baron Colmar von der Goltz was one of a number of German military thinkers who emerged from that institution of genius, the German General Staff, during its heyday under Moltke and Schlieffen. In his two best-known works, *The Nation in Arms* (1887) and *The Conduct of War* (1908), he refers frequently, if somewhat vaguely, to the theory of war and to its principles. He may not deserve to be included in the intellectual company on this list, other than as a representative of an extremely prolific and thoughtful group of German writers from the General Staff. His work had great influence in Germany, in France, and particularly in Britain.

Ferdinand Foch was a disciple of both Clausewitz and Ardant du Picq. He probably understood Clausewitz as well as anyone ever has—certainly better than most Germans. Paradoxically, he misread his countryman, Ardant du

Picq. He did try to think and write in scientific, theoretical terms, and there was much that was sound in his approach to analyzing military history. However, his influence and his devotion to the moral significance of *l'offensive à outrance* nearly ruined the French army at the outset of World War I. But his leadership in the recovery from that near disaster was brilliant.

Giulio Douhet was the first and most important theorist of air warfare. Like many other early adherents of airpower, he greatly exaggerated the potential of the military aircraft of his time. What distinguished him from others was his development (in his book *Command of the Air*, published in 1921) of a coherent, consistent theory of air warfare that correctly anticipated (even if it overestimated) the dominant role of airpower in all subsequent wars. Douhet's name is often linked with the contemporary air warfare apostles of Britain and the United States: Marshal of the Royal Air Force Sir Hugh Trenchard and U.S. Maj. Gen. William Mitchell. Neither of these men, however, had the influence, even in their own countries, that Douhet exercised upon airpower development and trends through the twentieth century.

John F. C. Fuller was perhaps the greatest military thinker of this century and probably the most important since Clausewitz (Trythall 1977). In his earlier writings he tended to downgrade Clausewitz, but in later years he began to recognize that his own approach to military theory was essentially Clausewitzian. He was immodest enough to compare himself (and Clausewitz) with Copernicus, Newton, and Darwin. Fuller was the first important armored warfare tactician and theoretician as a combat staff officer in World War I. He was the first to codify the "principles of war" as they have been known for most of this century. Underlying this seminal production was a conviction that there must be laws of combat, or a science of war. Fuller knew that there should be more content and more scientific rigor to a theory of combat than just the principles of war, but he never quite succeeded in formulating such a theory.

Fuller wrote extensively on armored warfare, military theory, the science and philosophy of war, and military history in general. Despite his brilliance, Fuller was never fully understood or liked by the majority of his fellow officers in the British army. He continued to write and to criticize with acid pen and tongue after he was retired as a relatively youthful major general.

A fellow countryman and contemporary of Fuller, Frederick William Lanchester, was also concerned with the application of the "principle of mass" on the battlefield. An early aeronautical engineer, Lanchester wrote an article entitled "The Principle of Concentration," which was published in October 1914 in the British journal, *Engineering*. That article has had profound impact on the evolution of a theory of combat. Like Fuller, Lanchester's ideas (expressed in the form of two differential equations) about the "principle of concentration" (or mass) were based upon his analytical reading of military history. This is somewhat ironic in view of the fact that many who have exploited Lanchester's ideas have rejected the relevance of history to modern warfare.

In essence, the Lanchester equations show the effects of force concentration upon the loss rates of two opposing sides in a simple, uncomplicated combat situation under each of two general conditions of combat: (1) when one or both of the sides have only a general knowledge of the location of the other (as in a meeting engagement or as in the case of an attacker against defenders concealed behind prepared or fortified defenses); and (2) when one or both sides have accurate information of the location of the other (as, for instance, a defender in most prepared and fortified defense situations or as two forces opposing each other on a broad, flat desert). Whether these equations represent combat realistically and accurately is debatable. What is not debatable is that Lanchester profoundly influenced military theory in the late twentieth century.

Soviet Search for a Theory of Combat

Soviet military structure tends toward greater rigidity and conservatism than its counterparts in the West. The magnitude of the Soviet effort in pursuit of a theory of combat is impressive. Officers are schooled in the scientific method far more thoroughly than their Western counterparts. Quantitative analytical techniques are taught throughout the Soviet military educational system, not just as a specialty to a few officers. The Soviets have dozens of officers with doctoral degrees in military science conducting research and publishing treatises on all aspects of war.

Soviet planners apply the data derived from historical research to their operational plans. They press hard to avoid leaving anything to chance. They do not see themselves as practitioners of an art, but rather as scientists and engineers applying the scientific process.

The ultimate expression of the Soviet application of military history to contemporary military science is in what they call the *correlation of forces and means*. This is both a mathematical model of combat and a theory of combat. The official statement of this concept, in greatly abridged form (Belyakov 1979), is:

> The Correlation of Forces and Means is an objective indicator of the fighting power of opposing sides, showing the degree of superiority of one over the other. It is determined by comparison of existing quantitative and qualitative data of opposing forces.
>
> An analysis of the correlation of forces permits a deeper investigation into the essence of past battles and engagements.
>
> It is usually calculated during preparation for battle. An estimate is made of the quantity of forces and means necessary for accomplishing missions.
>
> A correlation of forces was estimated during the great patriotic war based on the combat and numerical strength of our own forces and the enemy's. This method of calculating the correlation of forces is also useful today.
>
> Where combat capabilities differ significantly, estimated coefficients of comparability of combat potentials are used. The following are also taken into account: opposing organizations, training, nationality, moral and fighting qualities, armament and equipment, leadership, terrain, etc. Factors are compared with the aid of coefficients.

Those factors which lend themselves to a mathematical expression are compared with the aid of one or another of the coefficients, while the rest are expressed in terms of "superior" or "inferior." Modern computer equipment is used for speeding up the computation of the correlation of forces and means. Possible changes in the correlation of forces and means during combat operations can be determined with the aid of modeling.

It would appear that Soviet theory skillfully integrates the past, the present, and the future.

AMERICAN SEARCH FOR A THEORY OF COMBAT

In general, and with only a few significant exceptions, American military theorists have shown little interest in the concept of a comprehensive theory or science of combat. While most Americans who think about such things are strong believers in the application of science to war, they seem not to believe, paradoxically, that waging war can be scientific, but instead consider it an art rather than a science. Even scientists involved in military affairs, who perhaps overemphasize the role of science in war, also tend to believe that war is a random process conducted by unpredictable human beings and thus not capable of being fitted into a scientific theoretical structure.

That aspect of the paradox relating the application of science to war became increasingly pronounced during and since World War II. This has been manifested in two principal activities: the application of technology to the design and development of improvements of weapons and the study of a wide variety of combat phenomena through military operations research.

American scientists have been generally successful in the first of these activities, but this success has not produced the results that might have been anticipated. Despite the unquestioned lead of the United States and its allies in technology, the Soviet Union, with its relatively inferior technology, has been able to produce comparable weapons just as rapidly.

The experience of American scientists in military operations research has been, if anything, even more frustrating. Despite brilliant success solving individual problems, operations research has not been able to verify its accomplishments or to distill them into a coherent theory. In fact, the opposite may be true, because the results of operations research tend to be confusing without an overall theory to place them into context.

The situation is particularly disappointing in the field of combat modeling. Elegant mathematical formulas abound, purporting to describe the battlefield operations and interactions of weapons and forces in detail, from duels between individual combat soldiers through engagements between small units to battles involving larger aggregations of units. Thousands of computers are used by the American defense research community to operate combat models and simulations, producing results designed to provide useful insights to planners and commanders on how to achieve success in battle. Unfortunately there is a major problem: no two sets of results agree. The combat models are not validated, and there is a general lack of confidence in them.

In 1978 an informal group (first called a Committee to Develop a Theory of Combat, later The Military Conflict Institute) was formed to foster a scientific understanding of the nature of military conflict. Its first goal was to produce a theory of combat, a draft of which was completed in early 1989. Concurrently, one group member found that, since the fundamental problem in any effort to generalize and formulate theories of combat was the influence of presumably unpredictable human behavior on outcomes of battle, the key to developing theories of combat was a systematic study of military history. A method for determining these human behavioral patterns evolved after a long and difficult review of the specifics of a large number of conflicts (Dupuy 1987).

Conceptual Components of Combat

Just as there are different levels in the waging of combat, and largely because of those different levels, there are also different levels in conceptualizing combat. Traditionally there have been two principal conceptual components or levels of combat: strategy and tactics.

About 1830 Clausewitz defined strategy as "the use of engagements to attain the object of the war." Tactics, he wrote, is "the use of the armed forces in engagements" (Clausewitz 1984). About the same time Jomini defined strategy as "the art of getting the armed forces onto the field of battle" and as comprising "all the operations embraced in the theater of war in general." Jomini went on to define tactics as "the maneuvers of an army on the day of battle; its contents, its concentrations, and the diverse formations used to lead the troops to the attack" (Jomini 1830, pp. 58–60). In theory the distinction between strategy and tactics was clear; in practice the line was slightly fuzzy.

As war became more complex and as its scope expanded early in the twentieth century, it became evident to military theoreticians, particularly those on the German General Staff, that strategy's scope was correspondingly expanded, dealing often with more than one theater of war and even embracing such nonmilitary considerations as economics and politics. This expansion, of course, was at the "upper end" of strategy. It also meant that the nature of the authority and responsibility for those concerned with the upper level of strategy at the national capital and in the headquarters of a commander in chief was very different from those of the theater and army commanders at the lower end.

The Germans began to refer to the lower level of strategy as *operations*, a term that—according to Gen. Hermann Foertsch in the late 1930s—was "frequently employed to indicate a sub-concept of strategy. Strictly speaking, operations are the movements of armed forces preparatory to battle, but the fighting itself is usually also included in the concept. There is no definite line of demarcation between the two in ordinary usage" (Foertsch 1940). Foertsch then provided a diagram to help clarify the distinctions among tactics, operations, and strategy as seen by the Germans at that time. For the Germans, warfare comprised three conceptual levels, divided by theoretically clear but practically fuzzy lines.

At the same time other theorists, particularly in Britain, had adapted a term used by Jomini—*grand tactics*—to deal with the area of warfare the Germans called "operations," and they coined the term *grand strategy* to distinguish that form of strategic thinking applicable to the conduct of war at the highest levels of government. There were, however, no generally accepted definitions of grand tactics or grand strategy. Furthermore, it was clear that the concept of grand tactics was really part of the realm of strategy as originally visualized by both Jomini and Clausewitz.

In the United States after World War II a clearer understanding of the relationships of the upper levels of strategy emerged, through the development of concepts of "national strategy" and "military strategy." This has led to a new set of definitions for strategy in general and for its upper levels, as follows:

Strategy is the art and science of planning for the use of, and managing, all available resources in the waging of war by those in high levels of national and military authority.

National strategy is the art and science of developing and using political, economic, psychological, social, and military resources as necessary during war and peace to afford the maximum support to national policies and—in the event of war—to increase the probabilities and favorable consequences of victory and to lessen the chances of defeat. Art predominates over science in national strategy.

Military strategy is the art and science of developing and employing in war military resources and forces for the purpose of providing maximum support to national policy in order to increase the probabilities and favorable consequences of victory and to lessen the chances of defeat. Science predominates over art in military strategy. The difference between military competence and military genius at the strategic level is greater artistry by genius. This definition covers a very broad range of the activities of warfare, from the global deployments of armed forces to the theater-level activities the Germans called "operations."

Soviet military theorists have also devoted their attention to the relationship between the lower and intermediate levels of strategy by characterizing the lower level as the conceptual area of the operational art. To end fuzziness of distinctions, they arbitrarily define tactics as that aspect of the art of war that is the responsibility of division commanders and lower; operational art is the responsibility of army and front (army group) commanders; strategy is the domain of higher commanders. This arbitrary distinction may have ended the practical fuzziness, but it tends to blur the concepts, since it is not possible to make a firm distinction among the concepts of strategy, operations, and tactics simply on the basis of command levels.

Despite the theoretical problems clouding the concept of the operational art, the United States early in the 1980s adopted the concept, following the Soviet example perhaps more closely than would be desirable for conceptual clarity. A definition of operations, or operational art, generally consistent with that recently adopted by the U.S. Army, is as follows:

Operations involves the control and direction of large forces (usually armies or army groups) in combat activities within a single, discrete theater of combat.

Operations can be considered a separate conceptual level of combat lying between strategy and tactics.

Thus, the classic duality of the conceptual components of combat as visualized by Clausewitz and Jomini has become in the twentieth century a trilogy in the current military doctrines of many major military powers. The classic definitions of tactics by Clausewitz and Jomini require some adjustment to fit into this trilogy:

Tactics is the technique of deploying and directing military forces (troops, ships, or aircraft, or combinations of these, and their immediate supporting elements) in coordinated combat activities against the enemy in order to attain the objectives designated by strategy or operations.

Another word often used in relation to the conceptual components of combat is *doctrine*. Interestingly, the Germans have no such term in their military lexicon, apparently because of its imprecision. However, it is a useful word and concept, and the following definition attempts to limit its inherent imprecision.

Military doctrine is the combination of principles, policies, and concepts into an integrated system for the purpose of governing all components of a military force in combat and ensuring consistent, coordinated employment of these components. The origin of doctrine can be experience, theory, or both. Doctrine represents the available thought on the employment of forces that has been adopted by an armed force. Doctrine is methodology, and if it is to work, all military elements must know, understand, and respect it. Doctrine is implemented by tactics.

APPLICABILITY TO AIR AND NAVAL WARFARE

Discussed earlier were 12 military theorists since the time of Napoleon whose writings have contributed to the inchoate effort to produce a theory of combat. Only one of the 12 was a naval combat theorist, although mankind has been fighting on, in, and over the water almost as long as it has on land; and only one was an air combat theorist.

If the list were expanded to include all possible contributors to significant military theory, the proportion of naval theorists would not rise much above 10 percent. The proportion of air theorists would probably be even smaller, in part because manned flight and air combat has been possible for less than a century. In any event, there is reason to believe that a general theory of combat for land warfare is likely to be applicable—probably with some modifications—to both naval and air warfare.

Clausewitz's Theory of Combat

To provide background for a discussion of Clausewitz's basic theory of combat, it is useful to survey what he wrote in *On War* about his philosophy of war.

CLAUSEWITZ'S PHILOSOPHY OF WAR

One of the three most profound theoretical statements that Clausewitz made about war had to do with his philosophy of war, that is, his statement of the relationships of war to politics.

War as a continuation of politics. This is perhaps the most fundamental element of Clausewitz's philosophy of war. War is, and must always be, subservient to politics.

"Absolute" war in theory and war in practice. In theory, Clausewitz points out, war is an act of violence to be carried out to the utmost limits of the lethal capabilities of the opponents. In practice, however, war will be carried out only to the degree of violence consistent with the politics motivating the opponents. This is mainly because war is an instrument of policy, but it is also because of the realities that led him to develop his concept of friction. From this duality of theory and practice emerge two more significant characteristics of war.

Total war or limited war. War can be conducted with as much force as is possible—thus approaching the theoretical absolute war—in order to overthrow an opponent, if that is the aim of policy. Or else it can be carried out in more limited fashion for the purpose of achieving lesser policy goals.

Ends and means in war. When the ends of war are total (i.e., the overthrow of the opponent or survival against such an effort), the means will be violent to the utmost capability of the contestants. If the ends of war are less than the overthrow of the enemy, then the means will be less violent.

The activities of war. Clausewitz divides the activities of war into two principal categories: fighting, or combat; and preparation for fighting, or administration.

In sum, Clausewitz thought in theoretical terms and saw war as having both quantitative and qualitative aspects. He also made it very clear that the general philosophy of war—dealing primarily with strategy—was essentially qualitative and probably not amenable to quantitative analysis. On the other hand, when he was writing about tactics—in other words, dealing with actual fighting or combat—he saw much in terms of scale, degree, or quantity.

Next to be examined is the concept that was the essence of Clausewitz's quantitative approach to combat theory.

THE "LAW OF NUMBERS"

It has been obvious to most soldiers and scholars who have studied *On War* that it is the most profound book on military theory ever written. Although it is an unfinished work, it is thought that if Clausewitz had been able to complete it in the fashion that he planned, he might have been able to integrate its many brilliant thoughts and concepts into a single, comprehensive theory.

One of the most important passages in *On War* was Clausewitz's discussion of numbers, the essence of which is a passage called the "Law of Numbers."

> If we . . . strip the engagement of all the variables arising from its purposes and circumstances, and disregard the fighting value of the troops involved (which is a given quantity), we are left with the bare concept of the engagement, a shapeless battle in which the only distinguishing factor is the number of troops on either side.
>
> These numbers, therefore, will determine victory. It is, of course, evident from the mass of abstractions I have made to reach this point that superiority of numbers in a given engagement is only one of the factors

that determines victory. Superior numbers, far from contributing every-thing, or even a substantial part, to victory, may actually be contributing very little, depending on the circumstances.

But superiority varies in degree. It can be two to one, or three or four to one, and so on, it can obviously reach the point where it is overwhelming.

In this sense superiority of numbers admittedly is the most important factor in the outcome of an engagement so long as it is great enough to counterbalance all other contributing circumstances. It thus follows that as many troops as possible should be brought into the engagement at the decisive point.

Whether these forces prove adequate or not, we will at least have done everything in our power. This is the first principle of strategy. In the general terms in which it is expressed here it would hold true for Greeks and Persians, for Englishmen and Mahrattas, for Frenchmen and Germans. (Clausewitz 1984, pp. 194–95)

Just as important as the actual numbers—or perhaps more important—are the variable factors describing the engagement, which must be "stripped out" for analysis. Clausewitz also states specifically that the fighting value, or effective-ness, of a military force is a given quantity (i.e., quite measurable), and he implies clearly that the quality of forces will vary from nation to nation and among units within national forces. Finally, he tells us that his formulation of the relationship of numbers to victory is historically timeless and applicable in any geographic setting. The "law of numbers" is a clear, unambiguous state-ment of a mathematical theory of combat, which Clausewitz asserts is valid throughout the course of history.

It is necessary to reconcile this interpretation of the law of numbers with the passages in Book Two of *On War*, where Clausewitz argues with himself the twin questions of whether war is a science or an art and whether or not war is amenable to theory. It is necessary also to reconcile this deterministic state-ment with the many references throughout *On War* to the role of chance in war, which has led many of his readers to assume that Clausewitz saw war as a random process with unpredictable results, rather than the mathematical pro-cess implied so clearly in the above quotation.

Despite some passages in *On War* that could be interpreted that way, Clause-witz did *not* think of chance as a roll of the dice determining victory or defeat. As is clear, for instance, in his famous quotation on "friction," he looked upon chance much as he did upon friction: it is one of many factors contributing to the confusion and chaos of battle. Indeed, the two concepts of chance and friction seem to have overlapped in his mind.

To Clausewitz the word *chance* meant that there will always be problems in battle that a commander cannot possibly foresee, problems that arise either because of the "innate perversity" of inanimate objects, or of nature, or of man himself. Even though not individually foreseeable, these problems of chance are things that a commander can—if he is ready—deal with and control by means of his "genius" in the same way in which his genius will enable him to overcome the even less predictable actions and reactions of his opponent.

What Clausewitz wrote about chance is fully reconcilable with his law of numbers. The outcome of the battle will be determined by the genius of the commander in bringing to the critical point on the battlefield a force superior in numerical combat power; by his genius in being adaptable and taking advantage of the "circumstances of the combat," including most of the variables of combat (not excepting friction and chance); and by his genius in ensuring the highest value (quality) of his troops.

Even though Clausewitz did not specifically say so, and even though he might not even have recognized the fact at the time of writing, his law of numbers is, indeed, a synthesis of a comprehensive theory of combat. Although Clausewitz never expressed that law as a formula, it is stated so clearly, and in such mathematical terms, that such a formula was unquestionably in his mind.

First we see Clausewitz's concept of battle outcome as a ratio:

$$\text{Outcome} = \frac{N_r \times V_r \times Q_r}{N_b \times V_b \times Q_b}$$

where:

N = numbers of troops
V = variable circumstances affecting a force in battle
Q = quality of force
r = red force identifier
b = blue force identifier

If that is a valid relationship—as Clausewitz asserts—then the following equation can be written for the combat power, P, of each of the opposing sides:

$$P = N \times V \times Q$$

Just as Newton's physics can be summarized by the simple equation $F = MA$, so, too, can Clausewitz's theory of combat be summarized in an equally simple equation: $P = NVQ$.

Future of a Theory of Combat

Although Clausewitz's Law of Numbers was published a century and a half ago, it has only recently been seriously proposed as the basis for a comprehensive theory of combat. This is probably because Clausewitz expressed his essentially mathematical concept in words rather than in equations. Therefore, it has been ignored by theorists seeking a theory expressed mathematically, because they have been looking for a mathematical form. It may be some time before the profundity and universality of Clausewitz's theory is accepted by those who have hitherto overlooked it in their search for *the* theory.

It may be safely predicted, however, that any alternative approach will have to take Clausewitz's theory into consideration and will have to come to terms with it, either consciously or unconsciously. Any alternative inconsistent with Clausewitz's theory, as presented above, will almost certainly be demonstrably invalid. Any alternative that is consistent with it cannot be fundamentally different.

TREVOR N. DUPUY

SEE ALSO: Friction; Strategy; Tactics.

Bibliography

Ardant du Picq, C. J. J. J. 1921. *Battle studies.* New York: Macmillan.

Belyakov, V. I. 1979. Correlation of forces and means. *Sovetskakila voennakila entsiklopedkila.* (Soviet military encyclopedia). Moscow: Voyenizdat.

Clausewitz, C. von. 1976 [1832]. *On war.* Reprint. Ed. and trans. M. Howard and P. Paret. Princeton, N.J.: Princeton Univ. Press.

Dodge, T. A. 1889–1907. *Great captains.* 6 vols. Boston: Houghton Mifflin.

Douhet, G. 1942. *The command of the air.* Trans. D. Ferrari. New York: Coward-McCann.

Dupuy, T. N. 1987. *Understanding war.* New York: Paragon House.

———, C. Johnson, and G. P. Hayes. 1986. *Dictionary of military terms.* New York: Wilson.

Earle, E. M., ed. 1971. *Makers of modern strategy.* Princeton, N.J.: Princeton Univ. Press.

Foch, F. 1970. *The principles of war.* Trans. J. de Morinni. New York: AMS Press.

Foertsch, H. 1940. *The art of modern warfare.* Trans. T. W. Knauth. New York: Veritas.

Fuller, J. F. C. 1961. *The conduct of war, 1789–1961.* London: Eyre and Spottiswoode.

Groener, W. 1927. *Das Testament des Grafen Schlieffen.* Berlin: E. S. Mittler & Sohn.

Jomini, A. H. 1830. *Tableau analytique des principales combinaisons de la guerre, et de leurs rapports avec la politique des états, pour servir d'introduction au Traité des grandes opérations militaries.* Paris: Anselin.

———. 1851. *Traité des qrandes opérations militaries, ou Histoire critique des guerres de Fréderic le Grand comparées au système moderne.* Paris: J. Dumaine.

Lanchester, F. W. 1914. The principle of concentration. *Engineering,* 2 October.

Mahan, A. T. 1884. *The influence of sea power on history, 1660–1783.* Boston: Little, Brown.

Paret, P., ed. 1986. *Makers of modern strategy.* Princeton, N.J.: Princeton Univ. Press.

Schlieffen, A. G. von. 1931. *Cannae.* Fort Leavenworth, Kans.: Command and General Staff School Press.

Sun Tzu. 1963. *The art of war.* Trans. S. B. Griffith. Oxford: Oxford Univ. Press.

Trythall, A. J. 1977. *"Boney" Fuller: The intellectual general.* London: Cassell.

U.S. Military Academy, Dept. of Military Art and Engineering. 1944. *Jomini, Clausewitz, and Schlieffen.* West Point, N.Y.: Dept. of Military Art and Engineering, U.S. Military Academy.

Wright, Q. 1942. *A study of war.* Chicago: Univ. of Chicago Press.

Yorck von Wartenburg, M. Graf. 1902. *Napoleon as a general.* 2 vols. London: K. Paul, Trench, Trubner.

TRANSPORTATION CORPS

Transportation in a military context classically refers to the loading and transport of materiel by men, animals, and vehicles from one place to another for supply and use.

In ancient times, transportation was an integral part of military movements over medium to long distances. Primarily, all weapons and war equipment that could not be obtained or captured on foreign soil were moved.

Thus, when Hannibal's troops crossed the Alps, they carried all their materiel by means of pack animals and the men themselves. The principle of carrying all that was needed for the battle and for self-preservation, however, could not be maintained for long. Wars of conquest into distant, roadless countries had compelled Alexander the Great, and later the armies of the Roman Empire, to depart from the procedure of drawing supply from the country through which they marched. The Roman legions had a very effective supply train with large bulk stores, which could be quickly replenished from the country if necessary. This remarkable logistic organization and the well-developed roads in those times contributed to the outstanding successes of the Roman armies.

During the centuries following the dissolution of the western Roman Empire, European armies generally moved ponderously, bound to rough roads in dry seasons and dependent on supply obtained from the country or from traveling vendors. Yet the Mongol hordes of Genghis Khan that swept over large areas of eastern Europe in the thirteenth century had an excellent system for carrying their supplies along with them.

Developments in the Last Three Centuries

European warfare regained a certain mobility from the innovations of Gustavus Adolphus II of Sweden at the beginning of the seventeenth century. He carefully organized and planned his supply. His armies were supported partly by fixed storage facilities, but also by the replenishment of stocks from the country.

In Prussia around 1740, Frederick the Great (Frederick II) established a permanent supply organization and introduced a transportation organization to carry provisions, field bakeries, and field hospitals. Because of his attempts at economizing, however, these arrangements were not always fully effective. For example, the transportation organization was mobilized only during wartime. Teams and wagons were registered, and on the day of mobilization the owner had to lease them to the state for a payment of 40 talers. The drivers received no military training and were merely supervised by retired cavalrymen. The Prussian army also employed river boats on the Oder, Havel, and Elbe for resupply purposes.

Even without real supply troops in the army of Frederick the Great, the supply services during the Seven Years' War were enormous. Transportation convoys of 1,000 vehicles were nothing out of the ordinary. These were so valuable that in 1758, when retreating from Olmütz, Frederick detached half of his army to escort his train of 4,000 vehicles and protect it from Austrian troops.

The armies of the French Revolution and of Napoleon brought mobility and depth to military operations in Europe, based on the stock they carried along and successful exploitation of the country by an outstanding supply organization. When a division invaded Russia, for example, the supply train carried provisions for 21 days. Important reasons for the defeat of Napoleon during the Russian campaign were that the large train could not keep pace with the advance and that the impoverished country could not provide enough to support the army.

Technical developments in the nineteenth century led to fundamental changes in the means and possibilities of warfare. A memorandum of Prince William (later King and Emperor William I) on 30 June 1851 established a "train cadre" for each of the nine corps of the Royal Prussian Army. In case of mobilization, each train cadre would provide five provisions columns, two field bakery columns, one horse depot, one stretcher company, and three light and three heavy field hospitals.

The order in council, dated 2 July 1860, budgeted nine train battalions that proved their worth in the campaigns of 1864, 1866, and 1870–71. A memorandum of the German General Staff about the Franco-German War of 1870–71 states in a few words the importance of the supply system: "It is due to the prudence and dutifulness of the officers and soldiers employed in the train that difficulties as to subsistence could be overcome without endangering the health of men and horses to a far higher degree than during other great wars."

Beginning in the nineteenth century, the effectiveness of resupply by means of the railway was proven. During the American Civil War, the rail transportation of soldiers, military equipment, and provisions was of decisive importance in many battles and for the final victory of the Union.

World War I to the Present

After the turn of the century, the advent of the motorized truck dramatically improved the possibilities of logistics.

World War I exceeded the scope of previous experiences in both qualitative and quantitative ways. Some figures will help to illustrate the scope of logistic requirements.

- In the years from 1914 to 1918, 13 million German soldiers were called up, compared with 1.4 million in the Franco-Prussian War of 1870–71.
- In 1870–71, a German army corps comprised approximately 30,000 men and 30 train vehicles. In 1914–18, the personnel strength had increased to 45,000 (i.e., by half) and the number of the train vehicles to 60 (double the size).
- During a single day of heavy battle in World War I, the German army expended more artillery ammunition than in the war of 1870–71 altogether.

The dimensions of these phenomena were hardly predictable, and the expansion of war naturally made them conspicuous in the logistics area.

In order to face the lack of resupply forces and to be able to concentrate forces, the German ammunition and train columns were separated from the corps and divisions and put under the command of the supreme headquarters of the army as internal units at the end of 1916. The standard vehicle was then the carriage and pair (still in service in the German Reichswehr until the

1930s). In addition, there were already motor vehicle forces. Organizational consolidation of the train and ammunition columns with these new units was only performed later on.

With the extension of World War II beyond the original strategic area and to several theaters of operations without immediate connection with each other, the requirements for supply and maintenance rapidly increased. Even more than during World War I the armed forces—including the air forces and the navies—faced an unprecedented organizational challenge.

The Transportation Corps Today

National and international developments of military logistics have taken slightly different paths, but objectives hardly differ. The overall objective is to make available to the troops the required quantities of supplies, equipment, provisions, fuel, weapons, spare parts, and especially ammunition as quickly as possible, in time and at the right place. Both supply and resupply are part of this global interpretation.

Today's logistic troops are the modern equivalent of the baggage and train that supplied the armies of ancient and medieval times.

In Fred E. Elam's *U.S. Army Transportation Corps*, he describes the tasks and principles of military transportation:

Purpose: to provide transportation services to the army, the Department of Defense, and other government agencies in peace and war.

Missions:
- develop transportation concepts and doctrine; develop unit organizations and the requirements to support acquisition of transportation systems for the army;
- provide training and professional development of active and reserve components and civilian personnel in transportation;
- plan, schedule, and supervise the use of each mode of transportation for the effective movement of personnel and cargo;
- perform transportation unit operations;
- provide terminal services for all modes of transportation and stevedoring services at fixed ports and unimproved beach sites;
- provide maintenance and supply for the army and rail equipment; and
- provide transportation engineering services.

Nearly the same principles apply to the French, British, Italian, and German logistic troops of the field armies.

Thus, *transportation corps* as a term is simple to define. It includes all actions that affect the transportation of goods, commodities, equipment, and men from one place to another in interlocking systems, convoys, or other transportation means. Its organization requires the composition of transportation units or integrated transportation systems to ensure military supply, loading, short-term storage, or delivery and replacement. Depending upon their role and the environment in which they operate, transportation units may be of different sizes, types, and compositions, such as air transportation, road transportation (trucks), railroad transportation, inland navigation, pipeline systems, pack animals in the mountains, and special transportation equipment.

The logistic troops of most Western military structures may be roughly broken down as follows (taking the German land forces as an example): resupply and supply units, transportation units, and maintenance units. These units may be fully mobile, via wheeled or tracked vehicles, or partly dependent on transportation assistance.

According to modern interpretation, *transportation* means not only the resupply and shipment of bulk supplies such as ammunition and fuel but also the supply of high-value, special, and deployed supplies via modern transportation and handling systems that have been adapted to the threat. Transportation vehicles must be adapted to the units to be supported, organized in appropriate units, and equipped with vehicles that have the necessary road and cross-country mobility and sufficient self-defense capability. To supply and support ground forces and to evacuate damaged materiel and casualties in emergencies, other methods of transportation may be employed. These include pack animals, helicopters, and tracked armored personnel carriers in the battle area as well as inland waterway craft. Firm arrangements among several allied nations provide for the rapid buildup of transportation and resupply forces; an example is the host nation support/wartime host nation support (HNS/WHNS) between Britain, the United States, and Germany.

According to James A. Huston (1988), the recognized principles of transportation may be illustrated by this list of requirements: principles of logistics, transportation, materiel precedence, forward impetus, mobility, dispersion, economy, feasibility, flexibility, relativity, continuity, timeliness, unity of command, and simplicity.

The need for modern armies to ensure the high availability of their forces and means in future wars will dictate changes and developments in army logistics. These developments will be driven by the need to: (1) make the most effective use of logistic troops so that they can achieve the increased handling and transportation efficiency that will be required during rapid operations; (2) present (and perhaps face) a permanent threat on the battlefield; and (3) ensure the survival of the fighting soldier.

Challenges to the System

The challenges to logistic troops have changed. Men may now be replaced by technological means, and resultant high materiel consumption rates must be balanced by effective transportation systems. The threat to resupply will increase during quick, intensive operations, thus increasing requirements. Transportation and transfer of supplies to the weapons systems now and in the future must be carried out in support assembly areas, in the fighting positions, or on the battlefield during mobile operations. Those in charge of army logistics must strive constantly to obtain better systems for rapid support of the troops. Rationalization, mechanization, and automation of air transportation means and the use of civil means of transportation and handling may enhance the effectiveness and efficiency of the supply troops.

Many armed forces already respond to the changed requirements of the 1990s with better performance and improvement of the payload of tactical transport vehicles. For example, the German "MULTI" palletized loading system already available will be developed so that its interoperability with the appropriate PLS (palletized load system) or DROPS (demountable rack off-loading and pickup system) of the U.S. and British armies is ensured. This multinational system possibly will be joined by the French army; with it, NATO will have a system that meets all tactical requirements for flexibility and high mobility and results in a considerable improvement of the efficiency of army logistics.

Aspects of the Future

The rapidly changing combat situation in modern warfare makes battlefield resupply and maintenance difficult. Weapons systems and equipment must be highly efficient and easy to maintain. This requires systems with the most up-to-date design and an even closer coordination between logistics and battlefield command.

The requirements of logistics must be considered at an early stage in the development of military materiel so that new equipment will not need technical adaptation but will meet requirements and can be employed effectively. Supply to the most forward battle line is required—without losses, quickly, and in sufficient quantities. Repairability and manageability of combat-essential supplies, allowing quick restoration of field use, are the top maxims of operative logistics.

Modern ground forces have ever-increasing requirements for capacity and flexibility in the transportation and handling ability of their logistic troops. Improvement of efficiency linked to an increased personnel demand can rarely be realized, because of the ever-tighter personnel and financial situation of most countries' armed forces. Therefore, every effort must be made to improve the efficiency of transportation capacity by increasing the payload per vehicle and to improve handling capacity by integration into the vehicle.

Both requirements are perfectly linked in the trilateral and interoperable transportation and handling system MULTI/PLS/DROPS. This system has proven its capability in numerous tests in the civil and military area, in all places where supplies had to be handled often and transported over short distances on hard-surface roads as well as over other terrain.

Changes in technology and tactics will require continuing innovations and follow-on developments as far as both combat and combat support troops are concerned.

The logistic troops are an indispensable part of an army. They ensure sustainability in wartime. In the near future, they will face the inevitable obligation to improve the ratio of efficiency between personnel and materiel and to heighten the flexibility and serviceability of the systems.

GÜNTHER NAGEL

SEE ALSO: Combat Service Support; Combat Support; Logistics: A General Survey.

Bibliography

Huston, J. A. 1988. 16 principles of logistics. *Army Logistician*, September–October, pp. 14–15.

Kasch, H., and F. Steinseifer. 1987. Vom Tross zur Nachschubtruppe. *Truppenpraxis*, May, pp. 488–92.

Scholl, W. 1989. Der Lkw MULTI kann viel. *Truppenpraxis*, January, pp. 52–56.

ADDITIONAL SOURCES: *The U.S. Army Transportation Corps.*

UNCONVENTIONAL WAR

The term *unconventional war* can be used to describe a wide variety of types of conflict not bound by the classical guidelines that normally shape the nature and use of military power.

Guerrilla warfare lies within the unconventional warfare category and is its most significant manifestation. When the strength of guerrilla forces has increased (in numbers, equipment, and training) to the point where they can engage conventional military power in direct confrontation, the terms *guerrilla* and *unconventional* no longer apply.

Unconventional warfare, including that involving guerrillas, may occur in peacetime (in a low-intensity-conflict environment) or in wartime. Clandestine and covert activities involving intelligence, counterintelligence, subversion, sabotage, psychological operations, terrorism, kidnapping, and establishment of evasion and escape mechanisms are integral elements of unconventional warfare.

A published work by Professor Friedrich August Frhr. von der Heydte entitled *Modern Irregular Warfare* (1986) provides an especially comprehensive and thoughtful examination of the phenomena within which unconventional warfare is included.

Guerrilla Warfare

The term *guerrilla*, which came into general usage during the Peninsular War (1808–14), means *little war* in Spanish. Spanish *guerrilleros*, whose roots were within the indigenous population, succeeded in impeding and frustrating the French invaders, eroding their position and forces to such a degree that the guerrillas were a significant factor in the defeat and withdrawal of Napoleon's forces from the Iberian Peninsula. By the latter part of the twentieth century, *guerrilla* had become an accepted part of the international military lexicon. Used as a noun it describes an individual, usually a volunteer, who is part of an organized band that uses unorthodox tactics against both civilian and military targets. Guerrilla warfare is a product of social, political, economic, psychological, and military factors that combine in varying degrees and under a wide range of circumstances to determine its character at any given time. Guerrilla warfare is the province of psychological warfare, terrorism, sabotage, and subversion.

Supporting Mechanisms

The emergence of a guerrilla force capable of carrying out irregular warfare missions is usually preceded by growth of an illegal underground organization. Cellular in nature, the underground structure is designed to avoid detection by the security and counterintelligence systems of the society within which it is implanted.

The steps and procedures that lead to the formation of a subversive infrastructure may involve a wide variety of activities that are not unique to guerrilla warfare. They include clandestine intelligence and counterintelligence strategies, tactics, and training.

The subversive underground may be supplemented by an auxiliary force of individuals who serve the gestating guerrilla movement in a variety of ways, while ostensibly pursuing normal lives within the civilian community. This support may include provision of intelligence, assistance in the conduct of psychological operations, spotting for recruitment, and both financial and logistic help. The underground is the incubating mechanism that the architects of revolution and resistance use to recruit, motivate, train, and launch the fledgling elements of guerrilla operational units capable of performing paramilitary tasks.

Guerrillas are most vulnerable to countermeasures by security forces during the early stages of guerrilla development. However, because of the restraints placed upon governmental investigative powers in some societies, the subversive underground may remain relatively undisturbed while it develops the vital components of a guerrilla force. When active guerrilla operational units begin to appear in the field, the infrastructure that spawned them within the civilian population continues to function as their principal lifeline.

General Characteristics of Guerrilla Movements

Distinguishing features of successful guerrilla movements have invariably included some or all of the following:
1. extraordinary motivation and willingness to accept extreme hardships and iron discipline
2. popular sympathy for the perceived goals of the guerrilla movement
3. charismatic leadership
4. suitable terrain
5. access to food
6. an efficient intelligence network
7. tactical aptitude together with training in weapons, demolitions, field medicine, and communications.

Any notion that discipline among guerrilla forces tends to be more casual and relaxed than that of conventional armies is misleading. Whereas the "spit-and-polish," military courtesy, and formality that are traditional in the military profession are not characteristic of guerrilla units, there are, however, rigid standards with regard to interpersonal behavior, devotion to duty, and tactical performance in the field. Violations of these rules and lapses or derelictions that lead to loss of life or equipment or that compromise security can result in severe summary punishment without possibility for appeal.

Guerrilla Warfare Goals and Objectives

Although the permutations and combinations of conditions, events, and personalities that give rise to guerrilla warfare are many, certain general scenarios are likely to reoccur. Among these are:
1. guerrillas fighting against their own unpopular government
2. indigenous guerrilla forces aligned with their own military and security forces against those of a foreign invader
3. indigenous guerrilla forces supporting their own military and security forces and those of a friendly foreign nation against a common enemy
4. two or more indigenous guerrilla forces struggling against each other to seize political control.

When a guerrilla movement surfaces as a result of deep and widespread discontent, the government held to be the culprit is not likely to survive, whether or not it receives massive assistance from foreign sources.

Guerrilla Tactics: Field Operations

Whether aimed at a foreign invader or against an unpopular indigenous government, guerrilla warfare has certain common characteristics. Among these is the requirement for terrain, rugged or otherwise difficult enough to provide cover and concealment at least for small groups. Guerrilla bases, although established in locations that are difficult to discover and to reach, are never meant to be defended at length.

Routes to alternate base areas are reconnoitered in advance of anticipated contact with the enemy. Such areas are occupied only as long as they are undiscovered and unmolested by the enemy. High mobility is indispensable to a guerrilla field unit. Guerrilla camps and bivouacs can be expected to be abandoned hastily and in good tactical order. Cached supplies and equipment are prelocated in the vicinity of alternate guerrilla bases or at mission support sites in areas where tactical operations may take place. A guerrilla attack calling for concerted action by several bands is followed by immediate post-action dispersal. Each band withdraws to its own prechosen mission support site in preparation for further withdrawal if pursued by the enemy.

Training in the use of demolitions equipment for sabotage and harassment of lines of communication is of particular importance to guerrillas. Such training usually includes emphasis on improvisation, using items and supplies normally found in civilian markets open to the public. Guerrilla workshops may also turn captured or stolen munitions into antipersonnel mines and booby traps.

Individual guerrilla bands must be relatively small to subsist, escape detection, and move quickly. Coordination among guerrilla tactical units for engaging important targets is achieved in various ways. Advances in overhead reconnaissance, together with sophisticated systems for locating and analyzing electronic emissions, make centralized control of dispersed guerrilla bands more difficult. Mission-type orders, use of couriers, and prearranged signals for general phases of an operation take the place of tight control.

Guerrilla tactics against conventional forces can be compared with those of a picador, the horseman with a lance who, in the course of a bullfight, sticks the bull repeatedly but is not expected ever to deliver the coup de grâce.

Through good intelligence, careful reconnaissance, mobility, and surprise, manageable elements of the enemy's system are engaged in short, sharp encounters. The aim is not to annihilate the more powerful enemy force but only those parts the guerrilla force is able to isolate and digest. Quick dispersal and withdrawal to safe areas following a guerrilla assault places a major burden upon the security forces of the enemy, especially when the guerrilla force, which was concentrated only for its attack, fragments into a number of small bands, each retreating in a different direction. Security forces often find themselves ill-prepared to cope with the concept of a nonlinear battlefield, let alone an evasive enemy who appears to have ephemeral but repeated life. Conventional pursuit forces become correspondingly more frustrated. Held hostage to a lack of intelligence, they are incapacitated from wielding their superior strength and firepower against the fleeting guerrilla, while simultaneously experiencing increased vulnerabilities to the guerrilla.

To shield themselves from the multiple pinpricks and bee stings inflicted by guerrillas, conventional forces are forced to allocate more and more of their effort to defense. Isolated outposts, way stations along lines of communication, and small groups traveling in rear areas become vulnerable to guerrilla attack. The psychological impact of a guerrilla presence on the morale of the conventional forces is increased through propaganda emanating from the underground, auxiliaries, and the guerrillas themselves.

Guerrilla actions become bolder and heavier as enemy formations show signs of waning resolve. In the words of Mao Tse-tung, the timeless guerrilla tactical philosophy framed first by Mao's ancestor Sun Tzu (400–320 B.C.) remains: "The enemy advances, we retreat; the enemy camps, we harass; the enemy tires, we attack; the enemy retreats, we pursue" (Griffith 1963, p. 51).

Of more recent origin but also reflecting the tactical military wisdom of the ages, the standing orders of the colonial American ranger commander, Maj. Robert Rogers, contain advice that modern guerrillas still find valuable. Written in the American vernacular of the time, the orders, dated 1759, instruct the rangers as follows:

a. Don't forget nothing.
b. Have your musket clean as a whistle, hatchet scoured, 60 rounds powder and ball, and be ready to march at a minute's warning.
c. When you're on the march, act the way you would if you was sneaking up on a deer. See the enemy first.
d. Tell the truth about what you see and what you do. There is an army depending on us for correct information. You can lie all you please

when you tell other folks about the rangers, but don't never lie to a ranger or officer.

e. Don't never take a chance you don't have to.

f. When we're on the march we march single file, far enough apart so one shot can't go through two men.

g. If we strike swamps, or soft ground, we spread out abreast, so it's hard to track us.

h. When we march, we keep moving till dark, so as to give the enemy the least possible chance at us.

i. When we camp, half the party stays awake while the other half sleeps.

j. If we take prisoners, we keep 'em separate till we have had time to examine them, so they can't cook up a story between 'em.

k. Don't ever march home the same way [you came]. Take a different route so you won't be ambushed.

l. No matter whether we travel in big parties or little ones, each party has to keep a scout 20 yards ahead, 20 yards on each flank and 20 yards on the rear, so the main body can't be surprised and wiped out.

m. Every night you'll be told where to meet if surrounded by a superior force.

n. Don't sit down to eat without posting sentries.

o. Don't sleep beyond dawn. Dawn's when the French and Indians attack.

p. Don't cross a river by a regular ford.

q. If somebody's trailing you, make a circle, come back onto your own tracks and ambush the folks that aim to ambush you.

r. Don't stand up when the enemy's coming against you. Kneel down, lie down, hide behind a tree.

s. Let the enemy come till he's almost close enough to touch. Then let him have it and jump out and finish him up with your hatchet.

Guerrilla Operations: Impact Upon Targets

From the viewpoint of conventional forces, guerrillas constitute a will-o'-the-wisp, appearing and disappearing, always to be guarded against. If ignored they can draw blood in increasing amounts until active countermeasures are instituted. These countermeasures in turn draw upon resources that would otherwise be available for the conduct of conventional warfare.

Although a guerrilla force may be outnumbered by an enemy that is on the strategic offensive, the guerrillas can be active in tactical offense. The cumulative effects of innumerable small tactical initiatives can become a major factor in changing the overall military posture of the enemy. This is especially true if the guerrilla actions are undertaken in coordination with the operations of a friendly conventional force.

Interaction Between Guerrillas and Friendly Conventional Forces

Guerrilla effectiveness can be increased if a friendly conventional force provides small detachments to assist the guerrillas with logistics, communications, intelligence, and fire support. Historical experience suggests that it may be wise for these detachments to refrain from interfering with the guerrilla command and control structure, which may differ substantially from that of the conventional forces.

If the roots of the guerrilla movement are firmly embedded in the indigenous population, the psychological effect of repeated guerrilla attacks together with the real damage stemming from sabotage and concurrent conventional military pressure may begin to turn the enemy's posture from the strategic offensive to strategic defensive. At this critical juncture, the commander of the friendly conventional force, who understands the complex nature of irregular warfare and its role with regard to his own strategy, will begin to give serious attention to raising the quality of the guerrilla forces. He must bring them closer to an organizational and training level that will permit them to engage effectively in conventional combat. In this connection, Mao Tse-tung (1966) warns that:

> If the commander of a main force has made the mistake of neglecting the interests of the local population and local governments as a result of a purely military approach, he must correct it in order that the expansion of the main force and multiplication of the local armed units may both receive due attention.
>
> To raise the quality of guerrilla units it is imperative to raise their political and organizational level and to improve their equipment, military technique and discipline so that they gradually pattern themselves on the regular force and shed their guerrilla ways. (p. 182)

Guerrilla Interaction with the Population

It is a cardinal principle that a guerrilla force can be successful only if it has the support of the population from which it has been raised; it follows that the guerrilla's attitude toward and actions having an impact on that population must be above criticism. To this end, Mao Tse-tung's famous Three Main Rules of Discipline and Eight Points for Attention were learned by heart, recited regularly, and even put to music and sung by his guerrilla forces.

THE GENERAL HEADQUARTERS OF
THE CHINESE PEOPLE'S LIBERATION ARMY
October 10, 1947

Our Army's Three Main Rules of Discipline and Eight Points for Attention have been practiced for many years, but their contents vary slightly in army units in different areas. They have now been unified and are hereby reissued. It is expected that this version will be taken as the standard one for thorough education in the army and strict enforcement. As to other matters needing attention, the high command of the armed forces in different areas may lay down additional points in accordance with specific conditions and order their enforcement.

The Three Main Rules of Discipline are as follows:

- Obey orders in all your actions.
- Do not take a single needle or piece of thread from the masses.
- Turn in everything captured.

The Eight Points for Attention are as follows:

- Speak politely.
- Pay fairly for what you buy.
- Return everything you borrow.
- Pay for anything you damage.
- Do not hit or swear at people.
- Do not damage crops.
- Do not take liberties with women.
- Do not ill-treat captives.

Foreign Forces and Indigenous Guerrillas

The extent to which an indigenous guerrilla movement may be of benefit to the national strategic posture of a foreign country is a function of several variables. These include the competence, charisma, and motivation of the principal guerrilla leaders; the causes that are seen to have given rise to their movement; the compatibility of their political aims with those of the outside power that seeks their cooperation; and the physical environment within which the guerrilla forces must operate.

Cooperation of indigenous guerrilla bands in tactical operations of foreign military forces may be influenced by liaison personnel who provide training in selective advanced skills and arrange for the delivery of equipment and supplies needed by the guerrillas. Attempts by foreign liaison officers to command guerrilla movements are apt to fail for the very reasons that set the guerrilla movement in motion. With feelings and convictions strong enough to result in subversion, insurrection, or rebellion, guerrilla leaders are not likely to abdicate their control in favor of a representative of a foreign power whose tactical and strategic objectives stem from completely different sources.

Historical experience indicates that foreign liaison with guerrilla movements calls for individuals who are mature; knowledgeable concerning the languages, culture, history, and mores of the guerrillas' homeland; and who can participate in the guerrilla councils as a responsible spokesman for the governments that sent them. In addition, liaison officers must be able to meet the punishing physical demands of the guerrilla environment and to share its dangers, frustrations, and hardships.

The liaison officer is of primary importance for achieving coordination between guerrilla warfare and regular military operations. He must, therefore, understand the art of war in all its applicable dimensions in addition to having a grasp of the political factors that govern the overall objectives of the conflict.

An important function of the liaison officer is keeping his own headquarters advised of supporting actions that may reasonably be expected of the guerrilla force. The liaison officer must also be a competent analyst of the guerrilla leadership so that his own government may be fully aware of the consequences of assisting a movement that could later become a serious political liability. He must keep in mind also that the purely military impact of hit-and-run tactics, light weapons, and limited defensive capabilities may be marginal.

On the other hand, guerrilla support for tactical operations of a friendly conventional force can yield much more than the benefits that accrue from harassing the enemy. They can also strike soft targets located deep in the enemy rear. They can provide flank protection from enemy patrols. They can collect critical intelligence from the local indigenous population, which results in enhanced security from infiltrators in the friendly rear areas.

The willingness of guerrilla leaders to accept and act upon orders from a friendly conventional force commander will vary greatly. Factors other than the accomplishment of a purely military mission will bear upon the guerrilla leader's decision to risk resources for which he has other plans and uses.

Political Factors Bearing upon Guerrilla Warfare

In the Soviet Union during the German invasion of World War II, there was no question as to whether the partisan guerrillas would place all of their efforts behind those of the Soviet armed forces. Through liaison officers from the Soviet army, Russian partisans received training, leadership, and instructions, which they normally carried out to the best of their ability. By contrast, differing political aims among the several guerrilla factions in Greece during the same period served to weaken their combined effectiveness against the occupying Axis armies.

Allied decisions to provide logistics support to specific Greek guerrilla groups were subject to hotly debated questions as to whether the military advantages that might accrue in each case took precedence over the possibly adverse political consequences of such assistance. The Allies faced a similar dilemma in Yugoslavia where two movements capable of conducting meaningful guerrilla operations against the German forces were also aligned against each other in what was essentially a political struggle. The Chetniks, under Col. Kosta Pecanac and later under Gen. Draza Mihailovic, were motivated mainly by their dedication to Serbian nationalism, while the irregular forces that had been brought together by Marshal Tito (Josip Broz) were Communist oriented. Indeed, Tito had been the leader of the Yugoslav Communist Party during the time it had been illegal in Yugoslavia. In effect, Mihailovic was widely seen to represent the "establishment," which was held responsible by much of the Yugoslavian population for a great many of Yugoslavia's prewar social and economic ills.

The charisma of Tito, together with the skillful use of propaganda and persuasion, served to rally to his cause large numbers of Yugoslavians who perceived the Communist formula as the key to a better life in their postwar nation. Moreover, the Communist expertise in organization of underground movements was directly applicable to the tasks involved in recruiting, training, motivating, and deploying guerrilla forces. Allied aid to Mihailovic netted little in the way of military returns, while assistance to Tito paid dividends, the ultimate cost of which would be predominantly political.

Whereas historic cases abound showing the extent to which guerrilla operations might supplement, complement, or even frustrate conventional military campaigns, strategic planners should be aware of the overriding influence of political factors on scenarios in which guerrilla warfare plays even moderate roles. While it is widely accepted that guerrilla warfare is the weapon of the weak against the strong, its strength relies on its application against the weakest elements of an enemy force.

WILLIAM P. YARBOROUGH

SEE ALSO: Low-intensity Conflict: The Military Dimension; Psychological Warfare.

Bibliography

Asprey, R. B. 1975. *War in the shadows: The guerrilla in history.* 2 vols. Garden City, N.Y.: Doubleday.

Blair, C. N. M. 1957. *Guerrilla warfare.* London: Ministry of Defence.

Broz, J., et al. 1970. *The Yugoslav concept of general peoples defense.* Belgrade: Review of International Affairs, Nemanjuia 34.

Challiand, G. 1982. *Guerrilla strategies: An historical anthology from the Long March to Afghanistan.* Berkeley, Calif.: Univ. of California Press.

Condit, D. M. 1961. Case study in guerrilla war: Greece during World War II. Washington, D.C.: American Univ. Press.

Griffith, S. B. 1963. *Sun Tzu, The art of war.* Oxford: Clarendon Press.

Jureidini, P. A., et al. 1962. *Casebook on insurgency and revolutionary warfare: 23 summary accounts.* Washington, D.C.: American Univ. Press.

La Charite, N. A. 1963. *Case studies in insurgency and revolutionary warfare: Cuba 1953–1959.* Washington, D.C.: American Univ. Press.

Lawrence, T. E. 1973. *The seven pillars of wisdom.* London: Jonathan Cape.

Lettow-Vorbeck, P. E. von. 1920. *My reminiscences of East Africa.* London: Hurst and Blackett.

Mao Tse-tung. 1966. *Selected military writings.* Peking: Foreign Language Press.

Molnar, A. L. 1963. *Undergrounds in insurgent revolutionary and resistance warfare.* Washington, D.C.: American Univ. Press.

Tanham, G. K. 1961. *Communist revolutionary warfare.* New York: Frederick A. Praeger.

Thomas, W. "R." 1981. *Guerrilla warfare, cause and conflict.* Washington, D.C.: National Defense Univ. Press.

Von der Heydte, F. A. 1986. *Modern irregular warfare.* New York: New Benjamin Franklin House.

Zawodny, J. K., et al. 1962. *Unconventional warfare.* Philadelphia: The Annals of the American Academy of Political and Social Science.

URBAN WARFARE

In developing nations, with their low level of urbanization, most armed conflicts culminate in fighting for the control of the few key cities. Whether in a war between neighboring states or during an insurrection, it is considered of paramount importance to seize, or hold, the urban centers to act as bases from which to exert influence on the whole country, although, of course, merely holding the cities will not necessarily ensure success.

This emphasis on urban warfare in developing countries contrasts with the renewed emphasis put by the Western military on maneuver warfare in Europe. Because Central Europe is one of the most urbanized regions on earth, skeptics have argued the focus should be more on urban warfare than on traditional open-terrain operations of heavy armor. Such critical arguments are explored below.

Reasons It Is Not Popular

Even experts critical of the mainstream concede that urban warfare has not been excluded from the process of developing doctrine for ground forces operations (Mahan 1984, p. 43). For instance, the increasing concentration of U.S. Army manuals on maneuver warfare has been supplemented by additional volumes dealing with "military operations on urbanized terrain" (MOUT).

These doctrinal statements have been transformed into detailed training and evaluation programs, although realistic training facilities are still scarce in Western armies. The facility of the German Bundeswehr in Hammelburg, for example, has been overbooked throughout the years. Obviously, official lip service paid to the importance of urban warfare has so far not resulted in an adequate infrastructure.

This apparent lack of pressure fits well with the fact that, cautiously put, the issue does not incite enthusiasm among professional soldiers. This was demonstrated by a quantitative content analysis of relevant professional journals of the U.S. Army (Mahan 1984, p. 44). In recent years, this picture has not changed significantly. For instance, after the Army Science Board (Ad Hoc Group on Military Operations in Builtup Areas [MOBA] 1978, p. 75) found a "curious lack" of interest in the development of MOBA-oriented equipment, related improvements have been moderate at best. This lack of interest could prove to be counterproductive because "antitank missiles [and] artillery . . . rounds do not arm themselves until they are a considerable distance from the firing weapon—commonly 30 to 65 meters' distance. Many situations in urban areas will call for effect at less than half of those distances" (Mahan 1984, p. 45).

Resorting to military and political psychology may, for the moment, provide a satisfactory explanation for this blind spot. John Keegan, a military writer who has advocated the reinstitution of first-class, dismounted infantry along with the integration of villages and urban sprawl into new schemes of fortification, remarks: "Fortifications lack glamour. Rommel is remembered and admired not for his construction of the Atlantic Wall but for his derring-do in the desert at the head of his panzers" (Keegan 1982, p. 53). In other words, mechanization is at the center of military attention, and professional careers are built around it.

In addition, many members of the military may feel that preparing for combat in built-up areas, and writing or talking about it, could frighten and badly irritate at least that part of the civilian community that war could directly affect.

Why Urban Warfare Is Important

Seriously preparing for urban warfare in central Europe is considered necessary for three basic reasons. First, take the example of the Federal Republic of Germany: by 1985 approximately 15 percent of its land area was urbanized, and that figure will certainly double by the end of the century (Jolley 1979, p. 28). For the average brigade commander this would mean about 25 towns and villages in his 12- by 25-kilometer sector (U.S. Department of the Army 1979, p. 1–3).

Second, an opposing division commander engaged in concentrating for a breakthrough would face a mirror image of the above density. At any one time he would have to deal with 10 to 15 towns and villages—his division's frontage varying between 8 and 12 kilometers.

Third, the other side's (former Warsaw Pact) forces train for urban combat. Their training programs may well meet Western standards, and the related infrastructure has been said to be superior. There are indications that Soviet military doctrine emphasized the need to avoid time-consuming battles in built-up areas (Donnelly 1977, p. 238). It seems to have been equally accepted, however, that in certain cases fighting for the control of a populated area could become unavoidable. In this context, one may think of road junctions and bridges whose control is vital for a mobile operation's success and that are, for natural reasons, located in the middle of a town or a city.

Advantages for the Defender

Those who propose to put more emphasis on utilizing built-up areas for defensive operations think of three main approaches (Bracken 1975; Canby 1980; U.S. Department of the Army 1988, p. 87).

The City as a Trap

This argument goes as follows: if those towns and cities that the aggressor needs to control to maintain the momentum of his armored advance quickly mounted a first-rate infantry defense, the outcome could be remarkable.

Storming such a place would require a significantly overproportionate number of airborne and/or crack motorized-rifle units capable of operating in small teams with considerable initiative, organized in a combined-arms mode with tanks acting as assault guns. Even if the assault were successful, it could turn out to be very costly for the victor. These costs might include delays in the overall attack plan, resulting in hasty improvisations and the diversion of notoriously scarce and therefore precious elite infantry forces from other vital missions (such as the taking of command posts and sensors out in the field or serving as a "penetration aid" for armor).

CHECKERED OR ARCHIPELAGO DEFENSE

The creation of area-covering schemes of interconnected, mutually supporting strongholds is well known from recent military history. The British did it against Rommel's forces with their "checker zone" at Alam Halfa (near El Alamein) in August 1942, and the Germans used this pattern of an *archipelago defense* (a term attributed to J. F. C. Fuller) to thwart a British breakthrough attempt, code-named "Goodwood," in Normandy, July 1944.

Similar proposals related to the situation in Central Europe envisage networks consisting of German villages and urban sprawl turned into fortified strongholds (Fig. 1). Each of these localities would house combined teams of infantry with mortars, antitank guided weapons, and an artillery component. If directly attacked, these teams could provide each other with fire support. Normally they would check the advance of mechanized—or other—forces seeking passage through the system. The intruding forces would have to expose themselves to fire at their flanks. As a consequence, they could get broken up and canalized to their disadvantage, delayed, or even stopped. In any case, they would suffer from attrition.

Many see the archipelago defense as an optimal combination of rugged stability and flexibility. Small wonder that it has been suggested for implementation mainly across the key axes of a potential adversary's advance!

AMBUSH, ANCHOR, ANVIL: COOPERATION WITH HEAVY COUNTERATTACK

A defender, who follows the prescriptions sketched out above, may be able to collect benefits beyond the immediate advantages inherent in the military control of built-up areas. It has been suggested that the features of urbanization be viewed as elements of a static structure that could protect and orient mobile

Figure 1. A German couple strolls by Bradley fighting vehicles parked in the town of Langgöns, Germany. (SOURCE: U.S. Air Force)

operations, thereby increasing the effectiveness of the overall defense effort. In this context, three assumed functions are especially noteworthy:

First, urbanized areas—particularly those defended by light troops—could serve to mask the assembly of friendly forces for a surprise counterattack on passing enemy formations.

Second, urban strongholds or a village-based area defense could provide heavy, mobile elements with flank protection, or an "anchor," or "pivot"—in other words: stable points of reference around which fluid forces could be organized.

Third, immobilizing the aggressor's forces in a city or in the cross fire of a defensive checker zone could lead to vulnerable buildups of their follow-on forces. This would create excellent conditions for hammer-and-anvil operations to be executed by the defender: his static elements forming the "anvil" and his mobile counterattack forces being the "hammer."

Disadvantages

The picture of urban warfare is not as rosy as it appears at first glance, however. Critical arguments of considerable weight suggest the military's reluctance to show more than the minimum necessary interest in the issue does not stem from psychological factors alone. Here are the arguments.

First, towns and, especially, cities are said to have the potential to absorb a lot of occupation manpower even if they are undefended. This seems to be a function of a city's size and complexity. In any case, guiding long marching columns through all the bottlenecks of an urban area could prove to be very time consuming, even without the normal engine breakdowns and accidents.

The introduction of civil resistance schemes, meaning low-risk strategies for the ordinary citizen, could additionally render a town or a city indigestible from an aggressor's perspective (Nolte and Nolte 1984).

Yet another idea to make attack formations abstain from storming densely populated places comes from the conceptual thinking of alternative defense. This school of thought strongly emphasizes defensive structures that cover the areas around towns and cities. In other words, there would be a penalty on entering as well as on leaving such places. As a result, the seizure of towns would lose much of its military value (Unterseher 1989, p. 253). If, as a consequence of these considerations, most of the urbanized areas remained undefended, collateral damage could be greatly reduced. And, even if that first-rate infantry, required for the defense of cities, could be overcome only by an overproportionate allocation of assault forces, their employment in other roles (i.e., manning natural or man-made obstacles out in the field) could be made equally cost effective.

Second, modern sensor technology appears to have reduced significantly the chances of armor moving and assembling in built-up areas without detection. Collateral damage—if buildings in areas of suspected movements are destroyed preemptively by air strikes or artillery fire—is another consideration, as is the problem of trying to rapidly maneuver armored troops through piles of debris.

And third, turning villages and urban sprawl into interconnected strongholds greatly facilitates an opponent's fire coordination simply because these easily identifiable localities constitute systematic, lucrative targets. This is all the more self-defeating since new kinds of "unconventional conventional" munitions (e.g., fuel-air explosives) render even the most solid German farmhouses useless as shelters for fire teams.

All this, however, does not deal the basic idea of a static, infantry-centered area defense a lethal blow. Such defense would be very survivable as well as effective if its combat teams were randomly dispersed in the field but capable of systematic fire coordination.

Richard Simpkin has called such a pattern a "universal net." "The net's task is . . . mobility denial in the broadest sense, based on the blocking of routes. The aim is to pose a sufficient threat to force the enemy to move up massed infantry, dismount it, and clear through the hindering terrain on foot." The defender "can create an instant anvil of fire wherever he wants just by thickening up the net . . . while his mobile force [the 'hammer'] has free play on surface routes" (Simpkin 1985, pp. 302, 303).

Lutz Unterseher

See Also: Air-land Battle; Defense; Doctrine; Infantry; Mechanized Warfare.

Bibliography

Ad Hoc Group on Military Operations in Builtup Areas (MOBA). 1978. *Final report*. Army Science Board.

Bracken, P. 1975. West European urban sprawl as an active defense variable. In *Military strategy and tactics*, ed. R. Huber. New York: Plenum.

Canby, S. 1980. Territorial defense in Central Europe. *Armed Forces and Society* 7:51–68.

Donnelly, C. N. 1977. Soviet techniques for combat in built up areas. *International Defense Review* (2):238–42.

Jolley, R. L. 1979. Military operations on urban terrain. *Infantry Journal*, July–August, pp. 27–29.

Keegan, J. 1982. Soviet blitzkrieg: Who wins? *Harper's*, May, pp. 46–53.

Mahan, J. 1984. MOUT: The quiet imperative. *Military Review*, 64:42–58.

Nolte, H.-H., and W. Nolte. 1984. *Ziviler Widerstand und Autonome Abwehr*. Baden-Baden: Nomos.

Simpkin, R. E. 1985. *Race to the swift: Thoughts on twenty-first century warfare*. London: Brassey's.

Unterseher, L. 1989. Ein anderes Heer: Wesentliche Einzelheiten. In *Strukturwandel der Verteidigung*, ed. Studiengruppe Alternative Sicherheitspolitik. Gerlingen: Bleicher.

U.S. Department of the Army. 1979. *Field manual 90-10: Military operations on urbanized terrain (MOUT)*. Washington, D.C.: Government Printing Office.

———. 1982. *Field manual 90-10-1: An infantryman's guide to urban combat*. Washington, D.C.: Government Printing Office.

WARRANT OFFICER

The emergence of the rank of warrant officer, which falls between that of the commissioned officer and the noncommissioned officer, resulted both from the fact that men of noble birth predominated among commissioned officers and that there was an increase in complexity of the occupational structure of military organizations. The distinction between a commissioned officer and a warrant officer is based on relative rank and utilization. In the United States, the majority of regular warrant officers hold commissions from the president. Junior warrant officers and reserve warrant officers are appointed by warrant of the secretary of the army, the secretary of the navy, or, in the case of the Coast Guard, the secretary of transportation. The United States Court of Claims has held that the words *warrant* and *commission* are synonymous because (in the navy) both warrants and commissions are signed by the president (*Brown v. U.S.*, 18 Ct. Cl. 543).

In seventeenth-century England, masters, boatswains, gunners, and men with similar technical naval skills (appointed by warrant of the Navy Board) were the first full-time personnel of the Royal Navy. Warrant officers provided continuity during the years before commissioned officers served full time and before the long-term service rating was introduced in the Royal Navy during the Victorian period (Lewis 1959). Not surprisingly, the Continental Navy in eighteenth-century North America and the Coast Guard of the new United States included boatswains, carpenters, surgeons, pursers, and others as warrant officers (Bourjaily 1965).

While usually considered a naval rank—the rank of warrant officer did not appear in the U.S. Army until the twentieth century—there is evidence that warrant officer was a rank in Napoleon's army. Warrant officers were used to pass orders from the commissioned officers to the ranks, thus serving to facilitate command from the noble-born officers to the peasantry, who were the common soldiers (Bourjaily 1965).

As the professionalization of commissioned officers developed and they began to serve full time, the opportunity for upward mobility among warrant officers became an issue. In England, the opportunity for warrant officers to advance to the rank of naval lieutenant was nonexistent in the mid-seventeenth century. It was subsequently the midshipman, taken on board as a protégé of the captain, who was in line for advancement to lieutenant and captain (Teitler 1977).

With further specialization of naval equipment and weapons, the role of the naval warrant officer continued to evolve. As commissioned officers began to specialize in the application of specific weapons and skills, some warrant officer classifications gradually disappeared. During the nineteenth century, for example, the warrant officer master was replaced by the specialist navigating lieutenant (Lewis 1948). While the opportunity for movement into the commissioned ranks remained limited for individual warrant officers, the professionalization in society at large of occupations that had been included in the warrant officer ranks resulted in certain warrant specialties becoming commissioned specialties (e.g., surgeons, chaplains, and engineers). Because of the limited possibility for movement into the commissioned ranks by warrant officers, the "operation of weaving [these new professions] into the pattern of the older officer-classes was not entirely painless" (Lewis 1948, p. 208).

In the twentieth century, with further specialization of military organizations and occupations, warrant officers serve as specialists, operators, and technical managers in relatively narrow career fields. In the United States, warrant officers were first authorized in the army in the Mine Planter Service in 1918. They served as masters, mates, and engineers on vessels of the army's Coast Artillery Corps. Two years earlier, the U.S. Marine Corps had authorized warrants as gunners and quartermasters. The numbers of warrant officers in modern military forces are small, representing less than 1 percent of total active military manpower in the United States.

Since mobility into the commissioned ranks remains limited, initial qualifications for appointment and subsequent training programs for warrant officers do not generally focus on factors associated with generalized leadership skills, as is the case with the selection and career management of commissioned officers. Thus the modern warrant officer is a highly skilled technical specialist serving in positions above the enlisted level that are too narrow in scope to permit the effective use and development of commissioned officers.

In the United States, it is typical for warrant officers to be appointed following a lengthy period of enlisted service. There are, however, significant exceptions. In the army, warrant officer helicopter pilots enter directly into the warrant program without a requirement for prior enlisted service.

FRANCIS M. RUSH, JR.

SEE ALSO: Noncommissioned Officer; Officer; Rank and Insignia of Rank.

Bibliography

Bourjaily, M. 1965. *The warrant officer in the military services.* Washington, D.C.: Army Times.
Lewis, M. 1948. *England's sea-officers.* London: Allen and Unwin.
———. 1959. *The history of the British navy.* Fair Lawn, N.J.: Essential Books.
Teitler, G. 1977. *The genesis of the professional officers' corps.* Beverly Hills, Calif.: Sage.

INDEX